THE
HISTORY OF
Ships

THE HISTORY OF
Ships

Peter Kemp

BLACK CAT

**Endpapers: The schooner *Alert* (right) lying in Whitby
upper harbour, North Yorkshire, photographed by Frank
Meadow Sutcliffe in 1880**
**Page one: Trial run of USS *Connecticut* off Maine,
1907, by E. Muller**
Page two: The oil tanker *Tactic*
**Page four: Ships of the French-Genoese fleet of 1390
from late fifteenth century French MSS**
**Page six: One of the entries in the Tall Ships Race,
New York, 1976**

ISBN 0–7481–0092–X

Printed in Czechoslovakia

52185

Contents

Foreword

'Ships and the sea, there's nothing finer made.' Thus did John Masefield express what countless shiplovers have felt for centuries. Today, when old sea ways are giving place to new, interest is greater than ever before, and the thirst for information has led to such a spate of books that their very number is bewildering, making wise choice daily more difficult.

The history of ships is a vast subject, extending for over five thousand years of man's endeavour, and to cover it fully is a daunting challenge. The knowledge needed is encyclopaedic and calls not only for an awareness of every stage in the development of the ship, from the age of the Pharaohs to that of the nuclear submarine, but also for a detailed understanding of the changes in man's lifestyle and habitat that have led to each new maritime advance. The author must supplement the expertise of the naval architect with the scholarship of the historian.

Additionally, and this is of the utmost importance, no man can truly evaluate or write convincingly of ships unless he is himself a seaman. And finally, the author must be somebody of vision and imagination who can explain a subject of immense complexity in words the reader can understand, and do this so powerfully that the story, as it unfolds, becomes difficult to lay down.

The success of this book, the best of its kind that I know, stems from the fact that in its author all these requirements are superbly, perhaps uniquely, combined. Add to this the wealth of illustration, illuminating every important detail of the text, and you have within the covers of a single magnificent volume what is in effect a distillation from the resources of a whole maritime university. A book to enjoy, a book to study, and a book to treasure.

FRANK CARR
Former Director of the National Maritime Museum

Chapter One
The Cradle of Seafaring

No contemporary picture of a truly primitive boat exists. The oldest known pictures of boats, in rock carvings or on pottery, show them at a much later stage of their development. Such knowledge as we have of earlier craft can only really be surmise. There is plenty to suggest what they were like, in present-day vessels in some less developed parts of the world. Men still bind branches together to make crude rafts beside some of the lakes and rivers of Africa; in South America people still take to the water in tree trunks, hollowed out with the aid of primitive implements or with fire. But the earliest actual pictures of boats that we have show them at a comparatively recent stage in their history. They date from about 6,000 years ago, and there were many thousands of years before then during which man ventured upon the water.

The rock carvings and pottery decorations which are the oldest known pictures of boats come from the Nile valley. They generally show some sort of long, narrow craft, with a steering paddle over the stern and men paddling amidships. Most are boats made of papyrus reed, since wood suitable for boatbuilding was scarce in the Nile valley, but some of them are constructed of numerous short wooden planks, held together with pegs or rope binding.

The earliest ship – for she was a great deal bigger than a boat – about which we have real knowledge is the funeral ship of the Pharaoh Cheops, the builder of the great pyramid at Giza, the first of the three pyramids built by his dynasty at Giza. It is generally accepted that he lived about 2600 B.C.

His funeral ship was carefully and lovingly made in prefabricated sections to be buried in

Left: Model of boat used by Tutankhamun on the Nile.
Above right: Earliest known picture of a vessel under sail, from an Egyptian pottery decoration of 3100 B.C.
Right: Egyptian river boat of 3300 B.C. on pottery.

a great pit hewn from the solid limestone of the Giza plateau, and when assembled was covered over by forty-one slabs of rock, each weighing around 18 tons. There she remained in her pit, ready to be used by Cheops if his soul should wish to embark on a voyage to the celestial regions. Since she was built more than forty centuries have gone by; 250 generations of men and women have lived and died. But this funeral ship of an ancient Pharaoh, preserved by the dry Egyptian air, has come to us out of the depths of time.

She is a wooden ship, constructed out of 600 separate pieces of wood, and considerably larger (133 ft (40·5 m) by 26 ft (7·9 m)) than any other ship of her day. This was undoubtedly because she was built purely as a funeral ship, and for the most powerful Egyptian ruler of his time. She was not built to go to sea, and, in fact, if she had tried to do so she would have been broken up by any moderate waves. Her importance in the history of the development of ships lies in the evidence that she furnishes about the skill of the Egyptian shipwright of 5,000 years ago in the working of wood to form a ship's hull. She was built with a made-up timber, rather like a keel, to which was attached a curved sternpiece and stempiece, but as yet there were no ribs, or timbers, to which to fasten the hull planking. In this ship they are held in place partly by wooden pegs and partly by small, shaped blocks of wood. The wood itself is cedar, imported for the purpose from Phoenicia.

Above: The interior of the cabin shows the fine workmanship.

Far right: The funeral ship of Cheops is the oldest and largest ancient ship to survive. It has been rebuilt from 600 parts and a further 624 fittings which had been carefully buried.

Right: Sewn cedar planks with elaborate scarfs held in position by rope fastenings.

Right: Relief from the tomb of Sahuré (about 2500 B.C.). It shows a keel-less boat with longitudinal bracing provided by a stout rope or hogging truss above the deck.

If we date Cheops's funeral ship at about 3000 B.C., we know from stone reliefs and hieroglyphics that by this time Egyptian ships were trading in the Mediterranean with Crete and Syria, and similar evidence records a war expedition to Phoenicia in 2700 B.C. We know also from these reliefs that the ships carried a single square sail on a bipod mast which could be lowered when the rowers took over. From the fact that this bipod mast was stepped well forward in the ship it is evident that the sail could only be used with a following wind, though early pictures on rock faces and pottery show ropes attached to the ends of the yard, which indicate that the yard could to some extent be braced round to the wind. There were still no ribs rising from the keel to support the outside hull planking and no deck beams to maintain the upper hull shape. Longitudinal support was provided by a large rope stretched from stem to stern and tensioned by a bar of wood in the manner of a Spanish windlass, and athwartship support by two ropes taken tightly round the whole upper hull and tensioned by a series of zig-zag racking turns with a smaller rope. Paddlers had by now given place to rowers, since the discovery of how to attach the oar to the ship's gunwale and use it as a powerful lever.

The rock temple at Deir el-Bahari at Thebes contains a long series of reliefs which tell the story of Queen Hatshepsut's expedition of five ships to the land of Punt, in search of such exotic imports as monkeys and greyhounds, myrrh and ivory. She was the co-regent and sister of Pharaoh Thotmes II, and the date is 1500 B.C. Judging from the temple reliefs, these ships were

Right and below: Modern
reconstruction and relief
of one of the ships from
Queen Hatshepsut's
expedition to Punt.
(Deir el-Bahari)

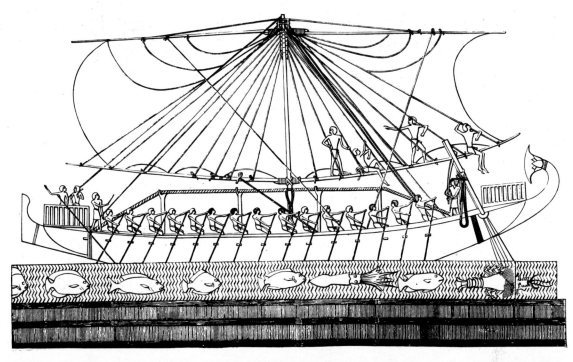

fairly large, around 100 ft (30 m) in length. They had fifteen rowers a side, thirty in all, and set one large square sail on a yard. The land of Punt is now thought to have been the present Somalia, or possibly even Rhodesia, a long voyage from Egypt down the Red Sea and around the horn of Africa, and an expedition undertaking a voyage of such long duration as this would obviously require larger ships than were necessary for the shorter Mediterranean voyages, since they had to accommodate larger crews. But the reliefs in the temple, which are remarkably detailed, show two points of interest which transcend the mere increase in size. They show the mast now stepped

amidships instead of forward, which meant that the yard could be braced to a beam wind, instead of only to a following wind, and they also show a row of deck beams carried through the hull planking, providing the essential athwartships stiffness which every ship needs if she is to be able to sail in any but the calmest of waters.

The temple reliefs at Deir el-Bahari also give a picture of another remarkable Egyptian vessel, a purpose-built ship for transporting obelisks, which were hewn straight from the granite at Assuan, down the Nile to Luxor. The obelisks stood about 95 ft (29 m) high when erected, and each weighed about 350 tons. The ship built to carry them loaded two at a time, and was about 180 ft (55 m) long with a beam of 60 ft (18·3 m), if we can believe the figures of a court official of Thotmes, though probably she had in fact to be somewhat larger if she was not to sink under the weight of the obelisks, possibly up to 200 ft (61 m) in overall length with a beam of about 75 ft (23 m). The temple reliefs show three levels of deck beams to provide support athwartships.

All these pictures of Egyptian ships provide evidence that, as long ago as 1500 B.C., the basic design of a ship was very similar to that of ships today. The long central keel had been developed, shaped stem and stern pieces had been attached at either end, and deck beams had been evolved to support the hull. All that was still missing were ribs, rising from the keel and shaped to take the hull planking.

Below: Egyptian river craft from the fifteenth century B.C. (Tomb of Sennefer)

It should not be thought that the Egyptians were the only Mediterranean people who built and used ships. It is convenient to describe the evolution of their ships only because a greater wealth of illustration remains, in the shape mainly of rock carvings and reliefs, recording Egyptian achievements at sea. There can be no doubt that, simultaneously, ships were being built and developed in Crete, Syria, Phoenicia and Greece, as well as outside the Mediterranean in a host of other lands which bordered the sea.

If it is possible to generalize about Mediterranean ships of this early period, it could be said that those of Crete and Greece leant more towards the making of war, and those of Egypt and Phoenicia more towards seaborne trade, although there were at the same time undoubtedly Cretan and Greek ships built as traders and Egyptian and Phoenician vessels built as warships. On certain circumstantial evidence it seems that much of the Egyptian trading around the shores of the eastern Mediterranean was carried out under the protection of Cretan warships, and the fact that the ancient Cretan cities were built without defensive walls has been attributed to the extent of Cretan control of the surrounding seas, denying their use to invaders.

That Egypt, too, had ships built for war is certain from the evidence of rock carvings, but their main purpose was to escort merchant ships in their search for trade, or to seize and hold a trading port on the Palestinian coast. In the fifteenth century B.C. the Pharaoh Thutmose III fought eighteen small wars to capture ports on the Phoenician coast, though the ships he used were probably large merchantmen temporarily adapted for purposes of war. Three hundred years later Ramses III, the last of the great pharaohs, won a significant naval battle against 'the northerners of the isles', and details of the action are depicted on the walls of his temple at Medinet Habu. The ships are shown with the traditional bipod mast, but now there is a distinct crowsnest at the masthead, though whether for a lookout or an archer is unknown. The square sail is fitted with brails so that it can be furled up to the yard when the rowers were required at their oars, and around the sides of the ships are high washboards to protect the rowers. There were no thwarts for them, indicating that they stood to their oars. But the most important feature of the ships as depicted on the temple walls is the absence of the usual girdle of two ropes to provide athwartships support for the sides. This would seem to indicate that the last step towards what has been basic shipbuilding practice ever since may by then have been taken, with the introduction of timbers, or ribs, rising at intervals from the keel to support the hull planking. (There is evidence that these ships of Ramses III were copied from the ships of his enemies.)

Left and below: Modern reconstruction and relief of Ramses III's great naval victory over the 'northerners of the isles'. (Medinet Habu)

Above: A fresco dating from about 1500 B.C. sheds new light on Minoan naval power. This is the first detailed representation of their seagoing ships. (Thera)

Evidence of the form of construction of Cretan ships is scarce, as it is only in comparatively recent years that the remains of the Minoan civilization have been uncovered, and there is nothing like the wealth of Egyptian rock carvings and temple decorations to provide any details of design or building. According to Thucydides, the Minoan kings were the first to build fighting navies, and since, unlike Egypt, there was no shortage of trees on the islands of the Aegean Sea we assume that they built their warships of wood. Such pictures as we have, mainly on rings, seals and scraps of pottery, show Cretan ships with a single mast and a bank of oars, and with a pointed bow which could have been used as a ram in battle. What does seem certain is that Cretan warships during the period of the Minoan civilization controlled much of the waters of the eastern Mediterranean and used their fighting power to clear those seas of the pirates who preyed upon the peaceful trade of the islands.

Some time before 1450 B.C. – the exact date is uncertain – the Cretan empire was invaded by the Mycenaeans from the mainland of Greece and completely and utterly overthrown. The entire Minoan civilization was obliterated; their cities burned to the ground. To mount an invasion such as this across the seas argues a very considerable development in the size and strength of the ships used, for this was a major operation of war, a far greater undertaking than any of the maritime battles in which the Egyptians had taken part. There is plenty of detailed evidence about the size and development of later Greek ships, both trading ships and warships, and it is probably safe to assume that, even by this early date, the Greeks had made significant advances in ship design and construction. They would hardly have ventured their attack on the Minoan empire if they had not.

A clear distinction between the ship built

expressly for war and the ship built for trade emerged with the Greeks, if at this stage we consider the Mycenaeans as Greek. They engaged in a long series of wars before finally they had to surrender their mastery of the Mediterranean to the Romans. The first of them was the Trojan War, of which we have many accounts in the writings of Homer. It is a nice, romantic idea that Agamemnon fought this long war against Troy in order to recover his brother's wife Helen, but it is much more likely that he did so to keep open the Greek trade routes in the Aegean Sea. Greece was by then trading extensively by sea. Her ships called regularly at the Black Sea ports for shipments of grain, and protection of the merchant shipping certainly called for a large navy. Homer talks about 1,200 ships engaged in the Trojan War. No doubt this was poetic exaggeration, but, whatever the exact number, there can be no doubt that there were a great many of them. Homer even provides some descriptions: almost all were 'black', which means that their hulls were covered, or payed, with pitch to make them watertight; they were 'hollow', which indicates that they still had no deck; they were 'benched', which shows that the rowers sat on thwarts at their oars. The largest of them rowed 50 oars, making them perhaps 80 ft (24·4 m) in overall length, and they lay low in the water, with a short wickerwork screen set forward to keep out the spray. There is some evidence that the largest were fitted with an *embelon*, or bronze beak for ramming an enemy, and, if this is so, they were the direct forerunners of the war galley which was to be the principal warship of the Mediterranean for the next 2,500 years.

However, for the next three or four hundred years, before the Greek bid for sea power, it is to the Phoenicians that the sea story of the Mediterranean really belongs. Centred on the ports of Tyre and Sidon, their ships ranged throughout the length of the Mediterranean and beyond, in search of trade. The Bronze Age had arrived, and the Phoenicians were notable workers in metal, so tin and copper (the ingredients of bronze) were the raw materials most in demand during the years of their maritime supremacy. At sea, the Phoenicians were, above all, great traders, though as their trade expanded over the seas they also had to build war galleys to protect their merchant vessels. They had a great reputation, too, as practical and skilled seamen. They built two types of merchant ship: the relatively small *gaulus*, for trade in and around the Aegean Sea, and the bigger *hippo*, or ship of Tarshish, for longer voyages. It was largely in their search for sources of tin that the Tarshish ships were built. Copper was obtainable locally from the mines in Cyprus, and could be brought to the ports of Sidon and Tyre in the smaller ships, but the nearest source of tin was Spain, and when the Spanish supplies began to run short, tin had to be brought from Cornwall and the Scilly Islands.

There were two distinct types of Tarshish ship, the earlier being a large ship with a single square mainsail set between upper and lower yards on a central mast, and with a steering oar on each quarter. The ship was decked, with two hatches for cargo and crew. The hull was built deep and roomy, on a length-to-beam ratio of about $2\frac{1}{2}$ to 1, with high, curved stempieces and sternpieces. There were no bulwarks, but along the gunwales were what today we would call stanchions and rails, to provide protection for the crew in rough weather and to keep the deck cargo from sliding overboard when the vessel rolled in a seaway. Cargo was normally carried both above and below the deck. (A mural painting in a thirteenth century B.C. tomb at Thebes, showing Phoenician ships at anchor in an Egyptian harbour, provides the details of this ship.)

It was with ships such as this that the Phoenicians traded the length of the Mediterranean and beyond, to southern Britain and the Canary Islands. There is evidence, too, that they operated them in the Red Sea and Indian Ocean, a canal between the River Nile and the head of the Red Sea providing the means of access to those waters. But, no matter in which direction they traded, their ships were always known as Tarshish ships. The site of this city has never been discovered, though references to it abound in the ancient records of all Mediterranean countries, and it was recognized as the richest city-state in the world. It almost certainly lay somewhere on the Iberian peninsula, probably outside the Mediterranean on the Atlantic coast of Spain or Portugal. It could be that even the Phoenicians never reached it, in spite of the fact that their ships were named after the city. For it is certain that they settled a colony at Gadir, now known as Cadiz, on the Atlantic coast of Spain and built it up into a rich and prosperous centre from which to stretch their trading tentacles into even more distant lands, but Gadir was not Tarshish.

The second type of Tarshish ship, a good deal later than the *hippo*, is of particular interest in the history of the development of the ship. Details of its rig were revealed on a carved marble sarcophagus which was discovered in 1914 in the Old Harbour at Sidon. It has two masts – or possibly one mast and a very high-steeved bowsprit – each carrying a sail laced to a single yard, the foresail being very similar to the spritsail set below the bowsprit carried by sailing ships up to about the seventeenth century A.D. Both yards could be braced to the wind, and there is no apparent provision for rowers. It seems unlikely at this very early stage that any ship was built exclusively for sailing, but with the two-masted rig as shown in the carving it is not entirely impossible. Alternatively, it may be that the carver of the sarcophagus had not the skill or the space to show oars as well as sails. The usual twin steering oars are shown, but a point of considerable interest is a sort of low aftercastle projecting beyond the sternpost, very reminiscent of the sterns of the typical Spanish carracks of 1,800 years later. Another interesting feature is a raised cargo hatch, as is generally found on merchant vessels today. The mainmast shrouds appear to be tensioned by deadeyes – another modern touch – and the carving shows a small ship's boat carried on deck.

To protect their merchant ships on their long voyages the Phoenicians built war galleys with two banks of oars, the forerunners of the Greek bireme. Indeed, they were the first true biremes, and the Greeks copied them almost exactly. On the waterline or just below it, they were fitted with a bronze, or occasionally wooden, beak, or ram, the traditional main weapon of the galley throughout most of its history. Unlike the merchant ships, they were built long and slim, with a length-to-beam ratio of 5 or 6 to 1, or sometimes even as much as 8 to 1, and under oars they were fast and very manoeuvrable. They carried archers on a central upper bridge for attacking enemy ships, and were rowed by slaves. The earliest known representations occur in two Assyrian reliefs of about 700 B.C., and these show a curious arrangement of the two banks of rowers. The rowers pulling the lower oars sit below the narrow central bridge which runs the whole length of the galley, while those pulling the upper oars sit in outrigger extensions to the hull on either side. The design shows not only considerable shipbuilding skill, but also an improvement on earlier designs in understanding of the principles governing a ship's stability in a seaway. The long, narrow hull ensured greater speed and power if the ram was to be used, while the outrigger extensions, which were fully planked, provided a reserve displacement and an effective counter to the risk of capsizing through excessive rolling, which is inherent in any long vessel of minimum beam. A typical square sail, set on a mast stepped in the longitudinal centre of the galley, gave relief to the rowers with a following wind, and the two traditional steering oars, one over each quarter, ensured adequate directional control. For their day, these biremes were formidable vessels of war.

Right: Two-banked
Phoenician warship of
about 700 B.C., showing
ram. (Palace of
Sennacherib)

Below: A Tarshish ship.
(From a sarcophagus found
in the Old Harbour, Sidon)

Even the Greeks, their traditional enemies, admitted that the men who manned the Phoenician ships were magnificent seamen. Their long voyages in search of trade, particularly of tin, proved that. They are reputed to have made an even longer voyage, circumnavigating Africa during the reign of Pharoah Necho II (the pharoah who started the construction of the canal to connect the River Nile with the Red Sea). It was, in fact, an Egyptian-organized expedition, though the men who undertook it were all Phoenician. Herodotus, who travelled in Egypt 150 years later, was doubtful about the authenticity of the story, but the reason he gave for his doubts is at least an indication that it could well have taken place. His account runs:

'Libya [the original name of all Africa] shows that it has sea all round except the part that borders on Asia, Necho a king of Egypt [610–594 B.C.] being the first within our knowledge to show this fact; for when he stopped digging the canal which stretches from the Nile to the Arabian Gulf he sent forth Phoenician men in ships, ordering them to sail back between the Pillars of

Right: Phoenician merchant ship of about 700 B.C., loading and towing timber. Cedarwood was a staple Phoenician export. (Palace of Sargon)

Below: Eighth century B.C. Greek warship. Opinion is divided about whether it is one- or two-banked.

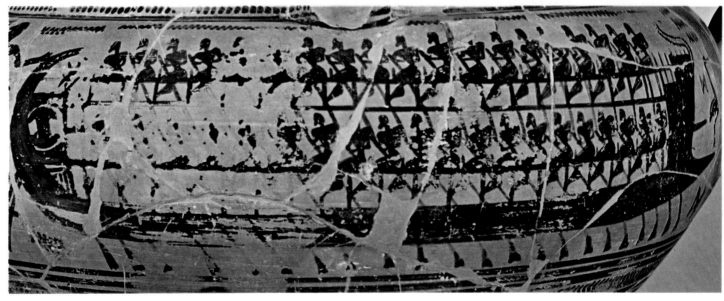

Hercules until they came to the Northern [Mediterranean] Sea and thus to Egypt. The Phoenicians therefore setting forth from the Red Sea sailed in the Southern Sea [the Indian Ocean], and whenever autumn came they each time put ashore and sowed the land wherever they might be in Libya as they voyaged, and awaited the reaping-time; having then reaped the corn they set sail, so that after the passing of two years they doubled the Pillars of Hercules in the third year and came to Egypt. And they told things believable perhaps for others, but unbelievable for me, namely that in sailing round Libya they had the sun on the right hand. Thus was Libya known for the first time.'

Herodotus can be excused for doubting the truth of the story, for all Mediterranean men knew that at midday the sun lay to the south of them, or on their left hand when they faced the sunset. If the Phoenicians did make this voyage, they sailed about 14,000 miles (23,000 km), a prodigious feat in 600 B.C., yet quite possible, even though it was to be nearly another 2,000 years before the magnetic compass was available to guide mariners across the seas. In those days few ships ventured out of sight of land during their voyages if they could help it, creeping round the coast by day and anchoring at night.

Unfortunately, Herodotus, in recounting this story which he picked up in Egypt, says nothing about the ships in which the Phoenicians sailed. We can only guess, but it is reasonable to assume that they were not designed specifically with this voyage in view, and, in fact, were the normal merchant ships of the period, still with the single central mast and square sail, and rowing probably 12 to 15 oars each side. The typical Phoenician *hippo*, in which they made their long voyages to the Canary Islands and southern Britain, was of exceptionally solid construction and would be the best ship available for such a voyage round Africa, particularly as they were built with a crowsnest at the masthead for a lookout, almost essential on a voyage such as this where it was necessary to keep the coastline in sight.

During the period of Phoenician dominance at sea, the city-state of Tyre was the richest in the world, and built mainly on extensive maritime trade. For three centuries Tyre, Sidon and the smaller Phoenician ports were the great clearing houses of world trade, importing great quantities of linen, cotton, wheat and papyrus from Egypt, silver, tin, iron and lead from 'Tarshish' (including Cornwall and the Scilly Islands), cedar and other timber from Cyprus and the Lebanon, brassware and slaves from Greece and Asia Minor. Their exports were mainly bronze articles, glassware (the Phoenicians are believed to have discovered the method of glass manufacture by fusing sand and nitre) and coloured dyes, of which the most desirable was Tyrian purple, reserved for the robes of emperors, caesars, and the richest and most desirable whores. To service this great trade not only was a great number of ships required, but also the finest and most robust ships that could be built, manned by the best seamen in the world. The Old Testament, in the words of the prophet Ezekiel, gives some of the details. Speaking of Tyre, Ezekiel says: 'They have made all thy ship boards of fir trees of Senir; they have taken cedars from Lebanon to make masts for thee. Of the oaks of Bashan have they made thine oars; the company of the Ashurites have made thy benches of ivory, brought out of the isles of Chittim. Fine linen with broidered work from Egypt was that which thou spreadest forth to be thy sail; blue and purple from the isles of Elishah was that which covered thee. The inhabitants of Zidon and Arvad were thy mariners; thy wise men, O Tyrus, that were in thee were thy pilots. The ancients of Gebel and the wise men thereof were in thee thy calkers [a Bible commentary translates this as 'stoppers of chinks' or, in the modern term, 'caulkers']; all the ships of the sea with their mariners were in thee to occupy their merchandise. . . . The ships of Tarshish did sing of thee in thy market; and thou wast replenished and made very glorious in the midst of the seas.'

All this was true enough, but Ezekiel was merely building up the picture for a prophesy of doom: 'Thy riches, and thy fairs, thy merchandise, thy mariners, and thy pilots, thy calkers, and the occupiers of thy merchandise, and all thy men of war, that are in thee, and in all thy company which is in the midst of thee, shall fall into the midst of the seas in the day of thy ruin. The suburbs [another version gives 'waves' for 'suburbs'] shall shake at the sound of the cry of thy pilots. And all that handle the oar, the mariners, and all the pilots of the sea, shall come down from their ships, they shall stand upon the land; and shall cause their voice to be heard against thee, and shall cry bitterly, and shall cast up dust upon their heads, they shall wallow themselves in the ashes. And they shall make themselves utterly bald for thee, and gird them with sackcloth, and they shall weep for thee with bitterness of heart and bitter wailing. . . . The merchants among the people shall hiss at thee; thou shalt be a terror, and never shalt be any more.'

Ezekiel prophesied that Nebuchadnezzar, king of Babylon, was to be the instrument of Tyre's downfall. Phoenicia was never a nation as such,

Above: The dock entrance at the old Phoenician port of Motya, Sicily, is so narrow that it confirms the small size of ancient warships.

merely a collection of independent city-states which never learned to combine against their enemies. Nebuchadnezzar subdued them one by one with great ferocity, but, although he besieged Tyre for thirteen years and captured the outer city whose inhabitants he put to the sword, he failed to take the harbour area. Nevertheless, Tyre took many years to regain its trading supremacy, and only did so through the constant realization that wealth depended on mastery of the sea. By building larger and better ships, and maintaining a yet more powerful force of warships, the Tyrians at last won back to their former trade pre-eminence.

But, many years later, Ezekiel's prophecy finally came true. The instrument of the city's fall was Alexander of Macedon – better known as Alexander the Great – who succeeded in breaching the city's walls after a siege of nine months. The slaughter of Tyrians was immense, and 30,000 of them were sold into slavery.

It was the end of Tyre as a city-state, the end of Phoenician mastery of the seas. For close on seven centuries their ships had ventured into waters as yet not penetrated by any other Mediterranean power, and had shown that the old belief of Mediterranean sailors that a ship sailing into the unknown ocean beyond the Pillars of

Hercules would fall over the edge of the world into the abyss was false. They had done this partly by building fine, strong ships and partly by an understanding of some of the rudiments of celestial navigation, an understanding not generally possessed by the seamen of other Mediterranean nations. Of their methods of navigation, and of the early attempts to map the ocean, an account is given at the end of this chapter; of their shipbuilding skills, the proof lies in the long voyages which they undertook.

They were probably the first of the Mediterranean nations to give their ships a continuous upper deck with hatches cut for the loading of cargo. The Egyptians had taken the first step, it is true, when they gave their ships transverse beams to provide athwartships support, but it was the Phoenicians who developed the idea to its logical conclusion, by raising the transverse beams to deck level and thus producing the basic pattern of keel, stempiece, sternpiece, possibly ribs, and deck beams to which every modern ship is built. Unlike the Egyptians, they were fortunate in having close at hand plenty of suitable timber for their ships. They were the first to experiment with two masts, for though the second mast looked perhaps more like a bowsprit than a mast it was cocked up, or steeved, so high that it acted more as a foremast than a bowsprit. On this they set a spritsail on a yard, which enabled them to sail with the wind on the beam, a tremendous advance on the single square sail of the Egyptians and Cretans that could only be hoisted and used to advantage with a following wind. They caulked the seams of their ships with wool and pitch to make hulls and decks watertight. They also realized that an expanding maritime trade could not be sustained without an efficient navy to protect the merchant ships, and so they developed the bireme with a bronze ram and an upper bridge deck for archers, so that the two banks of rowers below could pull their oars unhindered by the fighting men. The long, slim lines of the galley hull, with the added stability of the two outrigger extensions, either shows that the Phoenicians knew more about the modern science of hydrodynamics than many other seafaring nations a thousand years later or that they had a remarkable piece of good fortune, in hitting upon a design that was not simply revolutionary, but also ideal for the calm waters of the Mediterranean. Given the known skills of the shipbuilders of Tyre, Sidon, Gebel and Arvad, it seems reasonable to discount the element of luck and to assume that this particular design was the result of study of what a ship was required to do.

More important than the advances in shipbuilding and design which the Phoenicians initiated was the example that they set to the rest of the world by their trading ventures. By opening up new trade routes, first to the western Mediterranean and then out into the Atlantic, even as far as the green seas and grey skies of northern Europe, they proved that man had it in his power to overcome obstacles hitherto thought to be unassailable. Wherever their ships went, whether to Cornwall and the Scilly Islands or, by way of Red Sea ports, to India and perhaps beyond, their enterprise and courage formed the first link of a chain of maritime achievements which in the end was to lead man to the very last outposts of the earth. The sea was their dominion. They learned to be fine seamen, and their practical ability enabled them to profit by that learning in building fine, robust ships. But behind their skill lay the spirit of adventure and a determination to discover what filled the great unknown spaces of the world, by daring the wild waters. One of the great periods of maritime expansion came to an end with the fall of Tyre.

For a time the Phoenician tradition of trade was carried on by Carthage, a sister city-state colonized by the men from the Levant. But the true heirs to Phoenician sea power were the Greeks, whose maritime domination of the Mediterranean was about to begin. For a long time they did no more than follow closely the pattern set by the Phoenicians, both in their methods of trade – though they never ventured outside the Mediterranean, except to the Black Sea – and in the design of their ships. Only later in their history did they prove themselves to be even better seamen than the Phoenicians.

The Greeks traded to and from colonial settlements which they set up in Italy, Sicily, southern France, North Africa and the Black Sea. This last colony is interesting: not only was it a wheat-producing area which supplied most of the homeland of Greece, but there was gold in the rivers. The method of extracting the gold from the fast-flowing rivers was to pin down sheepskins on the river beds to catch the grains of gold washed down by the current. And here we find the basis of the legend of the Golden Fleece, the Argonauts and their ship, *Argo*.

We know quite a bit about the *Argo*. She was built of pine felled on the slopes of Pelion, the pine trunks being shaped into planks with an axe. She was built as a galley and her top strakes were pierced for fifty oars. Her whole hull was covered with pitch inside and out, except for her bows which were painted vermilion, the standard colouring for all Greek ships, and on either bow there was the traditional eye, so that the

Left: Model of
Phoenician trireme,
about 300 B.C.

ship could see her way across the waters. She was built on a beach, and when she was completed she was too heavy for the fifty Argonauts to run her down into the water, her keel sinking deep into the sand. So they cut more pines to make rollers, and got her up onto the rollers and so down to the water.

This is the traditional story of the building of the *Argo*, and it matches almost exactly the normal construction of a Greek *penteconter*, a sixth-century B.C. galley, with 50 oarsmen, a length of about 80 ft (24 m) and a beam of about 10 ft (3 m). Although the *Argo* was obviously built for trade – the fact that she was going to the Euxine (Black) Sea for the Golden Fleece, or, in other words, for a cargo of sheepskins which had been pinned down in the rivers to catch grains of gold, is evidence of this – we know from Herodotus that on many Greek trading voyages

the ships used were 'not the round-built merchant ship, but the long *penteconter*'. They were used not for defence against pirates, with whom the Mediterranean waters abounded, but for attack; for the Greeks were, above all, buccaneers in their trading ventures, and never averse to running a merchant ship aboard, plundering her cargo, and either enslaving her crew or leaving them to drown in their sinking ship.

The *penteconter*, based on the original design of the Phoenician galley, had a long history of buccaneering during the centuries of Greek dominance in the Mediterranean. They were of light construction and, pulling 25 oars a side, were fast enough to overtake any other vessel that they encountered. When the wind was favourable they set the usual square sail, laced to a yard hoisted on a central mast which was always lowered when the wind came ahead.

Below: Greek vase decoration showing Ulysses and the Sirens. The ship is of the *penteconter* type.

They were open ships, undecked except for a storming bridge (*kakastroma*, in Greek) which ran from stern to bow, providing the longitudinal strength needed for fighting purposes and making possible the light construction of the hull. The normal steering oars, one on each quarter, gave them their manoeuvrability.

The *penteconter*, built for the sort of aggressive trade which the Greeks pursued, was not the sole type of merchant ship used by them. There are few illustrations – no doubt Greek artists preferred to depict the more prestigious biremes and triremes – but one vase decoration shows a ship with an overhanging bow, not unlike a modern clipper bow, high bulwarks and a light central bridge running the length of the ship. She is shown under sail and with no oars visible. It is difficult to estimate her size, but if the length of the yard and the size of the sail approximate to

those in more detailed illustrations she would be 45 to 50 ft (13·7 to 15·2 m) long, and one would guess at a beam of about 14 ft (4·3 m). The vase shows her fairly high out of the water, and her distinct bulwarks indicate that she would carry a deck cargo in addition to that stowed in her hold. The clipper-like bow is interesting: a very similar shape of bow is found in Mediterranean fishing craft today, particularly in the waters around Italy and Malta. It would be wrong to conclude from this one illustration that all Greek trading vessels, except of course the *penteconters*, followed this pattern – each district no doubt had a more or less traditional design based on the type of cargo to be carried – but in general it could be said with some confidence that they were small, tubby ships built to carry the maximum amount of cargo with the minimum length of keel.

Above: A high-sided Greek merchant ship with deep draught. Contrast the lightly built war-galley on the left.

A whole series of wars, initially between the individual Greek states, against Carthage, against Persia, and finally against Rome, made it necessary for the Greeks to concentrate on warship building. The Phoenicians had already developed the bireme, the galley with two banks of oars on either side, and, with the *penteconter* proving too light in construction for purposes of outright war, the Greeks took the bireme as their warship. However, they built it lighter than the Phoenician model, with only a skeleton outrigger, instead of a solid one, on either side to provide a fulcrum for the upper bank of oars. The lower bank were pivoted on the edge of a round hole cut in the side planking. The upper and lower rowers sat on different thwarts, the upper rowers having a thwart level with the gunwale, the lower having one level with the holes in the sides. The main weapon of the bireme was the beak, or ram, fixed to the bow on or just below the waterline, and archers or stone-slingers were carried in addition to the rowers, using the *kakastroma* as their action station. To enable the hull to absorb the shock of ramming an enemy, the keel was slightly prolonged beyond the hull line aft and the thick wales, fixed to the hull near the waterline, were similarly prolonged to meet the end of the keel, where they were brought up together into a point or bunch, often decorated with the head of a bird or a stylized acanthus. The biremes all carried a mast, which was always lowered when the wind was ahead, and the traditional square sail on a long yard, with brails to furl it to the yard when not required.

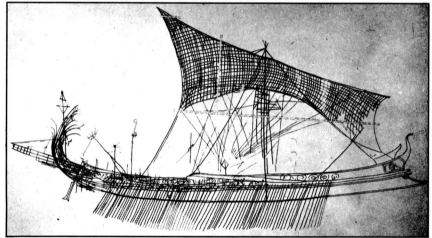

Above: Large rock carving at Lindos, Rhodes. The ship had to beach stern first, with steering oars raised.

Above left: Greek biremes under sail, sixth century B.C.

Left: Greek trireme of first century B.C. (Graffito from Delos)

Below left: Detail of an Athenian trireme, showing the upper oarsmen rowing through an outrigger. (Relief from Athens)

Over the course of a series of wars fought on the Mediterranean against increasingly powerful enemies, the Greeks discovered that they needed something stronger and heavier than the bireme, if they were to retain their control of the sea. Who it was that designed and built the first trireme is unknown. Thucydides suggests that it was the Corinthians, and that they used them in battle in 664 B.C. He may have been referring to some other form of warship, possibly using oars on three levels instead of two – his text is imprecise on this point – since 664 B.C. seems a very early date for the full development of this most famous of Greek warships. Much of the strength of the trireme was attributable to the solid outrigger. If we date this innovation sometime during the sixth century B.C., as is generally done, we arrive at a date for the first appearance of the trireme which is about a hundred years later than that given by Thucydides.

The arrangement of rowers in the trireme has been a matter for argument for centuries. Unhappily, there is no illustration· or drawing to settle the doubts. We know that the three banks of rowers had separate names: the rowers of the top bank were known as 'thranites', and the length of their oars has been put at 14 ft (4·3 m); the middle bank rowers were 'zygites', pulling an oar $10\frac{1}{2}$ ft (3·2 m) long; and the lower bank rowers were 'thalamites', and the length of their oars was $7\frac{1}{2}$ ft (2·3 m). How their benches were arranged is not known for certain, but one popular theory, put forward after considerable research by Dr. Graser, is that they were con-

structed in sets of three, with the thranite sitting on the top bench, his zygite sitting on a bench 2 ft (60 cm) lower and 1 ft (30 cm) behind him, and the thalamite on a bench another two feet lower and another foot behind. A different theory envisages only two benches, with thranites and zygites sitting side by side on the upper bench, their oars extending through two separate holes in the outrigger planking, one above the other, with the thalamite sitting on a lower bench, behind them and between them to give him space to swing his oar. The recent construction of a full-sized trireme by the Greek Navy has dissolved many uncertainties over the trireme's propulsion under oars.

But how the rowers were actually seated is of less importance than the design and structural details of the trireme herself. Once again the waterline wales were brought up to a point with the keel to form a decorated sternpost. The stern rose from the keel at an angle of about 70 degrees and curved backwards up to the level of the forecastle, or raised fighting bridge, then rose above it and curved forwards to finish in the acrostolion or ornamental decoration. The beak projected about 10 ft (3 m) beyond the stem, reinforced by the thick wales, and formed a three-toothed spur, with the centre tooth longer than the others. This was covered in metal, usually bronze. Above it, but not so long, was a second beak, formed by the upper wales meeting in a point. This, too, was covered in metal, and frequently shaped like a ram's head. The object of the upper ram was to give the coup de grâce to an enemy, after she had been pierced by the lower beak.

The trireme was rowed by 31 thranites, 27 zygites and 27 thalamites each side, giving a total of 170 rowers. Five officers and twenty-five petty officers and other specialists made up the total ship's company of 200. In the Greek triremes a few marines, fighting men in heavy armour, were stationed on the deck in battle. The captain had a sort of small deckhouse aft, just forward of the flagstaff. The discovery of the foundations of dry docks at Munychium and Zea give some idea of the overall dimensions of a trireme. The docks measure about 150 by 20 ft (46 by 6 m), and, allowing for a certain amount of spare room at the sides and each end, suggest figures of about 130 ft (40 m) for length, including the ram, and 16 ft (5 m) for beam. One would expect such a vessel to be capable of a maximum speed of around 7 to 8 knots in short bursts with the rowers giving their best. The trireme had two masts, or possibly one mast and a bowsprit steeved at an angle of about 70 degrees to the horizontal and called the artemon, but never used sail in battle, both masts being lowered before battle was joined.

Greek trireme
(c. 480 B.C.)

Length 130 ft (39·6 m) *Beam* 16 ft (4·9 m) *Complement* 200

The trireme, the capital ship of her day, was developed from the bireme during the sixth century B.C. Her principal weapon was the long ram projecting about 10 ft (3 m) from her bow. This was formed by bringing together the thick wales which ran down either side of the vessel to meet the keel. In this way the shock of ramming an enemy could be absorbed by the whole structure of the ship, not simply the keel. In addition to her 170 rowers, she had one or two masts with square sails, used when the wind was astern but lowered when the trireme went into battle. The most famous engagement in which triremes took part was the battle of Salamis in 480 B.C.

The reconstruction is of a Greek trireme of about the time of Salamis. The side is cut away to show the raised platform, or *kakastroma*, running the length of the ship. The diagram shows two possible arrangements of rowers.

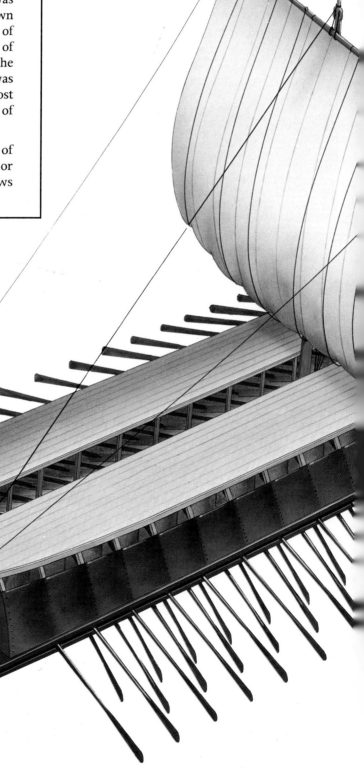

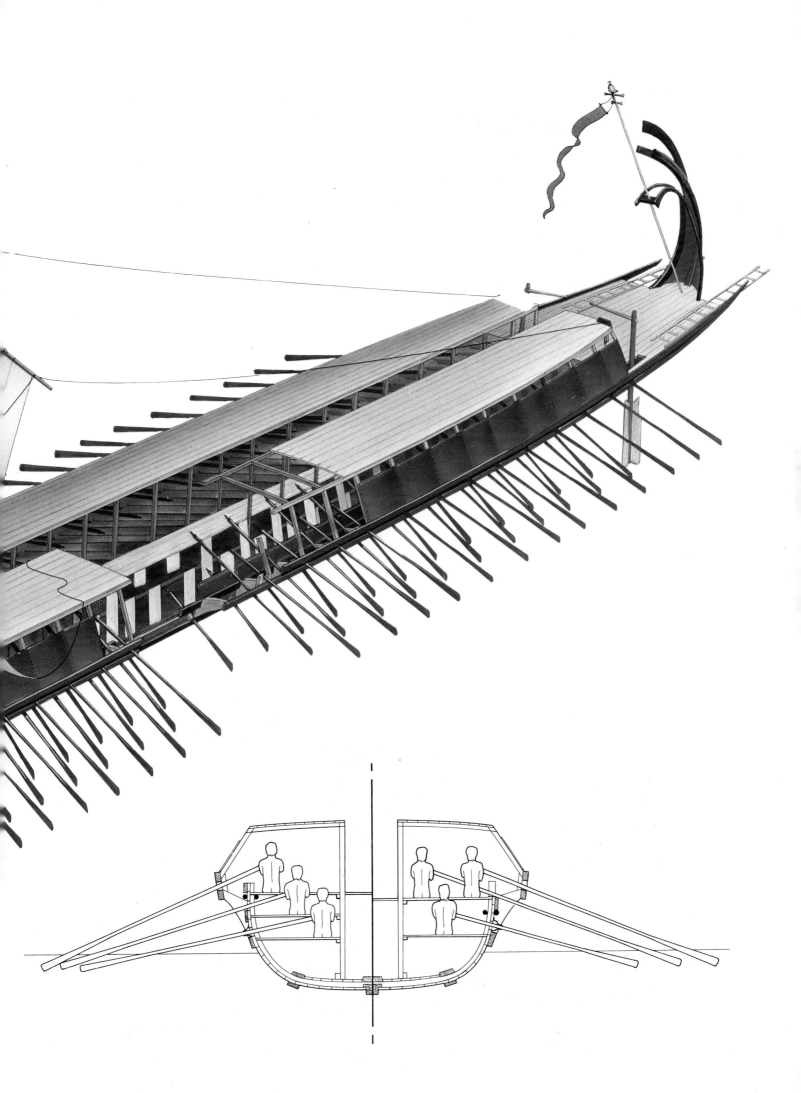

The battle of Salamis, fought in 480 B.C. against a Persian fleet, much superior in numbers, commanded by Xerxes, saw Greek triremes in action. The Greek fleet was commanded by Themistocles and he had drawn up his ships in the bay of Eleusis in the island of Salamis in the Aegean Sea. There they were trapped by the Persians who closed the two channels leading into the bay. It was the narrowness of these channels, combined with the great number of Persian ships, which led to the Persian defeat. Unable to use their numerical superiority in such restricted waters, and too impetuous in attack they jammed themselves in the narrow entrances, presenting a perfect target for the Greek triremes. After some hours of battle, over 200 Persian warships had been destroyed for the loss to the Greeks of about 40 vessels. Aeschylus, in his play *The Persae*, compares the Persian fleet with tuna fish, the traditional method of catching them being to drive them into shallow water where they could be killed with any available weapon.

Aeschylus was serving as a marine on board one of the Greek triremes and his words are those of an eyewitness. In Gilbert Murray's translation there is a graphic description of the battle, given by the messenger who brought the news of the defeat to Xerxes's mother:

'The first rammer was a Greek
which sheared away a great Sidonian's crest;
then close, one on another, charged the rest.
At first the long-drawn Persian line was strong
and held; but in those narrows such a throng
was crowded, ship to ship could bring no aid.
Nay, with their own bronze-fanged beaks they
  made
destruction; a whole length of oars one beak
would shatter; and with purposed art the Greek
ringed us outside, and pressed, and struck;
  and we –
our oarless hulls went over, till the sea
could scarce be seen, with wrecks and corpses
  spread.

One of the mysteries of Greek, also of Roman and Carthaginian, warships is the evolution of the trireme into the quadrireme and quinquireme. Until comparatively recently, the doctrine of 'one oar, one man' was widely accepted, and these vessels were visualized as rowing four and five banks of oars. But, on this theory, there are records of ships built with up to 16 banks of oars, which is plainly ridiculous. There is even an account of a 40-banked vessel, a *tesseraconteres* built for Ptolemy Philopator, which is even more ridiculous, if we accept the 'one oar, one man' theory. The upper rower in a *tesseraconteres* would be pulling an oar 53 ft (16 m) long (the longest oar used in the British navy is 18 ft (5·5 m)).

Today it is considered that the terms quadrireme and quinquireme referred to the number of men on each set of three oars. For example, two thranites, two zygites, and one thalamite on each set would make the ship a quinquireme.

These vessels were, of course, larger and more unwieldy than the trireme, and required larger crews. Ptolemy's *tesseraconteres* was said to be 400 ft (122 m) long with a beam of 50 ft (15 m), needing 4,000 oarsmen without counting the fighting men. It seems most unlikely that this immense ship ever existed, except in Ptolemy's imagination. Not unnaturally, perhaps, there came a revulsion against the big warship on the grounds of the expense of building and upkeep, and, even more, her unwieldiness, and by the third century B.C. the bireme was coming back into fashion.

Inevitably, as trade developed in the Mediterranean, there were other powers ready to challenge the supremacy of Greece. Carthage was always a thorn in her flesh, and Rome was growing into a major power, ready to expand east and west as the number of her legions grew. Although essentially a land power, Rome quickly discovered that she needed control of the seas if she was to keep her expanding empire. This lesson was learnt during the First Punic War when, in 269 B.C., the Carthaginians sent a fleet to invest the island of Sicily and threaten the coastal towns and ports into quick surrender. Fortunately for the Romans, a Carthaginian quinquireme was wrecked on the Italian coast and revealed the secrets of her construction. Using her as a model, the Senate in Rome decided to build a fleet of 100 quinquiremes and 20 triremes, the ships being built by Greek shipwrights who had settled in Italy. Always a methodical race, the Romans constructed rowing benches on scaffolding ashore and trained teams of rowers to be ready to man the ships as soon as they were launched.

Being soldiers rather than sailors, the Romans built their warships large and heavy, adapted more for a military style of action than conventional naval warfare. Not for them the swift galley relying on its ram to pierce an enemy's hull; not for them the *dickplous*, the sudden charge on a given signal to break through the enemy line of battle, wheeling right and left after breaking the line to take the enemy galleys in the rear; or the *periplous*, a move to outflank the enemy's line and fold it up on itself. The Romans preferred a straight fight, using marines as soldiers to capture enemy ships by boarding. For this purpose Roman triremes were fitted with a gangway 36 ft (11 m) long, hinged below and held vertical against the mast. Forcing their way alongside an enemy, they would let go the gang-

Above: First century B.C. Roman galley with two banks of oars. This was probably a quadrireme or larger ship. (Relief from Praeneste)

Right: Roman galley on a coin from the second century B.C.

For this purpose, the number of marines on board was increased from 40 to 120 or more.

This type of military warfare at sea was immensely successful at first, possibly because of its novelty and the unpreparedness of the Carthaginian fleet to counter such tactics, and at the battle of Mylae, fought in 260 B.C., Gaius Duillius shattered the Carthaginians, sinking or capturing more than forty of the enemy. A column adorned with the beakheads of the captured Carthaginian ships was erected in Rome to celebrate this.

Mylae set the pattern of Roman maritime dominance of the western Mediterranean, and by the end of the First Punic War there was no other navy to challenge her. She relied on the big galley, massively constructed, to maintain her power, accepting the loss of speed and manoeuvrability as of lesser importance than the weight of attack so heavy a galley could mount. When Roman galleys were sent into the eastern Mediterranean to meet the challenge of Philip of Macedon, they established control of those waters, too, in spite of the hordes of pirates who attacked at every opportunity. It took a naval

way from the masthead and it would fall across the enemy ship, a spike at the end, known as a *corvus*, holding it firmly on the enemy's deck like a grappling iron. The gangway was 4 ft (1·2 m) wide and across it poured the marines, armoured and carrying the Roman short sword.

31

Above: Part of the hull
of a huge Roman ship
raised from Lake Nemi,
showing the beams that
supported the lower deck.

force of more than 500 ships and a military force
of many legions to clear the sea and hold the
shores for Rome, but Pompey, in a masterly campaign which was begun in 67 B.C., achieved it.

The dominance of the extremely heavy warship, however, was not to last. Rome was torn
apart by a struggle for internal power with
Octavian's bid to become emperor. He selected
Agrippa as his commander at sea, and at the
battle of Actium, fought in 31 B.C., Agrippa was
able to demonstrate that victory did not always
go to the bigger, heavier ship. Mark Antony's
ships were considerably heavier and slower than
those of Agrippa, and that day proved that the
relatively small, fast ship had little to fear from
sheer weight, if handled intelligently. Agrippa
concentrated not so much on ramming his enemies as running alongside their galleys and
shearing off their oars.

Actium, having disposed of the challenge to
Octavian, set the seal on Rome's naval control
throughout the entire Mediterranean. For the
next two and a half centuries, Roman galleys
kept the peace at sea and Roman merchant ships
carried the bulk of seaborne trade. In 1932 a
chance came to examine Roman ships, when the
Lago di Nemi in the Alban hills was drained. In
the mud at the bottom of the lake lay two enor-

mous hulls, one of a warship and one of a merchant ship. They were dragged up out of the mud
onto the shore and a museum constructed around
them. The warship was about 235 ft (72 m) long
with a beam of 110 ft (33·5 m). These dimensions
suggest that it could have been a '15-banked'
galley, or a trireme with 15 rowers for each set
of oars. There was a recognizable ram, and the
traditional inward curve of the bow was still
intact, with part of the starboard outrigger and
the starboard steering oar. But the main interest
of the warship hull lay in the construction, which
indicated a very considerable skill in building,
with a keel, keelson, frames very closely set, and
the strakes of the hull planking pinned to each
other and attached to the frames. The underwater part of the hull was sheathed in lead, an
innovation in shipbuilding usually dated several
centuries later. The ship almost certainly had two
decks, a lower deck on which the rowers sat,
supported by pillars mounted on bilge stringers
at about waterline level, and an upper deck near
the top of the frames. No trace of the upper deck
remained when the ships were recovered, but
the frames rose so high above the lower deck that
a second must surely have been included.

The merchant ship, about 240 ft (73 m) long
with a beam of 47 ft (14 m) had the lines of typical
Mediterranean trading vessels. The hull which
was recovered was less complete than that of the
warship and there were no clues as to her rig, but

Above: Relief at Ostia showing Roman merchant ship with twin triangular topsails, entering harbour.

there is other evidence that the two-mast rig (main and *artemon*) was being supplemented about this time by a third mast aft, eventually to be called a 'mizen'. A contemporary account of a Roman grain ship gives her size as about 180 by 45 by 44 ft (55 by 13·7 by 13·4 m), somewhat stubbier than the Lake Nemi merchant ship. But that Roman merchant ships were large by the standards of the time is well documented: the ship in which St. Paul was wrecked is recorded as carrying 276 passengers and crew.

There are a number of contemporary illustrations of Roman merchant ships, the most interesting and detailed being that found at Ostia. They are thought to be ships of the third century A.D., and the illustration shows two triangular topsails set on the mast above the square sail. It also shows a strong forestay led to the stemhead and shrouds tensioned through deadeyes. The vessel herself looks broad and deep. She is two-masted, with mainmast and *artemon*, but no sign yet of a mizen. But perhaps more interesting still is the description given by Lucian of a Roman grain ship which he inspected when she put into the port of Piraeus during the second century A.D. 'What a tremendous vessel it was,' he wrote, '120 cubits [180 ft (55 m)] long, as the ship's carpenter told me, and more than 30 cubits [45 ft (14 m)] across the beam, and 29 cubits [44 ft (13 m)] from the deck to the deepest part of the hold. And the height of the mast and the

yard it bore, and the forestays that were necessary to keep it upright. And how the stern rose in a graceful curve ending in a gilt goosehead, in harmony with the equal curve of the bow and the forepost with its picture of Isis, the goddess who had given the ship her name. All was unbelievable: the decoration, paintings, red topsail, the anchors with their windlasses, and the cabins in the stern. The crew was like an army. They told me she could carry enough grain to satisfy every mouth in Athens for a whole year. And the whole fortune of the ship is in the hands of a little old man who moves the great rudders with a tiller no thicker than a stick. They pointed him out to me, a little, white-haired, almost bald fellow: I think they called him Heron.'

Just why the two ships discovered in the mud in 1932 were built on a lake high up in the Alban hills is a mystery. One opinion is that they were constructed as playthings of the Roman court. But, be that as it may, they revealed a great deal about the skill of contemporary Roman shipwrights in building large ships. It is a pity that the upperworks of the galley did not survive, since they might have revealed the reason for the one or two small wooden turrets, usually painted to resemble stone, which the Romans erected on the decks of their galleys. The museum for the two ships built on the shore of Lake Nemi was destroyed by fire during World War II, and the

Right: Two-banked *liburnian* depicted in a mosaic at Palazzo Barberini at Palestrina.

Far right: Roman shipwright shaping a rib before inserting it into the completed shell – a reversal of modern practice.

Below right: Trajan's Column showing the Emperor standing in the stern of a trireme flanked by two *liburnians*.

ships perished in the flames before the full extent of their secrets could be revealed. An attempt to date them on the basis of the earliest Roman coins discovered in them suggests that they were built during the reign of Caligula, the latest coin found being one of A.D. 164.

As the Roman empire consolidated and expanded, new forms of armament were provided for the heavier galleys. Catapults to sling stone and lead were erected on the upper deck, and it is recorded that the catapults of a large galley could throw up to half a ton of lead a distance of 600 to 700 yards. Greek fire (a mixture of naphtha, sulphur and pitch) was another new weapon. It was blown through long copper tubes with ends shaped like the jaws of savage monsters, or launched by hand by the marines onto the decks of enemies, as a sort of hand grenade.

Although the Romans continued to build large galleys for their fleet, the lessons of Actium were not ignored. At the same time they developed a smaller, faster galley, based on a design first produced in the Adriatic, to protect their merchant ships from the incessant attacks of pirates. This vessel was known as a *liburnian*, originally pull-

ing 25 oars in a single bank on each side. But in a later version, illustrated in a mosaic in the Palazzo Barberini at Palestrina, she had become a bireme, with two banks of oars. A larger version, known as a *dromon*, built to a length of 150 ft (46 m) and pulling 50 oars a side in two banks, was armed with catapults and fighting towers for the marines. Smaller, and possibly built for reconnaissance or as a fleet lookout, was the *galea*, though she was heavily enough armed to hold her own should need arise.

As Rome expanded her empire through northwest Europe, Roman ships penetrated northern waters. A fleet of warships was stationed in the English Channel during much of the Roman occupation of Britain; Roman merchant ships brought supplies and reliefs to the legions that held the land in sway. There was no competition for control of these seas as yet: northern European peoples were not yet awake to the wonders and riches that lay beyond the seas. Nor does it appear, when the northerners did at last begin to carve a way to new lands across the sea, that the Roman ships which they had seen had any influence on local design and construction. Development was entirely indigenous to the region, designs emanating from the Baltic out into the North Sea and more distant waters.

The Birth of Navigation

Navigation (a term derived from the Latin *navis*, a ship, and *agere*, to drive) is the art of taking a ship from one place on the earth's surface to another by sea, safely, speedily and efficiently. Today it is done by means of charts, compasses, logs (to record a ship's speed and distance run), accurate sextants (to measure the angle of heavenly bodies), automatic sounding machines to gauge the depth of the water, broadcast time signals, and a host of electronic aids, which give the navigator his exact position on the surface of the globe; the first navigators in history had none of these aids. It took hundreds of years for the first seaman to evolve as simple an implement as a lead and line to measure the depth of water under his ship. Usually, in this very early period of travel by sea, ships always sailed by day, and within sight of land, hugging the coast, then anchoring as night fell. When, occasionally, they were blown out to sea beyond sight of the shore, they were lost until they had the good fortune to make a landfall somewhere else. We read that, even as late as A.D. 61, when the ship in which St. Paul was voyaging from Caesarea to Rome was driven out to sea in a storm, no one on board knew where the ship was until the wind blew the ship to Malta and safety.

It is thought that it was the Phoenicians, during their voyages in the first millennium B.C., who first learned how to use the stars, or, at least, one of them, in plotting a course at night, though it is possible that the knowledge came from Eastern navigators. The Greek poet Aratus, writing about the constellation of the Little Bear, says, 'By her guidance the men of Sidon steer the straightest course,' 'the men of Sidon', of course, being Phoenicians. *Ursae Minoris*, the Little Bear, contains *Polaris*, the Pole Star, which always lies to the north, and this knowledge gave the Phoenicians a fixed point of reference by night. They knew, too, that at local noon the sun always lay due south, and this was especially useful knowledge when combined with another navigational aid – the wind-rose.

The wind-rose was a circular card, in the shape of a compass card, on which were drawn the directions of certain named winds. It is not known who first introduced it, but it is certain that by

the time of Homer, around 900 B.C., Greek seamen used four particular winds, which blew from the four quarters, as their principal means of navigation. These were Boreas, the north wind, Euros, the east wind, Notos, the south wind, and Zephinos, the west wind. Later, as voyages became longer and a greater degree of accuracy was needed to reach a given destination, four more winds were added. After one of the original four had been moved through 45°, the eight winds were (clockwise from the north) Boreas, Kaikias, Apeliotes, Euros, Notos, Lips, Zephuros and Skiros. By reference to the sun at noon or the Pole Star by night, a navigator would identify which wind was blowing, and shape his course accordingly.

The eight wind system was adopted by the Romans, who gave their own names to the winds which became Tramontana, Greco, Levante, Sirocco, Mezzodi, Garbino (later changed to Affricone), Ponente and Maestro. The system was later expanded to twelve winds, then sixteen, and finally thirty-two.

It is surprising that, in a developing world where more and more trade was being carried by sea and men were inquiring more and more into the shape and nature of the earth, very few attempts were made to map the sea. Homer, in his poems, envisaged the world as an immense disc surrounded by a broad, flowing river known as Okeanus. The earliest known map, moulded in clay and now in the British Museum, dated about 700 B.C., follows Homer's model, with Babylon at the centre of the disc. The earliest Greek maps share the disc concept, though they have Delphi at the centre. Later Greek geographers, noting the overall shape of the Mediterranean, thought that the world must be longer along the east-west axis than the north-south, and so drew the earth as a rectangle, with a prime meridian and a prime latitude passing through Rhodes, then considered to be the maritime centre of the world.

But even before these Greek geographers got to work, the idea that the earth was a sphere had already taken hold. Pythagoras, in about 580 B.C., was the first man to grasp this. Using the Pythagorean theory, a Greek from Cyrene in Libya, named Eratosthenes,

Above: Ptolemy, the Greek mathematician, astronomer and father of cartography.

set out in 200 B.C. to discover the circumference of the earth by calculation. He measured the length of the shadow of a gnomon, cast by the sun in Alexandria at the summer solstice, and, taking the distance due south to Aswan, on the Tropic of Cancer, where the sun is directly overhead (this distance was known from the existing cadastral surveys of the Nile valley), he arrived at a figure for the circumference of the earth which differs by less than 4 per cent from the modern one.

On the basis of this calculation Eratosthenes constructed a new world map, using meridians of longitude and parallels of latitude, adjusted to pass through places of importance, such as Meroe (in Abyssinia, the farthest known point to the south) and the Pillars of Hercules (the farthest known place to the west). These meridians and parallels were based on Rhodes.

Eratosthenes was followed by Marinus of Tyre, who in the first century A.D. began drawing charts for seamen. His meridians and parallels were equally spaced, though he still used Rhodes for the intersection of his prime meridian and prime parallel.

There was, therefore, by this time a considerable body of knowledge about the real shape of the earth and sea, at least in the Mediterranean and in Arabian waters. Where the great difficulty lay, so far as charts for navigators at sea were concerned, was in accurately translating a curved surface (the earth) into a flat surface (a chart). This problem was solved by Ptolemy, whom we recognise today as the real father of cartography. Although born a Greek, he lived and worked in Alexandria, as a mathematician and

Above: The earliest map of the world with the oceans and Babylon at its centre.

astronomer. In about 130 A.D. he evolved a simple conic projection whereby the features of a curved surface could, with reasonable accuracy, be projected onto a flat surface. Later he evolved a more sophisticated method of doing it with his equal-area projection. Using this projection he drew a map of the world, showing it as contained within 180 degrees of longitude, from the Canary Islands in the west to China in the east. The whole of the Mediterranean Sea, Red Sea and Persian Gulf are shown with fair accuracy, although he portrays Africa as a huge continent bending round to the east and finally joining up with China to enclose the Indian Ocean as a vast lake.

Only in one respect did Ptolemy really fail: for his world maps he accepted a figure, given by Poseidonius who lived in the first century B.C., of 18,000 miles for the earth's circumference, instead of the earlier and much more accurate measurement of Eratosthenes. This made one degree of latitude, the basis of all measurement of distance at sea, equivalent to 50 miles, instead of 60 miles as it should be, and led to considerable distortion.

Left: Ptolemy's world map drawn in 130 A.D. His works, rediscovered at Constantinople in 1400, formed a basis for the rebirth of ocean mapping in the two succeeding centuries, stimulated by the discoveries of navigators like Columbus, Diaz and da Gama.

Chapter Two
The Ship in Northern Waters

There are, in Norway, Sweden and Denmark, rock carvings of boats which, if not stretching so far back in time as those of Egypt, date back at least to the Stone Age. Some of them closely resemble the oldest Greek representations of boats, and this similarity has led to a theory that Mediterranean practice and design spread northwards through Europe and that this was how the boat found its way to northern waters.

Nothing could be further from the truth. The oldest Scandinavian rock carvings date back at least to 2000 B.C., and it is beyond normal belief that Mediterranean boat and ship design could have penetrated so far into the then-unknown world by that date. If it had done so, northern Europe could not possibly have remained unknown to the Greek geographers of 1,800 years later. It would seem perfectly reasonable to assume that the same solutions to the same problems were found in other parts of the world at the same time as in the Mediterranean.

The earliest Scandinavian rock carvings give no indication of the material from which the vessels were made, but it seems most likely that they were constructed of hides stitched across a wooden frame, somewhat in the manner of the modern Irish curragh. The frame is shown in the carvings as extending a little beyond the hull at bow and stern, probably to act as carrying handles for taking the boats across land, for they were longer than a curragh and less handy for carrying on the shoulders of the crew as is still the fashion in Ireland. But many of the later Bronze Age carvings show a sort of keel which projects appreciably beyond bow and stern, curved upwards at the forward end. The general opinion is that what at first looks to be a form of keel was, in fact, a runner, to keep the hull clear of the ground when it was hauled across land. This would imply that boats were by that time

Left: Warriors on their way to Valhalla by ship, on eighth century stone, Gotland, Sweden.
Above right: Late Bronze Age carving showing vessel with projections similar to the Hjortspring boat.
Right: Modern Irish curragh made with hides or canvas.

Above: A model of the Hjortspring boat, showing projecting runners at bow and stern.

Above right: Model of the Kvalsund boat, showing keel and overlapping planking.

Right: Crisscross lines on the sail of a ship on one of the Gotland stones may represent strips of leather reinforcing the linen sail.

made with wooden hulls: it would not be possible to haul a hide boat across the ground without damaging it, and it would have to be carried.

This opinion was vindicated when a boat was found buried in a bog on a farm called Hjortspring on the Danish Island of Als in south Jutland. This boat was constructed between A.D. 200 and 300, of wood, and is about 44 ft (13 m) long, with a beam of nearly 7 ft (2 m). Her hull consists of five overlapping planks, 20 in (51 cm) wide and $\frac{5}{8}$ inch thick, forming a rounded shape, with projections left on the inside of the planks to which thin ribs were bound. At the bow and stern these planks are stitched to two shaped endpieces, cut from solid blocks of wood, with the upper parts projecting with a long, gently upward curving sternpiece and stempiece. The most interesting part of the construction is a long piece of wood, which acts as a keel or runner, fixed to the outside of the bottom plank and extended some distance beyond the bow and stern. A short, vertical piece of wood connects each end of this runner to the projecting stempiece and sternpiece, obviously to give added strength to the whole structure. The Hjortspring boat had space for ten thwarts and accommodated twenty paddlers. It was presumably steered by a paddle over the stern as there is no fitting for the usual steering oar. From her long, slim shape, with a length-to-beam ratio of more than 6 to 1, it is unlikely that she was built for trade; more likely she was intended for raiding voyages against neighbouring settlements.

Another form of Scandinavian boat building was based on the dugout. Several hundred have been found, all over the Scandinavian countries, and, though we are apt to look on the dugout as one of the most primitive types of boat, the Scandinavians used it as a model for larger vessels. Examples of dugouts with outriggers in the form of horizontal bilge-keels, of two or more dugouts joined to form a double hull, of dugouts extended by fixing planks to their sides have all been recovered. One discovered at Bjorke in Sweden is a shallow, hollowed-out trunk, tapering towards each end, to which are fastened two overlapping sides. The shaped bow and stern-piece are attached to the trunk and sides with iron rivets. As in the Hjortspring boat, the inside of the dugout and its sides have been left with natural longitudinal projections to which the ribs of the boat were stitched. This boat, which has been dated around A.D. 100, is nearly 24 ft (7·3 m) long, and the hull takes the form of a shallow curve, not unlike the cross-section of a flat dish.

The shallow cross-section, with a considerable beam in relation to the depth, was a feature of most early Scandinavian types. Apart from the longitudinal runner found in the earliest boats, which may also have acted as a form of keel, the Scandinavian boats were keel-less, though in many cases the bottom plank of the hull, running down the centre of the structure, was thicker than the others. Another universal feature was the overlapping planking, known today as 'clinker' construction; whereas in contemporary Mediterranean vessels – and indeed for many centuries to come in that landlocked sea – the hull planking was invariably set edge to edge ('carvel' construction as we call it today).

The first indication of a true keel as an integral part of the hull construction can be found in one of two boats found at Kvalsund in Norway in 1920. There is the same basic shallow hull section, but the bottom plank has a short, downwards-pointing, vertical extension which would cer-

tainly act on the water as a short keel and give a bit more stability to the vessel. For the rest, the hull planking is carried appreciably upwards at bow and stern to form a distinct canoe shape, the earliest example of the actual planking being used to give this pronounced sheer at both ends. This boat is about 60 ft (18·3 m) long, with a length-to-beam ratio of about 6 to 1, and is estimated to date from the sixth century A.D.

Unlike Mediterranean vessels of similar dates, there is no indication of masts and sails in any of the early Scandinavian boats, and it seems clear that this method of propulsion did not come to northern Europe before about the seventh century. Scandinavian craft were all propelled by paddlers until about the fourth century, by which time we begin to get indications of oars pivoted on the gunwale, rowed by men sitting on thwarts and facing aft. Some earlier carvings on rocks and stones show something like a tree growing out of the boat amidships, and this is thought to show that leafy branches were used as temporary sails when the wind served.

Sometime around the seventh or eighth century, if we can believe the evidence of the Gotland pictorial stones, a new type of construction was introduced in Scandinavia, where the bow and stern formed almost a right angle with the keel, the hull planking tapering in to join a distinct stempiece and sternpiece. It would be reasonable to assume that this new hull form coincided with the introduction of a mast and sail, for the longer keel and pointed ends would provide a more efficient and stable sailing form than the shallow, keel-less hulls of earlier boats.

The Gotland stones show a sail set from a short central mast, with a yard at top and bottom and with sheets led to bridles on the lower yard, one each side of the mast. The sail itself, we know, was originally made from a coarse, homespun material which became unduly baggy when wet. For this reason it was usually reinforced with strips of leather, which is why the stone carvings show the sails with a diamond pattern of diagonal lines.

This type of hull was almost certainly designed for trade; the Scandinavian fighting, or raiding, ship was still a long, slim boat, propelled by oars, the rowers becoming the fighting men during an action. At this stage of development this vessel was the forerunner of the fighting longship with which the Scandinavians were later to rampage over most of north-western Europe, though as yet it had no sail and relied entirely on oars for propulsion. The sail trading ship also carried rowers, but few in number, and they can have been used only for short coastal voyages. The merchant ships were completely undecked, carrying their cargo on the boat's floor amidships, clear of the rowing thwarts forward and

Below: The hull lines of a longship, exemplified by the burial ship found at Gokstad, Oslo Fjord.

Bottom: The Oseberg ship showing her excellent state of preservation; note steering oar in the foreground.

42

aft. They mounted a single steering oar on the starboard quarter of the ship, the helmsman operating it by means of a short tiller set at right angles to the oar.

The Viking era of Norwegian history opens in about A.D. 800 and lasts for about five centuries. It was characterized by the famous longship, and an early example, or prototype, is the ship discovered on Gokstad Farm, near Sandefiord, in 1880. She was found in a 15 ft (4·6 m) burial mound of blue clay and was well preserved. But, although built on longship lines, her overall length of 76 ft (23 m), beam of 16 ft (5 m) and relatively high freeboard of 6 ft (1·8 m) show her to be too small for use as a war or raiding ship. Bows, stern and keel are each fashioned from a solid block of timber, and she has sixteen strakes of clinker planking fixed together with rivets. The caulking is of tarred rope, and the strakes are lashed to the ribs of the vessel by means of cleats, or projections, on the timbers. She carried a 40-ft (12·2 m) pine mast on which was set a square sail with a spread of about 16 ft (5 m). The hull is pierced for sixteen oars a side, and, though there are no built-in thwarts,

the holes for the oars are too low down for the rowers to have stood to their oars. It has been assumed that they sat on their sea chests, or on removable benches. The normal steering oar is fixed to the hull on the starboard quarter, and she exhibits the traditional high bows and stern of the longship.

The Gokstad ship is dated at about A.D. 900,

and when she was unearthed she had thirty-two overlapping shields on each side, the Norse feature beloved of all illustrators of Viking longships. These shields were in fact decorative only, or used in harbour for recognition purposes, and would never have been arrayed along the gunwales at sea. That they were found in the ship buried at Gokstad was almost certainly because she was furnished in full state as a burial ship.

That the ship was seaworthy was proved in 1893 when a replica was sailed across the Atlantic by Captain Magnus Andersen, to be put on show at the Chicago World's Fair held to commemorate the four hundredth anniversary of Columbus's discovery of America. It is strange that this particular ship should be at Chicago to honour Columbus's feat, for it was in a longship of similar construction, though larger, that Leif Ericsson may have made his voyage to the New World nearly 500 years earlier.

An earlier version of the longship – or, like the Gokstad ship, a direct prototype of the longship – is the famous Oseberg ship, discovered on Oseberg Farm, near Tonsberg, Norway, in 1904. Like the Gokstad ship, she was found in a burial mound and is remarkable for the beautiful decorative carving on her bow and stern. Her general constructional details are similar to those of the Gokstad ship and stand as a monument to the skill and precision of Norse shipbuilders of the period. She is reckoned to have been built around a century earlier than the Gokstad ship, around A.D. 800. The decorative carvings may have been added later.

She is smaller than the Gokstad ship, with an overall length of 70 ft (21·3 m), was built of oak and was pierced to row fifteen oars a side, again with the rowers probably sitting on their sea chests. She had a mast, a single square sail, and the usual steering oar operated with a short tiller. Again, she was not a warship but was probably a *karfi*, or *karv*, a vessel built light enough to be used on estuaries and lakes and manhandled along rivers.

That it was not only in Scandinavia, but also in other countries in north-western Europe that the ship was evolving is proved by the discovery of the English royal burial ship unearthed at Sutton Hoo, near Ipswich. She, like her Scandinavian sisters of the same date, was propelled only by oars, although mast and sail had been used in England for some centuries. The Sutton Hoo ship is dated at about A.D. 650. On the other side of the English Channel, in the early ninth century, the Emperor Charlemagne established naval forces at Boulogne and Ghent to check the

Above: The Oseberg ship during excavation of the burial mound in 1904.

Right: Detail of the carving on the stern.

ravages of the piratical Norsemen, who were now using their longships to overrun western Europe in search of women, slaves and plunder.

As has been seen from the construction of the Gokstad and Oseberg ships, Scandinavian shipbuilders were supremely skilled in their trade. As Norse eyes turned more and more seawards, the time came to build larger versions of these ships, able to face the longer voyages and steeper seas associated with more distant targets. The Norsemen invented a form of ship measurement to describe the varying sizes of their longships, based on the *rum*, which was the name given to the space between two adjacent crossbeams. Each *rum* contained one thwart on which sat a pair of rowers, one each side, and the longships varied between the *skuta*, a ship of about 15 *rum* to the *skeid* or *drakkar*, of 32 *rum*. Occasionally larger longships were built: Olaf Tryggvason had his famous *Ormrinn Langi*, which would be translated as *Long Serpent*, built to a size of 34 *rum*; Harald Hardrada's *Buza* was 35 *rum*; and King Haakon's *Kristsuden*, built about 1260, was 37 *rum*. The anglicized form of *rum* is 'room', and when, as frequently occurs in English writings, a longship is described as 'of 32 rooms', it means a 32-*rum* ship.

We know a great deal about these famous ships from the writings of the skalds, who composed the sagas in which so much of Norse history is enshrined. Of the *Long Serpent*, probably the best known of all Norse longships, Snorre, the skald, writes that 'of all the ships in Norway she was the best made and at the greatest cost', and describes how, when she was rowed away after battle, she looked like 'the flutter of an eagle's wings'. She was built by a shipwright named Torberg who introduced a considerable improvement in the fitting of stems and sternposts to the keels. Olaf Tryggvason was one of the great heroes of Norway, finally losing his life at the battle of Svolde in 1000; and his magnificent longship, which was the last of the Norwegian fleet to remain afloat in that decisive battle, is as famous in Scandinavian history as its owner.

By about the year 800, Norse and Danish longships were proving to all western Europe that, as well as being supremely well built and magnificent seaboats, they were a formidable seaborne foe. The Vikings ranged across the North Sea and down the English Channel to the coast of western France and northern Spain, raiding, plundering, and holding to ransom as they went. At first they met no opposition: no other north European country had ships which could match them for speed or manoeuvrability, or indeed possessed any sort of warship at all. But as the years passed, and French, English and Scottish kings realized that the only answer to the intolerable raiding and plundering of their nations was to meet the raiders at sea instead of waiting for them to come ashore and trying to engage them with land forces, some navies were built to oppose them, consisting almost entirely of copies of the existing Norse longships. The raiders' answer was to raise their freeboard a foot or two with additional longitudinal strakes, so as to enable their crews to fire their arrows and throw their darts downwards into any ship that tried to resist them. But it was this increase in freeboard that made possible, and perhaps even inspired, the longer voyages of the longships into the stormy waters of the northern Atlantic. Another development which made this possible was the invention of the *beitass*, a long pole, with one end held inside the ship in a chock abreast the mast and the other end secured to the weather leech of the square sail, holding it boomed out to windward. The use of a *beitass* enabled a ship to sail much closer to the wind, and so for the first time in northern waters a vessel could make way through the water to windward without having to depend on her rowers whenever the wind blew from before the beam.

The northern voyages began in 984 with Eric the Red, who fled to Iceland from Norway to escape trial on a charge of murder. Hearing from another Norse trader that he had sighted land still further to the westward he decided to investigate, verified its existence, and gave it the name of Greenland. Returning to Iceland he persuaded a group of local inhabitants to join him in setting up a colony there, and in the summer of 985 set sail with them to Greenland, rounded Cape Farewell, and landed in Ericsfjord, near the present Julianehaab, where he founded the settlement of Brattahlid.

Eric the Red had a son, Leif Ericsson, who in 999 returned to Norway, visited the Court of Olaf Tryggvason, and obtained from him a commission to proclaim Christianity in Greenland, returning there the following year. According to Norse sagas, and particularly the *Flatey Book*, a trader named Biarni Heriulfsson had been blown off course during a voyage to Greenland and had sighted land to the south-west, but had not investigated it. Leif Ericsson decided to discover whether there was any truth in this report, and in 1001 left Greenland on a voyage to the south-west. He claimed that he discovered the land and went ashore at places he named Helluland (now believed to be Baffin Island), Markland (probably Labrador), and Vinland (thought to be Newfoundland). At Vinland he reported finding self-sown wheat, vines and 'mosur' wood. Recently, these have been tentatively identified by Professor S. E. Morison as lyme grass, the wild red currant or mountain cranberry, and the white, or canoe, birch, all of which grow wild and prolifically in Newfoundland. Nor was this the full extent of longship voyages. Sagas of the same period also describe voyages of Viking fleets to Barcelona, Pisa, Rome, even Constantinople, during the ninth century.

If we can believe the saga of the *Flatey Book* — and most of the sagas have at least a foundation in fact — the first landing on the continent of America took place nearly 500 years before the great voyage of Columbus. But be that as it may, there is no doubt whatever that regular voyages to Iceland and Greenland were well within the compass of Norse ships: a tribute to the skill of their shipwrights and the soundness of their design and construction, for even at this date such ships probably had no continuous deck, but were open craft, or possibly half-decked, superbly built with long, flowing lines and manned by men who were seamen to their fingertips.

Viking longship
(c. A.D. 1000)

Length 150 ft (45·7 m) *Beam* 20 ft (6·1 m)
Complement 180

This longship is based on the famous *Visunden*, or *Ox*, built at Nidaros in Norway in 1026 for King Olaf Haraldsson, later known as Saint Olaf, patron saint of Norway. The largest longships were called *drakkars*. They were battleships of the Viking period, and the *Visunden*, at 30 pairs of oars, was part of the group of 'super-longships' which numbered only sixteen named craft in the period 995–1263. The longship was ideally suited to raiding, with a shallow draught that allowed her to penetrate a long way up estuaries and rivers. Her sailing performance was far superior to Mediterranean galleys and the square sail could be braced to windward so that she could make progress against the wind.

This reconstruction shows some of her oars shipped. At the masthead is one of the gilt wind vanes which have been found among Viking remains. The diagram shows the arrangement of rowers on one side, and an archer firing from a raised platform on the other.

Above: The remains of a Viking merchant ship, or *knorr*, recovered from the bottom of Roskilde Fjord.

The Scandinavian trading ship of the period was the *knorr*, modelled on the traditional long-ship, but bluffer in build with a length-to-beam ratio more like 3 or 4 to 1 than the 5 or 6 to 1 of the longship. An example of a *knorr* was recently excavated in the Roskilde Fjord, Denmark, and her construction closely follows the general pattern of the longship, with the same rounded bow and stern, and with stempiece and sternpiece carried well up above the level of the side planking. *Knorrs* were of course never built as big as a longship, being probably no more than 50 to 60 feet in overall length, and were almost certainly used only for coastal trading. Like the longship, they were undecked.

The development of the ship in Britain is always said to have started with the coracle, a wickerwork frame covered with animal hide. Small, crude vessels of this type were mentioned by Julius Caesar when reporting on his conquest, but he also mentions, though without specifying a type of ship, that there was maritime trade between Britain and Gaul long before his conquest, so it seems certain that something larger and stronger than a coracle was available. During his conquest of Gaul, Caesar records that British ships co-operated with those of the Veneti, and no coracle could have crossed the English Channel and the Bay of Biscay to reach the mouth of the River Loire, around which the Veneti lived. As the British and the Veneti fought together against the Romans, and as there had been mutual trade between them for several years before that, it seems probably that there was at

least a similarity between their respective ship types, particularly as Caesar describes the ships of the Veneti and not those of Britain, perhaps implying that his description covered them both.

In Caesar's words, the ships of the Veneti 'were built and fitted out in this manner. The bottoms were somewhat flatter than those of our vessels, the better to adapt them to the shallows and to enable them to withstand without danger the ebbing of the tide. Their bows, as likewise their sterns, were very lofty and erect, the better to bear the magnitude of the waves and the violence of the tempests. The hull of each vessel was entirely of oak to resist the shocks and assaults of that stormy sea. The benches for the rowers were made of strong beams of about a foot in breadth, and were fastened with iron bolts about an inch thick. They fastened their anchors with iron chains instead of with cables; and they used skins and a sort of thin, pliant leather for sails, either because they lacked canvas and were ignorant of the art of making sailcloth, or more probably because they believed that canvas sails were not so fit to bear the stress of tempests and the rage and fury of the winds, and to drive ships of that bulk and burden. Our fleet and the vessels of such construction compared as follows, with regard to fighting capabilities. In the matter of manoeuvring power and ready command of oars we had an advantage; but in other respects, looking to the situation of the coast and the stormy weather, all ran very much in their favour; for neither could our ships injure theirs with their prows, so great were the strength and solidity of the hostile craft, nor could we easily throw in our darts, because of the loftiness of the foe above us. And this last feature was also a reason why we found it extremely difficult to grapple with him, and bring him to close action. More than all, when the sea began to get up, and when the enemy was obliged to run before it, he, fearing nothing from the rocks and cliffs when the tide should ebb, could, in addition to weathering the storm better, trust himself more confidently among the shallows.' Nevertheless, Caeser's ships gained a decisive victory and the first navy possessed by Britain was completely destroyed.

The interesting point about this description of Caesar's is that it shows that the mast and sail were being fitted and used in English ships during the years before Christ, in contrast to the case in Scandinavia, where they came into use very much later. Not that this is surprising; it would be much more so if they had not been used. Centuries earlier, Phoenician ships had come to Cornwall and the Scilly Islands to barter for tin from the mines there, and, as we have seen, they had a mast and square sail. As trade developed between England and neighbouring France, the Phoenician practice would surely have been noted and followed. And, although the general standard of Roman shipbuilding was certainly far higher than in Britain, there was at least one type of indigenous vessel which impressed the Romans to the extent of their adopting it for their own purposes: this was the ship which the Romans named the *picta*, a long, fast-sailing pinnace, whose hull was smeared with wax to lessen the skin friction, and which carried a square sail on a centrally placed mast and rowed 10 oars on either side. When this type of craft was added to the Roman navy in the Mediterranean, the sail was dyed light blue and the crew clothed in the same colour, presumably to make the *picta* less conspicuous, since its main purpose in the Roman fleet was reconnaissance. (This is, perhaps, the earliest example of a naval uniform.)

Under Roman stimulus and command the Britons were encouraged to build and maintain small squadrons of warships for anti-piracy duties, and such few records as exist show that these were of sufficient strength to discourage any form of piracy in home waters. Since the pure galley design of the Mediterranean was obviously unsuitable for use in British waters, it is fairly certain that these ships must have been based on the longship, though perhaps improved by the use of Roman shipbuilding techniques.

When the Roman occupation came to an end, and Britain reverted to the tribal system, seaborne defence against piracy and invasion was neglected. In this defenceless state Britain was wide open to the ravages of the Vikings. Saxons, Angles, Danes, Jutes and Norwegians, all came and all conquered, and the Scandinavian longship became a common sight around British shores, though some of them had different local names, such as *ceols* (keels), *hulks* and *aescs*. Their size varied, but the largest were built up to about 50 tons.

The Vikings turned the country into petty kingdoms, each ruled by a Viking leader who proclaimed himself a local king. As they squabbled and fought among themselves, some went under; a few flourished. Those that did began to build themselves fleets of warships powerful and numerous enough to meet and defeat any invaders at sea. One such was Offa, King of Mercia, and we know from the Saxon Chronicle that, because of the size and fighting power of his fleet, he was able to treat with even so great a monarch as Charlemagne on equal terms. Unfortunately the Saxon Chronicle is silent about the size and design of Offa's warships but there can be little doubt that they followed the general pattern of the Scandinavian

Right: A bronze-gilt engraved wind vane from Heggen, probably fitted originally to the prow of a ship.

Below right: Thirteenth century carving from Bergen of the prows of a Norse fleet, some with animal figureheads and some with vanes like the bronze-gilt one shown above.

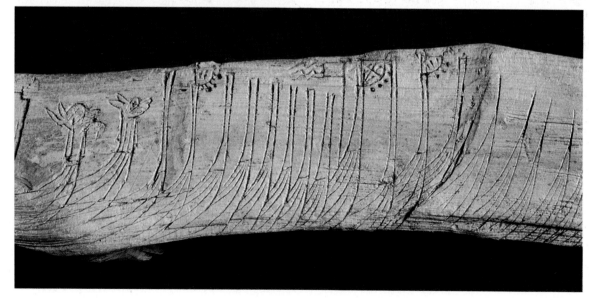

ET VENIT AD PEVENE SÆ :·

longship. Local English shipwrightry had not yet developed to a point at which it could make advances on the ships of its adversaries.

Alfred, king of the West Saxons, who by the end of the ninth century had extended and unified his kingdom until in effect it became England, built bigger and better longships to guard his ragged dominion against the continual Danish attacks. In the words of the Saxon Chronicle, his ships 'were full twice as long as the others; some had sixty oars and some had more; they were both swifter and steadier, and also higher than the others; they were shaped neither like the Frisian nor the Danish, but so as it seemed to him that they would be most efficient.' Longer and bigger they may have been, but they still embodied the essential longship design.

English warships were still longships at the time of the Norman conquest of Britain in 1066. So, too, were the warships of William of Normandy, if we can accept the evidence of the Bayeux Tapestry. The representation of the *Mora*, William's flagship, clearly shows the longship design, with a tall prow surmounted by a lion's head. The sail has three vertical stripes, red, brown or yellow, red. It has a single sheet, held by the steersman with one hand – unlikely in a ship as big as the *Mora* – while in the other he holds the *clavus*, or steering oar, operating it

with what looks like a yoke of the sort sometimes seen on small boats today. If we can accept the position of the men in the *Mora* as reasonably accurate, then she had a continuous upper deck. On the same evidence, the transports carrying fighting men and horses are undecked. Again, though it is impossible to be certain, the evidence of the tapestry suggests that the majority of the transports were smaller, and of considerably lighter scantling, than the warships.

Like all his forerunners in the history of England since the Roman conquest, William was really little more than a pirate. In fact, all the kings of England during this period, including the rulers of the petty kingdoms, were pirates, dependent on holding their lands by force. Cymbelene, Egbert, Offa, Alfred, Edward the Elder, Edgar, Canute, Harold – all were essentially pirates who happened, in their day, to command the strongest force of ships in the seas around Britain. Power derived from might, and though some of these piratical monarchs proved to be wise statesmen and capable of enlightened thought and action, in the last analysis their power rested on the number of fighting ships that they could muster. William was, perhaps, the last of the pirate kings of England, but he had learned the lesson well and took care to maintain his fighting fleet while he was consolidating his conquest and establishing his dynasty.

Above: Part of the
Bayeux Tapestry showing
the *Mora*, William of
Normandy's flagship.

In one respect, the old records of the time are strangely silent: all through these years fishing was a considerable industry, but there is no description of the craft which fished the North Sea or more distant waters. It is possible to reconstruct, probably fairly accurately, the sort of vessel which fished in waters where herring, mackerel and pilchards abounded. We know that they had surface nets, and any strongly built open boat of around 30 ft (9 m) in overall length could operate a seine net and remain safely at sea for the two or three days required to reach and return from the fishing grounds. But we also know that the whale was being hunted in northern waters round Greenland and in the Arctic Sea. During his reign Alfred sent two Danish seamen, Oddr and Wulfstan, to discover how far to the north the land of Scandinavia stretched. 'So he sailed north as far as whale hunters ever go, and thence north again three days. Then the land bent east and he sailed along it four days till the land bent south, and he sailed also to the south five days till he came to a great river, up which he dared not sail for it was all inhabited.' This must have been the White Sea and the mouth of the River Dwina. But in what sort of ship did he make this voyage? And in what sort of ships did the whale hunters operate? Probably basically the same kind, but it must have been reasonably large to withstand the gales of northern seas and to carry on board enough provisions for a long voyage, and must have been decked, for crews could not live long in those latitudes without shelter and warmth. In some respects, these voyages to the far north are even more remarkable than the Norse voyages to Iceland and Greenland, which were largely island-hopping voyages by way of the Orkneys, Shetland and the Faroe Islands. It is not difficult to imagine a sturdy decked boat of around 15 to 20 tons accomplishing these voyages into the Arctic Ocean, but it is intriguing to guess at its sail plan. It seems unlikely that the normal square sail, even with a *beitass* rigged, would have answered the purpose. Even when the *beitass* was replaced by a bridle on the leech of the sale and a bowline to haul it taut to the wind, the combination would leave much to be desired for a voyage into the White Sea. Perhaps, even by that early date, something like a lugsail was being developed from the normal crossyard and square sail. There is a description of something that might be a sort of lugsail rig as early as about 1050, but the voyage to the White Sea occurred more than 200 years before that date. Yet, so slowly did new ideas, developments and designs travel in those days that it is not entirely impossible that a form of lugsail had been developed as early as 850, especially for whaling.

Seamen would doubtless have experimented with the cut and setting of their sails in the light of their particular needs. A lugsail would have met the needs of the whalemen, while the normal square sail offered so little manoeuvrability that it cannot have been very suitable for whaling.

Meanwhile, development in the Mediterranean had not been standing still. Rome was still the dominant naval power, her fleet divided into thirteen squadrons under the control of the regents of the various districts, which together made up the great empire of Rome. The fleet was needed not so much to fight wars, for, although there were many small ones, there were few of any importance. The battle of Actium and the defeat of Mark Antony had removed the threat to Octavian's assumption of power in Rome, and, with the possible exception of the 30-year war against the Vandals from A.D. 440 to 470, there were only local wars to test the might of Roman sea power. The first serious challenge to Roman mastery of the Mediterranean came in A.D. 825 with the rise of Mussulman power. But the demands of both the war against the Vandals and the Mussulman threat had a considerable impact on the design of warships.

Actium had demonstrated that, for all its ponderous strength, the heavily built, multi-banked galley could be defeated by the versatile tactics of lighter and more mobile galleys. As has been seen, the lighter galleys used at Actium were based on a design evolved in the Adriatic and known to the Romans as *liburnians*, later further developed into *dromons* of two sizes, one pulling two banks of oars, the other single-banked. In the *Tactica* of the Emperor Leo, descriptions of three types of *dromon* are given, but in effect his first two descriptions refer to one type – the larger of the two main ones – merely specifying small differences in weapons and manning. Nevertheless, in spite of Actium, the heavy galley was still being built because it alone was large enough to mount the relatively new weapons of naval warfare – the catapult and the *corvus*, or boarding bridge.

The Roman war against the Vandals was very largely a land war, but Rome was taking no chances of losing her command of the sea through the heavy financial calls of a land war, and continued to devote a reasonable proportion of the national taxes to the building of warships. A new development was the replacement of the relatively small paddling oars, used on galleys for centuries, by longer sweeps, up to 30 ft (9 m) in length or even longer in some cases. The introduction of the longer oar brought with it the

51

necessity of pivoting it further from the rower, and this was solved by the invention of the *apostis*, a strong external timber running parallel to the gunwale and supported on a light longitudinal framework. This external timber carried the thole pins against which the oars were secured. Because, for reasons of strength, the loom of these long oars had to be thicker than that of the paddling oars and probably too thick for a rower to grasp comfortably in his hands, handles, known as *manetti*, were fixed to the loom, enabling three or four men to be employed on each oar. The rowers were arranged in steps, known as *alla scaloccio*, so that each man was at the right height to operate the oar comfortably. The longer oars provided greater leverage and therefore greater speed was attainable, possibly as much as 8 or 9 knots in short bursts, depending on the strength of the rowers.

The rise of Mussulman sea power in the Mediterranean during the ninth century A.D. created new problems for Rome. By 825 they had captured Crete and Sicily, and were consolidating their hold on the north African coast, which formed the southern boundary of the Mediterranean. To counter this Arab threat, Rome needed even faster galleys with better armament. A small increase in speed was achieved by lengthening the oar to 50 ft (15 m) and increasing the number of rowers to as many as seven. There were no radical developments in warship weaponry, beyond an increase in range and efficiency of the catapult and the further development of the *falcas* (a spar with a curved iron head shaped like a sickle to cut through an enemy's rigging). What was a new development was the provision of protective armour, for the Mussulmans were adept at the use of combustibles, including some mixtures which detonated when thrown on the deck of an enemy ship. Some of the Roman galleys were protected against such combustibles by a leather or felt lining on the upper deck, or thick woollen cloth soaked in vinegar.

The Mussulman fleet introduced a new dimension into naval warfare in the Mediterranean by introducing mixed squadrons of galleys and sailing ships. We have no firm date for the appearance of the lateen rig, but it is certain that, although it first appeared in the western world in the Mediterranean (its name is derived from the word 'latin'), it originated many years earlier among the Arab nations. Although in the lateen rig the sail is still set on a yard, the rig is essentially fore-and-aft, enabling a ship to sail about five points off the wind. It is indeed possible that these mixed Mussulman squadrons incorporated sailing ships rigged lateen-style, for Mussulman and Arab worked in very close co-operation. The Romans did, in fact, themselves build some sailing warships, though not as yet to mix with galleys in a fleet, but rather to attempt to contain the wave of Arab pirates.

More dramatic than the development of the Roman warship was that of the Roman merchant vessel, if size and rig is the criterion. Lucian, it will be remembered, gave the size of a Roman corn ship as 180 feet by 45 feet by 44 feet, but as the Roman era approached its end considerably larger cargo ships were built, particularly for the transport of marble and obelisks to Italy. These were the ships which introduced the three-masted rig, which became the standard big sailing ship rig for the next thousand years. They set a square sail on each mast, but on the mainmast an additional topsail, known as a *supparum*, was set, almost certainly a triangular sail with its apex at the masthead. Only the corn ships from

Left: Fourteenth century manuscript illustration of Greek Fire being used from a dromon.

Left: A third century
mosaic from Rome showing
a ship under sail at the
harbour entrance.

Alexandria were allowed to sail into Roman ports with their topsails spread; all other sailing ships had to strike them off the harbour entrance before coming into port. A further feature of these great merchant ships was a platform extending beyond the sternpost, rather in the fashion of the later stern gallery. It was covered with an awning for the comfort of the captain and important passengers.

In these last years of Roman dominance of the Mediterranean, a new sea power was arising in the Adriatic. The independent republic of Venice was becoming richer through trade than Rome herself, and skilled shipwrights were creating a formidable navy both to protect the fast-growing merchant fleet and to further Venetian interests, particularly in the eastern Mediterranean, through which flowed the great volume of trade brought by the overland caravans from the Far East. And at the same time, on the other side of the Italian mainland, the republic of Genoa was developing on very similar lines. The two were in time certain to fight each other for supremacy at sea. A series of naval campaigns was fought, mainly between galley fleets, although something approaching the galleasse, in which oars were subsidiary to the sail as motive power, began to make its appearance during these wars. This was a big step forward, for in the galley the sail was invariably lowered and the mast unstepped in battle so that the rowers should be unhindered in their task, and the hull design of the galley always reflected this pre-eminence of the rower. As a result, the galley hull had, for the times, an exaggerated length-to-

beam ratio, resulting in a vessel that needed a calm sea for maximum efficiency and was virtually useless in a fighting capacity when the waves began to rise. The design of the hull of the galleasse, on the other hand, resembled much more the sailing ship hull, with a length-to-beam ratio of about 4 to 1, sturdy and able to operate even in an angry sea. The fighting galley was essentially a Mediterranean warship, useless in other climates, but even in those usually calm waters storms could blow up with extreme rapidity, rendering the galley temporarily impotent even in its home seas. It was at times such as this that the galleasse proved a notable advance.

Venice has another small claim to shipbuilding skill: the design of the gondola, which dates back at least to the eleventh century and possibly earlier. It is of fairly typical eastern Mediterranean design with ornamental bow and stern pieces, but characterized by the *ferro*, an iron beak, in shape not unlike a halbard projecting upwards from the bow piece. This is a hull design which has not changed through the centuries, although up to the sixteenth century gondolas had a richly coloured awning supported on an arched framework, with both ends open, in place of the usual heavy black cabin of today.

A lack of contemporary illustration makes it difficult to assess the state of ship development in the more distant parts of the world, although it can be taken as certain that a great many far eastern countries were involved in maritime trade. Certainly, by the twelfth century the word *djong*, (meaning ship or large vessel) was an integral part of the Javanese language and spreading to China, Japan and southern India, indicating that ships in those areas had at least reached the large vessel size. The word is the origin of the term 'junk', used in the early days in western countries to describe many different types of eastern ship. The vessel which we now know as a junk (a flat-bottomed, high-sterned ship with square bows overhanging the water) may not necessarily have been anything like the vessels known as junks originally. But in most seafaring countries there is a continuity of design – at least, until some revolutionary advance, such as the invention of gunpowder or the introduction of the steam engine, necessitates radical change – and it is probable that, even in the earliest days, the basic junk design which we know today was found to answer best to the wind and sea conditions of the Pacific and Indian Oceans.

Between Europe and the Far East, particularly among the Arab nations bordering the Indian Ocean and the Persian Gulf, the dhow was deve-

Left: Venetian galleasse model of the thirteenth century.

Right: Arab astronomers at Constantinople and some of the navigational instruments which they developed.

Below: Illustrations from *Linschoten's Voyages* (1596) showing the Chinese junk as sixteenth century European explorers saw it.

loping. The general hull shape followed the Egyptian or Phoenician pattern, probably because both Egyptian and Phoenician ships had traded in those waters since the earliest years of maritime expansion and these had served as a model for local building. The great contribution of the Arabs, however, was the evolution of the lateen rig, which they certainly introduced very early on, though no approximate date has yet been established. It has been suggested that the normal light and steady winds of the area, combined with the tropical heat in which rowers became too quickly exhausted to serve as reliable motive power, provided the impetus for the evolution of a sail plan which was flexible

enough to provide forward motion to a ship even when the wind blew from forward of the beam. The Arabs were experienced seamen – for example, they were considerably quicker off the mark than the men of the West in the invention and practical use of navigational instruments, and they led the West in the use of charts – and the adaptation of a square sail to a lateen sail was a reasonably logical step, requiring no more than the slinging of the yard fore-and-aft, instead of athwartships, and setting it at an angle to the mast, instead of square. Be that as it may, the lateen rig originated among the Arabs, quickly spreading to the Mediterranean upon the realization that it was a highly efficient sail plan for small vessels.

About other types of Eastern vessel, the records are silent. The big outrigger war canoes of the Pacific Islanders certainly have a long history, and were described by the first men from the West to penetrate those waters in the sixteenth century as very much like they are today. Unquestionably, they pre-dated the arrival of western traders and explorers by a long time, possibly centuries. But there are no writings and no contemporary illustrations of the craft used by these peoples. One can only guess that their seagoing vessels developed on lines similar to those of other maritime countries.

The Hanseatic League

It is not possible to give an exact date for the formation of the loose but effective federation of German maritime towns which became known as the Hanseatic League. It was originally formed as a sort of alliance of German towns with a common interest in expansion eastward along the southern coast of the Baltic Sea – a political association, almost, to protect the rights of Germans who settled in the Baltic lands. But this initial loose federation quickly gave way to a stronger organization, based on the Wendish towns of Lübeck, Hamburg, Lüneburg, Wismar, Rostock and Stralsund, whose basic concern was the protection and growth of trade. The first meeting linking these towns was held in 1256, and although the initial objective was to stimulate seaborne trade in the Baltic and concentrate it as much as possible in the hands of the Hanse towns, interest very quickly spread to the growing trade with the west, particularly with Holland and England, and that, too, was brought as far as possible under the control of the league.

The main method of stimulating and attracting trade was to set up 'hansas' in the trading countries and, bargaining from federated strength, extract preferential treatment and, if possible, monopolies in certain classes of goods. As early as 1226 the merchants of Cologne set up a hansa in London, followed in 1266 and 1267 by hansas established by the merchants of Hamburg and Lübeck. Eventually, all three combined in 1282 to form the Gild-hall of the Germans, in order to speak with a single voice. Because of the rich Norwegian trade in iron, copper, timber and fish, a hansa was set up in Bergen in 1343. All these hansas enjoyed special trade facilities, the Gild-hall in London setting up 'counters', or trading settlements, in Lynn, Boston, Hull, York, Norwich, Ipswich, Yarmouth and Bristol, virtually controlling most of the foreign trade in these towns. By 1422 the London hansa had become known as the Steelyard because of the method employed of weighing merchandise by means of a pivoted steel beam, and it claimed right of jurisdiction over all the other counters in England.

Seaborne trade means ships, and under the strong, centralized control of the league, the building of ships in the

various Hanse towns proceeded apace. There was no attempt by the league to dictate to its members the sort of ships that they should build; there was just continual encouragement from the central organization to keep pace with the growth in the volume of trade. But, as the waters of the Baltic, North Sea and English Channel were as frequently rough as smooth, a new type of ship was evolved, designed to sail efficiently whatever the state of the sea. This was known as the 'Hansa cog', and it is pictured on the seals of many of the Hanse towns, those of Elbing, Wismar and Harderwijk being particularly interesting. They show a departure in design from the usual curved bow, which had been such a feature of ship design in those waters, and show instead a straight stem at an angle of about 60 degrees to the horizontal. This was carried down without any curve and fixed to a long, straight keel, which terminated in a sternpiece, also straight, set at an angle of about 75 degrees to the horizontal. The long keel would

obviously give a good grip on the water, ideal for sailing in rough seas, though, if used with a fore-and-aft sail plan, it would make a vessel very hard-headed to steer. But these Hansa cogs still set a single square sail, with braces and bowlines so that the sail could be trimmed to provide forward motion to the ship when the wind was abeam. With this square rig, the straight keel was the best answer in rough water for a deeply laden cargo ship.

It is impossible to estimate the size of a Hansa cog from the town seals, but from other evidence the average deep-water cog apparently had an overall length of about 100 ft (30 m), a beam of about 25 ft (8 m), and a draught of about 10 ft (3 m), which in modern measurement terms would mean a ship of around 280 tons. This was a fairly large size for a merchantman in those early days of the thirteenth century.

Another feature of the Hansa cog were castles built forward and aft, a small one forward and a large one aft. In the earliest seals they appear to have

secured with the points. Most sails were tanned with a solution prepared from bark, to prevent rot. Already the cordage used was hemp rope, where formerly it had been made from strips of hide.

Inevitably, the league's monopoly of trade brought national jealousy in its wake. The merchants of England saw no reason why their nation's trade should be dominated by this German federation, and as they grew in political strength they put pressure on their government to bring it to an end. The companies of Merchant Adventurers, set up in England in the sixteenth century to open up new trade routes, commanded sufficient political strength to force the withdrawal of the Hanseatic privileges in England, and, moreover, exacted a concession allowing the formation of an English counter in Hamburg, to compensate for the German retention of the Steelyard in London. Holland,

capturing the bulk of the North Sea fishery, the Baltic grain trade and the French salt trade, broke away from Hanseatic control in the early sixteenth century, and Bergen, in Norway, quickly followed suit.

The league itself lingered on, now completely impotent to enforce trade concessions in foreign countries, and growing less cohesive through the incessant quarrelling among its constituent German towns. In the end, it consisted only of Lübeck, Bremen and Hamburg, charged with upholding the name and inheritance of the league, even though the name now meant nothing in terms of trade and there was no inheritance worth upholding. All that was left were the empty buildings, erected in the foreign cities in the days of the Hanseatic ascendancy. In the end these were sold, the Steelyard in London in 1852, and the counters in Bergen and Antwerp in 1775 and 1863 respectively.

Above left: The town seal of Elbing.

Top and above: The seals of Wismar and Harderwijk. These Hanseatic towns' seals depicting the innovatory Hansa cog date from the fourteenth century.

Right: The Hanseatic cog of c.1380 which was unearthed from a Bremen mudflat in 1962, at the Deutsches Schiffahrts Museum.

been appendages added later to the basic hull, probably to provide observation platforms while the ship was under sail, but later seals seem to show them as integral parts of the hull, so they were probably incorporated in the design after they had proved their value. Following the early Egyptian pattern, the ends of the deck beams project through the hull planking, to provide additional strength.

The single square sail had an area of about 2,000 sq ft (185 m²), and was fitted with reef points, not in the normal fashion of a square sail which is reefed to the yard, but along the bottom so that the foot of the sail was bunched and

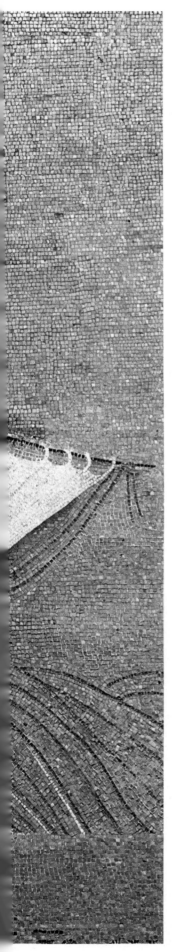

Chapter Three
The Development of the Sailing Ship

The most important development in ship design during the three hundred years from 1200 to 1500 was the substitution of a wooden rudder, hung from the sternpost by means of gudgeons and pintles, for the steering oar projecting over the starboard quarter of a ship. The exact date of this innovation is uncertain, but there is a relief carving of a ship on the font in Winchester Cathedral, which looks as though it is meant to depict a stern rudder. It is not easy to date the carving, but it is thought to be a Belgian work of around 1180. There is a school of thought which holds that the hanging rudder was introduced with the cog – probably with the Hansa cog – and so will not accept that the Winchester carving shows a rudder hung from the sternpost. It is true enough that the carving shows the front edge of the rudder – if it is, in fact, a rudder – projecting somewhat in front of the sternpost, but this could well be a vagary of the carver, not knowing how the new rudders worked.

There is a church in Gotland, called Fide Church, which has a picture of a ship carved into the wall plaster, and there is no question that this carving does depict a ship with a rudder hung from the sternpost. The carving is believed, with some degree of certainty, to have been made in the early years of the thirteenth century, perhaps no more than about forty years later than that in Winchester Cathedral. The hanging rudder is worked by a tiller which is curved round the upper part of the sternpost, and there are several other more or less contemporary paintings and carvings which show the same arrangement of the tiller. By making it curved, it was possible to retain the high Norwegian and Danish sternpost which was a standard design feature of all these early north European vessels.

The carving in Fide Church definitely predates the development of the Hansa cog, but it would appear reasonably certain that the initial deve-

Left: Thirteenth century Venetian ship with three masts and two oars for steering. (From a mosaic in St Mark's Cathedral, Venice.)

lopment of the hanging rudder at the stern took place in the Baltic or in west German waters around the Elbe estuary. And it could just as easily have originated in Hansa ships before the development of the cog. The seal of Dover, one of the most important of the Cinque Ports, is accurately dated 1284, and shows a ship still employing a steering oar, though on the port side of the ship instead of the starboard (unquestionably a mistake on the carver's part).

If we may take the ship in the seal of Dover as typical of the state of English development at this time, the Viking influence on the general lines of the hull is still abundantly evident. But forecastles and aftercastles, which began to come in during the last years of the twelfth century as separate structures built on deck inside the hull, have now become an integral part of the hull and project forward of the stem and aft of the stern. A third castle is shown built on the mast above the yard, and, in a miniature decorating a manuscript produced in 1279 for Queen Eleanore of Castile during the Crusades, fighting men are shown in this mast castle. The Dover seal, however, almost certainly shows a merchant vessel and the mast castle was probably used by a lookout. For the rest, the Dover ship shows the standard square sail on a central mast; however, it has a distinct bowsprit, by no means as highly steeved as in the Mediterranean where the purpose was to set a square spritsail under it, but mounted at a modest angle to the horizontal and obviously meant as an aid to trimming the mainsail. Most likely, the sail had bowlines on each leech which could be rove through a block or hole at the end of the bowsprit to hold the leading edge taut when close to the wind. There are no fittings for the use of oars in the Dover ship, and she was definitely built for use under sail alone, though, no doubt, she carried a few sweeps for temporary use in a flat calm.

Most north European ports of standing during

the thirteenth and fourteenth centuries had official seals showing contemporary ships, and from these it is possible to note small design changes as the centuries advanced. A similar source of information is the paintings on walls and ceilings of churches, devotional works calling on the Almighty to safeguard local sailors on their voyages. The most significant change is the gradual growth of the castle forward into a raised forecastle deck fully incorporated into the hull design, with the side planking carried up to the level of the castle floor. Simultaneously, we find the aftercastle expanded so that it terminates a few feet abaft the mast, forming a distinct poop deck fitting snugly onto the gunwale to provide a raised deck aft. The earlier representations of this period still show the Viking influence on hull designs, with the long extended bow and the familiar detachable dragon's head at the top of the sloping stempost, but they have been adapted to modern requirements by the addition of the three castles (the third at the masthead) and the hanging rudder fixed to the sternpost. Their general lines suggest that they were still shallow-draught vessels. Later illustrations, towards the end of the fourteenth century, show a very different kind of ship, approaching the typical medieval vessel in design, with raised forecastle and poop, low waist and obvious deep draught. It was this deepening of the draught, perhaps even more than the invention of the hanging rudder, that really separates the Viking design and the ocean-going ship of later centuries.

There was still only one mast and single square sail on these north European vessels – a surprising slowness in sail plan development in view of the fact that two- and three-masted ships were becoming common in the Mediterranean. After all, by the fourteenth century, a whole series of Crusades had been fought, in which armies from Germany, France and England had been carried to the Levant in Mediterranean ships on which two or three masts were the rule, rather than the exception. There is indeed a record of Richard I attacking a huge Saracen ship with three masts at Acre, so there was no lack of knowledge among north European nations of this extended rig. Richard's own ship, the *Trenchemer*, though sometimes described as a galley, was, in fact, a *dromon* with two masts, although there is no record to say whether she was square-rigged or had the more usual Mediterranean lateen rig of the time. She carried rowers, of course, to drive her along when the wind would not serve.

According to a list compiled during the reign of Richard I (1189–1199), English naval vessels of the period were of the species known as 'galleys', 'gallions', 'busses', 'dromons', 'vissers' or 'ursers', 'barges' and 'snakes'. The English galley was really the galleasse, of basic Mediterranean galley design, but having mast and sail as her primary means of propulsion and rowers who only took over when the wind was foul. The gallion was pure galley, but with only a single bank of oars, small and used only in calm seas. The buss was, with the dromon, the biggest ship in the fleet, of heavy build, deep draught and capacious holds. With single mast and square sail, she was slow and ponderous in the water. She was used in warlike operations as a

Right: Henry I returning to England by ship, possibly an *esnecca*.

transport, and a report made in March 1170 stated that at the foundering of a single buss 400 lives were lost. This statement has been questioned many times, but there seems to be no good reason for doubting its truth. Twelfth-century vessels were a great deal larger than many people imagine, and, as this particular buss was engaged in transport work at the time of her loss, she could well have been carrying as many men again as the number of her crew. And a crew of 200, or even more, was certainly not unusual at this period: Richard of Devizes, writing in about 1195, notes that a large buss could carry, besides her crew, up to eighty knights with their horses, eighty footmen, and twenty-eight servants, and on an expedition carried provisions for a year, as well as a very complete outfit of spare parts for self-refits, including three spare rudders, thirteen anchors, thirty oars, two sails, three sets of all kinds of ropes used on board and duplicates of all her gear, except for the mast and boat.

The dromon could, at this time, be almost any large ship of war. As mentioned in an earlier chapter, she originated in the Mediterranean as a double-banked galley, fast and manoeuvrable (in English her name means 'runner'). By the time of the Crusades, there were two distinct types, one of them being a very large, high-sided galley, with both sides flaring outwards at upper deck level. The evidence for this rests in the story of Rognvald's voyage from the Orkneys to the Mediterranean and Palestine. Off Sardinia his six longships sighted two Saracen dromons, and, after taking counsel with his captains, Rognvald decided to attack one of them by running as close alongside as possible. He and one other longship lay alongside the after quarter of the dromon, two more amidships, and the last two forward. The traditional defence against such boarding tactics was to pour brimstone and burning pitch onto the decks of the attackers, but when the dromon tried to do so, it all fell into the sea outside the longships, so great was the overhang of the dromon's sides. So the great dromon was captured, stripped, burned and her crew sold as slaves. The date was 1180.

Right: Ships taking
Crusaders to the Holy
Land in the thirteenth
century. Weatherly craft
were needed for the long
voyage from northern
Europe.

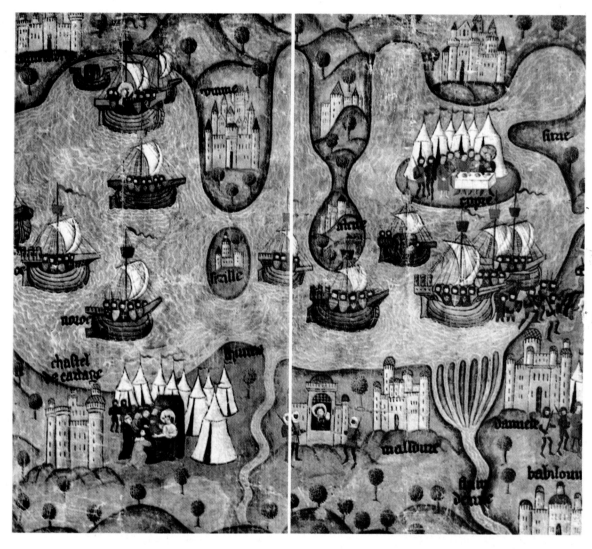

Right: Ships taking
Crusaders to the Holy
Land in the thirteenth
century. Weatherly craft
were needed for the long
voyage from northern
Europe.

The other type of Mediterranean dromon was a two- or three-masted sailing ship, again very large, often used as a transport for troops and with space for horses in the hold. She could be rowed when the wind failed. This was the type used in England, though solely as a fighting ship, not as a transport, and with only a single mast. Her fighting crew were archers and arquebusiers. She too could be rowed in calm weather or to bring her into the position in battle where her bowmen could perform most effectively.

A visser, or urser, was a flat-bottomed craft of shallow draught, used for the transport of horses, again having a single mast and sail. The barge was very similar to the barge of today, a ship of burden, flat-bottomed to take the ground when neaped by the tide. She was the direct ancestor of the barges still to be seen in the coastal waters of Holland and East Anglia today, a remarkable example of a design which has scarcely altered in the 800 years of its existence.

The snake was the English translation of the *esnecca*, a Scandinavian longship of the eighth to eleventh centuries. It first appeared in England as a despatch boat for taking messages from the commander of a fleet to other ships, but it quickly developed into a sort of royal yacht. Henry I and Henry II both had *esneccas* in which they made visits of state, and ambassadors were frequently sent to their stations abroad in them.

There is nothing to indicate that any of these ships had more than a single central mast, though there are some vague suggestions that they may sometimes have spread more than one sail on it. Roger of Wendover, writing in about 1190, mentions three sails set on the single mast, but unfortunately gives no details of how and where they were spread. If it were really so, it would be unusual, as, outside the Mediterranean and Arab waters, shipping generally had not yet progressed beyond the single square sail.

Other types of ship used in English waters were the schuyt, or schuit, and the cog. The name 'shuyt' was applied to any small sailing merchant ship, and was the Dutch word for a flat-bottomed river boat, built with a great breadth of beam and with a square tuck to the sides. The word was

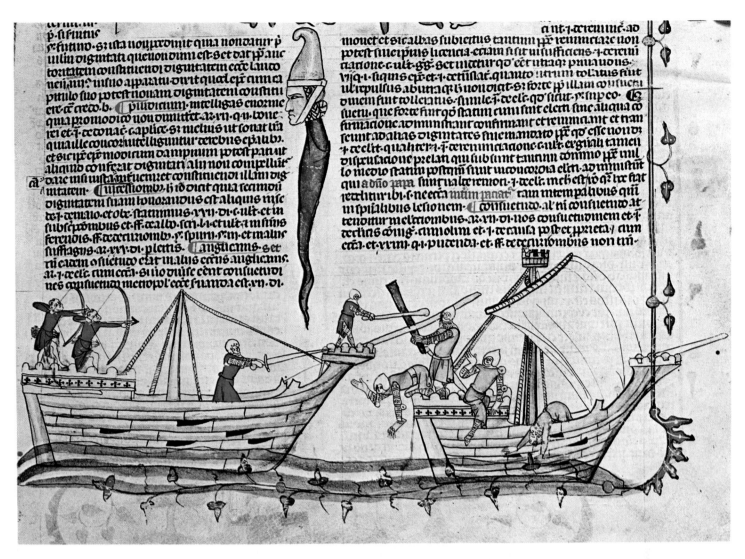

used of ships in England, not because of any particular similarity to the Dutch *schuyt*, but because the term described small Dutch vessels and it was convenient to apply the Dutch word to any merchant ship that was small.

There has been much argument about what a cog really was. In his uncompleted *History of the Royal Navy*, published in 1847, Sir Nicholas Nicolas said of the English cogs that 'they were short and of great breadth, like a cockle shell, whence they are said to have derived their name'. This might conceivably be true of the early thirteenth-century, as no description or illustration of so early a cog exists, but it was certainly not true of the second half of the thirteenth and the whole of the fourteenth centuries, when the term 'cog' was frequently applied to some of the biggest ships then sailing. Possibly the word came to be used to describe any sort of vessel indiscriminately, much as today we use the word 'ship' to describe a whole variety of seagoing vessels of different sizes and different functions. This might be a later application of the word, but the Issue Rolls for 1210 record that the King hired five ships for his service 'without a cog'.

The English cog was unlike the Hansa cog in that it did not have the straight stem and long keel. It was built with the traditional curved stem that joined the keel considerably further aft than in the Hansa variety. It certainly had the three castles, at bow, stern and masthead, and, while being designed as a sturdy and capacious merchant ship, was liable to be called up for war in an emergency, frequently forming the major constituent of a fleet. Thus, the Cinque Ports fleet employed in the war against Scotland of 1299 to 1300 consisted of fifteen cogs, eight ships, two snakes, and five other vessels whose names are given without any designation of type.

To celebrate his victory over the French at the battle of Sluys in 1340, Edward III had gold nobles struck which showed him standing in a cog. It is difficult to see, as it is in all contemporary seals, coins, etc., whether the ends of the deck beams project through the wooden hull, as they do in the Hansa cog, although there are a number of small circles shown on the strakes which could be taken as a medallist's conception of the ends of deck beams. Although no tiller is shown attached to the rudder, a good example of the noble shows quite clearly the method of attachment to the sternpost by gudgeons and pintles. There was no room on the noble to show any detail of the building of the forecastle and aftercastle, but the aftercastle is large and built forward in the nature of a poop deck.

Various new types of ship are mentioned in the reign of Edward III, but it is difficult today to be sure of what they all exactly were. The most interesting names used, in view of what the words were later to be associated with, were the 'carrack', which started as a description of ships of Spanish or Genoan origin calling at English ports, but later came to be used loosely in England as applying to any ship of large dimensions used as a trader, and the 'dogger', a fishing vessel which took its name from the Dutch word for a cod-fishing boat. Many people believe that this

Right: Gold noble commemorating the Battle of Sluys, showing Henry III standing on board a cog.

vessel took its name from the Dogger Bank, but it is more likely that the bank was named after the vessels which fished it, or the fish that they caught. An Icelandic report of the end of the fourteenth century mentions thirty English *fiski-duggur* fishing in Icelandic waters, and it is clear from many English accounts that this was a yearly custom. So the dogger must have been a fairly large fishing vessel to be able to venture annually into those inhospitable waters.

Among the Rolls at Carlton Ride, in Norfolk, there is a detailed account of the building, at King's Lynn in 1336, of the galley *La Phelipe*. Many of the items listed in this account are familiar to us today, including (to use the modern spellings) a capstan, hawsers, pulleys, stays and backstays, painters, sheets, bolt-ropes, cables, tow ropes, sounding lines, seizings and hatches. Other items with which she was fitted cannot be identified from the old English names (unless a

'david' could mean a davit, which is highly improbable). We know that the galley had one mast, which cost £10, and one bowsprit, costing £3. Her anchor was made from 1,100 lbs (500 kg) of Spanish iron, and she carried five smaller anchors, in addition, at a total cost of £23 10s. 3d. Her sail, dyed red, took 640 ells of cloth and to it were attached 'wyne-wews', dyed black, of 220 ells. Perhaps a 'wyne-wew' was a bonnet (an additional strip of cloth which could be laced to the foot of a square sail to increase its size, in order to take advantage of a following wind). Certainly bonnets were being widely used at that time and a sail might have two or even three bonnets. The galley had no pump, but water that had collected in her bilges could be lifted out by a 'winding-balies', into which the water was put by two 'spojours'. It is difficult to conjecture what this could be, but presumably it enabled the vessel to be kept reasonably dry. Her sides were caulked with 'mosso' and then covered with grease, and her bottom was paid with a mixture of tar, oil, pitch and resin. The accounts record that the master carpenter was paid 6d. a day, ordinary carpenters 5d., 'clinkerers' 4d., 'holderors' 3d. and labourers 2½d.

It is in these Norfolk Rolls that we find the first mention of an English ship with two masts. The date is around 1350, but there can have been very few of them as the largest cogs built – the cog *Thomas*, one of the largest, is recorded as having a tonnage of 240 – had only the single mast. No details of the two masts are given, though one might expect the second to have been a small mizen abaft the mainmast, to help balance the helm. The high forecastle, now fairly standard on larger ships, presented a lot of windage which tended to hold the ship's bows away from the wind, and a small sail aft would have done much to counter this effect. However, this is pure speculation in the light of modern knowledge of aerodynamics; the fourteenth-century navigator may not have appreciated the wind's effect on a built-up bow.

In the Mediterranean, Venice was arising as the chief maritime power, and for his Crusade to the Holy Land in 1268 Louis IX ordered most of his ships to be built in Venice, with rather fewer in Genoa. There are records of these ships and we know that those built in Venice had an overall length of 85 ft (26 m), keel of 57 ft (17·4 m), maximum beam of 21 ft (6·4 m) and depth from rail to keel of 22 ft (6·7 m). Internally they were fitted with two complete decks, upper and lower, and aft they had two short decks in the form of what we would now call a quarter-deck

Right: Detail from a painting by Carpaccio showing a Venetian carrack of the fifteenth century.

well reflect a desire of Mediterranean shipwrights to produce a more robust ship, better able than the current Mediterranean design to hold her own in waters more generally hostile than those of the Mediterranean. This is not to say that the lateen sail was suddenly discarded – it remained the most common sail plan in local use in the Mediterranean – but that, in an era of expanding trade, there was a growing recognition of the fact that, for use in more distant waters, distinct advantages were to be gained from the use of the square sail, mainly because of the difficulty of dipping the long lateen yard round the mast when tacking.

This reversion to the square sail in Mediterranean ships heralded the birth of the ship known as the 'carrack', which in its earliest days was a two-masted ship carrying one large square sail on the mainmast, with a smaller square sail on a mizen stepped well aft, though in some carracks the mizen sail was lateen instead of square. She was fairly bluff in the bows, with a rounded stern ending in a square counter, a fore castle which was so much an integral part of the ship's hull that it was virtually the same as the modern forecastle, and after castle which was unquestionably a quarter-deck. Following the Mediterranean pattern, her hull was carvel-built with the hull planks fixed edge to edge, whereas north European ships still retained clinker construction with overlapping hull strakes.

An important mid-fifteenth-century model of a Spanish ship in the Prins Hendrik Museum at Rotterdam – it originally hung as a votive offering in a church at Mataro, near Barcelona – gives us a good picture of a Spanish ship of the years just before the first great explosion of discoveries began with the Spanish and Portuguese voyages to west and east. The model was originally two-masted, with main and mizen, but although only a single mast remains today, the result of loss or breakage over the centuries, a most significant point about it is that in the early days of its existence someone tried to convert it into a three-masted ship by adding a third mast stepped on the forecastle. The model is described as that of a Spanish não, but as the word is the Spanish for 'ship', it does not get us very far. Today we can say with some certainty that it originally represented a two-masted carrack, and that later on in the fifteenth century someone tried to bring it up to date by adding a third mast.

The carrack design was more or less standard for all large ships in the Mediterranean from about 1400 onwards, the original two masts being increased to three as ships were built bigger. It was during the fifteenth century that, almost worldwide, warships took a great leap forward in size, and, whereas a ship of 250 tons was large

and poop deck. These were added to provide space for cabins for nobles and knights. From mosaics at San Marco in Venice it appears that these ships were three-masted, but it is not possible to be sure as the mosaics are highly stylized. The ships were fitted with a lateen rig and steered with a steering oar on either quarter.

The hanging rudder at the stern came later to the Mediterranean, and its arrival was possibly contemporary with the re-adoption of the square sail in place of the lateen. This gives a date of about 1350, which is to some extent confirmed by a Spanish miniature of that date that shows several ships with square sails and rudders fixed to the sternpost. There was by that time a fairly lively trade between the Mediterranean states and northern Europe, and the northern cog was no stranger in many Mediterranean ports. The ships in this Spanish miniature all bear a distinct resemblance to the northern cog, which could

Left: Contemporary model of a fifteenth century ship from Motaro, Spain.

Right: Late fifteenth century caravel.

S o we come to the caravel, one of the most discussed and controversial ships of the period. The word itself is Portuguese and was originally the generic term used in that country to describe small ships used mainly for fishing. This meaning of the term, however, died out quite early, and the word was reborn at the beginning of the fifteenth century and applied to various types of small ship. It earned a place in the history of the sea with the Spanish and Portuguese voyages of discovery of the last decade of the fifteenth century, almost all of which were made in caravels.

All that is positively known about true caravels is that they were relatively small, of sturdy build, with a maximum draught of 6 to 7 feet, and were variously rigged on three masts. One of their early-recognized characteristics was that they were handy ships which could beat to windward, and the early Portuguese voyages of exploration down the west coast of Africa were successful purely because of this. Although always encouraged by Prince Henry the Navigator, who had established himself at Sagres in about 1430, no Portuguese pilot had yet dared to round the Cabo de Não, on the western bulge of Africa, a short distance along the coast from Cape Bojador, because of strongly held superstitious beliefs that (a) a ship could never get back against the prevailing northerly winds, and (b) the sea at the equator boiled and would melt the pitch and tar with which the bottom of a ship was paid. A rough translation of a Spanish couplet of the time, using the English version 'Cape Nun' for Cabo de Não, runs:

When old Cape Nun heaves into sight
Turn back, me lad, or else – goodnight.

However, Gil Eannes, captain of a Portuguese ship and one of Prince Henry's trained pilots, successfully rounded Cabo de Não in 1434 sailing the new caravel which gave him full confidence in his ability to return home by tacking against the northerlies.

This Portuguese caravel used a full lateen sail plan, with a big lateen sail on the mainmast, a smaller one on the mizen, and a very small one on a mast stepped still further aft, which we would today call a 'bonaventure' mast or, perhaps, a 'jigger' mast. The full lateen-rigged caravel, known as a *caravela latina*, while admirable for making to windward in seas no more than moderate, was always labour-intensive, as the spars had to be dipped round the mast on every change of tack. Moreover, they were much more difficult to handle in a rough sea and required a much bigger crew to do so. So, for ocean voyages, the *caravela latina* adopted the main elements of

at the beginning of the century, by the end of it ships of four times that tonnage were being built. Indeed, an official report reached England in 1425 that a Spanish carrack of 1,300 'botts', or tons, was being built at Barcelona, with a second of 1,000 'botts' also under construction. If the report was true, these would be quite exceptional, and a long way in advance of the general run of shipping at that time. But by the end of the century, only seventy-five years later, ships of this size were becoming, if not commonplace, by no means remarkable. Obviously, so large a ship could not be efficiently operated with a two-masted rig, even with the addition of topsails above the large mainsail, and so a third mast, and frequently a fourth in the larger ships, became a necessity.

The early Mediterranean carrack, following the re-adoption of the square sail, appeared first with a smaller square sail set on the mizen, but in a very few years reverted to a small lateen sail on the mizen which was found to provide a better balance for steering the ship on a wind. The lateen mizen then became a standard feature throughout the whole life of the carrack, and, indeed, of its smaller sister the caravel, and was also adopted in north European waters, as soon as the third mast became a regular feature of a ship's rig.

Portuguese caravel
(c.1500)

Length 75 ft (22·9 m) *Keel* 50 ft (15·2 m) *Beam* 25 ft (7·6 m)
Draught 6 ft (1·8 m) *Hold* 9 ft (2·7 m) *Burthen* 65 tons
Complement 30

The caravel is the kind of ship most closely identified with the great voyages of discovery made by Europeans in the fifteenth and sixteenth centuries. Caravels accompanied Diaz, da Gama and Columbus on their expeditions, and Columbus's' favourite ship on his voyage of 1492 was the *Nina*, a caravel similar to the one portrayed here. The qualities that recommended the caravel to explorers were her size, large enough for ocean voyages but small enough to manoeuvre close inshore, her shallow draught, which made it safe for her to enter uncharted rivers and bays, her rig, especially the fore-and-aft rig which was very weatherly, and her general seaworthiness, inherited from her sturdy fishing-boat ancestors. She did not have much space for cargo, but she was light enough to be rowed if there was not enough wind to fill her sails.

The small drawing shows the *caravela latina* rig, while the large drawing shows the same ship as a *caravela redonda* with square sails on the foremast. This transformation might be accomplished by moving the middle mast of the *caravela latina* to the bows and re-rigging it with square sails, and restaying the forward-sloping mainmast in an upright position.

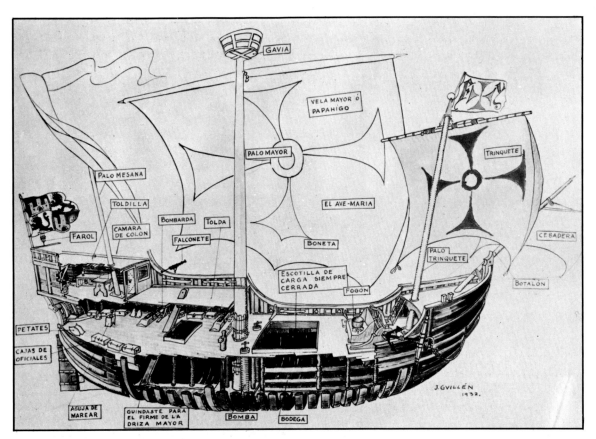

the carrack rig and became square-rigged on fore and main masts, a change of rig which gave her the name of *caravela redonda*. It was in a *redonda*-type vessel that Columbus made his voyage to the new world in 1492 and Ferdinand Magellan made the first circumnavigation of the world between 1519 and 1522.

There has been much discussion and argument about Columbus's ship, the *Santa Maria*, and many experts no longer recognize her as a caravel. About the other two ships in the expedition, the *Pinta* and *Niña*, there is no question at all: the *Pinta* was a *caravela redonda*, and the *Niña* started as a *caravela latina*, but was re-rigged in the Canary Islands as a *caravela redonda*, since the *latina* rig was soon found to be unsuitable for Atlantic waters, particularly when the little fleet picked up the north-east trade wind which square sails were able to make the most of.

Columbus himself described the *Santa Maria* as a '*nao*', which means very little. From about 1460 onwards, carracks were turning into large ships with towering stern galleries, with as many as four small decks being superimposed one above the other in the largest, and of one thing we can be certain: that in 1492 the *Santa Maria* was not a carrack. We also know that by the end of the century the large *caravela redonda* was being built up to a size of 110 or 120 tons. Although her tonnage is not known exactly, the *Santa Maria* may have been of as much as 100 tons burthen, though a more likely figure, on the

evidence of Bartolomé de las Casas in his *Historia de las Indias*, would be 80 to 90 tons. Her overall length was about 80 ft (24 m) and she drew about $6\frac{1}{2}$ ft (2 m) of water. According to contemporary accounts, she was 'somewhat' larger than the *Pinta* (about 60 tons) and the *Niña* (about 50 tons). Being a larger vessel, she carried a more extensive sail plan than the others, a small topsail above the main course and a small spritsail below the bowsprit. Apart from those two sails, she carried the normal *caravela redonda* rig. Perhaps, because she was the Admiral's ship, Columbus decided to call her a *nao* to distinguish her from the two caravels which accompanied her. No original building plans exist, and, though many models have been built and life-size reconstructions attempted, no one really knows with certainty what she looked like. The most convincing description is in the work of the distinguished Spanish marine archaeologist Admiral Guillén y Tato, *La Carabela Santa Maria*, on which was based the reconstruction for the Seville Exposition of 1929.

Meanwhile, a small revolution was taking place in England. As has been mentioned, there was virtually no difference here between the merchant ship and the warship, the trading cog being called up for military service in time of war. The task of the ship in war was merely to

Below: Naval engagement in the late fifteenth century, the Battle of Zonchio (1499).

carry the fighting men to battle, and a sea fight was really no more than a land battle fought at sea, with the same weapons and tactics. But by the fifteenth century it was being realised in England that the cog, generically known as a 'roundship' because of her very low length-to-beam ratio, was unsuitable for maritime warfare and that, for the defence of the seas around the kingdom, special ships designed for the purpose needed to be built. As there was no effective central government agency for defence, it fell to the king to build these ships. During Henry V's war with France he built the *Jesus*, a 'great' ship of 1,000 tons, and this was followed by the *Holigost* (760 tons) and the *Trinity Royal* (540 tons). By the end of the war the king owned

seventeen large ships, seven carracks captured from the Spanish, two barges and twelve ballingers, which were barge-type vessels of large build, capable of carrying 100 men or more. Henry's ships had to be sold on his death to pay his debts, but the practice of building his own ships for purposes of war was followed by his successors, though, being generally impecunious, they hired them out to merchants during the years of peace for use in seaborne trade. Within a few years France and Holland had followed the English lead: in France warships were built and owned by the king and in Holland by individual states.

Even more important in warship development was the introduction of gunpowder. It was first

used in land warfare in Italy in about 1326, and the first guns were issued to ships in England about fifteen years later. These were mainly hand guns, and, although the store accounts of the *Christopher of the Tower*, a cog belonging to Edward III, include three iron cannon with chambers, which means that they were breechloaders, they were not part of the ship's armament, for she had none. Possibly they were part of the equipment of the fighting men carried on board; they were certainly not mounted in the ship as a weapon to be used against other ships.

Gradually, however, the gun began to establish itself as a real naval weapon, no longer merely an adjunct of the fighting men or soldiers, who up to that time had made up what might be called the 'business end' of a warship. As soon as the gun became an integral part of the ship, it gave a new meaning to the term 'warship': it was the mariners, whose only commitment in naval battle had been to work the ship while the fighting men gave battle, who now became the fighting men as well. The whole art of naval warfare was to change, the land battle at sea giving way to a new type of battle, with an entirely different conception of both strategy and tactics. And it meant, too, that the old interchangeability of merchant ship in peace and warship in war was largely a thing of the past.

As the role of the warship changed, so the ship herself had to change to adapt to her new role. A whole series of interacting developments transformed her completely. The advent of the gun, and its own growth in size from the original small anti-personnel weapon to the first ship's cannon, which weighed about 2 tons and fired a 17-pound ball, dictated a significant increase in size of ship. The fifteenth century, during which these changes were taking place, saw the tonnage of the warship increase fourfold, from about 250 tons at the start of the century to about 1,000 tons at its close, much as merchant ships had grown during the same period. This increase in the size of the ship dictated the adoption of a more powerful and complicated rig, from the single mast of 1400 to the three or four masts of 1500, with topsails and topgallants above the courses. The handling of the new rig called not only for larger crews, but also for a higher degree of seamanship among the men, while the gun called for men trained in its use to be incorporated into the warship's crew. The whole concept of a navy was changed, and in every European country with any pretensions to control of the adjacent seas, a new skilled band of seamen arose to man and work the new warships.

For some years the ship's cannon created as many new difficulties as it solved old ones. The only places on board at which it could be mounted to command an adequate field of fire were in the forecastle and aftercastle, or poop. Smaller anti-personnel guns could be carried in the tops to fire down onto the decks of an enemy ship, and at the break of the forecastle and poop decks for use against anyone attempting to carry the ship by boarding her at the waist, where her freeboard was lowest. But, as naval cannon grew in size, so also did their weight, and it was quickly discovered that any ship's stability at sea was adversely affected by having these heavy objects mounted so high above the waterline. The basic elements of marine architecture demanded that all such heavy weights should be mounted as low as possible in the ship, but it took some years to work out that this could only be done by cutting gunports in the ship's side and making some sort of lid to seal them tightly whenever the sea was rough enough to threaten an entry into the ship

The invention of the gunport, cut in the ship's side and closed with a hinged, close-fitting lid of the same thickness as the side strakes, has been attributed to a French shipwright named Descharges, who worked at Brest. The year of the invention is given as 1500, but there is no doubt whatever that the gunport was incorporated in several warships some years before that date. It is possible that the idea came from Spain, where some of the larger carracks had guns firing through gunports cut in the sides of the forecastle and aftercastle. However, these ports do not seem to have been closed with port-lids, but instead usually with a painted shield in the form of a *pavesse* (the shield-shaped emblem which was used to line the gunwales of warships in the

Left: Fifteenth century warship development: guns project through ports cut in the hull. (Anthony Roll)

fifteenth and sixteenth centuries, ostensibly to provide some protection against balls fired by hand-guns, but more probably to accommodate the contemporary love of colour and display in ships of war).

As we have seen, the growth in size of the warship during the fifteenth century was accompanied by a similar growth in the size of the merchant ship (though not yet to quite the same extent). This was especially marked in the Mediterranean, which was still the only channel of trade with the Far East. Rich merchandise from China, Persia, India and Arabia still came to the Levant by the old overland caravan routes and from there was carried to western Mediterranean ports, particularly Venice, for distribution throughout a Europe hungry for the produce of the East. This was a trade that grew phenomenally during the fifteenth century and brought in its wake the need for larger ships to handle it. But trade was expanding elsewhere, too, and in all maritime countries the merchants and ship-owners were alive to the financial benefits which larger cargoes would bring. Larger cargoes meant larger ships, and, although the merchant ship of the period never quite approached the tonnage of the warship, there were many good businessmen who were prepared to venture their money in ships of 500 and even 600 tons, whereas a century earlier a 250-ton ship was considered to be something of a leviathan.

There was, too, a new art spreading across the sea – an art that was quickly to change the whole face of the maritime world. Ptolemy's geographical treatises, lost from sight for over a thousand years, had come to light again, and a new interest in navigation was being born. Many geographers knew that latitude could be calculated by observation of the sun at noon and the Pole Star at night, but it took many years to pass on the methods to the average pilot at sea, many of whom were uneducated and even illiterate. Much of the application of geographical knowledge to a ship at sea was embodied in the work of Prince Henry the Navigator, who set up an establishment at Sagres in 1430 to encourage ships' pilots to study the art, and the work of his nephew, Don Alfonso V, who took on the task when Prince Henry died in 1460. Catalogues were made of the major stars and constellations; charts were drawn up using degrees of latitude and longitude; and the theory of the precession of the equinoxes, originally the work of Hipparchus and preserved by Ptolemy, was revived and studied. During this same century the first astronomical tables, commissioned from learned

geographers by Alfonso X of Castille and known as the Alfonsine Tables, were published in 1483. With their aid, observation of the altitude of sun or star could be translated into latitude, and over the course of the century the astrolabe and the quadrant were introduced, the first of the navigator's tools to measure altitude. In 1475 Johann Muller published his *Ephemerides*, with tables of the sun's declination calculated for the years from 1475 to 1566. With the *Ephemerides*, the Alfonsine Tables and an astrolabe, a ship's pilot could discover his latitude by means of a very simple calculation.

All this was leading to a growing recognition of the fact that there must be a way by sea to every nation in the world whose shores were lapped by the ocean. For far too long most navigators had been content to accept Homer's idea that the earth was a large land mass or island totally encompassed by an immense river, to which he gave the name Okeanus. It was a convenient theory for the navigator whose longest voyages were still rarely made out of sight of land, even though by now all geographers, and probably some navigators, knew that the earth was a sphere. It needed a German geographer, who joined Prince Henry the Navigator for a time at Sagres, to demonstrate the fact to navigators beyond all question. He was Martin

Above: The Polo brothers setting sail from Venice at the start of their second voyage in 1270.

Behaim of Nuremburg, and he is credited with adapting the astrolabe, formerly only used in astronomy, as an instrument of navigation. But of much more importance, and his main claim to remembrance among navigators, is the great globe which he constructed and which showed beyond any doubt that there did indeed exist a route by sea to every country in the world which bordered the ocean. It was the first navigational document to show the existence of antipodes; the first which showed beyond question that there was a sea route to India and China, whose goods were becoming so highly prized in Europe. It is the oldest globe known to exist, and it represents the limit of geographical knowledge in the period which preceded Columbus's first voyage to the west in 1492.

This new navigational knowledge, disseminated from Sagres to the other European nations, was to have an immense impact on ship development, as great indeed as that of the gun. No longer could a merchant shipowner be content to build his ships for coast-hopping voyages; now he had to think of long voyages far out of sight of land, and to design his ships accordingly. Not only did he need a ship stout enough to withstand all that the sea could do to her over the course of a voyage that might last many months, but he had to plan his ship's accommodation to carry enough food, fresh water and essential stores to keep her and her crew in good shape for all that time. He did not yet realize how vast the world's oceans were – Columbus reckoned the distance from the Canary Islands to Japan to be

2,400 miles; in fact it is 10,600 – and when, in a very short space of years, the shipowner was brought face to face with the huge distances involved, he found that he needed still stouter ships, with even more experienced crews, to have some hope of success on these longer trading voyages.

It was not only on the construction and design of the ship's hull that this new concept of world navigation had an effect; it also influenced sails and rigging. It has been noted that even Columbus, Mediterranean-born and trained, had appreciated that the full lateen rig was unsuitable for long ocean voyages and had adopted a modified

Above: Navigation becomes a science: illustration from a sixteenth century treatise, de Vault's *Cosmografia* (1583).

Below: Globes become important aids to navigation because they showed relative distance accurately, without the need for elaborate methods of projection.

Right: A Venetian cog of the sixteenth century, showing the bluff bow and full form amidships.

Below: A near-contemporary seventeenth century print showing Stradanus's ship of the late sixteenth century.

square rig for his ships. This rig (square sail on fore and main masts, and a lateen sail on the mizen) was also adopted in northern Europe, although in those more stormy waters there was little love for the lateen because of the need to dip the yard round the mast every time the ship changed tacks. Nevertheless, it gave a good balance on the helm, the tall lateen sail counteracting the pressure of wind on the high forecastle, and so was accepted until something better should make its appearance. Fortunately, this was already to hand, although it was to be a few years yet before its great advantages over the lateen mizen for the three-masted rig were recognized. This was the sprit, a spar stretched diagonally across a four-sided fore-and-aft sail, with its heel, or forward end, held firmly near the base of the mast. It was not a new idea – Greeks and Romans had used it in small boats, if the evidence of reliefs at Thasos dating from the second century B.C. are to be believed – but it was not introduced into western Europe until the early fifteenth century, almost certainly by the Dutch, as a rig for small coastal craft, for which it proved

much more weatherly than the square sail in the shoal and tidal waters off the Dutch coast.

The sprit rig, where the luff of the sail is held close to the mast and the sail is spread by the spar, can be said to be the first true example of the fore-and-aft rig, more so than a lateen sail spread on a yard. There was nothing to be dipped round the mast when a vessel tacked, and shipowners of the period were quick to see that this led to a distinct saving in the number of men required to handle the ship. Within the space of fifty years, the lateen mizen had virtually disappeared from north European waters.

There can also be no doubt, in spite of some lack of pictorial evidence, that the development of ships in Far Eastern waters was progressing at much the same pace as in the western hemisphere. De Bry, in his many volumes of *Collectiones . . .*, has several illustrations of eastern ships, and they do not differ very greatly in general hull design from their western counter-

Below: A single-masted Javanese *fusta*, from *Linschoten's Voyages*, part of De Bry's *Collectiones.*

parts. In his *Collectiones . . . in Indiam Orientalem* he shows, as an example, a Javanese *fusta*, which is not all that different from a Mediterranean dromon, though shorter and rowed by fewer oarsmen. It has the same raised deck above the rowers to accommodate the fighting men, and the same rounded shelter over the after end of the deck to provide a cabin for the commander. The long pointed ram is mounted at the level of the gunwale, rather higher than in the Mediterranean galleys. A novelty is a stern gallery round the whole of the stern to provide the commander with a private walking place. The *fusta* has two masts, with a single lateen sail on each.

It is difficult to estimate her size from the illustration, because, in common with so many ship artists of the time, De Bry had little sense of perspective or relative sizes, the men pictured on board standing about as tall as one-third of the masts, but from their numbers the vessel could hardly be less than 120 ft (37 m) overall. She has a hanging rudder at the stern and the illustration shows four guns mounted on the gunwale between the rowers, and there was presumably a similar number mounted on the opposite side of the ship.

De Bry's illustration of a trading ship shows a vessel of comparable size, though with a pair of steering oars in place of a rudder. Again, the hull design looks fairly conventional through western eyes, though the whole centre of the ship, from abaft the single mast to the position of the steers-

men, is built up and roofed in, almost certainly to provide protection for the cargo. She carries a single lateen sail and rowers are accommodated in the forward end of the ship, facing forward instead of aft and pushing their oars instead of pulling them. De Bry also illustrates some sailing proas, in outline only, but there are no surrounding objects to permit even the wildest guess at their size. Again there is the single lateen sail, but with a very pronounced curve in the leech, strongly reminiscent of a modern Nile *felucca*, and a large outrigger to provide stability.

This evidence is little enough to go on, but it does offer some indication that in more distant waters the development of the ship was keeping pace, at least in size, with development elsewhere. And this was only to be expected, as seaborne trade in the east was growing in volume, just as it was in the west. There was a lively business, too, in piracy, an activity which has always stimulated the building of fast, weatherly ships, and one can be sure that, in this particular department, the pirates of eastern seas were at least as efficient as those of the west.

With these new ships, and particularly with the new sail plan which their increase in size had dictated, the unknown world was poised like an oyster, ready to be prised open. The century which followed was to witness many voyages of epic proportions, hear many new stories of distant, uncharted waters, and see many new islands and continents drawn in on the map of the world.

Right: An outrigger canoe and other Far Eastern craft. (From *Linschoten's Voyages*)

Henry the Navigator

Henry, Prince of Portugal, and known to history as the Navigator, was the third son of John I of Portugal and, incidentally, a grandson of England's John of Gaunt. He served with distinction in various wars and finally retired from the army to become governor of the Algarve, living at Sagres, near Cape St. Vincent, 'where endeth land and where beginneth sea' as the Portuguese poet Camöens put it. Being an ardent student of geography, he established there a naval 'arsenal' to which he attracted mathematicians and geographers to teach navigation, astronomy and cartography to Portuguese captains and pilots.

In 1455 a papal bull had granted Portugal exclusive jurisdiction over the west African coast of Guinea 'and past that southern shore all the way to the Indians'. Whether Prince Henry consciously accepted the implication in this papal bull that the way to India was round the continent of Africa is uncertain, but he certainly wanted to know what happened beyond the tip of Africa. So he made African exploration one of the aims of his naval 'arsenal' at Sagres, and used the royal revenues to fit out exploring expeditions to push down the African coast, mapping and observing as they went. When these expeditions proved profitable through the discovery of gold in Guinea and the sale of black slaves, as well as increasing knowledge of the globe, Henry found no lack of adventurers ready to sail in his ships into the unknown.

Already the magnetic compass and the chart had made their appearance at sea, though both had severe limitations for purposes of accurate navigation. No navigator, as yet, had any knowledge of the existence of a magnetic pole, to which a magnetic compass pointed, or realised that the north shown by the compass was not the same as that shown on a chart. His chart, if he had one, was a portulan chart drawn on a sheepskin or goatskin, which showed coastal outlines, with the positions of ports and cities and illustrations of their flags and banners, but no details of the hinterland. The sea areas of the charts were covered with compass roses, each with radiating rhumb lines, from which a navigator could read off his course from one place to the next. But since his ship's compass did not correspond accurately to the compass rose on the chart, his reading of the course was likely to be in error.

If he had no chart – and they were still rare and expensive items in the fifteenth century – a navigator may have had a *portolano*, which was a form of

pilot guide in notebook form, describing coasts, ports, anchorages, rocks and shoals, and the facilities available for trade at the various ports. A fortunate navigator had both, for the information in the *portolano* supplemented the information given on a portulan chart.

Apart from supplying all his pilots with the latest charts and information for the voyages that he called on them to undertake, Henry's great ambition was to improve the accuracy of the marine chart and the methods of determining a ship's position upon it. His own studies of geography had convinced him that there really was a solution to be found in the position and daily movements of the sun, moon and stars to the problem of establishing a ship's position at sea. He sent invitations to the best known astronomers and mathematicians in the world to come to Sagres, recruiting some of them from as far away as Arabia, whose seamen at that time were leading the world in the knowledge and practice of navigation. At a time of anti-semitism he recruited the greatest Jewish mathematicians, guaranteeing them immunity from persecution in the Algarve.

Amongst other contributions to the relatively new art of navigation, they produced the first accurate tables for the daily declination of the sun, with whose aid a navigator could always determine his latitude by means of a simple observation of altitude. One result of

this work was that, over the years, Portuguese pilots acquired so great a reputation for navigational skill that all organizers of voyages of exploration, whether Spanish, English or French, invariably tried to engage one of them for their ships. Another was that, by 1484 at least, when Henry the Navigator had been succeeded by his nephew Alfonso V, every Portuguese ship carried a chart with an accurate grid of lines of latitude.

No less important to the navigator than the astronomical tables which gave him his latitude was the chart itself, on which he could see where he was, relative to the land. The first great centres of production of portulan charts were Venice and Genoa, as might be expected from their commanding position in Mediterranean seaborne trade. The greatest of the portulan chartmakers was Petrus Vesconte, who, in the fourteenth century, ran a thriving cartographic workshop in Genoa. (Today, five of his original charts are still in existence, highly prized exhibits in museums and libraries.) From Venice and Genoa the art spread to Catalonia, and by the fifteenth century the Catalan school had become supreme in the chartmaking art. One of its greatest exponents was Abraham Cresques, who worked in Majorca, and there are several references in the Spanish royal archives to the King of Aragon ordering a number of special *mappamundi* from him. He died before Henry the Navigator established his naval arsenal in 1420, but one of Henry's first acts was to send for Abraham's son, Jafuda, who was glad to come to Sagres to escape the persecution of the Jews in the kingdom of Aragon. Jafuda founded the school of chartmaking in Sagres which was to make Portuguese charts renowned for their accuracy throughout the seafaring world in the fifteenth and sixteenth centuries.

Simultaneously with the work of preparing astronomical tables for seamen, and charts to plot their voyages, Henry the Navigator turned his attention to the design of nautical instruments with which his pilots could take accurate readings. Some were adapted from navigational instruments used by the Arabs on their long voyages across the Indian Ocean; others were marine versions of measuring instruments used

in land surveys. The first of real importance was the astrolabe, a heavy instrument worked by two men: one to hold it so that it hung vertically; another to sight an arm, pivoted at the centre, at the sun or stars and read off the altitude. It was a difficult instrument to use on the heaving deck of a ship, but useful ashore to calculate the latitude of new lands. For use at sea, the Arabic *kamal* was adapted into the cross-staff, and although it came on the scene a little later than the astrolabe, it arrived in time for all the major voyages of exploration of the sixteenth century.

With these aids to navigation, many of them made available through the interest and encouragement of Henry the Navigator, the Portuguese pilots were admirably equipped for the great surge of world exploration which took place in the sixteenth century. But such secret knowledge as the Portuguese navigators may have enjoyed at first did not remain secret for long. It spread rapidly throughout Europe, and within a very few years was helping the seamen of France, Spain, England and Holland just as much as it had done those of Portugal

Far left: The headland at Sagres in Portugal, home of Prince Henry and point of departure for his navigators.

Above left: Prince Henry the Navigator (1394–1460) in a detail from a triptych attributed to Nuno Goncalves.

Above: An astrolabe made by Arsenio Lovanio, a navigational aid in maritime exploration.

Chapter Four
The Age of Exploration

It has been mentioned earlier how the development of the *caravela latina* with its all-lateen rig, by enabling a vessel to make way to windward, had given Gil Eannes enough confidence to round the Cabo de Não, on the western bulge of the African continent, in 1434, and continue exploring along the coast. It has also been seen how Columbus discovered that the *caravela latina* rig was unsuitable for ocean voyages and put into the Canary Islands on his first voyage to the west, to convert his one *caravela latina*, the *Niña*, to a *caravela redonda*, with square sails on foremast and mainmast and a lateen sail on the mizen. It did not take very long for the Portuguese explorers along the African coast to reach the same conclusion as that reached later by Columbus. Once they had confidence in the caravel's ability to beat to windward, they switched over to the *caravela redonda* rig as one much more suited to long ocean voyages.

At the time when Prince Henry the Navigator died in 1460, his dream of African discovery had been hanging fire. There was so much money to be made out of voyages to the already known African coast, from the discovery of gold or the sale of the black population as slaves, that any urge to venture further towards the equator and beyond was stifled. This lack of incentive was effectively overcome by Alfonso V, nephew of Prince Henry and as interested in exploration as had been his uncle. He granted a Lisbon merchant, Fernão Gomes, a monopoly of all trade on the Guinea coast on the condition that each year he was to explore 100 leagues further. The bargain paid off on both sides. When Gomes's ships swung round the bulge of Africa and sailed east along the coast, they opened up yet richer districts of western Africa, the Gold Coast and Ivory Coast. When his monopoly ended in 1474, Gomes's ships had reached the island of Fernando Po, only three and a half degrees north of the

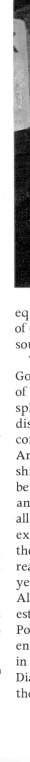

equator, and had ventured right across the Gulf of Guinea to where the African coast turns to the southward again.

These voyages brought great wealth to Fernão Gomes, but they brought to Alfonso V something of much greater importance. If the earth was a sphere – and no geographer of any repute now disputed the fact – the rounding of the African continent was bound to open a sea route to India. And if Africa could be rounded by Portuguese ships navigated by Portuguese pilots, it would be a Portuguese route by right of prior discovery and India would ostensibly be defensible against all comers. The national prize was immense, and expeditions, financed by the king, pushed further and further south. By 1484 Diogo Cão had reached the mouth of the River Congo, and four years later the great prize was itself achieved. Alfonso did not live long enough to see his greatest ambition realised, but his son, João II of Portugal, who was equally wholehearted and enthusiastic in his patronage of exploration, was in Lisbon in December 1488 when Bartholomew Diaz brought his three caravels home and sailed them proudly up the Tagus. They had rounded

Left: A fanciful impression of the battle between English ships and the Spanish Armada in 1588.
Above right: Portrait of Christopher Columbus.

81

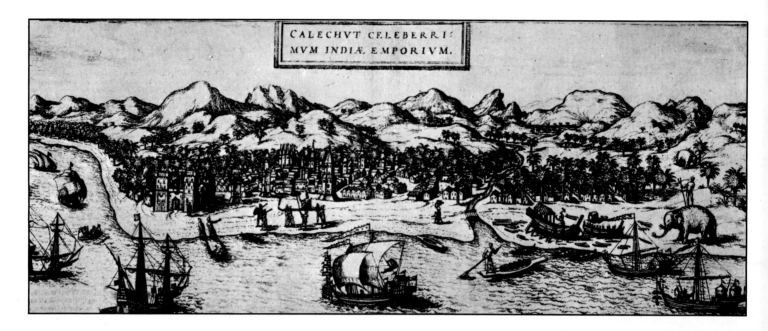

CALECHVT CELEBERRI: MVM INDIÆ EMPORIVM.

Above: Calicut, where Vasco da Gama landed in India. (From an engraving of 1572)

Right: Illustration of Columbus's discoveries in the 'Indies', from the 1493 edition of his letters to Don Luis de Santangel.

the southernmost cape of Africa, had been driven further south into a wide open sea by a great storm, had steered to the eastward when the storm abated after thirteen days, and on their return to Africa had sailed well up the east coast before a threat of mutiny by his crew had forced Diaz to return to Portugal. The seaway to India was now open, and João and all his navigators knew it. Diaz, remembering the great storm which had arisen off the southernmost cape and driven his ships so far to the south, had named it Cabo Tormentosa, Cape of Storms, but the king soon changed that: it was not Cabo Tormentosa to him but Cabo de Bona Speranza, Cape of Good Hope, for his next expedition would surely reach India, the greatest prize of all. And so it was: in May, 1498, a Portuguese squadron under the command of Vasco da Gama let go their anchors off Calicut on the mainland of India.

In the meantime Spain was chasing the same prize. Christopher Columbus, who had studied charts and globes and was an experienced seaman, had come to the conclusion that the western route to India was much shorter than the eastern route, especially since there was no great continent such as Africa blocking the way. He had a lot of difficulty in selling his navigational ideas to Ferdinand and Isabella of Spain, but in the end they were convinced and agreed to finance an expedition. Columbus's geography was of course, wildly inaccurate, but the world had long forgotten Eratosthenes's calculation of the earth's circumference 1,700 years earlier, and most contemporary geographers reckoned that 'Cipangu', modern Japan and the western gateway to the Far East, lay on about longitude 60°W.

On that reckoning Columbus was not far out when he claimed the western route to India to be shorter than the eastern; it was only the reality of his great voyage that proved contemporary geographers wrong.

His little fleet of three caravels dropped down the Rio Tinto from Palos at daybreak on 3 August 1492, put into Gomera in the Canary Islands for repairs to the *Pinta* and alteration of the *Niña* to the *redonda* rig, and on 6 September set sail for the west, picking up the north-east trade winds.

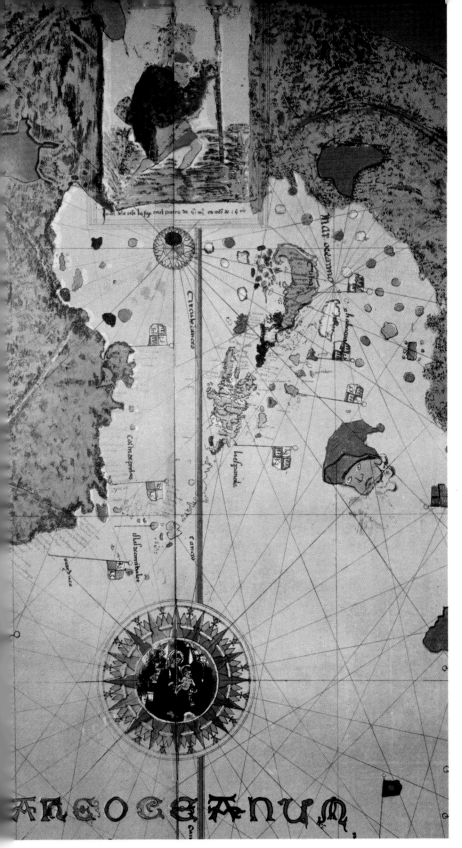

Above: Part of the world map drawn by Columbus's pilot, de la Cosa, showing Spanish discoveries in the West Indies.

Above right: Spanish caravels similar to Columbus's Pinta and Niña.

At two o'clock in the morning of 12 October the lookout on the *Pinta*, Rodrigo de Triana, sighted a white cliff shining in the moonlight and the cry *'Tierra! Tierra!'* echoed through the ship. Later that morning, with the three ships lying at anchor off a white coral beach, Columbus and the two brothers Pinzón of the *Pinta* and *Niña* went ashore in their longboats flying the royal standard of Castile and the banner of the expedition, a green crowned cross on a white field. 'And, all having rendered thanks to Our Lord, kneeling on the ground, embracing it with tears of joy for the immeasurable mercy of having reached it, the Admiral rose and gave this island the name San Salvador.'

Columbus was convinced that he had reached an outlying island off the mainland of India. As he sailed further west, discovering still more islands, but no land that even began to look like a continent, he underlined his belief that the mainland of India must lie just over the western horizon by naming the islands collectively as 'las Indias' (the Indies) and since India had to lie further to the westward, they became the West Indies, the name by which they are known today. It was not until his third voyage to the west, from 1498 to 1500, that Columbus came to the conclusion that what he had discovered was a new continent hitherto unknown to Europeans. By then he had coasted along the northern shore of the mainland of South America, and he knew by now that it was not India; he knew, too, that it was not China; so it had to be a new and unknown continent, although Columbus would not renounce his belief that India and China must still lie just over the horizon to the west. All the maps and all the globes that he had seen had told him so. They couldn't be all *that* wrong even though they were so obviously wrong over this new continent. How could he justify his assurances to Ferdinand and Isabella that it was *las Indias* which he had discovered in 1492? He was too proud to eat his words; there must be some other explanation that would not discredit the geographical assumptions on which his voyages had been financed. So Columbus decided that this new continent was the Garden of Eden, and that it stood at the top of a large protruberance projecting up from the earth's surface like a woman's breast, in order to bring it nearer to

83

Heaven than the surrounding land. Only thus could he account for all the miles he had sailed to the west without reaching India. If the earth's curvature had remained normal, he would already have reached India on the mileage that he had sailed; that he had not yet done so was attributable to the fact that his ships had been sailing up the curve of the breast.

Whatever explanation Columbus put forward, the fact remained that he had shown the world that new lands, ripe for commercial exploitation, lay across the ocean to the west. Merchants now had to adjust themselves to the existence of a New World and to design and build ships able to cope with the distances involved.

These great Spanish and Portuguese voyages – Spanish to the westward, Portuguese to the east – were made in small caravels, ranging from a maximum tonnage of 80 or 90 down to a minimum of 30 to 40. This does not by any means indicate that the caravel, in build, design or sail plan, was the 'master' ship of Europe; all it meant was that, for the purposes of discovery and the opening of new trade routes round the world, it was the sort of vessel that the explorers themselves preferred. They wanted, first of all, a ship that drew a minimum of water so that it could come close into unknown coasts and anchor just offshore, instead of further out in deep water. The average caravel, drawing about 6 ft (2 m), met this requirement admirably. Moreover, the explorers did not come to trade: they only needed a ship with enough room on board to carry a few chests of beads, bells and baubles which they could exchange with the natives for gold, silver, pearls and anything else of sufficient value to indicate to their paymasters that their discoveries were economically significant enough to warrant the financing of further voyages. The little caravel answered this purpose too. Above all, and most important, the explorers did not want large crews. The risk of discontent among the men, of a breakdown in discipline, even of mutiny, was always far greater among a large crew than a small one. The largest caravel carried about ten officers and officials, and about thirty men on the lower deck; the smallest about five officers and sixteen men. It was not too difficult to keep crews of this size in a reasonably good humour through a long voyage, and there was a good chance that morale could be kept up when things were going badly. Columbus himself had managed to do so during his first voyage in 1492, when there were signs of an incipient mutiny that might have forced the abandonment of the venture. A larger ship would obviously entail shipping a larger crew. Columbus recorded

Below: A carrack and two caravels locked in battle near the entrance to the Red Sea. (From Testu's *Cosmographie Universelle*)

in his journal during his first voyage that even the 90-ton *Santa Maria* was larger than he really wanted. Of the three ships in his little fleet, his favourite was the 50-ton *Niña*, the smallest of the three.

The impact on the other maritime nations of Europe of these voyages, to India in the east and to the new continent in the west, was profound. The doctrine of possession by right of prior discovery was accepted throughout Europe, and Spain and Portugal took immediate steps to get their discoveries registered by papal bull. Originally, Pope Alexander VI granted Spain possession of all land lying to the west of a line drawn from north to south 100 leagues west of the Azores, and to Portugal all land lying to the east of it. On a protest from Portugal that this line ran too near the west African coast and would jeopardize further Portuguese discoveries to the south and east, it was moved to 370 leagues west of the Azores. In the event, this paid off well for Portugal, for when, in 1500, Pedro Cabral touched the coast of Brazil during a voyage to India, the new land was found to lie to the east of the line and Portugal's claim to possession was confirmed. But, if Spain and Portugal welcomed the papal bull as providing legitimacy to their claims, the other European maritime nations would have none of it. England and Holland were not bound by papal edict as were Portugal and

Spain, and even France decided that her national interest in the scramble for trade which was bound to follow the new discoveries took precedence over her allegiance to Rome. So far as England, Holland and France were concerned, maritime exploration remained a free-for-all, and the tiny areas of land already visited by Portuguese and Spanish navigators still left a huge undiscovered area, ripe for exploitation under the doctrine of prior discovery.

Holland, at that time a province of Spain – though with an active independence movement backed by England – was at first relatively inactive in the quest for trade, but when she finally rebelled, as the result of a relentless policy of oppression, it was to beyond the Cape of Good Hope that she looked for an empire. France, on the other hand, looked to the west and for a way through the new continent to the Far East, while England tried both east and west. It was in fact Holland who chose the most promising alternative, reaching round the south of India and setting up her empire on the islands of the East Indies. The Frenchman, Jacques Cartier, having landed on the North American coast in 1534, sailed up the St. Lawrence in the belief that, at the centre of the continent, it must join up with another river flowing westwards, thus providing a direct route to China. The west-flowing river did not exist, of course, but the acquisition of

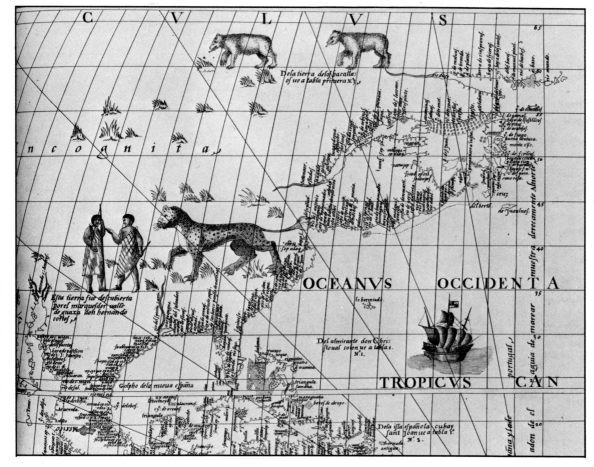

Left: Part of Sebastian Cabot's map of the east coast of North America, produced in 1544.

85

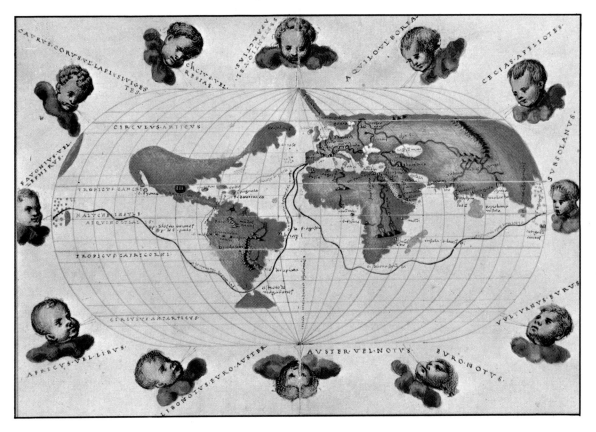

Above: The *Victoria*, the only ship of Magellan's squadron to complete the voyage around the world.

Right: World map showing the route of Magellan's expedition, dated 1545.

Canada for the French empire and the development of the fur trade paid a handsome dividend.

England's more northerly route across the Atlantic, pioneered by John Cabot's voyage of 1497, brought her the economically disappointing discovery of Newfoundland, though there was a temporary bonus in the form of the great cod fishery of the Newfoundland Banks. But a fishery well off the coast could not be claimed or defended as a national monopoly on the basis of prior discovery, and within two or three years it was the French and Portuguese who were exploiting its wealth far more energetically than the English ever did. English voyages to the east were more successful in establishing 'factories', or trading centres, on newly discovered parts of the coasts of India and the East Indies, though many of them had to be actively defended against Portuguese and Dutch attacks.

Within a few years of the discovery of the New World, as America was known in Europe, its approximate shape and rough limits northwards and southwards were known to geographers and incorporated in their maps and globes. Vasco Nuñez de Balboa had seen the Pacific in 1513, named it the Great South Sea, and claimed possession of it for the King of Spain. Many voyages, and particularly those of Giovanni and Girolama da Verrazzano starting in 1524, had searched the east coast of North and South America for a way through to the Great South Sea, all without success, and it was becoming more and more apparent that the New World was an unbroken land mass placed squarely across the direct sea route to the riches of 'Cathay', as China was then called, and India. The world's geographers showed it as such and the world's navigators reluctantly had to accept that there was no way through it by sea.

Even if there was no way through, there might still be ways round this huge land mass, both to the north and the south. Ferdinand Magellan discovered the southern way round it in his voyage of circumnavigation of 1519–22. Magellan was Portuguese, but having fallen out with the King of Portugal became a naturalized Spaniard and his voyage was made under the flag of Spain. As a navigational feat, it can be said to have been the greatest sea voyage ever made, even though Magellan himself was killed in the process and only one ship out of his original five came home to Spain. (Magellan lost his life in the Philippine Islands at the battle of Mactan in April 1521, but his claim to be the world's first circumnavigator still stands as he had reached that longitude on an earlier voyage to the east when in Portuguese service.)

Magellan did more for the geographers than place the southern route to the Pacific on the map of the world: his voyage made clear the huge

extent of the Pacific Ocean, very much greater than had been thought. Once the surviving ship of his expedition had reached home with her log of the voyage, the true size of the globe became known and far more accurate maps were drawn.

There remained the northern route round America, a heart-breaking search which was to occupy the English for the next 300 years. Martin Frobisher and John Davis both led expeditions in the mid-sixteenth century in search of the North-West Passage; both failed amid the ice of the Polar Sea north of Canada, as did many other expeditions through the centuries, until, in 1850, Vice Admiral McClure found a way.

Left: A squadron of Portuguese carracks, painted in the sixteenth century.

Below left: *Ark Royal*, Lord Howard's flagship at the time of the Armada.

Simultaneously, England was looking to the north-east for a passage to China, around the top of Europe and Asia. The idea that such a passage might exist was first put forward in 1527, in a letter written by Robert Thorne, as the best way of avoiding conflict with the Spaniards and Portuguese, who still claimed the possession of all unknown lands in the world east and west of Pope Alexander's north–south line in mid-Atlantic. English expeditions in search of this North-East Passage were led in mid-century by Sir Hugh Willoughby, Richard Chancellor, Stephen Borough and others, but like the corresponding voyages to the north-west, were all foiled by the polar ice. One thing that they did achieve, however, was a trading contact with Russia, which led to the formation of the Muscovy Company of Merchant Adventurers, to regulate trade between the two countries.

This huge expansion of the known world within the span of twenty to thirty years had a profound effect on the ships of the principal trading nations, for, while the smaller ship might be the ideal vessel in which to discover new worlds, it was the bigger ship that was required to bring home the rich cargoes from the new lands. As the sixteenth century developed, Spain and Portugal made the carrack their 'big ship' for trading purposes as well as war, and expanded her cargo-carrying capacity by building her up to 1,200 tons, and even larger in some cases. In the north European countries the carrack was never popular, even though some were captured from the Spanish and Portuguese and incorporated into the northern fleets. The tendency in England, France and Holland was to expand the cog, by doubling her overall length, adding two more masts to the existing one, and using carvel construction instead of clinker. This enlarged cog was known first as a *hourque* or hulk, and then, when built still bigger, as a *nef* or, in England, as a full-rigged ship. Smaller vessels, with both two- and three-masted rigs, were known as 'pinnaces', or sometimes as 'frigats' (though they should not be confused with later frigates, built by all the world's navies as small, fast and efficient warships).

On navies, too, the effect of the new discoveries was equally profound. Gone for ever were the days when a maritime nation required fighting ships only to uphold the sovereignty of its own territorial waters, to resist invasion by neighbouring powers, to protect its fisheries, to put down piracy in its own patrimonial seas. A national navy now needed the capability to safeguard the country's trade routes to newly discovered countries. Thus Spain needed a large navy, not only to maintain her trade with the West Indian islands and the mainland of America, but also, following Magellan's voyage, to police the Pacific which she claimed as her exclusive possession. Her subsequent lack of success in defending her new territories against freebooters and privateers is a measure of her failure to build a centrally controlled navy and reliance, instead, on hiring and arming privately owned ships. Portugal similarly required an expanded navy to guard her trade route to the east and to hold her African possessions, which she was developing not only as rich colonies in their own right, but also as staging posts for ships on the long voyage to India. So, too, did Holland, with her East Indian empire.

Only in England did this reason for a large navy not apply. She had come badly out of the search for new lands and had virtually no colonies worth protecting. But even in her case a growing navy was needed, partly because of the decision to fight for a share of the trade earmarked by Spain, Portugal and Holland for themselves, partly because the French had become so obsessed with Canada and the St. Lawrence River that they had neglected to occupy and claim that part of the North American continent which lay to the south. There was a wide belt of potentially rich land between the French possessions in Canada and the furthest extent of Spanish penetration of the mainland to the south, and into this gap the English stepped, planting colonies along the coastal strip.

The English navy really began to flower during the reign of Elizabeth I (1558–1603), mainly through her acceptance of the strategic concept that the most effective way to use a navy was to carry the fight to an enemy at sea, rather than to wait at home and fight defensively when the enemy attacked. Her father and grandfather had both built their own warships; Elizabeth added modestly to the number of royal ships, but those built in her reign were greatly superior in quality and endurance. It was during the Elizabethan period that the fight for a trading foothold amid Spain's western possessions began in earnest, not in any way as a national conflict, between the respective navies, but as a series of private struggles in which the crown had a financial interest, usually secured by lending a royal ship, and thus a warship, to the backers of the trading ventures. This was a not unusual course – both Henry VII and Henry VIII had done it – and it had the merit of confining the blame for any possible conflict to private adventurers, relieving the crown of any responsibility for an action which could be held as an act of war if performed openly by the sovereign.

Henry VIII's main contribution to what was the nucleus of a national navy was the *Henry Grace à Dieu*, laid down at Erith in 1512, launched in 1514, rebuilt in 1540, and accidentally destroyed by fire in 1553. She was built to replace the *Regent*, lost in action off Brest in 1512, and like her was a four-masted ship with a fixed topmast on her foremast and mainmast, possibly a fixed topgallant mast above her main topmast, a mizen and a bonaventure mizen. Volpe's famous picture, now at Hampton Court, depicting her at Dover in 1520 does not show her with all sails set, but a contemporary panel, which used to hang in Canterbury Cathedral and was later presented to Admiral Sir John Norris, does. According to this, she set three square sails on foremast and mainmast (course, topsail, topgallant sail), two lateen sails with a small topgallant sail on the mizen and a single lateen with a small topsail on the bonaventure mizen, and she also carried a spritsail on a yard slung from her bowsprit. This mass of sail, certainly unusual for the period, probably represents artistic licence on the part of the painter. Most Tudor warships, even the largest, set only two square sails on the foremast and mainmast, with single lateen sails on the two after masts, and a spritsail on the bowsprit.

The *Henry Grace à Dieu* was built by William Bond, the master shipwright at Erith, under the general directions of Robert Brygandine, Henry's Clerk of the Ships. Many contemporary accounts gave her a tonnage of about 1,500, but this is thought to be an exaggeration and her true tonnage is now given as about 1,000. Even this would make her a very big ship in the context of contemporary English shipbuilding, though by now Spain and Portugal, and possibly France as well, were building as large, if not larger.

Henry's second great contribution to the navy was the replacement of the small anti-personnel gun, of which very large numbers were carried on board, by the cannon, firing a heavy ball or stone shot and, by its nature, an anti-ship weapon. The lower gundeck, and gunports cut in the ship's sides, were natural corollaries of this increase in the size, and therefore the weight, of the cannon. The need to lower the gun's position in the ship for reasons of stability was, in turn, responsible for the pronounced tumble-home, which became such a feature of wooden warships. There is no tumble-home visible in contemporary pictures of the *Henry Grace à Dieu*, for the few cannon she carried were still mounted in the two castles fore and aft; fifty years later it was commonplace. Henry's *Mary Rose* is said to have been the first warship to have gunports cut in her sides; another, sadder, claim to fame is that she was the first ship to be lost by heeling over and having the sea enter her open gunports,

which were only 16 in (41 cm) above her waterline. This tragedy occurred off Spithead in 1545 as she was about to go into action against the French. (In 1982 her well-preserved hull was brought to the surface and has since provided much new data on Tudor naval techniques.)

At the same time, Henry VIII was unable to break away completely from the Mediterranean predilection for the galley as the supreme warship type, even though his introduction of the anti-ship gun was the complete answer to galley warfare and despite the fact that English and Atlantic waters were well recognized as unsuitable for the oared galley. During his reign he built about a dozen, and Queen Elizabeth, right at the end of her reign, had four built to a Mediterranean design. It is difficult to understand why they were built, for they did not incorporate the pointed ram which was always the galley's main weapon of attack, but relied simply on one or two cannon, or demi-cannon, firing ahead. Perhaps the reason for their construction was that neighbouring France had galleys in her fleet and it may have been thought wise to be able to meet like with like. The original square sail on a central mast, which the earlier English galleys inherited from the longship, gave way in the sixteenth century to a single large lateen sail.

If the maritime nations of northern Europe were lukewarm in their appreciation of the galley as a ship of war, the Mediterranean nations still swore by it, and indeed retained it as a warship type right up to the times of the Revolutionary and Napoleonic wars at the start of the nineteenth century, though it was rapidly losing favour by then. One of the greatest and best-known galley actions in naval history was fought at Lepanto, off the western coast of Greece, in 1571 between a combined fleet of Christian nations commanded by Don John of Austria and a Turkish fleet under the command of Ali Pasha. On the outcome of the battle depended the whole future of the Mediterranean, for victory would have assured the Turks not only of complete mastery of the Adriatic and possession of the vast wealth of Venice, but probably also maritime control of the western basin of the Mediterranean. Don John's force consisted of over 200 galleys, rowed by 43,000 oarsmen and manned by 12,000 seamen and 28,000 soldiers, with about thirty other ships attached, six of them huge Venetian galleasses. The Turkish fleet was even larger in numbers, though they had fewer of the large galleys and more of the smaller, and no galleasses. The battle lasted from dawn to midnight and ended in a Christian victory.

Right: Part of Henry VIII's fleet off Dover.

Below right: The Battle of Lepanto in 1571 between the galleys of the Turkish and combined Christian fleets.

We know a lot about the Venetian galley of the sixteenth century. There is a mid-sixteenth century relief of a galley under sail on the tomb of one of the Venetian admirals, Alexander Contarini, in the cathedral of San Antonio in Padua. Even more important are manuscript instructions for the building of galleys written at the same period by Pre Theodoro de Nicolo, one of the best of the galley builders in Venice, and now preserved in the Biblioteca Nazionale in Venice. He gives the dimensions of three types of galley, ranging from the small *fusta*, with a length of 88½ ft (27 m), a maximum beam of 13 ft (4 m) and a depth from deck to keel of 4½ ft (1·4 m), to the large galley, for which the corresponding

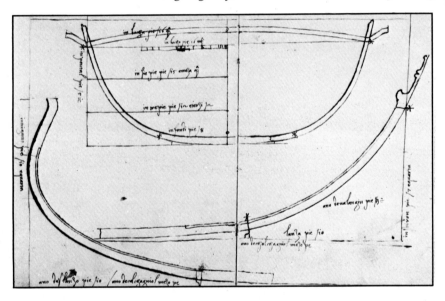

Above: Part of the building plans for a Venetian galley.

measurements are 151, 24½ and 10 ft (46, 7·5 and 3 m). He tells us that the *corsia* (the narrow raised bridge between the thwarts, running from stem to stern) was 2¾ ft (84 cm) wide and that the distance between the *corsia* and the *apostis* (the outrigger in the form of a longitudinal beam on which the oars rested) was 14¼ ft (4·4 m).

One result of this battle of Lepanto was to prove the value of the galleasse in battle. The Mediterranean galleasse was a very different ship from the north European galleasse, being based on a totally opposite conception. In England the concept of the galleasse was of the normal heavily-built sailing warship, adapted for using oars to provide additional manoeuvrability; the Mediterranean concept was the normal swift oared galley, adapted to sail and given an added robustness of build to permit a powerful all-round gun armament in addition to her ram. The Venetian galleasses used at Lepanto rowed twenty-six oars each side, with four rowers to each oar, had a three-masted lateen rig, mounted eight large guns in the forecastle, two more in the aftercastle and eight broadside guns, four each side, on the upper deck above

the rowers, and, finally, were provided with a powerful ram, reinforced and tipped with iron.

Until 1570 or 1580, the general type of sailing warship did not differ greatly between any of the western nations. Whether it was the enlarged carrack of Spain and Portugal or the expanded cog of England and Holland, it was in either case a so-called 'high-charged' ship, with a built-up castle overhanging the stern, surmounted by another, even higher castle at the after end, and sometimes another and another, so that in extreme cases there might be as many as four built-up decks, rising in steps, one above the other. In fact, only the very largest carracks, of 1,500 to 1,800 tons, were built with four: a big carrack would have three, and an average carrack two. English and Dutch ships were not built nearly as big as Spanish, and the largest of them had no more than two built-up decks aft.

The high-charged ship, standing high out of the water, was very difficult to sail, except directly before the wind. Once she came on to the wind, the large forecastle built out over her stem presented a large surface to the wind which forced her bows down to leeward and gave her a tendency to carry excessive lee helm. The lateen sail on the mizen, which should have counteracted this lee helm, was not large enough, in relation to the amount of canvas carried on the foremast, to do so. So this typical sixteenth century ship was apt to wallow in the waves at sea, her bows being continually pushed down to leeward and making it hard for the helmsman to hold her on course.

Sir John Hawkins realised this drawback in contemporary ship design during the last two of his three 'triangular' voyages, for which Queen Elizabeth hired him one of her ships in return for a share in the profits. The two voyages were made in 1564 and 1567, and the royal ship was the 700-ton *Jesus of Lubeck*, a typical high-charged ship of the period. With her went the *Judith* and *Minion*, two 50-ton vessels described as 'barks'.

The basic plan of all these 'triangular' voyages was to sail first to Sierra Leone with goods to exchange for a cargo of black slaves, carry the slaves across the Middle Sea (that area of the Atlantic lying between the west African coast and the Spanish possessions in the West Indies and Gulf of Mexico), sell the slaves to Spanish planters and load a cargo of sugar or other produce, return to England and sell it. These voyages were not without considerable danger: there was always a risk of meeting a Portuguese warship off the African coast, intent on upholding her country's monopoly of African trade, and Spanish colonists were forbidden by law to trade with any but Spaniards, so it needed a good deal of forceful persuasion to induce them to buy the slaves, even though they were always in great demand. It was the Spaniards' determination to restrict all trade to their own nationals that led to disasters for Hawkins on the third voyage. Stress of weather and a shortage of provisions had forced his little fleet to seek refuge in the anchorage of San Juan de Ulloa, and the Spaniards there agreed to Hawkins's request that his ships be reprovisioned for their voyage home. But on a given signal they were treacherously attacked. The little *Judith* and *Minion* managed to sail clear; the *Jesus of Lubeck*, a slow sailer and unhandy in the water, was unable to win free, and although Hawkins and a handful of seamen were rescued by the *Minion*, the rest of the crew were slaughtered to a man.

The disastrous loss of one of the Queen's ships, brought about in some measure by the deficiencies in sailing ability inherent in her design, made Hawkins consider how the design could be improved. He was a practical seaman and knew a lot about ship construction and the action of the winds on sails and hull. Moreover, the disaster had been precipitated by Spanish treachery and Hawkins, and the captain of the *Judith*, his young cousin, Francis Drake, vowed vengeance. We will see later how Drake fulfilled his vow; Hawkins did so by devoting the rest of his life to the naval service of his country and reshaping Elizabeth's navy with ships of a new design. In 1577 he became Treasurer of the Navy and his practical experience as a seaman brought him considerable influence on the naval affairs of his day. His views on construction and design were heard with respect, and his ideas for the improvement of the basic ship design were quickly put into effect.

The first of the new breed may have been the *Foresight*, a ship of 300 tons built in 1570, but it is more likely that the *Bull* and *Tiger* were the prototypes. They were both small vessels of 200 tons, both built some years earlier, and both taken in hand in 1570 for rebuilding. It would be a reasonable precaution, in launching a radical new design, to try it out on small, old ships, due in any case for a major refit. Hawkins's notion was to test whether a ship, made to lie lower in the water by cutting down her high sides, could be made more weatherly (that is, able to point higher into the wind when sailing close-hauled) by removing the high forecastle over the stem and replacing it by a lower structure, placed further aft on the foredeck. This gave the new ships a low beakhead with a distinct cutwater, and at the same time removed the large area forward of the bow which caught the wind and forced the bows down to leeward. And, in the course of this process of tidying up, the aftercastle was also reduced in height to make the ship low and snug overall, the length-to-beam ratio was increased from $2\frac{1}{2}$ to 1, to 3 to 1, and the rounded stern was changed to a square one. The new design quickly became known as 'low-charged', to distinguish it from the previous 'high-charged' type.

Above: Sir John Hawkins, who pioneered the new low-charged warship.

Left: The *Jesus of Lubeck*, captured by the Spanish at San Juan de Ulloa.

English galleon
(c.1580)

Length 140 ft (42·6 m) *Keel* 100 ft (30·5 m) *Beam* 37 ft (11·3 m)
Hold 18 ft (5·5 m) *Burthen* 500 tons
Armament 22 culverins, 16 demi-culverins
Complement 320 sailors, 100 soldiers

This is a typical English warship of the new 'low-charged' type introduced during the second half of the sixteenth century. The English fleet which defeated the Spanish Armada in 1588 included many vessels of this type, among them the flagship of Lord Howard, the *Ark Royal*. Being a large ship, she has four masts. Fore and main masts are square-rigged, carrying (in descending order) topgallants, topsails and courses. Her mizen mast and bonaventure mizen, stepped aft, are lateen-rigged, while she carries a square spritsail beneath the bowsprit. Steering in a ship of this kind would have been by means of a whipstaff. As well as having a much lower forecastle than earlier warships, she also has a more streamlined underwater hull shape, both of which would have contributed to her superior sailing performance. Her main armament, of culverins and demi-culverins, comprises guns with longer range and greater accuracy than the traditional cannon, though less sheer destructive power.

She is shown here with bonaventure mizensail, main topsail, fore topgallant and fore topsail set, and her guns run out through open gunports. The small drawing shows her hull profile superimposed, for comparison, on that of a slightly larger ship of the high-charged type. As well as being considerably lower, her forecastle is built further aft than that of the high-charged ship which actually overhangs the stem. The new arrangement presents less wind resistance at the bow, enabling her to sail better to windward, and gives rise to the pronounced 'beak', or cutwater. Her quarter-deck, on the other hand, is a no less lofty structure than that of the other high-charged type of vessel.

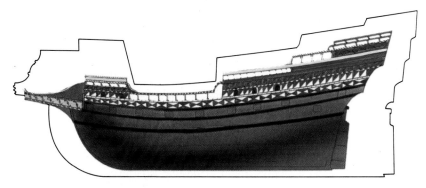

Above: An illustration from Matthew Baker's treatise on shipbuilding. Drawn in about 1585, it is the earliest technical drawing of an English ship to survive.

These radical changes made an immense difference to the sailing qualities of the warship, and within a very few years had spread to merchant shipbuilding as well. The new design was given the generic name of 'galleon', a term which never caught on in England even though the design originated there. It was discovered that the low-charged ship could not only hold a better wind than the old high-charged design, but was also faster through the water and much easier to handle, placing less strain on the helmsman. Once these qualities had been demonstrated, Hawkins pressed ahead with building new ships for the Queen, realising that the continual brushes with Spanish ships over the right to trade in the West Indies and the American continent was certain to end in war.

There is a contemporary manuscript on shipbuilding in the Pepysian Library at Magdalene College, Cambridge, unsigned and undated, but reliably believed to have been written by Matthew Baker, the Elizabethan shipwright, in about 1585. It contains several design drawings of the low-charged Elizabethan warship, including a typical sail plan. This shows the now normal four-masted rig, square on foremast and mainmast, with a topsail and topgallant sail set above the course, and single lateen sails on the mizen and bonaventure mizen. In several of Matthew Baker's profile designs he has superimposed a large fish on the underwater part of the hull, evidently a cod, possibly as an indication that the underwater hull design should conform to the shape of a cod's body.

Although the galleon design was introduced in England in the decade 1570 to 1580, it was some time before other maritime nations adopted it. The Dutch appear to have been the first: a model of a Flemish ship of 1593 in the Museo Navale in Madrid is of distinct galleon design. France did not take up the design in her warships until the early years of the seventeenth century, and Spain and Portugal adopted it at about the same time.

It is necessary to return briefly to Francis Drake to see how he achieved his vow of vengeance on Spain following the treachery at San Juan de Ulloa, as it was certainly due in part to his successes that the subsequent war with Spain was fought. He made two inconspicuous voyages to the West Indies in small vessels in 1570 and 1571 to gather information and make plans; then in 1572, sailing in the 70-ton *Pasha* and accompanied by the 25-ton *Swan*, he made his descent on the Spanish Main in search of plunder. He held the town of Nombre de Dios to ransom, crossed the Isthmus of Panama to become the first Englishman to sight the Pacific, and waylaid a mule train bringing treasure across the Isthmus. He returned to England in 1573, a very rich man through the gold and silver that he had captured.

His next venture against Spain was a circumnavigation of the globe between 1577 and 1580. Materially, the voyage was immensely successful owing to the capture of a Spanish treasure ship and the holding of towns to ransom up the length of the west coast of South America. The moral value of the expedition was even greater, for it proved to the English that there was nothing to fear from Spanish claims to control the Pacific. When Drake reached the Pacific through the Straits of Magellan, he had only one ship of his small squadron left, the 100-ton *Pelican* which he renamed *Golden Hind*, but he ran her like a warship. We get a picture of Drake in the Pacific from a letter written by Don Francisco de Zarata, owner of a captured Spanish ship, whom Drake entertained on board the *Golden Hind*:

'The English general is about thirty-five years of age, short of stature, with a red beard, and one of the best sailors that sail the seas, both in respect to boldness and to capacity for command. His ship is of near 400 tons burden, with a hundred men on board, all young and of an age for battle, and all drilled as well as the oldest veterans of our army of Italy. Each one is bound to keep his arquebus clean. Drake treats them all with affection, and they him with respect. He also has with him nine or ten gentlemen, the younger sons of great people in England. Some

Right: Francis Drake, whose exploits were partly responsible for bringing about the war between England and Spain.

Below right: Model of a Flemish galleon of 1593 in the Museo Navale, Madrid.

of them are in his counsels, but he has no favourite. These sit at his table, and he is served on silver plate with a coat of arms engraved on the dishes; and music is played at his dinner and supper. The ship carries about 30 pieces of artillery, and plenty of ammunition and warlike stores.'

On his return to England from this voyage Drake, like Hawkins, devoted himself to naval service. He approved wholeheartedly of the new warship design, and particularly of what might be called the middle order of size, the ship of about 500 tons carrying around forty-five guns of various sizes. Such a ship was the *Revenge*, in which he served as vice-admiral in the battle against the Spanish Armada.

War against Spain was declared in 1585 and Europe watched in wonder as England, still regarded as a ridiculously small naval power, prepared to challenge the maritime might of

Spain. It had to be a naval war, for England had no real army and Spain would have to cross the sea if she was to use her huge army to subdue England. It was Francis Drake who struck the first blow in the war, with his brilliant attack on Cadiz in 1587. His ship was the *Elizabeth Bonaventure*, originally a 600-ton high-charged ship, but rebuilt on galleon lines in 1581. The main naval significance of this Cadiz action lay in demonstrating the complete powerlessness of the typical Mediterranean war galley against the typical north European gunned sailing warship, even in enclosed waters in which the galley should have been at its most dangerous because of its speed and manoeuvrability under oars. Six Spanish galleys attacked Drake's squadron as it sailed into the harbour, but they were scattered by the first broadside and so knocked about that they could take no further part in the battle, nor do anything to stop Drake in his wholesale des-

Below: Contemporary map of Drake's expedition against Spanish possessions in America in 1585.

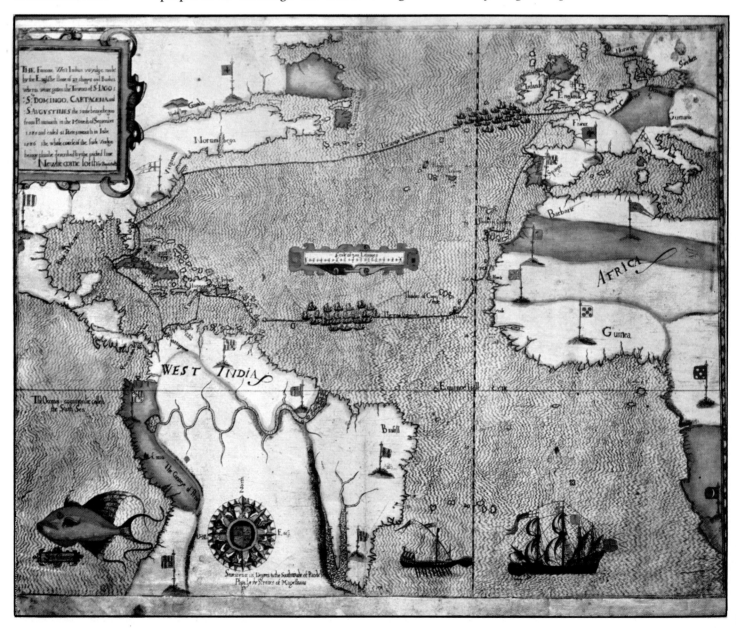

truction of Spanish ships assembled for the invasion of England.

The Cadiz raid paid one more big dividend to England, in the subsequent capture of the 1,500-ton carrack *San Felipe* off the Azores, homeward bound from the Far East with a rich cargo. The cargo was, of course, always welcome, but of infinitely more importance were the charts and papers captured with her, opening the eyes of English merchants to the huge profits to be made from systematic trade in Indian, East Indian and Chinese waters. It was the *San Felipe's* charts and papers that inspired the creation of the great East India Company, with all that this meant for the development of the ship.

One year later, in 1588, Philip of Spain launched his 'Enterprise of England', in the shape of his Invincible Armada. The running fight up the Channel, the attack by the British fireships off Calais, the subsequent battle of Gravelines, and the pursuit of the Spanish fleet up the North Sea until they were committed to a return to Spain round the north of Scotland – all have their place in maritime history. What is of more importance in the context of ship design is the comparison in performance between English and Spanish ships under battle conditions. For three centuries the general picture presented of the Armada campaign was one of large clumsy Spanish ships harried throughout the long action by smaller faster English ships, which kept their distance and drove the Spaniards on by their superior gunnery. Since then, many historians have tried to change the picture by asserting that, in general, the English ships were as large as the Spanish and that they mounted heavier guns. Neither picture is entirely accurate. Re-

garding the size of the ships, an analysis of the lists of those engaged shows that seven Spanish ships had a tonnage of above 1,000 tons, while of the English fleet two were of 1,000 tons or over. Of ships of 500 tons and over, the Spaniards had sixty-seven, the English thirteen. As to the number and size of guns, the advantage lay with Spain by a ratio of about 5 to 1, but the Spanish artillery was much the less effective because, size by size, the range of most of their guns was a good deal less than that of English guns, and because their gunports were so small as to allow no movement of the gun and, in many cases, even prevented the gunners from sighting their guns before firing them.

However, where the great strategic difference lay was in the actual design of the ships. The Spanish ships, although in some contemporary accounts they are described as 'galleons', were still carracks, high-sided, high-charged ships,

Below: Map showing the route of the Armada around the British Isles.

Bottom: Picturesque view of the Armada battle, seen through the eyes of an unknown contemporary English artist.

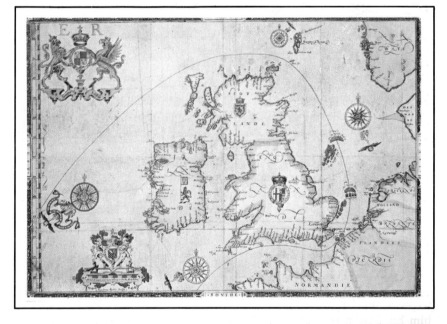

slow in the water, very slow in stays when tacking, and incapable of sailing closer than about 7 points off the wind. Their high sides and lofty fore and after castles presented easy targets for the English gunners. Most of the English ships, at least of the thirty-four that belonged to the Queen and formed the backbone of the fleet, had either been built to the galleon design or taken in hand and cut down from their original high-charged form into low-charged. They lay low in the water and thus presented smaller targets to the Spanish gunners, were at least a knot faster through the water and probably slightly more, fast in stays, and able to lay the wind closer than the Spanish ships when sailing close-hauled, to within about 6 to $6\frac{1}{2}$ points. The English guns had longer barrels and thus greater accuracy, while the gunners were better trained and, with the aid of large square gunports, were able to sight their guns before firing.

The defeat of the Spanish Armada has long been considered one of the world's most decisive battles (taking the nine days of fighting as one single battle), because it marks the start of the downfall of Spain as the world's greatest maritime power and the start of the rise of England to the same pinnacle. Although in her own eyes England had been great upon the seas ever since the battle of Sluys in 1340, in the eyes of the rest of Europe she had been something of a minnow in a pond dominated first by the predatory fish of Spain and Portugal, and by Spain alone when she combined the crown of Portugal with her own in 1580. Now the eyes of Europe were opened to a new spectacle: the coming of age of a new navy which had, at its first real blooding, overthrown the greatest fleet that the world had ever seen. For this had been Philip of Spain's boast to Europe: that his armada was so great and so powerful that its victory was assured. To give him his due, it was not Philip who gave it the name of 'Invincible'; he called it 'felicissima' ('most fortunate'). It was the young officers of the fleet who claimed it was invincible, but in Europe the name stuck.

Although the war with Spain dragged on until James I succeeded Elizabeth on the English throne, there was little naval action worthy of the name beyond periodic attempts by the English to waylay the annual Spanish treasure fleet bringing the gold and silver of America across the Atlantic. But the great trade war, east and west, was now on. The defeat of the Armada had proved that the exclusive commercial policy, which Spain had adopted and tried to enforce in respect of her settlements in the West Indies and on the American mainland, could not be upheld by her sea power, and, where Drake and Hawkins had earlier shown the way by their forceful trading techniques, a host of merchant adventurers were now ready to follow. And from the capture of the *San Felipe* in 1587 had sprung a new understanding of the rich trade to be found, and if necessary fought for, in Far Eastern waters. All this brought a great new impetus to merchant shipbuilding, almost all of it based on the English galleon design that had proved so successful in war. A much larger number of merchants were now building their own ships for trade than had done so before the Armada battle, arming them with guns, not only for self-defence against the piracy which still flourished in all the oceans, but also to underline their determination to trade wherever they might make a suitable landfall. Merchant shipowners trading to the same areas usually formed their ships into convoys, so that a trading expedition to the east or west might well consist of a dozen or more ships, each belonging to a different owner. Every ship on a long voyage went armed, and few of these joint expeditions returned to England without having had to fight somewhere along the way.

The profits of these joint ventures were so large that they attracted a growing number of merchants who were prepared to invest their money in ships, and by the end of the Elizabethan age the volume of traffic was growing rapidly. This increase was by no means confined to English ships: it was a worldwide movement, taking some advantage of the fact that the original claims to exclusive trade by right of prior discovery had been shattered by the outcome of the Armada battle. It led, too, to the formation in many countries of large trading associations of merchants interested in one particular area, as, for example, the various national East India Companies, which were formed within a very short time of the English victory in 1588. These grew to dominate trade, becoming over the course of years so powerful that they acquired complete monopolies and in the end had to be suppressed. But in their heyday they had a profound influence on the growth and design of merchant shipping all over the world.

This huge expansion in numbers was also reflected in the size of ships. Voyages under sail to India and China, to the Americas and round Cape Horn to the Pacific took a long time and entailed the carriage on board of large quantities of provisions and fresh water to sustain the ship's crew, quite apart from the trade goods for sale in the port of arrival. So ships had to be built larger, and the average merchant ship tonnage of ships employed on the longer trade routes rose to around 1,000 within a very few years. The four-masted rig, popular in the larger ships until near the end of the sixteenth century, quickly gave way to a more efficient, three-masted rig,

with a square topsail set above the lateen sail on the mizen to give a better aerodynamic balance.

It is easy, when faced with this huge expansion of merchant shipping, to concentrate on the big, important ships to the exclusion of the smaller ones used on the shorter trade routes. There is an official Dutch estimate, for example, that by the end of the sixteenth century there were no fewer than 10,000 merchant ships in Dutch ownership' While some of these were large ships engaged in the East Indian trade, the great majority were small, trading across the Baltic and the North Sea. This same story was true in England, France, Spain, throughout the Mediterranean and, indeed, across the world. There is no particular design which can be said to be common to all these small trading vessels. In England, for example, the pinnace was probably the most common, a vessel built with a square stern like a miniature warship, three-masted and single decked, generally, though a few of the larger pinnaces were built with two decks. In Holland the commonest small trading ship was the *fluyt*, three-masted like the English pinnace, but with a round stern instead of a square one. In the Mediterranean it was probably the *bergantina* two-masted and lateen-rigged, while in Far Eastern waters the junk, or local derivatives of it, was the universal coastal carrier.

With the exception of the *bergantina* with its two lateen sails, all these small trading vessels were square-rigged, although it was during the sixteenth century that the fore-and-aft sailing rig was introduced. If we discount certain evidence of Mediterranean rock carvings that the sprit (a long spar spreading a square sail from tack to peak) was used in those waters as early as the second century B.C., the earliest pictorial evidence of the sprit that we have, in Europe at any rate, shows that it was in existence in Sweden as early as 1525, although it is generally believed that it was first developed in Holland a few years earlier. Certainly it was the Dutch who developed the spritsail rig, with its long, heavy spar, into the gaff rig, with a gaff and boom instead of the sprit. For years, the gaff was known as a half-sprit until it acquired its own name.

No doubt, most of those 10,000 merchant ships with which the Dutch credited themselves at the end of the sixteenth century were small gaff-rigged vessels, much handier than the square-rigged fluyts for sailing in the shoal waters off the Dutch coast. It is probable that the upper size limit for the gaff rig in those days was about 50 tons and that these small vessels were used only for very local traffic, up and down the coast and in and out of estuaries and rivers.

Above: Dutch barges at Dordrecht, with their characteristic spritsail rig. (From a painting by Jan van Goyen)

East India Companies

By the end of the sixteenth century it had become common knowledge that the riches of the Far East, spices, silks and precious stones, outweighed those of the Spanish West, in the shape mainly of gold and silver. The Portuguese had been the first Europeans to reach India by ship, a century earlier. The Dutch had followed, to exploit the islands of the East Indies to the south. The British had arrived last of all, probably because they had wasted too much time looking for a new route to the East through the ice-bound seas north of Europe and America. Nevertheless, some English navigators had been employed as pilots on Dutch trading voyages to the East Indies, and they spread the good news when they returned home. This was strongly reinforced when Sir Francis Drake captured the great carrack *San Felipe* in 1587, complete with her valuable cargo of spices and charts of eastern seas. European countries anxious to have a part in this rich East Indian trade set up incorporated companies in order to exploit it to the full, on the realistic grounds that any sort of joint company acting together must be

stronger than its individual numbers acting singly.

In all, eight European nations set up East India companies – England, Holland, France, Denmark, Austria, Spain, Sweden and Scotland. Of these, only two became really significant, those of England and Holland, the French company following some way in the rear in importance. The others got nowhere and faded out early.

The English company, known officially as the Honourable East India Company, and colloquially as 'John Company', was founded towards the end of the sixteenth century and was incorporated by royal charter of Queen Elizabeth on 31 December 1600. It had a capital of £72,000 which was subscribed by 125 shareholders interested in trade in far eastern waters. The first trading expeditions, known as 'separate' voyages, were made by the individual shareholders who carried all the cost and took all the profit. But in 1612 a new system was introduced, which became permanent, under which the company as a whole owned the ships and organized the voyages, the profit

being shared out among all the shareholders. Already, by 1612, company ships had reached as far as Japan, with whom friendly relations had been established, and had set up two 'factories', or trading centres, on the mainland of India, at Masulipatam and Pettapoli. The company had also, in 1609, constructed its own dockyard at Deptford, on the River Thames, where it built its own ships. These were armed as warships, both to give protection against the chronic piracy at the time and, when necessary, to dispute the right to trade against the similarly armed merchantmen of the Dutch, Spanish and French East India companies.

The Dutch East India Company was incorporated as a company in 1602 by charter from the States-General, to bring together under single control all the existing Dutch trading ventures in the Far East. It was granted a monopoly of all Indian and East Indies trade, was given exemption from all import taxes, and authority to own land, maintain an army and a navy, build and fortify trading centres, to declare local wars and make local peace, to exercise civil

and criminal jurisdiction, and to coin its own money. These rights gave the Dutch company immense advantages over its competitors, and the English East India Company took steps to obtain the same privileges. It applied for a revised charter and received from the king the same rights as those exercised by the Dutch.

There was war from the start between the English and Dutch companies, with pitched battles taking place where they came into contact. In 1619 the two companies signed an agreement to stop these disputes, but it lasted less than an hour and renewed fighting broke out, even before the smoke from the guns saluting the signing of the agreement had cleared. This vicious squabbling reached its peak of horror in 1623, when English merchants at Amboyna, while under protection of a flag of truce, were tortured and massacred by the order of the Dutch governor.

At the height of its success, which lasted through most of the seventeenth century, the Dutch East India Company had its main capital in Batavia, with subsidiary stations in Ceylon, Malacca, Java, the Malay archipelago, Ternate and Amboyna. It also maintained a fortified post at the Cape of Good Hope, as a base for the protection and re-provision of its ships, on their way to and from the homeland. It had 150 armed merchantmen, 40 warships, and an army of 10,000 soldiers, and its word was law. But its rigid policy was, in the end, to bring it to disaster. Its aim was always a complete monopoly of trade, maintained by force of arms – an

ambition that was bound to bring it into constant conflict with the English and French East India companies. By the early eighteenth century the Dutch had been driven from the mainland of Asia and from Ceylon by the English and French, and the increase in military costs as the company fought to maintain its monopoly brought it to bankruptcy. It was wound up in 1798 when Holland was invaded by the revolutionary armies of France.

Meanwhile, the English East India Company prospered exceedingly. With the warlike Dutch expelled from the whole of India, an armed neutrality existed between the English, firmly entrenched in their 'presidencies' in Bombay and Bengal, and the French, whose main centre was Madras. But when the Seven Years' War between England and France broke out in 1756, the two East India companies were inevitably brought into the conflict. The end came for the French with the battle of Plassey in 1757, and with that victory the whole of India came under 'John Company's' direct control. This vast accession of power and of territory alarmed the British government at home, and it took steps to assume responsibility for this addition to the empire by making all the top company appointments subject to government approval – a change which eventually brought the financial, military, and political control of all India into the hands of the government in London.

By 1813, the Honourable East India Company was approaching the end of its long history. In that year its

monopoly of trade with India was dissolved, and although Company ships still traded there, competition from other shipowners began to cut it down to size. For another twenty years it was allowed to retain its monopoly of trade to China, but this, too, came to an end in 1833. But, because it was so well established in India, and controlled through its many centres the machinery of government, it was decided in London, as a matter of administrative convenience, to allow it to continue the operation of civil government. This came to an end with the Indian Mutiny of 1857, and particularly with the excessive punishments meted out by the company officers to the mutineers. The government in London was forced to take over complete control, and the Honourable East India Company was officially wound up in 1858.

In the times of their greatness the various East India companies built some of the finest ships the world has ever seen. At the Dutch shipyards at Rotterdam and Amsterdam, the French Biscay port of Lorient (specially constructed and named for this eastern trade), and the English dockyard at Deptford, a succession of magnificent ships slid down the slipways, larger and finer than any others in the world.

Left: An East Indiaman off Hong Kong. (From an 1837 painting by William John Huggins).

Below: East Indiamen under construction on the Thames. These proud, stately ships of any of the national companies were instantly recognisable as ocean aristocrats.

Chapter Five
Command of the Seas

'Whoso commands the seas commands the trade of the world; whoso commands the trade of the world commands the riches of the world.'

The words are those of Sir Walter Raleigh and they were beginning to be understood, if still a little dimly, by most European nations at the beginning of the seventeenth century, particularly by the English and the Dutch. Spain, too, was beginning to recognize this essential truth, though for her they had the opposite significance. She had already seen the command of European waters slip from her grasp with the defeat of her 'Invincible Armada'; now she was seeing her command of American waters and the Pacific continually challenged by English and French expeditions intent on settlement and trade, and was powerless to intervene because she was not prepared to spend money on a fleet of warships to defend the huge territories which she had claimed for herself. Almost her only naval operation during the years which followed the Armada defeat was an annual convoy, in which she deployed her entire fleet to escort the ships carrying the treasure that she had amassed in America and her East Indian possessions home across the Atlantic, and guard them against attack from the French and English squadrons which lay in wait off the Azores. Already she had virtually abandoned the Pacific. Drake, on his voyage round the world, had had no difficulty in capturing the annual treasure ship which brought the wealth, accumulated during a year's trading, from Manila to Acapulco for onward transmission to Spain in the annual convoy; Cavendish, during a similar circumnavigation a year or two later, captured another. These annual treasure ships had to cross the Pacific unescorted. There was no Spanish warship in that ocean to guard them and ensure their safe arrival in Mexico with their rich cargoes intact.

Left: *The Sovereign of the Seas*, a 1st rate launched in 1637. Although bigger than anything yet seen, she was not a success, and was rebuilt twice before being burnt. The portrait is of the co-designer Peter Pett, son of Phineas.

The Dutch, having been materially aided by the English in their struggle to win independence from Spain, took the opportunity offered by that friendship to expand their own trade in Europe and strive for a monopoly of the carrying trade at sea. They built good ships, well suited for trade, in large numbers, and were to be seen in every port in Europe, where they quoted freight rates that local shipowners could not touch. As the century wore on, the other European nations were more or less forced to pass Navigation Laws to safeguard their own shipping, under which a country's exports could only be carried at sea by her own ships. England passed her first important Navigation Act in 1651, and the Dutch were forced into war if they were not to see their pre-eminence in maritime trade wither and die.

The basic Dutch trading ship in European waters was still the *fluyt*, enlarged and modified into a sensible design of ship, incorporating a long, straight keel which gripped the water well when the ship was under sail. She had a straight stem joining the keel at an angle of about 45 degrees, and a vertical sternpost on which the rudder hung, while the stern rounded up into the counter. She had a 'no-nonsense' three-masted rig of courses and topsails, with an upper and lower spritsail set on the bowsprit. As *fluyts* never carried any sort of topgallants – even the largest of them and even in the most settled of weather – they were easy to handle at sea and needed a much smaller crew than ships of similar size belonging to other nations. It was reckoned that a small English ship of around 100 tons required a total crew of about 30 men; a *fluyt* of equivalent tonnage could be handled with a crew of one-third of that number. Because the beam measurement used in the calculation of a ship's tonnage was taken across the upper deck, the sides of Dutch *fluyts* in the first half of the seventeenth century were built with a pronounced tumble-home. This kept the beam measurement down, and with it the ship's calculated tonnage, reducing the harbour and other dues which the owner had to pay. When a new system of measurement was introduced in 1669 which took the ship's beam as the width at its widest point, the *fluyt's* sides were built straight upright instead, to give more width and accommodation on deck. The Dutch pinnace was similar to the *fluyt*, except that she had a flat stern on typical warship lines. Although pinnaces were included in the war fleets to act as fast reconnaissance ships and as convoy escorts, the type was also used for trading purposes. They were generally single-decked vessels, with a comparatively narrow hold, but they were faster through the water than *fluyts* and thus of value in some trades.

The largest Dutch merchant ship of the seventeenth century was the big East Indiaman, built very much along warship lines, though usually to lighter scantlings. These East Indiamen were

built up to about 1,200 tons in their largest form, though about 800 tons was a more average size. Like the warships, they had two gundecks, and were three-masted, full-rigged ships, setting topgallants above their topsails. The early Dutch East Indiamen were decorated with much more carving and gingerbread work than the early warships, but by the middle of the century Dutch warships had caught them up in fancy decoration, following the English pattern of embellishing a ship with carvings wherever there was room for them.

For their warships, the Dutch had been quick to appreciate the efficiency of the English galleon introduced by John Hawkins and they took it over as their basic naval design, though only rarely did they build a warship with more than two gundecks. This was probably on account of the generally shoal waters off the Dutch coast, in which vessels of deep draught would be at a

Below: Seventeenth century Dutch East Indiamen entering port. (From a painting by Vroom)

disadvantage. There was also a general lack of cohesion in the Dutch navy, as each of the seven States was completely autonomous in naval affairs. Each built its own navy, manned by its own seamen, and would only agree on an overall commander-in-chief after much bickering with its neighbours. During the First Anglo-Dutch War (1652–54) the largest and best Dutch warship was Marten Tromp's *Brederode*, a ship of about 800 tons mounting 56 guns. The Dutch Navy List of 1654 shows a total fleet of 131 warships, of which only nine mounted 50 guns and upwards. The great majority of their warships carried between 30 and 38 guns mounted on a single gundeck.

It was still the general practice of all maritime nations during a war to hire armed merchant ships to swell the fleet numbers and the Dutch were no exception. But in general these merchantmen were of little value, and many a battle was lost because the captains, having little stomach for fighting, stole away with their ships whenever opportunity offered.

In England, the general run of small merchant vessels was based on the pinnace design, flat-sterned and built up slightly higher aft than the Dutch *fluyt*. Like the *fluyt* they were three-masted, but set topgallants above their topsails, thus needing larger crews to handle them efficiently. They were more like small warships, mounting up to 28 guns on a single gundeck, ostensibly for defence against pirates, but ready to make their presence felt if obstacles were placed in the way of their trade. They had no generic name, being variously described as a 'ship' or a 'bark'.

The large English trading ship of the first half of the seventeenth century was, as in Holland, the East Indiaman, but it was several years before the English version equalled the Dutch in tonnage. A very few English Indiamen were built over about 500 or 600 tons, invariably to the galleon design, and of course armed with a battery of naval cannon, but it was not until nearly the end of the seventeenth century that they approached the Dutch either in numbers or size. One exception to this generality was an East Indiaman called the *Trade's Increase*, in which Sir Henry Middleton commanded a Company voyage in 1610: she was a ship of 1,000 tons.

In warships, on the other hand, England built larger than any other nation. Elizabeth, at her death in 1603, had left a flourishing navy which was held in considerable respect by the other European nations. Her successor, James I, who had brought the war against Spain to a close on his accession, let the navy slide into decay until, in 1607, there were only twenty-seven Royal ships left, of which the Venetian ambassador could report to his government that many were 'old and rotten and barely fit for service'. One year later, perhaps as a warning to other countries that the English navy was not moribund, James ordered the building of the *Prince Royal*, the largest warship yet to be constructed in England. She has been called the navy's first three-decker, in the sense that she carried her guns on three separate decks. While this is true, she could more accurately be described as a two-decker, in the proper sense of the term, since she had only two covered gundecks, the guns mounted on her upper deck not constituting a separate gundeck in the accepted sense of the word. She was built at Woolwich by Phineas Pett and William Bright, with a length of keel of 115 ft (35 m), a maximum beam of 43 ft (13 m) and a depth of 18 ft (5·5 m). According to the contemporary system of ship measurement, her gross tonnage worked out at 1,330, but a more modern figure would be 1,187.

There was tremendous criticism of her design throughout her building, partly because Phineas Pett's ideas were not shared by other well-known naval architects of the day, partly because she was considered a bit of a monstrosity. Pett does seem to have been less than clever in the building of this important ship. His original estimate of 775 loads of timber to build the ship was less than a half of the 1,627 loads actually used, adding £5,908 to her cost. Much of the wood used in her building was green and unseasoned, and in 1621 another £6,000 was required to make her fit for service. Her total initial cost was £20,000. She was built in a dry dock at Woolwich. When the time came to launch her in 1610 she was found to be too wide to pass through the dock opening and it had to be enlarged to allow her to get out.

There were two innovations in the building of the *Prince Royal*. She was the first English warship to be double-planked throughout her hull (built with an inner and outer wood skin) and she was also the first ship to have her bulkheads double-bolted with iron. A retrograde step was the decision not to sheathe her bottom. In Elizabeth's time Hawkins had sheathed his ships by double planking below the waterline, with hair impregnated with tar between them which acted both as a preservative for the timber and a deterrent to attacks by marine worms. Some merchant ships had had their bottoms sheathed with lead sheets to prevent attack by the teredo worm, but this practice was discouraged in naval ships, as it was found that in sea water the lead caused the iron of the pintles and rudder to corrode by galvanic action.

Above: The *Prince Royal,* with Charles I on board, at the head of an English fleet.

John Stow, in his *Annales of England*, described the *Prince Royal* thus: 'This year the King built a most goodly ship for warre, the keel whereof was 114 feet in length, and the cross beam was 44 feet in length; she will carry 64 pieces of ordnance [in fact she eventually mounted 55], and is of the burthen of 1,400 tons. This royal ship is double built, and is most sumptuously adorned, within and without, with all manner of curious carving, painting, and rich gilding.' Indeed, it was this carving and painting which was the most remarkable thing about this first of the great English warships. The Pipe Office accounts in the Public Records Office in London reveal that Sebastian Vicars was paid £441 for the carvings and Robert Beake and Pane Isackson £868 7s. for the painting and gilding – a considerable proportion of the overall building cost of £20,000. Her figurehead was a carving of St. George and the Dragon with, on top of the forerail, a large knight's helmet surmounted by an enormous crown. The three stern galleries were elaborately carved, with the Prince of Wales's feathers on the two lower galleries and the lion and unicorn crest on the upper gallery, all surrounded by gilded ornamental carvings.

Ship decoration was nothing new. Most nations had long embellished their ships with startling colours and decorative carvings. But the *Prince Royal* set a new standard of richness which was copied in their warships by other European nations, and also by private shipowners, notably the East India Companies. Decoration grew to ridiculous proportions later in the century: the *Sovereign of the Seas* when she was launched had more gilded carving on her stern, sides and bulkheads than there was plain timber.

Yet, in spite of her size and prestige, the *Prince Royal* was not a successful ship. She was badly designed and badly built, and showed no real advance on the Elizabethan warships that had preceded her. One of her novel features was three stern galleries, an adaptation of the Spanish carrack design introduced into the English navy for the first time. But in this respect the *Prince Royal* was exceptional. Three stern galleries did not become the rule until much later, when the size of the average first-rate ship of the line rose from around 1,000 tons to more than double.

The *Prince Royal*, though generally unsuccessful as a ship, was important because she marked a distinct step upwards in warship size, a lead which all other navies had to follow. She was followed twenty-five years later by a new warship nearly half as big again, the *Sovereign of the Seas*, built by Charles I for his ship-money fleet. Once again the designer was Phineas Pett, and she was built as something of a showpiece of English naval architecture. Her carving and decoration cost Charles no less than £6,691 out of a total cost of £65,586 16s. 9½d., inclusive of her guns – a fantastic sum even in comparison with the *Prince Royal* – and, as all her carving was covered with gold leaf, she glittered in the sunshine. The Dutch, whom she met frequently in battle, called her the 'Golden Devil'.

The *Sovereign of the Seas* marked a notable step forward in warship rig, for she stepped only three masts, instead of the four which had been more or less standard on all large warships.

Following her lead, all rated warships, and indeed most merchant ships of any size, were to be three-masted for the rest of the sailing era. She was the first true English three-decker in the sense that she had three covered gundecks, and she was also the first warship to carry royals above her topsails. Another important advance in design was the substitution of a round stern in place of the square stern, which was to remain a feature of English warships until the advent of the iron ship in the mid-nineteenth century.

The system of rates, under which warships were graded by the number of guns that they mounted, was brought in during the seventeenth century. By the end of the century, first-rates mounted from 90 to 100 guns, second-rates from 80 to 90, third-rates 60 to 80, fourth-rates 40 to 60, fifth-rates 28 to 40, and sixth-rates below 28. A list of the English Royal Navy (it had been given the prefix 'Royal' by Charles II upon the restoration of the monarchy) of 1660 shows nine first-rates, eleven second-rates, thirty-nine third-rates, forty fourth-rates, two fifth-rates and six sixth-rates. The various other types of ship making up the English navy were bombs, fireships, hoys, hulks, ketches, smacks and yachts, but, with the exception of the hulks, all were small and thought of more as naval auxiliaries than as warships. The hulks were fairly big ships, mostly merchant ships captured from the Dutch. Of the rated warships, no fewer than forty were ships of over 1,000 tons.

This increase in size was general, throughout the warships of all rates: while the first-rate had approximately doubled her tonnage, so had every other rate. It had happened within a span of about thirty years, reflecting experience gained in battle of the fact that a good big ship would always beat a good small ship. It took some time for this simple doctrine to spread to the navies of other countries, but in the end they were forced to follow suit if their maritime ambitions were ever to be achieved. And, as was so

Left: A model of a Dutch 64-gun ship of the seventeenth century. The foremast is raked slightly forward, and the lateen and spritsail topmast are still in evidence.

frequently the case, merchant ships followed the naval lead, doubling their average tonnage, though over a rather longer time span.

It was with fleets such as this, or with fleets very similar, that the three Anglo-Dutch wars of the seventeenth century were fought. They consisted of bitter, hard-fought battles with up to a hundred ships on either side engaged in a gigantic mêlée. The basic cause underlying each of the three wars was the struggle for trading supremacy, not only in European waters, but worldwide. Both countries had realized the truth of Sir Walter Raleigh's words, quoted at the beginning of this chapter, and both were disputing the command of the seas to enable their merchant ships to trade freely and advantageously in every part of the world where trade could be found. After the three wars it was the navy of England which emerged victorious, opening the oceans for unrestricted use by her merchant ships. It was the start of a huge expansion in English merchant shipping. In the course of a relatively few years it was to surpass that of all the other seafaring nations put together.

By the end of the third of these Anglo-Dutch wars in 1674, the sailing warship had attained the general design and rig which she was to retain more or less until the end of her useful life. The only major change still to come was a further increase in size, and even this was limited since there was a maximum size which could be propelled through the water, without raising masts to such a height that they became impossible to stay. There were, of course, minor improvements to be made in general hull design and in the rigging plan, but the basic ship design showed no significant change until new shipbuilding materials, particularly iron and steel, were introduced in the nineteenth century.

Throughout western Europe, both in fighting and merchant navies, the basic hull design remained firmly based on the English galleon. The original low beakhead projecting well beyond the cutwater gave way over the years to a shorter beakhead with a pronounced upward curve. The space inside the beakhead and forward of the forecastle bulkhead was floored with gratings and served as the crew's lavatory. Hopefully the sea would wash up through the gratings when the ship was under way and keep the area reasonably clean. The forecastle itself was built lower as the years progressed, almost disappearing completely in merchant ships in the eighteenth century, but retained in warships to provide a mounting for the chase guns that fired directly ahead at an enemy ship attempting to escape. Abaft the mainmast the largest ships had quarter-deck and poop deck, one above the other, to provide cabins and stern galleries for the officers.

A ship with quarter-deck and poop deck had three stern galleries, on upper, quarter- and poop deck levels; smaller ships, without a poop, had two. In the very largest ships, extra galleries were added on each quarter. These stern and quarter galleries were glazed with lights (windows), and were integral with the more important cabins, providing a private space for recreation for the occupant.

All warships, and a great majority of the larger merchant ships, were built with a pronounced tumble-home. This was to provide enough width on the lower gundecks for the guns to recoil when fired. These were mounted on wooden trucks with wheels and the force of the explosion of the firing charge forced them backwards at high speed across the deck until they were brought to a halt by the rope breeching attached to the ship's side. This width of deck was not required on the upper deck, which normally carried no guns, and so the sides were curved inwards to reduce it to more normal proportions. As most large merchant ships still went armed for self-defence, they too had the tumble-home. And that they still needed their guns is evidenced by an action fought as late as 1804: a convoy of British East Indiamen had to fight its way past a French squadron of one ship of the line and several frigates in the Malacca Straits before being able to continue its voyage home.

The standard rig of all these ships was three-masted, with square sails on all masts except the mizen, which only had square sails above the mizen course. At the start of the seventeenth century the lateen course was giving way to the fore-and-aft sail spread by a long sprit, and after another fifty years this spritsail gave way to a fore-and-aft gaffsail, at first loose-footed, but later with the foot of the sail laced to a boom. Although not technically a course, this gaffsail was generally known as the mizen 'course' until, much later, a square sail was spread as a true mizen course, the gaffsail then becoming known as the 'spanker'. The old bonnet, which used to be laced to the foot of a course to increase its size in a following wind, had completely disappeared, but the same enlargement of the sail area could be obtained by setting studdingsails on the topsail yard by means of studdingsail booms which temporarily prolonged the yards outwards. The old clumsy upper and lower spritsails, set on the bowsprit, gave way during the early eighteenth century to jibs and fore staysails, and additional staysails were set between the masts. Under full sail, with royals set above her topgallants, a full-rigged ship was a magnificent spectacle.

The basic method of shipbuilding had not changed since Phoenician times. The bones of a ship still consisted of a keel, a stempost and stern-

Right: The Texel (1673), last engagement of the Third Anglo-Dutch War.

Below right: Details of a seventeenth century man-of-war, showing the tumble-home (left) and the beakhead (right).

A new Table of all the names of the principal Parts and Rigging of a MAN of WAR Necessary for all sea-faring men and others that desire to be therewith acquainted. Also all the Prospects of a Section of a Ship cut thro' the Keel, both fore & aft with her Boats, Longboats and Sloops.

Flag Staf Cap
Stern
Upper Gallery

Stern of the Ship

Stem head
Bulk head of the fore Castle
Bowsprit
Stem

Sold by Daniel Midwinter at the three Crowns in St. Pauls Church Yard London.

post, scarfed in at either end, and frames or ribs, curved to the shape of the hull, fitted at intervals to the keel to take the side planking and held rigidly in place by the deck beams which ran laterally across the ship between each pair of frames. This general pattern provided a powerful structure which held the ship together longitudinally, laterally and vertically. The strength of the rig was assured by stepping all three lower masts into the keel, so they were held rigidly at deck level, as well as being held firmly in place above deck by shrouds, fixed to the sides of the ship and running up to the mastheads to stop any athwartships movement, and by forestays and backstays to prevent any fore-and-aft movement. Topmasts and topgallant masts were similarly supported by shrouds and stays.

The wooden warship of the seventeenth and eighteenth centuries was a vessel of immense strength. She had massive double-planked sides

of oak up to 18 in (46 cm) thick, strengthened longitudinally under the gunports by oaken wales which ran externally along the sides from bow to stern, adding another 6 to 8 in (15 to 20 cm) in thickness. The only real difference between the warships of Britain and those of other European nations was in the shape of the stern, the British retaining the rounded stern and other navies preferring the square stern. This difference lasted into the eighteenth century, when the rounded stern was adopted almost universally.

During most of the seventeenth century the guns with which the world's warships were armed were the cannon firing a 42-lb (19 kg) shot, the demi-cannon (32-lb (14·5 kg)), the culverin (18-lb (8·2 kg)) and smaller guns firing balls varying from 12 to 3 lb (5·4 to 1·4 kg). Later in the century, and throughout the eighteenth, warship guns lost their names of 'cannon', 'demi-cannon',

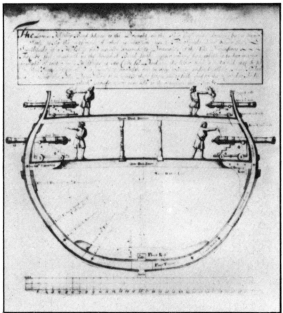

Left: A sectional drawing of a seventeenth century two-decker (Keltridge).

Far left: Lower gundeck of the salvaged Swedish two-decker *Wasa*. The guns were salved by divers after the sinking.

Below left: Broadside tactics involved close-range cannonading. This is HMS *Brunswick* engaging the French *l'Achille* and *le Vengeur* at the Glorious First of June, 1794.

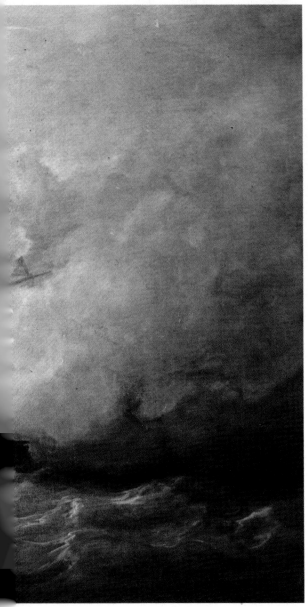

and so on, and were designated solely by the weight of the shot they fired, as '42-pounder', '32-pounder', etc. It was a formidable armament, particularly at the range at which naval battles were normally fought, colloquially known as 'half pistol shot', or about 100 yards (91 m).

With her massive oaken sides and the batteries of guns on her gundecks, the ship of the line had little to fear in broadside battle, which was almost the only form of action possible under the conditions of the age. There was no means of training the guns to fire at any angle forward or aft. They could only fire at right angles to the centreline, and so could only hit an enemy ship when she was directly abeam. As soon as the naval battle developed, from the disorganized *mêlée* of the First and Second Anglo-Dutch Wars to a more orderly form of combat, this limitation in gunnery obliged warships to fight in line ahead, and so forced them to attack their opponents at their strongest point. It was for this reason that, throughout this period, so few naval engagements ended in a clear-cut victory.

In only two directions did the ship of the line offer any defensive weakness – directly ahead and directly astern. Wooden ships were not built with strong transverse bulkheads, and there was nothing to stop a cannon ball, fired at a ship from one of these two directions, travelling the whole length of the deck. This was particularly true of the broadside fired from directly astern, where the target was large and the only obstructions were the glazed lights of the stern galleries and the relatively flimsy partitions separating the cabins from one another. It was a weakness exploited in battle, particularly by the British, from the second half of the eighteenth century until the end of the sailing warship era.

Royal George
(1756)

Gundeck 178 ft (54·3 m)
Keel 143 ft 5 in (43·7 m)
Beam 51 ft 9 in (15·8 m)
Tonnage 2,041 B.O.M.
Armament twenty-eight 42-pounders,
twenty-eight 24-pounders, twenty-
eight 12-pounders, sixteen 6-pounders
Complement 850

A first-rate ship of the line of 100 guns, H.M.S. *Royal George* was launched at Woolwich, on the Thames, on 18 February 1756. Three years later she took part in the battle of Quiberon Bay as the flagship of Admiral Hawke. She was lost, along with 900 lives, in a notorious accident at Spithead on 29 August 1782. She was being heeled for purposes of fitting a cock below the waterline, when water entered through her gunports and she filled up and sank.

She is seen here with her side cut away to show (in descending order) the half deck, middle gundeck, lower gundeck, orlop deck and hold. The small drawing shows her under sail. The long mizen yard served as a spare in case of damage to another spar.

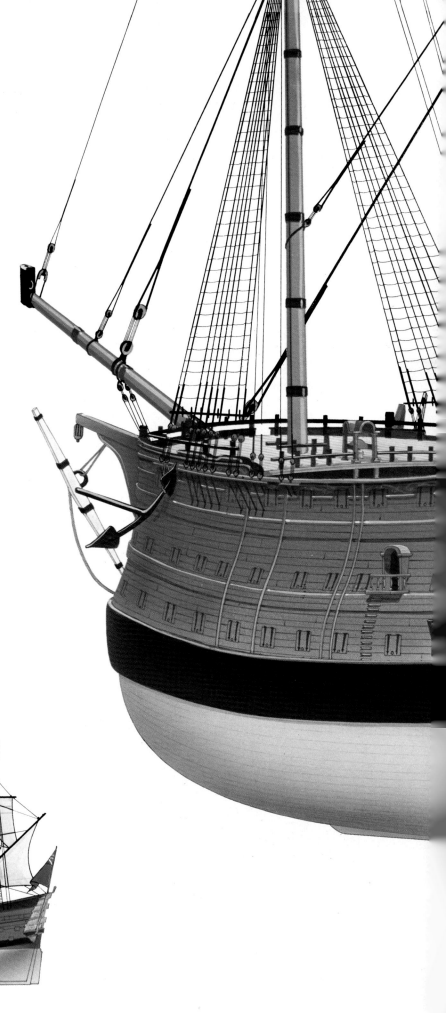

Right: Cross-section of a fireship. Loaded guns have been piled on deck, to explode and cause even greater destruction.

Below: Fireships in action against the Armada anchored off Gravelines. The danger they presented was enough to disrupt the best-organized formation.

Only warships of the first three rates were true ships of the line. Fourth-rates were described as 'cruisers', although they too fought in the line of battle occasionally (at the battle of the Nile, in 1798, H.M.S. *Leander*, a fourth-rate of 50 guns, stationed herself between two French ships of 74 and 80 guns, and engaged them both with broadsides). Fifth- and sixth-rates were classed as 'frigates' and never fought in the line, and it was an unwritten law no ship of the line would open fire on a frigate unless the frigate fired first.

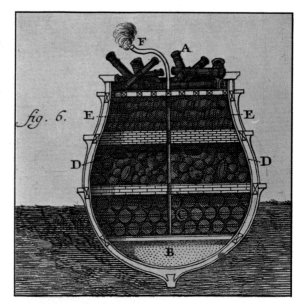

Apart from what might be described as true fighting ships, that is, ships rated by the number of guns they mounted, all navies included various other types of vessel for use in minor roles or as auxiliaries. Only two need to be considered at this stage: fireships and bombs.

Fireships were relatively old weapons of naval war, having been used in battle in various forms over the centuries. During the seventeenth century, and particularly in the three Anglo-Dutch Wars, they formed an integral part of every fleet that put to sea, to be used whenever the wind served to sail them down upon an enemy. There were no real naval tactics in those days. Ships of each squadron rallied round their admiral and in general fought in a bunch in as close combat as they could manage, thus presenting a good target for a fireship attack. The fireship herself was normally an old vessel, packed with barrels of gunpowder, tar, pitch and anything else that would explode or burn. The fuse was a powder trail that was ignited at the last possible moment. They were sailed by small, picked crews who were encouraged by the promise of a reward for a successful attack. Their method of operation was to sail down so close to an enemy that their grappling irons would inevitably become entangled in her rigging. They towed a longboat astern on a short warp. At the last moment the crew took to their boat, the master fired the gunpowder trail, jumped into the boat himself, and cast it off, and they pulled away as fast as they could, to win clear of the subsequent explosion.

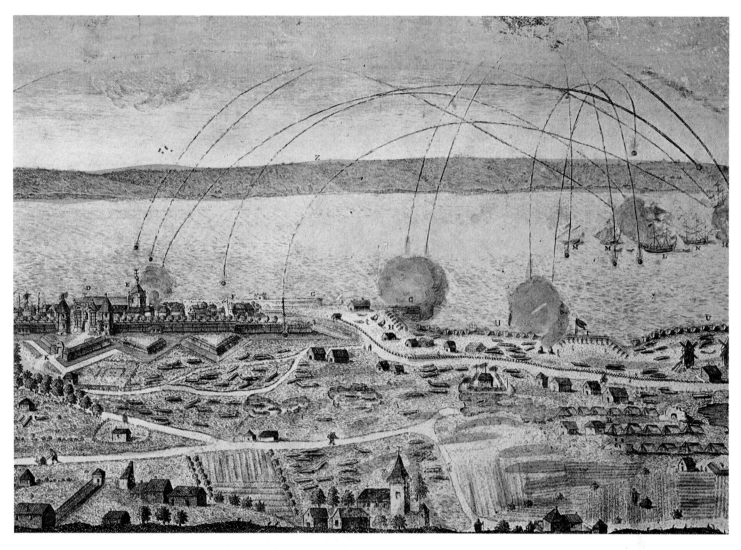

A paragraph in the British *Fighting Instructions* for 1714 reads:

'That if any of His Majesty's Fireships perform the Service expected from them, in such Manner That any of the Enemies Men of War of Forty guns, or more, shall be burnt by them, every Person remaining in the Fireship till the Service be performed, shall receive on board the Admiral, immediately after the Service done, Ten Pounds, as a reward of that Service, over and above his Pay due to him; and in Case any of them shall be killed in that Service, it shall be paid to his Executors, or next Relations: And the Captains of such Fireships shall receive 100l. or a Medal of Gold, with a Chain of the same Value, as he shall make Choice of, to remain as a Token of Honour to him and his Posterity; and shall receive such other Encouragement, by Preferment and Command, or otherwise, as shall be fit to reward him and induce others to perform the like Service. . . .'

Service in fireships was obviously a hazardous occupation in order to command such rewards as this at a time when the normal pay of an able seaman amounted to 19 shillings a month.

The 'bomb' took its name from the missile that it fired, and was a small naval vessel armed with a single heavy mortar which fired a bomb weighing up to 200 lbs (90 kg). It was a weapon used for the systematic bombardment of targets ashore, never against ships. The mortar had been developed as a land weapon towards the end of the sixteenth century. It was first taken to sea a hundred years later, in 1682, when the pirate stronghold of Algiers was systematically bombarded with mortars by a French fleet under the command of Abraham du Quesne. Later, most European navies adopted the bomb as an ingredient of their national fleet.

For the operation of a deliberate bombardment, the mortar was fixed in position in the ship, and the ship herself trained, to give the correct direction of fire. This was achieved by mooring the ship with two anchors and using springs on the cables to swing the ship as required to get the bomb onto the target. It was possible, with springs used thus, to obtain a very high degree of accuracy, which naturally made the bomb an extremely significant weapon in this type of naval operation.

Above: Le Havre under bombardment by British ships during the Seven Years' War.

117

The heavy mortar was mounted originally on the deck of a three-masted ship, with the foremast removed to provide sufficient space for the weapon. The resulting two-masted rig of mainmast and mizen became widely known in naval circles as a 'ketch' rig, although the only real resemblance to the traditional ketch was in the fact that there was no foremast. Apart from that, the rig and functions of the real ketch and the bomb ketch, were miles apart. Once the foremast of the ship destined to become a bomb had been removed, additional deck beams were added to provide enough structural strength to absorb the very heavy recoil of the mortar. Later, after the new weapon had proved its usefulness, conversions from small three-masted ships by removal of the foremast gave way to two-masted vessels specially built as bombs, with decks designed to take the force of the recoil. Later still, when the bomb ketch had ceased to be a viable naval weapon, they became the most popular type of ship used for polar exploration, their inbuilt strength proving invaluable in resisting the pressures generated by movements of pack ice.

It has been said that the main naval activity of the seventeenth century was the long struggle between the English and the Dutch for a mastery of the seas that would guarantee freedom and expansion of seaborne trade. The three Anglo-Dutch Wars had brought in their train a huge growth of English merchant shipping, and as a result of the wars English ships were able to pass freely and without dispute in waters which had formerly been strictly controlled by the Dutch on almost a monopoly basis. The eighteenth century was to see a similar series of wars fought for basically the same reason, between Britain and a resurgent France.

France was a comparatively late starter in naval shipbuilding in the seventeenth century, in part because the central government held little authority over the coastal provinces. In 1624, when Cardinal Richelieu came to power, he was quick to recognize that power in the world rested on control of the sea and in 1625 he had himself made Grande Maître, Chef, et Surintendant-Général de la Navigation et Commerce de France, a grandiloquent title which nevertheless gave him overall control of all shipbuilding and everything else maritime. One of his first acts was to order five warships from shipyards in Holland, which could be used as models by the naval shipbuilding yards which he was establishing in France. One of these five was the *Saint Louis*, of which the Dutch engraver of maps, Hendrik Hondius, has left us a picture. She was a two-

Left: A modern model of the bomb ketch *Granado* of 1742. Note the heavy timbering to withstand the recoil of the 10 inch mortar. (By R. A. Lightley from original plans)

Below left: The ornate stern of a model of the galley *Réale*.

Right: Hoisting the sternpost onto the keel of a ship under construction in the dockyard at Toulon. (From Colbert's *Atlas*)

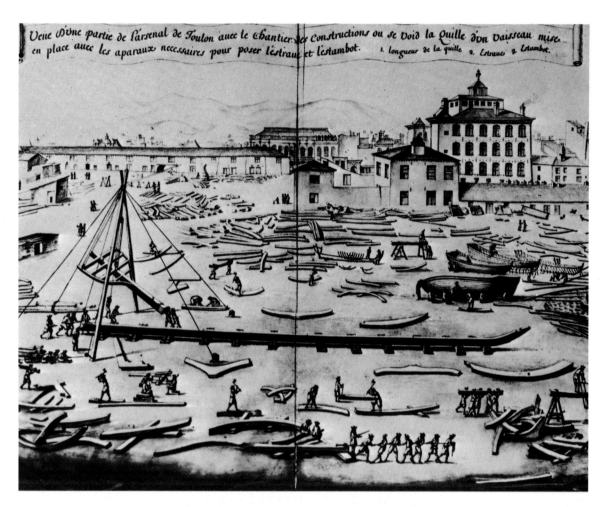

Veüe d'une partie de l'arsenal de Toulon auec le chantier des Constructions ou se void la Quille d'un vaisseau mise en place auec les aparaux necessaires pour poser l'estrau et l'estambot. 1. longueur de la quille 2. Estraue 2. Estambot.

decker of 56 guns and, according to Léon Guérin's *Histoire Maritime de France*, had a tonnage of 1,200, obviously an overestimate for a ship of her size. Using these Dutch ships as models, Richelieu began to build up a fleet and by the time of his death the French fleet consisted of sixty-three ships and twenty-eight galleys. What was missing, however, were officers and men of experience to command and fight them, for the social order in France made it impossible to appoint a commoner, which most of the experienced sea captains were, to command a fleet, or even a single ship, over the head of a member of the nobility. The French fleet, moreover, was divided geographically between the Mediterranean and the Bay of Biscay, and was woefully mismanaged in both places.

The best known of Richelieu's home-built warships was the *Couronne*, launched in 1638 and possibly the French reply to the English *Sovereign of the Seas*. She was a two-decker of 78 guns and, according to Guérin, a tonnage of 2,000, again an obvious overestimate. A model of her in the Musée de la Marine in Paris shows that she was built with the typical square stern of the Dutch, but an oddity of her design was a small flying poop built up over her stern, giving her the appearance of a carrack almost, abaft the

mizen. She was three-masted, setting topgallants above the topsails on fore and mainmasts, with the typical lateen mizen of the times.

Jean-Baptiste Colbert, Louis XIV's great minister, was the next to take a hand in building up a French fleet. Between Richelieu's death in 1642 and Colbert's ministry of 1663 the navy of France had been in the hands of Cardinal Mazarin, who had no knowledge of, and little interest in, the exercise of sea power. By the time of his death the navy had dwindled to twenty ships and six galleys, some of them dilapidated beyond repair. Colbert virtually had to start again and build a new navy. Nevertheless, at his death in 1683 he left a navy of 117 ships of the line (though included under that designation were some not strong enough to fight in the line of battle) and thirty galleys. To design his ships he imported naval architects from other countries, including the English shipbuilder, Anthony Deane, and one from Naples, Biagio Pangallo, who became famous as a ship-designer throughout France under the name of Maître Blaise. It was he who set a new pattern of French warship building which was to bring French naval architects a reputation for providing the best ships in the world, partly by increasing the beam by a foot or two and reducing the draught, which brought

LE SOLEIL ROYAL

Above: Stern of the three-decker *Soleil Royal*, pride of the fleet of Louis XIV.

was lateen-rigged on two masts, spreading some 8,000 sq ft (743 m²) of canvas, and carried five large guns, of which the largest was a 36-pounder, under the forecastle, which could only fire directly ahead, and twelve small swivel guns, six each side, on the catwalks which ran the length of the galley outside the oarsmen. The long protruding ram was tipped with an iron replica of a horse's head, with a spike between the ears. The usual narrow *corsia*, or bridge, known in France as the *coursie*, ran the length of the galley amidships between the thwarts, and was patrolled by drivers with long leather whips, to encourage the slaves and the criminals who had been condemned to the galleys in place of a prison sentence. The large poop deck aft was normally shaded by a fine, rich awning supported on a framework of light spars, under which the captain and other officers could take their ease while the rowers sweated below. Although there were a few galleys attached to the Biscay fleet, where they were of little or no use, the majority of them were stationed in the Mediterranean where the era of the galley was not yet over.

The pride of Louis XIV's French fleet was the *Soleil Royal*, a three-decker variously described as of 98, 102 and 106 guns – as big or bigger than any other warship in the world. There is a contemporary drawing of her by A. L. van Kaldenbach which shows her to have been as magnificently decorated, even, as the *Sovereign of the Seas*. The decorations which covered the stern and quarter galleries were carved by Pierre Puget. Her figurehead was a gilded mermaid bearing a golden orb, and the three lanterns on her poop rail were magnificently embellished and surmounted by golden crowns. Eventually she was forced ashore and was burned by the English at the battle of Barfleur in 1692 – a sad end for a ship of much magnificence.

increased steadiness as a gun platform, and partly by designing a slightly hollower bow and stern, which brought up to an extra knot in speed.

The galleys built for the French fleet were of two types: a smaller version rowing 26 oars on each side, with five men on each oar, and a larger version with up to 33 oars each side, usually with five men on each oar, but with seven on each in the largest galleys. They were known as '*gallées ordinaires*' and '*gallées extraordinaires*'. Among the *extraordinaires* was the galley flagship, traditionally named *La Réale* to indicate that she was the king's galley. The stern of one of these *Réales* is preserved in the Musée de la Marine, complete with the superb decorations carved by Pierre Puget, the leading French sculptor of the day. Her date was 1680, and she was one of the big galleys rowing 31 oars each side with seven men to each oar, giving a total of 434 oarsmen. She

Throughout the seventeenth and eighteenth centuries, the general design of the large ship, whether warship or merchantman, had altered very little. The largest of both had roughly doubled in size from about 1,500 tons to around 3,000 tons. All now had the three-masted rig, carrying royals above topgallants. The typical bluff bow remained virtually unaltered, even though the science of hydrodynamics was beginning to come in for study by some naval architects who realised that a square bow pushing its way through the water caused so much resistance and skin friction that speed was seriously affected. But this was a period of history in which speed was not generally of the first importance.

There was no great financial advantage to be gained by bringing in a cargo a week or two before that of a rival shipowner. The demand for the goods of other nations was insatiable and there were not enough ships of any design in the world yet to satisfy it. It was a golden age for trade in a world which was still expanding as new continents became settled and civilized.

Two important innovations, however, should be noticed. During the early eighteenth century, spritsails set above and below the bowsprit were superseded by the much more efficient jibs and fore staysails. Jibs were introduced in the British navy in 1705 for small ships and sloops, and in 1719 for the largest ships of the line. Merchant ships quickly followed the naval lead. It is probable that the jib originated in Holland some forty years earlier on the single-masted *jacht*, built for speed as a naval scout or despatch vessel. The second innovation was the substitution of the steering wheel for the tiller. As ships were built larger, so the tiller had to be made longer to provide enough leverage to move the rudder, and in strong winds it could take five or six men to control it and steer the ship. Another drawback of the tiller on large ships had been that it had to be on the same level as the rudder head, and a helmsman on the tiller found himself below the poop deck and quite unable to see how the sails were drawing. This crucial disadvantage was removed by the invention of the whipstaff (a vertical lever connected to the tiller, enabling the helmsman to move it from side to side through a pivot point below deck). But there was a penalty to be paid for the whipstaff, since it could only move the rudder through a total of about 15 degrees. The steering-wheel, geared to the rudder head by means of ropes or chains, did not necessarily have to be on the same level as the top of the rudder. It was introduced at the end of the seventeenth century and had been adopted for use in all large ships by quite early in the eighteenth. This was the complete answer to the limitations of the whipstaff or the oversize tiller, and when placed on deck at the break of the quarter-deck – its normal position in all sailing vessels – it gave the helmsman a clear view of the sails.

Yet, in spite of the relative lack of progress in the basic hull shape of ships, design changes were in the air. The great Swedish naval architect Frederik Hendrik af Chapman produced his *Architectura Navalis Mercatoria* in 1768, and some of his designs for merchant ships, as well as for small warships, show careful study of the relationship between hull form and speed through the water. He was the first naval architect to build a tank for testing ship models, which were drawn along the tank by a clever system of drop weights. The results of these studies convinced him, and many others who read his book and studied its superb illustrations and building plans, that the basic shape of existing ships was hydrodynamically unsatisfactory. His studies showed that, to achieve the most efficient shape, a ship's hull needed a fine entry and a clear run aft, qualities which were missing from almost all contemporary designs. In the gun sloops he built for the Swedish navy he adopted these lines to produce fast, stable vessels admir-

ably suited to their purpose. Writing about them, Chapman said, 'When these gun sloops had been built I armed one of them myself [they mounted two 18-pounder guns, one in the bows and one in the stern], took it up to Vartan in Stockholm where the King himself came on board, and then rowed it, fired salvoes, made for land and set out gangplanks, landed with the guns and advanced firing all the time, then retreated still firing until the guns were once more in position in the sloop, all finally coming to an end in that His Majesty made me a lieutenant-colonel.' In addition to gun sloops Chapman also designed and built smaller gun launches mounting a single 18- or 24-pounder. In addition to rowing 7 oars a side, they carried a simple lug rig on two masts.

In 1775 Chapman published his *Tractat om Skepps Buggeriet* (Treatise on Ship Building), a publication which over the next twenty or thirty

Above: A large rigged model of Admiral Balchen's flagship HMS *Victory* (1737). It was built after the ship was lost on the Casquet Rocks in 1744, to demonstrate her characteristics to a Board of Enquiry.

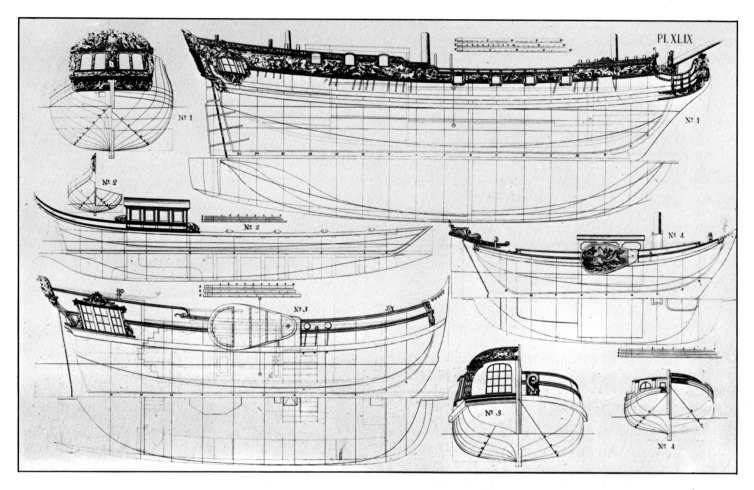

Pl. XLIX

Above: Some of
Chapman's plans from his
Architectura Navalis for
yachts and barges. The
art of depicting a
warship in the form of a
drawing advanced rapidly
in the seventeenth
century, and from 1704
the Royal Navy began to
keep plans on a
systematic basis.

years was to have a profound effect on ship
design in all western countries. Although it took
time for naval architects to absorb some of the
finer points of Chapman's designs, such as the
hollow bow and the tapering run of the hull aft,
the days of the tubby ship with a length-to-beam
ratio of 3 or 3½ to 1 were now numbered. The
longer ship with a more streamlined underwater
hull shape was on the way in.

Although the standard design of large
ships altered very little, apart from the fact that
they approximately doubled in size, there were
great advances, as well as a great variety, in the
design and rig of smaller vessels during the
seventeenth and eighteenth century. The most
notable of all the features of small vessels was the
gaff rig, which had, in fact, been introduced by
the Dutch during the sixteenth century. This was
much easier to handle than the square rig, and
demanded a much smaller crew. The earliest
known example of a vessel setting a full gaff rig
on two masts is the two-masted Dutch *jacht*, a
small shallow-draught craft used in Dutch inland
waters. Because she drew so little water, leeboards were fitted on each side, the one on the
lee side being lowered to prevent leeway.

The two-masted gaff rig was soon found to be
unnecessary in so small a vessel, so the foremast
was removed to make it a single-masted craft,
with a triangular fore staysail to balance the rig
and still with leeboards to deepen the draught
when sailing on the wind. As the single staysail
was insufficient in a strong wind, a running bowsprit was added from which a jib could be set
forward of the staysail. This final version was
known as a *bezaan jacht*. At about the same time
the Dutch produced the *staten jacht*, which had
virtually the same rig, but with a square topsail
added. This was built man-of-war fashion with a
quarter-deck to accommodate a cabin and was
used by important people as a private yacht.

Other European countries copied this fore-
and-aft gaff rig, though often with variations. In
England the Dutch *bezaan jacht* rig was used on
a deeper-draught hull – the coastal waters being
less shoal than those off the coast of Holland –
to become the English cutter, though a few years
later a single square sail was added. The rig was
then developed into a larger two-masted craft,
with gaff sails on both masts, the cutter's square
sail on the foremast, and square topsails on both
masts. It could perhaps best be described as a
'schooner' rig, though the term did not come into
use until many years later, having been coined
in the United States. A similar 'schooner' rig, but

without the square sails, can be seen in Dutch marine paintings of around the end of the seventeenth century, and Chapman has similar illustrations in his *Architectura Navalis Mercatoria*.

For coastwise trading and shorter sea voyages, snows, brigs and brigantines were the favoured vessels of the north European nations. They were all two-masted, with variations in rig to suit the particular needs of the trade for which they were built. The origin of the name 'brig' was the much older Mediterranean term 'brigantine'. This denoted a small ship, equipped like a galleasse with sails and oars, built for speed and therefore much in demand by pirates (the Italian '*brigantini*' means 'brigand'). This type of brigantine dates from the early sixteenth century; the trading brigantines of the seventeenth and eighteenth centuries were very different vessels.

At first the trading brig and brigantine were the same ship, 'brig' being merely an abbreviation of 'brigantine', but during the eighteenth century the two descriptions came to signify different rigs. The name 'brig' was given to a ship square-rigged on both masts, with the addition of a fore-and-aft gaff sail on the mainmast; a brigantine was square-rigged on the foremast and fore-and-aft rigged on the main. The snow was almost identical to the brig, except that it had a separate small mast, known in England as

the 'trysail mast', on which the gaff mainsail was hoisted. This mast was stepped immediately abaft the mainmast and brought an advantage in the ease of handling the gaff sail, which could thus be set or furled at will without interfering with the main yard from which the main course was set. Moreover, with a trysail mast, the gaff

Top: The Royal yacht *Mary,* painted by L. de Mann in the early eighteenth century.

Above: The cutter was a popular small man-of-war for inshore work. This is the *Hawke* of 1777.

Above right: Model of a Dutch mercantile brigantine at the end of the eighteenth century. The need to save manpower led owners to try simpler rigs.

Below: A snow with her gaff sail furled about the trysail mast, another variant popular among small trading vessels.

could be hoisted higher than the main yard to give a larger sail area and a better balance to the rig. In some snows, the trysail mast was replaced by a horse on the after side of the mainmast which served the same purpose. Brigs, snows and brigantines were built up to a maximum tonnage of around 1,000 and were the main workhorses of the short-sea trade.

Brigs were also widely used in European navies during the eighteenth-century wars, armed with up to 18 guns and known generically as 'gunbrigs'. Many naval officers looked upon them with suspicion, for they were considerably overcanvassed, having on their two masts as much sail as, say, a frigate of similar size carried on three. Being warships, they were often required to make ocean passages with the fleet, long voyages for which their hulls were not designed, and their losses through stress of weather were considerable. During the Revolutionary and Napoleonic Wars a large number of British gun-brigs were sent out to operate against the French in the West Indies, and though some of them performed extremely well in action, a larger number succumbed to shipwreck and foundering in the periodic tropical storms which swept the area. Later, when sailing men-of-war had been supplemented by steam-driven warships, brigs were widely used in most navies as training ships for boy seamen, and in the British navy were retained in this role as late as the first decade of the twentieth century.

Although there were brigs, brigantines and snows operating in the Mediterranean, the more popular types of small merchant ships there were the xebec and the polacre, both of them exclusive to those waters. The true xebec was a development of the pirate's brigantine, with a pronounced overhanging bow and stern, somewhat like a galley. They were built with a narrow floor to give them extra speed through the water, but with a considerable beam in order to provide a base for the extensive sail plan which they

Above: A polacre, with
lateen sails on all three
masts.

carried. They were also built with turtle decks to make water shipped on deck while sailing run down into the scuppers, and above these decks gratings were rigged to allow the crew to work dry-shod. The distinctive feature of the xebec was the variable rig which it set according to the weather and point of sailing. The normal rig was square on the foremast and lateen on the main and mizen, but with the wind abaft the beam the lateen yard on the mainmast was taken in and very long square yards swayed up from which immense square sails were spread. When sailing close-hauled, a lateen rig was spread on all three masts with outsized yards, and in strong winds these long yards were replaced by yards of normal length. It was a very complicated rig, which needed a very large crew to handle it. As Falconer, in his marine dictionary of 1771 puts it, 'By the very complicated and inconvenient method of working these vessels, it will be readily believed that one of their captains of Algiers acquainted the author, viz: That the crew of every Xebec has at least the labour of three *square-rigged* ships, wherein the standing sails are calculated to answer every situation of the wind.' Nevertheless, there was no other ship of the times to touch them for speed.

The polacre, also peculiar to the Mediterranean, took two forms, known as 'brig' and 'ship'. The brig polacre was two-masted, normally square-rigged on both masts, but occasionally lateen-rigged on the mizen; the ship polacre had three masts, lateen-rigged on fore and mizen and square-rigged on the main, but occasionally lateen-rigged on all three masts. She was altogether a bigger ship, being sometimes built up to a tonnage of around 1,200. They were called 'polacres' because their masts were formed from a single spar and they had neither tops nor crosstrees. The yards had no footropes and the crew

Right: A tartane, one of
several types of small
trading vessel common
in the Mediterranean.

Below right: Modern junks
off Hong Kong. The type
has remained virtually
unchanged for centuries.

stood on the topsail yards to loose or furl the topgallants, and on the lower yards to loose, furl or
reef the topsails.

Of still smaller vessels there was an almost in-
finite variety. The Baltic nations had the *jagt* and
the *galeas* as their main types of small trading or
fishing craft, but they were of different hull
design and rig in each nation. The Dutch had the
tjalk, and its many derivatives, the *kof* and the
bezaanschuit as their main types. In England
barges, keels and ketches carried the majority of
short passage trade, although in the coal trade
down the east coast a type of ship called a 'cat'
was used. The best-known of the French small
craft was the *chasse-marée*, originally three-
masted with square sails on the two forward
masts and lateen on the mizen, but later lug-
rigged on all three, using very large sails with all
three masts raked aft. It proved a weatherly rig
which produced a good turn of speed. They were
used extensively for smuggling and, in wartime,
as privateers. In the Mediterranean there was an
equally wide variety of types, of which the best
known were the Spanish *felucca*, the Portuguese
fregata, the Spanish and Italian *tartane*, the
Italian *trabaccolo* and the Greek *sacoleva* and

trekandini. None of these was large; in all of them
there were local variations in hull design and rig,
so that, for example, a *tartane* built in one port
would differ slightly from the *tartane* built in the
next port along the coast. About the only thing
that each type had in common was the number
of masts it stepped, and even here there could be
local variations.

The rest of the world was equally prolific in
the types of ship built and sailed. The Arab
nations used the *baghla*, a large ship with a hull
design of European parentage, no doubt influenced by the Portuguese, Dutch and English East
Indiamen which sailed those waters in the seventeenth and eighteenth centuries. A slightly odder
Arabian vessel was the *ghanja*, in which the
quarter-deck was extended to overhang the rudder head by a considerable distance. All used full
lateen rigs on two or three masts. Farther east,
until one comes to the south-western Pacific, the
junk is the dominant ship type, both large and
small, widely adapted to suit local conditions, in
some cases so radically that it might be difficult

to establish the junk parentage. One of the geographical features of this part of the world is the wide rivers which provide navigable water far inland, and it is in the river craft that designs have broken away from the junk model. But here again the local variety is enormous.

The junk herself has a history at least as long as, and probably very much longer than, any other type of ship. The earliest description of a junk known in the west – and, with some small modifications, it could be a description of a junk today – is that given by Marco Polo in his account of his voyage to China in 1298. He does not go into any details of the actual hull design – and early European attempts to illustrate a junk usually gave it a European-type hull – but there is no mistaking the authenticity of his description, or that what he saw then is remarkably similar to what he would have seen today. Chinese junks were built to a considerable size even in Marco Polo's time, and carried the trade of China throughout the Pacific and Indian Oceans. They also formed the Chinese war fleet, until the steamship and the long-range gun made their appearance. Today, although most junks are motorized, there are still some sailing junks in use for the local coasting trade.

One of the features of Marco Polo's junk – and one which it took the West centuries to appreciate – was its subdivision into watertight compartments by transverse bulkheads, specifically to prevent the ship from filling and sinking if she were holed by striking a rock or by any other cause (Marco Polo mentions in this respect a hungry whale!). Another was the fact that she had a single rudder, which could mean that the Chinese invented the hanging rudder attached to the sternpost well ahead of Western nations.

Another type associated with China is the *lorcha*, a sailing vessel with a European hull shape surmounted by the Chinese junk rig. It originated at Macao when it was first settled by the Portuguese in 1557. The name, oddly enough, spread to the Mediterranean where the traditional lateen rig was considered to resemble the junk rig, and many small Mediterranean vessels were described, quite wrongly, as *lorchas*.

The south-west Pacific islands remained, by and large, faithful to the canoe design. The Malayan word for boat or ship is *prahu*, and the word *prau* is still widely used to indicate any type of vessel local to those waters. The commonest sail rig was, and is still, the dipping or standing lug, in use around Indonesia and the south-west Pacific for centuries. Vessels designed to carry large cargoes often consisted of platforms constructed on two or three canoe hulls, with a variety of lugsail shapes carried on one or two masts.

Mercator and Harrison

One of the greatest problems facing the first geographers was how to make an accurate representation of a curved surface (the globe) on a flat surface (a chart). No attempt was made to do so in the early portulan charts, which merely set out to show an outline of the land using the positions of known ports and landmarks. Although these portulan charts were of exquisite workmanship and reasonably accurate in what they showed of the general shape of the land, they were of little use for navigation beyond that of a hit-or-miss variety.

Gerardus Mercator, who used the latinized form of his proper name, Gerhard Kremer, founded a geographical establishment in Louvain and began producing his own maps in 1537. His first map of the world, in two hemispheres, was produced in 1538 and showed him to be much influenced by the theories of Ptolemy. A change of religion from Catholicism to Protestantism was followed by a trial for heresy, but he escaped further religious persecution when the University of Duisburg offered him the chair of cosmography, which he eagerly accepted. Here he turned his back on the Ptolemaic theories and introduced his own projection, with parallels of latitude and meridians of longitude cutting each other at right angles. His first work on these principles, the famous world map in eighteen sheets, was published in 1569, and he followed this up with several other maps. In 1585 he issued the first part of his equally famous atlas. Two years later he produced a world map with his projection for inclusion in the atlas, and in the year of his death, 1594, his final world atlas made its appearance.

Mercator's projection proved invaluable to the navigator as it meant that the course that he wished to steer appeared on his chart as a straight line. The shortest route between any two points on the surface of a globe lies along the arc of the great circle passing through those points, but to sail this shortest distance means that a ship must sail a constantly changing course. This cannot be done without great difficulty or inconvenience, and so a navigator making a long ocean passage steers a series of straight courses, along chords of the great circle, which approximate to the shortest route and are much easier for the helmsmen to steer. These straight

Above: Mercator's map of India.

Below: Mercator, whose famous projection altered sixteenth century chart-making.

courses are known as 'rhumb lines', and one will cut all meridians of longitude at the same angle. On a chart produced on the Mercator projection all rhumb lines appear as straight lines, and, since ships normally steer rhumb line courses, such a chart would obviously be of immense navigational value.

Mercator's projection can be imagined as a cylinder encircling the globe, touching it at the equator and prolonged upwards and downwards (i.e. north-wards and southwards) to infinity. The lines of latitude and longitude, together with the features of the globe, are projected outwards onto the cylinder, at right angles to the surface of the globe, and the cylinder, when unrolled, forms a flat chart. Since the sides of the cylinder are parallel to the north-south axis of the globe, it follows that north and south poles can never be shown on Mercator's projection. Moreover, the size and shape of land masses becomes more and more distorted, the nearer they are to the poles, because north-south distances appear progressively greater than east-west distances. For this reason, on a Mercator chart, the land masses of the far north and south, such as Greenland or Tierra del Fuego, appear many times larger.

Nevertheless, for navigational purposes, the fact that a rhumb line always appears as a straight line on a Mercator chart gives it a unique advantage. The distortion does not worry the navigator, because he measures distances by the scale of latitude at the side of the chart.

* * *

How to measure a ship's latitude at sea had been known to navigators for centuries, almost certainly from the times when the Phoenicians were the great navigators of Europe between the eighth and second centuries B.C. A measurement of the sun's altitude at local noon, or that of the Pole Star at night, gave them the answer. But the calculation of longitude, the other co-ordinate of a ship's position at sea, baffled seamen for centuries, and, in fact, was responsible for innumerable shipwrecks simply because navigators did not know how far east or west they were when out of sight of land.

Once it was known that the earth was a globe and that it turned one complete revolution in relation to the sun every 24 hours – which was accepted very early in the history of navigation – navigators realised that they could easily calculate their longitude at sea, if they had a clock which could tell them the time at the prime meridian (longitude 0°). If it took 24 hours for the earth to revolve through 360 degrees, then in one hour it must revolve through 15. Each hour of difference, therefore, between the time of noon on longitude 0° and the time when the sun reached its highest point at the ship's position, must represent 15 degrees of longitude east or west of the prime meridian. It was easy enough to tell when the sun reached its highest point (by observation with an astrolabe, cross-staff or sextant); what was needed was a method of knowing the time on the prime meridian that would remain accurate over the course of a long voyage.

It was to solve this second problem

that, in 1714, an Act of Parliament in Britain set up a Board of Commissioners for the Discovery of the Longitude at Sea, which offered a prize of £20,000 for a solution, stipulating accuracy to within 30 miles (48·3 km). The offer attracted the interest of John Harrison, an estate carpenter in Lincolnshire. He and his younger brother James had, as a hobby, already constructed a number of long-case clocks of remarkable accuracy, including one with the first ever bimetallic pendulum, designed to overcome inaccuracy caused by variation in temperature. However, a pendulum clock was useless in a ship, as her motion in a rough sea would be enough to stop the pendulum.

With the £20,000 prize in view, Harrison gave up carpentry to devote all his time to devising new movements which would keep accurate time without a pendulum, and between 1735 and 1760 he constructed four chronometers, all of which proved accurate enough to qualify him for the prize. The first was a massive mechanism made of brass and wood which weighed 72 lb (32·7 kg) – far too large and unwieldy to be carried

about in a ship, although it was taken on a voyage to Portugal and back in 1736 in H.M.S. *Centurion*. But his fourth chronometer was about twice the size of the average pocket watch, ideal for use on board ship, and in two trials at sea in 1762 and 1764 it easily qualified in accuracy for the award. A copy of this watch, made by Larcom Kendall, was taken by Captain Cook on his second voyage round the world, and, when three years later he made his final landfall at Plymouth, his calculation of his longitude based on the watch's timekeeping proved correct to within 8 miles (13 km).

John Harrison was at first only paid half the £20,000 prize, the Board of Longitude requiring more proof of the accuracy of his chronometer than could be obtained from two voyages. The balance was finally paid in 1773, but the long wait for the full reward embittered Harrison in the last years of his life. He died in 1776, and generations of navigators since then have owed him a vast debt of gratitude for having solved the problem of almost the last of the navigational unknowns.

Right: John Harrison holding a chronometer.

Chapter Six
Frigates, Sloops, Yachts and Barges

It was noted in the last chapter that, in the days when warships were rated according to the number of guns which they carried, ships of the fifth and sixth rates were known as 'frigates'. But the name is much older than the ship under consideration: its history is a long one, going back to early times in the Mediterranean when the big galleys were equipped with a smaller tender, also oared, called a *'fregata'*. The *fregata* remained in attendance until the demise of the galley, latterly being lightly armed to enable her to intervene in battle when the opportunity presented itself.

In the fifteenth and sixteenth century a frigate could also be a sailing craft, two- or three-masted, usually with lateen sails on every mast. She was built for speed, was generally fairly small, and used mainly as a despatch vessel. It was this version of the frigate that Richard Lovelace had in mind when he wrote in *Lucasta*:

Have you not seen a charact [carrack] lie,
A great cathedral in the sea,
Under whose Babylonian walls,
A small thin frigot almshouse stalls.

Another use of the term, introduced around the end of the sixteenth century, was to denote a medium-sized merchant ship. This practice lasted into the eighteenth century, although, once the naval frigate was firmly established, the merchant version became known as a 'galleon-frigate'. All that this really meant was a merchant ship built frigate-fashion (that is, with a fore-castle and quarter-deck descending by steps to the waist of the ship).

The naval frigate as such, a rated warship of relatively modest armament, does not appear until the eighteenth century, though the name was used for some warships in the seventeenth. The first English naval frigate, for example, is widely considered to have been the *Constant*

Warwick. She was built in 1646 as a privateer for the Earl of Warwick, but was purchased for the navy three years later. She was a ship of 379 tons, mounting 30 guns when built – which was increased later to 42 – but on this scale of size and armament she can hardly be classed as a true frigate for her day. Perhaps her claim to be the first frigate rests on the fact that she was the prototype of a new trend in English naval architecture towards a longer keel and less freeboard in warships, producing a ship of finer lines, lying lower in the water, and thus slightly faster and stiffer. Although, after the *Constant Warwick*, several more medium-sized warships were built on these improved lines, the tendency to increase the length-to-beam ratio did not become general, and it was not until the eighteenth century that what we now recognise as the true naval frigate emerged – a fast, seaworthy ship, mounting a moderately heavy armament on a single gundeck.

It was during the wars of the first half of the eighteenth century that many navies realised the need for vessels answering to this description. They were required by the battle fleets as reconnaissance ships, and as escorts by mercantile convoys. In the early part of the century the smaller warships of 44 and 40 guns, of which a number had been built, were used for this purpose, but they proved unsatisfactory because they were too slow and, having two gundecks, their accommodation below was terribly cramped. In 1748 the first genuine naval frigates began to be built, mounting 28 guns on a single gundeck. Even they were not quite what was wanted since the largest guns which they could accommodate were 9-pounders, but a few years later a new design of frigate carrying thirty-two 12-pounder guns was produced, and this was much nearer the desired ship. Eventually, certainly by 1757, a 36-gun frigate made her appearance, and she proved to be the ideal vessel for both purposes, with a good turn of speed for fleet reconnaissance and a relatively heavy armament for the defence of convoys.

Left: The Battle of Lissa, fought in the Adriatic on the night of 13–14 March 1811 between four British frigates and ten French and Venetian ships. Captain Hoste won a brilliant victory over the French Commodore Dubourdieu.

Each nation had its own design of frigate, and it is interesting to see how the different national naval architects interpreted the requirements for such a vessel in terms of its dimensions. Oddly enough, the French considered British warships to be the best in the world, so far as construction and design were concerned, while the British had almost the exactly opposite opinion, holding that French design, though not construction, was the best. When, in 1758, the French 36-gun frigate *Aurore* was captured by the British, she was put into a dry-dock and carefully measured for comparison with the British 36-gun frigate *Brilliant*. The differences were surprising.

	Brilliant	*Aurore*
Date of launch	1757	1758
Length of gundeck	128 ft 4 in (39·12 m)	144 ft 0 in (43·89 m)
Keel	106 ft 2½ in (32·37 m)	118 ft 9 in (36·2 m)
Beam	35 ft 8 in (10·87 m)	38 ft 8½ in (11·8 m)
Depth	12 ft 4 in (3·76 m)	15 ft 2 in (4·62 m)
Burthen	718 tons	946 tons

It can be seen from this table that the French frigate, though she mounted exactly the same number of guns as the British, was more than a quarter larger in terms of tonnage, and all her other dimensions were also significantly greater.

Later in this same century, when the Americans began to build frigates during the War of Independence, these, too, were considerably larger, gun for gun, than the British. So also were Spanish frigates, but the Dutch approximated much more to British dimensions. One would be hard-pressed to say which was the better design for the frigate's role – the larger ships of the French, Spanish and Americans, or the smaller design of Britain and Holland. Each type had its successes and failures, and in general the quality of the crew probably counted infinitely more than the actual design of the vessel. Nevertheless, there were many British frigate captains who envied the larger size of foreign frigates and would have dearly loved to command one, mainly because they were marginally faster on certain points of sailing.

Right: Original plan for building the Royal Navy frigate *Brilliant* in 1757.

Below right: The French 74-gun *Droits de l'Homme*, is driven ashore by the frigates *Indefatigable* (44-gun) and *Amazon* (36-gun) in January 1797. The *Amazon* was also lost, but the action was Sir Edward Pellew's most famous exploit.

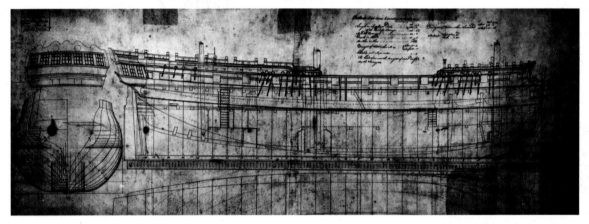

Above: The quarterdeck of the 6th rate *Deal Castle* in 1775. Awnings provided shade, for officers and men, as well as the goats and hens carried on deck.

battle line, if they looked like drifting down onto the enemy line where they could be boarded and captured. Independently, they were the best type of ship for escorting convoys, since they had a fair margin of speed over the merchant ships and could overhaul any ships straying from the convoy and round them up, and also had a fair advantage of firepower over any enemy privateer engaged in the *guerre de course* and looking for the easy capture of a merchant ship. Frigates were admirably suited, too, for use with blockading squadrons, since their speed and manoeuvrability enabled them easily to close the enemy port in order to count the warships inside and see whether they were making any moves to come out, such as crossing their yards or sending up their sails.

They were rigged exactly like a ship of the line, with the standard three masts and square sails on each, but with their finer lines – a length-to-beam ratio of nearly 4 to 1 compared with 3 to 1 in a ship of the line – they could sail as much as half a point closer to the wind than their larger sisters. Towards the end of the eighteenth century their 12-pounder guns were replaced by 18-pounders, and, to provide the extra constructional strength necessary, the scantlings of their bottom planking increased from 3 in (76 mm) to 4 in (102 mm). Towards the end of the century the traditional oak from which all warships had been built (except those built in India where teak was used) began to be replaced by fir in the case of smaller warships, and in Britain seven frigates were constructed of this wood as an experiment. They were found to be excellent ships for use in the West Indies, being very light and airy, but in home waters they were not popular.

Also at this time, a new version of the traditional frigate was introduced, known as a 'donkey-frigate' to distinguish it from the true frigate. Besides the single covered gundeck of the frigate, she had additional guns mounted on the forecastle and quarter-deck. Perhaps a more accurate description of her would have been 'ship-sloop'. The type was not considered a success, and few were built.

As, with succeeding campaigns, the value of the frigate in naval warfare became more and more evident, they were built in larger and larger numbers. Taking Britain as a typical example, in 1750 there were seventy-eight true frigates, that is, fifth- and sixth-rate ships; ten years later their number had risen to 115. By the end of the eighteenth century the number was 159, and this out of a total naval strength of 517 ships, including all the ships of the line and more than 200 smaller vessels, such as sloops, brigs, cutters, etc. Figures for other navies show much the same situation and indicate the importance attached to the frigate by all the navies of the world. They were what might be called all-purpose ships, serving the battle fleets both as scouts and, in action, as repeating ships, lying outside the battle line and repeating the admiral's signals so that all ships could see them without having to peer through the smoke of battle. They were also used to tow disabled ships out of the

The frigate was the favourite warship of the United States, and, although there was no official United States Navy until an Act of Congress of 27 March 1794 authorized six frigates to be built, the revolutionary Congress formed during the War of Independence had, in 1775, authorized the building of thirteen ships. These were small frigates, five of 32 guns each, five of 28, and three of 24. Later in that year, three more frigates were authorized, all of 32 guns. They

Far left: Contemporary model of the *Mermaid*, a 32-gun frigate. She was launched at Sheerness in 1784, having previously been laid down at Woolwich from where the timber frames were transferred in 1782.

Left: The *Constitution* as she is today at Boston. Like HMS *Victory* she is kept in commission as a naval vessel.

Right: The spar deck of the USS *Constitution*, the oldest man-of-war still afloat, as she looked in 1931 before restoration.

Below right: The capture of the 38-gun HMS *Guerrière* by the *Constitution* in August 1812, which created the legend of 'Old Ironsides'.

were all built to the conventional frigate design, the main armament on a single gundeck and chase guns mounted on forecastle and quarter-deck. Later, these frigates were altered by connecting the forecastle and quarter-deck with longitudinal gangways along each side, making the ships appear as though they had a continuous upper deck without a waist. Later still, the Americans mounted guns on these gangways, increasing the number of guns from 32 to 44 in their largest frigates. They were then known as 'double-backed' frigates and proved popular with their captains and crews.

Of these thirteen frigates, the best-known was the 32-gun *Hancock*, built at Newburyport, Massachusetts by Jonathan Greenleaf, Stephen Cross and his brother, Ralph. She was launched in 1776 and was generally considered to be the fastest frigate in the world. Nevertheless, in 1777, she was sighted and captured by the British 44-gun frigate *Rainbow* after a chase which lasted 36 hours. Taken into the British navy and renamed *Iris*, she was repaired and her bottom coppered at Plymouth, and under her new flag she captured another of the thirteen American frigates, the *Trumbull*. Finally, in 1781, she was taken by the French and finished her days as a powder hulk in Toulon, but not before the British had measured her very carefully and taken a draft of her lines as a model for future British frigate building.

As mentioned above, the U.S. Navy came officially into being with the Act of Congress of 27 March 1794 and the order for what were to become known as the 'six original frigates'. These were the *United States, Constitution* and *President*, all of 44 guns, and the *Chesapeake, Constellation* and *Congress*, originally of 36 guns, although this number was increased during building to 38. They were all good ships, built considerably longer and fuller than most of the frigates of corresponding firepower of other countries. The *Constitution*, built at Boston by Edward, Joseph, and Edmund Hart and launched in 1797, is perhaps the most famous warship in American naval history. She fought and won a notable action against the British 38-gun frigate *Guerrière* in 1812 – an achievement which earned her the nickname 'Old Ironsides' – captured the British *Java* later that year, and followed these victories with another in 1815, against the British *Cyane* and *Levant*. According to the normal American practice she was built very large for her 44-gun rating, with a displacement of 2,200 tons on an overall length of 204 ft (62·18 m), a beam of $43\frac{1}{2}$ ft (13·26 m), and a depth of hold of $14\frac{1}{4}$ ft (4·34 m). She was restored to her original condition in 1931 and is now berthed as a national memorial at Boston, where she was originally built.

The Americans did not begin to build ships of the line until after 1815, and then they did not enjoy much success with them. But to back up their frigates they built schooners, armed with carronades and long-barrelled 9-pounders and fast enough to overtake pirate vessels or slavers. Even more notably, they built ship-rigged sloops, with hulls based on the Baltimore clipper,

endowing them with both speed and good looks. It is these sloops which are said to have marked the transition of the U.S. Navy from the 'frigate theory' to the 'sloop theory'. Certainly they were excellent small warships, and probably the best form of navy for a nation which as yet had very little seaborne trade to protect.

Frigates, sloops and brigs remained the basis of the U.S. Navy until the sailing warship became a thing of the past. By mid-nineteenth century, steam propulsion was being incorporated in sailing warships, existing ships being cut in two and lengthened to accommodate the engine and boilers. They were still wooden ships, with the full ship rig on three masts, but they had an unfamiliar look because of the pair of collapsible funnels amidships. In 1854 the United States ordered five steam frigates and one corvette (normally smaller than a frigate), which proved to be the most remarkable ships yet built. They were of 3,200 tons (3,250 tonnes) – half as big again as the first-rate H.M.S. *Victory* – and mounted twenty-four 9-inch guns, fourteen 8-inch and two 10-inch. The corvette had a dis-

Above: HMS *Galatea* was one of six big wooden steam frigates built in 1857 to match American commerce raiders.

with twenty-four 10-inch guns on the gundeck and two 68-pounder pivot guns on forecastle and quarter-deck. The other four were smaller, of 3,800 tons (3,860 tonnes) displacement, though they, too, mounted 10-inch guns as their main armament. All six proved considerably faster than the American ships (12 to 13 knots as against 8 to 9), and they were the ultimate development of the wooden-hulled frigate.

The sloop (and her French equivalent, the corvette) stood immediately below the frigate in fighting strength. She was originally designed as a counter to the hordes of privateers which roamed the seas in search of merchant shipping in time of war. Any private citizen who owned a ship could become a privateer by obtaining from the naval authority of his country a Letter of Marque. It was a condition of a Letter of Marque that any merchant ship captured had to be brought before the Prize Court to be 'condemned' (a safeguard against outright piracy), and if she was properly condemned by the Court the owner of the privateer took 90 per cent of the value with the other 10 per cent being added to the national Prize Fund. It was an intensely profitable business, and many citizens formed themselves into syndicates to buy and operate

placement of no less than 4,580 tons (4,650 tonnes) – a third as big again as the frigates – and mounted fourteen 11-inch Dahlgren guns.

Faced with this challenge from across the Atlantic, Britain also ordered six steam frigates, in 1857. The two largest, the *Ariadne* and *Galatea*, had a displacement of 4,426 tons (4,497 tonnes) – very nearly as big as the largest first-rate yet built in Britain (H.M.S. *Wellington*) –

ships as privateers. Many of them were not too particular as to which merchant ships they attacked, and it was not unknown for a merchant ship to be captured and ransacked at sea by a privateer of her own country. Some privateers were no more than pirates, attacking every ship they encountered irrespective of her country of origin.

It was to the sloop or her equivalent that most navies looked to check the depredations of hostile privateers. She was smaller than the frigate, usually mounting eighteen guns or less on the upper deck, and was two-masted in contrast to the frigate's three. She was built for speed, with long, fine lines, and after 1796 was often constructed in fir instead of oak, mainly as an economy measure because of the huge wartime building programmes. Since she was not a rated ship, as she did not carry enough guns to qualify, she was usually commanded by a senior lieutenant, who was known as a 'captain', as opposed to a 'post-captain' who commanded a rated ship, and provided valuable command experience for officers on their way up the promotion ladder. Like the frigates, large numbers of sloops were built, and a measure of their usefulness in war can be seen in the fact that the total of forty sloops in the British Navy in 1793, when

the Revolutionary War against France began, grew to 107 by 1800, and this in spite of fairly substantial losses during the course of the war. The corvette was generally built a little smaller than the English sloop, but in just as large numbers. The average sloop ran to about 400 tons displacement, was designed with a length-to-beam ratio of better than 4 to 1, and had a complement of about 120 men.

The word 'yacht', in its meaning of pleasure craft, came to England in 1660 with the restoration of Charles II to the English throne. The word is derived from the Dutch 'jaght', and it was the gift to the king in 1660 of the jaght *Mary* by the burgomasters of Amsterdam that first introduced sailing for pleasure into England, and the word 'yacht' with it. Yet the original Dutch *jaght* was anything but a pleasure craft. The word in Dutch means 'hunt' or 'chase', and was at first applied to any armed, light sailing vessel with a good turn of speed, and frequently also to any fast pirate vessel. Later, as national navies developed, the small despatch and advice vessels used to serve the Dutch fleet as messengers, etc., which were roughly the equivalent of the English pin-

Above: The yacht *Mary* was one of a number of such craft built after the Restoration of Charles II. The first *Mary* was a gift to the King by the burghers of Amsterdam. (From a painting by van de Velde the Younger, 1677)

Far left: A British gun-brig captures the Spanish slaver *Marineito* in April 1831. Many brigs were used on anti-slavery patrols but they could be outrun by some of the faster slavers.

137

Above: 'Dutch Yachts Racing', a painting by van Ertwelt. The Dutch world *jaght* passed into the English language after 1660 to indicate, first a vessel of state, and second any sizeable craft used purely for pleasure.

nace, were called '*jaghts*' or '*jachts*'. Although, before 1660, the term was not used to describe any sort of English vessel, it was not unknown in England as a type of foreign vessel and occurs in English writings as early as 1557, when Stephen Burrough's account of his voyage in search of the North-East Passage mentions meeting three or four Norway 'yeaghes'. Other early English versions of the term were 'yoathe', yaught', 'yolke' and 'zaught'.

In many countries there had for centuries been yachts in the sense of Falconer's *Dictionary of the Marine* definition: 'vessels of state usually employed to convey princes, ambassadors, or other great personages from one kingdom to another.' These were almost invariably highly ornamented varieties of the type of warship then in current use, be it galley, longship, cog, carrack, or whatever. In England the earliest vessel built entirely for pleasure was probably a miniature warship

which James I ordered Phineas Pett to construct for Prince Henry, his eldest son. In his autobiography Pett describes the vessel: 'About January 15th 1604 a letter was sent post-haste . . . commanding me with all possible speed to build a little vessel for the young Prince Henry to disport himself in about London Bridge, and acquaint his Grace with shipping, and the manner of that element; setting me down the proportions and the manner of garnishing, which was to be like the work of the *Ark Royal*, battlementwise. This little ship was in length 25 ft (7·6 m) by the keel, and in breadth 12 ft (3·7 m), garnished with painting and carving, both within board and without, very curiously, according to his Lordship's directions.' She was named *Disdain*, but as Prince Henry died in 1612 he had only a few years in which to enjoy her.

The Dutch *Mary*, Charles II's first real yacht in the sense of a pleasure craft, was a vessel of 100 tons, not unlike the present-day Thames barge, though with a large cabin superimposed on the deck aft. She had the typical Dutch fore-and-aft rig with gaff mainsail and single jib and, another typical Dutch feature, was fitted with leeboards to prevent leeway when sailing close-hauled. Charles was a great lover of the sea and sailing, and in all owned twenty-five yachts, of which the smallest was the *Jamie* of 25 tons and the largest the *Saudadoes* of 180 tons.

Charles's example set a pattern in England that was followed by succeeding monarchs, though none equalled him in the number of yachts that he owned. It was followed, too, by many noblemen and courtiers, and the sport of yachting grew steadily over the years. The first recorded yacht race was sailed in 1661 between Charles's *Katherine* and the Duke of York's *Anne* over a course on the River Thames from Greenwich to Gravesend and back, and this sport, too, prospered over the years. The Dutch took to pleasure sailing with almost equal enthusiasm, but other countries seemed to be less keen.

Most royal yachts were included in their country's national navy, possibly because the cost of their building was paid out of funds voted for the navy or because they were manned by naval personnel. In wartime many of them served in their traditional role as fast despatch vessels, and there are records of some being captured and sold in the Prize Court.

Another small craft was the barge, and it is difficult in the earliest years to distinguish between a barge and a yacht. The essential feature of the barge was that it was always propelled by oars, with a minimum of eight, even in the days of sail, but it was ornamented and decorated with every bit as much splendour as the most regal of the royal yachts. One of the earliest recorded examples is Cleopatra's barge which she used on the Nile and which, in Shakespeare's words,

> . . . like a burnished throne
> Burnt on the water; the poop was beaten gold,
> Purple her sails; and so perfumed, that
> The winds were love-sick with them. The oars
>   were silver
> Which to the tune of flutes kept stroke, and
>   made
> The water which they beat to follow faster,
> As amorous of their strokes . . .'

Equally famous was the *Bucentaur*, the traditional name of the barge used by the doges of Venice in the annual procession on Ascension Day, commemorating the victory of Doge Pietro

Orseolo II over the Dalmatian pirates in the year 1000 and the subsequent conquest of all Dalmatia. The name *Bucentaur* is an adaptation of 'buzino d'oro' (barque of gold), an apt enough description as the doge's barge was gilded from the waterline up. The traditional name first occurs in a decree of 1311 as *Bucintoro*, and the barge of this decree remained in commission for over 400 years, until replaced in 1728. She was two-decked like a galley and rowed 42 oars, with four *arsenalotti*,

Above: Contemporary model of a late seventeenth century British royal yacht.

139

Bucentaur
(1728)

Length 115 ft (35·1 m) *Beam* 22 ft (6·7 m) *Depth* 26 ft (7·9 m)
Complement 168 rowers

This was the last in a line of sumptuous Venetian state barges and surpassed even her predecessors in magnificence. She was the second to bear the name *Bucentaur*, or *Bucintro* (a contraction of *buzino d'oro*, meaning 'barque of gold'). She was designed by Michele Stefano Conti on the lines of a war galley with a ram at the bow, although her function was entirely ceremonial. Four free artisans from the Arsenale, known as *Arsenalotti*, pulled each of her forty-two oars. The rowers occupied the main deck, while the upper deck was a continuous long saloon, adorned with crimson velvet and gold embroidery, and paintings and carvings of mythological characters. At the aft end stood the throne of the doge, surmounted by a canopy in the form of a huge shell supported by two cherubs. The *Bucentaur* was used on state and religious occasions, the most notable of which was the annual Wedding of the Sea ceremony, and there was a special window at the stern through which the doge threw a gold ring into the sea to symbolize the union. This ceremony took place for the last time in 1796. In the following year the doge was overthrown by the French. The *Bucentaur* was beached, stripped of her decoration, and, under the name *Idra*, was turned into a battery and sailors' prison. She was eventually broken up in 1824, nearly a hundred years after her launching.

This reconstruction is based on the model of the *Bucentaur* in the Arsenale museum at Venice. There are two beakheads at the bow, the higher and more prominent of which supports the lion of St. Mark. The tall figure in the group immediately over the stem is that of Justice. Undoubtedly there were alterations made to the decoration at various stages in the vessel's career. The detail from a painting by Canaletto depicts the *Bucentaur* surrounded by an armada of smaller craft on the day of the Wedding of the Sea ceremony commemorating Doge Pietro Orseolo II's victory over Dalmatian pirates in the year 1000.

who were privileged citizens, manning each oar. The annual procession was led by the *Bucentaur* to the island of Sant'Elena, where the Doge received a bunch of damask roses in a silver vase in exchange for an offering of peeled chestnuts and red wine before throwing a ring into the open sea with the words 'We wed thee, O Sea, in token of our perpetual dominion.'

The next *Bucentaur*, the last of the line, was designed by Michele Stefano Conti and launched in 1728. She was 100 ft (30·5 m) long, 24 ft (7·3 m) high, and like her predecessor was rowed by 21 oars on each side. In 1798, during Napoleon's campaign against the Italian states, she was taken by the French when Venice capitulated. The gold with which she was covered was stripped off and melted down, and she was used as a floating battery, first by the French and then by the Venetians, until she was broken up in 1824. A fine model of this last *Bucentaur* and part of her mast are in the Arsenale Museum in Venice.

In almost every capital in Europe, up to about 1800, the river on which it was built was the main highway for city travel. Individuals could hire skiffs or 'pair-oars' rowed by licensed watermen, to travel up or down river to the nearest landing place to their destination, but important personages travelled on the river by barge which, perhaps inspired by Cleopatra's example, grew increasingly ornate and sumptuous.

In London, for example, the Thames was used not only for the day-to-day travel of citizens, but also for the ceremonial welcome of important visitors, when a procession of decorated barges would provide a spectacular reception. All the London livery companies had their own barge, used on formal occasions and for junketing, as when the liverymen of the Clothworkers Company used to take their ladies to Chelsea to dine (a regular outing which in 1694 led to a restriction to 'a pint of Lisbon' for each liveryman since the earlier 'distribution of wine' had led to 'considerable inconveniences' – perhaps the understatement of the year).

From about 1422 the Lord Mayor's annual procession to Westminster went by water, in decorated barges with musicians on board, a custom which was retained until 1857 when the Lord Mayor and his procession took to the streets. When Anne Boleyn was crowned as Henry VIII's queen in 1533 she was escorted on her voyage upriver from Greenwich by fifty barges, all of which were required to have 'mynstrelsie' on board. Charles II brought Catherine of Braganza by river to London as his queen on 23 August 1662, and John Evelyn, writing in his diary, considered it 'the most magnificent triumph that ever floated on the Thames; considering the innumerable boates and vessels, dress'd and adorned with all

imaginable pomp, but above all the thrones, arches, pageants, and other representations, stately barges of the Lord Mayor and Companies, with various inventions, musiq, and peales of ordnance both from the vessels and the shore, going to meete and conduct the new Queene from Hampton Court to White-hall, at the first time of her coming to towne. In my opinion it far exceeded all the Venetian Bucentoras, etc. on the Ascension, when they go to espouse the Adriatic.' An etching by Theodore Stoop records the gay scene on the Thames that day.

We know some details of these state barges from the records of the livery companies. For example, the Merchant Taylors built their first barge in 1640 at a cost of £120 4s 0d. She was built by Abraham Tue, a shipwright of Southwark, and was manned by a crew of seventeen watermen, sixteen to row and one to steer, who wore sky-coloured plush caps lined with calico. Their fourth barge, built in 1764 by Thomas Searle of Lambeth, rowed nine oars each side and was built of 'white English oak free from Redness, Rot, Sap, and Prejudicial Knotts.' The 'house', or decorated canopy, where the Master and liverymen sat, was 35 ft (10·7 m) long and had sash windows between fluted columns. It was elaborately carved and painted. Their final barge, built in 1800, was 79 ft (24·1 m) long with a beam of 14 ft (4·3 m), and the 'house' was 37 ft (11·3 m) long and 6 ft (1·8 m) high, containing a pantry (no doubt always well stocked to sustain the passengers during their river trips) and – a modern touch – a water-closet. During the 1840s, when her upkeep was becoming too expensive for the Company, she was sold to the Oxford

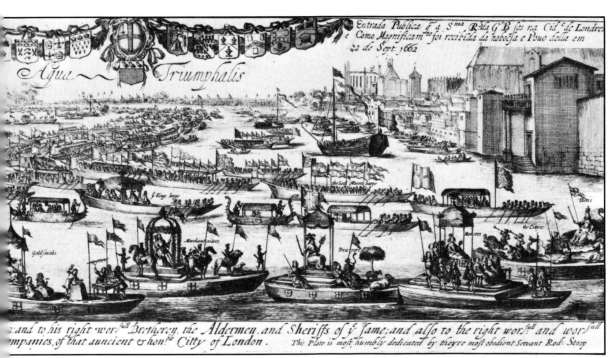

University Boat Club.

The last of the great river processions took place in January 1806 when the state barge originally built for Charles II carried the body of Lord Nelson, which had been lying in state at Greenwich, to the Admiralty office in Whitehall, where it was to rest for the night until the burial in St Paul's Cathedral the following day. All the state barges were out on the river, led by the College of Heralds in two barges, with the King's, Admiralty and Navy Board barges following immediately after the state barge bearing the coffin, and all the livery companies' barges bringing up the rear, the whole procession being attended by hundreds of other river boats which lined the route to Whitehall. The state barges 'had all their masts hoisted half-staff-high; the river glittered with the rich assemblage of colours which was displayed, while the innumerable multitude assembled on its banks beheld the pomp with mingled sensations of curiosity and sorrow.' Fortunately the sun shone on this January day to show off the rich decoration of the state barges.

River processions, not only in London, but also in other European capitals, fell into disuse around the middle of the nineteenth century. An entirely new generation of river craft was driving out the graceful barges, and, in the words of Nathaniel Hawthorne, 'the high streets of the metropolis' were now befouled by 'a multitude of smoke-begrimed steamers'.

143

Ship Models

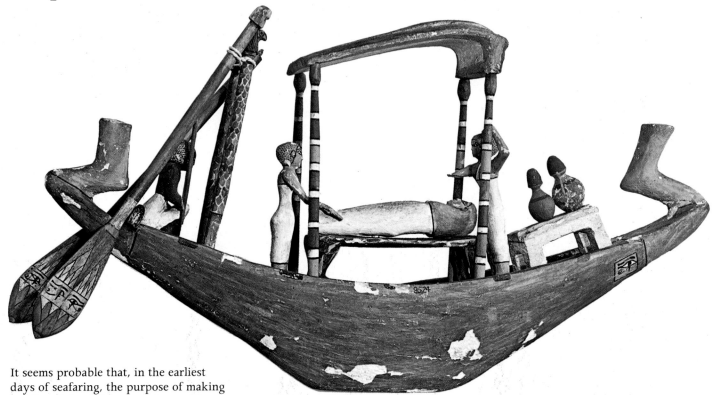

It seems probable that, in the earliest days of seafaring, the purpose of making small models of ships was almost entirely religious. Models of Nile ships and boats have been found in several of the tombs of the Pharaohs, dating back to around 2500 B.C., and other models of very early Mediterranean vessels have been found in tombs excavated in Cyprus, Crete and other early centres of eastern Mediterranean civilization. That there was some religious significance in burying these models with bodies in tombs is obvious, probably a physical representation of the widely held belief that upon death the spirit embarks upon some form of journey. It would not be surprising if similar models were made as toys for children. But such children's models, if they existed, have not survived the centuries.

The practice of making models for religious purposes continued throughout the ages, and in many churches in ports and fishing villages ship models hang from the beams, often as a thanks-giving for deliverance from shipwreck and drowning, sometimes commemorating great national events. In the church of Notre Dame de la Garde, which over-looks the port of Marseilles, there are many models given as votive offerings, most of them made or carved by sailors who have come safely home after facing perils on the sea. The church of St. Bavo at Haarlem has some beautiful models of

early Dutch ships hanging above the nave, to commemorate the breaking of the boom at Damietta during the Fifth Crusade. Other such votive offerings sometimes take the form of bench-ends and popey-heads in village churches.

During the seventeenth century, when shipbuilding was becoming a more exact science than the rough and ready methods of medieval builders, many naval architects made a model of a ship that they proposed to build, to show their clients before laying down the ship herself. In 1607 Phineas Pett, a master shipwright of the well-known family, wrote in his journal:

'After my settling at Woolwich I began a curious model for the Prince [Henry] my master, most part whereof I wrought with my own hands, which being most fairly garnished with carving and painting, and placed in a frame arched, covered, and curtained with crimson taffety, was, the 10th day of November, by me presented to the Lord High Admiral at his lodging at Whitehall . . . [The King made a] journey from Whitehall to Richmond to see the same model, whither he came in the afternoon about 3 of the clock, accompanied only with the Prince, the Lord Admiral, and one or two attendants.

Above: An Egyptian funerary boat from a tomb in Thebes, now in the British Museum.

Below: The elaborate carving of a model of HMS *Prince* (1670), incorporating in miniature all the decoration which would be found on the finished ship.

Right: A bronze-gilt nef clock attributed to Hans Schlottenheim.

His Majesty was exceedingly delighted with the sight of the model, and spent time in questioning me divers material things concerning the same, and demanding whether I would build the great ship in all points like to the same . . .'

So what started as a model to delight a prince became a new 'great ship' for the navy. She was launched in 1610 as the *Royal Prince*, one of the most famous ships of the Stuart navy.

This started the practice, which was always more pronounced in England than in other countries, of building a model in advance of construction. Charles I's great ship, *Sovereign of the Seas*, the largest warship in the world when she was launched in 1637, was built from a preliminary model 'of exquisite workmanship, curiously painted and gilt with azure and gold. So contrived that every timber in her might be seen, left open and unplanked for that purpose, very neat and delightsome.' Later in the same century, the British Admiralty officially required naval architects to submit scale models of many warships before confirming the building order.

It is from these models, many of them exact records of ships actually built, that we are able to trace advances in design and building techniques from the seventeenth century onwards. Often they were skeletal below the waterline so that details of the ship's framing could be seen by the purchaser before placing a firm order.

Many other ship models were made individually, not necessarily representing any particular named ship, but representative of a type. The best-known are the models made by French prisoners-of-war during the long years of the Revolutionary and Napoleonic Wars, which are made from bone, ivory or boxwood. They were made partly to occupy the long hours of detention in prison hulks, partly for sale to augment the meagre rations. Most of them are inaccurate models of French warships made by the prisoners from memory, and, often enough, given the name of a British ship to increase the chances of a sale, but nevertheless they are very beautiful and command high prices today when they come up for sale.

Another form of ship model, and even more highly prized today than the

French prisoner-of-war models, were the silver and crystal models used on the tables of the nobility in the fifteenth and sixteenth centuries, usually to hold salt (in those days a rare and precious commodity, and thus thought worthy of an ornate receptacle). They were known as 'nefs', as this was the type of ship most usually represented. The work of the finest silversmiths and glassworkers, they were incredibly elaborate, and in many cases had clockwork figures which performed at intervals. One of the most

famous is a bronze-gilt nef clock made by Hans Schlottenheim (1574–1625). The enamelled dial of the clock is under the mainmast, and when the hour struck, a miniature gun on the forecastle was fired and a tune played on a tiny organ. The men standing on deck were dressed as electors and heralds of the Holy Roman Empire, and they moved in procession in time to the organ, filing past the seated figure of the Emperor and each turning towards him and bowing as he passed.

Chapter Seven
The Mechanical Revolution

The desire for some means of mechanical propulsion for ships is nearly as old as the use of sails for propulsion. The sail, particularly in the days before man had learned to brace the yards to the wind when it was ahead, always placed a limitation on the course that a vessel could steer. She could only sail a course which the wind direction allowed, which was not necessarily the most direct, and to reach her destination if the wind headed her might mean sailing three, or even four, times as far as the straight course. And if her course took her across the equator she might lie motionless for days in the doldrums, without a breath of wind to fill her sails.

The Romans are said to have invented a form of paddlewheel, operated manually by means of a crank, but they discovered, not surprisingly, that rowers with oars were more efficient. During the Middle Ages the Chinese are supposed to have built a junk with paddlewheels attached to the keel and driven by slaves on a treadmill, but this, too, appears to have been a failure, since the invention was not followed up. What was needed – and the innovators soon recognized it – was some means of turning the paddlewheel other than by manpower. In 1685 a French inventor put forward the theory that air pressure would force a piston down a cylinder if a vacuum could be created below it, and that the resultant power could be used to turn a paddlewheel. The vacuum was to be formed by condensing steam injected beneath the piston. Twenty-seven years later, in 1712, this idea was, in fact, to be the basis of the first working steam engine, built by Thomas Newcomen, but even this had no application to ships because it proved impossible to generate enough power to drive a paddlewheel.

The first breakthrough came in 1765 when James Watt, in an attempt to eradicate the chronic inefficiencies of Newcomen's engine, invented the condenser and made the cylinder

double-acting, by admitting steam both above and below the cylinder. Here, at last, was a steam engine which developed reasonable power and, with the further invention of a centrifugal governor, power at a constant speed. This was what was needed if mechanical power was to replace the sail. In 1768 Watt went into partnership with Matthew Boulton, who had an engineering workshop at Birmingham, and it was Boulton and Watt engines which powered most of the world's first steamships.

Strictly speaking, the world's first steam vessel was the *Pyroscaphe*, a large clinker-built boat with an engine which turned a pair of small paddlewheels. It was invented by the Marquis Claude de Jouffroy d'Abbans, and in 1783 was tried out on the River Saône in France. The engine worked for 15 minutes before breaking down, and during that time the *Pyroscaphe* moved forward through the water under power. It would be equally correct to say that the second steam vessel in the world was the *John Fitch*, a small barge-like hull with an engine which operated, through linking beams, six vertical oars on each side. This vessel, named after its inventor, made a short trip on the River Delaware in the United States in 1786. However, since neither of these two was reliable enough to prove that steam was a viable method of propulsion for ships, it was left to a later vessel to demonstrate the steamship's potential.

The vessel which really inaugurated the era of the steamship was the *Charlotte Dundas*, which made her first voyage in March 1802. She was built on the River Clyde in Scotland to the order of Lord Dundas, a governor of the Forth and Clyde Canal, and he named her after his daughter. She was a wooden vessel 58 ft (17·7 m) long, with a beam of 18 ft (5·5 m) and a draught of 8 ft (2·4 m), with a single tall funnel amidships. Lord Dundas wanted her to replace the horses which towed the barges up and down the canal, and he gave the order for her to William Symington, an engineer with a workshop on the Clyde. She had a single paddlewheel at the stern, driven

Left: The *William Fawcett* (1829) started a mail service across the Irish Sea, thus founding the Peninsular and Oriental Steam Navigation Company, the 'P&O'.

by a single-cylinder steam engine which developed about 12 horsepower. On her first voyage she towed two 70-ton barges up the canal for a distance of 20 miles (32 km) at a speed of over 3 knots, which would have been higher but for a strong headwind. She ran steadily up and down the canal towing barges for three or four weeks, but was then taken out of service as it was feared that the wash from her paddle-wheel would cause the banks to fall in.

With the *Charlotte Dundas* proving that a steam-driven ship was a commercial proposition, the race for steam propulsion was on. Robert Fulton, an American inventor who had lived in Paris, and of whom we shall hear again later in connection with the birth of the submarine, was the next to construct a steam-driven ship. He had been on board the *Charlotte Dundas* during one of her canal trips, and decided to attempt a similar feat on the River Seine in Paris. His first attempts were a failure, as the wooden hull which he constructed was not strong enough to take the weight of the engine and boiler. It broke in two and sank. Undeterred, Fulton built a

stronger hull, recovered his engine from the bottom of the Seine, and in August 1803 gave a demonstration by towing two boats upriver for an hour and a half.

Convinced that the steamship had a commercial future, Fulton returned to the United States and, in co-operation with a financier named Robert Livingston, who lived at Clermont, built a wooden hull, with a length of 133 ft (40·5 m) and a displacement of 100 tons, on the East Hudson River. As there were no engineers in the United States with sufficient experience of building steam engines he sent over to Britain, to Boulton and Watt, for an engine to be shipped across the Atlantic. The engine had a single vertical cylinder, 24 in (60 cm) in diameter, with a stroke of 48 in (120 cm) and, through bell cranks and spur gearing, drove two 15-ft (4·6 m) paddlewheels, one on each side of the hull. She was named *Clermont*, after Livingston's home town, and on her maiden voyage in 1807 she covered approximately 240 miles (390 km) by steaming to Albany and back in 62 hours, at an average speed over the whole distance of 3·9 knots, though her best speed was 4·7 knots. She continued in commercial service on the East Hudson River for two seasons, eventually prov-

Left: Robert Fulton's steamer *Clermont* inaugurated a commercial service on the Hudson River in 1807.

Below left: The *Charlotte Dundas* had a brief career in 1802, towing canal barges. However her wash damaged canal banks.

ing too small for the crowds that thronged the landing stages to take a passage in her. She was so successful commercially that Fulton built a second steam vessel, which he named the *Phoenix* to operate similarly on the Delaware River. Since she was built at Hoboken and had to steam down the coast of New Jersey to reach the Delaware, she can claim to be the first steamship to make a voyage in the open sea, though she hugged the coastline the whole way.

The financial success of the river steamers in the United States inspired a Scottish engineer, Henry Bell, to enter the steamship business. He built the *Comet* at Glasgow in 1812 for a ferry service on the Clyde between Glasgow, Greenock, and Helensburgh, which proved so successful that he extended it up the west coast of Scotland to Oban and Fort William, 200 miles (320 km) away. The *Comet* was smaller than Fulton's *Clermont*, but her engine produced a better average speed of 6·7 knots. Two years later Henry Bell had five similar ferries running services on the River Thames from London as far down as Margate. The biggest ferry of this early steamship period was the *James Watt*, operating a coastal service between London and Leith. She had an overall length of 141 ft 10 in (43·23 m) and

a maximum beam over her paddle-boxes of 47 ft (14·32 m). Each paddlewheel was 18 ft (5·5 m) in diameter.

By 1816 a steamship passenger service was in operation across the English Channel between Brighton and Le Havre, and in 1820 a service between London and Paris was opened with the *Aaron Manby*. She had an engine designed by Henry Bell which gave her an average speed of between eight and nine knots. After a few regular passenger trips she was purchased by a syndicate of French shipowners and used for pleasure trips up and down the River Seine.

All these vessels were, of course, relatively small; all had paddlewheels driven by single cylinder engines (occasionally, as in the *James Watt*, with one cylinder to each paddlewheel); and all were used only for river or coastal passages. But they opened the way to more ambitious steamship operations, across the oceans, with bigger ships and greater horsepower. In fact, by the year in which the *Aaron Manby* made her passage from London to Paris, the Atlantic had already been crossed by a ship with a steam engine, though she did not really rank as a steamship. This was the American *Savannah*, a full-rigged ship with an auxiliary

Below: Henry Bell's *Comet* (1812) ran a ferry service on the Clyde.

Inset: Transverse section of the *Comet* showing the 3 h.p. engine.

engine and detachable paddlewheels. She crossed the Atlantic in 1819 from Savannah to Liverpool in 21 days, but used her engine for only 8 hours during the passage. A similar voyage, and much more noteworthy because steam propulsion was used to a significant extent, was made in 1825 by the *Enterprise*, a ship of 470 tons, which made a passage of 11,450 miles (18,430 km) in 103 days from London to Calcutta. She was still primarily a sailing ship, but used her engine on sixty-four days of the 103.

The great problem still facing marine engineers and designers was the accommodation of sufficient coal on board to feed the boiler throughout a long ocean passage. By the 1830s the steam engine itself, still a single-cylinder reciprocating engine, was reliable enough to be used for ocean passages, but in general the ships themselves were still too small to accommodate the amount of coal required and still to provide sufficient space for passengers or cargo to make the ship commercially viable.

The answer to this particular problem was, of course, one of ship design, and it was finally solved in a somewhat dramatic fashion. The directors of the Great Western Railway Company in Britain decided in 1837 to extend their railway line to Bristol and called in for consultation their company engineer, Isambard Kingdom Brunel. At the meeting one of the directors complained that the line, when extended to Bristol, would be too long, whereupon Brunel said he thought it would be far too short and ought to be extended to New York by building a passenger steamship. The idea was discussed, approved, and as a result Brunel was told to go ahead and build an Atlantic liner, to be named the *Great Western*.

There was at the time a steamship company in existence called the British and American Steam Navigation Company, and as soon as it was learned that the Great Western Railway were building a steamship specially for an Atlantic crossing, they decided that they would beat them to it. It was known that the *Great Western* was to be a ship of 1,340 tons with an engine developing 750 horsepower, and the British and American company placed an order for a larger ship, to be called the *British Queen*.

There were many delays in her building, and before long it became apparent that the *British Queen* would not be ready before the *Great Western*. British and American, therefore, looked round for a ship to charter, and chose the *Sirius*, built for a passenger and cargo service between London and Cork. She was a ship of 700 tons with an engine developing 320 horsepower, and in the race across the Atlantic she was the first away, leaving Cork on 4 April 1838 with 40 passengers on board. Every available space

Far left: The *Savannah* – first steamship to cross the Atlantic. The passage, made in 1819, took 21 days although she only used steam for 8 hours, relying on sail for most of the journey.

Left: The *Great Western* was Brunel's masterpiece, a steamship with ample endurance for crossing the Atlantic. She made the crossing on 23 April 1838.

Below left: To beat the *Great Western* the *Sirius* was chartered by a rival company, but she only made the crossing from Cork to New York by burning all the wood on board.

below decks was packed with coal, and she carried two large heaps of it on the upper deck as well. Out in the Atlantic she ran into a severe storm which slowed her up and entailed the use of more coal than had been planned. As a result she ran out of coal before she could complete her crossing, but, by feeding the furnace with all the cabin furniture, the wooden doors throughout the ship, all her spare yards and one of her masts, she reached New York. She was greeted by an immense throng of cheering people eager to greet the first ship in the world to make an ocean crossing entirely under steam power. She had taken 18 days, 10 hours and her average speed for the whole passage was 6·7 knots.

She was followed into New York a few hours later by the *Great Western*. The latter had left Bristol four days later than the *Sirius*, carrying only seven passengers, and her time across the Atlantic was 15 days, 5 hours, giving her an average speed of 8·8 knots. What was far more important, however, was the fact that when she arrived in New York she still had 200 tons of coal in her bunkers – proof that, with a proper allowance of bunker space in their design, transocean passages were well within the capability of the new steamships.

Although during these early years of development of the marine steam engine the principle of the compound engine was well enough known, it was impossible to incorporate it in a ship because the problem of generating steam at a high enough pressure had not yet been solved. In a compound engine the steam is used twice: first in a high-pressure cylinder and then in a low-pressure cylinder, connected in line on the same shaft. It is a much more efficient and less wasteful engine than the single-cylinder low-pressure engine, but requires steam at a minimum pressure of 60 lb/sq in (4·2 kg/cm^2) to operate it. During the first half of the nineteenth century steam pressure in ships had risen from an initial 2 lb/sq in (0·14 kg/cm^2) to as much as 50 lb/sq in (3·5 kg/cm^2) by 1850, but it was not until the second half of the century that improved boiler design allowed steam to be generated at pressures suitable for the compound engine.

By the middle of the nineteenth century the wooden ship had reached her maximum size, with tonnage approaching 7,000 on waterline lengths of about 340 ft (100 m). These huge wooden ships, built only as warships, drew so much water that they could not be used inshore for the classic naval operations of close blockade and bombardment, required immense crews to man them, and were popular only with commanders-in-chief afloat, who found superb personal accommodation in the immense cabins aft. One such ship was the last three-decker of the British navy, H.M.S. *Victoria*, launched in 1859. In her, the wooden hull had been taken to its limit, and there was not enough strength in wood to extend any further, or to support the huge array of masts and yards required to drive so large an object through the water.

Some other shipbuilding material was obviously necessary, if ships were to develop beyond the limitations imposed by wood, and the only obvious alternative was iron. In the late eighteenth century an iron lighter had been constructed on the Thames, and confounded the sceptics when she did not sink. Nonetheless, there were far more doubters than believers, and resistance to the new material was considerable, even in the face of demonstrable success.

The first true ship to be built with an iron hull was the *Aaron Manby*, the first steamship to operate a service between London and Paris. She was a relatively small vessel of 116 tons, and in spite of many gloomy prognostications, she lasted until 1855, when finally she became unsafe through the rusting of her plates. She was followed by a few other iron-hulled vessels,

but they were all small and another twenty years were to pass before reluctant shipowners could be convinced that iron had so many advantages over wood that it was worth adopting for large ships as well as small.

Apart from the obvious fears that iron, because it is heavier than water, was an unsuitable material for shipbuilding, there were other reasons for the delay in its adoption. The science of engineering had yet to perfect a method of bending iron to a desired shape, and the only methods available at the beginning of the nineteenth century were casting in a mould or working when red hot by hammering. These methods frequently led to fractures because of the uneven quality of the iron. There was no knowledge as yet of any means to prevent rusting, which was accelerated by contact with seawater, and it was also quickly discovered that encrustation of the bottom by barnacles and weed occurred considerably faster on an iron hull than on a wooden

Top: HMS *Victoria* was the last three-decker to go to sea, and served until 1867. The ironclads soon replaced these splendid anachronisms.

Above: The *Aaron Manby* began a regular service between England and France in 1820, but was soon relegated to running on the Seine only.

one. And finally there was the effect of the iron hull on the magnetic compass. So great a mass of magnetic material was certain to throw a compass out, and as yet there was insufficient scientific knowledge of the behaviour of compasses to provide an antidote.

Yet the advantages of iron were so obvious that many shipbuilders did not share the conservative views of shipowners, and devised a means of incorporating it in a wooden hull in what was known as 'composite' building. One of the great drawbacks of the standard wooden hull was the massive framing needed to provide adequate longitudinal and athwartships strength. This framing was a great source of unnecessary weight in a ship. The composite ship had an inner framework consisting of iron keelson, frames, knees and deck beams to which the outer wooden planking, keel and decks were secured, thus providing not only a considerable saving in weight, but also a big increase in stowage space through the elimination of the thick wooden framing. It was a compromise that lasted only until shipowners at last overcame their reluctance, and went all-out for the iron ship.

The first sign of a decline in the continued dominance of wood for large ships came in 1838, with the building of the 400-ton iron ship *Rainbow* for trade between London, Ramsgate and Antwerp. Her immediate advantage was that she could stow in her holds nearly twice as much cargo as a wooden-hulled ship of the same size, and she proved herself to be a good ship at sea, safe and easy to handle. And with her iron hull she was not subject to the perpetual small leaks endemic in all wooden vessels due to the working of the hull planking. But the final seal of approval was set in the following year, when

Isambard Brunel persuaded the directors of the Great Western Railway Company to follow up their successful *Great Western* with an even larger ship, to have an iron hull. This was the *Great Britain*, and her keel was laid at Patterson's shipbuilding yard at Bristol in 1838.

With the *Great Britain* Brunel showed all contemporary naval architects how to design their ships in metal and how to use the new material to provide enough hull strength for ships of rapidly increasing size. In the *Great Britain* he stipulated an iron keel of great strength, nearly 1 in (25 mm) thick and 21 in (53·3 cm) wide, and her hull plating varied in thickness between $\frac{3}{8}$ in (9·5 mm) and $\frac{3}{4}$ in (19 mm). The plates were rivetted to frames made of angle iron, and longitudinal hull strength was provided by two fore-and-aft bulkheads carried up to the level of the main deck, and athwartships strength by five bulkheads across the whole width of the ship. These athwartships bulkheads were made watertight so that the hull was divided into six watertight compartments, as an additional safety measure.

Only in warships was the use of iron delayed, for tests carried out at Portsmouth in England had shown that, while a cannon ball fired at short range at iron plating $\frac{3}{4}$ in (19 mm) thick had no difficulty in penetrating it, 8 in (20 cm) of oak would stop it. And, as the average thickness of a wooden warship's hull planking was 18 in (45 cm), the advantages of retaining wood for warships was obvious. Moreover, wrought and cast iron, the only known methods at the time of bending iron to the desired shapes, showed a tendency to crack or shatter under gunfire – a fatal flaw in a warship. Yet, even in these early days of the iron ship, forces were at work which would compel navies to make the change, par-

Above: The iron-hulled *Rainbow* was built in 1838, and proved her worth. She could stow more cargo than a wooden ship and was equally seaworthy.

ticularly the development of the gun from a short-barrelled weapon discharging a solid ball at a relatively short range to a longer-barrelled piece firing an explosive shell over greater distances. But the day for this transition had not yet arrived, and, until it did, the wooden warship remained in many ways just a larger version of the warship of 200 years earlier.

All these early steamships, whether with wooden or iron hulls, were driven through the water by paddlewheels, either a single one at the stern, as in the *Charlotte Dundas*, or by a pair of wheels, one each side of the ship. There were considerable disadvantages in the use of paddlewheels, the principal one being that when a ship rolled in a seaway, each paddle-wheel (if she had two), would alternately be lifted out of the water, putting a tremendous strain on the engine. And, as they projected outside the hull of the ship, they were easily damaged by careless handling or by other accidents. For warships they were largely useless, since a single hit on a paddlewheel would at once cripple the ship. It was these obvious disadvantages which led several inventors to try to devise a means of ship propulsion which would be permanently submerged, and thus capable of driving the ship without putting a varying strain on the engine or providing an easy target for an enemy gun.

The principle of the Archimedes screw was well known, and it was an adaptation of this principle which finally produced the answer. A very early attempt to produce a marine propeller was John Shorter's invention of 1800, but it suffered from a clumsy form of chain drive and a very long shaft which required a buoy at the end to support it in the water. Four engineers are usually credited with the invention of the ship's propeller, the Englishman Robert Wilson, the Frenchman Frederic Sauvage, the Swede John Ericsson, and another Englishman Francis Pettit Smith. They all took out patents for their inventions between 1833 and 1836. It was Francis Smith's propeller which was at first most widely used by shipowners, though an improved design patented by Ericsson in 1838 was the final winner, when he demonstrated its efficiency in a small steamer aptly named the *Archimedes*.

Isambard Brunel, who had laid the keel of his *Great Britain* in 1839, had designed his ship for propulsion by paddlewheels, but he attended the trials of Ericsson's propeller on the *Archimedes* and was quickly convinced of its superiority as a means of ship propulsion. The building of the *Great Britain* was stopped while Brunel prepared new plans and began a series of experi-

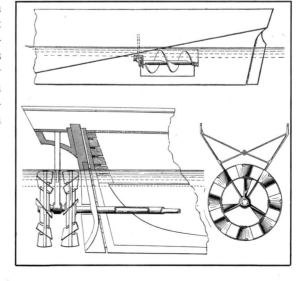

Left: Isambard Kingdom Brunel was a far-sighted engineer but he had a fatal knack of inspiring commercial backers to ruin themselves.

Below left: Illustration from a mid nineteenth century *Treatise on the Screw Propeller* by John Bourne showing (above) the Smith propeller and (below) two views of the Ericsson propeller. Several men were working in this field at the time and the parentage of the screw propeller is disputed.

Below: The *Great Britain* lies on the rocks in Dundrum Bay. Only her iron hull saved her from breaking up.

ments on various models of propellers to find the one most suited to his ship. The *Great Britain* was a large ship for her day, displacing 3,620 tons (3,680 tonnes), on an overall length of 322 ft (98·1 m) and a maximum beam of 50 ft 6 in (15·4 m). As a result of his experiments, Brunel gave her four engines, developing 1,500 horsepower, which drove a six-bladed propeller of 16 ft (4·9 m) diameter at 53 revolutions per minute. Steam from the boilers was fed to the engines at a pressure of 15 lb/sq in (1·1 kg/cm^2).

Like all steamships of her time, except for the smallest, the *Great Britain* was fitted with masts and sails. By 1840 the steam engine had proved itself on thousands of voyages, long and short, but in general most shipowners, and almost all passengers, felt less happy than the engineers about trusting their ships and themselves entirely to mechanical propulsion. So sail was carried, mainly as an insurance against breakdown. The *Great Britain* could spread 15,000 square feet of canvas on six masts, but although she crossed and recrossed the Atlantic many times during her service as a passenger ship, only once did she have to rely on her sails to complete a passage, when her propeller dropped off in mid-ocean.

If there were still any who doubted the superiority of iron over wood as a shipbuilding material, the *Great Britain* put their anxieties to rest. In September 1846 she ran aground on the rocky coast of Ireland at Dundrum Bay, due it is said to excessive deviation of her compass caused by the iron of the hull. She went ashore at the top of spring tides, and it was not until six months later that there was another tide high enough to float her off. All through the winter she lay on the rocks, battered by the winter gales, conditions which would have reduced any wooden ship to matchwood. When she was refloated and docked, it was discovered that her hull was hardly strained at all.

To avoid some of the loss caused by having her off the Atlantic service for so long, the Great Western Railway Company sold the *Great Britain*. Her new owners refitted her with smaller and more economical engines, and until 1886 she operated steadily between Liverpool and Australia. During that year she was damaged in a heavy storm off Cape Horn and was towed to the Falkland Islands and grounded in Port Stanley, to act as a coal hulk. Finally, in 1970, enough money was raised in Britain to salvage her and bring her home to Bristol, where she is preserved as a monument to the genius of her brilliant designer.

Great Britain
(1843)

Length 322 ft (98 m) *Beam* 50 ft 6 in (15·4 m) *Draught* 18 ft (5·5 m)
Displacement 3,443 tons (3,498 tonnes) *Speed* 12½ knots
Sail area 15,000 sq ft (1,400 m²) *Crew* 130
Cargo capacity 600 tons *Passenger capacity* 252 (designed)

The *Great Britain* is chiefly remembered as the first vessel of any
real size to be built wholly of iron, but she was also the first
screw-driven vessel to cross the Atlantic and was in her day the
largest ship afloat. Several features of her construction became
the pattern for future shipbuilding in iron, including the division
of her hull by watertight bulkheads and the absence of an external
keel. The second great shipbuilding project of Isambard Kingdom
Brunel, she made her maiden voyage to New York in 1845. The
following year she ran aground on the Irish coast and the fact
that she had sustained so little damage when she was finally
floated off 11 months later did much to promote the use of iron
for ship construction. She ended her working career as coal
hulk in the Falklands in 1886. In 1970 she was raised to be
returned to the same dry dock at Bristol where she was built, as a
memorial to Brunel and the days of the first iron ships.

She is seen here as she was when first built. The cross section
and cutaway show two of her 88-in (2·1 m) cylinders and the
chain drive to the propeller shaft. The small drawing shows her
under full sail.

Above: The tug-of-war between the screw-driven *Rattler* (left) and *Alecto* (right) was more of an exhibition to convince public opinion than a scientific test, as the Royal Navy had already ordered seven screw ships by March 1845.

So far as the merchant ship was concerned, the propeller was almost universally recognised as the most efficient means of ship propulsion, but the warship in general remained wedded to sail. This was to some extent understandable, particularly in Britain, which had emerged from the last great war as undisputed mistress of all the oceans. She still maintained the largest fighting fleet in the world, and the officers and men who had manned that navy in war were still serving in it. A radical change from wood and sail to iron and steam meant starting the navy again from scratch, with the present superiority of numbers wiped out at a stroke. But with the invention of the propeller the overriding objection to steam propulsion in warships, the vulnerable paddlewheel, had been removed, and the steam engine at last had to be admitted into naval ships.

But it was not admitted without a struggle by traditionalists, and there was still much argument in naval circles in all countries as to whether the propeller was really superior to the paddlewheel. The argument was finally settled in 1845, when two virtually identical frigates of 880 tons, H.M.S. *Rattler* and H.M.S. *Alecto*, were both fitted with engines of 220 horsepower, that in H.M.S. *Rattler* driving a propeller and that in H.M.S. *Alecto* a pair of paddlewheels. In March of that year the two ships had a race over 100 miles (160 km), which the *Rattler* won by

several miles. In a later test, the two ships, tied together with a towing hawser, set off under full engine power in opposite directions. The *Rattler* with her propeller towed the *Alecto* stern first at a speed of 2·7 knots – conclusive proof that a propeller not only drove a ship faster, but also exerted considerably more power.

So wooden warships, or at least those of Britain, were fitted with steam engines, although they still retained their full complement of masts and sails. The installation was achieved by bringing the ships into drydock, cutting them in half, and lengthening them to accommodate engines and boilers. But, whereas in the merchant ship masts and sails were fitted as an auxiliary source of propulsion, for use if the engine failed, in the warship it was the engine that was an auxiliary source of power, for use if the wind were blowing in the wrong direction. In France, the only other nation with a comparable navy, the adoption of the steam engine, even as an auxiliary source of power, progressed much more slowly. By 1854, only nine years after the *Rattler-Alecto* trials, the entire British fleet sent into the Baltic at the start of the Crimean War was fitted with engines; the entire French fleet in the Baltic still relied entirely on sail.

Although the propeller had emerged as the best means of transforming engine power into motion through the water, one problem remained unsolved. The fitting of a propeller entailed making a hole for the shaft in the ship's sternpost, and technology could not yet ensure watertight fitting. There were cases where ships leaked so badly through their stern gland that they had to be beached to save them from sinking. (Wooden-hulled ships faced an additional hazard. Since the vibration of the propeller could shake the sternpost to such an extent that the seams of the planking near the stern opened up and let the sea in.) It was not until 1854 that this particular problem was solved by John Penn, an engineer whose marine steam engines were widely used in ships. Penn discovered that *lignum vitae*, the hard, smooth wood of the guaiacum tree, which grows in the West Indies and has self-lubricating properties, was ideal for the purpose of lining stern glands. It also suffered very little wear as the propeller shaft revolved inside it. It was used for lining stern glands for the next forty years, until the more modern metallic packings were introduced.

It has been mentioned earlier that, in general, navies were slow to implement the advances in shipbuilding which the first half of the century brought, but this does not mean that no improvements in naval shipbuilding were made. The best wooden warships were still those built by France, mainly because, with the exception of the United States, she built appreciably larger than other maritime nations. As late as 1845 the British laid down a 74-gun ship of the line on the exact model of a French ship which they had captured in 1794, so great was their belief in the superiority of French design. But in the meantime the Royal Navy had found a naval architect of genius. As a commander, William Symonds had been given permission by the British Admiralty in 1825 to build a corvette to his own design, and the resulting ship, *Columbine*, of 18 guns, was so outstandingly successful that Symonds was promoted. His success as a designer might have ended there had not the Duke of Portland given him a commission to build a yacht. Named *Pantaloon*, she was such a success that she, too, was purchased for the navy and adapted as a 10-gun brig. Symonds was then instructed by the Admiralty to design more ships, including a fourth-rate of 50 guns, and their general excellence resulted in his being knighted and made Surveyor of the Navy, responsible for all warship design. Within the next fifteen years he was responsible for the design of more than 180 warships.

Symonds's designs owed their great success

Below: Captain Sir William Symonds, Surveyor of the Navy, designed many fine sailing warships for the Royal Navy, but could not adapt his skill to cope with steam propulsion.

Bottom: The corvette *Columbine*, designed by Symonds in 1825.

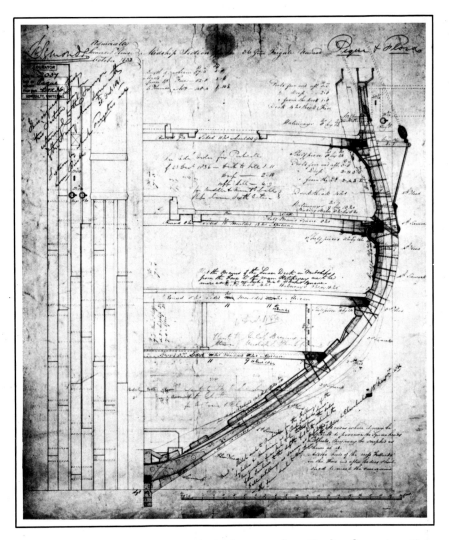

Above: The midships section of the 36-gun frigates *Pique* and *Flora* – sister ships built to the same plan (1832). This is a typical 'Symondite' hull-form.

Although, in general, the fighting navies of the world turned their backs on the revolution in shipping brought about by the introduction of the steam engine, there were some small exceptions. The young United States Navy led the way with the *Demologos*, launched in 1814, but completed too late to take part in the war then being fought against Britain. Designed by Robert Fulton (later she was renamed *Fulton*), she was a queer-looking vessel with two wooden hulls abreast, in one of which was the engine and in the other the boiler, and a paddlewheel mounted between them. She carried an armament of 30 guns designed to fire red-hot shot. She finally blew up in a dockyard explosion.

Britain adopted steam for her navy only reluctantly and, at first, purely for auxiliary services. It was Brunel who at last talked the Lords of the Admiralty out of their ultra-conservative attitude, and in 1822 the *Comet*, a wooden paddle steamer of 238 tons equipped with a Boulton and Watt engine of 90 horse-power, was built by contractors in the dockyard at Deptford. She was joined later by the *Monkey*, a similar paddle steamer of 212 tons, which had been built commercially at Rotherhithe and was purchased into the navy. The two vessels were used solely to tow the sailing men-of-war out of harbour when the direction of the wind made it impossible to sail out. In fact, the British Admiralty carried its disapproval of the steam engine to the extent of refusing to include the names of the engineers in the official Navy List, and requiring the contractors who built the ships to supply engineers with them.

France, Russia and Italy followed the naval lead of Britain by building or acquiring small steam vessels for use with their navies as auxiliaries, but, since in the world strategic situation their navies were of less account than that of Britain, they could afford to experiment. Not that their experiments produced anything revolutionary in the naval sphere; in general they were, like Britain, reluctant to tinker with their capital ships until they knew that they could be sure of the effect. Nevertheless, in Britain, the Surveyor of the Navy was instructed in 1832 to design a steamship, the first to be built in Britain in a naval dockyard by naval personnel. She was the *Gulnare* of 306 tons, mounting three guns, built of wood with paddlewheel propulsion. She was followed by other small steam gunboats, but until 1840 none was built above 1,000 tons, or with anything but a small armament. As they drew very little water, less than 5 ft (1·5 m), they were thought to have a naval use for inshore bombardment purposes, the risk of damage to their paddlewheels by enemy gunfire being accepted.

not only to improved methods of construction, which brought a great increase in structural strength, but also to an improved underwater shape, much less full and heavy than had been previously the case. To some extent he followed the French lead in building large, not so much in overall length as in beam and depth, so that his ships, though shorter than the French, were broader, roomier, and higher between decks. The loss of speed which a shorter overall length might have incurred was more than made up for by the improvement in shape of bottom, which gave his ships a much cleaner run through the water. Another of his improvements was the introduction of a system of standard sizes for masts and yards, so that they became interchangeable, not only between ships of the same class, but also between ships of different classes, though not of course for the same purpose. Thus, for example, the topsail yards of a second-rate ship of the line were cut to the same size as the main yards of a frigate, and so on. By this means the eighty-eight different sizes of masts and yards maintained for the Royal Navy were reduced to twenty, with no loss of efficiency.

Left: Turner's *Fighting Temeraire tugged to her Last Berth to be Broken Up* is a fitting contrast between the old and the new. During the Crimean War steamers had to stand by to tow the lumbering three-deckers in and out of action.

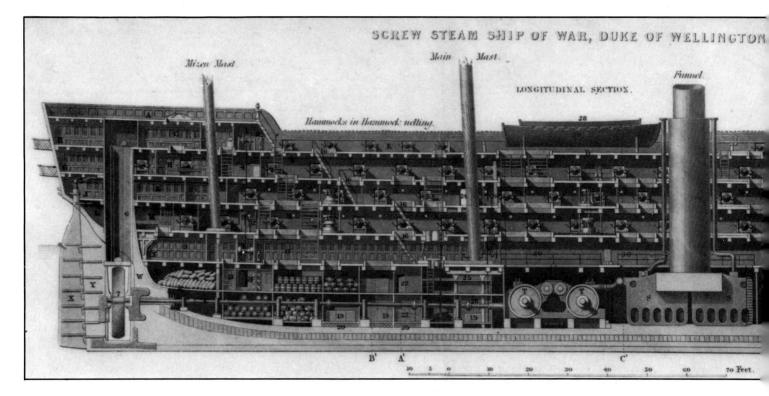

SCREW STEAM SHIP OF WAR, DUKE OF WELLINGTON

Mizen Mast. *Main Mast.* *Funnel.*

LONGITUDINAL SECTION.

Hammocks in Hammock netting.

Above: Inboard profile of the 131-gun 1st rate *Duke of Wellington* (1852). The addition of a propeller and machinery to a three-decker's hull made for cramped conditions between decks.

Right: Drawings of a typical Paixhans shell gun, showing how the powder-flash ignited the time-fuse of the shell.

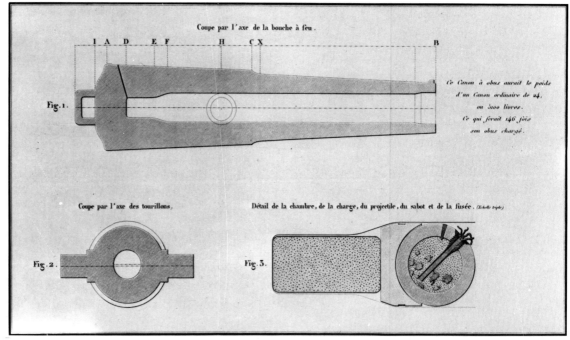

Coupe par l'axe de la bouche à feu.

Fig. 1.

Ce Canon à obus aurait le poids d'un Canon ordinaire de 24, ou 5400 livres. Ce qui ferait 146 fois son obus chargé.

Coupe par l'axe des tourillons.

Fig. 2.

Détail de la chambre, de la charge, du projectile, du sabot et de la fusée.

Fig. 3.

Not all British naval officers were as reluctant as the Board of Admiralty in London to face the implications of the marine steam engine, and in 1825 Lord Cochrane submitted a memorandum asking for 'six steam vessels, having each two guns in the bow and perhaps two in the stern, not less than 68-pounder long guns'. Such a squadron would have proved a formidable weapon against fleets of sailing men-of-war, and if built might well have speeded up the change-over from the sailing to the steam navy, which in fact took another half century. Only one of the six, the *Perseverance*, was built, and not for the British navy, but for the Greek. She played a useful, if fairly unspectacular, part in the Greek War of Independence against Turkey.

Iron did not enter into the Royal Navy's calculations until 1840, when the Admiralty purchased the iron-hulled steam packet *Dover* for no very clear purpose. No trials were carried out with her, and she was not used with the fleet. In the same year, three small iron gunboats were built, each mounting 2 guns, and with paddle-

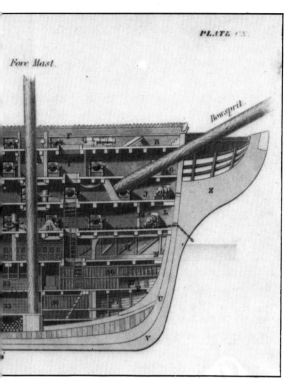

Fore Mast.

PLATE

Bowsprit

be designed from the start to incorporate an engine and propeller was the 80-gun second-rate *Agamemnon*, laid down at Woolwich in 1849 and launched in 1852. But in every case, except for that of the smallest vessels, a British warship converted to steam still retained her full complement of masts, yards, and sails as her main means of propulsion. Her engine was a very secondary affair, and elaborate and time-consuming arrangements were made to enable the propeller to be raised out of the water whenever she was to use her sails, in order to eliminate the drag exerted by the screw and retain the ship's sailing performance. It was not until 1861 that the lifting propeller was abandoned in the Royal Navy.

It was no sudden change of heart about the properties of iron that in the end forced every navy in the world to drop the use of wood for warship building; it was the development of a new form of gun and the outcome of its first use in actual conflict that brought the change. The naval gun during the first half of the nineteenth century remained the gun with which Nelson

Below: The troopship *Simoon* was originally an iron-hulled frigate.

wheel propulsion. But they were not followed up with anything larger, even though the way had been shown by John Laird, the Birkenhead shipbuilder, who had designed and built an iron frigate which he offered to the British Admiralty. (On the refusal of the Admiralty even to consider the purchase, she was sold to the Mexican navy.)

Yet the time was coming when the force of public opinion, particularly that of the shipping companies, would drive the Admiralty to begin using iron for warships larger than small gunboats. Orders were placed in 1846 for three iron steam frigates of 1,400 tons, the *Birkenhead*, *Simoon* and *Megaera*, the first fitted with paddlewheels and the other two with propellers. They never made it as warships, for gunnery experiments with an iron hull indicated that iron was still liable to break up and fracture when hit with solid shot, and the three were completed as troopships. (The *Birkenhead*'s tragic end off Danger Point, between Simonstown and Cape Town, in February 1852 is still well remembered.)

So it was back to the wooden hull for the British navy, even though some other navies were persevering with iron, backed with a thick lining of teak or oak to provide additional resistance against damage by solid shot. In Britain, the wooden ships of the line continued to be brought into the dockyards to be lengthened to take an engine and propeller, even the oldest ships being converted to steam. The *Ajax* and *Horatio*, both launched as long ago as 1809 and thus relics of the Napoleonic War, were two of the oldest; another was the *Nelson*, launched in 1814. The first British wooden ship of the line to

had won his battles – big muzzle-loading cannon, firing solid round shot. Explosive shells, fired parabolically from mortars, were used solely for bombardment and never considered as a ship-to-ship weapon. But in 1822 a French general of artillery, Henri-Joseph Paixhans, wrote a book called *Nouvelle Force Maritime et Artillerie*, in which he advocated the firing of explosive bombs from the normal naval gun, giving them a flat trajectory instead of a parabolic one, and thus converting the explosive shell into a ship-to-ship weapon. His gun was given its first serious tests in 1824, against the old, moored frigate *Pacificateur*, and proved remarkably successful. In 1853 Paixhans' guns were used for the first time in battle, when a Russian squadron of wooden-hulled ships armed with the new French guns encountered at Sinope, in the Black Sea, a Turkish squadron of wooden-hulled ships armed with conventional naval guns firing solid shot.

It was not just the defeat of the Turkish squadron which opened the eyes of the world's navies, but the fact that the explosive shells fired by the Russian ships set all the Turkish ships on fire and they burned down to the waterline.

The lesson of Sinope was underlined two years later at the bombardment of the Kinburn forts in the Crimea. After Sinope the French constructed a flotilla of floating batteries, protected with iron armour, and at the Kinburn bombardment three of them, the *Devastation*, *Tonnante* and *Lave*, steamed to within 1,000 yards (914 m) of a fort. It turned out that they were relatively impervious to the Russian fire, and they emerged unscathed from a position in which any wooden-hulled warship in the world would have been blown to bits. This demonstration of the advantages of iron construction in modern war conditions could not be ignored, and Britain was the first to put this experience to use by building, in 1856, the first iron-hulled armoured warships in the world – the *Terror*, *Thunderbolt*, *Erebus* and *Aetna*. They were designated 'armoured batteries' and built to a tonnage of 1,950, with an overall length of 108 ft 10 in (33·12 m), a beam of 48 ft 6 in (14·78 m), and a draught of 8 ft 10 in (2·69 m). They mounted 16 smooth-bore muzzle-loading 68-pounder guns, and their 200-horse-power engines gave them a speed of 5·5 knots. It was perhaps a small beginning, but the navies of the world had learned their lesson and began to catch up with merchant navies, which

had taken to iron with enthusiasm more than twenty years earlier.

Before leaving the iron warship, mention should be made of the British East India Company, which also built warships to protect and enforce their trade monopoly in India and China. It was in 1839 that the Company first considered using iron for their warship hulls, and in that year they approached the Birkenhead shipbuilder John Laird to build iron warships for service in the Far East. One of these was the *Nemesis*, a ship of 660 tons, armed with two 32-pounder pivot guns (at that time an innovation in the mounting of guns, when the normal practice was to mount them on wooden carriages in broadside batteries). Although the *Nemesis* only drew 5 ft (1·5 m) of water she made her way out to India under her own steam via the Cape of Good Hope, and during the First China War (1841–42) was taken over by the British Navy and gave excellent service during the naval operations.

Although during the first half of the nineteenth century the world's trade was expanding fast, it was not yet at a stage where shipowners, except monopoly companies like the East India Companies, could contemplate the building of fleets of ships. It was an event in Britain that first introduced this possibility. Until 1838 the mail

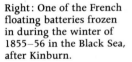

Right: One of the French floating batteries frozen in during the winter of 1855–56 in the Black Sea, after Kinburn.

for overseas had been carried in Post Office 'packets' (small ships built and run by the government solely for the purpose). These were sailing ships, but by this time it was obvious that the steamship was superseding the sailing ship in the commercial sphere and that, in any service where speed and reliability were essential, the day of the sailing vessel was over. Rather than bear the cost of constructing new steamships to carry the mails, the British government decided to put the carriage out to tender by any ship-owner able to guarantee a regular steamship service that would carry the mails to their destination. The value of the contract was enough to provide the shipowner with a sound economic basis for starting a regular ferry service.

The Government offer of the transatlantic mail service attracted two bidders. One was the Great Western Railway Company, which already owned the *Great Western*, on a regular run between Bristol and New York, and had laid down a larger ship, the *Great Britain*, destined for the same service; the second bidder was a Canadian merchant from Halifax, Samuel Cunard, who owned a number of sailing ships. When the terms of the mail contract were advertised, he

crossed to Britain and joined forces with Robert Napier, one of the best known marine engineers of the day, to bid for the contract. His tender for it included a clause that, if successful, he would build four ships and would guarantee to operate a regular service between Liverpool and Boston of two voyages a month, summer and winter. With his tender accepted, Cunard formed a company with the shipowners George Burns, of Glasgow, and David McIver, of Liverpool, and placed orders with Napier for four wooden paddle steamers, each with an overall length of 207 ft (63·1 m) and a tonnage of 1,156, and with an average speed of 8·5 knots. These were the *Acadia*, *Britannia*, *Caledonia* and *Columbia*, and they began their transatlantic service in 1840. It proved so popular and profitable that four years later the company built the *Hibernia* and *Cambria*, both of them larger and faster than the first four. The *Hibernia*, in fact, was the first ship to cross the Atlantic in less than ten days, and was also the first to use the port of New York instead of Boston.

Four years later, with the transatlantic trade still growing, another four ships were built, each of them having a tonnage of 1,820 and a

Above: The Cunard paddle steamer *Britannia*, which began a transatlantic service in 1840. This was beginning of the 'liner'.

Above: The paddle liner
Persia (1863) gave the
Cunard Line mastery of the
North Atlantic. She was
the biggest ship in the
world for a time and also
the first liner with an iron
hull, but she was one of
the last of the big paddle
steamers.

service speed of over 10 knots. So much of the trade was now coming to the Cunard Line that the United States decided to encourage their own shipowners to compete by offering their own mail carriage contract. It was given to the Collins Line, which built four new steamers of over 3,000 tons each, the *Arctic*, *Atlantic*, *Baltic* and *Pacific*, all of them with a small margin of speed over that of the Cunard ships. But though they were fine ships, Cunard replied to the challenge by building the *Africa* and *Asia*, both of around 2,000 tons, and now with twelve ships in his shipping line he was able to offer a much more frequent transatlantic service. Moreover, tragedy befell the Collins Line when the *Arctic* collided with the French steamer *Vesta*, and sank with the loss of 323 lives, and when the *Pacific* sailed from Liverpool with 156 people on board and was never seen or heard of again.

In the face of these disasters the Collins Line built the *Adriatic*, larger and faster than the other Collins ships, but so expensive to build that the company went heavily into debt. And it was at this moment that Cunard unveiled his

master stroke, the *Persia*. She was the first transatlantic liner to be built with an iron hull, and at her launch was the biggest ship in the world. Her appearance on the Atlantic killed the Collins Line dead.

It was a government mail contract which gave birth to another of the great shipping lines, the Peninsula & Oriental Steam Navigation Company. It began with Robert Bourne, who had a contract for the carriage of the internal mails in Ireland, which he operated with stage coaches based on Dublin. Bourne bought a small 206-ton steamer, the *William Fawcett*, to carry the mails across the Irish Sea. The company he formed was the City of Dublin Steam Packet Company, and in 1826 he appointed two young men, Brodie Wilcox and Arthur Anderson, who ran a shipping agency, as his London agents. A second small steamer bought by the company was the *Royal Tar*, and she was used to carry cargoes to Spain and Portugal during the Spanish and Portuguese civil wars. Her reliability and regularity so impressed the Spanish government that they asked for a regular steamer service to

Above right: The *Iberia* (1836) was the first ship owned by the Peninsular Steam Navigation Company.

Below: The P&O *Hindustan* leaves Southampton on 24 September 1842 to start the company's mail service to India.

be inaugurated and, with the British Government offering a contract to carry the mails to the Iberian Peninsula in 1837, Wilcox and Anderson formed the Peninsula Steam Navigation Company, whose first ship was the *Iberia*, a paddle steamer of 516 tons with an engine developing 180 horsepower. In 1840 the Peninsula Steam Navigation Company was offered the mail contract to Egypt and India. 'Oriental' was added to the Company's name, and two more steamers, the *Oriental* of 1,674 tons and the *Great Liverpool* of 1,311 tons, were built to carry the mails through the Mediterranean to Egypt. In 1842 the Suez-Calcutta service was inaugurated by the *Hindustan*, of 2,017 tons, and

in the same year the company gained the government mail contract for Australia. With this extension of their Indian route to Singapore, they were now poised to become the most powerful shipping force throughout the Far East.

There were other shipping lines starting to operate to different parts of the world around the same time, for these were the years which saw the beginning of the industrial revolution with its immense upsurge of world trade. It was the start of a golden age for shipping, and the next fifty years were to see more changes and more developments in the size, design, and power of ships than had occurred during the whole of the previous 2,000 years.

The Great Ship

In the early 1850s three brilliant engineers gathered together to air their views about the future of the merchant ship. One of them was Isambard Kingdom Brunel who, with the successful *Great Western* and *Great Britain* already to his credit, was the most influential ship designer in England. He realised that, although there was a limit to the size to which a wooden ship could be built because of the strength, or lack of it, in the building material, this limitation did not apply when a much stronger building material was used. Iron was this stronger material, and with it ships much bigger than the biggest wooden ship ever built could be constructed.

In Brunel's estimation there was, too, a definite need for a very big ship. Emigration was on the increase, the main destinations at this time being the United States and Canada. On the other side of the world, in Australia and New Zealand, there were immense areas of uninhabited land which, it seemed to Brunel, were ready and waiting to receive Europe's dispossessed multitudes. They would need ships to take them there and ships to bring their produce back to Europe after the land had been cultivated. And as the numbers grew, so also would grow the volume of trade with Europe, all of which would have to be carried across the oceans in ships.

The second engineer concerned was John Scott Russell. He had become interested in the maritime side of engineering in 1834 when he was

consulted on the possibilities of introducing steam navigation on the Edinburgh and Glasgow Canal. He owned a shipbuilding yard at Millwall, on the River Thames, but his greatest interest lay in the study of wave-formation. From many experiments, carried out both with models in a tank and with full-sized vessels on a canal, he established that there was a connection between a vessel's wave-making properties and her resistance to forward motion, and that a ship could be driven faster and more economically by designing her underwater hull shape to create the least possible wave disturbance.

The third engineer associated with the new ship, albeit to a lesser extent than the other two, was William Froude, who had been an assistant of Brunel in 1837 when he was principally a railway engineer. After nine years, Froude left the railway to devote himself to the study of ship behaviour and hydro-dynamics, working on very similar lines to Scott Russell.

The new ship was therefore designed with an underwater shape that

Above left: Scott Russell (left) and Brunel (second from right) at the first attempt to launch the *Great Eastern* in 1857.

Above: The incomplete *Great Eastern* awaiting high tide ready for a sideways launching – the final attempt – in 1858.

Right: The *Great Eastern* at sea.

conformed to the principles of Scott Russell and Froude, and an overall size that met Brunel's requirement for accommodation for 4,000 passengers, and space for 6,000 tons of cargo and enough coal for a voyage to Australia or India. The result was an overall length of 692 ft (210·9 m), a beam of 82 ft (25 m) and a loaded draught of 29·3 ft (8·9 m). Her designed measurement tonnage was 18,914, and her displacement tonnage 27,700 (28,145 tonnes). Because of her great size she was to be named *Leviathan*, and an idea of just how revolutionary was the increase in size which Brunel had proposed can be gained from the fact that the biggest ship in the world hitherto had an overall length of 375 ft (114·3 m) and a designed tonnage of 3,300. In tonnage terms, *Leviathan* was to be more than five times as large as any ship yet built.

Brunel persuaded the Eastern Steamship Navigation Company that her construction was a feasible commercial venture, and her keel was laid in Scott Russell's shipyard at Millwall. Because of her great length, it would be impossible to launch her in the normal way, stern first, as the Thames at Millwall was not wide enough, and so she was built broadside on to the river, and would eventually have to be launched sideways.

During building, her name was changed from *Leviathan* to *Great Eastern*. So many difficulties arose during construction that her cost rose enormously. More than one company associated with it was forced into bankruptcy, including Scott Russell's shipyard, and Brunel's own health broke down as a result of the constant worries associated with her building. She was finally ready for launching in 1858, but even this went wrong. After moving a few inches down the slipway, she stuck. Large hydraulic presses had to be built, to push her, and wire cables on winches mounted on the opposite bank of the Thames, to pull her. Finally, weeks later, she floated off on a very high tide.

Her new owners (the original company having gone bankrupt) decided to use her on the Atlantic run, and her cabins and saloons were fitted out at considerable expense, and with great luxury, for the period. By the time she was ready for her maiden crossing, Brunel himself had died from a heart attack. He was, perhaps, fortunate in not living to see the unhappy fate of his great ship. On her first voyage to America, she attracted no more than thirty-six passengers, instead of the 4,000 for which she had been built, and once at sea she rolled so heavily that prospective passengers refused to travel in her. She was taken out of service after a short period, and found no employment until 1865, when Sir Daniel Gooch chartered her to lay the first electric telegraph cable across the Atlantic. In all, she laid four cables across the Atlantic, and another from Aden to Bombay.

At the end of her cable-laying career, she lay at Milford Haven for twelve years, until she was bought by a firm in Liverpool as a summer attraction for visitors. She was refitted more or less in her original state, her grand saloon was used as a music hall, and there were side-shows in her cabins and a merry-go-round with a steam organ installed on her upper deck. It was a sad end for a once proud ship, but even in her new guise she did not pay. At the end of the summer she was laid up, and two years later sold for breaking-up.

Yet, commercial failure that she was, the *Great Eastern* marks a very important milestone in the history of ships. She proved Brunel's theory that with iron as a shipbuilding material there was no limit to the size of ship that could be built. Her construction introduced the principle of the cellular double bottom, and she was the first ship to fit a steering engine, at that time a novel means of overcoming the pressure of water on the rudder, but now a universal feature in all ships of any size. And, perhaps most important of all, she was the first large ship whose underwater shape was designed according to the principles of hydrodynamics. It was, at this time, admittedly an inexact science, but after the *Great Eastern* both Scott Russell and William Froude continued their work on the wave-line theory, and it is on this theory that all modern ship design is based.

Chapter Eight
The Growth of the Steamship

It was the improvement of the marine steam engine, through the development of more efficient boilers, that made possible the huge increase in the size of merchant ships during the second half of the nineteenth century. And it was the great expansion of world trade, coupled with a surge of emigration to the New World, which accounted for the simultaneous explosion in their numbers.

The theory of the compound steam engine (in which the steam is used twice in each cycle of the engine, first in a high-pressure cylinder and then again in a low-pressure cylinder, before being drawn off to a condenser to be turned back into boiler feed water) was first propounded in 1783. But to put it into practice demanded a higher pressure than, until later in the nineteenth century, was obtainable with the normal marine boiler. Between 1850 and 1860 new designs of boiler were introduced and steam pressure, which until about 1850 could not be produced at more than about 25 lb/sq in ($1 \cdot 75$ kg/cm^2), rose to between 50 and 60 lb/sq in ($3 \cdot 5$ to $4 \cdot 2$ kg/cm^2). Such pressures made the compound engine a reality for ships, and in 1853 John Elder, a Scottish engineer, took out a patent on a marine version of the engine. Naturally, the new engine aroused keen interest among shipowners, for using the steam twice in a single cycle brought not only a considerable saving in the amount of coal burned, but also a large increase in the power of the engine.

The Cunard Line was the first of the big shipping companies to install compound engines in their ships, and in 1868 the *Parthia* and *Batavia* were both built with compound engines for the transatlantic service. Other big companies followed Cunard's lead, and a great many smaller shipowners, attracted by the saving in fuel costs which could be as much as 30 per cent, installed the compound engine in their new ships and brought in their older ones to have their single-

Left: The destroyer HMS *Viper* symbolized the enormous progress marine engineering made in the nineteenth century.

expansion engines removed and the new engine fitted in their place.

Further boiler development followed, and, with the introduction of the Scotch return-tube marine boiler, the next step in engine development became possible. This was a very reliable forced-draught boiler which generated steam at a pressure between 120 and 160 lb/sq in ($8 \cdot 4$ and $11 \cdot 25$ kg/cm^2), and with this amount of pressure it became possible to make the steam work three times in one engine cycle by adding an intermediate-pressure cylinder between the existing high- and low-pressure cylinders. The first engine of this new design to be fitted in a ship was made by Dr A. C. Kirk for the steamer *Propontis* in 1874, but it was not a success because he used the old type of boiler and as a result lacked sufficient steam pressure. But, as soon as the new forced-draught boilers became available, the whole picture was changed: the triple-expansion engine was born – even more economical than the compound engine and developing still more engine power – and it was this combination, the Scotch return-tube boiler allied to the triple-expansion engine, which was to remain the standard power plant for ships, both passenger and cargo, across the world for the remainder of the century. Right at the end of the century, the Germans introduced a quadruple-expansion engine for their four great liners of the *Kaiser Wilhelm der Grosse* class, built between 1897 and 1902. These were the biggest marine reciprocating engines ever built, but even as they were being fitted they were being made obsolete by the next development in marine propulsion.

The big increase in engine power during the second half of the nineteenth century made larger ships possible, and tonnages rocketed. Until 1850 the largest steamship yet built was the *Great Britain*, of 3,270 tons (3,322 tonnes); during the half century which followed, the size of ships increased nearly tenfold, and, in the case of some passenger liners, more than that. A contributory cause was the introduction of steel in place of iron. The Siemens process of steelmaking was introduced at about the same time as the triple-expansion engine, and as it cut the cost of manufacturing steel dramatically, it made economic sense for shipowners to turn to steel as a building material. With its high tensile strength, steel meant that thinner plates and smaller scantlings could be used in shipbuilding without any diminution of hull strength, producing a saving in weight of up to 25 per cent. This, in its turn, meant lower coal consumption or, in the case of the prestigious liners, an extra knot or two of speed with the same engine power.

The most radical design changes in merchant shipping were to be seen in the big passenger ships. The cargo ship, except in size, did not alter greatly in design, the main consideration remaining the amount of cargo that she could conveniently stow. There was little call for anything beyond a moderate sea speed for a cargo vessel, for in those days of trade expansion on a huge scale there was never a lack of cargoes waiting to be carried. An increase in speed meant an increase in costs, and the successful cargo ship was the one which could quote the lowest freight rates. Gradually, as engines and boilers grew in reliability and power, the merchant ship shed her auxiliary sails, and little was to be seen of the square rig after about 1865, except in the case of passenger ships, which kept their sails, though on a diminishing scale, for another ten years or so, mainly as a reassurance to travellers who had not as yet learned to put their trust in steam.

In 1850 the cargo ship generally still had her sailing ship-type flush deck, except for a central bridge built across the tops of the paddle boxes. When the paddlewheels were replaced by the propeller, the central bridge remained, as it had been found a convenient place from which the captain and watchkeepers could control the ship, even though the steering wheel and the helmsman were still exposed on the upper deck aft. This after steering position was always a place of some danger in a heavy sea, and, since helmsmen were periodically washed overboard, most shipowners began to specify the inclusion of a poop deck in their new ships, to raise helmsman and steering wheel to a safer level. At roughly the same time, a forecastle deck was added to provide living quarters for the crew without having to use valuable cargo space below, while the bridge structure was raised to provide a better command post. Thus the typical flush-decked cargo carrier of the 1850s evolved into the typical well-decked carrier of the 1900s ('wells' being the names given to the two lower

deck levels, between forecastle and bridge and between bridge and poop deck). The increase in size of the cargo ship during the second half of the nineteenth century was certainly nothing like as spectacular as that of the passenger liner. But whereas a cargo ship of 2,000 gross tons would have been considered a very big ship in 1850, such tonnages were commonplace fifty years later, and some cargo carriers were being built up to 6,000 gross tons, and in a few cases even larger. The biggest of them were probably the colliers, for the demand for coal was incessant, not only for the growing industrial needs of the world, but also to establish coaling stations around the globe to refuel the world's ships. By the end of the nineteenth century an ocean-going collier could carry as much as 6,000 tons of coal in bulk in her capacious holds, and still the worldwide demand remained unsatisfied.

It was during this half century that the specialized cargo ship, designed to carry one type of cargo only, made her appearance. In 1870 a merchant ship with refrigerated holds sailed from Britain to New Zealand, to return with a cargo of lamb carcases frozen in her holds. The meat arrived in England in excellent condition and thus began a new trade in fresh foods from all parts of the world. In 1886 the *Gluckauf*, built in Britain, became the world's first true oil tanker, with separate tanks for the oil built into her hull. Until her appearance, oil had always been shipped in barrels or drums; now it could be pumped on board directly into the tanks. She, too, started a new trade which was to grow enormously over the years.

The phenomenal growth in passenger liner size was caused mainly by the huge immigration programme of the United States. Her desire for immigrants arose partly from the development of the transcontinental railway from the Atlantic to the Pacific coast, and partly from the rapid growth of the steel industry around Pittsburgh. Both these industries were hungry for cheap labour, and both sent recruiting parties to scour Europe for men to fill the vacancies. What they found in Europe were conditions where emigration often offered the only escape from misery and deprivation. In England, the economics of the industrial revolution had put tens of thousands of men out of work; in Ireland, the periodic failure of the potato crop brought famine to the population; in many countries of Europe, racial or religious persecution had made hundreds of thousands of families destitute. To these millions of people the promise of work on the railways or in the steel mills was a

Above: The collier *Eastwood* and smaller craft in winter ice on the Thames, February 1895.

Right: The *Timaru*, the first refrigerated cargo carrying ship.

Below right: The *Gluckauf* (1886) was the first ship designed to carry oil fuel in bulk.

powerful incentive to emigrate. (Between 1851 and 1905, 4,028,589 emigrants left Ireland alone, the vast majority going to the United States.) That the work when they got there was hard, ill-paid and frequently degrading was discovered too late; by then the great step had been taken and they had crossed the ocean, usually accompanied by their families. However, no matter how mistaken were their reasons for going, there were literally millions of people eager and waiting to cross the oceans to a new life.

It was a problem which only the big ship-owners could tackle – and they only in a somewhat roundabout fashion. Building a new ship is a long-term proposition: she has to repay her building cost, as well as her running costs, over several years of profitable operation. As no ship-owner could foretell for how long the surge of emigration would last, the building of one-class ships to handle this traffic could well have proved to turn out a financial disaster. Moreover, the vast majority of the emigrants were the poorest of the poor, and they could not afford to pay high enough fares to make a one-class ship profitable. The only way to handle the traffic was to build passenger ships in which the revenue from the first- and second-class passengers alone was enough to cover the running costs and the amortisation of the building cost, and to provide additional space for as many steerage passengers as possible at a fare which the emigrants could afford. And that meant big ships.

Brunel had shown the way with his *Great Eastern*. Although she was a great financial failure, she proved that with iron as a building material there was no limit to the size to which ships could be built, as there was with wood. And she had proved the soundness of the iron hull when, in 1865, she grounded on a reef in Long Island Sound and ripped a hole 75 ft (23 m)

long in the outer skin of her double bottom without sinking. It only remained to find an engine powerful enough before shipowners could build as big as they liked and, as we have seen, the solution of that problem came in the 1870s.

In the meantime, the interior design of passenger liners was changing. The general pattern in most liners had been to have the main passenger lounge and the first-class cabins accommodated in wooden deckhouses built aft on the upper deck, with the less expensive cabins and the steerage accommodation on the deck below. In 1871 the White Star liner *Oceanic*, built in Belfast by Harland and Wolff, made her first crossing of the Atlantic with her first-class accommodation amidships, with larger cabins and scuttles (windows) than ever before. She also had a promenade deck extending the full width of the ship above the cabins and lounges, and thus set a pattern which was to be followed in all future liner design. She was built very long for her beam, 420 ft (128 m) overall with a beam of 41 ft (12·5 m), to give her a speed of over 18 knots.

Another great step forward was made by the Inman Line in 1888, with their two ships *City of Paris* and *City of New York*. By now steel had largely replaced iron as the preferred shipbuilding material, and both ships were built of steel. The triple-expansion engine, also well established by now, was fitted in both ships. But the most impressive novelty in their design was the fact that they had two engines, driving two shafts, with two propellers, one on each quarter. As well as greater efficiency, this arrangement produced considerably less vibration than a single propeller on the centreline of the ship. When the ships came into service they were voted the most comfortable and the most handsome ships on the Atlantic run. They had a displacement tonnage of 14,500 (14,730 tonnes) on an overall length of 560 ft (170·7 m), a beam of 63 ft 2 in (19·25 m), and a draught of 41 ft 11 in (12·78 m). From their maiden voyages they held the speed record across the Atlantic with a passage time of less than 6 days at more than 20 knots until, in 1893, the Cunard Line's *Campania* made the crossing at a slightly higher speed.

Although these and their sister ships were what one would call the 'crack' liners on the Atlantic run, they were by no means the only ones to make regular crossings. There were hosts of other shipping lines, large and small, to carry the growing trade. While they all depended, more or less, on the first- and second-class passengers to cover their costs, none disdained the emigrant traffic, now in full flood, and all had large amounts of steerage accommodation, into which they crammed an astonishing number of men, women and children, eager to begin a new

life in a new country. Even the crack liners, which took the cream of the first- and second-class passengers, could carry as many as 2,000 souls in their steerage compartments at almost no additional cost to the shipping line. While the price of a steerage passage was small – as little as £3 on some ships – all that the shipowner had to provide was a bunk. These were erected in long tiers extending the whole length of the steerage compartment, with a space of about 5 ft (1·5 m) between the tiers. The bunks generally consisted of a wooden frame, with wooden slats or wire netting as a mattress, and there were usually three bunks to a tier. The emigrants provided their own bedding and food, though stoves were erected on the upper deck for the passengers to cook the food that they had brought. Inevitably they were always overcrowded, and in bad weather the lot of the steerage passengers, most of whom had never seen a ship, or even the sea, before, was miserable in the extreme.

The two great ports which handled the bulk of this emigrant traffic were Liverpool, to which the Irish came, and Hamburg, which was the gathering place of the mainland Europeans, and

Top: The liner *Oceanic* set new standards of comfort when completed in 1871.

Above: The Cunarder *Campania* won the Blue Riband in 1893 and ended her days as a seaplane carrier in 1918.

Above right: Steerage passengers aboard the Red Star liner *Pennland* in 1893. Conditions varied, but at best were spartan.

Right: The crack liner *Kaiser Wilhelm der Grosse* won the Blue Riband in 1897. She became an armed merchant cruiser in 1914, and was sunk.

these were, naturally, the terminal ports of most of the transatlantic lines. Cunard, White Star, Inman and many others were based on Liverpool, and the great Hamburg–Amerika and other continental lines on Hamburg.

Although the tonnage of the *Great Eastern* had been surpassed by several liners in the 1880s, it was not until 1897 that a ship with a greater overall length was built. This was the Hamburg–Amerika Line's *Kaiser Wilhelm der Grosse*, the first of four great German liners which were to bring that country into serious competition with the established giants of the transatlantic trade. These were ships of more than 648 ft (197·5 m) overall, and with her huge quadruple-expansion engine the *Kaiser Wilhelm der Grosse* broke the Atlantic speed record with an average of 22·35 knots. They were built mainly with an eye on the European emigrant trade then in full flood, and, although they offered a very high standard of luxury in their first- and second-class accommodation – equal in fact to the best on offer by Cunard, White Star, and the other great lines – they could also carry immense numbers of steerage passengers, who were packed in with the

minimum of space between the tiers of bunks. There were two steerage compartments – one for men, the other for women and children.

It was not only to North America that this great European emigration movement was directed, though it was that continent that attracted the greatest proportion of it. Gold had been discovered in Australia, and a gold rush developed. But in this case the distances involved were very much greater, and the problems facing the shipowner entirely different to those presented by the Atlantic trade. At the start of the 1850s, steamships had not yet reached a size at which they could stow on board enough coal for the whole passage, and, although there were coaling stations en route, at St Helena and Cape Town, the last leg of the voyage from South Africa to Australia, where gales and heavy weather were the rule rather than the exception, was still beyond their capacity without refuelling. So this trade, at least until the 1880s, was one of the last strongholds of the big sailing ship, and it was not until the last two decades of the nineteenth century, following the opening of the Suez Canal, that the steamship was able to compete with, and eventually replace, the sailing ship for the emigrant trade.

An unhappy story of a sailing emigrant ship on the Australian run was that of the *Dunbar*, specially built by Duncan Dunbar, a London shipowner, to carry passengers attracted to Australia by the gold rush. She was a ship of over 1,000 tons (big as sailing ships went). On her maiden voyage she left London with her captain making the boast 'Hell or Sydney in eighty days'; for the *Dunbar* was expected to be a flyer among sailing ships because of her high length-to-beam ratio. Seventy-nine days out of London she sighted Sydney Heads, but on the eightieth day, instead of lying at anchor in Sydney Harbour, she was no more than a torn mass of wreckage on the rocks of North Head, her captain having tried to pass them too close in the night. Only one man survived out of nearly 850 carried on board.

The half century 1850 to 1900 saw the beginning of the heyday of ocean travel and trade. Men's horizons were expanding at an unprecedented rate, and with the advent of a reliable marine steam engine and the great reduction in the time taken by an average voyage, a taste for foreign travel was growing fast. This was the foundation on which a number of shipping fortunes were made, backed up by the apparently never-ending emigrant movement of millions of Europe's poor and dispossessed. It was this huge expansion which kept marine engineers and naval architects on their toes, always striving for improvements in the reliability and power of engines, on the one hand, and improvements in hull form on the other.

Below: The immigrant trade to Australia was tougher than on the transatlantic route, because distances were so much greater. Here the Albyn Line *Otago* waits for the tide, her decks crowded with passengers.

John Scott Russell and William Froude, the two engineers who collaborated with Brunel on the design of the *Great Eastern*, were responsible for some highly important research into hull forms, with particular reference to the effects of skin friction and eddy-formation on a ship's forward progress through the water. Froude was the more influential of the two, and in 1870 the British Admiralty gave him a grant to build a tank for testing ship models near his home at Torquay, the prototype of the sophisticated test tanks of today. From his experiments Froude developed the wave line theory, to explain differences in the patterns of waves and eddies caused by bodies as they move through the water. When he applied his theory to the hull of a ship, Froude found that it was the wave pattern produced by the ship, which became more pronounced as the vessel's speed increased, that was responsible for most of the resistance to forward motion. This meant that a naval architect could test the efficiency of a new hull shape, at the planning stage, by measuring the amount of wave disturbance created by a scale model in the tank, and, by finding the shape which created least disturbance, could produce a ship that could be driven faster and more economically.

As the century wore on, the influence of Froude's theories became more and more marked, as evidenced by longer, cleaner runs aft, and a big increase in length-to-beam ratios, in even the humblest cargo-carriers. This increase was one of the main developments in ship design of the period, the old 4 or 5 to 1 ratio being replaced by 8 or 9 to 1 in the case of passenger liners, in which the main consideration was the speed that could be maintained over a long passage. Another important development in ship design at this time was a change in the placing of ships' propellers, again a direct result of Froude's wave-line theory. He had shown in the experiments that, at the stern of a ship moving through the water, there is a partial vacuum, and that a propeller revolving in this partial vacuum loses a proportion of its forward drive. With this knowledge

Below: In 1867 William Froude built two models, the *Swan* and *Raven*, to test his theories.

Bottom: Froude's testing tank, showing the dynamometer carriage at the end of its run.

Inset: William Froude FRS proved that accurate testing of hull-forms could be done with models towed in a tank.

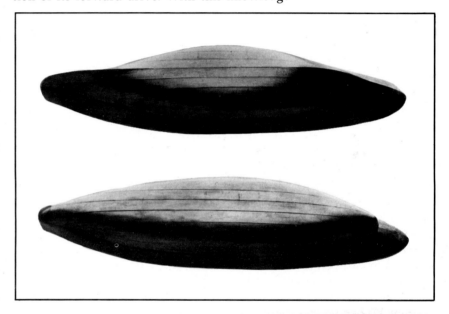

naval architects were able to position their propellers, in relation to the ship's hull, where they avoided this area of partial vacuum and so acted with greater efficiency. All these developments can be summed up by saying that during the fifty years before 1900 the science of hydrodynamics became a live and vital factor in the naval architect's work and that, with the growth of this scientific knowledge, ships improved, both in performance and in the economical transfer of engine power into speed through the water.

One other feature of this period was the development and growth of the steam yacht, a symbol of wealth and leisure that appealed greatly to many rich men of the nineteenth century. In 1827 the members of the Royal Yacht Club at Cowes, Isle of Wight (not yet named the Royal Yacht Squadron) had expressed their opposition to the marine steam engine in a resolution 'that the object of this club is to promote seamanship to which the application of steam is inimical, and any member applying steam to his yacht shall be disqualified hereby and shall cease to be a member.' One of the club's members, Thomas Assheton-Smith, considered the resolution an unwarrantable interference with personal liberty, resigned from the club, and in 1829 built the 400-ton yacht *Menai*, in which he installed an engine driving a pair of paddlewheels. She was the first steam yacht to be built in Britain. A few more British owners followed his lead, all their yachts being paddlers, and fitted with one or two oscillating or walking-beam engines and fire-tube boilers.

With the introduction of the propeller during the decade 1840 to 1850 the power plant changed to the single-stage steam reciprocating engine, still with the fire-tube boiler, to be replaced by the compound engine between 1860 and 1870, and by the triple-expansion engine about ten years later. The new water-tube boiler began to be seen in steam yachts in about 1865, but it was not until Sir Alfred Yarrow designed the three-drum variety of water-tube boiler in 1889 that the older fire-tube boiler finally disappeared.

The first steam yacht built in the United States, which made her appearance in 1853, was the 1,876-ton *North Star* built for Commodore Cornelius Vanderbilt. She set a pattern which caught on rapidly in a country where great fortunes could be made in a very short time. A steam yacht became something of a status symbol, a great many were built, and the desire to display evidence of personal wealth crossed the Atlantic to Europe, where many rich men followed the American fashion.

The great steam yachts, some of them ranging up to 3,000 tons displacement, were always fitted out with extreme luxury. Staterooms were equipped with every conceivable convenience, even to the extent of marble baths and washbasins in some notable yachts; saloons were enriched with gold leaf and massive carvings; and below the upper deck there was thick carpeting to add comfort and help to deaden the sound of the engines. These palatial yachts were symbolic of a period of great and rapidly increasing prosperity for those who were lucky enough to make quick fortunes.

The greatest changes of all, in this half century of change and development in ship design, took place in the world's navies. The lessons of the battle of Sinope in 1853 were quickly learned. It proved that warships could not survive in battle without armour on their sides, to keep out shells fired by the new rifled guns.

The French were the first to act when, in March 1858, they ordered four ironclad warships. Designed by the great naval architect Dupuy de Lôme, three of them were wooden-hulled ships of 5,617 tons (5,707 tonnes), with hulls plated with iron up to the level of the upper deck, $4\frac{1}{3}$ in (110 mm) thick on the upper strakes and $4\frac{2}{3}$ in (120 mm) on the lower. The wooden hull behind the armour was 26 in. (66 cm) thick. The three were the *Gloire*, *Invincible* and *Normandie*. The fourth, designed by Audenet and

Above: *La Gloire* was the world's first seagoing ironclad, developed from the floating batteries of the Crimean War.

and main masts, and fore-and-aft on the mizen only). She was designated a 'frigate', as were the three other ironclads, simply because they carried all their guns on a single gundeck, but by some they were known as 'ironclad frigates' to distinguish them from the sailing frigates, of which there were many still in commission.

The British reply to the *Gloire* was H.M.S. *Warrior*, launched in 1860. She was a ship of 9,210 tons (9,358 tonnes), designed by Isaac Watts, and was armoured with $4\frac{1}{2}$ in (115 mm) iron, backed by 18 in (76 cm) of teak. The armour extended for 213 ft (65 m), and stretched to a height of 21 ft (6·4 m) above the waterline and 6 ft (1·8 m) below it. This covered the length of the gundeck, which was closed at both ends with a $4\frac{1}{2}$ in (115 mm) bulkhead to form an armoured citadel inside which all the guns were mounted. Bow and stern, both projecting 85 ft (25·6 m) beyond the central citadel, were unarmoured. They consisted of plating alone, without any teak backing – a dangerous experiment, since there was no transverse watertight bulkheads to prevent the whole stern or bow section flooding, if the ship were hit on or below the waterline.

Initially, H.M.S. *Warrior*, like the *Gloire*, was designated a 'frigate', again because all her main guns were mounted on a single deck. And, since on completion she had 40 guns, she naturally fell into the fifth rate, even though she was more than a match for any first-rate in the fleet. Eventually, the Admiralty resolved this dilemma by changing the basis of the rating system, from the number of guns mounted to the number of men carried on board. The crew of the *Warrior* numbered 707, and that of the average third-rate ship of the line 705, so the classification of the *Warrior* and her sister ship, H.M.S. *Black Prince*, was changed from 'frigate' – or 'armoured frigate', as some called them – to third-rate ship of the line. Later still, their generic name was altered to 'second-class battleship'.

built at the suggestion of Dupuy de Lôme, was the 6,428-ton (6,531-tonne) *Couronne*. She was an iron-hulled ship, whose sides were composed of 4 in (100 mm) of armour plating, backed by 4 in of teak, then an iron lattice work $1\frac{1}{3}$ in (34 mm) thick and another 11 in (300 mm) of teak, fastened to a $\frac{3}{4}$-in (20 mm) skin of iron. This sandwich construction proved more satisfactory than that of the *Gloire* and her sister ships, and it was adopted by the French for all subsequent naval shipbuilding, until the invention of steel made the iron warship obsolete.

Launched in 1859, the *Gloire* was the first of these vessels to be commissioned. She was rigged initially as a barquentine (square sails on fore-mast and fore-and-aft on main and mizen), but later she was remasted as a full-rigged ship. Later still she became a barque (square sails on fore

Left: The British reply to *La Gloire* was HMS *Warrior*. Also an ironclad frigate, she differed in being faster and having a completely iron hull.

179

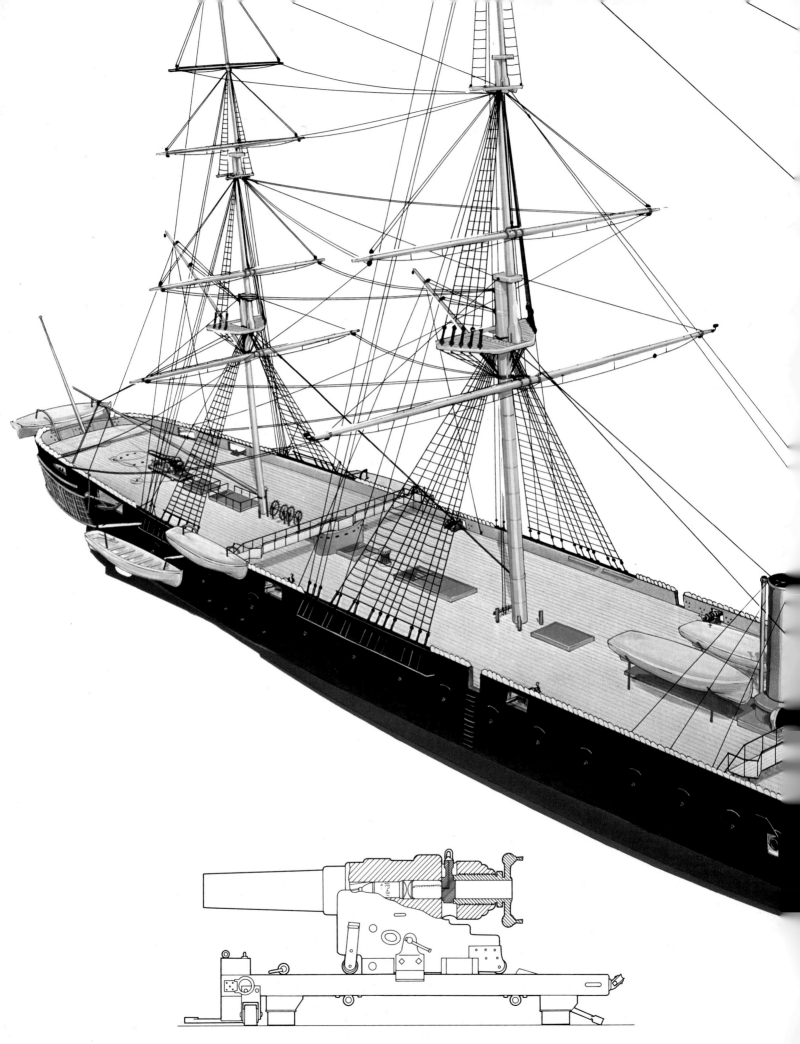

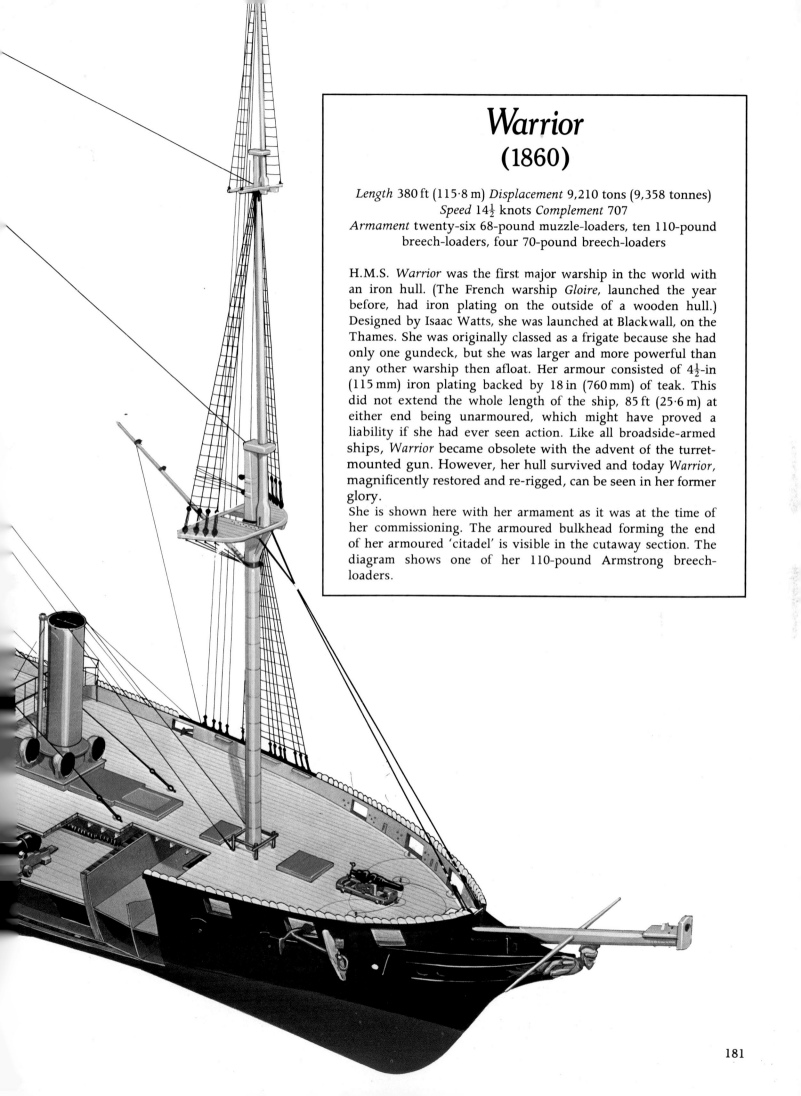

Warrior
(1860)

Length 380 ft (115·8 m) *Displacement* 9,210 tons (9,358 tonnes)
Speed 14½ knots *Complement* 707
Armament twenty-six 68-pound muzzle-loaders, ten 110-pound
breech-loaders, four 70-pound breech-loaders

H.M.S. *Warrior* was the first major warship in the world with
an iron hull. (The French warship *Gloire*, launched the year
before, had iron plating on the outside of a wooden hull.)
Designed by Isaac Watts, she was launched at Blackwall, on the
Thames. She was originally classed as a frigate because she had
only one gundeck, but she was larger and more powerful than
any other warship then afloat. Her armour consisted of 4½-in
(115 mm) iron plating backed by 18 in (760 mm) of teak. This
did not extend the whole length of the ship, 85 ft (25·6 m) at
either end being unarmoured, which might have proved a
liability if she had ever seen action. Like all broadside-armed
ships, *Warrior* became obsolete with the advent of the turret-
mounted gun. However, her hull survived and today *Warrior*,
magnificently restored and re-rigged, can be seen in her former
glory.
She is shown here with her armament as it was at the time of
her commissioning. The armoured bulkhead forming the end
of her armoured 'citadel' is visible in the cutaway section. The
diagram shows one of her 110-pound Armstrong breech-
loaders.

The term 'ironclad' was used to describe any armoured warship until the launching of H.M.S. *Dreadnought* in 1906. These first ironclads, apart from their armour, showed few advances in design upon the wooden warships that preceded them. The *Warrior* even had a 15-ft (4·6-m) figurehead, which made her look a handsome ship, but was an expensive concession to tradition, adding 40 tons of useless weight at a point where she could least afford to carry it. (Later she had to have an open shelter deck added aft, to counterbalance the weight of the figurehead and correct her trim.) Moreover, there were still those who mistrusted iron because of its tendency to rust and its surprising proneness to fouling with weed and barnacles, and periodic attempts were made to bring about a return to the good old days of wood and canvas. But, after the events at Sinope in 1853, the superiority of iron could never really be in question. For a moment in 1860 it appeared that the sceptics might win the debate, that immunity from rust and barnacles would be thought more important than strength and size; but the moment passed when, as a result of trials with the *Gloire*, the French government announced a building programme for thirty ironclads and eleven armoured floating batteries. In the face of a French bid to achieve the naval supremacy that had been denied them during the Napoleonic Wars, the opponents of iron in the British navy were overruled. The iron warship had come to stay.

But an even bigger revolution than the acceptance of iron for warship construction was about to sweep through the world's navies. Already the explosive shell had ousted the older solid shot, and the big gunfounders were introducing the rifled barrel to give the shell a predictable trajectory through the air, greater accuracy and longer range. But the new gun was still mounted on the old wooden carriage, and could still only fire on the broadside. What was now to alter the whole conception of warship design, more, indeed, then all the improvements in the gun itself, was a new gun mounting.

Two men are associated with this revolutionary advance, Captain Cowper Coles of the British Navy and John Ericsson, the Swedish engineer who had been closely associated with the introduction of the propeller and who had become a United States citizen in 1848. It is not possible to say which of the two was first to develop the idea of mounting the naval gun in a revolving turret so that it could fire in whatever direction the turret was trained, and there is a distinct possibility that neither of them was the real originator and that the credit should go to Prince Albert, the consort of Queen Victoria.

Coles's idea of a gun in a revolving turret, which he called a 'cupola', had its origin in a small armed raft which he designed and built for coastal operations in the Sea of Azov in 1855. This was the *Lady Nancy*, 45 ft (13·7 m) long, by 15 ft (4·6 m) broad, constructed on twenty-nine casks in six rows of cradles, the whole being held together by a framework of spars. On the centreline was mounted a long 32-pounder. With a draught of only 20 in (50 cm) she could be towed by boats close inshore, and she bombarded the dockyard town of Taganrog with great accuracy. Realising the advantages offered by a very low freeboard and an armament mounted on the centreline, Coles followed up the *Lady Nancy* by designing a larger armoured raft, 150 ft (46 m) long, with an engine and propeller and a single 68-pounder gun, centrally mounted and protected by a fixed hemispherical iron shield that had small gunports dead ahead and on either beam. It was not yet the revolving turret, but to an inventive mind such as Coles's, this was but a short and obvious step. Although the British Admiralty expressed no interest in Coles's armoured raft, which he had intended for attacks on the forts of Sebastopol and Kronstadt, Coles filed his first patent for a revolving turret in 1859. In the same year he submitted to the Admiralty a design for a 'cupola ship' of 9,200 tons (9,350 tonnes), in which twenty of the largest guns of the period were to be mounted in ten cupolas, eight of them on the ship's centre-

Below: Captain Henry Cowper Coles, a gifted but unfortunate designer.

Bottom: In 1855 Cowper Coles designed a gun-raft for use in the Sea of Azov, from which he developed the revolving turret.

line and the other two abreast on a low forecastle deck to provide axial fire on either side of the foremast. Captain Coles, in his description of the ship, admits that Prince Albert gave him 'advice of the greatest benefit . . . for he had previously turned his attention to the same subject and was thoroughly conversant with all the mechanical details involved in the execution of my plan.' In fact, according to Scott Russell, Prince Albert 'had matured an analogous system long before the adoption of the turrets of Coles or of Ericsson.'

Be that as it may, the old broadside gun was now replaced by the gun mounted in a revolving turret, and, as a result, the warship changed her shape again, having already done so when iron took over from wood for hull construction a year or two earlier. In Britain, Coles's ideas were embodied in H.M.S. *Prince Albert*, a coastal defence ship of 3,880 tons (3,940 tonnes) displacement which was laid down in 1862. Her four 9-inch guns each had a centreline turret, which was trained manually by rack-and-pinion gear and by a system of handspikes on the main deck. It took eighteen men about a minute to make one full revolution of the turret, but, as none of the eighteen men, either inside or outside the turret, could see the gunnery control officer, training of the turret was apt to be somewhat haphazard. Nevertheless, it was a start.

More or less simultaneously, the same development was taking place in the United States Navy, though under the more compelling stimulus of actual warfare. In 1861 the American Civil War broke out, and, when the navy yard at Norfolk, Virginia, was abandoned by the North in 1861, all ships which could not be moved away were scuttled. One of them, the wooden frigate *Merrimack*, was raised by the Confederates, given an engine, and a wooden penthouse with sloping sides over her entire deck. This was then covered with iron plates to a total thickness of

4 in (100 mm), with gunports cut in the sides of the penthouse through which her ten guns fired. She was also fitted with a large ram on her bow. Although she was renamed *Virginia* by the Confederates, it is as the *Merrimack* that she is always known and remembered. Two days after her conversion, on 8 March 1862, she went into action against Northern ships blockading the York and James rivers at Hampton Roads, rammed and sank the *Cumberland*, and forced the *Congress* to capitulate by the weight of her gunfire. Although she was heavily engaged by the guns of Federal warships and shore batteries, all the shells which hit her were deflected by the sloping sides of her armoured penthouse, and bounced harmlessly into the sea.

The North, however, had already built a completely new kind of ship, the brainchild of John Ericsson. Named *Monitor*, she was laid down in the Brooklyn yard in October 1861 and was completed in a little over three months. She was an iron ship with a very low freeboard of no more than a few inches, and on her heavily armoured deck she carried two 11-inch Dahlgren guns mounted in a revolving turret 9 in (230 mm) thick.

She reached Hampton Roads on the day after the *Merrimack*'s attack on the *Cumberland* and *Congress*, and for six hours the *Monitor* and *Merrimack* engaged in a gun duel, with neither inflicting much damage on the other. At the end of the day both ships withdrew, and, in fact, never met each other again. In May 1862, when the Confederates were in their turn forced to abandon Norfolk, Virginia, the *Merrimack* was burned and sunk, as she drew too much water to be evacuated up the James River, and in the following December the *Monitor*, which because of her almost non-existent freeboard could never have been considered a sea-going ship, foundered in a gale while on passage up the coast.

Above: HMS *Royal Sovereign* was a 131-gun three-decker cut down and armed with four Cowper Coles turrets. She and the iron-hulled *Prince Albert* were a big step towards the modern battleship, with gun mountings on the centreline.

This *Monitor-Merrimack* duel was certainly the first action between ironclad warships, but claims that it was these two ships which ushered in the era of the ironclad are demonstrably false. Several European nations had ironclad warships in their navies well before 1862, and, of American countries, Brazil already had a battleship under construction in a British yard. Nor was the *Monitor* the first of the new turreted ships, for Denmark was experimenting in 1861 with a two-turreted gunboat, the *Rolf Krake*, designed by Cowper Coles and mounting two 68-pounder guns in each turret. The Russian and German navies also ordered turreted ships, again to Coles's design. The real importance of the *Monitor-Merrimack* duel, apart from the interest that it aroused, being the first meeting of ironclads in war, was that it focussed the attention of the world's navies on the need to improve the effectiveness of the naval gun. That two ships could hammer each other for six hours without causing any serious damage pointed not so much to the defensive value of armouring the ships, for that was already well recognized, as to the inefficiency of the gun itself in being unable to penetrate the armour and inflict decisive damage.

Over the next thirty years the gun was developed, in size, range and accuracy, from the short-barrelled muzzle-loader to the long-barrelled breech-loader. The development, in the 1870s, of slow-burning powder made a big increase in muzzle velocities possible, and the adoption of breech-loading removed the need to bring the gun inboard on its mounting every time it had to be reloaded, increasing the rate at which it could fire. But the increase in the efficiency of the gun was answered by an increase in the thickness of armour, to withstand the penetrative power of the new long-barrelled weapons. From 1862, the next two or three decades saw warships mounting guns of ever-increasing calibre – latterly up to 18 in (450 mm) – and protected by iron armour of ever-increasing thickness – as much as 24 in (730 mm) by the end of the period. Eventually, the introduction of hardened steel removed the need for armour of excessive thickness and weight, and improvements in gun design mitigated the need for huge pieces weighing over 100 tons each. By the end of the nineteenth century the calibre of the average battleship big gun had stabilized at around 12 in (300 mm), and the thickness of Krupp steel armour at about the same figure.

It was an odd fact of battleship design during these years that only in Britain, which had pioneered the principle of turret-mounting ships' guns, did the turret fail to find favour. The reason was the British Navy's addiction to masts and sails, and its desire to retain them long after other navies had discarded them. The typical British naval officer was an ultra-conservative who wished to retain the old order at all costs, and there was also a widely held belief that the only efficient sailors were those trained under sail. Although British shipbuilding skill was producing some of the best battleships in the

Right: Sailors relaxing on the *Monitor's* deck, with 11 inch gun turret behind them. Note the dent from one of the *Merrimack's* shells.

Below: The Royal Navy's first seagoing turret ship was HMS *Monarch*. She carried full sailing rig, but her high freeboard gave more seaworthiness than the American *Monitor*.

world, until the late 1870s every British battle-ship was fitted with the heavy masts and extensive sail rig of the old three-decked ship of the line. With masts and rigging it was impossible to provide a clear arc of fire for a gun in a turret, and a compromise was found in what was known as a 'central battery'. This was basically a heavily armoured box, built amidships, from which the guns could fire through ports cut in the sides. Though it did give a reasonable arc of fire on the broadside, it had nothing like the flexibility of the turret.

In the end, though it was not until the beginning of the 1880s, even British naval officers had to accept the fact that their beloved masts and sails could no longer be justified. They were in fact a serious liability, for, apart from interfering with the firing arcs of the main guns, their windage cut down appreciably the ship's speed under steam power, and they concentrated a great weight aloft in the position where a steamship can ill afford it. It was, perhaps, the disaster that befell H.M.S. *Captain* in 1870 which hastened their end. She was a battleship of 7,767 tons, built to a design by Cowper Coles in order to vindicate his faith in turret-mounted guns and low-freeboard ships. On completion H.M.S. *Captain's* freeboard was not more than 6 ft 6 in (2 m). On a relatively small hull (320 ft × 53 ft × 23 ft / 97·5 m × 16·2 m × 7 m) Coles decided for some reason to erect the heaviest masts and spars, and maximum sail area then in use, perhaps as a gesture of his supreme confidence in her stability and her ability to carry as much sail aloft as any other ship in the British navy. She capsized in a gale off the coast of Spain, with the loss of the whole of her crew except seventeen men and a gunner who reached the Spanish coast in one of the ship's boats. Captain Cowper Coles was on board as a privileged observer on this, her first cruise with the fleet, and was among those lost. It was the last experiment with low-freeboard battleships.

As was to be expected during such a rapid revolution in major warship design as was then taking place – from sailing three-decked ship of the line to armoured steel battleship, all within the span of thirty years – the second half of the nineteenth century was a time of experiment. All navies had to face the problems posed by the simultaneous development of guns, armour, engines and boilers, and attempts to reach a satisfactory design of ship that would embody the best of all the technical advances in a single hull. It was extraordinarily difficult, for in each country which boasted a navy there were plenty

of inventors, designers and shipbuilders, 'all with their inventive and constructive powers in the high state of activity, each of them intent on his own point, and none of them under such control as could harmonize their work with that of others.' And at the same time 'there was an immense public opinion clamouring for, and forcing on, the adoption of each nominal advance in offensive and defensive power, and those who clamoured loudest had least thought out the nature of an excessively complex problem.' These words were written by Vice-Admiral Colomb in 1898, and, though he was thinking of the British Navy, they were equally true of all the others. It was through this maze of, often conflicting, advice and experiment, of pet theories and political pressures, that the world's admiralties had to pick their uncertain way. That the occasional white elephant should be produced from time to time in most countries in their search for battleship perfection was probably inevitable. By the end of the century there had evolved a reasonable international consensus on

Above: Cowper Coles was bitterly critical of the *Monarch*, and was allowed to design a turret ship of his own, HMS *Captain*.

Above: The layout of the *Captain* was the same as the *Monarch*, but she had low freeboard amidships as well as a full set of masts and yards.

Left: The immense strength of iron hulls led to a revival of ramming tactics. This is the specially-strengthened ram bow of HMS *Minotaur* (1868).

the correct components of an efficient battleship, designed to uphold a nation's power and influence at sea. Obviously there were some differences from nation to nation, since there were differences in the purposes for which battleships were required, and while it is not possible to be specific about size, guns, armour, etc., the average battleship was a steel armoured ship of around 15,000 tons, driven by triple-expansion engines at a speed of about 18 knots, and mounting about four 12-inch guns in turrets and sixteen or more smaller guns.

In only one respect could one say that this average ship was retrograde. With the introduction of the iron ship and mechanical propulsion there had been a revival of belief in the ram as a naval weapon – harking back to the days of the oared galley. Perhaps the idea of the ram as a viable weapon of war in the nineteenth century owed its origin to the theories of Admiral Sartorius, an old sea-dog, born in 1790, who was bewildered by steam propulsion and could think of no use for it other than hurling one ship

against another. His initial plans for the ram concerned no less a ship than Brunel's *Great Eastern*, and involved cutting her down to little above the waterline, covering her with shot-proof iron plates, fitting propellers at each end, installing a heavy gun battery on board, giving her pointed ends and using her hull as a ram. To guard against her being boarded by an enemy, he proposed the construction of towers from which boiling water could be pumped onto the boarders. His proposition was seriously made and, coming from an admiral, was seriously considered, but in the British admiralty it met with the reception which, perhaps, it deserved.

Nevertheless, mainly as a result of Sartorius's advocacy, the ram was brought within the orbit of naval weaponry, and it stayed there for the remainder of the century. It was odd that it attracted so much enthusiasm in naval circles in so many countries, for its record in battle was appalling. It was true that the ironclad *Merrimack* had holed the wooden *Cumberland* with her ram at Hampton Roads, but on the following day

187

Above: Ramming was used by the Austrian Fleet at the Battle of Lissa, but it only worked because the Italians were badly led and untrained.

both she and the *Monitor* failed to do any damage to each other by continual ramming attacks. At Mobile Bay, the Confederate ironclad *Tennessee*, attempting to ram, missed the *Hartford*, missed the *Brooklyn*, missed the *Lackawanna*, and, when she was herself rammed by the *Monongahala*, received only a glancing blow that did no damage. And when the Northern gunboat *Sassacus* rammed the *Albemarle*, all that she did was smash up her own bow.

The battle of Lissa, fought in 1866, was hailed as a vindication of the ram, though any real analysis would have revealed the opposite. It was a ramming battle if ever there were one, with the Austrian fleet steaming backwards and forwards through the disorganized Italian fleet trying to ram. True, the Austrian flagship, *Erzherzog Ferdinand Maximilian*, struck the Italian ironclad *Re d'Italia* and sank her, but the Italian ship was lying stopped at the time with her rudder damaged. All the other attempts to ram – and there were many of them – missed their targets.

The occasional unfortunate accident, too, was always hailed as a vindication of the ram. With fleets manoeuvring under steam, sometimes at night or in fog, there had inevitably been the occasional collision in which a ship had been sunk. In the ten years between 1869 and 1878 the Russian ironclad *Kreml* had rammed and sunk the frigate *Oleg*, the Russian ironclad *Admiral*

Spiridoff had rammed her sister ship the *Admiral Lazaroff* which was only saved from sinking by being beached in Kronstadt harbour, the Spanish ironclad *Numancia* had rammed and sunk the corvette *Fernando el Catolica*, the French ironclad *Jeanne d'Arc* had rammed and sunk the despatch vessel *Forfait*, the British battleship *Iron Duke* had rammed and sunk her sister ship, H.M.S. *Vanguard*, the French ironclad *Thetis* had rammed the ironclad *Raine Blanche* which managed to beach herself ashore before she sank, and the German ironclad *König Wilhelm* had rammed and sunk the turret ship *Grosser Kürfurst*. All these were hailed as evidence that the ram was an important, if not the most important, weapon of the battleship. The voice of sanity, pointing out that any ship with way upon her could manoeuvre so that a ramming ship would miss, or at best deliver only a glancing blow, remained unheard amid the excited clamour of the rammers. And later in the century, when the gun had been developed into a weapon of real power, those who held that a ship approaching another with the intention of ramming would be blown out of the water were equally ignored. So the ram was built onto the bows of every battleship, making them difficult to steer and reducing their speed.

During the last decades of the nineteenth century, another naval weapon made its appearance. It was to have an immense influence on the

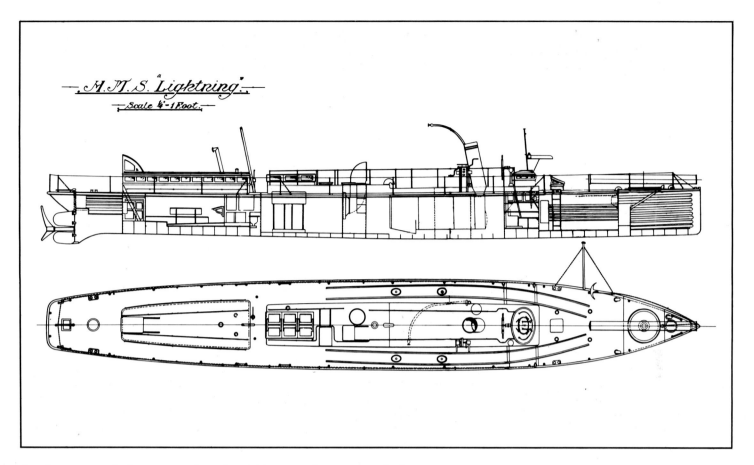

H.M.S. "Lightning".
Scale ¼″=1 Foot.

development of future navies. In 1865 an Austrian artillery captain named Luppis devised a boat-shaped craft, with an explosive charge in the bow, which was driven by clockwork and guided by lines attached to its rudder. He took it to Robert Whitehead, the English manager of a marine engine factory at Fiume, who developed the device into what is now known as the 'locomotive torpedo', an underwater weapon with a charge of explosive in its head which, by 1877, was capable of a range of 1,000 yards at a speed of 7 knots. Further development increased both range, speed and reliability, making the torpedo an important and powerful naval weapon.

In 1879 the British torpedo boat H.M.S. *Lightning*, originally designed to carry spar torpedoes, was modified by the addition of two above-water tubes for launching the Whitehead torpedo. She was such a success that in 1880 the British Admiralty ordered twelve more like her, and other navies were quick to adopt the type. Between 1881 and 1885 torpedo boats were built in large numbers for the navies of Russia, France, Holland, Italy and Austria, and in 1886 Chile, China, Greece, Spain, Portugal, Sweden and Turkey followed suit.

Having produced the weapon, which in the hands of so many continental navies was now a threat to the naval supremacy of Great Britain, it fell to the same country to devise the antidote. This, it was decided, should take the shape of a larger torpedo boat, carrying a 4-inch gun, with enough speed to catch the smaller torpedo boat and stop her by gunfire before she could make an attack. In 1886 H.M.S. *Rattlesnake*, the first of these new vessels, was launched, but did not have sufficient speed for the job. Finally, in 1893, H.M.S. *Havock* and H.M.S. *Hornet* were launched as torpedo-boat destroyers. With a displacement of 250 tons, a speed of 27 knots, and an armament of four guns and three torpedo tubes, they not only proved more than a match for any existing torpedo boat, but they even usurped their function. Thus was born the destroyer, which by the turn of the century had become an integral part of every navy. Completely unarmoured, she relied on her speed for protection from attack, and this was attained by an increase in the length-to-beam ratio to about 12 to 1, and in some cases even more.

Right at the end of the nineteenth century a new development in marine propulsion made its appearance. This was the steam turbine, invented by the Hon. Charles Parsons. It is a rotary-propulsion engine in which a jet of steam, is directed through a nozzle on to blades set at an angle in a drum, connected either direct or through gearing to the propeller shaft. The action of the steam on the angled blades revolves

Above: The builders' plans of HMS *Lightning*, the first torpedo-boat. These craft were developed from fast steam launches, the only hulls with the right power-weight ratio to give a sea speed of 20 knots.

the drum, and by this means the drive is transmitted to the propeller. After passing through the first set of moving blades, the steam is forced through a set of fixed blades, mounted on the casing of the turbine and angled the other way, to increase its speed before it hits another set of moving blades. And so on, until the steam is exhausted into a condenser to be turned back into boiler feed water.

Parsons introduced his turbine in dramatic fashion, calculated to obtain the maximum amount of publicity for his new engine in a single demonstration. He built a small yacht and installed in her three of his turbines, each driving a shaft on which three propellers were fixed. He selected the naval review, held at Spithead in 1897 to celebrate Queen Victoria's diamond jubilee for his demonstration, knowing well that representatives of all foreign navies would be present in honour of the occasion. On the day of the review he took his yacht, which he had named *Turbinia*, into the review area and steamed her up and down the lines of anchored warships. As the review area was meant to be kept clear for the passage of the Royal Yacht with Queen Victoria on board, the steam picket boats of the fleet were sent in pursuit to warn the *Turbinia* away, but none of them could look at her for

speed. At top speed, she was said to have achieved 34·5 knots – quite unheard of in those days – and her performance so impressed the various naval authorities and shipowners present that the future of the turbine as the new motive power for ships was assured. Its advantages over the reciprocating engine were considerable, not only in occupying much less space in the engine room, but also in the simplicity of construction and an extremely favourable power-to-weight ratio. That the British Admiralty were impressed

Below: The steam yacht *Turbinia*, test-bed for the Parsons steam turbine which made higher speeds possible.

Inset: The Parsons turbine achieved greater power than the triple-expansion engine, with less vibration and wear and tear.

Above: The great
Mississippi Steamboat
Race in July 1870, with
the *Robert E. Lee* beating
the *Natchez*.

by these advantages was witnessed by the launch, in 1899, of H.M.S. *Viper*, a destroyer of 325 tons (330 tonnes), with Parsons turbines driving four shafts, on each of which were two propellers. She was the first warship in the world to use this new form of propulsion, and she attained a speed of 36·58 knots on her trials.

Before we leave the nineteenth century, it is of interest to take a look at another type of craft, developed for use on the rivers of the United States. Many of the great rivers, and particularly the Mississippi and Ohio, formed magnificent natural highways for the transport of passengers and goods, and a special type of vessel was built for use on them. The hull form resembled a shallow, elongated dish, giving a draught of water of little more than 4 ft (1·2 m), in even the largest of them. Some of these steamboats were built as large as 5,000 tons gross, with as many as five or six decks rising above the flat-bottomed hull to provide saloons and cabins. All of them were paddle steamers, the larger with two side paddlewheels, the smaller with a single sternwheel.

A remarkable feature of all of them was the engine. With homespun ingenuity, a form of walking beam engine was developed, in which the moving beam and the trusslike structure on which the engine was mounted were built up largely from timber struts and locally wrought iron supports. The moving beam was in full and open view from the top deck, and the engine turned paddlewheels of up to 40 ft. (12 m) in diameter. A pair of tall black funnels was mounted abreast to carry the boiler smoke clear of the top deck and the wheelhouse, and these were decorated with a sort of serrated crown on top, a characteristic feature of these river paddlers. Up to the 1850s wood alone was burned in the boilers; between 1850 and 1880 wood was supplemented by coal; and after 1880 coal alone was burned, owing to the introduction of high-pressure boilers in an attempt to increase speed.

Inevitably, races were organised for these great vessels along certain stretches of river for the title of 'Fastest Boat on the River'. The best remembered of all these races was that held in 1870 between two of the real 'dandies' – the *Natchez*, which held the title, and the *Robert E. Lee*. (The race, won by the *Robert E. Lee*, with a speed of 19 knots on the stretch between Natchez and New Orleans, is depicted in a well known coloured lithograph of Currier and Ives.)

The First Submarines

'And also it is possible to make a ship or boat that may goe under the water unto the bottome, and so come up againe at your pleasure, as this, . . . that anything that sinketh, is heavier than the proportion of so much water, and if it be lighter than the magnitude of so much water, then it swimmeth or appeareth above the water.' The words are those of William Bourne, written in 1578, and they are followed by a description of how such a ship could be constructed. Whether his boat was ever built is not known, but the description is clear enough to show that he was the first to appreciate the principle on which a submarine operates.

To be able to make a ship disappear under water and return to the surface at will was a dream of many inventors, for its advantages for naval war were manifold. But, although Bourne, in his writing, had shown clearly enough how positive buoyancy in a ship might be removed to make it sink and restored to make it rise to the surface again, future inventors concentrated their efforts on an alternative method – that of ballasting a boat until she lay awash, and then forcing her under the surface with oars or other means. Cornelius van Drebbel, a Dutch inventor, used this method in building a 'submarine' in 1620, which was demonstrated on the River Thames in the presence of King James I. It made the journey from Westminster to Greenwich, either just awash or just submerged, but proved nothing beyond the fact that, at the end of the trip, the rowers inside were in poor shape because there was no provision for replacing the oxygen which they had breathed.

Van Drebbel had many imitators. In 1653 a Frenchman named de Son built a submarine at Rotterdam in which forward motion under the sea was to be provided by a paddlewheel revolved by clockwork. He announced his invention in no uncertain terms: 'he doeth undertake in one day to destroy a hondered ships, can goe from Rotterdam to London and back againe in one day, and in 6 weeks to goe to the East Indiens, and to run as swift as a bird can flye, no storme, no bullets, can hinder her, unless it please God.' Unhappily, when the submarine took to the water, the clockwork was not powerful enough to turn the paddle-

wheel and the craft remained motionless.

In 1747 another submersible boat, designed by Symons, was tried out on the Thames, but failed to submerge. In 1773 a ship's carpenter named Day built a boat, ballasted with rocks hanging from her keel, which reached a depth of 30 ft (9 m) in Plymouth Sound, and surfaced safely after Day had released some of the rocks by a mechanism inside the boat. On the second attempt the mechanism failed to work, and Day and his boat were taken to the bottom in 132 ft (40 m) of water, where the pressure of water crushed the boat.

The next steps in submarine development were taken by two Americans, David Bushnell and Robert Fulton, who are generally regarded as the fathers of the modern submarine boat. Though neither man's craft was particularly successful, both were produced under the spur of war, and Bushnell's craft was actually used in action.

David Bushnell graduated from Yale in 1775. Young, ardent and patriotic, Bushnell looked for a new weapon which could break the stranglehold of British sea power, and reckoned that he had found it in the submarine. He constructed an iron hull shaped like an egg, which was held upright in the water by a lead keel of 700 lb (318 kg), of which 200 lb (91 kg) was detachable in an emergency. Two small tanks were fitted in the bottom of the submarine, to which seawater was admitted by a foot-operated push valve and ejected by two hand-operated pumps. The submarine was operated by one man, who produced

vertical movement through the water by means of a small hand-operated propeller mounted on top of the submarine, and horizontal movement by means of a similar propeller mounted laterally. The method of attack was to flood the two tanks, which would make the submarine submerge until the top propeller was awash, then bring the submarine alongside the enemy ship with the aid of the horizontal propeller, and, when alongside, to make the submarine dive under water with the vertical propeller. Once the submarine was underneath the ship, a magazine containing 150 lb (68 kg) of gunpowder was attached to the ship's bottom by a screw, worked from inside the submarine. A clockwork fuse gave a delay of 30 minutes, during which the submarine was to make her escape. The submarine was given the name *Turtle*.

After successful trials in Long Island Sound the first real attack was made, on H.M.S. *Eagle* in 1776, with Sergeant Ezra Lee as the operator of the submarine. He reached the ship unobserved and forced the *Turtle* under the vessel's hull, but was unable to screw the charge home, for it had not been realised that the bottoms of British warships serving in foreign waters were covered with copper sheets, as a protection against the Teredo worm. Lee and the *Turtle* managed to escape, and later two more attacks on British warships were attempted, but were foiled by the good lookout maintained on board.

Robert Fulton's submarine, *Nautilus*, was conceived more as a means of making a fortune for her inventor, than for patriotic reasons. He constructed a model of his proposed submarine, offered it to France for use against the British fleet during the Revolutionary War of 1793–1801, and, when turned down by that country, spent the next three years travelling across Europe offering it to various governments, though with no success. By 1800 he was back in France, where Napoleon Bonaparte had now become First Consul. Napoleon, anxious for any new weapon which might break the British naval blockade, gave Fulton 10,000 francs with which to build a full-scale version of his *Nautilus*.

Laid down at the end of 1800, the *Nautilus* was launched in the River Seine in May 1801. Built of copper on an iron frame, in the shape of an imperfect ellipsoid, she was 21 ft 4 in (6·5 m) long and 7 ft (2·1 m) in diameter, with a small hemispherical conning-tower. As did Bushnell's *Turtle*, she submerged by taking seawater into internal ballast tanks, and was propelled under water by a hand-operated propeller. On the surface she carried a mast and sail, hinged and laid flat along the deck when she submerged. She carried a very similar weapon to that used by the *Turtle*, though it was to be attached to the target's hull by a spike instead of a screw.

After successful trials on the Seine, much admired by Napoleon, she was taken to Brest for a full demonstration. An old schooner was anchored in Brest Roads. The *Nautilus* set out to attack her, dived underneath her, attached the charge to her hull underwater, and withdrew. A few minutes later the schooner was blown sky-high. But his very success damned Fulton in France. Napoleon had by then given up his plans for invading England and was marching to new adventures in central Europe, and the French Navy found themselves with a troubled conscience in the contemplation of so terrible a weapon. Without Napoleon to urge him on, the French Minister of Marine washed his hands of the affair.

From France Fulton took his *Nautilus* to England in an attempt to interest the British Navy. He found an enthusiastic ally in William Pitt, the prime minister, who set up a commission of eminent men to examine the project. For a demonstration, the brig *Dorothy* was anchored off Walmer on the coast of Kent, and Fulton was invited to attack her. Again, he was completely successful, and the *Dorothy* was blown in two at the first attempt. But, as in France, his success appalled the commission set up to examine the invention. In spite of Pitt's protest, they refused to have anything to do with this diabolic weapon. Admiral Lord St. Vincent passed the final judgment: 'Pitt', he said, 'was the greatest fool that ever existed to encourage a mode of warfare which those who commanded the seas did not want, and which, if successful, would at once deprive them of it.'

Fulton then returned to America, became a successful steamship operator, and in 1810 managed to interest Congress (to the tune of 5,000 dollars) in a new, steam-driven submarine, 80 ft (24·3 m) long with a beam of 21 ft (6·4 m) and a draught of 14 ft (4·3 m). Fulton himself designed the steam engine, and the submarine was named *Mute* because of the silent way in which the engine worked. Unfortunately, Fulton died during the *Mute's* trials in 1815, and there was no one experienced enough to carry on his work.

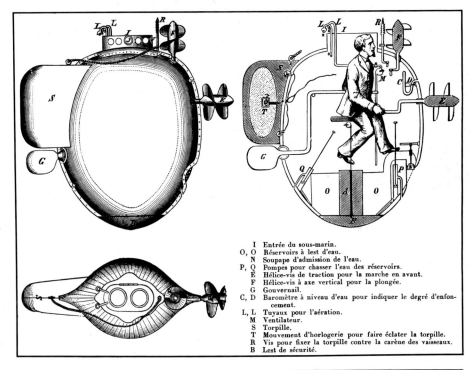

I   Entrée du sous-marin.
O, O   Réservoirs à lest d'eau.
N   Soupape d'admission de l'eau.
P, Q   Pompes pour chasser l'eau des réservoirs.
E   Hélice-vis de traction pour la marche en avant.
F   Hélice-vis à axe vertical pour la plongée.
G   Gouvernail.
C, D   Baromètre à niveau d'eau pour indiquer le degré d'enfoncement.
L, L   Tuyaux pour l'aération.
M   Ventilateur.
S   Torpille.
T   Mouvement d'horlogerie pour faire éclater la torpille.
R   Vis pour fixer la torpille contre la carène des vaisseaux.
B   Lest de sécurité.

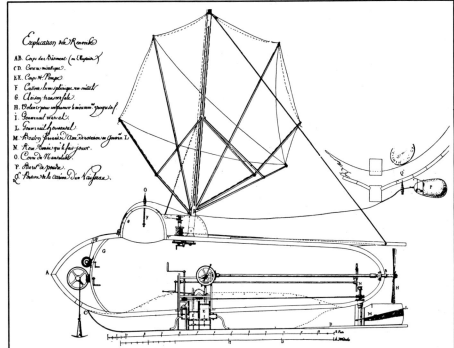

Far left, above: Robert Fulton (1765–1815).

Above left: An 1885 representation of Bushnell's *Turtle*. From the inventor's own description it now seems unlikely that the propeller was an Archimedes' screw; it was probably more like a vane in design.

Left: The *Nautilus*, Fulton's submarine.

Wilhelm Bauer, a non-commissioned officer in the Bavarian artillery, was the next man to build a submarine. His design was an advance on those of Bushnell and Fulton in that it dived at at angle, under forward propulsion. Once negative buoyancy had been achieved, by flooding internal ballast tanks with seawater, Bauer gave his craft a bow down attitude by means of a sliding weight which, when moved to the forward end of the submarine, produced a sufficient angle of dive to take the craft down. Forward motion was produced, as in the earlier submarines, by hand-operated propeller.

Bauer had grasped, too, another principle of submarine operation in his recognition of the fact that the pressure of water increases with depth. When, in February 1851, his submarine, *Plongeur-Marin*, with Bauer and two assistants on board, accidentally reached a depth of 60 ft (18 m), during exercises at Kiel, and began to buckle under the pressure, he realised that the only possible way of escape was to flood the submarine until the air inside it was compressed to the same pressure as that of the water outside. Once that was achieved, it would be possible to open the hatch of the conning-tower against the water pressure outside, and rise to the surface in the bubble of air thus released. He managed to persuade his two terrified

assistants that this was their only hope of survival. The hull was gradually flooded until the pressures of air and water were equalized, the hatch was opened, and the three men escaped exactly as Bauer had planned it.

Bauer next interested the Russian Navy in submarine construction and his next model, the *Diable-Marin*, was built at Leningrad in 1855 – an iron submersible with a length of 52 ft (15·8 m). She was a success and it is recorded that Bauer made 134 dives in her, including one in September 1856 during a naval review in honour of the coronation of Czar Alexander II, when he embarked a small orchestra which played the Russian national anthem while submerged. The sound carried through the water, and was clearly heard on board the ships at the review, creating a tremendous impression.

By now the submarine had evolved into something reasonably reliable, far advanced from the haphazard inventions of earlier days which were weighted down with rocks and stones. The use of iron as a building material gave a flexibility of design impossible with wood, and the nineteenth century submarines were beginning to take on the cigar-shaped hull design which promised a better underwater performance. What was still needed before they could be regarded as viable

warships was a weapon less crude than the keg of gunpowder to be attached somehow to the bottoms of ships, and a means of underwater propulsion more efficient than a hand-operated propeller.

The weapon made its appearance during the American Civil War, in the shape of the spar torpedo, a copper case containing 134 lb (60·7 kg) of gunpowder, carried on the end of a 30-ft (9·1 m) wooden spar. With one of these weapons mounted on their bows, submarines began to have an important part to play in naval warfare. It was invented in the Southern States, and in order to exploit it to the maximum they built a series of small submarines, averaging about 50 ft (15 m) in length, which were generically known as Davids, no doubt by way of a comparison to the goliaths of the Federal navy. Most of them had a crew of nine men, eight of them turning a propeller by means of a series of connected cranks and the ninth steering. A few were built with a small steam engine.

The best remembered of the hand-operated Davids is the *H. L. Hunley*, built in Mobile, Alabama, by officers of an Alabama volunteer regiment to plans provided by Horace L. Hunley, James R. McLintock and Baxter Watson. Her midships section was made from a cylindrical iron steam boiler. Tapered ends, containing ballast tanks which could be flooded or pumped dry, were added. On her bows she carried a spar torpedo. On the night of 17 February 1864, she attacked the Federal sloop *Housatonic* which was anchored in about 27 ft (8 m) of water, off the channel entrance to Charleston. When the lookouts on the *Housatonic* saw the *Hunley* coming, they slipped the cable to back away, but the eight men on the crank handles, cheered on by the ninth, redoubled their efforts and the *Hunley's* spar torpedo struck home and exploded, blowing a large hole in the *Housatonic's* side. She sank quickly, and probably took the *Hunley* down with her, for the David never returned.

It was this exploit, the first sinking of a warship in action by a submarine, that really put the submarine on the map. And an ideal submarine weapon, the locomotive torpedo, was already in view in the shape of Captain Luppis's clockwork contraption, which was about to be turned over to Robert Whitehead at Fiume for development as an underwater weapon. The submarine's other requirement, a means of propulsion other than a hand-operated propeller, was also on the horizon, in the shape of the internal combustion engine for surface propulsion and the electric motor, which used none of the precious oxygen in the vessel, for propulsion when submerged.

During the next thirty years there were several inventors in the submarine field, but only four were serious contenders for the prize of designing a submarine which the navies of the world would accept – Holland and Lake,

of the United States, Nordenfelt, of Sweden, and Goubet, of France. It was these four who contributed most to the development of the submarine into a recognised factor in any future naval warfare. In the end, it was the Holland boat which was preferred by the world's navies, although Lake's boat was the greatest advance, in that it had two pairs of hydroplanes, one pair forward and one aft. With these hydroplanes Lake demonstrated that a submerged vessel could remain at a constant depth, even at very slow speed, without the need of constant alteration in her internal ballasting. But Lake failed to win the contract, even though his submarine was of stronger and sounder design than the Holland craft, because he failed to appreciate the true function of the submarine. His idea of the submarine's role in war was sitting on the bottom, and sending out a diver to cut telegraph cables or the mooring wires of mines, or

telephoning back to base the movements of enemy ships. For this reason, he fitted two large external wheels to his submarine, so that she could run along the bottom, and it was this feature which made her unacceptable in naval eyes.

By the end of the century the submarine had established herself as an integral part of every navy in the world, except that of Britain, and Britain, too, was forced to adopt it in 1901.

Far left: Wilhelm Bauer's submarine *Seetaucher* or *Plongeur-Marin*. A bucket dredger raised it 36 years after sinking and it was put on display as an example of early submarine development.

Below: The *Holland*, the US Navy's first submarine, purchased in 1900.

Bottom: The Confederate 'David', *H. L. Hunley*, which sank the Federal *Housatonic* with a spar torpedo in 1864.

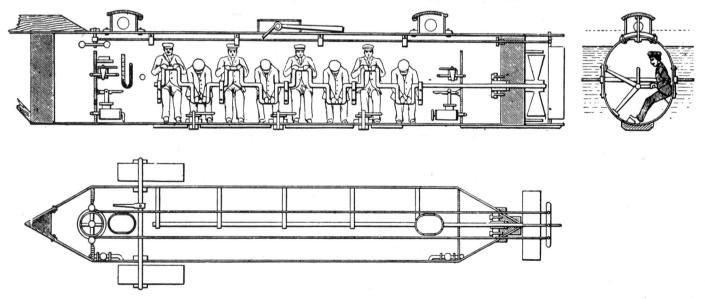

196

Chapter Nine
The End of an Era

It should not be thought that the introduction of steam propulsion during the nineteenth century meant the end of the sailing ship. Steam did, indeed, make prodigious strides throughout that century, not only in terms of the volume of shipping built with engines and boilers, but also in the improvement of the marine steam engine, culminating in the introduction of the turbine – the ultimate in steam propulsion – just before the century ended. But for most of the century the sailing ship still prospered, though on longer routes, and underwent equally dramatic developments in hull design and rigging plans.

For the first thirty or forty years of the century, the introduction of steam made very little impression on the supremacy of the pure sailing ship, both in the passenger and cargo-carrying trades. Where steam was used in ships during these early years it was almost entirely as an auxiliary means of propulsion, to keep a sailing ship moving when there was no wind to fill her sails. Later in the century, when steam propulsion had proved its reliability and efficiency and had ousted sail completely in those vessels in which it had earlier been installed only as an auxiliary, there were still a number of long trade routes beyond the range of the marine steam engine. On these there was no alternative to the sailing ship, and the keen competition for cargoes guaranteed continuing progress towards the ultimate in design and sail power.

The model on which British merchant ships were based at the start of the century was the naval frigate. Built to heavy scantlings, with a blunt and rounded bow, carrying a long bowsprit and jib-boom, a heavy, overhanging stern, very little sheer, and full in the bilge, they were typically sturdy and strong ships, slow through the water, but with a big carrying capacity. The British shipowner was not looking for speed. Often brought up in the tradition of the East

India Company, whose stately ships had enjoyed for two centuries the monopoly of trade to India and China, power, strength and cargo capacity were the qualities most sought after in a merchant ship by the British shipowner. And when the East India Company lost its trade monopoly in India in 1813 and in China in 1833, the owners who stepped in to take advantage of the new free-for-all remained faithful to the old design.

The challenge to the British model came from America. During the War of 1812 against Britain, the United States had built a large number of privateers, mainly schooner- or brig-rigged. Since superior speed was a *sine qua non* for a privateer, they were built with a higher length-to-beam ratio than the British ships on which they preyed, and the hulls were round-bottomed. This hull shape, admirable for speed, was poor in terms of cargo capacity, and when the war ended the Americans found that, though they had an edge over the competition in speed, most traders preferred a big carrying capacity for their goods. But there were two trades in which these American ships (which earned themselves the generic name of 'clipper', because they could 'clip' the time taken on a passage by a packet ship on a regular run) could prosper: one was the so-called 'blackbird' trade, shipping vast numbers of negroes from Africa for sale in the southern states of America, and the other was the Chinese opium trade. In both of these trades speed was essential, and the erstwhile privateers, ranging from 100 to 300 tons displacement, with a shallow draught, but deeper aft than forward, were ideally suited to outrun any ship whose duty it was to prevent this questionable traffic.

As a large number of these American vessels, particularly those constructed after the end of the war, were built in Virginia and Maryland, they were known as 'Baltimore clippers', although they were not true clippers in the sense of the term that eventually came to be accepted. They had the sharply raked stem – the true mark of a clipper – but not yet the hollow bow,

Left: The Boston clipper *Flying Cloud* made a record passage from New York to San Francisco in 1851, averaging 9 knots for the whole journey.

197

a characteristic feature of clipper design. They also had an inclined overhanging counter stern, and they owed their speed to the reduction of wetted surface area at bow and stern.

In 1832 an enlarged Baltimore clipper, the *Ann McKim*, was built at Baltimore and given a square rig, and many have claimed that she was the first of the real clippers, but in fact that honour belongs to the *Rainbow*, designed by John Griffiths, built by Smith and Dimon in New York, and launched in 1849. She had the hollow bow of the true clipper and created such a stir in shipping circles that her unorthodox design was followed by many other builders. Although her hull lines and deep keel were indicative of speed through the water, her length-to-beam

ratio of under 5 to 1 prevented her from reaching the speeds achieved by later clippers.

This first of the true clippers represented a great leap forward in the development of sail. British shipowners, still wedded to the practice of building their trading ships 'frigate-fashion', found themselves losing out to the faster American ships. The competition really began to bite in 1850, when the American clippers discovered the China tea trade, in which the first cargoes to arrive in England each year commanded a substantial premium. In 1849 the British government repealed the deep sea Navigation Act, under which no goods might be imported into Britain and her colonies except in British bottoms or in those of the producing countries, and it was the repeal of this act that opened the China–England tea trade to all comers. The first American clipper to bring tea to England from China was the *Oriental* in 1850, and because of her speed she secured nearly

double the freight rate offered to British tonnage. For the next five years American clippers secured the cream of this lucrative traffic.

The most famous American builder of clipper ships was Donald Mackay, of Boston, whose first clipper was the revolutionary *Staghound*, launched in 1850, and the first of a long line of world-famous Mackay clippers. His *Flying Fish*, *Flying Cloud* and *Sovereign of the Seas*, built for the New York–California run after the discovery in California of gold in large quantities, were all 'flyers', and in 1851 the *Flying Cloud* sailed the 17,597 nautical miles from New York to San Francisco, round Cape Horn, in 89 days, 21 hours, an average speed for the whole passage of something like 9 knots. These ships were built to a length-to-beam ratio of just over 6 to 1, giving them a useful advantage in speed over the shorter, tubbier clippers which had preceded them. But, having to withstand the stormy seas of the South Atlantic and South Pacific, they were very

Left: The *Sovereign of the Seas*, a Mackay clipper.

Below left: The American privateer brigantine *Rambler*, one of a series built to prey on British commerce in the 1812 War.

Bottom: The *Glory of the Seas* ready for launch in 1869 at Boston.

Inset: Detail from a photograph of Donald Mackay, the Boston clipper-owner.

strongly built, and rigged to achieve their maximum speeds in hard winds, and few of these Mackay-built ships were seen on the trade routes where gentler winds prevailed, such as the tea trade from China. And they were not long-lived ships, for they were built with the soft woods which abounded along the American coast, close to the shipbuilding yards. After about five years, particularly in the hands of skippers who were notorious for driving their ships to the utter limit, their hulls became strained and leaky, and the soft wood water-logged and sluggish. But, in comparison to the English practice of building hulls of hard woods such as oak or teak, they were cheap to build, and many enterprising traders found that they could cover the entire

building cost and make a very handsome profit from them during the span of their short lives, sometimes even in one year.

The American competition spurred British owners to try to improve their own designs and rigs. The best of the British ships were those known as 'Blackwall frigates', which got their name because many of them were built at Green and Wigram's yard at Blackwall, and because they were said to be 'frigate-built', though in no way did they resemble the naval frigate design. They were built mainly for the India trade, with a finer run, and therefore faster, than the typical

Above: The Blackwall frigate *True Briton*, an example of ships built on the Thames to meet the challenge of the American clippers.

East Indiaman of Company days, and for many years they dominated this trade after the East India Company had lost its monopoly. The first of the Blackwall frigates was Green and Wigram's *Seringapatam*, of 818 tons, which was launched in 1837, and she set a new record of 85 days from London to Bombay. But these Blackwall frigates were still far removed from the true clipper design, and, if British shipowners wanted to compete with the Americans, they would need to do a great deal better than the Blackwall frigate.

The first British attempt to build a ship to compete with the Americans in speed was the little *Scottish Maid*, built by Alexander Hall at Aberdeen, but, although she once did the Leith–London run in 33 hours – a remarkably fast time – she did not have the essential features of clipper design. The first real English clippers were the *Stornoway* and *Chrysolite*, also built by Hall at Aberdeen, to compete in the China tea trade. Another builder of clippers, and one who was to become in Britain the best known of them all, was Robert Steele, of Greenock. After the decline of American shipbuilding during the American Civil War (1861–65), he was to produce some of the most famous ships of the whole clipper era,

particularly for the China trade.

But as yet, certainly up to 1858, the American clippers reigned supreme. They dominated the New York–California trade, triggered off by the gold discoveries, with magnificent ships driven to their limit by 'hard-case' skippers and 'bucko' mates, who drove their crews as hard as they drove their ships. Inevitably some were lost in the fierce storms of Cape Horn simply because skippers and mates refused to shorten sail and literally drove their ships under, but it was an immensely profitable trade and the occasional ship loss was quickly recouped from the profits of the others. Everything had to go by sea, the gold miners themselves, their tools and machinery, their food, drink and building materials, even the girls specially imported to separate the miners from their earnings in the saloons. There was as yet no transcontinental railway, and a covered wagon from the eastern states to California would take very much longer than a clipper round Cape Horn. There was really no alternative to the clipper, and the entire trade, down to the last nut and bolt, was in their hands. This shipping boom lasted until 1857, when a railway built across the Isthmus of Panama, with steamship connections at its east and west terminal points, so shortened the time from New York to San Francisco that the clipper could no longer compete. One of the oddities of this clipper traffic was the huge quantity of port and sherry shipped for the voyage round Cape Horn and back. There was a theory prevalent among the wealthy New York wine-drinkers that these fortified wines were much improved by a good shaking up, and what better way to shake them up than in the holds of a clipper ship as she battled her way around Cape Horn.

The largest of the American clippers built for the New York–San Francisco trade was Mackay's *Great Republic*, a four-masted barque with an overall length of 325 ft (99.1 m) and a beam of 53 ft (16.2 m). She never had a chance of showing her paces, for after a fire on board while she was fitting out for her maiden voyage her hull and rig were both cut down to more modest proportions, removing her original promise.

In 1848 gold was discovered at Ballarat in Australia, and another gold rush developed across the world. The Australian trade was very largely in the hands of James Baines's Black Ball Line, of Liverpool, who hitherto had been content to use the slower Blackwall frigates for this traffic. But, with a new gold rush developing, speed was essential. Baines had a new ship, the *Marco Polo*, built on clipper lines at St John's, New Brunswick, and she broke all records for passages to and from Australia in 1852–53. In 1853 he chartered Donald Mackay's *Sovereign of the Seas* for the Australian run and in the following year ordered four more big clippers from Mackay – the *Lightning*, *Champion of the Seas*, *James Baines* and *Donald Mackay*. The *Lightning* and *James Baines* were considerably larger than the average clipper, of over 2,500 register tons, and were among the fastest vessels in the world at that time. In 1854, the *James Baines*, on her first voyage to Australia, sailed the 14,034 nautical miles from London to Melbourne in $63\frac{1}{2}$ days, carrying 700 passengers, 1,400 tons of cargo and 350 mail bags. She did the return trip, loaded with cargo, in $69\frac{1}{2}$ days. Some of the speeds credited to these Baines clippers were phenomenal: the *Sovereign of the Seas* was said to have achieved 22 knots at times during her record passage from New York to Liverpool of 13 days, 14 hours; in 1856 the *James Baines* recorded in her deck log 'ship going 21 knots with main skysail set'; the *Lightning's* log during her passage from Boston to Liverpool records that from noon on 28 February to noon on 1 March she ran 436 nautical miles, 'lee rail under water and rigging slack', giving her an average speed throughout the 24 hours of over 18 knots. And this was surpassed later that year when the *Champion of the Seas*, on her maiden voyage to

Melbourne for the Black Ball Line, logged 465 nautical miles in 24 hours while running her easting down. As she was sailing east, the difference in longitude cut her noon-to-noon period from 24 hours to 23 hours 17 minutes, to give her an average speed over the whole period of just on 20 knots. It is speeds and endurances such as these which testify to the supreme skill of Donald Mackay as a designer and to the sturdiness of his ships.

The Civil War gave Americans preoccupations other than the building of large clipper ships, and by the time it was over they had lost their superiority, never to regain it. It was now the turn of British shipbuilders to produce sailing vessels which were the wonder of the world. They retained the essential clipper features of raked stem, hollow bow and overhanging counter stern, but their ships had finer and more delicate lines, and an improved sail plan that enabled them to 'ghost' in light airs, yet was still marvellously efficient in a gale. These ships were a distinct type of their own, not just copies of the American clippers, and, although they never

Above: Model of the Mackay clipper *James Baines*, which once logged a speed of 21 knots under full sail. In 1854 she sailed 14,000 miles from London to Melbourne in $69\frac{1}{2}$ days.

quite managed the amazing bursts of speed of the Americans, they had a better all-round performance in that they were as much at home in light weather as in heavy. In general, they were smaller than the Americans, with a gross tonnage of around 1,000 to 1,200. Their high average length-to-beam ratio of between 7 and 8 to 1, with the raked stem rabbeted on to a long, straight keel, gave these clippers a very good grip of the water when sailing on the wind. They were wet ships in a head sea, but then so were the Americans, and indeed any ship with so fine a bow would be.

These British ships were built specifically for the China tea trade, and the best of them were built by Robert Steele, by now in his prime as a designer. During the 1860s he produced a number of very fine ships, of which the *Taeping*, *Ariel*, *Sir Lancelot* and *Serica* were world-famous for their speed and beauty. His ships were mainly of composite construction, the wooden hull planking being bolted to frames, deck beams and stringers of iron. The hull was sheathed with copper below the waterline to provide extra protection against marine growth and wood-boring worms.

By 1865 the China tea trade, which had earlier threatened to become an American monopoly through the speed of their ships, was firmly back in the hands of the British. British clippers, better designed and better rigged for the particular conditions to be expected during the 16,000 nautical miles between China and London Docks around the Cape of Good Hope, could put up considerably better passage times than the fastest of the American clippers. Each year the English ships raced home from China with their holds stuffed with cases of the new crop of tea, and it was a race well worth winning, for the premium paid by merchants for the first cargo to arrive was considerable. The most famous of these annual races was that of 1866 when five clippers were engaged. The *Fiery Cross* left Foochow on 29 May, the *Ariel*, *Taeping* and *Serica* on 30 May, and the *Taitsing* on 31 May. The first to arrive in London Docks was the *Taeping*, at 8.45 p.m. on 6 September. The *Ariel* arrived half an hour later and the *Serica* at 11.45 p.m., after a voyage halfway around the world that took just 99 days. The other two clippers docked in London two days later. It is remarkable that the first three were all Robert Steel ships and that they were of such equal excellence that only three hours separated them after 16,000 miles of sailing. (The average time for the clipper passage from China to London was around 110 to 112 days.)

The competition to build still faster clippers continued until about 1870. In 1868 Walter

Hood of Aberdeen built the *Thermopylae* of 991 gross tons to a design by Bernard Waymouth. She was claimed to be the fastest sailing clipper in the world, and her owner gave her a golden cock to be secured to her mainmasthead as evidence of her supremacy. On her maiden voyage she sailed with passengers and cargo from London to Melbourne in 59 days – a record for a sailing ship that has never been beaten – then sailed in ballast to Foochow to load tea, and brought her cargo home from Foochow to London in 101 days. It was specifically to challenge the *Thermopylae* that, in 1869, John Willis commissioned the Dumbarton firm of Scott & Linton to build him a clipper of 963 tons gross, to be named *Cutty Sark*. She made her first voyage with tea from China in 1870, taking 109 days from Shanghai to Beachy Head – no very remarkable passage. But in fact both she and the *Thermopylae* came too late for the 'Flying Fish

Top: The clipper *Fiery Cross*, one of five tea clippers to take part in the famous race in 1866.

Above: The clippers *Serica* and *Lahloo* at Foochow in 1868. The clipper, with her small cargo-capacity, depended on high-value cargoes like opium and tea for her profit, and her brief reign ended as soon as steamships could match her speed by better timekeeping.

202

Above: The *Cutty Sark* was one of the greatest of all clippers, but arrived when the tea-trade was dying. Like other clippers she survived by going into the Australian wool trade.

on board for the long voyages; but, as the century wore on, more and more coaling stations were established at strategically placed ports around the world, and this obstacle was gradually removed.

The biggest of the British composite clippers, and in some ways the most remarkable, was the 2,131-ton *Sobraon*, which was built by Hall of Aberdeen in 1866 for the firm of Lowther, Maxton & Company, trading to Australia. She was remarkable in that she was designed as a steamship but completed as a clipper. Her maiden voyage was made as a passenger ship in 1867, and until 1891 she made regular voyages between London and Sydney – a very popular ship with all who sailed in her. In 1891 she was taken over by the New South Wales government, as a reformatory ship in Sydney Harbour. She was surveyed in 1911 for recommissioning as a training ship and was found to be sound throughout after forty-five years of service. She was paid off as a training ship in 1916 and became the floating clubhouse of an Australian charity. In 1937 she was again surveyed, and once again her hull was found to be sound throughout – a remarkable tribute to the excellence of British shipbuilding during the second half of the nineteenth century.

By the early 1870s, the composite-built clipper was giving way to the iron clipper, the introduction of an anti-fouling composition for bottom painting having overcome shipowners' opposition to a building material which attracted more marine growth than wood. The first tea clipper of wholly iron construction was the *Lord of the Isles*, built by Scott of Greenock, and notwithstanding the longevity of the composite-built *Sobraon*, mentioned above, the iron clipper hull was undoubtedly stronger and more durable than the composite. Half way through the twentieth century, there were many iron clipper hulls still trading vigorously, shorn, alas, of masts and sails and fitted with engines instead.

It is not easy to estimate the effect of the opening of the Suez Canal on the decline of the sail trading ship, for the steam-driven passenger and cargo ships were at that time already proving their reliability and regularity, and were fast becoming an automatic choice for enterprising shipping companies anxious to increase their profits. Up to 1870, the clipper was a certain money-spinner, mainly because the marine steam engine was still in the early stages of its development, and the compound engine had not yet made its appearance on the oceans. The profits which a good clipper could make were enormous: Donald Mackay's *Staghound* not only repaid her entire building cost in her first year's trading, from New York to San Francisco, Canton

Trade', as the China run was known to seamen, for in 1869 the Suez Canal was opened and the steamships took over. With a much shorter route through the canal and more regular sailings, they could well afford to undercut the sailing ships, bringing tea to London in less than half the time taken by a clipper.

Yet as the tea trade ceased to be viable for the clippers, another trade presented itself. This was the wool trade from Australia, which involved an outward passage round the Cape of Good Hope and a homeward passage round Cape Horn, to take advantage of the prevailing westerly winds on both legs. The wool trade lasted until about the end of the century, though with returns steadily diminishing as, once again, the steamship companies stepped in and undercut the clipper rates. That it remained profitable for sailing ships as long as it did is attributable to the difficulty for a steamer of carrying enough coal and back, but showed a profit of over $80,000 over and above that. Similarly, the *Sovereign of the Seas* earned more than $84,000 in freight rates on her maiden voyage, and the average earnings of a single clipper voyage from New York to San Francisco during the gold rush were estimated at $78,000. The Suez Canal was opened to traffic in 1869 and, as has been seen, almost at once took the China tea trade out of the clipper's hands. But the Canal made little difference to the Australian trade, and it was simply the development of the steamship herself over the next twenty years which was to take that trade, too, away from the sailing ships. By 1880, steamships were making the London–Sydney run in around 50 days, compared with about 65 for the fastest of the sailing vessels.

Some figures of the period show that in 1868, the year before the canal was opened, world tonnage of sailing ships was 4,691,820; that of steamships was 824,614. In 1873, four years after the opening of the canal, sail tonnage had dropped to 4,067,564, while that of steam had more than doubled to 1,680,950. Within ten years, steam tonnage had overtaken that of sail, due to the development, first, of the compound, and then of the triple-expansion steam engine.

In the natural course of ship development, steel took over from iron as the prime shipbuilding material from about 1885 onwards, and this applied to sailing ship construction just as much as to steamships. The higher tensile strength of steel enabled shipbuilders to build larger, and so to introduce the final stage of the development of the sailing ship and the epitome of grace and power – the big four- and five-masted barques and schooners with which the age of commercial sail came to an end. Steel was used for more than just the hull: masts and yards were also made of steel, saving much weight aloft, and wire rope replaced the cordage of the standing rigging, saving yet more weight and reducing windage.

There were still some profits to be made by sailing ships. It is recorded, for example, that in the late autumn of 1891, there were 77 big sailing ships loading wool in Sydney Harbour for the London wool sales which were held in the first three months of every year. They carried immense cargoes, for screwjacks were used to compress the bales into the holds until the ship was almost bursting at the seams. The medium-sized clipper *Mermerus* once screwed 10,000 bales worth £132,000 into her holds, and in 1894 the smaller *Cutty Sark*, loading at Brisbane, carried 5,304 bales screwed home until the wool was almost solid.

Another good trade was wheat, barley and corn from the west coast of Canada and the United States to European ports – a long passage around Cape Horn. In 1882 one and a quarter million tons of wheat and barley were shipped in 550 sailing vessels from California and Oregon alone. This, too, lasted until about the turn of the century, before the steamship took over.

There was one other profitable trade remaining open: coal and manufactured goods round Cape Horn to the south Pacific coast of South America, and hides, nitrates and guano from there back to Europe. No steamship owner could even consider the Cape Horn run yet, mainly because of the lack of coaling stations along this long and distant route, but partly also because they lacked the flexibility and steadying influence of sail in the tumultuous seas that prevailed in those waters. While it lasted, it was a good trade for the big sailing ships, but some of the smaller ones, though Cape Horn weather held no fears for them, found cargoes progressively more difficult to obtain. This was because, being about the only employment now left for sailing vessels, the trade attracted almost every sailing ship available, and most shippers preferred to use the ship with the largest capacity.

Whereas the clipper had made her fortune by her speed, accepting a diminished cargo capacity because of the fine lines of her hull, the new generation of sail trading ship, always faced with

Above: Hands reefing sails aboard the *Garthsnaid*. Another reason for the decline of the big sailing ship was the number of men needed to man her.

Right: The five-masted barque *France II* was built in 1911, the largest sail merchantman ever.

growing competition from steam, had to shift the emphasis from speed to capacity, and so had to adopt the more or less square cross-section of the steamship in order to provide the large square holds in which a maximum of cargo could be stowed. This sometimes made them a bit slab-sided. Gone were the graceful lines of the clipper hull, but the beauty of the barque and schooner rig made up, to some extent, for the ugliness of the hull. However, not all this last generation of sailing ships were ugly in their hull design: some builders managed to combine the large holds and a beautiful hull, but there were many more built like elongated boxes with a raked bow and counter stern tacked on at either end.

These last trade sailing ships were much bigger than the clippers which preceded them. Two thousand five hundred tons was big for a clipper, the great majority being considerably smaller, but if the new sailing ships were to be able to earn their keep in competition with steamers, they needed to carry very much larger cargoes. In 1890, Henderson of Glasgow built the *France*, a five-masted steel barque, for the A. D. Bordes Line, with a deadweight tonnage of 5,900 (3,784 tons gross). At that time she was the largest trade sailing ship ever built, and also one

of the fastest, once returning from Chile round Cape Horn to France with a cargo of nitrates in 63 days. In March 1901 she was struck by a pampero off South America, took on a list of 45 degrees as a result of her cargo shifting, and sprang a serious leak. She staggered on for two months, but in the end had to be abandoned, her crew being rescued by a German barque.

Even larger was her successor, *France II*, built in 1911 by Chantiers de la Gironde, Bordeaux, for the Société des Navires Mixtres. A five-masted barque, she had a deadweight tonnage of 8,000, and was the largest sail trading vessel ever built, just exceeding in size the German *Preussen*, which had been built nine years earlier. She, too, came to a sad end, drifting in July 1922 onto a coral reef in the Pacific near Noumea because of lack of wind. Although it would have been possible to salvage and refit her, the depressed state of the freight market made it an unprofitable proposition and her hull was sold for £2,000 for breaking up. The days of the sail trader were fast coming to an end.

Two events hastened this end. The first came in 1897 when Lloyd's, the world centre for shipping insurance, introduced a big increase in insurance rates for sail tonnage. Some owners,

Preussen
(1902)

Length 438 ft (134·5 m) *Waterline* 407 ft (124 m)
Beam 54 ft (16·5 m) *Registered tonnage* 5,081
Sail area 54,000 sq ft (5,000 m²)
Cargo capacity 8,000 tons

The *Preussen* was the largest full-rigged ship ever built and the only one ever to have five masts. These, like her hull, were made of steel. There were two steam engines on deck providing power for winches, pumps, anchor handling, etc. She was built for the nitrate trade and once made a run of 370 miles (595·5 km) in 24 hours (an average speed of 15$\frac{1}{2}$ knots). In October 1910 she was run down by a Newhaven-Dieppe steamer, who underestimated her speed, and went ashore on the Kent coast.

The diagram below shows two of the brace winches, situated behind the mast, which swung the three lowest yards simultaneously when the ship tacked or altered course. (Only the port side braces are shown.)

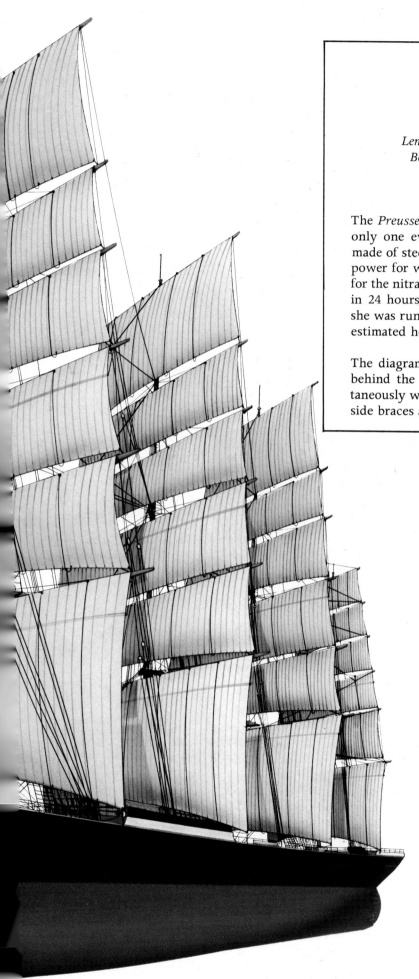

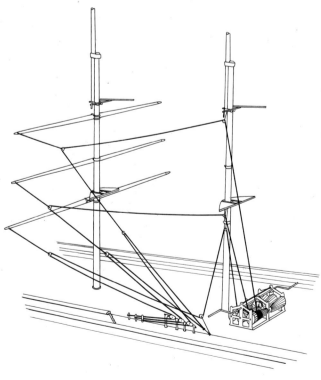

unable to pay the new rates and still make a profit in a declining freight market, sold some of their ships; others tried to economize on running costs by undermanning, or by taking apprentices on board in place of paid crew. This racket began to give these hips a bad name, for there were some captains who did nothing to teach their apprentices the seaman's trade, but used them purely as unpaid ordinary seamen.

The second event to hasten the end was the opening of the Panama Canal in 1914. Just as the opening of the Suez Canal in 1869 had taken the China tea trade out of the hands of the clippers and given it to the steamships, so the opening of the Panama Canal did the same to the South American nitrate trade, the last stronghold of sail. Some other cargoes were still available to the sailing ships, non-perishable bulk cargoes such

as steel rails, timber, coal and grain, but they were growing progressively fewer and less remunerative for sailing ships, as the numbers of steamships continued to mount. There were far too many sailing ships competing for a dwindling share of the market, and many owners were forced to pay off their crews, strip their ships down to the last gantline, and leave them where they lay. Many harbours of the world had a collection of sailing ship hulls, left by their owners to decay.

But the steam come up and the sail went down,
And them tall ships of high renown,
Was scrapped, or wrecked, or sold away.

A few owners, still in love with their graceful ships, tried to sail against the tide, by tramping. By taking cadets, who paid a premium to the

Above: Despite fierce competition a large number of sailing ships survived into the twentieth century. This is Port Blakely, Washington, in 1905.

Above right: The deck of the *Passat*, one of the famous 'Flying P' Line.

Right: The *Pamir*, which sank during a hurricane in the Atlantic in September 1957, with a loss of 80 lives.

owners to learn the seaman's trade, and the occasional enthusiast, who would even pay for the privilege of working a passage in a tall ship, they just about covered the costs of a voyage, or even made a small profit. But all the time freight rates were being undermined by the ubiquitous steamship, and as the years went by the going got harder.

The last British windjammer in active commission was the four-masted barque *Garthpool*, built in 1891 as the *Juteopolis* by W. B. Thompson of Dundee. She was bought in 1912 by Sir William Garthwaite, who ran her until 1928 in the Australian grain trade. He felt a deep love for the old, square-rigged ships of the last days of sail, and it was more through sentiment than the profit motive that he kept her running. When she was wrecked on Ponta Reef, in the Cape Verde Islands, in November 1929, it was the end of Britain's participation in commercial sail.

There were one or two others who kept it going. In Germany, Ferdinand Laeisz of Hamburg, who in the 1870s founded the famous 'Flying P' line of sail trading ships, kept his flag flying until the outbreak of World War II, though with a greatly depleted fleet. His ships, *Preussen*, *Penang*, *Pamir*, *Passat*, *Potosi*, *Pommern*, *Padua*, *Priwall* and others, were among the queens of commercial sail during the last forty years of its existence. In the eyes of many people, the *Potosi* was the finest sailing vessel in the world. She was built in 1895, a five-masted barque big enough to carry 6,000 tons of cargo in her holds, and she was one of the fastest sailing ships engaged in the nitrate trade and never made a bad passage. The biggest ship of the Flying P line was the *Preussen*, built in 1902, with an overall length of 407 ft (124 m) and beam of 54 ft (16·5 m). With a registered tonnage of 5,081 tons, she had room in her holds for just on 8,000 tons of cargo. She was remarkable for being square-rigged on all of her five masts – the only ship in the world ever to carry such a rig. Under full sail she spread 54,000 sq ft (5,000 m²) of canvas.

Another owner who kept his flag flying on sailing ships to the end was Captain Gustaf Erikson, of Mariehamn, Finland. His connection with the sea started when he was a boy serving on a North Sea timber barque at the age of nine, was a sea-cook at thirteen, then able seaman, bosun, and finally mate of a timber ship at the age of eighteen. After two years as a captain (aged nineteen), he decided that the North Sea and Baltic runs were not for him and went deep sea, as mate of big square-riggers for five years and as master for eleven, his final command being the Finnish 1,753-ton barque *Lochee*. He then came ashore to become an owner and began to build up a fleet. Perhaps the best-known

209

of his many ships was the lovely *Herzogin Cecilie*, a four-masted barque of 3,111 gross tons built in 1902, tragically lost in 1936 when she went ashore on Bolt Head, Devon.

Today, sailing ships still exist as training vessels, and many maritime countries have one or two in commission to give their young people a taste of the seafaring life. Others have been taken in hand as permanent memorials of the last and greatest days of the sail trading ships, so that men and women can still see and wonder at the beauty that has had its day.

The demise of the great sail traders coincided with the end of two other, very different, types of sailing vessel. One of these was the Banks schooner, a type of small schooner evolved purely for line fishing for cod on the Grand Banks off Newfoundland. They were built almost entirely in the fishing ports along the Massachussetts coast, particularly at Gloucester, which became the headquarters of the cod fishing industry in the United States. The type was originally based on the Baltimore clipper, and was inaugurated in 1847 with the small schooner *Romp*, built with a clipper bow and overhanging counter

Above: J-class yachts racing between the two World Wars.

Above left: The beautiful four-masted barque *Herzogin Cecilie*, which ran aground on the Devon coast in 1936.

Left: The fishing schooner *Elsie*, racing in 1921. Like the clippers, these Banks schooners needed speed to get the best price for their catch, and they were among the best-looking of all sailing craft.

The other type of sailing vessel which succumbed at about the same time was the victim not of steam or the internal combustion engine, but of excessive specialization. Big racing yachts had a well-established place in history running back to the early years of the nineteenth century, but the visit of the schooner *America* of 170 tons measurement from the United States to sail in English regattas in 1851 gave the sport a great fillip in Britain. In a race at Cowes sailed on 22 August of that year, she finished first out of a fleet of fifteen yachts to win the 'one hundred guinea cup' presented by the Royal Yacht Squadron, later to become an international challenge trophy as the America's Cup, and it was these races that stimulated competition among yacht designers to produce huge racing machines which could move faster through the water than any of their contemporaries. It would not be correct to lay the blame for this extreme development wholly on the America's Cup races, for the national competition between individual owners was also intense, but the effect of the glamour and publicity which surrounded the periodic races for the America's Cup certainly did work back to the drawing boards of the great designers and spur them on to greater lengths in the search for speed.

The final developments of this international competition for speed in big racing yachts were the J-class yachts of the 1920s and 1930s, each one being more extreme in design than her predecessors. They were all, of course, the toys of extremely rich men, but they nevertheless set an unhealthy trend in the yacht design world that did no service to yachting as a whole. It was forgotten that a yacht, even a racing yacht, is basically a small ship, and needs to have some of the sturdy seaworthiness that characterises a ship. Of these ultimate in racing yachts, with their slim hulls and immensely tall masts, it used to be said, perhaps rather unkindly, that before turning in for the night owners would set a lighted candle on the main boom, and that if it was still burning in the morning they would agree that there was not enough wind for racing, and, that if it had gone out, that there was too much wind to race. This may be an exaggeration, but they were always essentially light-weather craft and could not stand up to winds of force 5 and above. They ceased to exist as a racing class in 1936, though some of them were converted into useful cruising yachts, with their extreme rig cut down to a handier size. By that time the rising costs of construction, maintenance, professional crews and endless new ideas in equipment intended to give them another fraction of speed, had combined to price them out even of the very exclusive market they had hitherto catered for.

stern. But, as in other occupations, speed was at a premium, for the first vessels home with the catch commanded the best prices in the fish markets. The 'plumb stern' schooner, setting two jibs, a staysail and jackyard topsails above the foresail and mainsail was the next development, but in 1910 Thomas McManus, the best known of all the fishing schooner designers, launched the 98-ton schooner *Elsie*, which was hailed as one of the most beautiful small vessels ever to sail the seas. She had the rounded bow and long, sloping entry of the modern yacht, ending in a long keel drawing more water aft than forward. Her length-to-beam ratio of just over 4 to 1, allied to a hull shape with its maximum beam forward of the mainmast, was indicative of speed and power, and with jackyard topsails and a main topmast staysail set above the conventional gaff schooner rig, she was very quick through the water. These Gloucester-built Banks schooners were the ultimate sail fishing vessels, with beautiful yacht-like lines, complemented by a powerful, balanced sail plan. When they, in their turn, were overtaken by technological progress – not so much by steam in this case as by the internal combustion engine – some of the loveliest of all small working sailing ships vanished from the oceans.

The Dreadnought Battleships

By the opening year of the twentieth century the battleship had evolved into a more or less stereotyped form that was common to all navies – a steel ship of around 17,000 tons, mounting four big guns (usually of about 12-in (300-mm) calibre) in two turrets, and up to forty smaller guns, ranging from about 9-in (230-mm) to small quick-firing 3-pounders, protected along her sides and around her turrets by about 12 in (300 mm) of case-hardened steel, and propelled by two triple-expansion engines which produced a maximum speed of 18 to 19 knots. There were, of course, local variations, but these figures are a fair approximation for the average battleship. They were known generically as 'mixed-armament' ships, because of the variety of gun sizes they mounted.

With so little difference in gunpower, speed and armour protection between the battleships of the various maritime nations, sea power depended largely upon numbers, and the country which had the most could be said to dominate the oceans. In 1900 this happy condition was enjoyed by Great Britain, whose policy was to maintain a 'two-power standard' of naval strength (i.e. her navy was equal in numbers to the combined fleets of any two other nations). Britain had good reason for wanting a navy of such proportions, for she had dominions and colonies all over the world, and the British empire depended for its survival on command of the sea routes which linked them together. In this situation she was fortunate in having a shipbuilding

capacity unexcelled throughout the world, being able to build better and faster than any other country, and well able to maintain her lead in numbers over all other navies.

In the early years of the new century the serene calm of British naval supremacy was ruffled by a chill breeze, which was to be felt all round the world. It began with an article in the 1903 edition of Jane's *Fighting Ships*, by Vittorio Cuniberti, the foremost Italian warship designer of the day. Under the title 'An Ideal Battleship for the British Navy', he outlined a design for a battleship of about 17,000 tons, carrying twelve 12-inch guns, protected by 12-in (300 mm) armour, and capable of steaming at 24 knots. The basis of his argument for such a radical departure in battleship design was that her twelve 12-inch guns could bring a devastating volume of fire into action at long range.

The one great disadvantage – more so in the case of the British navy than any other – was that the introduction of this powerful new battleship design would make all the mixed-armament battleships in the world obsolete. British naval supremacy, which was based on numbers, would be removed at a stroke, and she would have to start rebuilding her battle fleet from scratch, on a par with other countries.

Yet, even before Cuniberti's article, Britain was already beginning to move towards this new conception of battleship design, though with different reasoning. In 1903 the fighting range of battleships was still only 3,000 yards

(2,750 m), though Admiral Sir John Fisher, when Commander-in-Chief in the Mediterranean, had experimented with much longer ranges. Improvements in gun control were coming in, and Fisher's experiments were suggesting that the battleship's fighting range should be more like 6,000 yards (5,500 m) than 3,000, and even that a good proportion of hits could be achieved at 8,000 yards (7,300 m).

At this range, the only reasonable method of achieving accurate gun control was by firing salvoes, and, since it was impossible to distinguish between the splashes made by 12-inch and 9·2-inch shells, corrections to range and direction were made for the salvo as a whole. If some of the shells fell short and some fell beyond the target, it was likely that at least one would hit it. But if all the guns were of the same calibre, the likelihood of one shell hitting the target was increased, and exactly the same corrections to the elevation of the gun would apply to all.

Thus, for its own reasons, the British navy was coming round to Cuniberti's point of view.

In 1904 Fisher, one of whose major preoccupations was gunnery efficiency at long ranges, was appointed to the Admiralty as First Sea Lord, and thus principal naval adviser to the government. He had made up his mind that the new type of battleship was essential if Britain was to retain her naval supremacy, simply because other navies would build them if Britain did not. If Britain were to get in first, her proven ship-

building capacity would ensure victory in any numerical race that might follow.

Fisher wasted no time, and the keel of H.M.S. *Dreadnought* was laid at Portsmouth dockyard on 2 October 1905. She was launched just four months later, on 10 February 1906, and was ready for trials on 3 October 1906. She joined the fleet in December of that year. She had ten 12-inch guns in five turrets, 12-in (305 mm) armour, a displacement of 17,250 tons (17,527 tonnes), and a speed of 21 knots.

She was greeted with a chorus of abuse, from naval officers, designers and publicists who were advocates of the mixed-armament ship and could not conceive of a naval battle fought at a range of more than 3,000 yards (2,750 m). They were also aghast at her price, £1,783,883, even though it was not much more than her mixed-armament predecessor, the *Lord Nelson*, still not completed, would cost. It was not until a paper was published in the United States, written by Lieutenant-Commander

W. S. Sims (later Admiral Sims), drawing attention to the overwhelming advantages which a fleet of *Dreadnoughts* would enjoy over a fleet of mixed-armament ships, particularly in the concentration of heavy fire against an enemy battle line, that criticism of the *Dreadnought* in Britain finally died away.

Fisher's gamble paid off. Because the *Dreadnought* was built in great secrecy and record time, it was not until she made her public appearance when she joined the British fleet that the rest of the world's navies knew what they were up against. In appearance, she was awe-inspiring, with an impression of uncompromising efficiency and colossal power, overshadowing every other battleship afloat. All other navies had to stop their battleship building programmes and take stock of this new phenomenon. For Germany, already emerging as the principal challenger to British naval supremacy, it was a particularly severe blow. She had already embarked upon building a series of 'Deutschland' class battleships, 18-knot mixed-armament ships of 13,400 tons (13,615 tonnes), but it would be obvious folly to complete them, in view of the British *Dreadnought*. But to build large enough to carry an armament comparable to *Dreadnought's* meant enlarging the Kiel Canal, only recently completed, but unable to take ships above 16,000 tons. It also meant enlarging their naval dockyards and rebuilding their dry-docks.

While Germany and the other maritime nations pondered the problems, Britain went ahead with her building programme, and so kept herself well ahead of the competition.

H.M.S. *Dreadnought* marked the beginning of a worldwide revolution in naval design and building. Fisher was cock-a-hoop at the stroke which he had dealt to the rest of the naval world. In a official paper which he prepared for the Admiralty he proclaimed 'We shall have ten "Dreadnoughts" at sea before a single foreign "Dreadnought" is launched.' And his paper was headed:

New Name for the Dreadnought:
'The Hard-Boiled Egg'
Why? Because she can't be beaten.

Far left: The launch of the *Dreadnought* at Portsmouth in February 1906.

Left: Stern view of the *Dreadnought*.

Chapter Ten
Big is Beautiful

During the early years of the twentieth century there was a great revolution in marine engineering caused by the introduction of the steam turbine, demonstrated so dramatically by Charles Parsons at the Spithead Naval Review of 1897. It had so many advantages over the reciprocating steam engine – a considerable saving of space and weight, greater efficiency, less maintenance, virtually no vibration when running – that it received general acceptance remarkably quickly for such a radical invention.

The turbine was first used on British destroyers, but its usefulness was by no means restricted to naval ships, and merchant shipowners were

Left: The *Mauretania* and her sister *Lusitania* were the first liners to use the Parsons turbine. The former is shown here with the *Turbinia* alongside.
Below: The *Mauretania*'s dining saloon.

quick to grasp its advantages for commercial purposes. As early as 1904 the Cunard Line ordered two new passenger ships, with a gross tonnage of 38,000 each, to be powered by four steam turbines, driving four propellers and producing a total of 70,000 horsepower. The ships were the *Mauretania* and *Lusitania*, both launched in 1906. On her maiden voyage the *Mauretania* crossed the Atlantic at an average speed of 27·4 knots, beating the previous record set up in 1897 by the *Kaiser Wilhelm der Grosse*.

The *Mauretania* was, perhaps, the most successful transatlantic liner ever built, and a favourite with passengers for over thirty years. With an overall length of 790 ft (240·8 m), a maximum beam of 88 ft (26·8 m), and drawing 36·2 ft (11 m) of water, on seven decks she could accommodate 560 first-class passengers, 475 second, and 1,300 third, all in reasonable

comfort, and the 560 in the first class in extreme luxury. Fifteen transverse bulkheads divided her into 175 watertight compartments, giving her a wide safety margin should she be holed.

The comfort and luxury of the passenger accommodation was one of the major attractions of ocean travel, and they reached a peak on the great liners of this period. The first was the *Oceanic* in 1871, which had an extra deck built above the upper deck to provide lounges across the whole width of the ship. The *City of Paris* and *City of New York* of 1880 had gone a bit further in this direction, and also proved especially popular because their twin screw installation provided a smoother passage. Now the *Mauretania* improved on the *City of Paris* and *City of New York* by having two passenger decks above the upper deck, providing space for more and bigger passenger lounges and larger cabins and staterooms, with scuttles and port-holes open to the outside air. In addition to the luxury of staterooms and lounges, the *chefs de cuisine* produced meals equal to those served in the world's finest hotels, and there was a small army of stewards and stewardesses to look after the comfort of the passengers. Every big liner had an orchestra to provide music during meals and for dancing. There was almost no limit to the luxury and, it seemed, no limit to the number of passengers who, wishing to cross the oceans, were prepared to pay a substantial premium to do so in style. It was the start of a golden age of ocean travel and the beginning of tourism, though as yet it was restricted to the very wealthy, who were ready and indeed eager to travel, regardless of the cost.

This valuable trade attracted shipowners of many countries, and almost every nation with a tradition of maritime trade had at least one, and often several, major steamship lines, operating across the Atlantic and other oceans of the world. Those who wanted a major share of this business had to have at least one of these palatial liners, if they were to stand a chance in the competition for the cream of the traffic. The design of the big ocean liner was now becoming more or less standard, and she was a ship with at least two passenger decks above the upper deck, a cabin and steerage capacity of around 2,500 to 3,000 passengers, turbine propulsion to eliminate the vibration associated with the reciprocating engine, and a speed of more than 25 knots. This meant a ship of about 40,000 tons to provide the passenger accommodation, and an installation of four turbines geared to four propellers, in order to drive a ship of this tonnage fast enough to attract the high fares (in the first class) required to cover overheads. To run a ship of this sort on a regular schedule required a very large crew on deck, in the engine and boiler rooms, in the kitchens, and in the cabins and lounges, and it required also a large and efficient back-up organization of dockworkers, office staff, and a miscellany of officials to ensure a rapid turn-round at the ship's terminal ports. All this, in a way, was an extension of the ship herself, the means by which she could justify her existence and the faith of her owners in putting up the money to cover the costs of building and fitting-out. In the *Mauretania*, for example, the shipboard crew totalled 812.

What was true of the Atlantic was as true of the other oceans, and there were similar, though usually slightly smaller, liners operating regular services to India, China, Australia, South Africa, South America, and across the Pacific from the west coast of Canada and the United States. They were just as luxuriously fitted to attract the passengers who could afford to pay for comfort, and, in fact, the major steamship line serving India and China, P & O, charged a premium on the already high fare to those who wanted a cabin or stateroom on the shady side of the ship while crossing the Indian Ocean. The glare of the sun on the water was something to be avoided if possible, and a cabin on the port side of the ship on the outward voyage and the starboard side on the homeward voyage avoided the worst of it. Those passengers who could afford to pay a bit extra for this particular comfort had the letters 'POSH' (Port Outwards Starboard Homewards) printed on their tickets, adding a new word to the English language.

These great liners, wherever they operated, were the queens of the ocean passenger trade, majestic ships designed to carry very large numbers of passengers across the oceans, at great speeds and in a maximum of comfort. Resplendent in their company livery, they sailed proudly across the seas – moving symbols of grace and power. It was to the invention of the turbine that they owed their ever-increasing size, for, with the four big German liners of the *Kaiser Wilhelm der Grosse* class, the steam reciprocating engine had reached its ultimate development. Each of these four liners had two immense quadruple-expansion engines, standing 40 ft (12 m) high, each with eight cylinders, two for each stage of expansion. An impression of their immense size can be gained from the fact that each low-pressure cylinder was no less than 9 ft 4 in (2·85 m) in diameter. They were the largest marine reciprocating engines ever built, and to accommodate their huge bulk and weight in the

Right: The launch of the *Lusitania*. Her sinking in 1915 has been hotly debated ever since.

Below right: The liner *Olympic* was much luckier than her sister *Titanic* and survived until 1936. The White Star Line emphasized comfort rather than speed in its ships.

ships' engine rooms created many problems of design. The total output of each pair of engines was 42,500 horsepower, sufficient to drive these 20,000-tonners at 22 knots. That was in 1897; but only ten years later the biggest liners had added nearly another 20,000 tons to their gross tonnage and 5 or 6 knots to their speed, needing another 30,000 or so horsepower; and no reciprocating engine which could produce that range of power would fit inside an acceptably sized engine room of a ship. In some of the big liners, designed before the turbine had fully proved itself, but still on the stocks when it was generally accepted, a compromise had been reached: the existing big triple-expansion engines drove the outer propellers and turbines drove the inner ones, or in some cases there was a single turbine driving an additional centreline propeller. This was the machinery layout in the two new White Star Atlantic liners *Olympic* and *Titanic*. They had been designed originally as 21-knot ships with two reciprocating engines only, but a central turbine had been added while they were still on the stocks.

In one respect, all these great liners were very much less than perfect. Most maritime nations exercised control over their national shipping through the provisions of a Merchant Shipping Act, or its equivalent, which laid down certain conditions, concerning safe levels of loading, etc., with which their ships had to comply before being given a certificate allowing them to operate. One of the provisions of the British Merchant Shipping Act – and those of other countries were similar – was that ships of over 10,000 tons had to carry a minimum of sixteen lifeboats on davits. As the largest ship's lifeboat could accommodate about sixty-five passengers, the total capacity of the life-saving equipment of a big liner was somewhere around 1,000, while she probably carried on board a total of some 3,000 or more passengers and crew. It was to take a great disaster to get the safety regulations tightened up.

This came in 1912. In 1907 the White Star Line decided to build two new ships for the Atlantic trade, to be followed by a third if the first two proved profitable. They were to be the biggest ships yet built, with an overall length of $852\frac{1}{2}$ ft (259·8 m) and a beam of $92\frac{1}{2}$ ft (28·2 m), giving them a gross tonnage of 46,328 tons. In accordance with White Star policy of sparing no expense in the building and fitting out of their liners, these ships were to be the epitome of comfort and elegance. White Star had never competed with other transatlantic steamship lines in the quest for speed, placing the comfort of their passengers first, and 21 knots had been put down as the specification for the service speed required. The

addition, during building, of a centreline turbine undoubtedly gave them a speed well in excess of 21 knots if required, but these ships were not built with an eye on breaking records across the Atlantic. Like her sister ship the *Olympic*, the *Titanic* was built with three passenger decks above the upper deck and seven decks in all. Below the upper deck there was a transverse watertight bulkhead approximately every 60 ft (18 m) along her length.

The *Titanic* sailed on her maiden voyage from Queenstown, Ireland, for New York on 10 April 1912 amid a great fanfare of praise and excitement ov   the world's newest and largest ship and, as suc ι, an example and advertisement of British shipbuilding skills. There was speculation when she sailed as to whether she would be trying to make a record crossing, and later, indeed, a belief that she was trying to do so, when it was revealed that she had been taking an extreme northerly course, as near as possible to a great circle, and therefore the shortest route between Britain and the United States. But, in fact, she maintained a steady speed of about 22 knots throughout her passage. Fortunately, cabins were not filled to capacity: she had on board 1,318 passengers, out of a total capacity of 2,435, and a crew numbering 885.

Shortly before midnight on her fourth day out, in the vicinity of the Grand Banks off the Newfoundland coast, she struck an iceberg which tore a hole 300 ft (90 m) long in her starboard side some 30 ft (9 m) below the waterline. Just over two and a half hours later she sank, leaving 916 passengers and 673 of the crew to die in the icy water. The results of the disaster were far-reaching, the most important being that new regulations were enacted requiring ships to carry sufficient lifeboats to accommodate everyone carried on board. Other effects were the institution of a more southerly track for liners crossing the Atlantic, and an ice patrol which continues to this day.

This tightening up of lifesaving requirements for all ships was, of course, long overdue, but the original requirements had been framed with a view to improving the structural design of large ships. Because the average-sized freighter of the times was of necessity built with large cargo holds and, as a result, could not be split up internally into a large number of watertight compartments, the lifesaving regulations required her to carry enough lifeboats on each side of the ship to accommodate the entire crew – in other words, twice the capacity to embark everyone on board. The less stringent regulations for passenger liners were designed to encourage owners to build additional watertight bulkheads into their big ships, on the argument that if they were made virtually unsinkable, large numbers of lifeboats would never be needed. It was certainly an odd way of encouraging improvements in the structural design of ships, and it took a disaster on the scale of the *Titanic* to show that this was not the right way of achieving the best and safest in ship design.

Beneath the exalted level of the big prestige liners, there existed an enormous variety of smaller commercial ships. The massive emigration movement of the second half of the nineteenth

Above: The *Titanic* suffered terrible damage when she collided with an iceberg on her maiden voyage. Despite rumours to the contrary, her design ensured that she sank slowly and on an even keel. This kept the loss of life lower than it might have been.

Right: The Hamburg-Amerika Line's *Cleveland* was one of the first cargo-liners, carrying a mixture of luxury passengers, emigrants and refrigerated cargo.

century was still in progress and, if anything, more extensive than ever, as the masses of underprivileged in Europe struggled towards a new life in the wide-open spaces. As a still very profitable trade, it attracted some ship-owners who built one-class ships specifically for emigrants but with space in their holds for a substantial cargo in addition. Examples of these special emigrant ships were the 4,900-ton *Gerania*, built specially for the Austria-United States run with a cargo capacity of 8,000 tons and space for 1,000 emigrants, and the 8,000-ton *Ancona*, built for the Italian emigrant trade, able to carry 8,200 tons of cargo and 2,500 emigrants. Germany, though she did build ships expressly for the emigrant trade, did not exclude passengers of other classes as well, those travelling in the steerage being kept more or less out of view of those who paid higher fares. A ship of this nature was the Hamburg-Amerika Line's 17,000-ton *Cleveland*, which was built with accommodation for 250 first-class passengers, 392 second-class, 494 third-class, and steerage space for 2,064 emigrants.

These were the good ships, with a good standard of accommodation and safety, but unhappily there were others, old ships which had had their day, but had been bought cheaply and patched up to operate for a few more years. Into these ships men, women and children were packed like animals and carried to their dream world overseas in conditions of utter squalor. It was still a period of social irresponsibility whenever there were quick profits to be made, and few national shipping authorities bothered

to inquire too deeply into the seamier side of the emigrant traffic. Perhaps fortunately, in this age of marine steam propulsion, voyages did not take long to complete, and even in the worst emigrant ships the state of destitution on board was, in many cases, no worse than the destitution these people had left behind them in their homes. It was to take a world war to eliminate these undesirable and worn-out ships, partly because during the war years they rusted away or were broken up, partly because after the war, when emigration was again in full spate, new worldwide regulations were in force, laying down minimum standards of safety and accommodation.

During the first twenty years of the twentieth century the great trade expansion, generated by the industrial revolution of the nineteenth, continued, and the world tonnage of merchant shipping grew in proportion. Ignoring all warships and ships of less than 100 tons gross, the registration figures for 1900 amounted to a worldwide total of 29,093,728 tons; ten years later it had grown to 41,914,765 tons, an increase of close on seventy per cent. A breakdown of these figures by nationality of ownership showed that in 1910 forty-five per cent of the world tonnage was registered in Great Britain, twelve per cent in the United States, ten per cent in Germany, with smaller proportions owned by Norway, France, Italy, Japan, Holland, Sweden, Russia, Austria, Spain and Denmark, in that order.

Right, below: The *Christine* (1890) was the first Danish oil tanker.

Far right, top: The *Royal Sovereign* was typical of the excursion paddle steamers built to run on the River Thames.

Far right, centre: The *Hendrick Hudson* (1906), a passenger steamer built for the Great Lakes.

Far right, bottom: The *Laketon* (1903) was a Great Lakes grain carrier. She is seen loading grain and has her bridge right forward, a characteristic of Lakes steamers.

It was during the first decade of the twentieth century that the movement towards designing ships specially for a particular trade accelerated. The first ship built specifically to carry oil in bulk was the S.S. *Gluckauf*, built in Britain in 1886; a ship fully refrigerated to carry frozen meat began to operate in 1870. As world trade expanded, so bigger cargoes, particularly of food and raw materials, were needed, and shipowners quickly realised that a bigger bulk cargo of any one given commodity could be stowed in a ship specially designed for it. Ships were designed and built especially to transport mineral ores (mainly iron and copper), grain, fruit, oil, and indeed any similar cargo suitable for transport in bulk.

As a generalization, it would be correct to say that the normal merchant ship of this period, even one specially designed for a particular trade, was of what was known as the 'three-island' type. Unless she was very small or very big, she would be built with four cargo holds, two forward of the central bridge structure and two aft. The masts were placed between the two forward and between the two after holds, to the heels of which derricks were fixed to load or unload the cargo in each hold. The 'islands' of the three-island freighter were the forecastle deck, the bridge structure and the poop deck, all rising some feet above the upper deck level so that, of a ship hull down on the horizon, the only parts visible were the three islands. About the only notable variations on this design were the big ore and grain ships on the Great Lakes, where the bridge was usually constructed well forward on the forecastle, thus removing the need for the centre island and providing space for additional cargo holds. This design, which would be considered unseaworthy on the open ocean, is acceptable on inland waters, even those as vast as the Great Lakes, and the additional cargo space is an economic bonus.

The American Lake steamers, in waters more placid than the open sea, were remarkable ships during this period, having a length-to-beam ratio of 10 to 1 to accommodate six large holds and a whole series of cargo hatches along the length of the upper deck. They were built with a short forecastle deck to provide quarters for the crew and a deckhouse aft for the officers. Below the deckhouse were the engine room, boiler room and coal bunkers. All the rest of the ship was taken up by holds. A typical Great Lakes ore carrier of the period had an overall length of up to 600 ft (180 m), a maximum beam of 60 ft (18 m), would draw 19 ft (6 m) of water, and have a cargo capacity of 11,000 tons. She was virtually no more than a long rectangular steel box, pointed at bow and stern.

No less interesting in design were the passenger ships on the Great Lakes and on some rivers. A typical example was the *Hendrick Hudson*, built in 1906. On a hull 380 ft (116 m) long, a beam of 45 ft (14 m), and drawing 8 ft (2·4 m) of water, the passenger decks were built out from the hull to the full width of the paddle boxes, 82 ft (25 m), supported beyond the ship's side by steel struts. With five passenger decks above the level of the upper deck, she could carry no less than 5,000 passengers – a phenomenal load for a hull of such modest size. Her feathering paddlewheels, 24 ft (7·3 m) in diameter and 16 ft 6 in (5 m) wide, gave her a speed of 22 knots.

Small passenger ships abounded in all parts of the world, some for short sea passages, more as ferries. Before World War I, road bridges were not considered an essential way of saving time when the water to be crossed was navigable. The world still moved at a relatively slow pace, and a ferry across a river or estuary served well enough to keep the traffic moving. Many of them, particularly at river crossings in the United States, were relatively large ships, carrying up to 2,000 passengers in saloons built out beyond the hull, with the midships part of the main

deck reserved for horses and carts or the occasional motor car. Most of them were double-ended with a wheelhouse at each end, a simple enough arrangement with paddle-wheels, when a simple reversal in the direction of rotation would enable the vessel to proceed equally efficiently in the opposite direction, but rather more complicated with screw propulsion. An example of the latter type was the *Guanabacoa*, built by Cammell Laird in Britain for service in Havana Bay. She was 140 ft (42·7 m) long, 38 ft (11·6 m) in beam, with a moulded depth of 13 ft 3 in (4 m) from deck to keel, and had two engines with screw propellers at each end driving the ship at a speed of 11 knots. Saloons along the sides of the vessel gave accommodation for 1,000 passengers, and between them was space for forty carts and horses. She made the passage from Britain to Havana under her own steam and ran successfully there for many years.

Another type of passenger ship, as yet not replaced by the motor car, was the excursion steamer, immensely popular among city dwellers who had few other means of transport for a day out. Typical of such ships was the Thames paddle steamer *Royal Sovereign*, which ran day

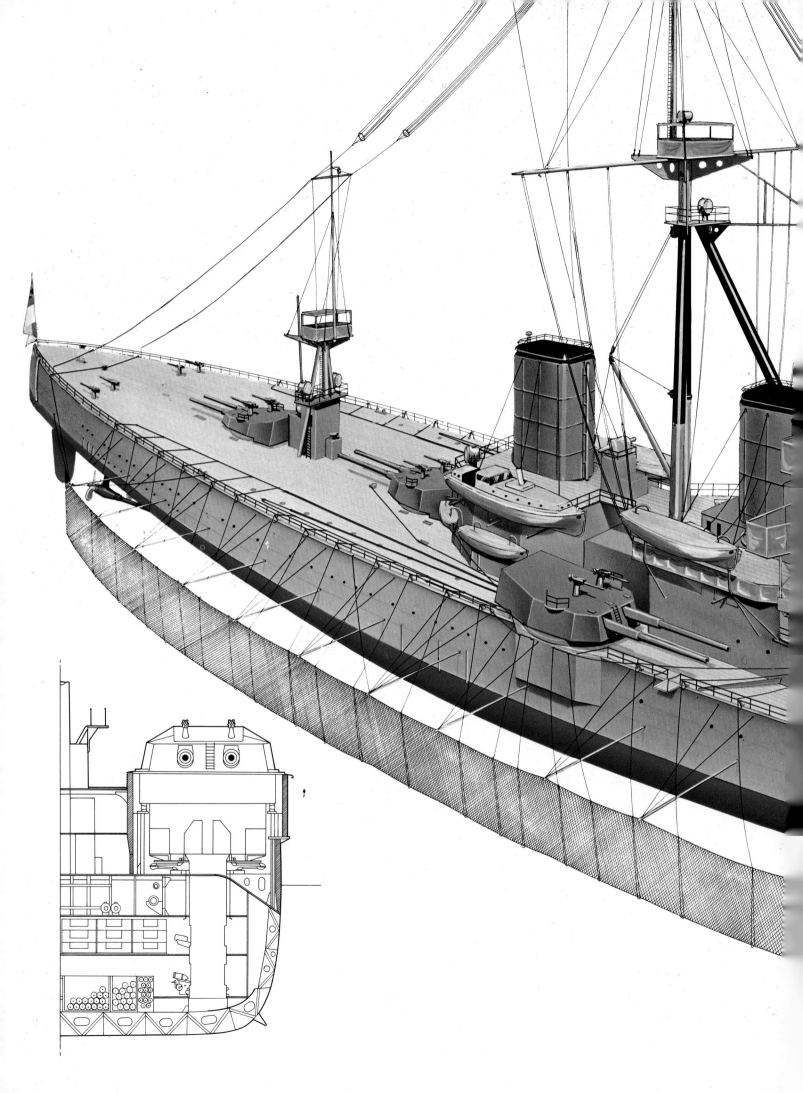

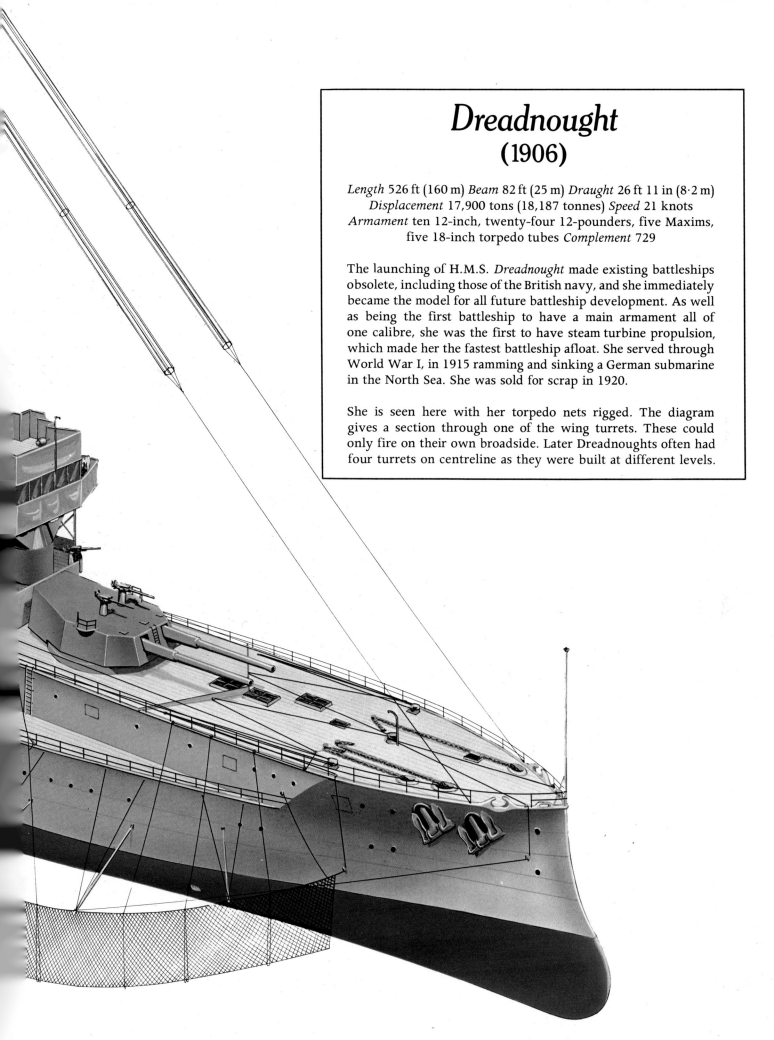

Dreadnought
(1906)

Length 526 ft (160 m) *Beam* 82 ft (25 m) *Draught* 26 ft 11 in (8·2 m)
Displacement 17,900 tons (18,187 tonnes) *Speed* 21 knots
Armament ten 12-inch, twenty-four 12-pounders, five Maxims,
five 18-inch torpedo tubes *Complement* 729

The launching of H.M.S. *Dreadnought* made existing battleships obsolete, including those of the British navy, and she immediately became the model for all future battleship development. As well as being the first battleship to have a main armament all of one calibre, she was the first to have steam turbine propulsion, which made her the fastest battleship afloat. She served through World War I, in 1915 ramming and sinking a German submarine in the North Sea. She was sold for scrap in 1920.

She is seen here with her torpedo nets rigged. The diagram gives a section through one of the wing turrets. These could only fire on their own broadside. Later Dreadnoughts often had four turrets on centreline as they were built at different levels.

trips from London to Margate and back. Her length overall was 300 ft (91·4 m), her beam 33 ft (10·1 m), and her draught 6 ft 6 in (2 m), giving her a gross tonnage of 891 tons. She could carry 2,320 passengers at a speed of 21 knots. She was typical of thousands of others, up and down coasts and along the rivers of the world, invariably well patronized by a public ready to pay a modest fare for a day trip on the water.

The first train ferry had appeared before 1900, on Lake Constance, but the majority that were built in the nineteenth century were for services between the Danish mainland and the outlying islands. The early ones had a single railway track along the deck, but, as they began to prove their value, larger ferries with double tracks were built. As the service expanded, still larger train ferries were built to operate between Denmark and Germany, and the *Drottning Victoria*, of 3,050 gross tons, carried trains on two tracks between Trelleborg and Sassnitz, a distance of 65 nautical miles. She had to be specially strengthened in the bows to act simultaneously, at times, as an icebreaker and train ferry.

One of the more difficult orders for a train ferry came from Russia to the firm of Armstrong Whitworth in Britain, for a ferry with four tracks for service on the River Volga. The Volga itself presented great problems, for the difference in water level between spring and summer is as much as 45 ft (14 m), owing to the huge additional volume of water in spring from melting snow. This particular problem was solved by fitting hydraulic hoists in the bows of the train ferry, which could lift the wagons 25 ft (7·6 m) above deck level, and by having the railway lines at the landing places built on two levels. Another problem was the thickness of the ice on the river in winter, rarely less than 2 ft (60 cm), and in some winters as much as 3 ft (0·9 m). This

could only be solved by building two ships – one an icebreaker to precede the ferry up and down the river in winter. But the biggest problem of all was caused by the Marinsky Canal system, through which both ships had to pass to reach the river at all. The locks were not wide enough to allow either ship to pass through, so the icebreaker (147 ft × 37 ft 6 in × 16 ft 6 in) (44·8 × 11·4 × 5 m) was built with an amidships longitudinal bulkhead from bow to stern, and on arrival at the canal system was divided longitudinally into two halves, each of which went through the locks on their own, to be joined up again when they reached the Volga. The train ferry (252 ft × 55 ft 6 in × 14 ft 6 in) (76·8 × 16·9 × 4·4 m) had to be built with a similar longitudinal bulkhead to allow division into two halves, and, in addition, an amidships transverse bulkhead to allow each half to be divided again. She went through the canals a quarter at a time, and was joined up again at the end of her passage to the Volga. Such a thing could never have been done before the days of the iron or steel ship – an example of the great flexibility of the new shipbuilding material.

Steam propulsion also came to small fishing

Top: The Swedish train ferry *Drottning Victoria* was built in 1909, and lasted until the 1970s.

Above: The two halves of the Russian icebreaker *Saratovski Ledokzl* which preceded the train ferry *Saratovskaia Pereprava*. Both were built by Armstrong Whitworth for use on the Volga, and launched in 1895.

Top: The Hull trawler
Asia on the Dogger Bank
in 1912. The sail on the
mizen was hoisted to
steady her while trawling.

Above: One of the first
British submarines
Holland No. 3 in
September 1902, with HMS
Victory in the background.

vessels around this period, both trawlers and
drifters. It had started when some enterprising
trawler-owners had purchased some old paddle
tugs and fitted them out with nets. In spite of
their age, they proved remarkably profitable,
encouraging other owners to change over entirely
to steam fishing, building new vessels with
steam engines especially for the purpose. In
comparison with the distant water trawlers of
today, they were very small craft, averaging
about 50 tons net, but, even at that size, very
much larger than the fishing boats that still used
sail. A British census of fishing vessels held in
1910 found that there were 3,000 steam fishing
craft totalling 150,000 tons, compared with
23,000 sail fishing boats with a total tonnage of
200,000.

The internal combustion engine, using either
petrol or naptha gas, was beginning to make its
appearance on the seas, though as yet in a very
small way and in very small vessels. The fire
risk inherent in a petrol engine in those early
days of development was considerable, and
only in very few types of ship, such as small
yachts, lifeboats, and occasionally as an auxiliary
engine in a big sail trading ship, were they used.

To take figures for Britain again, there were
three petrol-driven lifeboats employed around
British coasts in 1910, compared with four
steam-driven lifeboats. Of the total of 281 in
service, all the remainder relied on oars to
reach the scene of disaster.

Only in one type of vessel had the internal
combustion engine proved a real break-through:
this was the submarine, which needed some
alternative form of propulsion on the surface to
the battery-driven electric motor used when
submerged. This was provided first by the petrol
engine and later by the heavy-oil engine, which
removed the fire hazard. An electric motor, the
only form of propulsion which did not consume
valuable oxygen, was essential for underwater
use; when used on the surface it ran down the
batteries, considerably reducing the submarine's
radius of action. The internal combustion engine
changed all this. It produced a positive drive on
the surface when the conningtower hatch was
open and oxygen freely available, thereby con-
serving the batteries, and it could also be used
to drive the electric motors as dynamos and
recharge the batteries without recourse to an
external power supply. The introduction of the
internal combustion engine, particularly in its
heavy-oil form, made the submarine into a
viable weapon of war.

In the world of warships, development during
this period was stimulated largely by national
rivalry. In Europe, until about 1898, the main
competitors were Great Britain, on the one hand,
and France and Russia, on the other, with Italy
playing a significant part in the Mediterranean.
Every European nation kept a keen eye on the
naval developments of the others, particularly
in the spheres of gun development and armour
protection, and each new move in one of these
directions by any of the main naval powers was
either copied by the others or the balance was
redressed by some compensatory design improvement. Outside Europe, the principal naval powers
were the United States and Japan, and while
they naturally kept an eye on all European
warship developments, the need for them to
compete was much less pressing.

In 1898 a new protagonist appeared on the
European scene. Until that year Britain's 'two-
power standard' of naval strength had been
balanced against the combined navies of France
and Russia, which were bound together by a
treaty of alliance. In 1898 Germany passed the
first of her Naval Laws, giving notice to the
world that she was entering the naval world by
building a modern navy that would, within ten

or twelve years, bring her up to the status of the second naval power in Europe. This decision was to start a naval armaments race among the European nations, not only in numbers of warships built, but also in their design and development, each advance in this sphere being calculated to frustrate the naval aspirations of the other nations. The German decision had less effect on the navies of the United States and Japan, as they were still reasonably remote from the European scene, but some ripples from the European arms race did reach them across the oceans. This was particularly true of Japan, when Russian aspirations for naval bases on the eastern coast of Siberia brought her into direct contact with the European power struggle.

The closing years of the nineteenth century and opening years of the twentieth saw a complete change in the whole philosophy of warship design. In the days of the wooden warship, and the iron ship which succeeded her, the objective of the naval architect had been to design a ship of whatever size was required and stuff her as full of guns as was possible in the deck space available. She then fought her battles at a range of about 100 yards (90 m) hoping to succeed by the intensity of her gunfire at almost point-blank range. The development of the gun during the second half of the nineteenth century, particularly in the type of missile fired (explosive shell instead of solid shot), put an end to that conception of battle, and all naval tacticians accepted that future battles at sea would have to be fought at greater ranges – about 1,000 yards (900 m) by 1860, 2,000 (1,800 m) by 1880, 6,000 yards (5,500 m) by 1900, and up to 18,000 yards (16,500 m) by 1914. In the face of this progress in weaponry, naval architects realised that it was now necessary to design and build the warship around the weapon, rather than adapt the weapon to the ship. And by 1900 the gun was not the only form of armament to be considered; the torpedo and the mine had both been developed by then into significant naval weapons.

As has been noted, the naval big gun at the end of the nineteenth century was of 12-in (305-mm) calibre, but it was mounted in battleships in conjunction with big guns of slightly smaller size – 10-in (254-mm), 9-in (229-mm), and so on – and the basic design of battleships was arranged to accommodate these big guns of different sizes in the best positions for producing the maximum intensity of fire on various bearings – ahead, on the bow, abeam, on the quarter and astern. Admiral Fisher revolutionized battleship design when, at the end of 1906, H.M.S. *Dreadnought* was launched with an all-big-gun armament of ten 12-inch guns and nothing between them and small quick-firing 12-pounders carried as anti-torpedo boat weapons. The *Dreadnought* was designed wholly around her 12-inch guns, primarily to provide a steady gun platform for them at sea, with masts, funnels and bridge structure placed so as to produce the minimum interference with their arcs of fire. Even her turbine propulsion was designed to increase the effectiveness of her armament, by making her fast enough to overhaul other ships and bring them within range of her big guns.

Below: Although Admiral Fisher did little more than provide political backing for the *Dreadnought* his dynamic energy ensured that she was built in only fourteen months, and thereby stole a march on the Royal Navy's rivals.

Bottom: The revolutionary battleship *Dreadnought*. Many of her features were merely extensions of ideas tried in preceding ships, but the adoption of the Parsons turbine was a great improvement.

Development of the naval gun over the next eight years increased calibres, in Britain, from 12 in to 13·5 in (343 mm), and finally to 15 in (381 mm), and in other navies by a similar amount. Battleship design reacted accordingly. The main effect was on tonnage, for as guns and their mountings increased in size they also increased in weight, and so required a bigger and heavier hull to support them. It was realized, too, that the small quick-firing guns with which the *Dreadnought* had been equipped, as an anti-torpedo boat weapon, were no longer big enough to deal with the new destroyers, and so a bigger secondary armament, usually of guns of a calibre around 6 in (150 mm), was now required. The big 15-inch turrets of the later battleships posed further problems for the naval architect, for to get a maximum concentration of all-round fire the turrets needed to be mounted on the ship's centreline, and to provide enough space along the centreline to enable them to be trained across wide arcs on either side of the ship called for very long ships indeed, adding to cost, displacement and engine power needed to maintain speed. This particular problem was solved in the United States with the battleships *Michigan* and *South Carolina* where the forward and after turrets were super-imposed, saving an appreciable amount on the overall length of the ships. This arrangement was quickly followed by other navies, the advantages being considerable, without any loss of efficiency. These two ships, the first American all-big-gun battleships, were, in fact, better designed than the *Dreadnought*, but did not come into service until September 1909.

The development of the locomotive torpedo also had an effect on battleship design. During the thirty-odd years since its introduction, it had developed from a small underwater weapon, with a range of 1,000 yards (900 m) at 7 knots or 300 yards (275 m) at $12\frac{1}{4}$ knots, to a big underwater weapon, with a range of 4,000 yards (3,700 m) at 44 knots or 10,000 yards (9,000 m) at 28 knots. One hit with a torpedo in a vulnerable position could well be lethal to a battleship. Many ways were tried of minimizing the danger from underwater explosions against the hulls of battleships, the first of them being to build ships with their coal bunkers lining the insides of the hull, on the assumption that the coal in the bunkers would be the equivalent of an extra 2 or 3 in (63 mm) of armour plate. A test of this assumption was made in Britain in 1904, when an 18-inch torpedo was fired at the old battleship *Belleisle*. The coal in the bunkers was found to provide no protection, the force of the explosion blowing a 12-ft (3·7-m) hole in the side of the *Belleisle*, bursting the upper deck, and scattering 400 tons of coal all over the ship. The problem was never fully solved, but underwater vulnerability was mitigated by the introduction of longitudinal armoured screens inside the armoured hull plating, by more internal watertight subdivisions, by the provision of an extra 2 or 3 knots of speed to enable the ship to turn away from torpedoes and outrun them, and by the provision of steel anti-torpedo nets rigged round the ship at a distance of a few yards and held in position by booms projecting from the ship's side. This latter precaution, however, was mainly for harbour use.

Below: Had the US Congress been less dilatory, the USS *South Carolina* might have had the same impact as the *Dreadnought*. However she appeared two years later, and did not have turbine propulsion.

Left: Aerial view of HMS *Queen Elizabeth* in 1918. She introduced oil fuel and the 15 inch gun, in one of the most balanced and successful designs ever produced.

Below left: The French 2nd class cruiser *Du Chayla* was built in 1895 for scouting and commerce-raiding.

With the increase in gun size from 12 in (305 m) to 15 in (381 mm), battleship displacement increased from the 18,000 tons of the *Dreadnought* in 1906 to the 28,000 tons of the German *Baden*, laid down in 1913 – an enormous increase in so short a time. Main engine horsepower similarly increased from 23,000 *(Dreadnought)* to 53,000 *(Baden)*, though in the British *Queen Elizabeth* class, laid down a year before the *Baden*, it reached 75,000. The increases in speed were less dramatic, from about 18 knots in 1900 to 24 or 25 knots in 1914 (a reflection of the scientific fact that to raise a vessel's speed by 1 knot requires a very much larger increase in engine power at 20 knots than it does at, say, 10 knots).

Many people, not only in Britain, would agree that probably the ultimate in battleship design and grandeur during this period was the British *Queen Elizabeth* class. They were designed in 1912 by Sir Philip Watts as a new class of fast battleship, and when they made their first

appearance at sea in 1915 they stood out by virtue of their majestic appearance and exceptional fighting qualities. The five *Queen Elizabeths* were the first battleships to mount 15-inch guns, the first big ships to be completely oil-fired, and the first to be given the then high battleship speed of 25 knots. Their 15-inch guns could each fire a shell weighing 1,920 lb (860 kg) over a range of 23,400 yards (21 km) at the rate of 2 a minute. Many regarded them when they first went to sea as the most perfect example of the naval constructor's art yet seen afloat, and without any question they were most handsome and powerful fighting ships. Moreover, while their speed meant that they could fulfil the role of the battle-cruiser (fleet reconnaissance to within sight of the enemy battle fleet), they lacked the great drawback of that hybrid warship, and could take their place in the line of battle as fully protected by armour as any other battleship in existence.

The cruiser came next below the battleship in importance, approximating roughly to the fourth-rate ship of the line in sailing navies,

Above: Admiral Fisher wholeheartedly supported the 'dreadnought armoured cruiser', later known as the battle-cruiser. He believed that it could replace the battleship but heavy losses in battle showed how wrong this was. HMS *Inflexible* was one of the first of the type.

battleships), with a wide radius of action and medium-sized guns which packed a good punch. France inaugurated her cruiser programme with armoured ships carrying 7·5-inch guns, unique as cruisers at that time, and continued to develop these powerful ships, both in size and armament. Until 1898 the British had no answer to them, but during that year the new Krupp process of making case-hardened steel made possible the introduction of modest side armour in British cruisers, sufficiently strong to keep out a 6-inch shell. And from this was developed a new generation of big cruisers carrying 9·2-inch guns, all designed to counter the French armoured cruisers on the trade routes.

Apart from reconnaissance before, during, and after battle, the cruiser really had no place in the battle fleet. Yet battle fleets surrounded themselves with them, mainly because they were now carrying such big guns that they were assumed to have real value in battle. So much so, that by about 1910 the biggest armoured cruisers had been renamed 'battle-cruisers', a description that had no basis in fact and was probably responsible for their wide-spread misuse in battle. Apart from her commerce raiding and commerce protection, another role for which the armoured cruiser had been developed – and for which eventually she carried guns of the same calibre as battleships – was to serve as a reconnaissance unit, able by the power of her guns to sweep aside the outlying forces with which a battle fleet screened itself at sea, and by her superior speed escape before she could be brought to action and annihilated by the superior firepower of battleships. In terms of modern naval warfare this was a reasonable enough proposition during the early years of the twentieth century, but the change in generic name from 'armoured cruisers' to 'battle-cruisers' led many admirals to believe that they had a place in the actual line of battle. The battle of Jutland, fought between modern navies in 1916, was tragic proof of the fallacy of this argument.

In all the larger cruisers, it was the gun which was the dominant weapon; in the smaller light cruisers, the gun had to share its pre-eminence with the torpedo, discharged above water from tubes mounted on the upper deck. There was therefore very little difference between this small cruiser and a destroyer, and in many navies flotillas of destroyers were led by a cruiser.

In displacement tonnage, the armoured cruiser grew from the 13,000 tons of the *Duke of Edinburgh* (1906) to the 26,500 tons of the *Renown* (1916), in gun size from the six 9·2-inch guns of the former to the six 15-inch of the latter, and in propulsion from 23,000 horsepower and

smaller than the first three rates which were designed to lie in the line of battle, but larger than the frigates. Of all classes of warship, it was this one which was most diverse, ranging from big armoured cruisers carrying a battle-ship's armament to unarmoured light cruisers that were little more than glorified destroyers. Originally, the cruiser was a class of ship developed for trade protection and for general policing work at sea, largely unarmoured except for the main deck and applicable at first mainly to nations that maintained large overseas empires or depended economically on a large volume of overseas trade. But, particularly in France, where Admiral Aube was preaching a new doctrine of war, backed by an enthusiastic chorus of young naval officers who christened themselves the *'Jeune Ecole'*, it was becoming widely held that wars at sea could be won by the destruction of merchant shipping and the paralysis of a nation's trade, without the need ever to fight a major naval battle. And the best means of destroying commerce was by cruisers (which could be built far more economically than

23 knots to 126,000 horsepower and $32\frac{1}{2}$ knots. The light cruiser eventually stabilized at around 4,000 tons, with 6-inch guns and above-water torpedo tubes. A very similar advance was to be seen in destroyer development, with a growth in tonnage from around 350 to 1,000, in speed from 30 to 36 knots, and in armament from the 12-pounder to the 4-inch gun. The destroyer's main armament, however, was the torpedo, with triple-tube mountings on the upper deck.

Perhaps the most significant warship development of the period was in the submarine, where the successful solution of problems attendant on the heavy-oil engine completely revolutionized its role in naval warfare. The early submarines of the twentieth century, relying on the petrol engine for surface propulsion, had a role limited to coastal defence, as they were small boats with a very limited radius of action, and, with the risk of fire always present with the petrol engine, were obviously unsuited for distant-water operation. The heavy-oil engine changed all that. It was reliable and economical in its use of fuel, and with a relatively small increase in size to accommodate the necessary fuel tanks, changed the submarine from a short-range, tactical weapon into a long-range, strategic weapon, with great endurance and a wide radius of operation. This particular development was more or less simultaneous in all the navies of the world, but no one as yet could appreciate the devastating effect which this new weapon was to have upon all the carefully planned navies of maritime nations, or indeed upon the whole nature and philosophy of naval warfare. What was, within fifty years, to become the queen of the oceans was not yet even a small princess.

One other naval weapon was also emerging during these years, though it was not to reach real operational status by the time of the conflict which then lay only just beyond the horizon. This was the naval aircraft, with which the first experiments were beginning in 1910. By the end of 1911 an American, Eugene Ely, had demonstrated the possibility of flying off and landing an aeroplane on a platform erected on the deck of a cruiser, and in Great Britain the same feat was achieved by Lieutenant Samson using a platform over the bows of the battleship *Africa*. These feats led to the development of seaplanes, and from there to the development of seaplane carriers (old warships or merchant ships with a flight deck built above the forecastle from which seaplanes, mounted on trollies, could take off directly into the air, landing on the sea alongside the carrier ready to be hoisted aboard when their flight was over). These seaplane carriers, ready for use very shortly after war was declared, were direct ancestors of the aircraft carrier.

There is one more major revolution in ship development in the early part of the twentieth century to be described – the substituion of oil for coal as fuel for the marine steam engine. At first it was used only in warships, and then only in conjunction with coal, for the oil industry was not yet geared to a large enough scale of production for a complete transition to be possible. There was still a lot of ignorance in the world as to the extent of oil deposits, and, in his comment on a British Admiralty paper of 1906 pointing to the advantages of oil fuel for naval ships, a First Lord of the Admiralty could write: 'The substitution of oil for coal is impossible because the oil does not exist in the world in sufficient quantities.' Yet by 1914, in almost all the world's navies, virtually every ship up to and including battleships burned oil, at least in conjunction with coal, in their boilers, while many smaller warships, such as destroyers, gunboats, etc., carried no coal at all.

Above: Eugene Ely showed by 1911 that he could fly an aircraft off a wooden platform on board the cruiser *Pennsylvania*. When he landed as well, the foundations of naval aviation had been laid.

Thus, the first decade or so of the twentieth century saw a procession of new warships make their way down the slipway. The race had been started by the announcement of the German naval building programme in the Naval Law of 1898, which had galvanized every shipyard in the world into non-stop production. With the utmost ingenuity, naval constructors and architects were able to progress a step or two further with each successive design that came from their drawing boards, so that every year something new, something faster, something more powerful than the last, slid down into the sea. The world had never before seen fleets so big, so powerful, so widely dispersed across the oceans. And, so keen was the competition, internationally, for naval supremacy that very little was needed to set them all in motion.

It was, in a way, an irony that these immense fleets, representing an investment of thousands of millions of pounds, had been built without any experience of modern naval war, with no practical guidance as to how these expensive monsters would stand up to actual armed combat. The two small wars which had been fought at sea since the coming of the armoured ship taught very few worthwhile lessons. During the Sino-Japanese War (1894–95), a naval battle had been fought at the mouth of the Yalu, but all that it demonstrated was that a well-led superior modern fleet would always have the advantage over a poorly led, inferior, out-of-date fleet, even when the latter possessed a few larger ships. Perhaps the battle proved that a good margin of speed over an enemy allowed tactical flexibility, and that the offensive role was more likely to be successful than the defensive, but it offered no conclusions about warship construction and design.

The second small war, the Russo-Japanese War

(1904–05), provided two naval actions for the world's navies to study, one off Port Arthur and one in the Tsushima Straits. The first, off Port Arthur, indicated the ranges at which modern naval battles were likely to be fought, the Russian battleships opening fire at 20,000 yards (18,280 m) and dropping their shells 200 yards (180 m) beyond the Japanese ships. A little later in the action the Japanese flagship *Mikasa* was hit by a 12-inch shell at a range of 14,000 yards (12,800 m). A second notable lesson – and this lent support to the radical design of the British *Dreadnought* – was that in naval battle only the big gun counted. Both Russian and Japanese ships carried secondary batteries of 8-inch and 6-inch guns, as well as main batteries of 12-inch and 10-inch, and an eyewitness opinion expressed after the battle was that 'for all the respect they instill, 8-inch or 6-inch guns might just as well be pea-shooters.' The result at Tsushima, like that on the Yalu, again proved that the course of a naval battle, and its result, could be dictated by the admiral commanding the faster fleet, though there were other features of this battle which suggested that the Japanese success was not entirely attributable to this factor. In any case Tsushima had no real effect on battleship design, because, by the day it was fought (28 May 1905) the British Committee on Warship Design had long since reached its decisions and their new battleship, H.M.S. *Dreadnought*, was already in frame on her building slip in Portsmouth Dockyard. And she, with her all-big-gun armament of 12-inch guns and speed of 21 knots, already anticipated any of the lessons which could be learned from the actions of the Sino-Japanese and Russo-Japanese Wars, even though in fact her radical departure from previous battleship design owed nothing in its conception to either of them.

The conflict which was to set these vast fleets of warships in motion came in 1914, and the four years of war provided an acid test of the validity or otherwise of developments in warship design, construction and armament which had occurred throughout the previous years. Perhaps the hardest of the lessons which this new war had to teach was the proof that the big armoured cruiser was already an anachronism, less than twenty years from her original conception. So much had been hoped from her, so many dreams of naval glory embodied in her design, that her failure was a sad blow to the thousands who had believed that she held in her hands the keys to naval victory. What had happened was that in her short life she had already been overtaken by the new 'fast battleship' design and she had no fleet function to fulfill.

Another lesson that this war was to teach – a tremendously frustrating lesson to almost everyone who had anything to do with navies – was that so much money and power was locked up in each individual battleship that they had become too valuable to risk unduly in battle. The one extended naval battle of the war, that of Jutland on 31 May 1916, had seen the battleships of both sides turn away from the battle line whenever they were seriously threatened.

A third lesson, which took a lot more time to learn than it should have done, was that the big naval gun was no longer the dominant weapon at sea: it had been overtaken by the torpedo and the mine. They, and new weapons still to come, were strong factors in the eventual elimination of the battleship as a viable warship. But, until that lesson was learned, there were still some years of life ahead for this type of ship.

The last important lesson to be demonstrated in World War I was the power of the submarine, far beyond anything that had been predicted. Thanks to the heavy-oil engine it had been able to make its influence felt far out in the world's oceans, and its powers of destruction appeared to be virtually unlimited. It was still among the smallest of the world's warships, but by far the most lethal, and its effect upon the overall shape of the world's navies had already been immense, and through the next three or four decades was to become greater. During World War I, it was responsible for several new designs of ships, some whose sole purpose was to hunt and destroy this one type of vessel, others whose purpose was to screen and protect ships from underwater attack. Its huge depredations, particularly in attacks against merchant vessels, filled the world's shipbuilding and repair yards with orders and led also to a search for new shipbuilding materials as the call for steel, particularly for warship building, began to outrun the supply. A number of small merchant ships, required quickly to replace the many coasters which had fallen victim to the submarine, were built of concrete, reinforced with steel rods, but although useful temporarily to fill the gap, concrete proved to be too inflexible and too heavy a material with which to build a satisfactory ship. As yet, there was nothing to replace steel.

When the war ended, the exhausted combatants stood back to count the cost and to replan their shipping future. The first and most obvious task was to replace the immense tonnage of commercial shipping that had been lost in the war, for it was certain that, although the war had restricted the operation of seaborne

Above: The Russian battleship *Tsarevitch* was interned at the German port of Tsingtao after sustaining damage in the Battle of the Yellow Sea in August 1904.

could foresee that one result of the experience of war was a coming boom in the transportation of oil. Uses were also being developed for new raw materials, and for these new ships would need to be specially designed and built. If the first decades of the century had seen the introduction of many types of specialist ships, the following ones would see even more.

In warship development there were to be just as many changes. Right at the end of the war the first real aircraft carrier had emerged, taking the place of the seaplane carriers with which navies had been equipped when the war started. There was no one as yet who could foresee all the directions in which this new weapon would affect the traditional warship but that it would do so profoundly was accepted worldwide without question. The first aircraft carriers were no more than adaptations of existing ships, with a flat flight deck built over their entire length, but it was certain, even on the limited experience gained from these conversions, that purpose-built ships would inevitably be needed in due course.

However, in spite of all the lessons which had been learned, it was to be some time before the experiences of war were translated into warship development. The chief obstacle was a general lack of enthusiasm for military projects, not surprising in a world that had just endured four years of war, but the delay was going to cost the nations dear when another war loomed over the horizon.

Above: Artist's impression of Admiral Beatty's flagship, the battle-cruiser *Lion*, in action at Jutland. She escaped destruction from a cordite fire in one of her turrets, but her sister *Queen Mary* was lost with nearly all hands.

trade, there was still no alternative to the oceans as the main highway along which international trade could pass. And as the smoke cleared, it became equally certain that the volume of trade would grow at least as fast as it had done during the years before the war, and probably much faster, for the whole world was now hungry for the commodities which the war had denied it. But, though new ships were required in great numbers, they would not necessarily be the same ships as ten years earlier. Shipowners

Freak Ships

The old wooden sailing ship did not lend herself to experiment. Being entirely dependent on the wind for her motive power, she had to have a more or less conventional hull shape in order to make forward progress, and a more or less conventional sail plan in order to harness the power of the wind and convert it to forward propulsion. There were, of course, certain limits within which a ship designer was free to try and improve her performance – by altering the shape of her hull underwater, increasing the length-to-beam ratio, or changing the cut or arrangement of her sails – but basically she was always the same ship. However, with the introduction of the steam engine, which was able to impart motion to a ship in any direction, regardless of the wind, and iron construction, which gave much more flexibility to designers, there was almost no end to the possibilities for experiment with the design of special ships for special purposes. Not all of them were successful, and many were extremely odd.

One of the oddities was a collier, designed to bring coal down the east coast of England, from Newcastle to London, and built on the Thames at Blackwall in 1863. She was named the *Connector*, and her owners were registered as the Jointed Ship Company. The inventor's ingenious idea was to produce a ship somewhat like a railway train with an engine and two trucks, so that when fully loaded with coal she could detach a 'truck' at any port requiring coal, as she passed. It was an

idea with great possibilities, if it could be made to work, for the *Connector* could be loaded with coal for three different destinations, and deliver it with the minimum loss of time through the ship having to enter port and wait until the coal was unloaded before proceeding to the next port. The empty 'trucks' would be collected on the return voyage to Newcastle, and connected up again.

The ship was built with three separate hull sections, joined together by huge metal hinges, so that in a seaway each hull could pitch independently of the others. The engine was in the aftermost hull, which pushed the other two ahead of it. The latter were fitted with masts and sails, so that when they had been detached they could sail independently to their port of destination.

The *Connector* was tried out on the Thames, but on the day of the trial there was no wind, and so the sailing part of the experiment could not take place. Nevertheless, the ship proceeded up the river, detaching her two forward hulls *en route*, one by one, which, because it was windless, were secured to buoys, while the stern section carried on upriver. When she turned and came back, she picked up the two hulls which were secured to buoys, connected them up successfully, and returned to her starting point.

However, what was possible on a windless day, on the flat calm surface of the Thames, was not necessarily possible in a rough sea. The ship might have managed to survive intact if motion in a

rough sea involved only fore-and-aft pitching, though even this would have put a very severe strain on the connecting hinges. But sideways rolling – and it was inconceivable that all three parts would roll as one – would shear the connecting hinges as though they were made of matchwood, no matter how massively they were built. Even the inventor realised that his ship would never be able to stand the strain, and, in fact, the *Connector* never ventured out to sea at all.

A very weird ship was a battleship of completely circular design, built in Russia in 1875. She was designed by Vice Admiral Popov, with the idea of providing a steady platform for her big guns, whatever the state of the sea. She was an iron ship of 3,553 tons with a diameter of 101 ft (31 m). She was built at Nicolaev, on the Black Sea, and being as long as she was broad, could neither pitch nor roll in the heaviest of seas. Her armament consisted of two 11-inch guns mounted in a central circular armoured barbette, and she was powered by eight steam engines driving six propellers. Her guns were aimed by revolving the ship, using the outer propellers to provide the turning movement. She was given the name *Admiral Popov*, after her designer, and was considered so successful that a second battleship, named *Novgorod*, was later built to the same design. These two battleships were known in naval circles in many countries as 'popoffkas'.

At this stage in the development of control of the big naval gun, a steady

platform was a considerable asset, and in this respect these two ships had considerable advantages over the conventional battleship design. They were reasonably robust, but in anything of a sea they proceeded with their circular deck awash, as they had no more than a foot or two of freeboard. This meant that they were apt to pound, sometimes quite badly, in a rough sea, and the stresses involved placed a severe strain on their plating. It was also discovered that, although when used in rivers they handled quite well when going upstream, they were completely unmanageable when coming downstream, the rudders failing to grip the water so that they revolved continuously.

The *Admiral Popov* was inspected on her trials by Czar Nicholas II, who was deeply impressed by the absence of roll and pitch, even in a seaway. As he suffered badly from seasickness, though fond of the pleasures of yachting, he gave Admiral Popov instructions to design him a royal yacht on the same principle, though it was to look like a yacht and not like a floating dinner plate. In conjunction with the builders, Popov solved the problem by designing a more or less circular, or turbot-shaped, underwater hull and constructing a conventional yacht's upperworks on top of it, so that only the upperworks were visible above the water. The yacht was named *Livadia* and was built in Scotland by John Elder and Company, being

completed in 1880. Three engines installed in the submerged part of the hull drove three propellers, each 16 ft (4·9 m) in diameter, to give her a speed of 17 knots, while the royal cabins and staterooms occupied the part of the hull above water. The *Livadia* had a tonnage of 3,900, and was 235 ft (71·6 m) long, with a maximum underwater beam of 153 ft (46·6 m), and proved to be a very comfortable and successful yacht, being broken up in 1926 after forty-six years service. She had an odd arrangement of masts and funnels, her five masts being placed in pairs athwartships, like goal-posts, with the fifth on the centreline halfway between the pairs, and her three funnels were placed abreast.

The avoidance of seasickness was the basis for the design of another ship – this one by Sir Henry Bessemer, more famous perhaps as the inventor of the Bessemer process in the manufacture of steel than as a naval architect. She was built in 1875 as a cross-Channel steamer and named the *Bessemer*, after her designer. She had a perfectly normal hull and engines, but the passenger saloon was mounted on metal guides and could be manipulated by hydraulic machinery so that it would always remain level, no matter what the angle of roll or pitch of the ship herself. This hydraulic machinery was controlled by an engineer, and was regulated by reference to a large spirit-level set in the deck of the saloon. The idea worked reasonably well on its first trial, as the sea was smooth and the roll was very small and slow. On her second trip from Dover to Calais, the sea was rougher, and the engineer on duty found that he could not produce counteracting movements from the hydraulic machinery fast enough to match the amount of roll. No more ships were built to this design, as it was at that time impossible to get a quick enough response from machinery to meet, or anticipate, the movements of a ship in a seaway. But it could be said that the seed of Bessemer's idea took root through the years, and eventually blossomed into the automatic ship stabilizers of today.

Far left: The articulated *Connector*.

Above left and left: The circular Russian *Novgorod*, and the *Bessemer*.

Chapter Eleven
The Legacy of War

When World War I ended, the nations which had fought in it, particularly the maritime nations, had to pause and take stock. The losses in terms of ships, both mercantile and naval, on both sides had been prodigious, but much more so in the case of the Allies (Britain, France, Italy, the United States) and neutral countries than in that of the central powers (Germany, Austria, Turkey). This was natural and to be expected, for the sea blockade, imposed by the Allies at the start of the war and maintained throughout it, virtually closed the oceans to any shipping but their own.

The enormous losses were mainly due to the new weapons, the mine and torpedo. Mines, it is true, had been first introduced as a naval weapon during the Crimean War (1854–56), but that particular mining operation had been on so small a scale that it had not called for any changes in ship construction to meet the danger, and indeed the mines themselves were too small to be the lethal destroyers that they had become sixty years later. But even more devastating, to warships as much as merchant ships, was the torpedo, especially when discharged from a submarine. It was this weapon which was responsible for the biggest proportion of the losses.

When, at the end of the war, a final count was made of allied merchant ships lost through enemy action, the total came to 5,531 vessels totalling 12,850,814 gross tons. To that figure must be added the tonnage lost during the war years through 'natural' causes, such as shipwreck, collision, stress of weather, etc., and the final loss figure comes to just over 15,000,000 gross tons. Against that figure should be set the tonnage of ships built during the war – and a massive effort was made, worldwide, to try to keep pace with the rate of wartime loss – so that

Left: Two American battleships lead a squadron of heavy cruisers into Lingayen Gulf in the Philippines, October 1944, to begin the bombardment before an amphibious assault against the Japanese.

the net loss of allied shipping amounted to 1,811,000 gross tons. British shipping had fared more disastrously. At the beginning of the war she owned and operated about 45 per cent of the world total. During the war she lost through enemy action 2,480 ships, totalling 7,759,090 gross tons, and her net loss, allowing for new ships built, amounted to 3,084,000 gross tons, or approximately 16 per cent of her pre-war total.

It was very much the same story with regard to warship losses. Great Britain, having borne the brunt of the naval war throughout the four years of its duration, had lost proportionately more than any other naval power, so that, both in terms of warship and merchant ship tonnage, she emerged from the conflict relatively worse off than any other nation. And if this were true of her shipping, it was equally true of her economy. Being more impoverished than most other combatants, owing to the magnitude of her war effort, the trident of sea power was about to leave her hands, not entirely because she could no longer afford the financial burden of retaining it, but in part also because of the deep revulsion of the British nation against warlike projects, caused by the massive slaughter of young men on the Western Front.

The normal course of events after a major naval war would have been to analyze and assess the performance of the various types of ships engaged, before dashing into placing repeat orders to make good the war losses. And one might expect this to be particularly the case after a major war in which new and untried types of warships had been engaged. The two previous wars fought between fleets of armoured ships, the Sino-Japanese and Russo-Japanese Wars, had been too small and localized, and between fleets too unequal in quality and training, for valid lessons to be learned; but when World War I ended in 1918, there existed an extensive fund of experience of large-scale naval conflict, detailed analysis of which would certainly have produced new lines for warship development in the future.

Above: The British battleship *Rodney* and her sister *Nelson* were built under the provisions of the Washington Treaty. Although outlandish in appearance they were in fact the only ships to incorporate war-experience adopting a very advanced design. They were the most modern capital ships in the Royal Navy in 1939.

Even as the war ended, two of the main maritime nations were already engaged on big warship building programmes, likely to perpetuate the existing types of capital ship. European eyes had, of course, been focussed on the North Sea and the Atlantic Ocean throughout the war, but other eyes were now looking at the Pacific. A gigantic building programme was getting under way in the United States with the authorization by Congress of the building of six new battleships of 43,200 tons, each carrying twelve 16-inch guns, and six new battle-cruisers of 43,000 tons, each carrying eight 16-inch guns. Japan had already built two 33,800-ton battleships carrying eight 16-inch guns, was building two more of 39,900 tons to carry ten 16-inch guns each and two battle-cruisers of 43,000 tons to carry eight 16-inch guns each, and had plans for building two or three 45,000-tonners, each with eight 16-inch guns, in the next year or two. Faced with this threat to her naval supremacy, Great Britain in 1921 ordered four 48,000-ton battle-cruisers mounting nine 16-inch guns each, to be followed by an unspecified number (probably four or five) of 48,500-ton battleships, also with a main armament of 16-inch guns and a designed speed of 32 knots.

Although the United States was the first in the field in ordering these immense new ships, the fact that Japan immediately followed suit, and later Great Britain, caused the Americans to pause in their plans. The estimated cost of these huge warships was the then astronomical

sum of £252 million. And that was only the start, for such ships would need to be supported by large numbers of cruisers and destroyers if they were to form a balanced fighting fleet. Appalled by the shipbuilding snowball which they had set in motion, and by the danger of a Pacific war if a naval race were to develop between America and Japan, politicians in the United States decided to try to stop it by calling a disarmament conference in Washington, in the hope of reaching an international agreement on the limitation of naval armaments. It was held in 1921–22, with the main naval nations, France, Great Britain, Italy, Japan and the United States taking part.

After a great deal of argument and bargaining, the Washington Conference resulted in the following agreements:

(i) The British and American battlefleets to be limited to 580,450 and 500,650 tons respectively, with the Japanese to 301,320, the French 221,170 and Italian 182,800.

(ii) Capital ships to be limited to 35,000 tons displacement, and guns to a maximum of 16-in. (301-mm) calibre.

(iii) Existing capital ships not to be replaced less than twenty years from their date of completion, and no new construction to take place in the meantime.

(iv) Reconstruction of existing capital ships not to add more than 3,000 tons, and to be restricted purely to defence against submarine and air attack.

There were a few small variations to allow for

the two completed Japanese battleships, Great Britain being allowed to build two new ones and the United States being allowed to retain three of the four already on the stocks, while scrapping the fourth. Nevertheless, the Washington Treaty hit the British Navy harder than any other, as it involved scrapping 657 warships, totalling 1,500,000 tons.

As a means of halting the threatened arms race the agreement reached at Washington succeeded admirably, but at the same time it removed much of the incentive for experiments in new types of warship better suited for modern warfare. The treaty merely ensured the survival of the existing type of battle fleet, and, in a way, set the seal of international approval on the continued organization of the world's navies as they had been constituted in 1914. Few nations were prepared to expend much energy in this field of research and development, if they were not permitted to put the results into practice in the building of new ships. But, more important, it appeared to substantiate, by its endorsement of the battleship and her big guns, the claim of the gun still to be the dominant weapon at sea. All the experience of the four years of war between 1914 and 1918 went to show that the importance of the big gun had been exaggerated in relation to that of the torpedo and the mine, which had, between them, claimed so many more ships than had the gun.

Nevertheless, the war had taught one or two unmistakable lessons, one of which was the vulnerability of the big armoured cruiser, on which so many navies had spent millions of pounds in the years leading up to the war. No more were built. Their place had been taken more efficiently and safely by the fast battleship, and although some nations continued to build what they called battle-cruisers, they were that in name only for they carried the same thickness of armoured protection as did the battleship.

Another unmistakable lesson was the lethality of an underwater torpedo hit, even upon heavily armoured ships. The British battleship *Formidable* was sunk in the English Channel by a single torpedo hit; the armoured cruisers *Aboukir*, *Cressy*, and *Hogue* were all sunk in the course of one morning by torpedo hits from a single German submarine off the Belgian coast. A partial answer to this danger was to increase the speed of ships, on the grounds that it was more difficult for a submarine to hit a fast-moving ship than a slow one, and this was reflected in the increase of battleship speed over the next twenty years from an average of about 19 or 20 knots in 1918 to

around 29 or 30 knots in 1940. Another was to build outward bulges on the underwater hull, so that when a torpedo hit the ship the main force of the explosion would be taken on the plating of the bulge, leaving the inner hull, it was hoped, more or less undamaged. This was the solution chosen by many navies for existing battleships, under the clause in the Washington Treaty allowing reconstruction up to a limit of 3,000 tons. But, in cases of new construction, the practice of adding an outer bulge sometimes produced serious problems. Great Britain, for example, was permitted to build two new battleships, as mentioned above, and naturally designed them to the full 35,000-tons maximum. The effect of adding anti-torpedo bulges outside the armoured hull would have been to make them too wide to enter most of the existing dry-docks in the country. The difficulty was overcome by retaining the planned hull dimensions, but sloping the main armoured belt inwards, so that a space was created between the outer skin and the armour – in effect an inwards bulge instead of an outwards one. These changes in design, with some local variations, became a feature of battleship design throughout the world. Although it could not remove all the danger from a torpedo hit, it did make it more difficult to sink a battleship by a single torpedo, or even a salvo of torpedoes unless, by a lucky chance, two torpedoes hit consecutively in exactly the same place along the hull, or the flash of a torpedo explosion found its way into a cordite magazine.

Defence against the mine was much more

Above: The cruiser HMS *Endymion* and her three sisters were specially 'bulged' against torpedo-attack to allow them to provide fire support off the Gallipoli beaches in 1915.

difficult. The conventional double bottom, a feature of all shipbuilding for the previous seventy years, offered virtually no protection. The new battleship *Audacious*, only completed in 1913, struck a mine off the north coast of Ireland in 1914 and sank before she could be towed to the shore and beached, in spite of her extensive division into watertight compartments and double bottom. A countermeasure to the moored mine was achieved later in the war with the invention of the paravane, but, even as it was being introduced, a new design of mine, against which the paravane was useless, was being produced. This was the magnetic mine, first used operationally in 1918, which was to pose an immense threat to shipping twenty years later. The mine remained a menace against which no measures of defence in the design or construction of ships was adequate. It called instead for a new type of warship to be developed, in the shape of the minesweeper.

World War I ended before the full potential of aircraft in a fighting role at sea could be developed, although enough was by then known to indicate that they were certain to have a very profound effect indeed. Already, aircraft had flown off and landed on the flying decks of converted ships under way at sea; a ship at sea had been sunk by a torpedo dropped from a seaplane; a seaplane had been launched from a carrier for reconnaissance duties (during the early stages of the battle of Jutland in May 1916). When all these were considered in the light of the limited evolution which the flying machine had undergone in the few years since the Wright brothers had demonstrated the possibilities of heavier-than-air flight, it was quite clear that, as the aeroplane evolved further, its influence on naval warfare was bound to be enormous.

The first essential step along this new road was to design and produce a ship capable of stowing and handling its own aircraft, with hangars below deck for stowing and servicing them, and a flight deck for flying off and landing on. As has been seen, the first ships designed to handle aircraft were the seaplane carriers developed at the beginning of World War I, each operating up to a dozen seaplanes, used purely for fleet reconnaissance duties. These were all ships converted for the purpose, for the most part small liners or cross-Channel ferries, with the speed required to keep up with a battle fleet at sea. As the war progressed, some larger naval ships were similarly converted, not for seaplanes, whose value for many naval duties was restricted by the large floats that they had to carry, but for aircraft with conventional wheeled undercarriages, whose radius of action was always greater than that of a seaplane. All these early

carriers had a large flight deck forward of the bridge structure, quite suitable for an aircraft to fly off, but almost impossible for one to land on. It was occasionally done – one was successfully landed on the flight deck of H.M.S. *Furious* in 1917 – but it was an operation fraught with danger, and most pilots who attempted it finished up over the side and in the sea.

Part of the problem was solved when the *Furious* was taken into the dockyard and an after flight deck constructed abaft the bridge structure, giving her in effect two separate flying decks, one forward and one aft, the after deck being used for landing. But this again was unsatisfactory, as there was not enough length of deck to bring the aircraft to a stop before it hit the bridge structure. The next obvious step was to bring in another ship and give her an unobstructed deck over her whole length. This

Top: The dreadnought battleship *Audacious* sinking after running into a German minefield.

Above: The answer to mines was the paravane, a cutting device which could be towed on either side of a ship. Here sailors hoist the port paravane out on a boom.

Top: The aircraft carrier *Argus* was converted from a liner, and commissioned late in 1918. She was the first flush-decked carrier and proved successful.

Above: Squadron Commander Dunning made the first deck-landing on the deck of HMS *Furious*, but on his second attempt the aircraft skidded overboard and he was drowned.

was realised in H.M.S. *Argus,* but not without the need for a great deal of ingenuity to achieve the desired result. Her navigating bridge, an obvious necessity in every ship, was linked to a hydraulic system whereby it was raised or lowered as required, providing the flush deck while aircraft were being operated. Her funnels were replaced by a system of trunking which discharged the boiler smoke and hot gases over the stern.

This arrangement of bridge and funnels was moderately successful, but the retractable bridge was plainly not ideal, while the hot boiler gases discharged over the stern affected the stability of the aircraft just at the moment that they were coming in to land. So another carrier, H.M.S. *Eagle,* was brought in for reconversion. She had started life as a battleship, the *Almirante Cochrane,* being built in Britain for the Chilean

navy, but had been taken over during the war while still on the stocks and completed as a carrier. She was now reconverted, with a flight deck running the whole length of the ship, but with her bridge superstructure, mast and funnels as a permanent structure on the starboard side. Although this narrowed the flight deck amidships, it was not so much that aircraft met with any interference. She emerged in her new shape in 1920, and this design was endorsed in 1923 when H.M.S. *Hermes,* the first ship to be built from the keel up as an aircraft carrier, also emerged with her bridge and funnels offset to starboard. These two ships were known as 'island' carriers, the island being the bridge superstructure, and it was this that became standard carrier design in all the world's navies.

The American and Japanese navies both commissioned their first small aircraft carriers, the *Langley* and *Hosho* respectively, in 1922. Both were flush-decked, with funnels offset to one side and lowered to deck level when flying operations were in progress. No more aircraft carriers were built until after the signing of the Washington Treaty, when Britain, the United States and Japan each converted two more ships (battleships or battle-cruisers) which would otherwise have been scrapped under the terms of the Treaty. All of them were converted to the island design.

The Washington Naval Treaty was due to expire at the end of 1936, and although there had been comparatively little naval building around the world, except of the smaller classes of warship, most navies had their plans ready for quick expansion once the treaty limitations

were removed. Little that was radically new in design or development had emerged during the treaty years, except perhaps in the case of the destroyer where there was a fairly large increase in overall size, while, in Britain, the memory of the mine warfare of 1914–18 had produced a minelayer of radical design. In World War I minelaying had been undertaken by fast liners converted for the task, or by destroyers similarly converted, and Germany had adapted some of her submarines to lay mines while submerged. The essence of surface minelaying was speed, for if a minefield in enemy waters was to be effective it had to be laid under the cover of darkness, with the ships engaged well clear of the area both before and after the actual lay. Great Britain built H.M.S. *Adventure* in 1926 as a cruiser-minelayer, a new type of ship, but instead of being fitted with steam turbines which could have provided the speed essential for the task, she was given instead heavy-oil diesel engines which could not. She was a failure. Britain also built minelaying submarines, but they, too, turned out to be a doubtful investment, for by the time the next war came to be fought most minelaying in enemy waters was better and more expeditiously done by aircraft.

During the years of the Washington Treaty, with virtually no new building of capital ships taking place, a protracted argument raged about the vulnerability of the battleship to bombs. There were some who held that the advent of the aeroplane made the battleship obsolete, since so large a ship was a sitting target to an aeroplane with a bomb. The other side of the argument was that a bomb dropped from 12,000 ft (3,660 m) takes 28 seconds to fall, that a battleship at 21 knots moves 1,000 ft (300 m) during that time, that she would therefore be

very difficult to hit even if she held a straight course, and that if she were steering a zigzag course it would be virtually impossible. So an old battleship, the *Agamemnon,* had her guns and other valuable gear removed, and was fitted with radio-control for her steering gear, worked from an attendant destroyer. A series of exercises were held in which aircraft attacked her with bombs, in varying conditions of wind and sea and at heights of from 12,000 to 5,000 ft (1,520 m). During these exercises, 114 bombs were dropped, but not a single one hit the ship. Similar results were obtained in bombing trials carried out by other navies. Nevertheless, the threat of attack from the air was taken seriously, and an anti-aircraft armament was added to the gun establishment of all large warships.

By the beginning of 1937, when the limitations of the Treaty were lifted and the world's navies again began to build big warships, there was again, as in the years before World War I, a threat to the naval balance of power, and again it was Germany. As a result of her defeat in 1918, her navy had been limited to six old battleships, with an age limit of twenty years, and no replacement was allowed to exceed 10,000 tons (10,160 tonnes) displacement. In 1929 she laid down the first of three heavy cruisers, and as the details gradually became known, it was clear that she was of a novel and most provocative design. Although declared as being within the tonnage limit of 10,000, she was actually of 12,000 tons (12,200 tonnes), the first of a long list of deliberate underdeclarations by which Germany consistently built larger ships than permitted by the treaty. She mounted a heavy armament of six 11-inch guns, eight 5-inch, and six 4·1-inch, and she was powered by three sets of diesel engines which gave her a maximum speed of 28 knots, and a radius of action of 10,000 nautical miles at 20 knots. It was obvious from her armament and range that she was designed purely for commerce raiding, and with her 11-inch guns she could out-shoot any other cruiser in the world. Even her construction was novel, for in order to save the weight of rivetting her hull plates, bulkheads and decks were welded.

Although officially described as a 'cruiser', the rest of the world coined a new name for her, describing her as a 'pocket-battleship'. She was the *Deutschland,* later renamed *Lützow,* and in 1931 and 1932 she was followed by two larger sisters, the *Graf Spee* and *Scheer,* of the same design, but with thicker armour protection, bringing their displacement tonnage up to 12,500 tons (12,700 tonnes).

More was to follow. In 1934, with Hitler established as German chancellor, two fast battleships, the *Scharnhorst* and *Gneisenau,* were laid down. They were declared at 26,000 tons (26,400 tonnes) displacement, but were in fact 32,000 tons (32,500 tonnes), and, with a maximum speed of 32 knots and a radius of action of 10,000 miles, they were immensely versatile and powerful. In the same year, Hitler denounced the Treaty of Versailles, under which the naval limitations had been imposed, and announced the building of two more fast battleships to the maximum tonnage agreed around the world, 35,000 tons. These were the *Bismarck* and *Tirpitz,* which eventually emerged as 31-knot battleships of 42,000 tons (42,800 tonnes) displacement each. Since, at the same time, it became known that Germany had secretly built twenty submarines in contravention of the Treaty, it was obvious that she was already deeply engaged in rapid naval rearmament and thereby threatening the naval balance round the world, so painstakingly engineered at Washington. By 1939 she was also building heavy cruisers, declared at the agreed world maximum of 10,000 tons, which, in fact, when completed had a displacement of 15,000 tons (15,200 tonnes). All these ships were part of what was known in Germany as the 'Z' plan, designed to create a navy by 1945, consisting of 13 modern battleships, 4 aircraft carriers, 33 cruisers, 250 submarines, and a large force of destroyers. In 1939 two more 'Z' plan battleships were laid down at Hamburg, to be named *Friedrich der Grosse* and *Gross Deutschland.* They were to be monsters of 50,000 tons (50,800 tonnes) displacement, but with diesel engines instead of the steam turbines of the *Bismarck* and *Tirpitz.* The remaining battleships of the 'Z' plan, which never got beyond the drawing board, were even more extreme in conception, ranging from 84,000 tons (85,300 tonnes) to 120,000 tons (121,900 tonnes). It was perhaps fortunate for the Allies that World War II broke out in 1939 and not in 1945, when the 'Z' programme of naval building might have been complete. Another fortunate event occurred on 31 December 1942, when an escort group of British destroyers drove off a superior German force, including the pocket battleship *Lützow,* which was trying to attack a convoy of merchant ships. This action completely destroyed Hitler's faith in the battleship. All building work on the 50,000-ton leviathans at Hamburg was stopped, and the remainder of the 'Z' plan building cancelled.

The main interest in these German battleships, actual and projected, lies in the fact that, unlike all other battleships in the world, they were not designed for battle, but for commerce raiding. That was the reason for fitting them with diesel

243

Below: The Japanese battleship *Mutsu*.

Bottom: The *Bismarck* in a Norwegian fjord. Her destruction in 1941 marked a turning point in the naval war.

propulsion which, being a more economical user of fuel than a steam boiler, almost doubled their radius of action. The impact of these monsters, had they ever been loosed on the world's trade routes, defies imagination, especially in the light of the fact that it needed forty-eight surface warships to hunt down and destroy the *Bismarck* in 1941.

On the other side of the world Japan was also entering the monster battleship stakes. Two ships of 65,000 tons (66,000 tonnes) displacement, each mounting nine 18·1-inch guns, were laid down in 1936 under conditions of great secrecy, being both concealed from the public gaze behind a mile of sisal matting. Contrary to the German philosophy of battleship warfare, these two, the *Musashi* and *Yamato*, were designed for battle against other battleships, and it was ironic that both of them were sunk by air attack before they could fire a single shell from their immense guns at another ship of their own breed.

Right at the other end of the scale of naval developments was the landing craft, a box-like vessel with a hinged ramp in place of the conventional bow. Propulsion was by internal combustion engine and the small craft drew so little water that they could reach a shelving shore and land their occupants dryshod, or through only a few inches of water, when the ramp was lowered. These military landing craft were first developed by Japan for war in Manchuria, although the germ of the idea had been formed in 1915 with the Anzac landings on the Gallipoli beaches in the eastern Mediterranean. The Japanese craft were seen in action in Manchuria by several foreign observers who were so impressed by their obvious value in amphibious assaults on an enemy-held coast

that they persuaded their own governments to introduce similar craft. Until 1939 this was done on only a tiny scale, both in Britain and in the United States, but by 1941, after two years of war, the original small landing craft, with its capacity for landing perhaps one platoon of men, had been developed into a whole complex of ships designed for this one purpose. They ranged from big infantry and tank landing ships, for carrying troops and all their fighting equipment in bulk, to small assault craft, slung from davits on the landing ship, to put them ashore with their varied assault weapons. The smaller craft were of simple construction to allow for rapid production – steel, box-sided craft with a diesel or petrol engine, designed to ground themselves bows-on to a shelving shore-line and discharge their burden, human or mechanical, directly on to the shore over the lowered bow ramp. Many of the big infantry landing ships were converted liners, their role in an assault landing being to lie offshore and land their troops in their own assault craft.

So, under the stimulus of war, a completely new species of ship was developed, and, although the initial design was concerned entirely with the requirements of amphibious warfare, it was found after the war was over that there were a number of peacetime operations where they could prove of enduring value. The wartime tank assault craft made an admirable short-haul car ferry for access to small island communities, and adaptations of these craft served well for the carriage of supplies and for inter-island trade where the use of a larger conventional merchant vessel would prove uneconomic.

Before leaving naval development, a word needs to be said about the submarine problem, in relation to the defence of trade in wartime. As has been mentioned, the losses of merchant shipping during World War I to submarine attack were prodigious and the answer to it was only produced towards the end of the war, in the shape of the convoy system. The greatest sufferer in terms of merchant ship losses during that war had been Britain, and if a second similar war were to take place, she would again, by reason of her geographical position and dependence on overseas trade, be worst hit. During the years of peace a means of underwater detection of submarines, known as 'Asdic', had been developed, and so great was the faith put by Britain in this new invention that she felt able to neglect the building of destroyer-type ships suitable as escorts for convoys. But, as the war clouds gathered over Europe in 1937 and 1938, and a period of feverish naval rearmament began, it became obvious that, once again, merchant shipping would need to be organized into convoys, if it were to have any defence at all against attack by submarine or surface raiders. It was a problem that affected Britain more than any other nation, and in 1937 and 1938 she found herself remarkably unprepared to meet it. Her faith in the Asdic submarine detectors was waning as a result of the experience of many fleet exercises, and she had to face the stark reality

Below: US infantrymen wade ashore from a Landing Craft Medium (LCM). Thousands of these ungainly but vital craft were used in amphibious operations.

of a repetition of her World War I experience of unrestricted submarine warfare directed against merchant shipping. A new type of small warship was therefore developed during the last years of peace, designed especially for this type of warfare and known generically as an 'escort vessel'. She was something less sophisticated than a destroyer, but larger and more robust than the trawlers which, fitted with Asdic and anti-submarine weapons, were adequate escorts for coastal and short-range convoys. Under this one generic name, three new types of escort were developed during the next four or five years – the frigate, the sloop and the corvette. Of these, the largest was the frigate, first put in hand in 1940, a ship of around 1,500 tons displacement with a good speed, fairly long endurance, and an impressive array of anti-submarine weapons in the shape of 4-inch guns and depth-charges. The sloop, smaller and slower, did not have the range required for full ocean convoy duty, but was a valuable ship in anti-submarine warfare, particularly when it became possible to form support groups to reinforce the escort group of a convoy coming under actual submarine attack as required. The last of the trio was the corvette, a small vessel of 860 to 900 tons based on the design of the whalecatcher, sturdy little ships of great endurance and able to stand up to the stormiest weather. They were simple, easy to build, and were produced quickly in very large numbers. With a maximum speed of only 16 knots, they were too slow to catch a submarine escaping on the surface, but nevertheless did yeoman service in escort work until the larger and more powerful frigates and sloops were built. Being based on the whale-catcher design with its rounded hull sections, they rolled horribly in a seaway, and were very uncomfortable ships in rough weather, but at least they helped to hold the fort until the bigger escorts came along.

Just as warships were changing rapidly, so was merchant shipping. The pattern of world trade had much to do with the change, for the manufacturing industry was turning even more quickly to new methods of mass production to satisfy the needs of an increasingly affluent

Below: Over 300 'Flower' class corvettes were built in British and Canadian shipyards as cheap convoy escorts. The design was based on a large whalecatcher.

world, and this higher level of production meant that ships were urgently needed for its distribution. The first task was to replace the tonnage sunk during the war, which was done mainly with fewer ships of larger individual tonnage, the majority being mixed cargo carriers and passenger liners of the type which had borne the brunt of the sinkings. At the same time, new specialist ships had to be built on a large scale to serve new industries. An example is provided by the motor car. Under the spur of war the internal combustion engine underwent rapid and extensive development, for application to aircraft as well as motor vehicles, and when the war ended it was possible to mass-produce cheap motor cars, bringing them within the price range of a huge new public. Although as yet its transport from maker to market did not call for a specialized design of ship, the petrol that it consumed necessitated a very large increase in tanker tonnage. With the main oil producers concentrated in the Middle East and the main consumers concentrated in the West, the overall size of tankers was generally limited by the maximum that could use the Suez Canal. In the third and fourth decades of the twentieth

Above: Fifty elderly destroyers were handed over to the Royal Navy by the US Navy in September 1940. They served with distinction until 1945, when the survivors were returned.

century, when the oil boom was growing almost daily to keep abreast of soaring car production, a tanker of around 25,000 tons was a big one. Oil was not the only trade affected by the car boom: rubber, for tyres, from Malaya and Borneo was another commodity that shared in the boom and required ships to transport it.

Tankers were built with longitudinal, as well as transverse, bulkheads, to provide a large number of separate tanks for the oil – a precaution to minimize the escape of oil in the case of the

vessel being holed. Transverse cofferdams were built right across the ship both forward of and abaft the tanks to isolate the oil from the dry cargo space forward and the engine room aft, as a safety measure. Steam pump rooms, also built transversely across the ship between every section of tanks (usually containing about twelve), acted as additional cofferdams. The majority of tankers had dry cargo space under the forecastle deck, and the engine room below the poop deck, crew accommodation being in the poop with, officers' cabins in the bridge structure. In most tankers built between the wars, the bridge structure was amidships, with a longitudinal monkey bridge connecting the forecastle, bridge and poop deck.

Probably the most important single development in merchant shipping during the years between the wars was the changeover from coal to oil as the main bunker fuel for ships. It was a cleaner fuel than coal, with a distinctly greater thermal efficiency, and, at the same time, much easier to handle, being pumped into fuel tanks on board instead of manhandled from a collier or coaling wharf across the deck into coal bunkers, where sweating stokers had to trim it to fill all the corners. At the same time, a great many shipowners adopted the heavy-oil diesel engine as the propulsion unit on board their ships, again because it was more economical to run, especially in manpower, doing away with the need for boilers and the stokers to fire them. Here again, this was largely a legacy from World War I, for it was the needs of the submarine which had stimulated research into the production of powerful and reliable diesel engines.

But the biggest of the post-war revolutions in shipping was in the passenger trade, particularly the luxury liner, which was to grow to an unparalleled size. The huge rush of emigration which had had such an influence on the passenger trade in the late nineteenth and early twentieth century had eased off considerably. There were many people still eager to start a new life in another part of the world, but whereas in earlier years they had been counted in millions, now they were counted only in hundreds of thousands. And the days of crowded steerage spaces were passing; would-be emigrants were richer, or were helped by subsidized passages to countries needing immigrants. Passenger ships were now built with cabins for all they carried. A few shipping lines, in particular some of those of Mediterranean nations operating to South America, still ran a few elderly passenger ships with the old-fashioned steerage accommodation, because of local poverty and the inability of some emigrants to afford cabin accommodation. As the world grew richer, even these few ships quickly became obsolescent, and were withdrawn, either for scrapping, or conversion to all-cabin accommodation, or for sale to another shipping line further down the social scale.

At the top end of the passenger liner business, the most important attractions were still luxury and speed, as they had been in the years before the war. Several of the pre-war luxury liners had been sunk, either in action against other ships, after they had been converted into armed merchant cruisers, or by torpedo from a submarine. One of the best-known to suffer the latter fate was the *Lusitania*, sister-ship of the *Mauretania*, which was sunk off southern Ireland in 1915 by the German submarine U.20. Replacement tonnage was quickly built after the war, still with the same degree of luxury as before, but with more modern machinery capable of producing higher speeds.

Although fine, luxurious, and fast liners were built for all the main passenger trade routes, to South Africa, India, China, Australia, and South America, and across the Pacific from the west coast of America to Far Eastern and Australian ports, it was still the North Atlantic route which carried the most prestige and attracted the most competition. The race for the largest and most prestigious liner was begun by France when, in 1932, the mighty *Normandie* was launched. She was the first ship over 1,000 ft long, and her dimensions of 1,029 ft (313·6 m) overall, 117·8 ft (35·9 m) beam, and 36·6 ft (11·2 m) draught gave her a gross tonnage of 86,496 tons. To drive this huge bulk through the water at a record average speed of 31·3 knots eastbound, with which for a short time she held the Blue Riband of the Atlantic, required an engine horsepower of 160,000. She was built with a total of eleven decks and had cabin accommodation in three classes for 2,170 passengers, who required a crew of 1,320 to look after them.

Two years later, in 1934, the Cunard Line launched their reply, in the shape of the *Queen Mary*. She was slightly smaller than the *Normandie*, her dimensions of 1,019·5 ft. × 118·7 ft × 39·6 ft (310·7 m × 36·2 m × 12·1 m) giving her a gross tonnage of 81,237 tons. With engines of the same horsepower as the *Normandie* she proved fractionally faster, with an average maximum speed of 31·69 knots eastbound. She had twelve decks, with a passenger capacity of 776 in the first class, 784 in the tourist class, and 579 in the third class – a total of 1,939.

The *Queen Mary* was followed four years later by the *Queen Elizabeth*. Of similar design,

but slightly larger, she had an overall length of 1,031 ft (314·2 m) and a gross tonnage of 82,998 tons. Although launched in 1938, her fitting-out was overtaken by the outbreak of war in 1939, and it was not until October 1946, when the war had been over for a year and a half, that she made her first appearance on the Atlantic as a passenger liner operating between Southampton and New York.

Other maritime nations joined in the race for size, speed and luxury, the United States, Italy and Germany all building transatlantic giants in their desire to capture the cream of the passenger traffic. As yet there was no competition except from other liners, and, if a liner had a slight edge in the comfort of her cabins, the quality and variety of her cuisine, a fraction of a knot in speed, or a faithful following of passengers who would prefer her to any other ship, she would never sail empty. But already the writing was on the wall. Alcock and Brown, Lindbergh,

Left: The giant hull of the liner *Queen Mary* under construction on the Clyde.

Below: The *Queen Elizabeth* serving as a troopship during wartime.

Bottom: The *Queen Mary* in her peacetime livery.

Amelia Earhart, and one or two others had piloted flimsy aircraft across the Atlantic; Cobham, Mollison and Amy Johnson had pioneered the way by air to South Africa and Australia. After another world war, with its intensification of research and development, these isolated achievements would turn into a new era of mass air travel, in which the mighty ocean liners could not survive.

Before leaving these magnificent ships it is of interest to see what happened to them during the war which engulfed the world in 1939. Some were unfortunate, the *Normandie,* lying in New York harbour when France was overrun by the Germans in 1940, was taken over by the United States for conversion into a troop transport, being renamed the *Lafayette.* In 1942 she caught fire alongside her fitting-out wharf, and capsized under the weight of water pumped into her to extinguish the fire. She lay on her

side where she capsized for four years, being then sold for a small sum to be broken up for scrap. The German *Bremen,* flagship of the German Norddeutscher-Lloyd Line, escaped from New York at the outbreak of war, evaded the British fleet, and eventually reached Germany safely by sailing a northerly course and sheltering for a few weeks in the Russian port of Murmansk. However, when she reached Germany there was no useful employment for her, and she finally had her back broken when she was hit by bombs during an air raid.

The British *Queen Mary* and *Queen Elizabeth* were converted into troop transports at the beginning of the war, with a carrying capacity of 8,200 each, and until 1943 were based in Sydney Australia, and employed continuously worldwide in the carriage of troops. In April 1943 they were both brought into the Atlantic, their troop-carrying capacity increased to over 15,000 during the summer months and 12,000–13,000 in the winter, and were used for the build-up of American and Canadian troops prior to the invasion of Europe in 1944. Of the 865,000 American and Canadian troops brought to the United Kingdom across the Atlantic, 320,000 were carried in these two ships alone. Other liners, American, Belgian, Canadian, Dutch and Norwegian, as well as British, were converted for this type of war service, and because of their great speed they made their passages across the Atlantic unescorted, because of the virtual impossibility of a submarine, restricted in her movements by her slow underwater speed, reaching an attacking position before the liner had disappeared over the horizon.

Other liners were taken into navies for

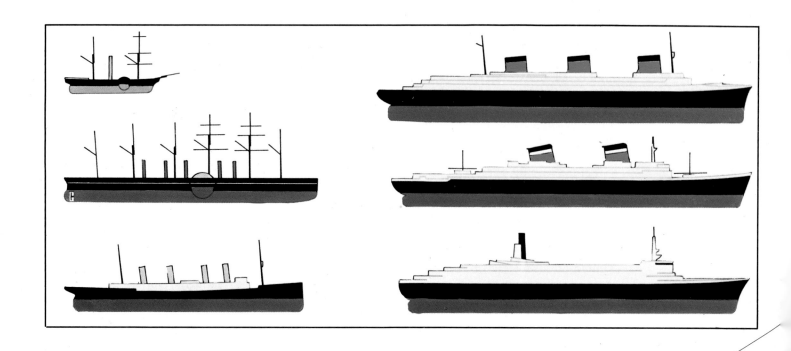

Normandie
(1932)

Length 1,029 ft (313·6 m) *Beam* 117·8 ft (35·9 m)
Draught 36·6 ft (11·2 m) *Gross tonnage* 86,496
Speed 32 knots *Crew* 1,320 *Passenger capacity* 2,170

The *Normandie*, the first ship ever to exceed 1,000 ft in length, was for a time the largest ship in the world and the holder of the Blue Riband of the Atlantic with an average speed of 31·3 knots. Although she soon lost both titles, the first to the *Queen Elizabeth* by a mere 2 ft (60 cm) in 1938 and the second to the *Queen Mary* in 1936, she was virtually the ultimate development in size of the ocean liner. She was built for the Compagnie Générale Transatlantique and had turbo-electric propulsion. She operated on the Atlantic run until France fell in 1940. Renamed the *Lafayette*, she underwent conversion to a troop ship in New York in 1942 but caught fire, capsized and then was sold for scrap.

She is shown here with her side cut away to reveal her machinery, cabins and the first-class dining room. The six ships in profile are the *Sirius*, *Great Eastern*, *Kaiser Wilhelm der Grosse*, *Normandie*, *United States* and *Queen Elizabeth II*, showing the changing scale and appearance of ships on the Atlantic run.

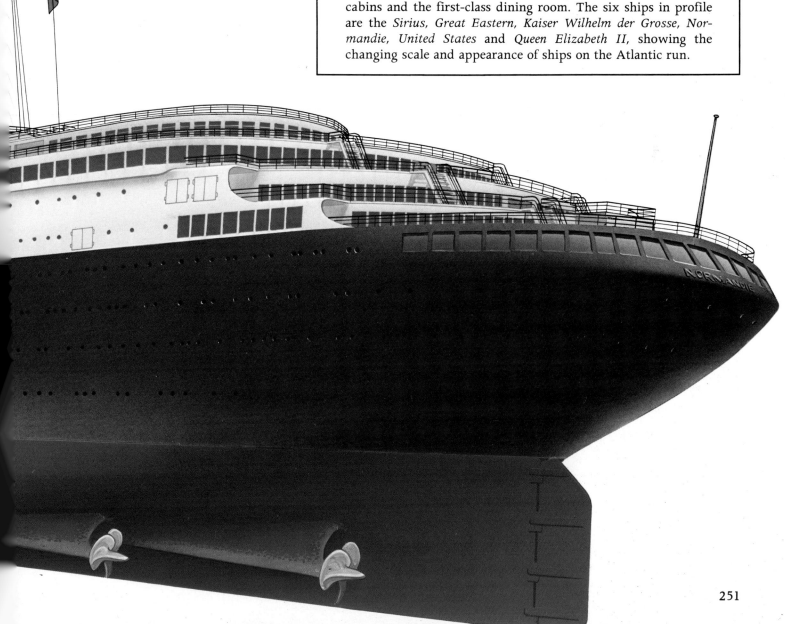

conversion to armed merchant cruisers, which helped to enforce the blockade of the enemy's trade, into command ships for amphibious operations, into landing ships for infantry and tanks, and for a variety of other auxiliary naval purposes. Some were sunk in action, others survived to be reconverted to their original use when the war ended.

In modern maritime warfare the merchant navy of a belligerent nation is often no less important than its fighting navy. The general modern practice is for a nation at war to assume responsibility for the operation of its merchant navy as a whole, fitting it into a co-ordinated war effort, so that every ship is used in the best national interest. More often than not, the experience of war produces new ideas for application in peacetime, new short cuts to

maximum efficiency, and new operating techniques, which, in turn, lead to new developments in ship design. Moreover, the need for urgency in replacing ships lost and repairing ships damaged through enemy action brings in its train new, faster, and more efficient methods of shipbuilding and ship repair. War can bring dividends for peacetime, and this was particularly so in the case of some of the smaller ships, especially ocean-going tugs which had a major role to play during the war, and an equally important one in the years of peace which followed.

It is not within the scope of this book to follow the various events of World War II, except in so far as they affected the development of existing ships or the design of new ones. After the invasion of Poland at the outset of war in September 1939, there was not much fighting on land for the first six months, but the war at sea began at once. On the very day war was declared, a British liner was sunk in the North Atlantic by a German submarine, giving notice that submarine warfare against merchant shipping was to be as much a feature of this war as it had been of the previous one. This was a crushing blow to Britain, for it meant that all her shipping had to be organized at once into convoys, in spite of the severe shortage of escorts and the non-existence of any escort with sufficient endurance to

Below: Albacore torpedo bombers taking off from HMS *Indomitable* during the 'Pedestal' convoy to relieve Malta in August 1942.

remain with a convoy for the whole duration of a transatlantic passage. It therefore entailed the start of an intensive emergency building programme for corvettes, sloops and frigates, and an intensive programme of research into new and more powerful anti-submarine weapons, a better means of illuminating an area of sea at night than with the old-fashioned starshell, the most efficient convoy formation for defence purposes, and similar problems. This lack of preparedness was, in part, a legacy of the Washington Treaty, in part a lack of understanding of the lessons taught by World War I, and in part caused by diversion of so large a part of the money voted for naval rearmament to the building of big battleships. It was to be 1943 before the emergency building programmes had produced enough escorts for the job, but by the time the goal was reached the actual ships produced, particularly the frigates, were fine sturdy vessels with all the weapons and equipment required to carry the war to the submarine and defeat her utterly.

The Norwegian campaign of 1940 highlighted another problem, one that had been guessed at, but not fully appreciated in any of the world's navies. This was that a warship could not survive in waters within range of enemy aircraft unless she was accompanied by fighter aircraft to cover her during operations. The answer was to hand, of course, in the aircraft carrier, introduced in most navies during the years between the wars, but development had been slow, and they were still very thin on the ground. Being a very big ship, the building of a new carrier was a long-term project, hardly suitable for a wartime emergency building programme. An answer to the problem for the Allies did not appear until the United States was drawn into the war in 1941, and, with her immense industrial potential, was able to initiate a crash programme of carrier construction, using modern methods of prefabrication to speed up output. These were small carriers of two main types,

known as 'light fleet carriers' and 'escort carriers', and what they lacked in aircraft capacity they more than made up for in numbers. They began to become operational in 1942 – an incredibly short building time for ships of that size – and by 1943 they were appearing in a steady stream. Inevitably, they became known as 'Woolworth' carriers. The simultaneous application of new fast building techniques and a large measure of prefabrication which produced the aircraft carriers required also held immense promise for rapid ship production in the years to come.

In 1940 and 1941, before the small American carriers arrived on the scene, the British had produced a partial solution to the problem by the adaptation of merchant ships. Their solution was aimed entirely at convoy protection. In 1940 convoys were being attacked by German long-range aircraft, as well as by submarines, and to protect them some merchant ships were fitted with a small launching platform and a catapult, and carried a fighter aircraft on board. They sailed in convoy in the normal way, and on the appearance of an enemy aircraft the fighter was catapulted into the air. On completion of its task, and being unable to land on deck, it ditched itself alongside the nearest ship and the pilot was picked up. They were known as 'camships' (Catapult Aircraft Merchant Ships). A more sophisticated conversion was the 'macship' (Merchant Aircraft Carrier). These ships, usually tankers or grain ships because they were longer and had an uncluttered deck, were fitted with a temporary flight deck above the superstructure, where fighter aircraft could be flown off and land. When, as a result of these measures, attacks by German aircraft ceased, macships were used with naval Swordfish aircraft, adapted to carry depth-charges instead of a torpedo, and used in an anti-submarine role. They lasted until the American escort carriers arrived to take over the task, and, although they were only makeshift and temporary substitutes for the real thing, they filled the gap.

Just as World War I had demonstrated the weaknesses of the battle-cruiser, so World War II demonstrated the deficiencies of the battleship in fleet action. Very occasionally there was a meeting of battleship with battleship, but in the major actions fought between fleets of which battleships formed a part, the two sides never came within 100 nautical miles of each other. These major fleet actions, all fought in the Pacific, were long-range affairs between carrier air groups, showing that the capital ship of the period was now the big aircraft carrier and no longer the battleship. Indeed, the battleship's main role in a fleet action was to serve as an

Below: CAM-ships were merchantmen equipped to launch a single Hurricane fighter from a catapult on the forecastle. The pilot had to 'ditch', but the measure provided a much-needed antidote to air attacks on Gibraltar convoys.

anti-aircraft support to the carriers – a sad descent from their previous position of pre-eminence. True, they had a subsidiary role, for bombardment in support of amphibious assaults, in which they proved themselves to be still a potent weapon, but this was hardly a justification of the huge cost of building them. And, as the war progressed, they increasingly fell prey to concentrated attack from the air. The loss of the British *Prince of Wales* and *Repulse* to Japanese air attack, and of the Japanese giants *Musashi* and *Yamato* to American air attack, spelled the end of these big ships. Since the end of World War II, apart from those already too far advanced on the building stocks to be cancelled, no maritime nation has built a battleship and, with the exception of one or two preserved in mothballs in the United States, all have been broken up for scrap.

Alongside the aircraft-carrier, it was the submarine which emerged as the other most significant weapon in naval warfare. Apart from an increase in size and more sophisticated methods of torpedo fire control, there had been little basic development between the wars. The submarine of 1939 was still limited when submerged by the capacity of its electric batteries for propulsion, and when the batteries were exhausted she had no alternative but to come to the surface and recharge them with her diesel engines, driving her electric motors as dynamos. And a submarine on the surface is highly vulnerable to attack, for being low in the water her range of visibility is restricted, and it is difficult to identify enemy craft and evade them. What was recognized as the true submarine, a vessel completely independent of the surface of the sea at all times, had been dreamed of for years, but in the current state of research and development there appeared to be no way of supplying energy without burning up oxygen.

During the war, German scientists came near to it. They had a piece of good fortune, when Holland was overrun in 1940, in coming across a Dutch invention, a long breathing tube which, fitted to a submarine, enabled the diesel engines to be run while the submarine was submerged. Development was completed by 1944, and the first operational submarines using it put to sea in that year. This was still not the ultimate submarine, but it was a step in the right direction as it enabled the submarine to recharge her batteries without having to come to the surface, and even enabled her to use the diesel engines for propulsion when submerged. The depth at which this could be done was limited by the length of the tube, or 'schnorkel' as it was named. It had a disadvantage, too, in that the exhaust fumes of the diesels also had to be discharged up the schnorkel, and more than one submarine was sunk because its diesel smoke, betrayed its presence near the surface.

Although the schnorkel was not the final answer, it went some way towards making the submarine invisible for longer periods, particularly at night – the normal time for surfacing and recharging – when radar was sweeping the darkness. Having developed the schnorkel, German scientists went a step further in the evolution of the submarine by providing oxygen for the diesel engines while submerged, without using the oxygen in the submarine's atmosphere, all of which the crew needed to breathe and keep alive. They did this by designing a closed-circuit diesel installation, using a catalyst with liquid hydrogen-peroxide to provide the gaseous oxygen to mix with the diesel fuel, thus making combustion possible without using the boat's atmosphere. Later, this was changed to a closed-circuit gas-turbine installation, which was more efficient and produced a very high underwater speed. They were known as Walther boats, from the name of their designer Dr. Walther. It was, perhaps, fortunate for the Allies that the war came to an end before this new design of submarine became operational, for it would have posed tremendous problems for the anti-submarine units.

The German submarine offensive, directed against trade, was even more devastating in World War II than in World War I. It sank 2,828 merchant ships, totalling 14,687,231 tons. To this figure must be added the tonnage sunk by raiders, mines and aircraft. These huge losses were far beyond the capacity of the Allied shipyards, using normal shipbuilding methods, to replace, and for four years the final outcome of the war hung in the balance, with the submarine seeming gradually to gain the upper hand. But even when the U-boat was finally defeated in 1943, there was still the tremendous loss of merchant tonnage to be made good, and indeed more was needed than before to carry across the oceans all the weapons and supplies needed for the final assault.

The answer was a vessel with the generic name of 'Liberty ship'. She was the brainchild

Above: A 'Liberty ship' bound for Murmansk wallows in heavy seas. Heavy losses were sustained when the Allies undertook to send convoys to Russia.

of Henry Kaiser, a businessman who had never run a shipyard before. In 1941, he reorganized a number of shipyards in the United States to undertake the construction of a standard merchant ship with a deadweight tonnage of 10,500 and a service speed of 11 knots. They were built to spartan standards, without frills, and by laying down a procedure for quantity production on a massive scale, Kaiser arranged for the continuous provision of these ships throughout the remaining four years of the war.

The chosen design had been produced as long ago as 1879 by the Sunderland Company of Newcastle-upon-Tyne, England, and Kaiser adopted it because the plans incorporated simplicity of construction and operation, rapidity of building, large cargo-carrying capacity, and a remarkable ability to withstand damage. To these qualities Kaiser added prefabrication, which was undertaken in factories away from the shipyards, and welding together instead of rivetting the prefabricated parts. Because the entire production of turbines and diesel engines in the United States was earmarked for naval and other essential construction, these Liberty ships were powered with triple-expansion engines and steam-driven auxiliary machinery.

During the four years between 1941 and 1945, no fewer than 2,770 Liberty ships, of a total deadweight tonnage of 29,292,000, were produced, of which twenty-four were equipped as colliers, eight as tank carrier ships, thirty-six as aircraft transports, and sixty-two as tankers. They proved to be sturdy, reliable ships, perhaps unglamourous in their complete lack of frills and their uncompromising design for the humbler tasks of war, but they helped turn the tide for the Allies and proved to be a remarkably successful experiment in rapid, large-scale shipbuilding.

Electronics and the Navigator

World War II saw many developments and new inventions of great value to ships. Without doubt, two of the most important and far-reaching were radar, which makes it possible to see the objects around a ship at a comparatively long range, in darkness or fog, and hyperbolic navigation systems, by which a navigator knows exactly where he is, without having to perform the long calculations and observations involved in the older processes of navigation. Both these modern aids can have dangers if used to the complete exclusion of older, and usually more laborious, methods: radar because it cannot predict the future course and speed of a ship depicted on the radar plot; hyperbolic navigation because of what is known as the occasional 'crumb in the set'. The wise navigator uses both radar and, if his ship is fitted with the equipment, hyperbolic navigation, but he also keeps a continuous check on his ship's position by the older and more primitive methods of determining his position.

Radar (RAdio Direction And Range) was known in its earliest days as RDF (Radio Direction Finding), but the name was changed in 1941 to 'radar', to avoid confusion with high-frequency direction finding (H/F D/F), an entirely different system in which a bearing is taken on the source of a high-frequency radio signal. The conception of radar is very nearly as old as the invention of wireless telegraphy itself, and the first experiment in reflecting radio pulses off a solid object was made by Christian Hülsmeyer of Dusseldorf in 1903. His idea, which is, in fact, the whole basis of radar, was that, knowing the speed at which radio waves travel, it would be possible to calculate the distance of an object by measuring the time which elapsed between transmitting a signal and receiving its echo, while its direction, or bearing, could be obtained by noting the direction in which the transmitting aerial was pointing at the time of the echo. Herr Hülsmeyer's experiments were inconclusive, but in 1922 Senator Marconi suggested that further experiments along these lines should be performed, as the science of radio telegraphy had by then advanced considerably further.

Serious development was started in Britain, France and Germany during the decade 1930–1940, and the first ship-

borne radar aerials, forerunners of the modern ship arrays, were fitted in the British battle-cruiser *Repulse* and the German pocket-battleship *Admiral Graf Spee* in 1936. But they proved to have a very short range, were not very accurate, and were cumbersome in operation and appearance. In 1937 a radar set was installed in the French transatlantic liner *Normandie*, but its maximum range was no more than 5 miles (8 km) – still too short to be of use for navigation. Nevertheless, progress continued to be made, and during the first years of the war reasonably accurate sets were used in warships for shadowing enemy ships and for gun aiming. The first time these were used in actual naval operations was during the pursuit of the German battleship *Bismarck* in 1941, when the British cruiser *Suffolk* used radar to shadow the *Bismarck* while keeping out of sight and range. The *Bismarck* also used her radar, to find the range of the British battle cruiser *Hood*.

The great breakthrough came in 1940 with the invention, in Britain, of the magnetron, by means of which very short wavelengths could be produced – a great step forward in range, accuracy and definition. By 1941 the wavelength had been reduced to 10 cm, and by 1943 to 1·9 cm, which enabled a radar set to obtain a definable echo from as small an object as the periscope of a submarine.

Radar sets were installed in merchant ships after the war, as aids to navigation, and they became standard equipment after 1950. The maximum range of a radar set depends on the height of the aerial above sea level, but would hardly be less than 25 nautical miles in a modern merchant ship.

It was assumed at first that radar would enable ships to use full speed even in poor visibility. It took a series of what became known as 'radar-assisted' collisions to prove that radar alone is not enough to tell the course and speed of another vessel even if it is visible on the radar screen.

Hyperbolic navigation originated from systems evolved during World War II, by which bombers flying over enemy-held territory could fix their positions accurately and keep to a pre-determined flight path to their target. The British system, introduced in 1940, was known as 'Gee', and in 1942 the United States introduced a similar system known as 'Loran'. These were then developed for application to ships, and one of the resulting systems known as 'QM', which later became Decca Navigator, was used in 1944 during the Allied invasion of north-west Europe, which called for extremely accurate navigation in the difficult tidal conditions of the English Channel.

After the war an international maritime conference was held in Great Britain where it was agreed to develop four hyperbolic navigational systems eventually to cover the whole world. The four systems selected were Consol, Decca Navigator, Loran and Omega, each varying slightly in operation and in the frequencies used. Very high frequencies give great accuracy up to a distance of about 50 miles (80 km), and are therefore used for coastal systems where a ship's need to fix her position continuously and accurately is greater. Very low frequencies give rather less accuracy, but have a very long range, and cover the mid-ocean areas, where pinpoint navigational accuracy is less vital.

Hyperbolic navigation is so-called because a ship's position is expressed in terms of two co-ordinates that are hyperbolic (i.e. curved) lines, not straight ones. A typical system consists of four transmitter stations, one 'master' and three 'slaves', at different locations on shore. By measuring the interval between the arrival of radio signals transmitted simultaneously by master and one slave station, a co-ordinate of the ship's position is obtained, which appears on the chart as a curved line passing through the gap between the two stations. By repeating the process, using a transmission from another of the slave stations, again in conjunction with the master, the vessel's position can be fixed precisely at the intersection of the two curves. (The transmitters are located so that there is always a good 'angle of cut' at the point of intersection.)

In practice the two co-ordinates are displayed automatically and continuously by the shipborne receiving apparatus, and all that remains for the navigator to do is to read off his position on an overprinted lattice chart.

Far left: Foremast of a modern ferry, showing the navigation radars.

Below: Decca chart of the English Channel with red and green 'decometers' (inset) that give co-ordinates of ships' positions.

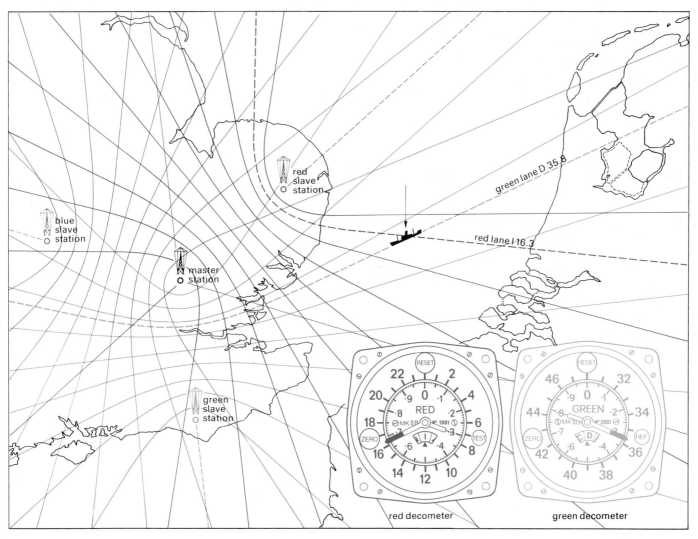

red decometer   green decometer

Chapter Twelve
Ships and Technology

When, in 1945, World War II came to an end both in Europe and the Far East, there was as much work to be done by planners, naval architects, shipowners and shipbuilders as there had been at the end of World War I, although in some respects the maritime nations were better prepared for it. One factor was the great advance in ship construction techniques which the impetus of war had encouraged; another was the emergence of the United States from her years of isolationism, ready now to play a greater and more influential part in world affairs.

So far as merchant shipping was concerned the immediate problem, as after 1918, was to get seaborne trade moving again. Because of the early successes of the U-boats in the battle of the Atlantic and the heavy losses of the Mediterranean and Russian convoys, the Allied merchant navies were all very short of ships. Many that had survived the war were damaged, or worn out by six years of continual hard work without the chance of a refit. There was a fairly simple answer to this particular problem in the mass-production methods evolved for the Liberty ships, and an immediate programme was put in hand to build a new series known as 'Victory ships', standardized merchant vessels of substantial cargo-carrying capacity. They followed much the same design as the Liberty ships, though built more strongly with a longer hull and a forecastle deck added. They were less austere than the wartime Liberty ships, and steam turbines replaced the latter's triple-expansion engines. They had, like their predecessors, an all-welded hull and were built to a gross tonnage of 7,607 (about 12,000 tons deadweight), their turbines giving them a top speed of 16 knots. Like most standardized products they had their drawbacks, especially in so varied a business as the carriage of cargo at sea, but they served well to tide over the immediate shortage of tonnage until individual shipowners could design and build ships better adapted to their particular trade requirements.

By 1946 most of the surviving passenger liners, taken over during the war for conversion into troop transports, armed merchant cruisers and so on, had been reconverted to their original role and were reappearing as luxury liners on the oceans. Because of the loss of the French *Normandie* during the war, the British *Queen Mary* and *Queen Elizabeth* were the largest passenger liners still in commission, although France was already planning another transatlantic giant and Holland, Sweden, Norway, Italy, Greece, Canada and the United States were again competing in the passenger business. Their ships were not comparable in size to the new French liner *France* and the two British *Queens*, but were very big ships nevertheless. The shipyards in Britain, too, were busy building new passenger liners to replace the many that had been sunk or damaged on wartime service.

For the next ten years this passenger trade was booming, for the world was opening up more rapidly than it had ever done before and there was a growing demand for travel, as much for holidays and recreation as for practical and business purposes. With the steady expansion of trade to keep pace with the opening up of new markets all round the world, there was no lack of revenue to pay for luxury in the new ships, and at this level of the passenger trade the new liners were fitted out in a style to match their older sisters. There was generally little increase in speed beyond the 30 to 31 knots of the *Queen Mary* and *Queen Elizabeth* until 1952 when the new American liner *United States* crossed the Atlantic at a record average speed of 35.59 knots. However, this was generally regarded among the shipping fraternity as an expensive stunt (the *United States* cost $74 million to build, a colossal price in those pre-inflation days) in order to acquire a mark of prestige that in fact carried little weight among the *élite* passenger ships; the extra 4 knots in speed made no apparent impression on the ability of the other big transatlantic liners to attract passengers in profitable numbers. Indeed, the very high initial cost of achieving this fast service speed did little more than make the *United States* commercially uneconomic, even though

Left: The *Queen Elizabeth II*, the first liner built to combine the tasks of transatlantic passenger liner and holiday cruise ship. During the Falkland Islands operations of 1982 she was used by the Ministry of Defence as a fast troopship to ferry an entire brigade 8,000 miles (12,875 km) non-stop to the fighting front.

her alternative wartime role as a fast troopship had made her eligible for a sizeable government subsidy towards her cost of construction. But in one respect she was notable, being the first really big ship to have her superstructure fabricated in aluminium alloy in order to save weight above the waterline, an innovation quickly followed by other ship designers and builders and still being put to use nowadays.

But already the competition from the air was building up and shipowners were not slow to recognize the writing on the wall. The war had seen the development of the big four-engined bomber and had provided a substantial fund of experience in their operation. With their considerable payload they were the natural prototype for the long-distance airliner, and by 1952 the big national airlines were already operating many long-distance air routes, of which the Atlantic was the most profitable and promised the greatest growth potential. The jet engine, developed for military purposes shortly before the end of World War II, had also become a reality in the world of civil aircraft, and as it increased the speed of aircraft by well over fifty per cent at a single stroke, it meant that would-be transatlantic passengers now had the choice of crossing the Atlantic at 600 knots in an aircraft in six to eight hours or at 30 knots in a liner in four to five days. And exactly the same choice was being offered on all the other main passenger routes – to South Africa and South America, to India and the Far East, to Australia and New Zealand, and across the Pacific Ocean – which until then had been the monopoly of ships. Shipowners, taking the long view, knew that their days of reliance on passenger traffic alone to produce profits were numbered.

One or two of the big shipping companies looked for a way out by buying a controlling interest in an existing airline and trying to run the two together as a complementary service. Actual operating experience proved that this was not really an answer as it did nothing to help the ships to hold their own against the aircraft and most of the companies engaged in this dual role discovered that it did not pay. What did emerge as an answer was the conversion, or building from new, of ships designed for a dual purpose – passenger transport and holiday cruising. On the transport side, no matter how many millions of passengers may prefer to save time on their journeys by flying, there has always been a hard core, recently estimated at about six per cent of the whole market, who accept the longer travelling time because they prefer to go by ship, a more

leisurely and relaxing method of ocean travel. On the other hand, holiday cruising is a boom industry, and the combination in one ship of the two distinct roles has given the liners a new lease of life.

During the 1960s all the very big liners built between the two world wars and immediately after the second, such as the *France*, found the competition from the airlines too fierce for them and they were gradually withdrawn from service – the *Queen Mary* in 1967, the *Queen Elizabeth* and *United States* in 1969, and the *France*, subsidized for some years by the French government until the cost became prohibitive, in 1975. They no longer had any role to play at sea, being too large and of too deep a draught to serve as cruise liners. The *Queen Mary* still exists at Long Beach, California, as a tourist museum and hotel, and the *Queen Elizabeth* was to have served as a university at Hong Kong until she was set on fire and sank in harbour. No decision has as yet been taken on the future, if any, of the *France*.

A good example of a dual-purpose ship is the Cunard Line's *Queen Elizabeth II*, launched in

Right: The *United States* was not only the largest American liner ever built but also the fastest in the world, crossing the Atlantic at an average speed of over 35 knots.

Below: The *France* was the last liner built purely for the transatlantic trade but like all the others found the competition from the airlines too fierce for economic operation. She was withdrawn from the Atlantic in 1975.

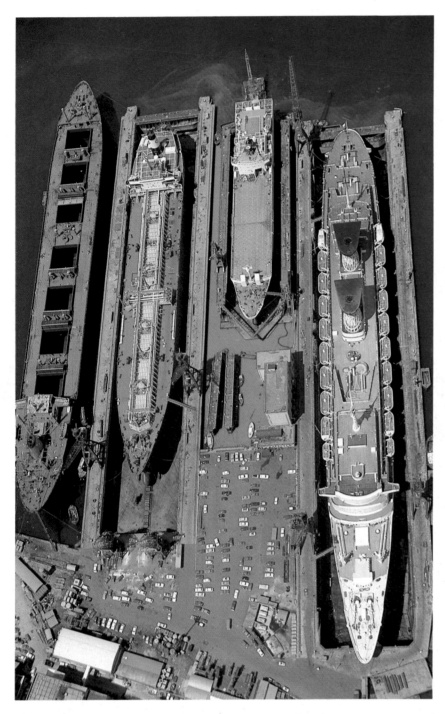

Above: An aerial view of merchant ships being fitted out in a shipyard in Genoa, Italy. After their launch, the hulls of new ships are towed to the fitting-out yard for the installation of engines and all other internal and deck gear.

Right: The *Queen Mary*, after the end of her career as a transatlantic liner, was sold for conversion to a floating hotel and conference centre. She now lies alongside a wharf in Long Beach, California.

1970 as a replacement for the *Queen Mary* and *Queen Elizabeth*. Although smaller than her two predecessors, she is still a very big ship at 65,000 tons gross. A great deal of preliminary planning went into her design, largely to produce a draught of less than 32 ft (9·75 m) so that, in her cruising role, she would be able to enter some of the more exotic foreign harbours which had insufficient depth of water for a normal ship of her tonnage. During the summer months she makes up to a dozen or so direct crossings of the Atlantic as a passenger liner, and for the remainder of the year operates as a luxury cruise liner. And, as we have seen in the recent turmoil in the South Atlantic, she still has the same role to play in

times of war as her sisters during World War II, operating as a fast troop carrier. Adopting the naval techniques of refuelling at sea, she carried a brigade of troops, 3,000 men, and delivered them to the seat of war, 8,000 miles (12,900 km) away, in a non-stop voyage and at a speed considerably faster than any other ship could have maintained. She was not the only one with a different role to play in times of conflict; other cruise liners were taken up as troop carriers and hospital ships, civilian ferries, container ships, tankers, and other general types were quickly adapted to a wartime role, to speed supplies of all varieties required by the troops fighting in the Falkland Islands. As in all previous wars, the versatility of merchant shipping to adapt quickly to different requirements and different roles was again proved beyond question.

The *Queen Elizabeth II*, as well as providing an economic answer to the competition of the transatlantic airlines, is also an excellent example of the technical engineering and shipbuilding advances of the last thirty years. She has a very refined hull design and, like the *United States* before her, all her superstructure above the upper deck is constructed in light alloy. Her engine room shows even more startling advances. The *Queen Mary*, launched in 1934, had twenty-four Yarrow boilers delivering steam at 400 lb/sq in (28 kg/cm²) to drive her four sets of Parsons turbines at 180,000 horsepower. Four years later the *Queen Elizabeth* had twelve Yarrow boilers delivering steam at 450 lb/sq in (32 kg/cm²) to drive similar machinery at the same speed and horsepower. The *France*, which made her maiden voyage in 1962, had eight boilers delivering steam at 910 lb/sq in (64 kg/cm²) which drove four sets of turbines geared to two propellers to give a comparable speed. The *Queen Elizabeth II*, launched in 1970, produces about the same speed with only three Foster-Wheeler boilers which deliver steam at 650 lb/sq in (46 kg/cm²) to two of the most powerful sets of turbines ever constructed for a ship. They had been made possible by new advances in metallurgy, particularly in the development of nickel-chrome steel with its better heat-resisting qualities.

As, in the face of competition from air travel, the liner has become progressively smaller, so the average merchant ship has become progressively larger. They have had to primarily because of the great increase in the volume of world trade since the end of World War II, the great majority of which is still carried in ships because there is virtually no competition from

Above: Until 1976 the ULCC *Globtik Tokyo* was, at 484,000 tons, the largest oil tanker in the world but has since been overtaken in size. The present slump in the world's oil demands has raised some questions of the economic viability of these huge tankers.

the airlines in bulk transport. Another important reason for this growth in size is that it makes more economic sense to carry large cargoes in fewer ships than small cargoes in a large number of ships.

The biggest growth in size has been in oil tankers, due very largely to extraneous reasons. These were the two periods of closure of the Suez Canal, the first in 1956 after the Suez Crisis, the second in 1967 after the Six Day War between Israel and Egypt. Until the first closure the normal route for tankers bringing oil from the Middle Eastern oilfields to the Western industrial nations was through the Suez Canal, which put a physical limitation on the size of any tanker using this route as the Canal was not wide enough, or dredged to a suitable depth, to take very big ships. The maximum size of a tanker using the Suez Canal was about 30,000 tons gross. After the Canal was closed in 1956, all oil brought from that source to the Western countries had to be carried by the very much longer route round South Africa. With so much further to steam, the existing size of the average tanker made the longer voyage uneconomic in terms of the cargo able to

be carried, and was the cue for the introduction of what became known as the 'supertanker'.

The growth in size of the average tanker during these years can perhaps best be illustrated by taking actual examples. Although there was the occasional tanker up to about 24,000 tons deadweight built between the two world wars, the average size of the large tanker was from 10,000 to 15,000 tons deadweight. In 1950 a tanker named the *Velutina* of 28,000 tons deadweight was launched, and in 1953 she was followed by the *Tina Onassis* with a deadweight tonnage of 45,750. Six years later, after the first closure of the Suez Canal, a tanker with a deadweight tonnage of 68,840, the *W. Alton Jones*, was built in the United States.

The second closure of the Suez Canal in 1967 was a much longer affair and occurred at a time when there was an unprecedented world demand for oil, partly because world trade, and therefore manufacture, was buoyant and partly because of the huge explosion in numbers of the motor car and aeroplane, both completely dependent on oil for their motive power. The combination of these two – the closure of the shorter route to the West and the great surge in demand – gave an enormous boost to the design and construction of new and bigger tankers which made the earlier supertankers look almost like midgets. Thus a new generation of tankers was born, to be known as VLCCs (Very Large Crude Carriers) ranging up to between 250,000 to 275,000 tons deadweight. There were at first some doubts whether so huge a ship could be built strong enough to withstand the strains, especially of hogging and sagging, which all ships undergo when steaming in a rough sea. But the experience of actual operation of such large ships proved that they were viable both in terms of economic transport and of safety at sea. And as the proof of their strength and viability was recognized, so the next generation took its place on the building slips. They were known as ULCCs (Ultra Large Crude Carriers) and were first built up to a deadweight tonnage of around 400,000. With the world demand for oil still increasing at a large rate, it was not long before even larger tankers were deemed to be necessary, and designs of ships of up to 800,000 tons deadweight were on the drawing board. With the success of the VLCCs and the first of the ULCCs as far as hull strength was concerned, it seemed that there could be no limit to the size to which a ship could be built using the modern methods of construction and modern metals. While this is no doubt a fact of modern ship design and building, the imagination shudders at the size of the disaster if one of these ultra large tankers should break up in mid-ocean or run ashore when approaching the coast. The extent of the damage caused by the stranding of the smaller tankers *Torrey Canyon* off Land's End in 1967 and *Amoco Cadiz* off the coast of Brittany in 1978 was severe enough to be still remembered.

By 1976 the largest of the ULCCs in commission was the *Globtik Tokyo* of 483,664 tons deadweight, although since then several larger tankers have been completed, including in 1981 the *Seawise Giant* of 564,763 tons deadweight. Converted by Nippon Kokan of Japan from another tanker (to which an extra midship section was added), the *Seawise Giant* is at present the largest ship in the world with a length of 1,504 ft (458·5 m), a beam of 226 ft (68·8 m) and a draught of 98 ft (29·8 m). Whether she will prove to be an expensive white elephant or an economic unit of the oil-carrying trade only the future will reveal. But even before she began her career as a tanker, things in the oil market had begun to change. In the mid-1970s the oil-producing countries raised the price of their oil to four times what it had been previously, and a year or two later doubled it again. This huge increase in price started a chain reaction throughout the world, with consumer nations adopting policies of energy conservation to reduce their consumption of expensive oil – policies which helped to lead the world into a trade depression which still further reduced the oil consumption. Consequently, shipowners around the world found themselves with an excess of tanker tonnage, leading to a cancellation of building orders and the laying-up of a large number of existing tankers, particularly the biggest ones. One result of this decrease in consumption, which looks as though it could well become permanent as the nations of the world become more conservation-conscious, is that the average size of the modern tanker, particularly in the case of new vessels being built, has gone into reverse and is dropping to more modest dimensions.

Below: An aerial view of the oil tanker *Torrey Canyon* broken in two after running aground on the Seven Stones rocks off Land's End, England, in 1967 as a result of faulty navigation. The resultant pollution around the neighbouring coasts was a local disaster.

Right: A merchant ship unloading in Hong Kong harbour. She is lying at a mooring buoy and discharging her cargo into barges secured alongside, which will then ferry it to the shore.

Below: The oil tanker *Tactic* labouring in a heavy sea. It had been thought that the stresses set up in the hull under such conditions would have proved critical in such large ships but modern methods of construction have overcome this problem.

Another factor which is influencing this reduction in size has been the worldwide exploration for new sources of oil. Large deposits have been found in Africa, under the North Sea, in Alaska and in many other parts of the world. So geography now has to come into the calculations of the oil companies when working out the requirements for transporting their crude oil to the world's refineries. The days of almost total dependence on the Middle East, with long voyages round the south of Africa to the west, are no longer the prime consideration in the determination of tanker size. The two great canals in the world, Suez, which has been widened and deepened, and Panama, which can take ships of up to 100,000 tons, are again exerting an influence in tanker design and size. The possibility, for example, of being able to transport Alaskan oil from the Pacific to the Atlantic through the Panama Canal is obviously a more attractive project than doing so around Cape Horn. A tanker of up to 100,000 tons can make such a passage

through the Canal; bigger tankers are forced into a voyage three times as long with the added cost of more fuel consumed on the voyage, a larger wage bill for the crew, and all the additional costs of ship maintenance and wear and tear.

All large tankers are steam driven with turbines, although some of the smaller ones are fitted with diesel engines. Steam propulsion in tankers has an added advantage as a ready producer of inert gas, mainly carbon dioxide, which all tankers need in order to minimize the risk of explosion, particularly from the mixture of air and petroleum gas which is present when the oil cargo is being discharged or has recently been discharged. Inert gas is readily available in steam-driven tankers from the boiler uptakes and, when amalgamated with the air and petroleum gas mixture in the empty tanks, makes them safe from explosion. Steam in tankers is also required for heating the crude oil cargo to make it fluid enough to be pumped, and to drive the pumps, capstan, and winches on board, as

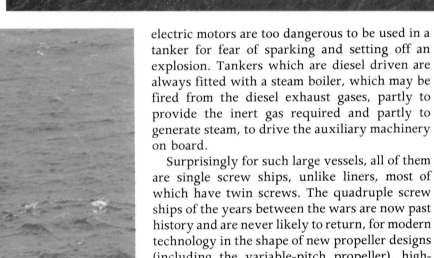

electric motors are too dangerous to be used in a tanker for fear of sparking and setting off an explosion. Tankers which are diesel driven are always fitted with a steam boiler, which may be fired from the diesel exhaust gases, partly to provide the inert gas required and partly to generate steam, to drive the auxiliary machinery on board.

Surprisingly for such large vessels, all of them are single screw ships, unlike liners, most of which have twin screws. The quadruple screw ships of the years between the wars are now past history and are never likely to return, for modern technology in the shape of new propeller designs (including the variable-pitch propeller), high-pressure steam and turbines of increased power, has enabled the single propeller to drive even the largest ship at a reasonable speed with, at the same time, a considerable increase in overall efficiency.

Tankers do not necessarily all transport oil. Some are designed to carry water, some small ones are used for the transport of wine, others carry molasses, liquefied gas, or liquid chemicals. But whatever their cargo, the basic tanker design is the same, the cargo being carried in insulated tanks, or compartments, within the main tank which forms the largest part of the hull.

The post-war development of the cargo ship has followed a similar pattern of growth in size, due not so much to the two closures of the Suez Canal as to the phenomenal growth in world trade throughout the years following World War II. Modern technology allied to intensive research has resulted in vast increases of production in almost every sphere of man's endeavour, from agriculture to manufacturing, and virtually the whole of the export and import of this greatly increased production has to be handled by cargo ships. The general post-war trend has been to build large ships to handle imports and exports in bulk to world centres of distribution and to use smaller cargo vessels to act as feeders to and from these centres. The general increase in size has not been nearly so dramatic as in the case of oil tankers, and a cargo ship today of 60,000 to 80,000 tons is a very big ship. Developments in the method of cargo carrying, rather than in the cargo ship itself, have dictated most of the changes in merchant ship design during the last twenty or thirty years. There were ships built specifically to carry one type of cargo – coal, wheat, mineral ores, etc. – from the last century onwards, and virtually the only change to be seen in today's ships of this type is in their size, now very much larger to compete economically with the growth in demand. There have also, of course, been some changes to adapt to more modern methods of loading and unloading these bulk cargoes, but the basic essentials of the ship engaged in this trade have not changed overmuch. There are new standards of crew accommodation, more efficient installations for ship propulsion and better handling methods on board, but these are the normal improvements which are to be found in virtually every modern ship operating on the seas today.

The most radical new method of cargo handling today is that of containerization, and this has

Below: A multi-user container terminal at Tilbury Docks, London. The containers are picked up by travelling gantries using a spreader which locks onto the four top corners. They are then lowered into the hold or onto the deck stowage of the ship.

brought about one big change in cargo ship design since the end of the war. The use of metal containers of standard size throughout the world has revolutionized the stowage of cargo on board ship and has also changed the overall shape of the ship from the typical cargo carrier of forty years ago. In those days the average cargo ship was what was known as the 'three island type' – a forecastle where the crew had their accommodation, a forward well-deck for the forward holds, a midships bridge structure, an after well-deck for the after holds, and a poop, below which was the boiler and engineroom; the forecastle, bridge

and poop formed the three islands. The growth of containerization has changed all that.

Most dry cargo, except of course those carried as bulk cargoes such as grain, coal, sugar, etc. can be packed, or 'stuffed', into standard-size containers in depots ashore and easily transported by rail or road to the nearest container-loading port. There they are picked up by travelling gantries or special container cranes equipped with a 'spreader' which fits on top of the container to be lifted and, by remote control from the crane driver, engages in twist locks on each corner of the container so that it can be hoisted and

lowered without fear of it being dropped. Knowing the exact size of the container, the naval architect can design his cargo-carrying ship with holds of the right size needed to take the containers, and with a clear deck space of the right size to take an additional deck cargo of containers. The holds have wide hatchways, and the sides are lined with angled steel guides into which the containers are lowered vertically so that they are unable to move. Deck cargoes, stacked two, three, or even four deep, are held solid by the four corner twist locks on each container. With the steel guides in the holds and the twist locks on deck, there can be no danger of the cargo shifting in a rough sea (so often the cause of disasters at sea in past years) and of course no problems, as also in the past, of fitting items of different size and shape in the holds so that they are not damaged in transit. In order to create unobstructed space on deck for the containers, the central island of the conventional 'three island' ship containing the bridge structure has been removed to the poop deck aft, and the forecastle as such has disappeared, with the crew quarters also moved aft to the poop. The new deck layout makes for an efficient ship, even if not a handsome one, generally somewhat slab-sided and with a bulbous bow (see p. 303) which does not add to good looks. These ships are officially described as cellular container ships, are driven either by steam or diesel and are normally fast ships with a service speed (average speed when fully loaded) of over 20 knots.

The stowage of cargo containers on deck sometimes causes problems of stability through the reduction of the ship's metacentric height, at times to as little as a few inches. A ship's metacentric height, which is the vertical distance between her centre of gravity and a theoretical point above it known as the 'transverse metacentre', is an important element in determining the righting movement which is exerted to bring a ship back on an even keel when she rolls under the influence of the sea or the wind. The greater the metacentric height, the greater the righting movement, and stowing cargo on deck obviously raises the position of a ship's centre of gravity and thus reduces her metacentric height. In the case of container ships fully loaded with a heavy deck cargo of containers, this problem is accentuated during the course of her voyage by the consumption of fuel and other stores, which reduces the weight normally carried low down in the ship and thus raises further the centre of gravity. This possible danger is only lessened at the first port of call where the top layers of containers forming the deck cargo are unloaded, thus lowering the centre of gravity and increasing the metacentric height. This is a problem which is

well recognized by naval architects and allowed for in their initial calculations, so that there is no real danger of such a ship actually capsizing under the weight of her deck cargo. The main effect on a ship of a small metacentric height is that she will probably have a very slow period of roll in a seaway.

Although in its essentials the merchant ship of today does not vary greatly from her sisters of yesterday except in the case of overall size, there has been a considerable revolution in what one might describe as the infrastructure of the shipping world. The navigational work of a ship has been considerably eased by the introduction of both long-range and short-range hyperbolic navigation systems (see pp. 256–7), by the adoption of separation zones in restricted areas carrying heavy traffic such as the English Channel, equivalent perhaps to a motorway on land, and to the compulsory fitting of radar in all ships of any size. Automation on board has also greatly eased the amount of manual work in a ship normally carried out by the crew. The effect of this can be seen in the average size of a modern ship's crew as compared with a similar-sized ship of the

Above: The container ship *Kowloon Bay* at sea with her cargo of containers. Computerized loading ensures that containers are stowed on board in the correct order for unloading when the ship reaches her destination.

269

years between the two world wars. Today, even the big tankers of a quarter of a million tons are operated by a crew of between thirty and forty men. If one could imagine a similar ship of that size between the wars, she would have needed a crew running into hundreds of men. Today, boilers can be automatically stoked, engines can be automatically operated, and ships steered on a pre-set course, all electronically monitored.

It is the same story in cargo handling. Forty years ago ships were loaded and unloaded by cranes on the dockside which hoisted items of cargo into the air, usually in a net, and swung them over the ship's side to be lowered into the hold where a swarm of dockers manhandled them into position, wedging them in so that they would not move about during the ship's passage. In some ports, where dockside cranes were not available, this was done by the ship's own derricks. Today, many merchant ships are built on the roll-on, roll-off (Ro-Ro) loading principle so that cargo does not have to be hoisted and lowered by cranes or derricks to reach the hold. This kind of loading is usually done by pre-packing the cargo onto pallets, which are then lifted by fork-lift trucks to a large loading port in the ship's side or bow, from where they are taken by an inboard fork-lift truck direct to the hold.

Modern port installations also play a large part in this infrastructure. New commercial ports have been built, older ones expanded and modernized, and all designed to provide a quicker turn-round of the ship in harbour – faster unloading and faster loading – so that she spends as little time as possible lying in port and more time at sea earning her keep. The organization of a modern port is a complex affair, all computer-based, so that there is a constant supply of essential information of when ships are due, what stores they will need to take on board, what cargo is due to be loaded and unloaded, the order in which it is to be loaded according to destination and the ship's planned voyages, and so on. Work goes on day and night so that the ship, the main essential factor in the whole operation of sea transport, is not needlessly held up in her task of distributing the world's agricultural and manufacturing produce from its points of production to the points of its consumption.

One other small design change is the attention

Above: An aerial view of the Northfleet Hope container terminal at Tilbury Docks, London. Containerization has revolutionized the transport of mixed cargoes.

now paid in all new shipbuilding to the accommodation of the crew on board. The reduction in the size of crews in modern ships allied to the general move of crew accommodation from the old-fashioned forecastle to the new poop structure, has resulted in widespread improvements both in comfort and in the general standard of living. Instead of the crowded bunk space under the forecastle deck in which the crew slept, ate and spent their time off watch in the old days, the men now have cabins, single in the big ships and perhaps two-berth or four-berth in the smaller ones. The modern seaman's food is good, served in a general mess-room and usually on a cafeteria basis in the larger ships; he has a library; a games room; and even perhaps a swimming pool. He can expect mail and newspapers not only at the ports of call during the ship's voyage but also, on some big ships with built-in helipads, delivered by helicopter from ports close to the ship's route. In many large ships he can also expect his quarters to be air-conditioned. It is all a part of the new look of today's shipping industry.

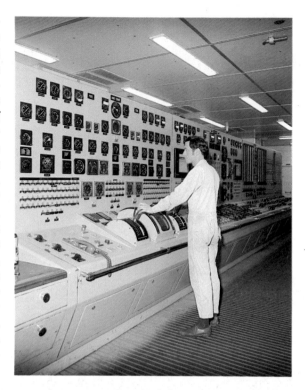

Left: The control console in the engine-room of a modern merchant ship. The visual display of information allows remote control of all engine-room operations by a single engineer.

Below: The roll-on, roll-off ferry *Seaspeed Arabia* seen at anchor at Suez.

The speed with which ships can reflect in their design the public moods and requirements of the immediate present is quite remarkable, particularly since World War II when this change has been more rapid than ever before. As has been seen, the explosion in oil tanker building followed quickly on the first closure of the Suez Canal, grew even greater after the second, and almost as quickly faded out again as the price of oil shot up and the main consuming nations became conservation-minded. A similar example was the case of the big whale-factory ships which made their appearance in the South Atlantic and North Pacific during the years after the end of World War II. There had in fact been whale-factory ships in the Atlantic in the 1920s, but they were relatively small and not particularly well adapted to their task. It took the world shortage of food during the years immediately following the end of World War II to transform them into large ships of up to 26,000 tons, specially designed and built to process whales on almost a production-line basis. This was made possible by their open stern with a sloping ramp up which the whales could be hauled directly onto the flensing deck. The huge post-war demand for whalemeat, both for human consumption and the production of pet foods, and for other whale products such as candles, soap, margarine and cosmetics, led to a great increase in the design and building of whale-factory ships and smaller whale catchers, with many nations attracted to this very profitable trade. After a very few years the resultant overfishing almost led to the extinction of this gentle mammal, to an extent where the conscience of the world became revolted by the slaughter. An International Whaling Com-

mission was set up to agree on measures of conservation, together with some national decisions to ban the use of whale products, both of which steps have brought the overfishing to an end. The main result has been that the whale-factory ship is a dying breed, only just kept alive by Russia and Japan who still send annual expeditions to the whaling grounds. The other nations, including Britain, who used to take part in this trade, have broken up their whale-factory ships and adapted their whale catchers for other purposes.

But the general efficiency of the design has not been lost, and is seen today in some of the new fishing trawlers. The traditional trawler, known as the 'beam trawler', worked its trawls from the vessel's sides, using a single trawl which was brought up alongside, hoisted over the fish well with a derrick, emptied of its catch, and then shot (let out) again for another catch. The more modern development is the stern trawler, not unlike a miniature whale-factory ship, which works two trawls through a square opening in the stern, one trawl being shot as the other is hauled, so that no time is lost between trawls while she is on the fishing grounds. Distant water trawlers are relatively large vessels of up to about 3,000 tons and are equipped to stay as long as five weeks on the fishing grounds, often with a fish-factory processing ship in attendance.

One area of phenomenal post-war growth is in ferries. There have, of course, always been ferries, ranging from quite small boats carrying passengers across rivers to large, long-distance ferries carrying passengers, cars and cargo. The earliest large development, before the days of cars and lorries, were train ferries, normally with a single train deck with from one to four rail tracks and usually converging to one track at the bow and three at the stern. The early train ferries

Above left: The carcass of a slaughtered whale is winched up the stern ramp of a whale-factory ship.

Above: A modern type of deep-sea motor trawler, the *Norina*, built at Goole in Britain, with a stern ramp for the more efficient shooting and hauling of trawls.

Above right: Nets (trawls) being handled on the stern of a trawler after being hauled.

Below right: A Russian fish carrier off Dakar, on the west coast of Africa. These ships either accompany their own trawler fleet or purchase the catches of local fishing vessels for bulk transport to Russia.

loaded and discharged over the stern, but more modern ones are double-ended with an opening bow door and stern ramp. As rail cars have to be loaded over a comparatively level track, the rise and fall of the tide necessitates the use of a link span at train ferry terminals with facilities for elevation and depression. Ships which carry trains, and some car ferries, are fitted with equalizing tanks with automatic flooding and pumping to correct any angles of heel which may be caused when loading or off-loading heavy railway vehicles or cars and coaches.

The fastest area of growth, however, has been in passenger/car ferries, mainly due to the roll-on, roll-off system of loading developed since the war. In the older car ferries cars were slung on board with a four-point chain bridle, one leg to each wheel, and lifted into the ferry's hold by a dockside crane. The immense worldwide explosion in car ownership and the resultant demand for touring holidays in foreign countries called for a much more efficient method of loading and off-loading, and this problem was quickly solved using wartime experience of tank and infantry landing craft. Initially, the roll-on, roll-off facility was embodied in the introduction of a stern door opening onto a ramp along which cars could be driven directly onto the ship's car deck. It was only a short step from this to the introduction of a hinged, lifting bow section in addition to the stern doors so that cars could be

driven into the ferry and off again without having to turn round – the full, modern, roll-on, roll-off facility. Some car ferries, which operate from ports which have no modern car terminals so that they have to lie alongside a jetty, load and off-load through large doors cut in the ship's side, from which a ramp leads down to the jetty. They are mostly to be found in the Mediterranean and Baltic seas, where the very small rise and fall of the tide does not affect the level of the side door in relation to the level of the jetty.

Most ferries are powered today by the medium-speed, V-form diesel engine driving

Above: The car and passenger ferry *Finnjet* photographed at Helsinki, Finland. She is the largest and fastest car ferry in the world and is powered by two gas turbines.

twin variable-pitch propellers which can be controlled directly from the bridge. In medium-sized ferries, up to about 5,000–6,000 tons gross, this machinery will give a service speed of about 20–24 knots. In the earlier post-war car ferries steam turbines were the most popular form of propulsion, but they are now being gradually withdrawn. A typical car ferry, such as those which cross the English Channel, would have a capacity of around 1,250 passengers, 200–250 cars, and about 50–60 commercial vehicles.

The largest car ferry yet built is the Finnish *Finnjet*, which operates between Helsinki and Travemünde in West Germany, a passage of 600 nautical miles which she covers in 22 hours. She can carry 1,532 passengers, all accommodated in two-berth and four-berth cabins, and 350 cars. She is a monster ferry at 24,605 tons gross, and is remarkable by being powered by two Pratt and Whitney gas turbines which give her a speed of over 27 knots. Her consumption of fuel on each round trip is over 600 tons, an indication of the great thirst of gas turbines. With the aid of

powerful bow thrusters (see p. 303) she can turn in her own length without the assistance of tugs. Today she is the ultimate development in car ferries; whether she can remain profitable depends on her being able to maintain an economic level of passengers and cars.

Given the flexibility and strength of modern shipbuilding materials and the versatility of modern engineering methods, there are few demands that a good naval architect allied to a good shipbuilder cannot meet. Not all the craft which they produce fall into the conventional categories of warships and merchant ships; exploitation of the sea's resources has called upon the shipbuilder to adapt to the new demands of specialist constructions. Exploitation of the seabed, and particularly the search for offshore oilfields, has produced specially designed drilling ships and production platforms (see pp. 295–301); the new demand for specialist oceanographical surveys has stimulated the design and building of the bathyscaphe, a sophisticated development of the bathysphere, which is in its essentials a small free-moving submarine constructed and armoured to withstand tremendous pressures as it explores the ultimate depths of the sea. In 1960 a bathyscaphe descended to a depth of 36,000 ft (11,000 m) in the Guam Deep Trench. The pressure of the water on the hull at this depth is over 8 tons per square inch, which gives some impression of the strength of her construction. These are but one or two examples of the versatility of the modern shipbuilder; given the particular problems to be faced, he can more often than not produce a solution.

There are, naturally, still some limitations which restrict the naval architect and shipbuilder, of which the most important is probably initial cost in relation to the market which the ship is designed to serve. Every shipowner, for example, would like his ships to be fast in order to cut down the length of time spent on their voyages, but the cost of additional speed, in the shape of fuel consumption and engines of greater power, rises astronomically for every extra knot achieved above a ship's economical speed. Additionally, if cost were no criterion in construction, aluminium alloy would almost certainly replace steel as the prime shipbuilding material, for it has the strength to bear the normal strains imposed on a ship in a seaway, is much lighter in weight than steel, thereby achieving a saving in fuel consumption, and is also much more resistant than steel to corrosion. It can be welded as easily as can steel, which makes it an attractive material for shipbuilders. All steel ship construction is now welded and the sound of the rivetting hammer, so long the noisy accompaniment of work in the shipyards, is no longer heard in the land. Welded construction, as strong if not stronger than rivetted, has the advantage of saving weight through the elimination of rivets and of providing a more streamlined hull with no overlapping plates. Aluminium alloy is used for the construction of some small warships, where economy in initial cost is not the prime consideration, and for the superstructure of liners and some other large ships where the saving of weight is an important asset. But it is still too expensive a material to be used for most merchant ships where the initial cost is very much a factor of their economic life. Similarly, if the cost were not

to be counted, most merchant ships would be propelled by gas turbines, as their power-to-weight ratio is so much greater than any other form of marine propulsion. Their great drawback lies in their inordinate thirst for fuel, which makes them very expensive to operate.

Another restriction on the naval architect and shipbuilder lies in the limiting strength of metals and their liability to fracture under pressure. The most economical means of ship propulsion today, in terms of fuel consumption and running costs, is the diesel engine and many shipowners prefer it above all others for that reason. In theory there

Below: A merchant ship under construction on a building slip on the River Tyne, England, towers above the houses in an adjacent street.

275

T he post-World War II years also saw the development of the hydrofoil as a very fast short-haul passenger carrier. The basic idea of a boat's hull lifting itself clear of the water onto planes, or foils, when driven fast is not new; the first experiment along these lines dates back to 1891, and in 1906, in trials on Lake Maggiore in Italy, Enrico Forlanini demonstrated a small craft fitted with ladder foils which reached a speed of 38 knots. Until 1927 these craft operated with their foils submerged, but in that year German engineers evolved what became known as the surface-piercing foil, in which the foils rise completely to the surface and the craft skids across the top of the water. By lifting the hull in this way completely out of the water, all drag and skin friction is eliminated, enabling very high speeds to be achieved. It was not until 1956 that this new revolutionary method of marine propulsion was put to commercial use with the establishment of a fast passenger ferry service operating between Sicily and Italy. This was quickly followed a year later by Russian passenger-carrying hydrofoils built at the Krasnoye Sormovo shipyard for use on the Russian rivers. Since then hydrofoils have been introduced as fast ferries on a number of relatively short sea crossings. They have also been tested for possible naval use, mainly in the fields of anti-submarine warfare and minesweeping.

There are two basic types of hydrofoil, those fitted with the *canard* type foil in which thirty per cent of the vessel's weight is supported on the forward foils and seventy per cent on the after foils, and the conventional type in which the percentages are reversed. In the *canard* type the foils are surface-piercing so that the whole vessel and its foils ride on the surface; in the conventional type, the foils remain submerged although the hull of the vessel is lifted clear of the water. The *canard* type produces a very high speed but less control, the conventional type less speed but greater stability. Powered by gas turbine engines, many hydrofoils can attain speeds of over 60 knots.

Both types of hydrofoil burn fuel at a very high rate, which limits them to comparatively small size and short range. Some visionaries have produced designs for ocean liners built on the hydrofoil principle to carry up to 500 passengers at 60 knots, but a realistic examination of such ships' plans indicates that they would probably need to carry additional fuel tanks to the exclusion of all passenger accommodation in order to reach their destinations.

Exactly the same considerations limit the uses to which the hovercraft can be adapted, for here

Above: A VLCC oil tanker under construction in a Japanese shipyard. In many such large ships the deck crew are issued with bicycles.

Above right: The hovercraft is the first really radical innovation in sea transportation since the introduction of steam.

Right: The hydrofoil is another quite recent innovation. As it picks up speed the angled foils raise the hull clear of the water, thus reducing drag and making high speeds possible.

was no reason why it could not be developed in size and power to drive even the largest ships, but its limitation lies in the size of the crankshaft required to stand up to the enormous pressures generated when the engine is a very big one. This has restricted the engine to a power output of around 16,000 to 17,000 shaft horsepower, suitable for a ship of around 18,000 to 20,000 tons. Recent engineering advances, coupled with variable-pitch propellers, now make the diesel engine a possibility for larger ships, and it may well be that its use in the future will be extended in the field of marine propulsion. Nevertheless, the larger merchant ships still rely on the steam turbine, almost always with single or double reduction (a form of gearing), as the main source of motive power, with a few using turbo-electric drive in which the turbines are used to drive dynamos which, in turn, produce current to drive electric motors geared to the propeller shaft. Some diesel-engined ships do the same thing in a diesel-electric drive.

again the fuel consumption is too high to permit long-distance operation. Like the hydrofoil the idea of the hovercraft is not new, for the principles on which it operates were first investigated in Holland in 1875. Constructional difficulties prevented its development then and it was not until 1950 that these were overcome, when a practicable design was produced by the British engineer Christopher Cockerell. It took another eight years to get official sponsorship and funds to develop it.

The hovercraft is a vehicle (there is still argument as to whether it should be ranked as a ship or an aircraft, although as it has to obey the International Navigational Rules of the Road at Sea it must surely be nearer a ship than an aircraft) which rides on a cushion of air between it and the surface over which it is travelling. The largest hovercraft at present in commercial operation as a passenger/car ferry is the SRN-4, a vessel of 165 gross registered tons with an overall length of 130 ft (39·6 m) and a beam of 77 ft (23·5 m). As a car/passenger ferry it has a capacity of 256 passengers and 30 cars, or as a passenger-only ferry 610 passengers. Its power unit consists of four gas turbine engines which drive four variable-pitch aircraft propellers to provide forward movement and four 12-bladed centrifugal fans to provide the cushion of air on which the vessel rides. This cushion of air is prevented from escaping sideways by a neoprene skirt which hangs down to the water all round the vessel. The SRN-4 has a cruising speed of 55 knots and a maximum speed of 65 knots. It has two considerable advantages over the conventional car ferry. With its high speed it can make many more passages a day and it does not need any car terminal facilities since it can ride ashore for loading and off-loading on any hard area of beach. Smaller versions of the SRN-4 have been evaluated for military purposes, particularly in the field of amphibious warfare. US hovercraft were used operationally in Vietnam, and proved especially useful in transporting troops across boggy ground.

While steel remains the major, and virtually the only, building material for the hulls of ships of any size, there has been a revolution since World War II in the construction of smaller craft by the introduction of completely new building materials. The most widely used of these is glass reinforced plastic (GRP), more commonly called 'fibreglass'. This has almost completely revolutionized small boat construction, replacing the original individual wooden hulls of earlier days by mass production in modern plastics.

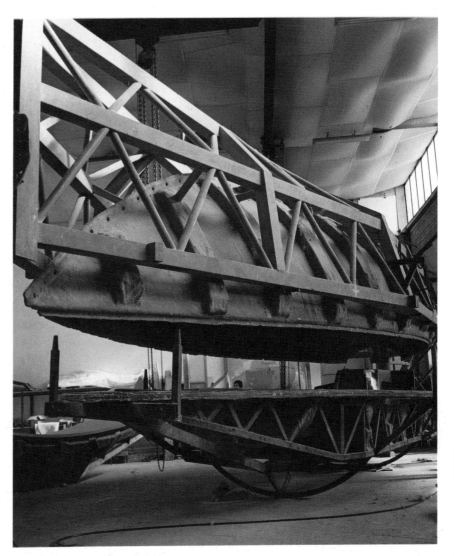

Glass reinforced plastic consists of a mat of very fine fibres of glass saturated with a liquid polyester resin and laid in a pre-formed mould. A catalyst, such as methyl-ethyl ketone peroxide, together with a hardener, is then applied as a liquid and causes the resin to set rock hard. The outside of the hull has an extra layer or skin, known as a 'gel coat', which contains the colour pigment and gives an exceptionally hard, smooth and shiny surface. One of the many advantages of this method of hull construction is that it lends itself to the mass production of small craft of all varieties, from dinghies to sailing and motor yachts, by the use of moulds onto which the GRP is applied. Other advantages of GRP are its lightness in relation to its strength, its complete freedom from rust, corrosion, and rot, and its resistance to all the marine organisms which attack wood and to knocks and minor collisions. All these advantages are such that today something approaching ninety per cent of all dinghies, yachts, and other craft up to about 75 ft (23 m) in length are constructed of it. Some of the modern life-saving craft are also made of GRP, and because of its non-magnetic properties several

Above: Hulls of smaller vessels can be moulded in glass reinforced plastic (GRP or fibreglass). This material does not decay or corrode and for minesweepers it has the added attraction of being non-magnetic.

navies have adopted it for the construction of minehunters, as minesweepers are called today.

Another new material developed for small craft production is ferrocement. Ships made of cement are not new; during World War I some small merchant ships were constructed in Britain of this material as quick replacements for some of the horrifying losses caused by the German U-boat attacks, and it was also used during those years, though in small numbers, for the building of dumb lighters for use in loading and unloading ships lying out at anchor in the stream. The modern method of cement construction, however, is much more refined than the crude methods of World War I. Several layers of wire mesh, usually of the welded type, are wired to the intersections of steel rods and tubes to form a close-knit framework for the vessel's hull. This is then made waterproof by the application of a semi-liquid mortar mix, applied simultaneously from both inside and outside the hull structure. The mortar is made with cement, very fine sand and *possolano* or volcanic ash to make it more

workable. When this has set and cured over a period of about a week, it produces a very hard, smooth, and resilient hull. Ferrocement can be used for hulls of up to about 80 ft (24 m) in length, and in addition to thousands of harbour launches, yachts, and other small craft most modern Chinese sampans are mass-produced in ferrocement, replacing the traditional wooden sampans of earlier days. The same material is widely used for building ashore; the roof of the Sydney Opera House is constructed of ferrocement, for example.

There has been a revival, too, in the multi-hull theory of construction, almost exclusively in the yachting world. A multi-hull is a type of vessel with two or more hulls, or floats, propelled by paddles, sails, or mechanical power. The inspiration for the modern multi-hull was undoubtedly provided by the outrigger canoes of the Indian and Pacific Oceans which date back hundreds of years, but its appearance in European waters is of more recent date. With a view to eliminating rolling in choppy seas, a twin-hulled ferry of

Below: Second World War experience gave birth to the design of the frigate, mainly for anti-submarine warfare but also armed with a gun and/or anti-ship and anti-aircraft missiles. The design of this Mark 10 frigate, capable of 30 knots, dates from 1962.

Nautilus
(1954)

Length 324 ft (99 m) *Beam* 28 ft (8·5 m)
Standard displacement 3,530 tons *Speed* 25 knots (submerged)
Armament six 21-inch torpedo tubes *Complement* 105

The launching of the U.S. submarine *Nautilus* marked the beginning of a new era not only for submarines but for ships in general, since she was the first vessel of any kind to have nuclear propulsion. Her nuclear reactor powers two steam turbines giving 15,000 h.p. She also has conventional diesel and electric propulsion units. Because the nuclear reactor consumes no oxygen, the only effective limitation on her ability to remain submerged is the endurance of her crew and their oxygen requirements. On one occasion without refuelling she covered 91,324 nautical miles, 78,885 of them under water. She can dive to a depth of 720 ft (219·5 m). On 3 August 1958 the *Nautilus* passed under the North Pole on her way to becoming the first submarine to travel from the Pacific to the Atlantic beneath the ice-cap, succeeding where the earlier submarine of the same name had failed in 1931.

This reconstruction of the *Nautilus* is based on the information that is available. The cutaway section shows (from bow to stern) the torpedo room, crew's quarters, officers' quarters, operations and control rooms, radiation shield, nuclear reactor and engine room. The diagram gives a cross section through the hull amidships, showing operations room (above) and control room, and the cylindrical pressure hull. The photograph shows the *Nautilus* under way on the surface.

Above: The ferrocement yacht *Petralis* under construction at St Katharine's Dock, London. The work of amateur shipbuilders, she is the largest ferrocement yacht to be built in Britain. The photograph shows the projecting mesh webs for bulkhead attachments and as supports for the cabin floors.

1,533 gross tons, named the *Castalia*, was built in 1874 for crossing the English Channel from Dover to Calais, and she was followed a few years later by a similar but larger ferry, the *Calais-Douvres*, of 1,820 gross tons. Both consisted of two identical hulls joined at deck level by a platform carrying the bridge and upperworks. They were propelled by a paddlewheel working between the hulls. The twin hulls provided extra stability and reduced the rolling in rough seas, but added quite considerably to the fuel consumption as the resistance to two hulls was considerably more than to one.

The experiment was not a commercial success and the multi-hull concept remained in abeyance until after World War II when it was revived for sailing yachts. The main advantage is that with lightweight sailing boats there is a smaller area of wetted hull surface when under sail, and this will produce a considerably greater speed for any given sail area. There is also an added stability, and these two factors have made them very popular as leisure craft. Large numbers of catamarans (two identical hulls connected by a central platform) and trimarans (one central hull with two outrigger-type floats) have been built. In heavy seas the structural stresses on catamarans and trimarans are considerable, but many long voyages, including circumnavigations of the world, have been successfully accomplished by multi-hulls.

In Europe World War II came to an end in the traditional and long-established pattern, with sea power, in this particular case allied to air power, providing the conditions in which armies could establish themselves on the battlefield for the decisive thrust. The same pattern heralded the end of the war in the Pacific a few months later, even though the final surrender was perhaps hastened a little by the explosion of atomic bombs at Hiroshima and Nagasaki. But even before these bombs were dropped, Allied sea power had already opened the way for armies to establish themselves on the final battleground. No doubt the two atomic bombs saved the lives of thousands of American and Japanese soldiers which would otherwise have been lost in the subsequent land campaign, but they had little or no effect on the inevitability of Japanese defeat which sea power had brought about. That the cost in civilian lives was horrific must remain on the conscience of us all.

The normal reaction at the end of any war is for those involved to relax through national exhaustion, to disarm and to indulge in a period of little or no progress in the development of new armaments. The lessons of the war are largely forgotten in the euphoria of victory or the bitterness of defeat, for the urgency of war is no longer operative. But at the end of World War II this normal pattern was reversed as the world split into two mutually antagonistic ideological camps, forcing the nations into a fairly large-scale arms race instead of the expected post-war disarmament. There was also the revelation, during the very last hours of the war, that an entirely new weapon had made its appearance on the military field, a weapon of incalculable power with an application to navies, armies and air forces alike. It was not something to be left in limbo while nations relaxed.

With hindsight, it is interesting to pick out the features of World War II which were truly indicative of the changes to come. The small rocket carrying an explosive was used operationally both by aircraft and by warships, and was developed by Germany into a big medium-range missile called the V2. With the achievement of atomic fission in the shape of the two atomic bombs dropped in Japan, scientists could not only see the way ahead to nuclear fusion, which would produce explosions beside which those in Japan in 1945 would seem almost like pinpricks, but could also see a marriage between the nuclear explosion and a development of the V2 rocket. Naval architects could perhaps see a little further: yet another marriage between this new weapon and the submarine. The application of these new weapons to ships would be purely as a purpose of carriage and delivery, for such a huge and instantaneous release of energy in an explosion had no application as an anti-ship weapon. There was, however, one intermediate step to be taken before the two could come together in a virtually foolproof weapon of immense strategic power.

The fission of uranium atoms was accompanied by intense heat, and if this fission could be slowed down and controlled, the heat produced could be harnessed to the production of steam for normal ship propulsion. The great advantage of such a form of steam production was that it would be achieved in a reactor without the need of oxygen from the surrounding air. This at once made it particularly attractive as a means of propulsion for submarines, giving them for the first time the ability to proceed indefinitely underwater without the need to come periodically to the surface in order to recharge their batteries.

The decision to go ahead with the harnessing of nuclear fission for ship propulsion was taken by the United States in 1948 when the U.S. Atomic Energy Commission awarded a contract to the Westinghouse Electrical Company to develop a nuclear propulsion plant suitable for use in a submarine. Progress was rapid, and the keel of what was to be the world's first nuclear-powered submarine, the U.S.S. *Nautilus*, was laid on 14 June 1952. She was launched in January 1954

and commissioned in September of the same year. Built by the General Dynamics (Electric Boat) Corporation, she was a large submarine as submarines went at that time, with a length of 324 ft (98·8 m), a beam of 28 ft (8·5 m) and a surface displacement of 3,530 tons (3,586 tonnes).

The controlled nuclear reaction in a reactor takes the place of a marine boiler in a conventional ship's steam propulsion unit, and the heat produced is used through heat transformers to generate steam for the turbines which either drive the propellers direct or through electric motors. The reactor has to be totally encased in a heavy safety shield to prevent the escape of radiation. The *Nautilus* at first used Uranium 235 as fuel, but was refuelled two years later with enriched uranium, now the standard fuel for all nuclear propulsion units.

One of the immense advantages of nuclear propulsion for ships is the length of time it takes to use up one charge of uranium fuel and the consequent ability to run a ship at full speed for a vast distance before it is necessary to refuel her. On a single fuelling of her reactor, the *Nautilus* was able to cover a distance of 91,300 nautical miles, of which nearly 80,000 were submerged.

The advantages of nuclear propulsion for

Left: The hinged caps over the vertical tubes of a Polaris sea-launched ballistic missile submarine. These missiles are propelled by a two-stage solid-fuel rocket motor and are effective at ranges up to 2,500 miles (4,000 km).

submarines are incalculable. The conventional submarine, using its diesel engine for surface propulsion and its electric batteries for operating when submerged, has many limitations. It is dependent on its oil fuel capacity both for its radius of operation and for the length of time it can stay out at sea on operations. It is limited in speeds to the power of its diesel engine on the surface – perhaps 16 to 18 knots – and on its batteries for submerged speed – perhaps 10 or 11 knots for a very short time or a much slower speed for a longer period of dive. Submerged propulsion exhausts the capacity of its batteries quickly, and to recharge them using its diesel engine, the submarine has to come to the surface, or else lie submerged just below the surface and obtain oxygen for the engine through its schnorkel breathing tube. In either case she is very vulnerable to discovery and attack as modern radar can obtain a reflection from the top of a schnorkel tube as easily as it can from the above-water hull. Nuclear propulsion changes all this. In the case of the *Nautilus,* one charge of nuclear fuel in the reactor lasts, on average, about two years, giving the submarine a virtually unlimited radius of operation. Without the need of oxygen for combustion, she can use her steam turbines for propulsion both on the surface and submerged and, with these turbines producing 15,000 horsepower, she has been able to maintain a submerged speed of over 25 knots.

The success of the *Nautilus* opened the way to a wide expansion in nuclear propulsion, mainly in submarines where it has revolutionized the practice of submarine warfare, and also in some surface warships. As far as submarines are concerned, development has concentrated largely on obtaining increased underwater speed by streamlining the hull and adopting a teardrop hull shape, which has produced underwater speeds of up to 35 knots, greatly in excess of anything previously obtained.

Nuclear-propelled submarines normally fall into two distinct categories. There are those whose weapon is still the torpedo, though a much more sophisticated torpedo than that used in World War II. Modern torpedoes have a considerably greater range of up to around 20 miles (32 km) and are guided towards their target until their own guidance system can take over and lock itself onto the target so that it cannot miss. The other category is an alliance between the nuclear-propelled submarine and the long-range guided missile carrying one or more nuclear warheads. These are much larger, normally over 7,000 tons, so that they can accommodate a battery of large missiles of the Polaris and Poseidon type, giving reality to the post-war vision of a combination of submarines and long-range

rockets. Although Polaris and Poseidon are classed within the intermediate range of rockets, they are nevertheless effective up to 2,500 miles (4,000 km). Following the remarkable feat of engineering by the U.S. in solving the problems of firing the missiles while the submarine remains submerged, large missile-firing submarines of this type have also been built by Britain, France and Russia.

No weapon, however efficient it may be, and the Polaris/Poseidon weapon is remarkably efficient, is immune from refinement and further development. Today a new submarine-launched weapon in this family is under development; it is larger so that each rocket can carry several warheads which can be targeted individually on different objectives, and range is increased to 4,000 miles (6,400 km). This is the Trident missile, and its considerably larger size will call for a

Above: The Polaris submarine-launched missile has been one of the most effective elements in the defence armoury of the West. Although superseded by the Trident system it is likely to remain in service for some time.

revolution in submarine building. Submarines of around 14,000 to 16,000 tons or even more will be necessary to carry these new weapons, far larger than anything envisaged in the past. With their increased range allied to the vast expanse of ocean available in which to operate, no target on earth will be beyond their reach.

The cost of this new weapon, mainly in its requirement of new and very large submarines, is of course, very heavy, but it has strategic advantages. Unlike a similar land-based missile, its firing position from somewhere in the vast expanse of ocean is mobile and unknown, and, being submerged, is invisible. It is, therefore, essentially a second-strike weapon, always available for use if a sudden enemy attack should be made on the land-based missiles whose firing positions are known. The strategic argument used to justify its existence is that fear of the vast scale of destruction which would be caused by unlimited nuclear war has kept the world free from nuclear war for the last thirty-eight years and that an efficient and reliable second-strike weapon is a sufficient deterrent to any would-be opponent to keep it so. It must of course be realized that these missile-carrying submarines are not really warships in the accepted sense of that term; the weapons they carry have no role to play in naval warfare. Their missiles are essentially land weapons fired in the last extremity at a shore target. The submarine which carries them is no more than a submersible and mobile launching pad for nuclear weapons intended to make all-out war unthinkable.

Below: USS *Bremerton*, one of a recent class of large nuclear-powered submarines designed mainly to operate against enemy submarines. She carries Subroc and anti-submarine torpedoes and tube-launched Harpoon missiles.

Nimitz
(1975)

Length 1,092 ft (332 m) *Beam* 134 ft (40·8 m)
Draught 37 ft (11·3 m) *Flight deck width* 252 ft (76·8 m)
Standard displacement 81,600 tons; 91,487 tons deep load
Speed 30+ knots *Complement* 3,300 + 3,000 assigned to air wing

U.S.S. *Nimitz* is the world's second nuclear-powered aircraft carrier, following U.S.S. *Enterprise* which was commissioned fourteen years earlier. She has two pressurized water-cooled reactors compared with the eight fitted in the earlier *Enterprise* but the nuclear cores for her reactors are designed to provide enough energy to keep the ship operational for at least thirteen years, with the ability to steam up to one million nautical miles between each refuelling. The *Enterprise*'s reactors needed refuelling every two to three years, providing energy to steam up to about 300,000 miles, though after her last extensive refit the endurance of the new nuclear cores for her reactors is expected to be longer, probably from ten to twelve years.

The *Nimitz* carries an air wing of over ninety aircraft capable of all normal carrier duties of attack, defence, reconnaissance and early warning. The wing is divided into two squadrons of fighters, two light attack squadrons, one medium attack squadron, two anti-submarine squadrons of which one is of Sea King helicopters, and detachments of reconnaissance aircraft, electronic warfare aircraft, early warning/control aircraft and tanker aircraft for in-flight refuelling. The illustration above right is of a Grumman F.14A Tomcat fighter. The *Nimitz* is fitted with over thirty radar sets to cover a variety of purposes, and also with satellite communications antennae. Her deck armament consists of three multiple launchers for Sea Sparrow missiles.

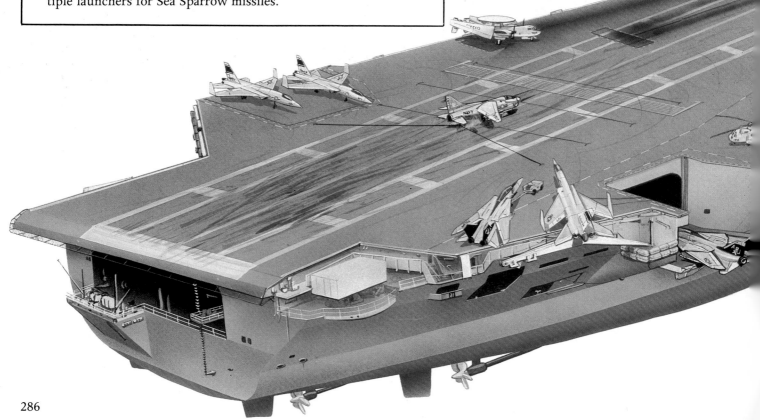

287

Nuclear propulsion, so successfully developed for the submarine, has many obvious advantages for the warship, most notably in the long life of the fuel element which obviates the necessity of frequent refuelling and provides an almost unlimited radius of action at continuous high speed. The United States uses it to power their new and large aircraft carriers and some of their larger cruisers. It has some disadvantages, in its high initial cost and in the extra weight of the reactor's heavy shielding, necessary as a safeguard against radiation leaks. All modern warships have to be extremely weight-conscious because of the heavy installations of modern weaponry and ancillary services, such as radar and essential counter-measures, mounted on and above the upper deck. The overall weight of a nuclear propulsion unit can therefore become a critical factor in warship design, particularly in the case of smaller ships.

Another naval lesson of World War II was the influence of the large aircraft carrier both on tactics and strategy. Misreading the lessons of World War I, which indicated that the torpedo

Far left below: Fleet Air
Arm Buccaneers from
the aircraft carrier HMS
Ark Royal which has since
been paid off out of the
Royal Navy and sold for
breaking up.

Left: USS *Enterprise*, the
world's first nuclear-
powered aircraft carrier, at
sea. She has a displacement
of 76,700 tons and at the
time of her construction
was the biggest warship
ever built. Her maximum
speed is 35 knots and she
carries an air wing of
eighty-four aircraft.

and the mine were more destructive weapons
than the gun, all the maritime nations entered
World War II still pinning their faith to the
battleship armed with the big naval gun. Their
vulnerability to attack from carrier-borne
aircraft made them virtually useless in naval
battles at sea and they were soon relegated to the
sidelines of sea warfare. Only in one aspect of
naval warfare could they still prove their value,
when their support fire in amphibious assault
landings proved devastatingly effective, but this
relatively minor role was not enough to justify
their retention in the post-war naval world. No
country has built a new battleship since the war
ended, although a few of them have been preserved in care and maintenance status by the United
States. It seems that, in the face of modern airborne and shipborne weapons, they will never
again find a fighting role at sea.

The aircraft carrier, developed after the war to
a size undreamed of by wartime naval architects,
has had a chequered career over the years that
followed. With the development of new
weapons, and particularly of the smaller guided
missiles carried in ships and aircraft, many navies
came to the conclusion that the big carrier was
too vulnerable a target to roam the oceans and
that her aircraft, too, might well be excessively
vulnerable to the target-seeking anti-aircraft
weapons mounted in ships. These navies gradually phased out their carriers, relying on the
helicopter to do some of the tasks of the carrier-
borne fixed-wing aircraft and deciding to dis-
pense with the others.

Only the United States Navy differed from this
policy. Instead of phasing out their carriers they
have developed them to more than twice their
original size. Their latest ships in this category
are nuclear-propelled and, with a displacement
of around 95,000 tons (96,500 tonnes), are capable of operating up to about 100 aircraft each. In
recent years Russia, too, has built carriers of
about 40,000 tons (40,640 tonnes) and, even more
recently, Britain has re-entered the carrier field.
Her new ones, however, are comparatively small
ships of around 20,000 tons (20,300 tonnes) and
capable of operating only helicopters and vertical
take-off aircraft in small numbers. While these
are extremely versatile aircraft, they are comparatively slow and lack the range of normal
fixed-wing aircraft.

It is the technological advance in weapon
development during recent years which appears
to have given the conventional aircraft carrier a
new lease of life. For some years missiles have had
guidance systems which virtually ensure them
hitting their target, initially discharged along a
radar bearing until they approach near enough
for their own guidance system to take over and
lock onto the target. This final guidance system
is frequently visual in the form of television pictures sent back from the missile to an operator on
the launching vessel. It was this threat of an almost certain hit which caused the temporary lack
of confidence in the carrier by so many navies, a
very big and expensive target whose loss might
well be a naval disaster. But the development of
the missile has in more recent years been matched

by the development of the anti-missile-missile, which can track and intercept an incoming missile, destroying it before it can reach and hit its target.

In a somewhat roundabout way the anti-missile-missile has again justified the large aircraft carrier operating fixed-wing aircraft. The maximum range at which the anti-ship missile can be fired is about 20 miles (32 km), because it can only start its run on a radar contact and a radar beam cannot be bent round the curved surface of the earth. But these missiles, most of which skim the surface of the sea, travel so fast that there is not sufficient reaction time to bring an anti-missile-missile to bear if the original discharge has not been detected. It is here that the carrier with fixed-wing aircraft earns part of her keep, for she can fly air patrols out to a range of about 200 miles (320 km) and detect the incoming enemy long before he comes within his firing range. The fixed-wing aircraft can also use their own missile armament to attack enemy ships and aircraft while they are still far distant unless the enemy fleet also has an aircraft carrier which is flying air patrols.

For some years after the ending of World War II it was possible in very general terms to say that the main effect of modern weapon development on warship design was a reduction in the size of the ship, in spite of the obviously contrary experience in the case of carriers and submarines. The post-war years saw the end of the battleship and the big cruiser, and the general run of naval shipbuilding was concentrated on the smaller warships such as destroyers, frigates, fast patrol craft and minehunters. In those days the general pattern was to build the ship, place her weapons on board and give her a good radar installation, and that was that. Technology has today advanced far beyond that. Although many warships still carry a gun, it is a far more sophisticated weapon than it was even a few years ago, being fully automated with a very rapid rate of fire and not even requiring a gun crew to operate it. Modern warships are also armed with anti-air and anti-ship missiles, and the most modern ones with anti-missile-missiles. Radio and radar decoys and counter-measures are also accommodated on board, so that in recent years the actual sizes of frigates and destroyers have had to be increased to carry the new weapons and their associated electronics. Thus the destroyer, which during World War II averaged perhaps 1,800 tons (1,830 tonnes) is now a ship of approaching 5,000 tons (5,080 tonnes), with the frigate a ship of perhaps half that size or a little more.

The big amphibious assaults which were such a feature of World War II are now operations of the past; any assault on such a scale on an enemy-

held coast would today almost certainly draw a nuclear response. But, on a smaller scale, such as in the Falklands, an amphibious capability is too valuable a weapon to throw away and it calls for a ship of special design to combine all the elements of amphibious warfare on a smaller scale. The British solution is perhaps typical of the skill of the naval architects when faced with such a problem. Basically it takes the form of a small streamlined floating dock within the hull of a ship, used to carry landing craft which can put a full commando unit ashore. To launch the landing craft, water ballast is taken on board to lower the ship in the water until the dock is flooded and the landing craft can be floated out. They are re-embarked in the same way, with the water ballast pumped out when the landing craft have been floated into the dock, allowing the ship to rise and the dock to drain. Smaller landing craft are carried additionally on davits to add to the troop-carrying capacity, and the ship has a small flight deck capable of operating large helicopters. All this is contained in a ship of 20,000 tons (20,320 tonnes) with twin turbines giving her a speed of over 20 knots.

Apart from weapons, the greatest advances of these post-war years have been in the field of ship propulsion and naval engineering. As has been seen, nuclear propulsion is a huge if expensive step forward, particularly in the case of submarines, transforming them into a particularly lethal weapon of naval warfare. Advances in metallurgy have also played a large part in the development of the modern submarine, by

Above: The Type-21 frigate HMS *Antelope* exploding after being hit by a 500-lb (226-kg) bomb during an Argentine air attack in San Carlos Bay.

Far left above: The loss of British ships to the missiles and bombs of the Argentine air force during the Falklands War of 1982 was mainly due to the lack of extensive air cover. Here a Royal Navy Sea King helicopter hovers over liferafts from the blazing landing ship *Sir Galahad* after the devastating Argentine air attack during the landing at Bluff Cove.

Far left below: The destroyer HMS *Sheffield*, armed with a gun, Sea Dart missiles and helicopter-launched anti-submarine missiles. During the Falkland Islands operations she was hit and sunk by an Argentine air-launched Exocet missile.

Above: A Rolls Royce Olympus gas turbine being hoisted aboard the Thai frigate *Makut Rajakumarn*. Although gas turbines have a shorter life than steam turbines, the ease with which they can be replaced means less time in harbour for repairs.

Above right: Radar is probably the greatest gift which modern technology has given to seamen. It is an invaluable aid to navigation, particularly in darkness and fog, but is also vital in modern sea warfare.

producing steels whose strength enables submarines to dive to depths of up to 1,000 ft (305 m) where they are well below the reach of surface-borne sonar detecting devices. (It has recently been claimed that by using additional titanium in the steelmaking process a steel has now been produced that is strong and flexible enough to enable a submarine to operate at 3,000 ft (915 m). If this steel has in fact been produced, there is no reason why submarines built with it should not dive to this depth.) In the larger steam-driven warships, advances in engineering have produced vastly more efficient marine boilers and engines, considerably reducing the number of boilers needed to produce the required steam output, and at the same time increasing the power output of the engines.

More important than the modern steam installation, particularly for warships such as destroyers and frigates, and, indeed, for all but the largest ships, is the gas turbine. All the experimental work on it was done by the aircraft industry, the marine version being an adaptation of the aircraft engine. It was first used at sea in conjunction with the steam turbine, originally to give an additional boost to the engines when a sudden burst of speed was required for tactical reasons. With its reliability proven at sea it became the sole propulsion installation for many of the smaller ships until, with extended experience of its operational value, it was adopted in the British Navy for all major warships; even the new 20,000-ton carriers are being powered by gas turbines developed from the Concorde engine. Although pioneered by Britain, many other navies have adopted it as the prime means of propulsion.

The gas turbine has many distinct advantages. Its power-to-weight ratio is far superior to any other form of marine propulsion. Power for power, it takes up less space in a ship even than a conventional marine diesel engine, which is itself a great space saver. And it has the inestimable advantage for a warship that, from cold, it can develop full power within a very few minutes so that in an emergency a ship can get under way in a very short time, at full speed if necessary, without having to go through the long process of warming through the engines. Its main disadvantages, however, are its high cost (though this is modest compared with that of a nuclear reactor) and fuel consumption, and the fire risk caused by its highly volatile fuel.

It is a rough and ready rule that a warship's design is dictated largely by the weapons she carries rather than the other way round. This has posed some problems for modern naval architects ever since the missile rather than the gun became the main above-water weapon of all navies. Missile technology calls for extensive radar back-up both for detection of the enemy and for guidance to the target, and this in its turn means that a considerable weight has to be accommodated on and above the upper deck. To compensate for this extra weight the modern practice has been to substitute the lighter aluminium alloys for the heavier steel for all the vessel's superstructure, although in some warships even this is not enough to preserve their essential stability, making it necessary to carry additional ballast low down. Some small warships remain stable only by topping up their fuel tanks when half-empty, a requirement that drastically reduces their range. The new generation of warships will probably be built broader, sacrificing streamlining for the stability needed to carry extra armament for attack or defence.

Warships are designed and built to incorporate the lessons and the theories of naval warfare. Many of these lessons have had to be painfully re-learned over the past 20 years. In the Vietnam war, air attacks from offshore carriers proved so costly against sound AA defences that the US Navy recommissioned its 'Iowa' class battleships, to bombard inland targets with heavy-calibre shellfire. The Falklands War of 1982 proved a particularly hard school, showing that AA missile capacity can be costly and fallible alternative to carrier-borne airborne early warning and fighter cover. In the light of the Falklands experience the rapid-fire gatling gun, guided by its own radar, has been adopted as a potent counter to surface-skimming missiles of the Exocet type. Perhaps the most convincing warning against the dangers of modern 'technology mania' came in 1987. This was the use of contact mines, one of the oldest of all naval weapons, in the Iraq-Iran Gulf War. Only when several ships had fallen victim to this 'old technology' weapon did it emerge that the US Navy, the world's biggest, had virtually no conventional minesweepers for the location and removal of these simple but deadly weapons, which can be deployed wherever a small boat can venture. The new generations of warships will, no doubt, be better and even more efficient once these re-learned lessons have been thoroughly studied, analysed, and put into practice.

Left: A practice firing of the British Sea Slug surface-to-air guided missile from HMS *Kent*, one of four guided-missile destroyers of the 'County' class.

Below: HMS *Broadsword*, a Type-22 destroyer of the Royal Navy, armed with Exocet (surface-to-surface) and Sea Wolf (surface-to-air) missiles in addition to anti-submarine torpedoes.

Chapter Thirteen
Oil from the Seas

The tenfold rise in the price of crude oil over the last few years brought new problems to ship designers and builders. It meant that deposits of oil which were in difficult or inaccessible places, and therefore uneconomic in the days of cheap oil, became economic almost overnight. One of those difficult places was the North Sea, under which it was known that there were deposits of oil, and the rise in price made it apparent that there were good profits to be won if the difficulties of drilling and processing there could be overcome at not too large a cost.

There are three essential stages in the production of oil, whether below the sea or the land. The first and obvious one is to discover by a seismic survey the rock formations which indicate the probable presence of oil. At sea, this normally involves two ships, one fitted with seismic equipment for firing the charges, using compressed air instead of explosives to reduce the risk of killing too many fish, the other towing a string of microphones to record the echoes of the charges from the different rock formations. This process calls for exact navigation on the part of both ships since the readings must be related exactly to the seabed, even to within a few yards, in order to determine the exact position in which to drill. Special seismic survey vessels have been built to accommodate the equipment required for this first step in the discovery of oil.

With a potentially favourable seismic survey, the second stage is to drill an exploratory well to discover whether in fact the survey has been correct in forecasting the presence of oil and, if so, that the oil is of a quantity and quality worth recovering. It is at this stage that the costs of production begin to escalate at a prodigious rate, and an oil production company will expect to see at least ten years of prolific life from a well in order to justify the immense capital expenditure which is involved in recovering oil from fields under the sea.

Left: The Shell-Esso production platform Cormorant 'A' at the start of a long tow to Norway.

Two basic kinds of drilling rig are used today, a mobile jack-up rig which can be used in depths of water up to about 50 fathoms (90 m) and, for waters of greater depth, a self-propelled drilling ship or a semi-submersible rig. A jack-up rig has four legs with a drilling platform which can ride up and down them, a device developed as a result of experience in the Mulberry harbours erected for the invasion of Normandy in World War II. It is towed into position with its four legs raised, and when in the exact position the legs are lowered until they rest firmly on the seabed, the platform being lifted up the legs to the necessary height above sea level. The derrick which operates the drill is then erected on the platform, if it is not already in place, and drilling begins. The other type, drilling ship or semi-submersible, is not attached to the seabed with legs but is held in position by four or more anchors, together with an electronic monitor which adjusts the position automatically. This consists of a 'bleeper' placed in position on the seabed and instruments in the drilling ship or semi-submersible which listen continuously to the 'bleep' to detect every small change in position of the rig. If it does move, motors are automatically switched on to bring the rig back to its exact position. The drilling ship follows more or less the conventional hull shape of all ships, but adapted internally for its job of operating an oil drill, usually with the derrick amidships and, of course, the drill itself working through the ship's bottom. The semi-submersible is a specially designed drilling platform supported on large, tubular steel legs attached to pontoons, which are submerged to a depth of around 60 ft (18·3 m) and support the weight of the platform. They are very large and complex floating structures with all the necessary machinery for turning the drill and pumping the mud down the drill pipes, with full accommodation for the drilling crew and a deck for helicopters to land and take off. They represent the first large escalation of cost, for they can cost up to £20 million to build and £20,000 a day to operate. But they are

North Sea Oil-Rigs

Oil wells under the sea are no new phenomenon; there has been offshore production of oil for many years in relatively shallow waters. It is only in the last few years that the tenfold increase in the price of oil has made the exploration of deeper and less hospitable waters financially viable. The oil-producing companies have therefore been faced with new problems of constructing drilling and production rigs able to withstand greater extremes of wind and weather. The North Sea rigs illustrated here are the successful product of this engineering challenge.

The rig below is the *Ocean Benloyal*, a self-propelled Aker H-3 type twin-pontoon semi-submersible. It is used to drill exploratory wells to test for quality and quantity after a seismic survey has indicated a potential oilfield. Its drilling derrick reaches 160 ft (48 m) above deck level and it has accommodation for seventy-eight men. *Ocean Benloyal* is held in position by anchors, and can drill to a depth of 25,000 ft (7,620 m) in 1,200 ft (365 m) of water. The section diagram on the right gives some idea of the massive extent of a single oil-rig's possible field of drilling.

The illustration on the far right is B.P.'s *Forties Charlie*, a jacket rig which is fixed on the seabed after an exploratory rig has located a substantial oilfield. *Forties Charlie* has a deck area of 170 × 175 ft (52 × 53.5 m), stands in 416 ft (127 m) of water, and measures 285 ft (87 m) from sea-level to the top of the drilling derrick. It has accommodation for ninety-six people and a nominal production capacity of 125,000 barrels a day (1 barrel = 159 litres).

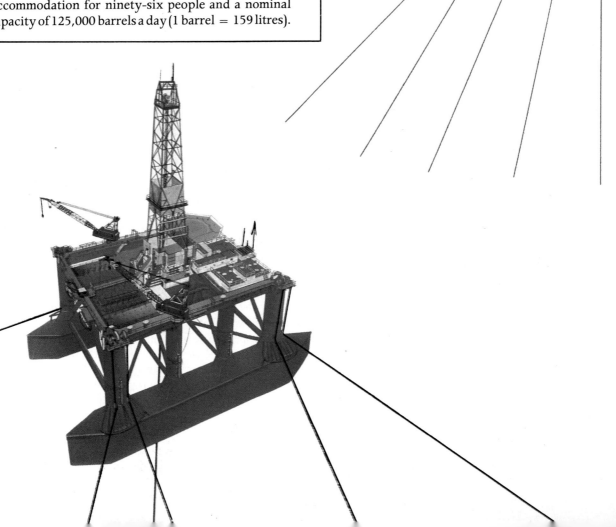

Above: The Shell-Esso Brent 'B' production platform during a North Sea storm with winds gusting up to 90 knots. The bottom of the platform is 75 ft (23 m) above sea level, which gives some indication of the height of the waves during the storm.

mobile and when sufficient exploratory wells have been drilled on one site to prove the extent and capacity of the field, they can be towed to other promising sites to continue the exploration work. When a field has proved itself worth developing, the modern drill stem can be made to operate outward into the seabed by means of ball and socket joints so that it can reach oil lying as much as two miles (3 km) from the site of the rig.

The design of a drilling rig, either fixed like a jack-up, or mobile like a semi-submersible, presents constant problems to the naval architect. For locations in areas such as the North Sea, where the weather is unpredictable and storms of considerable violence can spring up quite suddenly, the main problem is to build sufficient strength into the rig to withstand the pressures exerted at times by enormous waves and gales of 60 knots or more.

The final stage is the erection of production platforms to extract the oil and process it for transport to the refinery after the field has been proved and drilled. Although plans exist to use semi-submersible platforms to perform this part of the task, and indeed in very deep waters to do the job permanently underwater from production chambers on the seabed, almost all modern extraction is from platforms supported by concrete legs or piled steel jackets (scaffolding-like

structures) resting on the bottom.

Platforms on concrete legs have three of them, all hollow so that additional wells can be drilled through them. They are constructed ashore in their final, vertical position and then towed out by tugs, still upright, to the position in which they will operate, where they are sunk so that the concrete legs stand on the bottom with the actual platform well above sea level. They rely on their great weight to hold them fixed solidly to the seabed. Around the bottom of each leg is a cluster of storage tanks for the oil as it is forced out of the field, preparatory to its being processed on the platform to remove the gas and salt water that is dissolved in it. Some of the gas separated from the oil as it comes from the well can be used as fuel for the auxiliary machinery on the production platform, the remainder is flared off unless there is a sufficient quantity to make it worth piping ashore for commercial and domestic use.

Steel jacket platforms, also constructed ashore, are built in a dry dock lying on their side and resting on flotation tanks. When the dock is flooded on completion of the building, the platform is floated out on its tanks and again towed, still lying horizontally on its side, to its destination in the oilfields. On arrival, the flotation tanks are flooded, starting with those at the foot, so that it gradually tips upright and settles on the seabed. Once in position it is anchored to the bottom with steel piles driven through the feet of the uprights at each corner. The platform is then constructed on the top of the jacket with prefabricated parts lifted into position by cranes mounted on barges or ships.

A production platform is a vast structure. The platform itself, supported on top of its concrete legs or steel jacket, is the size of a large football ground. It is covered not only with all the machinery for drilling further wells and for the actual processing of the oil, but also with living accommodation for the platform crew, a mess hall and recreation room, facilities for a team of divers, and a helicopter deck for the daily delivery of supplies, the transference ashore of any sick or hurt members of the crew and the fortnightly relief and replacement of the crew. Some of the larger platforms also accommodate a small cinema, and all, of course, have a communications centre.

As with the drilling rigs, the complexity of the design and the inbuilt strength required cause many problems for the designers, virtually a complete departure from the design of a ship. It is the structural strength required, both to support the weight of the platform and to withstand the pressures of the elements, that makes the construction of a platform a real challenge to the skill of a designer. Although a great many of them have been built to service the many offshore oilfields around the world, only very occasionally does one hear of collapse due to a faulty design or damage caused by the failure of a platform to withstand the enormous stresses of rough seas and high winds.

The larger offshore oilfields are connected to an oil terminal or refinery ashore by a pipeline run along the seabed, an operation which requires specially designed ships to lay the pipes. Smaller fields pipe the processed oil either to a large tank on the seabed about a mile clear of the platform, or direct to a buoy known as a single buoy mooring. The seabed tank, if that is the method used, is also connected to a single buoy mooring. The distance of the buoy from the production platform is necessary to allow tankers, which come to collect the oil and take it to a terminal ashore, to have plenty of room to swing round the buoy clear of the platform while loading their cargo of oil. Unless the sea is very calm, it would be unsafe for a tanker to moor directly alongside a platform.

The whole business of extracting oil from an offshore field has given birth to a new generation of specialist ships and other craft designed purely for the purpose of servicing the industry. In addition to lifeboats for the emergency evacuation of a rig or platform, safety capsules have also been designed which are self-propelled and capable of going safely through a belt of fire on the sea should the oil escape and ignite. The laying of a pipeline, which consists of lengths of steel pipes welded together and covered with a coating of tar and cement, calls for a special pipe-laying barge, where the welding and coating is done, and a ship carrying a trenching machine which follows the barge. As the pipe is welded and coated it is paid out over the stern of the barge, and as it reaches the seabed the trenching machine takes it between two vertical arms and digs a trench in which the pipe rests, the movement of the sea filling the trench as the trenching machine moves on. Both these vessels are specially adapted to carry out this task.

There is a considerable variety of special support ships for the offshore oil industry, including converted trawlers on permanent standby to evacuate the platform crew in an emergency, supply and repair ships bringing essential stores and machinery or providing seaborne repair facilities, and specially designed fire-fighting vessels. Once an offshore site is in full production it becomes an economic necessity to keep it running at maximum capacity because of the heavy

Below: An aerial view of the accommodation rig *Treasure Finder* en route to its North Sea location alongside the Brent 'B' production platform. It provides facilities for rest and relaxation and has a medical centre with a flying-doctor service.

Above: An underwater
construction support
platform demonstrates its
fire-fighting potential.
Known as 'Uncle John', it
is one of the most
sophisticated support
platforms in the world. In
the background is the
Brent 'D' production
platform.

Right: *Semac I*, a semi-
submersible pipe-laying
barge engaged in laying a
gas pipeline in the East
Shetlands basin of the
North Sea. In the
background is the
Cormorant 'A' production
platform with a supply
vessel (left) and a
surveying ship (right).

highest rates of pay on board a production platform, any other methods of avoiding such lost
working time are eagerly sought in a constant
economic struggle to make a worthwhile profit
from an oilfield.

One such answer is to use armoured diving
suits with articulated joints modelled on those
developed to recover the gold in the sunken liner
Egypt in 1930–35. In these the diver works at
normal atmospheric pressure and so is not affected by compression disease. But they are heavy,
clumsy suits with very limited movement and,
although tools can be operated through the
articulated joints by remote control inside the
suit, there is a limit to the number of repair operations which can be performed by the diver inside. Miniature two-man submarines offer more
facilities for submerged repairs, adjustments and
inspections, and like the armoured suit the divers
inside work in a normal atmospheric pressure.
They are much more mobile and are equipped
with a variety of tools designed to be able to carry
out most of the predictable tasks which can be
expected in such a submerged installation, all of
them remotely controlled from inside the submarine. These small submarines are, again, a
legacy of World War II experience, their
prototypes being the British X-craft and the German Biber boats.

Nevertheless, there will always be some tasks
below water which only the individual diver can
perform. Modern diving techniques enable these
divers to work at depths greatly beyond those
achieved in the years between the wars, and with
the presence of a diving bell for periods of rest
and sustenance, individual divers can remain
operational for long periods at a time. There are
some tasks, too, which call for the use of free
divers with the normal aqualung equipment,
such as period inspection of the rigs and platforms for signs of corrosion or malfunction or
excessive growth of weed and barnacles.

Drilling rigs and production platforms fixed
to the seabed with concrete legs or steel jackets
can hardly be designated as ships, although they
are generally built in shipyards or equivalent
establishments and call for the knowledge and
expertise of naval architects and marine engineers. A better case can perhaps be made for class-
ing semi-submersible rigs as ships in spite of their
non-shiplike appearance, for they are at least
free-floating with a capability of self-propulsion
within a very limited compass. But the whole
offshore industry of winning oil from below the
seas is essentially a maritime concept in its
execution and support back-up, and calls in large
measure for the skills and experience of men
whose knowledge is of the techniques that apply
to ships and the sea.

capital cost involved in the development of a
difficult site under the sea in comparison with the
generally easier sites on land. In a great many
cases these vessels are adaptations of existing
ships to the specialized services required, but
some are designed and built from the keel up for
particular oilfield duties.

The most interesting of the specialized vessels
are probably the miniature submarines which
many oil companies use today in place of divers,
or in collaboration with them. All complicated
underwater systems, such as those established
for the offshore extraction of oil, require constant
inspection and repair. Some of these systems are
laid at a depth of as much as 150 fathoms (274 m),
where the pressures are very high, calling in the
case of individual divers for a long period in a
decompression chamber, sometimes for as much
as a week, to avert the danger of compression
sickness, or the 'bends'. Such long periods of
decompression obviously limit the diver's time of
working on the seabed, and since they earn the

Epilogue
Beyond the Horizon

Looking back over the development of the ship from its earliest days, perhaps the most striking feature is how soon man hit upon the best overall hull shape for the ship. In very broad terms there is not a great deal of difference between the early Egyptian trading boats or their war galleys and the warships and merchant vessels of today, as far as the general shape of the hull is concerned. This would seem to indicate that there is little room for any radical advance in the hull design of ships, except in those cases where ships are built purely for specialized tasks, such as fast ferries using the hydrofoil principle. But in small ways there may well be design advances to be made on the more or less standard hull design of today. Who, a few years ago, would have thought of adding a large bulbous protrusion to the bows of a ship as an aid to efficiency? Yet this is what a bulbous bow does, giving a smoother passage of water along a ship's sides, therefore causing less resistance to her forward movement and reducing fuel consumption. At today's high fuel costs even a small saving is attractive to every commercial user of ships, so all the new designs of merchant ships of any size today incorporate the bulbous bow.

Another innovation of ship design in the years following World War II is the ship stabilizer, first introduced by the shipbuilding firm of Denny-Brown in the 1930s. It has a particular relevance to large ships, particularly liners, although it is fitted in some smaller vessels where extra stability is required. One of the first of the big liners to fit Denny-Brown stabilizers was the *France*. Their object is to reduce rolling at sea to a minimum, and this is achieved by fitting one or two retractable fins of aerofoil design on each side of the ship. They are pivoted at the base and act in very much the same way as the hydroplanes of a submarine. They are automatically controlled by gyroscopes, and as the ship

begins to roll the stabilizing mechanism automatically adjusts the angle of the fin to counteract the roll. In narrow channels or in harbour the stabilizing fins are retracted into spaces inside the hull below the waterline. Ship stabilizers are today fitted to most liners, some warships (where they provide a steadier gun platform, especially in smaller warships when operating in a seaway) and some fishing vessels, particularly those which do their fishing off the south-west coast of Africa where the sea conditions often produce excessive, and sometimes dangerous, rolling. In these smaller vessels one stabilizer is normally sufficient to control the rolling, and it is non-retractable. It can be fitted on either side of the vessel as circumstances and design dictate. In addition to their anti-roll properties, always appreciated by passengers prone to seasickness, stabilizers have a bearing on the economics of running a ship. A ship which is rolling heavily increases her resistance to forward movement through the water, thus slowing herself down, but if the rolling can be controlled she can maintain her speed with a lower consumption of fuel, or make a better speed for the voyage with the same consumption.

It is no loss that the other type of movement of a ship in a seaway, longitudinal pitching, cannot be automatically controlled except by the exertion of some force so gigantic as to be impossible to produce. All ships pitch when steaming into a head sea, and this is a big factor in ensuring the safety of their construction. If a ship were to be held rigid in these conditions she would be subjected to intolerable hull strains, and the seas would sweep over her with such force that they could damage, or even carry away, her bridge and superstructure.

Another post-war invention is the fitting of one or two lateral thrust propellers, often described as 'bow thrusters', driven by an auxiliary engine at right angles to the fore and aft line of a ship. Today most big ships, and many ferries, have bow thrusters as an aid to manoeuvrability in narrow waters and in ports. The lateral thrust

Left: The container ship *Table Bay*. The bulbous bow is a modern innovation which eases the flow of water along the hull and reduces fuel consumption.

303

Above: Artist's impression of a diver lock-out submersible, in effect a midget submarine, mating onto a work chamber on the seabed.

tankers and container ships, but the practice continues to spread in general cargo ships. Again, efficiency is the key; the easier handling of cargo in loading and unloading, the chances that this affords for the more efficient use of the ship's crew, even the ability to work the ship with a smaller crew than in the past. These are some of the things which the shipowner of today is looking for and which keep the naval architect on his toes.

As we have seen, nuclear propulsion of ships was born out of the research into the atomic bombs which were dropped on Japan at the end of World War II. It has proved to be of extreme value for warships, having now been operated by them on a growing scale for thirty years without any serious mishap. It has provided the only solution to the dream of the true submarine, one which can operate submerged for long periods without needing to come to the surface to recharge batteries or renew the internal air supply. It has been proved, too, in surface warships where the advantages of an immense radius of action without the need to refuel are obvious. Although it is a costly system of propulsion to instal, one would have thought that its many and great advantages would have made it commercially attractive to the shipowner.

An attempt was made by the United States in 1962 to demonstrate its commercial possibilities with the building of the *Savannah*, a cargo ship of 22,000 tons fitted with a nuclear propulsion engine which gave her 21 knots on her trials, a very good speed for a merchant ship. Although only built for demonstration purposes and never operated as a commercial venture, she was not a success and was very quickly withdrawn and laid up. Germany built and launched a nuclear-powered cargo/passenger liner in 1968, the *Otto Hahn*, but she, too, has not caught the attention of modern shipowners as the way into the future.

The Russians have been more successful in their adoption of nuclear propulsion for icebreakers on the northern sea route between Novaya Zemlya and the Bering Sea, north of Siberia. The first of them, the *Lenin*, was commissioned in 1959 and was built with three nuclear reactors as her power plant. She was followed by the *Arktika*, which in August 1977 penetrated as far north through the ice as the Pole itself. Icebreakers, of course, are very specialized ships, only of real commercial interest if they can open up, and keep open, new and shorter sea routes between East and West, like for example the Arctic Ocean–Pacific Ocean route north of Russia or the notorious North-West Passage from Atlantic to Pacific north of Canada. With their nuclear-powered icebreakers the Russians have been able to keep open, at least during the

propeller is housed in a tunnel which runs laterally through the forward part of the ship below the waterline and, as it revolves, it draws water from one side of the ship and thrusts it out on the other, creating a turning force which assists sideways movements by pushing the bow round. Some ships also have a similar tunnel aft which acts as a stern thruster, so that when both are used simultaneously the ship can come alongside a harbour jetty broadside on. Many large ships can, with the aid of bow and stern thrusters, enter and leave port without having to call on the assistance of harbour tugs, an expense well worth saving in the modern economic climate of the shipping industry.

Any further innovations are most likely to take place inside the hull, however. Already, in the past two or three decades, there have been considerable changes, the main one being the move of the bridge superstructure from amidships to aft to permit a more sensible arrangement of the holds. This is particularly the case in summer months, their northern sea route, but so far no attempts have been made to open up the Atlantic–Pacific North-West Passage. There should, in theory at least, be no real difficulty in keeping this route open for at least a part of each year, given sufficient engine power such as a modern installation can provide and the strength of modern steels to withstand the forces entailed in breaking through the ice. Who can foretell how much that greatly shorter sea route between East and West might mean as an economic stimulus to increased world trade? It is a possibility for the future and if it were to come about, naval architects would be called upon to design, perhaps, a new breed of specially strengthened and equipped ships to take advantage of the new routes.

Apart from such specialized uses, and in spite of the wealth of experience gained from its naval operation, nuclear propulsion has not been seriously considered as a commercial proposition, even in the largest ships. The initial installation is very expensive, and the shielding which must enclose the reactor is massive and heavy, but one would think that the advantages of being able to operate a ship for up to two years without the need of refuelling her would outweigh the costs of installation and make this form of propulsion an attractive alternative for shipowners continually faced with spiralling increases in the cost of conventional fuel. The main reason against its installation in merchant ships lies in the size and political clout of the anti-nuclear lobby and the reluctance of many commercial ports around the world to accept and handle ships with this form of propulsion in the face of public disapproval and fears of radioactive leakages. Until or unless that element of public opinion changes, it is unlikely that commercial operators would risk the banning of their ships from many of the ports they serve.

Another form of ship propulsion, largely rejected commercially in spite of naval enthusiasm for its use, is the gas turbine. Its advantages lie in its

Below: The German nuclear-powered merchant ship *Otto Hahn* lying in Hamburg harbour. Nuclear propulsion has not yet proved itself as an economic method of propulsion for seaborne trade.

Right: The giant Russian icebreaker *Lenin* is one of the few non-military ships which justify the vast expense of nuclear propulsion. The power is needed to punch a way through the ice in order to keep open the northern sea route from Novaya Semlya to the Bering Sea.

weight and space-saving properties and its ability to produce full power within minutes of starting from cold – important assets for a warship. No other means of propulsion can equal its power output in relation to its overall weight. But additional speed, except in certain ships or short-haul passages, such as passenger and car ferries, is not so important commercially on long-haul voyages as fuel economy, and the gas turbine is a heavy 'gas guzzler'. Apart from specialized fields when speed is economically important, the gas turbine would therefore appear to have little commercial future in merchant shipping.

During the early 1970s four large 31,000-ton container ships were built, powered by gas turbines, to provide a fast transatlantic service to compare with that of the big passenger liners. They achieved a service speed of 28 knots, but when the price of oil rocketed in the middle and end of that decade, they were proved uneconomic and the gas turbines were run at reduced power to save fuel, providing a speed of 18 knots. Today the ships have been withdrawn from service so that their gas turbines can be replaced with diesel engines, an eloquent indication that speed in merchant ships can be too expensive in economic terms.

In the field of marine engineering the technological advances in the design and performance of steam and diesel engine propulsion have been enormous, and it is in the nature of all progress that these advances will continue. They are, between them, the most economical of all means of propulsion, with the steam turbine the more popular for the larger ships. In earlier years, as ships grew larger, the single engine developed into two, three, and four to drive that number of propellers; today more and more big ships are reverting to the single propeller without much loss of speed and with much greater fuel efficiency. This has been made possible by the design of engines with greater power output than was thought feasible ten or twenty years ago. Because diesel fuel is very costly, the tendency today is to produce engines with a longer stroke, which makes them slow revving and enables them to burn a heavier and less refined oil. In this way the essential power is maintained at a reduced fuel cost. In some smaller ships these engines are used with controllable-pitch propellers, which simplify the overall control of the ships as they are operated directly from the bridge. Although some shipowners today look upon these propellers as an expensive luxury, others have discovered that the extra control they confer has resulted in a saving of engine-room staff. As experience with them builds up, they may well be more widely adopted.

It is in this aspect of ship management, the more economic use of crews, that the greatest changes have been seen in the last few years, and this process is likely to continue well into the future as new techniques are evolved. Automation in ships is a relatively new technology, but already it has drastically reduced the large crews which were carried on board during the days when much of the essential work on board was performed by manual labour. Today much of it is done by machines which are remotely controlled, not necessarily by human decisions but by electronic sensors which adjust to optimum efficiency. The days of the fully

automatic ship with minimal crew have not yet arrived, and probably never will, but every advance in automation pays a dividend in the reduction of operational costs through the more economic use of manpower on board.

One small experiment carried out in Japan, which at first might look like a partial return to the practices of days long past, may well have a considerable influence on modern design. About three years ago a Japanese shipyard, Nippon Kokan, built a small tanker to which they fitted square sails controlled by a computer. The sails are spread, furled, and trimmed to the wind entirely by the computer, which decides when the wind is strong enough and blowing in a direction which will help the ship along. After several voyages over the course of a year, the tanker has cut her fuel costs by just over ten per cent without any loss of service speed or efficiency. The idea may look a little far-fetched, but the figures speak for themselves and the saving of fuel by using the wind when it is favourable may

Left: This jack-up rig was fitted with 200-ft (61-m) sails to assist it on its voyage from Louisiana to the Esso-Shell Leman Bank gasfield, near Great Yarmouth, England. With one tug towing the rig, the sails shortened the voyage by five days.

Below: The Japanese tanker *Shinaitoku Maru* is fitted with computer-controlled square sails for setting when the wind is favourable. A saving of ten per cent in fuel costs has been achieved without loss of speed or efficiency.

well prove an example that others will be tempted to follow.

Today, as for the last hundred years, steel remains the principal material for the construction of ships, though invariably welded instead of rivetted as in past years. It has some drawbacks, as it is prone to rust and corrosion, and it is heavy in comparison with some of the light alloys now available, which have great resistance to corrosion and can be welded as easily as steel. The reason for its almost universal use in preference to alloys lies in the comparative costs of the two materials, for aluminium alloys are still very expensive. Some small craft, mainly yachts, have been built of aluminium alloy and have been very successful, but these are the toys of the rich who are not concerned with the economics of shipbuilding for commercial purposes. There have been suggestions that a ship's hull built of these alloys could be additionally used as a means of trapping solar energy to provide extra energy for propulsion, but this is probably to approach the land of make-believe. Unless the cost of these alloys can be considerably reduced, which seems unlikely in the foreseeable future, steel is likely to remain unchallenged as the material for the building of ships. Glass reinforced plastic, so widely used for small craft today, has the strength, lightness, and complete resistance to corrosion that makes it an ideal material for shipbuilding, but it can never compete in the large shipbuilding industry because, by reason of its quick-setting property, hulls made of it have to be moulded as a whole and cannot be built in sections and subsequently joined together. This limits its practical use to hulls of less than 100 ft (30·5 m) overall.

It has been seen in a previous chapter how two closures of the Suez Canal have influenced the size of oil tankers, making it economically necessary to build very large tankers to carry immense cargoes on the longer sea passages. It has been seen, too, how the present glut of oil all over the world has caused many of these very large tankers to be laid up until the world demand picks up again. There are many who believe that world demand will never pick up enough in the future to justify these immense ships and that the price increases over the last few years have made nations, and individuals, so conservation-conscious that adequate world distribution can be assured more economically by tankers of moderate size. Others believe that the opposite scenario could well be the correct one, that political uncertainties among the Middle East oil producers may well produce a world shortage and that the very

large tanker will again come into its own in the economic transport of large cargoes of oil from the more distant fields, such as Alaska and the East Indies.

There is one aspect of the very large tanker which could well lead to a change in design. A ULCC, fully loaded, will have a draught of around 65 ft (20 m) or more (the *Seawise Giant*, for example, the biggest ship in the world, draws 98 ft /29·8 m when fully loaded), and there are in the world very few oil terminal ports which can guarantee that depth of water at the bottom of the tide. As a result it is often necessary for such

tankers to lie off their ports of arrival in deep water and pump enough of their cargoes into smaller tankers until the reduction of draught makes it possible for them to enter and discharge the remaining oil direct. To make these harbours capable of handling such large ships direct would entail an immense and continuous programme of dredging, and therefore one might expect to see large tankers of the future built with separate sections which on arrival off a terminal could be floated off independently and towed in for delivering the oil. The ship herself would remain anchored in deep water, saving her owners the cost of harbour dues which, being calculated on tonnage, are quite considerable for big ships.

It has been reported that one tanker design, for a ship even bigger than the *Seawise Giant*, incorporates a hinge device halfway down her length to enable her to ride more easily over waves at sea. If true, this would appear to be harking back to 1863 when such a ship, named the *Connector*, was built on the Thames at Blackwall (see p. 234). That ship did not work because the strain on the 'hinges' was too great when she rolled, but perhaps with modern engineering skills and the strength of modern metals it is a possibility

The world's largest tanker, *Seawise Giant*, of 564,763 deadweight tons. She has been converted from another tanker by the insertion of an additional midship section. Constructed in Japan, she is shown in this photograph in two parts ready to be joined together. On completion she will have an overall length of 1,504 ft (458·5 m).

today. She will be a novel ship if built.

A post-war development, designed to operate among the smaller ports of the world, is the stowage of independent barges or lighters within a ship's hull for ocean transport to smaller destinations where they can be floated off for direct delivery of cargoes. The best-known systems are LASH (Lighter Aboard Ship), BACAT (Barge aboard Catamaran) and SeaBee (Sea Barge). All operate on similar principles, though with different methods of loading and unloading. In the LASH system, loaded lighters, each of about 400 tons deadweight, are floated into the open stern of a single deck carrier. The lighters are lifted with a 500-ton travelling gantry crane and carried by it to their stowage position in the ship. On arrival off the port of discharge the reverse process unloads the lighters to be towed into port. BACAT, like LASH, has barges which are floated into the stern and positioned so that they then bed down onto a metal transporter, which can be drawn up to the final stowage position. The transporters are also given lateral movement by wheels operating on a rail so that the barges, on reaching their stowage level, can be moved sideways to enable them to be stowed abreast

within the hull of the catamaran. SeaBee is much the same as LASH except that the carrier ship normally has three decks and a 2,000-ton capacity elevator platform. The barges are larger than the lighters used in LASH, each with a capacity equal to thirty-six standard containers. When loaded the barges are towed, two at a time, to the open stern of the carrier ship and floated above the elevator platform. This lifts them to the level of the deck where they are to be stowed; then they are winched onto a wheeled transporter and drawn into their final position for the voyage. A typical SeaBee ship is the *Almeria Lykes*, which with a gross tonnage of 21,667 can carry thirty-eight barges stowed on her three decks. On the upper deck stowage, the individual barges can carry additional containers on their own decks.

These new developments are still in their infancy, but the ability to carry small cargoes to a number of adjacent ports and even deliver them, if required, to destinations served by rivers or canals, carries with it the promise of considerable expansion. It also brings within the range of seaborne trade a large number of small ports too shallow to accommodate ships of any size.

Below: A cargo barge carrier and dock ship, familiarly known as a 'SeaBee'. Barges loaded with up to thirty-six standard containers each are floated into the stern dock. They are then lifted on a 2,000-ton capacity elevator platform to the correct deck level, where they are winched onto a wheeled transporter on deck tracks for stowage. On arrival at their destination the reverse procedure floats them out for local dispersal. There is room on board for thirty-eight barges.

It seems likely that, in the not too distant future, naval architects will be confronted with the problems of extended exploitation of the seabed and its resources. Some of the problems of oil exploration and production from undersea fields have been examined in the previous chapter, but with the price of oil already very high and tending always to rise higher, it makes economic sense to the oil companies to exploit possible sources at depths of water too deep for the erection of a fixed production platform. One solution is the use of semi-submersible production platforms on the same principle as the semi-submersible drilling rig; another is the use of individual wellhead chambers positioned on the seabed above the wells and serviced by a capsule lowered from a ship on the surface. An umbilical cord brings fresh air pumped from above so that the crew can work in normal atmospheric pressure inside the chamber. Relief crews travel up and down in the service capsule.

A more ambitious production scheme is for the use of fixed chambers anchored on the bottom. Wells are drilled by a semi-submersible rig in which the drill string passes through the fixed chamber and drills the wells below it. When the oil begins to flow it is processed inside the chamber and the waste gas led to a flare-stack which takes it above sea level for burning off. The oil, when processed inside the chambers, is pumped to a module on the seabed made up of several cells, and from these is led to a single buoy mooring for collection and transport ashore by tankers. There are living quarters in the chambers and periodic relief of the crew is by mini-submarine which homes in to an access hatch much as a capsule connects with an orbiting laboratory in space. Air inside the chambers is at normal atmospheric pressure.

Oil is not the only source of wealth below water. In many areas of the ocean, the bed is strewn with nodules of valuable minerals, mainly manganese, and plans are afoot to recover them, perhaps by some sort of trawl, perhaps by other means. But collecting them, by whatever means are ultimately employed, will call for ships specially adapted for the process, another future task to test the skills of the naval architect and the shipbuilder.

For many years there have been those who prophesy a commercial future for the submarine. Speeds underwater can be very much higher than speeds on the surface, without any of the stresses suffered by the surface ship as she pounds into a heavy sea at speed. There is no rolling or pitching under water, and no inherent difficulties in the design or construction of a submarine able to carry an economic cargo. Navigation below water with an inertial system

is just as exact as navigation on the surface. Trans-ocean voyages could be made at speeds in excess of 30 knots with much less wear and tear on the hull. But the sort of submarine which might have this sort of commercial future is inevitably nuclear-powered – the conventional battery-powered submarine has no such capability – and the reluctance of so many ports to give access to any ship with a nuclear installation would appear to be a complete bar to any development along those lines.

There are many directions in which ships can develop in the future, largely dependent on the nature and condition of world trade as it expands through the years ahead. New products of industry often call for new means of transport, and ships are no exception to this demand. Perhaps the one stable condition of advance in the design and building of ships is economic reality. Throughout the centuries in which the ship has developed, there has been no lack of enterprise on the part of owners, designers, and builders to try to produce the best vessel for each particular task in view. Many of the dreams they have had have come true, some have ended in failure. But for all of them, successful or not, the urge to create has been guided by an economic need. It is still so today, although the risks of failure are much reduced. Feasibility studies, the testing of models, advances in technology and computer analysis are the new tools which guide the shipbuilders of today, so that very few vessels are built now or will be built in the future without the fore-knowledge that their economic success in their particular fields is virtually assured.

Above: A diver from a lock-out submersible. With the considerable development of underwater exploration for oil and gas, divers are needed for the continuous inspection of production rigs to ensure their safety and proper maintenance.

Some Maritime Definitions

ARTICLES The conditions of service signed by a seaman in the merchant service when joining a ship. They normally set out rates of pay, scale of victualling, hours of work, etc., and, signed also by the ship's master, form a contract binding on both sides. The ship's discipline on board is based on the articles and the master has the right of punishment when the articles are transgressed.

BEAUFORT SCALE A scale indicating the varying states of wind and sea first developed by Sir Francis Beaufort when he was Hydrographer of the British Navy between 1829 and 1855. The wind scale varies from 0, calm, to 12, hurricane, and each number, as it indicates a rising wind strength, is accompanied by a description of the sea state produced by a wind of that strength. The Beaufort Scale has been universally adopted as a quick and accurate means of general weather measurement. A similar scale is used to indicate the state of the sea based on the height of the waves. It varies from 0, flat calm, to 9, waves with a mean height of over 45 ft (14 m).

BILGE The almost horizontal floor of a ship on either side of her keel. The point where the hull starts to round upwards from its flattish bottom is known as the turn of the bilge.

BILGE KEELS Steel-plate projections running fore and aft along each side of a ship's hull just below the turn of the bilge, also known as docking keels. They were first introduced in the design of Brunel's *Great Eastern* in 1854 as a roll-damping device but their main use today is to take the weight of a ship on the launching ways as she is being built and to support the ship on lines of chocks when she enters a dry dock.

BOTTOMRY A mortgage raised on a ship by her master when he is out of contact with her owners and needs to raise money for repairs or to complete a voyage. Money raised by a bottomry bond must be used only for the exact purpose stated, and the bond takes priority over all other mortgages on a ship.

BURTHEN The older term for expressing the carrying capacity of a ship, based on the number of tuns (casks) of wine she could stow in her holds. See also TON, TONNAGE.

CLASSIFICATION The degree of seaworthiness of a ship as determined by a survey on her construction and the size (scantlings) of the materials used in her construction. An original classification lasts for a definite period of years and a ship must be resurveyed when this period expires if she is to retain her classification. After a disaster, such as fire or shipwreck, another survey is required to re-establish her classification. The best known body which issues ships' classifications is Lloyd's Register of Shipping, which has committees for this purpose in every maritime nation in the world.

DRAUGHT Sometimes written as draft, the depth of water which a ship draws, obviously varying according to her load. When loaded down to her Plimsoll Line she is said to be at her deep load draught. Most ships have draught marks painted on both sides of the bow and stern, normally in Roman figures, each figure indicating 1 ft (30 cm) of draught measured to the bottom of the painted figure.

FLAGS OF CONVENIENCE A term applied to ships registered in certain small countries by owners who are not nationals of those countries. The practice started during the shipping slump of 1920–30 when some owners wished to operate their ships without the need to submit them to the inspections and regulations of the recognized maritime countries. The practice grew considerably after the Second World War when many Greek and Italian shipowners bought up war surplus tonnage and registered it in Panama, Honduras, Liberia, or Costa Rica, thus avoiding most of the conditions imposed by the main maritime nations, particularly in seaman's rates of pay, and also paying minimum taxes. Until about 1960 many of these ships were sub-standard, but by then such large profits had been made that the older ships were replaced by modern ones as good as any in the world.

At the same time Liberia became what was known as a 'flag of necessity' for many U.S. ships, reflecting the American stake in the international oil industry and her inability to compete economically because of the high rates of pay of American seamen in comparison with those of other nations. As a world maritime power the U.S. recognized the strategic need to maintain large tanker and cargo fleets on the world's trade routes, which added very considerably to the tonnage being operated under flags of convenience. While the real ownership of such ships is disguised, approximately half are U.S.-owned and many of the rest U.S.-financed.

GUNWALE (pron. gunnel) The thick plank of wood used to cover the tops of the timbers in a wooden ship.

KNOT The unit of speed of a ship at sea, one knot being a speed of one nautical mile an hour. Because of the difference in length between a nautical mile and a land mile, one knot at sea is equivalent to 1·15 m.p.h. (1·85 km/h) on land. The name comes from the early forms of speed measurement at sea when a wooden board to which a line was attached was cast overboard and the ship's speed estimated from the amount of line which ran out during a given period. After the adoption of the nautical mile during the fifteenth century as the unit of distance at sea, the line was marked with knots spaced uniformly in the same proportion to a nautical mile as was the running time of a sandglass to an hour. The smallest sandglasses issued to ships ran for about 30 seconds, so the knots were placed at intervals of 47 ft 3 in, approximately the same proportion to a nautical mile as was 30 seconds to an hour. The number of knots which ran out while the sand in the glass emptied itself gave the ship's speed in nautical miles an hour and was always reported as so many knots.

LLOYD'S An association of marine underwriters whose origin lies in a daily meeting of London merchants in Edward Lloyd's Coffee House in the City of London. It has a continuous history of marine underwriting from 1601 to the present day. It is also a centre of marine intelligence of the daily movements of merchant ships, marine casualties, etc. published every day in *Lloyd's List*.

In 1760 a number of Lloyd's underwriters formed a society to draw up rules regarding the construction of merchant ships. Known as Lloyd's Register of Shipping, the rules cover the size (scantlings) of the materials used in the construction, method of building, etc., and it issues Lloyd's classifications for all ships built to these rules. It publishes annually a list of all ships which are still afloat and have received the Lloyd's classification. See also CLASSIFICATION.

NAUTICAL MILE The unit of distance used at sea, being the length of an arc on the earth's surface subtended by an angle of one minute of latitude at the earth's centre. Because the earth is not a perfect sphere this length varies from place to place, being shortest at the equator and longest at the poles because the earth is flattened across the polar caps. The arithmetical mean of a nautical mile measured at the equator and one measured at the poles is 6,077 ft (1,852 m) but for the purpose of ships' navigation this figure is rounded up to 6,080 ft (1,853 m). Thus the nautical mile differs considerably from the land mile of 5,280 ft (1,609 m).

PLIMSOLL LINE A series of six lines painted on the sides of all British, and many foreign, merchant ships to show the maximum depths to which a ship may be loaded in various conditions. The six lines indicate the depth of loading in tropical fresh water, fresh water, tropical seawater, summer seawater, winter seawater, and winter North Atlantic. The Plimsoll Line is accompanied by a circle with a horizontal line through the centre and letters indicating the registration society; in all British ships and many foreign ones the letters are LR for Lloyd's Register.

The Plimsoll Line became compulsory in Britain under the terms of the Merchant Shipping Act of 1876 after a long parliamentary struggle by Samuel Plimsoll, M.P., who was campaigning against the so-called 'coffin ships', vessels often unseaworthy and overloaded and heavily insured against loss. Violent opposition to the parliamentary campaign was mounted by many shipowners who saw in the proposed legislation a threat to their livelihood by limiting the loading of their ships to below their total capacity.

PROPELLER The rotating screw of a powered ship which forces her through the water. The earliest propellers, introduced in 1835 – 40, had two blades, long and thin like early aircraft propellers, but with the building of larger ships and more research in hydrodynamics, three-, four-, five-, and six-bladed propellers have been introduced, with greater efficiency in the shape and the pitch of the blades.

The pitch of a propeller is the distance which one revolution moves the ship forward in still water. A recent innovation is the hydraulically operated variable-pitch propeller. This allows the angle at which the blades are set on the shaft to be altered while the ship is still in motion, giving the captain on the bridge control of his ship's movements from full speed ahead to full speed astern without the need of stopping and restarting the engine or altering the speed at which it is running. The advantage of the variable-pitch propeller, besides giving a quicker and more flexible control of the ship's movement through the water, is that the engine can be run at the constant speed at which it performs most efficiently and economically.

RULE OF THE ROAD An internationally agreed set of 31 rules compiled by the International Convention for Safety of Life at Sea, which lay down the required conduct of ships at sea to prevent collisions between them. The rules are divided into six main groups which cover such points as the lights and shapes to be carried by night or day so that vessels and their employment, such as fishing, etc., can be recognized; sound signals in fog; steering and sailing rules to keep ships apart; distress signals; etc.

The most important group of rules are those which lay down the required conduct of ships approaching each other when there is a danger of collision if they maintain their original courses. They indicate which ship has the right of way in such circumstances and which has to give way so that collision is avoided. In general, under the Rule of the Road, ships keep to the right when at sea.

SEPARATION ZONES The introduction of one-way lanes for ships in narrow waters and channels which carry heavy traffic. As an example, the English Channel, which is the main waterway between northern Europe and the rest of the world, has separation lanes in which all eastbound traffic uses a lane off the coast of France and all westbound traffic one off the coast of England. The lanes are monitored by radar stations along the coast and ships are warned when there is one proceeding in the wrong lane.

STEEVE The angle made by the bowsprit of a sailing ship in relation to the level of the deck; a high-steeved bowsprit is one which is well cocked up towards the vertical.

TIMBERS The ribs of a ship, connected at their lower end to the keel and at their upper end to the deckbeams, which give the hull of a ship its shape and its strength. In steel ships they are more usually known as frames.

TON The unit of measurement of the capacity of a ship, being 100 cu ft (2·83 m³) of her internal volume. The origin of this measurement was the tun, a cask holding 252 old gallons of wine, and a ship's tunnage was measured by the number of tuns of wine she could hold. See also BURTHEN, TONNAGE.

TONNAGE A measurement used to indicate the capacity of a merchant ship for carrying passengers and/or cargo. The original measurement of capacity was the number of tuns (casks) of wine which a ship could stow in her holds but as ships grew larger during the sixteenth and seventeenth centuries with the growth of seaborne trade, it became necessary to devise a new and more accurate method of measurement on which the harbour dues payable by ships using them could be calculated. The formula agreed by shipowners and harbour officials was the product of length multiplied by breadth multiplied by depth of hold to give an internal capacity in cubic feet, and this was then divided by 100 to provide a figure known as tonnage on which harbour dues were calculated.

As ships developed through the years, becoming larger with finer lines, this formula was revised in 1773 to provide a more accurate tonnage measurement. Known as the Builders' Old Measurement, the new formula was much more complicated, but served its purpose well until, during the nineteenth century, iron, and later steel, became the accepted building material for ships, introducing an entirely new design of hull to which the Builders' Old Measurement had little relevance.

With these new ship designs a system was adopted of calculating from internal measurements the actual capacity in cubic feet of the hull below the upper deck and dividing the result by 100 to give a gross tonnage figure. But since this gross figure bore little relation to a ship's actual carrying capacity, a second figure was calculated on the same formula in which allowance was made for all space below the upper deck – boiler rooms, engine rooms, bunkers, living spaces, etc. – which could not be used for the stowage of cargo, and this figure gave the net tonnage. Both these figures, gross and net, are known as register tons as they are entered on the ship's certificate of registration. Harbour dues, salvage and towage dues, and light and buoyage dues are calculated on a ship's net register tonnage although merchant ships are normally quoted for size on their gross register tonnage.

Another tonnage calculation, known as displacement tonnage, is measured by the volume of water a ship displaces with her fuel tanks or bunkers full and all stores on board. This again is calculated in cubic feet but is divided by 35 as this volume of sea water weighs one ton. The size of warships is always indicated by their displacement tonnage.

Deadweight tonnage is the tonnage of cargo carried on board a ship to trim her down to her Plimsoll Line. It is measured in cubic feet by the difference between the volume of water displaced when she is unloaded but with fuel tanks or bunkers full and stores aboard and that displaced when she is down to her Plimsoll Line. The difference is, as in displacement tonnage, divided by 35. The size of oil tankers is often designated by their deadweight tonnage.

TRINITY HOUSE The body in England and Wales which is responsible for the erection and maintenance of lighthouses, lightships, buoys, and other aids to navigation around the shores. It is also the licensing authority for pilots. It was founded by King Henry VIII in 1517 as a guild to encourage the 'relief, increase, and augmentation of the shipping of this our realm of England', and its duties were extended by Henry's daughter, Queen Elizabeth I, to the erection of seamarks to aid ships in their inshore navigation. In 1604 the guild was reorganized into Elder and Younger Brethren, of whom the former are responsible for the day-to-day duties of Trinity House and also act as nautical assessors in the Admiralty Division of the High Court. There are thirteen Elder Brethren, eleven elected from the merchant service and two appointed by the Royal Navy.

Other nations have their own authorities who are responsible for the lighting and buoyage of their shores.

WALE An additional thickness of timber which was bolted to the sides of wooden ships to provide protection where required. A wale running the whole length of the ship just below the gunwale on both sides of the vessel protected the hull when lying alongside the quay where the rise and fall of the tide might cause damage to the hull planking by rubbing against the piers. In wooden warships wales were fixed between each row of gunports to protect the portlids from damage when coming alongside an enemy ship to board her. Shorter wales, known as chain-wales, were fixed opposite each mast to prevent the shrouds rubbing against the gunwale.

313

Bibliography

Abell, Sir W. S. *The Shipwright's Trade* (Cambridge University Press, 1948)

Anderson, R. & R. C. *The Sailing Ship* (Evelyn, London 1971)

Archibald, E. H. H. *The Wooden Fighting Ship in the Royal Navy* (Blandford, London 1968)

Barnaby, K. C. *Basic Naval Architecture* (Hutchinson, London 1963)

Bathe, B. W. *Seven Centuries of Sea Travel* (Barrie & Jenkins, London 1972)

Bonsor, N. R. P. *The North Atlantic Seaway* – Vol. I (David & Charles, Newton Abbot 1975)

Bradford, E. *Southward the Caravels* (Hutchinson, London 1971)

Brinnin, J. M. *The Sway of the Grand Saloon* (Macmillan, London 1971; Delacorte Press, New York 1971)

Butler, T. Harrison *Cruising Yachts, Design and Performance* (R. Ross, Southampton 1945)

Chapman, F. H. *Architectura Navalis Mercatoria* – 3 vols (Svenska, Stockholm 1768; Adlard Coles, London 1971)

Corlett, E. *The Iron Ship: History and Significance of Brunel's 'Great Britain'* (Moonraker Press, London 1975)

De Mierre, H. C. *Clipper Ships to Ocean Greyhounds* (Harold Starke, London 1971)

Dugan, J. *The Great Iron Ship* (Hamish Hamilton, London 1953)

Dunn, L. *The World's Tankers* (Harrap, London 1956)

Emmons, F. *The Atlantic Liners 1925 – 1970* (David & Charles, Newton Abbot 1972)

Gibbs, C. R. V. *Passenger Liners of the Western Ocean* (Staples Press, London 1957)

Grant, Sir A. *Steel and Ships* (Michael Joseph, London 1950)

Griffiths, M. *Man the Shipbuilder* (Priory Press, London 1973)

Hardy, A. C. *Book of the Ship* (Sampson Low, Morston, London 1949)

Herrmann, P. *Conquest by Man* (Hamish Hamilton, London 1954)

Hobbs, E. W. *Sailing Ships at a Glance* (Architectural Press, London 1925)

Humble, R. *Aircraft Carriers – the Illustrated History* (Michael Joseph, London 1982)

Humble, R. (Ed.) *Naval Warfare – an Illustrated History* (Orbis, London 1983)

Hurd, Sir A. (Ed.) *Britain's Merchant Navy* (Odhams Press, London 1943)

Hyde, F. E. *Cunard and the North Atlantic 1840 – 1973* (Macmillan, London 1975)

Jobe, J. (Ed.) *The Great Age of Sail* (Patrick Stephens, London 1967; Viking Press, New York 1971)

Johnson, R. F. *The 'Royal George'* (Charles Knight, London 1971)

Kemp, P. (Ed.) *Oxford Companion to Ships and the Sea* (Oxford University Press, London 1976)

Kihlberg, B. *The Lore of Ships* (Heinemann, London 1964)

Landström, B. *Sailing Ships in Words and Pictures* (Allen & Unwin, London 1969)

Longridge, C. N. *Anatomy of Nelson's Ships* (P. Marshall, London 1955)

Lyon, D. & H. *World War II Warships* (Orbis, London 1976)

McKay, R. *Some Famous Sailing Ships and their Builder: Donald McKay* (7C' Press, New York 1970)

McDowell, W. *The Shape of Ships* (Hutchinson, London 1961)

MacIntyre, D. *The Adventure of Sail 1520 – 1914* (Paul Elek, London 1970; Random House, New York 1970)

Moore, J. E. *Warships of the Royal Navy* (Jane's, London & New York 1981)

Parkes, O. *British Battleships* (Seeley Service, London 1957)

Preston, A. *Sea Combat off the Falklands* (Willow Books, London 1981)

Rowland, K. T. *Steam at Sea* (David & Charles, Newton Abbot 1970)

Selincourt, A. de, *The Book of the Sea* (Eyre & Spottiswoode, London 1961)

Smith, E. C. *A Short History of Naval and Marine Engineering* (Cambridge University Press, 1938)

Spratt, H. P. *The Birth of the Steamboat* (Griffin Press, London 1958)

Spurling, J. & Lubbock, A. B. *Sail: the Romance of the Clipper Ships* (Blue Peter Publications, London 1927)

Tavernier, B. *Great Maritime Routes: an Illustrated History* (Macdonald, London 1972)

Watts, C. J. *Practical Yacht Construction* (R. Ross, Southampton 1947)

Wettern, D. *The Decline of British Seapower* (Jane's, London 1982)

Index

Acknowledgments

Admiralty Experiment Works: 177; American Museum in Bath: 184; Archivo B: 53; Associated Press: 257 (bottom); Beken of Cowes: 211, 277 (bottom); Bergens Sjofartsmuseum: 41 (top); C Bevilacqua: 22, 65, 79 (bottom), 188; Biblioteca Nacional, Madrid: 52; Bibliothèque Nationale, Paris: 74 (top), 86 (bottom), 120; Biblioteca Nazionale, Venice: 92; Bodleian Library: 60; A Bollo: 19 (top); Borras Edistudio: 14; British Library: 4–5, 63; British Museum: 85, 88 (bottom), 145; David Brown Gear Industries Ltd: 293 (bottom); Brunel University Library: 154 (top), 168 (left and right); Cees van der Meulen: 257 (top); Cement and Concrete Association: 282 (top); Central Office of Information: 290 (bottom); Chambre de Commerce de Boulogne: 273 (top); Chicago University: 16 (top and bottom); Richard Cooke: 288 (bottom); A C Cooper: 20 (bottom), 99 (bottom), 136 (bottom), 155, 201, 203, 210 (top); G Costa: 39 (top and bottom), 41 (bottom), 48, 70–1, 72, 91 (bottom), 116 (top), 117, 124 (bottom), 125, 128 (bottom), 178–9; G Dagli Orti: 70, 79 (top), 81; Daily Telegraph Colour Library/Mike Hardy: 276 (top left); Daily Telegraph Colour Library/P Ward: 262 (top left); Daily Telegraph Colour Library/ J Young: 292 (top right); Deutsches Archaologisches Institut, Rome: 32, 33; Deutsches Schiffahrtsmuseum, Bremen: 57 (bottom); C M Dixon: 26 (bottom), 27, 35, 37; Laurence Dunn Collection: 220, 221 (bottom), 224 (top), 255, 261 (top); Earl Beatty Collection: 233; Esso Petroleum Co. Ltd: 173 (bottom), 307 (top); Robert Estall: 78; Mary Evans: 36 (top), 194, 195 (bottom); Fathy: 15; Finnish Tourist Board UK Office: 274; W Forman: 38–9, 42, 42–3, 49 (top and bottom); Fox Photos: 247; Gilardi: 34–5 (bottom); Globtik Tankers Ltd: 264; Goole Shipbuilders Ltd: 272 (top right); Handford Photography: 310 (bottom); Robert Harding Associates: 8–9; Michael Holford: 9 (top and bottom), 25, 50–1, 64, 144 (top); Robert Hunt Picture Library: 226 (bottom), 236–7, 238, 245; ICP: 258–9; IGDA: 20 (top), 24, 26 (top), 62, 82 (top and bottom), 83 (left), 84, 87 (bottom), 128 (top); Illustrated London News: 182 (top and bottom), 234; Imperial War Museum: 136 (top), 179, 217 (top), 225 (bottom), 226 (top), 228 (top), 229, 239, 240 (top and bottom), 241 (top and bottom), 242 (top and bottom), 244 (top and bottom), 246, 252, 253; Istanbul University Library: 55; Lessing/Magnum: 12–13; Library of Congress, Washington: 1, 185 (top), 230–1; Jan Lukas: 6; William Macquitty: 134 (right); Mansell Collection: 86 (top), 235 (bottom); Mariner's Museum, Virginia: 153, 198 (top); Maritiem Museum 'Prins Hendrik', Rotterdam: 66; Masters and Fellows of Magdalene College, Cambridge: 93 (bottom), 96; F Arborio Mella: 74 (bottom); Merseyside County Museum: 150–1 (bottom); Metropolitan Museum, New York: 198 (inset); Musée de la Marine, Paris: 26 (middle), 111 (top), 118 (bottom), 119, 127, 164; Museum of City of New York/Byron Collection: 175 (top); Mystic Seaport, Connecticut: 196–7; National Archaeological Museum, Athens: 16–17; National Archives, Washington: 135 (top); National Gallery, London: 140–1, 161; National Maritime Museum, London: 80, 88 (top), 98, 99 (top), 103, 104–5, 106–7, 108–9 (top), 111 (bottom), 112–13 (bottom), 113, 116 (bottom), 118 (top), 121, 123 (top), 130–1, 132 (top and bottom), 133, 137, 138, 142–3, 143 (bottom), 148 (top and bottom), 149, 151, 152 (top), 158, 159 (top and bottom), 160, 165, 166, 169, 172–3, 173 (middle), 174 (top and bottom), 175 (bottom), 176, 189, 191, 200, 202 (top and bottom), 204, 205, 209 (top and bottom), 212, 213, 217 (bottom), 219, 221 (top and middle); National Museet, Copenhagen: 22–3, 40–1; National Portrait Gallery, London: 97 (top); Naval Photographic Center, Washington: 285 (bottom), 286–7; Nippon Kokan KK: 307 (bottom), 308–9; Novosti: 306; N R Omell: 102; Orion Press: 272 (left); Orbis: 54–5, 61 (courtesy of Dean and Chapter, Winchester/ E A Sollars), 76, 77, 93 (top right), 97 (bottom), 154 (bottom), 162 (bottom); Overseas Containers Ltd: 269 (top), 271 (top), 302–3; P & O Photo Library: 146–7, 167 (top and bottom); Peabody Museum, Massachusetts: 198 (middle left), 199, 210 (bottom); Photri: 271, 283, 284, 289; R Pittaglia: 36–7; Popperfoto: 183, 185 (bottom), 186–7 (top and bottom), 215, 228 (bottom), 235 (top), 248, 254, 256, 260–1 (bottom); Port of London Authority: 268 (bottom), 270 (top); Press Association: 290 (top), 291 (top right); Publifoto: 218; F Quilici: 126–7; Real Photos: 249 (top); Reproduced by gracious permission of HM The Queen: 91 (top); Reale Accademia di San Fernando, Madrid: 87 (top); Rex Features: 293 (top); B Richner: 109, 124 (top), 278; Rijkesmuseum, Amsterdam: 101; A Rizzi: 54 (top), 75 (top), 83 (right); Roger-Viollet: 73; Rolls-Royce: 292; Ronan Picture Library: 149 (inset), 162 (top); John Ross: 10 (top and bottom), 11; San Francisco Maritime Museum: 208; Scala: 34–5 (top), 57 (top), 59; Science Museum, London: 12, 13, 67, 75 (bottom), 122, 129, 144 (bottom), 150 (top), 152 (bottom), 170, 190, 190 (inset), 192, 193 (top and bottom), 214; Shell Photo Service: 294–5, 298 (top), 299 (bottom), 300 (top), 301; Staatsarchiv Hamburg: 56, 57 (top and middle); Submarine Museum, Connecticut: 195 (top); Sutcliffe Gallery: endpapers; Titus: 19 (bottom); John Topham Picture Library: 265; US Navy: 227; US Navy Photo/MARS, Lincs.: 289 (top); Universitets Oldsaksamling, Oslo: 44 (left and right); Vasa Museum, Stockholm: 112–3 (top); Vatican Museum: 31 (top); P A Vicary/Maritime Photo Library: 163, 225 (top), 232–3; Vickers Ltd: 224 (bottom); VO Offshore Ltd: 304 (top left), 311 (top right); Vosper Thornycroft (UK) Ltd: 279 (bottom); Woodmansterne: 123 (bottom), 134 (left), 139; Zefa/Helmut Adam: 305 (bottom); Zefa/M. Pitner: 263; Zefa/Skyphotos: 266–7.

CLARENDON STUDIES IN THE HISTORY OF ART

General Editor: Dennis Farr

CLOISTER DESIGN AND MONASTIC REFORM IN TOULOUSE

THE ROMANESQUE SCULPTURE OF LA DAURADE

KATHRYN HORSTE

CLARENDON PRESS · OXFORD

1992

Oxford University Press, Walton Street, Oxford OX2 6DP
Oxford New York Toronto
Delhi Bombay Calcutta Madras Karachi
Petaling Jaya Singapore Hong Kong Tokyo
Nairobi Dar es Salaam Cape Town
Melbourne Auckland
and associated companies in
Berlin Ibadan

Oxford is a trade mark of Oxford University Press

Published in the United States
by Oxford University Press, New York

British Library Cataloguing in Publication Data
Data available

Library of Congress Cataloging in Publication Data
Horste, Kathryn.
Cloister design and monastic reform in Toulouse : the romanesque
sculpture of La Daurade / Kathryn Horste.
(Clarendon studies in the history of art)
Includes bibliographical references (p.   ) and index.
1. Sculpture, Romanesque—France—Toulouse. 2. Sculpture, French—
France—Toulouse. 3. Christian art and symbolism—Medieval,
500–1500—France—Toulouse. 4. Daurade (Monastery : Toulouse,
France) I. Title. II. Series.
NB551.T6H67 1992
730'.944'86209021—dc20 91–43385
ISBN 0–19–817508–6

Typeset by Pentacor PLC, High Wycombe, Bucks.
Printed in Great Britain by
Butler & Tanner Ltd
Frome and London

ACKNOWLEDGEMENTS

STUDY of the Romanesque cloisters of Toulouse has involved a range of exploratory efforts—travel, field work, photography, archival research, and the reconnoitring of museum collections and storage rooms. My completion of this research has depended upon the assistance and expertise of many individuals and institutions in France.

I owe most sincere thanks to Denis Milhau, director of the Musée des Augustins in Toulouse, for opening to me the entire resources of this great museum during my initial year of study there and in many subsequent visits. His willingness to discuss with me the problems of the Toulousan sculptures, whether practical or theoretical, was a welcome stimulus to my work. Most important, his personal graciousness and generosity will not be forgotten. Daniel Cazes, now curator of the Musée Saint-Raymond, gave me much practical assistance while I worked at the Musée des Augustins. I wish to thank him for making available to me the photographs of fragments from La Daurade excavated in 1976. I would also like to thank the photography staff of the museum for giving me valuable help with lights and equipment when I photographed the Romanesque sculpture collection in 1979. Also deserving special thanks is Monsieur Robert Saint-Jean, curator of the collection of the Société archéologique de Montpellier, for his help with my study of that collection.

Among the many libraries and archives opened to me, I owe particular thanks to the staff of the Archives départementales de la Haute-Garonne in Toulouse, especially to Geneviève Douillard, to the staff of the Bibliothèque municipale de Toulouse, the Archives du Tarn-et-Garonne at Montauban, and to Christian Cau, director of the Archives municipales de Toulouse.

Portions of this book were written in Pittsburgh, Ann Arbor (Michigan), Durham (North Carolina), and Los Angeles. During these peregrinations I had the pleasure of discussing some of my ideas at various stages of realization with John Williams of the University of Pittsburgh, Marjorie Panadero, now of Cambridge, Massachusetts, Edson Armi of the University of North Carolina at Chapel Hill, Brigitte Buettner of Smith College, and Conrad Rudolph of the University of Notre Dame, a Fellow at the Getty Center for the History of Art and the Humanities in 1987–8. I owe special thanks to Professor Rudolph for his help with my Latin translation. Two other colleagues, Stephen Gardner of Santa Barbara, California, and Kathleen Nolan of Hollins College, have brought me untold hours of enjoyment and enrichment through our discussions of twelfth-century problems.

I am sincerely grateful to Thomas Lyman of Emory University for consenting to read my finished manuscript and for his thorough comments on it. I am also indebted to him for sharing with me his photographs of capitals at Saint-Sernin, as well as his incomparable knowledge of this basilica and its sculptural ambit. I would like to extend special thanks to William Broom of the Department of Art and Art History at Duke University for helping me to create the reconstruction drawing of the chapter house of La Daurade.

Acknowledgements

To Ilene Forsyth, Arthur A. Thurnau Professor of the History of Art at the University of Michigan, I owe a special debt for my early training in Romanesque studies. Her profound respect for the work of art and its making demands that her students know the work of Romanesque carvers intimately and at first hand, whether in rural churches or little-known lapidary museums and private collections. This has remained an ideal for me and has inspired my own travels through the French countryside with camera and tripod. Finally I would like to extend a special recognition to the late John Fitchen. During the years I spent in Hamilton, NY, visits to his house were special occasions. Knowledge that he must have worked for most of his career in near isolation from other architectural historians made it seem doubly a privilege to know him at the end of his life.

This book would never have been written had it not been for the support of my parents and my brothers. I owe them the greatest thanks of all.

K.H.

CONTENTS

Contents

LIST OF PLATES

LIST OF FIGURES

xix

LIST OF ABBREVIATIONS

GC	*Gallia christiana in provincias ecclesiasticas distributa . . .*, ed. Dom Denis de Sainte-Marthe and Dom Paul Piolin, 16 vols. (Paris, 1856–99)
HGL	Dom Claude Devic and Dom Joseph Vaissète, *Histoire générale de Languedoc*, 2nd edn., continued to 1890 by Ernest Roschach, 15 vols. (Toulouse, 1872–93)
Mesplé or M.	Paul Mesplé, *Toulouse, musée des Augustins: les sculptures romanes*, Inventaire des collections publiques françaises, 5 (Paris, 1961)
Paris, AN	Paris, Archives nationales
Paris, BN	Paris, Bibliothèque Nationale
PL	*Patrologiae cursus completus. Series latina*, ed. J.-P. Migne, 221 vols. (Paris, 1844–65)
RHGF	*Recueil des historiens des Gaules et de la France*, ed. M. Bouquet *et al.*, 24 vols. (Paris, 1738–1904)
Toulouse, ADHG	Toulouse, Archives départementales de la Haute-Garonne
Toulouse, AMT	Toulouse, Archives municipales de Toulouse

To my Mother and Father and to Joe and Ken

INTRODUCTION

W̲ʜᴇɴ Arthur Kingsley Porter posed the question 'Spain or Toulouse?' in the title of his famous article of 1924, he was addressing himself to Émile Mâle's newly published *L'Art religieux du xiième siècle en France* and the presumptive framework on which Mâle had built his history of monumental sculpture in the Romanesque period.[1] The 'old and crumbling theory', the unproven assumption, as Porter deemed it, of Mâle's entire account of the rebirth of monumental sculpture was the French scholar's identification of Toulouse as the generating centre of this rebirth, the source from which regional developments in all the schools of Romanesque sculpture had had their beginnings. Porter rejected this Franco-centric view, arguing instead for the priority of Spain, as well as other regions of Romanesque Europe and the East, over Toulouse in the origin of specific developments in Romanesque art.

In his astonishingly comprehensive *Romanesque Sculpture of the Pilgrimage Roads*, published a year earlier, Porter himself had assumed an entirely different theoretical framework for his own history of the Romanesque art of monumental sculpture.[2] Here he had shown his impatience with concerns about regional priorities by elaborating his theory of the pilgrimage roads as promoters of an international and interregional development of Romanesque sculpture. In Porter's compelling and poetic schema, the road itself is the central character, overshadowing the individual sculptural enterprise or regional artistic centre. Great abbeys and priories, smaller churches and monasteries are strung along its route like beads on a string—some more lustrous than others, to be sure—but all participating in a great network of communication that reached to Italy and the Holy Land and along which artistic ideas and motifs moved freely, in the company of pilgrim travel. In Porter's account, 'It was from the pilgrimages that the art was born; it was by the pilgrimages that it lived; and it was only in the pilgrimage churches that it really flowered.'[3]

By proposing a universal explanation for the generation as well as the spread of Romanesque sculpture, Porter had obviated the need to probe the individual historical circumstances that obtained in centres where Romanesque sculpture had appeared earliest and where its accomplishments were of an especially high order. It is clear, from the reassessment

---

[1] Arthur Kingsley Porter, 'Spain or Toulouse? and Other Questions', *Art Bulletin*, 7 (1924), 3–25 (review article of Émile Mâle, *L'Art religieux du xiième siècle en France: étude sur l'origine de l'iconographie du moyen âge* (Paris, 1922)). An English edition of Mâle's classic work with updated bibliography and illustrations has been edited by Harry Bober (*Religious Art in France, the Twelfth Century: A Study of the Origins of Medieval Iconography*, Bollingen Series, 90/1 (Princeton, 1978)).

[2] Arthur Kingsley Porter, *Romanesque Sculpture of the Pilgrimage Roads* (Boston, 1923). In his article 'Spain or

Toulouse?' Porter acknowledged the work of Georgiana Goddard King for bringing to his attention the notion of the pilgrimages as an influence on Romanesque sculpture (see her 'French Figure Sculpture on Some Early Spanish Churches', *American Journal of Archaeology*, 2nd ser., 19 (1915), 250–67). However, it was the French scholar, Émile Bertaux, who probably first formulated this idea ('La Sculpture chrétienne en Espagne des origines au xive siècle', in *Histoire de l'art*, ed. André Michel, ii/pt. 1 (Paris, 1906), 214–95).

[3] Porter, *Pilgrimage Roads*, i. 198.

of Porter's contribution to the field of Romanesque studies that went on throughout 1983 at symposia occasioned by the hundredth anniversary of his birth, that scholarly opinion today would not give the overwhelmingly dominant role to pilgrimage that it played in Porter's schema of generation and transmission.[4] Where Toulouse is concerned, questions of its precedence in the origins of monumental sculpture are again being raised in the literature, especially since the 1960s, with the intense scrutiny that has been turned on the workshops of the basilica of Saint-Sernin.[5] Yet for Toulouse in particular, more than for any other site of Romanesque France, Porter's characterization of the city as a pilgrimage centre continues to fascinate. It is the complex of issues that unites Toulouse with Santiago that has claimed the largest share of attention in the considerable literature generated since the 1960s on the beginnings of Romanesque sculpture in Languedoc and northern Spain. Porter's postulation of a causative link between the phenomenon of devotional pilgrimage and the spread of artistic ideas is now treated with reservation in this literature. Nevertheless, the term 'pilgrimage style' continues to be employed to refer to the commonly recognized style, and the repertory of subject matter that goes with it, that links Toulouse by a complicated web of relationships to sculptural ensembles on both sides of the Pyrenees, at Jaca, Loarre, León, Fromistà, Santiago, and elsewhere in Spain, on the one hand, and at Saint-Sever-sur-l'Adour, Saint-Gaudens, Mazère, Saint-Sever-de-Rustan, and other sites in France.[6]

This emphasis on its part in the formation of a 'pilgrimage style' has produced, for art historians at least, a certain picture of Toulouse in the Romanesque period, one in which its importance as a stopping place on the route to Santiago and its involvement with artistic developments in Spain are paramount. But this describes only one aspect of Toulouse as a generating centre of monumental sculpture in the Romanesque period and one that played itself out largely within the construction of the basilica of Saint-Sernin. Our own approach acknowledges the value of a broadly interregional and intercultural perspective that is the legacy of Porter. At the same time it is one that looks with scepticism on theories of artistic exchange or 'influence' that span great geographic distances without defining in precise terms

---

[4] The following institutions commemorated Porter's centenary with symposia assessing his work and the current state of research on the monuments to which he devoted much of his career: Department of Art and Archaeology, Columbia University, 'Arthur Kingsley Porter and the Pilgrimage Roads', The Medieval Art Forum, Second Annual Spring Workshop, held at Barnard College, 10 Apr. 1983; Department of Fine Arts, Harvard University, 'Abstraction and Rationality in Romanesque Art', The Arthur Kingsley Porter Centenary Symposium, 27–9 Oct. 1983; Art History Department, Emory University, 'The Arthur Kingsley Porter Centenary: A Summation', 24 Mar. 1984.

[5] For the extensive bibliography on the construction of Saint-Sernin in Toulouse and its sculpture workshops see below, Ch. 2 nn. 2–5 and Ch. 5. Most of the literature to 1974 is noted in Abbé Jean Cabanot, 'Le Décor sculpté de la basilique Saint-Sernin de Toulouse. Sixième colloque international de la Société française d'archéologie (Toulouse, 22–23 octobre 1971)', *Bulletin monumental*, 132 (1974), 99–145.

[6] Thomas Lyman's article, 'The Pilgrimage Roads Revisited' (*Gesta*, 8 (1969), 30–44) played a major role in reframing, in subtle and precise terms, the issues involved in the Spain–Toulouse connection that were left unresolved by the pre-war debates within French and American scholarship. In his ongoing studies of the basilica of Saint-Sernin, he has consis-

tently proposed the most rigorous criteria by which the artistic kinship and the patterns of transmission among the monuments traditionally discussed under the rubric of the 'pilgrimage style' can be more precisely defined. See his 'Terminology, Typology, Taxonomy: An Approach to the Study of Architectural Sculpture of the Romanesque Period', *Gazette des beaux-arts* 88/1295 (1976), 223–7. Marcel Durliat questions the entire notion of a 'school' of Romanesque sculpture that can be associated with the pilgrimage routes. In his review of Lyman's article of 1969, he makes some pointed criticisms ('The Pilgrimage Roads Revisited?', *Bulletin monumental*, 129 (1971), 113–20). Nevertheless, he and Lyman are essentially in agreement in emphasizing the widely dispersed influence of the style of Saint-Sernin over the entire northern slope of the Pyrenees to the south and west of Toulouse. Both Lyman and Durliat acknowledge the early importance of the work of Georges Gaillard for insisting upon the complexity of the relationships among the early Romanesque monuments north and south of the Pyrenees (see Georges Gaillard, *Les Débuts de la sculpture romane espagnole* (Paris, 1938); id., 'De la diversité des styles dans la sculpture romane des pèlerinages', *La Revue des arts*, 1 (1951–2), 77–87. The latter article is included in Gaillard's collected essays, *Études d'art roman*, Publications de la Sorbonne, 'Études', 3 (Paris, 1972), 64–78.

the actual processes by which Romanesque art was made and the concrete mechanisms by which ideas could have been generated or transmitted.

Porter had suggested in 1923 that, if one wanted to represent in graphic terms the history of Romanesque sculpture in Spain and France, one might take a fully inked pen and trace out on paper the Way of St James.[7] If we go back to Porter's map of Romanesque Europe, our own approach might be explained as one of inscribing with the same pen a heavily inked circle around the city of Toulouse and then cutting a cross section through its historical and material past. In the chronological sense, we will be taking a longitudinal section as well, through the whole of the city's history from about 1070 to 1170. When the Romanesque history of Toulouse is viewed in this extended section, a marked shift to the north—away from Spain—in the artistic orientation of its second generation of sculptors is the most significant fact of the second quarter of the twelfth century. This shift, which corresponds to a reorientation of political and cultural concerns as well, was to be a permanent one, culminating finally in the incorporation of Toulouse and the Languedoc into the French royal domain in the late thirteenth century. Hence when the mature phases of Toulouse's artistic development are considered, a fuller and rather different picture emerges than the one encompassed by its role as a centre of 'pilgrimage' sculpture.

This approach recognizes that historical circumstances were singular in every centre in which Romanesque sculpture produced its master works and that the situation that obtained in Toulouse was not that of Cluny or Conques or Saint-Gilles. Most singular, where Toulouse is concerned, is the fact that early developments there in Romanesque sculpture were produced in conditions that, by the end of the eleventh century, can unquestionably be called urban. This is not to deny that the sculptural programmes forming the primary subject of our study were produced in and for the cloister—the heart of the monastic complex—nor that the themes with which they deal are decidedly those that were of concern to reformed monasticism.

What needs to be underlined, nevertheless, is the very scale and above all the pace of building activity in Toulouse between the years 1075 and 1140. A vivid picture of Toulouse in the eleventh and twelfth centuries, an urban agglomeration in the process of defining itself as a medieval city, has been drawn by John Hine Mundy in *Liberty and Political Power in Toulouse, 1050–1230*, and in his article, 'Charity and Social Work in Toulouse, 1100–1250'.[8] In terms of its social make-up and its commercial activities, Toulouse at this period had much in common with other southern cities orientated towards the Mediterranean that were in the process of undergoing their most rapid physical and demographic expansion. As historic capital of the Midi, Toulouse, however, was first city of the region and favoured seat of the counts of Toulouse, the 'uncrowned princes of Languedoc'. Its importance was to grow during the twelfth century, along with the fame of its counts.

The Early Christian history of the city was preserved in three great and proud churches, all founded by the fifth century and each with its special lustre—the church of St Saturninus or Saint-Sernin, where the tomb of the martyred Early Christian bishop of the city was preserved,

---

[7] Porter, *Pilgrimage Roads*, i. 181.

[8] John Hine Mundy, *Liberty and Political Power in Toulouse, 1050–1230* (New York, 1954); id., 'Charity and Social Work in Toulouse, 1100–1250, Part I', *Traditio*, 22 (1966), 203–87. The latter is an expanded version of Mundy's 'Hospitals and Leprosaries in Twelfth and Early Thirteenth-Century France',

in John H. Mundy, Richard W. Emery, and Benjamin N. Nelson, *Essays in Medieval Life and Thought Presented in Honor of Austin Patterson Evans* (New York, 1955), 181–205. On early medieval Toulouse, see also Philippe Wolff, 'Civitas et burgus: L'exemple de Toulouse', *Die Stadt in der europäischen Geschichte: Festschrift Edith Ennen* (Bonn, 1972), 200–9.

the cathedral of Saint-Étienne which stood close to the Gallo-Roman rampart, and the ancient church of La Daurade, earliest sanctuary in Christian Gaul dedicated to the Virgin. When Cluniac monasticism penetrated the Midi in the mid-eleventh century, the bishop of Toulouse, Durandus, and his successor, Isarnus, actively pressed its reforms. This expansive Cluniac monasticism entered Toulouse at the same moment that the ideas of the Gregorian reform were taking hold in the Toulousan Church. The upheavals of the Gregorian reform movement were felt all over Christian Europe. In Toulouse the struggles to free the Church from lay domination were played out with particular intensity, erupting into open conflict not only between the lay lord and the adherents of Gregorian independence, but between the rival ecclesiastical powers of the city as well. It was the energy of this determined expansion and reform of the Church which, though climaxing in conflict, also impelled the remarkable building activity in Toulouse before and after 1100.

Evidence of the sharing of sculptors among widely dispersed workshops, along with what can be gained from the study of hands within individual projects, strongly suggests that the number of skilled carvers capable of executing important figural sculpture was remarkably small during the early decades of sculptural activity in Languedoc and northern Spain and probably remained so for the duration of the Romanesque period.[9] The competition for accomplished artists from the surrounding regions and their concentration within an active working environment must go far to explain the rapidity with which Romanesque sculpture matured at Toulouse during the formative period of the style.

The accomplishments of Toulousan artists are part of what is commonly referred to as the rebirth of monumental sculpture in stone, an eleventh-century phenomenon that was Europe-wide but which did not proceed everywhere at the same pace. It is now recognized that this rebirth was long in preparation and accompanied an increasing tendency towards the three-dimensional definition of skeletal members such as ribs and shafts in the masonry architecture from which it emerged.[10] None the less, the eleventh-century beginnings were modest and have their representatives in Toulouse in the first tentative essays in the three-dimensional treatment

[9] If scholars are still divided about the relative chronology of major monuments of the pilgrimage style on both sides of the Pyrenees, there is considerable agreement in detecting the work of some of the same sculptors at many of these sites. Projects at Saint-Sernin, Moissac, Jaca, Loarre, and Santiago, among others, seem to have shared some artists, though workshops at these sites evolved over the course of their existence. For my assessment of these relationships, see below, Ch. 5. Although I do not accept his methods for the distinction and identification of hands, it is significant that Edson Armi has reached similar conclusions about the relatively small number of individuals who seem to have executed the major Romanesque sculptural projects of Burgundy (C. Edson Armi, *Masons and Sculptors in Romanesque Burgundy: The New Aesthetic of Cluny III* (University Park, Pa., and London, 1983), i, 14 and *passim*).

[10] The phenomenon of the decline of monumental sculpture in stone at the end of Antiquity and its 'rebirth' in the 11th cent. remains one of the least understood processes in the history of Romanesque sculpture. As with other controversial issues in architectural sculpture of the Romanesque and early Gothic periods, answers will come only with more penetrating studies of a larger proportion of individual monuments. The 10th and 11th cents. are a critical and difficult area of this study (see Christian Beutler, *Bildwerke zwischen Antike und*

Mittellalter: Unbekannte Skulpturen aus der Zeit Karl des Grossen (Dusseldorf, 1964); and Louis Grodecki, 'La Sculpture du XIᵉ siècle en France: état des questions', *L'Information d'histoire de l'art*, 3 (1958), 98–112). On the role of freestanding cult statues in the Romanesque rebirth of monumental sculpture see Ilene Forsyth, 'Origins: The Throne of Wisdom Statue and the Revival of Freestanding Sculpture', *Kolloquium über spätantike und frühmittelalterliche Skulptur*, 3 (Mainz, 1974), 161–86 (repr. from ead., *The Throne of Wisdom: Wood Sculptures of the Madonna in Romanesque France* (Princeton, 1972), Ch. 3). M. F. Hearn's *Romanesque Sculpture: The Revival of Monumental Stone Sculpture in the Eleventh and Twelfth Centuries* (Ithaca, NY, 1981), the most recent attempt to treat this issue in comprehensive fashion in an English language publication, is inadequate as an explanation for the rapid and Europe-wide developments in architectural sculpture at the end of the 11th cent. Hearn has here revived the old theory that Romanesque monumental sculpture was initially generated by artists who worked in other media, primarily metalwork. This notion, however, takes no account of the essential gulf that lies between the practice of the minor arts collectively and the masons' yard and stone cutters' chantier on the other hand, in regard to modes of production and the transmission of artistic ideas.

of the human form, the capitals of the Portes des Comtes at Saint-Sernin, carved in the 1080s.[11] Within the space of three decades, barely more than a generation in the probable working lives of sculptors of the period, Toulousan carvers mastered the challenge of figural sculpture, creating an art of remarkable expressive power, sure elegance, and iconographic profundity.

It was during the second generation of building activity in Toulouse that the monks of La Daurade and the regular canons of Saint-Étienne and Saint-Sernin constructed their Romanesque cloisters, as part of the larger monastic complexes required to serve these newly reformed and expanded communities. What happened to these cloisters in modern times is one of the most grievous chapters in the story of destruction and vandalism of the medieval monuments of France. With the nationalization and sale of Church properties that followed the Revolution of 1789, all three were pulled down in the early years of the nineteenth century. Major portions of their sculptural programmes escaped destruction, however, and are preserved in the Musée des Augustins in Toulouse. The number of surviving Romanesque cloisters is few. That three sculptural ensembles of such richness, all produced between 1100 and 1140, have been preserved from a single artistic centre is itself extraordinary. No other such concentration of examples exists from the Romanesque period. The Toulousan cloisters are, moreover, of special importance because they stand at the beginning of developments in the historiated cloister as a principal context for monumental sculpture.

Because of the accidents of loss and the deficiencies in requisite documentation, it is not possible to form a complete picture of all three Toulousan cloisters. In the case of La Daurade, the documentation is more abundant because of certain information that was recorded about its monastic structures at the time of the eighteenth-century rebuilding of its church. For this reason La Daurade is the major focus of this study. Its surviving sculpture is more fully representative of the programme of decoration of its cloister and chapter house than are the remains from Saint-Sernin or Saint-Étienne. Moreover, its decorative programme constitutes a summation of developments in the sculpture of Toulouse over most of the twelfth century. Three workshops succeeded each other in the cloister of La Daurade, representing three stylistic generations, from the sculptors who began the cloister about 1100 and had their artistic formation in the eleventh century, to the workshop responsible for the chapter house portal, a surprising late work produced in the second half of the twelfth century, well after the creative high point of Romanesque sculpture in Toulouse. Equally important, the cloister of La Daurade is a key representative of the role that Toulousan projects played at the beginning of the twelfth century in defining the uses to which monumental sculpture could be put in the cloister.

Though it is one of the most inventive creations of Romanesque art, no fundamental study of the historiated cloister has been written,[12] and no sufficient basis exists from which to argue,

---

[11] For the issues involved in the dating of the Porte des Comtes see Marcel Durliat, 'La Construction de Saint-Sernin de Toulouse au XIe siècle', *Bulletin monumental*, 121 (1963), 151–70; id., 'Les Données historiques relatives à la construction de Saint-Sernin de Toulouse', *Homenaje a Jaime Vicens Vives*, 1 (Barcelona, 1965), 235–41; and Thomas Lyman, 'The Sculpture Programme of the Porte des Comtes Master at Saint-Sernin in Toulouse', *Journal of the Warburg and Courtauld Institutes*, 34 (1971), 12–39.

[12] Ilene Forsyth has recently analysed the problems and issues that need to be addressed in the study of the cloister in 'The Monumental Arts of the Romanesque Period: Recent Research. The Romanesque Cloister', The Study of Medieval Art in the Last Half Century: A Symposium on Romanesque and Gothic Art Celebrating the Fiftieth Anniversary of the Cloisters, New York, 21–2 Oct. 1988. The 'Septième journées romanes de Cuxa' of 1976 were devoted to various aspects of the Romanesque cloister in the Midi. Among the conference papers, published in *Les Cahiers de Saint-Michel de Cuxa*, 7 (1976), see esp. Marcel Durliat, 'Les Cloîtres historiés dans la

either for or against, the often expressed apprehension that Romanesque cloister ensembles are unprogrammatic or random in their selection of subject-matter. In 1972 the now famous symposium, 'Paradisus Claustralis: What is a Cloister?', convened in New York at the Metropolitan Museum of Art and the Cloisters, was addressed to this very real, perceived need for a comprehensive study of this monastic creation.[13] The scope of the symposium was broad, encompassing the origins of cloister design in earlier building types, its meaning and function in monastic life, and the character of its architecture and decoration until the end of the Middle Ages.

If the papers that resulted from this symposium, all exemplary in their scholarship, and provocative throughout, fall short, as a collection, of their intended aim, it is not for want of posing the proper questions. What is lacking as a basis for the symposium papers is the serious study of individual cloister ensembles. Indeed, this is a principal drawback, in the present state of our knowledge, to any attempt to draw general conclusions about cloister programmes. It is startling to realize that even the ensemble at Moissac, cited again and again as the early model for the uses of monumental sculpture in the cloister, has never been treated to a systematic study of the origins of its workshop or the relationship of its imagery to the Cluniac ideals and values of the eleventh century.[14]

The search for guides to the meaning of cloister iconography has most often turned to literary sources, in which certain repeated metaphors turn up in medieval writers who spoke of the cloister as a meaning-laden image. Most frequently cited are Honorius Augustodunensis (active *c*.1095–1135), Sicard of Cremona (lived 1160–1215), and William Durandus (lived 1230–96), who variously speak of the cloister as an equivalent of the Portico of Solomon, as an image of the heavenly Paradise, as a symbol of the contemplative soul, and an embodiment of monastic virtues.[15]

For two reasons, efforts to uncover universal meanings in the medieval cloister through such texts have remained largely unsatisfactory for the study of Romanesque sculptural ensembles. To begin with, excepting the treatises of Honorius Augustodunensis,[16] the surviving texts that specifically speak of the cloister as invested with symbolic meaning post-date the formative and mature Romanesque examples of the historiated cloister that are of such interest to the art historian. More frustratingly, texts like those of Honorius, Sicard, and William Durandus

France méridionale à l'époque romane'; Thomas Lyman, 'Portails, portiques, paradis: rapports iconologiques dans le Midi'; Mireille Mentré, 'L'Apocalypse dans les cloîtres romans du Midi'; and Pierre Ponsich, 'Chronologie et typologie des cloîtres romans roussillonnais'.

[13] The symposium papers were published in a special double issue of *Gesta*, 12 (1973).

[14] Raymond Rey's chapter on the cloister of Moissac in *L'Art des cloîtres romans: étude iconographique* (Toulouse, n.d. [1955]) could be taken as a point of departure for a more penetrating study of the choice of themes in this Cluniac cloister. A colloquium held at Moissac in 1963 dealt with many aspects of Moissac's relationship to Cluny, but the observations of Jacques Hourlier ('La Spiritualité à Moissac, d'après la sculpture') are too general to be of much usefulness in explaining the iconographic choices that went into the ensemble at Moissac. See Hourlier's paper and the others of the symposium in *Moissac et l'occident au XIᵉ siècle: actes du colloque international de Moissac, 3–5 mai 1963* (Toulouse, 1964); also published as a special issue of the *Annales du Midi*, 75/64

(1963). More promising is the work of Leah Rutchick. In her forthcoming Ph.D. thesis for the University of Chicago she is preparing a major study of the cloister programme at Moissac. She has presented some of her ideas under the title, 'Cross-currents of Imagery: Oral Memory and Benedictine Literacy in the Moissac Cloister', Annual Conference of the College Art Association of America, New York, 15–17 Feb. 1990.

[15] See the special issue of *Gesta* devoted to the cloister (n. 13 above), in particular, Paul Meyvaert, 'The Medieval Monastic Claustrum'; Wayne Dynes, 'The Medieval Cloister as Portico of Solomon'; and Léon Pressouyre, 'St. Bernard to St. Francis: Monastic Ideals and Iconographic Programs in the Cloister'.

[16] Honorius has been associated with collegiate and monastic centres in England and southern Germany and may have spent his career in both countries. See V. I. J. Flint, 'The Career of Honorius Augustodunensis: Some Fresh Evidence', *Revue bénédictine*, 82 (1972), 63–86; id., 'The Chronology of the Works of Honorius Augustodunensis', ibid. 215–42. His writings may or may not have been known to French clerics of the early 12th cent.

seem to have little discernible application to sculptural programmes that actually exist. Both of these observations arouse the suspicion that the allegorical and moralizing images in which the cloister was cast by these writers should most accurately be seen as literary conceits, applied after the fact.[17]

More promising is the approach of Léon Pressouyre, who has brought the subject of cloister iconography into direct relationship with the issues of the monastic reform movement and the debates within the monastic world about the nature of communal life, debates that reached their height in the twelfth century.[18] A primary issue for the art historian concerns religious affiliation and its possible influence on the choice of themes for cloister decoration. Can we speak, for example, of a distinctively Benedictine or a Cluniac iconography of the cloister, or identify themes that may have been considered appropriate to the cloisters of the newer reforming orders, including the orders of regular canons, the nature of whose communal life presented a challenge to traditional monasticism? This leads to the even more fundamental question of whether the iconographic programmes of cloisters can be shown to be essentially different from their counterparts found outside the claustral setting in churches and cathedrals.

These issues are emerging as major concerns in the literature.[19] A more promising base from which to explore them could hardly be proposed than the group of Romanesque cloisters produced in Toulouse in the first half of the twelfth century. In our attempts to penetrate the meaning of Romanesque cloister programmes, our difficulties are considerable, for we do not know enough about the role of those who devised the themes of Romanesque sculpture—the abbots, priors, and canons who initiated monastic building in this period—or about the possible directives handed down from the heads of orders. What we do find through study of examples like the three Toulousan cloisters, is that ideas of compelling concern to individual monastic communities were incorporated into sculptural programmes in specific instances. For this reason there is a need to investigate much more systematically the history of individual monastic communities, their liturgical practices and their patrons, as well as their affiliation with a particular monastic order, before we can know whether it is legitimate to draw broad conclusions about cloister iconography.

Where the formal aspects of inventiveness in the cloister are concerned, there can be no question that, in the decorated cloister as a type, we are dealing with a new creation of the Romanesque period. By conjoining monumental sculpture with the idiosyncratic architectural framework of the cloister, and in particular by extending sculpture to load-bearing members of this framework, Romanesque artists generated a new form, a monumental scheme that is unique in type. The remarkable diversity and inventiveness—even the seeming 'untidiness'—of many extant cloister ensembles of the twelfth century are evidence of experimentation by Romanesque craftsmen in dealing with a new and special kind of architectural scheme, one in which major and minor sculptural accents and the iconographic themes they carry are necessarily experienced by the viewer in cumulative fashion, rather than simultaneously. The accomplishments of the Toulousan workshops between 1100 and 1140 stand at the beginning

---

[17] Wayne Dynes acknowledged this difficulty in 'The Cloister as Portico of Solomon', *Gesta*, 12 (1973), 68.

[18] See Pressouyre, 'St. Bernard to St. Francis', 71–92.

[19] I first raised these issues in regard to the Toulousan cloisters in my paper of 1980, 'A Sculptural Program in the Benedictine Cloister: The Passion Series from La Daurade',

delivered at the Fifteenth International Congress on Medieval Studies at Western Michigan University, Kalamazoo. More recently Ilene Forsyth has discussed the ideas of monks about their own monastic profession, as expressed particularly in cloister art, in 'The *Vita Apostolica* and Romanesque Sculpture: Some Preliminary Observations', *Gesta*, 25 (1986), 75–82.

of this creation of the decorated cloister as a type. In defining this process, a picture also emerges of the circumstances that made Toulouse an urban centre of the Romanesque and gave it the same role as receiver and generator of artistic forms that the Paris region would play a generation later in the emergence of the Gothic style.

Los Angeles
April 1989

1

TOULOUSE AND ITS REGION IN
THE PERIOD OF REFORM

TOULOUSE, CAPITAL OF THE DOMAIN

THE densely populated city of Toulouse that today embraces both banks of the Garonne river is a city of architecturally distinctive streets, urban quarters, boulevards, and public squares that harmonize with remarkable success the legacy of its past history with the needs and tastes of modern life. The periods of Toulouse's greatest prosperity and ambitions have left their unmistakable imprint on the profile and layout of the city, from the red brick walls of its medieval churches of Saint-Sernin, the Dalbade, and the Jacobins rising from among their surrounding streets, to the secluded courtyards of its splendid Renaissance town-houses and the grand panoramas of its eighteenth-century boulevards and formal gardens.[1] Situated in the Garonne river valley on the approach to the Pyrenees, Toulouse had been an early Celtic settlement and later a Roman provincial town, important in the defence of the southern perimeter of the Empire. Extensive excavations have revealed the course of the Gallo-Roman rampart that encircled the city during the Late Empire. The remains of this fortification were used as the foundation for the later medieval rampart, so that the boundary of the original Gallo-Roman settlement continued to define the perimeter of the walled city until the end of the Middle Ages.[2] During the Visigothic occupation of southern Gaul in the fifth century, Toulouse had been the capital city of that kingdom and in the Carolingian period it had served as capital of the extensive March of Gothia or Realm of Aquitaine.[3] By the eleventh century Toulouse was the favoured seat of the extensive domains of the counts of Toulouse, held in fief from the French king. The domains extended from the borders of Gascony in the west to the Rhône valley in the east and from Quercy to the Pyrenees.[4] Prior to the twelfth century,

[1] For a comprehensive history of the streets, civic structures, and historic architecture of Toulouse, organized by *capitoulat*, see Jules Chalandes, *Histoire des rues de Toulouse*, pts. 1–3 (Toulouse, 1919–29); repr. in one volume by Laffitte reprints (Marseilles, 1982). For the modern alterations to Toulouse and their implications for urban studies see the essays published by the Institut français d'architecture, *Toulouse: les délices de l'imitation* (Brussels, 1986).

[2] On Gallo-Roman Toulouse and the excavations of the rampart, see Michel Labrousse, *Toulouse antique des origines à l'établissement des wisigoths*, Bibliothèque des écoles françaises d'Athènes et de Rome, 212 (Paris, 1968), 238–76 with bibliography.

[3] See ibid.; Michel Labrousse and Philippe Wolff in *Histoire de Toulouse*, Histoire des villes, under the direction of Philippe

Wolff (Toulouse, 1974), 48–61; and John Hine Mundy, *Liberty and Political Power in Toulouse, 1050–1230* (New York, 1954), 3–5.

[4] As counts palatine, the counts of Toulouse held their lands directly from the French king. Yet such was their power and independence in their own domains, and so distant was the Midi from the reach of the Crown, that their allegiance to the king, by the 10th cent., was nominal, invoked only in the formulas of their charters. See John H. Hill and Laurita L. Hill, *Raymond IV, Count of Toulouse* (Syracuse, NY, 1962), 6; Jacques Flach, *Les Origines de l'ancienne France*, iv. *Les Nationalités régionales: leurs rapports avec la couronne de France* (Paris, 1917), 603–4; Augustin Fliche in Ferdinand Lot and Robert Fawtier (eds.), *Histoire des institutions françaises au moyen âge*, i. *Institutions seigneuriales* (Paris, 1957), 71–3.

Toulouse was a relatively populous but loosely agglomerated provincial town on the right bank of the Garonne. The decades of interest for this study, approximately 1070 to 1170, constitute the period of greatest demographic and civic change, when Toulouse first took on its identity as a genuine medieval city.

In terms of its ecclesiastical and political jurisdictions, the primary division within this agglomeration throughout the eleventh and twelfth centuries, as John Mundy has described it, was the distinction between the city itself (referred to variously in eleventh- and twelfth-century documents as the *civitas*, *urbs*, or *villa*) and the Bourg or suburb (*burgus* or *suburbium*) of Saint-Sernin.[5] These were separated from one another by the so-called Saracen wall, the *Fig. 1* northern perimeter of the old Gallo-Roman rampart.[6] An extension of the rampart was constructed in the early twelfth century to enclose the suburb of Saint-Sernin.

Within the jurisdictions of city and suburb a number of distinct quarters or neighbourhoods had grown up around the three most venerable churches, all founded by the fifth century. The episcopal see had its cathedral of Saint-Étienne on the east side of the city, close to the rampart. The western boundary of the city, at least until the expansions of the twelfth century, was formed by the Garonne river, on whose bank the ancient church of La Daurade and its commercial quarter stood. The southern boundary was defined by the Chateau Narbonnais, the fortified residence of the counts of Toulouse, adjoining the Narbonne Gate. The ancient Capitol, with its role in the *vita* of the early third-century bishop of Toulouse, St Saturninus, occupied the northern edge of the city, next to the Saracen wall.[7] Beyond this wall to the north was the large and important suburb or Bourg which had grown up around the basilica of Saint-Sernin and its enclosure.[8]

It was the increasing tension between the city and the Bourg in the late eleventh century that precipitated the most serious conflicts in the history of the Gregorian reform in Toulouse. These tensions culminated in the efforts of the bishop of Toulouse, aided by the count, to bring the church of Saint-Sernin under his ecclesiastical control. The story of this turbulent period in the reform of the Church in Toulouse, the period just before and after 1100, has been recounted in recent studies by John Mundy, Elisabeth Magnou, and H. E. J. Cowdrey, though each of these authors has assessed rather differently the motives of the various parties to the conflict.[9] None of these accounts has been told, however, from the point of view of La

On the domains and the titles of Count William IV and his brother, Raymond de Saint-Gilles, see Dom Claude Devic and Dom J. Vaissète, *Histoire générale de Languedoc*, ed. Ernest Roschach, iii (Toulouse, 1872), 415–17.

[5] As Mundy has pointed out, the terms used to refer to the jurisdictions of city and Bourg were not consistently applied in documents of the 11th and 12th cents. (Mundy, *Liberty*, 5 and n. 5).

[6] The Saracen wall took its name from its role in repelling the Arab armies of El Samah in 720 or 721 (Labrousse, *Toulouse antique*), 238.

[7] See the *Passio sancti Saturnini* in Mgr. Griffe, *La Gaule chrétienne à l'époque romaine*, i (2nd edn., Paris, 1964). According to his legend, the Capitol was the place where St Saturninus was tied to a bull, to be dragged to his death.

[8] New quarters arose during the course of the 12th cent. (e.g. around the church of the Dalbade) or were absorbed into the city, as in the case of the former allodium of Saint-Pierre-des-Cuisines. The foundation of important hospitals in the 12th cent. spawned new suburbs outside the Narbonne Gate and on the left bank of the Garonne, which grew into the district of Saint-Cyprien (see John Hine Mundy, 'Charity and Social Work in Toulouse, 1100–1250', *Traditio*, 22 (1966), 211–12, 217–18; id., *Liberty*, 8).

[9] The history of the conflict can be read in the documents of Saint-Sernin, as published by Célestin Douais, *Cartulaire de l'abbaye de Saint-Sernin de Toulouse (844–1200)* (Paris and Toulouse, 1887) and in the archives of the archbishopric and of the chapter of Saint-Étienne (series 1G and 4G, respectively, in the Archives départementales de la Haute-Garonne, Toulouse). These sources have been utilized by Mundy (*Liberty*, esp. 14–16) and Elisabeth Magnou, *L'Introduction de la réforme grégorienne à Toulouse (fin xie-début xiie siècle*, Cahiers de l'Association Marc Bloch de Toulouse: Études d'histoire méridionale, 3 (Toulouse, 1958), chs. 2–4; id., 'Le Chapitre de la cathédrale Saint-Étienne de Toulouse (fin xie-début xiie siècle)', *La Vita comune del clero nei secoli XI e XII. Atti della settimana di studio, Mendola, settembre 1959*, ii (Milan, 1962), 110–14. Also see H. E. J. Cowdrey, *The Cluniacs and Gregorian Reform* (Oxford, 1970), 113–18. The account of the conflict in *HGL*, vol. iii, pp. 437–40, is based primarily on Guillaume de Catel, *Mémoires de l'histoire du Languedoc*

Daurade, which served as headquarters for the Cluniac reform in Toulouse. The role that this newly reformed priory played in these ecclesiastical disturbances is, in part, difficult to decipher. The relative silence of the documents on this point, compared to the fuller picture that emerges of the antagonisms between the cathedral chapter of Saint-Étienne and the canons of Saint-Sernin, would suggest that the Cluniac monks at La Daurade bided their own time during the worst of the conflicts of the later eleventh century, when the attempts of the bishop, the count, and the chapter of Saint-Sernin each to exert their own will were at their most heated.[10]

What does emerge from the documents of the eleventh and twelfth centuries is the special relationship that the Cluniac community at La Daurade enjoyed with the house of Toulouse-Saint-Gilles, most particularly the count, William IV. This relationship is central to an understanding of the prestige of the monastery of La Daurade within the city into the twelfth century and, as we will see, it bears on many aspects of the Romanesque cloister, from its date to its iconography. Furthermore, it is clear that William IV was a major supporter of the introduction of Cluniac reform into his domains and into Toulouse itself. For these reasons, our history of La Daurade will begin by focusing on its role as an important Cluniac installation within the city of Toulouse and on the patronage of the counts of Toulouse as a factor in the constructions that were carried on there after the monastery was incorporated into the Cluniac fold.

THE COUNTS OF TOULOUSE AND CLUNIAC REFORM IN SOUTHERN FRANCE

The real opening of the Midi to Cluniac influence began with Cluny's reform of the great abbey of Moissac in the mid-eleventh century.[11] Even before this, the order of Cluny was already a presence in the region, following the donation to Abbot Odilo of Cluny of the church of Sainte-Colombe in the diocese of Toulouse by Petrus Rogerus, bishop of Toulouse.[12] A Cluniac priory had also been founded at Carennac in the Quercy, through the donation of a church there by the bishop of Cahors.[13] From the time of the installation of a Cluniac abbot at Moissac in 1048, however, Cluny assumed a leadership of the monastic reform movement in this region that it was to retain until the end of the eleventh century.[14] And from the beginning,

curieusement et fidèlement recueillis de divers auteurs (Toulouse, 1633), and id., *Histoire des comtes de Tolose* (Toulouse, 1623).

[10] Relations between the Cluniacs at La Daurade and the canons of Saint-Étienne were not without their tensions, however. See below for claims by the cathedral chapter to the church of La Daurade, settled in favour of the Cluniacs in 1130.

[11] For the history of Cluny's expansion into south-west France see Noreen Hunt, *Cluny under Saint Hugh, 1049–1109* (Notre-Dame, Ind., 1968), 124–6; S. Berthelier, 'L'Expansion de l'ordre de Cluny et ses rapports avec l'histoire politique et économique du xe au xiie siècle', *Revue archéologique*, 11 (1938), 319–26; Jacques Hourlier, 'L'Entrée de Moissac dans l'Ordre de Cluny', *Annales du Midi*, 75 (1963), 353–63.

[12] Auguste Bernard and Alexandre Bruel (eds.), *Recueil des chartes de l'abbaye de Cluny: collection de documents inédits de France*, v. *1091–1210* (Paris, 1894), no. 2882b. 834–6. Bernard and Bruel date this donation to 18 June 1032.

[13] Bernard and Bruel, *Chartes de Cluny*, iv. *1027–1090* (Paris, 1888), nos. 2856 and 2857, pp. 55–7. These donations are not dated. Both 1031 and 1041 have been suggested (Hourlier, 'L'Entrée de Moissac', 356 n. 15).

[14] For a critical discussion of the date of affiliation of Moissac with the order of Cluny, see Hourlier, 'L'Entrée de Moissac', 353–63. As Hourlier shows, this affiliation was achieved in stages under Abbots Odilo and Hugh of Cluny. See also Jean Dufour, *La Bibliothèque et le scriptorium de Moissac*, Centre de recherches d'histoire et de philologie, ser. 5: Hautes Études médiévales et modernes, 15 (Geneva and Paris, 1972), 3–7. The essential sources for the history of Moissac and its role in the Cluniac reform in south-west France are the documents in the extensive Collection Doat (Paris, BN, vols. 127–31); the G series in the Archives départementales du Tarn-et-Garonne at Montauban; Bernard and Bruel, *Chartes de Cluny*; GC, vol. i, cols. 157–72 and Instrumenta; the Chronicle of Aymeric de Peyrac (Paris, BN, MS lat. 4991-A); A. Lagrèze-Fossat, *Études historiques sur Moissac* (Paris, 1870–4); and Ernest Rupin, *L'Abbaye et les cloîtres de Moissac* (Paris, 1897).

the reform of the monasteries of Toulouse and its region was undertaken with the encouragement and at the invitation of the counts of Toulouse.[15]

According to the Chronicle of Aymeric de Peyrac (abbot of Moissac 1377–1406), it was during a journey of Abbot Odilo of Cluny through the Midi that the bishop of Cahors, Bernard, appealed to the abbot of Cluny to undertake the reform of Moissac. Bernard was joined in this appeal by Gausbertus, the secular abbot of Moissac.[16] Odilo was persuaded to undertake the reform, and in 1048 he installed as abbot a monk of Cluny, Durandus, who had been accompanying him on his travels through south-western France, to head the reform of the monastery.[17]

The most immediate concern of Durandus, as it was of the monastic reformers in general, was to free the abbey from secular control by reclaiming the exclusive right of the monastic community to elect its own abbot.[18] This was achieved and the affiliation of Moissac with the order of Cluny was confirmed in an act of 9 June 1053 in which the count of Toulouse, Pons, along with his wife Almodis, renounced his control of abbatial elections and solemnly delivered the abbey of Moissac to Abbot Hugh and the order of Cluny.[19]

This encouragement of Cluniac reform in the region of Toulouse by Count Pons and the Countess Almodis was taken up even more enthusiastically by their son, Count William IV, whose devotion to the Church and to the Cluniac Order in particular made him a faithful supporter of Moissac. The most important act in solemnizing the relationship of William IV to the abbey was the ceremony of 9 June 1063, in which the authority of William and his male successors over the abbey was decreed. As Devic and Vaissète expressed it, in their quality as counts of the Quercy, William IV and his successors were recognized as protectors and, in effect, as *de facto* secular abbots of the monastery.[20] Though in one instance, discussed below, William's enthusiastic backing of the monks of Moissac brought down upon him a papal reprimand, his lifelong support of the reform efforts of the Church in his region drew in general the affection and praise of the papacy and earned him the title *très-chrétien* from his ecclesiastical biographers.[21]

In 1061, shortly after succeeding his father Pons as count, William IV ceded to the monasteries of Cluny and Moissac a church dedicated to St Peter the Apostle and SS Justine and Ruffina in the diocese of Cahors.[22] In 1067 William and his mother Almodis donated to

[15] Prior to his consent to the reform of Moissac, Count Pons had already shown his interest in and liberality towards Cluny by 3 separate acts of donation of lands to the order (Bernard and Bruel, *Chartes de Cluny*, iv, nos. 2947, 2948, and 2951, pp. 147–51). For the dates of these donations see Hourlier, 'L'Entrée de Moissac', 355. For an analysis of the motives behind lay encouragement in general of monastic reform in the 11th cent., particularly on the part of the nobility, see Hunt, *Cluny under Saint Hugh*, 132–49.

[16] Aymeric de Peyrac, Chronicle (Paris, BN, MS lat. 4991-A, fo. 157ᵛ, cols. 1 and 2); Hourlier, 'L'Entrée de Moissac', 354 and 358.

[17] Hourlier, 'L'Entrée de Moissac', 359.

[18] In the case of the community of Moissac, one of the few monasteries affiliated with Cluny that was permitted to retain its status as abbey, the right to approve or veto the community's choice of abbot actually devolved to the abbot of Cluny (Hunt, *Cluny under Saint Hugh*, 163).

[19] *HGL*, vol. iii, pp. 318–19 and vol. v, *Preuves*, cols. 470–1; GC, vol. i, Instrumenta, no. 18. Abbot Hugh was present at this ceremony. The original of this act does not exist. See,

however, Bernard and Bruel, *Chartes de Cluny*, iv, Additions, no. 3344b, 827 n. 1, for their justification of the date of 29 June 1053, which is also maintained by Devic and Vaissète (*HGL*, vol. iv, n. 32, no. 4, pp. 166–7) and by Hourlier ('L'Entrée de Moissac', 358). Despite this measure of reform by Cluny, Moissac retained until the 13th cent. a secular abbot or *defensior* (called the *Abba nominatus* in the document of 1053). In an act of 9 June 1063 Gausbert de Gourdon renounced his defence of the monastery and confirmed its attachment to Cluny, while retaining his title of secular abbot (Bernard and Bruel, *Chartes de Cluny*, vol. iv, no. 3392, pp. 495–7; *HGL*, vol. iii, pp. 342–3 and vol. v, *Preuves*, cols. 522–3). For the definition of secular abbots and their role in the history of the monastery see Elisabeth Magnou, 'Abbés séculiers ou avoués à Moissac au XIᵉ siècle', *Annales du Midi*, 75/64 (1963), 123–32; and Rupin, *L'Abbaye de Moissac*, 13–19.

[20] *HGL*, vol. iii, pp. 342–3. For the act of 9 June 1063 see n. 19 above.

[21] See Catel, *Comtes de Tolose*, 122.

[22] Catel has calculated that William IV assumed the title of

Abbot Durandus of Moissac the alodial lands they held in the rural estate of *sancti Petri de Coquinis* or Saint-Pierre-des-Cuisines,²³ and Cluniac monks were installed there. This was the beginning of an important Cluniac presence in Toulouse. The district of Saint-Pierre-des-Cuisines was, at the mid-eleventh century, a relatively undeveloped locale at the western edge of the suburb of Saint-Sernin, running along the river. It experienced considerable commercial growth and seems to have been absorbed into the agglomeration of Toulouse by the early twelfth century.²⁴ The Cluniac presence also made itself felt when the important abbey of Lézat, directly south of Toulouse, was reformed by Moissac in 1073.²⁵ In 1115 the Cluniac monks of Lézat founded a *salvetat* (or new population centre) just outside the Narbonne Gate on the south side of Toulouse and constructed a chapel there dedicated to St Anthony.²⁶

The close intertwining of affairs between the Toulousan Church and the Cluniac monastery of Moissac increased when Abbot Durandus was elected bishop of Toulouse about 1059. Durandus continued to rule simultaneously as bishop and as abbot of Moissac until 1071.²⁷

The real ascendancy of Cluny's influence in the religious life of the city occurred, however, during the long episcopacy of Isarnus, successor of Durandus as bishop of Toulouse, beginning in 1071.²⁸ Isarnus is a complicated figure in the history of Toulouse. The language of the acts that he issued during his ambitious programme to reform all aspects of religious life in his diocese show him to have held many ideals and objectives in common with the Gregorian reformers. Yet he has been called un-Gregorian in his conservative insistence upon the absolute autonomy of the bishop as the ecclesiastical power to which all others must answer in the affairs of his diocese, to the point that he resisted papal intervention in these affairs.

Elisabeth Magnou, in her portrait of Isarnus as reforming bishop, cites his deep admiration for the Benedictine discipline and for the saintly Abbot Hugh of Cluny as the factors that prompted him to enlist Cluniac aid and inspiration from the beginning in his comprehensive reform of the Toulousan Church.²⁹ In this introduction of Cluniac influence into the religious life of Toulouse, Isarnus had a willing ally in Count William IV. Catel claims that it was, in fact, William IV, along with Abbot Hugh of Cluny and Abbot Hunaldus of Moissac, who persuaded Bishop Isarnus to undertake the reform of the cathedral chapter of Saint-Étienne by placing the canons there under a new rule of regular life.³⁰ Mundy has also called this reform of the cathedral chapter 'Cluniac inspired'.³¹ Indeed, the text of the act of foundation of the

---

count of Toulouse in 1061, since acts issued by his father exist for 1060, while those naming William as count begin in 1061 (Catel, *Comtes de Tolose*, 120). On the donation of the church of SS Peter, Justine, and Ruffina, see ibid. 122 and Montauban, Archives départementales du Tarn-et-Garonne, Cartulary of Moissac (10th–12th cents.), G 569. Rupin also cites a chapel dedicated to St Saturninus donated by William to Moissac in 1061 *(L'Abbaye de Moissac*, 54).

²³ Catel, *Comtes de Tolose*, 120, 122; *HGL*, vol. v, *Preuves*, cols. 544–6; *GC*, vol. i, col. 162. Pierre Cabau has recently argued that this was a confirmation of an even earlier donation of the alod of Saint-Pierre to Moissac in c.1054 by William's father, Pons. See Pierre Cabau *et al.*, 'L'Ancienne Église Saint-Pierre-des-Cuisines à Toulouse', *Mémoires de la société archéologique du Midi de la France*, 48 (1988), 1–181.

²⁴ Mundy, *Liberty*, 7–8.

²⁵ Bernard and Bruel, *Chartes de Cluny*, iv, no. 3454 (from the Cartulary of Lézat, Paris, BN, MS lat. 9189). See also Paul Ourliac, 'L'Abbaye de Lézat vers 1063', *Annales du Midi*, 75 (1963), 491–501.

²⁶ Paris, BN, MS lat. 9189 (Cartulary of Lézat), fos. 182ᵛ and 218ʳ; *HGL*, vol. v, *Preuves*, cols. 847–50.

²⁷ On the career of Durandus, see Rupin, *L'Abbaye de Moissac*, 46–57. According to Rupin's calculations, Durandus probably died in 1072, but he may have relinquished the episcopal throne at Toulouse the year before his death, in 1071. On this, see also *HGL*, vol. iv, n. 19, p. 101.

²⁸ *GC*, vol. xiii, col. 13, no. 30. See also *HGL*, vol. iv, n. 19, p. 101. The end date of Isarnus's tenure as bishop is more difficult to fix. Devic and Vaissète believe the date 1098 given by Catel (*Mémoires du Languedoc*, 876) is wrong. They cite acts of 1100, 1102, and 1105 that still name Isarnus as bishop (*HGL*, vol. iv, n. 19, p. 102).

²⁹ Magnou, *Réforme grégorienne*, 6–9. She cites the letters that passed between Gregory VII, St Hugh, and Isarnus as evidence of the closeness of their ideals at the beginning of Isarnus's introduction of Gregorian reform into Toulouse.

³⁰ Catel, *Comtes de Tolose*, 123.

³¹ Mundy, *Liberty*, 15 n. 8.

chapter, dating most likely to 1073, states explicitly that the reform was undertaken in consultation with Count William IV and Abbot Hugh 'the propagator of monastic discipline'.[32] Both Abbot Hugh and Hunaldus of Moissac were present at the foundation, as signatories to the act. In Chapter 7 we will look closely at the language of this important document for indications of the ideals of monastic life which the Cluniac rule and the new order of regular canons at Saint-Étienne can be seen to have held in common.

THE REFORMED MONASTERY OF LA DAURADE

The influence of Cluniac reforming ideals within the religious life of Toulouse was assured when Isarnus made the decision to donate the ancient church of Sancta Maria to Abbot Hugh and the monks of Cluny for reform. The church was called, in the earliest documents, simply Sancta Maria or Sancta Maria infra muros.[33] Later, in tenth-century documents, it was to be called Sancta Maria Fabricata; it is not until the late eleventh century that the appellation Sancta Maria Deaurata or Beata Maria Deaurata (Blessed Mary the Gilded), a reference to the glittering mosaics of its sanctuary, began to be applied to the church, undoubtedly to distinguish it from the church of Notre-Dame la Dalbade, a Toulousan dependency of the Deaurata, which also became prominent in the documents at this time.[34]

The church of Sancta Maria Deaurata (or Notre-Dame la Daurade) had stood on the right bank of the Garonne river at least since the fifth century, making it one of the most venerable churches in Toulouse, tied, like the cathedral of Saint-Étienne and the basilica of Saint-Sernin, to the Early Christian history of the city. The church had originally been a centralized building, ten-sided in plan. A portion of this primitive church, still serving as the eastern sanctuary, survived down to the eighteenth century.[35] According to local tradition repeated in all the early histories of Toulouse, this centralized church had originally been constructed as a pagan temple and had been rededicated to the Virgin as a Christian shrine about AD 400 by St Exupery, bishop of Toulouse.[36] Recent studies of its architecture and decoration, however, at

[32] Magnou, who has analysed the 4 existing copies of the act of foundation in great detail, has arrived at the 'almost certain date' of 1073 for the foundation of the cathedral chapter, the date also reached by the 18th-cent. paleographer and archivist of the records of Saint-Étienne, Claude Cresty (see Magnou, *Réforme grégorienne*, ch. 1, esp. 24–5 and 30). Magnou's date differs from that of 1077 given by Devic and Vaissète (*HGL*, vol. iii, pp. 391–2) and in the *GC*, vol. xiii, Instrumenta, no. 8, cols. 7–11. In the exact words of the act, Isarnus states that he obtained: 'immunitate gloriosissimi nostri comitis dompni Willelmi, consultu sequae monasticas disciplinae propagotoris Cluniensium abbatis Hugonis, auxiliante quoque et cooperante reverendo Hunaldo abbate Loci Moysiacensis' (Magnou, *Réforme grégorienne*, Recueil annexe, no. 1, p. 2, ll. 1–3). The role of William IV is explicit elsewhere in the document as well. See the section in which he renounces his right to elect the bishop of the see of Toulouse (a segment missing, however, from Copy A, probably the oldest of the texts) (ibid., 6, Copy C). In all 4 texts, William joins with Bishop Isarnus in placing his concession under the protection of Abbot Hugh of Cluny (ibid., 6–7). William's brother, Raymond de Saint-Gilles, is also named briefly in the document as consenting to the regularization of the canons (ibid. 3, ll. 6 and 7).

[33] See the appellation Sancta Maria Tolosae in the 6th-cent.

Historia francorum of Gregory of Tours, vii. 10 (*PL* 71, col. 422) and the charter of Charles the Bald of 5 Apr. 844 in favour of the churches of Toulouse, discussed below.

[34] See a grant of land made by Bishop Hugh of Toulouse in 960 in which the church is called Sancta Maria Fabricata (*HGL*, vol. 5, col. 238) and another grant of the same year from Raymond, count of Rouergue (*HGL*, vol. v, col. 244). In a letter from Urban II to Count William IV which I have dated c.1090 (see below) the pope refers to the church as Sancta Maria Deaurata (*HGL*, vol. v, *Preuves*, col. 730), and it is likewise referred to in a document of 1130 from the archives of Saint-Étienne, published by Catel (*Mémoires du Languedoc*, 864).

[35] For a summary of the early writers on the primitive church of La Daurade and the evidence for its decoration, see Paul Mesplé, 'Recherches sur l'ancienne église de la Daurade', *Mémoires de la société archéologique du Midi de la France*, 31 (1965), 41–56. See especially Dom Martin for a plan, elevation, and description of the primitive sanctuary before its destruction (*La Religion des Gaulois, tirée des plus pures sources de l'antiquité*, i (Paris, 1727), 147–58 and pl. 4).

[36] The priest and early historian of La Daurade, Jean de Chabanel, cited a collection of letters by Sidonius as the source for his claim that the church of La Daurade was a converted pagan temple (*De l'estat et police de l'eglise Nostre Dame dite*

least what can be known of these from early descriptions and a few surviving fragments, have revealed no basis for this tradition of a pre-Christian date for the building. Rather, its centralized plan would seem to place it early in the series of martyria dedicated to the Virgin which became a popular type following adoption of the dogma of the Theotokos at Ephesus in 431, as several authors have recently suggested.[37] G. Boyer has proposed that the centralized church may, in fact, have been built as a palace chapel for one of the fifth-century Visigothic rulers of Toulouse. He argues that this would explain both the richness of its interior mosaic programme and the control by its clerics, at least from Carolingian times, of prime properties along the banks of the Garonne, as well as the water and portage rights themselves, usually reserved to the public domain.[38]

Gregory of Tours, writing in the sixth century, acknowledged the early prominence of the church of La Daurade in the history of Toulouse, in recording that the wife of a Merovingian duke, Ragnovald, had taken asylum in the church from King Chilperic and was joined in residence there in AD 584 by Chilperic's daughter, the princess Rigonthe.[39]

A monastery had been attached to the ancient church of Sancta Maria at least since the Carolingian period, when it is mentioned for the first time in a charter of 5 April 844 issued by Emperor Charles the Bald. La Daurade is here referred to as 'monasterio sanctae Mariae, quod est infra muros ipsius civitatis, cum omnibus appenditiis'.[40] The documents are almost completely silent concerning the history of La Daurade between the Carolingian period and the eleventh-century reform, though its possessions must have grown, since records of at least two donations have survived from the late tenth century.[41]

In short, the eminent position that this church held in the city was assured by its importance as a shrine of the Virgin and object of pilgrimage to her cult, by its claim of imperial privileges dating from the Carolingian era, and, equally important, by its prime location on the bank of the Garonne, an advantage that was to bring it increasing wealth as this quarter of the city began to expand rapidly in the eleventh and twelfth centuries.

In 1077 Bishop Isarnus recognized the prestigious role of this venerable church of the Virgin

la Daurade a Tolose . . . , (2nd edn., Toulouse, 1623), 1). According to one tradition, cited in the *Gallia christiana*, the foundation of a church of the Virgin at La Daurade dated as early as the reign of Theodosius I, while another tradition attributed its foundation to the Visigothic king, Theodoric, whose ashes were said to have been contained in an urn in the high altar (see *GC*, vol. xiii, col. 100). Jean-François de Montegut, an amateur archaeologist present at the demolition of the medieval church of La Daurade, reported the presence of bricks with Roman imperial stamps in the masonry of the eastern sanctuary as evidence that the original fabric of this portion of the church may have been of Gallo-Roman construction ('Recherches sur les antiquités de Toulouse', *Mémoires de l'académie des sciences, inscriptions et belles-lettres de Toulouse*, 1st ser., 1 (1782), 65–110). These bricks, however, could have been reused ones.

[37] André Grabar, *Martyrium: recherches sur le culte des reliques et l'art chrétien antique*, i. *Architecture* (Paris, 1946), 411–12; Raymond Rey, 'Le Sanctuaire paléochrétien de la Daurade à Toulouse et ses origines orientales', *Annales du Midi*, 61 (1949), 249–73; Étienne Delaruelle, s.v. 'Daurade', in *Dictionnaire d'histoire et de géographie ecclésiastique*, ed. Alfred Baudrillart *et al.*, 14 (Paris, 1960), col. 98; Étienne Delaruelle, 'Toulouse, capitale wisigothique et son rempart', *Annales du Midi*, 67 (1955), 205–21. Also see Richard

Krautheimer, 'Sancta Maria Rotunda', in *Studies in Early Christian, Medieval and Renaissance Art* (New York, 1969), 108–10.

[38] G. Boyer, 'Une hypothèse sur l'origine de la Daurade', *Annales du Midi*, 68 (1956), 47–51.

[39] Gregory of Tours, *Historia francorum*, vii. 10 (*PL*, 71, col. 422). Also see May Vieillard-Troiekouroff, *Les Monuments religieux de la Gaule d'après les œuvres de Grégoire de Tours* (Paris, 1976), no. 305, 300–1.

[40] For a transcription of this document, along with a critical analysis of its authenticity and the dates of all existing copies (the original is lost), see François Galabert, 'Un diplôme de Charles le Chauve en faveur des églises de Toulouse et sa confirmation par Louis VII', *Le Moyen Age: revue d'histoire et de philologie*, 2nd ser., 27 (1914), 185–214. Variants have been published in many source books, including Catel, *Mémoires du Languedoc*, 850; *GC*, vol. xiii, Instrumenta, cols. 1–2; Douais, *Cartulaire de Saint-Sernin*, 5–6; and *HGL*, vol. ii, *Preuves*, cols. 219–20. Delaruelle hypothesized that a monastery was most likely to have been established at La Daurade at the beginning of the 9th cent., during the important Carolingian reforms instituted in this region of the Empire by St Benedict of Aniane (Delaruelle, 'Daurade', col. 99).

[41] See n. 34 above.

in the spiritual life of the city in his decision to give over the community there to comprehensive reform by the Cluniacs. During the troubled period of decline between the late Carolingian age and the mid-eleventh century reform, the Toulousan Church, like others in the former Carolingian realm, had fallen under the control of the local feudal lords, its lands usurped, and its observance of religious life and custom compromised by the practice of simony. In the words of Bishop Isarnus in his act of donation, the clergy of La Daurade had fallen into just such a decline, their virtual abandonment of all semblance of divine worship and of the service of God constituting a particular offence against this most ancient church of the Virgin.[42] With its submission to Cluny, the monastery of La Daurade was made a priory, directly dependent on the abbey of Moissac,[43] and a contingent of monks from the nearby mother house was sent to reform the Toulousan dependency.

Isarnus's act of donation attaching La Daurade to the congregation of Cluny is a dated document of 1077. There is at least some evidence, however, that Isarnus's predecessor, Durandus, may earlier have tried to install Cluniac monks at La Daurade during his episcopacy (1060–71). This information comes from a document of 1130 published by Catel and which he identifies as having been in the archives of Saint-Étienne. The document chronicles complaints of the canons of Saint-Étienne going back to the eleventh century, when they claim that clergy of the see of Saint-Étienne were wrongfully expelled from the church of La Daurade by Durandus, who was then both bishop of Toulouse and abbot of Moissac. According to the history of the dispute given in the document of 1130, the clergy of Saint-Étienne had attempted to reclaim the church of La Daurade during the episcopacy of Isarnus but were again expelled 'by the monks' (presumably the Cluniac monks already in residence there).[44]

The question of whether Cluniac monks were already installed at La Daurade, however tenuously, even before Isarnus's recorded donation of 1077, is not without importance to our study. Marie Lafargue pointed to the document of 1130 from the archives of Saint-Étienne as evidence that it was Abbot Durandus who donated La Daurade to Cluny and that Isarnus's act was simply a confirmation of that earlier donation.[45] She took this to support her argument that construction of the Romanesque cloister, along with its sculpture, could have begun at the Toulousan monastery as early as 1067.[46]

Lafargue's use of the date 1067 as a *terminus post quem* for the earliest series of capitals

---

[42] *GC*, vol. xiii, Instrumenta, col. 9; Bernard and Bruel, *Chartes de Cluny*, iv, no. 3514; Catel, *Mémoires du Languedoc*, 871–2 (with lacunas); Jean de Chabanel, *De l'Antiquité de l'église Nostre Dame dite la Daurade a Tolose, et autres antiquitez de la ville* (2nd edn., Toulouse, 1625), 113.

[43] *HGL*, vol. iii, p. 391; *PL* 151, no. 9, col. 292, and no. 196, col. 466 (confirmations of the possessions of Moissac by Urban II in 1088 and 1096).

[44] Catel, *Mémoires du Languedoc*, 864–5. The *Gallia christiana* also makes reference to this dispute (vol. xiii, col. 101). The provost of Saint-Étienne had intended to present the claims of the cathedral chapter to the church of La Daurade at the Council of Clermont of 1130 but was dissuaded by William, archbishop of Auch, who referred him to Peter the Venerable, abbot of Cluny (*HGL*, vol. iii, p. 677). The document of 1130 is the history of the dispute as presented by the provost of Saint-Étienne to the abbot of Cluny. The canons of Saint-Étienne did not win their claim, and La Daurade remained a Cluniac priory under the abbey of Moissac.

[45] Marie Lafargue, *Les Chapiteaux du cloître de Notre-Dame la Daurade* (Paris, 1940), 14–16; ead., 'Les Sculptures du premier atelier de la Daurade et les chapiteaux du cloître de Moissac', *Bulletin monumental*, 93 (1938), 213–14.

[46] Lafargue based her theory of an earlier donation in the time of Durandus in part on an unpublished history of the Toulousan monastery by the 17th-cent. Maurist scholar, Dom Claude Chantelou, who had been for a period a monk at La Daurade (Paris, BN, MS. lat. 13.845, fo. 55ᵛ–56ʳ). Chantelou, however, cited no documentation for his claim that Isarnus's donation of 1077 was a confirmation of an earlier act. In fact, he may have based his own history on the Chronicle of Aymeric de Peyrac, who specified that La Daurade was affiliated with the order of Cluny, as a dependency of Moissac, in the year 1067 (Paris, BN, MS lat. 4991-A, fo. 158ᵛ, col. 2). Aymeric's Chronicle, while valuable in some respects, is nevertheless replete with instances of dates wrongly recorded or transcribed. His recording of a date of 1067 rather than 1077 for the donation to Cluny can hardly be taken as conclusive.

from the cloister has been seriously questioned in more recent literature.[47] The fact that Isarnus's lengthy act of donation of 1077 makes no reference at all to an earlier affiliation of La Daurade with Cluny throws doubt on Lafargue's interpretation of the documents. It was frequently the case that resident clergy or monks initially resisted the imposition of reform from the outside by Cluny. The abbey of Lézat, located outside Toulouse and mentioned earlier, is a case in point (see n. 25 above). There were also, particularly during the early years of Cluny's expansion into the Midi, different degrees and types of Cluniac affiliation, short of outright administrative dependence of a church or community on Cluny. The language of the document of 1130 from the archives of Saint-Étienne, indeed, suggests that, if there was an attempt to reform the community of La Daurade according to Cluniac customs prior to Isarnus's act of 1077, there was a period of considerable resistance before this was accomplished. This is far from the conditions of stability and administrative responsibility that would seem necessary for the undertaking of an ambitious programme of construction at La Daurade such as Lafargue suggests was begun in 1067.

The text of the act of donation of La Daurade to Cluny is revealing in several respects. It makes clear the degree to which Isarnus counted on the power of Abbot Hugh and Cluniac discipline to restore the spiritual life of this venerable centre of worship of the Virgin. It also says something about Isarnus's view of his own role in the revitalizing of the Toulousan Church. In it he invoked the names of the most venerated Early Christian bishops of Toulouse, the martyred St Saturninus, along with the Bishops St Sylvius and St Exupery, with whose stature as founders of the Christian faith in Toulouse he explicitly wished to associate his own episcopacy.[48] By invoking the sainted personages and founding ideals of the Early Church in the context of his own reform objectives, Isarnus here revealed an attitude that is very distinctly consistent with the broad ideals of both the Gregorian and monastic reform movements, and one that is repeatedly expressed in the writings of both papal and monastic reformers of the eleventh and twelfth centuries.[49]

In light of the later claims to rightful ownership over the church of La Daurade that were to be pressed as late as 1130 by the chapter of Saint-Étienne, it is also interesting that the donation of La Daurade to Abbot Hugh was made, according to the act of 1077, with the advice and corroboration of the canons and that the act was signed by the provost and the principal canons of the cathedral. This is another indication that it was the strong personality and determined ambitions of Isarnus that in large part impelled the successful reforms of the eleventh century in Toulouse. With the decline of reforming zeal and the weaker position of the bishop that characterized the episcopacy after the death of Isarnus (1105/6), the canons of the cathedral were prepared to attempt a recouping of certain losses of their own possessions that had occurred during the earlier period.

Finally, the act of donation of 1077 is testimony to the active role played by William IV, count of Toulouse, in the reform of La Daurade, and it is this role that we wish to explore in some depth, since it bears directly on the issue of William IV and his successors as patrons of

---

[47] William Forsyth, review of Lafargue, *Chapiteaux de la Daurade*, in *American Journal of Archaeology*, 49 (1945), 392–3; Marcel Durliat, 'La Date des plus anciens chapiteaux de la Daurade à Toulouse', *Estudios dedicados a Duran y Sanpere: cuadernos de arqueologia e historia de la ciudad de Barcelona* (Barcelona, 1967), 196–8; Kathryn Horste, 'The

Passion Series from La Daurade and Problems of Narrative Composition in the Cloister Capital', *Gesta*, 21 (1982), 33–4 and n. 25.
[48] Magnou makes this point (*Réforme grégorienne*, 8).
[49] On the nostalgia for the Early Church as an inspiration for the reformers of the 11th and 12th cents., see below, Ch. 7.

the Romanesque building programmes at La Daurade. Isarnus's donation of La Daurade to Abbot Hugh was made, as he tells us, with the advice (*consilio*) of Count William. Later in the document Isarnus praises the count for having liberated the Church of Toulouse from 'the hand of its enemies'. All William's actions, as recorded in the documents of the last quarter of the eleventh century, indicate a commitment, equal to Isarnus's own, to the reform of the Toulousan Church. Magnou, in fact, concludes that, from all appearances, it was by the choice of the count that Isarnus was named to head the diocese of Toulouse.[50] Given the early support that William IV showed to Moissac and the Cluniac community there, it is probable that Isarnus's admiration for Abbot Hugh and the model of Cluniac monasticism strongly influenced the count to select Isarnus as successor to the energetic Bishop Durandus. For it was to the Cluniacs of Moissac that the count looked as the initial agents of reform of the Church in Toulouse.

THE ROLE OF WILLIAM IV

With a strong Cluniac presence in Toulouse consolidated by the installation of monks from Moissac at both Saint-Pierre-des-Cuisines and La Daurade, William IV consorted with Bishop Isarnus and the abbot of Moissac in an attempt to extend this presence into the Bourg as well. The aborted effort of the count and the bishop to install monks from Moissac at the church of Saint-Sernin in the Bourg has been described in detail by Magnou, Mundy, and Lyman, among others.[51] The canons of this most venerable pilgrimage church of Toulouse had undertaken a reform of their own chapter according to the prescriptions of the *Institutiones Patrum* (that is, the writings of the Church Fathers that deal with the canonical life) at a date that can be placed sometime between 1073 and 1080.[52]

The bishop's attempt to expel the regular canons and to introduce Cluniac monks into the cloister of Saint-Sernin in 1081 or 1082 was the climax of a long-simmering dispute over jurisdictions between the cathedral chapter of the episcopal see and the newly reformed canons in the Bourg.[53] Though the motives of the various parties involved in this crisis were complex, there seems little doubt that the actions of Bishop Isarnus were precipitated in great part by his unwillingness to accept the independence of the chapter of Saint-Sernin from his episcopal jurisdiction. In their disputes with the cathedral chapter of Saint-Étienne, the canons of Saint-Sernin claimed papal protection and a direct allegiance only to Rome.[54] Isarnus's view of the

[50] Magnou, *Réforme grégorienne*, 8.

[51] Ibid., chs. 3 and 4; Mundy, *Liberty*, 15; Thomas Lyman, 'The Sculpture Programme of the Porte des Comtes Master at Saint-Sernin in Toulouse', *Journal of the Warburg and Courtauld Intitutes*, 34 (1971) app., 35–9.

[52] The date of adoption of a regular life by the canons of Saint-Sernin is much disputed and has a bearing on the probable date of the beginning of construction of the Romanesque basilica there. Magnou places the reform of the chapter conservatively between 1073 and 1080 (*Réforme grégorienne*, 33–4). Devic and Vaissète (*HGL*, vol. iii, pp. 437–8) conclude that the canons were following a regular life at least by 1076, and Lyman agrees, citing references to their regular life in documents concerning their missionary activities 'towards 1076–80' at Saint-Cyprien and Vigan in Quercy (Lyman, 'Porte des Comtes Master', 37). See the documents referred to by Lyman in Douais, *Cartulaire de Saint-Sernin*, nos. 293 and

295, where the clergy of Saint-Sernin are described as following the institutions of SS Augustine, Gregory, and Jerome. Also see Marcel Durliat, 'Les Origines de la sculpture romane à Toulouse et à Moissac', *Cahiers de civilisation médiévale*, 12 (1969), 349, and id., 'La Construction de Saint-Sernin de Toulouse au xie siècle', *Bulletin monumental*, 121 (1963), 152.

[53] The immediate causes of the crisis are enumerated in the letter of Pope Gregory VII instructing his legate Cardinal Richard, abbot of St Victor of Marseilles, to settle the dispute (see Cowdrey, *Cluniacs*, 114–15, and Magnou, *Réforme grégorienne*, 45–7 and Recueil annexe, no. 6, 19–20). The letter is reproduced in Gregory VII, *Registrum*, in E. Caspar (ed.), *Monumenta germaniae historica epistolae selectae*, ix (Berlin, 1920–3) no. 30, 615–17.

[54] On the authenticity of a privilege of Gregory VII supposedly granting this papal protection, see Magnou, *Réforme grégorienne*, 38–40, and Cowdrey, *Cluniacs*, 114 n. 3.

prerogatives of the bishop could not countenance such independence from his episcopal control. In a bold action in which he fully recognized the possibility of papal excommunication, he formed a pact with Abbot Hunaldus of Moissac and the count of Toulouse in which he donated the church of Saint-Sernin to Moissac and to Abbot Hugh of Cluny.[55] The accord provided that the community of Saint-Sernin would follow monastic rule and would be headed by a prior—hence would be submitted to the abbots of both Moissac and Cluny. With the force of the count behind him, Isarnus was able to have the canons of Saint-Sernin expelled from their cloister and replaced by a contingent of monks from Moissac. These events occurred between the end of 1081 and the middle of 1083.[56]

This attempt on the part of the bishop and the count to replace canonic with monastic reform at Saint-Sernin was short-lived. The appeals for redress by the ousted canons were heard by Pope Gregory VII and, through the intervention of his legate, Cardinal Richard, abbot of Saint-Victor of Marseilles, and of Abbot Hugh himself, the occupation by the monks of Moissac was broken and the basilica of Saint-Sernin was returned to its canons.[57]

The role and motives of the count of Toulouse in this crisis can be surmised from Isarnus's act of donation of Saint-Sernin to Moissac, to which the count was a party, and from an act of contrition which the count issued on 23 July 1083.[58] While his zeal for the reform of the Toulousan Church seems unmistakably genuine, William IV's concept of the proper course for this reform seems to have matched the conservative views of Isarnus rather than those of the true Gregorians, which were radical by comparison. Both William's and Isarnus's ideas of reform were rooted in the eleventh-century movement towards purification of the Church through the abolition of simony and the return of ecclesiastical properties usurped by the laity. At the same time, they both saw the advantages of the traditional concept of the bishop as autonomous and hegemonic within his own diocese. Both resisted the threat to local control posed by the proliferation of reformed communities like that at Saint-Sernin, which sought direct submission to the Roman see. They viewed with concern, as well, the parallel phenomenon of papal intervention in diocesan affairs that marked the policies of Gregory VII and his successors. Thus the count's aims in regard to Saint-Sernin were entirely compatible with those of the bishop and he, too, as Magnou has put it, preferred to see the church in the hands of monks who could be brought under episcopal control than in those of an independent community of canons.[59]

In the accord of 1081/2 in which Isarnus donated Saint-Sernin to Cluny, William had pledged to stand firm with the bishop even in the face of excommunication by the pope or his legate. Nevertheless, his quick repentance of his actions when faced with the universal censure of the ecclesiastical authorities suggests that the historical descriptions of this count as a devoted and sincerely pious upholder of the Church are probably justified. In his act of

---

[55] Transcribed in Catel, *Mémoires du Languedoc*, 873–4. For an analysis of this accord, see Magnou, *Réforme grégorienne*, 47–53. Isarnus claimed broad episcopal rights in this document, including one-quarter of all offerings and the key to the tomb of St Saturninus.

[56] Magnou, *Réforme grégorienne*, 47. Devic and Vaissète place Isarnus's pact at the end of 1082 or 1083 (*HGL*, vol. iii, p. 439). The height of the crisis was certainly in 1082 when numerous letters passed between Gregory VII and his legate.

[57] Gregory's letter to Richard mandated that Saint-Sernin was indeed submitted to his papal authority and that the

canons there were living a regular life (Gregory VII, *Registrum*, ix. 30, as in n. 53 above). In a separate letter the pope reprimanded his legate for overstepping his assignment by excommunicating the monks of Moissac who had occupied the basilica of Saint-Sernin (*PL* 148, *Epistolae extra registrum vacantes*, col. 701).

[58] See n. 55 above for the act of donation. William's act of contrition is preserved in the Cartulary of Saint-Sernin (Douais, *Cartulaire de Saint-Sernin*, no. 290, and Magnou, *Réforme grégorienne*, Recueil annexe, no. 9, 24–5).

[59] Magnou, *Réforme grégorienne*, 53.

contrition of 23 July 1083, the count declared himself gravely penitent for the 'sacrilege' he had perpetrated upon the church of Saint-Sernin by ousting the canons, who were living a regular life there, and he pledged never again to try to introduce monks into their cloister. It is probable that William was moved as much by the harsh condemnation of the archbishops of Narbonne and Lyons, of Abbot Hugh of Cluny himself, and 'above all' of the venerable Geraldus, bishop of Cahors, all of whom he cites, as he was by the threat of excommunication from Rome.[60]

In his act of contrition, William claimed that it was Hunaldus, abbot of Moissac, who had incited him to expel the canons of Saint-Sernin and to introduce monks there. The crisis of 1081–3, in fact, should more accurately be seen as a personal defeat for Abbot Hunaldus and for Isarnus, than as a general setback for Cluniac interests in Toulouse. If our interpretation of the documents below is correct, Abbot Hunaldus was disgraced by his actions in regard to Saint-Sernin, and all the evidence suggests that Abbot Hugh of Cluny himself condemned these actions and probably did not know of them in advance.[61]

We do not hear of any part played by the Cluniac community at La Daurade in this crisis, and the silence of the documents suggests that the community there took a back seat during the period of the attempted take-over of Saint-Sernin. Considering the outcome of events, this was probably a wise policy. The venerable monastery at La Daurade seems to have lost no prestige during this period of collusion between the bishop, the count, and the abbot of Moissac. Indeed, events after 1083 suggest that its position within the city was strengthened, due to the renewed favour which William IV showed to this monastery during the last years of his life.

William IV, by his act of contrition and his subsequent actions in defence of the Church, remained on excellent terms with the papacy. Though its mother abbey at Moissac might have been temporarily out of favour with the Gregorian reformers, the community at La Daurade benefited from the special relationship it maintained with the count of Toulouse. This is evident in an undated letter, full of praise for William's devotion, addressed to him by Gregory's successor as pope, Urban II (1088–99).[62]

This papal bull has been often cited, since it concludes with Urban's concession to a request of William IV for permission to establish a dynastic cemetery and burial place for himself and his successors next to the church of La Daurade. Yet the date of this bull has never been fixed, and the meaning of its references to trouble at Moissac have been variously interpreted. Since the granting of a family burial place to the counts of Toulouse and the date at which this occurred are of major importance in the history of the building programmes at La Daurade, this letter of Urban II to William IV deserves close attention.

A number of writers have concluded that Urban's letter, and hence the establishment of a dynastic burial place at La Daurade, must date from the end of 1093 or from 1094.[63] This is

[60] William's confession here that Abbot Hugh had condemned his action, along with the testimony of the letter of Gregory VII to his legate, Cardinal Richard (*PL* 148, col. 701, letter 57), support Cowdrey's opinion that St Hugh had not condoned the installation of monks from Moissac at Saint-Sernin and probably had not known of the action in advance (Cowdrey, *Cluniacs*, 116–18). In the latter letter, Gregory states that the improperly installed monks were withdrawn from the church of Saint-Sernin by command of the abbot of Cluny.
[61] See n. 60 above.
[62] *HGL*, vol. v, *Preuves*, col. 730; *PL* 151, cols. 392–3.

[63] *HGL*, vol. iii, p. 464 and vol. v, *Preuves*, col. 730; *PL* 151, col. 392; Delaruelle, 'Daurade', col. 100; and Carl D. Sheppard, Junr., 'An Earlier Dating for the Transept of Saint-Sernin, Toulouse', *Speculum*, 35 (1960), 588–9. Magnou seems to be the only historian who has questioned the traditional dating of this letter to 1093/4 (*Réforme grégorienne*, 67, and Recueil annexe, no. 11, where she gives a date of 'environ de 1090'). There is an unexplained contradiction in her text, however, since on p. 75 she dates the establishment of the dynastic cemetery of the counts at La Daurade to around 1094.

based on the assumption that the papal bull must supersede an accord reached in late 1093 between the canons of Saint-Sernin and the cathedral chapter of Saint-Étienne in which the right of burial of the noble family of Toulouse was at issue. This accord, dated 2 December 1093, granted exclusive right in perpetuity to the canons of Saint-Sernin to bury 'the bishop, the count, all knights and their wives, sons, and daughters' in their cemetery.[64] Magnou points out that Saint-Sernin had, in fact, enjoyed the privilege of burying the nobles of the city in its cemetery since about 1050, though this privilege had long been challenged by the canons of Saint-Étienne and was a source of much friction between the two chapters.[65] According to Devic and Vaissète, the sepulchral niche next to the Porte des Comtes contains the tombs of two young sons of William IV, as well as that of William's father, Pons (d. 1061), and two earlier counts of Toulouse, Guilhem Taillefer (d. 1037) and Raymond Bertrand (d. before 1050).[66] William's sons were probably buried in the niche at the time of their death (*c.*1088?), while the bodies of Pons, Guilhem Taillefer, and Raymond Bertrand would have been transferred there from an earlier burial location.

Why the count of Toulouse should have requested from the pope the right to establish a new family burial place at La Daurade can only be conjectured, since the documents are not explicit on this matter. To be sure, in granting the new cemetery to William IV, Urban's letter cites the love and honour which the count had for Sancta Maria Deaurata 'among all the churches of Toulouse'. Given the fact that two of his infant sons were earlier buried at Saint-Sernin, however, an explanation of William's change of heart seems called for. Despite his public apologies for his part in the events of 1081–3, William's decision to move his family burial place to La Daurade would seem to indicate a certain disaffection with the chapter of Saint-Sernin following those events and a reaffirming of his close loyalties to the Cluniacs. If this was the motive in his request for a dynastic cemetery at La Daurade, then Urban's letter granting him the cemetery may date from significantly before 1093–4.

The dispute over the installation of an abbot at Moissac referred to in this letter, while open to more than one interpretation, may also speak for an earlier date for this papal bull. The letter opens with the pope's praise of William for not allowing the abbots of Moissac and Lézat to be unjustly expelled from their abbeys and others unfairly substituted in their place. He then notes that the monk Ansquilinus (Ansquitil),[67] whom he has duly consecrated as abbot of Moissac, has been kept from assuming his office by the usurper (*invasore*), Hunaldus. Urban goes on to say that he has instructed the bishop of Cahors, in whose diocese the abbey of Moissac is situated, to have the usurper withdrawn, and he calls on William to aid in the carrying out of this decree. The letter concludes with the pope's grant of permission to William to establish a burial place at La Daurade and grants plenary indulgence to anyone buried there. The other important primary document for these events is another letter from Urban II, also

[64] The accord was reached through the mediation of the bishops of Toulouse, Carcassonne, and Agen. Douais, *Cartulaire de Saint-Sernin*, no. 2, 4–5.
[65] Magnou, *Réforme grégorienne*, 65.
[66] *HGL*, vol. iii, p. 291. The 5 bodies are contained in 3 reused sarcophagi still in place in the niche. For a lithograph of the sepulchral niche prior to its restoration in the 1860s, see Alexandre Du Mège, 'Archéologie Pyrénéenne', v, 'Atlas', pl. 49. This 5th vol. of his *Archéologie pyrénéenne* was not completed before Du Mège's death in 1862. The unfinished

work is in the Bibliothèque municipale de Toulouse (Rés. A XIX 95). Also see Mariotte's drawing for the 1st edn. of *HGL*, vol. ii (Toulouse, 1733), opposite p. 173. The sepulchral niche is discussed in Sheppard, 'Transept of Saint-Sernin', 584–90, and Lyman, 'Porte des Comtes Master', 20 n. 27 and *passim*.
[67] For the various spellings of this abbot's name in Latin documents, see Rupin, *L'Abbaye de Moissac*, 62. The French transliteration, Ansquitil, is often found in English language publications.

undated, to the bishop of Cahors, in which the pope says that Hunaldus was made abbot of Moissac against the will of the Roman Church.[68]

Differences in the interpretation of the troubles at Moissac described here have centred around the identification of the usurper, Hunaldus, named in Urban's two letters. A member of one of the most illustrious families of the Midi, Hunaldus of Gavarret (called Hunaldus of Béarn by some historians) had been elected abbot of Moissac in 1072.[69] It was this Hunaldus who conspired with Bishop Isarnus and William IV forcibly to install monks from Moissac at Saint-Sernin. Ernest Rupin, in his history of the abbey of Moissac, maintains that Hunaldus retired to his priory of Layrac in 1085, shortly after the defeat of his ambitions *vis-à-vis* Saint-Sernin,[70] and it is in 1085 that we have the earliest documents mentioning a successor to Hunaldus as abbot, Ansquitil (spelled there Ansquitinus).[71] Rupin then goes on to relate that the early abbacy of Ansquitil was threatened by a pretender to the office, one Hunaldus, whom Rupin identifies as a monk of Moissac of the same name as the former abbot.[72]

An interpretation of these documents which accords just as well with their contents and which is further supported by the fourteenth-century Chronicle of Aymeric de Peyrac, is that Ansquitil's abbacy was threatened not by Rupin's 'faux Hunaud', a monk of the monastery, but by the attempted return of the ambitious former abbot, Hunaldus of Gavarret. This is the interpretation maintained by Magnou,[73] and it seems to us, for reasons given below, to provide for an earlier and hence for a more credible date for Urban's letter to William IV concerning the cemetery of La Daurade.

Though Hunaldus of Gavarret had been very successful as abbot in the aggrandizement of Moissac (it was during his tenure from 1072–85 that Moissac acquired its most considerable properties), his designs on the church of Saint-Sernin in Toulouse had obviously carried him too far, at least in the eyes of the papacy. The triumph of the canons of Saint-Sernin, Hunaldus's temporary excommunication, and his rebuke by the pope must have been a humiliating defeat for such an ambitious and apparently able administrator. The fact that Abbot Hugh himself intervened to discipline his over-zealous abbot and that both Aymeric de Peyrac and the *Gallia christiana* state that Hunaldus retired from his abbacy well before his death,[74] suggests that this retirement was not a voluntary one.

Though there are donations from as early as 1085 naming Ansquitil as abbot of Moissac,[75] Aymeric de Peyrac gave the date of Ansquitil's 'possession' of the abbey of Moissac as 1091, during the papacy of Urban II.[76] Aymeric's meaning may be that the abbatial office of Moissac

[68] *PL* 151, col. 393, letter 121. This letter, in which Urban orders Bishop Geraldus of Cahors to expel Hunaldus from Moissac and reinstate Ansquitil, obviously dates from shortly before the one to William IV granting the cemetery, since in his letter to William Urban makes reference to his instructions to the bishop of Cahors concerning the matter of Hunaldus.

[69] Rupin, *L'Abbaye de Moissac*, 57. The earliest mention of Hunaldus as abbot of Moissac dates from 1073 (GC, vol. i, col. 163). His election in 1072 can be surmised, however, by the probable death of his predecessor Isarnus in that year (*HGL*, vol. iv, n. 19, p. 101). On Hunaldus's descent from the house of Gavarret, not of Béarn, with which Aymeric de Peyrac associated him, see Rupin, *L'Abbaye de Moissac*, 57.

[70] Rupin, *L'Abbaye de Moissac*, 62.

[71] GC, vol. i, col. 163 (in a donation of Gaufredus di Roviniano).

[72] In identifying this second Hunaldus as a monk of

Moissac, supported by his own faction within the monastery, Rupin has 2 bases. One is an undocumented passage in the *Gallia christiana* in which the invading Hunaldus is identified as a monk (GC, vol. i, col. 164). The other is the letter of Urban II to the bishop of Cahors (n. 68 above).

[73] Magnou, *Réforme grégorienne*, 66–7.

[74] Rupin gives the date of Hunaldus's death at Layrac as 1095 without any documentation (*L'Abbaye de Moissac*, 62), while the *Gallia christiana* states that Hunaldus was said to have died in 1091 at Layrac, where he was buried (GC, vol. i, col. 163).

[75] See n. 71 above and Rupin, *L'Abbaye de Moissac*, 62 n. 4, and p. 67.

[76] 'Ansquilinus preest monasterio Moyssiaci anno Domini millegesimo nonagesimo primo . . .' (Paris, BN, MS lat. 4991-A, fo. 160ʳ, col. 2).

was under dispute until that date. Indeed, we have seen that the documents show there were two claimants to the office, each backed by his own adherents. According to Aymeric, who clearly identifies Hunaldus with the former abbot, the dispute reached a climax when Hunaldus, angered that Ansquitil had carried the issue directly to the pope, went on a rampage with a band of mercenaries, burning and vandalizing the monastery and the town of Moissac before retiring to Layrac.[77] These violent acts must have just preceded or just followed the two letters of Urban II to the bishop of Cahors and to William IV, and Magnou's proposal of a date of 1090 for the expulsion of Hunaldus referred to in these letters fits the historical picture better than a date after December 1093.[78] This is especially so, since it seems probable that William IV died in the year 1093 or very shortly thereafter. The latest surviving document naming him as count of Toulouse is a restitution of properties to the abbey of Sorèze dated to the year 1093.[79] Devic and Vaissète cite 'an ancient author', Gaufridus Vosiensis, who reported that William died in the Holy Land,[80] but there is no substantiating documentation for this claim. There is, on the other hand, no evidence that William was ever entombed in the cemetery at La Daurade founded at his behest.[81] It is, moreover, entirely consistent with what we otherwise know about the character of William that this pious and—by the 1090s—elderly count might well have undertaken a pilgrimage to the Holy Land at the end of his life, dying there or *en route*.

The granting by Pope Urban II of a cemetery at La Daurade has traditionally been interpreted as a rectification, at the request of William IV, of the episcopal accord of 2 December 1093 which named the cemetery of Saint-Sernin as the official burial place of the counts of Toulouse, as well as the other noble families of the city. That is to say, according to this interpretation, Urban II's letter to William must date from after this accord of 2 December 1093. It is our belief, on the grounds cited above, that the letter dates from before 1093, most probably from 1090, just before the expulsion of the rebellious Abbot Hunaldus from Moissac. Might the accord of 1093, then, be seen as an attempt on the part of the canons of Saint-Sernin to reclaim the privilege of burying the count and his family immediately after the death of William IV?

The monks of La Daurade were, ironically, denied the honour of receiving the remains of any of the twelfth-century counts of Toulouse subsequent to William IV, since all died and were buried outside Toulouse. William's brother, Raymond IV (Raymond de Saint-Gilles) and Raymond's two sons, Bertrand and Alphonse-Jourdain, successive holders of the title of count of Toulouse, all chose the greater honour of dying while on the Crusade in the Holy Land,

---

[77] Ibid.

[78] Magnou, *Réforme grégorienne*, 67. There are contradictions in Magnou's text. On pp. 11 and 12 she dates Urban's letter requesting help from William in expelling Hunaldus 'vers 1094 (?)' while on p. 67 she questions this date and proposes 1090. Cowdrey, in his account of the reform of the Toulousan Church, also interprets the 2 letters from Urban II discussed here as referring to the abbot of Moissac, Hunaldus. In his words, 'Urban II regarded Abbot Hunald . . . as a contumacious rebel, who had opposed the Roman Church. The Pope himself saw to his deposition and to the consecration of his successor, Ansquelinus . . . ' (Cowdrey, *Cluniacs*, 118). Cowdrey's history of events at Toulouse is, as he states (113 n. 1), based closely on Magnou, and, like her, he does not broach the issue of a purported second Hunaldus, monk of Moissac, named in the *Gallia christiana*, vol. i, col. 164.

[79] *HGL*, vol. v, *Preuves*, cols. 729–30.

[80] Gaufridus Vosiensis in *Bibliotheca nova mss.*, ii. 304 (cited in *HGL*, vol. iii, p. 465).

[81] In an article of 1784, Jean de Montégut, a local antiquarian and member of the Académie des sciences de Toulouse who was present during the demolition of the medieval church of La Daurade in the 1760s, discussed a sarcophagus which he identified as the probable tomb of Count William IV. On the basis of his description, however, the tomb could not have dated earlier than the 13th cent., because of the presence on it of armorial devices. See Jean de Montégut, 'Mémoire sur un Tombeau qui étoit dans l'ancienne Eglise de la Daurade, et sur une Epitaphe gravée sur un marbre attaché au mur de cette Eglise', *Mémoires de l'académie des sciences de Toulouse*, 2 (1784), 100–14, and pl. 3, fig. 2.

while Raymond V is buried in the cloister of the Cathedral of Nîmes, where he had died in 1194.[82]

Nevertheless, the cemetery of La Daurade must have remained the family burial site at least into the rule of Alphonse-Jourdain (d. 1148), since the epitaph of the tomb of an unnamed son of this count, who died as a child, was preserved at La Daurade until after the destruction of the medieval church in the eighteenth century.[83] According to Catel, this epitaph was transferred from the cemetery into the cloister, where it could formerly be seen addorsed to the wall of the church near the chapter house.[84] In the verse on this marble tomb slab, the eulogy for the young son of Alphonse-Jourdain was followed by the statement that Pope Urban II had ordered that 'this cemetery of the Counts' be created.[85]

The community at La Daurade was confirmed in its possession of this cemetery in a letter of 1105 from Pope Paschal II to Abbot Hugh of Cluny, at which time the pope decreed that any secular persons desiring to be buried there could not be excluded.[86] This opening of the cemetery to the general populace must have meant the acquisition of important additional revenues for the Cluniac community at La Daurade after 1105, particularly since Urban's original grant of the cemetery had included the award of a plenary indulgence to anyone buried there.

The date of this cemetery and the honoured position it gave to La Daurade as the burial place of the counts and their family are of first importance to the history of the building activity that took place at the newly reformed monastery at the end of the eleventh century and beginning of the twelfth. The significance of this cemetery for estimating the most likely dates for the construction of the cloister has never been proposed, nor has the special relationship of the Cluniac community to the counts of Toulouse been explored for what it has to reveal about the Romanesque sculptural programme of La Daurade. In the coming chapters, we mean to show that the iconographic programmes of both the cloister and the chapter house testify to a continued close association between the ruling family of Toulouse and the building projects at La Daurade well into the latter half of the twelfth century.

The history of Toulouse after the death of William IV provides a further framework within which to define the most likely period of the construction of the cloister. William IV died without surviving male progeny and was succeeded as count by his brother, Raymond IV (Raymond de Saint-Gilles), who already held title in his own right to property of the eastern domains of the dynastic inheritance along the Rhône.[87] Raymond was as steadfast a supporter

---

[82] For Raymond IV see Hill and Hill, *Raymond IV*, 157; for Bertrand see *HGL*, vol. iv, n. 50, p. 218; for Alphonse Jourdain see Catel, *Comtes de Tolose*, 197; for Raymond V see *HGL*, vol. vi, p. 160.

[83] Montégut reported seeing the epitaph in 'one of the chapels of the cloister', to which it had apparently been moved at the time of the 18th-cent. demolitions. He provided a drawing of the tomb slab (his pl. 3, fig. 1) and a transcription of the verses on it (Montégut, 'Mémoire sur un tombeau', 111).

[84] Catel, *Comtes de Tolose*, 198.

[85] 'Vir sacer Urbanus Romanus Papa Secundus / Esse cimeterium praecipit hoc Comitum', ibid. 198; *HGL*, vol. v, *Preuves*, p. 12, no. 40. Jean de Chabanel, priest and early historian of La Daurade, reported the arms of Count William IV painted against the wall of the cemetery, above a sepulchre (*L'Antiquité de la Daurade*, 77).

[86] *GC*, vol. xiii, Instrumenta, cols. 13–14, no. 13.

[87] See Hill and Hill, *Raymond IV*, 7–8, for the patterns of inheritance of the ruling family of Toulouse in the 11th cent. Provision for Raymond's succession to the county of Toulouse, should his older brother William die without male heirs, was made as early as 1063 (see the charter of Gauzebert, abbot of Moissac, in *HGL*, vol. v, cols. 522–3, and ibid., vol. iii, p. 342). Two acts of donation of 1088 give Raymond's titles as Count of Toulouse, Duke of Narbonne, and Marquis of Provence (*HGL*, vol. v, *Preuves*, cols. 707–8). Devic and Vaissète have taken this as evidence that William IV had ceded or sold the county of Toulouse to his younger brother even before his death (*HGL*, vol. iii, pp. 452–5). William of Malmesbury states that this was the case (*Gesta regum Anglorum* in *PL* 179, col. 1343). His reliability is, however, questionable (see Flach, *Origines*, iv, 589). This interpretation of the documents can be challenged, moreover, since William IV himself continued to be called count of Toulouse in charters dating from after 1088.

of Cluniac foundations during his lifetime as had been his brother William. John and Laurita Hill, in fact, stress Raymond's good relations with Cluny as a contributing factor in the successful consolidation of his power and good will within his domains.[88] In 1065 he donated the abbey of Goudargues to Abbot Hugh of Cluny for the benefit of his soul and the souls of his family and in 1066 he subscribed, along with his mother Almodis, to a grant by the abbey of Saint-Gilles to the congregation of Cluny.[89] In 1074 he and his brother William acted together in donating the important abbey of Figeac in the Rouergue to Cluny.[90] Though Raymond, like his brother, showed an interest in many churches within his domains, it is the enthusiastic support for Cluniac establishments over the lifetime of both these Languedocian princes, most especially during the early period when Cluny was in full expansion in the region, which, in the words of Hill and Hill, 'form a pattern of great influence exerted by the Order over both William and Raymond'.[91]

At the Council of Clermont, convened on 18 November 1095, Raymond de Saint-Gilles became the first of the princes of Europe to take up Pope Urban II's call to recover the Holy Sepulchre. After receiving the pope during his visit to Toulouse in 1096 and later at Nîmes, where a second council was convened, Raymond and his armies departed for the Holy Land late in 1096.[92]

Chapter 7 will consider in some detail Raymond de Saint-Gilles's central role in the First Crusade and the possible reverberations of heightened crusading consciousness in the iconography of the cloister capitals being carved at La Daurade about 1120–30. Our concern here, however, is the impact which the absence of its count and defender had for events in Toulouse and the Toulousan Church during the first decades of the twelfth century.

THE POITEVIN OCCUPATION AND THE RESTORATION OF THE HOUSE OF TOULOUSE-SAINT-GILLES

Though the triumphs of Raymond de Saint-Gilles in the Holy Land were to bring glory to Toulouse and raise its crusading count to mythic stature, his departure in 1096 marked the beginning of a politically troubled period for the city which did not end until his son, Alphonse-Jourdain, was firmly in control of the county of Toulouse in 1123. According to Devic and Vaissète, Raymond resigned his estates to his son Bertrand upon his departure for the Crusade,[93] and it is probable that the count, then in his sixties, did not expect to return from the Holy Land. Bertrand, however, did not command the authority in Languedoc that his

See *HGL*, vol. v, *Preuves*, col. 715 (1090); letter of Urban II to William IV, ibid., col. 730 (*c*.1090); restitution to the abbey of Sorèze, ibid., cols. 729–30 (1093). Raymond, in fact, may have begun to be designated count in documents following the deaths of William's 2 young sons, as an enunciation of his presumed succession to the county. While there are later instances of an heir being identified by his presumptive title in charters issued by the counts of Toulouse, our ignorance of William's activities during the final years of his life leaves open the issue of his possible renunciation of his lands and title in favour of his brother prior to his death. (See the discussion of this issue in Hill and Hill, *Raymond IV*, 18–19.)

[88] Hill and Hill, *Raymond IV*, 8.
[89] Bernard and Bruel, *Chartes de Cluny*, iv, nos. 3404 and 3410.
[90] *GC*, vol. i, Instrumenta, cols. 44–5, no. 36.

[91] Hill and Hill, *Raymond IV*, 8 n. 19. These authors broach the issue of possible Cluniac influence on Raymond's enthusiasm to take up the cross against the Muslims but cite the difficulty of documenting the nature of this influence. The precise role of Cluny in fostering or encouraging the Crusade is itself a subject of difference among scholars (cf. e.g. Hunt, *Cluny under Saint Hugh*, 133; Cowdrey, *Cluniacs*, 180–3); Étienne Delaruelle, 'The Crusading Idea in Cluniac Literature of the Eleventh Century', in Noreen Hunt (ed.), *Cluniac Monasticism in the Central Middle Ages* (London, 1971), 191–216; Frederic Duncalf in Kenneth M. Setton (ed.), *A History of the Crusades*, i. *The First Hundred Years*, ed. Marshall W. Baldwin (Madison, 1969), 235–6.
[92] *HGL*, vol. iv, n. 42, pp. 202–3.
[93] Ibid., p. 203.

father had done, and he soon found his succession to the county of Toulouse challenged from Aquitaine. In 1094 the powerful William IX, duke of Aquitaine and count of Poitiers, had married Philippa, daughter and only surviving child of Count William IV of Toulouse, a marriage that was motivated, according to Flach, by the duke's plan eventually to absorb Toulouse and its region into a reconstituted duchy of Aquitaine.[94] Challenging the Toulousan tradition of exclusive male succession, Philippa claimed to be the only legitimate heir to her father's domains. The departure of Raymond de Saint-Gilles and his armies from the Midi provided the duke of Aquitaine with the opportunity to launch what was to be the first of two attempts to claim his wife's inheritance by force.

Differing dates are given by various historians for the first occupation of Toulouse by Poitevin forces. Devic and Vaissète maintain that it was brief, lasting from shortly after Raymond's departure on crusade in 1096 until the end of 1099 or the beginning of 1100.[95] William IX and Philippa were certainly in possession of the city in July 1098, when they issued an important charter in favour of the church of Saint-Sernin.[96] Mundy cites 1108 as the date Bertrand 'reentered his capital'.[97]

It seems unlikely, however, that William IX was in control of the city after about 1100. Bertrand seems to have been able to marshall the necessary support for his succession among the clergy and local nobles within a relatively short time, so that this first challenge by William IX and Philippa was not a serious one. Devic and Vaissète cite two charters in which Bertrand, whose titles are given as Count of Toulouse, Rouergue, and Albi, confirmed the privileges given earlier by Philippa and William IX to Saint-Sernin.[98] One of them was offered on the altar of Saint-Sernin and was subscribed to by the archbishop of Narbonne and by Guillaume-Jourdain, count of Cerdagne. Though neither is dated, as Devic and Vaissète point out, they must have been issued before 1102, the year in which the count of Cerdagne himself departed for the Holy Land.[99]

During his brief reign as count of Toulouse, Bertrand displayed the same interests in furthering the Cluniac cause as had his father and uncle. He repeated his uncle's earlier attempt to oust the canons from Saint-Sernin and replace them with monks, presumably Cluniac ones. Like William IV, he was unsuccessful in this attempt. The acts cited above, in which Bertrand confirmed privileges and donations accorded the church of Saint-Sernin by Philippa and William IX, were also acts of restitution, in which Bertrand swore to defend the canons and never to introduce monks into their cloister.[100]

With Bertrand's own departure on crusade in 1109, following in his father's footsteps, and his death in the Holy Land in 1112, a clear power vacuum was created in Toulouse, and this time Philippa and her husband made a serious effort to take the city. Bertrand's young half-brother, Alphonse-Jourdain, born in the Holy Land in 1103, was still a minor and unable to defend his claim to the county.

[94] Flach, *Origines*, iv. 589–90.
[95] *HGL*, vol. iii, pp. 507 and 543–4.
[96] Ibid., vol. v, *Preuves*, cols. 754–6. William IX here signed himself Count of Poitiers and Toulouse. The signatures of 2 local viscounts, Bernard, viscount of Béziers, and Adhémar, viscount of Toulouse, show that some of the local nobility had joined with the Poitevins against Bertrand's succession to the county.
[97] Mundy, *Liberty*, 16 and n. 17, citing Flach for the date 1108. Flach, however, says only that William IX 'was no longer master of Toulouse' in 1108 (*Origines*, iv. 599).
[98] *HGL*, vol. v, *Preuves*, cols. 767–8. See also Douais, *Cartulaire de Saint-Sernin*, no. 435.
[99] *HGL*, vol. iii, p. 544.
[100] Ibid., vol. v, *Preuves*, cols. 767–8. See also Bertrand's authorization of a sale in favour of Moissac in 1104 (ibid., cols. 788–9).

The period of the occupation of Toulouse by the Poitevin dynasty was important for bringing the powerful influence of the reforming monk and preacher, Robert d'Arbrissel, founder of the order of Fontevrault, to the region of Toulouse. Robert d'Arbrissel accompanied Philippa and her husband during both their occupations of the city. His name appears as witness to the charter of privileges issued to Saint-Sernin in 1098 by Philippa and William IX and again on a document of accord between Philippa and the viscount of Béziers, issued during the second occupation.[101] With Philippa's support, Robert d'Arbrissel was very active in the region, founding in 1114 the important priory of Lespinasse a short distance to the north-west of Toulouse.[102] His follower, Géraud de Sales, founded the monastery of Grandselve, also to the north-west of Toulouse, which subsequently became Cistercian.

The second Poitevin occupation lasted from 1112 to 1119. William IX's claim to the county of Toulouse seems not to have gained popular support, and when his wife Philippa herself took up the habit of Fontevrault and retired into a convent of that order about the year 1116,[103] this ended any legitimate basis for his designs upon the county. He soon became absorbed in other concerns, notably a crusade against the Saracens in Spain. In 1119 the citizens of Toulouse rose against the castellan whom William had left in charge of the city, and publicly recognized the young son of Raymond de Saint-Gilles, Alphonse-Jourdain, in exile in his lands along the Rhône, as their lord. The Poitevin castellan, William of Montmaurel, was forced to flee to the Chateau Narbonnais, where he was held under siege by the townspeople. In 1123 the rule of the counts of Toulouse was officially restored in the city when an army of Toulousans marched to Orange to deliver Alphonse from siege by the count of Barcelona and escorted him triumphantly back to Toulouse.[104]

The restoration of the house of Toulouse-Saint-Gilles to the lordship of the city meant a resumption of the pattern of favour shown to the priory of La Daurade and the Cluniac community by this family before the Poitevin interregnum. Most important of the acts of Alphonse-Jourdain in assuring the growth in wealth and temporal power of the priory of La Daurade over the course of the twelfth century was the charter in which he granted to the monastery of La Daurade and its prior the right to build a toll-free bridge across the Garonne, 'inter hospitale Beatae Mariae et Vivarius' for the use of all inhabitants of the city and Bourg.[105] This was a singular privilege, since at the time there was only one other bridge over the river at Toulouse. The New Bridge, or Daurade Bridge, as it came to be called, effectively connected the monastery of La Daurade on the east bank of the Garonne (called the Vivarius) directly with its Hospital of Notre-Dame in the growing suburb of Saint-Cyprien on the west

---

[101] Ibid., col. 756, and ibid., col. 845.

[102] Ibid., col. 846. Besides Lespinasse, Robert d'Arbrissel founded monasteries of the order of Fontevrault throughout the diocese of Toulouse (see ibid., vol. iii, p. 624). On the life and spirituality of this influential reformer see R. Niderot, *Robert d'Arbrissel et les origines de l'ordre de Fontevrault* (Rodey, 1952); J.-M. Bienvenu, *L'Étonnant Fondateur de Fontevraud, Robert d'Arbrissel* (Paris, 1981); Jacques Dalarun, *L'Impossible Sainteté: la vie retrouvée de Robert d'Arbrissel* (Paris, 1985); id., *Robert d'Arbrissel: fondateur de Fontevraud* (Paris, 1986).

[103] Mundy (*Liberty*, 16), following some early authors, says that William IX divorced Philippa. Devic and Vaissète, however, deny this, and claim that Philippa died in retirement at Fontevrault or in the monastery of Lespinasse which she had founded outside Toulouse, before William IX remarried in 1119. See *HGL*, vol. iii, p. 627, for the early writers on this issue.

[104] Alphonse-Jourdain probably did not take physical possession of the city until 1123, although Devic and Vaissète cite documents indicating that he was widely recognized as count in the region from 1120 on (see *HGL*, vol. iv, n. 50, pp. 219–21).

[105] The charter is transcribed by Catel (*Mémoires du Languedoc*, 156, and id., *Comtes de Tolose*, 196). The original is in Toulouse, ADHG, 102 H 145. The prior of La Daurade, Raymond, to whom the donation was made, died between 1128 and 1130 (see *GC*, vol. xiii, col. 104). On this basis Mundy dates the granting of the bridge to between 1119 and 1130 ('Charity and Social Work', 212 n. 26).

bank. This hospital itself testifies to the expanding charitable activity of the Cluniac community of La Daurade within the city in the twelfth century.[106]

The bridge granted by the count of Toulouse must have been important in stimulating commercial activity both in the parish of the Daurade and in Saint-Cyprien. This is one more way in which the privileged position of the monastery on the banks of the Garonne contributed to its wealth and rendered it a certain autonomy. As the historical *seigneurs* of a sizeable stretch of the Garonne, the monks also controlled portage and fishing rights and benefited from the revenues of mills along the river.[107]

As to the continued patronage of La Daurade by the counts of Toulouse in the twelfth century, we have already seen that the Cluniac priory continued to be the burial place of the dynasty at least until the end of the first half of the century. The charters of Raymond V and Raymond VI indicate that both La Daurade and the other Cluniac priory in Toulouse, Saint-Pierre-des-Cuisines, were favoured locations of these counts for the holding of councils in the later twelfth century.[108]

What did the turbulent events of the crusading period and the occupation of Toulouse mean for artistic activity at La Daurade during the course of the twelfth century? With its traditional benefactors, the counts of Toulouse, absent or, in the case of Alphonse-Jourdain, in exile, and with most of the dynastic fortunes being converted to finance the enormous costs of the Crusade, the ambitious building programme underway at La Daurade at the beginning of the twelfth century may have been left without substantial support during the years 1109 to 1123.[109] This is the best explanation for the evident separation in time between the activity of the first and second workshops in the cloister of La Daurade during the first decades of the twelfth century. Though completion of cloister programmes in successive stages, by successive workshops, was common practice in the twelfth century, the stylistic gulf between the first and second ateliers at La Daurade is so complete that an actual hiatus in work for several years appears probable. The sculptors who began the cloister of La Daurade, probably shortly after 1100 with the dispersal of the Moissac cloister workshop, can have completed no more than two arcades when their part in the programme came to an end. The cloister was completed by a workshop whose style is not at all rooted in the earlier Pilgrimage Road tradition and has many characteristics of an importation from outside Languedoc. Not only are the first and second workshops clearly separated in style and date, but the initial iconographic programme was abandoned in the second campaign of decoration. The stylistic, iconographic, and historical evidence is consistent in suggesting a break in work, of perhaps as much as fifteen years, during the course of construction of the cloister of La Daurade.

It is significant, however, for artistic activity at La Daurade in the later twelfth century that

---

[106] 'Charity and Social Work', 211–12.

[107] See Germain Sicard, *Les Moulins de Toulouse au moyen âge* (Paris, 1953), 56–61, and Boyer, 'L'Origine de la Daurade', 47–8. In a document of 1190 the prior of La Daurade claimed that the rights and properties of the monastery along the Garonne went back to a Carolingian donation (see Sicard, *Moulins*, 57–8 and n. 20. The document is in Toulouse, Archives de la Société toulousaine d'électricité du Bazacle, vol. 1, p. 1, confirmation of 1190).

[108] See Ch. 9 for councils held in the cloister of La Daurade. See Toulouse, AMT, AA 1, doc. 8 (6 Jan. 1189) for an oath of fealty sworn between Raymond V and the Common Council of

Toulouse in the church of Saint-Pierre-des-Cuisines. The oath was affirmed by Raymond VI on 6 Jan. 1195, also in the same church (ibid., doc. 10).

[109] As I have noted elsewhere, there is no evidence that the Poitevin invaders, Philippa or her husband, had special interest in or gave donations to the Cluniac community at La Daurade (Horste, 'Passion Series', 34 and n. 32). On the contrary, they supported religious establishments that were rivals to Cluniac influence in Toulouse. As Mundy put it, 'if the policy of Bertrand and his predecessors [Count William IV and Raymond de Saint-Gilles] had been "Cluniac", that of Philippa and the Poitevins was "Fontevrault"' (Mundy, *Liberty*, 17).

this eclipse of the fortunes of the monastery was a temporary one. Mundy has cited the period of the Poitevin occupation and the ascendancy of the order of Fontevrault in the region as a turning-point, when Cluny clearly lost its monopoly on monastic reform in Toulouse and its region to the newer reforming orders and to the Knights Templar and the Hospitallers, who began to be important presences in the city in the early twelfth century.[110] Not only in southern France but throughout Europe, Cluny was never again to exert the dominant spiritual influence that had characterized its dynamic period of expansion in the eleventh century. Nevertheless, many individual houses of the order retained locally influential positions. The priory of La Daurade must be counted as one of these. As the resident religious community of one of the most revered churches of the city, and as custodians since the time of William IV of a dynastic cemetery of the counts, the Cluniacs of La Daurade continued to profit from a certain conservatism on the part of the ruling family of Toulouse in its solicitude for its old beneficiaries. This is manifest in the terms of the charter in which Alphonse-Jourdain granted to the priory of La Daurade the right to construct a bridge across the Garonne. In exchange for this privilege the clergy were to perform an annual office and mass for the souls of Alphonse-Jourdain's father and grandfather (Raymond de Saint-Gilles and Pons), and the monks were to pray for the count as long as he lived.

The sculptural decoration that survives from the Romanesque building programmes at La Daurade preserves something of this sense of historical continuity in the dynastic ties that bound the ruling family of Toulouse to the venerable Cluniac priory. This is particularly so in the iconography of the Passion series and in the royal tone of the chapter house portal. To explore the influence of historical context on the sculptural programme at La Daurade is one aim of this study.

[110] Ibid. 16–17.

2

BUILDING ACTIVITY IN TOULOUSE, 1070–1140

THE EVENTFUL DECADES between 1070 and 1140, turbulent though they were, fostered the accelerated building activity of the Romanesque period in Toulouse, and with it a new art of monumental sculpture. This unprecedented fever to build was initiated by the ecclesiastical and lay powers of the city who were responding, within the local sphere, to the pressures for reform that had been preached throughout Europe within monastic and papal circles, since the mid-eleventh century. In Toulouse these pressures were particularly intense because of the respective strengths and conflicting interests of the key promoters of the reforms. These comprised two successive and ambitious bishops, Durandus and Isarnus, who were committed to the spread of a revitalized Cluniac monasticism in their diocese, a powerful ruling family favouring the more conservative elements of the reform, and the newly regularized canons of Saint-Sernin, who claimed their independence under papal protection and immunity.

The picture that emerged in the previous chapter is decidedly one of competition for rights, privileges, and prestige among the great religious houses of Toulouse. The communities of Saint-Sernin, Saint-Étienne, and La Daurade all undertook the rebuilding of their churches during this period, as well as the construction of cloisters and conventual buildings to serve their newly reformed and revitalized regular life. Besides these major undertakings, the movement towards reform encouraged the foundation of new churches and priories and the reform of existing ones, through new donations of land or the return to ecclesiastical control of properties that had fallen into lay hands. The existing Romanesque structures in Toulouse and its immediate environs only partially reflect the building activity of these years, since the number of destroyed foundations, known to us from documents, is considerable.

There is no documented date for the beginning of the most ambitious construction project of this period, that of the pilgrimage church dedicated to St Saturninus. Plans to build an enlarged church on the site of the martyr's tomb may have been in mind as early as the first half of the eleventh century.[1] Most scholars believe that work actually started, however, only after the canons of Saint-Sernin adopted a regular life, some time between 1073 and 1080.[2] Construction

---

[1] In a bull of 20 July 1096 Urban II ascribed the new basilica to the efforts of Bishop Petrus Rogerius (1020–c.1040) (Toulouse, ADHG, Ser. O, 'Urbanus papa secundus ecclesiae Sancti Saturnini possessiones et privilegia'. Transcribed in Célestin Douais, *Cartulaire de l'abbaye de Saint-Sernin de Toulouse (844–1200)* (Paris, 1887), app. 3. 475–7).

[2] Marcel Durliat, 'La Construction de Saint-Sernin', *Bulletin monumental*, 121 (1963), 152; id., 'Les Donneés historiques',

Homenaje a Jaime Vicens Vives, i (Barcelona, 1965), 235–41; id., 'Les Origines de la sculpture romane à Toulouse et à Moissac', *Cahiers de civilisation médiévale*, 12 (1969), 349; Thomas Lyman, 'The Sculpture Programme of the Porte des Comtes Master', *Journal of the Warburg and Courtauld Institutes*, 34 (1971), 36–7; id., 'Raymond Gairard', *Journal of the Society of Architectural Historians*, 37 (1978), 71 n. 5. For the adoption of regular life by the canons of Saint-Sernin, see above, Ch. 1 n. 52.

proceeded rapidly during the four decades between 1080 and 1120. Much of the literature since 1960 has sought to establish a more accurate chronology for this construction, but important differences of opinion have emerged.[3] The most widely accepted chronology, in which the consecration date of 1096 and the death of Canon Raymond Gayrard in 1118 have been regarded as important milestones in the project, has been most compellingly elucidated in a succession of publications by Marcel Durliat.[4] This view, widely adhered to in French and Spanish publications, is not universally accepted, however. In studies of the building that span twenty-five years, Thomas Lyman has argued for a different building sequence and has interpreted the role of Raymond Gayrard in very different terms from those of other writers on the building programme.[5]

Durliat places the beginning of construction close to 1080, basing his argument on both the probable date of reform of the canons and the relationship of the plan of Saint-Sernin to that of the cathedral of Santiago, whose beginning date is more securely fixed in 1078.[6] Durliat defines a first building campaign at Saint-Sernin, beginning on the south side of the hemicycle with the exterior wall of the ambulatory and its radiating chapels, and comprising the lower storey of the apse, choir, and transept, including the north and south transept portals. Capital decoration in this portion of the early project was under the charge of the Master of the Porte des Comtes and his workshop. Durliat dates the sculpture of the Porte des Comtes itself to between 1082 and 1090.[7] He perceives a definite halt or break in construction at this stage, as

[3] See Carl D. Sheppard, Jun., 'An Earlier Dating for the Transept of Saint-Sernin', *Speculum*, 35 (1960), 584–90; David Scott, 'The Miègeville Portal of the Basilica of Saint-Sernin of Toulouse', Ph.D. thesis, University of California at Berkeley (1960), esp. 31–42; id., 'A Restoration of the West Portal Relief Decoration of Saint-Sernin in Toulouse', *Art Bulletin*, 46 (1964), 271–82; Serafín Moralejo Alvarez, 'Une sculpture du style de Bernard Gilduin à Jaca', *Bulletin monumental*, 131 (1973), 7–16; Willibald Sauerländer, 'Das sechste internationale Colloquium der "Société française d'Archéologie": die Skulpturen von Saint-Sernin in Toulouse', *Kunstchronik*, 24 (1971), 341–7; Abbé Jean Cabanot, 'Le Décor sculpté de la basilique Saint-Sernin de Toulouse', *Bulletin monumental*, 132 (1974), 99–145. A useful synopsis of the older opinions on construction campaigns at Saint-Sernin, going back to the late 19th cent., as well as the current controversies, has been provided by Lyman, 'Raymond Gairard', 72–4, esp. n. 8.

[4] Durliat, 'Construction de Saint-Sernin', 151–70; id., 'L'Atelier de Bernard Gilduin à Saint-Sernin de Toulouse', *Anuario de estudios medievales*, 1 (1964), 521–9; id., 'Données historiques', 235–41; id., 'Le Portail occidental de Saint-Sernin de Toulouse', *Annales du Midi*, 77 (1965), 215–23; id., 'Origines de sculpture à Toulouse et à Moissac', 349–64; id., 'Les Cryptes de Saint-Sernin de Toulouse: bilan des recherches récentes', *Les Monuments historiques de la France*, NS 17 (1971), 25–40; id., 'La Construction de Saint-Sernin de Toulouse: étude historique et archéologique', *Actes du congrès de la société des historiens médiévistes de l'enseignement supérieur public* (Besançon, 2–4 June 1972), *Annales littéraires de l'université de Besançon* (Paris, 1973), 201–11; id., 'Les Chapiteaux de la Porte Miègeville à Saint-Sernin de Toulouse', *Économies et sociétés au moyen âge: mélanges offerts à Edouard Perroy* (Paris, 1973), 123–9; id., *Haut-Languedoc roman* (La Pierre-qui-vire, 1978), 47–77.

[5] Thomas Lyman, 'The Romanesque Capitals of Saint-Sernin in Toulouse and Related Sculptures', Ph.D. thesis, University of Chicago (1964); id., 'Notes on the Porte Miègeville Capitals and the Construction of Saint-Sernin in Toulouse', *Art Bulletin*, 49 (1967), 25–36; id., 'The Pilgrimage Roads Revisited', *Gesta*, 8 (1969), 30–44; id., 'Porte des

Comtes Master', 12–39; id., 'Terminology, Typology, Taxonomy', 223–7; id., 'Raymond Gairard', 71–91; id., 'Motif et narratif: vers une typologie des thèmes profanes dans la sculpture monumentale de los Romerías', *Les Cahiers de Saint-Michel de Cuxa*, 10 (1979), 59–78; id., 'Le Style comme symbole chez les sculpteurs romans: essai d'interprétation de quelques inventions thématiques à la Porte Miègeville de Saint-Sernin', ibid. 12 (1981), 161–79; id., 'La Table d'autel de Bernard Gilduin et son ambiance originelle', ibid. 13 (1982), 53–73; id., 'Bernard Gelduinus, the Jaca Master and the Spain-Toulouse Issue Today', paper read at 22nd International Congress on Medieval Studies, May 1987, at Western Michigan University.

[6] Durliat, 'Origines de sculpture à Toulouse et à Moissac', 349–50. On the beginning date of Santiago de Compostela, based on the most recent excavations there, see R. Louis, 'Fouilles dans la cathédrale Saint-Jacques-de-Compostelle', *Bulletin de la société nationale des antiquaires de France* (1954–5), 152–3. See also John Williams, ' "Spain or Toulouse?" A Half Century Later: Observations on the Chronology of Santiago de Compostela', *Actas del XXIII. congreso internacional de historia del arte: Espana entre el Mediterraneo y el Altantico* (Granada, 1973), sect. 2, 557–67.

[7] In his recent monograph on Saint-Sernin Durliat has refined his dating of the Porte des Comtes. In this publication of 1986 he maintains that the portal was sculpted as early as around 1082, with the main lines of the portal—its projecting *avant-corps* with recessed jambs supporting multiple archivolts —certainly having been established by that date (Marcel Durliat, *Saint-Sernin de Toulouse* (Toulouse, 1986), 71). In his earlier publications he had placed the appearance at Saint-Sernin of this new portal type at 'around 1090' (cf. Marcel Durliat, 'L'Apparition du grand portail roman historié dans le Midi de la France et le nord de l'Espagne', *Les Cahiers de Saint-Michel de Cuxa*, 8 (1977), 9–10; id., 'Origines de la sculpture à Toulouse et à Moissac', 352). His modification of that date is presented in the recent monograph without explanation. In effect, it brings his chronology for the portal closer to that of Lyman, who suggests that work on the Porte des Comtes was under way by 1081/2.

indicated in the masonry fabric of the south transept façade, at the level of the tribunes.[8] This coincides with the evidence of the interior capital decoration, which indicates that a new workshop was in charge during the construction of the transept tribunes, headed by Bernard Gelduinus and his team. According to Durliat, Bernard Gelduinus and his marble carving shop must have been called to Saint-Sernin not long before the dedication of 1096, specifically to carve the signed altar table and related marble reliefs now enwalled in the ambulatory. These sculptors were subsequently employed in the decoration of the transept tribunes, whose completion Durliat assigns to the last years of the eleventh century.[9]

Durliat defines a final Romanesque campaign, now under the administration of Canon Raymond Gayrard, which began about 1100 with the laying of the nave perimeter wall. This campaign would have included the decoration of the Porte Miègeville. In Durliat's view, by the time of the death of Raymond Gayrard, recorded in 1118 in the necrology of Saint-Sernin,[10] the side aisles would have been complete, the main nave vessel raised to the height of the upper windows, and the three eastern-most nave bays vaulted. After the death of the canon, work on the basilica would virtually have come to a halt in the second quarter of the twelfth century, leaving the west façade incomplete above the level of the sculptured portal.

There are points of common ground between Durliat and Lyman in their respective analyses of the building's fabric and the important stylistic groupings of its capital decoration. Lyman, however, has elaborated a history of the Romanesque building campaigns that differs in fundamental respects from the orthodox view propounded by Durliat and others. The most important of these differences concerns the role of Canon Raymond Gayrard during the first decades of construction and the laying out of the perimeter of the building in one unified campaign which, he proposes, corresponds to Raymond's leadership.[11] Moreover, Lyman rejects the evolutionary view of sculptural styles at Saint-Sernin, arguing that stylistic distinctions among types of capital decoration are not necessarily linked to the chronological progress of construction itself.[12]

In Lyman's view, the reform of the chapter of canons and their adoption of regular life provides for the beginning of construction in the 1070s.[13] He sees construction of the hemicycle and choir and the lower storey of the transept as a first campaign, ending above the level of the transept portals. In a departure from traditional thinking, however, he identifies the significant historical event delimiting this first campaign not as the consecration of 1096 but the disturbances of 1081–3 when the canons were expelled and Cluniac monks temporarily installed.[14] Given a starting date in the 1070s, he argues, the lower storey of the hemicycle and transept, including the transept portals, could have been under way by the time of the ousting of the canons in 1081/2. The restoration of the canons in 1083 would have marked the resumption of work, with a campaign to complete the transept tribunes, a campaign in which Bernard Gelduinus and his assistants participated. This would also have been the period when the altar table signed by Gelduinus would have been carved. Lyman has hypothesized that the altar table was commissioned specifically to replace an earlier (tenth-century ?) one destroyed

[8] Durliat, *Haut-Languedoc roman*, 75.
[9] Ibid. 75; id., 'Construction de Saint-Sernin', 170.
[10] *HGL*, vol. iv, col. 524.
[11] Lyman, 'Raymond Gairard', 71–91.
[12] Lyman, 'Terminology', 223–4. Lyman's definitive publication on Saint-Sernin will be his forthcoming monograph, *Saint-Sernin of Toulouse: The Art of the Romanesque Builder*.

I am indebted to Professor Lyman for allowing me to read the conclusion to his book before it went to press.
[13] Lyman cites suggestions that the canons were leading a regular life in documents that date 'toward 1076–80' ('Porte des Comtes Master', 36–7).
[14] Lyman, 'Porte Miègeville Capitals', 32.

or desecrated during the troubles of 1081–3.[15] Hence in Lyman's chronology the Gelduinus-style figured capitals of the transept tribunes, which are concentrated in the two outermost bays of each transept arm, and which have long been associated with the altar table, were carved, like the altar itself, between 1083 and 1096, not in the years immediately after the consecration of 1096, as Durliat's chronology would have it.[16]

Lyman's new interpretation of the role of Raymond Gayrard in the construction of Saint-Sernin is based on his perception of the building sequence as revealed in the fabric of the building and its sculptural decoration, in conjunction with a new reading of the often-quoted passage describing Raymond's role that is contained in his fifteenth-century *Vita*.[17] Most readers have interpreted the passage to assign construction of the nave to Raymond and specifically to exclude any of the eastern portions of the building (the *capitis membrum*) from his tenure.[18] Lyman, on the other hand, has speculated that the wording of Raymond's *Vita* could have been intended to affirm, rather than to deny, the saint's participation in the construction of the *capitis membrum* (the crypt and aisles in his interpretation). As an alternative reading, then, Lyman has suggested that the passage may mean to say that Raymond completed the lower nave walls *in addition* to completing the *capitis membrum*.[19]

Based on the masonry evidence and this alternative reading of Raymond's *Vita*, Lyman's conclusions regarding the building sequence are as follows: a first building campaign up to 1081/2 saw the construction of the crypt, the lower storey of the hemicycle, and the ambulatory that would enclose the transepts. He proposes that solid stone piers had been set up as far as the first several bays of the nave beyond the crossing when the expulsion of the canons caused the interruption of work. Upon the return of the canons in 1083 construction resumed, now under the administration of Raymond Gayrard, with a campaign to complete the aisle around the transepts, vault the choir and crossing, and construct the transept tribunes, beginning with the bays closest to the crossing. At the same period—that is to say, between 1083 and about 1093 —Raymond enclosed the nave by carrying a wall around the remaining perimeter of the building, up to the height of the side aisle windows and including the western tower façade to the height of a few metres. Lyman proposes that there was an accelerated campaign to complete the transept tribunes by the Gelduinus workshop prior to the visit of Urban II in 1096, which employed some already-carved capitals left behind by the workshop of the Porte des Comtes Master.[20]

In Lyman's chronology, then, Raymond Gayrard's stewardship of the project corresponds to the activity of the Porte des Comtes Master and Bernard Gelduinus in the decades before 1100, rather than to the sculptural projects of the Porte Miègeville and the west façade portal. This

---

[15] Lyman, 'Table d'autel', 61 and 63. In an article of 1967, Lyman had speculated that Bernard Gelduinus and his team were at Saint-Sernin working on the signed altar table even before 1081/3 ('Porte Miègeville Capitals', 33). In his later publications he has renounced this possibility.

[16] Ibid. 32–3. Lyman has held to this chronology in his subsequent publications. See, however, 'Raymond Gairard,' 89–90, for considerable refinements and precisions in his account of the progress of work before 1096.

[17] The *Vita Sancti Raimundi*, quoted in Lyman, 'Raymond Gairard', 72, after Célestin Douais, 'La Vie de Saint-Raymond, chanoine, et la construction de l'église Saint-Sernin', *Bulletin de*

la société archéologique du Midi de la France, 17 (1894), 154 (also published in *Mélanges sur Saint-Sernin de Toulouse*, fasc. 1 (Toulouse, 1894), 7–22). This is the 15th-cent. version of the *Vita*. Cf. this same passage quoted by Guillaume de Catel (*Histoires des Comtes de Tolose* (Toulouse, 1623), 177) from a later text of the *Vita* then in the Collège de Saint-Raymond in Toulouse.

[18] See Douais, 'Vie de Saint-Raymond', 150–63. Also see Marcel Durliat, 'La Construction de Saint-Sernin de Toulouse au XIᵉ siècle', *Bulletin monumental*, 121 (1963), 168–9.

[19] Lyman, 'Raymond Gairard', 89.

[20] Ibid., 71–91.

has caused him to question the date of 1118 given for Raymond's death in the necrology of Saint-Sernin.[21]

Lyman's reading of the progress of construction at Saint-Sernin is the most precise and analytical of all the studies that have been devoted to this building. It is based on an original analysis of the masonry fabric and the vast capital decoration of the interior, that recognizes a greater complexity in the building sequence and working practices within the chantier than has been acknowledged by other observers. At the same time, the texts that exist for the history of Saint-Sernin in the eleventh century remain too ambiguous to support the chronology of events in the building enterprise that Lyman has proposed. This makes his efforts to tie his archaeological observations to the course of known events in the eleventh-century history of the chapter highly conjectural. For example, in the act of donation of Saint-Sernin to Hugh of Cluny and Hunaldus of Moissac, Bishop Isarnus made reference to an altar of St Ascicles to which, as a prerogative of his authority, he retained the key. For Lyman this becomes the inspiration for his idea that the altar was desecrated during the Cluniac occupation and that this (conjectured) event necessitated the carving of a new one by Bernard Gelduinus and his workshop.

Despite the differences of opinion concerning the building sequence, there is no disagreement that the pace of construction on the pilgrimage church at Toulouse during the years between about 1075/80 and about 1120 was rapid. While the nave and western block were to remain unfinished until work was taken up again towards the end of the thirteenth century,[22] the entire pilgrimage choir with its crypt-confessio and enormous galleried transept had been raised and vaulted in little more than forty years. The scale of the building was almost unprecedented for the period—only the great abbey church of Cluny III, rising during the same decades in Burgundy, was larger—and the sculptural programme at Saint-Sernin was vast. Three richly sculptured portals with ambitious iconographic programmes were produced during these four decades, though the west portal remained incompletely realized, and an astonishing 260 sculptured capitals were carved for the Romanesque interior of the building.[23] Clearly the desire to complete and vault the hemicycle and transept, the focus of liturgical worship and relic veneration, and supply it with sanctuary furnishings, had been the chief priority of the canons. Once this was realized, the canons seem to have turned their attention to the needs of their communal life, since, on the basis of its surviving sculpture, the Romanesque cloister at Saint-Sernin was probably constructed about 1120–40.[24]

What all of this means is that funds must have been abundant, at least at the outset of the project, in order for construction to progress so rapidly; enthusiasm and the determination to go forward must have been high, and, very importantly, the chantier must have been one of the largest of the period, at least during those brief decades when work was going forward apace.

---

[21] Lyman, 'Raymond Gairard', 88–9.

[22] On the original design for the tower façade and its vaulting, see Lyman, 'Raymond Gairard', 78–9 and fig. 15. The disinterring of the relics of St Saturninus in the late 13th cent. seems to have inspired a renewed interest in completing the church. The vaulting of the nave space and erection of an upper storey for the west façade, which never received the double towers anticipated in its plan, extended into the 14th cent., along with the completion of the crossing tower (see Durliat, *Haut-Languedoc roman*, 70 and 75–6).

[23] The figure is from Cabanot, 'Le Décor sculpté', 106. See Jules de Lahondés, 'Les Chapiteaux de Saint-Sernin', *Mémoires de la société archéologique du Midi de la France*, 14 (1891), 258–83, for Lahondés's enumeration of 394 capitals on the portals and interior of Saint-Sernin. His list includes the post-Romanesque members.

[24] For the cloister of Saint-Sernin, see below, n. 58.

We know the latter must have been true, since the diaspora of the sculpture atelier of Saint-Sernin on both slopes of the Pyrenees and west towards Santiago suggests it was the dominant workshop of the region during the course of several decades.

Despite the enormous demands for stone masons, sculptors, and marble carvers that would have been generated at the building site of Saint-Sernin over a forty-year period, during these same years two other building projects, less grandiose but still of major scale, were under way in Toulouse at La Daurade and at the cathedral complex of Saint-Étienne. The building programme at La Daurade, which consisted of the addition of a monumental forechurch with monks' choir to the existing church, and the construction of a decorated cloister, will be discussed in the following chapter. The third project, the rebuilding of the cathedral of Saint-Étienne, was undertaken by Bishop Isarnus shortly after his reform of the cathedral chapter in the 1070s. Its site was on the extreme eastern edge of Toulouse, close to the old Gallo-Roman rampart, in one of the oldest quarters of the city.[25]

Fig. 1

Nothing is known about the character of the earliest pre-Romanesque cathedral of Saint-Étienne or its exact location on the site, though its foundation was attributed by legend to St Martial.[26] Élie Lambert suggested that it may have been an Early Christian cathedral, perhaps constructed about AD 400 by the bishop, St Exupery.[27] In the same act in which Isarnus laid out the statutes for the reform of the cathedral canons according to the Rule of St Augustine, he proclaimed his intention to rebuild the cathedral, which was in a deplorable state of delapidation.[28] As we saw in Chapter 1, this act can be dated to some time between 1073 and 1077, and Magnou has presented the most convincing arguments for placing it in 1073.[29] Construction of the new cathedral must have begun shortly after this date.[30]

The Romanesque cathedral of Isarnus no longer exists, having been replaced in subsequent rebuildings on the site. What can be deduced from the archaeology of the cathedral precinct makes it clear, nevertheless, that, in comparison with the vast five-aisled basilica of Saint-Sernin with its pilgrimage choir, the plan and dimensions of the eleventh-century cathedral of Isarnus must have been decidedly more modest. The repeated rebuildings, along with elusive documentary references that are difficult to attach to distinct structures, have left a confused and difficult picture. Nevertheless, despite the little that is known of Isarnus's cathedral and possibly other projects at the site, it cannot be ignored in judging the volume of building activity in Toulouse during the decades before and after 1100.

The earliest surviving plan of the cathedral precinct is that of Joseph-Marie de Saget, part of his monumental plan of the city of Toulouse dating from 1750.[31] Our illustration is a lithograph by Délor in the Musée Paul Dupuy at Toulouse, drawn after the plan of Saget. It shows the cathedral and the adjacent structures essentially in the state in which they existed until shortly after the Revolution. The Gothic cathedral still stands today, but all the other

Fig. 2

[25] NB Fig. 1, reproduced after Mundy, contains an error. The cathedral of Saint-Étienne should be oriented, with the great Gothic choir closest to the rampart.

[26] See Auguste d'Aldéguier, 'Notice sur l'église de Saint-Étienne, de Toulouse', *Mémoires de la société archéologique du Midi de la France*, 1 (1832–3), 24–5.

[27] Élie Lambert, *Abbayes et cathédrales du sud-ouest* (Toulouse, 1958), 89.

[28] Elisabeth Magnou, *L'Introduction de la réforme grégorienne à Toulouse* (Toulouse, 1958), Recueil annexe, no. 1, p. 2, ll. 4–6.

[29] See above, Ch. 1 n. 32.

[30] Lambert gave 1078 as the date of the beginning of work on Isarnus's cathedral, without providing any justification (*Abbayes et cathédrales*, 89). Presumably he based this date on the act of reform, which is dated *c*.1077 by the authors of the GC (vol. xiii, Instrumenta, 8, col. 7).

[31] Toulouse, Bibliothèque municipale, Plan no. 34. A detail of the Saget plan showing the cathedral precinct has been reproduced by Linda Seidel, *Romanesque Sculpture from the Cathedral of Saint-Étienne, Toulouse*, Outstanding Dissertations in the Fine Arts (New York, 1977), fig. 8; her Ph.D. thesis, Harvard University (1964).

Fig. 3   structures shown in Saget's plan have been destroyed. The cathedral itself is a hybrid building. Its Gothic choir, begun by Bishop Bertrand de l'Isle in 1272 and completed in the fifteenth century, is appended to an earlier single-aisled nave begun in the early thirteenth century.[32] The Romanesque cloister is shown in the Saget plan to have adjoined the Gothic choir on the south. There is no documentation for the date of the cloister, but it was probably constructed shortly before or at the same time as the chapter house of the canons, which I date on the basis of its sculpture to about 1125–35.[33] Hence it must have been put up under the successor to Isarnus, Bishop Amelius (called Amélius Raimond du Puy by Devic and Vaissète), whose long episcopacy lasted from 1106 to 1139.[34] Flanking the cloister along its opposite (south) walk was a smaller church dedicated to St James. This church, pulled down along with the cloister in the early nineteenth century, was a rebuilt fourteenth-century structure.[35]

Fig. 3   The location of Bishop Isarnus's cathedral has long been considered to have corresponded approximately to the nave of the existing building. This is Lambert's conclusion.[36] This, however, would have placed it in a very curious relationship to the Romanesque cloister, which lay well to the east of Lambert's proposed location for the eleventh-century cathedral

Fig. 2   and would have been unconnected to it. He explained this arrangement by hypothesizing that the cloister of the canons was built to communicate with the old, pre-Romanesque cathedral which Isarnus had preserved to the east of his new church.[37]

Lambert's identification of the site of Isarnus's cathedral is based on several kinds of evidence. Most important are the remains of Romanesque brick masonry and two oculi with parti-coloured mouldings of alternating brick and stone of Romanesque type that have been incorporated into the walls and buttressing of the thirteenth-century nave of the existing building on the north side. Lambert identified these as vestiges of vaulted side aisles of Isarnus's cathedral. He reconstructed this church in plan as having had a simple, transept-less nave, flanked by single side aisles and terminating at the east end in a principal semicircular apse, flanked by two smaller apses.[38] He drew on a seventeenth-century description of the cathedral of Toulouse by Guillaume de Catel to calculate the eastern extension of Isarnus's three-aisled basilica and the form of its triple-apsed chevet, which he believed was still standing until 1610.[39] He placed the easternmost extension of the chevet at the so-called *pilier d'Orléans* of the present Gothic choir, the over-sized pier separating the westernmost side

Fig. 3   aisle bay from the choir on the south side. Finally, Lambert pointed to two series of reused Romanesque capitals that have always been visible on the interior of the thirteenth-century nave, incorporated into rectangular pilasters that receive the transverse arches of the vaulting,

[32] Plan by G. Debré and J. Braunweld, published in Lambert, *Abbayes et cathédrales*, 84, fig. 10. The most exhaustive study of the architecture and archaeology of the cathedral, with critique of earlier bibliography, is by D. Cazes, Y. Carbonell-Lamothe, and M. Pradalier-Schlumberger, 'Recherches sur la cathédrale Saint-Étienne', *Mémoires de la société archéologique du Midi de la France*, 43 (1979–80), 7–165 (review by Marcel Durliat in *Bulletin monumental*, 142 (1984), 105–6).

[33] On the Romanesque cloister see Chs. 6 and 8.

[34] *HGL*, vol. iv, n. 66 p. 353, and *GC*, vol. xiii, cols. 14–15.

[35] See Lambert, *Abbayes et cathédrales*, 87. In post-Revolutionary documents it is referred to as the Eglise de Saint-Jacques et Sainte-Anne. By 20 Dec. 1811 it had been demolished. For the documentation on its destruction and that

of the adjoining cloister of the cathedral see Kathryn Horste, 'A New Plan of the Cloister and Rampart of Saint-Étienne, Toulouse', *Journal of the Society of Architectural Historians*, 45 (1986), 11 n. 25.

[36] Lambert, *Abbayes et cathédrales*, 89. This study of the cathedral virtually repeats that contained in Lambert's earlier publication, 'La Cathédrale de Toulouse', *Mémoires de la société archéologique du Midi de la France*, 21 (1947), 137–63. Linda Seidel accepted Lambert's hypothesis about the location of Isarnus's church (*Sculpture from Saint-Étienne*, 6–7). See her drawing, ibid., fig. 4.

[37] Lambert, *Abbayes et cathédrales*, 89.

[38] Ibid. 90–2 and fig. 11.

[39] Ibid. 91. See Guillaume de Catel, *Mémoires de l'histoire du Languedoc* (Toulouse, 1633), 164.

and into the arcade of the tribune gallery on the interior west wall. According to Lambert, these capitals were carved for Isarnus's church (whether or not they were ever set into place there) and are contemporary, in his judgement, with the capitals of the hemicycle, transept, and side aisles of Saint-Sernin.[40]

The evidence pointed to by Lambert does indicate that the present thirteenth-century nave was built on the site of an earlier Romanesque church, a portion of whose walls it incorporated. That this earlier structure was the cathedral of Isarnus is, however, contradicted by the sculptural evidence cited by Lambert. The reused capitals and imposts incorporated into the interior of the Gothic nave do not belong to the period of this bishop (c.1071–1105/6).[41] *Pls. 5 and 6* Their style suggests a later twelfth-century date, during the period of Isarnus's successor, Amelius Raimundus (1106–39) or later. While their Corinthian format and ornamental repertory derive ultimately from the capital styles of the basilica of Saint-Sernin, that widely influential ensemble provided the basis for a prolonged meditation on its ornamental forms in the later Romanesque sculpture of the region. This is obvious even within the basilica of Saint-Sernin itself, in the latest of the Romanesque-style capitals of the interior, those of the western bays of the nave side aisle walls. The capitals in the nave of Saint-Étienne appear to belong to *Pl. 1* the latter end of this protracted development, not to its beginning.

Of the reused capitals on the interior of the cathedral of Saint-Étienne, those incorporated into the tribune gallery of the inner west wall compare most closely to specific sculptures at *Pl. 2* Saint-Sernin. What they compare to are not the early Romanesque capitals of the eastern parts of the pilgrimage church, however, but those of the western bays of the nave (against the outer aisle walls) and on the west façade, which I date to the end of the Romanesque building programme there, about 1115–20. The capitals of the nave walls at Saint-Sernin make use of many of the palmette and acanthus leaf forms that make up the staple repertory in the eastern parts of the basilica, but they introduce new forms as well. Large upright palmettes with ruffled or scalloped edges, a row of scallops fringing the astragal, and a plump berry motif, attached to a stem, are all new motifs that appear in the latest aisle wall capitals at Saint-Sernin and help to lend a rich, ornate effect to these latest interpretations of the Corinthian capital. *Pl. 1* Compared to the style of the eastern parts of Saint-Sernin, the foliate capitals of the western nave walls exhibit an increasing diversification of vegetal forms; leaves are more variegated, with more ruffled members and with the intermixing of more elongated and more curvilinear forms. The points of the large palmettes which define the registers of the capital curve outward and downward in more pronounced arcs, and the volutes are more springy and tightly wound.

These features also define the reused capitals of the western arcade on the interior of Saint-Étienne and separate them from the powerful early Romanesque style of the hemicycle and transept of Saint-Sernin. Capitals with stemmed berries, tightly wound volutes, and foliage with scalloped edges in the western arcade of Saint-Étienne should be compared to specific *Pl. 2* capitals along the outer aisle walls at Saint-Sernin, for example in the eighth bay from the east on the north side or the twelfth bay on the south side. The way of finishing the astragals in the *Pl. 1* series of capitals at Saint-Étienne also indicates their more advanced twelfth-century date. The standard astragal in the capitals of the eastern parts of Saint-Sernin is either a simple rounded torus or, most often, the astragal is sharply chamfered. This form is replaced, however, in the

---

[40] Lambert, *Abbayes et cathédrales*, 93–4.
[41] For additional illustrations of these capitals, see Cazes *et* *al.*, 'Saint-Étienne de Toulouse', pls. 20–3 and 25–30.

capitals of the west façade portal of Saint-Sernin, where a more complex astragal is introduced, composed of a narrow, projecting torus of rounded profile sandwiched between finer rings. This is also the form used in the capitals of the west arcade at Saint-Étienne. In the only figured example among the group, the feet of the nimbed angels lap over and grasp the astragal, as do those of the lions and monkeys on the capitals of the west façade of Saint-Sernin. The scalloped foliate forms on the historiated capital at Saint-Étienne are close to the nave aisle capitals on the interior of Saint-Sernin, while the human masks with inflated cheeks resemble those of the howler monkeys on the capitals of the west façade of Saint-Sernin.

Pl. 3

Pl. 4

Pls. 5 and 6

Given the comparative material at Saint-Sernin, the capitals on the interior west wall of Saint-Étienne should probably be dated no earlier than about 1115–20. The nineteen Romanesque-style capitals incorporated into pilasters of the nave were probably carved even later in the twelfth century.[42] They have the Corinthian form and some of the motifs, such as paired birds, of the eastern portions of Saint-Sernin, but they are remote in style from those early capitals. They carry further the evolution towards a greater diversity, multiplication, and ornateness of leaf forms, in particular the preference for scalloped and curvilinear forms, described in the outer aisle capitals of the nave of Saint-Sernin. The treatment of imposts is equally ornate in these reused fragments. One motif of large plastic rosettes held within the scotia of the impost moulding can be compared to similar motifs on bases from the Romanesque chapter house of Saint-Étienne that date from the second quarter of the twelfth century.[43]

Clearly, nevertheless, the reused capitals in the present nave of Saint-Étienne are the remains of an earlier Romanesque church. If not Isarnus's cathedral, then what was this structure? Though the evidence is ambiguous, certain authors have maintained that the cathedral of Saint-Étienne once shared the site with a church dedicated to Notre-Dame. The bases for this belief are early references—one dating from 1190—to two altars maintained by the chapter, one dedicated to the Virgin and the other to St Stephen.[44] According to Catel, the high altar of the parish was dedicated to the Virgin in 1386, as if to preserve thereby the memory of an earlier church with this dedication.[45] What is more, Catel believed that the most likely site for a cemetery of Notre-Dame in the parish of Saint-Étienne, to which there are numerous early textual references, was the Place Saint-Étienne, that is, the locale just in front of the west façade of the present nave.[46]

There is no consensus of opinion among the most recent authors who have considered this

[42] The authors of the 1980 study of the cathedral of Saint-Étienne concluded that the reused capitals betray an 'advanced' 12th-cent. date, without associating them with any specific late Romanesque ensembles of the region. The authors note that only 19 of the Romanesque style capitals are actually spolia (Cazes *et al.*, 'Saint-Étienne de Toulouse', 100). Five were carved at the time of the 13th-cent. resetting to provide the requisite 24. Likewise, only some of the impost fragments are reused remains. Durliat has dated the re-employed nave capitals of Saint-Étienne to about 1110–20 (*Haut-Languedoc roman*, 190), earlier than either I or the authors of the 1980 study would place them.

[43] Compare the impost in the nave at Saint-Étienne (Cazes *et al.*, 'Saint-Étienne de Toulouse', pl. 30) to the rosettes on bases in the Musée des Augustins (M. 4, 27, 47, and 48). Bases M. 173 and 175, attributed since the catalogue of 1912 to La

Daurade, may originate from Saint-Étienne, on the basis of their use of this motif. For my dating of the Saint-Étienne chapter house see Ch. 6.

[44] The donation of 1190 in favour of the chapter of Saint-Étienne for the maintenance of two lamps for altars to the Virgin and to St Stephen is cited in the inventory of Claude Cresty (Toulouse, ADHG, Inventaire Cresty, Saint-Étienne, vol. 2. 133ᵛ).

[45] Catel, *Mémoires du Languedoc*, 163, and Cazes *et al.*, 'Saint-Étienne de Toulouse', 113–14.

[46] Catel, *Mémoires du Languedoc*, 171. Catel described prayers and absolutions performed on this site, 'as in other cemeteries', by the canons of Saint-Étienne on the day after All Saints. A document of 1189 records a transaction made in regard to the cemeteries of Saint-Étienne and of Notre-Dame (Toulouse, ADHG, Inventaire Cresty, Saint-Étienne, vol. 2).

question.[47] None the less, the existence of a separate church with a dedication to the Virgin, sharing the functions of the episcopal *ecclesia* with a church of St Stephen, would have placed Toulouse within that large group of double cathedrals that were characteristic of the earliest episcopal foundations in Gaul, for example at Metz, Paris, Auxerre, and elsewhere.[48] What is more, the possible existence of such a church on the site of the present nave—its most likely location, in light of Catel's information about an ancient cemetery just to the west of this spot—would account for some of the most puzzling difficulties of the site.

More pertinent to the question of Isarnus's cathedral is the physical evidence that a Romanesque church occupied the site of the present Gothic choir. The south wall of this choir has been built on top of and incorporates the remains of a much earlier wall of thinner bricks which is easily visible on the exterior of the building and was signalled by Lambert in his study of the cathedral. That this wall is not later than the Romanesque period is attested by the line *Fig. 3* of corbels, also pointed to by Lambert, which mark the former roof line of the north cloister walk on this side, as well as a walled-up round-headed portal, which Lambert dated to the twelfth century, near the eastern end of this early wall.[49] Marcel Durliat, as well as the authors of the 1980 study of the cathedral, have all taken the existence of this wall, along with the location of the former cloister, as indications that an early church probably did exist on the site of the present Gothic choir and that the Romanesque cloister was constructed adjacent to it. None of these authors has suggested, however, that this destroyed church was the cathedral built by Isarnus.[50] Yet this is most likely to have been its location, with the cloister and chapter house of the canons communicating directly to it. If it replaced an earlier, primitive cathedral of Saint-Étienne on the spot, this location would have placed the original Saint-Étienne very close to the Gallo-Roman wall of the city, a situation often chosen for urban churches in the Early Christian period, for protection or physical buttressing. Isarnus's cathedral, then, would have hallowed the spot of the original sanctuary, a site perpetuated, in turn, by the enormous choir of Bertrand de l'Isle. To the west of it may have stood a second church dedicated to the *Figs. 2 and 3* Virgin, constructed under Bishop Amelius. This suggested reconstruction of the site makes more sense in light of the location of the twelfth-century cloister than does Lambert's.

The cathedral complex at Toulouse also included, from at least the twelfth century, a church or chapel dedicated to St James. Its location flanking the Romanesque cloister on the south is shown in the Saget plan. As already noted, the church that existed on this site down to the *Fig. 2* nineteenth century was of late Gothic date. But it, too, is almost certain to have replaced an earlier one, since, well before this period, a church of Saint-Jacques at Toulouse is associated with the cathedral of Saint-Étienne in the documents.

The earliest mention of it occurs in a copy of the famous diploma of Charles the Bald of 5

---

[47] Cazes, Carbonell-Lamothe, and Pradalier-Schlumberger believe the documentary evidence is insufficient to demonstrate the previous existence of a companion church of Notre-Dame near that of the cathedral of Saint-Étienne, and they conclude that the documents refer to a single edifice bearing, for a certain period, a double dedication ('Saint-Étienne de Toulouse', 114). Durliat, on the other hand, believes 2 churches existed from pre-Romanesque times at the site and that the more westerly one, reconstructed at the beginning of the 12th cent., was dedicated to the Virgin. The more easterly of the 2 churches, to which the cloister adhered, 'remplissait les fonctions de véritable cathédrale' (*Haut-Languedoc roman*, 190–1).

[48] Jean Hubert, 'Les "Cathédrales doubles" de la Gaule', *Geneva*, NS 11. *Mélanges d'histoire et d'archéologie offerts en hommage à M. Louis Blondel* (1963), 103–25. Hubert cites Saint-Étienne at Toulouse among his list of double cathedrals.

[49] Lambert, *Abbayes*, 86. The plan published by Lambert (our Fig. 3), shows the location of this wall in solid black, along the south side of the Gothic choir.

[50] Cazes *et al.*, 'Saint-Étienne de Toulouse', 109 and 114; Durliat, *Haut-Languedoc roman*, 190–1.

April 844 in which the Emperor confirmed privileges awarded by his father, Louis the Pious, to the three most venerable churches of Toulouse. The precise words of the document are that the immunities are made to Samuel, 'Tolosanae aecclesiae civitatis episcopus, quae est constructa in honore sancti Stephani seu et sancti Jacobi apostoli . . . cum monasterio sanctae Mariae, quod est infra muros ipsius civitatis, cum omnibus appenditiis suis, necnon et monasterium sancti Saturnini martiris . . . '.[51] The Carolingian original of this document has been lost. Galabert has dated the above copy (which he calls B) containing the double dedication to the late eleventh or early twelfth century.[52] A second copy, dating to 1155, has attached to it a confirmation by Louis VII of the privileges granted to the churches of Toulouse by the Carolingian Emperor. In this confirmation, the cathedral of Toulouse is identified only by the single dedication to St Stephen ('eclesia prothomartiris Stephani').[53]

As Lambert has pointed out, the cult of St James and the European pilgrimage to his tomb did not become current until the mid-tenth century.[54] Therefore, a church dedicated to his cult is unlikely to have been constructed at Toulouse before this date. Lambert suggested that the inclusion of the name of St James in the dedication of the cathedral may not have been present in the original document of 844 but may have been added at some unknown date, in order to associate a more recent church at the site with the cathedral of Saint-Étienne. This interpolation would then have been transcribed into the copy of the late eleventh or early twelfth century (Galabert's copy B). By 1155 (the date of the confirmation of Louis VII), Lambert has suggested, the two churches had become sufficiently independent for the cathedral to be identified only by its dedication to St Stephen.[55]

As its dedication would indicate, the church of Saint-Jacques must have been built as a pilgrimage chapel, and it was said to have preserved a relic of the head of St James under one of its altars.[56] The cult of St James was beginning to attain its height of popularity in the last quarter of the eleventh century, when the pilgrimage church centred on his presumed tomb at Santiago was begun. Construction simultaneously started on the sister basilica of Saint-Sernin in Toulouse, where St James is honoured as a pendant to St Peter above the Porte Miègeville. Since the earliest document in which a church of Saint-Jacques is mentioned at Toulouse dates from the late eleventh or early twelfth century (copy B of the diploma of 844), this church may very well have been constructed during the episcopacy of Isarnus, alongside his rebuilt cathedral of Saint-Étienne.[57] The two churches would shortly have been joined together by the Romanesque cloister and chapter house that must have been constructed by Isarnus's successor, Amelius.

---

[51] Toulouse, ADHG, H Saint-Sernin. packet 1, act 1. See Ch. 1 n. 40, and Galabert, 'Diplôme de Charles le Chauve', 185–214.

[52] Ibid. 188.

[53] Toulouse, ADHG, H Saint-Sernin, packet 2, act 1. See the full transcription in Galabert, 'Diplôme de Charles le Chauve', 188–9. He has designated this copy C. The transcription of the diploma of 844 and the confirmation by Louis VII attached to it were made at the time of Louis's sojourn in Toulouse in 1155 on his return journey from a visit to the tomb of St James at Santiago (discussed below, Ch. 9).

[54] Lambert, *Abbayes et cathédrales*, 88.

[55] Ibid. 87–8.

[56] Jules de Lahondés, *Toulouse chrétienne: l'église Saint-Étienne, cathédrale de Toulouse* (Toulouse, 1890), 37.

[57] The church of Saint-Jacques was unquestionably existing in 1119, when it was accorded several privileges by Pope Calixtus II at the council held in that year at Toulouse (Lambert, *Abbayes et cathédrales*, 88). At the time of its demolition in the early 19th cent., Alexandre Du Mège recorded the presence of antique black marble columns and capitals incorporated into the 14th-cent. piers of the Church of Saint-Jacques ('Mémoire sur le cloître de Saint-Étienne de Toulouse', *Histoire et mémoires de l'académie royale des sciences, inscriptions et belles-lettres de Toulouse*, 4 (1834–6), 255–6). Du Mège attributed these to a destroyed antique structure and suggested that marbles from the same structure may have been incorporated into the fountain of the cathedral cloister. On this fountain see Horste, 'Plan of Saint-Étienne', 11.

In summary, between about 1073 and 1140, during the episcopacies of Isarnus and Amelius, the episcopal see of the diocese of Toulouse was considerably altered by new construction. The old cathedral of St Stephen was rebuilt and a sculptured cloister and chapter house were constructed along its south flank, for the usage of the canons. On the south side of the cloister a church or chapel dedicated to St James may already have been erected for the worship of pilgrims on their way to the tomb of the Apostle. Finally, somewhat later in the twelfth century, a second episcopal church dedicated to the Virgin was very likely constructed to the west of the cathedral of St Stephen.

These were the same decades, as we have seen, in which the canons of Saint-Sernin were constructing one of the largest churches of Christendom outside the walls of Toulouse, and it is hard not to see these as rival projects. If the pilgrimage church of Saint-Sernin surpassed the cathedral church of the diocese in its architectural pretensions, the surviving remains indicate that the cathedral cloister and chapter house were richer in sculpture than the cloister of Saint-Sernin, and they were certainly more important artistically. The surviving capitals from Saint-Sernin present a marked contrast in their uniformity to capitals from the other two cloisters of Toulouse.[58] The repertory is limited to paired lions or birds in vine tendrils or pure foliage ornament. Only two of the surviving capitals have human figures (Mesplé 211 and 212) and these are diminutive in scale, depicting a battle of armed angels with winged dragons and an enigmatic scene of humans and animals caught in a vine interlace. *Pls. 7 and 8*

Pl. 9

The latter subjects can be seen to anticipate the general tendency to abandon ambitious narrative themes in the latest phase of Romanesque capital decoration in Toulouse (after 1140) and to adopt a precious and diminutive ornament of allegorical combat.[59] Yet the style and motifs of the cloister capitals are already presaged at Saint-Sernin as early as 1105–20 in the workshop that executed the *Lions* capital in the east jamb of the Porte Miègeville and in the capitals of the west façade. The salient characteristic of this style is its deep and extensive undercutting, which frees the highly plastic forms from the ground. The contrast between the three-dimensional volume of the figured forms and their simultaneous attachment to the drum by fibrous vine stems creates an interesting tension in these sculptures. Certain motifs, such as the humped backs of the lions and their long, claw-like feet also link the portal capitals of Saint-Sernin to those of the cloister. *Pls. 206 and 207*

[58] Little has been written about the sculpture of the cloister of Saint-Sernin. Durliat attributes 23 capitals in the Musée des Augustins to the structure (*Haut-Languedoc roman*, 134). In my judgement, only 19 of these can be assigned with certainty to the cloister (M. 211–29). The provenance of 4 others (M. 241–4) remains problematic. They are close in style to the *Lions* capital on the east jamb of the Porte Miègeville and to the capitals of the west portal of Saint-Sernin, and they may originate from somewhere within the Romanesque construction at Saint-Sernin. However, they appear to be later in date than the cloister capitals, their most striking feature being the false imposts, attached by vine stems to the drum of the capital. The incorporation of the impost into the drum is a feature of late Romanesque capital design in Toulouse and its region; see M. 309, as well as a capital in the Metropolitan Museum in New York (Charles T. Little, 'Romanesque Sculpture in North American Collections. XXV. The Metropolitan Museum of Art. Part V. Southwestern France', *Gesta*, 26 (1987), fig. 5). Two of the problematic capitals (M. 243 and 244) were acquired by the museum only in 1960, after having been in the collection of the marquis de Castellane since the 19th cent. (see

Paul Mesplé, 'Sculptures romanes et gothiques de l'église Saint-Sernin', *Revue du Louvre et des musées de France*, 11 (1961), 167–74). Durliat has identified 2 other capitals from the cloister in a private collection at Castres (*Haut-Languedoc roman*, 134). Two others in the collection of Raymond Pitcairn at Bryn Athyn, Pa., should be added to the group (New York, Metropolitan Museum of Art, *Radiance and Reflection: Medieval Art from the Raymond Pitcairn Collection*, exh. cat. by Jane Hayward, Walter Cahn, *et al.* (New York, 1982), nos. 13A and 13B). On the plans of the cloister and history of its destruction, see Françoise Abrial-Aribert, 'Le Cloître de Saint-Sernin de Toulouse,' *Actes du 96e congrès national des sociétés savantes, Toulouse, 1971*, ii (Toulouse, 1976), 157–74.

[59] The capitals from La Daurade that post-date the activity of the second workshop show this tendency (M. 172, 174, and 178). For the conservative character of this late Romanesque ornament at Toulouse see Kathryn Horste, 'The Capitals of the Second Workshop from the Romanesque Cloister of La Daurade, Toulouse', Ph.D. thesis, University of Michigan, (1978), 1, 346–53.

Though the carving is of high quality, in the repetitive animal and bird motifs there is nothing of the iconographic profundity and originality of the cloisters of Saint-Étienne and La Daurade or of other contemporary cloisters of the region, such as Moissac or Saint-Pons-de-Thomières. By banishing this category of sculpture from their cloister galleries, the canons of Saint-Sernin may have intended to emphasize the distinction between their own 'progressive' form of communal life and that of traditional Cluniac monasticism, whose most characteristic expression in the cloisters of south-western France was precisely the heavy enrichment of the galleries with narrative and hagiographic themes.

During the eleventh and twelfth centuries developments at Saint-Sernin had persistently been interlinked, in a complex give and take, with the activity of sculpture workshops at León, Jaca, Santiago, and elsewhere in northern Spain. The style of the cloister of Saint-Sernin represents a prolongation of this Spanish connection at Toulouse into the second quarter of the twelfth century. The animal repertory, the plasticity of the relief, and the strong detachment of the figured elements from the drum connect these cloister capitals with the style of sculpture practised at Santiago de Compostela on the Puerta de las Platerías and in certain capitals on the exterior of the castle church at Loarre.[60]

The passion for building that was an attendant phenomenon of the monastic reforms of the eleventh and twelfth centuries made of Toulouse 'a city of convents'. The masons, sculptors, and marble carvers working at Saint-Sernin, Saint-Étienne, and La Daurade represent only a portion of the building activity in progress in the city in the decades before and after 1100. The list of other churches founded or reformed and rebuilt during this period in Toulouse and its environs is an important one. One of these was Saint-Pierre-des-Cuisines, located in the former allodium of Saint-Pierre at the north-western edge of the city, near the banks of the Garonne. The church and allodial lands of Saint-Pierre had been donated to Moissac in 1067 by Count William IV and his mother Almodis as part of their support for Cluniac reform in the region.[61] Saint-Pierre was made a dependency of La Daurade after the reform of that priory in 1077 and toward 1100 the Cluniacs of La Daurade undertook the rebuilding of Saint-Pierre. This building is now largely in ruins but has been reconstructed with a simple unaisled nave, a square choir roofed with a cross vault and surmounted by a tower, and with a semicircular apse.[62] The surviving masonry, characterized by decorative stone and brick work, and the use of oculi above round-headed windows, indicates a date close to the eastern portions of Saint-Sernin. About 1180 a second nave, parallel to the early Romanesque one, was added along its south flank. The surviving Romanesque portal, remounted in the Gothic period,[63] dates from this second Romanesque campaign.

In 1073 the important abbey of Lézat, located just to the south of Toulouse, was also united with Cluny and reformed by Moissac. In 1115 monks of Lézat founded a *salvetat* (or new population centre) at the southern edge of Toulouse, outside the Narbonne Gate. They

[60] For illustrations see Lyman, 'Pilgrimage Roads Revisited', figs. 27 and 28; Georges Gaillard, *La Sculpture espagnole de Saint Isidore de Léon à Saint-Jacques de Compostelle* (Paris, n.d.), pl. LX, nos. 1 and 2.

[61] Catel, *Comtes de Tolose*, 120 and 122; *HGL*, vol. v, *Preuves*, cols. 544–6.

[62] Durliat, *Haut-Languedoc roman*, 224; Pierre Cabau *et al.*, 'L'Ancienne Église Saint-Pierre-des-Cuisines à Toulouse',

Mémoires de la société archéologique du Midi de la France, 48 (1988), 1–181.

[63] Durliat, *Haut-Languedoc roman*, 224. In the first half of the 14th cent., the double nave was unified into a single space and the Romanesque portal remounted in its south wall. On the portal see also Jules de Lahondès, 'Le Portail de Saint-Pierre-des-Cuisines', *Bulletin de la société archéologique du Midi de la France*, NS 37 (1907), 70–80.

constructed there a priory church dedicated to St Anthony (now destroyed) and, at a later date, a hospital.[64]

Further out, small Romanesque churches, surviving wholly or in part at Saubens, Venerque, Belberaud, Gémil, and Roquesérière, testify to the influence of Toulousan workshops on building in the rural vicinity of Toulouse in the first decades of the twelfth century.[65] The most important sculptural work of this group survives from the church of Saint-Rustice, located just 20 kilometres to the north of Toulouse in the municipality of Fronton. The church itself was entirely destroyed in the nineteenth century, but its remarkable series of sculptured window capitals was preserved and incorporated into the modern church that replaced it on the same site. These little-known capitals, twenty-five in all, have recently been moved to the Musée des Augustins in Toulouse, where they were exhibited for the first time in 1984.[66] Closely related in style and motifs to capitals in the cloister of Moissac, the capitals of Saint-Rustice were probably carved by members of the Moissac workshop who dispersed after 1100 or sculptors trained by them.[67] An important component in the make-up of that workshop came from sculptors who had worked earlier in the hemicycle and transept arms of Saint-Sernin. The capitals of Saint-Rustice employ the motifs of confronted lions or birds, eagles with deployed wings, and modified Corinthian designs that became the standard 'pilgrimage' repertory under the influence of Saint-Sernin. Even the figured capital with Christ held aloft in a mandorla from Saint-Rustice owes much in its composition and structure to the Master of the Porte des Comtes.[68]

La Daurade Pls. 78 and 79

With the number of monasteries, priories, and collegiate chapters, not to mention their rural dependencies, actively engaged in building in the decades following the reform of the Toulousan Church, the demand and, indeed, the competition for skilled masons and sculptors must have been high. The large workshops, namely those of Moissac and Saint-Sernin, must have exerted substantial claims on the pool of available talent, but, as the list of other projects in Toulouse and its immediate region has indicated, they can by no means have monopolized the desirable craftsmen of the area. What is more, workshops evolved over the lifetime of these projects, as new sculptors, bringing their own particular training, were constantly being attracted to the abundant work in the capital of Languedoc. This is evident in the sculptural styles at Saint-Sernin, where Bernard Gelduinus and his assistants, and one or more sculptors with experience in Spanish workshops, changed the character of the monumental sculpture being produced at the pilgrimage church.

It would be a distortion, in short, to envisage Toulouse in the Romanesque period as something of a great syphon, draining off the best talent from a wide region and leaving minor carvers to produce mediocre works in the countryside. As its own sculpture testifies, wealthy

[64] Paris, BN, MS lat. 9189, Cartulary of the abbey of Lézat, fos. 218ʳ and 182ᵛ; Jules Chalandes, *Histoires des rues de Toulouse* (Toulouse, 1919–29; repr. Marseilles, 1982), pt. 1, no. 102, 206–8; John Hine Mundy, 'Charity and Social Work in Toulouse', *Traditio*, 22 (1966), 218 and nn. 53 and 54.

[65] For brief notices on these little-studied churches, see Durliat, *Haut-Languedoc roman*, 28–42.

[66] See the catalogue of the sculptures by Daniel Cazes in Toulouse, Musée des Augustins, *Musée des Augustins, 1969–1984. Nouvelles acquisitions*, exh. cat. (Toulouse, 1984), nos. 34–69. Marcel Durliat signalled the importance of these capitals in 1978 in *Haut-Languedoc roman*, 41. The capitals

that can now be seen on the exterior of the church are casts of the originals.

[67] See my discussion of their relationship to the Moissac workshop in 'A Romanesque Capital from the Region of Toulouse and Moissac', *Bulletin of the University of Michigan Museum of Art*, 7 (1984–5), 26–46. Saint-Rustice is listed as a possession of Moissac in a bull of Urban II of 1096 confirming the privileges of that abbey (*PL* 151, no. 196, col. 467).

[68] Toulouse, *Musée des Augustins, 1969–1984*, no. 57. A second fragmentary capital from Saint-Rustice (no. 58) displayed a similar theme.

43

Pls. 71–7 abbeys like Moissac, and undoubtedly others that were famous at the time but whose buildings are lost to us, such as the priory of Saint-Martin at Layrac or the abbey of Lézat, could well compete with Toulouse for craftsmen. What is more, the capitals from Saint-Rustice, as well as others in the region at Bruniquel and Lescure, illustrate that sculpture of high quality, especially technical quality, could be and was produced for small churches, even those that were architecturally modest in their ambitions.[69]

Toulouse is well known for two sculptors who signed their work: Bernardus Gelduinus and Gilabertus, who called himself 'vir non incertus'. The pride evident in the latter signature suggests that the well-financed projects of the capital, which benefited in part from aristocratic patronage, must indeed have been able to attract sculptors of unusual reputation. At the same time, during the period of its greatest artistic growth and vitality, there were many talented but anonymous stone carvers who contributed to the formation of Romanesque sculpture, men with a powerful three-dimensional sense who worked with great facility in their medium. These stone carvers must have developed their skills in moving about from one modest project to another, where the entire sculptural embellishment might amount to half a dozen capitals, imposts, and some decorated cornices. In projects of this scale one or two carvers specializing in sculptured elements would have been sufficient to carry out the work. In this sense the great chantiers at Moissac and Saint-Sernin should not be seen as starting-points in the formation of monumental sculpture in south-west France. Chapter 5 will address this issue in a discussion of the formation of the Moissac cloister workshop.

What Toulouse did offer as a creative environment was an exceptional concentration of craftsmen of unquestionably differing backgrounds, working with dispatch on major building projects in each of the old ecclesiastical quarters of the city. What is more, the projects of construction and embellishment that were launched in the last quarter of the eleventh century and first decades of the twelfth made demands on these artists of a far more challenging nature than previous projects in the region could have required. Figurative sculpture developed so rapidly in Toulouse because artists who had elsewhere proved their ability to work in three dimensions on iconographically modest projects were challenged by their monastic and episcopal patrons to produce figural work. The simple moral lessons of the jamb capitals of the Porte des Comtes and the primitive heraldic grouping honouring St Saturninus designed for the space above it quickly gave way at Saint-Sernin to a sanctuary programme of complex liturgical meaning. In the Porte Miègeville which immediately followed, Toulousan sculptors created what is probably the earliest portal of the region to employ a sculptured tympanum as the focus of a many-layered theophanic message.

To summarize, the remarkably rapid development of figurative sculpture in Toulouse between the years 1075 and 1140 was the result of an unusual climate favouring such development. The concentration of artists of differing backgrounds working in close proximity, the accelerated pace of building activity, and the spiritual climate in the Toulousan Church during the period of reform, all contributed to the leadership of Toulouse during the formation and coming to maturity of Romanesque sculpture in south-west France. With this picture in mind of Romanesque building in Toulouse, we turn now to the Cluniac monastery of La Daurade and the history of construction there from the time of its reform until the mid-twelfth century.

[69] On the sculpture of these churches, see below, Ch. 5.

3

THE ARCHITECTURAL CONTEXT:
THE DESTROYED CHURCH AND CLOISTER
OF LA DAURADE

ALL THREE ROMANESQUE CLOISTERS of Toulouse were, in great part, still standing at the turn of the nineteenth century. The story of their destruction has been inseparable in the literature from that of the formation of the Musée des Augustins in Toulouse (called at the beginning of its history the Musée de Toulouse) and from the career of its enthusiastic early curator, the Toulousan antiquarian, Alexandre Du Mège.[1] From the standpoint of our understanding of cloister programmes in Toulouse, this fact has been a mixed blessing.

The way in which the great Romanesque ensembles from La Daurade, Saint-Étienne, and Saint-Sernin have been discussed in the literature has, to a remarkable degree, been moulded by the way they have been exhibited in the museum.[2] In 1891 the curator Roschach dismantled the 'reconstructions' Du Mège had created in the 1830s from the remains of the cloisters. Photographs of the medieval galleries taken after Roschach's remodelling show the sculptures treated and displayed as *disjecta membra*—capitals and imposts stacked on long shelves with little regard for distinctions of provenance and serving as pedestals for the larger figured reliefs. *Pl. 10* In 1928 Du Mège's fanciful installations were recreated by Henri Rachou. These, in turn, have been dismantled once again, in apparent response to the recent critical literature. The statues

---

[1] The most comprehensive study of Du Mège and his role in forming the collections of the Musée des Augustins is the exhibition catalogue by Marcel Durliat (Toulouse, Archives départementales de la Haute-Garonne, *Exposition Alexandre Du Mège, inspecteur des antiquités de la Haute-Garonne* (Toulouse, 1972)). See also id., 'Alexandre Du Mège ou les mythes archéologiques à Toulouse dans le premier tiers du XIXe siècle', *Revue de l'art*, 23 (1974), 30–41. The principal document collections for the history of the museum are preserved in the Archives du Musée des Augustins, in the Archives de la Haute-Garonne at Toulouse (L series), the Archives municipales de Toulouse (in the Registre des délibérations du bureau d'administration de l'École des sciences et des arts de Toulouse) and in the papers that Du Mège transmitted to the Académie des inscriptions et belles-lettres de l'Institut de France (now held in the Archives and the Bibliothèque de l'Institut at Paris in the H series). For a bibliography of the early catalogues of the museum, the first of which was edited by the curator François Lucas in 1794 or 1795, see Henri Rachou, *Catalogue des collections de sculpture et d'épigraphie du musée de Toulouse* (Toulouse, 1912), pp. xvi-xviii.

[2] For a history of the installations under the directorships of Du Mège, Roschach, and Rachou see Henri Rachou, *Pierres romanes toulousaines: Saint-Étienne, la Daurade et Saint-Sernin* (Paris, 1934). In her studies of the chapter houses of Saint-Étienne and La Daurade, Seidel concluded that the uncritical acceptance of Du Mège's reconstructions had for years inhibited the formation of alternative hypotheses about how the figurative sculpture from these ensembles might have functioned together with architecture (Linda Seidel, 'A Romantic Forgery,' *Art Bulletin*, 50 (1968); ead., 'The Façade of the Chapter House at La Daurade,' *Art Bulletin*, 55 (1973)). In a turnabout in methodology, however, her most recent study of Toulousan sculpture in the Musée des Augustins lauds the current installation of capitals from La Daurade as a spur to new ways of thinking about them ('Installation as Inspiration: The Passion Cycle from La Daurade', *Gesta*, 25 (1986), 83–92). In fact, the present installation to which Seidel attributes so many revelations is not new. It reproduces the arrangement established for the exhibition of 1971 for the 87th Congrès national des sociétés savantes de France, an arrangement maintained until the museum closed for refurbishing in 1976. Nor can the installation be considered free from historical bias. It perpetuates the assumption, implicit in all the early publications on La Daurade by Mâle, Lafargue, and Mesplé, that the capitals formed a chronological Passion cycle.

from the chapter houses of La Daurade and Saint-Étienne are today exhibited as individual elements, like the capitals, and many fragments from the two ensembles are now in storage.

If the sculptures of La Daurade are to be rescued from the status of *objets* which they inevitably assume within the great exhibition hall of the Musée des Augustins, then it must be recognized that their original meaning and purpose were played out within a functioning monastic complex that comprised church, cloister, chapter house, and conventual buildings. As an ensemble, the Daurade sculptures were the artistic focus of some of the most intimate spaces of the monastery. Here, the evidence would indicate, certain liturgical and sepulchral rites took place, as well as the meditation, the reading, and the more mundane daily business of the monastic discipline.

Since 1971 the archives of Toulouse have yielded up documents, mostly of the eighteenth century or later, that enable us to conclude a good deal about the physical situation of the cloister in relation to the medieval church, its cemeteries, and the other conventual buildings of the monastery.[3] This picture is not only revealing of the architecture of the cloister but constitutes some of the best evidence for its dating, which has been controversial. What the documents do not provide is precise information about the grouping and sequence of the surviving sculptures within the complex of cloister and chapter house—in a word, programming. Indeed, only a single document pre-dating its destruction even mentions the existence of sculpture in the cloister of La Daurade, an architect's report of 1760, which is discussed below. Nevertheless, that testimony is precious, since it establishes beyond a doubt the existence of a figured portal at the entrance into the chapter house, of which the column statues and large reliefs of kings, queens, and prophets now in the Musée des Augustins are the remains.

As for the two series of Romanesque capitals surviving from La Daurade, on the basis of their shape and dimensions there is little question that they originated from the cloister arcades. A remarkable find of fragments discarded from among those brought to the museum by Du Mège in the nineteenth century, discovered during excavations in 1976 in the convent of the Augustins, adds small but important details to our knowledge of the cloister ensemble. In addition, new documentary material permits us to situate certain medieval chapels within the cloister, and these provide a possible provenance for the unlocalized capitals of diverse dimensions and styles that have been associated with La Daurade since their entry into the museum (see Inventory). The most provocative new evidence we can bring to bear on the medieval context of the Daurade sculptures is a missal of 1415 for the usage of La Daurade, describing Holy Week ceremonies within the cloister. Published with brief comments when it was acquired by the Bibliothèque Nationale in Paris in 1902, the evidence of this manuscript has been overlooked in the history of the cloister and its functioning in the liturgical life of the monastery.

The following pages will examine what we know about the cloister of La Daurade, its plan and architecture, and its physical situation within the monastic complex. We will discuss the

---

[3] The exhibition of 1971 prompted new investigations into the archival resources of Toulouse, through the efforts of Henri Blaquière, Odon de Saint-Blanquat, Mme Sansen, and Robert Mesuret (Toulouse, Musée des Augustins, *Les Grandes Étapes de la sculpture romane toulousaine* (Toulouse, 1971)). See my discussion of new documentary material in 'The Capitals of the Second Workshop', Ph.D. thesis, University of Michigan (1978), 12–102; ead., 'An Addition to the Documentation on the Façade of the Chapterhouse at La Daurade in Toulouse', *Art Bulletin*, 59 (1977), 618–21; ead., 'A New Plan of the Cloister and Rampart of Saint-Étienne', *Journal of the Society of Architectural Historians*, 45 (1986), 5–19.

historical evidence for the date of the cloister and will trace the history of its destruction and the entry of the sculptures into the Musée des Augustins. Our knowledge of the plan of the cloister and chapter house, as well as their relationship to contemporary structures at Moissac and Saint-Étienne, can contribute to our conclusions about programming. Important testimony must come from the sculptures themselves, however, through the iconographic interrelationships among them and their interactions with the larger spatial environment as suggested by their formal properties. Consequently our final surmises about the sculptural programme of cloister and chapter house must wait for our discussions of their meaning in Chapters 7 and 8.

THE CHURCH AND MONASTERY

The medieval church of La Daurade, as well as the adjoining north walk of the cloister, were demolished in the 1760s to make way for the new and larger church in the Neo-classical style which now occupies the site on the banks of the Garonne river.[4] The remainder of the cloister, as well as the chapter house and its chapels, were destroyed following the Revolution, casualties of the nationalization and sale of Church properties that claimed many of the medieval monuments of Toulouse. The nineteenth-century École des Beaux-Arts now covers the site formerly occupied by these structures.

The most valuable document for the appearance of the monastery prior to the demolitions is a seventeenth-century engraving published in the *Monasticon gallicanum*. Important features *Pl. 11* of the church and the conventual buildings shown here are confirmed by written sources, also of the seventeenth century, and by a drawing of the monastic complex included on Joseph-Marie de Saget's giant plan of the city of Toulouse of 1750. Most of what we know in specific *Fig. 7* terms dates, however, from the period of the demolitions, when a certain amount of information was recorded by architects engaged in the design of the new church, and by the Benedictines themselves.

In 1627 the monastery of La Daurade was affiliated with the congregation of Saint-Maur and underwent reform. The engraving from the *Monasticon gallicanum*, one of a collection of topographical views of Benedictine monasteries of Saint-Maur executed before 1694,[5] shows the monastery after this reform. Though the view is distorted in scale and summary in some of its details, architectural styles are sufficiently distinguished in it to identify the large five-storeyed wing in the foreground as modern in date. Labelled C on the engraving, it contained dormitories, a refectory, and kitchen facilities. Its construction undoubtedly reflects the revival of the fortunes of the monastery and an increase in the monastic population that accompanied affiliation with the Maurists.[6] The medieval church, cloister, and adjacent cemetery still stood at this time, as the ancient core of the monastery.

At the top of the engraving of the *Prioratus Beatae Mariae Deauratae* is the church,

---

[4] On the demolition of the medieval church see Horste, 'Capitals of the Second Workshop', 27–55.

[5] The engravings were intended to accompany a volume of notes on each of the monasteries by Dom Michel Germain, but the whole was not published until 1871 (Dom Michel Germain, *Le Monasticon gallicanum*, ed. M. Peigné Delacourt (Paris, 1871), pl. 140). For the history of this publishing venture, see the reprint edition (Brussels, 1967) with preface by Léopold

Delisle. My illustration reproduces the impression owned by the Musée Paul Dupuy in Toulouse (engraving D 60–6–22).

[6] The Maurists carried out renovations and alterations to the church as well. A history of the monastery written by Dom Odon Lamothe, a member of the Maurist community there, records renovations and additions to the church in 1683 (Paris, BN, MS lat. 12680, fos. 213–40 and 249–75). An accompanying letter of 22 Mar. 1684 mentions 'considerable repairs in the

identified as 'Ecclesia Conventualis et Parochialis'. Its western end faced the Garonne. It is shown in the engraving to have consisted of a polygonal sanctuary and a longitudinal nave, preceded by a massive forechurch of two bays. Flanking the church on the south was the double-storeyed cloister (labelled *B*: 'Claustrum Inferius et Superius'). The chapter house, which opened into the east walk of the cloister, is not identified, but above it, according to the legend, were more dormitories and their refectory (*D*). The west side of the cloister at the upper level was flanked by a *hospitum* or guest quarters. Immediately to the west lay a cemetery, indicated here as the cemetery of the parish ('Caemesterium parochiae') and beyond it, down to the river, were gardens and terraces. The enormous entrance gate of the monastery (*I*) permitted public passage across the cemetery and through the porch of the church to the busy Place de la Daurade on the north side, as other evidence tells us below.

The earliest portion of the church, the eastern sanctuary, has been the object of considerable discussion in the literature, representing, as it did, a very early example in the western Christian Empire of what had originally been a centralized church with eastern-inspired mosaic programme. It was a decagon of three stories, covered by a dome that was pierced at the apex by an oculus.[7] Its mosaic cycle, set within a rich frame of architectural decoration, has been reconstructed in some detail, on the basis of early descriptions, and from the marble columns and capitals that were salvaged from its demolition.[8] Its architecture and decoration have suggested to most recent historians a date in the fifth century for the construction of this first church.[9]

As our engraving shows, at some point in the Middle Ages this ten-sided centralized church was opened up to the west so that a longitudinal nave could be added to it. No documentary evidence exists for the date of this addition. In fact, the architecture of this portion of the church has hardly been discussed in the literature, though dates in the tenth or the eleventh century have been proposed for it.[10] Nevertheless, the engraving provides a surprising amount of information about this western addition. What is more, two seventeenth-century publications by Jean de Chabanel, a priest of La Daurade, clarify and substantiate a number of architectural features of the church indicated in simplified fashion in the topographical view.

The publications of Chabanel are among the earliest sources for the history of the monastery, and other early authors, such as Guillaume de Catel, based their information in part on Chabanel's writings.[11] Though he was more than willing to accept the colourful legends surrounding the church of La Daurade, Chabanel appears to be reliable when

monastery' during the preceding year (ibid., fo. 296). Excerpts from this MS were published by Abbé Degert, 'Démolitions et reconstructions à la Daurade au dix-septième siècle', *Bulletin de la société archéologique du Midi de la France*, 2nd ser., 32–6, meeting of 28 Mar. 1905, 296–8.

[7] On the centralized church of La Daurade see Dom Martin, *La Religion des Gaulois* (Paris, 1727), i. 147–58; Marquis de Castellane, 'Notes sur les rois Goths', *Mémoires de la société archéologique du Midi de la France* (1834–5), 109–41; Paul Mesplé, 'Recherches sur l'ancienne église de la Daurade', *Mémoires de la société archéologique du Midi de la France*, 31 (1965), 41–56.

[8] See Paris, BN, MS lat. 12680, fos. 231ᵛ–235ʳ; Abbé Degert, 'Les Mosaïques de l'ancienne Daurade à Tolose', *Bulletin de la société archéologique du Midi de la France*, 2nd ser., 32–6, meeting of 20 Dec. 1904, 197–215; Helen Woodruff, 'The Iconography and Date of the Mosaics of La

Daurade', *Art Bulletin*, 13 (1931), 80–104; May Vieillard-Troiekouroff, *Les Monumens religieux de la Gaule d'après les œuvres de Grégoire de Tours* (Paris, 1976), 300–1.

[9] See the bibliography in Ch. 1, nn. 37 and 38. See also Toulouse, *Musée des Augustins 1969–1984, Nouvelles acquisitions*, exh. cat. by Daniel Cazes, Denis Milhaun, *et al.* (Toulouse, 1984), 15–16.

[10] Jules Chalandes, *Histoire des rues de Toulouse* (Toulouse, 1919–20; repr. Marseilles, 1982), pt. 2, 170. Durliat attributes the nave to the Romanesque period (Marcel Durliat, *Haut-Languedoc roman* (La Pierre-qui-vire, 1978), 140).

[11] Jean de Chabanel, *De l'estat et police de l'eglise Nostre Dame dite la Daurade a Tolose* (2nd edn., Toulouse, 1623); id., *De l'antiquité de l'eglise Nostre Dame dite la Daurade a Tolose, et autres antiquitez de la ville* (2nd edn. Toulouse, 1625).

describing what was well known to him at first hand, namely the architecture of his priory church and the liturgical practices and customs of its monastic community.

In chapter XXII of *De l'antiquité de l'église Nostre Dame*, Chabanel describes not one but two additions to the original centralized church of La Daurade. The first of these he attributes to Ragnachilde, wife of the Visigothic king Theodoric II (453–66). Chabanel clearly confused this Visigothic queen with the mythical *Regina pè d'Auca* or duck-footed queen of Toulousan legend, who was widely believed to have been buried at La Daurade.[12] According to Chabanel, in this first enlargement the western half of the rotunda was pulled down, and the church was extended to the west 'by constructing and drawing out in length the two aisles or walls which extend from the remaining hemicycle as far as the chapel dedicated to the name of Jesus, adjoining the portal of the Cemetery of the Counts, on which [or above which] this queen had her tomb placed, which shows that it was she who had had the church enlarged out to there'.[13] In *De l'estat et police de l'église Nostre Dame*, Chabanel makes reference to this same enlargement under Queen Ragnachilde, 'who had this church enlarged and lengthened on the side of the Garonne up to the little portal of iron, on which [or above which] one sees her sepulchre, as we have elsewhere remarked . . .'.[14]

Since the cemetery (O in the engraving) is elsewhere clearly identified in eighteenth-century documents as the Cimetière des Comtes,[15] there can be no mistake that Chabanel meant to mark this first addition to the church only as far as the little structure inscribed with a cross which is seen in the engraving projecting into the cemetery and which Chabanel identified as 'the chapel dedicated to the name of Jesus, adjoining the portal of the Cemetery of the Counts'. Indeed, the difference in style between this portion of the church—a simple longitudinal nave with no bay articulation—and the two westernmost massive, buttressed bays, does suggest that the nave and the western block (or forechurch) belong to quite distinct periods of construction. The nave itself is seen to be slightly higher than the two western bays, and its original termination is marked by the easternmost salient buttress and by the curious pediment that rises above the roof of the church at this point.

Chabanel's theory that the first western extension of the church should be ascribed to Queen Ragnachilde, 'surnamed Pied d'oye', was evidently inspired by the presence of what he believed to be her tomb, affixed to or above a small portal of iron located at the juncture of the nave and

[12] On this confusing local legend, see Alexandre Du Mège, 'Mémoire sur les monumens romains attribués, dans Toulouse, à la reine aux pieds d'oie, ou à *Regina pè d'Auca*', *Mémoires de l'académie royale des sciences, inscriptions et belles-lettres de Toulouse*, 3 (1847), 165–203. 'La Reine aux pieds d'oie' was identified with a figure from popular Toulousan history, the legendary 'princesse Austris', daughter of Marcellus, supposedly a Roman ruler of Toulouse in the time of St Saturninus. This princess was given her name for her fondness for bathing. Her purported role in the life of St Saturninus was, from the evidence of early descriptions, celebrated on the west façade of Saint-Sernin, in the never-completed sculptural programme, of which only fragments now remain in the Musée des Augustins. According to Antoine Noguier and Guillaume de Catel, she was shown being baptized there by St Saturninus in the presence of St Martial (see David Scott, 'A Restoration of the West Portal Relief Decoration of Saint-Sernin of Toulouse', *Art Bulletin*, 46 (1964), 275–7). Another early writer, the Abbé Leboeuf, further added to the confusion surrounding this legendary queen of Toulouse by identifying her with the queen of Sheba, the *Regina Austri* or queen from the south, who was also fond of bathing and who is identified in her image on numerous Early Gothic portals by a webbed foot (see Du Mège, 'La Reine aux pieds d'oie', 189).

[13] 'Laquelle [Queen Ragnachilde] . . . fit abbattre le demy-ronde de l'Eglise qui regardoit l'occident, et l'allongea de ce costé là, y faisant construire et tirer en long les deux aisles ou murailles qui s'etendent depuis le demy-rond restant, iusques à la Chappelle du nom de Iesus, ioignant la porte du cimetiere des Contes; sur laquelle cette Reyne fit colloquer son tombeau, qui monstre que c'est elle qui a fait accroistre iusques là l'Eglise', Chabanel, *L'Antiquité de la Daurade*, 72.

[14] 'Car ceste Princesse [Ragnachilde] ayant faict accroistre & alonger ceste Eglise du costé de Garonne iusques à la petite porte de fer, sur laquelle on voit son sepulchre, comme nous avons ailleurs remarqué', Chabanel, *L'Estat et police*, 18.

[15] See among other documents in the H series the 'Mémoire Pour les Religieux Benedictins de la Daurade de Toulouse,' 2 (Toulouse, ADHG, 102 H 4), dated 22 Nov. 1766.

forechurch. A number of early references to this 'Tomb of the Queen Pédauque' were recorded by local observers, who also described it as having been above a portal within the Cemetery of the Counts.[16] This 'tomb', in fact, had no demonstrable connection with either Queen Ragnachilde or the duck-footed queen of Toulousan legend. It was the reused lid of an Early Christian sarcophagus depicting *Scenes from the Miracles of Christ* and is preserved in the Musée des Augustins, where it can be identified from the early catalogue of the curator Lucas.[17]

It is unclear from any of the descriptions just where the portal with this reused tomb above it was located. Chabanel cannot mean that it was affixed above the large round-headed portal in the western forechurch, visible in the engraving from the *Monasticon gallicanum*, since that part of the construction belonged, in Chabanel's account, to a later building history. If we are to make sense of Chabanel's two descriptions, he must mean that the tomb was placed above a portal opening into the little chapel which supposedly marked the western end of Queen Ragnachilde's nave. The Toulousan antiquarian, Du Mège, evidently believed this to have been its location. In a plan of the church and monastery he published in 1836, Du Mège shows an opening in the south face of the small chapel that extends into the cemetery, an opening identified in his legend as 'Porte et tombeau de Regine Pedauque'.[18] While all of Du Mège's archaeological writings must be treated with caution, it is clear that his plan was redrawn from

Fig. 7 the much more reliable Saget plan of 1750 cited earlier.[19] And Saget does show a portal at this location in the chapel, communicating directly with the Cemetery of the Counts.[20] The location of the chapel in immediate communication with both the church and the cemetery and the embellishment of its portal entrance with an Early Christian sarcophagus lid featuring *Christ Raising the Widow's Son at Nain*, suggest that it was a sepulchral chapel.

This small chapel abutted and communicated with the great western block that preceded the nave of the medieval church. In speaking of these two western bays in his chapter entitled 'Of the Second Enlargement of the Church of La Daurade and the Cemetery of the Counts', Chabanel again took up the question of patronage. He maintained that this second addition to the church was undoubtedly due to the beneficence of the counts of Toulouse, speculating that it was specifically William IV who was responsible for its construction, on the basis of the special favour shown to the church of La Daurade by this powerful eleventh-century count.[21]

Chabanel's speculations would hardly be worth treating seriously, except that they record the impression of a cleric who used the church daily that the nave was much older than the western forechurch. And the engraving from the *Monasticon gallicanum*, naïve as it is in its rendering, records details that reinforce this impression. Based on the history of La Daurade

[16] The most important is the record of an expedition to view and draw the tomb in 1718 (Toulouse, AMT, AA 28, nos. 265 and 266).

[17] *Catalogue des tableaux et autres monumens des arts formant le muséum provisoire établi à Toulouse* (Toulouse, l'an III de la République (1794–5)), no. 157. See also the catalogue of 1818/19, [Alexandre Du Mège], *Notice des tableaux statues, bustes, bas-reliefs et antiquités composant le musée de Toulouse* (Toulouse, n.d.), no. 109.

[18] Alexandre Du Mège, 'Le Cloître de la Daurade', *Mémoires de la société archéologique du Midi de la France*, 2 (1834–5), pl. VII.

[19] A comparison of Du Mège's plan with others produced in the 18th cent. makes it obvious that his version is based

directly on the Saget plan and no other. This is most evident from the fact that, following Saget, Du Mège shows only the medieval structures at La Daurade and the streets bounding the monastery, while specifying nothing of the modern buildings, aside from the boundaries of the terrain they cover.

[20] Curiously, the only other surviving plan of the medieval church, one drawn by François Franque about 1764–5 (Toulouse, ADHG, Plan ancien 102) shows the only portal into this chapel to have been on its west face (Figs. 4 and 5). It is not possible to resolve this discrepancy, and the 17th-cent. engraving does not indicate the location of a portal into this chapel.

[21] Chabanel, *L'Antiquité de la Daurade*, 74.

during the early Middle Ages summarized in Chapter 1, the most likely date for the nave would be a Carolingian one, probably in the ninth century. We know that by 844 there was a monastic community attached to the church of Sancta Maria and that it must have been flourishing. Certainly the requirements of monastic worship would have provided the most likely motive for the transformation of a small martyrium or palace chapel into a basilican church. And the nave as represented in the engraving looks Carolingian, with its large mural surfaces, absence of bay divisions on the exterior, and simple oculus window. Considering the general decline of monastic establishments in the former Carolingian realm in the late tenth and early eleventh centuries, a major building programme at any time subsequent to the tenth century seems unlikely, though no documentary evidence exists on either side of the question.

It has been suggested in the literature that the nave dates from the period following the reform of 1077 and is contemporaneous with the construction of the cloister.[22] This is highly unlikely, in my view. Beyond the obvious observation that the nave was very different in style from the western forechurch and therefore probably earlier, the relationship of the cloister to the south nave wall as represented in the engraving argues against the idea that they are contemporaneous. While the upper storey of the cloister does not appear from the engraving to be Romanesque, it undoubtedly replaced an earlier second storey, probably of wood. Other twelfth-century cloisters with wooden or masonry upper storeys were constructed at Saint-Lizier, Silos, and Saint-Guilhem-le-Désert. That the cloister of La Daurade was planned from the beginning to be double-storeyed is suggested by the function of the upper storey as a passage-way leading from the monks' dormitory over the chapter house to the western end of the church (something we again learn from Chabanel, as we can see below). What is more, it appears clear from the engraving that construction of the two-storeyed cloister required changes in the illumination of the nave. The two round-headed windows of Romanesque type directly above the roof of the cloister are not symmetrically positioned in relation to the Carolingian-style oculus between them. The most likely explanation is that these two windows were let into the wall as an *ad hoc* solution to the cutting off of light to the nave at the lower level, occasioned by the addition of the two-storeyed cloister along its south flank. This necessity would hardly have arisen had the nave been constructed immediately prior to the cloister as part of the same Romanesque building campaign.

An anonymous architect's report describing the church of La Daurade in 1760 or 1761, a document we will examine below in relation to the cloister, provides the important information that the nave of the church was vaulted. According to this description, the vault was a pointed barrel, constructed of brick and two feet thick, and reinforced with transverse arches.[23] The nave, if Carolingian, was almost certainly originally wooden roofed. It is likely, then, that the pointed barrel vault was added in the twelfth or thirteenth century. On the evidence of the architect's report, it is probable, in fact, that the ancient nave walls were more than once reinforced during the history of the church to accommodate an increased load.[24]

As for the two westernmost bays, they have the character of a massive addition to the front

[22] Durliat, *Haut-Languedoc roman*, 140. Though Lafargue summarizes the older literature on the date of the eastern sanctuary, she gives no opinion about construction of the nave (Marie Lafargue, *Les Chapiteaux du cloître de Notre-Dame la Daurade* (Paris, 1940), 7–14).

[23] 'La voute qui nest proprement quun Berçeau en tierspoint Sans lunette ni fenêtre, portant en plein dans toute Sa Longueur sur Les Murs Lateraux, toute de Brique et epaisse par tout de deux pieds non compris les arcs doubleaux qui Sont de Meme epaisseur, est parsemée dune infinité de petites fentes' (Toulouse, ADHG, 102 H 3, 'Observations Sur Le Dome De La Daurade Et Sur Le Reste De Leglise', fos. 1ᵛ–2ʳ).

[24] The architect describes the lateral nave walls as being formed of 3 thicknesses (ibid., fo. 2ʳ).

of the church, strongly articulated by salient corner buttresses and a colossal order of arched pilaster strips of early Romanesque style. The style as pictured in the engraving, in fact, agrees entirely with Chabanel's suggestion that this portion of the church was built under William IV, count of Toulouse from about 1061 to about 1093. Construction some time after the reform of the monastery in 1077 and prior to the death of the count would mean that this major addition to the church of La Daurade was exactly contemporaneous with the eastern portions of the basilica of Saint-Sernin, rising just outside the walls of the city.

Why should we find Chabanel more credible on this point than in his statements about the Visigothic Queen Ragnachilde as benefactress? Chabanel's opinion fits the history of the monastery. The fact that the noble cemetery, requested of the pope by William IV, lay immediately adjacent to the western block on the south side suggests that the two may have been planned together and that the count attached some special significance to burial at this particular location.[25] Within Toulouse there seems to have been a tradition of burials in proximity to portals from an early date. The burial niche in the south transept arm of Saint-Sernin, next to the Porte des Comtes, is another indication that this was considered to be a privileged position. The present sepulchre dates to the restorations of the 1860s by Viollet-le-Duc, but it replaces a small sepulchral chapel at this spot described in 1623 by Catel.[26] The tombs of three early counts of Toulouse, William III Taillefer, Raymond-Bertrand, and Pons were moved to this sepulchre from earlier burial places whose location is uncertain, while Count William IV had two young sons entombed there.[27]

Pl. 12 Next to the church of Saint-Pierre-des-Cuisines in Toulouse, a priory of Moissac donated to Cluny by William IV in about 1054, there is another such elaborate burial niche in association with an entrance portal.[28] Built of brick, the sepulchral niche now forms a kind of free-standing gateway perpendicular to the main portal of the church on the south side, but it was originally the entrance way into a walled cemetery on that side of the church.[29] Above the free-standing arch, a recessed niche holds a stone sarcophagus elevated on short columns with carved capitals. An arcade of three arches resting on columns with foliate and animal capitals screens the niche, while an open lunette lights the niche from above and lends it added monumentality.

The date of this sepulchral niche at Saint-Pierre-des-Cuisines, and the identity of the burial contained within it, are uncertain. The capitals of the arcade and the tomb pediment, while Romanesque in style, are of differing dates, and Durliat's characterization of the whole as a montage of re-employed elements, mounted in a Gothic structure, is probably accurate.[30] The south doorway of Saint-Pierre-des-Cuisines, near which this tomb stands, is also a remounted

---

[25] This is Chabanel's conclusion. At the time of his writing, the Cemetery of the Counts may have been larger than it appears in the engraving, for he says, 'ce Cimetiere privilegié, nommé le Cimetiere des Comtes, qui est du costé de Gronne [*sic*], s'estend par dehors depuis la petite porte de fer, où est le tombeau de la Reyne dicte de Pedauque, iusques à la riviere, le long du choeur; son assiette seule monstre evidemment que le Comte Guillaume qui le choisit là, plustost qu'ailleurs, avoit fait construire le choeur, à costé duquel il voulut que ce Cimetiere nouveau fut pris, et beny pour sa sepulture', Chabanel, *L'Antiquité de la Daurade*, 76–7.

[26] Guillaume de Catel, *Histoire des comtes de Tolose* (Toulouse, 1623), 110.

[27] On the sepulchral niche and the burials there, see Ch. 1 n. 66.

[28] A recent issue of the *Mémoires de la société archéologique du Midi* has been devoted to the history, archaeology, and architecture of Saint-Pierre-des-Cuisines. See Pierre Cabau *et al.*, 'L'Ancienne Église Saint-Pierre-des-Cuisines à Toulouse', *Mémoires de la société archéologique du Midi de la France*, 48 (1988), 1–181. See also the review by Marcel Durliat in *Bulletin monumental*, 147 (1989), 348–51.

[29] An undated plan in the Archives de la Haute-Garonne indicates that the 'porte et entrée principale du cimetière de St. Pierre des Cuisines' was located on the south side of the church (Toulouse, ADHG, Plan ancien l b).

[30] Durliat, *Haut-Languedoc roman*, 226.

structure.[31] Though the brick fabric and archivolts of both the doorway and the tomb structure at Saint-Pierre-des-Cuisines may be Gothic in date, their reuse of Romanesque sculpted elements, including bases and billet mouldings, and their employment of the round-headed arch with simple roll moulding in the archivolts, indicates a determination to preserve the salient characteristics of an earlier arrangement, undoubtedly for symbolic or associational reasons.

The Toulousan tradition of burials adjacent to portals returns us to the problem of the small chapel adjacent to the western forechurch at La Daurade, erroneously identified by Chabanel as the tomb of the Queen Pédauque. Could this structure, in fact, have been built as a sepulchral chapel for the counts of Toulouse? Unfortunately, the evidence for this long demolished structure is too scanty to permit more than speculation on this point. In the engraving it has the appearance of an addition to the western forechurch. In both the Saget plan, however, and one of 1764–5 by François Franque, discussed below, it is seen to communicate directly with the ground storey of the forechurch, and it could have been constructed as part of the original fabric of the Romanesque outer wall.

Pl. 11
Fig. 7
Figs. 4 and 5

What do we know about the burial place of the counts at La Daurade? In fact, very little. As noted in Chapter 1, after a family burial place was granted to William IV late in the eleventh century, there is no evidence that he was interred at La Daurade, nor were any of his twelfth-century successors, all of whom died outside Toulouse. However, a young son of Count Alphonse-Jourdain was buried in the cemetery at La Daurade, since his epitaph, which mentioned the grant of the cemetery by Urban II, was recorded by several early historians of Toulouse.[32]

Chabanel has some provocative words to say on this subject. At the beginning of chapter XXIV of *De l'Antiquité de la Daurade*, he maintains that everything he has concluded in the preceding chapter about William IV as the donor of the new western forechurch is verified 'by the arms of the Count painted against the great wall of this cemetery, above a sepulcher of stone enclosed within a niche [*arceau*]; as well as by the epitaph of a young child, son of Count Alphonse, written and engraved in old Gothic letters on a block of marble, which, having fallen some time ago, was carried into the cloister, where it was affixed against a wall'.[33] This tells us only that some members of the ruling family of Toulouse were buried in the cemetery of La Daurade but not that they maintained a sepulchral chapel there. Moreover, the painted arms, which Chabanel presumes to be those of William IV, cannot have dated from earlier than the thirteenth century, when dynastic armorial devices came into use.

The most convincing indication that the western forechurch pictured in the engraving dated from shortly after the reform of 1077, and hence from the time of William IV, is the function ascribed to it by Chabanel. According to him, this western addition was built as a monks' choir, to allow the monks to carry on their own offices without having to enter the nave of the church itself or to mingle with the parishioners who were served by secular clerics performing Mass in the eastern sanctuary. The first monks sent to the church of *Sancta Maria* from Cluny were, in Chabanel's words, strictly devoted to the perfection of the monastic life,

[31] Its figured capitals belong to the style of the late Romanesque in Toulouse and were probably carved during a second campaign of construction on the church, about 1180. The entire portal was probably mounted in its present location at the time of alterations to the nave in the first half of the 14th cent. The sepulchral niche may have been erected at the same period (see Durliat, *Haut-Languedoc roman*, 224).

[32] The epitaph is transcribed by Catel (*Comtes de Tolose*, 198). See also Ch. 1 above.

[33] Chabanel, *L'Antiquité de la Daurade*, 77.

saying their Psalms day and night and chanting the divine offices and their conventual Masses in the Chapel of St. Michael which was erected in the choir, built up high on six heavy piers at the base of the church . . . and to which they could pass (as they still do at present) from the dormitory which is above the cloister, nearly flush with it[.] One mounted [to the chapel of St. Michael] from the cloister the length of a covered stairway made between two walls, without entering into the nave of the church; [the nave] was closed off at this side by two doors, so that the monks who wished to ascend to the choir by this stairway, could not enter into the church to mingle with the people nor interpose themselves in the affairs of the parish.[34]

According to Chabanel, then, the choir, with its chapel of St Michael, could be entered directly from the monks' dormitory. This dormitory, in conformity with the common layout of the medieval monastic complex, probably lay to the east of the cloister, above the chapter house, as it did in the seventeenth century, as shown in the engraving *(D)*. Chabanel's text suggests that the monks could enter the western choir and chapel either from the monks' dormitory (by travelling along the passageway at the second storey of the cloister, along the south flank of the church) *or* from the lower level of the cloister via a stairway which may have been located either at the north-west or north-east corner of the north cloister walkway.

The liturgical function of this western forechurch as the choir of the monastic community can be documented as early as 1415. A missal for the usage of La Daurade, dating to this period, describes Holy Week ceremonies and processions performed in part in the cloister and in the western monks' choir.[35] Extracts from the missal were published by Camille Couderc in 1902 at the time it was acquired by the Bibliothèque Nationale in Paris, and it was evidently known to Catel.[36] Nevertheless, it has effectively been ignored as a source of information about the architecture and liturgical practices of the monastery of La Daurade. On the basis of its hand, Couderc dated the missal to the beginning of the fifteenth century, and he cited evidence that convincingly dates it even more specifically to 1415.[37] Leroquais agrees with the early fifteenth-century date.[38]

The portion of the Holy Week ceremonies most revealing for the topography of church and cloister at La Daurade is contained in the rubrics for the liturgy of Holy Thursday, describing the ceremony of the benediction of the new fire. According to the missal, the ceremony is to take place after Nones, when

a procession is made through the community, which is vested only in albs, to the new fire which is prepared by the servant of the sacristan in the cloister next to the chapel of St. Vincent. . . . The community, advancing one after the other, then descends by the choir stairs to the aforesaid chapel, reading the Psalm: *Miserere mei Deus, secundum magnam* . . . And then holy water is aspersed over the flame.

The rubrics then instruct the members of the choir (processing in two lines which carry candelabra, serpent, and lantern) to approach and light these objects, as well as the thurible, from the new fire.

[34] Chabanel, *L'Estat et police*, 40–1.

[35] Paris, BN, nouv. acq. lat. 2387.

[36] Camille Couderc, 'Note sur un missel à l'usage de l'église de la Daurade', *Annales du Midi*, 14 (1902), 541–50. (See Catel, *Comtes de Tolose*, 124, where he mentions the purported dedication of La Daurade by Theodosius, as recorded in the dedication ceremony in a missal of La Daurade 'written in 1415'.)

[37] Couderc believed the missal to be identical with one cited in a finding of the early 17th cent., dealing with a dispute between the prior and the perpetual vicar of La Daurade over their respective offices. The authority drawn upon in this dispute (and from which a passage was quoted) was described as a dated missal of 1415. This is almost certainly the same one of 1415

mentioned by Catel (n. 36 above). The missal now in the Bibliothèque Nationale carries no date. However, a substantial portion of the MS is missing. Only 85 fos. have survived, out of an original that may have numbered over 237, and the surviving portion commences in the middle of the office for Tuesday of Holy Week. It is possible, then, that the manuscript as it existed in the 17th cent. may, indeed, have carried a date of 1415. (See Couderc, 'Note sur un missel', 545; also Victor Fons, 'Notre-Dame la Daurade', *La Semaine catholique de Toulouse*, 2 (1862), 381.)

[38] Abbé V. Leroquais, *Les Sacramentaires et les missels manuscrits des bibliothèques de France*, iii (Paris, 1924), no. 566, 11–12.

When all of these [objects] have been lighted [and when] the community, still in procession in the above mentioned manner, returns to the choir through the other part of the cloister and ascends by the stairs which lead to the refectory and dormitory, having entered the gallery (*porticus*) which is over the cloister, the Psalms which are abridged should be said: Ps. *Deus in nomine tuo . . .* And with the community in the choir prostrate on the ground, [the prayer] should be said: *Kyrie eleison.*[39]

One must imagine, then, the entire monastic community gathered after Nones in the monks' choir at the upper level. An initial procession of monks proceeds down a stairway connecting the choir to the lower level of the cloister and the chapel of St Vincent. This chapel was located in the north-west corner of the cloister, as the plan of François Franque, examined below, tells us.[40] The remainder of the community, carrying candelabra, serpent, lanterns, and thurible, then joins them. We should imagine the monks processing, as customary, in two lines, but having to proceed single file as they descend the stairway. The passage seems to imply that, after all the objects have been lighted from the new fire, the entire community processes around the cloister, since they must 'return to the choir through the other part of the cloister and ascend by the stairs which lead to the refectory and dormitory'. This stairway was most probably located at the north-east corner of the cloister. The passage must mean that the monks ascended these stairs and processed along the gallery above the north cloister walk, to return to the monks' choir, where they prostrated themselves.

see Fig. 4 and its tracing, Fig. 5

The missal then goes on to describe the ceremony of the *mandatum* performed in the cloister and chapter house (also on Holy Thursday), followed by the ceremony of the Adoration of the Cross, performed at La Daurade on Good Friday.[41] The significance of these latter two liturgical rites in the function of the cloister and in the meaning of its sculptural programme is discussed in Chapters 4 and 7. There is no certainty that the liturgy as performed at La Daurade in the early fifteenth century had remained unchanged since the twelfth. Certainly the chapel of St Vincent did not exist when the cloister was first constructed, as evidence below reveals. At the same time, the details of the Holy Week ceremonies for the lighting of the new fire and the Washing of the Feet as set out in the missal of 1415 are very close to the prescriptions for these rites in the Cluniac customs of Ulrich of about 1079–82 and in the so-called Farfa customary of about 1042–9 (now known to be Cluniac).[42]

Most important, it seems clear that the reason for the construction of the western choir at La Daurade was to serve the liturgical needs of the monastic community. Such an elevated liturgical space, creating, in effect, a double-ended church, is not a familiar feature of monastic church design in eleventh-century southern France; nor is it characteristic of Romanesque churches of the Pilgrimage Road type, as the contemporary design of Saint-Sernin in Toulouse

---

[39] Missal for the usage of La Daurade (Paris, BN, nouv. acq. 2387, fo. 7ʳ–7ᵛ). I am indebted to Conrad Rudolph of the University of Notre-Dame for his assistance in the translation of this passage. For the Latin text see Couderc, 'Note sur un missel', 546.

[40] The location of this chapel is also established in the anonymous architect's report of 1760–1 on the church and cloister, probably written by Franque (see below).

[41] Paris, BN, nouv. acq. 2387, fo. 8ʳ and fos. 14ʳ–15ʳ (see Couderc, 'Note sur un missel', 546–8).

[42] Antiquiores Consuetudines Cluniacensis Monasterii collectore Udalrico Monacho Benedictino (Customs of Ulrich, Bk. 1, ch. 12), *PL* 149, col. 658; *Liber tramitis aevi Odilonis abbatis* (Customs of Farfa), ed. K. Hallinger, *Corpus consuetudinum monasticarum*, 10 (Siegburg, 1980), Bk. 1, ch. 7: 55.3, 55.5,

and 55.7 (pp. 74–8). The ceremonies of the lighting of the new fire and the *mandatum* of the poor also compare in many particulars to the Customs of Lanfranc of the late 11th cent. These customs were drawn up for the monastic community of Christ Church, Canterbury, and were themselves closely based on Cluniac rites. See *The Monastic Constitutions of Lanfranc*, ed. David Knowles (London, 1951), 43–4, where the lighting of the new fire takes place on Holy Saturday. But Lanfranc specifically states that in many monasteries (e.g. Cluny), the processional ceremony is also made on the Thursday and Friday of Holy Week. As in the missal of La Daurade, this rite takes place after Nones. In Lanfranc's customs, the meaning seems to be that the new fire is kept in the cloister, as at La Daurade, but the sacristan goes out and brings it in to the others in the choir.

illustrates. It must be viewed at La Daurade as a response to a particular situation, namely the liturgical needs of a reformed and expanded Cluniac community constrained by circumstances to share a much older church of restricted space with an urban lay parish and its secular clergy.

At the same time, the elevated western choir was a solution that had a venerable tradition in much earlier monastic planning, going back to the Carolingian period. Carol Heitz has argued for the liturgical function of such western forechurches in such influential Carolingian models as Saint-Riquier (Centula) and Corvey on the Weser. At Saint-Riquier, where the western sanctuary was dedicated to the Saviour, Heitz has demonstrated that this liturgical space was principally devoted to the cult of the Saviour and his Passion and that its primary role was in the liturgy of Holy Week.[43] In the monastic tradition, the Carolingian forechurch had Romanesque descendants in the tower-porches of the Loire valley and the Limousin, as in the well known examples at Saint-Benoît-sur-Loire and Moissac, and also in Burgundy, in the double-storeyed narthex of Saint-Philibert at Tournus and in the Cluniac 'Galilée porches', such as those of Vézelay or Cluny II and III.

It is difficult to associate the western forechurch of La Daurade with any of these specific models, since we do not know the function of its lower storey. At Saint-Riquier, the great hall or *crypta* below the elevated western sanctuary served for the display of relics.[44] At La Daurade the location of the dynastic cemetery immediately adjacent to the south side of the forechurch and its direct communication with a sepulchre or sepulchral chapel suggests that the lower storey may have functioned in funerary ceremonies for the laity, in particular those of Toulouse's ruling family.

William IV's preference for a burial place at or adjacent to the western entrance of the church suggests associations with another Carolingian tradition, that of the burial of Pepin the Short at the western entrance of Saint-Denis, a site that was later hallowed by his son Charlemagne, who constructed a western addition to Fulrad's basilica over the site of Pepin's tomb.[45] But preference for the western entrance as a privileged burial place also had a contemporary expression that must have been known to the counts of Toulouse, namely the Pantheon of the kings of Leòn-Castile. On the basis of the excavations there, John Williams has convincingly argued that this royal mausoleum was added to the western end of the church of San Isidoro at León towards the end of the eleventh century, under the patronage of Doña Urraca.[46]

Figs. 5 and 7 As shown in the eighteenth-century plans of the church of La Daurade by Saget and Franque the two bays of the western forechurch were dissimilar. The easternmost bay was rectangular in plan and equal in width to the nave but with intermediate supports in the form of massive compound piers. It is this inner bay with which the cemetery chapel communicated and, in the

[43] Carol Heitz, *Recherches sur les rapports entre architecture et liturgie à l'époque carolingienne* (Paris, 1963), 21–8, 77–113, 121–8, and 143–5; id., 'More romano. Problèmes d'architecture et liturgie carolingienne', *Roma et l'età carolingia. Atti delle giornate di studio, 3–8 maggio 1976 a cura dello istituto di storia dell'arte dell'Universita di Roma. Instituto nazionale di archeologia e Storia dell'arte* (Rome, 1976), 27–37; id., *L'Architecture religieuse carolingienne: les formes et leurs fonctions* (Paris, 1980), 51–62 and 148–56.

[44] Heitz, *Architecture religieuse carolingienne*, 54; S. Berger, 'Les Reliques de l'abbaye de Saint-Riquier au xᵉ siècle', *Revue de l'orient latin*, 1 (1893), 467–74.

[45] See Sumner McKnight Crosby, *The Royal Abbey of Saint-Denis from its Beginnings to the Death of Suger, 475–1151*, ed. Pamela Blum (New Haven and London, 1987), 53, 56, and 67–8. Crosby notes that numerous other burials have been excavated in the vicinity of the western end of the Carolingian basilica. On Pepin's tomb see also Alain Erlande-Brandenburg, *Le Roi est mort: étude sur les funérailles, les sépultures et les tombeaux des rois de France jusqu'à la fin du XIIIᵉ siècle* (Geneva, 1975), 71–2.

[46] John Williams, 'San Isidoro in León: Evidence for a New History', *Art Bulletin*, 55 (1973), 170–84.

Saget plan, appears to have shared space. The westernmost bay of the forechurch was open on the north and south sides, forming a 'portal passage' as it is labelled on an earlier survey plan of the monastery by Jouvin de Rochefort, dating from 1692.[47] Franque's plan also clearly indicates the 'public passage' cutting through the cemetery, which permitted local inhabitants to pass from the south side of the walled monastery to the commercial Place de la Daurade on the north.[48]   *Figs. 4 and 6*

If the westernmost bay of the church was initially as open as it appears to have been in later times, then it may have had the character of a true *église-porche*, comparable with that of Saint-Benoît-sur-Loire, serving as a vaulted protection for the portal entrance into the church. The massive round-headed opening into the forechurch visible in the seventeenth-century engraving suggests that this openness may, indeed, have been part of the original Romanesque design.   *Pl. 11*

That the western forechurch was probably constructed in the last quarter of the eleventh century, after the reform of 1077 and in conjunction with the dynastic cemetery, is important for our dating of the cloister. Marie Lafargue, whose monograph is still quoted on this point, maintained that the construction of the cloister at La Daurade began immediately after the donation of the monastery to Cluny, which she placed in 1067, on the basis of the Chronicle of Aymeric de Peyrac, written about 1400.[49] Hence she considered it to be earlier than the cloister of its mother abbey at Moissac, carved by the same workshop. As we saw in Chapter 1, the surviving act dates the donation of La Daurade to Cluny to 1077, and there is no documentary basis on which to accept the earlier date claimed by Lafargue. What is more, as I argued in 1982, it is unlikely that the construction of the cloister began immediately after the reform.[50] The construction of a substantial western addition to the church, if its purpose was to serve the liturgy of the reformed monastic community, would have been the highest priority following that reform. The construction of a decorated cloister probably followed the completion of the western choir about 1100 when, coincidentally, the workshop active at the mother abbey at Moissac would have become available upon completion of the cloister there.[51] This hypothesis is borne out by the style of the first series of capitals from La Daurade, examined in Chapters 4 and 5 below.

---

[47] Toulouse, AMT, CC 116, *Cadastre 1680* by Jouvin de Rochefort, Daurade ville, 10th *moulon*. The plan for the 10th *moulon* has been dated to 1692 by Odon de Saint-Blanquat, former curator of the Archives municipales, chiefly on the basis of the names of property owners which accompany the plan (see Toulouse, Musée des Augustins, *Grandes Étapes*, 100; François Galabert and Odon de Saint-Blanquat, *Répertoire numérique des archives: Ancien Régime-Revolution*, pt. 1, ser. AA-FF (Toulouse, 1961), 46).

[48] Records of disputes between the Benedictines and the inhabitants of the parish indicate that this passage through the cemetery existed at least from 1653, when the Benedictines unsuccessfully attempted to close it (Toulouse, ADHG, 102 H 100, documents of 1634, 1653, 1661, and 1764). In the document of 1764, the parish traced its claims to public ownership of the cemetery back to the bull of Paschal II of 1105 which opened the Cemetery of the Counts to the general lay population. It is clear from this and the earlier documents that the parishioners considered the cemetery to belong to

them, not to the monks of La Daurade. According to these documents, the monks were required to construct their guest hospice (G in our Pl. 11) up on high piers, so as not to encroach on the ground of the cemetery (see the plan of Franque, Fig. 6, which shows the supports of this hospice along the outer west wall of the cloister). The burial ground of the Cemetery of the Counts ran directly up to the west wall of the cloister beneath the hospice of the monastery.

[49] Marie Lafargue, 'Les Sculptures du premier atelier de la Daraude', *Bulletin monumental*, 93 (1938), 212–14; ead., *Chapiteaux de la Daurade*, 14–15; Paris, BN, MS lat. 4991-A (Chronicle of Aymeric de Peyrac), fo. 158ᵛ, col. 2.

[50] See Kathryn Horste, 'The Passion Series from La Daurade', *Gesta*, 21(1982), 34. I have discussed the other arguments against Lafargue's dating above in Ch. 1.

[51] For the inscription dating the cloister of Moissac to 1100 see Ernest Rupin, *L'Abbaye et les cloîtres de Moissac* (Paris, 1897), 314.

THE ARCHITECTURE OF THE CLOISTER AND CHAPTER HOUSE

Fig. 4

Much of what we know about the architecture of the cloister is based on the surviving plans in the Archives de la Haute-Garonne and the Archives municipales de Toulouse.[52] The plans date from two periods: (1) the demolition of the medieval church, which began in 1761, (2) the years following the Revolution, when the cloister was sold to a private industrialist and finally to the state. The most informative of those from the period of the demolitions is an undated plan by the 'architecte du roy', François Franque (hereafter referred to as Plan ancien 102).[53] Franque was called from Paris by the Benedictines first to inspect the deteriorated condition of their medieval church and then to design a new one. He was involved with the project from 1760 until some time after 1765, and Plan ancien 102 can be dated to 1764 or 1765 on the basis of other dated plans from the same series.[54]

Fig. 5

Franque's drawing shows, in dotted line, the plan of the medieval church as it still stood in the 1760s with the projected new church, in pink, superimposed on it. The north cloister walk, slated for destruction along with the old church, is indicated in dotted line. In solid black are the structures of the monastic complex that were to be preserved: most of the cloister, the chapter house and its chapels (with the exception of the apsidal one at the north-east corner, which had to make way for the new sanctuary), and most of the conventual buildings. Because of the difficulty of reading the outlines of the medieval church in dotted line, I have provided a tracing taken directly from a photograph of the plan, ignoring Franque's projected new church and showing clearly the juxtaposition of the medieval church, cloister, and chapter house. The cloister adjoined the church on the south side and, as all the surviving plans indicate, it was highly irregular in plan. The north arcade ran parallel to the flank of the church but the south arcade did not align with it. The east and west arcades both diverged from the parallel, while the north and west arcades did not meet but approximated a trapezoid at the cloister's north-west corner.

Franque's plan appears to be accurate in its representation of the scale and disposition of the church and surrounding conventual buildings, since it is confirmed by the Saget plan and the later series of post-Revolutionary plans. His chief concerns were obviously the location, axis, and proportions of the proposed church, relative to existing structures. Probably for this reason, smaller features of the cloister and chapter house, such as structural supports and portal openings—details of the most interest to us for a reconstruction of the sculptural programme—are represented in highly schematic, even arbitrary fashion.

Fig. 6

This is most disappointing in regard to the cloister supports, since Plan ancien 102 is the only plan from the pre-Revolutionary period that purports to show these supports. Unfortunately, Franque's drawing cannot be considered accurate for this crucial feature. The surviving capitals make it clear that single, double, and triple columns supported the arcades at La Daurade, while Franque shows only double and triple members. Moreover, Franque shows the paired columns aligned parallel to the wall plane. This suggests a fundamental

---

[52] I have discussed some of these plans in 'Passion Series', 34–7.

[53] Toulouse, ADHG, Plan ancien 102 ('Plan General de la maison des RR. PP. Benedictins de Toulouse & Ses environs, avec les projets tant de la nouvelle Eglise que de l'Entrée de ladite maison l'église faite sur les desseins du Sieur franque architecte du roy') (1/309. 96.5 × 65 cm.). This plan appeared as no. 194 in the catalogue of the exhibition of 1971 (Toulouse,

Musée des Augustins, *Grandes Étapes*). See Marcel Durliat, 'Le Portail de la salle capitulaire de la Daurade à Toulouse', *Bulletin monumental*, 132 (1974), 201–11 and fig. 3.

[54] Toulouse, ADHG, Plan ancien 77 (dated 1765) and Plan ancien 48–2 (dated 7 Nov. 1765), both by Franque (nn. 55 and 56 below). On the dates of Franque's involvement with the project, see also the 'Cahier pour la Construction de l'Eglise de la Daurade commencé en 1761', Toulouse, ADHG, 102 H 2.

misunderstanding of medieval arched construction. The rectangular bedding surface of Romanesque capitals and bases of the type from La Daurade, whether for single or double columns, is meant to provide a broad base of support for the thickness of Romanesque walls. The alignment of paired columns perpendicular to the wall plane never varies in medieval construction, except in special circumstances in which paired columns perform a decorative or symbolic function rather than providing true structural support.

What is more, Franque has shown triple column groups at the corners of the Daurade cloister. Two triple capitals survive from La Daurade, but neither has the L-shaped configuration shown in Franque's drawing, one being rectangular like the double and single capitals, and the other being square in plan. Furthermore, the slender colonnettes corresponding to these capitals could not have provided sufficient support at the corners of the arcades. Romanesque masonry construction demanded heavy pier support at the angles of a cloister arcade, even when the galleries were wooden-roofed. A more detailed nineteenth-century plan, discussed below, confirms the presence of such pier support at the corners of the Daurade cloister.

Fig. 11

Franque's representation of the chapter house, like that of the cloister, may be accepted in its general outlines and dimensions,[55] while his indications of structural details must be considered as conventionalized. The rectangular chapter room is shown to have communicated with the east walk of the cloister by three openings, a highly typical scheme in Romanesque chapter house design. Flanking it on the south and also opening into the east cloister walk was a large rectangular chapel, labelled here Chapelle des Tailleurs. According to Franque's plan this chapel communicated directly with the chapter house by means of an arched doorway in their common wall. Three smaller chapels were aligned along the east wall of the chapter house and opened into it. Of these, the one at the north-east corner had an apsidal termination, while the others had flat end walls. A fourth square chamber to the east of the Chapelle des Tailleurs did not communicate directly with the chapter house or its chapels.

Fig. 6

Franque's plan has represented all the openings into the chapter house and its chapels uniformly, as recessed portals whose innermost arch appears to have rested on a cylindrical column to either side. But can these details be taken literally? It seems not, since two other plans from the same series drawn by Franque differ in their representation of these openings. Plan ancien 77[56] and Plan ancien 48–2,[57] both dated 1765, include drawings of the chapter house precinct. They agree with each other in showing the entrance into the Chapelle des Tailleurs to one side of its west wall, rather than in the centre, as it appears in Plan ancien 102.[58] Plan ancien 48–2 is more precisely drawn than either of the other two, as far as the chapter house is concerned. It shows three orders of recessed archivolts framing each arched opening, while Plans 102 and 77 both indicate only two. Nevertheless, the uniformity with

Fig. 8
Fig. 9

[55] Interior dimensions of the chapter house on Franque's plan: L. about 6.55 toise (or 12.76 m.); W. about 3.77 toise (or 7.35 m.). Length of façade on exterior about 7 toise (or 13.643 m.).
[56] Toulouse, ADHG, Plan ancien 77 (1/381. 48 × 33 cm.). Titled at the lower left, 'Plan de leglise de la Daurade. 1765'. This plan is not signed by Franque, but it is essentially the same project presented in Plan ancien 102. Franque was still providing drawings for the new church as late as 1766 (see the letter of 9 Apr. 1766 from Franque to Dom Uteza, prior of La Daurade, Toulouse, ADHG, 102 H 7). See also Horste, 'Capitals of the Second Workshop', 28 nn. 46–8.

[57] Toulouse, ADHG, Plan ancien 48–2 (1/763. 99 × 52 cm.). In the lower right margin: 'Plan general de l'église de la Daurade avec les changements projettes tant sur l'église que sur la nouvelle entrée de la maison. Ne varietur Fr. Jean Bapt. Uteza prieur de la Daurade Signé a l'original deposé au greffe du Controlle duquel le present a ete Extrait par le Greffe et Controlleur du domaine de la Ville de Toulouse soussigné Virebent' and, under the scale: 'Ne varietur le 7. 9bre 1765. Garipuy Capitoul Signé. Ne varietur. Lagane Procureur de roy Signé.'
[58] The chapel is labelled with its dedication, Chapelle de St Sebastien, on Plan ancien 77.

which the openings are represented in Plan 48–2 invites suspicions that Franque has here, too, employed conventional schema throughout, rather than recording the actual portal design. This seems likely because the openings into the dependent chapels are shown with exactly the same scheme as those in the chapter house entrance. It is most improbable that the portals of these modest spaces should have been as elaborately treated as the chapter house façade itself.

Fig. 7   The plan of Saget, drawn in 1750, contradicts certain elements of Franque's plans, while presenting its own difficulties of interpretation. Saget shows a solid wall between the chapter house and the Chapelle des Tailleurs. Like Plans 77 and 48–2, however, his plan specifies that the western entrance into this chapel was not centred. Most important, Saget's representation of the three openings in the chapter house façade indicates that they were not uniform. Though the drawing is very deteriorated and difficult to read in this detail, it is clear that Saget meant to distinguish in some manner between the central opening and the ones that flanked it on either side. Are these side openings meant to indicate windows? Among surviving Romanesque chapter houses, a common design is one in which the three spacious openings are equal in width and height, but the two lateral openings are partially screened by tympana supported by a central upright (commonly, paired colonnettes) resting on a low parapet wall. An example of

Pl. 187   this design close in date to the Daurade chapter house survives at Saint-Caprais, Agen. In other examples, such as the Romanesque chapter house of Beaulieu-sur-Dordogne, the side openings

Pl. 184   are only partially screened, since the parapet wall is omitted. The only certain conclusion that can be drawn from the Saget plan is that he meant to indicate that the side openings were treated differently from the central one. However, this may mean only that the side openings had been partially blocked up at some time prior to 1750.

Fortunately, valuable details are added to our knowledge of the chapter house at La Daurade by a written document from this period, the report of a visit to the church and cloister precinct by an anonymous architect. Entitled 'Observations Sur Le Dome De La Daurade Et Sur Le Reste De Leglise',[59] it dates from 1760 or 1761, when several experts were called by the Benedictine community to pronounce on the stability of a new dome that had been constructed in 1759 directly on the ancient piers and supporting walls of the medieval sanctuary. In the context of the plans discussed here, the interest of the report is enhanced, since its most likely author is François Franque himself.[60]

I published the passage from this document relevant to the chapter house in 1977,[61] but it is worth quoting a longer extract here, since the report also records important information about the cloister. Beginning with the interior of the church and proceeding into the cloister, the architect recorded in minute detail the evidences of stress in the fabric of these structures caused by the dome of 1759. In the following passage the architect leaves the church and enters the north cloister walk from the corridor which passed between the wall of the ancient

cf. Fig. 5   polygonal sanctuary and the wall of the longitudinal nave on the south side of the church:

[59] Toulouse, ADHG, 102 H 3.

[60] Franque was first called from Paris in 1760 or 1761 to examine the dome. At least 2 other architects were consulted, Jean Dartain, whose brief report of 2 folios (signed and dated at Toulouse, 17 Nov. 1760) is preserved (Toulouse, ADHG 102 H 4), and a Sr. Richefort, architect of Bordeaux, who recommended against demolition (ibid. 102 H 4, 'Reponse Aux Memoires et Lettres anonimes sur le Dome de la Daurade', p. 6). It was on the basis of Franque's report, however, on which

he was engaged for 3 weeks, that the decision to demolish the church and dome was made (ibid. 102 H 3, 'Memoire historique et precis de ce qui s'est passé relativement a la demolition et Reconstruction de l'Eglise De La Daurade', fo. 1ʳ, and record of the ceremony of the laying of the first stone, ibid. 102 H 3, fo. 2ʳ). It is, therefore, likely that the lengthy and detailed 'Observations Sur Le Dome De La Daurade' should be attributed to Franque.

[61] Horste, 'Chapterhouse at La Daurade', 620.

At the end of the cloister to the right on going out of the church is a chapel of Gothic construction adhering to the wall of the church. Its first transverse arch has been considerably cracked by the dropping down of one of the voussoirs to which still clings the light plaster which covered it and the joint. The next diagonal rib and the second transverse arch show a gap to the right of this crack. At the other end of this same gallery of the cloister is a small arch [*arceau*], supported on one side against the wall of the sanctuary, traversed on its three faces by a crack some small distance from its springing from the said wall. In the three large arched openings of the chapter house are seen several cracks, crevices and swellings, one of which traverses entirely an infilling [*remplissage*] under the principal arch at the right above two subordinate arches; the other [cracks] follow entirely, or in very large part, the circular contour of the mouldings of which the large arches are composed. The head of one of the figures which ornaments this portico began to detach itself from the trunk eight days ago. In putting it back into place, it became apparent that this was the wholly recent effect of the collapse of a capital up above at its point of bonding with the masonry course. Finally, the wall of the church in the gallery of the cloister which is applied to it there from one end to the other, from the vault of the said cloister down to the pavement, is so replete with crevices, swellings and cracks in the plastering and between the bricks that it would be difficult to assign them a number. All the springers, with half corbels, of the vault are encircled [with cracks], as though ready to break loose from the said wall. That [wall] on the side [of the cloister] on the return under the guest quarters [i.e. the west wall of the cloister] is not exempt from these sorts of cracks and swellings in the plastering.[62]

The most important testimony in this passage is its reference to figures ornamenting the portal of the chapter house, figures which had capitals above them. In fact, this is the earliest textual reference to sculpture in the cloister of La Daurade and the only reference that describes such sculpture *in situ*, as it appeared before the pieces entered the Musée des Augustins. There is no question, then, that at least some of the large-scale figures attributed in the early catalogues to the 'portail du chapitre de la Daurade' did, indeed, form a monumental decorated portal into the monks' chapter room. Since the column statues and relief slabs now in the Musée des Augustins form an iconographic ensemble (Mesplé 66–101), it is safe to say that the entire group formed a portal arrangement, though no reliable evidence exists, apart from the sculptures themselves, for a reconstruction.

If the disposition of the sculptures on the façade is still a matter of speculation, the architect's report does help to visualize some of the larger features of the façade design. He tells us that the chapter house had 'three large arched openings'. His observation of a crack traversing 'an infilling (*remplissage*) under the principal arch at the right above two subordinate arches' can best be interpreted to describe a tympanum filling the arch of the right lateral opening and probably supported on paired columns or colonnettes, which thus divided the opening into 'two subordinate arches'. In other words, his description very much suggests the general design of existing twelfth-century chapter house façades at Marcilhac-sur-Célé (Lot), Catus (Lot), Beaulieu (Corrèze), and Agen (Lot-et-Garonne). That is, it suggests that the *Pls. 184–7* lateral openings were distinguished from the central one by their subdivision into paired arches supporting a tympanum. That the large arches are said to be 'composed' of mouldings suggests recessed openings with multiple archivolts. Finally, the architect's use of the word 'portique' (portico) to refer to the ensemble as a whole suggests an open but partially screened arrangement of the sort that characterizes the twelfth-century chapter houses in south-west and south central France cited above.

Besides its information about the chapter house, this excerpt from Franque's report also reveals the existence of a chapel 'of Gothic construction' in the north-west corner of the

---

[62] Toulouse, ADHG, 102 H 3, 'Observations sur le Dome de La Daurade et sur le Reste de l'Eglise', fos. 3ʳ⁻ᵛ. For the French text see Horste, 'Capitals of the Second Workshop', app. 3, and an excerpt in ead., 'Chapterhouse at La Daurade', 620.

Figs. 5 and 6

cloister of La Daurade.[63] The presence of this chapel not only explains the irregular configuration of the north and west cloister arcades shown on all the plans of La Daurade, but it provides a possible provenance for some of the unlocalized capitals in the Musée des Augustins that have been loosely attributed to the cloister, in particular Mesplé 183–90. The chapel is, in fact, shown on Plan ancien 102, though its presence is almost masked by a projected stair tower superimposed on it in Franque's plan for the new church.

Clearly the chapel must post-date the Romanesque construction of the cloister, since the unorthodox meeting of the north and west arcades must be a modification of the original scheme to permit passage around the chapel. This chapel existed at least as early as 1415, since it was mentioned in the rubrics for the Holy Week ceremonies in the missal of La Daurade which we looked at earlier for its references to the monks' choir. In the excerpt quoted from that missal, it will be recalled that the ceremonies for Maundy Thursday called for the community in solemn procession to descend by the stairs of the monks' choir to the new fire, prepared by the servant of the sacristan, 'in the cloister next to the Chapel of St. Vincent'.

No earlier sources mention the chapel. Other documents, however, reveal that, at least from the seventeenth century, the structure served as a sepulchral chapel for the illustrious Bertier family of Toulouse. A dated document of 4 May 1653 records the ceremony of the burial of 'Messire Jean du Bertzier' in the cloister of La Daurade, 'in the chapel of St. Vincent, sepulchre of his ancestors', in the presence of the monks of La Daurade and the Court and *Parlement* of Toulouse.[64] Plan ancien 102 shows that this chapel was slated to be demolished, along with the north cloister arcade, to make way for the new church designed by Franque. Other records of this period tell us something about the architecture of the chapel. A memorandum dating from 1764 or 1765 records that, in as much as the Benedictines had been forced to demolish 'a chapel dedicated to St. Vincent in which the tomb of the family of Monsieur Bertier had been located for several centuries', the monks agreed to rebuild the chapel and tomb to the west of the old location, in such a way that the chapel would still be addorsed to the walls of the new church.[65] A related document from the rebuilding specifies that the chapel 'is in the corner of the lower cloister'.[66] A feature of the chapel was a subterranean crypt in which the burials themselves were contained. According to the stipulations of the agreement, the new chapel was to be constructed as completely as possible in the same taste as the old one, 'and notably that it should be vaulted, that on the key of the vault should appear in relief the arms of the said Seigneur de Bertier' and that the keystones of the small arches and the balustrade of iron should be preserved and put back into place.

Though the document does not say so, the keystones of the small arches were probably singled out for preservation because they also carried the arms of the Bertier family and this would indicate that the chapel had been constructed from the beginning as a family sepulchral

[63] See Horste, 'Capitals of the Second Workshop', 36–41.

[64] Toulouse, ADHG, 102 H 1. Transcribed in Horste, 'Capitals of the Second Workshop', app. 1.

[65] Toulouse, ADHG, 102 H 1. Transcribed in Horste, 'Capitals of the Second Workshop', app. 12. The memorandum is untitled and undated and is probably a copy or a draft for an original.

[66] Toulouse, ADHG, 102 H 2. Transcribed in Horste,

'Capitals of the Second Workshop', app. 13. See also ibid., ch. 1 n. 64. This list of observations on the 9th project of François Franque notes that 'We [the Benedictines] think it possible to place the chapel of Mr. de Bertier which is in the corner of the lower cloister, under the new sacristy which will be elevated by 9 to 10 feet above the level of the lower cloister'. Franque's Plan ancien 77 shows this projected new location, identified on the legend as '15. Chap. de Bertier'.

chapel. Its location suggests as much, and though Franque's plan does not show this, another document of the period tells us that the chapel was entered by way of the cemetery.[67]

The details revealed above are consistent with the description of the chapel of St Vincent contained in the anonymous architect's report of 1760. There, the chapel was said to be 'of Gothic structure', and the architect's terminology suggested it was roofed with ribbed vaulting of pointed section. On the basis of this report, it is indisputable, in fact, that the entire north gallery of the cloister, as it survived to the eighteenth century, was vaulted.[68] The architect described the wall of the church on the side to which the cloister was joined as being replete with cracks and fissures 'from one end to the other, from the vault of the cloister to the pavement', and he described the vault springers with their corbels as appearing ready to come loose from the wall.

There is no evidence one way or the other for vaulting in the other three galleries of the cloister. As constructed in the twelfth century, the entire cloister is most likely to have been wooden roofed, like that of the mother abbey at Moissac. The construction of a vaulted Gothic chapel in the north-west corner would have been the occasion to vault the north and probably the west cloister walk as well. Even so, it is still not possible to date these major constructions in the cloister, except to say that they occurred before 1415, when the chapel of St Vincent is known to have existed. This opens the possibility that some of the unlocalized pieces attributed to La Daurade in the Musée des Augustins may have originated from this chapel.

In particular, several capitals for corner columns (Mesplé 183–90) form a stylistic group that could have decorated either a portal or an interior. These capitals, foliate or with charming genre subjects, such as a sculptor at work on a capital (M. 188) or a woman combing a child's hair (M. 184), belong to the acanthus variety introduced at La Daurade with the chapter house programme, which I date in Chapter 8 to the third quarter of the twelfth century. The more elegant profile of these capitals, their bolder corner volutes, deeper undercutting, and more naturalistic foliage show them to be later than those of the chapter house, however. They reflect the much stronger impact of northern Gothic forms and ideas finally embraced by Toulousan sculptors near the turn of the year 1200, and they may date to the late twelfth or early thirteenth century. They could have originated from any of the chapels dependent on the chapter house. At the same time, their evident later date, compared to the other fragments that survive from La Daurade, suggests a possible origin in the Gothic chapel of St Vincent.[69]

Pl. 13
Pl. 14

[67] '[C]ar le terrain du Cloître appartient aux Familles qui y ont acquis de temps immémorial leur Sépulture, & sur-tout à l'illustre Famille de Bertier originairement Paroissienne, qui y a la sienne & même audit Cloître vers le Cimitiere, une Chapelle à ses Armes dans laquelle on entroit autrefois par le Cimetiere', Toulouse, ADHG, 102 H 100, 'Acte d'Opposition signifié à Messieurs les Capitouls et conseil de Bourgeoisie, avant la tenue du conseil', fo. 1ᵛ (dated 3 Nov. 1764, typeprinted).

[68] The 'Cahier pour la Construction de l'Eglise de la Daurade' (n. 54 above) lists payments for the quarter Apr.–June 1765 'to demolish the vault of the cloister' ('plus jusque la fin de juin pour journées a demolir la voute du Cloître' (fo. 44ʳ)). See also in the 'Moin Courante des Mises faites pour la demolition de Lencienne Eglise et Construction de la Nouvelle' (p. 13), a payment in Mar. 1765 'pour assurer les materiaux du Cloitre ou pour la Demolition des planches et voute du Cloitre' (Toulouse, ADHG, 102 H 4). Two 19th-cent. engravings of the cloister of Moissac in Nodier and Taylor show the galleries

roofed with an arched vault of wood (Charles Nodier, J. Taylor, and Alphonse de Cailleux, *Voyages pittoresques et romantiques dans l'ancienne France* i, pt. 2, *Languedoc* (Paris, 1834), pls. 63 and 65). The 18th-cent. writer who recorded the demolition of the cloister of La Daurade could have chosen the word 'voute' to describe such a wooden roof there. For the other reasons cited, however, it seems likely the 'vault' over the north walk at La Daurade was a masonry one.

[69] The capitals form a stylistically coherent group and several were inventoried in the earliest catalogue by Du Mège, *Notice des tableaux*, 1818/19, nos. 156–61. The 2 with the *Sculptor Carving a Capital* and a *Woman Combing a Child's Hair* are identifiable by their subjects, and Du Mège cites the origin of all of them as La Daurade. If this group of capitals survives from the chapel of St Vincent, they must have been preserved somewhere on the premises, since the chapel was destroyed in the 1760s. The agreement with the Bertier family specified that decorative materials from this chapel were, in

Figs. 10 and 11

The plans of François Franque show in general terms what structures were still standing in the cloister precinct up to 1765 and indicate projected demolitions. Comparison with the post-Revolutionary Plan géométrique 965, indicates that the entire north cloister arcade and a portion of the west, as projected in Plan ancien 102, were indeed lost through the destructions of the eighteenth century. The date of 1761 commonly given for the destruction of the north cloister arcade is not accurate.[70] The authoritative source is the account book for the construction of the new church. This indicates that the principal demolitions in the cloister occurred between January and June 1765.[71]

By 1773 Franque was no longer head of the project. In that year construction of the new church, which had been delayed by disputes with the province of Lanquedoc over the alignment of the church's west façade, was entrusted to a local architect, Philippe Hardy. Had Hardy's final plan for the new church, dated Paris, 1 July 1781, been carried out as projected, it would have meant even more extensive demolitions in the cloister.[72] Fortunately for the survival of the Romanesque sculpture, Hardy's ambitious project never progressed as far as the rebuilding of the cloister. The new church itself was still under construction when the Revolution halted work on the project.[73]

DESTRUCTION OF THE CLOISTER AND CHAPTER HOUSE AFTER THE REVOLUTION

The history of the cloister and chapter house after the Revolution and the chronology of their destruction can be pieced together from official documents in the Archives municipales and Archives de la Haute-Garonne in Toulouse. This material is important in our effort to establish the state of these medieval structures at the time the sculptures were removed and in determining what could have been visible at the time Alexandre Du Mège visited the cloister precinct in 1811. It also throws light on a post-Revolutionary plan of the cloister (Toulouse, ADHG, Plan géométrique 965) that presents many problems of interpretation.

Figs. 10 and 11

Following the Revolution, the monastery of La Daurade was nationalized under the law of 14 May 1790 and was subsequently acquired from the State by the city of Toulouse.[74] On 31 May 1791 the city ceded the buildings of the former monastery to François Bernard Boyer-

fact, to be preserved for incorporation into the new one. The chapel was never rebuilt and the materials might have been stored, possibly within the chapter house. See the deliberations of 24 May 1791 of the Conseil Général de la Commune de Toulouse on the petition of Boyer-Fonfrède to establish a cotton factory within the buildings of the former convent of La Daurade. Specifically excluded from occupation by Boyer-Fonfrède were the portions of the monastery 'dans lesquelles sont deposés tout les materiaux et decorations de lanciene eglise que plusieurs objets destinés a la perfection et decoration de la nouvelle' (Toulouse, AMT, BB 61). Transcribed in Horste, 'Capitals of the Second Workshop', app. 15.

[70] Mesplé, *Musée des Augustins*, n.p.; Lafargue, *Chapiteaux de la Daurade*, 16.

[71] Toulouse, ADHG, 102 H 2 (as in n. 54 above). For the full documentary record of the course of demolitions, see Horste, 'Capitals of the Second Workshop', 43–6.

[72] Toulouse, ADHG, Plan ancien 48–3 ('Plan de la Nouvelle Eglise de la Daurade') (1/703. 69 × 54 cm.). This plan shows that Hardy had intended to replace the medieval cloister with a smaller one, square in plan. A comparison of Hardy's drawing

with Franque's Plan ancien 102 indicates that the south tower of Hardy's church required the sacrifice of most of the Cimetière des Comtes and the demolition of the guest quarters (*hoteleries*) and the exterior west wall of the cloister. These destructions are confirmed in a memorandum dating probably to 1786 (Toulouse, ADHG, 'Mémoire pour les Religieux Benedictins de la Daurade'. Transcribed in Horste, 'Capitals of the Second Workshop', app. 14).

[73] The last entry in the 'Cahier pour la Construction de l'Eglise de la Daurade' is for Dec. 1787 (Toulouse, ADHG, 102 H 2). According to Roschach's edn. of Devic and Vaissète, *Histoire générale de Languedoc*, construction of the church was still not completed as of 1875 (vol. iv, p. 695), and the building as it now stands only partially fulfils Hardy's ambitious design.

[74] Toulouse, AMT, 5 N 3, 'Extrait du procés verbal de Vente faitte En Vertu de la loi du 28 Ventose an 4 au citoyen Francois Bertrand [*sic*] Boyer Fondfrede negt a Toulouse, (copy of 19 ventôse an 12 [12 Mar. 1804] of the record of sale of 22 germinal an 6 [11 Apr. 1789]).

Fonfrède, an industrialist from Bordeaux who intended to install a cotton mill on the premises. Specifically excluded from this initial transaction of 1791 were 'the new church, the terrain necessary for the sacristies [i.e. an area to the north-east of the cloister and chapter house] and the residues of the former cemeteries as well as [the residue] of the cloister contiguous to the said church'.[75] It was not until 1798 that Boyer-Fonfrède was able to purchase the cloister, chapter house, and their dependent chapels, in addition to the other buildings of the monastic complex.[76]

Boyer-Fonfrède's cotton mill was forced to shut down by 1810.[77] On 12 June 1812 he sold the buildings of the former monastery, including the cloister, back to the State which, by decree of Napoleon, undertook to install an imperial tobacco factory on the premises.[78] An important series of twenty-five plans depicting projected changes to the monastic buildings necessary for the installation of the tobacco factory survives in the Archives de la Haute-Garonne. Plan géométrique 965 has been identified in the archival inventory as part of this series, and in the exhibition catalogue of 1971 it was titled 'Plan (de la Manufacture des Tabac)'.[79] In actuality Plan géométrique 965 carries no title, and I have elsewhere identified it as a plan of the monastic buildings before their conversion into a tobacco factory.[80] It is evident from other plans in the series that the site occupied by the cloister and chapter house was slated to be cleared to form an open entrance court and loading areas.[81] Since Plan géométrique 965 depicts the cloister and chapter house before their demolition, it must record the state of the monastic buildings at the moment they were acquired by the State or shortly afterwards.

But exactly what does this plan represent and should it be treated as more than a simplified schema of buildings slated for destruction? The plan carries no legend and the scale at the bottom is only sketched in. Despite this, it contains a remarkable amount of detail, far more than any of the eighteenth-century plans. It shows precisely the portions of the cloister arcade demolished in the previous century, and the curious configuration of the north-west corner, buttressed by two angle piers, is at last made clear. It also shows that the north side of the cloister had not been entirely destroyed in the 1760s. It is more than likely, based on this plan, that the parapet wall and piers had been left standing to form a boundary between the church property and the abandoned cloister. *Fig. 11*

As for the remaining three galleries, the author of the plan has indicated what can only be the cloister supports, yet it is difficult to reconcile what is shown here with the sculptures that survive in the museum. If the architect meant the squares and rectangles to differentiate single and double supports, then he has not been accurate, since twelve single capitals in the Musée des Augustins can be reliably placed in the cloister of La Daurade,[82] while the plan shows only

[75] See the deliberations of 23 Apr. and 24 May 1791 of the Conseil général de la Commune de Toulouse (Toulouse, AMT BB 61, no. 52, 390–410 and 414–21). The deliberation of 24 May is transcribed in Horste, 'Capitals of the Second Workshop', app. 15. The date of 31 May 1791 is confirmed in a petition of 23 messidor an 13 (11 July 1805), 'Pour le Sr. Boyer Fonfrède Contre le Sr. Anglade Chauderonier' (Toulouse, ADHG, 10 Q 1).
[76] Toulouse, AMT, 5 N 3, 'Extrait du procés verbal de Vente' (n. 74 above).
[77] Toulouse, ADHG, 12 M 6, letter of 17 Aug. 1810 from the Préfet de la Haute-Garonne to the Ministère de la police générale.
[78] On the sale, see Toulouse, ADHG, 10 Q 1 and 10 Q 2 (Arzac, *Établissement d'une succursale de la manufacture des*

tabacs [n.p., n.d.], 2 [8]). On the designation of the former monastery of La Daurade as the site of an imperial tobacco factory, see Paris, AN, AF IV 532 [4150], 'Conseil d'Etat. Extrait du Registre des Délibérations. Séance du Cinq Mars 1811', *Minutes des Décrets du Conseil d'Etat*, 8 Mar. 1811, nos. 39–45.
[79] Toulouse, Musée des Augustins, *Grandes Étapes*, no. 199.
[80] Horste, 'Passion Series', 36.
[81] See e.g. Toulouse, ADHG, Plan géo. 943–2, 'Plan du Rez-de-Chaussée de la Manufacture Royale des Tabacs de Toulouse sur lequel sont tracés les divers changements et Nouvelles Constructions Deliberées par le Conseil d'administration de ladite Manufacture'.
[82] See the Inventory.

six. If the rectangles represent twin supports, then a number of double capitals never reached the museum, since ten at most survive from La Daurade, while the plan shows eighteen or nineteen.

In the light of these discrepancies, it would be easy to dismiss the plan as arbitrary or simply inaccurate in its representation of the cloister supports. There are two reasons why this does not seem justified. First, the position and nature of these supports are details on which the architect expended considerable attention and which it was considered important to record. This is clear from the fact that there are multiple prick marks in the plan outlining the corners of every cloister support—columns and piers—as well as prick marks defining the semicircles of the twin columns engaged to the north-east corner pier. The most logical explanation for these prickings is that they betray the method used to produce a copy. The way they are clustered at points of detail like the corner piers, rather than as guide posts along extended horizontal lines, suggests they were meant for copying, rather than for constructing the drawing. Given the method of pricking through from a top sheet (original) to a bottom sheet (copy), the surviving example in the Archives de la Haute-Garonne could be either the original or a copy.[83] Since the remainder of the plan and the scale are unfinished, it is more likely that Plan géométrique 965 is a copy, meant to record specifically the cloister and chapter house only.

But what was the purpose of this exercise? Why represent in such detail structures that were slated for demolition? The best explanation is that the plan does, indeed, represent the cloister precinct at the time of its acquisition by the State, and that its primary purpose was to designate those elements—the cloister supports—that had been promised to the museum and which were not to be disposed of in the demolition of the medieval structures.

When it became clear in 1811 that Boyer-Fonfrède was preparing to demolish the cloister of La Daurade and dispose of its materials, Alexandre Du Mège, then Commissaire aux recherches sur les antiquitiés de la Haute-Garonne, and Jacques Paschal Virebent, director of the École spéciale des sciences et des arts, made a hasty visit to the site to salvage what they could for the new collection of antiquities being formed at the Musée de Toulouse. The results of their expedition were announced at the meeting of 26 March 1811 of the administration of the École spéciale des sciences et des arts:

Monsieur le Secretaire reports to the Bureau that upon his request M. Boyer-Fonfrède held back at the time of the public sale of the materials of a chapel and the cloister of the convent of La Daurade all the objects of antiquity which could be found there so that the Bureau should be able to place them in the museum.

MM. Virebent and Du Mège took themselves to the premises of M. Boyer-Fonfrède to examine these objects, the result was that several were well preserved and will be very useful to the collection being formed; Monsieur le Secretaire proposes to draw on the funds which are at the disposal of M. Virebent to furnish transportation for these various pieces of sculpture.[84]

Though the official sale of the cloister to the Government of Napoleon was not finalized until 1812, records indicate that by August of 1811 the State, for all practical purposes, was

---

[83] See Stephen Murray's analysis of the drawing technique and the use of prick marks in the famous 'Reims Palimpsest' ('The Gothic Façade Drawings in the "Reims Palimpsest"', *Gesta*, 17 (1978), 51–5 and fold-out). The method of reproducing an architectural drawing as Murray reconstructs the process from sheet B of the Reims Palimpsest reveals a 13th-cent. Gothic technique. Nevertheless, the use of prick marks in

Plan géo. 965 closely resembles that evidenced in the Reims drawing.

[84] Toulouse, AMT, 'Registre des délibérations du Bureau d'Administration de l'Ecole spéciale des Sciences et des Arts de Toulouse', no. 2 (28 Aug. 1808–21 Aug. 1818), meeting of 26 Mar. 1811, 65.

already in possession of the property. In a letter of 21 August 1811 from Monsieur Dorey, the Inspecteur général en mission à Toulouse for the Administration des droits réunis, Division des tabacs, to a Monsieur Langlade, Dorey refers to the former convent of the Benedictines as 'aujourd'hui manufacture impériale'.[85] And in an earlier letter, Dorey wrote to M. Dessolle, Conseiller de préfecture de l'École spéciale des arts et du Musée de Toulouse, to reassure him that 'the objects of art and antiquity which you claim will be carefully preserved to be deposited in the museum'.[86] Plan géométrique 965 is evidence that Boyer-Fonfrède did not pull down the cloister before vacating the property.

It does not seem possible, without more information, to reconcile what is shown in Plan géométrique 965 with the *proportions* of single, twin, and triple capitals in the museum. At the same time, there is a close correspondence between the *number* of supports shown in the plan and the number of capitals surviving from La Daurade. If the small circles adhering to the north-east and south-west corner piers and next to the opening in the east gallery are seen to represent denuded bases which have lost their columns, then twenty-four surviving supports can be counted on this plan. If double engaged capitals are assumed to have decorated the two inner faces of the south-east and south-west piers, then twenty-seven supports might have existed when this plan was drawn. Since I, along with Lafargue and Mesplé, firmly attribute twenty-six capitals to the cloister, with a twenty-seventh remaining problematic, the plan accords almost exactly with the number of capitals that actually reached the museum.[87] This fact tends to substantiate the conclusion that the drawing is not arbitrary in this detail.

The most logical conclusion, then, is that Plan géométrique 965 accurately records the number of sculptured supports that still stood in the cloister in 1811, to be preserved for the museum, but that the drawing cannot be taken as a guide to the sequence of single and double supports in the arcades. Perhaps the author of this plan did not himself carefully distinguish between types of supports in the cloister. Both single and double capitals from La Daurade are rectangular at the upper surface, as are their imposts; only their bases are differentiated. The triple capital M. 131 is square in plan, as is its base, while triple capital M. 151 is rectangular at the upper surface, like all the others. Any of these factors could have caused confusion in the recording of the supports. It is even possible that the four supports surrounding the fountain at the centre of the cloister are among those that reached the museum, though we have no means of knowing whether this structure was Romanesque in date. But certainly the architect took care to record it.[88]

A further body of documents in the Archives municipales de Toulouse from the years between 1791 and 1806 confirms other significant details of Plan géométrique 965, particularly regarding the chapter house. These documents reinforce the conclusion that the plan is not a simplified sketch but, in important details, can be taken literally. For example, a lengthy description of the property, based on an on-site visit by the expert Antoine Gasc in

[85] Toulouse, ADHG, 10 Q 1, letter of 21 Aug. 1811.
[86] Toulouse, Archives du musée des Augustins, dossier for 1811–16, folder 1811–12, letter of 5 Aug. 1811 from Dorey to Dessolle.
[87] See the Inventory. The double foliate capital (M. 169) (Pl. 139) is the problematic member. It had earlier been attributed to Saint-Étienne, but Lafargue placed it with the Daurade second series and Mesplé retained this attribution. I agree that it most likely belongs to the cloister of La Daurade. While its ornament of loosely interlocked circles is close to capitals from

Saint-Étienne (M. 9 and M. 20), its dimensions associate it with the other capitals of the Daurade cloister, both historiated and foliate. Moreover, the pattern of interlocking circles matches that on M. 44, one of 4 small corner capitals I have reassigned to La Daurade.
[88] That this was, indeed, a fountain is confirmed by other drawings from the series of working plans for the tobacco factory which show a pump at this location (Toulouse, ADHG, Plan géo. 943–2).

Fig. 11

1791, confirms the blocking off of the cloister and chapter house from the main body of the monastic buildings, as shown in Plan géométrique 965, by the non-structural walls thrown up at numerous points across the cloister walks.[89] These documents also include two unpublished drawings dating from the period when Boyer-Fonfrède still owned the property.

In the act of sale of 17 germinal an VI (6 April 1798) Boyer-Fonfrède had been specifically prohibited from demolishing the monastic buildings, 'in whole or in part except that which could be expedient for the activity of his factory'.[90] Nevertheless, he did make certain modifications to the property that appear to have included the chapter house. These changes, actual and proposed, were the subject of lengthy legal disputes that began in 1805 and were still not settled by the time Boyer-Fonfrède divested himself of the property in 1812. They concern the rights to the terrain just to the north and east of the former chapter house, the area

Figs. 10 and 11

in the upper left corner of Plan géométrique 965, where the north wall of the chapter house lay close to the south transept arm of the new church.

The details of the dispute are not important for us here, but two unpublished drawings offered as evidence by the opposing parties are revealing. Together with the accompanying documents, they tend to substantiate what appears to be shown in Plan géométrique 965, namely that significant alterations had been made to the interior of the chapter house and to its façade before the property was sold to the State in 1811. Consequently, the representatives of the Musée de Toulouse, Du Mège and Virebent, can hardly have seen the chapter house in anything like its original state when they visited the site in 1811, notwithstanding the two 'descriptions' of the façade Du Mège has left in his writings. The documents generated by the property dispute also help to explain some of the more perplexing details of Plan géométrique 965, such as the apparent subdivision of the interior of the former chapter house into 'cells'.

Fig. 12

The first of the drawings, attached to a report by two experts called to examine the disputed terrain in 1804, shows, in the lower right quadrant, the outline of the church's south transept arm.[91] Attached to it and extending diagonally towards the south-east is the 'Nouveau Mur Bati par M. Fonfrède' (in pink on the plan). The direction of this wall, attached to the south transept arm, can also be seen in Plan géométrique 965. Separated by a vacant parcel of land

Fig. 10, upper left

Fig. 12, upper right quadrant

from Boyer-Fonfrède's new wall was the former chapter house, only the north outer wall of which is shown in the plan of 1804. The location of the chapter house is clearly labelled, 'Salle du chapitre au Rez du chaussée. La Bibliothèque au dessus'. Extending behind the chapter house, to the east, the plan of 1804 shows the 'Petite chapelle dépendante de la salle du chapitre'. This small apsidal chapel had not, then, been demolished as planned in the 1760s. Plan géométrique 965 also shows that a portion of that chapel was still standing. Also labelled in the plan of 1804 are a break in the north wall of the chapter house 'Made by M. Fonfrède' and, most important, affixed to the north-west corner of the chapter house, the 'Pilier Existant

Fig. 12, far right, marked no. 1

Bati Selon le Plan de Mr. Francque' (in pink). As seen in the drawing, this pier is one of several

---

[89] Toulouse, AMT, 5 N 1, no. 2, fos. 2ᵛ and 4ʳ (report of a visit of 5 Jan. 1791 to the former convent of the Benedictines at La Daurade). The purpose of the report was to assess the value of the property preparatory to its sale.

[90] Toulouse, AMT, 5 N 3, 'Acte de vente de 17 germinal an 6 [6 Apr. 1798] de la Republique française', fo. 2ᵛ.

[91] Toulouse, AMT, 5 N 3, 'Plan des Lieux contentieux annexé à son Rapport qui a Servi de Base au Jugement'. The accompanying report by Jacques Barthe and Antoine Gasc was submitted 28 vendémiaire an XIII (19 Oct. 1804) (Toulouse, AMT, 5 N 10, no. 6). The Gasc active here is the same individual who filed the report on the property in 1791 (n. 89 above).

vestiges of the foundations of the church laid out but never finished by François Franque and allowed to stand in the vacant terrain to the south of Hardy's church.[92]

The other drawing of this period, submitted by Boyer-Fonfrède in defence of his claim, shows, in the right half, a plan of the same terrain.[93] In the left half of the drawing is the *Fig. 13* exterior elevation of the structures that defined the vacant terrain on its south side, namely the chapter house and, behind it to the east, a range of three-storeyed modern structures built by Boyer-Fonfrède. These were erected in part on the walls or foundations of the small chapels that still existed to the east of the chapter house.[94] That the elevation shown in this drawing is, indeed, the north side of the Romanesque chapter house is clear from the vestige of Franque's uncompleted church attached to its north-west corner, labelled *E* on the elevation and on the accompanying plan, where the legend identifies it as 'Vieilles Demolitions' (cf. the location of the 'Pilier Existant Bati Selon le Plan de Mr. Francque' on the other plan of 1804). These two drawings of 1804 are important, then, for confirming the accuracy of Plan géométrique 965, where the vestige of Franque's eighteenth-century pier is carefully recorded in the curious configuration of the north-west corner of the chapter house. *Fig. 11*

As for the chapter house itself, Boyer-Fonfrède had evidently converted it for use as a stable. In the ground plan accompanying the elevation of 1804, the former chapter house is labelled *H*, 'Ecurie appartenant a Mr. Fonfrède'. This explains one of the most puzzling features of Plan géométrique 965, where it appears that the interior has been divided up along its east wall into small cells that must, indeed, be horse stalls. The architect took care to represent this seemingly *Fig. 11* insignificant detail, yet he shows no other interior supports dividing the space of the chapter house. Nor do any of the eighteenth-century plans indicate interior supports. The thick outer walls suggest that the chapter house was vaulted, as we would expect it to have been, on the basis of Romanesque practice in the region.[95] But the absence of interior supports would rule out groin vaulting. It is probable, therefore, that the chapter house had a barrel vault, most likely divided by transverse arches into three bays, corresponding to the widths of the three eastern chapels.[96] Plan géométrique 965 shows that the entrances to all of these dependent chapels had been heavily walled up by the early nineteenth century.

We can only regret that the contentious parties to the dispute over a minor parcel of ground to the north of the chapter house did not see fit to demand an elevation of the west façade as well! As it stands, the only post-Revolutionary record of this façade is Plan géométrique 965, and the architect's rendering of the openings as they appeared in 1811–14 is not easy to interpret. When compared with the eighteenth-century plans of this structure, the later drawing seems to be completely schematic, indicating only the central opening and the thickness of the walls, without defining details of the jambs or the lateral openings. Nevertheless, on the basis of its attention to detail in other regards, I would interpret Plan géométrique 965 as an accurate representation of the façade as it appeared in the early nineteenth century. Effectively, the original design had probably been obscured by modern

[92] See the report by Barthe and Gasc (AMT, 5 N 10, no. 6, fos. 1^v–2^r).

[93] Toulouse, AMT, 5 N 3, 'Batisse de la Maison de la Daurade Possedée par Mr Boyer [*sic*] a la Place de la Nation'.

[94] Toulouse, AMT, 5 N 1, no. 6, undated reclamation of Boyer-Fonfrède to the Minister of Finances, with ruling by the Minister dated 30 germinal an XIII (19 Apr. 1805).

[95] In Ch. 8 I date the chapter house to the third quarter of the 12th cent., by which time it had long been standard to vault the chapter room in Romanesque practice generally. The earliest surviving examples in the region at Beaulieu, Catus, and Marcilhac, all constructed around mid-century, are vaulted.

[96] Seidel envisioned a vaulting system very like this for the chapter house of Saint-Étienne in Toulouse (see our Pl. 192 after her drawing).

alterations meant to shore up the structure or to put it to expedient use. The architect's report of 1760 described the chapter house façade as being riddled with cracks. Though the sculptured figures were still in place, the architect recorded the loss of the head of one statue as evidence of the strains to which the façade was subjected by the outward thrust of the dome over the crossing. The Benedictines must have abandoned the structure for use by the 1760s, since it is referred to in Franque's plans as the 'ancien chapitre', the former chapter house.

What is more, a working plan by Philippe Hardy for the new church indicates that a wall had already been thrown up to close off the east cloister walk before the Revolution.[97] This wall, abutting the north-east cloister pier on one side and the chapter house on the other, is
Fig. 11 also recorded in Plan géométrique 965. It must have considerably disarranged the sculptural programme of the façade, as would the beginning of the construction of Franque's church, the vestiges of which adhered to the north-west corner of the chapter house as we have seen. Plan géométrique 965 may be interpreted to indicate that the two lateral openings of the façade had been blocked up on the inner side, as had the doorway between the chapter room and the Chapelle des Tailleurs next to it.

All of this indicates that the entrance wall of the chapter house had probably been substantially altered by the time this plan was drawn. It seems likely, in fact, that the sculptured elements had already been removed. The sculptures could have been preserved within the cloister precinct or in the chapter house itself, perhaps since the 1760s.

This is conjectural, of course. Yet the appearance of the chapter house as represented in Plan géométrique 965 makes it highly unlikely that the original façade programme was intact at the time the building was demolished. As we saw, Alexandre Du Mège visited the cloister precinct in 1811, and he has left two substantially different 'descriptions' of the chapter house façade. These have already been the subject of considerable analysis in the literature, probably more than their intrinsic value justifies, and the relevant passages have been published by Seidel and Durliat.[98] In 1977 I published the extract from the anonymous architect's report, quoted above, that describes the chapter house as it stood in 1760.[99] My purpose was to present a piece of textual evidence for the façade—indeed, the only such evidence prior to its destruction —that stood free of the suspicions and controversies that surround the writings of Du Mège. As I acknowledged in 1977, the earlier of Du Mège's two descriptions, written about 1820, is more compatible with the architect's report of 1760 than is his later description of 1834–5, which describes a heavily decorated central portal, projecting saliences (also decorated with sculpture), and 'two small flanking doors'.[100] This seemed to lend at least some credence to Seidel's conclusion that Du Mège's earlier description, never published, was the more reliable of the two.

Today, however, the additional testimony of Plan géométrique 965, in conjunction with the other evidence discussed above for the vicissitudes of the chapter house between 1760 and the

[97] Toulouse, ADHG, Plan ancien 48–1, '4ᵉ Projet d'Eglise Pour La Paroisse Notre Dame De La Daurade de Toulouse' (illustrated in Horste, 'Capitals of the Second Workshop', vol. ii, pl. 12). This wall is also shown in an unpublished plan in the Archives de la Haute-Garonne, 102 H 99, showing the state of the cloister before the construction of Hardy's church.

[98] Seidel, 'Chapter House at La Daurade', 328–33; Durliat, 'Salle capitulaire de la Daurade', 202.

[99] Horste, 'Chapterhouse at La Daurade', 618–21.

[100] The earlier of Du Mège's 2 descriptions of the portal is contained in his 'Monasticum Gallicanum. Haute-Garonne', i. 111–15, which remains in manuscript in the Archives de l'académie des inscriptions et belles-lettres de l'Institut de France in Paris (3 H 46). It was transmitted to the Académie by the Minister of the Interior on 27 June 1823. Durliat dates it about 1820 (Toulouse, ADHG, *Exposition Alexandre Du Mège*, 63). The considerably altered later description was published by Du Mège in 'Le Cloître de la Daurade', *Mémoires de la société archéologique du Midi de la France*, 2 (1834–5), 246–9.

time of its demolition, make it unlikely that confidence can be attached to either of Du Mège's descriptions. Durliat expressed just this opinion in his critique of Seidel's work, although he did not examine Plan géométrique 965 nor the documentation relating to it.[101] In this particular instance, my own scepticism is based not only on Du Mège's unreliability as an historian, but also the likelihood that the chapter house had been altered beyond recognition when he saw it.[102]

As for the cloister arcades, these were not entirely destroyed when Plan géométrique 965 was drawn. I have already hypothesized that the plan was intended to record what remained of the cloister, to be held back from the sale of the property in 1812. Hence Du Mège would have seen at least portions of the cloister intact during his visit of 1811. Unfortunately, his descriptions of this structure are even more vague than those of the chapter house. The only new information provided in any of these is that the colonnades were supported on round-headed arches, an observation noted in his earliest description of about 1820.[103] In this description, and in the one of 1834–5, Du Mège seemed only to be interested in the subject matter of the capitals, which allows us to identify the *Story of Job*, the *Arrest of Christ* and the *Flagellation*, the *Entry into Jerusalem*, the *Transfiguration*, the *Entombment*, the *Last Judgement with Resurrection of the Dead*, the *Death of John the Baptist*, the *Four Rivers of Paradise*, and the *Last Judgement with Weighing of the Souls*. These are all capitals inventoried in Du Mège's catalogue of 1818/19, where their origin is given as the cloister of La Daurade.

THE SURVIVING SCULPTURE

Elsewhere I have concluded that the cloister and chapter house were finally torn down some time between 1811 and 1814.[104] Whatever the exact date of the destruction, it is probable that the sculptures were preserved on the premises of the former monastery and did not enter the Musée de Toulouse until after 1813. They are not included in the *Notice des tableaux, statues, bustes, dessins, etc. composant le musée de Toulouse*, published in 1813. Moreover, in a manuscript note, written in the third person by Du Mège and explaining his own part in the editing of the series of catalogues of the museum's collections, he states that proceeds from the sale of the 1813 catalogue were used in part to pay for the transport 'of a large number of objects which M. Du Mège had obtained without cost from various individuals and among others, the entire former cloister of La Daurade, columns, capitals, bases, statues, and that which remained of the former cloister of Saint-Étienne'.[105] Though Du Mège's published

[101] Durliat based his arguments against Seidel on the Saget plan of 1750 and those of Franque and Hardy in the Archives de la Haute-Garonne. Durliat has maintained his scepticism about Du Mège's reliability in his publications since 1974. See his catalogue on the career of Du Mège (Toulouse, ADHG, *Exposition Alexandre Du Mège*) and *Haut-Languedoc roman*, 181–4.

[102] Du Mège claimed in his catalogue of 1835 that, at the time he visited the cloister precinct of La Daurade, he 'drew the monuments, took a cross section of the portal of the chapter house and drew up the plan' (Du Mège, *Description du Musée des antiques de Toulouse* (Paris, 1835), 191). He made similar claims, demonstrably false, regarding his installation of the chapter house sculptures of Saint-Étienne, described in the same catalogue: 'In the plan, in the width of the portal, in the

height of the arch, the placement and disposition of the figures, what existed had been followed entirely. This is a reconstruction of this monument' (ibid. 200). See my comments on Du Mège's credibility regarding the Saint-Étienne sculptures in 'Plan of Saint-Étienne', 13–14, and below, Ch. 8. In fact, the plan that Du Mège used to illustrate his article of 1834–5 on the cloister of La Daurade is not a new one but is visibly redrawn after the plan of Saget (Du Mège, 'Cloître de la Daurade', pl. VII).

[103] Du Mège, 'Monasticum Gallicanum' (as in n. 100 above), 109.

[104] Horste, 'Passion Series', 36 and nn. 49 and 50; ead., 'Chapterhouse at La Daurade', 618–19.

[105] Toulouse, Archives du musée des Augustins, dossier for 1826–30, folder for 1827, no. 2. The note is in Du Mège's handwriting. A title has been added at the top of fo. 1^r in a

writings are unquestionably suspect, given to rhetoric and exaggeration as they are, there is no reason to suppose that he would deliberately falsify information of the sort quoted above, which comes from his business correspondence concerning museum affairs.

The sculptures of La Daurade were unquestionably in the museum by 1817, when they are mentioned for the first time. At the meeting of 12 March 1817 of the museum administration, Du Mège gave a report on the new sculptures acquired from the cloisters of La Daurade and Saint-Étienne and on his plans for installing them in the former cloister of the Augustins. The new acquisitions were listed as follows in Du Mège's report:

These monuments consist:
  1. of statues representing Clovis and several princes and princesses of the *première race*
  2. of figures of prophets
  3. of capitals (numbering 44) and of several imposts and friezes; the whole originating from the cloister of La Daurade. These monuments are of the seventh or eighth century.
  4. of twelve figures of Saints or Prophets and of 15 or 20 capitals, imposts, and friezes, the whole originating from the cloister of Saint-Étienne.[106]

The first inventory of the sculptures appeared in the catalogue of 1818/19 of the Musée de Toulouse, written by Du Mège.[107] Republished with minor variations in Du Mège's catalogues of 1828 and 1835, this earliest inventory has remained the basis for all later attributions of sculpture to La Daurade, from the catalogues of Roschach, Rachou, and Mesplé to the monograph of Marie Lafargue.[108] Since serious questions have been raised about so many of Du Mège's writings, how much value should be attached to his early catalogues? Du Mège's greatest aptitude was collecting, an end he pursued with inexhaustible energy and persistence. Though his historical writings display pretensions to professionalism, his curiosities and methods were those of the enthusiastic amateur. His inventories are unsystematic and his knowledge of iconography flawed.

None the less, these are not reasons to discard the early catalogues *in toto*. Du Mège's attributions of the larger ensembles to La Daurade and Saint-Étienne make sense. He had visited both cloister precincts to reconnoitre sculptures for the museum. If the post-Revolutionary documents indicate that neither sculptural programme was intact by the time Du Mège visited the sites, he must still have recalled the origin of at least the prominent pieces from each ensemble. Du Mège was responsible for designing and supervising their installation in the museum's remodelled Gallery of Antiquities in the cloister of the former convent of the Augustins.[109] It is not difficult to imagine that some capitals and fragments from these closely allied programmes became intermingled while being transported or after their arrival at the museum. Nevertheless, iconographic, stylistic, and historical bases permit us to situate key pieces within the cloister and chapter house of La Daurade. Around these fixed points other fragments can be grouped on the basis of style, iconography, and dimensions. The

different hand: 'Iere Note de M. Du Mège sur la comptabilité du Musée. 1827'. Du Mège also states here that he was the author of the catalogue of 1813.

[106] Toulouse, Archives du musée des Augustins, dossier for 1817–19, no. 6, 'Rapport sur quelques monumens français appartenant au musée de Toulouse et sur la manière de les placer dans la partie du cloître contigue à l'Ecole des arts. Direction du Musée—Séance du 12 mars 1817'.
[107] On Du Mège as the author of this catalogue and its date, see my Ph.D. thesis, 'Capitals of the Second Workshop',

ch. 1 n. 133. See also Toulouse, ADHG, *Exposition Alexandre Du Mège*, 50.
[108] Ernest Roschach, *Musée de Toulouse: catalogue des antiquités et des objets d'art* (Toulouse, 1865); Henri Rachou, *Catalogue des collections de sculpture et d'épigraphie du musée de Toulouse* (Toulouse, 1912); Mesplé, *Musée des Augustins: Les sculptures romanes*; Lafargue, *Chapiteaux de la Daurade*, 'Liste descriptive'.
[109] See Toulouse, ADHG, *Exposition Alexandre Du Mège*, 37–57.

correspondences with Du Mège's inventories show that his catalogues are generally reliable in so far as they preserve the origin of prominent pieces in the cloisters of La Daurade or Saint-Étienne.

Where the chapter house of La Daurade is concerned, we know from the architect's report of 1760 that it had a figured portal. The ensemble centring on the Virgin and King David that Du Mège attributed to La Daurade is, in fact, highly appropriate to the chapter house of that monastery, dedicated, as it was, to Sancta Maria, since the Virgin was not otherwise honoured within the cloister programme. There is no reason to doubt that this ensemble, including its statues of prophets and 'princes and princesses of the *première race*', originated from La Daurade.

As for the cloister capitals, how can we be certain that any of those attributed by Du Mège to the monastery of La Daurade actually originated from there? As we will argue in the next chapter, the eight capitals that have come to be known as the 'first series' from La Daurade were carved by the same workshop that produced the much larger series at Moissac. Even without the inventories of Du Mège, these eight should be attributed to La Daurade on the basis of the Toulousan monastery's historical dependency on the mother abbey at Moissac. Eighteen slightly later capitals (the so-called 'second series') can be attributed with certainty to a second campaign to complete the cloister, on the basis of their dimensions and the style of their imposts, which associate them with the first series. Thirteen of these can also be identified in the early inventories of Du Mège, where they are attributed to La Daurade.[110] Seven other capitals said by Du Mège to come from La Daurade are credibly attributed to the monastic complex there, because they show motifs and stylistic features in common either with the second workshop or the sculptures of the chapter house.[111] Based on their dimensions and later twelfth-century style, these seven capitals did not originate from the cloister but could have decorated the chapel on the south side of the chapter house, the interior of the chapter room, or, as suggested above, the chapel of St Vincent.

The Inventory lists all the pieces that I believe can be reliably attributed to the Romanesque construction at La Daurade. All are in the Musée des Augustins. There are no startling departures from the catalogue of 1960 by Paul Mesplé. This should not be surprising, since the only pieces in question over the years have been a small number of foliate capitals and imposts for which no objective evidence exists to associate them with one or another of Toulouse's Romanesque cloisters. Four small ornamental capitals (M. 44, 45, 46, and 48), assigned since 1912 to Saint-Étienne, more closely match in foliate and animal motifs the work of sculptors at La Daurade, and I have reassigned them to the Cluniac priory.[112] These corner capitals could have been recessed into the jambs of a small portal (for example, the entrances into any of the chapels on the eastern side of the chapter house), or they could have been situated in the corners of these chapels.

My inventory also includes the new fragments discovered since publication of Mesplé's catalogue. During excavations in 1976 in the convent of the Augustins, where the museum has been installed since the nineteenth century, a quantity of fragments of medieval stone sculpture from various Toulousan monuments were uncovered. From the inventory numbers painted on

---

[110] See the Inventory for a collation of sculpture now in the Musée des Augustins with Du Mège's earliest catalogue.

[111] Mesplé 172, 174, 176, 178, 180, 184, and 188.

[112] The first 3 belong to the style of the second workshop at La Daurade. M. 48, on the other hand, is probably later. Its acanthus foliage and drilled ornament on the spine of the acanthus leaves matches it with capitals carved for the chapter-house façade.

some of these, it is clear they were fragments that had entered the museum early in its history but were judged at some point to be too insignificant for preservation and were tossed as rubble fill into the foundations of a nineteenth-century wall then being constructed.[113] A number of these clearly belonged to the Romanesque cloister ensembles transported to the museum by Du Mège. Three of the newly discovered fragments turned out to be missing portions of broken imposts by the first workshop of La Daurade previously catalogued by Mesplé (M. 193, 194, and 195). An additional impost fragment, cut for a corner placement (M. 192), is most surely from La Daurade and a product of the first workshop, but may not originate from the cloister.

see Pls. 15–17

The most spectacular recovery from La Daurade in the find of 1976 was the missing half of a capital of the first series showing *Christ and the Canaanite Woman* (Inv. 76–13–3; missing portion of Mesplé 113). This find confirms that the capital in question was double and meant for applied columns. Only two capitals for applied columns survive from La Daurade, the *Canaanite Woman* and the *Musicians of King David*, both by the first workshop. As Plan géométrique 965 illustrates, these would have been backed against corner piers, in the mode familiar in Romanesque cloister construction, as for example at Moissac.

Pl. 37

Based on the documentary evidence and the Inventory of surviving pieces, we can summarize our knowledge of the cloister of La Daurade as follows: the cloister was small and irregular in plan.[114] It had arcades with round-headed arches and corner piers with double applied columns on their inner faces. The six large blocks in the Musée des Augustins described by Mesplé as friezes (Mesplé 200–5) are, I hypothesize, the fragments of giant imposts for the three corner piers that survived from the Romanesque work—the north-east, the south-east, and the south-west.[115] Their motifs, relief technique, and the upper moulding of three narrow, overlapping bands link these giant imposts to the smaller ones of the second series and identify them as products of the second workshop.[116] At least the north aisle of the cloister, and probably the west as well, had vaulting at the time the cloister was pulled down, though this would have replaced an earlier wooden roof. The vaulting and the alterations to the intersection of the north and west galleries most likely took place at the time a Gothic chapel was constructed in the north-west cloister walk, certainly before 1415.

Pls. 10 and 18–19

It may reasonably be supposed that, before the north and west galleries were altered to

[113] See *Musée des Augustins*, 1969–1984, nos. 20–33; Denis Milhau, 'Haute-Garonne: découvertes archéologiques aux Augustins de Toulouse', *Bulletin monumental*, 135 (1977), 157–8; id., 'Découvertes archéologiques au monastère des ermites de saint Augustin à Toulouse et données nouvelles sur l'histoire du couvent', *Mémoires de la société archéologique du Midi de la France*, 41 (1977), 39–88.

[114] Based on the most detailed of the plans, Plan géo. 965, the cloister had the following dimensions: east arcade, 15.5 m. long; south arcade, 16.94 m.; west arcade, 14.84 m. + 2.94 m.; north arcade, 17.5 m. The scale on this plan was not completed; nevertheless, the subdivisions are clear and, given the date of the plan, the unit of measure must be the metre. The scale of François Franque's Plan ancien 102 is given in toises (an archaic unit of measure equivalent to 1.949 m.). Based on his plan, the cloister measured east, 15.59 m. long; south, 16.72 m.; west, 15.59 m. + 1.95 m.; north, 18.63 m. Of the two plans, I believe Plan géo. 965 to be more precisely measured, just as it is more precise in all its details than the plans of Franque.

[115] Based on their ornament and dimensions, I believe M. 200 and 201 are the 2 fragments of a single impost, as are 202 and 203. Likewise, M. 204 and 205 belong together. With the exception of the broken fragment (M. 201), all the large imposts have carved decoration on 3 faces and, again with the exception of M. 201, all measure 22 cm. high and 90 cm. long, while they vary in depth from front edge to back. I have elsewhere suggested a reconstruction of the pairs as imposts for L-shaped corner piers ('Capitals of the Second Workshop', fig. 16, 339–46). Based on Plan géo. 965, I could no longer support the other alternative I suggested in 1978, that the pairs might have served as imposts for square piers located at the midpoints of the cloister arcades.

[116] Cf. e.g. the motif of delicate intersecting circles on M. 200 and 201 to the small impost M. 167 from the second series. The crows in rinceaux on M. 202 and 203 find their duplicates in another of the imposts of the second series (M. 152), while M. 204 and 205 closely approximate the interlace on another face of M. 152.

accommodate the chapel of St Vincent, the plan of the cloister was more regular, approximating to a rectangle. The north and west arcades would have had the same number of bays and columnar supports as their counterparts on the south and east. Based on Plan géométrique 965, this would have meant 13 supports in the two longer north and south arcades and 11 in the east and west, assuming that all the piers had double engaged capitals. This would have given a total of forty-eight supports. I attribute twenty-six capitals with certainty to the cloister, with a twenty-seventh remaining problematic.[117] Consequently, as many as twenty-one or twenty-two capitals have been lost, mostly from the north and west arcades.

Imposts survive for all the capitals of the first series with the exception of the two double-engaged capitals. In the second series, three imposts are lacking among the eighteen capitals I firmly attribute to this series. Since all the imposts of the second series, whether for single or double capitals, have the same dimensions at the upper surface (approximately 60 × 50 cm.), the matching of any particular impost to any capital on the basis of size is arbitrary. The sole exception is the triple capital of the *Arrest of Christ*. This capital is square at the upper surface *Pl. 91* (52 × 52 cm.) and the only square impost of the series (M. 132) (61 × 61 cm.) clearly belongs with it. As for the bases, the matching of these with specific capitals is even more arbitrary than in the case of the imposts, since they cannot easily be divided into the products of a first and second workshop. The only certain matches are the two bases for triple columns, one square (M. 133) and one rectangular (M. 153), which can only belong with the two triple capitals, the square one of the *Arrest of Christ* and the rectangular one of the *Ascension*. No bases have survived for the two double engaged capitals of the first series (the base, M. 103, exhibited with the capital of the *Musicians of King David* in Mesplé's catalogue is for free-standing double columns and does not belong with that capital).

I have made some changes in Mesplé's attribution of bases, removing two double ones from the cloister (M. 106 and M. 168) on the basis of their dimensions, profiles, and style, which differ from all the others. On the other hand, bases M. 177, M. 179, and M. 182, all double, belong, in my judgement, to the cloister. Mesplé had matched them with the capitals of *The Boats*, *The Bear Hunt*, and the *Story of Job*, which are later in style than the cloister capitals and probably originated from the chapter house or its chapels. Bases M. 173 and 175 (both for double-engaged capitals) were assigned to La Daurade by Mesplé. On the basis of their decoration they belong, I believe, to Saint-Étienne. Both feature rectangular rosettes held within the scotia, a motif found on two of the bases for standing Apostles from Saint-Étienne (M. 4 and M. 27). In addition the zigzag ribbon on M. 173 is a common motif on the imposts of Saint-Étienne (cf. M. 7, M. 10, M. 14, M. 17 and 18, and M. 23). Finally, a base for a single column (M. 43), assigned since 1912 to Saint-Étienne, matches in dimensions and profile the bases of the Daurade cloister and belongs with that ensemble. There is no evidence on which to assign it to Saint-Étienne, since there are none with the same profile surviving from the ensemble there.

The result of these exchanges is that one or possibly two double bases, as well as two bases for the double engaged capitals, are lacking for the total of twenty-six cloister capitals

---

[117] See the Inventory. The certain attributions are the 8 capitals of the first series, the 13 historiated capitals of the second series, a capital with *Lions* (M. 160) pl. 135, one with *Birds* (M. 166) pls. 133 and 134 and 3 foliate capitals (M. 163, 170, and 171). For the problematic foliate capital (M. 169), see above, n. 87.

surviving from La Daurade. The existing bases are of two closely related profiles: (1) a fat cushiony torus at the bottom, separated by a wide and deep scotia from a fat cushiony torus at the top, smaller in diameter than the lower torus; (2) three fat, cushiony toruses of diminishing diameter from bottom to top, with no scotia between. Two examples (M. 159 and 179) differ slightly from these two basic profiles in having taller and shallower scotia, but their dimensions and the shaping of the bottom of the base indicate that they belong with the other bases of the cloister.[118] Some of the bases, those with both two and three toruses, have corner 'nails' or claws.

The most striking feature of the series of bases, nevertheless, is their uniformity in profile and shaping. In other words, no evolution in profiles can be discerned in the series of bases, despite the fact that the capitals and imposts are clearly the products of two different workshops and are separated in time. On the basis of these observations, I venture the hypothesis that all the bases were carved by the first workshop and that ready-carved examples left at the building site were used later by the second workshop. Hence the scheme of alternating single and double columns was settled upon at the outset of the project and was foreseen for the cloister as a whole. The second workshop honoured the essentials of this scheme in its completion of the cloister, while introducing minor adjustments in the proportions of capital to impost in its own series.

Is it possible to conclude in what sequence the capitals were arranged in the cloister arcades? This, of course, is the question of most significance to a reconstruction of the iconographic programme. Unfortunately, the surviving plans do not provide the evidence we need. Nevertheless, on the basis of Romanesque cloister design in closely related examples in the region, it is most likely that the cloister of La Daurade used an alternating scheme of single and double columnar supports, with triple column clusters at prominent locations in the arcade, either at the centre or flanking an opening in the parapet wall. This conclusion is based on the design of the Moissac cloister, constructed by the same workshop that began the cloister of La Daurade.[119] As I have pointed out elsewhere, the Moissac design is atypical for Romanesque cloisters, the vast majority of which employ either uniformly double or uniformly single columnar supports.[120] As the earliest surviving Romanesque cloister in south-west France, in the leading Cluniac monastery of the region, the cloister of Moissac, with its alternating scheme, influenced cloister design in Toulouse, as well as at Saint-Lizier (Ariège) to the south and probably at Saint-Pons-de-Thomières (Hérault), to the south-east of Toulouse.[121] My recent discovery of a plan of the Romanesque cloister of Saint-Étienne at Toulouse adds to this *Figs. 14 and* constellation of examples. The plan shows a scheme of alternating single and double supports
15

---

[118] M. 179 differs from all the others of the cloister in the presence of a small stemmed berry at the conjunction of the lower toruses. This motif appears on certain bases of the later 12th-cent. chapter house. But M. 179 is otherwise very different from these, which show a marked change toward flatter, less cushiony toruses and sharper lines.

[119] The cloister arcades at Moissac were rebuilt in the 13th cent., but as I conclude below (Ch. 7), there is every evidence that care was taken to preserve the original order of the capitals. Furthermore, the existence at Moissac of both single and double capitals in equal numbers is the best evidence that they were meant to alternate.

[120] Horste, 'Plan of Saint-Étienne', 16–17. See below, Ch. 7, for a discussion of sequencing in cloister supports.

[121] Surviving capitals of the destroyed cloister of Saint-Pons are of both single and double varieties. One of its workshops was powerfully influenced in style and iconography by Toulousan sculpture at La Daurade and Saint-Étienne. I would therefore suggest it likely that an alternating system based on that of Toulousan cloisters existed at Saint-Pons. For recent discussions of the Toulousan connections of Saint-Pons, see Walter Cahn and Linda Seidel, *Romanesque Sculpture in American Collections*, i. *New England Museums* (New York, 1979), 154–60; K. Horste, 'Romanesque Sculpture in American Collections. XX. Ohio and Michigan', *Gesta*, 21 (1982), 130–2.

in the cathedral cloister, which was contemporary with the second campaign in the cloister of La Daurade and was closely related to its sculpture workshop.[122] The alternating system settled upon at Moissac should be seen, then, as an original design feature, one that would have important implications for the structure of historiated capitals in its kindred offshoots at Toulouse and elsewhere in the region.

In summary, the plans and written documents from La Daurade help us to visualize the structure of the cloister, the chapels that opened into it, and, very importantly, the schema of communication between the church, the cloister, and the chapter house that indicate a significant role for the cloister of La Daurade in the liturgical life of its community. The more problematic issue of how the sculptural programme functioned within this structure can only be approached by scrutinizing closely the sculptures themselves, in an effort to penetrate the ways in which they would have addressed their meaning to the viewer.

[122] See Horste, 'Plan of Saint-Étienne', 5–19. For the close relationship between the cloister workshops of La Daurade and Saint-Étienne and their possible sharing of some sculptors, see below, Ch. 6. There is little evidence for the other Romanesque cloister constructed in Toulouse between 1120 and 1140, that of Saint-Sernin. A plan by the architect Esquié shows alternating single and double supports in the 3 Romanesque arcades that were still surviving in the 19th cent. This plan was not published until 1881, however, long after the cloister had been destroyed between 1803 and 1808 (see the illustration in Françoise Abrial-Aribert, 'Le Cloître de Saint-Sernin de Toulouse', *Actes du 96ᵉ congrès national des sociétes savantes, Toulouse, 1971*, ii (Toulouse, 1976), 162–3 and fig. 1). All the capitals reliably attributed to the cloister of Saint-Sernin are single ones. Small and of cubic dimensions (30 x 30 x 30 cm.), it is most likely that the surviving drums were paired to form twin capitals, as in the cloister of Arles.

4

THE FIRST SERIES OF CAPITALS FROM LA DAURADE

THE MOISSAC WORKSHOP IN TOULOUSE

The cloister of La Daurade is of special importance in the discussion of Romanesque sculpture in Toulouse in part because its surviving capital decoration so clearly represents the work of two successive generations of sculptors of very different artistic formation and allegiances. The workshop that began the cloister belongs to the eleventh century, though individual members of the workshop, or others they had trained, were still actively decorating churches in the region as late as 1120. The cloister was completed by a different group of sculptors whose style appeared in Toulouse shortly after 1120, introducing a wholly new aesthetic and fresh sources of artistic inspiration.

The eight capitals that should be attributed to the first workshop at La Daurade are enumerated in the Inventory, along with their imposts. It has long been recognized that this group of capitals is very closely associated with the much larger ensemble in the celebrated cloister of Moissac, located 65 kilometres to the north-west of Toulouse. What this association means for the definition of first-generation Romanesque sculpture in Toulouse is complicated by the ties that exist between the cloister of Moissac and the successive workshops that decorated the basilica of Saint-Sernin during the last decades of the eleventh century and the beginning of the twelfth. The dynamics among these three projects during the formation of the first figurative sculpture in south-west France provides the context in which the earlier capitals of La Daurade will be discussed in this and the succeeding chapter.

The similarities between the capitals of the first series from La Daurade and the large ensemble at Moissac leave little room for doubt that some of the same sculptors were employed in the decoration of both cloisters. All scholars who have recently considered the question have arrived at this conclusion.[1] The similarities, examined below, encompass

---

[1] Lafargue concluded that 'the capitals of La Daurade and those of Moissac are the work of the same workshop, but the first are anterior to the second' ('Les Sculptures du premier atelier de la Daurade', *Bulletin monumental*, 93 (1938), 212). She did not, however, define what she meant by a workshop. Durliat, who reached the opposite conclusion to Lafargue regarding the relative dates of the 2 ensembles, was more precise, concluding that 'The differences, where they exist, never exceed those that one can observe between the productions of the various hands that collaborated on the work of Moissac' ('La Date des plus anciens chapiteaux de la Daurade', *Estudios*

dedicados a Duran y Sanpere (Barcelona, 1967), 200). He cited Vidal's distinctions of 5 or 6 different carving modes among the Moissac capitals (Marguerite Vidal, Jean Maury, and Jean Porcher, *Quercy roman* (La Pierre-qui-vire, 1969), 131), and he credited the great Cluniac abbey with developing the large workshop on which the community of La Daurade then called to decorate its own cloister. Denis Milhau embraced the same conclusion: '. . . the workshop of Moissac transported itself, at least in part, to La Daurade once the cloister of the mother abbey was completed . . .' (Toulouse, Museé des Augustins, *Les Grandes Etapes* (Toulouse, 1971), 14). Ruth Capelle Kline

everything from the overall shape and dimensions of capitals and imposts, to the figure style and repertory of gestures, and the use of repeated compositional formulas. Moreover, the ambitious use of historiated themes in both cloisters, in which relatively complex narrative sequences are attempted, draws these two groups of capitals together and suggests a common guiding conception behind both sculptural programmes.

While there is wide agreement that some sculptors participated in both projects, the more difficult issues of the relative dates of the two cloisters and the origin of the workshop remain controversial. Stylistic and formal criteria have been used to argue variously that the capitals of La Daurade are earlier or later than the ensemble at Moissac. In her study of the first series of capitals from La Daurade, Marie Lafargue argued that the Toulousan capitals must be earlier than those of Moissac, because the Moissac carvings show 'progress' *vis-à-vis* La Daurade in terms of their figure proportions, modelling of the body, and their 'freer' and more skilful compositions.[2] In his review of Lafargue's book, William Forsyth framed the issue in different terms but implicitly accepted the sculptures of Moissac as more successful than those of La Daurade. As he expressed it, 'La Daurade was rebuilt as a dependency of Moissac under the order of Cluny, and it might be that the finer work of Moissac inspired the more provincial work of its dependent priory. It is in large part a question of what is "provincial" and what is "primitive" '.[3] The distinction Forsyth urged can hardly be valid in this case, however. Notwithstanding its administrative status as a dependency of Moissac, the Cluniac priory in the Toulousan capital could in no sense be considered provincial.

Though formal analyses of the Moissac–La Daurade relationship have been undertaken previously in the literature, what follows is an attempt to show how much is still to be learned by this method.[4] The primary aim is not to date the two ensembles, though the intimacy between them revealed through formal and technical analysis contradicts Lafargue's conclusion that they are widely separated in time (she proposed 1080 for the completion of La Daurade and 1100 for Moissac).[5] The objective is to place the discourse about these sculptures within a wider theoretical framework. The basis for this discourse was opened up by Meyer Schapiro in his brilliant study of 1931 of the Moissac cloister. Since then discussion has been carried forward on an equally theoretical plane only by Otto Werckmeister, in his review of Schapiro's collected works.[6]

In his long review article, Werckmeister criticized the published version of Schapiro's Moissac study (extracted from his longer doctoral dissertation) for excluding any reference to

concluded that the first series of capitals at La Daurade was carved by sculptors who then moved on to Moissac ('The Decorated Imposts of the Cloister of Moissac', Ph.D. thesis, University of California at Los Angeles (1977), 151–2 and n. 26).

[2] Marie Lafargue, *Les Chapiteaux du cloître de Notre-Dame la Daurade* (Paris, 1940), 38–9; ead., 'Premier atelier de la Daurade', 207. Lyman, for his part, implies that the ensembles from Moissac and La Daurade are very close in date, if not contemporaneous. He identifies the years 1093–8 as the moment of greatest activity at Moissac, 'and also perhaps at La Daurade' (Thomas Lyman, monograph on Saint-Sernin, forthcoming).

[3] William Forsyth, review of Marie Lafargue, *Les Chapiteaux du cloître de Notre-Dame la Daurade*, in *American Journal of Archaeology*, 49 (1945), 391–3.

[4] In addition to Lafargue and William Forsyth see Durliat,

'Plus anciens chapiteaux de la Daurade', and Ilene Haering [Forsyth], 'Narrative Order in Romanesque Sculpture', MA thesis, Columbia University, (1955). See also the lengthy analysis of formal relationships among the imposts of La Daurade, Moissac, and Saint-Sernin by Kline ('Decorated Imposts').

[5] Lafargue believed that the cloister of La Daurade was begun as early as 1067. Since the cloister of Moissac is dated by inscription to 1100, this would imply a span of 33 years for the activity of the workshop in the 2 cloisters. Add to this the 2 decades or more during which the hand of Moissac sculptors can be identified in the region after 1100, and the career of the workshop as well as the tenacity of its style achieve astonishing longevity, according to Lafargue's chronology.

[6] Otto K. Werckmeister, review of Meyer Schapiro, *Romanesque Art, Selected Papers*, in *Art Quarterly*, 2 (1979), 211–18.

the capitals of La Daurade or to other regional sculpture. Indeed, as Werckmeister characterized it, Schapiro's study made of the Moissac cloister a self-contained microcosm, within which figurative compositions ranging from symmetrical and abstract to asymmetrical and more realistic could be observed. The most abstract and symmetrical solutions were denoted by Schapiro as the most archaic and hence, by implication, as anterior in conception, if not in execution, to the more varied, detailed, and asymmetrical solutions of other capitals. In Schapiro's study Werckmeister saw 'the model of the dynamic stylistic transition from abstraction to realism which continued to fascinate Schapiro in his later work'.[7]

For Schapiro's stylistic dynamic, Werckmeister substituted the observation that abstraction and realism were coeval and autonomous values of Romanesque art, not the opposite ends of a stylistic continuum. If this is the case—and this seems to be Werckmeister's point—then arguments for the relative dating of two works of Romanesque sculpture cannot be made on the basis of their supposed distance from or proximity to a stylistic ideal defined as realism.[8]

The premise of my comparisons in this chapter between Moissac and La Daurade is that formal analysis is, indeed, capable of revealing a process and direction of change within the workshop of Moissac. But this exercise cannot be productive, for the reasons Werckmeister has elucidated, if it takes as the measure of this change degrees of abstraction or realism. I propose instead to analyse the process of change in terms of the particular problem presented to the sculptors in the cloisters of Moissac and La Daurade. The problem was to create an art of visual narration that would be effective within a specialized architectural context, and it was a demand for which the sculptors very likely had no useful precedents to draw upon.

I perceive the variations between and within the two series of capitals to be the results of a learning process among the team of sculptors within a very brief span of time, as they worked through the task of carving capitals for one very large project and a second, considerably smaller one. During the process they came to realize the advantages *for narrative purposes* of abstracting the framework (the capital structure) into a simpler and simpler form while conversely increasing the complexity, asymmetry, and realistic detail of the story-telling components (the figures, the scenic props, the compositions).

In the case of the capital framework, the decision to work towards simplification and abstraction is clear and unswerving. On the other hand, where the compositional solutions and mobility of the human figure are concerned, a decisive linear development cannot be tracked. Instead the simultaneous impulses towards abstraction and realism observed both by Schapiro and Werckmeister within the ensemble at Moissac—and often, indeed, within a single capital —are present, as well, in the figural compositions of La Daurade. Only the most 'archaic' solutions were dropped in the Toulousan cloister. This indecisiveness and its mixed results are measures of the exploratory character of these capitals. The problem of visual narration was one with which the new art of cloister sculpture continued to grapple during the twelfth century. When we come to analyse the second series of capitals from La Daurade in Chapter 6, we will see that the later workshop embraced it with a different kind of ingenuity and with different results.

---

[7] Otto K. Werckmeister, review of Meyer Schapiro, *Romanesque Art, Selected Papers*, in *Art Quarterly*, 2 (1979), 212.

[8] Werckmeister does take the position in his review that the capitals of La Daurade appear to pre-date those of Moissac, citing the work of his student, Ruth Capelle Kline, as the demonstration of this proposition (Kline, 'Decorated Imposts'). Elsewhere in the article he refers to the 'less consistently symmetrical compositions of the capitals of La Daurade, which the sculptors at Moissac apparently corrected through more intricate designs of balanced symmetry . . .' (212).

THE STYLE OF THE FIRST SERIES

The sculptors who began the cloister of La Daurade employed a simple and weighty capital shape which, with minor variations in detail, is essentially the same as that used in the cloister of Moissac. This shape is usually described as an inverted and truncated pyramid, but, in fact, capitals of both cloisters are differently shaped at the bottom, depending on whether they were carved to top single or double colonnettes. The single capitals taper more dramatically towards the astragal than the double ones, which are broader at the bottom. The double capitals have twin astragals, but there is otherwise no indication of double 'heads' or drums comprising the capital, and they are treated identically in all other respects to the single ones. The shape of the capitals, whether single or double, is essentially rectangular at the upper surface, to receive the rectangular bed of the impost block. The treatment of the upper zone, with a single pair of volutes, deeply concave abacus, and powerfully projecting central modillion, betrays the ultimate derivation of this capital shape from the antique Corinthian type, as many observers have noted. Nevertheless, the forms have been so highly abstracted that the shape of the capital is more immediately reminiscent of the rectangular block from which the sculptor began his work than it is of the graceful outline of the Corinthian capital. The astragals of the Daurade capitals take the form of a simple, rounded torus moulding or, in one case (M. 104), a champfered profile. Both types of astragals are represented, among others, at Moissac.

cf. Pls. 32 and 47

This bold and simple shaping of the capital, along with a correspondence in basic dimensions, is among the indications of shared workshop practices which most clearly link the capitals of La Daurade to those in the Moissac cloister. Nevertheless, there are small but important differences in proportions between the two groups of capitals. Both groups measure 52 × 40 cm. at the upper surface, but the capitals of La Daurade are somewhat taller, measuring 35–6 cm. in height, while those of Moissac range from 29 to 31.5 cm., with the average height being 30 cm. On the other hand, the imposts at Moissac are somewhat larger and thicker.[9]

Pls. 40 and 26

The simple elements of the upper zone of the Moissac capitals show considerable variation in detail, such as the shape of the modillion, the presence of foliate ornament or inscriptions on it, and the decorative detailing of the volute stems. The capitals of La Daurade, while employing the same formula for the parts, lack this variation in details. It must be kept in mind that only a small sample of the early-style capitals remains from La Daurade. Chance survival may not give a true picture of what the first workshop produced there. It is striking, nevertheless, that the eight capitals of the first series show almost no variation in the details of the upper zone, while at Moissac almost no two capitals are alike. Only two modillion shapes occur among the surviving Daurade capitals: a rounded cushion shape with concave under surface (M. 104, *Daniel in the Lions' Den*) and a variant of this in which the centre of the modillion projects to create a tripartite cushion (M. 102, *Musicians of King David*). In all cases the volute stems are treated simply as V-shaped troughs with an incised line down the centre. Most significant at La Daurade is the thin triangle or wedge which springs from between the volute stems and seems to penetrate the modillion above, as if by its sharp point. With minor

Pl. 23
Pl. 20

---

[9] The respective dimensions are: L. 60–1 cm.; W. 49–50 cm.; and H. 15–16 cm. for the intact imposts of La Daurade and L. 63.5–64 cm.; W. 51.5–52 cm.; H. 16.5–17.5 cm. for the Moissac imposts.

exceptions, this configuration of the upper zone is used uniformly on the capitals of La Daurade.[10]

In contrast, at Moissac a wedge that slices into the central modillion is only one of numerous ways in which the modillion and volute configuration is treated.[11] Modillions may have the cushion shape like La Daurade, but just as often they are wedge-shaped or rectangular. They may be ornamented with a second pair of volutes, a single rosette, or a spray of pointed

Pl. 29   leaves.[12] In some instances, elements carved on the modillion play an iconographic role in the

Pl. 26   scenes below, as in the capital of the *Adoration of the Magi*, where a curious tiny coffer in the centre of the modillion may represent the manger of the Nativity or possibly the gifts of the Magi. The volute stems of this and other capitals at Moissac are raised, rather than concave, and have *tituli* inscribed on them. Others are ornamented with a fine pattern of vertical hatchings.

Beneath this abstract upper zone, the lively narrative themes are played out with equal charm and animation on the capitals of Moissac and La Daurade. The characteristic postures and gestures, the details of costume and facial type, reveal that they were carved by members of the same workshop, sculptors who had trained together to produce a distinctive and unique style. For all its naïvety, it is a style that conveys with considerable success the essential messages of Old and New Testament stories and parables enacted by its diminutive and energetic players. It relies on high relief and strong, simplified silhouettes to disengage the individual figures from the uniform wall of the background. Meyer Schapiro, in his unequalled analysis of the Moissac style published in 1931, compared the Moissac figures to pictographs indeterminate in their situation in space.[13] And, indeed, for all their relief projection, there is a sense in which these figures are perceived as silhouettes projected against a blank wall. The Moissac silhouette, moreover, is one that sticks very vividly in the mind. It is made up of oversized oval head, child-like body with small shoulders and short legs, accentuated often by a knee-length triangular skirt or a three-quarter length flaring mantle that broadens the

Pl. 22   silhouette to either side.

The larger elements of the Moissac capitals, namely their clear pyramidal shape, simplified upper zone, and elimination of foliage, create a clarified field of activity for the figured scenes portrayed on them. The essence of the Moissac style lies in the visual tension between the abstractly conceived and powerfully delineated structure of the capital and the intimate character of the scenes occupying its circumference. Here a world of diminutive detail and engrossing activity is laid out. The signature of the Moissac workshop is found in a wealth of distinguishing details, in costume and hairstyle, and in the way that figures hold themselves, move, and gesture. Bodies and legs are very short, while heads and hands are enlarged. Feet are

Pl. 44   tiny and often point in the same direction in profile to indicate walking figures. Figures seen

Pl. 28   from the front have feet pointing straight downwards. The holy figures of Old and New Testament—prophets, apostles, Christ himself—wear full length under-robes, often with a three-quarter length mantle thrown dramatically back from the shoulders and held at the front

Pl. 27   or on one shoulder by a circular brooch. Secular figures of the lowest rank most often wear

---

[10] Cf. the *Transfiguration* (Pl. 39), the *Adoration of the Cross* (Pl. 54), and the *Weighing of the Souls* (Pl. 49).

[11] This configuration appears most commonly at Moissac in the south gallery (see Meyer Schapiro, 'The Romanesque Sculpture of Moissac. I', *Romanesque Art*, Selected Papers (New York, 1977), figs. 24–6 and 35; repr. from 'The Romanesque Sculpture of Moissac. I', *Art Bulletin*, 13 (1931), 248–351).

[12] For other examples, ibid., figs. 61, 62, and 75.

[13] Ibid. 173.

short tunics, flaring at the knees into a triangular skirt and with the neckline finished in a bordered notch. If royal, as in the persons of Nebuchadnezzar and Herod, secular figures may also wear a long mantle clasped together with a brooch. Sleeves are most often full and open, sometimes exposing a tighter shirred sleeve beneath. But in another characteristic treatment *Pl. 28* seen in both the Moissac and Daurade capitals, sleeves may form an enflated ball at the elbows, repeating the bulbous form of the abdomen which is the most prominent feature of many figures, for example in *Daniel in the Lions' Den* at La Daurade and in the west gallery at Moissac or the angel with a cross and book from La Daurade. *Pls. 23 and*

25 The rounded and plastic forms of the body are overscored with the characteristic Moissac *Pl. 51* drapery folds delineated by a double incised line. On the torso these drapery folds, in their concentric patterns, resemble plates of armour closely encasing the figure. Hairstyles are varied, but the most characteristic styles are a short, thick 'pudding-bowl' cut, with a bluntly cut fringe, or a long style that curls up at the ends into a roll. Moissac figures are distinguished by their very large halos, which accentuate the figures' top heavy character and short stature. Almost uniformly, the haloes are very plain, with only a single incised line creating a narrow edge, but occasionally, as in the capital of *St Peter led from Prison*, an extra row of tiny *Pl. 30* beading may decorate the edge.

Throughout the capitals of Moissac and La Daurade, there is a predominance of round and bulbous or oval forms for prominent body parts of the human figure. This motif is carried into the drapery forms already described, in the recurrence of the inflated elbow roll, the concentric bands of drapery outlining torsos and abdomens, and in the liberal use of circular jewellery clasps. The use of broad bands to edge the borders of sleeves and mantles also produces a preponderance of smooth and curving drapery lines.

Selective variations in the treatment of drapery, however, produce dramatic effects. Occasionally fan-shaped and pleated patterns are created by the grouping of flatly pressed folds. In capitals from La Daurade these can be seen, for example, in the mantle that flares across the torso of Christ in the *Maestas* image or in the overlapping skirt of *Daniel in the Lions' Den*. Such *Pl. 52* configurations appear throughout the cloister of Moissac as well, in the fanning cloak of the angel *Pl. 23* in the *Vision of St John* from the south gallery, for example,[14] or in the pleated hem of the table-cloth in the *Wedding at Cana* in the east gallery. In the delineation of drapery, contrasting levels of *Pl. 28* relief are used skilfully by the Moissac carvers to highlight dramatic action. In the scenes of the *Arrest of Christ* from La Daurade or the *Transfiguration from Moissac*, the high relief and *Pls. 47 and* rounded forms of Christ's figure are set off against the flaring outline of his cloak, pressed flat and *40* barely raised from the surface of the drum, a contrasting of plastic and linear values that lets the cloak swing free of the body of Christ in its own independent movement.

This particular device, the calculated contrasting of very aggressive and very subtle relief, represents an essential characteristic of style in the Moissac cloister capitals. Such subtlety and control reveal that these capitals, however naïve they appear initially, are not 'first works'. They imply a considerable sculptural practice behind them. The contrasting of levels of relief was used with greatest effectiveness by the master who did many of the capitals of the south gallery at Moissac,[15] for example the *Temptations of Christ* or the capital of the *Vision of St John*. His

---

[14] For capitals not illustrated here, see Schapiro, 'Romanesque Sculpture of Moissac. I'.

[15] Schapiro has distinguished at least 3 hands among the sculptures of the Moissac cloister ('Romanesque Sculpture of Moissac. I', 191–8). On the innovative character of the south-gallery master in particular, see ibid. 169–72.

Pl. 30

Pl. 27

Pls. 28 and 29

Pl. 31

control of relief was such that he could achieve very subtle and delicate effects of projection, as in the spread wings of the angel in the capital of *St Peter led from Prison* or the drapery patterns of the striding Christ administered to by angels after the *Temptation*. Other capitals at Moissac, for example the *Miracle at Cana*, the *Washing of the Feet*, or the *Fall of Adam and Eve*, all in the east gallery, show a more uniformly high projection and thick rendering of drapery.

Pl. 30

Pl. 34

The preference for visually contrasting shapes and patterns that underlies so many aspects of the Moissac cloister style shows itself in the motif of miniature architecture developed by the Moissac sculptors as an element of narrative condensation. The diminutive gateways and towered walls that identify a scenic locale for many of the scriptural subjects are constructed by the piling up of rectangular blocks and pyramidal turrets, often with many window openings, detailed portal fixtures, and several levels of roofing. The shapes of these architectural props are made to contrast in the strongest terms with the rounded and inflated forms with which the human figures are put together. At the same time, in their unrealistically miniature scale they appear like inanimate equivalents of the mobile, doll-like figures, conforming as they do to the same principles of abstraction (compare the pose of the dancing Salome to the vertical tower next to her in a capital of John the Baptist from La Daurade or the three standing pavilions prepared for Christ, Moses, and Elijah in the *Transfiguration* from the same series (illustrated in Mesplé, no. 110)).

Pls. 23 and 24

Of all the elements that summarize the style of the early Moissac workshop, none so clearly distinguish it as the postures, gestures, and characteristic ways of moving of its active, short-legged figures. And no other traits so clearly identify the Daurade cloister capitals as creations of the Moissac workshop. The predominant conception of the figure in both these groups of capitals is one in which the body as a whole, or major subdivisions of it, such as the head, the torso, or the legs, can only be presented in strictly frontal or strictly profile view, a common formula observed in many artistic styles and periods when a comprehension of foreshortening is lacking.[16] Among the capitals of the Daurade series, the most 'primitive' in appearance, because of its strict adherence to this prescription, is that of *Daniel in the Lions' Den*. Here the sense of formality is heightened by the fact that Daniel is presented as an object of veneration by the pairs of recumbent lions who flank him. Far from offering a descriptive narrative of Daniel's trials, the sculptor adheres to the ancient mode of representing the deliverance of the Prophet, the heraldic representation whose iconographic tradition goes back to the Early Christian catacomb paintings. The seated Daniel has his arms raised parallel to the front plane, palms outwards, in the ancient posture of prayer. His knees, rather than projecting straight forward towards the viewer, are also aligned parallel with the front plane of the relief, thus presenting his legs and feet in profile, in what is visually their most comprehensible configuration.

Pls. 20 and 21

The capital of *King David and his Musicians* from La Daurade shows the sculptor combining both strictly frontal and profile views within a single figure. In the representation of David's musicians, it is the action of plucking or striking the instrument that is essential to the narrative. Consequently the shoulder, arm, and hand of both the harpist and the tambourine player are shown in true profile, affixed to a body represented in frontal view. Similarly, while

---

[16] Schapiro described in detail the working of these principles in the capitals of Moissac ('Romanesque Sculpture of Moissac. I', 182).

the body of the tambourine player belongs partially to the side and partially to the front of the capital, his face is turned outwards towards the viewer, giving it a flat, two-dimensional appearance that repeats the form of the corner volute directly above it.

This tendency to adhere simultaneously to inconsistent viewpoints within a single image is more marked in some capitals of the Moissac cloister than in others and was one of the criteria Schapiro used to distinguish what he described as the more naïve and archaic master of the east gallery capitals from a more sophisticated and experimental sculptor in the south. Many capitals of the east gallery are indeed distinguished by the abrupt way in which they switch from profile to frontal viewpoints numerous times within the same image. In the *Wedding Feast at Cana*, for example, the members of the wedding party are aligned behind the table *Pl. 28* with shoulders turned frontally to face the viewer. Their pairs of feet are, likewise, viewed uniformly from the front and hands are either turned palm outwards, parallel to the front plane, or are shown in strict profile, so that the arm and shoulder attach themselves awkwardly to the frontal body. The dining table with its draped cloth is shown as a visitor would observe it from the front, but we are shown the objects which should be resting on its top as if they were arrayed along its side. This same 'mixed perspective' is the rule in comparable scenes on the capitals of La Daurade, for example the *Feast of Herod*. Objects on the table best *Pl. 32* comprehended when seen from a bird's eye view, such as the round loaves of bread and cutting knives, are pictured from above, while the footed serving vessel is shown as though seen from the side.

There are, among the capitals of both Moissac and La Daurade, individual figures which exhibit a more sophisticated understanding of the movements of the human body in three dimensions and a more flexible ability to represent figures who are striding or turning in space. This concept of the figure is found more abundantly in the south gallery than elsewhere in the cloister of Moissac, as Schapiro has already observed.[17] The Moissac sculptor most successfully achieved the illusion of movement within three-dimensional space by means of the figure who strides with crossed legs or, as a variation of this type, the figure who directs his attention backward while striding forward (the 'equivocal posture', in Schapiro's terminology).[18] Figures with this kind of expressive torsion in their pose are seen in such capitals of the south gallery as the miracle of *Christ and the Centurion of Capernaum*, *St Peter led from Prison* and *Pl. 30* another with the *Transfiguration*. In the latter example, Christ strides energetically forward as *Pl. 44* his entire head and upper body pivot backward to address Peter, James, and John descending the mountain with him after the Transfiguration. In another capital from this gallery, showing *Angels Administering to Christ*, the greater ease of this sculptor in dealing with the third *Pl. 27* dimension is evident in the movement of Christ, at once energetic and fluid. In place of the awkward assemblage of frontal and profile body parts, the sculptor of this capital fashions a Christ whose body turns within a cylinder of space, striding legs in a scissors pose, and shoulders and torso in a true three-quarter view.

The sculptor or sculptors who migrated to La Daurade in Toulouse were also capable of carving figures with this expressive and flexible posture, giving them leading roles in the scene of *Christ and the Canaanite Woman* and the *Arrest of Christ*. The latter figure grouping is the *Pl. 37* most dynamic among the surviving capitals of the first series from La Daurade. The pivot of *Pl. 47*

---

[17] Ibid. 170–1 and 197.
[18] Ilene Forsyth has explored the narrative uses of such

'contraposed' movement in her study of the Moissac cloister capitals (Haering [Forsyth], 'Narrative Order').

the scene is the figure of Christ, impelled simultaneously in opposing directions, while the upper body and crossed legs of Judas work together in presenting a profile view.

Among the eight capitals that survive from the first workshop at La Daurade, figures of this more flexible and dynamic type may be found side-by-side on the same capital with others that display the naïve conjunction of profile and frontal views that indicates adherence to more archaic formulas. Schapiro observed a similar phenomenon of divergent stylistic tendencies among the capitals of Moissac,[19] a fact that links the two ensembles even more closely as products of the same workshop. In other words, the picture presented by the figure style is not that of a linear stylistic development over the course of the project at Moissac or even from one of the projects to the next. A sculptor such as the south gallery master may have introduced more experimental postures and figure groupings into the repertory of the workshop. At the same time, there seems to have been a reluctance among all members of the workshop to abandon tried and proven formulas for posture and gesture. In this way, the freest and most mobile figures, like the interacting pair of Christ and Judas in the *Betrayal* scene at La

Pl. 47 Daurade, could appear on the same capital with the stiff disciple bearing a palm in the *Entry*
Pl. 46 *into Jerusalem*. The scene of *Christ and the Canaanite Woman* from La Daurade juxtaposes, in the cross-legged Christ, one of the most expressive figures of the entire ensemble, while two apostles, on the converging short face, repeat in their frontal torsos and profile legs, the most
Pl. 38 conservative formulas of the Moissac cloister.

Schapiro's close and astute analysis of the Moissac sculptures led him to distinguish at least three hands among the historiated capitals there.[20] While one might dispute his assignment of this or that capital to one master or another, the variations he has observed within a common workshop style are sound and wonderfully revealing. Because of the powerful conservative tendencies among the Moissac sculptors and the stylistic inconsistencies observable within a single capital, it is difficult to assign each capital of the first Daurade series to a clearly defined master or to match each of these to the stylistic groupings distinguishable at Moissac. What does seem clear is that Schapiro's most 'archaic' master is not represented at La Daurade. Schapiro found this sculptor largely responsible for the east gallery as well as the engaged capitals of the piers. His figures have the most doll-like and unnatural proportions, being only about three heads high, while at the same time they are the most bulbous and strongly
Pls. 29 and projecting of any in the cloister. Their thick and heavy draperies are without the subtlety of
31 surface and detail observed in other capitals at Moissac, and the drapery folds themselves seem often to assume no logical or comprehensible pattern that can be related to movements or postures of the body (in the Prefect Emilianus on the capital of the *Three Spanish Saints*, for example).[21]

Most telling is the unusually prominent role given to inscriptions in the work of this east gallery master in capitals of the *Washing of the Feet*, the *Marriage at Cana*, the *Adoration of*
Pls. 31, 28, *the Magi*, and the *Parable of Dives and Lazarus*, for example. Letters may be inscribed on
and 26 almost any surface of the capital, including the modillion and the volute stems. In Schapiro's words, the inscriptions of this master are the most 'vagrant and decomposed',[22] with letters often enlarged or stretched to fill a vacant space between figures or with some letters or even entire words written in reverse. Three of the eight capitals from La Daurade include

---

[19] Schapiro, 'Romanesque Sculpture of Moissac. I', 196.
[20] Ibid. 191–3.
[21] Ibid., fig. 64.
[22] Ibid. 156. See also ibid. 194.

inscriptions (*Daniel in the Lions' Den*, the *Canaanite Woman*, and the *Transfiguration*), but they are used much less obtrusively there, where they appear only on the neutral background surface of the drum, in small-scale letters of relatively uniform size.

Only one capital from La Daurade shows the confused drapery patterns characteristic of Schapiro's east gallery master, in the lap of King David in the scene of him seated with his musicians. But the bodies do not have the broadened and squat appearance of those on capitals like the *Washing of the Feet* or the *Miracle at Cana* from the Moissac east gallery, or the overwhelming predominance of the frontal orientation. *Pl. 20*

Two capitals from La Daurade, on the other hand, may be the work of Schapiro's south-gallery master. These are the pair with Apocalyptic imagery. The character of the subject-matter makes close comparison with the art of the Moissac master difficult. The two Daurade capitals feature themes that are visionary and emblematic, while the forte of the south-gallery master is his facility with narrative themes that depend upon an expressive interaction between figures. Even so, the distinguishing hand of this master can be recognized in his delicate and subtle wielding of the chisel, which produces a fine gradation of relief planes not found in the work of the other sculptors of Moissac. This is especially evident in the capital with the *Christ in Majesty* from La Daurade. Here, too, the figure proportions of the south-gallery master—more slender and somewhat taller with a small, oval head— make a marked contrast with other capitals from the Toulousan cloister. In the detailed jewelled ornament on the mandorla of Christ and in the delicate feathering of the angels' wings (both here and on the adjacent face with the *Resurrection of the Dead*) there is a subtlety of relief projection comparable to the most refined capitals of the south gallery at Moissac, as in the scene of *Angels Administering to Christ*. The interest in a rich surface and ornamental detail is another characteristic of this master, seen in the exquisite jewelled cross and pleated veil displayed by angels on the face opposite to the *Christ in Majesty* on the capital from La Daurade. *Pls. 49–54* *Pl. 52* *Pl. 27*

Similar figure proportions and refinement of relief appear on the other capital with the *Weighing of the Souls* and *Blessed Entering Paradise* from La Daurade. The angel holding aloft a cross and book from one short end of this capital can be closely compared to the angel with a sickle from a south-gallery capital at Moissac. Though the angel on the Daurade capital lacks the complex mantle wrapping the upper body of his counterpart at Moissac, the diagonal roll of drapery cutting across the legs and the decorative flourish blown up from the hem of both garments is nearly identical in the two figures. Such windblown drapery flourishes are highly unusual among the capitals of La Daurade, appearing elsewhere only on the capital of the *Canaanite Woman*. This kind of motif, however, is a hallmark of the more individual and expressive use of drapery by the master of the south gallery at Moissac (for example, in the flying cloak of the Apocalyptic Rider from the same capital as the *Angel with a Sickle* at Moissac). *Pl. 51* *Pl. 37*

The remaining six capitals from La Daraude, with their more stumpy figure proportions and simplified drapery patterns, are not comparable to the style of the two *Last Judgement* capitals. These six may be the work of Schapiro's third master at Moissac, active mainly in the north and west galleries. The style of this master may be distinguished by figures that are built up of rounded and ovoid forms. He is more concerned in general with the third dimension than is Schapiro's east-gallery master, and he perfects a finer delineation of hair and drapery folds.

None the less, we do not necessarily perceive an exact correspondence between the hands distinguished by Schapiro in the Moissac cloister and the stylistic groupings that suggest themselves at La Daurade. The Moissac workshop may, in fact, have been somewhat more numerous than Schapiro's distinction of hands would suggest, something he himself acknowledged.[23] We have already concluded that one of the sculptors at Moissac—Schapiro's east-gallery master—is not represented at La Daurade. This could mean either that the small sample of surviving capitals from La Daurade simply does not include his work or that the Moissac workshop did not move *in toto* to Toulouse after the completion of the larger cloister in 1100. We have concluded that two of the Daurade capitals (M. 116 and 119) distinguish themselves from the rest of the group by their taller figure proportions and refined control of relief, and we have associated these most closely with the master of the south gallery at Moissac. We would prefer to characterize the remaining capitals of the series as the work of a sculptor or sculptors influenced by the more experimental approach to figure groupings and narrative composition employed by the south-gallery master but one who nevertheless failed to exploit fully the narrative potential of these devices.

It is his skilled narrative method that most clearly distinguishes the work of the south-gallery master within the larger ensemble at Moissac. This master exploited the four faces of the capital in ways very different from his fellow sculptors. In his pioneering exposition of narrative method in the cloister of Moissac, Schapiro defined the dominant compositional approach as one in which the sculptor treated each face of the capital as a 'closed field' with its own compositional midpoint or axis. This compositional mode, in Schapiro's analysis, reflects the premium that the Moissac sculptors placed on the decorative unity of each discrete face of the capital, the boundaries of which are defined by the corner volutes and zigzag upper frame, topped by the four-sided impost block.[24] Nevertheless, a majority of the capitals in the south gallery display a different approach to composition, in which the four faces of the capital are not so self-sufficient. In this more complex mode, the narrative has a dominant direction of movement and continues around two or more faces of the capital without the repetition of the key protagonists, which is an essential element of the first mode. An example is the capital of the *Transfiguration*, where activity extends from left to right across three faces of the capital devoted to that scene, while the remaining long face shows the subsequent episode of *Christ and the Apostles Descending the Mountain*.

Pls. 40 and 44

Several capitals from La Daurade take this approach of uniting two or more faces of the drum by means of an uninterrupted horizontal composition. In the double capital of the *Entry into Jerusalem* and the *Arrest of Christ*, the surface is apportioned equally between the two scenes, with each scene occupying an adjacent long and short face. The sculptor of this capital was less imaginative in focusing the narrative activity than his compatriot in the south gallery at Moissac, however. In both the *Entry into Jerusalem* and the *Arrest* scenes Christ, the central protagonist and actor in the drama, is positioned in predictable fashion in the very middle of a long face of the capital. A certain dynamism is effected in the scene by the torsion of Christ's backward turning movement. Nevertheless, the attendant figures on the adjacent short face— soldiers with lances in the *Arrest*; Apostles with palms in the *Entry into Jerusalem*—easily

---

[23] Schapiro, 'Romanesque Sculpture of Moissac. I', 194.

[24] Schapiro defined other refinements and variations within this dominant compositional mode, e.g. the subtle asymmetries introduced into some compositions and the indeterminate sequence of episodes in many of the narrative capitals. See my comments on narrative composition at Moissac in 'Passion Series', 39–40.

drop out of mind, and the compositional focus is essentially on a single face of the capital, as in the more conventional compositions at Moissac.

The sculptor who composed the scenes of *Christ and the Centurion's Servant* and the bold *Transfiguration* in the south gallery at Moissac, on the other hand, caused the long face and the adjacent short face in each instance to participate equally in the dynamics of the narrative activity by his cunning placement of figures and scenic props. In the *Transfiguration* James and John, overcome by their fear, face the vision of the transfigured Christ on the adjoining face, while St Peter is pushed forward to participate in the space belonging to Christ and the two Prophets. Just as the upright figure of Christ serves to pivot narrative activity from one *Pl. 40* adjoining face to the next in the scene of the *Centurion's Servant*, the sculptor of the *Transfiguration* has planted a strikingly ornate tree as a vertical axis on which the composition turns. The overlapping of Peter's lower legs and mantle in front of this tree enhances the continuity of activity from the short to the long face of the drum.

The same scene on a capital for a single column at La Daurade is so similar to the version at *Pls. 39, 41,* Moissac that one is tempted to assign them both to the same sculptor. Nevertheless, subtle *and 42* alterations in the composition produce a result that is less dramatic than the Moissac model. Individual figures in the two capitals are almost identical in their poses (compare the dialogue of Christ and the foremost Prophet in both scenes). At La Daurade, however, the kneeling St Peter is placed behind, not in front of, his two companions, so that the three are more isolated as a group from the transfigured Christ on the adjacent face. And the composition, in effect, has been rotated 90° on the capital drum, so that the disciples occupy a long face and Christ stands at the centre of the short one. This seems a less effective use of the surface than in the capital from Moissac, since the figures of Moses and Elijah cannot now occupy the same space as Christ. Narrative unity is further interrupted in unexpected fashion in the capital from La Daurade. The remaining short face is devoted, not as it is at Moissac to the subsequent episode of *The Descent from the Mountain after the Transfiguration*, but to the post-Resurrection scene of the *Incredulity of Thomas*.[25]

With the exception of *Daniel in the Lions' Den*, no composition from Moissac, in fact, is reproduced identically at La Daurade, even when the subjects are the same, as most of them are.[26] Rather, there seems to have been a deliberate effort, as in the *Transfiguration of Christ*, to achieve a different scenic arrangement of each subject, though all the compositions from La Daurade are based on formulas that appear repeatedly in the Moissac cloister. Closest of the capitals from La Daurade to the compositional ingenuity of the south gallery master is the badly damaged capital of *Christ and the Canaanite Woman*. Recovery of the missing portion *Pls. 37 and* in 1976 has revealed a distribution and interaction of figures very close to those of *Christ and* *38* *the Centurion's Servant* at Moissac. At La Daurade, however, the scene has been fitted to the three faces of an engaged double capital, and the figure of Christ has been moved slightly to the

[25] This pairing of scenes at La Daurade suggests that the *Transfiguration* and *Incredulity of Thomas* were brought together here not for their narrative content but as parallel events in the pre- and post-Resurrection life of Christ in which his supernatural body is made manifest to his disciples. The centrality of the Resurrection in the iconography of the cloister of La Daurade and in Cluniac spirituality is discussed in Ch. 7.
[26] The capital from La Daurade is very similar to the *Daniel* in the north gallery at Moissac, but on the latter capital only a

single pair of lions flanks the Prophet. As for the scene on the opposite face from *Daniel*, the Toulousan capital is different from both of the versions at Moissac. At La Daurade, Daniel's deliverance from the lions is paired with a scene of his accusers devoured (Pl. 24). In the north gallery at Moissac the corresponding scene is *Daniel and Habakkuk*, while in the second Daniel capital in the west gallery it is the *Annunciation to the Shepherds*.

left of the corner volute, not placed directly beneath it. The full eloquence of this figure at La Daurade, deprived of much of its meaning when the capital was broken in half, is now restored, and it was surely one of the masterpieces of the first workshop in the cloister.

Interestingly, the other subject which shares half the capital with the *Centurion's Servant* at Moissac is the *Miracle of the Canaanite Woman*. The composition of this theme at La Daurade, while essentially replicating the elements of the Moissac version, takes the pose of Christ from his pose in the scene of the *Centurion's Servant*. This kind of calculated play with compositional components and narrative structures is testimony to the intimate relationship that existed between the workshops of Moissac and La Daurade.

The *Musicians of King David* and the *Death of John the Baptist* from La Daurade both duplicate subjects that appear in the Moissac cloister but, as we have seen in the other instances, compositions have been varied so that an exact replication of either Moissac capital has been avoided. The composition of the *Musicians of King David* at Moissac is not one of the more imaginative in that cloister, although the twirling skirts and lively movements of the *Pl. 22* musicians give the scene a visual excitement. In effect, a single musician or dancer has been spotlighted on each face of the capital, as they converge on the seated King David, placed directly on the angle of the south short face. The large areas of bare, uncarved ground play an unusually important role on this capital, isolating each figure more distinctly and giving visual emphasis to the silhouettes of the whirling, dancing musicians.

At La Daurade the same imagery and same cast of characters have been arranged on a double capital for engaged columns. The Moissac version belongs to the type in which each face of the capital demands a separate attention as a closed, visually complete composition, with the result that there is no obviously prescribed order in which to view the four faces. At La Daurade, this has been traded for a composition with a strong processional movement from *Pls. 20 and* right to left. This sense of procession is heightened by the spacing of the musicians much more *21* closely together than they are at Moissac, so that the pace of their approach towards David seems quickened. The strict isocephalism, which includes the seated David, enhances the perception of the composition as a series of regularly repeated verticals. Nevertheless, interesting variations are introduced, in the positioning of the foremost musician just to the right of exact centre, and in the different shapes of the musical instruments and the heights at which they are held.

The capital of the *Death of John the Baptist* from La Daurade is the most unimaginative of the series in terms of its narrative composition. The story of John's execution has been conceived as four distinct images which may be read in counter-clockwise sequence around the capital, one scene per face: *Salome's Dance*, the *Feast of Herod*, the *Beheading of John in* *Pls. 32 and* *Prison*, and *Salome presenting Head of St John to Herodias*. This represents a reordering of the *34–6* subject as it is presented in the Moissac cloister, where it has been fitted to a double engaged capital. At Moissac Salome has centre stage on the long face, but her dancing pose with upraised hand is nearly identical to La Daurade, though the image has been reversed on the *Pl. 33* Toulousan capital. At Moissac the feast table of Herod, with the severed head of the Baptist from a bird's eye view, wraps around the angle of the capital, and Herod points spiritedly towards his guests around the corner from him on the engaged half-face. Though the figure style and mixed perspective of the Moissac capital show it to be the work of the most naïve of the Moissac carvers, it has more liveliness and sense of climax than the corresponding

90

rendition from La Daurade. The immense potential drama of the subject has been dissipated at La Daurade by the segmenting of the narrative into separate incidents, visually and conceptually isolated from each other by their neat assignment to discrete faces of the capital. Curiously, the *Feast of Herod* is not presented in narrative fashion at all, as a banquet in progress among feasting guests. Instead the king is presented to the viewer as an evil emblem, hands flat on the table and flanked symmetrically by two of his subjects. Even the round loaves of bread, the knives, and the serving bowl are arranged as perfectly pendant pairs to either side of an enormous tureen.[27] Clearly the story-teller at La Daurade was not the same sculptor who carved the *Miracle of the Canaanite Woman* or the *Arrest of Christ*, with their dynamically interacting protagonists.

This mixed picture of compositional modes, in which more exploratory directions were tempered by strongly conservative tendencies, means that a definition of ideal compositional formulas continued to elude the sculptors of the Moissac workshop. The picture is much clearer where the relationship of the narrative zone to the abstract framework of the capital is concerned, when the two series of Moissac and La Daurade are compared to each other. The pattern observable here clearly suggests that sculptors at La Daurade were profiting from their previous experience on the very similar project at Moissac. An increase in the height of the drum in the capitals of La Daurade (from a standard of 30 cm. at Moissac to one of 35–6 cm.), while all other proportions remained the same, suggests one such alteration in working methods on the part of the Moissac sculptors when they began the project at Toulouse. In the capital shape employed by the Moissac workshop at Moissac a large proportion of the drum is absorbed by the upper zone of volutes and central modillion. The difficulties of disposing complex narrative sequences peopled by numerous figures on the remaining area of the drum are evident. The increase of 5–6 cm. in the height of the capitals from La Daurade appears to be an adjustment aimed at giving the sculptors a larger carving area for the figured scenes, in response to difficulties encountered in the earlier cloister at Moissac.

The greater uniformity in the treatment of the upper frame at La Daurade, as well as the particular configuration it assumes, both argue for the later execution of the Daurade series. As described earlier, this upper zone takes the form of a cushion-shaped modillion with rounded corners or a tripartite shape, penetrated by a triangular wedge between the volute stems. The uniformity of this configuration suggests a move to simplify and standardize the form of the capital by reducing even further the references to Corinthian capital design still perceptible at Moissac. It is clear that the evolution was indeed in the direction of a greater abstraction and simplification of the *structural* elements of the capital, when the inspiration for the forms used at Moissac and La Daurade is realized. The triangular wedge penetrating the console, a form that appears on some of the capitals at Moissac as well, is the last remote echo of the foliage decoration of a Corinthian capital.

The process of abstraction which produced the form can be observed at Moissac. The numerous foliate capitals with two rows of curling palmettes are the closest derivatives of the Corinthian acanthus capital at Moissac. Here, the curling forward of the large central palmette between the volute stems still has a close formal kinship with the upper row of foliage on a   *Pl. 57*

---

[27] It is possible that the central serving vessel is meant to represent the head of John the Baptist displayed before Herod. If so, this would change significantly the order of narrative sequence, making this the climactic scene on the capital. This is not consistent, however, with the depiction of the Baptist's head from a bird's eye view on another face of the capital, where Salome presents it on a salver to Herodias, or with the corresponding capital at Moissac.

Pl. 22; cf. Pls. 39 and 49 from La Daurade
Pl. 33
Pl. 27

classical Corinthian capital. This organic basis of the zigzag upper frame is clear in the historiated capitals, in that many of those at Moissac retain this central pointed palmette, curling forward to expose its dorsal surface. Others of the Moissac series further reduce the leaf to a simple triangle, while in others (the models for the Daurade series), all reference to the organic origin of the device is disguised as the central wedge is embedded in the modillion.

Significantly, the most literal quotations from the Corinthian capital are found at Moissac in the carvings of the most conservative and archaic of the sculptors, the master of the east gallery,[28] while his more experimental colleague in the south gallery used the motif of the disappearing wedge more frequently than did the other sculptors. This relationship is reversed, however, where the concept and treatment of the human figure are concerned. The figure style of the east-gallery master is the most abstract and remote from natural human proportion and movement, while the art of the south-gallery master points in the general direction of an increased naturalism.

One more aspect of the capitals from La Daurade reinforces these observations. I have noted in the historiated capitals that virtually no visual distinction has been made by the Moissac sculptors between single and double capitals, apart from a twinning of the astragals in the latter type. Nevertheless, within the total ensemble at Moissac, the double capitals by the east-gallery master consistently show more marked reminiscences of double drums than do the others. I agree with Schapiro in assigning to this master, as well, all the double-engaged

Pl. 26
Pl. 33

capitals of all the piers. In capitals such as the *Adoration of the Magi* and the engaged capital of the *Death of John the Baptist*, there is a definite crease or depression down the centre of the capital and a rounding of the lower portion into two distinct cylinders suggesting a double-headed capital. What is more, this artist, whom we have characterized as the least imaginative in his compositions, frequently positions figures in a symmetrical fashion that tends to leave a gap at the centre of double capitals, as though mentally he conceived of the drum as double. Examples are the *Washing of the Feet*, where the disciples tend to divide themselves into pairs

Pl. 31
Pl. 29

on either side of the centre axis, the *Miracle at Cana*, and the engaged capital with the *Annunciation* and *Visitation*.

The total rejection of the double drum by the other sculptors of the Moissac cloister may reflect the realization that the simplest, unsubdivided surface provided the best field for the presentation of complicated narrative themes. The vertical enlargement of this field in the capitals of La Daurade and the simplification of the upper frame to its most abstract and unobtrusive configuration point to the same realization. All of these fine adjustments in the capitals of La Daurade suggest an attempt to arrive at an ideal through trial and error, since none of the compositional solutions or stylistic niceties remained the exclusive property of one individual within the workshop.

We are inhibited from forming a complete picture of the relationship of the workshop at La Daurade to its parent workshop at Moissac, because no decorative capitals of animal or foliate motifs have survived from the Toulousan cloister. Nevertheless, a number of the imposts of the first Daurade series carry foliate motifs based on the repertory of decorative capitals and imposts at Moissac. The imposts, then, attest to the presence in the Daurade workshop of at least one sculptor who had carved foliate capitals at Moissac. Considering how closely the

[28] See the *Wedding Feast* and *Miracle at Cana*, where double pairs of volutes and some foliage points on the console have been retained (Pls. 28 and 29).

surviving capitals from La Daurade reflect the programme at Moissac in other respects, it is very likely that the Toulousan cloister also included foliate and animal capitals within the arcades decorated by the first workshop, though none of these has survived the destructions of the eighteenth and nineteenth centuries.[29] Without the evidence of decorative capitals, the imposts are our best testimony that the composition of the Daurade workshop reflected very closely the mix of sculptors who had worked together earlier at Moissac.

In a manner parallel to what we have seen in the historiated capitals, the imposts of the first Daurade series do not copy precisely any of those in the Moissac cloister. Rather, they play upon the same repertory of motifs that occur over and over at Moissac, regularly varying them but employing all the compositional formulas that control the decoration of imposts in the latter cloister. Six largely intact imposts survive from the first building campaign at La Daurade, along with fragments of five others.[30] Their decorative motifs have been minutely described by Kline in her study of the imposts at Moissac,[31] but a few general observations should be made about them here. The visible edge of each impost has a horizontal upper band and a bevelled lower one which are distinguished from each other by their decoration. The upper band is characteristically ornamented with very simple patterns of scallops in shallow relief or with three overlapping horizontal bands, lightly incised, while the bevelled zone carries a great variety of human, animal, and foliate motifs that are intricately detailed and very deeply undercut.

Pls. 15–17 and the Inventory

At Moissac, the most common ornamentation of the upper band is a pattern of overlapping imbrications, and these appear on one of the Daurade imposts (M. 117). But other patterns of scallops in a single row or as interpenetrating half-circles also appear (M. 105, 108, and 111), just as they do at Moissac. The other frequently occurring motif on this upper band is a series of three overlapping horizontal bands. This is found on three of the imposts from the first campaign at La Daurade (M. 193, 194, and 198) while another (M. 120) shows a variation on it, in which actual concave channels are separated by a narrow fillet. Interestingly, this manner of finishing the impost at the top was used uniformly in the second series of capitals from La Daurade, including the giant imposts which probably decorated the L-shaped corner piers (M. 200–5). In this subtle way, a debt of influence to the working practices of an earlier generation of sculptors was acknowledged by the workshop that completed the cloister of La Daurade.

Pl. 50

Pls. 56 and 36

Pls. 15 and 16

Pl. 54

Pls. 18 and 19

---

[29] The fact that only historiated capitals have survived does not necessarily imply a predominance of this type of capital in the programme. Given the higher value usually attached to figurative sculpture, it may be that these were singled out for preservation, while decorative capitals were discarded.

[30] Three fragments of what are obviously imposts from the first campaign at La Daurade were recovered during excavations in the cloister of the Augustins in 1975–6 (Inv. 76–13–6; 76–13–9; and 76–13–10). All of these proved to be additional pieces of fragmentary imposts that have been in the Musée des Augustins at least since 1912, when they were catalogued by Rachou (see M. 193–5). I also assign M. 192 to La Daurade. A fifth fragmentary impost (M. 198) resembles those of the first Daurade series in its dimensions (H. 16; L. 59; W. 50 cm.) and its 3 overlapping horizontal bands. It should be noted, however, that its ornament of beaded meander does not appear on the Moissac imposts, although it is common on the somewhat later imposts from the cloister and chapter house of Saint-Étienne (see M. 18, 23, 35, and 58–62).

[31] Kline, 'Decorated Imposts of Moissac'; ead. [Ruth Maria Capelle], 'The Representation of Conflict on the Imposts of Moissac', *Viator*, 12 (1981), 79–100. Kline's descriptions and classification of the decorative motifs on the respective imposts of Saint-Sernin, La Daurade, and Moissac provide data which could aid in an analysis of the sculptors active at these sites. Nevertheless, the value of her study is undercut by its methodology. I do not believe it is possible to draw the conclusions Kline draws about the relationship among these 3 sculptural programmes on the basis of the imposts alone. It is obvious that foliate imposts and foliate capitals in Toulouse and Moissac drew upon the same repertory of motifs. In most cases, capitals and imposts were clearly carved by the same workmen who were particularly skilled at ornamental devices. It therefore makes no sense to study the imposts in isolation from a general discussion of ornamental capitals at these sites, their origins, and the dispersion of the repertory in the region.

Though the capitals of this second workshop are otherwise so different in style from the earlier series, the characteristic and uniform manner of finishing the impost block seems to reflect the decision by the second group of sculptors to maintain a consistency in the larger architectural features with those already established by the first workshop. This has already been seen in the overall dimensions of the capitals and the choice of alternating supports.

Pl. 17
Pl. 16
In the decoration of the lower impost band, much of the flora and fauna of the Moissac decorated imposts appears again in the first series from La Daurade. Deeply undercut palmettes with seven points, arranged as a row of single medallions within circling vine stems (M. 195) or as a repeated tripartite group with upright central palmette embraced by a half-leaf to either side (M. 193), appear in numerous closely similar patterns in the Moissac cloister. The specific pattern of two upright palmettes embraced by a half-palmette on the long face of M. 193 compares to the same pattern on the impost above the capital of the *Martyrdom of St Saturninus* at Moissac.[32] Like the comparable Moissac foliage, these leaves have a deeply depressed centre which gives the form a strikingly plastic character, while the deep undercutting around each leaf and stem creates a stencilled or perforated effect. There is a powerful emphasis on the optical play of dark and light in the ornament of the imposts, enhanced by the selective use of the drill to create circular punctuations where tightly wound leaf points curl back upon themselves.[33]

Pls. 40 and 63
Pl. 51
Another foliate motif of asymmetrical fan-shaped leaves, enclosed in a continuous rinceau of vine circlets, appears on an impost from La Daurade (M. 192) and on both imposts and capitals at Moissac. On one of the imposts of La Daurade (M. 116), the foliate ornament opens like an oculus to reveal a moon-like human face. This curious motif has its prototype at Moissac in an impost above the capital of the Beatitudes in the west gallery. There, too, the face appears only on the two short ends of the impost. At La Daurade, however, the face emerges from an intricately interlaced vine tendril that is different from the usual Moissac foliage types.

Pls. 36 and 15
The animal and bird motifs that appear in decorative groupings on several imposts of La Daurade are all drawn from the menagerie of natural and fantastic species that ornament the imposts of Moissac. Most of these are arranged heraldically as simple affronted or addorsed pairs, flanking a central foliate motif or devouring a quadruped victim between them. Two such imposts from La Daurade (M. 108 and 194) employ lions and griffins with curled serpent tails, the latter motif closely similar to the decoration of an impost in the north gallery at Moissac, above the capital of the *Calling of the Apostles*. In yet a different arrangement at La Daurade (M. 115), stags, collared dogs (or possibly bears), and riderless, saddled horses led by grooms with hunting horns form a continuous frieze, moving counter-clockwise in procession around the impost. Such motifs drawn from the hunt, specifically the riderless horse and the stag, also appear on an impost at Moissac,[34] but there the arrangement is a more conventional heraldic one.

Pls. 45 and 46
Two imposts from La Daurade are carved with enigmatic and amusing vignettes that do not find exact parallels in any of the impost ornament at Moissac. In his early catalogues of the sculptures from La Daurade, Du Mège singled out these two imposts for description, giving them the fanciful titles by which they are usually identified today: *The Prince's Toilette* (M.

---

[32] Schapiro, 'Romanesque Sculpture of Moissac. I', fig. 53.

[33] See my dicussion of the imitation and conventionalization of Moissac foliage patterns in the 12th-cent., dispersion of the style in 'A Romanesque Capital from the Region of Toulouse and Moissac', *Bulletin of the University of Michigan Museum of Art*, 7 (1984–5), 26–46.

[34] Illustrated in Lafargue, *Chapiteaux de la Daurade*, pl. IX, fig. 10.

105) and *Scenes of Domestic Life* (M. 111).³⁵ The first pictures a seated man drying his head with a towel while having his shoe put on or removed by a kneeling figure to his right. Three *Pl. 56* other male figures carrying staves kneel to either side of this central group. All the figures wear short-skirted tunics with notched necklines and the bluntly cropped hairstyles that denote secular figures throughout the capitals sculptured by this workshop. The other faces of the impost carry more familiar animal imagery, including the predatory birds (here with curling head combs) who bite their own wings, similar to those on another impost of the series (M. 120). The so-called *Scenes of Domestic Life* in fact depicts figures engaged in a variety of *Pls. 39 and* popular amusements, which include board games and, perhaps, spelling or rhyming games. *43* The frieze of diminutive players, some dressed in the headgear of popular *jongleurs*, includes tumblers and musicians.

This incongruous intrusion of secular amusements into the sculptural programme of a monastic precinct is not at all unique in Romanesque practice, but the two imposts of La Daurade are nevertheless remarkable for the minutely detailed attention they give to these secular pastimes. As is usual in the marginal contexts in which such vignettes are portrayed, whether in sculpture or manuscript illumination, the figures disport themselves with none of the decorum of the protagonists of the sacred imagery. In fact, the freedom with which these tiny figures tumble, gesture, and dispute illustrates the full expressive power of which the Moissac style was capable but applied here to subjects wholly lacking in serious tone. The mobile and varied postures and, above all, the delicacy of detail in the two figured imposts suggest the hand of the south-gallery master of Moissac, the probable author, as I have proposed, of two of the surviving capitals of the Daurade series.

Figure style, composition, and ornament are consistent, then, in revealing the intimate relationship between the sculptures of Moissac and La Daurade. At the same time, the nature of this relationship is not that of imitation. Rather, there is a thoroughgoing adherence to the same compositional formulas and principles on the basis of which variation is developed. The kind of practised ease seen here in working with the same repertory of figure types and ornament in the two groups of capitals indicates that they are products of the same workshop. Since the cloister of La Daurade was considerably smaller than that of its mother abbey, it is probable the entire Moissac shop was not required for the Toulousan project. Nevertheless, what survives is a good representation of the particular talents of the Moissac carvers.

THE ICONOGRAPHY OF THE FIRST SERIES

The intimate institutional links between Moissac and its dependent priory within the city of Toulouse are revealed not only by their sharing of the same workshop in the construction of their cloisters. In its choice of themes and imagery, the first series of capitals from La Daurade is an abridged version of the much larger ensemble at the mother abbey. Six of the eight surviving capitals are literal repetitions of subjects at Moissac—the *Musicians of King David*, *Daniel in the Lions' Den*, the *Death of John the Baptist*, the *Transfiguration*, *Christ and the Canaanite Woman*, and the *Adoration of the Cross*. The Toulousan priory showed itself dutiful in following the spiritual leadership of the mother abbey, by populating the early arcades of its cloister with themes that are eminently representative of the Cluniac theology of

³⁵ [Du Mège], *Notice des tableaux* (1818/19), nos. 167 and 166.

the period. In the larger context of monastic reforming ideals of about 1100, discussed in Chapter 7, this spiritual outlook may be characterized as decidedly conservative in its exposition of a Cluniac theology that belongs firmly to the eleventh century.

The range and mix of subjects in the cloister of Moissac have so far frustrated attempts to discern an overriding lesson or programme of meaning that unites the whole and explains the presence of individual images.[36] The subjects range from typological and moralizing themes from the Old and New Testaments to hagiography, parables, and miracles extracted from the Gospel story, as well as visionary images that allude to the cosmic world of Judgement and the end of time. It has been suggested that our inability to perceive a comprehensive programme at Moissac could be due to a disruption of the original order of the capitals, since the cloister of Moissac was rebuilt in the thirteenth century, when the existing Gothic brick arcades replaced the earlier Romanesque ones. What little evidence exists for the capital sequence at Moissac, however, suggests that the thirteenth-century builders took some care to maintain the Romanesque structural elements in their original order. The alternation of single and double capitals at Moissac cannot be proven to have existed in the original design, but I have elsewhere argued that it is the most feasible arrangement of the existing elements.[37] There is the further evidence that in those cases in which an inscription or iconographic motif indicates that a specific capital and impost were designed as a unit, care was taken to maintain this pairing (see, for example, the *Dream of Nebuchadnezzar* and *Story of St Martin*). Finally, the designation of hands at Moissac arrived at by Schapiro in 1931 revealed a concentration of identifiable sculptors' work in specific galleries or segments of galleries. For example, Schapiro identified a master of the south gallery, a master of the east gallery, and a third hand, the master of the pier reliefs, whom he associated with most of the north and west galleries. My own observations have been largely in agreement with Schapiro's, with some exceptions. The distribution of hands that emerges suggests, then, that individual sculptors were assigned responsibility for decorating one or another side of the cloister. Surely such concentrations of hands would not be distinguishable today unless the original positions of the capitals had been kept largely intact.

If no single programme of meaning seems to unite all the capitals at Moissac, the clear preference for certain types of themes is a true reflection of the character of Cluniac liturgy and monastic ideals in the eleventh century. The same kinds of preferences are evident in the much smaller sample of themes that survives from La Daurade. The importance of Psalmody and the cult of the saints in Cluniac liturgy is reflected at both Moissac and La Daurade. King David, author of the Psalms, was celebrated in both cloisters in memorable capitals that picture him accompanied by musicians and dancers. The rich hagiography of Cluny is prominently featured in the iconography of Moissac and an echo of this is found at La Daurade. Ten

---

[36] Those who have approached the problem of iconography in the cloister of Moissac are Émile Mâle, *Religious Art in France, the Twelfth Century* (Princeton, 1978), 10–14; Raymond Rey, *L'Art des cloîtres romans: Étude iconographique* (Toulouse, n.d [1955]), 37–67; Dom Jacques Hourlier, 'La Spiritualité à Moissac', *Annales du Midi*, 75 (1963), 395–404; Étienne Delaruelle, 'The Crusading Idea in Cluniac Literature', in Noreen Hunt (ed.), *Cluniac Monasticism in the Central Middle Ages* (London, 1971), 212–16; Vidal *et al.*, *Quercy roman*, 130–3. Leah Rutchick has recently presented some very interesting ideas about meaning in the cloister of Moissac,

based on her forthcoming doctoral thesis for the University of Chicago. She also points to the absence of a unified programme at Moissac. She finds it more important that individual images act as spurs to contemplation. Leah Rutchick, 'Cross-Currents of Imagery: Oral Memory and Benedictine Literacy in the Moissac Cloister', paper delivered at the annual conference of the College Art Association of America (New York, 16 Feb. 1990).
[37] Kathryn Horste, 'A New Plan of the Cloister and Rampart of Saint-Étienne', *Journal of the Society of Architectural Historians*, 45 (1986), 15.

capitals of the Moissac ensemble are devoted to saints either venerated by the order or of more local significance to the devotions at Moissac. SS Peter and Paul, John the Baptist, Benedict, Martin, and Lawrence were all saints whose feasts were celebrated with special solemnity in the liturgy of Cluny by being accorded an octave and special offices.[38] Individual capitals are devoted to all these saints within the ensemble at Moissac, with the *Martyrdoms of SS Peter and Paul* being depicted together on a capital situated in the east gallery, next to the corner pier with the paired images of these two titular saints of Cluny. In addition, St Peter, titular saint of Moissac, is honoured in two other capitals showing his miracles and his deliverance from prison. St John the Baptist, whose Nativity and Decollation were both celebrated with special solemnity at Cluny, has a capital devoted to his beheading at Moissac. The virtual repetition of its sequence of episodes on a capital from La Daurade shows how closely the Toulousan priory modelled its hagiographic narratives on capitals of the mother abbey. At Moissac, locally venerated saints, St Saturninus of Toulouse and the three Spanish saints, Fructuosus, Eulogius, and Augurius, are given their own capitals. We can only regret that more capitals of the first building campaign have not survived from La Daurade, since they might have told us what other saints were particularly honoured in the twelfth century by the Cluniac community in Toulouse.[39]

Of the Old Testament themes at Moissac, the Book of Daniel was given particular prominence in the cloister. Four capitals are devoted to the writings of this Prophet, with images of *Nebuchadnezzar's Dream* and *Daniel's Interpretation* (south gallery), the *Three Hebrews in the Fiery Furnace* (north gallery), and two separate capitals devoted to *Daniel in the Lions' Den* (north and west galleries). We have already noted how the powerful and emblematic image of Daniel flanked by lions was copied virtually without alteration in the cloister of La Daurade (with the image at Toulouse being closest to the version in the north gallery at Moissac). The archaic quality of its imagery is arresting among the more complex narrative compositions found in these two cloisters. In fact, the Daniel theme is one of the few historiated subjects that had a prior history in the region of Toulouse and Moissac in the eleventh century. One of the earliest instances appears to be a capital at the entrance to the apse of the church of Saint-Michel de Lescure, dating to the last quarter of the eleventh century,[40] but the theme also appears in the hemicycle of Saint-Sernin at Toulouse, the oldest part of the construction there.[41]
Pl. 74

Daniel in the Lions' Den has a particularly long history, going back to the very beginnings of the representation of biblical themes on stone capitals with its appearance on a capital of the seventh century in the Visigothic church of San Pedro de la Nave.[42] The Daniel theme belongs to a limited category of Old Testament subjects, among them the *Fall of Man* and the *Sacrifice of Isaac*, that were repeated over and over again by the earliest sculptors of Romanesque capitals in the regions to the north-east and north-west of Toulouse for two decades or more

[38] Guy de Valous, *Le Monachisme clunisien des origines au XVᵉ siècle* (Archives de la France monastique, 39), i. *L'Abbaye de Cluny: les monastères clunisiens* (Paris, 1935), 363–4. See also the calendar of Cluniac liturgical feasts during the 10th and 11th cents. compiled by Valous (ibid., app. III A). The customs for the 11th-cent. observances of these feasts can be found in the Customs of Ulrich (*PL* 149, cols. 654–6).

[39] See Ch. 6 for the special attention given to St Martial in the capitals of the second series.

[40] The important capitals at Lescure will be discussed below

in Ch. 5 in the context of the formation of the Moissac workshop.

[41] See Lyman's discussion of this capital and its place in the iconography of Saint-Sernin ('The Sculpture Programme of the Porte des Comtes Master', *Journal of the Warburg and Courtauld Institutes*, 34 (1971), 27–31 and fig. 13b).

[42] Pedro de Palol and Max Hirmer, *L'Art en Espagne du royaume wisigoth à la fin de l'époque romane* (Paris, 1967), fig. 7.

after the completion of the Moissac cloister. The restricted character of this imagery will be discussed in the following chapter on the formation and dispersion of the Moissac workshop.

The repetition, in two capitals at Moissac and again at La Daurade, of the orant Prophet as an image of divine salvation reflects the primitive hold this imagery had in Christian iconography, going back to the earliest catacomb paintings. But at Moissac this ancient image was made part of a larger Daniel iconography that indicates a particular interest in this Old Testament Prophet. An inventory of the books in the library of Moissac during the abbacy of Ansquitil (who constructed the cloister, the pier inscription tells us), lists a commentary by St Jerome on the Book of Daniel, which could well have inspired the interest in this theme as a subject for cloister sculpture.[43]

This inventory indicates an interest at Moissac not only in Daniel but in eschatology in general and the prophecies of the last things. The Moissac library of the turn of the twelfth century, scanty as the surviving record is, also included commentaries by St Jerome and St Gregory on Ezekiel and one by Jerome on Isaiah. The interest at Moissac in the cosmic world of Judgement and the world to come is vividly represented in the cloister where, in addition to the capitals of *Nebuchadnezzar's Dream* and *Daniel's Prophecies*, are capitals of *Babylonia the Magnificent, Jerusalem the Holy, Og and Magog* and the *Chaining of the Devil, Symbols of the Four Evangelists with Beasts' Heads*, the *Vision of John the Evangelist, St Michael Slaying the Dragon, Christian Knights before the Walls of Jerusalem*, and the *Triumph of the Cross*.

Émile Mâle long ago made this particular selection of images the basis for his belief that the iconographers of Moissac must have been inspired by an illuminated copy of Beatus's commentary on the Apocalypse. He suggested that it must have been very like the Apocalypse from Saint-Sever, which has St Jerome's treatise on the Book of Daniel appended to it.[44] Since Mâle's time, the presence of a Beatus manuscript at Moissac has been frequently hypothesized,[45] though it need not have been an illuminated one, since, as Mâle himself acknowledged, the capitals of Moissac are only analogues of the illustrations of the Saint-Sever manuscript, not copies of them.

An image that does not appear in the illuminated Beatus manuscripts is the *Triumph of the Cross*, celebrated in two pendant images on the north and south faces of Schapiro 58 in the west gallery at Moissac. In both images an erect jewelled cross is adored by attendant angels, the cross on the south face revealed by a veil of honour. The first series of capitals from La Daurade duplicated the powerfully cosmic tone of this imagery in two capitals devoted to Judgement and the triumphant Second Coming of Christ. Mesplé 119 depicts *Christ in Majesty*, seated within a lozenge-shaped mandorla upheld by flanking angels and with his hands outspread in judgement. Pendant to him on the opposite face of the capital, a jewelled cross descends from the clouds and is displayed by two angels. On the two long faces, other angels sound their horns, calling the dead, who emerge from their tombs.

Pl. 55

Pl. 52
Pl. 54
Pl. 53

---

[43] Paris, BN, lat. 4871, fo. 160ᵛ; published in Jean Dufour, *La Bibliothèque et le scriptorium de Moissac* (Geneva, 1972), app. 1. For Dufour's dating of this inventory to the abbacy of Ansquitil, see ibid. 13–14.

[44] Mâle, *Religious Art, the Twelfth Century*, 8–14. See the papers from the recent colloquium on the Saint-Sever Apocalypse: *Saint-Sever: millénaire de l'abbaye. Colloque international 25, 26 et 27 mai 1985*, ed. Jean Cabanot (Mont-de-Marsan, 1986).

[45] See Rey, *Cloîtres romans*, 37; Vidal *et al., Quercy*

roman, 130. Mâle also associated the tympanum of Moissac with the tradition of the Beatus illustration, in particular the manuscript of Saint-Sever. The more penetrating study of Mézoughi rejects, however, important elements of Mâle's interpretation, as Schapiro had already done in 1954 (Noureddine Mézoughi, 'Le Tympan de Moissac: Études d'iconographie', *Les Cahiers de Saint-Michel de Cuxa*, 9 (1978), 171–200; Meyer Schapiro, 'Two Romanesque Drawings in Auxerre and Some Iconographic Problems', *Romanesque Art*, 306–27).

The eschatological subject-matter is continued on the second Daurade capital, Mesplé 116. Pls. 49–51 Here a standing angel holds aloft a book and the cross-staff of Resurrection, an image that has its counterpart in a capital in the west gallery at Moissac.[46] On an adjoining face of the capital from La Daurade, St Michael, holding the scales of judgement, confronts two demons, one of whom displays a scroll with the inscription: IN IGNEM ETERNU[M]. On the face opposite, in a rare iconography for this period, two robed and nimbed figures of the Elect make their way towards the Heavenly Jerusalem, depicted as a gated and towered structure of crenellated walls.

There could not be a more explicit statement than these of the Cluniac doctrine of resurrection and the triumph of Christ within the language of early Romanesque imagery. This doctrine was made explicit in the sermons of St Odilo of Cluny (994–1049) on the triumph of the cross and on the resurrection.[47] In Odilo's Sermon 15, 'De sancta cruce', the cross is presented not as an emblem of Christ's human suffering and mortification but as the symbol of triumph, 'the sign of the son of Man' that would come at the end of time, as promised in Matthew 24: 30. Étienne Delaruelle has contrasted the spirituality of eleventh-century Cluny, a theology that emphasized Christ's passion and resurrection as glorious mysteries, to that of the pilgrims and Crusaders to the Holy Land.[48] Those Christian devotees, as we will describe in Chapter 7, were drawn to the Holy Land by their desire to see and experience the very sites where Christ had suffered and been resurrected, while the sermons of St Odilo make no mention of the locations of the Passion story or of Christ's last days as historical, human events.

The images of the *Crux invicta* in the cloisters of Moissac and La Daurade must have been given special resonance by the devotion to the cross in the liturgy of Cluny. The *Exaltatione S. Crucis* was celebrated at Cluny with special offices on 14 September.[49] As for La Daurade, we know that a ceremony of the Adoration of the Cross was being performed there on Good Friday in the early fifteenth century, since it is described in the missal for the usage of La Daurade that we have looked at earlier.[50] In a ritual that seems to combine reminiscences of the finding of the true cross by St Helena with primitive ritual measures against flooding, the ceremony involved a procession to the banks of the Garonne below the church, where a fragment of the true cross was repeatedly displayed and plunged into the waters of the river.

In their emblematic and visionary language, the two capitals of the *Adoration of the Cross/ Christ in Majesty* and the *Last Judgement* from La Daurade stand apart from the other six of the first series, which, though diverse in theme, are all based on scriptural narrative. Mesplé's numbering of the capitals has the effect of placing the two eschatological themes at the termination of the series, as though they summed up the iconography of the whole. It is tempting to see these powerful images in just such a climactic role, and yet we do not know what their original sequence was within the cloister arcades. Both are capitals for single columns; it is unlikely, therefore, that they did stand next to each other in the cloister of La Daurade. No matter where situated, however, their impact would have been considerable, since their visual language is of a different order than that of the other capitals of the series.

[46] Schapiro, 'Romanesque Sculpture of Moissac. I', fig. 85.

[47] Odilo of Cluny, 'De sancta cruce', Sermon 15 for the feast of the finding of the true cross (*PL* 142, cols. 1031–6); Sermons 5–7 on the resurrection (ibid., cols. 1004–11).

[48] Delaruelle, 'Crusading Idea', 209–11.

[49] Valous, *Monachisme clunisien*, app. IIIA; Customs of Ulrich, *PL* 149, cols. 684–5; *Liber tramitis aevi Odilonis* (Customs of Farfa), ch. 68, cols. 99–100 (Inventio sanctae crucis).

[50] Paris, BN, nouv. acq. lat. 2387, fos. 14ʳ–15ʳ.

First Series of Capitals from La Daurade

The emblematic images of the *Maestas Domini* and the *Crux invicta* have venerable traditions in early medieval art, in countless ivory and metal book covers, manuscript pages, and altar frontals. The artistic and iconographic recensions behind these images give them a focus and weight not present to the same degree in the other six capitals of the series.

Of these, we have already tied the Daniel and the John the Baptist to closely conceived capitals in the Moissac cloister. The remaining capitals from La Daurade depict scenes from the life of Christ. An important number of capitals in the Moissac cloister are also devoted to Christ. Three have scenes drawn from the Epiphany cycle: the *Annunciation and Visitation*, the *Annunciation to the Shepherds*, and the *Adoration of the Magi*. The overwhelming majority, however, are concerned with Christ's Public Life and Ministry: his *Temptations*, his *Baptism*, the *Calling of the Apostles*, *Christ's Miracle at Cana*, the *Healing of the Centurion's Servant*, the *Canaanite Woman*, the *Samaritan Woman*, the *Transfiguration*, and the *Raising of Lazarus*. Curiously, Christ's Passion is unrepresented at Moissac, with the exception of the *Washing of the Feet*, which precedes the Passion *per se*.

At La Daurade, Christ's Ministry is also represented, in two of the same themes included at Moissac, *Christ and the Canaanite Woman* (M. 113) and the *Transfiguration* (M. 110). We have already seen that the latter image is a nearly literal reproduction of the same subject at Moissac, though shifted by 90° on the surface of the capital. Though the Daurade series seems in every way so dependent on the earlier ensemble at Moissac, it does broaden the range of themes treated in the two cloisters by adding three important episodes from the Passion and post-Resurrection cycles: the *Entry into Jerusalem* and the *Arrest of Christ* (on the same capital) and the *Incredulity of Thomas*, paired at La Daurade with the *Transfiguration*.

That the Moissac sculptures represent an initial effort, essentially unprecedented, towards the enrichment of narrative vocabulary within the realm of capital sculpture is clear from the mixed results that were achieved. Many of the capitals are difficult to decipher, particularly those that deal with narrative themes, as distinct from symbolic or emblematic imagery. Many or most of the themes treated in the Moissac cloister obviously have iconographic traditions behind them in manuscript painting and the minor arts. Nevertheless, regardless of what pictorial or other models might have been accessible as inspiration for the sculptors, the task presented to them was a new one, that of structuring effective visual stories on three-dimensional and spatially dispersed elements of architecture. Pictorial sources or ivories have frequently been proposed as the models for the cloister capitals, and much speculation has centred on just what models might have been available in the library or treasury of Moissac.

To my mind, such speculations are really of secondary significance in penetrating the creative process at Moissac, since two-dimensional models of whatever kind would still have left the Moissac carvers without guidance in the difficulties of narration on a free-standing pyramidal form. By virtue of its functioning within an idiosyncratic architectural space, the cloister capital presents special problems for the comprehension of narrative subject-matter that do not exist in the two-dimensional arts. Many of the narrative compositions of the Moissac capitals have the character of uneasy constructs, suggesting they were *ad hoc* solutions to a set of compositional problems for which precedents did not exist.

Compounding these problems, both for the sculptors and for viewers, was the evident premium placed on narrative discursiveness, whether the story being told was that of a saint's life or one of the miracles or parables of Christ. This is perhaps the most distinctive feature of the historiated capitals of Moissac. Whereas the naïve story-telling methods more characteristic of other Romanesque capitals in the region might summarize the Fall of Man in the simple image of the Tree flanked by Adam and Eve (as at Lescure, Moirax, Cadalen, Roquesérière, and Bruniquel),[51] at Moissac the story must be pictured in detail, in successive images of the Temptation, the Lord's Reproach, the Expulsion, and the Labours of Adam and Eve. Similarly, the parable of Dives and Lazarus, one of the most popular themes in capital sculpture in the region, was most often epitomized in the emblematic figure of the Rich Man, crouching and weighed down by his money bag, as he is tormented by demons, for example in the capitals at Lescure (west portal), Cénac (apse), and Cadalen (south portal), as well as in the famous capitals of the Porte des Comtes. At Moissac, in contrast, fully four individual episodes are crowded on to the capital devoted to this theme, with Dives Feasting, Lazarus before the Gates of the Rich Man (his wounds licked by dogs), Lazarus in the Bosom of Abraham, and Dives Punished in Hell. The result, in visual terms, is nearly indecipherable on a first viewing. Clearly the imperative of narrative detail took precedence here over visual or conceptual clarity.

Pl. 71 left
Pl. 77

Pl. 72

The same imperative is unmistakable throughout the programme of sculptured capitals at Moissac. In earlier Byzantine and Western medieval art the theme of the Transfiguration is most often transformed into an image of great symbolic power in which the transfigured Christ is presented as a frontal icon, flanked symmetrically by Moses and Elijah. At Moissac, in contrast, we are given a dramatic acting out of the narrative, in which Christ is engaged in dialogue with the two Prophets. On the other side of the capital we see him later descending the mountain with his disciples. Many of the capitals at Moissac present the viewer with difficulties in identifying the beginning or end point of the narrative or in disentangling one episode from another. The capitals devoted to hagiographic themes, such as the lives of St Benedict and St Stephen, may be counted among these. The difficulties stem from the preferred method of narration at Moissac, one that gives equal weight to sequential episodes of a story, rather than selecting a climactic image to epitomize the whole.

Schapiro perceptively characterized this narrative method at Moissac when he described the capital of Adam and Eve, in which the primary characters are repeated in each of four episodes. In his words, 'we are asked to view the figures in a sequence in time as well as space, and to read them as we read the text they illustrate'.[52] His observation appears to have considerable pertinence for the process of invention that lies behind the more than fifty historiated capitals of the Moissac cloister. The great majority of the narrative compositions give the appearance of being constructed *ad hoc* according to textual modes of thinking, rather than taking their inspiration from a previous pictorial tradition. This is suggested by the unmistakable preference for discursive narration, as distinct from methods that might epitomize a story in a single episode selected for its dramatic action or might telescope several activities into a single picture. Because existing image models in the pictorial arts were in many ways ill-suited for adaptation to a four-sided capital, the sculptors, in most cases, may have constructed their narratives on the immediate basis of a written text or, more likely, on the basis of verbal instructions from a member of the monastic community. Like others of the monastic profession, this monk-iconographer would have been overwhelmingly textual and verbal in his training and orientation.

[51] See Ch. 5 for these churches.   [52] Schapiro, 'Romanesque Sculpture of Moissac. I', 156.

In the capitals produced for La Daurade by the Moissac workshop, the discursive mode also determined narrative structure in the historiated capitals. A narrative focus or climax is difficult to identify in any of the capitals. On Mesplé 107, for example, we are shown, on successive faces, Salome Dancing, the Feast of Herod, the Execution of John the Baptist, and Salome presenting the head to Herodias. Even on capitals devoted to more than one theme, as in the double capital of the *Entry into Jerusalem* and the *Arrest of Christ*, activity is dispersed around the circumference in a figure-by-figure description of the episode that suggests a verbal exposition.

The sense of the simultaneity of action—action as it is really taken in by the viewer who witnesses a dramatic event—is eminently capable of being reproduced in the visual arts, but such simultaneity can only be *suggested* by verbal means, whether written or oral. A narrator can inform his readers or listeners that more than one activity occurred at the same time or that more than one person took part, but these elements of the narrative, by necessity, can only be described or recounted in sequence. In their descriptive approach to narration, the capitals of the first series from La Daurade and their counterparts at Moissac seem more closely tied to such verbal models than they do to pictorial ones.

That the invention of visual narration at Moissac was closely bound up with textual thinking is also implied in the liberal use of tituli and inscriptions as prominent elements of the historiated capitals. These inscribed words name the players pictured in the religious dramas, or occasionally excerpt portions of Scripture which describe the players' actions or record their speech. The role of these inscriptions can hardly be explained as purely informational, nevertheless. As Schapiro observed in his early study of the cloister, in the most archaic of the capitals, the forms of the letters or word segments are made to play the role of abstract elements of the design as they are inscribed directly on to the drum in the interstices between figures.[53] Indeed, individual letters may be turned in reverse or entire words made to read backward to serve better the ornamental or compositional aims. This suggests that word and picture elements are viewed as interchangeable, an attitude that gives text a strong role to play in these early historiated capitals. Two of the eight capitals from the first Daurade series, *Daniel in the Lions' Den* and *Christ and the Canaanite Woman*, make text a part of their pictographic method as well. Schapiro referred to the liberal use of inscriptions as one of the more archaic aspects of the Moissac cloister capitals. It seems, indeed, to be allied to the more abstract (that is, textual) conception of narration which these capitals exhibit. Such inscriptions were repudiated altogether in the second series from La Daurade, where they would have insinuated an abstract order of signification entirely at odds with the concrete realism of the Passion scenes.

The varied and inventive exploitation of narrative themes in the cloisters of Moissac and its dependent priory in Toulouse are exceptional in the region for the early Romanesque period. The following chapter will explore the formation of this art by looking into the origins and make-up of the Moissac workshop.

[53] Schapiro, 'Romanesque Sculpture of Moissac. I', 160–1.

5

FORMATION OF THE FIRST WORKSHOP

THE LITERATURE on the Moissac cloister, when it has dealt with questions of origins and stylistic connections, has traditionally framed the investigation in terms of the relationship between Moissac and the vast programme of decoration undertaken at the basilica of Saint-Sernin in Toulouse.[1] This has tended to tie the cloister of Moissac into the discussion of the origins and dispersion of the so-called 'pilgrimage style' shared by a network of early Romanesque monuments distributed on both slopes of the Pyrenees to the west and south of Toulouse.[2] It is clear that the foliate and animal ornament of Moissac and Saint-Sernin does belong to a common repertory associated with the 'pilgrimage style'. In fact, so close are many of the ornamental capital types of the two monuments that the Moissac workshop must have drawn some of its sculptors from the larger chantier at Saint-Sernin. And Moissac carvers, again on the basis of foliate capitals, seem to have participated in projects as far afield as the castle church of Loarre in Aragon.

Yet important components of the Moissac workshop cannot be explained by the 'pilgrimage style' and its international diffusion. Specifically, the most striking aspect of the Moissac cloister programme, its remarkable series of narrative capitals, has little in common with the figured capitals of Saint-Sernin, which are few in number and show little interest in narrative imagery. Nor can parallels to the Moissac figure style and narrative originality be found in workshops that either fed into or profited from the art of Saint-Sernin at sites such as Jaca, Fromistà, Nogal de las Huertas, Leòn, Santiago, Saint-Sever-sur-l'Adour, and Saint-Gaudens, among others. Instead, the origin of the distinctive figure types of the Moissac capitals and the early interest these capitals exhibit in narrative themes from the Old and New Testaments, should be sought in local carving traditions which did not participate in the diffusion of the 'pilgrimage style'. These traditions had their home in the Tarn and Garonne river valleys to the north and north-west of Toulouse. The Moissac workshop, in brief, reveals a distinctive

[1] See especially Marcel Durliat, 'Les Origines de la sculpture romane à Toulouse et à Moissac', *Cahiers de civilisation médiévale*, 12 (1969), 349–64; Thomas Lyman, 'Notes on the Porte Miègeville Capitals', *Art Bulletin*, 49(1967), 33–5; Ruth Capelle Kline, 'The Decorated Imposts of the Cloister of Moissac', Ph.D. thesis, University of California at Los Angeles (1977), *passim*. Schapiro's study ('The Romanesque Sculpture of Moissac, I', *Romanesque Art* (New York, 1977)) does not deal with the question of origins.

[2] On the current use and definition of the term 'pilgrimage style', see my comments in the Introduction. Gaillard, Durliat, and Lyman have all rejected the notion of a school of Romanesque sculpture fostered by the pilgrimage routes, but the term continues to be applied to the constellation of

monuments whose style was formed in the workshops of Jaca, Saint-Sernin, and Santiago. See also the recent contributions of Katherine Watson, 'The Corbels in the Dome of Loarre', *Journal of the Warburg and Courtauld Institutes*, 41 (1978), 297–301; Serafín Moralejo-Alvarez, 'La Sculpture romane de la cathédrale de Jaca: état des questions', *Les Cahiers de Saint-Michel de Cuxa*, 10 (1979), 79–106; David Simon, 'Le Sarcophage de Doña Sancha à Jaca', ibid. 107–24; id., 'L'Art roman: source de l'art roman', *Les Cahiers de Saint-Michel de Cuxa*, 11 (1980), 249–67; Marcel Durliat, 'Les Pyrénées et l'art roman', ibid. 153–74; and John Williams, 'San Isidoro in Leòn', *Art Bulletin*, 55 (1973), 170–84; id., '"Spain or Toulouse"', *Actas del XXIII. Congreso internacional de historia del arte* (Granada, 1973), 557–65.

character and make-up in which the contribution of sculptors who had taken part in the vast programme of decoration at Saint-Sernin was only one component.

That Toulousan component is, nevertheless, an important one in the Moissac cloister, and we shall look at it first. The preference for the Corinthian-derived foliate capital, ornamented with a varied but distinctively Toulousan repertory of surface decoration, betrays the presence at Moissac of one or more sculptors who had been engaged in the first construction campaign at Saint-Sernin. At Moissac the pure foliate capitals constitute almost a quarter of the ensemble —eighteen capitals. Every type represented there has its counterpart in capitals of the eastern parts of Saint-Sernin. The same repertory of foliage motifs decorates the majority of the seventy-six imposts and the pier mouldings at Moissac. In addition, the capitals with birds and fantastic beasts take their motifs from the pilgrimage repertory of animal ornament employed by the first workshop at Saint-Sernin.

THE CONTRIBUTION OF SAINT-SERNIN AND THE 'PILGRIMAGE STYLE'

The relative chronology of Moissac and Saint-Sernin remains a matter of some disagreement in the literature and, in general, the artistic relationship between the two workshops has not been satisfactorily defined. The confusion stems in great part from the ambiguity of the documents that refer to construction at Saint-Sernin in the eleventh and twelfth centuries and what these texts mean for the absolute chronology of the various parts of the building. The only certain date in this history is the consecration of the church and the altar of St Saturninus during a visit by Pope Urban II in 1096.[3] Chapter 2 summarized the issues that remain controversial in regard to the vast building programme of the basilica. When did construction actually begin— about 1080, shortly after the laying out of the hemicycle of Saint-Sernin's sister basilica at Santiago de Compostela, or perhaps as early as 1073–5, when, the documents imply, the canons had already undergone reform and were living a regular life? How far had work proceeded when the canons were temporarily ousted from the church by the bishop and count of Toulouse in 1081/1082? When did Bernard Gelduinus and his workshop join the chantier at Saint-Sernin? Had the transept tribunes been constructed and was the nave perimeter wall standing at the time of the ceremony of 1096? And is the leadership of Canon Raymond Gayrard to be associated with the first or the second major campaign of construction?

As I concluded in Chapter 2, the significantly different, even contrary, meanings that have been extracted by scholars from the same few written documents indicate just how ambiguous are these texts for the history of Saint-Sernin. Their value for establishing an absolute chronology for the building campaigns has yet to be convincingly demonstrated, though it is unquestionably important to go back to them with a mind open to fresh interpretations as other kinds of evidence emerge. Our concern here is the formation of the Moissac cloister workshop, components of which came from Saint-Sernin. Important insights into this formation can be gained by examining the sculptural decoration of those parts of Saint-Sernin that are universally recognized to be the oldest, the apse hemicycle and its chapels and the lower storey of the transept.

---

[3] See the *Chronicon Sancti Saturnini Tolosae* in *HGL*, vol. v, cols. 49–50. The consecration is confirmed in a letter of 20 July 1096 from Urban II to the canons of Saint-Sernin (Célestin Douais, *Cartulaire de l'abbaye de Saint-Sernin* (Paris and Toulouse, 1887), app. 3. 475–7). The dedication of the altar was to SS Saturninus and Asiseclus and to All Saints.

From any point of view, the task of unravelling the building campaigns and progress of decoration at Saint-Sernin is a daunting one, in a basilica whose interior sculpture comprises more than 300 capitals, of which approximately 260 are Romanesque.[4] Modern studies of the basilica have sought a more precise system for the description, classification, and analysis of, in particular, the vast ensemble of ornamental capitals. The colloquium convened at Toulouse in 1971 by the Société française d'archéologie produced reports aimed at such classification,[5] but the imprecisions and confusions concealed in those and earlier studies have been elucidated by Thomas Lyman through the structure of his own analysis.[6]

It is not my objective here to undertake a critique of the terms in which these classifications have been defined nor to present an alternative system for distinguishing capital types or their evolution at Saint-Sernin. All the ornamental capital types elaborated within the ground storey of the hemicycle and transept of Saint-Sernin are represented in microcosm at Moissac, though accommodated to the substantially different architecture of the cloister capital. The vocabulary and grammar of this ornament come from Saint-Sernin, as, so I believe, did the sculptors who carved the Moissac capitals, and it is the nature of this relationship that I am concerned to define here. Much of what I observe has been observed by others, but its significance for the make-up of the workshop at Moissac has not been put into perspective.

With few exceptions, all of the foliate capitals on the interior of Saint-Sernin, no matter what the individual vegetal motifs from which their ornament is constructed, are derived in varying degrees of kinship from the classical Corinthian capital, as Lyman's taxonomy has tracked them.[7] Even those that are universally recognized to stand apart as a primitive first series, namely small window capitals in the oldest parts of the outer hemicycle wall and the south apsidiol,[8] take their essential elements from the structure of the Corinthian capital—corner volutes, central console, and distinctly defined, overlapping registers of ornament (Pls. 58 and 59). At the same time, these early capitals aggressively assert anti-classical sympathies in the small birds and rampant quadrupeds, confronted or addorsed, that perch in the upper registers of foliage.

Most important to our study, some of the individual foliate motifs that were rapidly to be worked into the full-blown ornamental style of the first campaign at Saint-Sernin are already present in the vocabulary of the earliest ambulatory capitals and their imposts, though on a modest scale. Some of these motifs, then, must have had a prior history of usage in the region. The extraordinary technical brilliance in the exploitation of this ornament at Saint-Sernin and in the cloisters of Moissac and La Daurade suggests that this was, indeed, the case. Distinctly

---

[4] This is Cabanot's figure ('Le Décor sculpté de la basilique Saint-Sernin de Toulouse', *Bulletin monumental*, 132 (1974) 106). For an early inventory of the capitals, see Jules de Lahondés, 'Les Chapiteaux de Saint-Sernin', *Mémoires de la société archéologique du Midi de la France*, 14 (1891), 258–83.

[5] See Cabanot, 'Décor sculpté', esp. 106–19; also the review of the colloquium by Willibald Sauerländer, 'Das sechste internationale Colloquium der "Société française d'archéologie"', *Kunstchronik*, 24 (1971), 341–7.

[6] See, in particular, Thomas Lyman, 'Terminology, Typology, Taxonomy: An Approach to the Study of Architectural Sculpture of the Romanesque Period', *Gazette des beaux-arts*, 88 (1976), 223–7. Lyman's nearly 25 years of work on the basilica of Saint-Sernin, represented in numerous scholarly articles (see above Ch. 2 n. 5), will see its definitive publication

in his forthcoming monograph, *Saint-Sernin of Toulouse: The Art of the Romanesque Builder*.

[7] Lyman, 'Terminology', fig. 1.

[8] Durliat, along with others, has localized the beginnings of construction at Saint-Sernin on the south side of the apse hemicycle and the westernmost apsidiol on the south side (see 'La Construction de Saint-Sernin', *Bulletin monumental*, 121 (1963), 154–5; id., 'Origines de sculpture à Toulouse et à Moissac', 350). Based on the capital sculpture, however, I believe work may have started simultaneously on the north and south sides of the hemicycle perimeter wall (see the 2 capitals in the westernmost window of the ambulatory wall on the north side). Cabanot also points to these as belonging to the primitive series ('Décor sculpté', 107 and n. 1).

Pls. 58 and 60

Pl. 59

productive for the full-blown ornamental vocabulary of Saint-Sernin are the delicate foliate sprays in which each tendril terminates in a curl and the bunches are held together by a band of chevrons, seen in two capitals of the south-west apsidiol. Also to be exploited in the full-blown Saint-Sernin ornament was the plant form that Lyman calls the running stem rinceau, a version of which appears already on the small window capital and its impost on the south side of the axial bay of the ambulatory. This motif, comprised of a five-pointed curled leaf within a vine circlet, star-like in form and with a deeply depressed centre, may be based on the ivy plant.[9]

The regional—or extra-regional—origins of the sculptors who carved these earliest ambulatory capitals at Saint-Sernin have not been investigated. Both Sauerländer and Cabanot describe the capitals as belonging to a 'pre-Romanesque' tradition.[10] It is not wholly clear what they mean to imply by this term, however, within the context of eleventh-century sculptural development in the region. Durliat, who describes a rapid evolution of style at Saint-Sernin, away from the small-scale motifs and limited repertory of the primitive series, towards the more forceful and three-dimensional forms of the later hemicycle and transept, says only that the small ambulatory capitals at Saint-Sernin 'belong to the past'.[11] Unquestionably they do, but given their importance to the understanding of the full-blown first style at Saint-Sernin, it is legitimate to wonder what the precursors to these carvings in the region looked like.

Their sculptors, and the team of masons who constructed the fabric of the building, must have worked somewhere before being called to Saint-Sernin. Monastic expansion began in earnest in the Midi in the late 1040s and 1050s, as we saw in Chapter 1. Virtually the entire first generation of building in the region has been lost to us, most regrettably the eleventh-century church of Moissac, spearhead of the reform, consecrated by Abbot Durandus in 1063. Durandus was one of the great builder abbots of Moissac, making it his mission to clear forests and found new churches in the lands that came into the possession of the abbey as the result of the Cluniac expansion. Vast new properties and churches also came under the administration of Moissac during the abbacy of Durandus's successor, Hunaldus (1072–c.1085).[12] In 1064, before becoming abbot, Hunaldus had founded the priory of Saint-Martin at Layrac, just to the west of Moissac. He later retired to it and was buried there.[13] The present Romanesque church on the site undoubtedly replaces an earlier one of Hunaldus's time,[14] and it may be assumed that many of the churches brought under the administration of Moissac during his abbacy were rebuilt, renovated, or added to, including the important abbey of Lézat, to the south of Toulouse, united to Cluny in 1073 and reformed by Moissac.

Were it possible to recover any of these buildings from the years between 1045 and 1080, they would almost surely reveal regional preparation for the early sculptural style at Saint-

---

[9] A third motif, Cabanot's 'double palmette', may also have its origin in the early series of ambulatory capitals. It appears in a window capital of the north ambulatory (see Cabanot, 'Décor sculpté', fig. 9).

[10] Sauerländer, 'Sechste internationale Colloquium der "Société française d'archéologie"', 343; Cabanot, 'Décor sculpté', 107. The only regional associations cited by Cabanot for these types are in the north apsidiol of Saint-Sever-sur-l'Adour, which he describes as slightly later than those of Saint-Sernin (ibid. 107 n. 2).

[11] 'Construction de Saint-Sernin', 154; id., 'Origines de sculpture à Toulouse et à Moissac', 350. Durliat believes that the full-blown style of the Porte des Comtes Master and his workshop (the style of the vast number of figured and foliate capitals in the hemicycle, the transept, and the Porte des Comtes) evolved rapidly at Saint-Sernin as work progressed around the hemicycle. He seems to imply that it evolved out of the earliest essays in the sculptured capitals, those of the south ambulatory and its chapels, but he does not say whether he believes the same sculptors were involved from the inception of building to the emergence of the full-blown Porte des Comtes style.

[12] See the Chronicle of Aymeric de Peyrac (Paris, BN, MS lat. 4991-A, fo. 158ʳ, col. 2) and Ernest Rupin, *L'Abbaye et les cloîtres de Moissac* (Paris, 1897), 52 and 59–61.

[13] *GC*, vol. i, col. 163.

[14] Pierre Dubourg-Noves, 'L'Église Saint-Martin de Layrac', *Congrès archéologique*, 127, Agenais (1969), 279–82.

Sernin. Some of the early ornament at Saint-Sernin, in particular the palmette of five or seven lobes inscribed within a frame, has been associated with Spanish Romanesque sculpture since the studies of Gaillard and can be found at churches as far flung as León and Sainte-Foy at Conques.[15] Nevertheless, the regional interpretation of this motif has a very distinctive character at Toulouse and Moissac, being very crisply cut and less thick and fleshy than the Spanish ornament. Other major components of the workshop responsible for laying out the hemicycle and transept of Saint-Sernin have no relationship to the work of Spanish Romanesque sculptors or to those of Conques, specifically the style of the Porte des Comtes Master himself and his assistants in the figural carvings. On this evidence, it seems likely that the first workshop at Saint-Sernin was drawn together not from far afield but from sculptors who had been constructing and decorating churches in the region for a generation. The style of the early ambulatory capitals could thus hardly be considered pre-Romanesque. Rather, these capitals should be considered the culmination of the first generation of architectural sculpture produced by the eleventh-century monastic expansion between Moissac and Toulouse.

Pl. 62, impost

That this first Romanesque sculpture was dominated by ornament and not figurative work can be surmised from the inventiveness of the ornamental capitals in the hemicycle of Saint-Sernin. The facility with which the first workshop played upon and used to its artistic ends the diverse foliage repertory contrasts strikingly with its much more inhibited definition of the human form. Within the confines of the hemicycle and the lower transept at Saint-Sernin, the first workshop elaborated all of the foliate capital types that appear in the smaller programme of the Moissac cloister. The predominant groups are those with pure acanthus foliage (represented at Moissac by Schapiro 8, 23, 34, 36, 59, 62, and 70) and those whose ornament is built up of foliate 'medallions'—a single leaf contained within a vine circlet attached to a running stem. Their counterparts at Moissac are Schapiro 21, 31, 33, 41, 45, 55, 68, and 74.[16] The leaves that comprise the individual motifs of the running stem ornament are of three basic forms: a bilaterally symmetrical, heart-shaped palmette of five lobes, upright or reversed; a star-like five- or seven-pointed leaf with depressed centre that we suggested earlier may be based on ivy; and a highly stylized, tightly curled leaf with great torsion. All of these motifs also form part of the common ornament on the imposts of Saint-Sernin and Moissac.[17]

Pl. 61

Pl. 62

Pl. 65

Pl. 65
Pl. 64

A third type of capital is not found in the eastern parts of Saint-Sernin but does appear in the ground storey of the south transept (west arcade of the south transept arm, second pier from the crossing). Not common in the repertory of the Toulousan basilica, it is represented in only one example at Moissac (Schapiro 65), although related motifs are found on imposts there (Schapiro 23, 29, and 51). The larger design of this capital is based on symmetrical bifurcation. Enlarged sprays of pointed leaves resembling accordion pleating form twin fans, bundled together at the centre by chevron bands. Below the bands, the stems of the upright foliage fans bifurcate and curl upward in opposite directions. The effect is strongly formal and remote from organic growth. Next to the example in the south transept at Saint-Sernin, a hybrid variation

Pl. 66

[15] See Georges Gaillard, *Les Débuts de la sculpture romane espagnole* (Paris, 1938), 19–21; Cabanot, 'Décor sculpté', 107–10.
[16] All the foliate capitals of Moissac are illustrated in Rupin, *L'Abbaye de Moissac*, though he uses a different numbering system than that shared by Schapiro and Vidal (see Rupin, *L'Abbaye de Moissac*, 27, fig. 4).

[17] See the Ph.D. thesis by Kline ('Decorated Imposts'), who developed a precise descriptive terminology to distinguish foliate motifs and their evolution on the imposts of Moissac and Saint-Sernin.

of the type appears, in which the bifurcated fans are combined with a lower collar of upright, heart-shaped leaves alternating with human heads in pure Porte des Comtes style.[18]

In the final type of foliage capital at Moissac (Schapiro 26), the drum is enclosed by large leaves resembling those of the fern, arranged so that the central spine of a leaf defines each angle of the capital. Prototypes for this variety at Moissac may be found at Saint-Sernin in the choir, on the south side (first bay to the east of the crossing).

Lyman's analysis of the capital variations at Saint-Sernin has made clear how important is the morphology of the capital structure to our understanding of the processes of invention within the vast programme of decoration there. Considerations of two and three register variants, the proportions of the registers to each other and to the drum as a whole, and the degree of kinship each variant bears to the antique Corinthian model are essentials of his analysis. The foliate capitals of Moissac diverge much more markedly in these respects from the classical Corinthian model than do any of the variants at Saint-Sernin. The Moissac capitals are broad at the top and narrow rapidly towards the astragal, giving them a much squatter shape than those of Saint-Sernin. On the broadened and squat Moissac drum, three rows of foliage could hardly have been accommodated without destroying entirely the proportions of foliage to capital. Hence only one and two row varieties occur in the cloister. In some of the capitals of Moissac, emphasis on the abstract and ornamental properties of the
Pl. 64   pattern has been enhanced by suppressing other references to the Corinthian capital. In these examples there are no overlapping rows of foliage. The drum has been simplified to bevelled planes that produce an eight-sided pyramid. In its geometric shape, the form of the drum here most nearly approaches the simple pyramid used for the historiated capitals of the cloister.

The dimensions and shaping of Romanesque capitals are often essential clues in the identification of a workshop, particularly when there is the suspicion that large numbers of capitals may have been blocked out and produced in series before placement, as Lyman has suggested was the case at Saint-Sernin.[19] But in this case, the substantial difference in capital structure between Saint-Sernin and Moissac cannot be taken to indicate a difference in workshop, so close are certain of the capitals, in their motifs, patterns, and fine details of execution. Rather, the distinctive capital shape employed at Moissac is an accommodation to its function within the architecture of the cloister arcade. In order to provide a broad and uniform support for the cloister wall above and to effect the transition to the slender colonnettes below, the Moissac capitals were required to be broad and flaring at the top while narrowing rapidly at the neck. The cylindrical bell of the Corinthian capital is not at all suited to serve within a cloister arcade, unless two drums are paired to form a true twin capital. A number of Romanesque cloisters do, in fact, adopt this solution to the problem of broad support, for example at Saint-Trophime at Arles, where the twin drums are closely modelled
Pl. 191   on the classical Corinthian bell capital.[20] In the tribunes of Saint-Sernin itself, where double columns perform a supporting function similar to the paired supports in the arcades of Moissac, the double capitals are formed of two separate drums, thus maintaining a close kinship to the Corinthian bell capital throughout the decoration of the interior.

At Moissac a different choice was made. It seems probable that the decision to use a broad

---

[18] This is one of the capitals at Saint-Sernin that suggests the carvers of the foliate and figural capitals were not necessarily different individuals.

[19] Lyman, 'Terminology', 223–4.

[20] See also the cloister gallery and tribune at Serrabone, where single cubic drums are paired to form double capitals (Marcel Durliat, *Roussillon roman* (La Pierre-qui-vire, 1975), pls. 55 and 59).

pyramidal capital not subdivided into twin drums was dictated there by the decision to introduce complex historiated themes into the capital decoration, though this can only be speculation. As we saw in the previous chapter, the complexities of composing on a four-sided capital were formidable for sculptors who may have had no prior experience with this challenge.[21] The difficulties of the task set for these sculptors, then, probably determined the design of the capitals for the entire cloister, with the structure of the foliate capitals following suit. Twin capitals of such ornate beauty as Schapiro 50 in the north gallery show how ingeniously the foliate capitals were accommodated to the structural requirements of the cloister, while maintaining the suggestion of a true double capital through the subtleties of the decorative pattern.

Pl. 65

The different capital shapes at Saint-Sernin and Moissac are functions, then, of their architectural roles. At the same time, the common bases used for constructing ornamental pattern in the two groups of capitals betray them as the productions of sculptors who worked at both sites. The Moissac foliate capitals, which are more uniform in execution than those in the eastern parts of Saint-Sernin,[22] correspond most closely in style and motifs to examples in the south transept and in the transept tribunes of the Toulousan basilica. Lyman has rightly cautioned that strict correspondences cannot be drawn between the progress of construction at Saint-Sernin and the evolution of its sculptural decoration, since many capitals may have been carved in advance and left over for later use.[23] At the same time, broad patterns of change from the capitals of the hemicycle piers to those of the lower transept and the transept tribunes do seem to reflect an evolution in the interpretation of ornament as large numbers of capitals were produced. Some motifs drop out of use and new ones are introduced. For example, a motif of a single upright flower with rounded petals, poised at the top of a vertical stem, initially appeared on some of the earliest capitals and imposts of the ambulatory, sometimes in conjunction with the asymmetrical curled leaf. This type of leaf, as we saw, became a staple of Toulousan and Moissac ornament, while the upright flower was dropped, as were the linked spirals on early double capitals in the ambulatory of the choir at Saint-Sernin. We have already mentioned the new capital type with bifurcated fans of foliage that does not make its appearance until the western arcade of the south transept at Saint-Sernin. This late arrival was, however, included in the Moissac repertory.

Pls. 58 and 59

Pl. 66

The foliate capitals of the transept tribunes at Saint-Sernin continue to employ the repertory of capital types and motifs established in the ground storey. An unmistakable movement towards finer detail and greater complexity in some ornamental patterns is observable in the tribunes, however. For example, the use of fine striations on volute stems, a frequent refinement in the Moissac cloister, is absent in the earliest construction at Saint-Sernin but appears several times in the tribunes. The motif of the eight-pointed rosette contained within a roundel on the console of the tribune capital illustrated here was a late introduction into the repertory at Saint-Sernin, as was the tightly coiled, stylized leaf that appears on some imposts of the tribune, but both are common in the Moissac cloister (see Schapiro 21, 31, and 55). The

Pl. 65

Pl. 67

---

[21] A possible inspiration exists for the kind of double capital devised at Moissac, in the interior of Saint-Michel de Lescure, in the capitals of *Daniel in the Lions' Den* and the *Meeting of Jacob and Esau* (Pls. 74 and 75). This could be one more clue that the sculptors who had worked in this small church contributed to the formation of the Moissac workshop (see below).

[22] I take this unity in style among the Moissac capitals to indicate that they were produced within a relatively short time span.

[23] Lyman, 'Terminology', 223–4.

Pl. 65

Pl. 68

combining of two different ornamental motifs or two different-sized leaves on a single capital or impost was a common method of achieving greater complexity and enrichment of pattern by the Moissac workshop. This degree of free inventiveness with pattern is not seen in the eastern parts of Saint-Sernin, but some capitals and imposts in the transept tribunes exhibit this free play. Finally, the affectation of certain fine details of finish, such as the frequent use of chamfered astragals or ones decorated with a narrow fillet, also betrays the close kinship in workshop practices and training between sculptors at Moissac and the workshop of Saint-Sernin.[24]

What do these observations permit us to conclude about the relationship between Moissac and Saint-Sernin? They do not enable us to date precisely the beginning of work at Moissac or to say exactly when a sculptor or sculptors of ornamental capitals broke off from the Toulousan workshop to journey to the Cluniac abbey. But they leave little doubt that the basic repertory of motifs and range of capital types in the Moissac cloister were created in the chantier of Saint-Sernin. There is universal agreement that the lower storey of the hemicycle and transept of Saint-Sernin was laid down very rapidly in a continuous campaign. The most conservative dating for this portion puts its completion, up to the tops of the transept portals, at no later than 1090 and Lyman believes this portion may have been under way as early as 1081/2.[25] If the Moissac cloister was completed in 1100, as its inscription tells us, its workshop would hardly have been forming before 1090 and the investiture troubles at the abbey in the 1080s (described in Chapter 1) make this even more unlikely. Moreover, given the subsequent urgency to complete the transepts of Saint-Sernin before the visit of the pope in 1096, it seems unlikely that the chantier at Toulouse would have been ready to give up a sculptor or sculptors to Moissac before that date. I will have more to say about this below when I discuss the relationship of the Gelduinus workshop to sculpture at Moissac.

While the preceding evidence indicates that the Moissac workshop recruited a sculptor or sculptors of ornamental capitals from among the sizeable team at Saint-Sernin, it is equally important to distinguish what Moissac did not borrow from the larger project. No figural work by the Master of the Porte des Comtes himself is found in the Moissac cloister. The historiated capitals by the Porte des Comtes Master and his workshop on the interior of Saint-Sernin are few in number compared to the decorative varieties. They are, nevertheless, important as some of the earliest essays into sculptural definition of the human figure by Romanesque carvers in Toulouse, at the same time as they attempted a relatively sophisticated iconography.[26] The *Incredulity of Thomas* on the axial pier inside the north transept portal is

Pl. 69

the most ambitious historiated capital by this workshop in the interior of Saint-Sernin. In the figures of Christ, Thomas, and the Apostles, the facial features, with their broad, wedge-shaped noses and wide, slit-like mouths, have a coarseness that is unlike the carefully incised facial features of Moissac. The drapery folds are similarly coarse and rudimentary in their definition, and do not exhibit the characteristic patterns found throughout the Moissac capitals, such as the overlapping, plate-like folds on the torso or the shirred or bulbous sleeves that identify Moissac drapery style. A comparison with the identical subject of the *Incredulity*

---

[24] See Lyman, 'Porte Miègeville Capitals', 33–4, for his analysis of the relationship between ornamental capitals in the tribunes of Saint-Sernin and in the cloister of Moissac.

[25] See Ch. 2 for a summary of Lyman's account of the building campaigns at Saint-Sernin.

[26] On the iconography of the historiated capitals of Saint-Sernin see Lyman, 'Porte des Comtes Master', 12–39. Lyman has proposed that the historiated capitals of the interior were meant to be seen in a planned sequence that extends the programme of the Porte des Comtes.

on a capital by the Moissac workshop from La Daurade highlights the greater animation and   *Pl. 43*
more expressive gestures of the Moissac style, as figures incline and look towards one another.
The figures by the Porte des Comtes Master are, by contrast, curiously incommunicative, as
their heads are uniformly turned towards the viewer. What is more, the *Incredulity of Thomas*
is the only capital by the Porte des Comtes workshop at Saint-Sernin that attempts a
complicated grouping of figures in narrative interaction. The other figured capitals by this
workshop employ heraldic and repetitive compositions that feature a crouching or seated
figure at the angle of the drum, flanked by menacing griffons or, in the iconography of the
Porte des Comtes itself, held fast by other flanking figures or tormented by demons.[27] The
other figured compositions by this workshop are equally simple, featuring an armed combat
between warriors and the theme of *St Michael Slaying the Dragon*, repeated in twin images on
two capitals at Saint-Sernin.[28] The capital of the *Sacrifice of Isaac* in the upper storey of the
north transept is the only historiated capital at Saint-Sernin that shows the facility to engage
figures in narrative interaction of the type characteristic of Moissac, and, as Lyman points out,
this capital is anomalous in the programme of Saint-Sernin.[29]

Two capitals at Moissac do indicate a knowledge on the part of Moissac carvers of the
favourite themes encountered at Saint-Sernin. In the east gallery, a capital with crouching male
figures menaced by griffons (Schapiro 29) was obviously influenced by the capitals of the Porte
des Comtes workshop in its imagery and use of the corner placement.[30] Similarly the curious
device of repeating the *Combat of the Archangel Michael and the Dragon* in a mirror image
was reproduced in a capital on the north-east pier at Moissac (Schapiro 39). Nevertheless,
there is no question of the participation of a Saint-Sernin sculptor in the carving of either
capital. The figure style and drapery patterns are those of the Moissac workshop. Typical is the
balloon-like inflation of the sleeves at the elbow, in the Moissac capital of the crouching men, a
motif not encountered in the style of the Porte des Comtes Master.

In short, the Moissac workshop did not take its figure style from the sculptors of the Porte
des Comtes. Nor could the limited imagery and formulary compositions of the first workshop
at Saint-Sernin have provided the source for the wealth of biblical themes and their more
demanding figure groupings that decorate the capitals of Moissac.

More difficult to define is the role that Bernard Gelduinus or members of his team may have
played in the sculptural programme of the Moissac cloister. Bernard Gelduinus, the individual
who signed the famous altar table of Saint-Sernin, has been identified as the head of a marble
carving workshop that also executed the seven reliefs now enwalled in the apse (facing into the
ambulatory), as well as historiated capitals and imposts, not of marble, in the tribunes of the
pilgrimage church.[31]

---

[27] Lyman, 'Porte des Comtes Master', pls. 9a–e.

[28] The 2 capitals of *St Michael Slaying the Dragon* occur on
the axial pier inside the Porte des Comtes and in the south
gallery of the sanctuary (ibid., pls. 11b and 15a).

[29] Lyman, 'Porte Miègeville Capitals', 31, and figs. 30 and
31. Stylistically the *Sacrifice of Isaac* is closest to 2 capitals in
the transept tribunes with the double image of *St Michael and
the Dragon* and the *Maestas Domini*. Also atypical for Saint-
Sernin is the presence of foliage behind the figures in the
Sacrifice of Isaac capital.

[30] Rupin, *L'Abbaye de Moissac*, fig. 114.

[31] In addition to the studies by Lyman and Durliat already

cited, there is an extensive literature on the art of Bernard
Gelduinus and his workshop. See Paul Deschamps, 'L'Autel de
Saint-Sernin de Toulouse et les sculptures du cloître de
Moissac', *Bulletin archéologique* (1923), 239–50; Étienne
Delaruelle, 'Les Bas-reliefs de Saint-Sernin', *Annales du Midi*,
41 (1929), 49–60; Friedrich Gerke, *Der Tischaltar des Bernard
Gilduin in Saint-Sernin in Toulouse*, Akademie der Wissen-
schaften und der Literatur in Mainz, Abhandlungen der
geiste-und sozialwissenschaftlichen Klasse, 1958, 8 (Wiesbaden,
1958), 453–513; M. F. Hearn, *Romanesque Sculpture* (Ithaca,
NY, 1981), 69–80.

Since no evidence of the style of Gelduinus is visible in the sculpture of the first campaign at La Daurade, the question of his possible participation in the workshop at Moissac might seem tangential to our study here. It should be borne in mind, however, that the sample of surviving sculptures from the first workshop at La Daurade is small. We have no knowledge of possible large-scale sculpture in marble in the Toulousan cloister. Nevertheless, given its close relationship to the sculptural programme at Moissac, it could be expected that the cloister of La Daurade might also have had reliefs on its piers, like those at the mother abbey.[32] Moreover, the question of Gelduinus's influence or activity at Moissac, where marble carving is a prominent element of the programme, has implications for the chronology of the project, the date at which the workshop was forming, and the impact on it of what was being done in the chantier at Saint-Sernin.

Close similarities in format and conception between the Saint-Sernin ambulatory reliefs and the Apostles on the piers of the Moissac cloister have been noted by every scholar who has dealt with the subject. Adding to the association between the two monuments is the presence at Moissac of three decorated imposts, one of them done exceptionally in marble (Schapiro 25),

Pl. 70 whose iconography and style closely parallel the decorated edge of the Gelduinus altar table. How these observations should be interpreted is a controversial issue. The question of which ensemble is earlier, the plaques at Saint-Sernin or the Moissac pier reliefs, is still unsettled. Moreover, it is difficult to decide how far the analogy extends between the two series of standing figures, since we are still ignorant of the original function and context of the marble plaques now in the ambulatory wall at Saint-Sernin.[33]

The three imposts at Moissac distinguish themselves from all the others in the cloister by their striking association in imagery with the altar table of Saint-Sernin (Schapiro 25, 53, and 75, in the east, north, and west galleries respectively). Only the examples in the east and west galleries are actually close to the style of Bernard Gelduinus, as represented by the altar table edge. The other example in the north gallery is very different in style from the altar at Toulouse.[34] The deeply undercut figures with small, pea-like heads lack the pronounced abdomen of Bernard Gelduinus's angels, and are more to be compared with the impost called the *Toilette du Prince* from the first workshop at La Daurade.

Pl. 56 Nevertheless, though different in style, every detail of the iconography of the Moissac impost in the north gallery links it closely to the imagery on the Gelduinus altar.[35] Overlapping imbrications, recalling the decoration of Early Christian sarcophagi, ornament the vertical upper edge, while the triumphal imagery of paired angels bearing a clipeus between them, also modelled on late antique and Early Christian funerary art, ornaments all four faces of the Moissac impost.[36] The way in which the angels' legs emerge from banks of wavy clouds at the corners of the impost also imitates a device used repeatedly by the Gelduinus workshop (see

[32] Analysis of Plan géo. 965 suggested that the north and west arcades of the Daurade cloister had been significantly disturbed some time after the 12th cent. and had probably been rebuilt. If so, the original decoration of the piers, if there was any, may not have survived to the 19th cent.

[33] Hearn has given a useful summary of the various functions that have been suggested over the years for the ambulatory reliefs (*Romanesque Sculpture*, 76–7). These have ranged from cloister pier decoration, to portal arrangements, an altar retable or antependium, a ciborium, and the crypt arrangement suggested by Hearn himself.

[34] Illustrations in Gerke, *Tischaltar des Bernard Gilduin*, figs. 43 and 47.

[35] Ibid., figs. 38–40.

[36] On the altar table edge, the clipeus held aloft by angels encloses a bust of the beardless, blessing Christ. On the impost of the north gallery at Moissac, each face of the impost bears a different emblem: a bust of God the Father, the Lamb of God, a dove, and the blessing hand of God.

the altar table edge and the image of Matthew in the ambulatory relief of Christ in Majesty), while the framing of each impost band by miniature columns placed at the angles appears on the decorated altar table of Lavaur, a work also associated with the workshop of Bernard Gelduinus.[37]

The other two imposts at Moissac show an obvious effort to imitate or approximate the style of Bernard Gelduinus but may be the work of an assistant to that master, since they do not match precisely the stylistic details of the altar table. The carving of the angel faces and bodies, for example, is more abstract and two-dimensional on the Moissac imposts, when compared to the inflated anatomy and the rounded, heavy-jowled faces of Gelduinus's angels.[38] The Moissac imposts seem to exhibit a simplified and streamlined version of Gelduinus's style, using the same double-lined convention to represent drapery folds, but reducing the number of folds and emphasizing longer sweeping lines, for example in the sleeves. Wings are tucked more unobtrusively out of sight in the Moissac reliefs, rather than contributing to the complexity of movements, as they do in Gelduinus's compositions. In fact, in its heightened abstraction and its emphasis on angular, sharp-edged forms, the style of the two Moissac imposts is more akin to the altar table of Lavaur, a work that should be attributed to sculptors trained in the Gelduinus workshop, rather than to the master himself.[39] In addition to the imposts with triumphal imagery, three other imposts at Moissac are carved with an ornament of paired birds standing within vine rinceaux that is closely akin to the decoration on the back edge of the Gelduinus altar, without being the work of the same hand.[40]

Pl. 70

In short, the evidence of the imposts suggests that a sculptor with intimate knowledge of the Toulousan altar table and its imagery, probably an assistant trained in the carving techniques of the Gelduinus workshop, was briefly present in the workshop of the Moissac cloister. It is even possible that this sculptor carved the single marble impost in the east gallery, in the material in which he was used to working, as a kind of model or demonstration piece for other members of the Moissac workshop to follow.

A similar kind of relationship exists between the marble pier reliefs at Moissac and the reliefs in the ambulatory of Saint-Sernin.[41] Though undeniably close in general conception and format, the style and approach to relief carving do not permit the attribution of these two ensembles to the same sculptors. Most observers have recognized that the seven reliefs at Saint-Sernin are not themselves uniform in style and may represent the work of two different sculptors, probably Bernard Gelduinus himself and one or more assistants exhibiting a more classicizing version of his style.[42] The latter approach, visible in the four larger reliefs depicting

---

[37] See Marcel Durliat, 'La Table d'autel romane de Lavaur', *Anuario de estudios medievales*, 2 (1965), 479–84; id., *Haut-Languedoc roman* (La Pierre-qui-vire, 1978), 283–7 and pls. 135–8.

[38] Gerke, *Tischaltar des Bernard Gilduin*, figs. 38–40.

[39] Durliat concluded that the altar table of Lavaur was carved by one of the sculptors of the Moissac cloister and represents an expansion of the Moissac workshop style in the direction of Albi (*Haut-Languedoc roman*, 285). I do not agree. The altar at Lavaur does relate closely to the 2 imposts in Gelduinus style at Moissac, but these are atypical in the cloister. The altar therefore reflects the movements of the Gelduinus workshop, not the workshop of Moissac.

[40] Schapiro 26, 43, and the central pier of the east gallery.

See Gerke, *Tischaltar des Bernard Gilduin*, figs. 27 and 30. At Moissac the birds are more slender and much more deeply undercut than their counterparts on the Gelduinus altar, and the vine roundels that enclose them are bound by slip knots. In fact, the bird and vine motif at Moissac may not be modelled on the altar table at all. The motif was introduced at Saint-Sernin by the workshop of the Porte des Comtes Master, probably before 1090. It appears on the impost topping the capital of *St Michael Slaying the Dragon* inside the south transept portal (Lyman, 'Porte des Comtes Master', pl. 11b).

[41] For illustrations of the Moissac Apostles, see Schapiro, 'Romanesque Sculpture of Moissac, I', and for the Toulousan ambulatory reliefs, Hearn, *Romanesque Sculpture*, figs. 49–55.

[42] Most observers, myself included, associate the 2 small

two angels and two saints has nothing in common with Moissac. The stolid proportions of these figures, the three-dimensionality of the heads (almost approaching sculpture in the round) and the ample space within which the figures stand, have all been seen as self-conscious efforts to associate these images with an Early Christian past, represented in Toulouse by abundant Gallo-Roman remains.[43]

The two smaller of the standing figures from Saint-Sernin, a cherub and a seraph, are, on the other hand, much closer to the Moissac pier reliefs in their two-dimensionality and emphasis on linear surface pattern, ornamental detail, and spatial confinement.[44] Nevertheless, the figure proportions, the facial types, the articulation of drapery, and even the stance of the figures, distinguish the Toulousan reliefs as the creations of different sculptors from those who carved the Moissac piers. In general, the heads of the Moissac Apostles are smaller in proportion to their height, giving the impression that they are taller and more slender than the cherub and seraph at Toulouse. The latter two figures, as well as the *Christ in Majesty*, have eyes that are pushed up close to the hair line, giving an unnatural elongation to the nose and the lower portion of the face. In the Moissac Apostles, in contrast, the brow bone and eye socket are beautifully defined by a single semicircular ridge which arches above the eye.[45] A number of the Moissac heads are turned in three-quarter view, so that the more distant eye and line of the cheek merge with the plane surface of the marble, while the heads of the two Saint-Sernin reliefs are turned in strict profile.

A comparison of the head of Christ at Saint-Sernin with that of Abbot Durandus, the only frontal face among the Moissac pier reliefs, shows a very similar formula for definition of the mouth, characterized by puffed out upper and lower lips, strongly defined to either side by depressions which separate the mouth from the cheeks. Other aspects of the abbot's face, however, exhibit a more refined definition than does the face of Christ, from the extremely high and rounded cheekbones and the strong but elegant brow ridges, to the oval pad of the chin.[46]

None of the Moissac Apostles, or the frontal Abbot Durandus, shows the widely spaced feet of the seraph at Saint-Sernin. Nor do their feet rest on a pyramidal base with real projection, as do those of the cherub at Toulouse. The spatial location of the feet of the Moissac Apostles is ambiguous, due to the tipping upward of the background plane at the bottom of each figure. All are shown to be standing either on a rectangular carpet or pedestal or on a short flight of steps. None of the Moissac Apostles shows the conventionalized rendering of the long underrobe as a regular series of vertical folds falling over the weight-bearing leg. This formula

reliefs of a cherub and a seraph with the *Maestas Domini*, while seeing in the 4 larger reliefs a second stylistic mode. Even so, not all authors have recognized in these distinctions the hands of different sculptors. See the summary of opinions offered at the sixth international colloquium of the Société française d'archéologie (Cabanot, 'Décor sculpté', 135). Along with Cabanot, Hearn has recently argued in favour of a single authorship for all 7 reliefs (*Romanesque Sculpture*, 71–5).

[43] For a distillation of the older views about the influence of antique sculpture on the ambulatory reliefs, see Gerke, *Tischaltar des Bernard Gilduin*, 494–508. See also Marcel Durliat, 'L'Atelier de Bernard Gilduin', *Anuario de estudios medievales*, 1 (1964), 528. Lyman has linked the style and iconography of the reliefs in a more direct way to the Early Christian history of the martyr's cult at Saint-Sernin and the revivalist elements of

the reform there (see 'La Table d'autel de Bernard Gilduin', *Les Cahiers de Saint-Michel de Cuxa*, 13 (1982), *passim*).

[44] Cf. Hearn, *Romanesque Sculpture*, figs. 50 and 51 from Saint-Sernin to the Apostles from Moissac (Schapiro, 'Sculpture of Moissac, I', figs. 4–13). The imposing weightiness of the *Maestas Domini* is manifestly a function of the iconography. This relief, then, stands apart from all the others, though on the basis of facial type, treatment of the hair, and ornamental detail, I would attribute it to the sculptor of the cherub and seraph, who was probably Bernard Gelduinus.

[45] See Schapiro, 'Romanesque Sculpture of Moissac, I', figs. 15–20.

[46] Cf. ibid., fig. 20, and Durliat, *Haut-Languedoc roman*, pl. 28.

was used in the two smaller Saint-Sernin reliefs to signify a contrapposto that stops at the waist of the figures. The legs of the Moissac Apostles take the same conventional stance, but the bordered hemlines of their robes assume more varied patterns of flatly pressed folds.

None the less, essential similarities between the two groups of reliefs cannot be denied when attempting to define their artistic relationship. Both present the standing saintly figure beneath a framing arch in a formula that has a long iconographic tradition extending back to late Antiquity. Both include telling details, such as the tiny rosettes in the upper corners of the reliefs and the identifying inscriptions incised on the arches, that have been rightly associated with the small-scale precious arts of ivory and metalworking of the earlier eleventh century and the Carolingian period.[47] Nevertheless, the essential artistic leap that these sculptures share is the rethinking of this formula in monumental terms and within architectural contexts in which the monumental figure had probably not been used in the region prior to these works.

That the two workshops simultaneously arrived at this new conception of a traditional iconography seems unlikely. The question then is, which of these two early works of monumental sculpture inspired the other? The inscription in the west gallery of Moissac tells us that the cloister was made in the time of Abbot Ansquitil.[48] As we saw in Chapter 1, he did not assume his office until 1085 at the earliest and may have been prevented from taking the abbot's seat until some years later, in 1091, because of the disputes over investiture that followed his election. No mention is made in the inscription that the cloister was begun under Ansquitil's predecessor, Hunaldus, although the disgrace that seems to have marked the final years of his tenure might have prevented him from being so honoured in the cloister. Nevertheless, the time of troubles in the abbey between the supporters of Hunaldus and Ansquitil in the years 1085–91 seems an unlikely period for the community to construct and decorate a new cloister. A time after 1091, when the supporters of Ansquitil had finally consolidated control and order was restored, would have been more propitious. The inscription and the iconographic programme may be intended to underline this new restoration of order. The new cloister for the community was built by Ansquitil, and the nimbed image of Durandus may be seen to recall the now 'sanctified' period of the abbey's history when it was first reformed under Cluniac rule. The rule of Hunaldus is ignored in the sculptural programme.

Based on this historical picture and on its relationship to the chantier at Saint-Sernin, it is most probable that the Moissac cloister workshop was forming about 1096, just after the completion of the transept tribunes and their sculpture at Saint-Sernin.[49] This would have been the appropriate time for the large chantier at Toulouse to spare one or more sculptors of foliate

---

[47] The ultimate source for the conception must have been Early Christian images like the famous 6th-cent. ivory of the *Archangel Michael* in the British Museum, London (New York, Metropolitan Museum of Art, *The Age of Spirituality*, ed. Kurt Weitzmann (NY, 1979), no. 481. 537) (cf. the positioning of the Archangel on a flight of steps and the ambiguity between the upper and lower parts of his body in space). The conception is most likely to have been transmitted to monumental sculpture via later Carolingian and Romanesque ivories, however. Cf. the Apostles in ivory from the 11th-cent. reliquary of St John the Baptist and St Pelayo, now in the Treasury of San Isidoro at León (Pedro de Palol and Max Hirmer, *L'Art en Espagne* (Paris, 1967), pls. 66 and 67) and the images of archangels flanking the standing Christ on the Carolingian

ivory cover of the Lorsch Gospels (Vatican, Biblioteca Apostolica, Museo sacro).

[48] The inscription is transcribed in Rupin, *L'Abbaye de Moissac*, 314.

[49] In an article of 1967, Lyman speculated that the cloister of Moissac was already under way in the 1080s, when members of Gelduinus's marble carving workshop would have travelled to the abbey to execute imposts there during the period of the Cluniac occupation of Saint-Sernin in 1081–3 (Lyman, 'Porte Miègeville Capitals', 33–4). In the years since then he has rejected this idea and now believes the period of greatest activity at Moissac was between 1093 and 1098 (monograph on Saint-Sernin, Conclusion, forthcoming).

capitals to join the cloister project at Moissac. A four-year period for the construction and decoration of the Moissac cloister—between 1096 and 1100—is commensurate with the nature of the project. Compared to the enormous and essentially unprecedented architectural undertaking of the basilica of Saint-Sernin, the erection of an unvaulted cloister of simple pier and arcade design would not have presented the kind of construction problems that would have made it difficult or time-consuming to complete. Moreover, our stylistic analysis has indicated that close to five or six sculptors were engaged on the decorative programme at Moissac—at least three who carved the historiated capitals, perhaps one, and probably more than one, who produced the foliate and animal capitals, and perhaps others who carved the marble pier reliefs.[50]

One of the marble carvers of the Gelduinus team was very likely also present in some capacity at Moissac, though his actual contribution in terms of sculpture produced was very small. It appears to have been limited, in fact, to the single marble impost in the east gallery, perhaps carved, as I have suggested, as a demonstration piece. This sculptor could have been sent as an adviser to the workshop that was about to embark on the ambitious decorative programme at the Cluniac abbey. The monks of Moissac, having settled upon a scheme for the cloister piers, may have called for consultation a sculptor from nearby Toulouse who had just participated in executing what was probably the only ensemble of monumental figures in marble to be found in the region. This would explain the intimate relationship in format, iconography, and even ornamental details between the Moissac reliefs and their counterparts at Toulouse.

That the invention of the format, in fact, belongs to Gelduinus and his workshop at Saint-Sernin cannot, of course, be proven, but it seems more likely that the initial step of monumentalization was taken in this ensemble and that the Moissac pier reliefs were inspired in some measure by them. We know that the altar table was finished by 1096, when it was consecrated, and the seven reliefs may all have been finished by that time as well. With their allusions to the celestial liturgy and to the triumph of Christ and his martyrs, they are intimately tied in iconography to the altar table and must have been devised as part of a single programme of enrichment and service to the liturgy.[51] Suggestions that the seven reliefs may have been intended for cloister piers, in the manner of Moissac, or for location on a façade must be rejected, because they are iconographically inseparable from the altar table. Everything about the ensemble—its revival of a centuries-long regional tradition of altar carving in precious marble, the liturgical and funerary references of its iconography, its self-conscious calling up of an Early Christian past in the style of the reliefs—suggests an original and essentially unique artistic enterprise, devised to serve a particular set of circumstances, namely the veneration of the tomb of a local Early Christian martyr and the practice of his cult.

---

[50] Schapiro believes the pier reliefs were carved by one of the sculptors who carved the unengaged capitals of the north gallery and a few in the west and south. He distinguished a separate authorship for the relief of Simon ('Romanesque Sculpture of Moissac, I', 192–3). I also distinguish 2 hands among the reliefs but see the stylistic groupings this way: one sculptor for Peter, Paul, Simon, Bartholomew, Matthew, and Abbot Durandus; a second who carved Philip, John, James, and probably Andrew. Unlike Schapiro, I find the Apostles so dissimilar in format and conception from the historiated capitals that it is very difficult to compare them. The piers may

be the work of marble carvers who had nothing to do with the capitals.

[51] Lyman has revealed this most convincingly in 'Table d'autel de Bernard Gilduin', 58–64. The suggested reconstruction of the altar table and reliefs in association with a shrine in the crypt of Saint-Sernin recently put forward by Hearn and Gillian Cannell has been shown to be unfeasible by Lyman (ibid. 55–6; see Hearn, *Romanesque Sculpture*, 77–8). On the iconographic sources of the altar table, see also Gerke, *Tischaltar des Bernard Gilduin*, 470–81.

Many, if not most, monastic churches of early foundation centred on the tomb, or at least the relics, of a saint of the early Church. However, the monumental size of the Saint-Sernin reliefs, the combining of frontal and profile figures in one ensemble, and the close interdependence of the figures implied by their reciprocal gestures, suggests that these reliefs were accommodated to an architectural space with special qualities. Thomas Lyman's suggested reconstruction of the ensemble, while conjectural, acknowledges the unique *Fig. 16* characteristics of the reliefs and accommodates them to the architecture of the crypt-confessio and sanctuary of eleventh-century Saint-Sernin.[52]

Lyman's reconstruction of course offers the advantage of providing a precedent for the positioning of monumental figures on weight-bearing members of the architecture, as they appear on the corner piers at Moissac. Lyman situates the four larger reliefs in pairs (each of the two angels paired with an Apostle or martyr) at right angles to each other at the entrance leading into the subterranean crypt-confessio of Romanesque Saint-Sernin. The possibility that the standing marble figures might have been associated in some such way with structural walls or supports at Saint-Sernin should not be construed as robbing originality from the Moissac ensemble. The sculptures of Saint-Sernin are still tied by their function, style, and iconography to funerary and liturgical arts usually associated with the furnishing of a sanctuary or crypt space. A conceptual leap would have been required to envision a proper context for such figures within the community space of the cloister. If, however, some liturgical practices did take place within the cloister, then a further inspirational link between the Saint-Sernin reliefs and the Apostles of Moissac may exist.[53] The identity of format and the choice of a precious material—marble—for the Moissac figures suggests as much.

The surviving capitals and imposts from the first campaign at La Daurade show no evidence of the presence or the influence in the Toulousan cloister of Bernard Gelduinus or sculptors trained in his marble carving tradition. Moreover, the movements of the Moissac workshop, or at least those of dispersed members of it, can be detected in the region to the north of Toulouse for perhaps two decades after 1100, and none of their work shows the influence, much less the participation, of Gelduinus-trained sculptors in these projects.[54] This, together with the stylistic differences we have drawn between the monumental marble figures at Moissac and Saint-Sernin, suggests that Gelduinus or Gelduinus-trained sculptors were never part of the Moissac workshop. Their participation in the sculptural programme at Moissac would have been limited to the consultation that they provided to a newly forming workshop that may have lacked sculptors with skills in what was at that time the rather specialized regional tradition of marble carving.

[52] For Lyman's suggested reconstruction of the ensemble see 'Table d'autel de Bernard Gilduin', and Durliat's review of his ideas in *Bulletin monumental*, 141 (1983), 86–7.

[53] See Thomas Lyman, 'Portails, portiques, paradis', *Les Cahiers de Saint-Michel de Cuxa*, 7 (1976), 35–43, where he draws a link between thresholds and porticoes (cloister galleries) in Romanesque iconology.

[54] The only other reverberation in the region of the marble carving tradition represented by Bernard Gelduinus is the altar table now in the Gothic church of St Alain at Lavaur, a work that may have been carved for the Romanesque predecessor of that church, founded in 1098 (see Durliat, *Haut-Languedoc roman*, 286). No other sculpture survives from this destroyed church. While there are enough differences in the style and relief technique of the altar table to exclude its attribution to Bernard Gelduinus or his identifiable assistants at Saint-Sernin, it obviously belongs to the specialized art of carved altar furnishings revived by Gelduinus at the end of the 11th cent. which seems to have come to an end once again with the demise of his workshop.

REGIONAL ASSOCIATIONS OF THE WORKSHOP

Fig. 17

It still remains to define the last component that went into the make-up of the Moissac workshop. If the ornamental capitals and imposts were carved by sculptors borrowed from the chantier at Saint-Sernin, the historiated capitals have no such origins in Toulouse or the churches of the pilgrimage network.[55] Instead the sculptors who produced the figured narratives of the Moissac cloister seem to have emerged from a more localized regional tradition in the vicinity of Moissac. The region in question lies to the north of Toulouse and is roughly delimited by Albi to the east and Agen to the west, the region drained by the Tarn and Garonne rivers on their westward flow towards Bordeaux. Chapter 4 defined the most characteristic features of the Moissac historiated capitals: their bold and simple treatment of the upper zone with coiled corner volutes and strongly projecting central modillion, the rejection of foliage decoration as a background for historiated themes, an immediately recognizable figure type featuring a short and small body and over-large head, distinctive hand gestures featuring the outward-turned palm, and the frequent use of inscriptions incised on the drum or console. These are all regional characteristics of Romanesque historiated capitals at Saint-Caprais d'Agen, Mas d'Agenais, and Moirax (all in the Lot-et-Garonne), at Cadalen (Tarn), Roquesérière, and others in the Agenais and Albigeois. In the case of Cadalen and Roquesérière, their portal capitals have been linked to the protracted heritage in the region of the Moissac workshop.[56] Where Agen and Moirax are concerned, Jean Cabanot hypothesizes the direct intervention of sculptors from both Moissac and Toulouse after the earliest portions of these buildings had already been constructed.[57]

An influence, either direct or indirect, from the workshop at Moissac is one possible explanation for the recurrence of common themes and ways of animating the figure that are found in all these ensembles. However, the differences in degree of similarity to Moissac suggest another explanation. The ensembles at Saint-Maffre de Bruniquel or Saint-Rustice, for example, appear to have been carved by one or more sculptors who must have dispersed from the Moissac cloister workshop itself. At the same time, the more distantly related sculptures in the Agenais and Albigeois may only resemble Moissac because they all share origins in a set of common regional approaches to the definition of capital shape, figure style, and narration.

Pls. 76 and 77
Pls. 78 and 79

Indeed, the forceful character of the Moissac figure style and the differing levels of sophistication among its capitals in their use of the human figure in narrative contexts strongly suggest that the Moissac programme does not mark the beginning of the historiated capital in the region, even if it represents the earliest accommodation of this type of capital to the cloister. What the prior experience and formation of the Moissac sculptors might have been like is suggested by the earliest capitals on the interior of the church of Saint-Michel de Lescure (Tarn), located just a few kilometres to the north of Albi and formerly a priory of the Benedictine abbey of Gaillac. On the evidence of changes in the design during the course of

---

[55] I cannot agree with Francis Salet, as he echoed the conclusions of Durliat, that sculptors at Moissac profited from the experience of Saint-Sernin in the composition of historiated scenes. As I have tried to show, the historiated capitals of Moissac have nothing in common with Saint-Sernin. (See Francis Salet, review of Marcel Durliat, 'Les Origines de la sculpture romane à Toulouse et à Moissac', in *Bulletin monumental*, 128 (1970), 143–4.)

[56] Durliat, *Haut-Languedoc roman*, 31–2 and 37–8.

[57] Agen, Mas d'Agenais, and Moirax have recently been discussed by Cabanot within a larger group of churches which he situates geographically on an oblique axis cutting through the valleys of the Adour and the Garonne rivers between Agen and Hagetmau (see Jean Cabanot, *Les Débuts de la sculpture romane dans le sud-ouest de la France* (Paris, 1987), esp. 120–76 and his catalogue of examples). See also the studies of these three monuments by René Crozet and Pierre Dubourg-Noves in *Congrès archéologique*, 127, Agenais (1969).

work, as well as that of an evolution in moulding profiles, Durliat has concluded that the construction of this simple church began with the apse and progressed rather slowly from east to west through the non-projecting transept and the two bays of the nave.[58] The fine series of sculptured capitals of the west portal can probably be identified as the product of sculptors dispersed from the cloister of Moissac after 1100, but an evolution towards somewhat taller proportions in both the capitals and the figures and a certain diminishing of relief projection, especially evident in the foliate ornament, classes them among the late works of the Moissac workshop, dating from about 1115–20.[59]

Pls. 71 and 72

The capitals of the interior, on the other hand, give many indications that they are earlier than those of the Moissac cloister. The most archaic of the group, located in the nave, depicts the *Sacrifice of Isaac*. The undefined character of the carving and the visually confusing relationship among the figures surely reflects a groping for narrative expression that precedes the solutions of the Moissac cloister. Nevertheless, it is worth noting that essential elements of the historiated capital as interpreted at Moissac are already present in the *Sacrifice of Isaac*, in the reminiscences of Corinthian elements (the corner volutes and strongly defined modillion) which are nevertheless highly abstracted. Corinthian foliage is banished altogether from the drum, as it was to be in the historiated capitals of Moissac.

Pl. 73

The two historiated capitals that face each other at the entrance to the choir, that on the south showing *Daniel in the Lions' Den* and that on the north, the *Meeting of Jacob and Esau*, would seem, by virtue of their location, to be even earlier than the capital of the *Sacrifice of Isaac* and to be by a different hand.[60] Both are very close in figure style, relief carving, and capital structure to the examples in the Moissac cloister. The capital with Daniel seated, hands raised in prayer, is identical in conception to the representations of this theme by the Moissac workshop, even to the arrangement of the flanking pairs of lions, one beast astride another, as they appear on the Daniel capital from the cloister of La Daurade. This double capital at Lescure also has the chamfered astragal that characterizes many capitals by the Moissac workshop.

Pls. 74 and 75

Pl. 23

The double capital with the *Meeting of Jacob and Esau* is equally suggestive of Moissac carvings, from the short bodies of the figures, showing the characteristic bulbous abdomen, to their poses, with feet aligned on the astragal, one behind the other, and the characteristic pudding-bowl hairstyle of Esau at the right. The corner volutes here curl into the delicate pointed leaves in which they terminate on most of the Moissac capitals, and the abbreviated tituli incised on the bare surface of the drum—IA at the left and IU at the right—are used in identical fashion at Moissac. The curious coffer-like symbol carved on the console above the heads of the brothers recalls a similar curious detail on the capital of the *Adoration of the Magi* at Moissac. Finally, the structure of the capital and the way the figured scenes are composed on its surface associates these capitals with the style of the simplest and most 'archaic' narrative compositions of the Moissac cloister, those of the east and north galleries. Both the Daniel and

Pl. 26

[58] Marcel Durliat, 'Aux origines de la sculpture romane languedocienne', *Cahiers de civilisation médiévale*, 5 (1962), 411–18; id., 'Saint-Michel de Lescure', *Congrès archéologique*, 140, Albigeois (1982), 355–9.

[59] Durliat dates the west portal capitals to about 1120. I have discussed the evolution of the Moissac cloister style after 1100 in 'A Romanesque Capital from the Region of Toulouse and Moissac', *Bulletin of the University of Michigan Museum*

of Art, 7 (1984–5), 34–6. Here at Lescure, iconography from the workshops of Saint-Sernin has been appropriated for 2 of the capitals, the *Sacrifice of Isaac* and the *Punishment of the Rich Man*.

[60] On the iconography of these 2 capitals see Durliat, 'Origines de la sculpture romane languedocienne', 413. The theme of the *Meeting of Jacob and Esau* had a precedent in the region at Saint-Sernin, in the north transept.

the Jacob and Esau capitals at Lescure top paired columns but, as in the capitals of the Moissac workshop, they are treated as if single, in the arrangement of figures on the surface and the single pair of volutes embracing the figures. Only the double astragals, along with a slight definition of double drums in the lower zone of the *Jacob and Esau* capital, contradict the definition of the upper part, a conception of the drum that should be compared, again, to the *Adoration of the Magi* and other capitals of the east gallery at Moissac.

What the two capitals of *Daniel* and of *Jacob and Esau* display is evidence that stone carvers from this region not far from Moissac could deal with figurative and even narrative themes at a date when few such themes were being attempted, and with less success, by the workshop of the Porte des Comtes Master or that of Bernard Gelduinus at Saint-Sernin. Marcel Durliat, in the first serious study of the sculpture at Lescure, singled out two of the fourteen capitals in the interior—one with quadrupeds and human masks, the other depicting the *Sacrifice of Isaac*— as more archaic-looking than the others. These, he concluded, reflect 'the state of sculpture in the region before the opening of the great atelier [of Moissac]'.[61] He suggested that certain of the Moissac sculptors may have been working at Saint-Michel de Lescure 'shortly before 1100' and that the contribution of these local carvers may be recognized in the coarsest of the sculptures of the Moissac cloister. In his interpretation, continuing contacts with the Moissac workshop allowed the modest programme at Lescure to benefit from the discoveries of the larger and more progressive atelier.[62]

I tend to see the importance of the capital sculpture at Lescure as more fundamental than this to the formation of the Moissac workshop. The two primitive capitals singled out by Durliat are both located in the nave (that of the *Sacrifice of Isaac* on the westernmost pier of the south arcade). It seems likely that the two historiated capitals in the oldest part of the church, those of *Daniel* and the *Meeting of Jacob and Esau* at the entrance to the apse, also represent the state of Romanesque sculpture in the region before the opening of the chantier at Moissac. In the latter two capitals, I believe we are seeing the work of sculptors who went on to join the team at Moissac and who substantially shaped the figure style of that workshop.

The ability to treat human figures in narrative interaction in modest compositions such as these must have been the necessary preparation for the much more varied and ambitious figure groupings that characterize many of the Moissac cloister capitals. No capitals at Lescure approach the narrative complexity of such scenes as *Christ and the Centurion's Servant* or the *Transfiguration* by the south gallery master at Moissac; rather they employ the simple, symmetrical formulas of the most archaic capitals of the east and north galleries. This strengthens the conviction that these Lescure capitals should be seen as a preparation for the cloister of Moissac in the earlier Romanesque sculpture of the region, rather than as a reflection of its influence. Limited as they are, their contribution was none the less essential. Suggestions that the art of the Moissac cloister might have been born out of manuscript illumination ignore fundamental eleventh-century experiments such as these in the plastic definition of the human figure in capital sculpture.

No other historiated capitals that could have served as preparation for the Moissac cloister have been identified in the region. Nevertheless, it is more than likely that the modest ensemble

---

[61] Durliat, 'Origines de la sculpture romane languedocienne', 415. He repeated this conclusion in *Haut-Languedoc roman*, 311.

[62] Durliat, 'Origines de la sculpture romane languedocienne', 415–16.

at Lescure does not represent the only early effort by local sculptors which the great abbey at Moissac could have drawn upon in the formation of its workshop. Unfortunately, the loss of Romanesque monuments from the early period of expansion and reform has been great. Durandus's church at Moissac and Hunaldus's priory at Layrac are but two important eleventh-century structures which must have played a role in the early formation of masonry and sculpture workshops in the region but whose evidence is lost to us.

The ensembles we have already cited in the Agenais and Albigeois suggest that by the first decades of the twelfth century there existed, in capital carving in those regions, a developed tradition of interest in Old Testament narrative themes in particular. This interest need not be traced directly to Moissac. The sculpture of numerous rural churches here is characterized by small programmes of capital decoration in which the same few historiated themes appear again and again, while foliate and animal capitals play the larger role. The Old Testament subjects of the Sacrifice of Isaac, Daniel in the Lions' Den, and the Fall of Man appear repeatedly.[63] In addition, the parable of Dives and Lazarus, depicted in a notable capital at Moissac, was one of the most popular themes, most often abbreviated to the Punishment of the Rich Man.[64] Just a few kilometres to the north of Toulouse at Saint-Rustice, a church decorated by sculptors of the Moissac workshop, figurative subjects are limited to the affronted birds and lions which also occur in the Moissac cloister. The exception is the important image of *Christ in Majesty*, which virtually reproduces the capital of that subject from the cloister of La Daurade.[65] Among the Romanesque churches to the north-west of Toulouse, only the large twelfth-century ensemble at Mas d'Agenais (church of Saint-Vincent, interior) has a diversity of Old and New Testament themes and hagiographic subjects that could be considered reminiscent of the Moissac cloister.[66]

Within their own region, then, including Toulouse, the cloister of Moissac, together with that of its cosmopolitan dependency of La Daurade, are remarkable in the period 1080–1120 for the pre-eminence they give to the historiated capital within their schemes. This observation is essential in understanding the special character of the Moissac workshop and its accomplishments. The case of Moissac illustrates the prime role that great monastic patrons played in the creation of the rich iconographic language of Romanesque monumental sculpture. The artistically ambitious programme at La Daurade reflects its character as the urban daughter of the great Cluniac abbey, as well as the benefits it received from the count of Toulouse. The special character of its iconographic programme, as reflective of Cluniac interests, is the subject of Chapter 7.

Pls. 78 and 79
Pl. 52

[63] The *Sacrifice of Isaac* appears at Lescure (both in the nave and on the west portal) and at Mas d'Agenais; *Daniel in the Lions' Den* is found at Lescure (apse entrance), Cénac (Dordogne), Montpezat (Lot-et-Garonne), and Mas d'Agenais; and the *Fall of Man* at Lescure (west portal), Cénac, Montpezat, Moirax, Cadalen, Roquesérière, and Bruniquel.

[64] See Lescure (west portal), Cénac, and Cadalen. The related theme of the *Chastisement of Luxuria* appears at Cénac and Roquesérière.

[65] On Saint-Rustice, see Ch. 2. The theme of *Christ in Majesty* occurs twice among the surviving capitals from this church (see Toulouse, *Musée des Augustins*, 1969–1984, nos. 57 and 58).

[66] See Pierre Dubourg-Noves, 'L'église du Mas d'Agenais', *Congrès archéologique*, 127, Agenais (1969), 223–36.

6

THE SECOND GENERATION
THE NEW STYLE OF LA DAURADE AND SAINT-ÉTIENNE

THE SECOND SERIES OF CAPITALS FROM LA DAURADE

THE SCULPTURE WORKSHOP that was brought together at Moissac and continued its work at La Daurade around 1100 introduced a host of new narrative themes into the art of capital sculpture at a time when there was little sophistication in treating such themes elsewhere in the region. Salient characteristics of the Moissac style suggested to us in Chapter 4 that the sculptors of this workshop may have generated their narrative imagery largely along the lines of verbal and textual models.

When we turn to the capitals created by the second workshop at La Daurade, it is clear that a wholly new conception of visual narration rules the art of these sculptures. The new style is startling in the precipitous pace of its narrative, in its emotional intensity, and its powerful claims on the viewer's attention. The style draws on all the devices of simultaneous action, exaggeration of gesture and posture, and the exploitation of climax to heighten narrative excitement. Figures are crowded into close interaction with one another, often huddled around the physical objects of Christ's Passion, such as his tomb and shroud or the skirted table of the *Pls. 105 and* Last Supper. These few but prominent scenic props, along with the miniature arches and *85* towers that overhang most of the scenes, lend a powerful sense of place and moment that draws the viewer into the dramas of Christ's Passion. Most striking of all, this art is achieved by remarkable sculptural means, by the aggressive projection of relief and the cunning exploitation of the capital's three-dimensional properties.

The only features that the capitals of the second series hold in common with the first are the dimensions of the capitals and imposts at their top surface and the occurrence of single and double capitals within both series.[1] This suggests that the second team of sculptors who completed the cloister after 1120, while introducing their own highly distinctive style at La Daurade, were interested in maintaining a consistency in those larger elements of cloister design that have to do with structure and support. They may even have made use of prepared stone blocks that had been left unused at the building site by the first workshop.

---

[1] See the Inventory for the dimensions of individual elements of each series. The imposts of the first series are somewhat thicker than those of the second (ranging from 15–16 cm. high, as compared to 12–13 cm. for the second series). The dimensions of length and width are, however, the same for both series of imposts, as are these dimensions for the bedding surface of the capitals on which the imposts rested. All the imposts of the second series are decorated on the vertical edge with three narrow overlapping horizontal bands, a motif that appears on several of the imposts of the first series (M. 193, 194, and 198). Cf. also the closely similar M. 120 from the first series.

In all other essential aspects—in their figure style and approach to visual narration, in their ways of distributing activity on the capital surface, and in the thematic interrelation of the capitals as a series—the later capitals of La Daurade depart dramatically from the work of the older sculptors who began the decoration of the cloister. The sculptors of the second series represent a new generation whose artistic formation must have been very different from that of the first workshop, which was grounded in the eleventh century. Neither can the formation of the second style of La Daurade be found in the immediately preceding Romanesque sculpture of Toulouse itself, as it was practised in the Porte Miègeville and the west façade sculptures of the basilica of Saint-Sernin. The second Daurade style seems to break upon Toulouse without preparation. This suggests that fresh outside influences, ones not formulated within the network of 'pilgrimage' churches, must have entered Toulouse around 1120. Are we to see in these sculptures, then, the work of imported artists from outside Languedoc? Or were Toulousan sculptors sufficiently masters of their craft by the second decade of the twelfth century to respond to new ideas from elsewhere and fashion them to their own devices? To approach this question, this chapter will attempt to define the artistic properties of the new style and will then look to its associations outside Toulouse.

The historiated capitals of the second Daurade series, when viewed as an ensemble, relate with remarkable fullness the Passion of Christ and his post-Resurrection appearances to his disciples, in a total of twenty-four episodes distributed over twelve capitals.[2] This in itself sets the series apart from all previous cloister sculpture in the region. In our discussion of the first series from La Daurade and its much more extensive model at Moissac, we remarked on the wide diversity of subject-matter represented there, reflecting the liturgical Psalmody, the cult of the saints, the eschatological thinking, and the moralizing exegesis that characterized eleventh-century Cluniac spirituality.

In contrast to these, the capitals of the second series have great thematic coherence. Whether these images, as originally arrayed within the cloister arcades, were asked to function as a historical (that is to say, chronological) Gospel narrative is a question that will be taken up in the next chapter when we discuss the meaning and function of the sculptures. But no matter how they were put to use when mounted in the cloister, the fullness of the Passion story gives the dismounted capitals the quality of a cycle. In the absence of prior models in sculpture, this is a powerful indication that the ultimate inspiration for the subject-matter comes from the pictorial arts, where cycles of the life of Christ and of saints' lives modelled on his Passion were developed at a much earlier date in manuscript illumination and wall painting. Nevertheless, imagery functions very differently in the cloister than it does on a manuscript page or a wall, both in isolation and in concert with the other images around it. The question of capital sequence, of how the capitals functioned in concert with one another and with the architectural spaces of the cloister, cannot be addressed apart from the meaning that the

---

[2] See the Inventory. In chronological order the distribution of scenes is as follows: (1) *Washing of the Feet* (M. 122) (single capital) (Pls. 80–3); (2) *Last Supper* (M. 125) (single capital) (Pls. 84–8); (3) *Christ in Gethsemane*: Christ Praying/Christ Rousing his Disciples/Christ Confronting the Soldiers/the Disciples Fleeing (M. 128) (single capital) (Pls. 89–90); (4) *Betrayal and Arrest of Christ/Flagellation/Judgement of Christ/ Way to Calvary* (M. 131) (triple capital) (Pls. 91–6); (5) *Deposition/Entombment* (M. 134) (single capital) (Pls. 97– 102); (6) *Christ in Limbo/The Elect Led to Paradise* (M. 140) (single capital) (Pls. 103–4); (7) *Resurrection/Holy Women at the Tomb* (M. 137) (single capital) (Pls. 105–7); (8) *Apostles at the Tomb/Noli me tangere* (M. 143) (double capital) (Pls. 108–13); (9) *Journey to Emmaus/Supper at Emmaus* (M. 145) (double capital) (Pls. 114–16); (10) *Incredulity of Thomas/ Traditio legis* (M. 148) (double capital) (Pls. 118–21); (11) *Ascension* (M. 151) (triple capital) (Pls. 122–6); (12) *Descent of the Holy Spirit* (M. 154) (double capital) (Pls. 127–9).

images must have held for the monastic community of La Daurade. Only after we have considered the meaning and function of these sculptured images in the life of the cloister—the subject of Chapter 7—will we return to the question of their arrangement as a programme.

Much of the impact of the Daurade capitals comes from the way narrative action is made to converge at salient points of the drum. While this is achieved according to various compositional strategies within the series of twelve capitals, six members of the series exhibit a most original approach by concentrating narrative activity on opposite short faces of the capital. This compositional solution is seen in the *Deposition/Entombment*; the *Resurrection/Holy Women at the Tomb*; the *Apostles at the Empty Tomb/Noli me tangere*; the *Journey* and *Supper at Emmaus*; the *Incredulity of Thomas/Traditio legis*; and the *Descent of the Holy Spirit*. In these capitals figures are not clustered, as might be expected, on the long faces of the capital, even though these surfaces would have provided a larger field of activity. Indeed, the narrative is virtually unreadable when viewed from either long face. Since it is the two short sides of these capitals that would have faced, respectively, the cloister walk and the garth, it seems clear that the compositional scheme used in these six capitals was calculated to achieve the highest legibility from these two vantage points (see, for example, the four faces of the *Deposition/Entombment*).

Pls. 97–102

This compositional solution is a hallmark of the second series and was used on capitals for both single and double columns. The triple capital with its more complex structure, representing scenes of the *Arrest of Christ*, *Flagellation*, *Christ before Pilate*, and *Way to Calvary*, employs other imaginative devices for concentrating and heightening narrative activity. Here climaxes of high drama and with numerous interactive figures erupt on the salient points of the three-part drum (exemplified by the *Arrest of Christ* and the *Way to Calvary*). They are linked by scenes of less intense climax, the *Flagellation* and *Christ before Pilate*, which intervene. Several of the other capitals—the *Washing of the Feet*, the *Last Supper*, the *Ascension*—exhibit a single point of high climax on what may be considered the primary or 'front' face of the capital. As in the capitals with paired scenes discussed above, the climax is focused on a short face of the drum, most likely the side that faced the cloister walk, while the opposite short face, of diminished narrative interest, probably faced the garth (see, for example, the *Ascension*).

Pls. 91 and 96

Pls. 81, 84, 88, and 122

Pl. 125

I have elsewhere defined these approaches to narrative composition in the second Daurade series in greater detail and have proposed reasons why they were employed.[3] When the capitals are studied from this standpoint, the conclusion emerges that the sculptors of the second series gave forethought to the way in which narrative images 'read' when disposed on the continuous surface of a three-dimensional capital. They deliberately sought compositional solutions aimed at narrative clarity, dramatic focus, and scenic unity. And, most remarkably, the solutions indicate that the sculptors of La Daurade recognized the special problems that the viewing conditions of the cloister space present for the legibility of historiated capitals.

Disposed, as they are, within an extended arcade that rests on a continuous parapet wall, four-sided cloister capitals conceal a blind face from the viewer, no matter from which of its

---

[3] Kathryn Horste, 'The Passion Series from La Daurade', *Gesta*, 21 (1982), 37–51. In addition to the 'dual-directed' and 'frieze' compositions described above, I distinguished in that article a third mode of composition used for 2 of the capitals, the *Christ in Gethsemane* and *Christ in Limbo*. In this compositional type, essentially similar to more archaic modes that appear within the first series and in the cloister of Moissac, each face of the capital is devoted to a single episode that constitutes a discrete vignette.

two sides he traverses the arcade. The sculptors of the earliest cloister capitals in the region, those of Moissac and the first series from La Daurade, either ignored this reality or, more likely, failed to see it as they carved the rich variety of historiated themes that populate these capitals. For those artists, there was no question of concentrating dramatic activity on certain visible points of the drum. When two or more themes were disposed on a single capital, as in one with the *Adoration of the Magi* and *Massacre of the Innocents* in the cloister of Moissac or the *Entry into Jerusalem* and *Arrest of Christ* from the first series at La Daurade, narrative activity commonly links a long and a short face in a continuous reading. Similarly, in a capital such as the *Parable of Lazarus and Dives* in the east gallery at Moissac (Schapiro 27), four distinct episodes are disposed around the circumference, as though the viewer were able to read them in a continuous sequence. In reality, a disruption of the narrative is inevitable in all these capitals, since none can be viewed in its entirety from one or the other side of the cloister arcade. As I concluded in my earlier publication, even Romanesque capitals from the later twelfth century, such as the several styles from the destroyed cloister of Saint-Pons-de-Thomières or the important series from the cathedral cloister of Pamplona, give evidence of only limited and unsystematic attention to the problems of narrative legibility in the historiated cloister capital.[4]

Pls. 45–7

The sculptors of the second workshop at La Daurade are, in fact, exceptional within their region and period for their ability to perceive the historiated capital as a functioning element of an integrated architectural whole that has an idiosyncratic spatial and structural configuration. In order to achieve narrative legibility within the restrictions of this architectural space, the highly dispersed compositions of the earlier workshop were rejected in favour of congealed figure groupings massed on focal points of the drum.

Pls. 99 and 91

The scenic unity and dramatic focus achieved in the capitals of the second series are functions of more than compositional ingenuity, however. All the elements of style, including the expressive interaction among figures, as well as the remarkable definition of relief, function together to distil action and emotion into scenes of vibrating intensity. The figures are precipitous in their movements, exerting an excess of energy to perform their dramatic tasks, as in the stooping figures of Nicodemus and Joseph of Arimathea who rush forward to lower the body of Christ into the tomb or the Doubting Thomas, falling to one knee to probe the wound of Christ, who draws in violent response in the opposite direction. The extremities are abnormally enlarged in most of the figures, giving greater emphasis to the emphatic hand gestures.

Pls. 99–101
Pl. 120

The effect of exaggerating the movements and gestures is to raise the emotional pitch of these scenes. In this sense the style is a component of meaning, since the story of Christ's Passion is one of high emotion, pushed forward by brutal events that rush one upon another and by the turmoil of Christ's followers in response to them. Expressive distortion and exaggeration are ingeniously exploited in the scene of Judas's Betrayal, for example. Here the reverse perspective, in which the heads of arresting soldiers in the rear of the crowd are nightmarishly enlarged, heightens the sense of oppression and entrapment. In other scenes of the series, however, the use of exaggerated posture and gesture seems less calculated to convey a specific emotional content than to make clear, as a consummate narrative device, what is transpiring between figures, as for example in the *Washing of the Feet* or the *Ascension of*

Pl. 91

Pl. 80

---

4 Ibid. 51–3. See also my remarks on the cloister capitals of Saint-Trophime at Arles in those pages.

Pl. 126 *Christ.* By these means there is created a sustained urgency of action throughout the series that may be described as its most distinguishing feature. It is this urgent narrative pace, more than anything else, that is so remarkably new in the second series of capitals from La Daurade, and it points the way to the origins of this imagery in a Romanesque tradition outside the region of Toulouse.

The figure style itself bears a distant family resemblance to the earlier style of the Moissac workshop in Toulouse, in the frequent use of the open-palmed hand gesture, the enlarged heads of the figures, their short proportions, and the appearance that they are composed predominantly of ball-like and ovoid forms. The figures of the second series move within a wholly different kind of spatial field, however, created by the new conception of relief in this series. The figures of the Moissac workshop, as Schapiro observed, exist in the absence of a spatial field. Their movements are essentially restricted to one plane, with the result that their gestures appear doll-like and artificial. The neutral surface of the drum at Moissac, and in the cf. Pls. 27 and 36 first Daurade series, implies not space but a solid wall from which the figures project forward. The dispersal of figures against this essentially neutral ground tends to emphasize the silhouette at Moissac, despite the substantial projection of some figures. As we noted in our analysis of the first Daurade series, the architectonics of the capital are powerfully defined by the sculptors of the Moissac workshop, and the figured scenes on its surface are for the most part highly regulated to emphasize, not to obscure, the capital's four-faced structure.

In contrast to this older Romanesque capital type of the Moissac workshop, the conception of the drum in the second Daurade series is revolutionary.[5] The role that was played in the Moissac capitals by the stereotypical upper zone of corner volutes and central modillion is now assumed by an upper canopy of miniature architecture, comprised of arches supporting diminutive towers and crenellated walls.[6] A primary function of this arcuated zone is to define the four-sided, rectangular plan of the capital at the upper surface. As such, its structure recognizes the role of the capital as a functioning element of an architectural system which includes the rectangular impost block and the arch resting on it. The arcuated zone provides the visual and structural transition between the heavy arcuated wall of the cloister arcade and the cylindrical columns on which it would have rested.

But this is not its only role. For all the scenes, the suspended character of the miniature baldachin permits it to define an actual, three-dimensional compass of space within which the small-scale dramas of Christ's Passion and Resurrection are enacted with complete freedom and with a startling sense of reality. Below the level of the arcuated register, the drum of the capital is profoundly eroded and its structure dissolved. In the double capitals like the *Traditio legis/Incredulity of Thomas* or the *Apostles at the Empty Tomb/Noli me tangere*, a vestige of Pls. 112 and 118 the structure of earlier twin capitals is visible on the long faces, where the twin drums part into a V of space, accentuated on the *Traditio legis* capital by the termination of the decorative diaper pattern. Here the drums have been reduced to slender cone-like shapes, however, far from the blocky pyramids of the earlier Moissac capitals. Interestingly, the treatment of the double drums in capitals like the *Traditio legis* seems to have been anticipated in the Moissac cloister in certain of the most stylized foliate capitals. A foliate capital in the

---

[5] See my comments on this in 'Passion Series', 40–2.
[6] In her article, 'Installation as Inspiration', *Gesta*, 25 (1986), 84, Linda Seidel pointed to the upper zone of miniature architecture as one of the defining features of the Daurade capitals. She saw in it references to contemporary, secular architecture. But above all she explained its function as one of defining 'concrete spaces' within which scenes occur.

north gallery, for example (Schapiro 50), illustrates how the ornament carpeting the surface is parted by a deep wedge that separates the cone-like drums. In Chapter 5 I described foliate *Pl. 63* capitals of this variety at Moissac as being farthest from a Corinthian prototype, and their shape is, in fact, highly original. The possibility that these abstract ornamental capitals were the inspiration for the new shape at La Daurade should be considered.

The device of a suspended architecture, sheltering and isolating a zone of dramatic activity beneath it, creates a powerful sense of place and moment in the episodes of the Daurade Passion that is equally new in Romanesque sculptured capitals. In scenes such as the *Entombment* we can enter a momentarily self-sufficient and self-defined world in which the poignancy of emotion is remarkably distilled in the intimate grouping of the figures. Nevertheless, only in some of the capitals—the *Washing of the Feet*, the *Last Supper*, the *Apostles at the Empty Tomb*—can the miniature architecture be interpreted literally in the context of the Passion story. Other scenes—the *Way to Calvary*, the *Journey to Emmaus*—are similarly sheltered, even though the context of the Gospel story calls for them to have taken place in exterior space. In this way, the sculptors of the Daurade capitals have engaged in a witty and artful play in which the 'reality' of the arcuated zone as an environment for the religious dramas enacted beneath or within it is constantly ambiguous.

This ambiguity exists even in those scenes in which the miniature architecture would seem to play an iconographic role in the episode and in which the figures are seen interacting with it. In the capital of the *Washing of the Feet*, for example, the miniature architecture, as it is applied to a pyramidal form, encourages the viewer to read the implied space in multiple ways. The example of other capitals in the series, such as the *Entombment*, predisposes the viewer to interpret the arcuated zone as a baldachin enclosing a void within which the figures move and act. The *Washing of the Feet*, on the other hand, belongs to a variant compositional type based upon a frieze, which invites the viewer to interpret the architecture as a continuous, horizontally extended arcade. The figures are seen to gesticulate and move in front of the miniature columns. In this way the figures are not at all confined within a miniature circuit of space sheltered by the upper zone of the capital. Instead they occupy an expansive space that extends outward from the front plane of the capital to include the viewer. If read in this way, the core of the capital then becomes exterior space, of which we are afforded limited glimpses through the openings in the arcade. The capital of the *Last Supper* sets up similarly shifting demands on the viewer's perception, since the conventional iconography for the scene in Western art is that of a horizontally extended frieze.

The ambiguities of reading seem meant to disconcert the viewer's expectations and to charge the architecture with a meaning that is metaphorical rather than literal. More will be said about this meaning in Chapter 8. Talented and imaginative as were the sculptors of La Daurade, they did not invent miniature architectural devices as frames for narrative scenes. At the time these capitals were carved, such devices had a considerable tradition in the pictorial arts, particularly in the tradition of Gospel illustration and in the illuminated lives of saints. The prominent use of this motif at La Daurade in conjunction with the qualities of narrative style that we have already pointed to in the second series, offer clues to the origin of its striking imagery.

THE ORIGINS OF THE NARRATIVE STYLE

Just where this new style came from is one of the critical questions for the history of Romanesque sculpture in Toulouse. It is clear that it did not emerge directly from the previous generation of Romanesque sculpture in the city, represented by the evolving pilgrimage workshop at Saint-Sernin and by the work of Moissac sculptors at La Daurade. Nor did the new style originate in the wider regions around Toulouse, Albi, or Agen, where local workshops were dominated by the style and the themes of the two great chantiers of Saint-Sernin and Moissac from 1100 to 1120.

So completely does the new style break with the immediately preceding sculptural work that we must suppose it to reflect an infusion of fresh artistic currents into Toulouse. The sophistication of its story-telling methods suggests that a deeply rooted tradition of narrative art, and specifically of narrative cycles from the life of Christ, lies behind the extended Passion–Resurrection series from La Daurade. It is in west central France, in the region of the Haut-Poitou and the valleys of the Loire and the Indre rivers, that a highly developed narrative art was already being practised in the early Romanesque period, in the second half of the eleventh century. This development is to be found, however, not in Romanesque stone sculpture but in the pictorial arts of wall painting and manuscript illumination that were brought to such a high level of brilliance in this part of Romanesque France.

Willibald Sauerländer first suggested that models in the medium of painting should be investigated as the source for the second Daurade style.[7] Linda Seidel, in her doctoral thesis of 1964, developed this idea more fully, pointing to central Aquitaine and, specifically, to the crypt paintings of Saint-Nicolas at Tavant (Indre-et-Loire) as the inspiration for the style of the second series and for the closely related sculptures by the workshop of Saint-Étienne.[8]

While the suggestions of these scholars recognize the link that exists between Romanesque painting in the Aquitaine and the art of the second Daurade style, I believe the nature of the relationship has been wrongly defined. Both Sauerländer and Seidel point, as the basis of their comparison, to what they see as the profoundly 'pictorial' quality of the style of La Daurade. In particular instances, most prominently in the scene of the *Arrest of Christ*, certain of the Daurade sculptures do show a debt to the conventions of spatial illusionism developed in the realm of Romanesque wall painting, in what Sauerländer described as the 'building up of figure *cf. Pl. 91* groups'. Seidel defined in more specific terms what she saw as the impact of the illusionistic devices of wall painting on the new style of sculpture in Toulouse. In her analysis of the capital of *Christ in Limbo* from La Daurade, she concluded that 'The surface of the capital functions in the scene as pictorial space', and she drew specific parallels between the scenic devices employed at La Daurade and those of the crypt paintings at Tavant.[9] The emphatically painterly effects of the frescos at Tavant, where forms are quickly and deftly sketched with a *Pl. 140* light hand and overlaid by fine strokes of translucent white highlights, prompted a comparison by Seidel with the surface treatment of forms in the sculptures of Saint-Étienne, *Pl. 166* with their fine and subtle drapery lines and receptivity to the modulations of light and shade.

It is dangerous, however, to conjecture about possible 'colouristic' or 'pictorial' effects

[7] Willibald Sauerländer, 'Chefs-d'œuvre romans des Musées de Province: Zu einer Ausstellung im Louvre', *Kunstchronik*, 11 (1958), 35.
[8] Linda Seidel, *Romanesque Sculpture from the Cathedral* of *Saint-Étienne* (New York, 1977), 155. See her overall discussion of fresco painting and La Daurade on 150–5.
[9] Ibid. 153–4.

sought by Romanesque sculptors through manipulation of the relief surface. Most Romanesque sculpture was itself highly painted, and there is no reason to suspect that the sculptures of either La Daurade or Saint-Étienne were exceptions to this practice. We can only imagine what this might have meant for the capitals of La Daurade. The effects of polychromy might have separated the clusters of relief figures even more dramatically from the ground. The diaper pattern, which catches and fragments light on a number of the capitals, suggests that this ground might have been painted with gold. The heavily jewelled borders and detailed pearling that highlight the drapery style at La Daurade may also have been picked out in white and jewel tones. Such rich ornamentation would have heightened the tension between plastic values and surface enlivenment that is already marked in the relief style of La Daurade.

More to the point, suggestions that the new style of Toulousan sculpture can be understood in terms of its pictorial quality or the degree to which it approximates pictorial effects misrepresents the profoundly original character of this new style as relief sculpture. The boldness of the Daurade sculptors can be gauged precisely in the degree to which they transcend the limitations to which the pictorial arts are subject. The space in which the miniature Passion episodes are enacted on the capitals of La Daurade is not conceived in pictorial or illusionistic terms. In scenes such as the *Entombment* or the *Apostles at the Empty Tomb*, the figures are held within an actual cavity of space, formed by the deep carving away of the drum behind them or, in the case of *St John at the Tomb*, by the situation of his figure at the junction of two faces of the drum that lie at right angles to each other. The figure groups are *Pl. 111* conceived entirely in sculptural terms. That is, their essential character is that of highly salient forms projecting outward from a ground whose role in terms of space is neutral. There is nothing to suggest a deeper space behind the figures and, indeed, the striking diaper pattern on a number of the capitals blocks such a suggestion.

Seidel was correct to point to central Aquitaine as a fruitful area of investigation into the origins of the new form of art that appeared in Toulouse about 1120. As distinct from Sauerländer and Seidel, however, I see the importance of this region for La Daurade not in any pictorial devices it might have bequeathed to the Toulousan workshop but in its supreme development of the narrative mode, as such, by means of visual language. Painters and illuminators of this regional school placed a premium on narrative vivacity and animation. In the service of their art they developed a distinctive language of fast-paced movement and gesture whose spirit can be recognized in the narrative dramas of the Daurade Passion cycle. There is no single existing programme of wall paintings nor fully illuminated Passion cycle from this region that can be pointed to as an obvious model for the sculptors of the Toulousan cloister. The fragility of wall painting as a medium and the chance survivals from what was originally a vastly richer production of illuminated manuscripts means that the examples we can point to for comparison are somewhat disparate in their subject-matter and their places of production. The pictorial cycles that do survive from the Loire and central France, nevertheless, speak of a tradition of visual narration in the art of this region that goes back to Carolingian times.

The deep roots of monumental narrative art in central Aquitaine are revealed by the early date of the frescos at Saint-Savin-sur-Gartempe (Vienne), just to the east of Poitiers, the most extensive and complex programme of wall paintings to survive in France from the Romanesque period. The early preference this region showed for covering vast areas of wall surface with episodic cycles from the Old and New Testaments and lives of the saints is epitomized at Saint-Savin. The programme here consists of several discrete cycles, now most commonly dated to between the late eleventh and early twelfth centuries.[10]

The boldness of this narrative art at Saint-Savin is most pronounced in the episodes from Genesis and Exodus in the nave vaults, where the scenes are framed in long rectangular panels and the figures are set against solid white or red ochre backgrounds. Despite the enormously tall proportions of the figures, they move with an energy and animation that are hallmarks of this central Aquitainian style. The cross-legged poses, backward turning postures, and emphatic hand gestures that signal dialogue were to become the stock in trade of high Romanesque figure sculpture later in the twelfth century in such familiar ensembles of Languedocian sculpture as the porch of Moissac and the reliefs of Souillac. In the wall paintings of Saint-Savin, however, the complex interaction of figures through directed gestures and highly articulate postures was already being exploited in the late eleventh century in the vivid narrative activity of these vault frescos.

Pl. 141

The gigantesque proportions of the figures, the feature that gives such grandeur to the nave frescos at Saint-Savin, located some 15 metres above the nave floor, make them seem initially remote as a source of comparison with the Daurade capitals, whose figures are short in stature, with enlarged heads. Nevertheless, the Toulousan capitals have so much in common with the paintings of Saint-Savin, both in spirit and in details, that their links with the tradition of this Aquitainian figurative art are compelling. The same vivacity of movement and liking for counter-directional postures animates the paintings and the sculptured capitals alike. A figure such as Christ in the *Incredulity of Thomas* from La Daurade, with his pointed, wind-born drapery ends and body that seems pulled in two directions can be compared to the backward-turning figure of God the Father in the *Construction of the Tower of Babel* from the nave vault at Saint-Savin.

Pl. 119

Pl. 141

The second series of capitals from La Daurade prominently features many specific details of style and motif that are hallmarks of the Aquitainian school and which are found at an early date here at Saint-Savin. These include characteristic elements of the drapery style, such as the broad bands of encrusted jewels that are such a prominent decorative element of the Toulousan style, both at La Daurade and Saint-Étienne. Jewelled borders of similar type hem the neck and sleeves of garments in the Saint-Savin style, in all the representations of God the Father in the nave and in the orant Christ who oversees the Apocalyptic cycle in the tympanum of the tower-porch. Flying drapery ends are a constant motif in Romanesque art, but they take many different forms, from fan-shaped to bell-like terminations. The most characteristic type at Saint-Savin is a single arc of drapery, swinging diagonally out from the body in a few firm and continuous lines and ending in two or three sharp points.[11] Drapery accents are used in

Pl. 141

[10] The cycles comprise an extended depiction of the Creation and Exodus in the vault of the nave, an Apocalypse in the lower storey of the tower porch, scenes from the Passion and Resurrection in the tribune above, and a cycle of the martyrdom of Sts Savinus and Cyprian in the crypt. There is still a significant difference of opinion among scholars regarding the order in which these various parts of the programme were completed at Saint-Savin. In the considerable literature that has appeared since the campaign of restoration at Saint-Savin in 1969, however, a consensus has emerged that the work of decoration was relatively rapid and continuous and that all the paintings date from between the late 11th cent. and the first

years of the 12th cent. For a recent summary of the state of the debate, see Janine Wettstein, *La Fresque romane: la route de Saint-Jacques, de Tours à Léon*, Études comparatives II; Bibliothèque de la société française d'archéologie, 9 (Paris, 1978), 6–8. The earlier thinking on the problem of chronology is summarized in Paul Deschamps and Marc Thibout, *La peinture murale en France: le haut moyen âge et l'époque romane* (Paris, 1951), 73–8.

[11] See other examples in the *Combat of Angels* in the porch of Saint-Savin, or the image of a mounted ruler in the Baptistry of Saint-Jean at nearby Poitiers (illustrated in Wettstein, *Fresque romane: la route de Saint-Jacques*, pl. IX, figs. 15 and 16).

exactly the same way in the figure style of La Daurade, highlighted against a blank ground and drawn with a few firm, continuous strokes terminating in downward-turning points. The images of *Christ in Limbo*, the *Noli me tangere*, *John and Peter at the Tomb*, the *Incredulity of Thomas*, and the Angels of the *Ascension* all exhibit this device.

Pl. 126

The undulating cloud-like forms that break along the upper edge of the *Ascension* from La Daurade and protrude into the scene of *Christ in Gethsemane* are a favourite motif in the Aquitainian school of wall painting, playing both a decorative and an iconographic role, as they do at La Daurade. In the Apocalyptic Christ of the tower-porch at Saint-Savin, they form a moving fringe at the outer edge of the mandorla, while another band decorates the arc of the lunette.[12] The visionary, cloud-bordered image of Christ ascending on the capital of La Daurade is particularly reminiscent of the painted image at Saint-Savin, where a diaper pattern also forms a resplendent ground for the figure, a device used repeatedly in the Daurade capitals.

Pls. 122 and 89

Pl. 122

Of all the paintings at Saint-Savin, the capitals of La Daurade are most closely related to those in the crypt, which depict the martyrdoms of the titular saint of the church, Savinus, and his brother, St Cyprian. These paintings are somewhat different in style and execution than those of the nave and tower porch.[13] Not superhuman or visionary like those of the nave and porch, the figures of these hagiographic scenes have shorter stature and more natural proportions. In part because of the subject-matter, the scenes display a sense of immediacy and an interest in anecdotal detail that make them close in spirit to the episodes from the Passion of Christ in the Daurade capitals. What is more, the miniature architectural framing devices that are such a prominent element of the capitals have their pictorial equivalent in these hagiographic scenes. The use of miniature architecture both to frame individual scenes and to create a sense of cyclic continuity was an important element in the pictorial tradition of hagiographic illustration in the region of central France, a point to be reiterated in our discussion of the manuscript of St Radegund. It is significant that these miniature architectural prospects, used in the crypt to frame hagiographic scenes, do not appear in the Old or New Testament epics of the upper parts of the church.

Pl. 142

The lively figure style of the Daurade cloister capitals is also strikingly close in some respects to the crypt paintings. The shape of the body, with small shoulders, curving waist, and pronounced rounding of the abdomen is a characteristic figure type in both cases. The shirred or tightly fitting sleeves and the short cloaks that fall back from the shoulders and stop just below the knees give similar silhouettes to many figures of both Saint-Savin and La Daurade. Even the drawing of head types shows a clear kinship, so far as the media of painting and sculpture can be equated in their means of delineation. The bold rendering of the head and facial features are among the most striking elements of the second Daurade style. The same can be said of the wide-eyed faces in the crypt paintings of Saint-Savin. A well preserved group of heads like that in the *Arrest of Christ* from La Daurade shows the same emphatic outlining of the eye, reinforced by a single sweeping stroke for the eyebrow and completed by a prominent

Pl. 91

---

[12] Ibid., pl. VIII, fig. 12. See also the *Creation of Adam* in the church of Saint-Jean Baptiste at Château-Gontier (ibid., pl. XXIV, fig. 15).

[13] Wettstein, nevertheless, has declined to attribute them to a different workshop (*Fresque romane: la route de Saint-Jacques*, 17–19). See ibid., pl. V, fig. 7, pl. XIII, fig. 28, and pl.

XXVIII, fig. 28. Gaborit-Chopin stresses the differences in style between the crypt paintings and those of the upper church but concludes that this does not imply a later date for them ('Gli affreschi de Saint-Savin e la miniatura in Aquitania', *Arte illustrata*, 30–3 (1970), 56–61).

Pl. 142 nose, that gives such an arresting quality to facial groupings like that of *SS Savinus and Cyprian before the Judge Ladicius* from the crypt of Saint-Savin. The conventions for rendering the hair, low on the forehead and swept straight back from the brow, or with a centre parting and delineated without curl in uniform, parallel streaks, are characteristic throughout the crypt paintings and in the capitals of La Daurade.

The close clumping of figures in some scenes from La Daurade, such as the *Arrest of Christ*, is not found anywhere in the Romanesque relief style of Toulouse or its region prior to the second workshop at La Daurade. This is the feature that prompted Sauerländer to suggest that the sculptors of La Daurade used paintings as models.[14] We have rejected the term 'pictorial' as an inappropriate descriptor of the essentials of the style. At the same time, a close look at the Arrest scene shows the Daurade sculptor using devices to represent the overlapping of heads that might, in this case, have been suggested to him by something he had seen in painting. In specific groups of figures, in particular the heads just to the left of Judas and in the crowded scenes of the *Gethsemane* capital, the sculptor represented heads in three-quarter view as though they were melding with those just behind them. Within the context of twelfth-century relief sculpture, this is a sophisticated attempt to represent in illusionistic fashion the manner in which the spherical form of the head and face are partially lost as they are turned away from the viewer. It can be compared to the painterly conventions used, for example, in the grouped heads of SS Savinus and Cyprian at Saint-Savin, pointed out above.

What of the Passion cycle itself at Saint-Savin as a source for the Toulousan capitals? Contained in the tribune of the tower-porch, the viewing conditions for this group are poor, and they have suffered the most from humidity and fading. It is clear, nevertheless, that, compared to the frescos of the nave and the crypt, the cycle in the tribune is not close in style to the Toulousan capitals. What is more, the Passion episodes at Saint-Savin were selected and orchestrated according to a complex theological programme that would seem to have little in common with the iconography of La Daurade. The focus of the programme is the enlarged *Descent from the Cross* in the eastern tympanum, below and to either side of which other episodes from the Passion and post-Resurrection appearances of Christ are arranged. Here pairs of images from the Passion and Resurrection story—the *Three Marys* and the *Angel Guarding the Tomb*; *Christ's Appearance to Mary Magdalene* and to the *Disciples at Emmaus* —are arranged as pendants framing the space of the eastern bay of the tribune or are paired in immediate juxtaposition on the side walls, as in the *Arrest of Christ* and the *Flagellation*. Completing the ensemble are themes from the life of St Denis and eschatological images, such as the Lamb of God held aloft by angels. It is the complex reverberations of meaning between and among the images as they reinforce the central message of Redemption, rather than any narrational intention, that have determined their inclusion here and their particular juxtaposition.

At the same time, there are enough distinctive iconographic details in common between this group of paintings and the Passion series from La Daurade to suggest that specific corresponding scenes in both series emerge from the same iconographic tradition. The powerful imagery of the *Arrest of Christ*, in which Christ is approached from behind by his betrayer while soldiers pull him forward, appears in this early series at Saint-Savin, which may

---

[14] Sauerländer, 'Chefs-d'œuvre romans' (as in n. 7 above), 35.

date from as early as the late eleventh century.[15] This distinctive iconographic type of the Arrest is separate from the older tradition, standard in Byzantine art, in which the scene is symmetrical and centrally focused, with the two main characters, Christ and Judas, facing each other in a ring of soldiers.[16] The scene of the Arrest as visualized in the capital from La Daurade and at Saint-Savin, in contrast, is full of tension and diametrically opposed movement. This variant of the Betrayal imagery gained particular favour in Passion cycles of Romanesque France and Spain, and its eleventh-century origins may be here in central France, a point to be discussed below. In the *Descent from the Cross* in the lunette of the east wall at Saint-Savin, a large jewelled cross with T-shaped terminals is the centrepiece of the image, a reference to Christ's triumph and return that links the iconography of this scene to its counterpart from La Daurade.[17]

Pl. 97

The scene in the large lunette above the triumphal arch that frames the *Deposition* may be the most significant iconographic link between this group of frescos and the capitals of La Daurade. It shows three standing figures, Christ flanked by two saints, in an architectural setting suggesting the Heavenly Jerusalem. The fresco is partly effaced, but the flanking saints have been tentatively identified as Peter and Paul, on the basis of a partial inscription reading 'S. P' next to the saint to the right of Christ. The scene has consequently been called a *traditio legis*.[18] If this identification is correct, then the inclusion of this theme within the context of the Passion bears comparison with the iconography of the Daurade capital series. One of the most unusual and telling images of the capitals of La Daurade is a scene of *Christ Delivering the Law to Peter and Paul*. This is the only scene of the twenty-one represented on the capitals that

Pl. 117

is not strictly narrative in character and not based on the Gospel accounts of the Passion and Resurrection of Christ. Chapter 7 discusses the Gregorian and Cluniac ideas we believe to lie behind the inclusion of this image within the Passion–Resurrection series from La Daurade. The possible earlier linking of this theme to Passion imagery at Saint-Savin may be another element pointing to a basis for the Toulousan cycle in the pictorial traditions of the Aquitaine.

The closest parallel to the narrative mode and figure style of the capitals from La Daurade is not a Passion cycle at all but an illuminated manuscript of the life of St Radegund (Poitiers, Bibliothèque municipale, MS 250), produced at Poitiers, probably for the convent of Sainte-Croix, at the end of the eleventh century.[19] Gaborit-Chopin and Wettstein have both related the style of this manuscript to the crypt paintings of SS Savinus and Cyprian at Saint-Savin.[20]

[15] For the date of the tribune frescos, see the bibliography in n. 10 above. For the *Arrest* scene, see the painted mock-up of the tribune cycle in Deschamps and Thibout, *Peinture murale*, pl. XXIX.

[16] See e.g. an 11th-cent. Byzantine Gospel book in the Biblioteca Apostolica (Vatican, cod. gr. 1156), fo. 194ᵛ (Émile Mâle, *Religious Art in France: The Twelfth Century* (Princeton, 1978), fig. 90). This variant also appears in the West, e.g. in the Evangelienbuch in St Peter (Salzburg, Stiftsbibliothek von St Peter, Cod. a. X. 6, fo. 80ʳ) and, in the Romanesque period, in the sculpted frieze of Saint-Gilles-du-Gard.

[17] For the significance of the jewelled cross in this context, see below, Ch. 7.

[18] Yvonne Labande-Mailfert, 'Nouvelles Données sur l'abbatiale de Saint-Savin: fresques, architecture', *Cahiers de civilisation médiévale*, 14 (1971), 46 n. 25. As this author notes, the standing figure of St Savinus appears on the curve of the vault, to the left of the *traditio legis* scene. Hence neither of the two

figures honoured by being placed with Christ in the lunette can be identified as the patron saint of the church.

[19] Émile Ginot, 'Le Manuscrit de sainte Radegonde de Poitiers et ses peintures du XIᵉ siècle', *Bulletin de la société française de reproduction de manuscrits à peintures*, 4 (1914–20), 9–79. Ginot's dating of the MS, to near the middle of the 11th cent., is earlier than most scholars would now support. See n. 20 below. A major article on the *Vita Radegundis* appeared while my book was going to press. I cannot do more here than refer the reader to its interesting discussion of the cult of Radegund and spiritual renewal in western France. See Magdalena Elizabeth Carrasco, 'Spirituality in Context: The Romanesque Illustrated Life of St Radegund of Poitiers (Poitiers, Bibl. Mun., MS 250)', *Art Bulletin*, 72 (1990), 414–35.

[20] Gaborit-Chopin, 'Gli affreschi de Saint-Savin' (as in n. 13 above), 57–8; Wettstein, *Fresque romane: la route de Saint-Jacques*, 7 and 31. Demus had earlier suggested such a

Whether the artists responsible for this common style were centred at Saint-Savin or at Poitiers, the key question is whether the style grew out of an indigenous regional context or has its origins outside the Haut-Poitou. Wettstein has concluded that we still lack sufficient knowledge about the formation of the artists who worked at Saint-Savin and Poitiers around 1100 to understand fully the origins of this Romanesque pictorial art.[21]

The illuminated *Vita Radegundis* contains full page and half-page miniatures illustrating scenes from the life and miracles of St Radegund, one of the most venerated saints of the Poitou region. Married by force in 536 to Clotaire I, king of the Franks, this Thuringian princess took refuge at Poitiers, where she founded the monastery for women of Notre-Dame and was buried after her death in 587 in the church of Sainte-Radegonde. Based on the text of her life by Bishop St Fortunatus, the full-page miniatures of the *Vita Radegundis* most often divide the page into an upper and a lower zone, depicting two successive episodes, as in St *Pl. 143* Radegund's washing the feet of the poor and, below this, serving the poor at table (fo. 29ᵛ). The style of the manuscript shows the same lively story-telling sense and the same impetuous movements that characterize the capitals from the cloister of La Daurade. The affinity with the Toulousan sculptures is apparent in the relatively stocky proportions of the figures and the way their silhouettes are strongly defined. The figures show a kinship in their large heads, prominent, enlarged eyes, and the similar treatment of the hair as luxurious and ornamental, often swept straight back from the forehead in a striated mass, as in the crypt paintings of Saint-Savin. Similar conventions for gestures are used throughout the two series. In the scene of *Pl. 144* St Radegund being consecrated as a deaconess (fo. 27ᵛ), for example, her kneeling posture with one open palm downward and the other raised in gesture can be compared to the kneeling *Pl. 113* Magdalene of the *Noli me tangere* at La Daurade. There is a similar liking for the dynamic figure in motion, often impelled in opposite directions, as in the scene of St Radegund retiring *Pl. 145* to her monastery (fo. 31ᵛ). This latter scene also shows the clumping or bunching of heads that we pointed to as a characteristic technique used by the sculptors of La Daurade to indicate a crowd of figures.

One of the most telling features that links the Toulousan capitals to the tradition of hagiographic illustration represented by the manuscript of St Radegund is the use of miniature arches and towers resting on framing columns that is such a striking aspect of the capitals from La Daurade. This kind of idealized architectural frame, used as an honorific device or to suggest the trappings of an imperial sanctity, has a long history in early medieval art. It has its origins ultimately in late Roman imperial imagery, from which it was transmitted to Early Christian and, later, to Carolingian art for both narrative and iconic images.[22] Nevertheless, the specific ways in which it is used in the *Vita Radegundis*, in the context of a figure style and narrative mode that are strikingly close to those of the Toulousan sculptures, suggest that the

relationship in passing (Otto Demus, *Romanesque Mural Painting* (New York, n.d.), 422 (German edn., Munich, 1968)). These authors are in accord in dating the *Vita Radegundis* to the end of the 11th cent. or c.1100. Gaborit-Chopin believes the same workshop executed the illuminations of the manuscript and the paintings of the crypt at Saint-Savin. Wettstein does not go this far. For a general discussion of the *Vita Radegundis* within the development of Romanesque painting in central France see C. R. Dodwell, *Painting in Europe 800 to 1200* (Harmondsworth, 1971), 184–5.

[21] Wettstein, *Fresque romane: la route de Saint-Jacques*, 31.
[22] See e.g. the ambo of the church of Hagios Georgios at Salonika with its scene of the *Adoration of the Magi* (Istanbul, Archaeological Museum) (ill. in André Grabar, *Christian Iconography: A Study of its Origins*, Bollingen Series 35, no. 10 (Princeton, 1968), ill. 122) or a 9th-cent. ivory of the Court School, depicting an Annunciation and a Crucifixion beneath portraits of the Gospel writers (Cologne, Schnütgen Museum) (ill. in Gertrud Schiller, *Iconography of Christian Art*, trans. Janet Seligman, i (Greenwich, Conn., 1971), fig. 76).

immediate source for this device at La Daurade may, indeed, have been some such manuscript as the life of Radegund produced at Poitiers.

In both the capitals and the miniatures, the architectural frames do not play a single assigned role. Rather, their roles are varied and complex. In the Radegund manuscript this results at times in the same ambiguity of reading encountered in the capitals of La Daurade. In a page such as fo. 24ᵛ from the Poitiers manuscript, the architectural devices clearly separate three episodes that are distinct from each other in time and location: Radegund at the table of her husband Clotaire, the saint praying in her oratory, and prostrating herself before the bed of the king. Here the figure groups are entirely confined within their frames, so that no portions of one scene intrude into the space of the next. In a later page (fo. 29ᵛ) with Radegund washing the feet of the poor in the upper register and Radegund serving the poor at table in the lower one, the role of the architecture is more ambiguous.

Pl. 143

In the latter scene figures gesture around and in front of the architectural elements, making of these elements a part of the architectural interior in which the scene is enacted, while they simultaneously function to divide the episode from the one above. The question—does the architecture belong to the reality of the scene or to the reality of the page?—apparently posed no confusion for the Romanesque artist of this manuscript. His use of architectural devices allows for a shifting perception of these elements to serve both orders of reading. We saw the miniature architecture similarly conceived and employed in the capitals of La Daurade, in particular in the *Washing of the Feet*, the *Last Supper*, and the *Apostles at the Empty Tomb*. In those examples, the architecture plays an active role in the dramatics of the narrative and at the same time performs the function of capturing the freely disposed figurative scenes within a uniform framework that is locked into the structure of the cloister arcade.

The sumptuous details of these architectural frames in the Toulousan capitals are also strongly suggested in the *Vita Radegundis*, in particular the spiral columns with parted curtains looped or knotted around them. Again the ultimate source for these motifs is late Antique art, as transmitted through Carolingian and Ottonian intermediaries, where they often appear in author portraits; but it is their function within an extended hagiographic, narrative cycle that is important here. Hagiographic cycles form a distinct genre within medieval literary and pictorial history.[23] That these medieval saints' lives, both in their textual and pictorial models, were patterned at least in concept on the miracles and Passion of Christ has been recognized. We have seen a pattern of similarities in the cycles of the Saint-Savin crypt and the *Vita Radegundis*. These Poitevin cycles in turn belong to a whole group of such Romanesque lives of SS Aubin, Martin, Amand, Omer, and Bertin that received pictorial treatment in the eleventh century, often in very similar format, as in the manuscript of the Life of St Aubin of Angers in Paris, which employs a very similar architectural frame to define

---

[23] See André Boutemy, 'L'Illustration de la vie de Saint Amand', *Revue belge d'archéologie et d'histoire de l'art*, 10 (1940), 231–49, and Francis Wormald, 'Some Illustrated Manuscripts of the Lives of the Saints', *Bulletin of the John Rylands Library*, 35 (1952–3), 248–66. Much recent work on hagiographic cycles has been done by younger scholars. See Barbara Abou-el-Haj, 'The First Illustrated Life of Saint Amand: Valenciennes, Bibilothèque municipale MS 502', Ph.D. thesis, University of California, Los Angeles (1975); ead., 'Consecration and Investiture in the Life of Saint Amand, Valenciennes, Bibl. Mun. MS 502', *Art Bulletin*, 61 (1979), 342–58; Rosemary Argent Svoboda, 'The Illustrations of the Life of St. Omer (Saint-Omer, Bibliothèque Municipale, MS 698)', Ph.D. thesis, University of Minnesota (1983); Magdalena Carrasco, 'Notes on the Iconography of the Romanesque Illustrated Manuscript of the Life of St. Albinus of Angers', *Zeitschrift für Kunstgeschichte*, 47 (1984), 333–48.

episodes.²⁴ It is possible that the immediate source for the *Vita Radegundis*, as well as for the Passion series from La Daurade, was an illuminated life of Christ, probably contained in a Gospel book, a missal, or as the preface to a Psalter.

Indications of what such a cycle might have been like, albeit in miniature format, is suggested by the extended narrative of the Passion and Resurrection depicted in an eleventh-century drawing from Tours, the artistic centre of the Loire valley. This drawing, discussed in a famous article of 1954 by Meyer Schapiro, is one of two surviving leaves detached from a Romanesque missal.²⁵ Both leaves are now preserved in the cathedral treasury at Auxerre, but Schapiro has assembled substantial evidence—iconographic, stylistic, historical, and paleographic—to show that the drawings were produced in the late eleventh century at Tours.

Pl. 146   Only one of the pair of drawings concerns us here. Most of the leaf is occupied by a large Crucifixion with Longinus and Stephaton flanking the cross and personifications of the weeping sun and moon above. Below the cross nude souls are seen rising from their sarcophagi. Forming a margin around this central image is a cycle of diminutive scenes from the Passion and post-Resurrection appearances of Christ, arrayed as horizontal friezes subdivided by architectural elements across the top and bottom of the page and framed as vertical strips of square panels down the sides.

The enlarged Crucifixion, the image of sacrifice and redemption, dominates the page and ultimately draws all meaning to itself. Nevertheless, the much smaller Passion and Resurrection scenes can be read as a coherent and self-sufficient cycle in their own right. There is a clear intention to present a historical progression of events, in the form of a succession of vignettes of approximately equal visual importance that reads in rough chronological order from left to right and top to bottom of the page.²⁶

The cycle is an extended one, comprising, so far as the iconography can be deciphered, fourteen individual episodes, including the Crucifixion.²⁷ Eight of the twelve legible scenes are episodes that appear on the capitals of La Daurade and in some instances the imagery is strikingly similar, notably in the *Arrest of Christ*, the *Flagellation*, the *Noli me tangere*, and the *Supper at Emmaus*. The scene of *Christ's Betrayal and Arrest*, the first episode of the cycle at

Pl. 147   the upper left margin of the page, provides the most powerful evidence of a connection between the imagery of this manuscript cycle and the Passion series from La Daurade. The iconography of the *Arrest of Christ*, in which Judas approaches Christ from behind while

²⁴ Paris, BN, MS nouv. acq. lat. 1390. For illustrations see Wettstein, *Fresque romane: la route de Saint-Jacques*, pl. XXVI, figs. 21 and 22, and pl. XXVII, fig. 23.

²⁵ Auxerre, cathedral of Saint-Étienne, treasury. Meyer Schapiro, 'Two Romanesque Drawings in Auxerre and Some Iconographic Problems', *Studies in Art and Literature for Bella Da Costa Green*, ed. Dorothy Miner (Princeton, 1954), 331–49; repr. in Meyer Schapiro, *Romanesque Art* (New York, 1977), 306–27. Maurice Prou had identified the leaves as originating from a missal in 1887 ('Deux dessins du XIIᵉ siècle au trésor de l'église Saint-Étienne d'Auxerre', *Gazette archéologique*, 12 (1887), 138–44). Prou, however, placed them in the first half of the 12th cent., somewhat late, according to Schapiro.

²⁶ The 2 small panels immediately to left and right of the large Crucifixion contain the *Good and Bad Thieves Crucified*; hence they are to be read as belonging to the central image. The marginal vignettes above the Thieves (who mark the precise centre of the page) depict scenes prior to the Crucifixion, while

those framing the lower half of the page depict episodes after Christ's death.

²⁷ Both the left and right margins of the vellum leaf have been cropped slightly, making identification of 2 of the scenes at upper right difficult. The scene in the uppermost right corner is surely *Peter's Denial*, although the cock has been shifted to the panel directly below this one, next to an image of Christ seated on an orb with his head bowed to one side against his hand, in a gesture of mourning. The 2 panels that occupy the lower right corner of the page have been nearly effaced. My reading of the legible scenes is as follows: (top, left to right) *Betrayal and Arrest of Christ*; *Christ Brought before Pilate*, who washes his hands; *Peter's Denial*; (left) the *Flagellation*; the *Mocking of Christ*; (right) the *Man of Sorrows as Judge of the World*; a second scene of *Christ's Mocking*; the *Good and Bad Thieves*; (left) the *Entombment*; the *Noli me tangere*; (right) *Christ in Limbo*, illegible; (bottom, left to right) *Way to Emmaus*; *Supper at Emmaus*; illegible.

soldiers pull him forward, belongs to that distinctive version of the theme that we have already singled out at La Daurade and in the tribune of Saint-Savin. Adelheid Heimann attempted to localize the origins of this western variant of the *Arrest* scene in Spain and south-west France.[28] The representation in the missal from Tours, however, pre-dates any of the examples she cites from these regions. The existence of the same distinctive iconography at Saint-Savin also suggests that the imagery has early roots in the Romanesque art of central France.[29]

The tiny drawing from the Auxerre leaf contains all the elements of the *Arrest* scene as it is visualized on the capital of La Daurade. The scene is strung out horizontally with the successive actions of Judas's betrayal, the taking of Christ, and Peter striking Malchus represented as if occurring simultaneously. As in the Toulousan capital, the figure of Christ is the axis of the opposing backward and forward movements, a compositional device that sets up a calculated tension lacking in the eastern version of the *Arrest*. As at La Daurade, Judas is made shorter than his master, thus heightening the directional tensions at the centre of the composition as he must pull the head of Christ backward and downward.

This liking for opposed movements pervades the activity of the figures in the Auxerre leaf, as it does in the Toulousan capitals, lending to a scene like the *Noli me tangere*, with its pivoting Christ and half-crouching Magdalene, a dramatic tension that belies the tiny size of the drawings. There is a similar energy level, a similar hurried and impetuous quality to the movements that unites the Passion series from La Daurade to the narrative tradition exemplified here in diminutive form. Even the figure style is reminiscent of La Daurade. Figures in the drawing have short bodies with rounded thighs and abdomens that are closer to the Daurade capitals than the monumental figures of the wall paintings of Saint-Savin.

Schapiro has concluded that 'the origin of these drawings in Tours permits us to locate in the Loire region in the late eleventh century one of the richest cycles of post-Passion and post-Resurrection scenes of the Romanesque period . . .'.[30] The developed character of the cycle and its early date, contemporary with the earliest wall paintings of Saint-Savin, suggest that this tradition was, indeed, deeply rooted in the region. The importance of Passion and post-Resurrection imagery in wall painting cycles of the region later in the twelfth century also supports the theory of an indigenous tradition of such imagery. Outstanding examples are the newly discovered fragments of a post-Resurrection cycle in the chapter house of the abbey of La Trinité at Vendôme (Loir-et-Cher), to the north of Tours,[31] and the famous programme in the tiny church of Saint-Martin at Vicq (Indre), on a line directly east of Poitiers and not far

[28] Adelheid Heimann, 'The Capital Frieze and Pilasters of the Portail Royal, Chartres', *Journal of the Warburg and Courtauld Institutes*, 31 (1968), 84–5.

[29] Lafargue made much of the resemblance between the *Arrest* scene from La Daurade and one in the Spanish Bible of Avila (Madrid, Biblioteca Nacional, MS Vit. 15-1 (formerly ER 8)). See Lafargue, *Chapiteaux de la Daurade*, 53. Her attempt to pinpoint this Romanesque bible as the principal source for the Passion series from La Daurade cannot be seriously entertained today, however, since the bible is now dated to the second half of the 12th cent. See Edward B. Garrison, *Studies in the History of Medieval Italian Painting*, i (Florence, 1953–4), 110 n. 1, and Council of Europe, *El Arte Romanico* (exh. cat.) (Barcelona, 1961), no. 9. Nevertheless, the unusual popularity of the dynamic *Arrest* imagery in Spanish Romanesque art gives the image from La Daurade a

close link to Romanesque cycles on the other side of the Pyrenees. The Toulousan capital shares an iconography strikingly close to the *Arrest* scene in the wall painting cycle from Bagüès now in the Musée diocésain at Jaca (Wettstein, *Fresque romane: la route de Saint-Jacques*, pl. XI, fig. 12) and in the cloister capital from the cathedral of Pamplona (Horste, 'Passion Series', fig. 21). While Wettstein has hesitated to tie Bagüès too closely to international currents, the iconographic links between all these images may be the 11th-cent. wall painting of central France.

[30] Schapiro, *Romanesque Art*, 317–18.

[31] See Jean Taralon, 'Les Fresques romanes de Vendôme. I. Étude stylistique et technique', *La Revue des arts*, 53 (1981), 9–22; Hélène Toubert, 'Les Fresques romanes de Vendôme. II. Étude iconographique', ibid. 23–38.

from Saint-Savin-sur-Gartempe.[32] The latter paintings, in particular, share important iconographic features with both the Auxerre drawing and the Daurade Passion cycle, such as the type of the *Arrest* scene, as well as the fast-paced excitement of the narrative, and the use of architectural framing devices for some scenes.

To find narrative cycles from the life of Christ of comparable pictorial development prior to the eleventh century, it is necessary to look to illuminated manuscripts of the later tenth and early eleventh centuries produced in the Ottonian Empire. One of the great accomplishments of Ottonian art was the imaginative iconographic elaboration it gave to New Testament cycles of the Infancy, Ministry, and Passion of Christ. Ottonian sources have, indeed, been suggested for both the style and the interest in pictorial narrative exhibited by central Aquitainian wall paintings like those of Saint-Savin. Nevertheless, the immediate sources for the Romanesque cycle of the Passion and Resurrection in this region may not necessarily have been imported from Ottonian centres. A major finding of Schapiro's study of the leaves from Tours was the continuity he established between the iconography of these Romanesque drawings and the prior tradition of Carolingian manuscript illumination as it was practised in this major artistic centre of the Carolingian Empire. This suggests the possibility that the Romanesque art of the Loire valley derived directly from an earlier and indigenous Carolingian art of the region, whether through revival or continuous tradition.[33]

Such a historical continuity within French medieval art, between the Carolingian period and the beginnings of Romanesque art, has been difficult to establish because of the scarcity of surviving French work from the tenth and early eleventh centuries. It is the extreme rarity and fragility of wall painting, with so few examples surviving from the ninth and tenth centuries anywhere in the old Frankish realm, that is, in part, responsible for the great lacunae in our knowledge of the relationship between the art of the ninth and the eleventh centuries in France. Given the brilliant development of wall painting as the art *par excellence* of this region in the Romanesque period, it is not unreasonable to suppose that its Romanesque flourishing was preceded by a considerable development of this medium in the previous centuries.

As for the Auxerre leaf itself, it is more likely to have derived from other illuminated manuscripts. The extended character of the cycle and the historical sequence of the scenes suggest this. Schapiro compared its arrangement of small marginal panels around a central iconic image to the famous Carolingian book cover at Oxford and to another divided between Paris and Dôle.[34] We would add to his examples a Carolingian ivory book cover of the ninth century with Crucifixion framed by Passion and post-Resurrection scenes, now in the cathedral treasury of Narbonne.[35] The format and iconography of the Auxerre leaf are so strikingly like this Carolingian piece that the Romanesque missal page suggests a revival or deliberate artistic reference to earlier Carolingian images of this sort. Nevertheless, the complexity of the figure groupings and narrative activity in the tiny Auxerre vignettes and the horizontal format of the larger scenes suggests that they were probably based on similar

---

[32] See Marcia Kupfer, 'Spiritual Passage and Pictorial Strategy in the Romanesque Frecoes at Vicq', *Art Bulletin*, 68 (1986), 35–53, with summary of earlier bibliography. Kupfer has presented new evidence here for dating the Passion cycle at Vicq to no earlier than the end of the third decade of the 12th cent.

[33] Wettstein has discussed the 'unknowns' involved in the issue of continuity vs. revival (*Fresque romane*), 46–9.

[34] Adolph Goldschmidt, *Die Elfenbeinskulpturen aus der Zeit der Karolingischen und Sachsischen Kaiser: VIII–XI Jahrhundert*, i (Berlin, 1914), no. 5, pl. III, and nos. 28–30, pl. XV.

[35] Ibid., no. 31, pl. XV.

pictorial models in somewhat larger format, probably the horizontal registers of a manuscript page with a sequence of framed or unframed scenes from the life of Christ.

LIMOGES

Though we have defined the Loire valley and the Haut-Poitou region as centres of the narrative tradition to which the Passion cycle of La Daurade belongs, it is possible that this new art may not have reached Toulouse directly from any of the sites we have already examined. Evidence suggests that the artistic centre of Limoges may have acted in some capacity as the intermediary in the transmission of this pictorial tradition southward. In the eleventh and early twelfth centuries, the scriptorium of the abbey of Saint-Martial de Limoges was the most flourishing and productive centre of manuscript illumination in central France, and its style was influential throughout Aquitaine.[36] Perhaps the most celebrated of the Romanesque manuscripts associated with Limoges, and certainly the most spectacular in its illuminations, is the Sacramentary of Saint-Étienne of Limoges.[37] Gaborit-Chopin has attributed this work to a Limousin artist not affiliated with the scriptorium of Saint-Martial but working for the canons of the cathedral of Saint-Étienne. The sacramentary can be dated quite precisely to between 1095 and 1105, on the basis of paleographic and historical evidence.[38] In addition to ornamented initials, its illuminations include eleven full-page miniatures with scenes from the life of Christ that have more than once been related in the literature to the iconography of the capitals of La Daurade.[39]

Those miniatures that particularly suggest iconographic links with the Toulousan Passion cycle are the *Ascension*, the *Pentecost*, the *Washing of the Feet*, and elements of the *Crucifixion*. The *Ascension* is particularly important in this linkage, since Romanesque sculpture in Toulouse prior to 1120 followed a different iconographic tradition for this theme, one that reflected the close ties between Toulouse and Spanish Romanesque monuments. The powerful figure of the frontal Christ with arms extended and flanked by gesticulating angels on the capital of the *Ascension* from La Daurade belongs to a different imagery for this theme *Pl. 122* than the way it was represented earlier in Toulouse on the Ascension tympanum of the Porte Miègeville, dating from about 1100–15. The great Christ hoisted to heaven by angels in the Porte Miègeville belongs to the type represented at San Isidoro de León, in the tympanum of the south transept portal.

The triple capital from La Daurade, on the other hand, dating from about 1120–30, is the

[36] Danielle Gaborit-Chopin has done a comprehensive study of manuscript production at Limoges. See *La Décoration des manuscrits à Saint-Martial de Limoges et en Limousin du IXe au XIIe siècle*, Mémoires et documents publiés par la Société de l'école des chartes, 17 (Paris, 1969).

[37] Paris, BN, lat. 9438. See Gaborit-Chopin, *Décoration des manuscrits*, 127–40 and 211–12; Victor Leroquais, *Les Sacramentaires et les missels manuscrits des bibliothèques de France*, i (Paris, 1924), 213–14; L. M. Michon, 'Le Sacramentaire de Saint-Etienne de Limoges', *Bulletin de la société nationale des antiquaires de France* (1956), 116–17; Jean Porcher, *Le Sacramentaire de Saint-Étienne de Limoges* (Paris, n.d.); id., *Limousin roman* (La Pierre-qui-vire, 1960), 245–6; Meyer Schapiro, *The Parma Ildefonsus: A Romanesque Illuminated Manuscript from Cluny and Related Works*, Monographs on Archaeology and the Fine Arts Sponsored by the Archaeological

Institute of America and the College Art Association of America, 10 (New York, 1964), no. 171.

[38] Gaborit-Chopin, *Décoration des manuscrits*, 137 and 211. Michon dates the script of the sacramentary to *c*.1100 ('Sacramentaire de Saint-Étienne', 116–17).

[39] Marie Lafargue, *Les Chapiteaux du cloître de Notre-Dame la Daurade* (Paris, 1940), 64. The full-page miniatures of the Sacramentary are these: *Nativity* and *Annunciation to the Shepherds* (2 registers); the *Stoning of St Stephen*; *Baptism* and *Miracle at Cana* (2 registers); *Presentation in the Temple*; *Christ instructing two disciples to search for an Ass* and the *Entry into Jerusalem* (2 registers); the *Last Supper* and *Washing of the Feet* (2 registers); *Christ in Majesty* surrounded by the tetramorph; *Crucifixion*; *Holy Women at the Tomb*; *Ascension*; and the *Descent of the Holy Spirit*.

earliest surviving example of a powerful new imagery of the Ascension in monumental sculpture from south-west France. This type was to become the centrepiece in a series of mature and late Romanesque portals of the Quercy, the region between Toulouse and the Limousin, at Cahors, Mauriac, Carennac, Collonges, and Saint-Chamant.

The Sacramentary of Limoges of 1095–1105, or at least the Limousin scriptorium that produced it, may well have been the source from which this powerful imagery of the Ascension was disseminated and taken up into Romanesque sculpture, first at Toulouse and then in the important Romanesque sites of the Quercy with which Toulousan sculpture had its closest ties after 1120. The full-page miniature of the Sacramentary of Limoges depicts the Ascension of

Pl. 148 Christ as a burning vision in colours of cardinal red and gold with patches of opaque white. The page is divided into an upper and a lower zone, with a towering Christ in a diamond-shaped mandorla separated by a narrow frame from the grouped disciples and Virgin in much smaller scale below. Two angels in the upper zone with Christ appear to dance at his side as they bend backward and downward in remarkably mannered and energized poses. Christ confronts the viewer hypnotically at the vortex of this activity. His arms are stretched wide, and he holds an open book in his left hand.

Though the *Ascension* capital from La Daurade lacks some of the details of the painted image—Christ is without mandorla, and he holds no attributes—the iconography belongs distinctly to this conception of the theme and is close to the Sacramentary in style and spirit.

Pl. 122 The way the upright frontal Christ dominates one entire face of the triple capital gives an iconic and visionary character to this Ascension type that is lacking in other Eastern and Western traditions for its representation, which may show a striding Christ in profile being pulled to heaven by the hand of God or, as in the Porte Miègeville of Saint-Sernin, a bulky Christ hoisted from beneath the arms by his attendant angels.[40] The extremely mannered, backward-bending postures of the angels in the Toulousan capital have their precedents in the imagery of the Limousin miniature. These angels exemplify the aesthetic preference for figures and compositions based on a tension of opposed movements that ties the style of the Toulousan capitals to that of the manuscript. Though figure proportions are quite different, the enlarged hands and feet, enormous eyes lined above by terrifying brows, and the long, striated hairstyles falling below the shoulders, create a strong resemblance between the style of the capitals from La Daurade and that of the Sacramentary of Limoges.

Even more strikingly like the Sacramentary is the distinctly ornamental quality that marks the style of the second series from La Daurade. The wide jewelled borders on the garments of the figures, the firmly drawn drapery folds, dominated by long continuous lines and oval forms, and the use of strongly contrasting diaper patterns on many of the capitals from La Daurade, create a visually rich and precious surface interest that is close in effect to the pages of the Limousin Sacramentary. The scintillating surface of Christ's mandorla in the *Ascension* miniature has its equivalent in the minutely detailed field of square and dot pattern above Christ in the *Arrest* scene from La Daurade, perhaps also meant to signify a nimbus of light. Likewise, the cross-hatched pattern on the interior of the angels' cloaks in the Limoges *Ascension* is a characteristic device on many of the figures in the series of Toulousan capitals.

40 For the distinction among the various iconographic types for the Ascension see Sophie H. Gutberlet, *Die Himmelfahrt Christi in der Bildenden Kunst von den Anfängen bis ins hohe Mittelalter*, Sammlungen Heitz Akademische Abhandlungen zur Kulturgeschichte. 3. iii. (Strasbourg, 1934); and Gertrud Schiller, *Ikonographie der christlichen Kunst*, iii (Gütersloh, 1971), 141–64.

The fact that the cloister capitals were very probably painted, and brightly so, must have increased their resemblance to the manuscript.

The dramatic iconography of the *Ascension* as it appears in the Sacramentary of Limoges was a hallmark of Ottonian art, particularly in manuscripts of the Liuthard group, where it appears in New Testament cycles from the life of Christ in some of the most splendid examples of Ottonian illumination.[41] The frontal ascending Christ with arms extended, as distinct from other Eastern and Western types for this theme, has its ultimate origin in an East Christian tradition represented by the sixth-century Rabbula Gospels.[42] It was Ottonian artists, however, who gave it the hypnotic, visionary quality that also distinguishes the image in the Sacramentary of Limoges. The differences in scale and the horizontal border that divides the upper from the lower zone in the Limousin *Ascension* mimic the compositional and conceptual separation of these zones introduced into the Ottonian images by horizontal cloud bands of different colours or, in examples such as the Bamberg Gospels at Munich, by a celestial 'wall' or screen from behind which angels peer down on the assembled disciples.[43]

Besides the *Ascension*, the pages of the Sacramentary of Limoges contain other iconographic peculiarities that are distinctive in Ottonian New Testament cycles. One that is especially rare in French Romanesque art is the peculiar imagery of the *Descent of the Holy Spirit*, represented in the Sacramentary (fo. 87) as undulating ribbons issuing from the head of Christ and branching into separate strands that attach themselves to the head of each Apostle represented below.[44] More commonly in French Romanesque art, the descent of the spirit is represented as tongues of flame or radiating beams of light, as in a Cluniac lectionary of the twelfth century in Paris.[45] The capital from La Daurade follows the more unusual tradition of the Limousin manuscript, in the peculiar undulating ribbons that attach themselves to the heads of the Apostles, though in the Toulousan capital the source of the Holy Spirit is not represented. Together with the Ascension, the Pentecost imagery is a strong iconographic link between La Daurade and the Sacramentary of Limoges.

Pl. 149

The images of the *Washing of the Feet* and the *Crucifixion* reinforce these links. The dramatic composition of the *Washing of the Feet* from La Daurade, with the prominence it gives to the curtain-draped column as a tense focus between Christ and St Peter, is highly reminiscent of the image in the Limousin Sacramentary. Also linking the two representations is the presence behind Christ of the disciple with a towel, perhaps St Martial himself, venerated both in Limoges and Toulouse. Finally, the jewelled cross of triumph on which Christ is crucified in the Sacramentary of Limoges appears again in the *Deposition* from La Daurade,

Pl. 150

[41] See e.g. the Reichenau Evangelistary (facsimile edn. *Reichenauer Evangelistar: Berlin, Staatlichen Museen Preussischer Kulturbesitz, Codex 78 A 2 aus dem Kupferstichkabinett*, Reihe Codices Selecti, 31 (Graz, 1972), fo. 45ᵛ; the Book of Pericopes of Henry II (Munich, Staatsbibliothek, Cod. lat. 4452), fo. 131ᵛ (ill. in Georg Leidinger, *Das Perikopenbuch Kaiser Heinrichs II (Cod. lat. 4452)*, Miniaturen aus Handschriften der Kgl. Hof- und Staatsbibliothek in München (Munich, n.d.), pl. 23); and the Evangelistary of St Gall, St Gall, Stiftsbibliothek, Cod. 340 (Gertrud Schiller, *Ikonographie der christlichen Kunst*, iii (Gütersloh, 1971), fig. 488).

[42] Florence, Biblioteca Medicea-Laurenziana, Syriac MS Plut. I. 56, fo. C 13ᵛ.

[43] Munich, Staatsbibliothek, Clm. 4454 (see Ernest T. Dewald, 'The Iconography of the Ascension', *American Journal of Archaeology*, 2nd ser., 19 (1915), fig. 18).

[44] An Ottonian Pentecost in which the descent of the spirit is represented as crinkled ribbons, similar in concept to the images from La Daurade and the Sacramentary of Saint-Étienne, is found in the Evangelienbuch in St Peter (Salzburg, Stiftsbibliothek von St Peter, Cod. a. X. 6, fo. 214ᵛ), ill. in Georg Swarzenski, *Die Salzburger Malerei von den ersten Anfängen bis zur Blutzeit des romanischen Stils* (Stuttgart, 1969), pl. XIX, fig. 62.

[45] Paris, BN, MS nouv. acq. lat. 2246, fo. 79ᵛ. On the significance of Pentecost imagery with the present or the absent Christ, see Michael D. Taylor, 'The Pentecost at Vézelay', *Gesta*, 19 (1980), 9–15. Taylor agrees with Schapiro (*Parma Ildefonsus*, 44) that the image in the Cluny Lectionary is a *Descent of the Holy Spirit*, not Christ's promise of the future Pentecostal descent.

the scene which may have substituted for the *Crucifixion* itself in the Toulousan series. Chapter 7 will discuss the significance of this triumphal imagery as one of the conservative elements in the iconography of the second series from La Daurade. The retrospective aspect of this image is shared by the Sacramentary of Limoges, which seems to take so much of its visionary quality from earlier eleventh-century art.

Iconographic as well as stylistic connections to Ottonian art have been claimed for the Sacramentary of Limoges by virtually all scholars who have discussed the manuscript.[46] It has been especially tempting to look to the extensive New Testament cycles of Ottonian art as a basis for this sacramentary because the eleventh-century manuscript art of Limoges itself does not provide precedents for the elaborate full-page narrative scenes from the life of Christ. Though the ornamentation of Limousin manuscripts is rich, it consists primarily of decorated initials and canon tables. Figurative iconography is present, but it most often takes the form of human and animal entanglements, individual images of saints or Prophets and, on occasion, small historiated vignettes contained within the text. The Sacramentary of Limoges stands alone among the Romanesque manuscripts of the Limoges school for its monumental cycle of New Testament pages.

On the other hand, we have given reason to hypothesize the existence of a pre-Romanesque tradition of narrative art indigenous to central France that may have been lost to us with the destruction of most of the early medieval wall paintings of the region. What is more, as Gaborit-Chopin has made clear, in the rinceaux, the interlaces, and the zoomorphic inhabitants of its ornamented initials, the Sacramentary of Limoges is firmly grounded in the indigenous art of Aquitaine and is tied by these elements to other Limousin manuscripts produced in the scriptorium of Saint-Martial.[47] In light of Schapiro's conclusions, we might ask if the narrative cycle of the Limoges Sacramentary also reflects a pre-Romanesque pictorial tradition in central France. Gaborit-Chopin has pointed out that the Ascension of Syrian type used in the Sacramentary of Limoges was not unknown to the region before 1100. She cites a drawing from the famous collection by Adémar de Chabannes, monk of Saint-Martial-de-Limoges from 988 to 1034, which probably copies an original of the ninth or tenth century.[48] Moreover, the recent discovery in the crypt of the cathedral of Saint-Étienne in Limoges of fragmentary wall paintings attributable to the same hand that produced the Sacramentary, presents the possibility that some of the originality of this artist may derive from his ties to the wall-painting medium.[49]

The ties to Aquitainian wall painting are evident in the style of the full-page miniatures of

[46] Porcher, *Sacramentaire de Saint-Étienne* (as in n. 37 above), *passim*; id., *Limousin roman* (2nd edn., La Pierre-qui-vire, 1974), 246. The most precise relationships with Ottonian manuscripts, in iconography and the technical processes of production, have been drawn by Gaborit-Chopin, *Décoration des manuscrits*, 128–9. She points to the Ottonian school of Salzburg and, in particular, the Pericopes of St Erentrud (Munich, Clm. 15.903) for its correspondences with the Sacramentary of Saint-Étienne. As Wettstein points out, the Pericopes of St Erentrud are commonly dated later than the Sacramentary of Saint-Étienne (*c.*1140) (*Fresque romane*: la route de Saint-Jacques, 75). Nevertheless, the Erentrud manuscript follows well-established iconographic conventions that are common to the Salzburg school of manuscript illumination (see Georg Swarzenski, *Die Salzburger Malerei* (as in n. 44 above)).

[47] Gaborit-Chopin, *Décoration des manuscrits*, 131.
[48] Leyden, Bibliothèque universitaire, MS lat. Voss. 8° 15, fo. 2. See Danielle Gaborit-Chopin, 'Les Dessins d'Adémar de Chabannes', *Bulletin archéologique du Comité des travaux historiques et scientifiques*, NS 2 (1967), 163–225 and fig. 19.
[49] A preliminary report on these newly discovered paintings, unavailable to me, was published by Marie-Madeleine Gauthier, 'Rapport sur les peintures murales de la crypte de la cathédrale de Limoges', *Bulletin de la Société archéologique et historique du Limousin*, 96 (1969), 89–105. The paintings are discussed by Gaborit-Chopin (*Décoration des manuscrits*, 127 and 130) who, along with Gauthier, assigns them to the same artist as the Sacramentary of Saint-Étienne. Wettstein (*Fresque romane*: la route de Saint-Jacques, 77) is more cautious, concluding that we lack firm evidence that Limousin painters worked in both media.

the Sacramentary of Saint-Étienne. The monumentality of the figures, the use of cross-legged poses, and the emphatic pointing or exclamatory gestures in scenes like Christ's instructions to his disciples and his Entry into Jerusalem (fo. 44ᵛ) betray a kinship with the narrative scenes of the *Story of Noah* in the vault of Saint-Savin-sur-Gartempe. Moreover, some of the characteristic motifs that give to the miniatures of the Sacramentary their visionary quality are favourite devices in the wall paintings of the Haut-Poitou region. Stylized cloud formations, which take several forms in the Sacramentary of Saint-Étienne and in other manuscripts of Limoges that have been attributed to this master, such as the Bible of Saint-Yrieix,[50] appear with the same frequency and in formations very like those of the frescos of Saint-Savin, Tavant, and other wall paintings of Aquitaine.[51]

Since such visionary aspects of both the wall paintings and the Sacramentary have been linked to Ottonian manuscripts, it could be argued that their similarity derives from their common use of Ottonian models. However, such kaleidoscopic cloud bursts, to indicate heavenly visions or visitations, appear as well in other manuscripts produced at Limoges, which have definite regional ties to Aquitainian fresco painting. A case in point is a miniature of *Elias and the Envoys of the King* in the great Second Bible of Saint-Martial de Limoges.[52]   *Pl. 151* The half-roundel of clouds with fringed edge above the heads of the envoys obtrudes into the scene and is ornamented with rosettes that recall both the *Christ in Majesty* (fo. 58ᵛ) and the *Vision of St Stephen* (fo. 20ᵛ) in the Sacramentary of Saint-Étienne. The clouds are set against a diaper pattern of tiny squares punctuated by dots that we have already pointed to as a common decorative device in the Sacramentary and in Christ's mandorla in the *Maiestas Domini* of the porch of Saint-Savin.

What is important for our study is that this locally common but idiosyncratic vocabulary of iconographic and decorative devices accompanied the transmission of a new narrative art to Toulouse in the 1120s, where it produced forms that have been considered enigmatic within the context of the Passion cycle of the capitals of La Daurade. Aureoles of bursting light with fringed edges like those that obtrude into the miniatures of *Elias and the Envoys* in the Second Bible of Saint-Martial or the *Vision of St Stephen* in the Limoges Sacramentary are surely the source for the strange formations that press in above the head of Christ in the scene of his prayers in Gethsemane on a capital from La Daurade. And as they do in the Limousin   *Pl. 89* manuscripts or the visionary scenes of Aquitainian wall paintings, they most probably represent a divine turbulence of the heavens associated with Christ's vision.

The figure style of the capitals from La Daurade has more in common with the pictorial art of Poitou than it does with Limousin manuscripts. Nevertheless, for a number of reasons Limoges may have been the intermediary for the transmission of the central Aquitainian style southward to Toulouse. The great abbey of Saint-Martial, the creative centre of manuscript production in Limoges, was Cluniac. Monks from Cluny had been installed there in 1063 with

---

[50] Gaborit-Chopin has attributed 4 manuscripts to the master of the Sacramentary of Saint-Étienne. Besides Paris, BN lat. 9438, these are: manuscript 18 in the collection of Chester Beatty in Dublin; the Bible of Saint-Yrieix (Saint-Yrieix, Mairie) and a bible in the Bibliothèque Mazarine in Paris (Lat. I and II). The exceptional character of the full-page miniatures in the Sacramentary of Saint-Étienne has been emphasized. At the same time, narrative images in other manuscripts produced by this master indicate that he shared regional characteristics with the rest of Aquitainian art. For example, an image such as

David and the Sunamite in the Bible of Saint-Yrieix (Gaborit-Chopin, *Décoration des manuscrits*, fig. 168) might be compared to the narrative images of the *Vita Radegundis* discussed above.

[51] See, e.g., the *Vision of Ezekiel* in the Bible of Saint-Yrieix (fo. 130) or the image of *Christ between Two Angels* in the same manuscript (fo. 304) (in Gaborit-Chopin, *Décoration des manuscrits*, figs. 177 and 167). See also the Apocalyptic vision of Christ in the wall painting of the porch of Saint-Savin.

[52] Paris, BN, lat. 8, vol. II, fo. 41.

the election of a new abbot, Adémar, whose long rule (1063–1114) marked the high point in the history of the abbey.[53] Textual documentation is lacking that might reveal whether particularly close relations existed between the community of La Daurade and the abbey of Saint-Martial in the eleventh and twelfth centuries. There is, none the less, an interesting suggestion of such a connection within the iconography of the Passion cycle from La Daurade itself. The capitals of the *Washing of the Feet* and the *Last Supper* both include imagery, rare in Romanesque art, in which St Martial, Apostle of the Gauls, is given a particular place of honour. According to a legend encouraged by the monks of the abbey of Saint-Martial, their patron saint was a contemporary of the disciples of Christ and served the meal at the Last Supper. The striding figure carrying the serving dish on the Toulousan capital of the *Last*

Pl. 86   *Supper* can probably be identified as St Martial, and he may also be the figure bearing a towel
Pl. 83   as an attendant to the *Washing of the Feet*.[54] By giving St Martial such a prominent place within the Passion cycle, the Cluniac community at La Daurade seems to have recognized and legitimized the apostolic claims for him of their great sister house of Saint-Martial.[55]

If historical relations between the monastery of La Daurade and the abbey of Saint-Martial are difficult to document, there does exist evidence for an artistic connection between the Romanesque scriptorium of Moissac, mother abbey of La Daurade, and contemporary Limousin manuscript decoration.[56] The scriptorium of Moissac was not truly organized until the abbacy of Ansquitil (1085/91–1115),[57] and this was, artistically, its most productive period. The decoration of manuscripts issuing from Moissac consisted predominantly of ornamented initials and letters, with only the occasional appearance of animals or figured elements and, rarely, simple drawings. Where foliate and animal ornament are concerned, however, the Moissac productions of the period of Ansquitil belong clearly to the *style aquitain* defined by Jean Porcher and Gaborit-Chopin.[58] This style, according to Gaborit-Chopin, appeared at Limoges in the early eleventh century and came to dominate not only the Limousin but the entire area neighbouring it to the south, in the manuscripts of the region of Moissac and Agen, as well as Gaillac and Albi. Jean Dufour, in his study of the Moissac scriptorium, has also pointed out that the decoration of Moissac manuscripts follows the Aquitainian vocabulary established by the scriptorium of Saint-Martial in the eleventh century. As examples of the connections between the two scriptoria during this period, he cites, among others, a lavishly ornamented Life of the Saints of the eleventh century from Moissac, and a copy of the *Collationes* of Odo of Cluny from the beginning of the twelfth century.[59]

[53] See Charles de Lasteyrie, *L'Abbaye de Saint-Martial de Limoges* (Paris, 1901); and Gaborit-Chopin, *Décoration des manuscrits*, 17.

[54] St Martial was officially awarded apostolic status in Church councils of the 11th cent. held at Poitiers, Paris, Bourges, and Limoges (*L'Art roman à Saint-Martial de Limoges: les manuscrits à peintures; historique de l'abbaye; la basilique* (exh. cat.) (Limoges, 1950), 13. Lafargue identified the figure with the serving dish on the *Last Supper* capital from La Daurade as St Martial (*Chapiteaux de La Daurade*, 103). Forsyth has also pointed out the special formal and iconographic emphasis given this figure in the Toulousan capital (Ilene Haering Forsyth, 'The Vita Apostolica and Romanesque Sculpture', *Gesta*, 25 (1986), 79–80).

[55] There is other evidence for the importance of St Martial in Toulousan hagiography. An image of St Martial baptizing the Princess Austris was reported by early writers to have shared equal place with the patron saint Saturninus in the destroyed sculptural programme of the west façade of Saint-Sernin (see above, Ch. 3 n. 12). According to legend St Martial founded the first cathedral of St Stephen at Toulouse.

[56] De Lasteyrie, in his monograph on the abbey of Saint-Martial, names Moissac as one of the abbeys with which Saint-Martial had particularly close spiritual ties, based on acts contained in Paris, BN, lat. 5243 (De Lasteyrie, *L'Abbaye de Saint-Martial* (as in n. 53 above), 249 and n. 1).

[57] The essential study of the scriptorium of Moissac is by Jean Dufour, *La Bibliothèque et le scriptorium de Moissac* (Geneva, 1972).

[58] Jean Porcher, 'Enluminures françaises du Midi', *La Revue française*, 56 (1954), 1ᵛ; id., *L'Enluminure française* (Paris, 1954), 23; Gaborit-Chopin, *Décoration des manuscrits*, 61–2.

[59] Paris, BN, lat. 17002 (Dufour, *Bibliothèque et scriptorium*

It is important to our study that the influence of Limousin decoration on the scriptorium of Moissac made itself felt at the end of the eleventh and beginning of the twelfth centuries. This means that the artistic influence of the Aquitaine, and specifically of Limoges, had already penetrated southward into the Midi prior to 1120. In other words, even before the major impact of new artistic ideas from regions to the north that marks the decade 1120–30 in Toulouse, the doors had already been opened and the receptivity to Aquitainian influences established. That the direction of influence should have been from north to south is not surprising, since, as our survey has shown, the manuscript and pictorial arts were much more highly developed at an early date in central France than they were in the Midi.

The relationship we have sought to establish between central Aquitaine and the new style of the 'second generation' in Toulouse is, in fact, confirmed in the realm of foliate ornament associated with this new style. Here, too, the route of transmission may have been the one already established in manuscript decoration between the scriptoria of the Moissac–Agen region and that of Saint-Martial de Limoges. The second workshop of La Daurade not only introduced a new narrative art and figure style into Toulouse, it also replaced the highly evolved foliate ornament so widespread in the sculpture of the pilgrimage workshops with a new repertory of foliate forms and patterns that had not previously been found in Toulousan sculpture. The basic repertory of vegetal ornament shared between the workshops of Saint-Sernin and Moissac at the end of the eleventh century does not appear in the decorative capitals and imposts of the second series from La Daurade. The repertory of the second workshop consists of fibrous vine stems worked into roundels or interlaces, terminating in small curled leaf spirals or in a variety of exotically formed flowers and tripartite leaves, some with pendant or upright fruits or berries. Many of these forms are based on the arum plant.[60] Isolated occurrences of this decorative ornament appear among the historiated capitals of the series as well (see the *Arrest of Christ*).

Pls. 136–8

Pl. 93

In the decorative ornament of the workshop of Saint-Étienne, which shares this same repertory, the ornament is treated with greater looseness and the forms become even more varied and exotic, breaking into fantastic flowers or fleshy cups with protruding stamens. These fleshy and freely mutating forms, so different from the elegant and controlled patterns of the first generation of ornament in Toulouse, find close parallels in some of the most richly decorated manuscripts of about 1100 from the scriptorium of Saint-Martial. Vine stems with abundant, flowering growth of similar curly and fleshy type, terminating in flowers with protruding, tongue-like stamens or with fruit-like centres exposing seeds, interlace with initial letters in a Life of St Martial dating from the beginning of the twelfth century.[61] Decorated initials in the Second Bible of Saint-Martial, attributed to the same artist by Gaborit-Chopin, show a similar repertory of verdant growth.[62] In both these manuscripts, the vine stems sometimes form into large roundels and two stems are sometimes linked by a short beaded band, as they are in the Toulousan vocabulary as well. A miniature of the *Vision of Ezekiel* in the Bible of Saint-Yrieix, a manuscript attributed to the same artist who illuminated the

Pls. 160 and 164

Pls. 153, 160, 189, and 190

de Moissac, cat. 100), and Paris, BN, lat. 2457 (ibid., cat. 71). According to Dufour, the latter could have originated either from Saint-Martial de Limoges or from Moissac. He finds the enclosed letters of its titles close to those of the lapidary inscriptions of the late 11th cent. in the cloister of Moissac.

[60] Denise Jalabert has distinguished these 2 generations of foliate ornament at Moissac and Toulouse as a 'première' and 'seconde flore languedocienne' (*La Flore sculptée des monuments du moyen âge en France* (Paris, 1965), 49–57).

[61] Paris, BN. lat. 529A (Gaborit-Chopin, *Décoration des manuscrits*, figs. 147, 154, 155, and esp. 151 (fo. 2ᵛ)).

[62] Paris, BN, lat. 8, vol. I, fo. 5ᵛ (Gaborit-Chopin, *Décoration des manuscrits*, fig. 150).

Sacramentary of Limoges, includes a large initial E entwined with flowering vine stems. The inverted, cup-like flowers with one or three long stamens belong to the same kind of foliate growth that covers some of the large decorative capitals that crowned the standing apostles from Saint-Étienne, as well as smaller capitals attributable to this sculpture workshop (see Mesplé 39, 44, and 45). The same species of foliage is the basis for ornamented initials in a Gospel book in the Bibliothèque Nationale produced in the region of Moissac-Agen at the end of the eleventh century.[63]

Pls. 160 and 164

THE ENCOUNTER BETWEEN SCULPTURAL AND PICTORIAL TRADITIONS AT TOULOUSE

The accumulation of evidence, then, indicates that the ornamental repertory and the narrative style of the new generation of Romanesque sculptors in Toulouse have their ultimate basis in the pictorial arts of wall painting and manuscript illumination, whether this influence was transmitted directly from as far north as the Loire valley and the Haut-Poitou region, or more indirectly, via Limoges, perhaps with contributions from Moissac and the Agenais. A major puzzle remains, however, concerning the actual mechanism of this transmission and the origins of the workshop responsible for the second series of capitals from La Daurade. Where is the evidence for the prior formation of these individuals as sculptors? Surprisingly, there is no such evidence in the regional school of Romanesque stone sculpture of the Poitou or in the limited examples of stone sculpture as it was practised in the Touraine or the region of Limoges prior to 1120. Indeed, one of the paradoxes to emerge from a review of Romanesque art in the Loire valley and central Aquitaine is how little congruence there appears to be between the brilliant art of wall painting that flowered there in the early Romanesque period and the regional school of stone sculpture that developed somewhat later. Exceptions are twelfth-century capitals at Airvault and Melle, both in the Deux-Sèvres. Anat Tcherikova has successfully tied the historiated capitals of the choir of Saint-Pierre at Airvault to the tradition of narrative painting in the Poitou. She specifically relates this series of capitals, in fact, to the vault paintings of Saint-Savin-sur-Gartempe and to the eleventh-century manuscript of the *Vita Radegundis*. Her arguments that the six choir capitals of Airvault date to the late eleventh century are not convincing, however.[64] I agree with Brooks Stoddard (and with most other scholars) in identifying them as twelfth-century work.[65] In the absence of other comparable sculpture in the Poitou region, a close study of the architecture of Airvault might yield evidence for determining just when the impact of the earlier tradition of Romanesque painting made itself felt on the architectural sculpture of the region.

The capitals of Saint-Pierre at Melle include some, such as the vivid *Entombment*, suggestive of a narrative sensibility equivalent to that of the Toulousan sculptors of the second

[63] Paris, BN, lat. 254. See esp. fo. 10 (Marguerite Vidal *et al.*, *Quercy roman* (La Pierre-qui-vire, 1969), fig. 63).

[64] Anat Tcherikova, 'Some Observations on Sculpture at Airvault', *Gesta*, 24 (1985), 91–103. Tcherikova's study exemplifies the pitfalls of argumentation based primarily on documents for the dating of medieval architecture. Besides the fact that consecration dates are notoriously ambiguous, it is hardly valid to expect that events recorded in the few surviving documents for a church necessarily correspond to observable

phases of a building programme. Tcherikova has also related certain figures on the façade of Saint-Jouin-de-Marnes (Deux-Sèvres) to Romanesque painting of Saint-Savin, although her comparisons are not as convincing as in the case of Airvault (see Anat Tcherikova, 'La Façade occidentale de l'église abbatiale de Saint-Jouin-de-Marnes', *Cahiers de civilisation médiévale*, 28 (1985), 361–83).

[65] Brooks Stoddard, 'A Romanesque Carver at Airvault (Deux-Sèvres)', *Gesta*, 20 (1981), 67–72.

generation. These capitals, however, date from the mid-twelfth century and indicate the appreciably later development of such themes in the Romanesque sculpture of this region.[66] In the Touraine, where wall painting was the art *par excellence*, and at Limoges, with its important monastic scriptoria, the surviving sculpture hardly gives evidence of an equal development of stone carving in these regions in the Romanesque period.[67]

More than one observer has suggested a connection between the capitals of La Daurade and the Romanesque art of metalwork. Given the artistic lines we have already drawn between Toulouse and Limoges, this suggestion might seem to present interesting possibilities. The richness of ornamental detail, and in particular the fondness for the bold diaper pattern that enlivens the surface of a number of the capitals, might be seen as reminiscent, in a general sense, of the techniques of metalworking. In more specific terms, there is no question but that the capitals of La Daurade have striking points in common with a whole class of metalwork and enamel objects from the famous Romanesque workshops of Limoges. A particularly close example is the enamel and gilt copper Chasse of Gimel with scenes from the *Martyrdom of St Stephen*.[68] Here the same enigmatic cloud-like forms, iconographically pertinent to the scene but highly stylized and ornamental, to which we have drawn particular attention in the capitals from La Daurade, are also a leitmotif of this and numerous other examples of the Limousin metalwork art. The figure style, the lively pace of the narrative, and animated communication between figures, even the use of high relief for the heads of primary figures, all bear close comparison to the style of the Toulousan capitals.

Unfortunately for the problem at hand, the whole body of Limousin metalwork art represented by the Chasse of Gimel and related works is too late in date to have inspired the style of the second generation in Toulouse. The Limousin metalwork ateliers that produced this reliquary and related works had their period of brilliance in the late twelfth and early thirteenth centuries. We are forced to conclude, along with Marie-Madeleine Gauthier, that the metalwork was inspired by earlier Languedocian Romanesque sculpture, not the other way around.[69] It is also possible that the parallels between the style of La Daurade and the later twelfth-century metalwork of Limoges are the result of their common grounding in the pictorial traditions of central Aquitaine that we have defined in the course of this chapter.

Investigation, then, will not sustain proposals that the vivid narrative art of central Aquitaine, the result of a long development in that region, was brought to Toulouse by Aquitainian stone sculptors or metalworkers. In the absence of other evidence, we are left with our original conclusion that this imagery reached Toulouse through the medium of manuscript illumination. It is legitimate to ask why the great tradition of narrative imagery fostered by the wall paintings and manuscripts of central Aquitaine should have made such an impact in Toulouse, when it seems not to have found expression in the school of Romanesque sculpture of its own region. Actually it is not surprising that this translation of an important narrative tradition into architectural sculpture should have taken place in Toulouse. The remarkable

[66] Raymond Oursel, *Haut-Poitou roman* (La Pierre-qui-vire, 1975), 268 and figs. 124–7.

[67] See the Romanesque fragments from the destroyed abbey church and conventual buildings of Saint-Martial de Limoges in *L'Art roman à Saint-Martial de Limoges* (as in n. 54 above), nos. 61–76.

[68] See Marie-Madeleine Gauthier, *Émaux limousins champ-*levés des XII*e*, XIII*e* et XIV*e* siècles (Paris, 1950), 152 and pl. 9. See also the closely related reliquary of St Stephen from Malval and one with scenes of the Resurrection at Nantouillet (ibid., pls. 10 and 11).

[69] Ead., *Émaux du moyen âge occidental* (Fribourg, 1972), 98–9.

capitals from the cloister of La Daurade represent the coming together of an extremely vivid and expressive story-telling mode, fostered by the pictorial arts, with the equally developed art of figurative sculpture in stone as it had evolved rapidly and with brilliance in Toulouse between 1075 and 1120. When Romanesque sculptors of Toulouse came into contact with this richly developed narrative art they were ready to receive it and to make use of it. The Toulousan contribution was in transforming this art through the powerful plastic sense that invests all Toulousan Romanesque sculpture. This deft and confident working of three-dimensional form is pronounced in the sculpture produced just prior to the appearance of the new style, namely in the reliefs of the Porte Miègeville and the west façade of Saint-Sernin.

This last point needs stressing since, as remarked earlier in this chapter, it is important not to misunderstand the nature of the convergence between this pictorially rooted art and the existing tradition of Romanesque sculpture in Toulouse. The capitals with Passion and Resurrection scenes from La Daurade represent profoundly sculptural solutions to the challenge of presenting narrative subject-matter in the cloister, both in their three-dimensional conception of the capital drum as a field for narrative activity and in their powerful sense of relief. In coming into contact with a lively pictorial art from outside their own region, what Toulousan sculptors took from this art was its episodic way of telling a story and its visually explicit means of dramatizing the narrative through actors who employ an expressive repertory of communicative gestures and body postures. This is very different from saying that sculptors of the new Toulousan style attempted to reproduce in relief sculpture pictorial effects that are germane to painting. What is more, it required a powerful sense of the three-dimensional to make these stories work on four-sided capitals that were locked into a monumental architectural framework.

The achievements of Toulousan sculptors in the capitals of La Daurade were not, as we have seen, the result of a gradual process of evolution or even of trial and error. The sculptors of La Daurade achieved their results in a startling master-stroke, as it were. This suggests both their technical sophistication, built upon an outstanding tradition of previous stone carving in Toulouse, as well as their conscious sensitivity to style and the expressive potential of various stylistic modes available to them. Toulousan stone carving, by 1120, was no longer a tentative art, working out first solutions to figural representation. Within approximately three decades Toulousan sculptors had achieved consummate control of relief sculpture and its special properties of expression.

It may not be possible to give more than broad reasons why the infusion of fresh artistic influences into Toulouse from neighbouring regions to the north should have occurred just at the moment when it did.[70] It is at least clear from the evidence of monastic scriptoria that the

---

[70] In 1964 Seidel suggested that it was William IX, duke of Aquitaine and count of Poitiers, who brought the new workshop of La Daurade to Toulouse during his second occupation of the city in 1113 (*Sculpture from Saint-Étienne*, 149–50 and 155–6). There are, however, problems with this theory. Seidel agrees that the new style first made its appearance in the cloister of La Daurade. Yet it is difficult to see how the occupation of William IX and his entourage could have exerted a concrete influence on the building programme already in progress at the Cluniac monastery. The deliberate policy of the duke and his wife Philippa was one of support for reforming movements that were in immediate competition with Cluny (see above, Ch. 1). In a paper of 1986 I suggested that

absence of recorded donations or privileges by Philippa to the Cluniac establishments in Toulouse may reflect a deliberate programme of opposition to her father's policies and loyalties. The only surviving child of William IV, Philippa, in effect, had been disinherited by the Toulousan tradition of exclusive male succession to the county. Her marriage in 1094 to the duke of Aquitaine was certainly an act of filial and political defiance of her father, who may have died in that year or in 1093 (Kathryn Horste, discussion of Thomas Lyman, 'The Male Audience and Female Patronage: The Iconography of the Fall in Early Romanesque Sculpture', Thirteenth Annual Medieval Colloquium, University of the South, Sewanee, Tenn., Apr. 1986). This suggests that the relationship between the 'foreign' entire region immediately to the north of Toulouse, that is, Moissac and the Agenais, Gaillac, and Albi, was already within the artistic sphere of Limoges and the *style aquitain* by the late eleventh century. What is more, other suggestions of an impact of the regional style of Aquitaine show themselves in the Romanesque sculpture of the Quercy at about the same time that the new changes were occurring in Toulousan sculpture. Notably, at Moissac there are dramatic differences between the sculptures of the cloister, completed in 1100, and the reliefs of the narthex, tympanum, and porch, commonly dated no more than 15–30 years after them.[71] This difference indicates the introduction of some new stylistic influence during the construction of the narthex and the decoration of its porch.

These changes are part of the same movement of artistic influences from central France to the Midi that is indicated in the capitals of La Daurade. The animated reliefs of the side walls of the Moissac porch, in scenes such as the *Presentation in the Temple* or the *Adoration of the Magi*, are under the sway of a new Romanesque canon of proportions and new sources of interior energy that relate directly to figures like those of Saint-Savin and other early Romanesque wall paintings of Aquitaine. The cross-legged poses and counter-posed movements that are hallmarks of the Romanesque style in its full-blown form at Moissac and nearby Souillac, were already characteristic of the figure style of Aquitaine some two to three decades earlier, as exemplified in figures like that of God the Father in the *Construction of the Tower of Babel* from the nave vault of Saint-Savin.

Pl. 152

Pl. 141

The transformations in mature Romanesque sculpture towards 1120 in south-west France appear to be part of the orientation of sculpture in this region away from its close involvement with Spain during the immediately preceding decades. The development of Romanesque sculpture in Toulouse and its region during the period 1075 to 1120 can be understood very largely in terms of mutual influences exchanged among churches of the so-called pilgrimage style linking the two sides of the Pyrenees. After 1120 this was no longer the case. The style of the second generation in Toulouse, represented by the sculptures of La Daurade and Saint-Étienne, reveals a disengagement of this region from its traditional southern network and a new openness to Romanesque developments from the centre of France.

THE WORKSHOP OF GILABERTUS AT SAINT-ÉTIENNE

The new involvement of Toulousan sculpture with Romanesque developments to the north of Toulouse after 1120 is confirmed in the sculptures of the cloister and chapter house of Saint-Étienne. This group is made up of five historiated capitals, large-scale reliefs of the twelve Apostles and the capitals, imposts, and bases associated with them, plus various foliate and figured capitals.[72] The sculptures are a great deal more heterogeneous in style than is the second series of capitals from La Daurade. This suggests that sculptors of different ages or artistic formation—perhaps an older and a younger carver—may have worked together at

---

occupying count and the conservative community at La Daurade may have been anything but warm. Added to this is the probability, discussed in the next chapter, that the imagery of the Passion cycle from La Daurade is at least in part meant to celebrate the role of the count of Toulouse, Raymond de Saint-Gilles, in freeing the tomb of Christ during his Crusade to the Holy Land.

[71] The south porch of Moissac and its sculpture have been dated to the abbacy of Roger (1115–31), whose effigy appears on the east spandrel of the façade. The narthex and tympanum are sometimes attributed to his predecessor Ansquitil on the basis of the Chronicle of Aymeric de Peyrac (see Schapiro, 'Romanesque Sculpture of Moissac. I', 137).

[72] M. 1–65. I have departed from Mesplé in attributing his nos. 44–6 and 48 to La Daurade rather than Saint-Étienne (see

Saint-Étienne. The name of one of the sculptors on the project, Gilabertus, is known, since he ostentatiously signed two of the pieces.[73] His style reveals the early participation of Toulouse in that maturing and 'calming' of Romanesque art in south-west France that has been described by some French writers as a *détente*.[74]

The sculpture workshops of La Daurade and Saint-Étienne have always been seen as closely associated, and, indeed, this association goes beyond a general stylistic kinship. It is contained in certain telling details that betray a training in common workshop methods on the part of sculptors engaged on the two projects. The sharing of ornamental details with La Daurade is particularly evident in the two Apostles signed by Gilabertus (Mesplé 5 and 22), and in the two historiated capitals I attribute to him, the *Death of John the Baptist* (Mesplé 31), and the unfinished capital of the *Wise and Foolish Virgins* (Mesplé 34). Identical ways of treating hair and beards, for example, recur in numerous instances among the two groups of sculptures. The hair, treated as individual locks, each ending in a tiny knob, on the seated male figure at the far left of Herod's banquet table, can be compared to the beard of Christ in the *Arrest* scene from La Daurade. Likewise the beard of Herod from the left short face of the Baptist capital can be compared to the identical short beard with decorative row of curls on the diminutive Simon of Cyrene in the *Way to Calvary* from La Daurade. The way in which the hair of Salome is arranged in large, loosely plaited or intertwined locks on the long face of the Baptist capital resembles closely the long, heavy locks of Christ in the *Last Supper* and those of Christ in the scene of him confronting the soldiers from the *Gethsemane* capital.

Pls. 156 and 157–8
Pls. 166–9
Pls. 170–3
Pl. 166
Pl. 91
Pl. 169
Pl. 168
Pl. 84
Pl. 90

There is a similar feeling for richly precious detail in the ornamenting of clothing and mantles in the two groups of sculptures. Even an identity of individual motifs can be seen in the heavily jewelled row of four-petalled flowers banding the neck and hem of Salome's garments and the sleeve of Herodias from Saint-Étienne, and the robe of one of the disciples to the right of Christ in the *Last Supper* from La Daurade. An identical four-petalled motif appears in the jewelled mantles of the paired Apostles from Saint-Étienne (Mesplé 24).

Pl. 168
Pl. 87
Pl. 163

The frequent use of shirred sleeves is also noteworthy, as is the vertical accordion pleating at the hems and necks of garments at Saint-Étienne and La Daurade. Certain formulas for the fall of drapery likewise are used by the two workshops, as when expansive areas of drapery, such as those covering backs and shoulders, are broken by only a few broadly treated folds (particularly in the figure seen from the rear or in profile), while drapery on hips and legs is defined by complex patterns. The stylistic intimacy between specific capitals from La Daurade and sculptures from Saint-Étienne prompted Linda Seidel to conclude in 1964 that the sculptor Gilabertus had trained in the workshop of La Daurade.[75] She laid emphasis on the artistic

Pls. 156 and 170
Pls. 121 and 124
cf. Pls. 124 and 167

the Inventory). None of the pieces attributed to Saint-Étienne can be situated with any certainty in specific structures of the claustral complex. They are ultimately attributed to the cathedral on the basis of Du Mège's report to the directors of the museum of 12 Mar. 1817 (see above, Ch. 3). Eight Apostle reliefs and 7 capitals are listed in the catalogue of 1818/19 (nos. 168–82), where they are described as originating from 'several chapels situated in the cloister of Saint-Étienne' (*Notice des tableaux* (1818/19), 89).

[73] The inscriptions which contained his signature no longer exist. They appeared on the lower edge of the figures of St Andrew and St Thomas (one reading VIR NON INCERTUS ME CELAVIT GILABERTUS and the other GILABERTUS ME FECIT). They were unaccountably broken off during the 19th cent. (Henri Rachou, *Musée des Augustins: pierres romanes de Saint-Étienne, La Daurade et Saint-Sernin* (Paris, 1934), 48). There is no reason to doubt that they existed, however, since they were recorded both by Du Mège (*Notice des tableaux* (1818/19), 87–8) and, later in the 19th cent., by Ernest Roschach (*Musée de Toulouse: catalogue des antiquités et des objets d'art* (Toulouse, 1865), 225). On their disappearance, see Seidel, *Sculpture from Saint-Étienne*, 46–52.

[74] Durliat, among others, has used this term, citing the much earlier study of Romanesque sculpture in Languedoc by Rey (Raymond Rey, *La Sculpture romane languedocienne* (Toulouse and Paris, 1936), 267). Cited in Marcel Durliat, 'La Cathédrale Saint-Étienne de Cahors: architecture et sculpture', *Bulletin monumental* 137, (1979), 324–5.

[75] Seidel, *Sculpture from Saint-Étienne*, 127.

dependency of the cathedral workshop on that of the Cluniac priory, going so far as to conclude that 'the style of Gilabertus is a logical development of the work of the second atelier of La Daurade'.[76] This latter claim is one I cannot agree with. While there are numerous indications of closely shared workshop practices among sculptures from the two sites, far from being a logical development of La Daurade, the art of Gilabertus turns away from some of the most essential elements of the Daurade style. Most notably, the energy and high excitement that invest the narrative imagery of La Daurade are traded by Gilabertus for a more reserved and psychological interplay between characters. The tension between plasticity and surface ornamentation that is so exaggerated in the second Daurade style is replaced by a much more subtle and muted handling of relief under the chisel of Gilabertus. As a concomitant of this new conception of relief, Gilabertus rejected the device of miniature architecture which so emphatically demarcates an upper and a lower zone in the capitals of La Daurade.[77]

The differences in conception are starkly revealed in comparing Gilabertus's capital of the *Death of John the Baptist* to the *Arrest of Christ* from La Daurade, both of which employ a frieze-like unrolling of multiple episodes around the circumference of the capital. The story of John the Baptist unwinds at a rhythmic pace across the surface of the capital in a very regular succession of actions, from the beheading at the far right, to the executioner's delivery of the Baptist's head to Salome and her presentation of it to Herodias. The latter episode, the climax of the narrative, is placed at the centre of the capital, while a fourth scene, Salome before Herod, is tucked behind a volute on the left half-face of the capital. This intimate scene in itself reveals a most original sense of narration on the part of Gilabertus. Rather than depicting a distinct episode from the Gospel story, it sets forth for the viewer the psychological relationship between the degenerate Herod and the youthful Salome. The introduction of such a vignette in place of an additional active episode represents a sophisticated mode of narration not encountered among the capitals of La Daurade. *Pl. 166* *Pls. 91–2* *Pl. 167* *Pl. 169*

There is a fluidity and a careful deliberation of movement from the right to the left side of the Baptist capital that is at once lyrical and distinctly formal. The rhythmic reappearance of key figures depicted at successive moments makes the beheading and the banquet scenes among the most complex and intimately knit narrative sequences in Romanesque sculpture.

In sharp contrast the narrative pace in the capital of the *Arrest of Christ* from La Daurade is violent and staccato. The complex contour of the capital is marked by eruptions of action as the narrative moves from one climax to another at projecting points on the undulant surface. The sense of lyricism and symmetry in the Baptist capital, embodied in the rhythmical and carefully paced succession of oval heads across the front surface of the capital, were obviously foreign to the sculptor of the *Arrest of Christ*. In the latter capital, asymmetry is inherent in the scheme, in which four scenes occupy a three-lobed capital. Narrative high points are situated off-axis and in completely idiosyncratic relationship to the regular rows of arched forms above. *Pls. 91–6*

The contrasting formality inherent in Gilabertus's sense of design is present in the unfinished capital of the *Wise and Foolish Virgins*. The coupled figures of Christ and Ecclesia on a short *Pls. 170–3*

---

[76] Ibid. 149.
[77] Those capitals from Saint-Étienne I attribute to Gilabertus are the *Feast of Herod* (M. 31) and the unfinished *Wise and Foolish Virgins* (M. 34). The fragmentary *Wise and Foolish Virgins* and the *Legend of Mary of Egypt* are not the work of his hand; nor is the *Magi* capital, which probably dates to the third quarter of the 12th cent.

face are matched by a cunning spacing of the Wise Virgins on the long face so that they organize themselves into two pairs. The fifth Wise Virgin on the adjacent small face is paired with a graceful equivalent of her own form, a budding tree whose sinuous stem coils around its own axis in imitation of the virgin's cross-legged pose. It is the subtle variation within the bounds of symmetry—the slight inclination of the heads, the crossed limbs—which gives to Gilabertus's figures their sense of poised equilibrium.

In the relationship between relief and ground and in his treatment of surfaces, the style of Gilabertus also shows sharp departures from the practices of the second workshop of La Daurade. The clumping of figures at particular points of the drum, for example in the *Arrest of Christ* and *Way to Calvary*, and the serious eroding of the ground, as in the *Entombment*, are alien to Gilabertus's sense of relief. In a capital such as the *Death of John the Baptist*, the projection of the figures is that of a uniform frieze. No portions of the relief project significantly forward from an even front plane.

Pls. 166 and 167

The difference between Gilabertus's relief technique and that of La Daurade is illustrated by the figure of the executioner directly beneath the right volute on the Baptist capital. Instead of emerging aggressively out of the core of the capital, as do the angle figures in the *Entombment*, the figure of the executioner is released entirely from the ground, his head, shoulders, and upper body almost completely in the round, and his figure is brought forward to the front plane, so that he forms a right angle with the contiguous front face of the capital. Gilabertus never piles up forms, several heads deep, as does the sculptor of the *Arrest of Christ* and the *Gethsemane* capitals, to suggest figures standing one in front of another. Instead he creates the impression of multiple and extremely shallow planes slipping with great fluidity one behind another while he maintains a comparatively discreet and even projection.

Perhaps the most striking departure by Gilabertus from the conception of the historiated capital that was pursued at La Daurade was his rejection of the range of arcades and miniature architecture that shelters the narrative zone. At La Daurade this upper zone replaced the earlier configuration of central modillion and corner volutes that terminated historiated capitals of the type of Moissac and the first series from La Daurade. By denying the existence of an underlying architectonic structure in the capitals of the *Death of John the Baptist* and the *Wise and Foolish Virgins*, Gilabertus avoided the constraints traditionally imposed by the block-like nature of the capital. In his hands the entire capital was made an unbroken field for the presentation of the figured themes, ranged in frieze-like fashion across the surface. The only tribute Gilabertus paid to the kinship of his capital form to earlier types are the discreet volutes at each corner, which assume the delicate form of curled leaves embracing a small cone or berry on the capital of John the Baptist.

The dissolution of the architecture of the capital is one of the indications that Gilabertus's work at Saint-Étienne followed in time the cloister at La Daurade. The complete absorption of the drum by the figures in Gilabertus's capitals represents a conceptual step beyond the second series from La Daurade, where this repudiation of the block-like form and solidity of the capital is achieved only in the lower zone. The drastic erosion of the drum, so that solid mass is

Pl. 100
Pl. 120

concentrated in the highly active figure groups (as in the *Deposition* and *Entombment*, or the *Incredulity of Thomas*, from La Daurade) was a necessary step prior to the complete disappearance of the cylindrical drum as the underlying basis of the capital and its replacement by the 'figure friezes' of the *Death of John the Baptist* and the *Wise and Foolish Virgins*.

The features that distinguish Gilabertus's capitals from those of La Daurade together constitute a new definition of the Romanesque in Toulousan sculpture—his abandoning of the strongly defined architecture of the capital, his calming of the high tension and agitation of the Daurade style in favour of a more lyrical narrative rhythm, his adoption of a figure type of elegant proportions and measured movements, along with a general softening of surfaces that encourages a diffuse and subtle play of light. These essential qualities bring into focus Gilabertus's participation in that phenomenon of mature Romanesque sculpture in south-west and south central France that has been described by the term *détente*, literally a relaxing of tension.

The decades 1135–65 saw the coming to maturity of the Quercy as one of the great foyers of Romanesque sculpture in its late flowering. A talented generation of sculptors, successors to the great workshops of Moissac, Souillac, and Beaulieu, produced sculptures of moving emotional appeal and technical refinement at Cahors (Lot); Brive-la-Gaillarde (Corrèze); Catus (Lot); Collonges (Corrèze); La Graulière (Corrèze); Serandon (Corrèze); Saint-Chamant (Cantal); and Ydes (Cantal), to name only some of the ensembles still remaining in this richly endowed region.[78] The sculpture of this generation has been considered by many writers to exhibit a quietening of the tension and agitation that define the great tympana of Moissac and Beaulieu or the trumeau of Souillac.[79] Certainly an essential aspect of the new works is their turning away from the supernatural and the abstract in favour of a more human scale and an emphasis on human response and sensibility.

Pl. 178
Pl. 177
Pls. 180 and 181
Pl. 179

Seidel has proposed a date between 1120 and 1140 for the carving of the Apostles from Saint-Étienne. She sees the conception of the figures as closest to other work within Languedocian architectural sculpture of about 1125.[80] I am in general agreement. On the basis of its relationship to La Daurade and to sculpture of the south porch at Moissac, I would place the work at Saint-Étienne between about 1125 and 1135. These dates, if accurate, would make the sculptures of Gilabertus among the earliest expressions in Languedocian sculpture of the new spirit of *détente* that characterizes the mature Romanesque of 1135–65. We have characterized the style of La Daurade, on the other hand, as one of highly charged energy and fast-paced narrative. At the same time, we have described as fundamentally new in the Daurade series the degree of intimacy in the Passion scenes, their interest in human emotional response, and their powerful evocation of place and moment. In these respects the capitals of La Daurade, like those of Gilabertus, may be seen to embody to a striking degree the new humanized spirituality and interest in individual psychological response that defined the mature Romanesque of the mid-twelfth century.

Toulouse, then, seems to have been important in the early definition of the more humanized vision that was to characterize the Romanesque sculpture of the second and third quarters of

---

[78] See Marie-Madeleine Macary, *Sculpture romane en bas-Limousin* (Périgueux, 1966); Rey, *Sculpture romane langue-docienne*, 259–80. Also, on individual monuments of the Quercy: Durliat, 'Cathédrale de Cahors', 285–340; id., 'Un chapiteau roman à Lasvaux (Lot)', *Bulletin monumental*, 129 (1971), 49–57; Elke Bratke, *Das Nordportal der Kathedrale Saint-Étienne in Cahors* (Freiburg im Breisgau, 1977); Pierre Quarré, 'Le Portail de Mauriac et le porche d'Ydes: leurs rapports avec l'art du Languedoc et du Limousin', *Bulletin monumental*, 98 (1939), 129–51; P. Lebouteux, 'Le Portail de l'église de Collonges-la-Rouge (Corrèze)', *Bulletin de la société des lettres, sciences, et arts de la Corrèze*, 74 (1970), 211–14; and Providence, Rhode Island, *The Renaissance of the Twelfth Century* (exh. cat.), ed. Stephen K. Scher (Providence, 1969), 50–8.

[79] I discussed this aspect of mature Romanesque sculpture in a paper entitled 'High Romanesque Sculpture: Developments in Southern France in the Generation after Saint-Denis', delivered at the Sixth Annual Symposium of the Robert Branner Forum for Medieval Art at Columbia University, 5 Apr. 1987.

[80] Seidel, *Sculpture from Saint-Étienne*, 157. She summarizes earlier opinions on the dating of Saint-Étienne.

the twelfth century. We have already pointed to the sculptures on the side walls of the porch at Moissac as another site where the two traditions of Languedocian stone carving and the pictorial art of central Aquitaine can be seen to come together in a monumental work. The important cross-fertilization between Toulouse and Moissac at this period, comparable to that which occurred in the earlier generation of 1080–1120, is suggested in the ensemble of Apostles from Saint-Étienne. Here a sculptor with stylistic associations to the Moissac tympanum worked side-by-side with Gilabertus and a third carver. Gilabertus's two signed Apostles, *St Thomas* and *St Andrew* (M. 5 and 22), are clearly distinguishable from the others. Another pair (M. 24), while not signed, is very likely also the work of this master. The work of an assistant to Gilabertus, highly influenced by his style, may be recognized in the pair of *SS Peter and Paul* (M. 15). Finally, six of the Apostles (two single figures and two pairs) (M. 1, 8, 11, and 19) are in a style suffused with Romanesque tension and distinctly opposed to the *détente* of Gilabertus's style.

Pls. 153–65 and 189–90

Pls. 156–8

Pl. 164

Pl. 165

Pls. 153, 159, 160, and 161

Pl. 155

Seidel has already dubbed the latter artist 'the St. James Master', after the Apostle holding an archiepiscopal staff and framed between cypress branches (M. 19).[81] She concluded that he had been trained in the workshop that executed the Moissac cloister and the first series of capitals from La Daurade. Hence, in her analysis, his formation as an artist belonged to the earliest beginnings of Romanesque sculpture in the region.

The figures by this artist seem to me much closer in spatial conception and relief definition to the style of the Moissac tympanum, probably executed about 1120–5,[82] and I believe him to have been a somewhat younger sculptor than the ones who worked in the Moissac cloister and during the first building campaign at La Daurade. The substantial plasticity of the Toulouse Apostles and the intricate layering of their heavy drapery folds, along with the wind-blown animation of the hems, have much in common with the tympanum of the south portal at Moissac, about twenty to twenty-five years later than the cloister. The long locks and swooping moustaches of these Apostles more closely resemble those of Christ and the Elders in the tympanum, or of Samson on the capital inside the narthex, than they do any of the heads in the Moissac cloister. What is more, the attempt by this sculptor to achieve a substantial projection through the bent knees of M. 8 results in an awkward ambiguity of posture similar to that of the enthroned Christ of the tympanum.

Pl. 159

These analogies reveal the presence in the workshop at Saint-Étienne of a sculptor who was close to developments at Moissac about 1120–5. I have suggested that it was about this time that influences from the Romanesque art of Aquitaine, probably transmitted to Moissac through manuscript painting, began to make an impact on sculpture at the abbey church. The St James master, as one of the collaborators on the project at Saint-Étienne, reinforced the

---

[81] Seidel, *Sculpture from Saint-Étienne*, 105–14 and 128–33 on the style of the St James master and 134–7 on the identification of this Apostle. In terms of her assignment of hands, I am essentially in agreement with Seidel, though I would not attribute the pair M. 11 to the same sculptor who executed the *Peter and Paul* (M. 15). I do not, on the other hand, agree with her analysis of the roles played by the respective sculptors nor her chronology of the execution. I believe Gilabertus was master of the project from the outset and established the form of the block turned on the diagonal. One master (M. 15) was strongly influenced by Gilabertus and

copied his drapery motifs closely. The third hand I interpret as an older sculptor (M. 8), probably with a considerable career behind him, who could not substantially alter his style and could only awkwardly adapt his fixed concept of the cross-legged figure to the new demands presented by Gilabertus's conception of the block.

[82] M. F. Hearn has summarized the evidence for dating the tympanum and side walls of the Moissac porch (*Romanesque Sculpture* (Ithaca, NY, 1981), 169 n. 1). Dates both earlier and later than 1125 are still claimed by various writers for the tympanum.

involvement of Toulousan sculpture at this period with developments in the region of Quercy, to the north of Toulouse.

The older literature on the Apostles from Saint-Étienne viewed them alternatively as Romanesque preparation for the portal with column statues of the Île-de-France or as southern reflections of this development that had already taken place at Saint-Denis and Chartres.[83] These theories hinged on the assumption that the Apostles had formed a figure-decorated portal with recessed jambs. In exposing the writings of Du Mège, which had formed the basis for their reconstruction as a portal, Seidel sought to remove the Apostles from a proto-Gothic equation and to return discussion of them to their place within the development of Languedocian architectural sculpture.[84] Even so, some scholars continue to maintain that the character of Gilabertus's work at Saint-Étienne presupposes the impact on him of the proto-Gothic sculpture of northern France. The calm demeanour of Gilabertus's Apostles, their oval facial structure, the delicate modelling of the figure through the softening effects of light, and the fine fall of drapery in vertical folds have all suggested to Denis Milhau that this Toulousan artist had experienced the sculpture of the Île-de-France or Le Mans in work that dates from between 1140 and 1160.[85]

From my own point of view, these are precisely the features of Gilabertus's art that herald the new direction in Romanesque sculpture of the Quercy, and there is no reason or necessity to presuppose an outside northern influence as the impetus for this phenomenon. The softening, the humanizing, as it were, of Romanesque sculpture that is discernible from about 1130, was a widespread phenomenon, appearing in portal sculpture earliest at Cahors, whose iconography, composition, and message are distinctly rooted in the indigenous artistic developments of the region and have little to do with northern portals of the period.[86] The impetus for the new directions in Romanesque sculpture that are observable at such an early date in Toulouse and, increasingly in the 1140s and 1150s, in the important monuments of the Quercy, is better sought in fundamental changes and new directions in Christian spirituality in the early decades of the twelfth century, and in particular in monastic spirituality, which generated these works. Only such fundamentally new conceptions of the nature of Christian devotion could explain the coherent and integral modifications of form and meaning that

---

[83] Vöge saw the workshop of Saint-Denis as the point of entry of Toulousan influences into the Île-de-France. He pointed in particular to Gilabertus's work at Saint-Étienne as a source of this influence, both at Saint-Denis and in certain of the sculptures of Chartres (Wilhelm Vöge, *Die Anfänge des monumentalen Stiles im Mittelalter* (Strasbourg, 1894), 80–90). Porter and Stoddard, on the other hand, saw the influence moving from north to south, concluding that Gilabertus of Toulouse benefited from the art of Saint-Denis, Chartres, and later northern portals of the 1150s and 1160s (Arthur Kingsley Porter, *Romanesque Sculpture of the Pilgrimage Roads* (Boston, 1923), i. 159, 241; Whitney S. Stoddard, *The West Portals of Saint-Denis and Chartres: Sculpture in the Île-de-France from 1140 to 1190, A Theory of Origins* (Cambridge, Mass., 1952), 45). In his recent amplification of his text of 1952, however, Stoddard has concluded that his dating of the Saint-Étienne sculptures was probably too late. He now agrees with Durliat's dating of them to 1135–40 and finds it questionable that there is any connection at all between Saint-Étienne and the portals of Saint-Denis or Chartres (*Sculptors of the West Portals of Chartres Cathedral: Their Origins in Romanesque and their Role in Chartrain Sculpture* (New York, 1987), 179–83).

[84] Linda Seidel, 'A Romantic Forgery', *Art Bulletin*, 50 (1968), 33–41. In a recent article on the *Virgin and Child* of Solsona, a work that he attributes to Gilabertus of Toulouse, Serafín Moralejo has pointed out that the debate over Gilabertus's relationship to the royal portals of the Île de France has done little to advance our understanding of his art. He has called for a broader investigation of Gilabertus's sources, one that would look to parallels in other geographic areas (Serafín Moralejo, 'De Sant Esteve de Tolosa a la Daurade: notes sobre l'escultura del claustre romànic de Santa Maria de Solsona', *Quaderns d'estudis medievals*, 23–4 (1983), 13–14).

[85] Denis Milhau in Toulouse, Musée des Augustins, *Grandes Étapes*, 34–5; id., 'Les Cloîtres romans de Toulouse: l'art des chapiteaux', *Archeologia*, 77 (1974), 55. Durliat has singled out the master of the west portal of Saint-Denis as the contemporary with whom Gilabertus has the most in common, without suggesting that either artist influenced the other (*Haut-Languedoc roman* (La Pierre-qui-vire, 1978), 205).

[86] On the dates of Cahors, see Durliat, 'Cathédrale de Cahors', 285–340.

transformed Romanesque sculpture in south-west France in the decades between 1130 and 1160. These transformations may parallel in certain ways what occurred in monumental sculpture in the north at the same period, since artists and iconographers in both regions were responding to some of the same currents in religious thought. The response of mature Romanesque art in southern France has a character of its own, however, and it is one that has not been particularly well defined in the traditional shift of attention away from this region and towards the Île-de-France after about 1140. The specific response of the Cluniac community at La Daurade to the new urges and aspirations in Christian spirituality of the twelfth century and to revivified monastic ideals, as expressed in the art of its cloister, is the subject of the next chapter.

7

MONASTIC IDEALS
THE ICONOGRAPHY OF A REFORMED CLOISTER

CONTRASTS between the first and second series of capitals already drawn in the previous chapters make it clear that a fundamental rethinking of the cloister programme occurred at La Daurade between the breaking off of work around 1105–8 and its resumption around 1120 or shortly afterwards. Whereas a systematic selection and ordering of subjects in accordance with an overriding message seems to be lacking in the early work, in the decoration of the later arcades a deliberate effort to draw the sculptured elements of the cloister together into a concerted programme of meaning is evident. While the programme cannot be known in its entirety, it can at least be seen that the surviving capitals of the second series collectively elaborate a theme central to the religious experience of twelfth-century monks, namely, the Passion of Christ and his charge to his disciples in his post-Resurrection appearances to them.

But the differences between the two series of capitals are more fundamental than this. The scenes of Christ's Passion, his Resurrection, and his appearances to his disciples that are vividly depicted in the later ensemble embody new spiritual values that transformed devotion and the definition of the religious life in many quarters during the course of the twelfth century. These new spiritual values were based on a quest for God through exploration of the 'inner man' (*homo interior*), achieved through solitude, private prayer, and the exploration of individual capacities for human response and moral transformation. Richard W. Southern and John Benton have described a new urge towards introspection and self-knowledge, what Colin Morris has termed 'the discovery of the individual', as the psychological transformation most prophetic for European humanism in this movement.[1] In distinction from those writers, Jean Leclercq and Caroline Bynum have offered a more refined definition of the new spiritual movement by emphasizing that the twelfth-century exploration of self was not concerned with the unique and singular qualities of the individual in the modern sense. Rather it was aimed at discovering and making contact with that aspect of the interior soul, the likeness to God, that all individuals share in common.[2] Bynum and Leclercq have stressed the proliferation of new

---

[1] Richard W. Southern, *The Making of the Middle Ages* (New Haven, 1953), 219–57; id., 'Medieval Humanism', in *Medieval Humanism and Other Studies* (New York, 1970), 29–60; John Benton, 'Individualism and Conformity in Medieval Western Europe', in A. Banani and S. Vryonis, Jun. (eds.), *Individualism and Conformity in Classical Islam* (Wiesbaden, 1977), 145–58; Colin Morris, *The Discovery of the Individual: 1050–1200* (1972; repr. edn., New York, 1973); id., 'Individualism in Twelfth-Century Religion: Some Further Reflec-

tions', *Journal of Ecclesiastical History*, 31 (1980), 195–206. For the shift towards the concern for interior attitudes see also Giles Constable, 'Opposition to Pilgrimage in the Middle Ages', *Mélanges G. Fransen I, Studia Gratiana*, 19 (1976), 142.
[2] Jean Leclercq, 'The New Orders', in Jean Leclercq, François Vandenbroucke, and Louis Bouyer, *The Spirituality of the Middle Ages* (New York, 1982), 127–61 (esp. 138–9); Jean Leclercq, 'La Crise du monachisme aux xiᵉ et xiiᵉ siècles', *Bulletino dell'istituto storico italiano per il medio evo e*

types of religious vocation in which devout religious and lay persons practised this spiritual quest, but practised it through affiliation with a group, whether traditional cenobitic monasticism or one of the many new eremitic communities that formed around a solitary, charismatic leader. In all these cases, the ideals of behaviour and moral life aspired to by the individual were based on a spiritual model held in common by the group. These models exhibit the strongly retrospective quality of the new spirituality, its desire to return to the fundamentals of primitive Christianity, to the example of the Apostles, and the communion of the Early Church.

The ultimate model for all these aspirants, of course, individual or group, was the humanity and moral example of Christ. The writings and actions of lay and religious devotees alike in the late eleventh century and, increasingly, in the twelfth, testify to an intense interest in the reality of Christ's life on earth, his interactions with his disciples and his personal suffering, crucifixion, and resurrection. This new preoccupation with the son of God as the exemplary model of humanity contrasts with the overwhelmingly supernatural concerns of earlier eleventh-century spirituality, with its emphasis on the inevitability of Apocalyptic judgement and the redeeming powers of miraculous interventions and relic worship.

The Gospel account of Christ's betrayal, condemnation, and crucifixion, and the spiriting away of his body by his followers, constitutes the episodes of his life on earth in which his humanity had been most intensely revealed. And for large numbers of Christian worshippers of the early twelfth century, the very spots where these events had been enacted were now accessible to personal experience, in a way they had not been before, as the result of the liberation of the holy places by the armies of the First Crusade. The cloister capitals of La Daurade are among the earliest works of monumental sculpture to give expression to this intensely felt interest in the holy places and in the human drama of Christ's Passion and Resurrection.[3] Since we have found no sources in prior Toulousan art for this vivid rendition of the Passion story, the Cluniac community at La Daurade must have actively sought a new workshop capable of distilling the drama of Christ's last days with the requisite power and immediacy.

In attempting to recover the process by which such a new artistic vision could have been realized in Toulouse, it is essential to recognize that the new directions in devotion and the religious life described here were already powerfully in evidence in the latter part of the eleventh century, linked, as they were, in numerous ways to the ideals of the early monastic reformers.[4] The growing desire to see and experience the holy places of Christ's life and death had been fuelled by the preaching and sermons that preceded the First Crusade, launched in 1096, and even more so by the recovery of the Holy Sepulchre by the Crusaders in 1099. Moreover, new religious orders of men and women embodying the new spirituality were

archivio Muratoriano, 70 (1958), 19–41; Caroline Walker Bynum, 'Did the Twelfth Century Discover the Individual?', *Journal of Ecclesiastical History*, 31 (1980), 1–17; ead., *Jesus as Mother: Studies in the Spirituality of the High Middle Ages* (Berkeley, Calif., 1982), 82–109.

[3] The interest in Passion imagery was to become increasingly pronounced in the 12th-cent. Romanesque art of southern France and northern Spain. Cycles such as those in the cloisters of Silos, Pamplona, and Arles, the frieze on the façade of Saint-Gilles-du-Gard and the wall paintings of Bagüés are among the most vivid examples of this heightened interest in the sphere of the monumental arts. All of these works, including, in my opinion, the pier reliefs of Silos (see n. 37 below), post-date the series from La Daurade.

[4] The humanity of Christ and the necessity of imitating his model are both themes of the writings of e.g. Peter Damian, the most influential 11th-cent. reformer. He also wrote of the importance of interior contemplation in the devotion to Christ (see Jean Leclercq, *Saint Pierre Damien: ermite et homme d'église*, Uomini E Dottrine, 8 (Rome, 1960), esp. 247–50).

already a prominent presence in western and south central France in the decades before and after 1100. Most significant for the region of the south-west were the order of Grandmont, founded in the Limousin by St Stephen of Muret (d. 1124), and the order of Fontevrault, whose charismatic leader, Robert of Arbrissel, was already active with his disciples in Toulouse by at least 1098.[5]

If the cloister of La Daurade was begun about 1100, as we concluded in Chapter 3, why was it not until the resumption of work there, two decades later, that the new spiritual ideals that had been growing since the mid-eleventh century were realized in the sculptural programme of the cloister? The explanation involves both a powerful conservatism in Cluniac spirituality (a point that will be raised again below) and the need for the new art of monumental sculpture to develop the artistic means to express the affective responses and psychological explorations of twelfth-century spirituality. The capitals by the first workshop belong to eleventh-century developments in monumental sculpture. Along with the capitals of Moissac, they are the work of the first generation of sculptors in the region to attempt demanding narrative themes and compositions within the format of the historiated capital. We have concluded that these sculptors were trained in regional carving traditions. At the time the cloister of La Daurade was begun, the application of historiated themes to the sculptured capital was in its infancy in the region, as illustrated by the few examples on the interior of Saint-Sernin, probably dating to the 1090s. Even the historiated capitals of the Porte Miègeville are no more sophisticated in narrative structure than those of Moissac. As we saw in Chapter 6, in the brief span of about fifteen to twenty years that separates the early capitals of La Daurade from those of the second campaign, influences had penetrated the region from areas far to the north of Toulouse. These helped to make possible, in the realm of monumental sculpture, the kind of developed imagery of story-telling that had had a much longer tradition in the pictorial arts of the regions of western and central France.

THE TOMB OF CHRIST AND THE TRIUMPHS OF THE FIRST CRUSADE

The iconographic programme of the second series from La Daurade embodies ideas that appear as persistent themes in the literature of monastic reform and renewal throughout the Christian Church of the late eleventh and twelfth centuries. The unusual importance of the Daurade sculptures lies in the concrete testimony they offer, within the most intimate cloistered spaces of the monastery, of the currency of these ideas for a particular community of Cluniac monks at the centre of the reforming movement in southern France. While sharing many of the ideas represented in their sculptural programme with reformed monasticism in general, there were, in addition, historical factors that gave special meaning to these images for the Cluniac community at La Daurade.

One of the contemporary preoccupations evident in the programme of the second series of La Daurade is the growing fascination with the holy places where Christ had endured his Passion and had appeared to his disciples after his Resurrection. More specifically, the imagery

---

[5] On Stephen of Muret, see J. Becquet, 'Les Institutions de l'ordre de Grandmont', *Revue Mabillon*, 42 (1952), 31–42, and Leclercq in Leclercq, Vandenbroucke, and Bouyer, *Spirit-uality of the Middle Ages*, 142–3. On Robert d'Arbrissel, see above, Ch. 1.

of the series gives a striking prominence to the tomb of Christ as the focus of events in the drama of his Resurrection. But this is only one of the remarkable aspects of the Daurade Passion cycle. The iconography gives an unmistakable prominence to the Apostles, both in their relationship to Christ during the events that preceded and followed his Crucifixion and in their role as the heirs of Christ's mission that began with his Ascension and departure from them.

The fascination and lure of the holy places that had fuelled the pilgrimages of the eleventh century was brought to a new pitch at the Council of Clermont in 1095 with the preaching of the First Crusade. Here, on 27 November, Pope Urban II launched his first great appeal to western Christendom to take up the cross and free the tomb of Christ from the infidel. There is every evidence that Urban's extended journey through France during the year 1095–6, before and after Clermont, was conceived in large part as a vehicle for promoting the Crusade, specifically in those Frankish territories where he expected his message would be most enthusiastically received.[6] And the Christian prince who was first to answer this appeal was the count of Toulouse, Raymond de Saint-Gilles. So immediately, in fact, did Raymond pledge his commitment of forces following Urban's address, that it seems likely he knew in advance of the pope's intentions at the Council and may already have given the pontiff assurances that he would answer his call for an army.[7]

When considering the pope's itinerary through France in 1095, it is clear that he planned his journey to travel first through the Rhône valley, then into the the Provençal and Languedocian domains of the count of Toulouse, sojourning with marked frequency at monastic houses under the protection or patronage of the count. This has suggested to John and Laurita Hill that the pope may have planned his campaign in France in the conviction that the wealthy and powerful Languedocian count was the most likely prospect to be the leader of a Christian army to the Holy Land.[8] In this he was not disappointed. When the departure of the Frankish forces for the Crusade was finally under way in the autumn of 1096, Raymond de Saint-Gilles led the largest army and he remained, until the capture of Jerusalem, the military leader of the expedition in its progress towards its ultimate prize. A contemporary historian of the Crusade, Baldric of Dol, likened Raymond and Bishop Adhémar, the pope's legate, to Moses and Aaron, leading their people.[9]

---

[6] On Urban's intentions, see John H. Hill and Laurita L. Hill, *Raymond IV* (Syracuse, NY, 1962), 29; Frederic Duncalf, 'The Pope's Plan for the First Crusade', in *The Crusades and Other Historical Essays Presented to Dana C. Munro* (New York, 1928), 44–56; id., in *A History of the Crusades*, i. *The First Hundred Years*, ed. Marshall W. Baldwin (Madison, Wis., 1969), 272; A. C. Krey, 'Urban's Crusade—Success or Failure?', *American Historical Review*, 53 (1948), 235–50. René Crozet stressed that Urban's trip did not have the preaching of the Crusade as its exclusive objective and saw within it Urban's wider plan of reform and consolidation of the French clergy ('Le Voyage d'Urbain II et ses négociations avec le clergé de France (1095–1096)', *Revue historique*, 179 (1937), 271–310; id., 'Le voyage d'Urbain II en France (1095–1096) et son importance au point de vue archéologique', *Annales du Midi*, 49 (1937), 42–69).

[7] Hill and Hill, *Raymond IV*, 30–2. It is possible that Urban and Raymond had met prior to Clermont during the pope's visit to Saint-Gilles. René Grousset also underlined the principal role assigned to Raymond de Saint-Gilles in the pope's plans (*Histoire des croisades et du royaume franc de Jérusalem, i: L'Anarchie musulmane et la monarchie franque* (Paris, 1934), 4–5).

[8] In their words, 'If we follow the movements of Urban before and immediately after his call at Clermont, we can feel it is possible that he journeyed to Gaul in 1095 with the knowledge or hope that the core of military aid for his program would come from the Languedoc and the Count of Toulouse . . .' (Hill and Hill, *Raymond IV*, 29). They note further that Urban's early contacts were with churchmen of the Midi, clerics who must have known the count of Toulouse and would have had influence over him. Among these was Adhémar, bishop of Le Puy, whom Urban was to name as vicar of the Crusade and who travelled with the count of Toulouse as ecclesiastical head of the expedition when it finally marched for the Holy Land.

[9] Baldricus Dolensis, *Historia Jerosolimitana*, in *Recueil des historiens des croisades: historiens occidentaux*, 4 (Paris, 1879), 16.

Urban II had set the feast of the Assumption, 15 August 1096, as the date of departure for the Christian armies. Preparations must have begun immediately after the pope's stirring speech at Clermont. Throughout 1096 he continued his travels through France to promote the Crusade, having already enlisted the aid of many prominent clerics to spread the fire of enthusiasm for the Crusade idea, among them the great Angevin reformer and preacher, Robert d'Arbrissel, who, as we have already seen, played a role in Toulousan history after the departure of the counts on Crusade. Urban spent the spring of 1096 in the Aquitaine and Languedoc. In May his itinerary brought him to Toulouse where he stayed for most of the month, residing for part of his sojourn at nearby Moissac, where he confirmed the privileges of the Cluniac abbey and consecrated an altar. On 24 May 1096, at a ceremony in Saint-Sernin at Toulouse attended by many prominent churchmen and where Raymond de Saint-Gilles himself spoke, the pope consecrated the altar of the partially completed basilica.[10]

The pope's presence in the region throughout this period and his meeting with Raymond de Saint-Gilles in Toulouse when preparations for the military expedition were accelerating, must have done much to fuel crusading consciousness in the domains of the count, as Urban had intended. This consciousness must have been high in Cluniac monasteries, which were particularly singled out as stopping-places by the French pope. During his year-long journey he also stayed at houses that did not have any particular ties to Cluny. Nevertheless, so clearly does his itinerary reflect his favour for the houses of the Order, that René Crozet has characterized Urban's journey as, above all, 'un voyage clunisien'. Himself a former prior of Cluny, the pope had made an extended stay at the great abbey church in 1095 a focus of his sojourn in Burgundy, and he was accompanied during much of his long trip through France by Abbot Hugh. Moreover, Crozet has noted the overwhelmingly large number of Cluniac houses included in the ceremonies of consecration and granting of privileges performed by the pope during his route through France. Among these, he has pointed to a notable concentration of such favours to Cluniac establishments in the Languedocian and Provençal domains of the count of Toulouse.[11]

The prominence of Cluniac houses in his itinerary may reflect the pope's special affection for the order that had formed his own spiritual outlook. At the same time, the pattern of his travels surely also reflects his political aim of spurring support in the Midi for the Crusade. In this he seems to have counted on the influence of an order to which Raymond de Saint-Gilles and his family had traditionally shown favour in their domains. Nowhere was the history of this relationship more important than at Moissac, where Raymond's father Pons had first exhibited his commitment to Cluniac reform in 1053 by renouncing the rights over the great abbey that the counts of Toulouse had traditionally claimed. As we saw in Chapter 1 the subsequent counts of Toulouse, William IV, Raymond de Saint-Gilles, and their mother Almodis had all confirmed this renunciation of lay control over the abbey of Moissac and had encouraged and supported its reforms in the region, notably within Toulouse itself, at the priories of La Daurade and Saint-Pierre-des-Cuisines. The special stature of Moissac in the region was acknowledged by Urban II in his choice of the abbey as a major stopping-place during his

---

[10] See above, Ch. 5 n. 3. The consecration of the altar at Moissac is recorded in a document of 1101 (François Galabert, *Album de paléographie et de diplomatique: xiie siècle* (Toulouse, 1912), pl. 1, no. 1).

[11] Crozet, 'Voyage d'Urbain II et ses négociations', 310. See Crozet's detailed enumeration of the houses visited by Urban during 1095–6 and the privileges granted. See also Duncalf, *History of the Crusades* (as in n. 6 above), 230.

journey through the Languedoc in May, sojourning a full week at the abbey and issuing two important bulls there in the presence of Abbot Hugh of Cluny and a prominent gathering of clergy.[12]

If Urban II granted privileges to Moissac's daughter house at Toulouse, the priory of La Daurade, no record of these has survived. Nevertheless, the presence of the pope in Toulouse and the leading role he was to elicit from its count, Raymond de Saint-Gilles, must have given special meaning to the crusading cause for the community of La Daurade. At the request of Raymond's brother, Count William IV, Urban II had only recently granted a noble cemetery for the ruling family of Toulouse next to the priory of La Daurade, in recognition of William's aid to the Church. None of the ruling counts was ever entombed there, since three successive holders of the title would take up the cross to die in the Holy Land. Nevertheless, the cemetery at La Daurade was the burial place of the ruling family well into the twelfth century,[13] and the Cluniac community there must have shared in the reflected glory of the counts.

The role of Raymond de Saint-Gilles in the successful capture of the Holy Sepulchre in 1099 and his military exploits before and after brought him near mythical stature in the Holy Land, as well as in the Midi. Consciousness of the Toulousan part in the winning of the Holy Sepulchre would have been high in the wake of these successes and perhaps especially so at La Daurade, given its special relationship to the counts and the apparent role that the Cluniac order had played in furthering the strategy of Urban II.[14] The eyewitness accounts of contemporary chroniclers who followed the progress of the Christian armies in the Holy Land give something of the flavour of the reports that reached those who had remained at home. Raymond's own chaplain, Raymond d'Aguilers, has left one such account, told from the point of view of the Provençal armies led by the Toulousan count.[15] The other major chronicles of the First Crusade are those of Fulcher of Chartres, follower of the northern armies and chaplain of Count Baldwin of the Lorraine, and the *Gesta Francorum* by an anonymous writer travelling with the Norman armies of Bohemond.[16] While these accounts vary with regard to the apparent accuracy, plausibility, and partisanship on the part of the authors, they are probably typical of contemporary reporting about the Crusades, both written and oral accounts, that must have circulated in the West after the taking of Jerusalem. Highlights of these accounts are the descriptions of the siege of Jerusalem, the rejoicing of the victorious Christians at their first sight of the Holy Sepulchre, stirring events like the wading of the Frankish armies into the Jordan river in a mass immersion, and the numerous miracles associated with the mission, such as the finding of a piece of the true cross by the Crusaders.[17] These, along with the descriptions of the topography of the holy places in and around

[12] Crozet, 'Voyage d'Urbain II et ses négociations', 303.

[13] See above, Ch. 1.

[14] Hill and Hill (*Raymond IV*, 34) and Crozet ('Voyage d'Urbain II et ses négociations', 281) believe that Cluny played a role in furthering the First Crusade. Delaruelle, however, challenges this idea ('The Crusading Idea in Cluniac Literature of the Eleventh Century', in Noreen Hunt (ed.), *Cluniac Monasticism in the Central Middle Ages* (London, 1971), *passim*).

[15] John H. Hill and Laurita L. Hill, Le '*Liber*' de Raymond d'Aguilers, trans. Philippe Wolff, Documents relatifs à l'histoire des croisades publiées par l'Académie des inscriptions et belles-lettres, 9 (Paris, 1969). The chronicle of Raymond d'Aguilers was

certainly finished before the death of Raymond de Saint-Gilles in 1105 and may date from soon after the taking of Jerusalem in 1099 (see ibid. 11).

[16] Fulcher of Chartres, *Chronicle of the First Crusade* (*Fulcheri carnotensis historia hierosolymitana*), trans. Martha Evelyn McGinty (Philadelphia and London, 1941); *The Deeds of the Franks and the Other Pilgrims to Jerusalem* (*Gesta francorum et aliorum hierosolimitanorum*), ed. Rosalind Hill (London, 1962).

[17] See, e.g., Fulcher of Chartres on the Holy Sepulchre and the finding of a piece of the true cross (*Chronicle of the First Crusade*, 70–2 and 78). The finding of the holy lance is reported by Raymond d'Aguilers (as in n. 15 above), 82.

Jerusalem and neighbouring villages, must have given a vivid reality to the sacred sites for those who could only read or hear about them at second hand.[18]

With the death of Raymond in the Holy Land in 1105,[19] the continuation of the work of the Crusaders became a dynastic ideal for the ruling family of Toulouse. In March of 1109 Bertrand, son and heir of Raymond, followed in his father's footsteps and, after participating in the siege of Tripoli, died in the Holy Land, probably in 1112.[20] The loss of their counts and the departure with them of the knights and vassals who formed their military support, left the Toulousans for an extended period without a defender. The ambitious duke of Aquitaine had twice taken advantage of this situation by occupying Toulouse, the second time from 1108 to 1121. We have attributed the suspension of work in the cloister of La Daurade during these troubled years to the absence of the traditional benefactors of the monastery and the appropriation of influence over the Toulousan Church by the invading count, William IX, his wife Philippa, and the new order of Fontevrault.

With the departure of William IX from Toulouse in 1119 his hold on the city was weakened and in 1123 a contingent of Toulousan supporters marched to Orange to fetch the young Count Alphonse-Jourdain and return him in triumph to his capital.[21] For the Toulousans, the aura of the young count must have been intimately linked with the dynastic adventures in the Holy Land. He had been born on the Crusade—some sources say at Constantinople, others at Mount Pilgrim in the Holy Land—and legend claimed that he had been baptized in the Jordan.[22] The triumphant restoration of the house of Toulouse-Saint-Gilles in the person of the young son of Raymond de Saint-Gilles must have reignited the memories of his father's leading role in the early successes of the Crusade and the glory this had reflected on the city, so long deprived of its count. The physical possession of the city by the son of Raymond de Saint-Gilles would have given a new reality to the near legendary triumphs of his father.

The two decades in which accounts of the holy places freed by the Crusaders had had time to grow, along with a rekindled consciousness of the central role the counts of Toulouse had played in the liberation of the Holy Sepulchre, are reason enough to explain some of the most unique features of the Passion cycle from La Daurade and its appearance in precisely this cloister in the 1120s. The remarkable vividness of scenes such as the *Resurrection of Christ* or *Pl. 106* the excitement of John and Peter's race to the empty tomb are unlike anything in previous *Pl. 111* Toulousan art. They suggest that interest in the holy places of Christ's death and resurrection, in the reality of place and time, and, most especially, in the physical shrine of his tomb, was stronger than ever in Toulouse.

Moreover, there was a sense in which the new sensitivity to the suffering, human Christ in the spirituality of the eleventh and twelfth centuries had found an intense expression in the aspirations of the Crusade. Canon Étienne Delaruelle has described this phenomenon:

The spirituality associated with the crusades is . . . marked above all by devotion to the passion. The crusader is seeking union with Christ who suffered for mankind, and he dwells on that agony in ways that are often very moving. It was to avenge the outrages which the savior underwent and which were more or less confused

---

[18] See the description of the holy places of Jerusalem in Fulcher of Chartres (*Chronicle of the First Crusade*, 65) and that appended as a pilgrim's guide to the *Deeds of the Franks*, ed. R. Hill, 98–101.

[19] Raymond died at his castle at Mount Pilgrim (Hill and Hill, *Raymond IV*, 157). Contemporary chroniclers reported an oath by Raymond never to return from the Holy Land

(Baldericus Dolensis, *Historia Jerosolomitana* (as in n. 9 above), 16.

[20] Guillaume de Catel, *Histoire des comtes de Tolose* (Toulouse, 1623), 157–8.

[21] *HGL*, vol. iii, pp. 648 and 654; ibid., vol. iv, n. 50, pp. 219–21.

[22] Catel, *Comtes de Tolose*, 183–4.

in the crusader's mind with the desecration of the holy places that the knight would set out in the cause of his Lord, and the first popular crusade would massacre the Jews. To suffer and die in the very place where Christ had suffered and died: such was the crusader's ideal, preached and grasped more or less clearly.[23]

The preaching that launched the First Crusade and the voices of the victorious witnesses at the taking of Jerusalem testify to this identification with the Christ of the Passion:

The lord pope [Urban II at Clermont] said also, 'Brothers, you must suffer for the name of Christ many things, wretchedness, poverty, nakedness, persecution, need, sickness, hunger, thirst, and other troubles, for the Lord says to his disciples, "You must suffer many things for my name"' (Acts 9: 16) . . . And when these words had begun to be rumoured abroad through all the duchies and counties of the Frankish lands, the Franks, hearing them, straightway began to sew the cross on the right shoulders of their garments, saying that they would all with one accord follow in the footsteps of Christ, by whom they had been redeemed from the power of hell.[24]

The reaction of the Crusaders at the tomb of Christ, as Fulcher of Chartres records it, expresses similar sentiments:

With the visit to this city, our labor of long duration was consummated. When we had looked at the most desired Holy of Holies, we were filled with an immense joy. Oh, how many times we recalled to memory that prophecy of David in which he said: 'We shall worship in the place where His feet have stood' (Psalm 132: 7).[25]

If the role played by Raymond de Saint-Gilles and the Toulousan armies in liberating the Holy Sepulchre gave special meaning to the veneration of the holy places within the community at La Daurade, it is also the case that fascination with the holy places was a widespread phenomenon that had manifested itself well before the First Crusade. With the opening up of the overland route between Western Europe and the Levant at the end of the tenth century, pilgrimage by Europeans to the Holy Land had become increasingly possible during the course of the eleventh century. The descriptions of the holy places brought back by the pilgrim travellers served to feed this enthusiasm and to make the experiencing of the sacred sites where Christ had lived and died a tangible goal for many thousands of Christian believers.[26] The interest in the topography of the Holy Land manifested itself in hand-drawn maps of the sacred sites, a few of which survive from this period. A twelfth-century example in the British Library locates numerous sites, featuring the church and cloister (enclosure) of the Holy Sepulchre.[27]

If this new accessibility of the sacred sites, and the pilgrimage literature that went with it, gave substantial reality to the events and places of Christ's Passion, what meaning can these phenomena have had for the cloistered monk? The audience, after all, for the dramatic images

[23] Delaruelle, 'Crusading Idea', 209. Also see on this subject, 'The Crusades and the Pilgrim Spirit', in Leclercq, Vandenbroucke, and Bouyer, *Spirituality of the Middle Ages*, 130–3.

[24] *Deeds of the Franks*, ed. R. Hill, 1–2.

[25] Fulcher of Chartres, *Chronicle of the First Crusade*, 78, par. 15.

[26] On European pilgrimage to the Holy Land and its spiritual meaning, see Jonathon Sumption, *Pilgrimage, An Image of Medieval Religion* (London, 1975). See Ralph Glaber's *Historiae* for a description of an 11th-cent. pilgrimage to the Holy Land (*PL* 142, cols. 611–98). For the writings of 12th-cent. pilgrims, see the summary provided by Bernard Hamilton, 'Rebuilding Zion: The Holy Places of Jerusalem in the Twelfth Century', *Studies in Church History*, 14 (London,

1977); repr. in *Monastic Reform, Catharism and the Crusades, 900–1300*, Collected Studies, 97 (London, 1979) no. XI, 106–16. Some of the earliest of the descriptions, following the taking of the Holy Sepulchre, were those of the pilgrim Saewulf (1103), the Russian Abbot Daniel (1107), and a guidebook known as *Fetellus* (c.1130) (see *Palestine Pilgrims Text Society*, 21 (1892), 6 (1888), and 19 (1892)).

[27] London, British Library, Add. MS 32343, fo. 15. See C. H. Krinsky, 'Representations of the Temple of Jerusalem before 1500', *Journal of the Warburg and Courtauld Institutes*, 33 (1970), 1–19. The interest in sacred geography and its possible relevance for the design of 12th-cent. cloister programmes was broached by Wayne Dynes, 'The Medieval Cloister as Portico of Solomon', *Gesta*, 12 (1973), 61–9.

of Christ's Passion and Resurrection depicted in the cloister of La Daurade was the community of Cluniac monks who lived and meditated there. The meaning of pilgrimage within the vocation of monastic life has been the subject of a number of recent studies by Jean Leclercq and Giles Constable, among others, and Ilene Forsyth has considered it in relation to the imagery of Romanesque sculpture.[28] These studies have revealed a considerable literature on the subject by medieval writers concerned with monasticism. Based on the directives voiced within traditional Benedictine and Cluniac monasticism, we can be certain that the images of the Daurade Passion cycle, vivid though they are with the presence of the holy places, were not intended to exhort the monks to leave their cloister and journey to the Holy Land.

It is clear from the rich literature brought together by Constable that some monks did go on pilgrimage in the eleventh and twelfth centuries, either on journeys of devotion and penance *ad loca sancta* or, in the tradition of the early Irish monks, as an act of voluntary exile and mortification that represented the ultimate cutting of bonds with all that was familiar in the monk's former life. It is also clear that many of these journeys were undertaken in that spirit of the *imitatio Christi* that we have also seen expressed by the Christian knights who actively sought hardship and possible martyrdom on Crusade to the Holy Land.[29]

Nevertheless, the official position of those who addressed themselves to the monastic life, from such leaders as Peter Damian and Peter the Venerable, to Pope Urban II himself, was to disapprove of and even to prohibit pilgrimage for monks.[30] According to traditional definitions of the monastic vocation, the monk's devotion to the religious life of prayer and his renunciation of the world outside the cloister represented the purest ideal of the Christian life and a higher calling than the exhortation to visit holy sites. If pilgrimage was encouraged for the lay public, who did not practise the higher spiritual life, for the cloistered monk the impulse to quit the walls of his cloister to visit the holy places was characterized by some writers as the inspiration of the devil.[31]

The superior calling of the monastic life over all other forms of Christian devotion and service was most persistently upheld by the Cluniac order, and this attitude shaped Cluny's own opposition to pilgrimage or Crusade for those who sought the highest spiritual perfection. It was their consistent espousal of this central meaning of monastic life and the single-minded dedication of their monastic day to a ritual of perpetual prayer that accounted for the enormous spiritual prestige of the Cluniac order among both lay people and the non-cloistered clergy, who wished to have the superior spiritual weight of these Cluniac prayers brought to bear perpetually on their own behalf.[32] Thus no act of devotion in the outside world, whether

---

[28] Jean Leclercq, 'Monachisme et pérégrination du IXᵉ au XIIᵉ siècle', *Studia monastica*, 3 (1961), 33–52; Giles Constable, 'Monachisme et pèlerinage au moyen âge', *Revue historique*, 258 (1977), 3–27; id., 'Opposition to Pilgrimage in the Middle Ages', *Mélanges Gérard Fransen*, i (1976), 125–46; Ilene Haering Forsyth, 'The *Vita Apostolica* and Romanesque Sculpture', *Gesta*, 25 (1986), 78–9.

[29] See Leclercq, 'Monachisme et pérégrination', 38–40, and Constable, 'Monachisme et pèlerinage', 12–13.

[30] On the views of Peter Damian and Urban II in the 11th cent., see Constable, 'Monachisme et pèlerinage', 17–19. The great Cluniac abbot of the 12th cent., Peter the Venerable, seems to have been more ambivalent about the value of pilgrimage. Compare his advice to a knight and an abbot in *The Letters of Peter the Venerable*, ed. Giles Constable,

Harvard Historical Series, 78 (Cambridge, Mass., 1967), i. 152, Epistle 51, and ii. 131–2 (nn. to Epistle 51). But his proscription against pilgrimage for monks is clear in Epistles 80 and 83 (ibid. i. 214–17, 220–1).

[31] Constable, 'Monachisme et pèlerinage', 16 and 22.

[32] On the role of Cluniac liturgical prayer as a form of intercession for the laity see H. E. J. Cowdrey, *The Cluniacs and Gregorian Reform* (Oxford, 1970), 121–5. On the superior vocation of the monk, see also Delaruelle, 'Crusading Idea', 200–1. On the relationship of Cluniac reform to the larger ecclesiastical reform movement of the 11th cent., see Raffaello Morghen, 'Riforma monastica e spiritualità cluniacense', in *Spiritualità cluniacense: convegni del centro di studi sulla spiritualità medievale, 1958* (Todi, 1960), 33–56.

visiting the tomb of a saint or following the route to Jerusalem, was equivalent to the total devotion of one's life to God within the world of the monastery.[33]

An important concomitant of this way of thinking for our own study was the belief that the monastery itself was the Paradise promised in the Old and New Testaments. Jotsald, biographer of Abbot Odilo of Cluny, writes that Odilo viewed the abbey of Cluny in this way.[34] The metaphorical way of thinking that produced the equation 'cloister or monastery = heavenly Jerusalem' also prompted medieval writers to liken the monastic life to a pilgrimage.[35] Though cloistered within a monastery, monks were thus engaged in an arduous spiritual journey, in which the goal, as for their counterparts, the pilgrims and Crusaders to the Holy Land, was to bring themselves closer to Christ by following in his footsteps and approaching the celestial Jerusalem.

It is within this complex of ideas about the holy places and the profession of monasticism that we approach the meaning of such vivid images as those of La Daurade within the closed walls of the cloister. Ilene Forsyth has illuminated the ways in which Romanesque sculpture within the cloister might aid or enhance the experience of monks in vicarious spiritual journeying, through the representation of certain subjects with which the monks could form an intimate identification.[36] Forsyth is surely right in linking the remarkable popularity of the Journey to Emmaus as a subject for twelfth-century monastic art to the contemporary directive that the monk's journey to and with Christ should be accomplished within the

Pl. 114 cloister. The Emmaus capital from La Daurade belongs among the earliest of these representations within the monastic setting.[37] The garbing of Christ here in the costume of a contemporary pilgrim, an often remarked-upon feature of these Romanesque images, seems clearly to reinforce the simile, as disciples and monastic audience alike join with Christ in a journey, at the conclusion of which they will be granted a vision of his divinity.

Among other examples of cloister imagery that must have encouraged monks to identify themselves with the followers of Christ, Forsyth singled out the capital of *John and*

Pls. 108–11 *Peter at the Empty Tomb* from La Daurade as a particularly powerful image. She pointed to some of the ingenious artistic devices that must have invited such self-identification, in particular the column and arches that play such a prominent part in the dramatic activity of this scene. As Forsyth observed, they are conceived here in forms that must have been very like the architecture of the cloister arcade within which the capital functioned.

The meaning and impact of the *John and Peter* capital are fully realized, however, only within the context of the other capitals of the series. Within the ensemble as a whole, the

---

[33] See the statement, probably attributable to St Hugh, that a vow to visit Jerusalem was accomplished if one entered a monastery (Constable, 'Monachisme et pèlerinage', 15).

[34] PL 142, cols. 899–900. St Bernard, writing about 1129, used the same metaphor in speaking of the abbey of Clairvaux as the celestial Jerusalem on earth (St Bernard, *Opera omnia*, ed. Jean Mabillon, i. (Paris, 1839), Epistle 64, cols. 208A–209B). For the literature on the monastery as Jerusalem, see Constable, 'Monachisme et pèlerinage', 15.

[35] See e.g. St Bernard of Clairvaux (PL 183, cols. 179, 183, and 186).

[36] Forsyth, 'Vita Apostolica', 78–9.

[37] I am not among those who accept the late 11th-cent. date for the first Romanesque workshop in the cloister of Silos, where the *Journey to Emmaus* is represented on one of the pier reliefs. In a paper read at the 22nd International Congress on

Medieval Studies at Western Michigan University (7 May 1987), John Williams reviewed the state of the question on the date of the Silos cloister. He presented the convincing conclusion that the church dedicated in 1088 was not the upper transepted church (with which the construction of the cloister has been linked) but the lower church. I agree with Williams in viewing the earliest capitals at Silos, produced by the same workshop that carved the pier reliefs, as reflections of developments in Toulousan Romanesque sculpture, most especially in the cloister of Saint-Sernin. A date closer to 1120–40 than 1088–1100 appears likely for the first workshop in the Silos cloister. The dating of the Silos cloister was the subject of strong debate in a colloquium on the Spanish abbey held at the 23rd International Congress on Medieval Studies at Western Michigan University (May 1988) but no consensus of opinion was reached.

prominence given to the tomb of Christ as a palpable focus can hardly be missed. The tomb is pictured in four of the scenes: the *Entombment*, the *Resurrection of Christ*, the *Holy Women at the Tomb*, and the already discussed scene of *John and Peter*. In all four scenes the physical details are rendered in a way that gives the tomb a bold presence. It is shown as a strigillated sarcophagus of the massive Gallo-Roman type, basin-like and raised on legs. Heavy marble sarcophagi of this type were abundantly reused in medieval times in the ancient cemeteries of Toulouse,[38] and the Early Christian associations of the type made the clear distinguishing of its physical details important to the iconography of the Passion series.

Two of the scenes, that of Christ's physical emergence from the tomb and the visit of John and Peter on Easter morning, while not totally unprecedented in earlier medieval art, are extremely rare and, in Romanesque monumental art of this period, virtually unknown elsewhere.[39] Their inclusion here underlines the insistent emphasis of this Passion series on the tomb of Christ as a physical relic sanctified by its role in Christ's death and Resurrection, much as the lance, the cross, and the crown of thorns are displayed as objects for veneration in the Romanesque tympanum of Beaulieu though not there within a narrative context. Finally, the *Pl. 176* remarkable use of architecture in the scene of Easter morning identifies the tomb of Christ as an actual sepulchre, a physical *place* into which John and Peter enter with astonishment and perhaps trepidation, as into a sanctuary.

Attempts have been made to link the iconography of the Resurrection and *Visitatio* scenes from La Daurade to the extra-liturgical enactments of the Resurrection and the *Visitatio Sepulchri* which had developed as accretions to the Holy Week Mass since at least the tenth century with the *Regularis Concordia* of St Dunstan of 967.[40] In the early twelfth century, however, these extra-liturgical ceremonies were not dramas in the sense of naturalistic theatre. Like the Mass itself, they were highly ritualized. Meaning was invested in powerful signs and symbols, such as a draped wooden cross to stand for the body of the crucified Christ. The players were monks and priests in habits and vestments. As we have repeatedly emphasized, the new element at La Daurade is precisely the dramatic realism and sense of immediacy of the Passion story. Liturgical drama is an unlikely inspiration for this vivid realism.

Bold architectural forms frame the majority of the scenes on the Daurade capitals and are one of their most distinguishing features. In prominent examples like the *Washing of the Feet* and the *Last Supper*, the figures interact actively with the architectural forms, as they do in the *Pls. 80 and 85*

---

[38] See the numerous examples of Gallo-Roman and Early Christian sarcophagi from local cemeteries now in the Musée des Augustins (Rachou, *Catalogue du musée de Toulouse*, 1912) and the Musée Saint-Raymond at Toulouse.

[39] A rare Western depiction of Christ's bodily resurrection prior to the 12th cent. appears in a Gospel book from Bamberg, where Christ is shown standing in the tomb (Munich, Staatsbibliothek, Clm. 4454, fo. 20) (see André Grabar, 'Essai sur les plus anciennes représentations de la "Résurrection du Christ"', *Foundation E. Piot: monuments et mémoires*, 63 (1980), 105–41). The depiction of Christ bodily climbing from the tomb, as he is shown at La Daurade, does not become common until the second half of the 12th cent., when it appears in the late Romanesque manuscripts of south Germany and the Rhine. Schiller illustrates numerous examples from these regions, as well as 3 from France. See Gertrud Schiller, *Ikonographie der christlichen Kunst* (Gütersloh, 1966), iii, figs. 176, 188, 190, 195, 197, and 200; also, an evangelistary in

Munich, Clm. 23 339, fo. 27ᵛ (G. Swarzenski, *Salzburger Malerei*, pl. LXXIII, fig. 241). John and Peter racing to the empty tomb is depicted in an initial of the 9th-cent. Drogo Sacramentary (Paris, BN, lat. 9428, fo. 56ʳ) and in the extensive Passion-Resurrection cycle of an English Psalter dating from about 1140, whose 4 remaining leaves are now divided (see C. M. Kauffmann, *Romanesque Manuscripts 1066–1190* (London, 1975), cat. 66 and fig. 180).

[40] *PL* 187, col. 493. Émile Mâle was the earliest spokesman for the role of liturgical drama as the inspiration for 12th-cent. iconography. His championing of this idea has had a prolonged life in the subsequent literature (see Émile Mâle, *Religious Art in France* (Princeton, 1978), 126–43). See also the more recent views of Thomas Lyman, 'Theophanic Iconography and the Easter Liturgy: The Romanesque Painted Program at Saint-Sernin in Toulouse', *Festschrift für Otto von Simson zum 65. Geburtstag*, ed. Lucius Grisebach and Konrad Renger (Frankfurt am Main, 1977), 72–93.

Pl. 96

capital of *John and Peter*. In other scenes, their function cannot be read literally, since they frame scenes clearly not enacted in an interior, such as *Christ's Way to Calvary* and *Peter Striking Malchus* on the triple capital of the *Arrest of Christ*. As I discussed in the previous chapter, the use of such frames for narrative scenes, particularly scenes from the life of Christ, had a long artistic tradition behind it. Their usage at La Daurade, I suggested, is one of the elements that helps to identify the sources of this series in pictorial narrative cycles of the tenth and eleventh centuries. Their meaning, then, in the capitals of La Daurade is not wholly without ambiguity, since they carry with them some of the meanings and associations acquired in this prior narrative tradition, where, as we saw in the manuscript of St Radegund, they are not always to be interpreted literally. Certainly the crenellated towers and walls that are delineated with such care on several of the capitals suggest the fortified and towered city of Jerusalem as the Crusaders knew and described it.[41] Nevertheless, details of some of the capitals, especially the splendid twisted columns and parted curtains of the *Washing of the Feet* and the scintillating diapered ground that backs many of the scenes, suggest that it is not the literal, earthly city of Jerusalem and its holy sites that are being represented here, but the super-terrestrial one. This interpretation is consistent with the express words of monastic writers from St Odilo to St Bernard,[42] that it is the celestial Jerusalem the community of brothers seeks within the perfect life of the monastery.

But does the powerfully lifelike quality of the Daurade Passion dramas belie this interpretation? In fact, the vivid sense of place and moment ignites a tension in these works that is part of their fascination. The intensity of human emotion conveyed by the narrative style is surely expressive of that new interest in the inner life and the quality of its experience that marked a change in the spirituality of the twelfth century. But as objects of meditation, the sacred dramas pictured on the capitals of La Daurade exist perpetually in a realm of introspection. The monk might know that the historical Jerusalem where Christ had walked as a man existed somewhere in the Holy Land, but this earthly place was linked only by the strands of appearance and simile to the Jerusalem in miniature of the cloister he could never desert.

THE *VITA APOSTOLICA* AS A MONASTIC IDEAL[43]

The prominence given to the tomb of Christ is only one of the notable aspects of the Passion and Resurrection cycle from La Daurade. As suggested above, this aspect of the programme may be tied to historical circumstances particular to the Cluniac community at La Daurade, namely the close intertwining of its history with that of the counts of Toulouse and their crusading activities in the Holy Land. Equally striking, at the same time, is the prominence given to the Apostles throughout the series. None of the episodes is totally unprecedented in earlier medieval art, and some of the scenes in which the Apostles play a central role, such as the *Washing of the Feet* or the *Pentecost*, were, individually, to find a frequent place within

[41] Towers play a prominent part in the descriptions of the siege of Jerusalem (especially the Tower of David). See Fulcher of Chartres, *Chronicle of the First Crusade*, 65 and 68.

[42] See above, n. 34.

[43] I first discussed the iconography of the Toulousan cloisters within the context of the monastic profession in a paper of 1980 delivered at the 15th International Congress on Medieval Studies at Western Michigan University, Kalamazoo. Here I pointed out the exceptionally prominent role given to the Apostles in the Passion series from La Daurade. I interpreted that phenomenon as a concrete expression of the exemplary model that 12th-cent. monks found in the role of the Apostles and their relationship to Christ.

subsequent cloister schemes of the twelfth century. What is unprecedented at La Daurade is the extended character of the cycle, which draws not only on the Gospel accounts of Christ's life on earth before and after his resurrection but also on the Book of Acts, in which the Apostles assume the central place as the heirs of Christ's Church on earth after his departure from them. Through the entire cycle, the theme of Christ's life with and among his disciples, their relationship to him, and their collective role as followers and perpetuators of his example, is sustained.

The *vita apostolica*, the communal life of the apostles in poverty and imitation of Christ, became a recurring motif in the reform of monastic life in the eleventh and twelfth centuries, for Benedictine and Cluniac monasticism, as well as the newer orders of canons and white monks. The power of this concept for the writers and practitioners of the reform has been increasingly emphasized by historians of the monastic movement.[44] More recently, historians of monastic art have begun to test the ways in which promotion of the apostolic model shaped the imagery of cloister programmes during the years of reform and revitalization of monastic life.[45]

Much has been written, in these recent studies, about the competitiveness among rival monastic orders that accompanied the proliferation of new forms of communal religious life in the late eleventh and early twelfth centuries.[46] As the new orders of monks, canons, and other cloistered religious sought to define their forms of communal life and as the older Benedictine monasticism sought to purify and to defend its own, all groups claimed the apostolic example as their ultimate model, regardless of the rule they followed. Indeed, it may have been the sense of need on the part of competing communities to explicate and to defend their way of life and their spiritual ideals that helps to explain the startling enrichment of cloister spaces with historiated programmes during the very decades of the most fundamental monastic reforms. Many of these reforms, particularly those imposed upon existing communities by the Cluniacs, were not carried out without resistance. Thus some of the more pointed iconography of reform within Romanesque cloister programmes may have been directed towards unwilling brethren or factions of the older community who needed to be reminded of the sources of authority for the new rule being imposed upon them.

If the influence of such concerns on the creation of cloister iconography is just beginning to

[44] Ernest McDonnell, 'The *Vita Apostolica*: Diversity or Dissent?', *Church History*, 24 (1955), 15–31; Charles Dereine, 'La "Vita apostolica" dans l'ordre canonial du IXe au XIe siècle', *Revue Mabillon*, 51 (1961), 47–53; Marie-Humbert Vicaire, *L'Imitation des apôtres: moines, chanoines, mendiants (IVe–XIIIe siècles)* (Paris, 1963); M.-D. Chenu, *Nature, Man and Society*, trans. Jerome Taylor and Lester Little of *La Théologie au douzième siècle* (Chicago, 1968), 203–21 and 239–41; G. W. Olsen, 'The Idea of the *Ecclesia Primitiva* in the Writings of the Twelfth-Century Canonists', *Traditio*, 25 (1969), 61–86 (with extensive bibliography); Caroline Walker Bynum, *Docere Verbo et Exemplo: An Aspect of Twelfth-Century Spirituality*, Harvard Theological Review, Harvard Theological Studies, 31 (Cambridge, Mass., 1979), 19–21.

[45] Léon Pressouyre drew attention to the theme of the apostolic model as central to the study of Romanesque monastic art in his article, 'St. Bernard to St. Francis', *Gesta*, 12 (1973), 71–92. His study stimulated my own thinking about monastic and canonic responses to this model in the iconography of the Toulousan cloisters. Ilene Forsyth has demonstrated how

widespread and compelling was the imagery of the apostolic ideal in Romanesque cloister sculpture ('*Vita Apostolica*', 75–82).

[46] Bynum, *Jesus as Mother*, 88–9. Bynum has looked at new kinds of evidence in the written sources for how canons themselves defined their spiritual vocation in ways that differed from monks. For the older literature see the acts of the 1959 conference at Mendola: *La Vita comune del clero* (as in Ch. 1 n. 9); also Charles Dereine, 'Vie commune, règle de Saint Augustin et chanoines réguliers au XIe siècle', *Revue d'histoire ecclésiastique de Louvain*, 41 (1946), 365–406; id., 'Le Problème de la vie commune chez des canonistes d'Anselm de Lucques à Gratien', *Studi Gregoriani*, 3 (1948), 287–98. Constable and Smith, on the other hand, in their introduction to the *Libellus de diversis ordinibus*, stress the searchings by its anonymous author and other contemporaries to find grounds for the acceptance of diversity in the forms of religious life (Giles Constable and B. Smith (eds. and trans.), *Libellus de diversis ordinibus et professionibus qui sunt in aecclesia* (Oxford, 1972)).

be defined, the Romanesque cloisters of Toulouse offer uniquely rich material for exploring these issues. The impact of the Gregorian and Cluniac reforms was real in Toulouse and fraught with conflict, as described in Chapter 1. The rivalries among the three great religious houses that accompanied their respective reforms make Toulouse a case-study in the contemporary debates about the nature and definition of monastic life. Pope Urban II himself took a protective interest in the canons of Saint-Sernin, newly reformed according to the Rule of St Augustine and the Church Fathers, and issued one of his most important bulls concerning the legitimacy of the *ordo canonicus* in response to a conflict there.[47] Earlier, as we saw, the bishop of Toulouse, Isarnus, with the help of Count William IV, had tried to expel the regular canons of Saint-Sernin in 1081/2 and replace them with Cluniac monks from Moissac, but the canons had been reinstalled in their cloister on the order of Pope Gregory VII, who praised the regular life the canons had been leading there.[48]

The clearest textual evidence that the apostolic model was a living ideal for the reformers of monastic life at Toulouse is the act of reform of the chapter of canons of Saint-Étienne, issued by the hand and in the words of Bishop Isarnus. The act is undated but can probably be situated in 1073.[49] It is a primary document for our knowledge of the spirit behind the eleventh-century ecclesiastical reforms in Toulouse and the roles played by the various parties to the reform. The wording of the act shows the powerful influence of both Cluniac and Augustinian visions of the spiritual life. The considerable weight that Cluniac influence carried in Isarnus's programme of reform in general is substantiated in this document, in which he places his act under the protection and defence of Hugh, abbot of Cluny, and his successors. Both Abbot Hugh, whom Isarnus calls 'propagator of monastic discipline', and the Cluniac abbot of Moissac, Hunaldus, were present at the ceremony of reform, which was undertaken, in Isarnus's words, with their counsel, aid, and co-operation.[50] Though no explicit mention is made of the precepts of St Augustine which the canons of Saint-Étienne adopted in their communal life, the preamble to the document contains language indicative of Augustine's influence, as Philippe Wolff has pointed out, in particular the language of individual emotional experience and reference to the contemplation of the interior man (*homo interior*).[51]

Isarnus's evocation of the apostolic ideal is, furthermore, unmistakable in the central passage of the act, in which the bishop committed the clerics of the cathedral to a regular life:

I [Isarnus] thus ordain, after deliberation, that any cleric who would wish henceforth to become a member of the body of this church, acknowledges himself [to be] submitted to the rigor of canonical life, notably that he possesses nothing of his own nor even calls anything his own. That all the clerics eat together, sleep together. That food and vestments shall be common to all according to the prescription of the Apostolic tradition. That the liberty to come and go to such and such place shall not be accorded except with the permission of their prior, in such a way that there exists one spirit, one soul for those who have but one God, one faith, one baptism.[52]

The prescriptions of individual poverty and of the sharing of meals and possessions in common that would form the basis of the regular life of the canons as laid out here are based

---

[47] Elisabeth Magnou, *L'Introduction de la réforme grégorienne à Toulouse* (Toulouse, 1958), Recueil annexe, no. 13.

[48] Célestin Douais, *Cartulaire de l'abbaye de Saint-Sernin de Toulouse* (Paris, 1887), app. 1. no. 3. 475–7.

[49] Magnou, *Réforme grégorienne*, Recueil annexe, no. 1; *HGL*, vol. v, cols. 626–31. See above, Ch. 1 n. 32 for the dating of the act.

[50] Magnou, *Réforme grégorienne*, Recueil annexe, no. 1. 2, ll. 1–3.

[51] Ibid. 1, l. 4; Philippe Wolff and Jean Dieuzaide, *Voix et images de Toulouse* (Toulouse, 1962), 45.

[52] Magnou, *Réforme grégorienne*, Recueil annexe, no. 1. 2, ll. 5–9.

on descriptions of the communal life of the Apostles in the Book of Acts 2: 42–7 and 4: 32–5. In the final sentence of the quotation above, Isarnus gave added power to his prescriptions by paraphrasing the very words in which the congregation of Christ's apostolic Church was described in the Book of Acts: 'And the multitude of believers had but one heart and one soul: neither did any one say that aught of the things which he possessed, was his own; but all things were common unto them' (Acts 4: 32).

The imitation of the apostolic life is one of the most persistent themes in the literature of eleventh- and twelfth-century monastic reform, and quotations from the Acts of the Apostles recur as a leitmotif in this literature.[53] The language of the act of reform of the canons of Saint-Étienne takes on rare importance, however, because we also possess, from the conventual buildings of the same cathedral, a remarkable ensemble of sculptures in which the canons gave concrete visual shape to the ideals expressed in this document. We are referring, of course, to the relief sculptures of the twelve Apostles that survive from the Romanesque constructions at Saint-Étienne. It is not possible to know with certainty whether these figures stood on the interior or the exterior of the chapter house, or whether, indeed, they may have been affixed in some manner to the cloister piers.[54] There is no question, however, but that they were meant to be seen as an ensemble—the college of the Apostles—and that they decorated the most cloistered spaces used by the canons during the comings and goings of their monastic day and in their chapter meetings.

Pls. 153–65

The last quarter of the eleventh century had been the period of greatest upheaval and universal reform in the Toulousan Church, when chapters of canons newly formed at both Saint-Sernin and Saint-Étienne had had to defend vigorously the legitimacy of their regular life alongside that of the established order of Cluny. The bull of 20 July 1096 of Urban II had spelled out in explicit terms that the canons of Saint-Sernin, by conforming to the prescriptions of a regular life, belonged to an order, that of *canonici regulares*, that was sustained and protected by the Church.[55]

While this bull, along with the earlier ones of Gregory VII during the crisis of 1081–3, had settled the immediate conflicts between the supporters of the *ordo novus* and the *ordo antiquus* in Toulouse, the literature of monasticism at large indicates clearly that the respective value and legitimacy of the canonic as distinct from the monastic life were subjects of deep concern to spiritual writers of the twelfth century. In Toulouse, these differences had stirred bitter rivalry, and charges by the canons of Saint-Étienne that their clerics had been wrongfully expelled from the monastery of La Daurade were indignantly revived as late as 1130.[56] All three religious communities must have felt an urgency to renew continually their own historical claims to represent the revival of the apostolic Church. And the themes that emerge most prominently in the surviving cloister programmes of Toulouse from the first half of the twelfth century are specifically those of apostolic imitation and the venerable Early Christian history of their respective houses.

Both these themes were promoted in the Romanesque programme of Saint-Étienne. The ensemble of the apostolic college formed only one part of the decoration there. Three early

---

[53] See ibid. 27; Vicaire, *Imitation des apôtres*, 15–19 and *passim*. As Bynum points out, however, the term *vita apostolica* did not have the same meaning for all writers (Bynum, *Docere Verbo et Exemplo*, 19–20).

[54] See below, Ch. 8.
[55] Magnou, *Réforme grégorienne*, 13.
[56] See above, Ch. 1 n. 44.

local historians, Noguier, Filère, and Catel, tell us that two corner piers of the cloister carried images of St Peter, St Sernin, St Exupery, and a deacon. While there are inconsistencies among the three early writers regarding the precise locations and the inscriptions accompanying these figures, all three writers agree on their identification.[57] St Saturninus, of course, was the earliest bishop of Toulouse and the most venerated martyr of the early Toulousan Church. Of St Exupery, bishop at the beginning of the fifth century, his legend claimed that he had turned back the tide of the invading Vandals from the city in 405 by the power of his prayers.[58] The presence of St Peter within a scheme devoted to the founders of the primitive Church requires no special explanation. As for the deacon, the descriptions of this figure by Noguier and Catel leave his iconography something of a puzzle. He is said to have been holding, with covered hands, a chalice and his inscription, according to Catel, read:

SACRAMENTA PARAT PIA PONTIFICIQUE MINISTRAT
OFFERAT VAS VITREUM, VIMITREUMQUE CANISTRUM.[59]

Since the inclusion of an allegorical type representing the office of deacon seems out of place in the scheme of the other pier figures, it is worth speculating that this image, in fact, represented St Stephen, named in the Acts of the Apostles as one of the first deacons of the apostolic Church, and the patron saint of the cathedral. The representation of him in the role of his profession as distinct from the more familiar iconography of his martyrdom may have made his identity obscure for the sixteenth-century writers who visited the cloister.

The programme at Saint-Étienne, so far as we are able to know it, appears to have been devoted, then, to the founders of the Early Christian and Toulousan Churches. In the lost west façade programme of Saint-Sernin, the sculptured images from the legend of St Saturninus underscored that collegiate community's equally venerable ties to the Early Christian history of Toulouse.[60] But within the private spaces of their cloister, the canons of Saint-Sernin honoured the titular founder of their own order in the splendid image of the seated St Augustine that was painted in fresco on the exterior west wall of the north transept within the east cloister walk. Now removed to the inside of the church, the monumental St Augustine, dictating his Rule to a scribe, was probably painted about 1140, near to the time in which the canons of Saint-Étienne were decorating their own cloistered spaces with the images of the twelve Apostles.[61]

Of prime interest to us is how the Cluniac order responded to these challenges to its prolonged dominance of the monastic reform. The canons and newer orders of monks that began to offer vital alternatives to traditional Cluniac monasticism in the latter decades of the eleventh century hardly had a monopoly on the concept of apostolic imitation, which had emerged as a fundamental ideal of the Gregorian reform as early as the councils of 1059 and

---

[57] Catel described the figures as 'statues ou images Gotthiques' in 'demi relief' (Guillaume de Catel, *Mémoires de l'histoire du Languedoc* (Toulouse, 1633), 165). The other early writers who mentioned these reliefs are Antoine Noguier (*Histoire tolosaine* (Toulouse, 1556), 60–1 and 77–8), and Alexandre Filère (Toulouse, Bibliothèque municipale, MS 694, 'Remarques Sur les Antiquités et autres Singularités de Tholoze', fos. 5ᵛ–6ᵣ, 9ᵣ–10ᵣ, and 37ᵛ–38ᵣ). In addition, Filère described 2 other figures 'au milieu du cloistre' that were not mentioned by Noguier or Catel. He described one as an enthroned king, crowned and holding a violin and sceptre, and the other as a statue in 'demy

relief' holding a sceptre with a fleur-de-lys at the top (fos. 5ᵛ–6ᵣ). By 'milieu du cloistre' Filère must have meant the middle of one of the cloister arcades, not within the cloister garth, which would have been a bizarre location for monumental sculpture.

[58] On St Exupery see Michel Labrousse, *Toulouse antique* (Paris, 1968), 558–66.

[59] Catel, *Mémoires du Languedoc*, 166.

[60] See Ch. 3 n. 12.

[61] Marcel Durliat, *Haut-Languedoc roman* (La Pierre-qui-vire, 1978), 128–9; Pressouyre, 'St. Bernard to St. Francis', 72 and n. 17.

1063 and in the writings of such eleventh-century reformers as Peter Damian.[62] The importance of this concept in Cluniac thinking is graphically evident in the series of standing Apostles in marble bas-relief that encircle the vast cloister of Moissac on the supporting piers. *Pl. 175* At their head stands the first Cluniac abbot of the reformed community, Durandus. His haloed tonsure (though, in fact, he was never canonized) and his position facing the chapter house seem to make him play, for the monks of Moissac, a role equivalent to the founder saints in the cloister of the canons of Saint-Étienne. The existence of the Apostle series at Moissac is proof that the model of the *vita apostolica* was a paradigm as powerful in Cluniac thinking as it was to the aspirations of the *ordo canonicus*. In fact, as an artistic expression of this concept, the images in the cloister of Moissac may represent the prototype in the region for the association of Apostle with pier support in the cloister, pre-dating by twenty-five to thirty-five years the sculptured Apostles from the cathedral close of Saint-Étienne.

As in the latter ensemble of figures, the prominence given to the Apostles in the Passion series from La Daurade makes it clear that the *vita apostolica* continued to be a vital theme into the first half of the twelfth century for those concerned with the definition of monastic life. As the energy and impetus of the eleventh-century reform came to fruition in the proliferation of successful new orders of men and women religious founded in the decades before and after 1100, there is no question but that Cluniac spiritual influence was under serious challenge in Toulouse and in the monastic movement as a whole. The order of Fontevrault had established a powerful presence in the vicinity of Toulouse during the period of the Poitevin occupation, as had the new order of Hospitallers. The spiritual life offered to women followers of the charismatic Robert d'Arbrissel and his disciples within the order of Fontevrault laid primary emphasis on personal religious experience as distinct from the older Benedictine monasticism represented by Cluny.[63] At the same time, the redemptive value of charity and the care for the poor and afflicted emphasized by the Hospitallers offered new means of salvation to concerned Christians who had previously bartered for the hope of salvation with the Masses and perpetual prayers of cloistered monks. John Mundy has charted the dramatic shifts in the character of lay giving within Toulouse during the course of the twelfth and early thirteenth centuries, as donations in support of hospitals and charitable institutions came more and more to supplant those traditionally made to Benedictine houses for the maintenance of perpetual prayer.[64]

John Van Engen has recently challenged the notion of a 'crisis of Benedictine monasticism' in the face of proliferating rival orders. He has pointed to economic solidity and the numbers of recruited monks as evidence that Benedictine monasticism held its own in competition with other orders at least until the middle of the twelfth century.[65] Nevertheless, where the character of its communal, and especially its liturgical, life is concerned, there can be no question but that by the first half of the twelfth century the black Benedictine monks represented the conservative arm of European monasticism and a brand of monastic spirituality that had its foot in the past, not in the future. Cluniac monasticism was

[62] Vicaire, *Imitation des apôtres*, 54 and 61–2. See Peter Damian's 'Contra clericos regulares propietarios' in *PL* 145, esp. cols. 487D, 488B, and 490AB.

[63] On Robert d'Arbrissel, see Ch. 1 n. 102.

[64] John Hine Mundy, 'Charity and Social Work in Toulouse', *Traditio*, 22 (1966), 203–87.

[65] John Van Engen, 'The "Crisis of Cenobitism" Reconsidered: Benedictine Monasticism in the Years 1050–1150', *Speculum*, 61 (1986), 269–304.

distinguished by a liturgy that had grown increasingly elaborate and protracted, a liturgy based on virtually continuous Psalmody and prayers for the dead that left little opportunity during the monastic day for the manual labour or private prayer and contemplation that assumed increased importance in many of the newer orders. This liturgy was itself highly conservative, having been given its most important shape and elaboration under the great eleventh-century abbots Odilo and Hugh.[66]

I have elsewhere commented on the conservative character that Cluny's spirituality gave to the theological message of some of the most powerful works of Cluniac monumental art of the twelfth century, such as the tympana of Moissac and Beaulieu.[67] Both works—the tympanum of Moissac is usually dated at about 1115–25 and that of Beaulieu in the early 1130s—have little to do with the humanity of Christ or his humility as models of exemplary Christian life that were so central to the theology of the newer forms of devotion in the twelfth century. These tympana evoke instead the cosmic, all triumphant Christ of the sermons of Abbot Odilo of Cluny (994–1049). This is clear in the choice of the *Maestas* theme at Moissac.[68] Yet even in Pl. 176 the vision of the resurrected Christ displaying his wounds at Beaulieu, the devotion to the Passion, which was one aspect of the liturgy of Cluny, is expressed in terms of Christ's triumph, not of his humanity and suffering. Angels present the instruments of his Passion, but it is a jewelled crown and jewelled cross of triumph that they display. Cluniac theophanies like this one sustained into high Romanesque art the image of the awe-inspiring Christ evoked by Abbot Odilo's sermon 15, a meditation on the *sancta crucis* as a symbol of triumph.[69]

In Chapter 4 we found the first series of capitals from La Daurade to be eminently representative of this essentially conservative Cluniac spirituality. The later Passion series, in contrast, reveals much that appears to respond to the newer directions of humanized Christianity in twelfth-century devotion. This can only be understood within the dynamics of the ecclesiastical and political life of Toulouse and the particular circumstances surrounding the cloister of La Daurade at the time of its creation. There was much about its status within the city of Toulouse that conspired to make the community at La Daurade subject to outside influences—artistic, spiritual, and political—that may not have been felt in more isolated monastic establishments. The priory of La Daurade was located in a rapidly growing urban centre, the capital of the domains of the counts of Toulouse. Though the religious life of its monastic community would have been kept separate from the duties of the secular clergy who served the lay worshippers, the priory still stood at the centre of one of the oldest and most populous urban parishes of Toulouse. The monastic community had large and wealthy temporal possessions to administer. Its position on the banks of the Garonne gave it enviable sources of revenue from the fishing and milling rights it controlled, while the Daurade bridge

[66] See Guy de Valous, *Le Monachisme clunisien des origines au XVᵉ siècle* (Paris, 1935), 327–72; Noreen Hunt, *Cluny under Saint Hugh* (Notre-Dame, Ind., 1968), 99–123. Hunt maintains that Cluny's liturgy, while onerous, was not more protracted than that of other Benedictine houses of the 10th and 11th cents. See also Philibert Schmitz, 'La Liturgie à Cluny', in *Spiritualità cluniacense. Convegni del centro di studi sulla spiritualità medievale, 1958* (Todi, 1960), 85–99.

[67] 'High Romanesque Sculpture: Developments in Southern France in the Generation after Saint-Denis' (paper delivered at the Sixth Annual Symposium of the Robert Branner Forum for Medieval Art, Columbia University, New York, 5 Apr. 1987).

[68] See Odilo's sermons in *PL* 142, cols. 991–1036. Delaruelle has connected the Cluniac emphasis on the sacred mysteries, as expressed in Odilo's sermons, to the iconography of the Moissac portal (Delaruelle, 'Crusading Idea', 210 n. 3). See also Yves Christe, *Les Grands Portails romans: études sur l'iconologie des théophanies romanes* (Geneva, 1969), esp. 29–33 for his interpretation of Odilo's spirituality and its relationship to the great Cluniac theophanic portals.

[69] Odilo of Cluny, Sermon 15, 'De sancta cruce' (*PL* 142, cols. 1031–6).

increased commercial traffic between the parish of La Daurade and the suburb of Saint-Cyprian. From at least 1119/30 it operated a hospital on the opposite bank of the Garonne, thus participating in the charitable activities that constituted one of the more progressive social phenomena of twelfth-century urban life in Toulouse.[70]

The monastery of La Daurade was, moreover, in direct rivalry with the most independent of the reformed communities of Toulouse, the canons of Saint-Sernin, for the favour of the counts of Toulouse. Its long history of benefaction from the ruling family of Toulouse may have encouraged a more than ordinary penetration of the life of the monastery by the political influence of the counts, for we know they held councils in the cloister of La Daurade from at least 1196.[71] Finally, from the artistic point of view, the monastery of La Daurade was located at the heart of the most progressive and creative centre in the Romanesque south-west of France. With the introduction of the second workshop into the cloister shortly after 1120, the building activity at La Daurade may be said to have revitalized Toulousan sculpture in the period after the restoration of the counts and determined the new direction of its second generation of sculptors.

Still, the monastery of La Daurade was subject to the authority of its powerful mother house at Moissac, spearhead of the eleventh-century Cluniac reform in the region. The close sway that the mother house must have exerted over its urban priory, at least in the early decades of its reform, is clear in the use by the Toulousan community of the same workshop that had decorated the Moissac cloister and by the adherence to an essentially conservative eleventh-century iconography in the first series of capitals carved for the cloister.

For these numerous reasons the imagery of the second series of capitals from La Daurade, while remarkably bold and responsive to new directions in twelfth-century spirituality in most respects, still shows some elements that appear linked to the conservative Cluniac spiritual values that were formed within the eleventh century. Both the conservative and progressive aspects of its iconography need to be explored.

We have already spoken of the ideal of the *vita apostolica* as one that was held to by all the orders during the period of reform. The vitality of this ideal for Cluniac monasticism in the twelfth century is exemplified in William of Saint-Thierry's *Liber de natura et dignitate amoris*. William was later to become a disciple of St Bernard of Clairvaux, but at the time of his composition of this treatise, around 1122, he was Cluniac abbot of Saint-Thierry near Reims.[72] In speaking of the foundations of monastic life, William wrote that, to praise adequately the discipline of regular life, 'it is necessary to go back to the time of the Apostles when it began to take flight'. He continued:

since it is the Apostles who instituted for their usage, according to the model that the Lord had taught them . . . a certain manner of living together, in which the many would have but one heart and one soul, where everything would be placed in common, where all would be continually within the temple in a unanimous spirit. Animated by a great love for this form of life instituted by the Apostles, certain men no longer want to have other house or lodging than the house of God, the house of prayer. Everything they do, is done at a common hour, under a common rule; in the name of the Lord they live together, possessing nothing of their own, not even their own body, not being any longer masters of their own will, they sleep together, they get up together, they pray, they sing Psalms, they study together. They have manifested their fixed and immutable willingness to obey their

---

[70] Mundy, 'Charity and Social Work', 211–12.

[71] Toulouse, AMT, Cartulaire du Bourg, AA 1, doc. 12, fos. 14ᵛ–15ʳ.

[72] Vicaire, *Imitation des apôtres*, 15.

superiors and to be submitted to them. They restrict their necessities to the minimum and live with very little; they have poor clothing, sober meals and limit everything in accordance with a very precise rule.[73]

Reverberations of the familiar verses from the Book of Acts that describe the communal life of the Apostles (Acts 2: 42–7 and 4: 32–5) sound throughout this passage of William's text, as they did in so many of the pronouncements of the reformers. This equation of the monastic community, headed by its abbot or prior, with the college of the Apostles in their devotion to Christ was more than an abstraction to the institution of monasticism. As William describes, it was sewn into the very structure and discipline of monastic life and, we might add, it was enacted in solemn rituals that were a part of the monastic *horarium*. The most vivid example of this, of course, was the ceremony of the *mandatum*, the washing of the feet. In the Gospel of John, after Christ had washed the feet of the disciples, he said to them, 'If then I being *your* Lord and Master, have washed your feet; you also ought to wash one another's feet. For I have given you an example, that as I have done to you, so you do also' (John 13: 14–15).

In the Cluniac discipline, a *mandatum* of the poor was performed daily in the monastery from June through the calends of November, during which the feet of three poor laymen were washed by selected members of the community and bread and wine were distributed to them.[74] During Holy Week, the *mandatum* became one of the central ceremonies of Maundy Thursday. On this day, two ritual foot-washings were performed, the monastic *mandatum* in which the members of the community, including the abbot or prior, washed one another's feet, and an elaborated *mandatum* of the poor. And, the Cluniac customaries of the eleventh century tell us, the location where the latter ceremony took place was the cloister.[75]

The missal of 1415 for the usage of La Daurade describes a *mandatum* of the poor on Holy Thursday that is very close in its ritual to that described in the Customs of Ulrich and the Farfa Customary. The foot-washing was to take place after the main meal of the day. At La Daurade eighty poor men were let into the monastery for this ritual, and it is specified in the rubrics that they were to be seated in the cloister. After their hands and feet were washed, they were to be brought barley soup, wine, and the bread of the convent and given one Toulousan *denario* and a fragment of fish. At the same time that the *mandatum pauperum* was taking place in the cloister, the missal specifies, a *mandatum* of the entire community was to be performed in the chapter house.[76]

Though we cannot be certain, there is little reason to doubt that the *mandatum* of Holy Week also took place in the cloister of La Daurade in the twelfth century, and its monastic counterpart in the chapter house, based on the early customaries. This ritual imitation of Christ's act of charity and humility, meant as an *exemplum* for his disciples, would have given vivid resonance to the memorable capital of the *Washing of the Feet* which stood in the cloister of La Daurade. The *Washing of the Feet* is, in fact, a frequently encountered theme in twelfth-century cloister art, and this fact may be tied to the performance of the Holy Week ceremony there.[77] The theme appears in the cloister of Moissac, even though no scenes of the Passion itself are included in that ensemble.

Pl. 80

[73] William of Saint-Thierry, *Liber de natura et dignitate amoris*, ch. 9 (*PL* 184, cols. 395B–396D).

[74] Customs of Ulrich, bk. 2, ch. 37 (*PL* 149, col. 730).

[75] Ibid., bk. 1, ch. 12 (*PL* 149, col. 658). See also the Farfa Customary (*Corpus consuetudinum monasticarum*, ed. K. Hallinger, x. *Liber tramitis aevi Odilonis abbatis*, ed. Petrus Dinter (Siegburg, 1980), bk. 1, ch. 7, 55.5 and 55.7 (pp. 75–8)).

[76] Paris, BN, nouv. acq. lat. 2387, fo. 8ʳ.

[77] On the occurrence of this theme in the cloister, see Pressouyre, 'St. Bernard to St. Francis', 75–6; Forsyth, 'Vita Apostolica', 80.

What is startlingly original at La Daurade is the simultaneous power and intimacy with which this vision of the apostolic ideal was set before the monks. In the cloisters of Moissac and Saint-Étienne at Toulouse, the college of Apostles was assembled as a metaphor for the monastic community. In the moving Passion series from La Daurade, it is the human bonds of the disciples to one another and to Christ that emerges as the primary theme. In the early episodes of the series, the *Washing of the Feet* and the *Last Supper*, the communion of the disciples with Christ is established, but in Christ's vigil at Gethsemane and in the rarely represented scene of the disciples fleeing the Arrest, they are shown in their human weakness and failure to live up to the example of Christ. In the scenes following the Resurrection, the period of Christ's post-Resurrection sojourn on earth and the preparation of the Apostles to receive their mission is detailed at unusual length.

The very style in which the Passion story is told at La Daurade creates the intimacy and lifelike quality that sets these capitals apart from anything in previous Toulousan sculpture. We have described the cunning of the Daurade narrative style in an earlier chapter, the dramatic interaction of the figures that establishes an emotional dialectic among them, as well as the powerful sense of place and moment, achieved through the small scale of the settings and the 'close-up' view we are permitted of these most intense moments of the Passion story.

Small details contribute to the sense of intimacy, such as the disciple who steps forward with a towel in the *Washing of the Feet* or the apocryphal figure of St Martial serving at the table of the Last Supper with a giant bowl before him. Details like this, not sanctioned by the scriptural accounts of the Passion, share some of the anecdotal and even sentimental flavour of contemporary saints' legends. At the same time, in the context of the highly charged narrative series of La Daurade, they provide relief from what might otherwise be intolerable levels of tension.

Pl. 83
Pl. 86

It is the emphasis given to the human *persona* of the disciples, their personal responses to the critical revelations of Christ's death and resurrection, that relates this series so closely to the Romanesque missal leaf at Auxerre. We singled out this leaf in an earlier chapter as perhaps the best representative of a narrative style in the pictorial arts that may lie behind the sculptures from La Daurade, even though every episode in the Daurade series does not find its match in the earlier manuscript leaf. The scenes of the *Arrest of Christ*, the *Noli me tangere*, and the *Journey to Emmaus* in the two series are, in fact, very close in the intimacy of their story-telling. Similarly, the rare scene of *Peter's Denial of Christ* included in the cycle of the Auxerre leaf may be compared to scenes such as the disciples fleeing or John and Peter at the Empty Tomb from the Daurade series in the focus it gives to the behaviour of Christ's followers at decisive moments in their relationship to him.

Pl. 146

The human aspect of the Passion story is most poignant in the pendant scenes of the *Deposition* and *Entombment* from La Daurade, in which his followers tend to the lifeless body of Christ in images of great emotional intimacy. At the same time, the scene of the *Deposition* is one of those within the series in which archetypal symbols, emergent from an early tradition of Cluniac devotion, are made to obtrude themselves into the very contemporary narrative language of the Passion story. We are speaking here of the commanding jewelled cross from which Christ's sagging body is detached, and whose associations of triumph and the return of the Son of Man belie the sorrowful emotions of the human drama.

Pls. 97 and 99

We have already referred to St Odilo's Sermon 15 on the *sancta crux* for revealing Cluny's

Pl. 54

devotion to the Passion of Christ as the consummation of his triumph. This idea was celebrated in the first series of capitals in the image of the *Adoration of the Cross*. In that capital a jewelled and veiled cross, its arms held aloft by angels, is presented as a pendant to the *Maestas Domini*. In the iconographic programme of the second series, it is as though the jewelled cross of the *Deposition*, as a visual image of great power, were meant to evoke the recollection of its symbolic counterpart in an earlier part of the cloister.

Pls. 117, 122, 129, and 130–2

In the quadrivium of the *Traditio legis*, the *Ascension*, the *Pentecost*, and the *Four Rivers of Paradise* from the second series, the Apostles are invested with their mission. Of these, the *Traditio legis* and the *Four Rivers* demand special interpretation. The Ascension and the Pentecost are described in the Acts of the Apostles (Acts 1: 9–11 and 2: 1–4), the postlude to the four Gospels in which Christ's mission is successfully transmitted to the apostolic Church on earth.[78] The *Traditio legis*, on the other hand, has no literal basis either in the Gospel text or in Acts. It belongs to the Early Christian iconography of the exalted Christ, an ahistorical, symbolic image in which Christ, as ruler of the cosmos, hands down the New Law to his Apostles, in the persons of SS Peter and Paul.

The image is a frequent one on Early Christian sarcophagi, commonly flanked by scenes from Christ's Public Life and Passion. The distinguishing features of the traditional iconography are the central position of Christ, seated or standing and extending a scroll to Peter on his left while Paul, sometimes holding a rolled scroll, stands as witness on the right. In some Early Christian versions, however, additional Apostles are assembled.[79] This suggests that it is to the entire community of the Apostles, who also represent the baptized (that is to say, the Church on earth), that Christ delivers the New Law. In fact, the occasional inclusion of other details indicates that this ahistorical scene may stand in place of or subsume the several scriptural appearances of Christ, both before and after his Resurrection, when he sent forth the disciples or invested them with powers (see Matthew 10: 1–14; Mark 16: 14–20; John 21: 14–17). For example, in the sarcophagus from Arles noted above, the presence of lambs clustered around the feet of Christ and the disciples recalls Christ's charge to St Peter at the Sea of Tiberias, 'Feed my lambs . . . feed my sheep' (John 21: 14–17).

The dramatic way in which the sculptor of the Daurade capital has modified the traditional iconography of the *traditio legis* has made identification of the scene problematic. In place of the symmetrical, essentially static arrangement of Christ flanked by Peter and Paul, the sculptor has given the scene a bold new focus by placing Christ (identified by his crossed nimbus) off axis in a half-crouching pose at the corner of the capital. This gives Peter the central position on the more prominent small face, while St Paul, his hand raised towards the scene, is placed behind Peter.

Émile Mâle, in the earliest iconographic study of the Daurade cloister capitals, had identified this scene as Christ's post-Resurrection appearance at the Sea of Tiberias, pointing out that this third appearance of the risen Christ to his disciples occurs in John's text immediately after the *Incredulity of Thomas*, with which the scene in question is paired on the Daurade capital.[80]

[78] Christ's Ascension is also referred to in the Gospels of Mark and Luke, but the iconography of the Daurade capital follows the fuller account in Acts.

[79] For examples depicting Christ flanked by Peter and Paul alone see the sarcophagus of Junius Bassus of AD 359 (Rome, Vatican Grotto) and a city-gate sarcophagus of Theodosian date in Verona. In a Theodosian column sarcophagus of *c*.400

(Arles, Musée lapidaire d'art chrétien) Peter and Paul stand at the head of other Apostles. All 3 sarcophagi are illustrated in Gertrud Schiller, *Iconography of Christian Art* (Greenwich, Conn., 1971), ii, figs. 2, 3, and 4.

[80] Émile Mâle, 'Les Chapiteaux romans du musée de Toulouse et l'école toulousaine du xiie siècle', *Revue archéologique*, 3rd ser., 20 (1892), 185.

None the less, the absence of the lambs, a usual requisite for this scene, argues against Mâle's identification.[81] Though the traditional positions of the three participants have been modified, the iconographic context of the scene within the series suggests that it is, indeed, the *traditio legis* that is represented at La Daurade, not Christ's specific charge to St Peter at Tiberias.

This is most strongly indicated by the inclusion within the second series of the *Four Rivers of Paradise*, the thirteenth capital whose presence greatly enriches the meaning of the series as a whole. The Four Rivers frequently appear in conjunction with the *traditio legis* in Early Christian art, where they are shown flowing forth from the Paradise Mount on which the exalted Christ stands.[82] In this sense they are part of the ancient cosmological imagery, along with the four winds and the four elements, that symbolized the universal and eternal character of Christ's rule. But in Christian art, the meaning of the Four Rivers is multivalent, as it is within the Daurade second series. The Rivers also frequently accompany images of the jewelled cross or the Agnus Dei to underline the cosmological and eschatological significance of Christ's death and resurrection.[83] On a sixth-century repoussé silver paten found at Berezov, Siberia, for example, two angels venerate the gemmed cross mounted on an orb and resting atop the Mount of Paradise from which the Four Rivers flow.[84] The image strongly recalls those of the *Adoration of the Cross* in the cloister of Moissac and in the first series of capitals from La Daurade. All these images have eschatological as well as triumphal implications, since the jewelled cross, the *crux invicta*, is the Sign of the Son of Man in heaven, which, according to Matthew 24: 30, will announce the end of time and the Last Judgement.

Pl. 55

Pl. 54

The *Four Rivers* capital from La Daurade depicts nude personifications seated at the four corners, each labelled with a titulus: Phison, Geon, Tigris, Eufrates. The nudes hold large trumpet-shaped horns from which streams of water gush. That capital must have been part of the cloister arcade and is the work of the second team of sculptors is clear from its dimensions, figure style, and use of the distinctive diapered ground, a hallmark of the second series. At the same time, its wholly allegorical discourse sets it apart from the rest of the series. It is as though the monks of La Daurade were not content with the novel intimacy and human focus that pulls together the twelve capitals of the Passion story. As an accompaniment to these images they could not resist inserting a symbolical note that recalls the language of an older eleventh-century Cluniac theology. The imagery of the *Four Rivers* capital may even have been suggested to the community at La Daurade by the remarkable capital of that subject that originally stood in the hemicycle of the mother abbey of Cluny, perhaps since the late eleventh century.[85] At Cluny, it functioned within a programme that was both learned and poetic

Pls. 130–132

[81] See the Carolingian ciborium of King Arnulf in Munich, Schatzkammer der Residenz (Jean Hubert, Jean Porcher, and Wolfgang F. Volbach, *The Carolingian Renaissance* (New York, 1970), fig. 239).

[82] See the Theodosian city-gate sarcophagus of *c*.AD 400 in Verona (n. 79 above). See also the apse mosaic of *c*.350 in Sta. Costanza in Rome, in which the sheep are also present beneath the *traditio legis* scene (André Grabar, *Christian Iconography: A Study of its Origins*, Bollingen Series 35, x (Princeton, 1968), fig. 101).

[83] See the Mosan book cover of open-work copper and gilt of *c*.1160 in the Musée de Cluny in Paris (Schiller, *Iconography of Christian Art*, ii fig. 404). In a chalice of *c*.1160–70 from the monastery of Wilten, now in the Kunsthistorisches Museum in Vienna, the Four Rivers are shown together with a Passion cycle (ibid., fig. 426). See also the Berthold Missal (*c*.1200–15),

in which personifications of the Four Rivers appear in roundels at the corners of a full-page miniature of the Pentecost (New York, Pierpont Morgan Library, MS 710, fo. 64ᵛ). The *traditio clavium* is also alluded to there, in the key held by St Peter (Stephan Seeliger, *Pfingsten: Die Ausgiessung des Heiligen Geistes am fünfzigsten Tage nach Ostern* (Düsseldorf, 1958), fig. 7).

[84] Leningrad, the Hermitage (Schiller, *Iconography of Christian Art*, ii, fig. 6).

[85] Kenneth John Conant, *Cluny: les églises et la maison du chef d'ordre*, The Medieval Academy of America, Publication 77 (Mâcon, 1968), pl. 68, figs. 134 and 135, and pl. 69, figs. 136 and 137. For a recent summary of the literature and the issues involved in the dating of the Cluny ambulatory capitals, see C. Edson Armi, *Masons and Sculptors in Romanesque Burgundy* (University Park, Pa., 1983), i. 22–3.

throughout. As an accompaniment to the Passion series at La Daurade, and in conjunction with the *traditio legis* theme, its symbolical language stands out as a decidedly archaizing note.

The presence of the *Traditio legis* at La Daurade and the prominence given to St Peter within it, also lend a distinctly Cluniac overtone to the series. The pairing of SS Peter and Paul, either in the dramatization of the *traditio legis* or as pendant images, is a frequent feature in the art of houses affiliated with the order, as are dedications of Cluniac houses to St Peter alone or to SS Peter and Paul together. The Romanesque popularity of the *traditio legis* image can be associated with ideas of return to the Early Church. As the Gregorian papacy's ideal example of 'Roman independence', no arm of the reform associated itself with the papacy's own objectives more faithfully than Cluny itself. The dedication of the abbey church to SS Peter and Paul reflects this fundamental identification with Rome and the Early Church. St Hugh's chapel at Berzé-la-Ville preserves one of the most monumental images of the *traditio legis* in Romanesque art, in the great fresco of the apse semi-dome.[86]

In the cloister of Moissac, the two princes of the Apostles are paired on the south-east corner pier, in close proximity to a capital of the east gallery depicting their martyrdom and glorification in heaven (Schapiro 20).[87] From an early period, Peter and Paul had become associated in hagiography because their feasts were celebrated on the same day (29 June), the day of their dual martyrdom. The Peter and Paul capital at Moissac contains a deep relic cavity, suggesting that the capital may have functioned in a liturgical ceremony devoted to the two saints.[88] On the south portal of the abbey church, Peter and Paul are again prominently paired, Peter on the west jamb and Paul on the west face of the trumeau, pendant to their Old Testament counterparts, the Prophets Isaiah and Jeremiah, on the east jamb and east face of the trumeau. On the closely related south porch of Beaulieu, a Cluniac dependency since 1095, monumental reliefs of Peter and Paul are again placed opposite each other on the jambs.

To name other prominent examples of the elevation of Peter and Paul within Cluniac iconography, the *Traditio legis* is the subject of a capital supporting the lintel of the small *Last Supper* portal of Cluny's Burgundian priory at Charlieu. The *Traditio clavium*, with St Peter at the head of a group of Apostles, is the subject of the tympanum of the Cluniac church of Saint-Sauveur at Nevers.[89] At Toulouse itself, the hagiography of Peter and Paul is the subject of two of the six capitals of the south portal of Saint-Pierre-des-Cuisines, the other Toulousan priory brought under the reform of Cluny in the eleventh century.[90] The *Martyrdom of St Peter* appears on the innermost capital of the east jamb, and on the outermost capital is the *Traditio clavium* and a pair of disciples who may be *Peter and Paul Departing on Their Mission*.

On the capitals of La Daurade, the themes of the *Traditio legis* and the *Four Rivers of Paradise* stand apart from the extended narrative of the Passion and the Resurrection. At the same time, in their conspicuous revival of themes strongly associated with Early Christian art, they reinforce the element of historicism and nostalgia for the Early Church that runs

[86] For the controversies over the date of this fresco, see the literature in Willibald Sauerländer, 'Gislebertus von Autun: Ein Beitrag zur Entstehung seines künstlerischen Stils', *Studien zur Geschichte der europäischen Plastik* (1965), 28 n. 23.

[87] Schapiro, 'Romanesque Sculpture of Moissac. I', 166, figs. 45 and 46. A nearby capital in the south gallery depicts the *Imprisonment and Deliverance of St Peter* (Schapiro 17).

[88] Vidal has referred to a ceremony honouring SS Peter and Paul that took place within the cloister of Moissac in the later Middle Ages. On the saints' feast day, the abbot led a procession through the cloister during which the capital with the relic cavity was censed (Marguerite Vidal, 'Le Culte des saints et des reliques dans l'abbaye de Moissac', *O Distrito de Braga*, 4 (1967), 9).

[89] Mâle, *Religious Art: The Twelfth Century*, fig. 299.

[90] For the affiliation of Saint-Pierre-des-Cuisines with Cluny see Ch. 1. I am in agreement with Durliat on the late 12th-cent. date of the south portal capitals (Durliat, *Haut-Languedoc roman*, 224–6).

throughout the series as a whole. The repeated use of twisted columns and swagged curtains, jewelled hems and strigillated sarcophagi in the style of La Daurade seems consciously evocative of Early Christian sumptuary and funerary arts. Recent publications have increasingly pointed to the importance of historicism in the art of Bernard Gelduinus and his workshop at Saint-Sernin, in his revival of Early Christian motifs and style as well as the choice of marble for the primary sanctuary furnishings for the new Romanesque basilica of the canons.[91] The nostalgia for the Early Church, then, can be read in every manifestation of the reform in Toulouse—in the language of reforming documents as well as the visual symbols with which the ecclesiastical communities of Toulouse surrounded themselves and interacted in the performance of their monastic rituals.

In discussing the revivalist intent of the *Traditio legis* and *Four Rivers* capitals at La Daurade, we have been carried away from that other theme of the monastic reform that explains the presence of these images in the cloister, namely the theme of apostolic investiture and mission that runs as a current through the series. The Book of Genesis (2: 10–14) describes the river that flowed out of Eden and split into four streams—Phison, Gehon, Tigris, and Euphrates—which were taken to signify the four cardinal points and the four corners of the world. In New Testament typology, this ancient cosmological symbolism was associated with the fourfold river of the Gospels, represented by the four Gospel writers themselves, and with the diaspora of the disciples whose mission it was to baptize and convert all the peoples of the earth.[92] This meaning can hardly be absent from the *traditio legis* theme at La Daurade either, which not only identifies the Apostles as Christ's heirs but subsumes all his commissions to them to preach, convert, heal, and evangelize that had been delivered in the text of the Gospels.

Yet if the monks of La Daurade were to take the apostolic life as their model, are we to believe that a teaching and converting role was being urged upon them in the capitals of the *Traditio legis* and the *Four Rivers of Paradise*? What we know from written sources about how monks themselves defined their profession in the twelfth century would make this seem unlikely,[93] although in our search for an understanding of this question, the material evidence of a work of art created to speak to monks within their own cloister can hardly be discounted as less pertinent than the testimony of written rules and treatises. Still, in our earlier discussion of pilgrimage, we saw that, within the realm of the cloister, some exhortations to a particular behaviour were understood to be intended metaphorically.

The goal of the monastic vocation was personal salvation through commitment to a religious life of poverty and prayer that was thought to be achievable only in seclusion from the world. Many monks in the twelfth century did, in fact, take clerical orders and performed pastoral duties. At the Council of Nîmes of 6–14 July 1096, Urban II, himself a former prior of Cluny, had adopted the canon that monks, like clergy, were entitled to administer the sacraments of baptism, communion, and penitence.[94] Nevertheless, even allowing that the Toulousan community at La Daurade was apparently more than usually open to certain new directions in devotion that were

[91] See in particular Thomas Lyman, 'La Table d'autel de Bernard Gilduin', *Les Cahiers de Saint-Michel de Cuxa*, 13 (1982), 57–73; M. F. Hearn, *Romanesque Sculpture* (Ithaca, NY, 1981), 79.

[92] Lafargue gave this interpretation of the *Four Rivers* capital (*Chapiteaux de la Daurade*, 75).

[93] Bynum has written illuminatingly on this question. She

has presented evidence that it was the orders of regular canons who perceived a special obligation to teach 'by word and example', a charge, she argues, that distinguished their vocation from that of monks. See Bynum, *Docere Verbo et Exemplo*, esp. 18–33, 77–98, and 181–99.

[94] Crozet, 'Voyage d'Urbain II et ses négociations', 272.

reshaping spirituality in the twelfth century, a literal preaching and teaching role such as that practised by the mendicant orders in imitation of the Apostles would hardly have been urged upon monks within the strict definition of the monastic vocation as interpreted by Cluny. Only the abbot was accorded a teaching role within the Rule of St Benedict,[95] a distinction that may have meaning for the frontal and commanding image of Abbot Durandus as he appears at the head of the college of Apostles on the piers of the cloister of Moissac.

Within the context of the second series of capitals from La Daurade, the *Traditio legis* and *Four Rivers* capitals may signify that the monks of this community viewed themselves as perpetuating the Gospel through their observance of the apostolic life (itself an imitation of the life of Christ recounted in the Gospel). Through their perpetual observance of the monastic office and the feasts of the liturgical year, they gave continual new life and re-enactment to the events of the Gospel and in particular to Christ's death and sacrifice.

With the introduction of the second workshop into its cloister around 1120, the Cluniac community at La Daurade seized the artistic initiative in Toulouse, an initiative it would hold into the third quarter of the twelfth century. Despite the obtrusion of certain conservative notes into the iconography, the essential character of its sculptural programme makes clear that this Cluniac community, for one, was distinctly open and responsive to the new current of humanized Christian devotion that was transforming twelfth-century spirituality in many quarters. We have seen that the capitals take as their theme the human bonds of the Apostles to one another and to Christ, as well as the individual responses of Christ's followers to the spiritual truths revealed by his Passion and Resurrection. In this they are different from anything in previous Toulousan sculpture. In fact, the Passion series from La Daurade may be identified as one of the earliest regional expressions of the new twelfth-century spirituality. In the area between Toulouse and Limoges, this new spirituality had a recognizable impact on Romanesque sculpture during the decades 1130 to 1160. This is apparent both in the kinds of themes that would gain importance during these decades, as well as in the increasingly concrete and immediate terms used by artists to express them.

The apostolic college and its mission as the heir and disseminator of Christ's teachings was to assume increasingly important attention in Romanesque sculpture in cloister programmes such as that of Saint-Guilhem-le-Désert (where reliefs of Christ among the college of the Apostles were featured on the piers of the upper cloister)[96] and in the Cluniac chapter house at Catus. At Catus the *traditio clavium* is depicted on a beautiful capital that stands at the centre
Pl. 177 of the chapter room. Though this was a theme with a long history in medieval iconography, its particular interpretation at Catus reflects the new spirituality of the twelfth century. The theological message here is concerned with the human life of Christ, with and among his disciples, and his mission to them, evoked through their intimate crowding and eager attention to the dialogue between Christ and Peter, as each registers his own response to the momentous meaning of the event.[97]

---

[95] *Benedicti regula*, ed. R. Hanslik, in *Corpus scriptorum ecclesiasticorum latinorum* (Vienna, 1960), chs. 2 and 4, 19–27, 149–52. See also Bynum, *Docere Verbo et Exemplo*, 107.

[96] The reliefs are now dispersed between the Musée de la société archéologique at Montpellier and the Musée lapidaire at Saint-Guilhem. See Robert Saint-Jean, Daniel Kuentz, and Philippe Lorimy, *Saint-Guilhem-le-Désert: la sculpture du cloître de Gellone* (Montpellier, 1990); also, Robert Saint-Jean,

'Le Cloître supérieur de Saint-Guilhem-le-Désert: essai de restitution', *Les Cahiers de Saint-Michel de Cuxa*, 7 (1976), 45–60.

[97] The chapter house at Catus, dating from *c*.1140, has been little studied. See Raymond Rey, *La Sculpture romane languedocienne* (Toulouse, 1936), 278–80; Marguerite Vidal *et al.*, *Quercy roman* (La Pierre-qui-vire, 1969), 11–12.

A similar turn towards human scale and intimacy is found in the portal sculpture of south-west France, even in major theophanic images like the Ascension which became a dominant theme for tympanum compositions during the period 1135–60. In the numerous renditions of this theme from these decades, for example at Cahors and Collonges, a new focus on the human bonds of the Apostles to one another, to the Virgin, and to Christ replaces the traditional emphasis on the supernatural. The moving descriptions of individual human response in images like those of Cahors and Collonges, or in Mary's reaction to the angel in a relief of the *Annunciation* of about 1160 on the porch of Saint-Georges at Ydes,[98] are anticipated in the reactions of the disciples to the Ascension on the capital from La Daurade or in the unforgettable image of St John discovering the empty tomb. The capitals of La Daurade opened up the realm of monumental sculpture to the more intimate scale and feeling that were to typify Romanesque work in the region between Toulouse and Limoges in the second and third quarters of the twelfth century.

Pls. 178 and 180–1

Pl. 179

THE APPREHENSION OF MEANING: THE FUNCTION OF SCULPTURE IN THE CLOISTER OF LA DAURADE

In considering the capitals that survive from La Daurade, both the earlier and the later series, the questions that bear on the meaning of Romanesque cloister sculpture transcend the interpretation of individual images and their sources in contemporary issues or in the preceding iconographic tradition. Ultimately more critical is the question of how these sculptures functioned in concert with each other and with the architecture of the cloister, a specialized construct that defined and ordered space for specific functions in monastic life. In light of the diversity and experimentation that characterize the use of monumental sculpture in Romanesque cloisters, we are far from being able to answer these questions yet in the broad sense. Nevertheless, the cloister programme of La Daurade can serve as a case-study that is unusually revealing for the period, produced, as it was, in a centre of monastic reform and in an intensely creative foyer of sculptural invention in the twelfth century.

What can be said, then, about how sculpture functioned in the cloister of La Daurade? This is not a question that can be answered on the basis of a single kind of evidence, and no category of information can be ignored or dismissed if it is useful. The surviving plans and documents for the cloister, the architecture of its nearest relatives in the region, the compositional schemes and narrative strategies employed by the sculptors, and the meaning that specific themes could have had for the Cluniac community in Toulouse have all been examined. A synthesis of this evidence has prompted me to conclude, as I did in an earlier publication, that the cloister arcades at La Daurade were most likely carried on a system of alternating single and double columns stabilized by L-shaped corner piers. The more complex triple supports may have flanked a passage through the parapet wall, perhaps at the midpoint of the arcade or at the end, facing a corner pier. New evidence for the plan of the closely related cloister of Saint-Étienne at Toulouse, which I discovered in 1984, has tended to reinforce the conclusion in favour of alternation I reached earlier.[99]

---

[98] For a bibliography on these portals, see above, Ch. 6 n. 78.

[99] See above, Ch. 3, and Kathryn Horste, 'A New Plan of the Cloister and Rampart of Saint-Étienne', *Journal of the Society of Architectural Historians*, 45 (1986), 5–19.

Because their subject-matter is so diverse, attempting to recapture the original sequence of the first series of capitals would seem to be a futile and probably unproductive enterprise. As with the much larger ensemble at Moissac on which they are based, there is no demonstrable pattern of thematic relationships that would suggest a premeditated grouping or positioning of subjects to enhance the meaning of the whole.

In the case of the later capitals from La Daurade, however, the question of sequence seems crucial to their meaning. They have always been discussed in the literature as a Passion-Resurrection cycle and, through several changes of installation, have, since the directorship of Paul Mesplé, been exhibited in the museum according to the chronology of the Gospel story.[100] The early scenes of Christ's Passion, from the *Washing of the Feet* to the *Resurrection*, are all depicted on single capitals, while scenes of the latter half of the Gospel story, Christ's post-Resurrection appearances to his disciples, are assigned to double ones, with the two triple capitals carrying intermediate scenes. Because of this distribution, a strictly chronological arrangement of the capitals would force the following sequence of supports: single, single, single, triple, single, single, single, double, double, double, triple, double. If such a pattern of supports existed in the cloister of La Daurade, it would have made that Toulousan structure unique in the twelfth century. Its intimate relationship to the cloisters of Moissac, Saint-Étienne in Toulouse, and later examples at Saint-Pons-de-Thomières and Saint-Lizier tells us that, on the contrary, La Daurade belonged to a closely related family of cloisters whose most distinctive design feature was the alternation of single and double columnar supports.

I have already given my reasons for believing that the present alternation of supports at Moissac preserves the original design, even though the arcades were rebuilt in the thirteenth century. As I have remarked elsewhere, the existence of single and double capitals within the scheme, and in equal numbers, is the most compelling evidence that they were meant to alternate.[101] As in the two series of capitals from La Daurade, all capitals at Moissac have the same dimensions at the upper surface, whether they are single or double. The single capitals, however, rest on columns of greater circumference than the twin columns. In this way, the twin and single columns were intended to receive uniform weight and to provide uniform support.[102] For this reason, they cannot be described as strong and weak supports in the literal sense. It is possible, however, that the alternation at Moissac preserves the memory of a functional system of bay division, perhaps in an earlier wood or stone cloister at the abbey.

Whether its origins are functional or aesthetic, the alternation of supports at Moissac should be recognized as a subtle and original element of design that created a preference for this scheme within an identifiable constellation of related examples. Alternation is not the usual pattern in Romanesque cloister design. By far the standard scheme on both sides of the Pyrenees was a system of uniformly double supports.[103] In Spain, only the partially surviving

[100] See Mâle, 'Chapiteaux romans', where he designated the Passion cycle as the 'first series'; Raymond Rey, *L'Art des cloîtres romans* (Toulouse, n.d. [1955]), 74–92; Mesplé, *Musée des Augustins: sculptures romanes*, nos. 122–56. Most recently, see Linda Seidel, 'Installation as Inspiration', *Gesta*, 25 (1986). The capitals were reinstalled in 1971 and again between 1976 and 1981.

[101] Horste, 'Plan of Saint-Étienne', 15.

[102] The circumferences of the astragals and bases tells us

that single and double supports were differentiated in this same way at La Daurade.

[103] See the cloisters of Saint-Bertrand-de-Comminges (Haute-Garonne), Saint-Gaudens (Haute-Garonne), Lombez (Gers), Elne (Pyrénées-Orientales), Saint-Trophime at Arles (Bouches-du-Rhône), Conques (Aveyron), and in Spain at Silos (Burgos), Pamplona (Navarre), Estella (Navarre) and the numerous late examples at Ripoll (Gerona), Estany (Catalonia), and elsewhere.

and heavily restored cloister of San Juan de la Peña in Aragon includes both single and double capitals within its ensemble, suggesting that an alternating scheme existed there.[104] Less common, but favoured in the Roussillon region, was a system of uniformly single columns, used at Cuxa, Canigou, and probably at Espira de l'Agly.[105]

As distinct from these more common schemes, those cloisters of south-west France that employed single and double supports are all closely related to one another. Furthermore, where both kinds of supports occur together, there is no evidence for any scheme other than alternation. The workshop that constructed the cloister at Moissac introduced its design into Toulouse at La Daurade, where, as we suggested in Chapter 3, an alternating scheme of supports was projected for the cloister as a whole from the outset of the project. It was carried through by the second workshop and probably influenced the design of the cathedral cloister of Saint-Étienne. At Saint-Pons de Thomières (Hérault), to the south-east of Toulouse, a   *Fig. 15* cloister was begun about 1140–50 by sculptors whose close dependence on the workshops of Toulouse has long been recognized in the style and iconography of some of its sculpture.[106] The scattered ensemble from the destroyed cloister there includes both single and double capitals, suggesting that its architectural design was also influenced by Toulouse.

Apart from Moissac, the only standing cloister of the region with a pattern of alternating single and double supports is at Saint-Lizier (Ariège), not far to the south of Toulouse on the   *Pl. 183* approach to the Pyrenees.[107] The dependence of this late twelfth-century example on the sculpture of Toulouse has also been recognized, in its repertory of interlaced vine ornament and small-scale animal and human combats that reflect the decorative style favoured at La Daurade in the third quarter of the twelfth century.[108] The regular pattern of alternation at Saint-Lizier was varied by the introduction of a four-column cluster in the west gallery. The tendency to introduce more complex supports at intermediate points in the arcade also reflects developments in Toulouse, where triple supports added variation to the later arcades at La Daurade and where compound supports were located at the midpoint of the arcades of the cathedral cloister of Saint-Étienne.[109]   *Fig. 15*

The occurrence of single and double capitals in the ensemble from La Daurade seems inseparable, then, from the conclusion that single and double members alternated. According to the distribution of scenes in the second series, however, alternation would have disturbed a

---

[104] The late Romanesque cloister of the collegiate church of Santa Maria la Mayor at Tudela (Navarre) has an unusual pattern of alternating double and triple columns. An influence on this Spanish cloister of the sculptural programme at La Daurade is a distinct possibility. The programme at Tudela includes an extended Passion–Resurrection cycle featuring numerous post-Resurrection appearances of Christ, as well as a *Bear Hunt*, a theme that appears among the latest capitals from the claustral complex at La Daurade (M. 178). See Anne de Egry, 'La Escultura del claustro de la catedral de Tudela', *Príncipe de Viana*, 20 (1959), 63–107.

[105] The vast cloister of Saint-Michel de Cuxa had single-column supports. There is some evidence, however, that the south-east segment of the arcades, later than the rest, may have been carried on double supports (see Marcel Durliat, *La Sculpture romane en Roussillon*, i (Perpignan, 1952), 26–7). For Espira de l'Agly, see Kathryn Horste, 'Romanesque Sculpture in American Collections. xx. Ohio and Michigan', *Gesta*, 21 (1982), 125–7.

[106] The capitals from Saint-Pons were inventoried by J.

Sahuc, *L'Art roman à Saint-Pons-de-Thomières* (Montpellier, 1908). For the more recent bibliography and discussion of workshops, see Seidel, in Walter Cahn and Linda Seidel, *Romanesque Sculpture in American Collections*, i. *New England Museums* (New York, 1979), 154–66.

[107] The north and south arcades at Saint-Lizier have been truncated by one bay at the east, but there is no evidence that the original design of the cloister has been disturbed. See Marcel Durliat, *Pyrénées romanes* (La Pierre-qui-vire, 1969), 144; Simone Henry, 'Les chapiteaux du cloître de Saint-Lizier', *Annales du Midi*, 54 (1942), 255–89.

[108] Cf. Mesplé 172, 174, and 178 from La Daurade.

[109] See the report of a visit to the cloister of Saint-Étienne in 1799, describing a central support 'formed by 5 columns' (Toulouse, ADHG, L2565 (formerly L2566), single sheet; Horste, 'Plan of Saint-Étienne', 10). The tendency towards more embellished supports was characteristic of later 12th-cent. cloister decoration in general (see e.g. the cloisters of Saint-Bertrand-de-Comminges, Saint-Denis, and Châlons-sur-Marne).

historical narration of the Passion story. But so, too, would the practice of placing chronologically sequential episodes on opposite faces of the same capital, as many of the scenes were distributed at La Daurade. The *Deposition* is paired with the sequential episode of the *Entombment*, the *Resurrection* with the *Visit of the Holy Women*, the *Apostles at the Tomb* with the *Noli me tangere*, the *Journey to Emmaus* with the *Supper at Emmaus*. It is only in the museum installation, where the viewer is free to move about the circumference of each capital, that the scenes appear to read in chronological order. When the capitals were locked into the structure of the cloister, the *Entombment* would not have been visible in sequence to the *Deposition*, nor the *Supper at Emmaus* to the *Journey*, because the paired episodes faced opposite sides of the parapet wall. Because of this practice of pairing sequential episodes, there is no possible arrangement of the capitals that would have created, visually, a historical sequence of Christ's Passion and Resurrection according to the Gospel account within the arcades at La Daurade. What is more, we have already suggested that foliate and animal capitals (five or possibly six of which survive) were very likely interspersed with the historiated members.

With its basis in an alternating system, and with post-Resurrection scenes possibly intermingling in a mixed scheme with Passion episodes and decorative capitals, would not the picture conjured up by such a reconstruction seem to violate the essential nature of the imagery at La Daurade? Would not the powerful story-telling impact of the scenes seem to compel a viewing of the images as successive climaxes in a sustained narrative? Seidel has argued that it would, concluding that 'the exceptionally detailed scenic definition given to each of the carvings in the La Daurade Passion series, in conjunction with both the dramatic rendering of particular scenes and the animated figure style, indicates to me that the capitals were intended to be seen in sequence and viewed as a series'.[110] For her, the 'historic immediacy' of the scenes is more compelling than any other category of evidence in considering the original arrangement of the capitals. She excludes arguments from analogy with other cloisters as a method of establishing a context of contemporary practice within which to consider the cloister of La Daurade. Such arguments can always be overwhelmed by claims that the Daurade cloister was unique, an unprecedented and unduplicated achievement. I would maintain, on the contrary, that when analysed in its entirety—capitals, imposts, bases—the surviving sculpture from La Daurade has revealed that the sculptors of the second workshop did not start from a *tabula rasa* in the cloister. We have enumerated concrete ways in which the team of sculptors who finished the cloister acknowledged their debt to the first workshop, even as they introduced exciting new approaches to the art of capital sculpture to Toulouse.[111]

Unquestionably, the fundamental expressive language of a work of art, the integral working in it of form and meaning that give it its power to move and inspire processes of response in the viewer, must stand at the centre of our understanding of an individual work. But in order to accept Seidel's analysis of the expressive power of the sculptures of La Daurade, one would need to accept her implication that the ordering of Passion episodes in continuous narrative sequence is the only order that would not violate their essential nature. When the special environment and functions of the cloister are taken into account, however, Seidel's interpretation does little to explain what could have constituted narrative art within such a context.

[110] Seidel, 'Installation as Inspiration', 84.   [111] See Ch. 3.

Certainly, throughout our analysis, we have emphasized the story-telling sophistication of the sculptors of the second series, the forethought they show in manipulating imagery to achieve a resolution of narrative activity into clearly focused episodes. At the same time, a strict programme of historical narration, sustained over a protracted sequence of capitals along the length of a cloister arcade, seems neither necessary nor even appropriate to the way in which sculptured imagery would have functioned in the monastic cloister. Because of the nature of the interplay between the architecture of the cloister and its sculptured elements, for the viewer the apprehension of meaning contained within those sculptured elements is, by necessity, a very active process. This is because the full sculptural ensemble can never be observed except over time, by a process of circumambulation, and the meaning of the whole can only be apprehended in retrospect, through a process of recollection, reassemblage, and mental concordance of images seen in many parts of the cloister. It is a process that is both abstract, in the sense that it is mental, but also highly active and demanding of involvement on the part of the viewer, specifically the monk in meditation.

Sculptures like those devoted to Christ's Passion from La Daurade must have functioned within the cloister at more than one level in the mental life of the monks who lived with them daily. They do in actuality constitute a cycle and a historical narrative in the sense that all the episodes of Christ's Crucifixion and Resurrection are present within the ensemble. But in order for them to function as such, they do not need to be physically arranged for the monk-meditator in anything approaching a Gospel sequence. The visual encounter with a single image distilled with the power, for example, of the *Entombment of Christ* would have been *Pl. 99* sufficient to call into vivid mental life for the monk all the other images of the story, intimately familiar to him from previous circuits of the cloister. It would have been possible for the monk-meditator to respond to the individual capital in a very powerful way, and he may very well have done so, perhaps meditating for prolonged periods in front of a single image, while calling to mind other images that were vivid and intimately known to him from other meditations within the same cloister. The intensely emotional and highly concentrated visual imagery of the Passion sculptures from La Daurade suggests that they were intended to function in this way.

I am suggesting that, because of the special and unique function that the cloister played in monastic life, as a place of ambulatory meditation, programming as such in the cloister may have taken place largely within the mind of the monk-meditators who used it. The expectation that the structure of the cloister itself would organize meaning for the viewer seems inappropriate both to the kind of space the cloister is and to how it was used by monks. It is just such an expectation of the ordering or sequencing of meaning for the viewer that is inherent in Seidel's suggested reconstruction of the capitals of La Daurade. One cannot disagree with her contention that the series of twelve Passion capitals, if viewed sequentially in their current museum installation, have a powerful narrative coherence. This fact, in itself, is the best indication that the source for the series was a narrative cycle, undoubtedly in pictorial form, as we have already concluded. But in their translation into cloister sculpture, the other kinds of evidence we have reviewed lead to the conclusion that the cycle was a disassembled one, in which ornamental and bestiary capitals also insinuated their varied forms among the Passion episodes at La Daurade.

Would not such a separation of episodes and climaxes seem to contradict the very nature of narration? There is no question but that this would be true if we were speaking of a written or oral narrative. One of the definitive qualities of story-telling, as distinct from other forms of discourse, is the hovering expectation it engenders in the audience, the anticipation of the next episode or event that impels the narrative forward. Both here and in my earlier analyses of the second series from La Daurade, however, I have resolutely discouraged any suggestion that the Passion images on the capitals can be equated in their functioning to a verbal narrative, either written or oral.[112] The sculptured cloister is not appropriate to this kind of narrative discourse. Cloister imagery presupposes and, indeed, requires a more active involvement of its audience in the igniting of meaning than does a verbal narrative of its listeners or readers. Cloister images were seen not once but perhaps hundreds of times by the monk who lived with them and who most likely spent his lifetime in a single cloister. When the images lived in his mental life in this way, any single image could, in a very real way, stand for and call up the whole.

The dispersed reliefs of the Apostles on the cloister piers at Moissac must have functioned very much in the same way in the mental life of the community of monks residing there. This ensemble, of course, does not involve narration, and so is different in nature from the collective episodes of the Passion from the cloister of La Daurade. Nevertheless, in the active work they demand of the viewer to bring them into relationship to each other, as an ensemble the pier reliefs are predicated on the same expectations. The Apostles at Moissac take their fullest meaning not in their individual identities but as a collective college, standing as the model for the monastic brothers of the community. Yet because of their dispersal among the corner and central piers, the apostolic assemblage could never have been literally brought into view at the same time. But for the monk-meditator who daily walked in the cloister, they need not have been. In his meditating upon them, they existed as a college, and, in their similarity of pose and form, any individual image from among them could and did stand in place of the whole. The Moissac reliefs, like the dispersed scenes of the Passion at La Daurade, presume the mental life of the viewer—the monk-meditator—as the medium in which physically dissociated images can be experienced in meaningful temporal relationship, whether sequential or simultaneous.

The kind of ordered narrative sequence that Seidel has reconstructed for the Passion series from La Daurade presumes a much more passive role for the monk-meditator in the cloister than the one I have suggested. If the power of the imagery on these capitals would seem to Seidel to have compelled a historical sequence for them, from episode to episode of the Passion story, they would also have compelled and manipulated the viewer. This makes the monk-meditator into a curiously passive respondent to what he would have seen in the cloister. Surely the monk did not need the sculpted images to tell or to teach him the story of Christ's Passion, and Seidel does not suggest this. But neither did he need to see them in narrative sequence in order to respond to the images as meaningful episodes of an ongoing story, when both the story and the sculpted images were as familiar to him as the recitation of his daily Psalms and prayers.[113]

[112] In my article of 1982 ('The Passion Series from La Daurade', *Gesta*, 21 (1982)) I avoided any suggestion that the Daurade second series could or should be analysed in terms of textual models.

[113] There are, to be sure, other ways in which sculpture must have functioned in the cloister besides as a catalyst for meditation. Léon Pressouyre has suggested something of the range of these functions (Pressouyre, 'St. Bernard to St. Francis', 71–92). Activities as mundane as washing went on in the cloister. At certain times of the year the cloister was the site of liturgical processions, and we have evidence for this at La Daurade itself. In the ordinary revolving of the monastic day, however, the most important activities in the cloister seem to have been reading, meditating, and, for the youngest boys, instruction (see Paul Maevert, 'The Medieval Monastic Claustrum', *Gesta*, 12 (1973), 54, and also the instructions in Bernard of Cluny, ed. Dom M. Hergott, in *Vetus disciplina monastica* (Paris, 1726), 202). But the notion that religious imagery had a primarily didactic function, to be used as a kind of visual catechism, is probably an inappropriate one for the cloister,

Because of the structure of the cloister and the absence of monumental precedents for its decoration, we should not expect to find imagery functioning within it in the same way it does in other kinds of monumental programmes of Romanesque art. One reason is because the cloister has no fixed centre, no beginning or end, in short, no obvious point of focus around which or in relation to which meaning can be organized in some hierarchical construct—centrifugal, centripetal, ascending, descending, heraldic or any of the other visual systems employed by medieval artists to express the relationship of subordinate elements to a dominant one. The garden or garth, while it lies at the centre of the cloister walkways, could not play the role of such a focus because the viewer was never in any fixed relation to it. The walkways were a place of transit and perpetual mobility.

It is in this sense that Romanesque sculptors were presented with new challenges and problems in the decoration of the cloister that they had not elsewhere faced, and this undoubtedly explains the creativity, experimentation, and seeming lack of system in the decorated cloisters of the Romanesque period. Complex portal and façade programmes and ensembles of sculpted and painted images in sanctuaries were developing at about the same time in the late eleventh and early twelfth centuries.[114] But portals, façades, and apses clearly do have a central focus—and an obvious 'above' and 'below'—around which and in relation to which meaning, and the sculptured elements that carry that meaning, can be organized. What is more, in even the earliest Romanesque portals that carry monumental sculpture, going back to early eleventh-century examples in the Pyrenees, such as Saint-Genis-des-Fontaines or Arles-sur-Tech, sculptors had numerous precedents to draw upon for the kind of imagery displayed there, whether from altar frontals, book covers, manuscript pages, or ivories, where hierarchical and centralized schemes for visually organizing meaning had long traditions.   *Pl. 182*

This is not to imply that Romanesque programmes of portal sculpture or apse decoration can be apprehended with a single glance or without a prolonged process of scrutiny. This is hardly the case. But even in the most complex programmes, the point of reference of every element of the programme, the focus of meaning, is usually clear. In the case of the sculptured portal, the meaning usually can be apprehended without changing substantially one's position, since the programme customarily addresses the viewer who is situated at an ideal physical vantage point.

In the decorated cloister, this cannot be the case, since the viewer's physical relationship to specific images is in constant permutation. The elements of time and of vision shifting through space are the most important determinants in the apprehension of meaning in the decorated cloister, and this discouraged the creation of prescribed arrangements of imagery in cloister programmes. The viewer to whom the images were primarily addressed, the meditating monk, was by definition in active rather than passive involvement with the images. It seems a misunderstanding of cloister imagery, then, to expect that one will find there prescribed

where the images could hardly have played this role for the adult community, most of whom were drawn from the literate classes. The issue takes on a different cast, of course, in situations in which it can be shown that the lay public was being permitted into the cloister, and what segment or social stratum of the public was included. In the case of La Daurade, at least during the period when the cloister was constructed and decorated, we must imagine that the primary aim of its community was to purge itself of lay involvement and to submit to a strict reform. As noted in the next chapter, by the

end of the 12th cent. the situation may well have been different, since official ceremonies enacted by the count in the presence of the council-men and other nobles of Toulouse are recorded to have taken place in 1196 and 1205 within the cloister precinct.

[114] See Thomas Lyman, 'Portails, portiques, paradis', *Les Cahiers de Saint-Michel de Cuxa*, 7 (1976), *passim*. He stresses the similarities, rather than the differences, between decorated cloister galleries and portals.

'pathways' of meaning, along which the viewer is compelled from image to image, like stations of the cross or like maps of sacred geography, as has been suggested for some cloister programmes.[115] Such thinking places the monk in the passive role of spectator or witness to the sacred dramas, a respondent to be acted upon. This is the stance that Romanesque imagery may, indeed, have presumed for the lay worshipper, but the function of the cloister disallows that this was the intended role of imagery for the professed monk.

In its choice of the second workshop and in its creation of a fundamentally new kind of iconographic programme for the cloister, the monastic community at La Daurade showed an independence from the mother abbey of Moissac that it had not exhibited in 1100 when the cloister was begun. This may reflect its achievement of a certain autonomous position within the city of Toulouse. Though the apogee of Cluniac power over the larger monastic reform movement had been passed by 1100, the priory of La Daurade, for its part, seems only to have increased its position of visibility and prestige in twelfth-century Toulouse because of its association with the ruling family of the counts and the unusual power its temporal holdings gave it. These factors worked together to ensure a role of importance for La Daurade within the politics and religious life of the city in the second half of the century. The most visible testimony to this is the ambitious decorative programme of its chapter house, in which the political ties of Toulouse to the north of France in the later twelfth century are clearly revealed. This is the subject of the following chapters.

[115] See Wayne Dynes, 'The Medieval Cloister as Portico of Solomon', *Gesta*, 12 (1973), 61–9.

8

THE LATE ROMANESQUE IN TOULOUSE
THE CHAPTER HOUSE OF LA DAURADE

For two generations, from about 1075 to 1140, architectural and sculptural activity in Toulouse was at a creative high. The same motives that drove the process of reform and renewal within the Toulousan Church also inspired the principal religious communities of the city with a passion for building. The enormous collegiate church of Saint-Sernin with its expansive pilgrimage choir, the newly rebuilt cathedral of Saint-Étienne at the centre of its episcopal complex, the recently enlarged priory church of La Daurade with its large monastic enclosure and properties bordering the river, were visible testimony to the influence and resources of their respective religious communities during a sustained period of revitalization. As we concluded in Chapter 2, the new kinds of demands shaped by these revitalized religious communities effectively generated an art of monumental sculpture in Toulouse during the decades on either side of 1100.

With the greatest period of monastic foundation and expansion in the Toulousan region largely over by 1140, evidence for only modest sculptural activity can be found in Toulouse in the last half of the century. John Mundy's work on charitable giving, cited in Chapter 2, suggests reasons why the sponsoring of new monastic art should have declined in Toulouse after the middle of the century, as hospitals, leprosaries, and houses of charity became the new beneficiaries of lay donors seeking the insurance of spiritual salvation.

The outstanding exception to the general falling off of sculptural activity in Toulouse after 1140 is the portal programme of the chapter house of La Daurade. The scale and the iconography of the ensemble make it one of the most ambitious portal programmes ever undertaken in Toulouse. Important elements of the ensemble, particularly its use of large-scale figures in relief, standing or seated within niches, link it with the tradition of monumental figure sculpture that began in Toulouse with the marble sanctuary reliefs of Saint-Sernin and which was newly interpreted in the Apostles by Gilabertus and his workshop for Saint-Étienne.

Nevertheless, a full generation separates the chapter house of La Daurade from the last monumental ensembles of high Romanesque sculpture in Toulouse. Its programme of decoration was a hybrid fusion of imported ideas, distant from the Romanesque experience of Toulouse, and conservative elements that seem bound to the successes of an earlier era in the Toulousan artistic past. This and the following chapter will argue that the portal has been compared to the wrong group of monuments, because it has been dated too late in the twelfth century. Traditionally dated to about 1180–96, the political, historical, and iconographic evidence indicates that the portal was most likely mounted between about 1165 and 1175.

The chapter house was the culmination of a building programme that began at La Daurade, we believe, under Count William IV in the late eleventh century. The monastery of La Daurade continued to maintain a special relationship with the counts of Toulouse over the course of the twelfth century. It will be argued here that important elements of the chapter house programme, including its mixture of the new and the traditional, can be attributed to this historical relationship. The style of the sculpture, its heavy plasticity, and the references to antique Mediterranean ornament suggest the influence of Provençal Romanesque, from the eastern domains of the counts, in this late style at La Daurade. The iconography of the portal, on the other hand, and its expression in the column statue—the most striking element of proto-Gothic portal design—reveal the overall conception to be imported from the Île-de-France. Based on what we learned in Chapter 3, the newer, imported elements were accommodated within an architecture that was thoroughly familiar in the Romanesque chapter house design of southern France.

THE DESIGN OF THE CHAPTER HOUSE FAÇADE

The elements of the architecture for which there is reasonably clear evidence—thick-walled construction, heavy pilaster buttresses, and the probability of barrel vaulting—all denote conservative Romanesque building practice in the design of the chapter house at La Daurade. We concluded from the architect's report of 1760 that the chapter house communicated with the cloister by three spacious openings of approximately equal height and width. The lateral openings were partially screened by tympana, and these were undoubtedly supported on a pair of columns that divided each lateral opening into the twin arches described by the architect. The testimony of the surviving plans is ambiguous in regard to other elements of the façade

Fig. 11 design. Based on the latest of the plans, we concluded, nevertheless, that the two lateral openings had been walled up from the inner side by the early nineteenth century. This suggests to us that these openings were not screened by a parapet wall in the original design. The absence of a parapet wall would have created a spacious and open effect at La Daurade

Pl. 184 closer to regional examples at Beaulieu-sur-Dordogne, dating about 1140, or at Catus, also
Pl. 185 about 1140, than to other chapter house schemes at Marcilhac and Agen.[1] At Beaulieu and
Pls. 186 and Catus the paired columns that frame the openings and support the tympana have the
187 monumental scale of a full architectural order. This brings the architectural definition of the lateral openings into scale with the central portal. In contrast, at Agen, where the height of the lateral openings is broken by a parapet wall, the small scale of the paired colonnettes and the responds of the arch mouldings gives a miniature and subordinate appearance to these openings.

The façades of Beaulieu and Catus have no figural sculpture, and it is precisely this feature that so dramatically separates the chapter house of La Daurade from other extant twelfth-century examples in southern France. The existence of true column statues (figures addorsed to a column) among the pieces from La Daurade—six complete statues and the lower portion of a seventh survive[2]— must mean that the openings into the chapter house were defined in some

[1] On the chapter house of Beaulieu see Eugène Lefèvre-Pontalis, 'Beaulieu', *Congrès archéologique*, Limoges 84 (1921), 388. On Catus see above, Ch. 7 n. 97. The chapter house at Agen is discussed below. On Marcilhac see M. Deshoulières, 'Marcilhac', *Congrès archéologique*, Figeac, Cahors, and Rodez 100 (1937), 77–81; Marguerite Vidal *et al.*, *Quercy roman* (La Pierre-qui-vire, 1969), 187–8.
[2] Mesplé 71, 74, 77, 85, 88, 91, and 100. See the Inventory.

manner by recessed jambs. In such a system, openings are stepped back into the thickness of the wall by means of graduated archivolts which rest on recessed columns below. The wording of the architect's description of 1760 of the chapter house suggested that this was the case at La Daurade.[3]

The details of the portal design at La Daurade are a matter of conjecture. Nevertheless, it is clear that its combination of figured jambs and multiple arched orders recessed into the façade would have given it a visual complexity, richness, and plastic definition remarkably different from the sober designs that survive in the region. The examples at Marcilhac, Beaulieu, and Catus eschew the visual subtlety of the recessed jamb. In each case the three openings through the façade baldly expose the thickness of the walls. The flat embrasures of the central opening are completely unadorned, while paired columns, supporting unmoulded arches, are backed directly against the window embrasures. A single recessed order serves as a framing device for each arched opening.

Pls. 184–6

The façade of the late twelfth-century chapter house of Saint-Caprais at Agen has more than once been suggested as a much reduced and sculpturally poorer version of what the chapter house at La Daurade might have resembled. It has been dated to the second half of the twelfth century.[4] It is, in fact, the only twelfth-century chapter house surviving in the region that incorporates monumental figural sculpture into the design of its façade. Certainly its recessed entrance way, with its integration of pilaster and columnar support for the orders, may hint at some elements of the jamb solution at La Daurade. The two figured reliefs, a standing *Angel* and *Virgin of the Annunciation* framed within architectural niches and supporting heavy ornamental pilaster capitals above, strongly call to mind elements of the figured ensemble from La Daurade. Nevertheless, the solution at Agen lacks the most remarkable feature of the Daurade programme, the monumental column statues. It is the integration of these, in company with the relief slabs, into the sequence of three openings that poses the most difficulties at La Daurade and which would obviously have made the entire programme very different from Agen.

Pl. 187

Pl. 188

So many monastic complexes have been wiped out without physical trace that it is dangerous to draw conclusions about the sculptural embellishment of twelfth-century chapter houses on the basis of surviving examples. Figure-decorated portals that do not survive may have prepared the way for the richly sculptured façade of the Daurade chapter house. In Toulouse itself, reconstruction of the chapter house of Saint-Étienne has remained hotly controversial. With speculations still being proffered for and against a figured portal at Saint-Étienne, the possibility cannot be excluded that this earlier Romanesque programme in some manner provided a precedent for the later portal of La Daurade.

The sculptured *Apostles* originating from the cathedral of Saint-Étienne have stood since the

Of the column statues, M. 91 (the crowned male with ampula) and M. 85 (the nimbed figure) are carved against columns that come to an angle at the back (Pl. 202). The columns of the others are more nearly cylindrical, though some are only roughly worked on the back. The fragmentary statue (M. 100) (Pl. 205) allows a clear view of how wedge-shaped all these figures are in plan. That is, the figures are broad across the front face but are backed against a column of small diameter, appropriate to their positioning within a recessed jamb.

[3] '. . . the other [cracks] follow entirely, or in very large part, the circular contour of the mouldings of which the large arches

are composed . . .' (Toulouse, ADHG 102 H 3, 'Observations sur le Dome de La Daurade', fo. 3ᵛ).

[4] Linda Seidel, 'The Façade of the Chapter House at La Daurade in Toulouse', *Art Bulletin*, 55 (1973), 328–9; Richard Hamann, *Die Abteikirche von St. Gilles und ihre künstlerische Nachfolge* (Berlin, 1955) i. 267–70; Raymond Rey, *La Sculpture romane languedocienne* (Toulouse, 1936), 360–2; René Crozet, 'Saint-Caprais d'Agen', *Congrès archéologique*, Agenais 127 (1969), 93–7; Marcel Durliat, 'Le Portail de la salle capitulaire de la Daurade', *Bulletin monumental*, 132 (1974), 211.

nineteenth century as companions to the statues of La Daurade in the vast exhibition hall of the Musée des Augustins. Until new archaeological or documentary evidence is found, the character of this sculptural programme is entirely up in the air. When he installed them in the Musée de Toulouse in the 1830s, Alexandre Du Mège assembled the fragments from Saint-Étienne as a monumental recessed portal with the figures of the twelve Apostles forming the jambs. Du Mège defended this 'reconstruction' in his publications on the chapter house of 1835 and 1837.[5] Until recent times it went largely unquestioned in the literature and was the basis for the modern installation by Henri Rachou, retained by the museum until 1976.

Pls. 189 and 190

In 1968, through an examination of his writings and career, Linda Seidel exposed Du Mège's 'portal' as a fabrication of the Toulousan antiquarian.[6] She proposed, instead, a hypothetical reconstruction in which the Apostles were dispersed on the interior of the chapter house, incorporated into pilasters beneath barrel vaulting strengthened with transverse ribs. She based her reconstruction in part on a little-known early reference to the Apostles published by Du Mège in 1823 before his installation of the sculptures in the museum. She judged this early description to be more reliable than the lengthy later ones. In the account of 1823 Du Mège made no mention of a portal and described four of the Apostles as having been positioned in the corners of the chapter house of Saint-Étienne.[7]

Pl. 192

While Seidel's scepticism about Du Mège's archaeological writings is now shared by most students of Toulousan history, her rejection of a figured portal at the entrance to the chapter house of Saint-Étienne is not accepted by all scholars. Marcel Durliat remains a critic of her theories and continues to discuss the Apostles within the context of monumental portal sculpture in the Languedoc.[8] In 1982 I was inclined to agree with Seidel's removal of the Saint-Étienne sculptures from this context.[9] As she pointed out, the pieces fit together awkwardly in Du Mège's arrangement of them as a stepped portal. Their juxtaposition in a continuous jamb ignored the visual isolation of the discrete figures within architectural niches and created impossible incongruities in the conjunction of the friezes and the imposts above them. In Seidel's reconstruction, on the other hand, the dispersed arrangement of the figures, which function as discrete supports, does seem more appropriate to the formal self-sufficiency of each of the single figures and each pair. The division of the chapter house interior into three barrel-vaulted bays divided by transverse arches would precisely accommodate the number of existing pieces—four single figures inserted in the corners and four pairs of Apostles facing each other across the space of the chapter room.

Pls. 189 and 190

Nevertheless, the Apostle figures themselves do not seem as visually suitable for the function Seidel gives them as her drawing would suggest. They are decidedly small in scale (about half-life size). Even in their earlier installation as a portal arrangement, they have always seemed to

---

[5] Alexandre Du Mège, *Description du musée de Toulouse* (1835), 199–201; id., 'Mémoire sur le cloître de Saint-Étienne de Toulouse', *Histoire et mémoires de l'académie royale des sciences, inscriptions et belles-lettres de Toulouse*, 4 (1834–6), 250–76; repr. in *La Mosaïque du Midi*, 3 (1839), 279–84.

[6] Linda Seidel, 'A Romantic Forgery,' *Art Bulletin*, 50 (1968), 33–44.

[7] 'To decorate one of the chapels of the cloister of Saint-Étienne, Gilabertus grouped together, two by two, eight statues of Apostles. They supported capitals; in the corners of the chamber (*sacellum*) were placed four other statues' (Alexandre Du Mège, in Étienne-Léon de Lamothe-Langon *et al.*, *Biographie toulousaine*, i. (Paris, 1823), s.v. 'Gilabertus', 477.

[8] Marcel Durliat, *Haut-Languedoc roman* (La Pierre-qui-vire, 1978), 196–205. See also Paul Mesplé, 'Le Portail de la salle capitulaire de la cathédrale de Saint-Étienne, est-il un mythe'?, *L'Auta*, 370 (Apr. 1970), 74–87. Léon Pressouyre has agreed with Seidel that the Apostles of Saint-Étienne should be removed from consideration as jamb sculpture ('Les Apôtres de la salle capitulaire de Saint-Étienne de Toulouse', *Bulletin monumental*, 127 (1969), 241–2).

[9] See my remarks in 'The Passion Series from La Daurade', *Gesta*, 21 (1982), 32 and n. 10.

this viewer too small for the massive and ornate friezes above them. A function for them as interior pilaster supports would have exaggerated this effect, particularly beneath weighty barrel vaulting. One can more easily imagine two pairs of Apostles facing each other across the lateral openings of the façade, as the Virgin and Gabriel do across the entrance of the chapter house of Saint-Caprais. Here they would have supported only small arches or tympana, while the single Apostles on diagonally turned blocks might have stood at a slight remove from the pairs, recessed into the wall at either side of the window openings to receive a moulding, as the recessed columns do in the façade of the chapter house at Beaulieu. *Pl. 188*

Pl. 184

As a different alternative, the Apostles may have been incorporated in some manner into the cloister piers. There are both iconographic and formal equivalents in Romanesque cloister decoration for this kind of scheme. The single figures on corner blocks from Saint-Étienne could have been inserted into the angles of the corner piers, in the manner of figures in the cloister of Saint-Trophime at Arles, for example.[10] While a role for the Toulousan Apostles as pier decoration is an attractive hypothesis, it is one that presents difficulties, since, if we are to believe the early writers on the cloister of Saint-Étienne, two of the corner piers were occupied by figures of St Peter, St Saturninus, St Exupery, and a deacon. One writer also reported seated figures carrying sceptres on one of the central piers.[11] *Pl. 191*

The foregoing are only suggestions, advanced to emphasize the fact that there are many possible ways in which the existing sculptures from Saint-Étienne might have functioned in conjunction with architecture. An archaeological reconstruction is now very difficult to achieve, since important evidence for the way in which the large rectangular capitals and their imposts would have bonded into the masonry has, I believe, been obliterated. Most of the capitals appear to have been hacked off at the sides or otherwise mutilated, probably during Du Mège's installation of them, to permit the Apostles to be fitted more closely together. Mesplé 9 and 20, for example, may be two pieces of the same capital. M. 2 and 25, in contrast, retain vestiges of angles that may originally have been a feature of all the capitals, to bond them into the surrounding masonry.

Without documentary evidence, one reconstruction of the Saint-Étienne sculptures is as conjectural as another. My own review of the documents from the period following the Revolution prompted me to conclude in 1986 that Du Mège probably never saw the chapter house of Saint-Étienne intact.[12] It is therefore likely that his 1823 description of Apostle figures standing in the corners of the chapter house is as much a fabrication as his later claims that they formed a portal. Du Mège said that he visited the precinct in 1812. But by that date the chapter house had already been substantially altered on the interior, having been divided up by partition walls into irregularly sized rooms. By the beginning of April 1812 it no longer existed, and it may have been demolished in 1811.[13] Du Mège's statement in the *Biographie* *Fig. 18;* *cf. Fig. 2*

---

[10] The full apostolic college was represented on the piers at Moissac and in relief in the upper cloister of Saint-Guilhem-le-Désert. Numerous Romanesque cloisters included selected Apostles within larger programmes of decoration, for example at Châlons-sur-Marne, Saint-Donat-sur-l'Herbasse, and Saint-Bertrand-de-Comminges. In his revised study of the sculpture at Chartres, Whitney Stoddard suggested a possible place for the Saint-Étienne Apostles on the cloister piers of the cathedral and cited them as a possible precedent for the solution in the cloister at Arles (*Sculptors of the West Portals of Chartres Cathedral* (New York, 1987), 179–80). Recently Forsyth has also revived the question of a reconstruction for the Apostles of Saint-Étienne ('Monumental Arts of the Romanesque Period', as in the Introduction n. 12).

[11] For the early descriptions of the Saint-Étienne cloister, see above, Ch. 7.

[12] See Kathryn Horste, 'A New Plan of the Cloister and Rampart of Saint-Étienne', *Journal of the Society of Architectural Historians*, 45 (1986), 13–14 and n. 37.

[13] Fig. 18 reproduces a post-Revolutionary plan of the structures flanking the east walk of the cloister (Toulouse, AMT, 2 M 3). Comparison of the plan with that of Saget (Linda

toulousaine that figures of Apostles stood in the corners of the chapter house was probably a conjecture on his part, as he attempted to call up a feasible context for them before hitting upon his idea of installing them as a portal. The article in which this statement appears is concerned with the style and genius of the sculptor Gilabertus, who signed two of the apostles. It can hardly have escaped Du Mège's notice when he first saw the sculptures that the apostles to which Gilabertus had proudly put his name were not flat relief slabs but vertical blocks turned on the diagonal. He may have conjectured that all four single apostles stood in corners on the basis of the shape of their blocks. In his later portal installation, he placed these blocks within the angles of recessed jambs.

The questions that continue to surround the role of sculpture in the chapter house of Saint-Étienne add to the difficulties of reconstructing the later programme at La Daurade. Whether they functioned on the interior or the exterior of the chapter house, the reliefs from Saint-Étienne did influence some components of the later ensemble at La Daurade. This is evident in the figured relief slabs. There are five surviving slabs from La Daurade with standing figures (one female and four males), all framed within niches, and two slabs with seated figures representing, respectively, the *Virgin and Child* enthroned and *King David Tuning his Harp*.[14] All must have been topped originally by massive, block-like capitals in the form of heavily ornamented friezes, six of which survive. The relief slabs were elevated on moulded rectangular bases, of which two complete examples and half of a third have been preserved.

Pls. 193–7
Pls. 198–200

The formula of standing figure contained within a shallow rectangular slab and carrying a massive frieze above clearly finds its precedent in the earlier figured ensemble from Saint-Étienne, where standing Apostles, elevated on bases and almost top-heavy under ornamented friezes, are paired within rectangular slabs. The monumental Daurade figures are sober and immobile, however, compared to their earlier counterparts from Saint-Étienne. They are, moreover, very different in sculptural conception. With the exception of the crowned female (M. 66) and one crowned male (M. 68) the standing figures from La Daurade are starkly frontal, and there is no depth to the niches in which they stand. These are little more than ceremonial frames from which the figures project forward in shallow relief, rather than being enclosed spatially within them.

At Saint-Étienne, in contrast, there is a sense of spatial enclosure, because of the way the paired figures are positioned on the rectangular slab. Each slab contains a pair of niches or architectural canopies, separated by a pseudo-colonnette that recedes into the depth of the block. The axis of each standing Apostle corresponds to a corner of the rectangular block, not to its planar front face, as the axes do in the reliefs from La Daurade. The result of this diagonal placement is the creation of a powerful three-dimensionality in the Saint-Étienne *Apostles*. The corner placement takes full advantage of the depth of the block, and the high relief figure is surrounded by real space on three sides. In the standing single figures from Saint-

Pl. 161

Seidel, *Romanesque Sculpture from the Cathedral of Saint-Étienne* (New York and London, 1977), fig. 8 and our Fig. 2) shows that the interior partitioning of this block of structures into chapter house, adjacent chapel, and stairwell had been completely altered by the post-Revolutionary period. The post-Revolutionary plan was attached to a petition of Pierre Roumieu, 'Entrepreneur des Travaux Publics', to the mayor of Toulouse, which clearly speaks of the chapter house as no longer standing (Toulouse, AMT, 2 M 3, dossier for 1791–1834, Église St-Étienne and Chapelle Ste-Anne, doc. no. 16).

The petition must date prior to Apr. 1812, when it was granted by the mayor (ibid. 2 D 29, 'Arrète [sic] du Maire', 2 Apr. 1812). A petition of 20 Dec. 1811 of the fabric of the cathedral to the mayor is ambiguous as to whether anything was still standing on the site of the cloister, but the church of Saint-Jacques that flanked it on the south is described as demolished (ibid. 2 M 3, dossier 1791–1834, Église St-Étienne and Chapelle Ste-Anne, doc. no. 17, fo. 2ʳ).

[14] See the Inventory for the surviving sculptures and their dimensions.

Étienne the sculptor's corner attack of the block is fully realized, for here the entire block is turned diagonally, so that the corner projects foremost towards the viewer. Among the relief slabs from La Daurade, only the *Virgin and Child* are distinguished by their envelopment within a three-dimensional space. But here three-dimensionality is created by very different means from the corner placement of figures in the sculptures from Saint-Étienne. Spatial enclosure is achieved by recessing the Virgin and Child deeply within a rectangular block that is thicker than all the others.[15]

Pls. 199 and 200

The Romanesque mobility of the Saint-Étienne *Apostles* also distinguishes them from the standing figures from La Daurade. Most have crossed legs, giving their posture a dramatic instability as their upper bodies turn in opposition to their pivoting lower limbs. The swinging fans of drapery agitate the figures, so that they appear to move restlessly in space beneath the massive, block-like friezes that would have locked their fragile niches into the wall.

The figures from La Daurade lack totally this mobility. It has been traded for a sober frontality, and the standing figures, at least, seem more willingly submissive to their function as pilaster support than do their counterparts from Saint-Étienne. The calming of the figures at La Daurade does not mask the similarity of the conception, nevertheless. At both La Daurade and Saint-Étienne, the function of these shallow slabs as components of a system of architectural support is clear from the survival of the bases and the rectangular capitals, the other components of an architectural order. In other words, the slabs cannot have been applied simply to the surface of a wall, in the manner of the reliefs of St Peter and Jeremiah addorsed to either side of the portal of Moissac, or even of the Apostles on the façade of Saint-Gilles, who are displayed within a kind of fantasy architecture with which they are not functionally integrated.[16]

The relief slabs from Toulouse, both Saint-Étienne and La Daurade, are all pilasters, and as such they could have been integrated in a number of ways into a Romanesque structural system. Seidel has suggested one way the *Apostles* of Saint-Étienne could have been so integrated, as responds for the transverse ribs of barrel vaulting. But we have no real evidence for this. In the case of La Daurade, we know the pilasters functioned within the façade of the chapter house, since they cannot be separated iconographically from the column statues, which were seen on the façade in 1760. The surviving scheme of the chapter house at Agen shows that the pilasters of a portal embrasure could carry monumental figured reliefs in the late Romanesque practice of the region. Seven reliefs survive from La Daurade. The three openings would accommodate at most six of these, if they were positioned in the embrasures. The other figure must have been placed elsewhere. Seraphín Moralejo has recently proposed a reconstruction of the ensemble at La Daurade that places six relief slabs in the embrasures of the three openings and two additional ones projecting as shallow buttresses at either side of the central portal. We will discuss Moralejo's reconstruction as a whole a bit later in this chapter, since it depends heavily on his iconographic reading of the ensemble. It can be stated here, however, that his suggestion of salient buttresses dividing the façade is entirely in keeping with other features of the architecture we have discussed. If the chapter room was barrel vaulted, as

Fig. 19

---

[15] The block from which the Virgin and Child were carved is 24 cm. in depth at the top and bottom. This compares to 21 cm. (top) to 21.7 cm. (bottom) for the depth of the David relief. The other reliefs vary from 14.7 to 17 cm. in depth.

[16] Illustrated in Schapiro, 'Romanesque Sculpture of Moissac II', figs. 129 and 131; Whitney S. Stoddard, *The Façade of Saint-Gilles-du-Gard: Its Influence on French Sculpture* (Middletown, Conn., 1973).

we suggest, such buttresses can have been expected on the exterior and would have reflected a three-bay division on the inside.

In the context of the Toulousan sculptural tradition, the niche figures of La Daurade are the most conservative element of the façade design. Their inspiration must have come in some respect from the earlier use of figured pilasters at Saint-Étienne, but the exact nature of the debt is unclear because of our uncertainties regarding the earlier programme. Moreover, the late Romanesque chapter house of La Daurade is separated by a generation or more from that of Saint-Étienne. These were decades during which little in the way of monumental sculpture seems to have been produced in Toulouse. Hence the two programmes are not linked by a continuous tradition of sculptural work in stone. Rather, the elements we have described as conservative in the Daurade ensemble have the character of sculptural quotations, intended, undoubtedly, to associate this portal programme with the sculptural legacy of the earlier twelfth century in Toulouse. In the relief slabs this is expressed not only in the formula of niche figure topped by a frieze but in certain components of the style. The sculptor who carved the king holding an unfurled scroll (Mesplé 68), for example, has employed striking ornamental details that quote the earlier style of the second generation in Toulouse. The broad jewelled bands on cuffs and necklines, the shirred sleeves, and the row of knob-like curls at the end of the beard are signatures of the style of 1120–35 as represented by the Passion series from La Daurade and the *Apostles* by Gilabertus. Likewise, the crowned women with pointing gesture (Mesplé 66) follows a female type that may be described as distinctively Toulousan, with its pronouncedly long-waisted figure, nipped in at the middle, broad shoulders, and long, braided hair. The models for her physical type can be seen in the representations of Salome and the Wise Virgins, in capitals from Saint-Étienne. Thus while there is no organic sculptural development connecting the sober and weighty forms of the Daurade chapter house to the style of the high Romanesque in Toulouse, the desire for a linkage is visible in the affectation of familiar motifs that would have been meaningful to contemporary viewers.

The type of ornament decorating the heavy friezes above the niche figures is another conservative feature. In fact, two distinctly different styles of foliate ornament appear in the portal ensemble and the two styles are given distinctly different functions. No attempt is made to harmonize them. The capitals that crown the cylindrical column statues are based on modified Corinthian forms. In keeping with this capital type, their foliage is a lush and organic acanthus growth. The ornament on the pilaster friezes, in contrast, employs the foliage repertory of the second generation of Toulousan sculpture, as we saw it in the cloister capitals of La Daurade and Saint-Étienne (compare, for example, Pls. 136 and 138 to Pl. 204). The basis of this ornament is a fibrous vine rinceau, whose stems break into varied obtrusions of curling leaves, berries, and cones. The type of relief itself links this ornament to the indigenous Toulousan tradition, for it employs the crisp *taille de réserve* so skilfully developed into a signature style by the closely allied workshops of La Daurade and Saint-Étienne in the 1120s and 1130s. The ornament is built up of repetitive motifs of interlocked 'medallions', as it was on the imposts of the second Daurade series, in sharp contrast to the unfettered growth of acanthus on the cylindrical column capitals. The human and animal combats that inhabit some of the pilaster friezes also have their origin in earlier Toulousan ornament, for example in the twin capitals with false imposts that can be attributed to La Daurade (M. 172 and M. 174). No specific location within the cloister or attendant chapels can be determined for these two

Pl. 194

Pls. 85, 91, and 122
Pl. 158
Pl. 193

Pls. 168 and 172

Pls. 201 and 203
Pls. 136 and 138 to Pl. 204

Pls. 136–9 and 189–90

Pl. 206 and 207

capitals, though the liking for cone and berry forms and the deep undercutting of the patterns links them to the earlier workshop practices of the second Daurade style. The qualities of miniaturization in M. 172 and 174 show the tendency towards preciousness in later Toulousan ornament, and they probably date from the middle of the century. Capitals like the *Hunt of the Siren and Centaur* (M. 178) and the *Story of Job* (M. 180) are even closer to the delicate relief on some of the pilaster friezes (cf. M. 69, 81, or 84).

Pl. 208
Pl. 209
Pls. 194 and 198

Against this background of conservative features—the traditional Romanesque chapter house design, the use of bas-relief elements, the indigenous ornamental repertory—the portal of La Daurade was given what must have been a more modern look by the introduction of the true column statue into the scheme, a form of jamb decoration that does not appear in the Midi prior to this chapter house façade. The imported character of this feature is underlined by the acanthus capitals of Corinthian-inspired type that top the column statues. This combination of elements follows proto-Gothic portal designs of the Île-de-France, the Loire, and Champagne. The liking for a natural vegetal growth of plastically defined, richly undercut leaves in these late-style capitals of La Daurade compares, for example, to the style of capitals from the late 1150s crowning the column statues of the south portal of the cathedral of Le Mans.[17] The introduction of figured motifs on some of the capitals of La Daurade, such as the animal musicians, the combats, or the addorsed griffins, recalls certain types of capitals on the west portal of Saint-Loup-de-Naud, or the south portal of Bourges cathedral, both from about 1160.[18]

Pl. 216

The contrast between the lush, antique-inspired foliage topping the column statues and the ornamentally repetitive vine patterns above the relief slabs is visually jarring. In a similar fashion, the abrupt juxtaposing of two different types of figured support within the design must have appeared uncomfortable at best, though the precise way in which the columnar and relief elements were incorporated into the design is a matter of conjecture. Moralejo, echoing similar observations by Durliat, has argued that, within the realm of southern Romanesque portal design, the integration of figured reliefs with column statues did not, in fact, produce difficulties for the Romanesque carver, because southern carvers tended to view these figured elements as 'interchangeable or even undifferentiated formats'.[19] As evidence of the latter way of thinking, Moralejo and Durliat cite the fragmentary *Annunciation* formerly in the church of the Cordeliers at Toulouse and the Spanish portals of San Vicente at Avila (west and south portals), San Pedro de la Guardia, and the Portico de la Gloria at Santiago.[20]

Unfortunately, the examples put forth by Durliat and Moralejo do not help us to understand the nature of the impact of northern Early Gothic forms on the sculpture of La Daurade. The portals of Avila, San Pedro de la Guardia, and Santiago date to the last quarter of the twelfth century, considerably later than the date of about 1165–75 that I propose below for the

[17] Willibald Sauerländer, *Gothic Sculpture in France, 1140–1270* (New York, 1972), pl. 17.
[18] For illustrations and bibliography see ibid., pls. 25 and 36 and pp. 393–4 and 399–400.
[19] Serafín Moralejo, 'La Fachada de la sala capitular de la Daurade de Tolouse: datos iconograficos para su reconstruccion', *Anuario de estudios medievales*, 13 (1983), 188; Marcel Durliat, 'L'Annonciation des Cordeliers au musée des Augustins', *Études de civilisation médiévale (IX–XIIe siècles): mélanges offerts à Edmond-René Labande* (Poitiers, 1974), 268–9; id.,

'La Dernière Sculpture romane méridionale: une mutation avortée', *La France de Philippe Auguste: le temps des mutations. Actes du Colloque international organisé par le centre national de la recherche scientifique, 29 Sept.–4 Oct. 1980* (Paris, 1982), 947–8.
[20] For the *Annunciation* of the Cordeliers, see Toulouse, Musée des Augustins, *Grandes Étapes*, fig. 48. For the Spanish portals see Pedro de Palol and Max Hirmer, *L'Art en Espagne du royaume wisigoth à la fin de l'époque romane* (Paris, 1967), pls. 204–9 (Avila) and pls. 212–17 (Santiago).

chapter house of La Daurade.[21] These Spanish examples show the impact of northern experiments with the column statue that were to lead ultimately to the strongly interactive figures on the north transept portals of Chartres cathedral around 1205–10. These experiments went on throughout the 1160s, 1170s, and 1180s in the workshops of northern France at Saint-Denis (Porte des Valois), Senlis, Mantes, Noyon, and Châlons-sur-Marne. The figures produced in these workshops are characterized by a restless mobility and torsion that many scholars trace to the legacy of the earliest column statues of Saint-Denis, on the west façade.[22] They represent a rejection of the taut and vertically elastic conception of the figure introduced by the Headmaster of the west portals at Chartres, a conception embraced in a whole series of portals that followed the Chartrain lead.

The line of northern Gothic jamb sculpture that would lead to the Chartres transept portals was aimed at exerting the independence of the figure as statuary from its column backing. It was these experiments with the moving figure that had such a strong impact on Spanish sculptors, appealing, as Moralejo puts it, to their preference for scenic interactions between and among figures. Statues on the flat inner jambs and on the columns in a portal like that of the Portico de la Gloria at Santiago do appear to be interchangeable or equivalent elements, precisely because those figures attached to the columns are not columnar, and they aggressively exert their freedom from this role by assuming the character of free-standing statuary.

The column statues of La Daurade, in contrast, conform to the role defined for the jamb figure on the Royal Portal of Chartres. This conception was adopted in a series of portals strongly influenced by the Chartrain type, at Le Mans, Ivry-la-Bataille, Paris (St Anne Portal), Provins, Saint-Loup-de-Naud, Bourges, and elsewhere. The kinship of La Daurade to this series may seem remote, because the Toulousan column statues have not much in common stylistically with those at Chartres, and only Mesplé 88, one of the crowned figures, exhibits the truly columnar fall of drapery that characterizes the Chartrain series. In fact, among surviving northern sculpture of the twelfth century, the figures from La Daurade probably have most in common stylistically with the monumental statues previously mounted in the apse and choir of the collegiate church of Saint-Martin at Angers. Comprising a Virgin, Apostles, and clerics, five of the original six figures are now in the Yale University Art Gallery at New Haven.[23] One suspects, nevertheless, that the features they hold in common with the Toulousan sculptures—the thick, broad forms swelling slightly at the hips, the low centre of gravity falling below the midpoint of the figure—stem from a common dialogue that both ensembles have with the late Antique. In the case of La Daurade this is more likely to have been garnered from Provençal Romanesque sculpture than from northern France.

Despite the stylistic disparities, those elements that connect the sculptures of La Daurade with the portals of the Chartrain series are the sobriety and frontality of the figures, the relatively narrow range of hand gestures, betraying an effort to keep the hands close to the

[21] On the dating of the Spanish portals see Georges Gaillard, 'Sculptures espagnoles de la seconde moitié du douzième siécle', *Studies in Western Art* (Acts of the Twentieth International Congress on the History of Art), i. *Romanesque and Gothic Art* (Princeton, NJ, 1963), 142–9; José Manuel Pita Andrade, *Escultura romanica en Castilla: los maestros de Oviedo y Avila* (Madrid, 1955), 16–20 and pls. 16–23.

[22] See Brouillette in Françoise Amanieux, Diane Brouillette and Alain Erlande-Brandenburg, 'Senlis: un moment de la sculpture gothique', *La Sauvegarde de Senlis*, 45–6 (1977), 4.

[23] Pamela Z. Blum, 'A Madonna and Four Saints from Angers: An Archaeological Approach to an Iconographical Problem', *Yale University Art Gallery Bulletin*, 24 (1974), 30–57; Konrad Hoffmann, *The Year 1200: A Centennial Exhibition at the Metropolitan Museum of Art* (New York, 1970), no. 8, 6–7. Blum has placed the Saint-Martin figures 'within the corpus of northern French sculpture of about 1170–1200'.

vertical axis of the figure, and, above all, the absence of torsion. The latter element most tends to disengage figures like those of Senlis or the transept portals of Chartres from their columnar backing. In the figures from La Daurade, an illusion of torsion is created by the pulling and tucking of the drapery diagonally around portions of the body, but the figures themselves remain static and their outer contours reveal the effort to restrict their forms to the constraints of a functioning column.

The slight disruption of the columnar pose that the Toulousan Romanesque sculptor introduced into the legs of two of the figures (Mesplé 71 and 91) is awkwardly achieved, *Pl. 201* indicating that this sculptor was not entirely comfortable within the new idiom of the northern column statue. It is the sense of conflicting forms inharmoniously brought together that separates the Daurade portal ensemble from the Spanish examples cited by Durliat and Moralejo. The Spanish group is characterized by a more aggressive shaping and manipulating of northern Gothic ideas into something expressive of southern Romanesque tastes and preferences.

In the ensemble from La Daurade, even if it is not wholly clear how the individual elements were assembled within the façade, the presence of conflicting formal impulses is unmistakable. The incongruities of the ensemble show in the determination to accommodate Early Gothic forms, conceived for a very different context, to the requirements of monastic chapter house design. In their earliest appearance in Abbot Suger's new west façade for the abbey church of Saint-Denis, the column statues took their place within a monumental scheme that spread across the width of the façade and united all three portals. The chapter house portal, in contrast to such a public façade, must have opened into a narrow space, the cloister walk, which is itself covered by a low wooden roof or a vault. What is more, the chapter house *Pl. 211* façade, in its much smaller scale, lacks the focal elements of church portal design, whether Romanesque or Gothic, namely, the sculpted tympanum and trumeau. At La Daurade, this meant that the focal thematic grouping, the enthroned *Virgin and Child*, had of necessity to be placed on the portal embrasure—undoubtedly the jamb of the central opening. The resulting ensemble would have mixed standing and seated figures, in relief and in the round, and at different scales.

THE ICONOGRAPHY OF THE PORTAL AND ITS NORTHERN GOTHIC GENEALOGY

If the incorporation of proto-Gothic forms at La Daurade is somewhat tentative in the overall design of the façade, this is not true of the iconography. Both in its larger meaning and in specific details of the imagery, the iconographic programme is a wholesale appropriation of an Early Gothic portal type centred on the Virgin that was made famous in twelfth-century portals at Chartres and Paris. It is the programmatic interpenetration of three powerful themes that reveals the direct links of La Daurade to these northern Virgin portals: the Incarnation of Christ as the fulfilment of Old Testament prophecy; Christ's royal ancestry through his descent from the House of David; and special veneration for the Virgin in her identity as the Throne of Wisdom.

The remarkable growth in the cult of the Virgin during the twelfth century found monumental expression in the proliferation of sculptured portals devoted to her. All schools of later twelfth-century sculpture exhibit this literal elevation of the Virgin in portal iconography, in the late Romanesque of France, Spain, and Italy. Previous discussions of the monumental *Virgin and Child* at La Daurade have linked the iconography of this image to southern Romanesque examples from Saint-Gilles-du-Gard, Fontfroide, Beaucaire, and Solsona.[24] Nevertheless, to include the Toulousan chapter house within that southern constellation of examples does little to illuminate its iconography. What distinguishes the northern Virgin portals at Chartres and Paris and their close relatives from the southern examples is the elaboration, through the jamb cycle, of Christ's royal genealogy and of his birth as the fulfilment of the Old Testament. It is to this distinctive progeny that the portal of La Daurade belongs. This iconographic association with the first generation of Virgin portals in the north contradicts the late date, between 1180 and 1196, that has traditionally been attached to the chapter house of La Daurade.

Pl. 199

Pl. 212

Among the features that reveal the models for the portal programme at La Daurade is the specific iconography of the *Virgin and Child* relief. Resemblances between the Virgin of La Daurade and the images of the enthroned *Virgin and Child* at Chartres and in the Portail Ste-Anne of Notre-Dame, Paris, have been noted in numerous references to the Daurade chapter house.[25] The significance of the relationship has gone undefined, none the less, because the role of these three important sculptural programmes within the twelfth-century elaboration of the Virgin portal has not been articulated.

At La Daurade, Virgin and Child are enthroned beneath an elaborate architectural canopy with pedimented gable, crenellations, and corner towers, the whole supported on columns that frame the mother and child. The two columns are not a pair: the one at the left is cylindrical, while its mate at the right is octagonal. The Virgin is veiled and crowned, and she turns her head and body slightly towards her left. The Christ Child sits diagonally on her lap, resting on the Virgin's right knee, while she steadies him gently with her right hand on his back.

Pl. 200

Photographs of the relief prior to 1976 show a pudgy-faced Christ Child who grasped the edge of the Virgin's veil with his right hand. They also show an apple fixed awkwardly to the front of the Virgin's mantle and seemingly held neither by her nor the Child (see the pre-restoration photograph in the Mesplé catalogue, no. 83). In 1935 Raymond Rey pointed to the head and right hand of the Christ Child as modern reconstructions.[26] The incongruous character of the apple, however, failed to draw his attention. He described the Christ Child as playing with the apple, as though it were a toy. During the examination and reinstallation of the sculpture collections of the Musée des Augustins between 1976 and 1981 it was revealed that the apple was not an original element of the iconography, as its inappropriateness had suggested. It was removed, along with the other plaster reconstructions, and the Virgin's left hand is now without an attribute.[27] What remains of the twelfth-century head of the Christ Child suggests that he, too, may have been crowned.

[24] See, e.g., Arthur Kingsley Porter, *Romanesque Sculpture of the Pilgrimage Roads* (Boston, 1923), i. 245–7; Hamann, *St. Gilles* (as in n. 4 above), 263; Moralejo, 'Sala capitular de la Daurade', 3 and n. 8; id., 'De Sant Esteve de Tolosa a la Daurade', *Quaderns d'estudis medievals*, 23–4 (1988), 106.

[25] Raymond Rey, 'Essai d'explication iconographique de l'ancienne porte capitulaire de la Daurade', *Bulletin de la société archéologique du Midi de la France*, 3rd ser. (1934–7), meeting of 19 Feb. 1935, 34–40; Hamann, *St. Gilles*, 263; Toulouse, Musée des Augustins, *Grandes Étapes*, 22; Durliat,

Haut-Languedoc roman, 184. For an illustration of the Incarnation portal at Chartres, see Sauerländer, *Gothic Sculpture*, pl. 6.

[26] Rey, 'Porte capitulaire de la Daurade', 36.

[27] The plaster additions to the *Virgin and Child* relief could have been made any time before the 19th cent. or even after the sculptures entered the museum. A drawing of the relief published in 1841 shows it with the plaster additions (Marquis de Castellane, 'Supplément aux inscriptions du vᵉ au xvIᵉ siècle', *Mémoires de la société archéologique du Midi de la*

Several authors have pointed to the similarities between the architecturally elaborate ciborium enframing the *Virgin and Child* at La Daurade and the corresponding structure beneath which they sit in the monumental tympanum of the St Anne Portal at Notre-Dame, Paris.[28] Clearly the Virgin and Child at Chartres also originally sat beneath a similar structure, vestiges of which are visible in the column base to the left of the Virgin's throne and in the shadow of a baldachin defining the upper zone of the central slab. There are other iconographic links between the Toulousan image and these two famous Gothic portals, however. In all three images the Virgin is crowned. Moreover, the position of the Virgin's left hand at La Daurade, with fingers bunched and pointing upward, is identical to that of the Virgin at Notre-Dame, Paris. Like her Toulousan counterpart, the Virgin of the Portail Ste-Anne has lost her attribute. The budding sceptre she now holds aloft is an addition by Viollet-le-Duc and his restorers.[29] As such, it is an iconographically acceptable completion of the image. In twelfth-century iconography the sceptre was the symbol of Christ's kingship and of his royal descent from the house of David, as prophesied by the Angel Gabriel in his annunciation to Mary: '. . . and the Lord God shall give unto him the throne of David his father; and he shall reign in the house of Jacob for ever; and of his kingdom there shall be no end' (Luke 1: 32–3). In a twelfth-century leaf from the *Speculum virginum* in Bonn, the Virgin holds such a sceptre as she sits enthroned in the Tree of Jesse.[30]

More commonly in twelfth-century iconography, however, the Virgin holds upright a flower or bud, the *flos* (referring to Christ) for which the Virgin is the shoot (*virga*), and both of which spring from the stem (*radix*) of Jesse, father of David, according to the well-known commentaries of Tertullian and St Jerome on the prophecy of Isaiah, 'And there shall come forth a rod out of the root of Jesse, and a flower shall rise up out of his root. And the spirit of the Lord shall rest upon him' (Isaiah 11: 1). Twelfth-century images of the Tree of Jesse frequently show the Virgin seated in the tree and holding aloft such a flower or bud, as in an illuminated manuscript of Jerome's commentary on the book of Isaiah, now at Dijon.[31] King David may be shown directly beneath her, to emphasize Christ's direct genealogical descent from the Old Testament ruler.

Pl. 213

The image at Chartres is damaged, but it can be seen that the arms and hands of the Virgin and Child were held in nearly identical poses to those of the Paris image. In an article of 1987 on the St Anne Portal, I concluded that the Paris tympanum was modelled directly on the slightly earlier image at Chartres, and that the Virgin there also held upright either a sceptre or flower like the Paris example.[32]

France, 4 (1840–1), pl. IV, no. 2. The style of the child's head suggests that the reconstructions might have dated from the 16th cent. (see the photo by James Austin in Toulouse, Musée des Augustins, *Grandes étapes*, fig. 43). The *Virgin and Child* relief is the only one from the chapter house to retain substantial polychromy on its surface. Considerable red paint remains over the entire surface of the Virgin and her niche and dark green is visible inside her right sleeve. On the back wall of the niche, to either side of the Virgin's head and next to the throne on either side, a delicate pattern of foliate branches, originally white or pink, is visible against a dark ground. Among the other figures only M. 85 (the nimbed column statue) retains faint traces of red clinging to the incisions of his hair and beard and black on the face, neck, and nimbus.

[28] See the bibliography in n. 25 above.
[29] See the lithograph of the Paris tympanum before restoration, published by Alexandre Lenoir, *Statistique monumentale de Paris* (reproduced in Paul Vitry, 'Nouvelles observations sur le portail Sainte-Anne de Notre-Dame de Paris', *Revue de l'art chrétien*, 60 (1910), 74).
[30] Bonn, Provincial Museum, no. 15326. Illustrated in Arthur Watson, *The Early Iconography of the Tree of Jesse* (London, 1934), pl. XXX.
[31] Dijon, Bibliothèque, MS 129, St Jerome, *Explanatio in Isaiam*, fo. 4ᵛ (ill. in Watson, *Early Iconography*, pl. v). See also an antiphonary in St Peter's abbey, Salzburg, MS a.XII.7, 383 (Watson, *Early Iconography*, pl. VIII). Among other 12th-cent. examples of the enthroned Virgin holding aloft a bud or flower see the Shaftesbury Psalter (London, British Libary, Lansdowne 383, fo. 165ᵛ) or the *Adoration of the Magi* in whalebone in the Victoria and Albert Museum.
[32] Kathryn Horste, '"A Child is Born": The Iconography of the Portail Ste-Anne at Paris', *Art Bulletin*, 69 (1987), 194–8.

The Virgin of La Daurade follows closely this same iconography. At the same time, the diagonal placement of the Christ Child and the graceful turning of his mother towards her left is a distinct departure from the strict frontality of the Paris and Chartres examples. This more informal posing of the Virgin and Child at La Daurade may be compared to another Early Gothic grouping, a *Virgin and Child* of about 1180 from the cathedral of Noyon, now in the *dépôt lapidaire*. Similar explanations have been given for the turning movement of both Virgins, namely that they were directing their attention to figures adjacent to themselves on a portal jamb, though, in fact, the original context of the Noyon *Virgin and Child* is still not known.[33]

The deviation from strict frontality in the Daurade *Virgin and Child* indicates an adjustment in formal aspects of the image relative to Chartres and Paris but does not necessarily reflect derivation from a different iconographic source. The Toulousan Virgin, after all, was not a central image that confronted the viewer on a tympanum. Placed, as it must have been, on the right embrasure of the entrance opening, the image would have lost much of its power had the Virgin and Child been facing strictly forward towards the empty space of the passage. Instead, the slight turning to the left of the Virgin's gaze towards the cloister walk would have drawn the viewer in the direction of the portal entrance. The seeming asymmetry of the Virgin relief would have been complemented by the relief of *King David*, which must have been the pendant image on the opposite embrasure. Positioned on the left jamb, his gaze would likewise have been turned towards the cloister walk. The two images would have embraced the monks as they passed into the chapter house.

It is Du Mège who tells us that the relief of *King David* was placed opposite to that of the Virgin on the portal of La Daurade. In Chapter 3 I expressed my scepticism that Du Mège had ever seen the portal of La Daurade intact, and I am not reassured by his claim that the Virgin was seen on the left jamb, a position that accords not at all with her pose.[34] Nevertheless, there is little reason to doubt that she and King David framed the entrance. As the only other seated figure within the Daurade ensemble, David is the logical pendant to the Virgin. Furthermore, his leading role in the Old Testament genealogy of Christ makes him the most appropriate choice for the place of honour opposite the *Virgin and Child*. Among the jamb statues on Early Gothic portals, King David is one of the few Old Testament personages who can often be identified with certainty, because he usually carries a musical instrument as an identifying attribute. He appeared within the cycle of eight jamb statues that still framed the St Anne Portal in the eighteenth century. The statues were removed in 1793 and replaced by copies in the nineteenth century, but the iconography and poses of the originals were preserved in an engraving published in 1729 by Bernard de Montfaucon.[35] Here King David can be identified by his crown and the viol that he holds against his chest. As both prophet of the Messiah and as royal ancestor of Christ, David would have taken his appropriate place within the portal scheme of Notre-Dame at Paris, where the primary meaning refers to the incarnation and Epiphany as the fulfilment of prophecy.[36]

[33] See Brouillette, 'Senlis: un moment de la sculpture gothique', 43.

[34] Alexandre Du Mège, 'Le Cloître de la Daurade', *Mémoires de la société archéologique du Midi de la France*, 2 (1834–5), 246.

[35] Bernard de Montfaucon, *Les Monumens de la monarchie françoise* (Paris, 1729), i, pl. 8. The accuracy of Montfaucon's engraving is revealed in the surviving fragments, most of which were only recently recovered in 1977–8 in the courtyard of the Hôtel Moreau (see Alain Erlande-Brandenburg, *Les Sculptures de Notre-Dame de Paris au musée de Cluny* (Paris, 1982), nos. 1–30 with bibl. on the pieces known before 1977).

[36] I have proposed this as the primary theological message of the Paris portal (Horste, 'Portail Ste-Anne', 187–210).

At La Daurade King David, by virtue of the physical location and iconography of his image, would have lent a special meaning to the portal as a whole. Placed opposite the Virgin, King David was shown not as a standing figure among other Old Testament royalty, as he appears on many Early Gothic portal jambs. Instead he is seated, cross-legged and tuning his harp, a guise that associates his image specifically with the twelfth-century iconography of the Tree of Jesse, as the Tree was depicted both in pictorial form and in the sculptured archivolts of Early Gothic portals. Closest to the depiction of David at La Daurade is his image within the Tree of Jesse in the archivolts of the centre doorway (west façade) of the collegiate church of Notre-Dame at Mantes. There he is seated in semi-profile, as at La Daurade, with his harp *Pl. 214* prominently displayed and with one leg crossed over in the dynamic pose that is a convention of the harping David in twelfth-century pictorial representations.[37]

The west portal at Mantes has customarily been dated to about 1180, although re-evaluations of related sculpture at Senlis and Saint-Denis (Porte des Valois) in the recent literature have given some reason for believing that the dynamic stylistic trend to which all these monuments belong may need to be dated earlier in the twelfth century.[38] The harping David also appears seated in the Tree in the archivolts at Senlis (*c.*1170) and directly above the seated Jesse in the archivolts of the centre doorway at Laon (*c.*1195–1205).[39] In all three portals, the Tree of Jesse theme frames a central image of the Coronation of the Virgin.

All of these archivolt treatments probably take their cue from the pictorial arts of manuscript illumination and stained glass, however, where the iconography of the Tree of Jesse was elaborated much earlier in the twelfth century. The theme in its fully elaborated form was chosen by Abbot Suger for the axial chapel (chapel of the Virgin) of his new choir at Saint-Denis, completed in 1144. Shortly afterward (*c.*1150) a closely similar image was installed as one of the three lancet windows of the west façade of Chartres cathedral. As Louis Grodecki has pointed out, it was Suger's formulation of the theme that gave new prominence to Christ's royal ancestry within the Tree, an iconography that may reflect Suger's preoccupation with the royal status of his abbey church that invests so many aspects of his writings and his art programme at Saint-Denis.[40] Suger's window and the lancet at Chartres, while differing in some details, were closely similar in their iconography of the Tree.[41] In both images the stem of the Tree rose vertically from the side of the recumbent Jesse. Kings were seated one above the next within its branches. Flanking them in the side panels were Prophets. The series of royal

---

[37] See the Romanesque example in the crypt of Saint-Nicolas at Tavant (P. H. Michel, *Romanesque Painting: The Frescoes of Tavant* (New York, 1944), pl. IV).

[38] Sauerländer challenged the late 12th-cent. date for Senlis (*c.*1185–90) in the older scholarship and argued instead for a date about 1170 (Willibald Sauerländer, 'Die Marienkrönungsportale von Senlis und Mantes', *Wallraf-Richartz Jahrbuch*, 20 (1958), 115–62). Diane Brouillette has also argued persuasively for the 1170 date ('Senlis: un moment de la sculpture gothique', 4); ead., 'The Early Gothic Sculpture of Senlis Cathedral', Ph.D. thesis, University of California at Berkeley (1981), i. 74–90, and 106–11. In a panel on the Porte des Valois of Saint-Denis, held at the International Congress on Medieval Studies at Western Michigan University in 1983, William Clark and Elizabeth A. R. Brown spoke in favour of an earlier dating of that portal to the 1160s.

[39] For illustrations, see Sauerländer, *Gothic Sculpture*, pl. 44 and ill. 48.

[40] Louis Grodecki with Catherine Brisac and Claudine Lautier, *Le Vitrail roman* (2nd edn., Fribourg, 1983), 95.

[41] Substantial portions of the Saint-Denis window, notably the 2 bottom-most panels with the figure of Jesse and the seated king above him, are modern, having been restored by Gérent and Viollet-le-Duc in 1848. Grodecki and others have concluded that, in these restorations, Viollet-le-Duc followed the 12th-cent. window at Chartres. A drawing of 1794–5 by Charles Percier, however, records the iconography of the lower portion of Suger's window with the recumbent Jesse and the stalk of the tree rising from his back. On the Percier drawing and the reconstruction of Suger's window see Louis Grodecki, *Les Vitraux de Saint-Denis*, i. *Histoire et restitution*, Corpus Vitrearum Medii Aevi, France, 'Études' 1 (Paris, 1976), 71–9; Jane Hayward in *The Royal Abbey of Saint-Denis in the Time of Abbot Suger (1122–1151)*, exh. cat. (New York, 1981), 72–3.

ancestors culminated in the seated Virgin and, above her at the top of the Tree, the enthroned Christ, her son.

King David's place in images that follow this vertically ascending formula is at the base of the Tree as the first king directly above Jesse. In abbreviated versions of the Tree David alone represents Christ's royal ancestry and is seated immediately between Jesse and the Virgin. These images express in the most direct terms Christ's descent from the house of David and his ascendance to the throne of David, as promised by Isaiah 9: 7 and by the Angel Gabriel in his annunciation to Mary. In the Shaftesbury Psalter of the mid-twelfth century, David alone *Pl. 213* appears below the Virgin, as he does in a late twelfth-century *Speculum virginum* in the British Museum.[42] In the more elaborate image of the Ingeborg Psalter (*c.*1210) David is shown at the base of the tree of ancestors, in the seated posture with his harp.[43]

The honoured position on the embrasure given to King David at La Daurade, and the iconographic context out of which his image emerges, give an unmistakable emphasis to Christ's royal genealogy in this ensemble, and to the Christ Child as the Messiah who ascends the throne of David. The throne itself is prominent in the David relief, its chiastic form paralleled by the crossed legs of the monarch. David and his seat together crush beneath them a bestial symbol of the enemies of the Messiah.

It has long been suggested that the kings, queens, patriarchs, and prophets on the jambs of the Early Gothic 'royal portals' refer to the Old Testament forebears of Christ. Wilhelm Vöge had tried to associate these figures literally with the genealogy of Christ as recited in the Gospel of Matthew 1: 1–17.[44] The now classic study of the early programmes at Saint-Denis and Chartres by Adolf Katzenellenbogen has tended to move away from such literal identification of individual statues. He has seen it as more valid to interpret the statues in generic terms, as Old Testament representatives of *regnum* and *sacerdotium*, the qualities of kingship and priesthood united in Christ.[45]

This is a more abstract and, in some ways, more elusive concept than the demonstration of Christ's literal human descent from the generations of the house of David as manifest in the image of the Tree of Jesse. The two themes of Christ's Old Testament genealogy and of his assumption of the mantles of *regnum* and *sacerdotium* are not the same. Nevertheless, the formulation of their imagery occurred simultaneously in Early Gothic iconography and in many of the same monuments.[46] It is surely significant that it is within the most elaborated versions of the Tree of Jesse, as this theme appeared in the 1140s in windows at Saint-Denis

[42] Shaftesbury Psalter, London, British Library, Lansdowne 383, fo. 15ʳ; *Speculum virginum*, London, British Library, MS Arundel 44, fo. 2ᵛ (Watson, *Tree of Jesse*, pl. xxix).

[43] On the Ingeborg Psalter see Florens Deuchler, *Der Ingeborg Psalter* (Berlin, 1967) and the review by Reiner Haussherr, *Zeitschrift für Kunstgeschichte*, 32 (1969), 51–68; Louis Grodecki, 'Le Psautier de la reine Ingeburge et ses problèmes', *Revue de l'art*, 5 (1969), 73–8. See also the sculptured *Tree of Jesse* on the trumeau of the Portico de la Gloria of the cathedral of Santiago de Compostela. There a harping David is seated immediately above the recumbent Jesse. Above David is Solomon with a sceptre (Watson, *Tree of Jesse*, pl. xxi).

[44] Wilhelm Vöge, *Die Anfänge des monumentalen Stiles im Mittelalter* (Strasburg, 1894), 173–5. For a recent revival of this theory see Marie-Louise Thérel, 'Comment la patrologie peut éclairer l'archéologie: à propos de l'arbre de Jessé et des statues-colonnes de Saint-Denis', *Cahiers de civilisation médiévale*, 6 (1963), 145–58.

[45] Adolf Katzenellenbogen, *The Sculptural Programs of Chartres Cathedral: Christ, Mary, Ecclesia* (New York, 1964), 27–36. Ernst Kitzinger was the first to propose that the Old Testament kings on the jambs of Saint-Denis stood as antecedents both of Christ and of the anointed kings of the Frankish monarchy ('The Mosaics of the Cappella Palatina in Palermo: An Essay on the Choice and Arrangement of Subjects', *Art Bulletin*, 31 (1949), 291–2).

[46] The Tree of Jesse appears in the outer archivolt of the central portal at Saint-Denis, while biblical royalty and leaders of the Jewish people were arrayed on the jambs. On the west front of Chartres, the lancet window with the *Tree of Jesse* in stained glass stands in the second storey of the façade, above the Old Testament royalty and Prophets in the portal zone.

and Chartres, that parallels are found to the sculptured jamb cycles. In other words, in visual representations of the Old Testament lineage of Christ, it is above all within twelfth-century images of the Tree that Prophets, patriarchs, and sometimes sibyls are shown together with royalty. When they are present in these images, as they are in the Jesse windows of Saint-Denis and Chartres, or in a later version like the miniature of the Ingeborg Psalter, the Prophets and patriarchs with their unfurled scrolls stand to the side, next to the Tree. They are present as witnesses to, and prophets of, the truth of the Incarnation represented there. Within twelfth-century jamb cycles they may play a similar role, arrayed there as witnesses to the truths of the images represented above.

A number of recent historians have been dissatisfied with the theory that the jamb cycles of the 'royal portals' represent the harmony of *regnum* and *sacerdotium*, and Early Gothic iconography is being subjected to new analyses as never before. The best that can be said at present is that there is surely no universal key to the meaning of Early Gothic jamb statues. Paula Gerson has taken this approach in her study of Saint-Denis, by suggesting that the statues should be read not collectively, as a horizontal zone of meaning, but vertically, as an extension on to the jambs of the subject-matter of the tympanum and archivolts immediately above.[47] Our inability thus far to penetrate fully the meaning of the earliest Gothic portals can be attributed in part to the probability that Saint-Denis, the earliest figured portal of the series, may also be unique in its meaning. There is no question but that the iconography of the jamb cycle at Saint-Denis was immediately altered in subsequent portals and continued to be modified in the diffuse examples of this enormously successful portal type as it spread to the regions contiguous to the Île-de-France.[48]

In the case of the sculptural programme of La Daurade, it is within the specific context of the Virgin portals of Chartres and Paris, along with the closely related variant at Bourges, that its iconography should be viewed. The great programmes at Saint-Denis, Chartres, and, in all probability, Paris as well,[49] were triple portal schemes. The iconography of La Daurade is not a conflation of some such larger programme. It focuses solely on the Incarnation as the climax of Old Testament prophecy and, as such, its iconography is properly analysed within the context of the Early Gothic Virgin portals that treat this theme. On the west façade of Chartres, Old Testament royalty (two kings and a queen) appear on the jambs below the image of the Incarnation in the south lateral portal, along with two nimbed figures who may be Prophets or patriarchs. In Paris, in the St Anne Portal, the programme I most closely associate with the iconography of La Daurade, the emphasis on Old Testament royalty was even more complete. The drawing published by Montfaucon indicates that David appeared within a series of six royal figures, to which were added the New Testament pair of Peter and Paul, who

[47] Paula L. Gerson, 'The West Façade of Saint-Denis: An Iconographic Study', Ph.D. thesis, Columbia University (1970), 140–61; ead., 'Suger as Iconographer: The Central Portal of the West Façade of Saint-Denis', *Abbot Suger and Saint-Denis: A Symposium*, ed. Paula L. Gerson (New York, 1986), 183–98. For other recent contributions to the iconography of Early Gothic sculpture see Pamela Z. Blum, 'The Lateral Portals of the West Façade of the Abbey Church of Saint-Denis: Archaeological and Iconographical Considerations', ibid. 199–227; Brouillette, 'Sculpture of Senlis' (as in n. 38 above), i. 167–245.

[48] Early Gothic figure-decorated portals in the wake of Saint-Denis saw the introduction of New Testament figures

such as Peter and Paul and John the Baptist into their cycles, as well as local saints, martyrs, and clerics. A useful catalogue of first-generation portals is contained in Michèle Beaulieu, 'Essai sur l'iconographie des statues-colonnes de quelques portails du premier art gothique', *Bulletin monumental*, 142 (1984), 273–307. Her conclusions regarding dating and the identification of individual figures should be approached with caution, however.

[49] I have concluded elsewhere that the Portail Ste-Anne was planned as a lateral portal in a triple portal scheme and that it was executed for the first (12th-cent.) façade design for Notre-Dame in Paris, which may never have been mounted (Horste, 'Portail Ste-Anne', 187–94).

Pl. 212

probably stood next to the portal entrance.[50] In the upper lintel, which is still preserved, the prophet Isaiah stands next to the Annunciation to make clear that the Son of God Incarnate fulfils the promise of the Old Testament. The heavy emphasis on royalty at Notre-Dame in Paris was given equivalent focus at La Daurade, where five royal figures appear within the cycle, and King David was given the prime position opposite the Virgin.

Pl. 205

Does its relationship to the Virgin portals at Chartres and Paris help us to identify the other figures that make up the ensemble from La Daurade? In addition to the rectangular slabs with the enthroned Virgin and Child and King David, the surviving elements consist of six relief slabs, six complete column statues, and the fragment of a seventh. The latter fragment (Mesplé 100) was first catalogued by Mesplé. It turned up in 1958 during excavations in the choir of the church of the Augustins. Mesplé hypothesized that it had been thrown there as rubble filler during restoration work in the church in 1831.[51] The fragmentary column statue, 32 cm. in height, consists of the lower legs of a draped figure, the feet, and the shaft of the column extending below the feet. The figure wore a long robe falling into vertical flutes with a mantle thrown over it. The drapery is very close in style to that of the other column statues from La Daurade, comparing most closely to Mesplé 74 and 85. The figure was clearly wearing sandals.

Pls. 201 and 203

Among the six complete column statues, two are crowned kings (Mesplé 88 and 91) and one is a nimbed male figure with beard, sandals, and unfurled scroll (Mesplé 71). The other three (Mesplé 74, 77, and 85) also have sandals and unfurled scrolls and are garbed like Mesplé 71 in long, vertically falling tunics with mantles draped diagonally over the top. They are without distinguishing attributes, except that Mesplé 85 retains most of his long and heavy beard. Mesplé 77 also shows the traces of a beard, but the head of Mesplé 74 has been largely destroyed. The sandals, garb, and scrolls could qualify any of these latter three figures for identification as Prophets or Apostles. But since they lack nimbi, while Mesplé 71 is distinguished by the presence of this attribute, it seems most likely they are Prophets.

Two of the reliefs depict a standing king (Mesplé 68) and standing crowned female (Mesplé 66). The other three reliefs are standing males. One of these (Mesplé 82), with heavy, full beard and unfurled scroll, is iconographically identical in his heavy toga to the three column statues we have identified as probable Prophets. The other two male figures wear different garb. One of them (Mesplé 94) wears a calf-length tunic like that of a twelfth-century ruler, with jewelled and shirred sleeves and long cloak thrown back from the shoulders. He wears the ribbed, helmet-like cap or *bonnet cotelé* associated with Old Testament leaders of the Jewish people in twelfth-century iconography, and he displays an open book, to which he points with his right hand. The other male figure (Mesplé 97), holding an unfurled scroll, wears a full-length tunic with shirred sleeves and long mantle held by a clasp at the throat. His feet are sandalled. His hair is elaborately curled and shaped to his head like a cap. A finely combed moustache and short chin whiskers identify him as a male. The costume and dressing of the hair of this figure,

[50] Bernard de Montfaucon, *Les monumens de la monarchie françoise* (Paris, 1729), i. pl. 8. Because the Portail Ste-Anne as mounted in the High Gothic façade brings together sculptures from at least 2 portals, it cannot be known for certain that the jamb statues recorded by Montfaucon represent the original 12th-cent. cycle for the Incarnation portal. Surviving fragments of several of the figures, however, including King David, match the upper lintel and are linked both to it and to the tympanum iconographically. For the newly discovered fragments of the Portail Ste-Anne see Alain Erlande-Brandenburg with Dominique Thibaut, *Les Sculptures de Notre-Dame de Paris au musée de Cluny* (Paris, 1982), 14–27.

[51] Mesplé, *Musée des Augustins: sculpture romane*, no. 100. A column base whose profile matches that of other bases known to come from the chapter house was among the fragments discovered in 1976 (see Inventory). As a base for a recessed column, it could belong with the fragmentary column statue.

as well as those of Mesplé 94 and 68, could be described as modish, while those of the other bearded figures conform to the traditional iconography of the Old Testament Prophet in heavy beard and classical drapery. Neverthless, Mesplé 94 and 68 have customarily been described as Prophets. Moses has been suggested for the figure in *bonnet cotelé* pointing to an open book, while Mesplé 97 has been called Daniel.[52]

Notwithstanding the suggestions given above, as with most of the jamb figures on Early Gothic portals in the north of France, it is difficult or impossible to give a specific identification to many of the figures from the Daurade portal. In fact, the very lack of attributes, which lends the figures the quality of generic types, is one of the peculiarities that associate the Daurade portal ensemble most strongly with the first generation of Early Gothic portals in the north. Toward the late twelfth century, the trend was to give explicit and distinctive attributes to figures, as in the jamb cycles of Senlis (west portal) and Saint-Nicolas at Amiens, or in the allegorical figures (probably from a cloister) now in the Musée municipal at Sens.[53] Those works date from between 1170 and 1200 and clearly the Daurade portal ensemble does not belong to that iconographic trend.

The presence of a nimbus on one of the figures from La Daurade (M. 71) and its absence on the others may be a good indication that the others can all be understood as belonging to the Old Testament. The lone nimbed figure with long unfurled scroll may be St Paul. If so, the fragmentary column statue with sandalled feet might be the remains of St Peter. Saints Peter and Paul frequently appeared as a pair on Early Gothic portals, as at Le Mans, Saint-Loup-de-Naud, Saint-Pourcain-sur-Sioule, and Saint-Bénigne at Dijon. But, most importantly, they appeared on the jambs of the St Anne Portal, within a scheme devoted to the Incarnation. None of the other examples are Virgin portals, and it is unlikely, therefore, that the two Princes of the Apostles carried the same meaning within all these programmes. Where they appear beneath a *Maestas* image among Old Testament personages, as they do at an early date at Le Mans, they may be present as the link between the Old and New Testaments.

At La Daurade, however, as in its northern relative in Paris, there is a very specific role within the iconography that would explain the presence of St Paul. In one of his epistles to the Romans Paul speaks of Christ as a sign and a fulfilment of prophecy, evoking the very words of Isaiah: '. . . and further Isaiah says, "The root of Jesse shall come, he who rises to rule the Gentiles; in him shall the Gentiles hope"' (Romans 15: 12).[54] The fact that the figure we propose as St Paul stands lower down on its column than, for example, the king with an ampula strongly suggests that this nimbed figure occupied the jamb closest to the portal entrance, as did Peter and Paul at Notre-Dame in Paris and Saint-Loup-de-Naud. In certain of the Early Gothic portals of the Île-de-France, for example at Chartres, the height of the column statues was graduated, increasing from the inner to the outer jambs. The nimbed *St Paul* turns slightly towards the viewer's right, indicating that he was probably situated on the left jamb, as we have positioned him in our reconstruction.

Pl. 201

Fig. 20

[52] Rey described the object held by M. 94, which has clearly indicated pages, as 'a book disposed like antique tablets' in support of his identification of the figure as Moses. He suggested Daniel for M. 97 because of the figure's youthful appearance and bare feet ('Porte capitulaire de la Daurade', 36–7).

[53] Illustrated in Sauerländer, *Gothic Sculpture in France*, pl. 43 (bottom) and ills. 53 and 29.

[54] I owe this observation about St Paul's role within the *Tree of Jesse* to a paper by Charles Scillia, 'The Saint-Denis *Stirps Jesse*: A Word, an Image, a Description', 22nd International Congress on Medieval Studies, Western Michigan University, May 1987.

Pl. 215 The north portal of the cathedral of Bourges, a work of about 1160–72,[55] must surely also be included within the group of early Virgin portals whose iconography was influential at La Daurade. The Virgin beneath her ciborium is closely related to those of both Chartres and Paris, and I have elsewhere described the tympanum at Bourges as a conflation of the tympanum and upper lintel of the St Anne Portal.[56] Only two badly damaged jamb statues remain on the north portal at Bourges, both identifiable as female figures. The south portal, however, also preserved from the twelfth-century programme, shows some similarities in its jamb cycle to the series of figures at La Daurade. Four crowned males, three bearded and one unbearded, are present. The cycle is completed by two male figures whose headgear and

Pls. 216 and 195–6 physical type somewhat recall the two male reliefs, Mesplé 94 and 97, from La Daurade. It will be recalled that these latter two were tentatively identified as Moses and Daniel by Raymond Rey. On the right jamb at Bourges, Moses can be definitely identified by the open tablets he holds. His ribbed cap and modish beard are similar to those of the figure pointing to an open book from La Daurade (M. 94) which we have provisionally accepted as Moses. The youthful appearance of Mesplé 97 from La Daurade prompted Rey to call him Daniel. The innermost figure on the right jamb at Bourges also has a youthful facial appearance, with ringletted hair and closely trimmed beard. He is clearly a Hebrew prophet or patriarch, because of his fitted skull-cap. The modish secular dress of the figures at both Bourges and La Daurade could indicate Daniel's royal blood, while his representation as a young prophet may refer to the scriptural story that he was filled with the Holy Spirit from an early age. We have already commented on certain general resemblances suggestive of a nearness in date between the figured capitals crowning the jambs at Bourges and the figured capitals of Corinthian derivation at La Daurade.

Pls. 193 and 194 As for the other figures from the portal of La Daurade, Serafín Moralejo is surely correct in identifying Mesplé 68 and 66, a crowned male and a crowned female, as Solomon and the queen of Sheba.[57] In formal and iconographic terms, the two reliefs have all the characteristics of a pair. The upward pointing gesture of the crowned female prompted Rey to suggest that she represented the Erythrian Sibyl, one of the pagan prophetesses whose pronouncements were accepted by Christian exegetical writers into the canon of Messianic prophecy. A crowned sibyl holding an unfurled scroll appears to the right of the Tree of Jesse, in the company of Old Testament Prophets and priests, in the late twelfth-century Ingeborg Psalter.[58]

Nevertheless, Moralejo builds a stronger case for the identification of the figure from La Daurade as Sheba, based on the reciprocity of her gesture with that of the crowned male he identifies as Solomon. On Early Gothic portals these two are among the most frequently represented royal pairs, and there is a medieval iconographic tradition, traced by Moralejo, for representing the two engaged in a kind of philosophic disputation.[59] According to 1 Kings, the queen of Sheba came from afar to learn for herself from the wisdom of Solomon, and she is

[55] Robert Branner, 'Les Portails latéraux de la cathédrale de Bourges', *Bulletin monumental*, 115 (1957), 263–70; id., *La Cathédrale de Bourges et sa place dans l'architecture gothique* (Paris and Bourges, 1962), 132–6; Sauerländer, *Gothic Sculpture*, 399–400. Ann New-Smith's dating of both lateral portals at Bourges to 1150–60 is difficult to maintain, in the light of the chronology of comparative monuments ('Twelfth-Century Sculpture at the Cathedral of Bourges', Ph.D. thesis, Boston University (1975), 396–422).

[56] Horste, 'Portail Ste-Anne', 201–2.
[57] Moralejo, 'Sala capitular de la Daurade', 190–1.
[58] N. 43 above. Illustrated in Gertrud Schiller, *Iconography of Christian Art* (Greenwich, Conn, 1971), i, fig. 33.
[59] Serafín Moralejo, 'La Rencontre de Salomon et de la reine de Saba: de la bible de Roda aux portails gothiques', *Les Cahiers de Saint-Michel de Cuxa*, 12 (1981), 79–109.

often portrayed in pictorial renditions of their encounter with scroll in hand, addressing a series of riddles to him.

A crayon drawing by Antoine Benoist of one of the lost female statues from the west portal of Saint-Denis has sometimes been identified as the queen of Sheba, because the position of her left hand suggests a pointing movement associated with medieval gestures of disputation.[60] This queen has the same long braids and unfurled scroll as the female in the relief from La Daurade, although these attributes are not solely associated with the queen of Sheba in the numerous representations of crowned females on Early Gothic portals.[61] In a few instances the queen from the south can be identified with certainty by her webbed foot, as in the destroyed portal of Nesle-la-Reposte.[62] The Toulousan sculptor did not avail himself of the opportunity to include this colourful detail. This may indicate that the confusion in Toulousan legend between the queen of Sheba and the duck-footed Visigothic queen supposedly buried at La Daurade post-dates the twelfth century.[63] The engraving of the destroyed portal of Saint-Nicolas at Amiens, published by Millin, shows on the outermost right jamb a disputatious queen of Sheba with upward pointing finger facing a king who must be Solomon across the space of the portal entrance.[64]

As Moralejo has rightly pointed out, the communication of gesture between the two reliefs from La Daurade comes vitally alive if the Solomon relief is placed to the left of the Sheba, and this is how they must have addressed each other in their original emplacements on the façade. In Moralejo's conjectural reconstruction of the Daurade chapter house façade, he places the *Fig. 19* Solomon and Sheba reliefs as pendants on the west face of salient buttresses, separated by the full width of the portal entrance but directing their reciprocal gestures towards one another. Based on the surviving plans and on what we were able to conjecture about the architecture of the chapter house in Chapter 3, we concluded that it was probably barrel vaulted. If so, the thrust would have been countered on the exterior by such salient buttresses. The Solomon and Sheba reliefs might well have been placed on the west faces of these buttresses.

With the exception of the *Virgin and Child* and *King David* reliefs, which I place on the inner embrasure of the central portal entrance, the other three reliefs (M. 82, 94, and 97) face strictly forward. Those three could either have been applied to the face of a buttress—hence facing directly outward—or they could have faced each other by having been placed on opposite embrasures of one of the lateral openings in the façade, as Moralejo shows them in his drawing. As he rightly points out, the communicative eloquence of the Solomon and Sheba, on the other hand, would have been significantly diminished had they been inserted in one of those openings.

I cannot agree with other important aspects of Moralejo's reconstruction, however, based on what we know of the chapter house design from the surviving plans of La Daurade and from comparable examples in the region. The most original aspect of Moralejo's study is his suggestion that an Adoration of the Magi, placed on the jamb of the entrance opening, was the

---

[60] Paris, BN, MS fr. 15634, no. 52, fo. 56. See Léon Pressouyre's discovery of the crowned head of this figure, whom he identifies only as a queen ('Une tête de reine du portail central de Saint-Denis', *Gesta*, 15 (1976), 151–60).

[61] See Gerson's association of long braids with the queen of Sheba in 12th-cent. representations ('West Façade of Saint-Denis', as in n. 47 above, 153–8).

[62] See the engraving of the portal of Nesle-la-Reposte in Montfaucon, *Monumens de la monarchie* (as in n. 50 above), i, pl. 15.

[63] See Ch. 3 on the legend of the Regine Pédauque.

[64] A. L. Millin, *Antiquités nationales* (Paris, 1790–1802), v, pl. 51, no. 2. See also Jacques Vanuxem, 'The Theories of Mabillon and Montfaucon on French Sculpture of the Twelfth Century', in Robert Branner (ed.), *Chartres Cathedral* (New York, 1969), 169–70.

core of the iconographic programme at La Daurade. Indeed, Moralejo's is the most serious effort to date to have been directed towards a formal and iconographic integration of the existing sculptural elements of the portal and for this reason it deserves to be examined here in detail. His analysis, however, associates La Daurade with a different constellation of monuments than those I have pointed to in the Île-de-France, and he places it in a different circle of developments in the twelfth-century history of the figure-decorated portal.

Departing from all previous interpretations, Moralejo believes that two of the column statues—the two males wearing crowns (M. 91 and 88)—represent not Old Testament kings but the Magi of the Adoration. He hypothesizes that a third Magus, who would have brought the number of column statues to an even eight, has been lost.[65]

His theory was prompted by the iconography of the two column statues. The most fully preserved, M. 91, exhibits a unique posture among all the surviving statues in that both his knees are noticeably bent. Moralejo interprets this as a signification that the figure was genuflecting, so far as such a posture could be conveyed within the restrictions of the column statue format. He interprets the movement of the left hand of this king in drawing up his mantle as a prelude to the genuflection, and he points to the ampula held in the right hand as obviously appropriate to the iconography he suggests. The other crowned male has lost his right hand, but a damaged area in the centre of his chest would seem to indicate that he, too, originally held an object of roughly globular shape. Moralejo has also pointed to the hem of the undergarment of both these figures. He interprets the separation of folds at the centre of both hems to signify that the kings are wearing divided trousers, a kind of loose pantaloon known in French as a *bliaut fendu*, that Moralejo associates with the equestrian Magi in representations of their Journey to Bethlehem. He points to a contemporary Toulousan use of this iconography in the capital showing the *Journey and Adoration of the Magi* from the

Pl. 217 cloister of the cathedral of Saint-Étienne, also in the Museé des Augustins (M. 28).

Fig. 19 In Moralejo's reconstruction, the trio of Magi would have stood in the right jamb of the entrance opening, in ceremonial approach to the Virgin and Child on the inner embrasure. Because he turns decidedly towards the right, Moralejo places Mesplé 91 at the inner edge of the recessed jamb, closest to the Virgin and Child. This is also commensurate with the posture of his knees, according to Moralejo, since, in contemporary representations of the Adoration of the Magi, the three kings are often shown in a kind of stop-action sequence, with the foremost Magus down on his knees, while the other two are still upright or about to genuflect. Moralejo's drawing shows the upright king (M. 88) immediately behind M. 91 on the jamb, with two additional column statues completing the jamb on that side (a lost Magus and a fourth figure, probably the *Prophet* M. 77, since this figure also turns and gestures slightly towards his right). The prominence given to Solomon and Sheba within the portal ensemble reinforces Moralejo's interpretation and gives support to his arguments. The visit of the queen of Sheba to Solomon was considered by medieval exegetes to be a prefiguration of the visit of the three Magi at Christ's birth, and the two events were frequently coupled pictorially in representations of the Epiphany, as Moralejo demonstrates.[66]

---

[65] Moralejo, 'Sala capitular de la Daurade', 183–4.
[66] Ibid. 191–2; Moralejo, 'Rencontre de Salomon' (as in n. 59 above), 84.

RECONSTRUCTION OF THE SCULPTURAL PROGRAMME:
PROBLEMS AND ISSUES

Moralejo's suggested iconography for the Daurade portal programme is enticing on several counts. Certainly his identification of M. 91 as a Magus has much to recommend it, although an approximated genuflection is not, it seems to me, the only possible explanation for the posture of this figure's knees. The nimbed figure (M. 71) also has one bent knee, in what may be an awkward approximation of contrapposto. In both cases, the sculptor seems to have been uncomfortable in dealing with the lower extremities within the unfamiliar columnar format, a difficulty that was not unknown to the earliest practitioners of this format in northern portals like Saint-Denis, where crossed legs appeared among some of the column statues. If we are to judge by the Montfaucon engravings, several of the figures from the central portal at Saint-Denis were also characterized by the slightly hunched shoulders and bowing head displayed by the king with the ampula from La Daurade. Furthermore, Moralejo may be correct that the two columnar kings from La Daurade are wearing *bliauts fendus*, but need these garments necessarily signify Magi? They might simply represent the exotic dress of oriental (hence Old Testament) biblical royalty. A column statue of a male figure from Notre-Dame des Doms at Avignon (probably originating from the cloister) wears a secular costume with mantle, belt, and parted pantaloon trousers with full legs. The authors of the Louvre catalogue describe this figure as a Prophet, and he does wear the skull-cap indicative of an Old Testament personage. He could represent Daniel, the Prophet of royal lineage, because of his rich secular costume. In another contemporary example, Plancher's engraving of the destroyed twelfth-century portal of Saint-Bénigne at Dijon shows the outermost figure on the left jamb (clearly not a Magus) as a crowned king with sceptre, differentiated from the others by his parted pantaloons.[67]

More troubling in Moralejo's reconstruction, however, is the jamb arrangement it would require. This is difficult to reconcile with the exigencies of chapter house design and with what we know of the architecture of La Daurade. An Adoration of the Magi would require at least three column statues to either side of the main entrance opening, and Moralejo has increased this by the addition of a fourth to either side. For this latter detail he calls up the testimony of *Fig. 19* Du Mège who, in an article of 1834–5, described the portal of the chapter house as having had 'eight statues taking the place of columns'.[68] Du Mège obviously meant to distinguish here the central opening alone, since, later in the same passage, he states that 'each of the small lateral doorways was decorated with four columns'. Our examination of the post-Revolutionary plans and documents in Chapter 3 prompted the conclusion, however, that the portal entrance and façade must have been gravely altered by the time Du Mège saw the structure.

Moralejo's decision not to deal with the architectural problems that his reconstruction presents leaves his suggested arrangement open to considerable challenge.[69] In my estimation, an entrance opening four columns deep in the façade of the chapter house is untenable from

[67] For the Avignon column figure see Marcel Aubert and Michèle Beaulieu, *Musée national du Louvre: description raisonnée des sculptures du moyen âge, de la renaissance et des temps modernes*, i. *Moyen Âge* (Paris, 1950), no. 103 and fig. 103. For Saint-Bénigne at Dijon, see U. Plancher, *Histoire générale et particulière de Bourgogne* (Dijon, 1739), i. plate foll. p. 502.

[68] Du Mège, 'Cloître de la Daurade', 246–7. The spectre of Du Mège and his unreliability still hang over Moralejo's article.

While he notes the debates in the literature over the writings of the Toulousan antiquarian, Moralejo himself seems reluctant to exclude entirely Du Mège's testimony about La Daurade. In fact, he has used both the earlier and later of Du Mège's descriptions of the chapter house façade, interpreted as contradictory by Seidel and myself, to check details of his own reconstruction (Moralejo, 'Sala capitular de la Daurade', 182, 184, and 194).

[69] See the caveat in his footnote 70 (ibid. 195).

several standpoints. The depth of such a portal and the height of the archivolts necessitated by the span of the embrasures would have given the portal a grandiose scale incongruous within the low-roofed cloister walkway into which the chapter house opened.

Moralejo does not discuss the scale of his drawing nor how he arrived at it. In fact, the only dimension of the chapter house façade that can be calculated with any reliability, based on the surviving plans, is the length of the façade wall. There are such discrepancies among the plans where smaller features are concerned, for example the relative widths of the three openings and the thickness of the walls, that we can only conclude that these features were not drawn from precise measurements on most of the plans. In the four plans that carry a scale, the length of the façade, from the north-west outer corner of the chapter house to the centre of the wall it shared with the Chapelle des Tailleurs on the south, is variously given as between 13.2 and 14.1 m.[70] The only post-Revolutionary plan of the group, Plan géométrique 965, which we have considered the most accurate in other regards, gives this dimension as 14.1 m. and this is the scale Moralejo seems to have accepted. His other dimensions must be considered hypothetical. His central recessed portal, including the decorated jambs, measures 4.8 m. wide from outer left embrasure to outer right embrasure. The outermost archivolt that spans this width in his drawing rises to a height of 4.7 m. from the pavement to the apex of the arch at the centre of the door. In other words, the dimensions of the portal almost exactly approximate a square in his drawing, with the height of the doorway nearly equal to its width, or even slightly less than the width.

In actual twelfth-century construction practice, however, the curve of the archivolts would hardly have been as shallow as Moralejo has drawn them. On the evidence of existing designs, the overall dimensions of the openings, including the central portal entrance, would have been based on a rectangle, not a square. That is to say, they would have been framed by arches more steeply curved than Moralejo's design suggests. At Agen, for example, where the central portal has only two flanking columns, the height of the portal to the apex of the outer archivolt (4 m.) is almost 15 per cent greater than its span (3.53 m. from outer left embrasure to outer right embrasure). The archivolts of the central opening at Agen are slightly pointed in section. The lateral openings, however, are round-headed, and these, too, are about 15 per cent higher than the openings are wide. We do not know whether the arches of the Toulousan chapter house were slightly pointed or not. Because the pointed section came into use early in the region and is standard in other surviving examples we have cited from as early as the 1140s or 1150s, such as the chapter houses of Beaulieu and Catus, I have drawn the arches with pointed sections in my reconstruction. In any event, the proportions I have described were standard for twelfth-century portals, even those with archivolts of rounded section.

Fig. 20

At La Daurade, where Moralejo gives the portal four splays to either side, an outer arc 5.5 m. above the pavement at the apex, or over 18 feet high, would have been required in proportion to the width of the doorway he envisions. This means there would have been an even greater disparity in height between the outer arc of the central opening and those of the two lateral openings than Moralejo has suggested in his drawing. The timber roof which in all probability covered the Romanesque cloister walks at La Daurade would have been supported on a row of projecting console blocks of the sort that are still in place on the façade of the chapter house at

---

[70] Plan ancien 102: length of façade = 7 toise (13.643 m.);   L. = 7.1 toise (13.838 m.); Plan géométrique 965: L = 14.1
Plan ancien 48–2: L. = 6.78 toise (13.21 m.); Plan ancien 77:   m. NB 1 toise = 1.949 m.

Agen. The relationship of the typical chapter house façade to the walkway can be envisioned in   *Pl. 187*
the chapter house of Pontaut, disassembled stone by stone and re-erected at the Cloisters in
Fort Tryon Park.[71] The similarity of Pontaut to the designs at Agen, Beaulieu, and Catus to   *Pl. 211*
which we have referred repeatedly, illustrates how essentially formulary and conservative were
the larger features of chapter house design across the orders in the twelfth century, at least on
the Continent.[72]

Whether wooden roofed or, as seems less likely, stone vaulted, the roofing of the cloister
walk at La Daurade would have been supported against the façade wall of the chapter house,
above the archivolts of the three arched openings. This would add another metre at least, and
probably more, to our calculation of the height of the façade wall at La Daurade. For such a
deeply splayed portal as Moralejo imagines, then, this would have required a façade wall of at
least 6.5 m. or more than 21 feet in height, with the central arched opening rising significantly
higher than the lateral ones. The cloister of La Daurade was small, with an east gallery only
about 15.5 m. long. Its cloister arcades must have been proportioned very similarly to those
now existing at Moissac, which are 3.65 m. (or almost exactly 12 feet) from the pavement to
the apex of the arches of the arcade.[73] Supporting a lean-to roof against it, it is difficult to
imagine how a chapter house façade wall, proportioned as Moralejo's reconstruction requires,
could have been appropriate to the modest dimensions of the earlier twelfth-century cloister
gallery at La Daurade.

In fact, the depth and height of the central opening and the concentration of sculptural
decoration around it that Moralejo pictures in his drawing would have made this façade
wholly exceptional within twelfth-century chapter house design. Moralejo's reconstruction has
the quality of a northern Early Gothic church portal displayed within the intimate confines of a
cloister space. It seems curious that such an extraordinary portal solution should have had no
close imitators in the region of south-west France.[74] Moralejo's portal recedes dramatically in
depth in relation to the lateral window openings, which are not as deeply set back. This would
have created a remarkable three-dimensional definition of the thickness of the façade wall on
both the exterior and interior of the building, since, on the interior side, the back wall of the
central portal would have seemed to project into the space of the chapter room (cf.   *Fig. 19 and
Fig. 6*
Franque's plan 102).[75]

Moralejo's conception, in fact, is an almost complete contradiction of the open, screen-like
front wall that characterizes the classic chapter house entrance in Romanesque and even in
later Gothic design. The essence of these classic screen façades is the resemblance they have to a
portico, mimicking, on a more elaborate scale, the elements of the cloister arcade. Distinctions

---

[71] James J. Rorimer, *The Metropolitan Museum of Art, the Cloisters: The Building and the Collection of Medieval Art in Fort Tryon Park* (New York, 1946), 31–5.

[72] The centralized chapter houses favoured in England of course form a special group. On this group and on Romanesque chapter house design in general, see Stephen Gardner, 'The Role of Central Planning in English Romanesque Chapter House Design', Ph.D. thesis, Columbia University (1976).

[73] The arcades at Moissac are of the 13th cent., but the intercolumniations and hence the height of the arches would have been about the same as in the original 12th-cent. design (the round-headed Romanesque arches being slightly shallower). The present intercolumniations at Moissac range between 1.41 and 1.48 m. Based on the measurements supplied by Plan géo.

965, intercolumniations in the cloister of La Daurade would have ranged from about 1.39 m. in the south gallery to about 1.56 m. in the east and west.

[74] The figure-decorated portal of Saint-Just at Valcabrère, dating from c.1200, illustrates the later arrival of the northern column statue to the region outside Toulouse. Its massive, broadly carved figures display no direct inspiration from the chapter house of La Daurade (see Marcel Durliat and Victor Allègre, *Pyrénées romanes* (La Pierre-qui-vire, 1969), fig. 61).

[75] For the depth of the central portal, Moralejo's dimensions, again, are only approximate. Based on the dimensions of the surviving bases of the column statues and relief slabs, Moralejo's reconstruction would require a façade wall 1.765 m. deep. He shows it as 1.7 m. deep.

between the central opening of the chapter house and the lateral ones were created through the use of tympanum walls or differences in sculptural elaboration, as we have seen, but these distinctions were subtle ones. The outstanding feature of the surviving designs is the integrity that is given to the façade as a planar wall, a wall that can be opened with spacious windows but which does not itself project or recede in space.

Could the design of the Daurade chapter house simply have been exceptional, considering its status as the most richly decorated building of its function surviving in the region? The sculptors who put together the façade were certainly using forms and ideas that were new to them. Nevertheless, we have seen how the exceptional aspects of the programme lie in its iconography and adoption of the northern column statue. In its larger architectural features, the evidence seems conclusive that this was not an exceptional design; indeed, its probable barrel vaulting, its thick-walled construction, its simple three-bay division, and even its figured bas-relief elements all mark it as distinctly conservative.

A more credible reconstruction of the façade programme, it seems to me, would treat the three-arched openings more uniformly. At least eight column statues must have been included in the programme, since seven have survived in part. There are several ways in which these might have been distributed within a more traditional Romanesque structural scheme. For the reasons I have already raised in objecting to Moralejo's reconstruction, it seems unlikely that more than two orders of column statues flanked the central portal. If all three openings were treated uniformly, then pairs of column statues could have flanked the lateral openings as well, where Moralejo shows bare columns. This scheme would have required twelve column figures, meaning that five have been lost. Equally possible would have been a scheme in which the central portal was given slightly greater elaboration, as at Agen, with two column statues to *Fig. 20* each side, while the lateral openings had only one. This scheme would have required eight statues and bears some resemblance to the possible portal arrangement we suggested above for the chapter house of Saint-Étienne.

We have already hypothesized that the lateral openings were not blocked by low walls, as Moralejo shows them. Our examination of the plans and architect's description instead *Pl. 184* suggested a scheme more like that of the chapter house at Beaulieu, in which the lateral openings are of the same scale as the central one and are closed only at the top by tympana. At La Daurade, the tympana would have rested at the centre on paired columns, as at Beaulieu. At either side of the lateral openings, the tympana would have been received by the rectangular relief slabs carved with single figures, but the whole would not have been elevated on a parapet wall as Moralejo pictures the scheme. Instead, all three openings would have been flanked by column statues brought down to the same level, most likely only slightly elevated on a low *Pl. 187* socle, as in the central opening of the chapter house at Agen.

Unlike Agen, however, the scheme I am suggesting at La Daurade would not have involved the combination of full-scale orders at the central portal and smaller elements in the window openings. Though their absolute dimensions make them smaller than life size (they vary from 1.09 to 1.13 m. in height), the heavy plasticity and bulk of the Daurade column statues and relief figures are not commensurate with a scheme like that at Agen. At La Daurade all elements would have been ranged at the same level. Though certain of the reliefs must have been distinguished by their honoured positions on the façade, the iconography of Incarnation and Prophecy binds all the figures into a single system of meaning. This iconography demands expression through figures whose visual impact is approximately equal. The reconstruction I suggest in Fig. 20 would achieve this.[76]   *Fig. 20*

If no more than two column statues flanked the central portal, does this rule out Moralejo's hypothesis that an Adoration of the Magi was the core of the programme? It is conceivable that only two kings were present in place of the usual three, although in twelfth-century Western art such an iconography would be highly exceptional.[77] Less rarely in the twelfth century, especially when the limitations of a particular compositional field demanded it, the Magi in veneration might be divided to either side of the Virgin's throne. Examples are the monumental fresco in the apse of Santa Maria at Tahull (Catalonia), where one Magus appears at the left and two at the right, or a Romanesque capital in the choir of Saint-Pierre at Chauvigny. The exigencies of portal structure at La Daurade could have required such a separation of the three kings, and the lost column statue postulated by Moralejo could have stood on the left jamb of the entrance portal, opposite the Virgin and his two companions.

It is also possible that Moralejo's identification is simply in error and that neither of the crowned column statues he singles out are Magi. Mesplé 91, the real pivot of his argument, might be Melchizedek, the priest-king. In this case, he would take his natural place among the other Old Testament forebears of Christ, as well as the Old Testament parallels invoked by Christian exegetes for the Epiphany.[78] We have already pointed out that the *bliaut fendu*, so crucial to Moralejo's argument, might have been a Toulousan iconographer's conception of an exotic oriental item of royal garb, rather than a specifically equestrian garment.

Without additional evidence of an objective nature, it is impossible to say with certainty whether the two crowned column statues in question represent Magi. Whatever the case, however, I have serious disagreements with the family of monuments with which Moralejo associates the destroyed portal of La Daurade. Rather than with the northern portals of the 1140s, 1150s, and 1160s I have referred to in my own analysis, he relates it to late twelfth- and early thirteenth-century portals in Burgundy and Spain. He cites in particular the portals of Saint-Lazare at Avallon (Yonne) and nearby Notre-Dame at Vermenton (Yonne), and, in Spain, San Pedro in La Guardia, Santiago de Compostela (the Portico de la Gloria), and both the south and west portals of San Vicente in Avila.[79]

What all these portals share is an attitude towards the jamb zone that permits that zone to be treated as a unified scenic space in which monumental figures may interact within dramatic narrative groupings.[80] Moralejo believes the scenic setting of jamb statues was probably a

---

[76] It should be remembered that a chapel flanked the chapter house on the south. It is significant that the doorway of this chapel was not in the centre of its west wall. Was this done to bring it into relationship with the other 3 openings in the façade for decorative or iconographic reasons? If so, this doorway may have participated in some way in the sculptural programme (Seidel suggested as much in 'Chapter House at La Daurade', 330 n. 15).

[77] Moralejo has drawn attention to the portal of Santa Maria de la Corticela at Santiago, where a single genuflecting Magus is shown to the left of the Virgin's throne, while the other 2 Magi are placed in the archivolt behind him (Moralejo, 'Sala capitular de la Daurade', 37).

[78] See e.g. the Klosterneuberg Altar where the visit of Abraham to Melchizedek and the visit of Sheba to Solomon are explicitly juxtaposed as parallels to the Adoration of the Magi (Helmut Buschhausen, 'The Theological Sources of the Kloster-

neuburg Altar', *The Year 1200: A Symposium* (New York, 1975), 119–38).

[79] Moralejo, 'Sala capitular de la Daurade', 186–9.

[80] Moralejo has recently proposed that the *Virgin and Child* of Solsona, along with other fragments attributed to the cloister there, shared in this meridional development of scenic narration in statuary format. At Solsona, however, he situates the statuary sequences on the cloister supports, where he reconstructs an Adoration of the Magi and an Annunciation. Such a use of 'historiated' supports places the Solsona pieces, in Moralejo's view, conceptually between Gilabertus's Apostles from Saint-Étienne and the chapter house portal of La Daurade (see Moralejo, 'Sant Esteve de Tolosa', 104–19). In my opinion the Solsona *Virgin* remains a very problematic piece. It clearly mimics certain signature motifs of Gilabertus, as well as the chapter house sculpture of La Daurade. In my judgement, however, it is a modern work of the 19th or 20th cent.

Burgundian invention and that monuments in Toulouse (La Daurade and the *Annunciation* of the Cordeliers), as well as the Spanish portals he cites, were inspired by the Burgundian innovations.[81]

Chronology is a problem that Moralejo largely sidesteps in his study. He accepts a date of about 1200 for La Daurade,[82] while the Burgundian and Spanish portals with which he compares it have been dated widely over the twelfth and thirteenth centuries, from about 1160 to the 1220s.

In opting for a date of about 1200 for La Daurade, Moralejo adheres to the traditional chronology. The *terminus ante quem* for the chapter house has always been given as 1196, the date when Count Raymond VI is recorded to have held an assembly in the cloister, *in aula prioris*, in the presence of the Common Council of the city and the Bourg.[83] However, a previously overlooked document provides sound evidence that a chapter house existed at La Daurade at least by 1179–84. The dated document of 1184, recording the act of donation to Moissac of a hospital and chapel located in Toulouse by one Bernardus Mandatarius and his wife, concludes with the formula, 'Hoc fuit factum in capitulo ecclesiae Mariae Deauratae cum concilio Guillelmi abbatis Lezatensis priorisque praedictae ecclesiae Mariae Deauratae et conventus eiusdem loci'.[84] The original of the act is lost. Mundy has identified the document of 1184 as a copy and has concluded that the original act may have dated from as early as 1179, on the basis of the dates of tenure of the bishop of Toulouse and prior of La Daurade named in the donation.[85]

Was the chapter house named in this act the same structure from which the surviving sculptures originate? If so, it undoubtedly replaced an earlier, perhaps temporary, one, since a chapter room would have been essential for the practices of the Cluniac community from the beginning of its foundation. The document of 1179–84 proves at least that the old date of 1196, long perpetuated in the literature, is without foundation.

In fact, the dating of the chapter house needs to be subjected to wholly new criteria. Political events in Toulouse, described in the next chapter, make it most likely that the figured portal of La Daurade was erected about 1165–75 under the strong influence of northern programmes at Chartres, Bourges, and, especially, Paris. Moralejo's late dating ignores the very powerful iconographic links the Toulousan sculptures have with this group of Virgin portals in the north.

The presence of an Adoration of the Magi on the jamb, if it did exist, would not contradict this family of associations. The iconography of the Adoration was an essential kernel in the genesis of the Early Gothic portals of the Incarnation, and its message resonates even in the

---

[81] Moralejo, 'Sant Esteve de Tolosa', 186.

[82] Ibid., n. 51.

[83] 'Hanc recognitionem et confirmationem fecit dominus prenominatus comes in claustro beate Marie, in aula prioris, in presentia consulum civitatis Tolose et suburbii et multorum aliorum proborum hominum qui ibi erant' (Toulouse, AMT, Cartulaire du Bourg, AA 1, doc. 12, fos. 14ᵛ–15ʳ). (In my article 'Passion Series', n. 33, I erroneously identified the depository of this document as the Archives départementales de la Haute-Garonne.) Also transcribed in R. Limouzin-Lamothe, *La Commune de Toulouse et les sources de son histoire, 1120–1249*, Bibliothèque méridionale, 2nd ser., 26 (Toulouse, 1932), 283–4; and in *HGL*, vol. viii, cols. 439–40 (after copy in Paris, Archives nationales, JJ XXI, fo. 29ᵛ, n. xv).

[84] Toulouse, ADHG, 114 H 193, fo. 5ʳ. Another document of 1214 in the same collection identifies the hospital as being located in the parish of Saint-Pierre-des-Cuisines.

[85] See John Hine Mundy, 'Charity and Social Work in Toulouse', *Traditio*, 22 (1966), 216 n. 46. On the basis of other documents bound with it which also concern the hospital of the Maynaderia, the document in the ADHG may be identified as a 17th-cent. copy of the copy of 1184. Catel published this document in his *Mémoires de l'histoire du Languedoc* (Toulouse, 1623), 215–16. Folcrand, named as bishop in the act, took the see of Toulouse in 1179. Guillelmus, named as prior of La Daurade and abbot of Lézat, became prior in 1177 and was succeeded in 1184 by Bernardus de Montesquive, who is identified as a simple monk in the act.

tympana of portals like Chartres and Paris where the Magi are not visibly represented.[86]   *Pl. 212*
Formally and stylistically the monumental figures of the Daurade chapter house are unique
conceptions in the region. The only other sculpture that can be associated with the same
workshop is the *Annunciation*, formerly in the church of the Cordeliers at Toulouse (Mesplé
248 and 249).[87] Now in the Musée des Augustins, the *Annunciation* is larger than the figures
from the Daurade chapter house and is carved in marble. The angel, far more fluid and graceful
in his movements than the Virgin, would appear to be the work of the same sculptor who
carved the animated relief of King David tuning his harp from La Daurade. The large heads
and over-sized hands are similar, as are the faces, with thin, compressed lips and long, almond-
shaped eyes. The expressive action of the angel's upraised right arm is recalled in the raised left
hand of King David and even more so in another of the kings, the one identified as Solomon,
with his right arm cocked in a gesture of teaching or declamation.   *Pl. 194*

The original function and place of origin of this *Annunciation* group are unknown. Du Mège
wrote in 1820 that the Angel and Virgin were formerly installed as part of a tomb monument
in a chapel of the church of the Cordeliers at Toulouse.[88] This cannot have been their original
emplacement, however, since the Franciscans did not establish a community in Toulouse until
1224, and the first church, a modest structure, was not under construction until 1235. Durliat
suggests that the *Annunciation* was most likely re-employed at the church of the Cordeliers
after 1522, when the Belbèze family established its sepulchre there.[89]

Given its workshop connection to the project at La Daurade, a possible origin for the
Annunciation group might be the church of Notre-Dame la Dalbade, which was rebuilt
between 1164/70 and 1200.[90] This is pure conjecture, since there is no evidence the group
comes from there. In favour of this hypothesis, however, is the fact that the church of the
Dalbade was, from the eleventh century, a Cluniac dependency of La Daurade, and it was
dedicated to the Virgin. It was rebuilt again between 1503 and 1540, when it was given its
present Renaissance design.[91] The sculptured *Annunciation* could have found its way at that
time to the church of the Cordeliers, where it was incorporated as spolia into the tomb of the
wife of Denis de Beauvoir.

No other evidence for the activity of the last Daurade workshop can be found in the region.
A Provençal influence on the workshop has frequently been claimed in discussions of the
sculptures, most determinedly by Richard Hamann.[92] The historical links between the two
regions are well known, united as they were within the domains of the counts of Toulouse,

---

[86] For a discussion of this phenomenon in 12th-cent. Virgin portals see Horste, 'Portail Ste-Anne', especially 194–204. Ilene Forsyth describes similar resonances in the iconography of the wooden Majesty figures of the enthroned Virgin and Child (*The Throne of Wisdom: Wood Sculptures of the Madonna in Romanesque France* (Princeton, 1972), 28 and 49–59). In addition, see her article 'Magi and Majesty: A Study of Romanesque Sculpture and Liturgical Drama', *Art Bulletin*, 50 (1968), 215–22, where she also proposes an association between the portable cult images of the Virgin and Child in Majesty and the theme of the Adoration of the Magi.

[87] Sauerländer, while noting the resemblances of this *Annunciation* group to the chapter house sculptures from La Daurade, does not associate them with the same workshop but with a phase of Toulousan sculpture immediately following the Daurade statues. He dates the latter to the late 12th cent. and

the *Annunciation* group to the first quarter of the 13th (Sauerländer, *Gothic Sculpture in France*, 450). Dating of the *Annunciation* group has traditionally depended in the literature on the supposed *terminus ante quem* of 1196 of the Daurade chapter house (see *Year 1200*, no. 18, p. 14).

[88] Paris, Archives de l'Institut, 3 H 50, Alexandre Du Mège, 'Notice sur les deux églises du couvent des Cordeliers de Toulouse', fos. 4ᵛ–5ʳ.

[89] Durliat, 'Annonciation des Cordeliers', 265–70. See also his discussion of this group in 'Dernière sculpture romane', 947–9.

[90] R.-C. Julien, *Histoire de la paroisse Notre-Dame la Dalbade* (Toulouse, 1891), 120–3.

[91] Jules Chalandes, *Histoire des rues de Toulouse* (Toulouse, 1919–20) pt. 1, 96.

[92] Hamann, *St. Gilles* (as in n. 4 above), 262–7.

who travelled frequently between their capitals at Toulouse and Saint-Gilles and generously supported churches and monasteries in both regions.

Nevertheless, I tend to see the links between the late style at La Daurade and Provençal Romanesque in rather general terms, in a shared affinity for antique Roman sculpture and architectural detail. Beyond this common use of antique vocabulary, it is difficult to demonstrate a link with any precision. Certainly there is no identifiable workshop active in Provence in the twelfth century whose style could be detected at La Daurade. The smoothed and slicked drapery lines of the Toulousan figures lack the deep gouging and channelling that create angular edges and sharp contrasts of light and shade in figures like those of the façade of *Pl. 191* Saint-Gilles or the cloister of Saint-Trophime at Arles. The Daurade figures also lack the expressive faces and head types of the Saint-Gilles and Arles masters. Instead, the facial features are extremely uniform, even formularized, among the range of figures, with long, almond-shaped eyes and with a classical regularity of proportion between eyes, nose, and mouth that make the Toulousan faces appear bland next to those of Arles or Saint-Gilles.

Nevertheless, quotations from antique Mediterranean sculpture are evident in both the Toulousan and Provençal work, in the liking for massive and weighty figures, deliberately made bulkier by the wrapping of heavy drapery around the mid-section of the body and the suspension of the arms in sling folds. The Daurade figures, like their Provençal counterparts, resemble Roman sculpture in their quality of physical presence, the way they aggressively occupy space and appropriate it with their dense solidity. The Daurade ensemble also shares with the Provençal school a common vocabulary of architectural details based on antique practice: the liking for Corinthian-inspired acanthus capitals and the use of classical mouldings, flutes, and channelling, as seen on the lateral faces of the *King David* relief. The relief of the *Virgin and Child* exhibits another antique decorative conceit, the pairing of unmatched columns of cylindrical and octagonal form. This same pairing is found in the twin *Pl. 199* columns of the cloisters of Saint-Trophime at Arles, Saint-Paul de Mausole, and elsewhere in Provençal practice.

Such stylistic features were not native to the Romanesque sculpture of Toulouse at the time the chapter house of La Daurade was decorated. It may be assumed that the Toulousan workshop was affected in some way by what was being done by Romanesque sculptors in Provence. According to the chronology now most widely accepted for the major monuments of Provence, Romanesque sculpture would appear to have flowered there rather later in the twelfth century than in Toulouse or Burgundy.[93] The richest and most ambitious programmes, at Arles and Saint-Gilles, were just being produced, at the earliest, in the 1140s and 1150s and some of the most richly decorated figured cloisters—Montmajour, Avignon, and Aix-en-Provence—were not erected until late in the century. Compared to the diminished level of sculptural production in Toulouse after about 1140, workshops in Provence were at the height of their activity throughout the second half of the century. The Toulousan carvers responsible for the portal of La Daurade may thus have been inspired in some sense by the vitality of

[93] For a summary of recent opinions on the chronology of Provençal Romanesque, see Willibald Sauerländer, 'Das 10. Internationale Colloquium der Société française d'archéologie: Die Fassade der Abteikirche in Saint-Gilles-du-Gard', *Kunstchronik*, 31 (1978), 45–54; Whitney Stoddard, *Façade of Saint-Gilles* (as in n. 16 above), 127–59. See also Jacques Thirion, 'Saint-Trophime d'Arles', *Congrès archéologique*, Arles (1976), 360–479; id., 'Le Décor sculpté du cloître de la cathédrale d'Avignon', *Fondation E. Piot: monuments et mémoires*, 61 (1977), 87–164.

Provençal Romanesque sculpture, but the ensemble is not the work of outside sculptors from that region. The links with the earlier Toulousan tradition, specified at the beginning of this chapter, are too prominent in this workshop, in the repertory of foliate ornament and in the quotation of specific motifs of drapery and jewelled ornamental details that were meaningful to Toulousan sculptors.

For all its incorporation of forms and iconography from contemporary northern sculpture, the prominent quotations from an earlier generation of Toulousan sculptors cultivate the qualities of retrospection and historicism in the programme of the chapter house façade. The period of Toulousan history recalled by these artistic associations, the first four decades of the twelfth century, is one of greatness for the counts of Toulouse. The reasons why it should have been important for the Cluniacs of La Daurade to cultivate such associations are suggested in the following chapter.

9

CAPETIAN POLITICS AND THE TRANSMISSION OF NORTHERN INFLUENCE TO TOULOUSE

THOUGH everyone who has looked at the portal of La Daurade has noted the northern features in it, remarkably, no one has broached the question of what a portal of this type and iconography is doing in the cloister of a Cluniac priory in the Midi, opening into the monks' chapter house. A special devotion to the cult of the Virgin, heavily promoted in the twelfth century by St Bernard and the Cistercian order, was already a developed aspect of Cluniac liturgy in the eleventh century.[1] The priory of La Daurade, like many communities reformed by Cluny, was dedicated to the Virgin. Its dependency, the church of Notre-Dame la Dalbade, was also dedicated to Mary, as was its hospital of Sancta Maria de Aurata, thus reflecting the Cluniac promotion of the cult of Mary in Toulouse. Beyond this, however, there was a widespread association between the Virgin and the monastic chapter house in the Romanesque period, as Stephen Gardner has pointed out.[2] There is evidence of such an association at Cluny itself from at least the abbacy of Odilo, who appended a chapel of Sancta Maria (rebuilt under St Hugh) to the chapter house of the great abbey in the eleventh century.[3]

Gardner has specifically associated the functions of the chapter house in communal spiritual renewal and in the enactment of the *Capitulum culparum* with monastic devotion to the Virgin as intercessor and regenerator.[4] Four of the five historiated capitals surviving from the cloister precinct of Saint-Étienne include the Virgin within their iconographic message. She is the intercessor to whom the repentant sinner directs her appeal in the *Mary of Egypt* capital (M. 33), and in the two versions of the *Wise and Foolish Virgins* she appears as Ecclesia at the side of her son in the judgement of the vigilant and the unvigilant (M. 34 and 37). A fourth capital shows the *Journey* and the *Adoration of the Magi* before the enthroned Virgin (M. 28). Iconography, then, may be the best evidence that some of these capitals should be situated within the sculptural programme of the chapter house.

The portal of La Daurade is surely the richest surviving Cluniac programme in which the

Pls. *170 and 174*
Pls. *217 and 218*

---

[1] See the Customs of Ulrich (*PL* 149, cols. 683–4 and 695–6); also Guy de Valous, *Le Monachisme clunisien* (Paris, 1935), 362–3).

[2] Stephen Gardner, 'The Role of Central Planning in English Chapter House Design', Ph.D. thesis, Columbia University (1976), 203–21.

[3] Kenneth John Conant, *Cluny* (Mâcon, 1968), 65 and pls. IV and V.

[4] Gardner, 'Role of Central Planning', 203–21. See in particular his linkage between the wording of a couplet above the portal of the 12th-cent. chapter house at Worcester and prayers of St Anselm, archbishop of Canterbury, in which the Virgin is described as the gateway of life and door of salvation (*PL* 163, col. 954).

veneration of the Virgin is given visible expression in the artistic decoration of the chapter house. What is remarkable in the ensemble from La Daurade is the emphasis this programme gives to the royal ancestry of Christ and the specific monuments of the Early Gothic north to which this iconography links it. The appearance of this northern-inspired portal in Toulouse cannot be equated with the widespread diffusion of the portal type into the regions immediately contiguous to the Île-de-France in the second half of the twelfth century. For its period, the chapter house at La Daurade is an anomaly in the Midi. Though it appeared in a venerable Cluniac establishment in the artistic capital of Languedoc, no wholesale adoption of northern forms was launched by this portal. This suggests that its appearance here, at this place and at this time, resulted from special circumstances. The political history of Toulouse in the second half of the twelfth century provides the best explanation for this phenomenon.

The great surge in building in Toulouse had been launched in the late eleventh century. By 1140, Toulouse was no longer producing new sculptural ideas. The few works that can be assigned to the years after 1140 have the character of small-scale musings on the familiar narrative devices and ornamental forms introduced by the generation of 1120–40.[5]

Despite this situation the Cluniac monks of La Daurade were able to sponsor, in their new chapter house portal, the richest and most ambitious sculptural programme in the city by reaching well outside the Romanesque Midi for a complex iconography and new sculptural forms. What is more, this occurred at a time when the ascendancy of Cluny in the region, as elsewhere in France, had long since passed, and its spiritual influence was in distinct decline after the great years of the eleventh century. What explains the appearance of northern, proto-Gothic forms in the cloister of La Daurade and, more especially, how do we explain a programme so uncharacteristic of Cluniac art as is this 'royal portal' in the Midi?

The best answer lies in the close relationship the community of La Daurade had maintained with the ruling family of Toulouse since the introduction of Cluniac reform in the eleventh century. This historical tie to the counts, described in Chapter 1, is at least partly responsible for the success with which the priory of La Daurade was able to maintain its position of prestige and temporal wealth in the city throughout the whole of the twelfth century. With the successes of the counts of Toulouse in the Holy Land, and the triumphant retaking of the city in 1123 by the son of Raymond de Saint-Gilles, Alphonse-Jourdain, it is a tie the Cluniacs of La Daurade chose to celebrate, as we suggested in Chapter 7, in the Passion series carved for their cloister in the decade 1120–30.

In the second half of the twelfth century the future of Toulouse took a historic turn when a new alliance was forged between the count of Toulouse and the Capetian king of France. The reasons for this alliance, on both sides, were political and military, but the means for ensuring it were matrimonial. In 1154, in the presence of Louis VII of France, Count Raymond V of Toulouse was wedded to the king's only sister, Constance. The Toulousans now had a countess of royal blood, who would produce a new count, Raymond VI. And in Louis VII the city had a royal protector who was militarily capable of performing that role. It is the esteem in which Constance was held in Toulouse and the personal link with the Crown that she continued to provide, even after her estrangement from Raymond V in 1165, that best

---

[5] Among the later sculptures from La Daurade that exhibit this trend, see M. 172, 174, and 178 and, from Saint-Pierre-des-Cuisines, the capitals of the south portal there, which appear as awkward interpretations of the narrative capitals of the second Daurade series.

account for the presence of the extraordinary figured portal in the cloister of La Daurade and its unmistakable overtones of royalty.

From the end of the Carolingian period until the mid-twelfth century, an outstanding factor in the political history of the Midi had been its nearly total independence from the French Crown. The Midi had been Romanized at an early date, and the orientation of its culture and its commerce had always been towards the east and the south, towards the old Roman cities of Provence and the Mediterranean. Toulouse, by virtue of linguistic and matrimonial ties, and by the steady migration of meridional peoples across the Pyrenees during the early Middle Ages, also had a powerful orientation towards Spain and had involved itself heavily in the Christian reconquest of the Iberian peninsula. Though it had been an important southern bastion of the Carolingian Empire, the Frankish culture of the north had never truly penetrated the Midi. With the disintegration of the Carolingian Empire in the tenth century, the independence of meridional culture and politics from the north was, for all purposes, complete.[6] The simple geographic distance of the Midi from the shrunken Crown lands helped to ensure this, as did the rugged and inhospitable Massif Central that lies between the two regions.

From the tenth century on, the counts of Toulouse ruled over their rich domains as virtual princes of their own realm. Jacques Flach dates the real birth of the Languedocian state to the death of Count William IV of Toulouse (*c*.1093/4), when his brother, Raymond de Saint-Gilles, earlier heir to the eastern domains of the dynasty of Toulouse-Saint-Gilles, claimed title to the county of Toulouse as well.[7] As count of Toulouse, duke of Narbonne, and marquis of Provence, Raymond de Saint-Gilles now ruled as suzerain over a domain that stretched from Gascony in the west to the Rhône Valley in the east and from Périgord in the north to the Pyrenees and the Mediterranean.

The political independence of the counts of Toulouse from the Capetian monarch is manifest in the total silence of the texts concerning any feudal relations between them during the centuries between 950 and 1150. Both Luchaire and Flach emphasize that documents of this period disclose not a single instance of feudal homage paid by a lord of the Midi to the Capetian monarch.[8] In July 1137 the count of Toulouse, Alphonse-Jourdain, and the king of France were by coincidence present at the same time in the city of Limoges. The young Louis VII was on the way to Bordeaux for his marriage to Eleanor of Aquitaine. Alphonse-Jourdain, attending the Feast of St Martial, was ignorant of the king's advent, so the chronicler, Geoffrey of Vigeois, tells us.[9]

This historical estrangement between Languedoc and the Île-de-France was dramatically brought to an end by political developments during the reign of Louis VII. The young Louis's marriage to Eleanor in 1137 had been arranged to bring her vast dower lands, the enormously rich duchy of Aquitaine, into the political control of the monarchy. The duchy stretched from the Loire Valley to Bordeaux, encompassing Poitou, the Saintonge, the Périgord, the Quercy,

---

[6] On the geographic, cultural, and commercial ties of Toulouse to the Mediterranean and Spain, see esp. John Hine Mundy, *Liberty and Political Power in Toulouse* (New York, 1954), 3–5, and Marcel Pacaut, *Louis VII et son royaume* (Paris, 1964), 19–22.

[7] Jacques Flach, *Les Origines de l'ancienne France* (Paris, 1917), iv. 613. On the date of the death of Count William IV, see above, Ch. 1. The best early source on the rise of the house of Toulouse-Saint-Gilles is still Dom Claude Devic and Dom

Joseph Vaissète, *Histoire générale de Languedoc* (Toulouse, 1872–93). See also Augustin Fliche in *Histoire des institutions françaises du moyen âge*, ed. Ferdinand Lot and Robert Fawtier, i. *Institutions seigneuriales* (Paris, 1957), 71–88.

[8] Flach, *Origines*, iv. 604–6 and 614; Achille Luchaire, *Histoire des institutions monarchiques de la France sous les premiers Capétiens (987–1180)*, i (2nd edn., Paris, 1891), 37–9.

[9] Geoffroi de Vigeois, *RHGF*, vol. xii, p. 435A.

the Agenais, and Gascony. It bordered, in Gascony, the western domains of the counts of Toulouse. Following the well-known events of the Second Crusade, Louis VII repudiated his wife, and their marriage was annulled in 1152. Two months later the strong-willed Eleanor married Henry Plantagenet, duke of Normandy, count of Anjou, and arch-rival of Louis VII. Eleanor brought with her in marriage her inheritance of Aquitaine. When Henry ascended the throne of England in 1154, Louis VII found himself in a very dangerous situation, his kingdom wedged between the duchy of Normandy and the vast lands of Aquitaine to his south, both now in the hands of his political enemy.

To counter the threat from the south, Louis VII launched a deliberate plan to bring the Midi, for the first time since the end of the Carolingian dynasty, into the sphere of influence of the Frankish monarchy. He embarked on a royal journey to the south in the autumn and winter of 1154–5 with several premeditated objectives intended to woo the region: a pilgrimage to the tomb of St James at Santiago de Compostela; closer relations with the clergy of the region through the confirming of privileges of numerous abbeys and churches; the giving in marriage of his sister, Constance, to Count Raymond V in a ceremony at Toulouse, and the revival, through his physical presence in the region, of the popular concept of the king as protector of the Church and the realm. This latter idea, despite the centuries-long estrangement from the northern reaches of the old Frankish kingdom, had survived in the Midi in the memories and legends of the great Carolingian rulers, Charlemagne, Louis the Pious, and Charles the Bald, whose actions had played such a powerful role in the earlier military and ecclesiastical history of the region. Feelings of national pride, according to Flach, continued to be invested primarily in the institution of royalty, as evidenced in the formulas invoking Frankish monarchs and their protection that appear in charters issued throughout the tenth and eleventh centuries in the Midi, even while no feudal allegiance to the monarch was exercised.[10]

It was during his sojourn in Toulouse in 1155, on his return from Santiago, that Louis VII issued his famous diploma confirming the privileges of the three most venerable churches of Toulouse: Saint-Sernin, Saint-Étienne, and La Daurade. The language of this diploma suggests that it was intended to link the Carolingian and the Capetian rights to bestow these privileges:

Ego autem Ludovicus, Dei gratia Francorum rex, rediens a Sancto Jacobo et per Tolosam transiens, viso privilegio Tolosane aeclesiae quod fecerat antecessor noster gloriosissimus rex Karolus magnus, predictam aeclesiam pretiosissimi martiris Saturnini, quae est in suburbio, cum eclesia prothomartiris Stephani et aeclesiam beatae Mariae quae est infra muros, petitione clericorum earumdem aeclesiarum sub eadem tuitione et emunitate posui. Hoc autem feci consilio et volunte Raimundi, Tolosani comitis, et in presentia Tolosanorum civium et burgensium in capitulo sancti Saturnini . . . anno ab incarnatione Domini M.C.L.IIII.[11]

It will be recalled that the ninth-century privileges granted to the churches of Toulouse, which this charter confirms, were originally bestowed by Louis the Pious and confirmed by Charles the Bald.[12] Through the *chansons de geste*, nevertheless, it was Charlemagne, with his legendary triumphs against the Saracens in Spain, who loomed larger in the local imagination. The erroneous attribution of the original privileges to Charlemagne in the diploma of 1155 seems a transparent effort to link Louis VII's protection of the Church and his right to exercise that protection with his most venerated Carolingian predecessor. The considerable list of other

[10] Flach, *Origines*, iv. 604–6.
[11] Toulouse, ADHG, H Saint-Sernin, bundle II, doc. I.

[12] For our discussion of the Carolingian charter, see above, Ch. 2.

Carolingian imperial charters of immunities and privileges that Louis VII confirmed in the following years for bishoprics and abbeys of Languedoc further illustrates his policy of engaging the Church in his effort to bring the region under the influence of the Crown.[13]

The alliance with the Frankish monarchy effected by Raymond V's marriage to Constance was clearly of great political advantage to the count, as well as to the king. Eleanor, now queen of England, was once again pressing the old Aquitainian claims to Toulouse and its region, through her grandmother Philippa, that had threatened the counts of Toulouse in the earlier twelfth century, when the city was occupied by a Poitevin army. The first test of the alliance came in 1159 when Henry II of England attempted to exert his wife's claims to Toulouse. Leading an army of Norman, English, and Aquitainian vassals, and allied with the count of Barcelona, Henry II marched into the domains of the count of Toulouse and prepared to lay siege to the city. Raymond V made appeal to his brother-in-law for help against their common English enemy. With his armies already in the vicinity, Louis VII reached Toulouse in advance of the invasion and garrisoned himself and his troops in the city. The action of the French monarch, along with the approach of the winter season, successfully discouraged Henry from continuing the siege, and he soon returned to England.[14]

The aborted assault of 1159 was only the first of repeated invasions of the Toulousan region launched by Henry II and his successor, Richard I, over the next twenty-five years. During this period, particularly in the 1160s, it was increasingly to the king of France that the citizens of Toulouse appealed for aid, rather than to their count. The journey of Louis VII to the Midi in 1154–5, the wedding of his sister to Raymond V, and his response to the threatened invasion mark the beginning of a wholly new relationship between the city of Toulouse and the heretofore distant Frankish monarchy. It was a relationship that was to grow in closeness and affection during the reign of Louis VII, and the documents indicate it was actively cultivated on both sides.

The abrupt flowering of this relationship where none had existed before could not be more clearly evinced than in the unexpected forms and the royal overtones of the chapter house ensemble at La Daurade. The key figure in the process of transmission of this northern portal scheme to Toulouse may have been Constance, sister of Louis VII. Constance was already a mature woman when she came to make her home in Toulouse, having been widowed in 1153 after twelve years of marriage to her first husband Eustache, son of King Stephen of England.[15] Referred to in a letter from the Common Council of Toulouse as 'our queen',[16] Constance was held in much warmer affection in Toulouse than was the errant count, her husband.

No records exist of donations by Constance or her husband to the monastery of La Daurade.[17] Nevertheless, in Chapter 1 we traced the history of protection for the order of Cluny on the part of the counts of Toulouse, a history that goes back to the mid-eleventh century. Under Count William IV this had meant a vigorous encouragement of Cluniac reform

---

[13] See Luchaire, *Histoire des institutions*, ii. 296–7, and Marcel Pacaut, *Louis VII et son royaume* (Paris, 1964), 100–1.

[14] See *HGL*, vol. v, pp. 809–11.

[15] Ibid. 794.

[16] *RHGF*, vol. xvi, no. 218, p. 69.

[17] See Émile Léonard (ed.), *Catalogue des actes des comtes de Toulouse*, iii. *Raymond V (1149–1194)* (Paris, 1932). *HGL*, vol. vi, p. 162 mentions a few specific donations to foundations

in the Midi. Numerous donations by Constance alone after her separation from Raymond are known (see, e.g., Jules Tardif, *Inventaires et documents publiés par l'ordre de l'empereur* (Archives de l'Empire: *Monuments historiques* (Paris, 1866), nos. 640, 646, and 700). She was especially generous to the Hospital Order of St John of Jerusalem, where she selected a tomb during a visit to the Holy Land in 1173 (*HGL*, vol. vi, p. 59).

in Toulouse. It was William IV who fused a special relationship between the monastery of La Daurade and the house of Toulouse. The documents do not tell us how this relationship fared under Raymond V. Clearly, however, his son, Raymond VI, favoured the cloister of La Daurade for the holding of councils and the issuance of official acts. We have already cited the assembly he called there in 1196.[18] Other important declarations were issued by Raymond VI in 1205 and 1210 before assemblies *in claustro Beatae Mariae*.[19]

In fact, the embracing of new forms and imagery in the chapter house portal of La Daurade, and the process of their transmission from the Île-de-France, probably had little to do with the count of Toulouse himself. Raymond V cannot have been enamoured by the Church of Toulouse. In 1166, in opposition both to Louis VII and to his enemy Henry II of England, Raymond V sided with the anti-Pope, Pascal III, against Alexander III. This placed Raymond in the camp with the Holy Roman Emperor, Frederick II. Raymond was promptly excommunicated and all the cities of his domains, including Toulouse and its churches, were placed under papal interdict.[20]

What is more, relations between the citizens of Toulouse and the count had been strained since the beginning of his rule, and these relations deteriorated during the course of the twelfth century. As Mundy explains it, and as their letters to the king of France clearly show, the citizens of Toulouse often felt deserted by their count.[21] Despite the periodic threats of invasion by the Anglo-Aquitainian forces of Henry II, Raymond V was far more occupied throughout his rule with the much older foes of the house of Toulouse-Saint-Gilles, the Trencavels, viscounts of Carcassonne and Béziers, who had allied themselves with the house of Barcelona. Raymond spent much of the 1160s and 1170s in continual warfare in his eastern domains along the Rhône, fighting to retake the cities of Nîmes and Agde from the Trencavels. During these years he favoured his Provençal capital of Saint-Gilles as his residence and administrative centre, leaving the citizens of Toulouse to feel increasingly abandoned. In the absence of their prince, the Toulousans looked more and more to the king of France as their potential protector. Threatened once more in 1163 with invasion by the Anglo-Aquitainian forces of Henry II, the Common Council of Toulouse itself initiated an alliance with the French king and petitioned his help during the numerous crises of 1163–4.[22]

The series of letters from the Common Council of Toulouse to Louis VII that survives from the years 1163–5 reveals the considerable affection in which the Toulousans held their countess, Constance. The letters repeatedly affirm the love and devotion of the city to her and appeal to the king's concern for her welfare in pleading for his protection.[23] It is significant that her quality of royalty, while not given more than customary acknowledgement in Constance's own letters and charters,[24] was a matter of pride for the Toulousans themselves and later was stressed by her son, Count Raymond VI. In a letter of 1163 or 1164 from the

---

[18] Toulouse, AMT, Cartulaire du Bourg, AA 1, doc. 12, fos. 14^v–15^r.

[19] Toulouse, AMT, Cartulaire du Bourg, AA 1, doc. 72; *HGL*, vol. viii, col. 499. See also R. Limouzin-Lamothe, *La Commune de Toulouse* (Toulouse, 1932), 403–4.

[20] *HGL*, vol. vi, p. 19–20.

[21] Mundy, *Liberty*, 52.

[22] See 2 letters of 1163 or 1164 from the Common Council of Toulouse and the city of Toulouse to Louis VII, warning of the impending invasion by Henry II (*RHGF*, vol. xvi, no. 217, pp. 68–9, and no. 337, p. 109).

[23] In addition to the 2 letters cited above, n. 22, see ibid., vol. xvi, no. 218, p. 69 and nos. 392 and 393, p. 127.

[24] Luchaire maintains that daughters of kings were referred to as queens following a custom going back to Merovingian times (Luchaire, *Histoire des institutions*, i. 157). The example he gives, however, referring to Constance, countess of Saint-Gilles, as 'regina', is dated 1245. The only charter in which she is so referred to during her lifetime, an act of sale of 1160, is known only in a copy of 1526 (see below, n. 26).

Common Council of Toulouse to Louis VII, the Council refers to Constance as 'our Queen (*nostra Regina*), your sister'.[25] Constance herself, in the charters issued in her lifetime, does not use this term in reference to herself but gives her own titles most often as 'soror Regis Franciae et Comitissa S. Aegidij'.[26] Her son, Count Raymond VI, who had his own reasons for stressing his royal lineage, almost invariably referred to his mother as queen in giving his own titles: 'Comes Tholosae, dux Narbonae, marchio Provinciae, filius reginae Constantiae'.[27]

In 1165 Constance was permanently separated from Raymond V. Her complaints of her husband's marital infidelities and his lack of care and concern for her are chronicled in numerous letters which Constance wrote to her brother, Louis VII.[28] The king dispatched envoys to Toulouse to escort his sister back to his court at Paris, where she was recorded as being present as godmother at the baptism of the long-awaited son of Louis VII, the future Philip Augustus.[29] The ceremony took place on 22 August 1165 in the chapel of St Michael near the royal palace. Raymond subsequently repudiated Constance and in 1166 married Richilde, widow of the count of Provence, to better ensure his claim to that county.

The separation of Constance from Raymond V did not end the newly forged relationship between the citizens of Toulouse and the Crown. The personal and political bonds are evident in two letters of 1165 addressed by the Common Council of Toulouse to Louis VII. In the first, the citizens of the city and Bourg of Toulouse give over their countess into the hands of the king, with the hope that he will protect her, her children, and the city of Toulouse, and that he will return her to them as soon as possible, 'because it is in her and with her that we place all our joy and all our strength'.[30] The second letter opens with thanksgiving for the news of the long-desired birth of Louis's son: '. . . in all our land both the clergy and the people, in the same spirit, offer the praises due to Almighty God and offer prayers to Him that God will preserve him [Philip] to you and to us for a long time.'[31] The letter then goes on to say that the Common Council of Toulouse is dispatching four chaptermen to the royal court at Paris, to attend to all business relating to Toulouse.[32]

When the papal interdict placed on the count of Toulouse and all the churches of his domain

[25] 'Serenissimam dominam nostram Reginam sororem vestram' (*RHGF*, vol. xvi, no. 218, p. 69). Devic and Vaissète (*HGL*, vol. iii, p. 794) claim that Constance kept the title *de reine* or *regina* after her second marriage because her first husband, Eustache de Boulogne, had been associated with the throne by his father, King Stephen, though Eustache died without ever having reigned. The authors of the *RHGF* also suggest this (vol. xvi, no. 218, p. 69 n. c). It is the case that queens, once crowned, retained their quality of royalty until their death (see Marion F. Facinger, 'A Study of Medieval Queenship: Capetian France 987–1237', *Studies in Medieval and Renaissance History*, v (Lincoln, Neb., 1968), 3 and 43). Modern historians disagree, however, that Eustache was anointed and crowned by his father before he died in 1153 (see John T. Appleby, *The Troubled Reign of King Stephen* (New York, 1970), 177–90; H. A. Cronne, *The Reign of Stephen 1135–54* (London, 1970), 63–4). There is no evidence that Constance herself was crowned. Her quality of royalty, then, officially acknowledged in the later charters of her son, Raymond VI, more likely attached to her as sister of Louis VII.

[26] See e.g. a donation by Constance to the church of St Victor at Paris (André Du Chesne Tourangeau, *Histoire généalogique de la maison royale de Dreux* (Paris, 1631), 230); a donation of 1171 by Constance to the abbey of Montmartre (Robert de Lasteyrie (ed.), *Cartulaire général de Paris*, i.

(Paris, 1887), 414, no. 497) and one of 1173 to the Hospital Order of St John of Jerusalem (Tardif, *Inventaires* (as in n. 17 above), 319, no. 646). In a donation to the Templars of 1172 or 1173, however, Constance gives her title only as 'soror regis Francie L [odovici]' (De Lasteyrie, *Cartulaire de Paris*, i. 422, no. 507), while in another of 1180 to the Hospitallers of Jerusalem, her title is 'Dei gracia Sancti Egidii comitisse' alone (ibid. 470–1, no. 578). In 1160 Count Raymond V sold property at Fontcouverte to the provost and the bishop of Nîmes. The act of sale was ratified by his wife, who signed herself 'Ego constantia Regina' (Toulouse, AMT AA 10, doc. 7, 20). The surviving act, however, is a copy of 1526.

[27] See Alexandre Teulet, *Layettes du Trésor des Chartes* (Inventaires et documents publiés par ordre de l'Empereur), i. (Paris, 1863), 230a, no. 623 (c.1201), 238a, no. 653 (15 Dec. 1202), and 268b, no. 726 (Sept. 1204). But see ibid., 171b, no. 405 (1193), where he refers to himself as son of Constance, countess.

[28] *RHGF*, vol. xvi, p. 126, nos. 389, 390, and 391.

[29] *Vie de Louis le Gros par Suger suivie de l'histoire du roi Louis VII*, ed. A. Molinier (Paris, 1887), 177.

[30] *RHGF*, vol. xvi, p. 127, no. 392.

[31] Ibid., no. 393.

[32] Ibid.

precipitated another crisis, it was Louis VII who intervened with the pope on behalf of the Toulousans.[33] A bull of 12 March 1168 addressed by Pope Alexander III to Géraud, bishop of Toulouse, to the councilmen and to all the clergy and people of Toulouse, declares that the pope is lifting the interdict against their city alone, 'because of their devotion to the Roman Church and the singular affection that King Louis has for them, and the prayers of this prince'. They were to be permitted to celebrate the divine offices in all the churches of the city and the Bourg, but only in the absence of the count.[34]

Despite the hopes of the Toulousan people, Constance never returned to the city, though as late as 1174 Pope Alexander III was still hoping for a reconciliation between the countess and Raymond V, as revealed in a letter of that year to Henry, archbishop of Reims, brother of Constance and Louis VII.[35] Nevertheless, her son, the future Raymond VI, would have continued to represent for the citizens of Toulouse a concrete filial tie to the countess and to the monarchy.

The timing of Constance's departure from Toulouse and her return to Paris in the 1160s may have been significant in setting in motion the process by which proto-Gothic forms and iconography were transmitted to the priory of La Daurade. When the countess presided at the baptism of the future Philip Augustus in 1165, work on a monumental Virgin portal for the west façade of Notre-Dame in Paris was just nearing completion, as I have argued in my study *Pl. 212* of the portal.[36] The primary theme of the portal was the Incarnation of Christ as the fulfilment of Old Testament history and prophecy. This theme had been given profound expression in the earlier Incarnation portal of Notre-Dame at Chartres (c.1145–55) and it was to have a considerable twelfth-century life in Virgin portals at Bourges, Loches, Laon, and as late as Germigny-l'Exempt (c.1220). At Notre-Dame in Paris, as I have suggested, the imagery of veneration for the Virgin and Child may be linked to certain concepts of history and prophecy promoted in the ideology of the Capetian monarchy.

Plans might already have begun for the chapter house of La Daurade when Constance left Toulouse for Paris in 1165. She, for her part, could hardly have been ignorant of the enormous new cathedral of Notre-Dame going up across the Seine from the royal palace, in the ancient heart of Paris. The kind of relationship we have observed between the portal programme of La Daurade and the proto-Gothic portals of the north is one of close similarity in iconography but not in style. In its use of the monumental figure the programme is characterized by a somewhat uncomfortable juxtaposition of imported and indigenous forms, and it gives an unmistakable emphasis to the imagery of royalty that is totally foreign to Toulousan sculpture other than this portal. All of this suggests the kind of knowledge of proto-Gothic portal programmes that would have been conveyed by verbal instructions, rather than the importation of northern workmen. The link between Toulouse and Paris effected through the presence of Constance at her brother's court presents the most likely means by which the unfamiliar forms seen in the Daurade chapter house might have been transmitted to Toulouse. This transmission would most likely have come through a prelate close to the circle around Constance, perhaps

[33] Louis's words are these: 'The city of Toulouse belongs to our realm: we love it specially, as well as the citizens whom you have submitted to the interdict' (letter of 1166 from Louis VII to Pope Alexander III (*HGL*, vol. vi, pp. 20–1)).
[34] Guillaume de Catel, *Mémoires de l'histoire du Languedoc* (Toulouse, 1633), 886.
[35] *RHGF*, vol. xv, p. 942, no. 370.
[36] Kathryn Horste, '"A Child is Born": The Iconography of the Portail Ste-Anne', *Art Bulletin*, 69 (1987). See this article for a summary of current debates about the chronology of 12th-cent. construction at Notre-Dame and the date of the St Anne Portal.

responding to a request for help from the prior of La Daurade with written suggestions for a Virgin portal suitable to the aspirations of the Cluniac community at Toulouse. Such a prelate might have been the priest of Saint-Pierre-des-Cuisines (La Daurade's dependent priory), who was named as one of the four emissaries dispatched to the court of Louis VII in 1165 to represent the interests of Toulouse.[37]

The particular character of the chapter house programme at La Daurade that I have tried to illuminate here has the quality of allusion to just such an archetypal monument as the Incarnation portals at Chartres or Paris would surely have been for contemporaries. Traditional methods of iconographic study train us to focus on specific details of what is present in the image as the key to the meaning and the artistic recension of works of medieval religious art. Yet for certain classes of religious art, in particular art that was very public and very monumental, meaning that was not explicitly signalled in the work by the recognized signs and symbols of iconographic language may yet, to contemporary viewers, have been a very palpable presence in the image. This meaning would have been ignited by virtue of the image's resemblance to specific archetypal works prominent in the minds of travelled observers. This must have been especially true of the processional entrance ways of the great cathedrals and abbey churches visited on the itineraries of the travelling churchmen and rulers along with their substantial entourages. These monumental portals would have been famous in their day. This is why, for twelfth-century viewers especially, there can have been reverberations of Vézelay in the portal of the Incarnation on the west façade of Chartres cathedral, despite the apparent iconographic dissimilarity of their central images. The right lateral portal of the narthex of Vézelay depicts a monumental *Adoration of the Magi*, in company with the Veneration of the Shepherds, above a register of narrative vignettes that complete the story of the Incarnation. I have argued that the Adoration portal at Vézelay has a distinct resonance in the Incarnation portal at Chartres.[38] Of course, through the omission of the Magi in the tympanum, the canons at Chartres deliberately selected a more abstract mode of conveying the mystery of the Incarnation, and it was not the approach that was followed in most other Virgin portals of the twelfth century. Nevertheless, the choice of *formal* language at Chartres—the frontal Madonna enthroned at the centre of the tympanum, the frieze of complementary narrative scenes below—betrays the allusion to Vézelay, and this allusion must have been a deliberate one. For contemporary visitors to the cult shrine of the Virgin at Chartres, the image in the tympanum would have taken extra meaning and impact from the great pilgrimage portal in Burgundy.

Pl. 212 I have described a similar process at work in the tympanum of the St Anne Portal of Notre-Dame in Paris. There, as I believe, an original *Adoration of the Magi* was replaced in 1165 or shortly after by an altered image which still continues to carry the resonance of the more familiar and expected iconography of the three kings.[39] For numerous reasons, it is the St Anne Portal in Paris with which I most closely associate the sculptural ensemble from La Daurade. Most of these reasons have been mentioned already: the specific details of the enthroned Virgin and her iconography, the prominence of King David in the cycle, and an overall tone that is both sober and decidedly royal. The evocation of the three kings implied in the image of the

---

[37] *RHGF*, vol. xvi, p. 127, no. 393.
[38] Horste, 'Portail Ste-Anne', 198–200 and figs. 6 and 7.

[39] Ibid. 204.

enthroned Virgin at La Daurade, whether the Magi were explicitly portrayed on the jamb or not, may be another indication that this portal should be linked with the one in Paris.

The second quarter of the twelfth century had seen a marked transformation in the monumental sculpture of Toulouse. A new kind of vivid narrative art in three dimensions had been created, along with new uses for the monumental figure within the cloister. This fundamental transformation occurred when Toulousan sculptors with a developed three-dimensional sense were exposed to the Romanesque pictorial arts of western and central France, whose roots were deep in the eleventh century.

In contrast, for Toulousan sculptors of the third quarter of the twelfth century, the encounter with ideas from the royal domain was time-specific and of quite restricted impact. The conjugal tie between the house of Toulouse-Saint-Gilles and the Capetian monarchy introduced a whole new dimension into the politics of Toulouse during the rule of Raymond V. Nevertheless, artistic ideas from the distant proto-Gothic north were received as a foreign importation, producing a resonance in the chapter house portal of La Daurade but igniting no creative processes within Toulousan monumental sculpture of the later twelfth century.

CONCLUSION

The abbey of Moissac, led by a succession of ambitious and reform-minded abbots—Durandus, Hunaldus, and Aquilinus—was the agent of the early and rapid expansion of Cluniac monasticism into south-west France, which began in the mid-eleventh century.[40] An essential factor in the success of this expansion was the support given to the order of Cluny by the counts of Toulouse within their domains and in the reform of the Toulousan Church. The early date at which the historiated cloister appeared in the Midi and the particular uses that were defined for sculpture in the early examples of this region are phenomena in which the abbey of Moissac played a decisive role.

As we observed in the Introduction, analytical study of cloister art is just beginning. But already scholars have asked whether it is legitimate to speak of a Cluniac art of the cloister. Is it fair to describe the cloisters of Moissac and La Daurade, in particular, as typically Cluniac?[41] We have seen that the sculptural programmes of Moissac and La Daurade communicated the reforming ideals of Cluniac monasticism, along with the beliefs of an older Cluniac spirituality, as embodied in the liturgy of the order. These included a devotion to Psalmody and the cult of the saints, as well as a view of the Divine Order that placed an emphasis on Judgement and the last things.

[40] The extent of the influence of Moissac can be judged by the list of abbeys, monasteries, churches, and other possessions submitted to its rule during the period of Moissac's initial expansion into the Quercy, the Rouergue, Languedoc, the Conserans, Béarn, the Bigorre, Gascony, and the Agenais between about 1048 and 1115. Some of these were former possessions of Moissac that were returned to the abbey by their lay lords. Ernest Rupin has detailed this expansion (*L'Abbaye et les cloîtres de Moissac* (Paris 1897), 53–62 and 67–70). During his sojourn at Moissac following the Council of Clermont in 1097, Pope Urban II issued a bull addressed to the bishops of Cahors, Agen, Toulouse, and Lectoure in which he exhorted these bishops to render to Moissac some 40 churches situated in their diocese and ordered them to excommunicate any detractors who resisted this order. The pope confirmed Moissac in its possession of a great number of abbeys and lesser monasteries in the Quercy, Languedoc, Rouergue, Gascony, Agenais, and elsewhere in the Midi and commanded that the abbots of these houses should be elected according to the will of the abbot of Moissac.

[41] Neil Stratford has raised this question in Lydwine Saulnier and Neil Stratford, *La Sculpture oubliée de Vézelay*, Bibliothèque de la société française d'archéologie, 17 (Geneva, 1984), 171 n. 47, as Ilene Forsyth has in her review of the state of research on the cloister ('The Monumental Arts of the Romanesque Period: Recent Research; the Romanesque Cloister', paper delivered at the international symposium, 'The Study of Medieval Art in the Last Half Century: A Symposium on Romanesque and Gothic Art', 21–2 Oct. 1988, New York, the Metropolitan Museum).

None of these themes can be considered the exclusive property of Cluny, however, since similar ones appear in cloisters not associated with the order, and they appear on the interior of many monastic and collegiate churches of the Romanesque period. In truth, nothing that can be defined as an official Cluniac cloister programme has been shown to exist among surviving Romanesque ensembles. It has repeatedly been observed in the debates about cloister imagery that the cloister of Cluny III itself was not historiated. Only foliate motifs and beading are found on the surviving fragments of capitals and archivolts.[42] Attributed by Conant to the abbacy of Pons (1109–22), the cloister has recently been redated by Stratford to the second quarter of the twelfth century, under Peter the Venerable.[43] The later date seems more appropriate for the highly decorative and deeply undercut capitals, which reflect developments in the late Romanesque of Burgundy that are also visible at Avallon and on the outer portals of the narthex of Charlieu.

It should be stressed, however, that the fragments from Cluny attest only to the appearance of the twelfth-century cloister that was standing at the time of the abbey's destruction. Of the earlier cloister constructed in the 1040s under Abbot Odilo (993/4–1048) nothing survives.[44] Odilo's biographer, Jotsald, tells us that the cloister, constructed near the end of Odilo's life, had columns of marble and was wonderfully decorated.[45] This is a tantalizing description, but it does not tell us whether the cloister decoration included figurative sculpture. If Odilo's cloister survived until the abbacy of Peter the Venerable, as now seems likely, then it is not impossible that St Bernard's famous diatribe against the presence of distracting monsters and animals in the cloister could have been aimed, at least in part, at Cluny's own programme of decoration.[46] It has been suggested, in fact, that the absence of figurative imagery in the later cloister of Cluny III may represent a defensive response on the part of Cluniac monasticism to the more puritan attitudes of the Cistercians.[47]

Other cloisters of Burgundy for which we have evidence, none dating from earlier than the second quarter of the twelfth century, also display a decoration limited to foliate and abstract ornamental forms. For Vézelay, the other important Cluniac cloister of the region, only a few fragments survive, but these carry decorative carving of the greatest elegance and richness, indicative of a date in the 1130s or 1140s.[48] Stratford has pointed to the cloister of Auxerre cathedral as the only standing cloister from which the structure and decoration of those at Cluny and Vézelay may be extrapolated.[49] Its capitals and column shafts, alternately single

[42] For illustrations of some of the fragments attributed to the cloister, see Conant, *Cluny*, pl. xcviii, figs. 224–6. All the fragments will eventually be published as part of a project begun in 1986 under the auspices of the CNRS. See the announcement in Neil Stratford, 'A Cluny Capital in Hartford (Connecticut)', *Gesta*, 27 (1988), n. 39. Conrad Rudolph has also discussed the implications of the absence of figurative imagery in the cloister of Cluny III in 'Bernard of Clairvaux's *Apologia* as a Description of Cluny, and the Controversy over Monastic Art', *Gesta*, 27 (1988), 125–32.

[43] Stratford, *Vézelay*, 169.

[44] See Conant, *Cluny*, 65–7, for the plan of the main cloister and the texts which mention it. As Conant reminds us, besides the main cloister, 2 other cloisters were constructed at Cluny in the 11th cent., the cloister of the chapel of Notre-Dame and the cloister of the novices, both destroyed completely.

[45] *PL* 142, col. 908A–B.

[46] Rudolph does not consider the possibility that the surviving fragments originate from a later cloister, not from the cloister that was standing at the time Bernard wrote his text

(about 1125). See Rudolph, 'Bernard of Clairvaux's *Apologia*', *passim*.

[47] Forsyth, 'Monumental Arts' (as in n. 41 above).

[48] See Stratford, *Vézelay*, cat. 289 (fig. 237), cat. 293 (figs. 239–41), and cat. 344 (fig. 269). See also the beautiful drawing by Viollet-le-Duc of cat. 293, a foliate capital (Paris, Archives des monuments historiques, 68 N 165, Viollet-le-Duc collection, p. 112ᵛ). It should be noted that 3 fragments now in the Fogg Art Museum at Cambridge were said by the dealer Joseph Brummer to have originated from Vézelay. All 3 can be related to yet another fragment with a rosette, uncovered in the diggings to the north of the nave and still at Vézelay. Seidel has tentatively suggested the Romanesque cloister at Vézelay as an origin for the 3 fragments in America. Notably, 2 of them carry figurative subject-matter. See Walter Cahn and Linda Seidel, *Romanesque Sculpture in American Collections*, i. *New England Museums*, Publications of the International Centre of Medieval Art, 1 (New York, 1979), 145–8.

[49] Stratford, *Vézelay*, 170.

and double, carry an elaborate decoration consisting of foliate ornament, spiral fluting, and beading.

For Romanesque Burgundy, then, and most notably for the abbey of Cluny itself, we are lacking evidence for cloister design and decoration during the early decades of sculptural development between about 1075 and 1125. The situation is different for south-west France. Here important sculptural ensembles from both Cluniac and non-Cluniac cloisters dating from between about 1096 and the 1140s are known from Moissac, La Daurade, Saint-Étienne, and Saint-Sernin in Toulouse, from Saint-Pons-de-Thomières in the Hérault, and, nearby at Narbonne, from the cloister of the abbey of Saint-Paul. Given the smallness of the sample, it would be unjustified to designate Moissac, the earliest of these, as a 'typical' Cluniac example. Rather, the cloisters of Moissac and the first building campaign at La Daurade represent the Cluniac cloister of the eleventh-century reform and the ascendancy of the order in the region of Toulouse—the period of Cluny triumphant. As we concluded in Chapter 3, the design of the Moissac cloister was apparently original to south-west France. Its outstanding features were its figured supports and extensive historiation in which narrative themes were given a privileged role. This prototypical solution would determine the development of cloister decoration in the region for several decades.

In Toulouse the chapter of cathedral canons was reformed, as we saw in Chapter 1, according to Cluniac ideals invested in the charter of reform by Bishop Isarnus and St Hugh of Cluny. The inscribed figures of founding saints in marble on its piers, along with its sensitive group of narrative and hagiographic capitals and its college of Apostles, could hardly constitute a clearer acknowledgement of the just uses of figured sculpture in the cloister according to the Moissac model, even if we are not altogether certain how these elements were situated within the whole.

The cloister of Saint-Sernin, on the other hand, stands apart from the others in Toulouse. Its canons had spent their early history resisting subjection to Moissac and the Cluniac order. The absence of thematic programming at Saint-Sernin seems deliberately intended to distinguish the cloistered spaces of the canons from those of the Moissac model, characterized by their heavy iconographic loading. The capitals of Saint-Sernin, of cubic shape and carved with repetitive images of lions, birds, and fantastic beasts, were probably paired back-to-back to form twin supports.[50] This design is very different from the true double capitals used at Moissac, La Daurade, and Saint-Étienne. There is no record of any pier decoration in the cloister of Saint-Sernin, only the sober portrait of the head of the order that once looked into the south walk—the effigy of St Augustine dictating his rule.

Decoration of the destroyed cloister of Saint-Pons-de-Thomières in the Hérault, about 52 kms. from Narbonne, was highly influenced by the iconography and style of the second workshop of La Daurade in Toulouse. The abbey of Saint-Pons had been founded in 936 by the count of Toulouse, Raymond Pons II. It was one of the ancient Benedictine abbeys of France that had maintained its independence during the period of the eleventh-century reforms, but it had important ties to Cluny. Abbot Pons (1109–22), successor to St Hugh as abbot of Cluny, had been a monk of Saint-Pons-de-Thomières.[51] Through the Toulousan workshop of La Daurade, the Saint-Pons sculpture is linked to the tradition of narrative and

---

[50] See above, Ch. 3 n. 122.
[51] Pons was of noble Languedocian lineage, a son of Pierre, the count of Melgueil, and had been pledged to the abbey of Saint-Pons in 1082 (*HGL*, vol. iii, p. 419).

hagiographic imagery that belongs to the Moissac model of cloister decoration. Its series of capitals, now dispersed among museums in Europe and America, included at least two with scenes from the Martyrdom of St Pons (*St Pons Thrown to the Bears* and his *Beheading*),[52] as well as another with the *Martyrdom of St Andrew* (Montpellier, Musée de la société archéologique). The series also included *Daniel in the Lions' Den* (London, Victoria and Albert Museum), an Old Testament theme that appears twice in the cloister of Moissac and which we identified as one of the most ubiquitous subjects in Romanesque capital decoration associated with the Moissac workshop. The tradition of narrative themes was elaborated at Saint-Pons in capitals of the *Entombment/Holy Women at the Tomb* (Paris, Musée du Louvre) and the *Journey* and *Supper at Emmaus/Noli me tangere* (Cambridge, Mass., Fogg Art Museum). The latter two were clearly inspired by specific narrative capitals of the Passion series from La Daurade, in the drapery style, the lively and exaggerated movements of the figures, and their narrative engagement with one another.[53]

Two double capitals attributed to the cloister of the abbey of Saint-Paul de Narbonne also show the influence of the Toulousan cloister of La Daurade in their figure style and narrative animation, as well as their interest in the post-Resurrection appearances of Christ. Now in the Musée des Augustins in Toulouse, they are probably the work of the same sculptors who carved the group from nearby Saint-Pons-de-Thomières. They depict, on one capital, the *Journey* and *Supper at Emmaus*, the *Noli me tangere*, and a scene of *Prophets and Evangelists* (Mesplé 263) and, on the other, *Scenes from the Life of St Nicholas* (Mesplé 264).[54] They are joined in the collections of the Toulouse museum by a monumental marble pier from the cloister of the cathedral of Saint-Just at Narbonne (Mesplé 261). The pier is carved with an enthroned Virgin and Child, two male martyrs, and a seated figure with crown and sceptre whose identity has not been satisfactorily explained (the figure has been called God the Father but it has the appearance of a secular ruler). The iconography of this decorated pier is reminiscent of the early description of a marble pier relief in the cloister of the cathedral at Toulouse, referring to a seated figure holding a violin and a sceptre. Together with the historiated capitals depicting hagiographic and Gospel themes, it seems clear that cloister sculpture at Narbonne was influenced in both style and iconography by the cloister programmes of the Toulousan capital. Seidel has already pointed to the occupation of Narbonne by the count of Toulouse, Alphonse-Jourdain, between 1134 and 1143 as a likely opportunity for the penetration of Toulousan artistic modes into the region.[55] This accords well with the chronology of the Toulousan workshops which, we have concluded, were active

---

[52] J. Sahuc, *L'Art roman à Saint-Pons-de-Thomières* (Montpellier, 1908); Kathryn Horste, 'Romanesque Sculpture in American Collections. XX. Ohio and Michigan', *Gesta*, 21 (1982), 130–2.

[53] Cf. the *Entombment* and *Emmaus* capitals from La Daurade, as well as the scenes of *The Last Supper*, *The Holy Women*, and the *Noli me tangere*. For the relationship between these capitals from Saint-Pons and the second workshop at La Daurade, see Linda Seidel in Providence, Rhode Island, *The Renaissance of the Twelfth Century*, ed. Stephen K. Scher (Providence, 1969), 90–1 and Horste, 'Romanesque Sculpture' (as in n. 52 above), 130–2.

[54] These 2 capitals have been discussed by Seidel, 'Romanesque Capitals from the Vicinity of Narbonne', *Gesta*, 11

(1972), 35–6. She has associated with them several small capitals with secular subject-matter now in the Musée Lamourgier at Narbonne. The twin capitals in the Musée des Augustins were associated with the abbey of Saint-Paul by Du Mège in his catalogue of 1835 (214, no. 546). They have been discussed by Henri Rachou, 'Un chapiteau roman du Musée des Augustins', *Bulletin de la société archéologique du Midi de la France*, 3rd ser., 3 (1938), 38–45; id., 'Sur un chapiteau du musée des Augustins', ibid. 223–6. In 1093 Pope Urban II had placed the abbey of Saint-Paul de Narbonne in the hands of a chapter of regular canons headed by an elected abbot (*HGL*, vol. iii, pp. 399 and 464, and vol. v, cols. 725–6).

[55] Seidel in *Renaissance of the Twelfth Century* (as in n. 53 above), 91.

in the cloister of La Daurade about 1120–30, while the programme at Saint-Étienne was probably completed about 1125–35.

The programmes of richly historiated capitals, the privileged role of narrative subject-matter, and the use of monumental figures on load-bearing members of the framework all point to the derivation of this important group of southern cloisters from the Moissac model. They may be distinguished from other nearby regional groups, most notably the Roussillonnais cloisters of marble that appear to have been carved by itinerant workshops active at Cuxa, Serrabone, and Espira de l'Agly, among other sites closer to the Pyrenees.[56] None of the cloisters in this Roussillonnais group was Cluniac. Serrabone and Espira de l'Agly were among a half-dozen Augustinian priories founded in the region in the late eleventh and early twelfth centuries, while Cuxa was one of the oldest Benedictine foundations in Roussillon.[57] With few exceptions the capital sculpture of these cloisters, technically brilliant and later by a decade or more than the Toulousan-Narbonnais group, is limited to repetitive images of rampant lions, eagles with wings deployed, or the occasional grinning mask.

The contrast between the Roussillonnais group and the historiated cloisters of the Midi illustrates that the connection between religious affiliation and cloister programming remains far from clear-cut. As in other aspects of Romanesque building, regional tradition and practice and the particular capabilities of locally trained workshops had a strong determining influence on the outcome of sculptural programmes. The uniformity of Romanesque sculptural decoration in Roussillon under the dominance of the Cuxa-Serrabone style could not more clearly illustrate this powerful regionalism, in cloister decoration as well as in sculptural production generally during the entire second half of the twelfth century.

It is interesting to note, on the other hand, that at least one sculptor of this Roussillonnais tradition was asked to participate at Saint-Pons-de-Thomières in the decoration of the cloister there. We have already seen that this was a sophisticated decorative programme with ties to the historiated cloister designs of Toulouse and Moissac. It is not without significance that, in this context, the Roussillonnais sculptor was prompted to produce figurative capitals of more challenging subject-matter than is found in the standard productions of the Cuxa-Serrabone style. The work of this sculptor is seen in capitals of Saint-Pons depicting the *Crucifixion of Christ* and the *Virgin and Child in Majesty* (Toulouse, Musée des Augustins, M. 264) and the *Traditio clavium* with Evangelist symbols (Paris, Musée du Louvre).[58]

In conclusion, there is no archeological evidence to support the notion that a Cluniac cloister programme existed in any official sense. At the same time, everything we have concluded in the foregoing chapters indicates that a distinctive type of sculptured cloister *was* created within the region of Cluny's southern expansion. What distinguishes this group is not the presence of hybrid monsters and other *exotica* of the type condemned by the Cistercians. Such fantastic imagery appears in every context in Romanesque art. Rather it is precisely the privileged role

[56] Marcel Durliat, *La Sculpture romane en Roussillon*, 4 vols. (Perpignan, 1952); Horste, 'Romanesque Sculpture' (as in n. 52 above), 125–30.

[57] See Pierre Ponsich, 'Chronologie et typologie des cloîtres romans roussillonnais', *Les Cahiers de Saint-Michel de Cuxa*, 7 (1976), 75–97.

[58] Four different sculptural styles can be differentiated among the surviving fragments from Saint-Pons-de-Thomières. The sculptor trained in Roussillon can be identified in at least 9 capitals among those catalogued by Sahuc. For analysis of the various workshops which participated in the decoration of the Saint-Pons cloister, see especially Seidel in *Renaissance of the Twelfth Century* (as in n. 53 above), 85–92, and Horste, 'Romanesque Sculpture' (as in n. 52 above), 130–2.

accorded narrative and hagiographic imagery that gives a special character to the early twelfth-century cloisters of south-west France. The particular success of this type in the region was due to the early monastic leadership of Moissac and the influence of its workshop from the beginnings of cloister design in the region. The cloister of Moissac itself and those of communities under its influence at Toulouse and elsewhere in Languedoc together exhibit a particular meridional expression of Cluniac monastic ideals in Romanesque art.

INVENTORY OF SCULPTURE FROM
THE CLOISTER AND CONVENTUAL BUILDINGS OF
LA DAURADE

Throughout this publication I have numbered the sculptures of La Daurade according to the catalogue of Paul Mesplé, *Toulouse, musée des Augustins, les sculptures romanes*, Inventaire des collections publiques françaises, 5 (Paris, 1961). The inventory numbers used by the Musée des Augustins are those assigned in 1912 by Henri Rachou, *Catalogue des collections de sculptures et d'épigraphie du musée de Toulouse* (Toulouse, 1912). The inventory below gives both Mesplé and Rachou numbers. It also signals those pieces which can be identified in the earliest of the catalogues by Du Mège, that of 1818/19, *Notice des tableaux, statues, bustes, bas-reliefs et antiquités composant le musée de Toulouse* (Toulouse, n.d.).

CLOISTER

CAPITALS

M. 102	Double capital for applied columns: *Musicians of King David* H. 33 L. 52 W. 25 cm. Cat. 1912 no. 473
M. 104	Double capital: *Daniel in the Lions' Den/The Accusers of Daniel Devoured* H. 36 L. 52 W. 40 cm. Cat. 1818/19 no. 134; Cat. 1912 no. 469
M. 107	Single capital: *The Feast of Herod* and *Death of John the Baptist* H. 35 L. 52 W. 41 cm. Cat. 1818/19 no. 151; Cat. 1912 no. 471
M. 110	Single capital: *Transfiguration/Incredulity of Thomas* H. 36 L. 52 W. 41 cm. Cat. 1818/19 no. 149; Cat. 1912 no. 472
Inv. 76–13–3 and M. 113	Double capital for applied columns: *Christ and the Canaanite Woman* Inv. 76–13–3: H. 34 L. 35 W. 25 cm. M. 113: H. 35 L. 25 W. 26 cm. Cat. 1912 no. 498
M. 114.	Double capital: *Entry into Jerusalem/Arrest of Christ* H. 35 L. 52 W. 40 cm. Cat. 1818/19 no. 143; Cat. 1912 nos. 474 and 499
M. 116	Single capital: *Last Judgement with Weighing of the Souls* and *Blessed Making their Way to Paradise* H. 36 L. 52 W. 40 cm. Cat. 1818/19 no. 145; Cat. 1912 no. 476
M. 119	Single capital: *Last Judgement with Resurrection of the Dead* H. 36 L. 52 W. 40 cm. Cat. 1818/19 no. 136; Cat. 1912 no. 475
M. 122	Single capital: *Washing of the Feet* H. 35 L. 52 W. 41 cm. Cat. 1912 no. 457

M. 125	Single capital: *Last Supper* H. 36 L. 52 W. 41 cm. Cat. 1912 no. 458
M. 128	Single capital: *Christ in Gethsemane* (Christ Praying/Christ Speaking to his Disciples/Christ Confronting the Soldiers/the Disciples Fleeing) H. 35 L. 50 W. 40 cm. Cat. 1912 no. 459
M. 131	Triple capital: *Arrest of Christ/Flagellation/Christ before Pilate/The Way to Calvary* H. 35 L. 52 W. 52 cm. Cat. 1818/19 no. 139; Cat. 1912 no. 460
M. 134	Single capital: *Deposition/Entombment* H. 36 L. 52 W. 40 cm. Cat. 1818/19 no. 140; Cat. 1912 no. 461
M. 137	Single capital: *Resurrection/Holy Women at the Tomb* H. 35 L. 52 W. 42 cm. Cat. 1912 no. 463
M. 140	Single capital: *Descent into Limbo/Blessed Led to Paradise* H. 35 L. 52 W. 40 cm. Cat. 1818/19 no. 135; Cat. 1912 no. 462
M. 143	Double capital: *Apostles at the Empty Tomb/Noli me tangere* H. 34 L. 51 W. 39 cm. Cat. 1818/19 no. 137; Cat. 1912 no. 464
M. 145	Double capital: *Way to Emmaus/Supper at Emmaus* H. 37 L. 52 W. 39 cm. Cat. 1912 no. 465
M. 148	Double capital: *Incredulity of Thomas/Traditio legis* H. 38 L. 52 W. 39 cm. Cat. 1818/19 no. 165 (on evidence of cats. 1828 no. 300 and 1835 no. 541); Cat. 1912 no. 466
M. 151	Triple capital: *Ascension* H. 37 L. 52 W. 39 cm. Cat. 1912 no. 467
M. 154	Double capital: *Pentecost* H. 36 L. 52 W. 39 cm. Cat. 1912 no. 468
M. 157	Double capital: *Four Rivers of Paradise* H. 36 L. 52 W. 38 cm. Cat. 1818/19 no. 144; Cat. 1912 no. 477
M. 160	Single capital: *Lions in Vine Stems* H. 35 L. 52 W. 40 cm. Cat. 1818/19 no. 162; Cat. 1912 no. 478
M. 163	Double capital: *Vine Interlace with Leaf Spirals and Cones* H. 35 L. 52 W. 40 cm. Cat. 1912 no. 480
M. 166	Double capital: *Fantastic Birds* H. 34 L. 52 W. 40 cm. Cat. 1818/19 no. 146; Cat. 1912 no. 479
M. 169	Double capital: *Vine Rinceaux with Cones* H. 36 L. 52 W. 39 cm. Cat. 1912 no. 396
M. 170	Double capital: *Vine Interlace with Leaf Spirals and Cones* H. 35 L. 52 W. 40 cm. Cat. 1912 no. 397

Inventory

M. 171	Single capital: *Vine Interlace with Tripartite Cones* H. 36 L. 52 W. 40 cm. Cat. 1912 no. 398

IMPOSTS

M. 105	'La Toilette du Prince' H. 16 L. 61 W. 50 cm. Cat. 1818/19 no. 167; Cat. 1912 no. 390
M. 108	*Affronted Beasts* H. 16 L. 60 W. 49 cm. Cat. 1912 no. 397
M. 111	*Scenes of Domestic Life* H. 15 L. 61 W. 50 cm. Cat. 1818/19 no. 166
M. 115	Reindeer and Saddled Horses H. 16 L. 61 W. 50 cm. Cat. 1912 no. 459
M. 117	*Vine Rinceaux Enclosing Human Masks* H. 16 L. 61 W. 50 cm. Cat. 1912 no. 398
M. 120	*Birds of Prey* H. 15 L. 60 W. 49 cm. Cat. 1912 no. 396
M. 193 and Inv. 76–13–9	Upright palmettes framed by half-palmettes M. 193: H. 16 L. 49 W. 37 cm. Inv. 76–13–9: H. 16 L. 50 W. 23.5 cm.
M. 194 and Inv. 76–13–6	*Fantastic Birds with Serpents' Tails* M. 194: H. 16 L. 50 W. 42 cm. Inv. 76–13–6: H. 16 L. 23.5 W. 26.5 cm.
M. 195 and Inv. 76–13–10	Paired upright palmettes enclosed in vine medallions; denticulated moulding M. 195: H. 15 L. 50 W. 44 cm. Inv. 76–13–10: H. 15 L. 49 W. 21.5 cm.
M. 123.	Ribbon H. 13 L. 61 W. 50 cm. Cat. 1912 no. 457
M. 126	Cones in running vine H. 14 L. 61 W. 50 cm. Cat. 1912 no. 464
M. 129	Vine stem with tripartite leaf shoots H. 13 L. 61 W. 50 cm. Cat. 1912 no. 472
M. 132	Running vine stem with curled, three-lobed palmettes H. 13 L. 61 W. 61 cm. Cat. 1912 no. 460
M. 135	Vine medallions enclosing upright, paired palmettes H. 13 L. 61 W. 50 cm. Cat. 1912 no. 461
M. 137	Intersecting circles H. 12 L. 60 W. 50 cm. Cat. 1912 no. 463
M. 141	Running vine stem with curled leaves enclosing cones H. 13 L. 60 W. 50 cm. Cat. 1912 no. 478
M. 146	Running vine with flowers of the arum plant H. 13 L. 61 W. 59 cm. Cat. 1912 no. 465

M. 149	Vine medallions enclosing upright palmettes
	H. 14 L. 61 W. 50 cm.
	Cat. 1912 no. 466
M. 152	Crows in vine stems; intersecting circles
	H. 37 L. 52 W. 39 cm.
	Cat. 1912 no. 467
M. 155	Running vine stem with five-lobed palmettes
	H. 13 L. 61 W. 50 cm.
	Cat. 1912 no. 468
M. 158	Palmettes in rinceau
	H. 13 L. 61 W. 48 cm.
	Cat. 1912 no. 477
M. 161	Basket weave
	H. 14 L. 59 W. 50 cm.
	Cat. 1912 no. 476
M. 164	Interlace
	H. 13 L. 59 W. 49 cm.
	Cat. 1912 no. 480
M. 167	Interlocking circles and semi-circles
	H. 14 L. 61 W. 49 cm.
	Cat. 1912 no. 479
M. 200 and M. 201	Impost with intersecting circles and semi-circles
	M. 200: H. 21 L. 90 W. 60 cm.
	M. 201: H. 21 L. 68 W. 29 cm.
	Cat. 1912 nos. 454A and 454F
M. 202 and M. 203	Impost with crows in vine circlets
	M. 202: H. 20 L. 90 W. 36 cm.
	M. 203: H. 21 L. 90 W. 54 cm.
	Cat. 1912 nos. 454B and 454C
M. 204 and M. 205	Impost with pearled straps; nude figures caught in arum rinceau
	M. 204: H. 21 L. 90 W. 35 cm.
	M. 205: H. 21 L. 90 W. 46.5 cm.
	Cat. 1912 nos. 454D and 454E

BASES

M. 43	Base for single column
	H. 22 L. 37 W. 37 cm.
	Cat. 1912 no. 395
M. 103	Base for double columns
	H. 23 L. 46 W. 30 cm.
	Cat. 1912 no. 473
M. 109	Base for single column
	H. 22 L. 36.5 W. 36.5 cm.
	Cat. 1912 no. 471
M. 112	Base for single column
	H. 22 L. 36.5 W. 36.5 cm.
	Cat. 1912 no. 472
M. 118	Base for single column
	H. 22 L. 37 W. 37 cm.
	Cat. 1912 no. 476
M. 121	Base for single column
	H. 22 L. 36 W. 36 cm.
	Cat. 1912 no. 475
M. 124	Base for single column
	H. 21 L. 36 W. 36 cm.
	Cat. 1912 no. 457

M. 127	Base for single column H. 17 L. 37 W. 37 cm. Cat. 1912 no. 458
M. 130	Fragmentary base for single column H. 18 L. 40 W. 30 cm. Cat. 1912 no. 459
M. 133	Base for triple columns H. 22 L. 48 W. 46 cm. Cat. 1912 no. 460
M. 136	Base for single column H. 21 L. 37 W. 37 cm. Cat. 1912 no. 461
M. 139	Base for single column H. 22 L. 37.5 W. 38 cm. Cat. 1912 no. 463
M. 142	Base for single column H. 21 L. 37 W. 37 cm. Cat. 1912 no. 474
M. 144	Base for double columns H. 23 L. 48 W. 31 cm. Cat. 1912 no. 464
M. 147	Base for double columns H. 22 L. 49 W. 30 cm. Cat. 1912 no. 465
M. 150	Base for double columns H. 20 L. 48 W. 31 cm. Cat. 1912 no. 466
M. 153	Base for triple columns H. 24 L. 50 W. 43 cm. Cat. 1912 no. 467
M. 156	Base for double columns H. 22 L. 49 W. 31 cm. Cat. 1912 no. 468
M. 159	Base for double columns H. 22 L. 48.5 W. 29.5 cm. Cat. 1912 no. 477
M. 162	Base for single column H. 21 L. 36 W. 35 cm. Cat. 1912 no. 478
M. 165	Base for double columns H. 20 L. 49 W. 31 cm. Cat. 1912 no. 480
M. 177	Base for double columns H. 20 L. 48 W. 30 cm. Cat. 1912 no. 470
M. 179	Base for double columns H. 23 L. 49 W. 31 cm. Cat. 1912 no. 484
M. 182	Base for double columns H. 21 L. 49 W. 29 cm. Cat. 1912 no. 483

CHAPTER HOUSE

RELIEFS

M. 66   *Crowned Female* (Sheba?)
               H. 112 W. 42.5 D. 15.5 cm.
               Cat. 1818/19 no. 118; Cat. 1912 no. 452C

M. 68   *King* (Solomon?)
               H. 108.7 W. 42.8 D. 17 cm.
               Cat. 1818/19 no. 120; Cat. 1912 no. 452G

M. 80   *King David Tuning his Harp*
               H. 112.7 W. 47 D. 21.7 cm.
               Cat. 1818/19 no. 113; Cat. 1912 no. 452B

M. 82   *Bearded Prophet with Unfurled Scroll*
               H. 113.5 W. 42.5 D. 16.5 cm.
               Cat. 1818/19 no. 119 (on evidence of Cat. 1828 no. 254); Cat. 1912 no.
               452D

M. 83   *Virgin and Child Enthroned*
               H. 113 W. 47 D. 24 cm.
               Cat. 1818/19 no. 123; Cat. 1912 no. 452A

M. 94   *Male in Ribbed Hat Pointing to Open Book*
               H. 109.5 W. 42.2 D. 16 cm.
               Cat. 1818/19 no. 122; Cat. 1912 no. 452F

M. 97   *Bearded Male with Unfurled Scroll*
               H. 112 W. 42.4 D. 15.3 cm.
               Cat. 1818/19 no. 121; Cat. 1912 no. 452E

COLUMN STATUES

M. 71   *Nimbed Male with Unfurled Scroll* (St Paul?)
               H. 111 W. 27 D. 23 cm.
               Cat. 1818/19 no. 115; Cat. 1912 no. 452I

M. 74   *Prophet with Unfurled Scroll*
               H. 109.5 W. 28 D. 22.5 cm.
               Cat. 1912 no. 452M

M. 77   *Prophet with Unfurled Scroll*
               H. 112 W. 27 D. 22 cm.
               Cat. 1912 no. 452K

M. 85   *Bearded Prophet with Unfurled Scroll*
               H. 112 W. 30 D. 25 cm.
               Cat. 1912 no. 452K

M. 88   *King*
               H. 112 W. 30 D. 24 cm.
               Cat. 1818/19 no. 116; Cat. 1912 no. 452J

M. 91   *King with Ampula*
               H. 109.8 W. 28 D. 19.3 cm.
               Cat. 1818/19 no. 114; Cat. 1912 no. 452H

M. 100   Lower portion of a column statue
               H. 32 W. 22.7 D. 23 cm.
               Inv. 59–7–4. Found 1958 on north side of choir of church of the Augustins,
               serving as rubble (see Mesplé, *Musée des Augustins: sculptures romanes*, no.
               100)

CAPITALS

M. 67   Pilaster capital
               H. 28.5 W. 51.8 D. 43 cm.
               Cat. 1912 no. 435E

M. 69	Pilaster capital
	H. 28.4 W. 51 D. 34.7 cm.
	Cat. 1818/19 no. 126; Cat. 1912 no. 453A
M. 81	Pilaster capital
	H. 29.1 W. 51.8 D. 42.7 cm.
	Cat. 1912 no. 453C
M. 84	Pilaster capital
	H. 31.4 W. 58 D. 26.5 cm.
	Cat. 1818/19 no. 125; Cat. 1912 no. 453B
M. 95	Pilaster capital
	H. 29 W. 53 D. 43 cm.
	Cat. 1912 no. 453E
M. 98	Pilaster capital
	H. 29 W. 52 D. 28 cm.
	Cat. 1912 no. 453E
M. 72	Capital for recessed column
	H. 29 W. 26.5 D. 26.5 cm.
	Cat. 1912 no. 490
M. 75	Capital for recessed column
	H. 29 W. 26 D. 26 cm.
	Cat. 1818/19 no. 153; Cat. 1912 no. 485
M. 78	Capital for recessed column
	H. 29 W. 26.5 D. 26.5 cm.
	Cat. 1912 no. 492
M. 86	Capital for recessed column
	H. 29 W. 26.5 D. 26.5 cm.
	Cat. 1818/19 no. 152; Cat. 1912 no. 486
M. 89	Capital for recessed column
	H. 29 W. 27 D. 26 cm.
	Cat. 1912 no. 488
M. 92	Capital for recessed column
	H. 29 W. 26.5 D. 26.5 cm.
	Cat. 1818/19 no. 148; Cat. 1912 no. 489

BASES

M. 70	Base for relief slab
	H. 16 W. 49 D. 19.5 cm.
M. 96	Fragmentary base for relief slab
	H. 16 W 24.4 D. 19.5 cm.
	Cat. 1912 no. 452F
M. 99	Base for relief slab
	H. 15.3 W. 50 D. 22.3 cm.
	Cat. 1912 no. 452E
M. 73	Base for recessed column
	H. 16.3 W. 27.2 D. 26.5 cm.
	Cat. 1912 no. 452I
M. 76	Base for recessed column
	H. 16.3 W. 27 D. 27 cm.
	Cat. 1912 no. 452M
M. 79	Base for recessed column
	H. 18 W. 27 D. 27 cm.
	Cat. 1912 no. 452L
M. 87	Base for recessed column
	H. 17 W. 27 D. 28 cm.
	Cat. 1912 no. 452K

M. 90	Base for recessed column
	H. 16 W. 27.2 D. 27.2 cm.
	Cat. 1912 no. 452J
M. 93	Base for recessed column
	H. 17.5 W. 26 D. 27 cm.
	Cat. 1912 no. 452H
M. 101	Fragmentary column base
	H. 11.5 W. 27 D. 18 cm.
	Inv. 59–7–5. Found 1958 on north side of choir of church of the Augustins, serving as rubble
Inv. 76–13–21	Base for recessed column
	H. 16.5 W. 26.5 D. 26.5 cm.

UNLOCALIZED PIECES

CAPITALS

M. 44	Engaged foliate capital for recessed column
	H. 32 W. 34 D. 27 cm.
	Cat. 1912 no. 399A
M. 45	Engaged foliate capital for recessed column
	H. 31.5 W. 33 D. 26 cm.
	Cat. 1912 no. 399B
M. 46	Capital for recessed column with lions in vine stems
	H. 31.5 W. 29 D. 29 cm.
	Cat. 1912 no. 399C
M. 48	Engaged capital for recessed column with masks in vine interlaces
	H. 32 W. 39 D. 27 cm.
	Cat. 1912 no. 400
M. 50	Engaged foliate capital for recessed column
	H. 31.5 W. 31.5 D. 37.5 cm.
	Cat. 1912 no. 401
M. 172	Double capital for applied columns: *Diminutive Men and Animals in Vine Interlace*
	H. 31.2 L. 54 W. 28.6 cm.
	Cat. 1818/19 no. 131; Cat. 1912 no. 481
M. 174	Double capital for applied columns: *Vine Interlace with Diminutive Animals and Humans in Combat*
	H. 31.1 L. 55 W. 26.7 cm.
	Cat. 1912 no. 482
M. 176	Fragmentary double capital: *Oarsmen in a Boat ('Les Barques')*
	H. 36 L. 46 W. 31 cm.
	Cat. 1818/19 no. 141; Cat. 1912 no. 470
M. 178	Double capital: *Bear Hunt/Hunt of the Siren and Centaur*
	H. 28 L. 53.8 W. 31 cm.
	Cat. 1818/19 no. 130; Cat. 1912 no. 484
M. 180	Double capital: *The Story of Job*
	H. 28.2 L. 52.3 W. 29.5 cm.
	Cat. 1818/19 no. 129; Cat. 1912 no. 483
M. 183	Fragment of double capital
	H. 31 L. 30 W. 28 cm.
	Cat. 1912 no. 496
M. 184	Capital for recessed column: *Woman Combing a Child's Hair*
	H. 51 L. 27.5 W. 27 cm.
	Cat. 1818/19 no. 161; Cat. 1912 no. 487

M. 185	Foliate capital for recessed column
	H. 29 L. 26.5 W. 27 cm.
	Cat. 1912 no. 491A
M. 186	Foliate capital for recessed column
	H. 29.5 L. 27 W. 27 cm.
	Cat. 1912 no. 491B
M. 187	Foliate capital for recessed column
	H. 28 L. 27 W. 27 cm.
	Cat. 1912 no. 494
M. 188	Capital for recessed column: *Sculptor Carving a Capital*
	H. 31 L. 25 W. 27.5 cm.
	Cat. 1818/19 no. 156; Cat. 1912 no. 493
M. 189	Capital for recessed column: *Figure with a Bull*
	H. 32 L. 27 W. 28 cm.
	Cat. 1912 no. 495
M. 190	Capital for recessed column: *Boar Hunt*
	H. 30 L. 26 W. 27 cm.
	Cat. 1912 no. 497
M. 191	Capital for recessed column: *Bird in Vine Rinceau*
	H. 28.5 L. 26.5 W. 25 cm.
	Cat. 1912 no. 616
Inv. 76–13–4	Fragment of a column capital
	H. 27 L. 27 D. 16 cm.

IMPOSTS

M. 181	Medallions enclosing birds and tripartite foliate sprays
	H. 12 L. 62 W. 44 cm.
	Cat. 1912 no. 483
M. 192	Impost fragment: Running vine with curled, four-lobed palmette
	H. 16 L. 33 W. 21 cm.
	Cat. 1912 no. 388

CATALOGUES OF THE MUSÉE DES AUGUSTINS

1794/5   *Catalogue des tableaux et autres monumens des arts, formant le museum provisoire établi à Toulouse* (Toulouse, an III (1794–5)).

1806   Lucas, J.-P., *Catalogue critique et historique des tableaux, et autres monumens des arts du musée de Toulouse* (5th edn., Toulouse, 1806).

1813   [Du Mège, Alexandre], *Notice des tableaux, statues, bustes, dessins, etc., composant le musée de Toulouse* (Toulouse, 1813).

1818/19   —— *Notice des tableaux, statues, bustes, bas-reliefs et antiquités, composant le musée de Toulouse* (Toulouse, n.d. [1818/19]).

1828   Du Mège, Alexandre, *Notice des monuments antiques et des objets de sculpture moderne conservés dans le musée de Toulouse* (Toulouse, n.d. [1828]).

1835   —— *Description du musée des antiques de Toulouse* (Toulouse, 1835).

1844   —— 'Description Du Musée des Antiques de Toulouse', in manuscript; November 1844 (Toulouse, Archives municipales de Toulouse 5 S 219 (formerly 5 S 157)).

1864   Roschach, Ernest, *Musées de Toulouse: antiquités, musée des Augustins, objets d'art, musée Saint-Raymond* (Toulouse, n.d. [1864]).

1912   Rachou, Henri, *Catalogue des collections de sculpture et d'épigraphie du musée de Toulouse* (Toulouse, 1912).

1961   Mesplé, Paul, *Toulouse, musée des Augustins: les sculptures romanes*, Inventaire des collections publiques françaises, 5 (Paris, 1961).

SELECTIVE BIBLIOGRAPHY

ABRIAL-ARIBERT, FRANÇOISE, 'Le Cloître de Saint-Sernin de Toulouse', *Actes du 96ᵉ Congrès national des sociétés savantes, Toulouse, 1971*, ii (Toulouse, 1976), 157–74.

AMANIEUX, FRANÇOISE, BROUILLETTE, DIANE, and ERLANDE-BRANDENBURG, ALAIN, 'Senlis: un moment de la sculpture gothique', *La Sauvegarde de Senlis*, 45–6 (1977), 3–55.

ARMI, C. EDSON, *Masons and Sculptors in Romanesque Burgundy: The New Aesthetic of Cluny III*, 2 vols. (University Park, Pa., 1983).

BERNARD, AUGUSTE, and BRUEL, ALEXANDRE, *Recueil des chartes de l'abbaye de Cluny: collection de documents inédits de France*, 6 vols. (Paris, 1870–1903).

BOYER, G., 'Une hypothèse sur l'origine de la Daurade', *Annales du Midi*, 68 (1956), 47–51.

BYNUM, CAROLINE WALKER, *Docere Verbo et Exemplo: An Aspect of Twelfth-Century Spirituality*, Harvard Theological Review, Harvard Theological Studies, 31 (Cambridge, Mass., 1979).

—— *Jesus as Mother: Studies in the Spirituality of the High Middle Ages* (Berkeley, Calif., 1982).

CABANOT, Abbé JEAN, 'Le Décor sculpté de la basilique Saint-Sernin de Toulouse. Sixième colloque international de la société française d'archéologie (Toulouse, 22–3 octobre 1971', *Bulletin monumental*, 132 (1974), 99–145.

—— *Les Débuts de la sculpture romane dans le sud-ouest de la France* (Paris, 1987).

CATEL, GUILLAUME DE, *Histoire des comtes de Tolose* (Toulouse, 1623).

—— *Mémoires de l'histoire du Languedoc curieusement et fidèlement recueillis de divers auteurs* (Toulouse, 1633).

CAZES, D., CARBONELL-LAMOTHE, Y., and PRADALIER-SCHLUMBERGER, M., 'Recherches sur la cathédrale Saint-Étienne', *Mémoires de la société archéologique du Midi de la France*, 43 (1979–80), 7–165.

CHABANEL, JEAN DE, *De l'estat et police de l'église Nostre Dame dite la Daurade a Tolose. . .* (2nd edn., Toulouse, 1623).

—— *De l'antiquité de l'église Nostre Dame dite la Daurade a Tolose, et autres antiquitez de la ville* (2nd edn., Toulouse, 1625).

CHALANDES, JULES, *Histoire des rues de Toulouse* (3 pts., Toulouse, 1919–29; repr. (3 pts. in 1), Marseilles, 1982).

CONANT, KENNETH JOHN, *Cluny: les églises et la maison du chef d'ordre* (Mâcon, 1968).

CONSTABLE, GILES, 'Opposition to Pilgrimage in the Middle Ages', *Mélanges Gérard Fransen*, i (*Studia Gratiana*, 19) (1976), 125–46.

—— 'Monachisme et pèlerinage au moyen âge', *Revue historique*, 258 (1977), 3–27.

—— SMITH, B. (eds. and trans.), *Libellus de diversis ordinibus et professionibus qui sunt in aecclesia* (Oxford, 1972).

COUDERC, CAMILLE, 'Note sur un missel à l'usage de l'église de la Daurade', *Annales du Midi*, 14 (1902), 541–50.

COWDREY, H. E. J., *The Cluniacs and Gregorian Reform* (Oxford, 1970).

CROZET, RENÉ, 'Le Voyage d'Urbain II et ses négociations avec le clergé de France (1095–1096)', *Revue historique*, 179 (1937), 271–310.

Deeds of the Franks and the Other Pilgrims to Jerusalem, The (Gesta francorum et aliorum Hierosolimitanorum), ed. Rosalind Hill (London, 1962).

DEGERT, Abbé, 'Démolitions et reconstructions à la Daurade au dix-septième siècle', *Bulletin de la société archéologique du Midi de la France*, 2nd ser., 32–6 (3 Nov. 1903–3 July 1906), meeting of 28 Mar. 1905, 296–8.

DELARUELLE, ÉTIENNE, 'Toulouse, capitale wisigothique et son rempart', *Annales du Midi*, 67 (1955), 205–22.

DELARUELLE, ÉTIENNE, 'Daurade' in *Dictionnaire d'histoire et de géographie ecclésiastique*, ed. Alfred Baudrillart *et al.*, xiv (Paris, 1960), cols. 97–107.

—— 'The Crusading Idea in Cluniac Literature of the Eleventh Century', in Noreen Hunt (ed.), *Cluniac Monasticism in the Central Middle Ages* (London, 1971), 191–216 (trans. from 'L'Idée de croisade dans la littérature clunisienne du xiᵉ siècle et l'abbaye de Moissac', *Annales du Midi*, 75 (1963), 419–39).

DEREINE, CHARLES, 'La "Vita apostolica" dans l'ordre canonial du ixᵉ au xiᵉ siècle', *Revue Mabillon*, 51 (1961), 47–53.

DEVIC, Dom CLAUDE, and VAISSÈTE, Dom JOSEPH, *Histoire générale de Languedoc*, 2nd edn., cont. Ernest Roschach, 15 vols. (Toulouse, 1872–93).

DOUAIS, CÉLESTIN, *Cartulaire de l'abbaye de Saint-Sernin de Toulouse (844–1200)* (Paris, 1887).

DUFOUR, JEAN, *La Bibliothèque et le scriptorium de Moissac*, Centre de recherches d'histoire et de philologie, 5; Hautes études médiévales et modernes, 15 (Geneva, 1972).

DU MÈGE, ALEXANDRE, 'Le cloître de la Daurade', *Mémoires de la société archéologique du Midi de la France*, 2 (1834–5), 241–51.

—— 'Mémoire sur le cloître de Saint-Étienne de Toulouse', *Histoire et mémoires de l'académie royale des sciences, inscriptions et belles-lettres de Toulouse*, 4 (1834–6), 250–76.

—— 'Mémoire sur les monumens romains attribués, dans Toulouse, à la reine aux pieds d'oie, ou à *Regina pè d'Auca*', *Mémoires de l'académie royale des sciences, inscriptions et belles-lettres de Toulouse*, 3 (1847), 165–203.

DURLIAT, MARCEL, 'Aux origines de la sculpture romane languedocienne: les chapiteaux et le portail de Saint-Michel de Lescure', *Cahiers de civilisation médiévale*, 5 (1962), 411–18.

—— 'La Construction de Saint-Sernin de Toulouse au xiᵉ siècle', *Bulletin monumental*, 121 (1963), 151–70.

—— 'Les Données historiques relatives à la construction de Saint-Sernin de Toulouse', *Homenaje a Jaime Vicens Vives*, i (Barcelona, 1965), 235–41.

—— 'La Date des plus anciens chapiteaux de la Daurade à Toulouse', *Estudios dedicados a Duran y Sanpere: cuadernos de arqueologia e historia de la ciudad de Barcelona* (Barcelona, 1967), 195–202.

—— 'Les Origines de la sculpture romane à Toulouse et à Moissac', *Cahiers de civilisation médiévale*, 12 (1969), 349–64.

—— 'The Pilgrimage Roads Revisited?', *Bulletin monumental*, 129 (1971), 113–20.

—— 'Alexandre Du Mège ou les mythes archéologiques à Toulouse dans le premier tiers du xixᵉ siècle', *Revue de l'art*, 23 (1974), 30–41.

—— 'L'Annonciation des Cordeliers au musée des Augustins', *Études de civilisation médiévale (ix–xiiᵉ siècle): mélanges offerts à Edmond-René Labande* (Poitiers, 1974), 265–70.

—— 'Le Portail de la salle capitulaire de la Daurade à Toulouse', *Bulletin monumental*, 132 (1974), 201–11.

—— 'Les Cloîtres historiés dans la France méridionale à l'époque romane', *Les Cahiers de Saint-Michel de Cuxa*, 7 (1976), 61–74.

—— *Haut-Languedoc roman* (La Pierre-qui-vire, 1978).

—— 'La Dernière Sculpture romane méridionale: une mutation avortée', *La France de Philippe Auguste: le temps des mutations. Actes du colloque international organisé par le CNRS, Paris 29 sept.–4 oct. 1980* (Paris, 1982), 939–53.

—— *Saint-Sernin de Toulouse* (Toulouse, 1986).

FLACH, JACQUES, *Les Origines de l'ancienne France, xᵉ et xiᵉ siècles*, iv. *Les Nationalités régionales: leurs rapports avec la couronne de France* (Paris, 1917).

FONS, VICTOR, 'Notre-Dame la Daurade', *La Semaine catholique de Toulouse*, 2 (1862), 379–81, 387–8, 395–7, 407–8, 415–17; 3 (1863), 445–7, 455–7.

FORSYTH, ILENE HAERING, 'Magi and Majesty: A Study of Romanesque Sculpture and Liturgical Drama', *Art Bulletin*, 50 (1968), 215–22.

—— *The Throne of Wisdom: Wood Sculptures of the Madonna in Romanesque France* (Princeton, 1972).

—— 'The *Vita Apostolica* and Romanesque Sculpture: Some Preliminary Observations', *Gesta*, 25 (1986), 75–82.

FORSYTH, WILLIAM, review of Marie Lafargue, *Les Chapiteaux du cloître de Notre-Dame la Daurade*, in *American Journal of Archaeology*, 49 (1945), 391–3.

FULCHER OF CHARTRES, *Chronicle of the First Crusade (Fulcheri Carnotensis historia Hierosolymitana)*, trans. Martha Evelyn McGinty (Philadelphia, 1941).

GABORIT-CHOPIN, DANIELLE, *La Décoration des manuscrits à Saint-Martial de Limoges et en Limousin du ixᵉ au xiiᵉ siècle*, Mémoires et documents publiés par la société de l'école des chartes, 17 (Paris, 1969).

Bibliography

GAILLARD, GEORGES, *Études d'art roman*, Publications de la Sorbonne, ser. Études, 3 (Paris, 1972).

GALABERT, FRANÇOIS, 'Un diplôme de Charles le Chauve en faveur des églises de Toulouse et sa confirmation par Louis VII', *Le Moyen Age: revue d'histoire et de philologie*, 27 (1914), 185–214.

Gallia christiana in provincias ecclesiasticas distributa . . . , ed. Dom Denis de Saint-Marthe and Dom Paul Piolin, 16 vols. (Paris, 1856–99).

GARDNER, STEPHEN, 'The Role of Central Planning in English Chapter House Design', Ph.D. thesis, Columbia University (1976).

GERKE, FRIEDRICH, *Der Tischaltar des Bernard Gilduin in Saint-Sernin in Toulouse*, Akademie der Wissenschaften und der Literatur in Mainz, Abhandlungen der geistes- und sozialwissenschaftlichen Klasse, 1958, 8 (Wiesbaden, 1958).

GERMAIN, Dom MICHEL, *Le Monasticon gallicanum*, ed. M. Peigné-Delacourt (Paris, 1871; repr. Brussels, 1967).

GERSON, PAULA L., (ed.), *Abbot Suger and Saint-Denis: A Symposium* (New York, 1986).

HAERING [Forsyth], ILENE, 'Narrative Order in Romanesque Sculpture', MA thesis, Columbia University (1955).

HAMILTON, BERNARD, 'Rebuilding Zion: The Holy Places of Jerusalem in the Twelfth Century', *Studies in Church History*, 14 (London, 1977); repr. in *Monastic Reform, Catharism and the Crusades, 900–1300*, Collected Studies, 97 (London, 1979), no. 11, 106–16.

HEARN, M. F., *Romanesque Sculpture: The Revival of Monumental Stone Sculpture in the Eleventh and Twelfth Centuries* (Ithaca, NY, 1981).

HILL, JOHN H., and HILL, LAURITA L., *Raymond IV, Count of Toulouse* (Syracuse, NY, 1962).

HORSTE, KATHRYN, 'An Addition to the Documentation on the Façade of the Chapterhouse at La Daurade in Toulouse', *Art Bulletin*, 59 (1977), 618–21.

—— 'The Capitals of the Second Workshop from the Romanesque Cloister of La Daurade, Toulouse', Ph.D. thesis, University of Michigan (1978).

—— 'The Passion Series from La Daurade and Problems of Narrative Composition in the Cloister Capital', *Gesta*, 21 (1982), 31–62.

—— 'A Romanesque Capital from the Region of Toulouse and Moissac', *Bulletin of the University of Michigan Museum of Art*, 7 (1984–5), 26–46.

—— 'A New Plan of the Cloister and Rampart of Saint-Étienne, Toulouse', *Journal of the Society of Architectural Historians*, 45 (1986), 5–19.

—— ' "A Child is Born": The Iconography of the Portail Ste-Anne at Paris', *Art Bulletin*, 69 (1987), 187–210.

HOURLIER, Dom JACQUES, 'L'Entrée de Moissac dans l'ordre de Cluny', *Annales du Midi*, 75 (1963), 353–63.

—— 'La Spiritualité à Moissac d'après la sculpture', *Annales du Midi*, 75 (1963), 395–404.

HUNT, NOREEN, *Cluny under Saint Hugh, 1049–1109* (Notre-Dame, Ind., 1968).

—— (ed.), *Cluniac Monasticism in the Central Middle Ages* (London, 1971).

KESSLER, HERBERT L., and SIMPSON, MARIANNA SHREVE (eds.), *Pictorial Narrative in Antiquity and the Middle Ages*, National Gallery of Art, Washington, Studies in the History of Art, 16, Center for Advanced Studies in the Visual Arts Symposium Series IV (Washington, DC, 1985).

KLINE, RUTH CAPELLE, 'The Decorated Imposts of the Cloister of Moissac', Ph.D. thesis, University of California at Los Angeles (1977).

LABROUSSE, MICHEL, *Toulouse antique des origines à l'établissement des wisigoths*, Bibliothèque des écoles françaises d'Athènes et de Rome, 212 (Paris, 1968).

LAFARGUE, MARIE, 'Les Sculptures du premier atelier de la Daurade et les chapiteaux du cloître de Moissac', *Bulletin monumental*, 93 (1938), 195–216.

—— *Les Chapiteaux du cloître de Notre-Dame la Daurade* (Paris, 1940).

LAGRÈZE-FOSSAT, A., *Études historiques sur Moissac*, 3 vols. (Paris, 1870–4).

LAMBERT, ÉLIE, *Abbayes et cathédrales du sud-ouest* (Toulouse, 1958).

LECLERCQ, JEAN, 'La Crise du monachisme aux XIe et XIIe siècles', *Bulletino dell'istituto storico italiano per il medio evo e archivio Muratoriano*, 70 (1958), 19–41.

—— 'Monachisme et pérégrination du IXe au XIIe siècle', *Studia monastica*, 3 (1961), 33–52.

—— VANDENBROUCKE, FRANÇOIS, and BOUYER, LOUIS, *A History of Christian Spirituality*, ii. *The Spirituality of the Middle Ages* (New York, 1982; trans. of *La Spiritualité du moyen âge*, 1961).

LÉONARD, ÉMILE (ed.), *Catalogue des actes des comtes de Toulouse*, iii. *Raymond V (1149–1194)* (Paris, 1932).

Bibliography

LIMOUZIN-LAMOTHE, R., *La Commune de Toulouse et les sources de son histoire, 1120–1249*, Bibliothèque méridionale, 2nd ser., 26 (Toulouse, 1932).

LOT, FERDINAND, and FAWTIER, ROBERT (eds.), *Histoire des institutions françaises au moyen âge*, i. *Institutions seigneuriales (les droits du roi exercés par les grands vassaux)* (Paris, 1957); ii. *Institutions royales* (Paris, 1958).

LUCHAIRE, ACHILLE, *Histoire des institutions monarchiques de la France sous les premiers Capétiens (987–1180)* (2nd edn., Paris, 1891).

LYMAN, THOMAS, 'Notes on the Porte Miègeville Capitals and the Construction of Saint-Sernin in Toulouse', *Art Bulletin*, 49 (1967), 25–36.

—— 'The Pilgrimage Roads Revisited', *Gesta*, 8 (1969), 30–44.

—— 'The Sculpture Programme of the Porte des Comtes Master at Saint-Sernin in Toulouse', *Journal of the Warburg and Courtauld Institutes*, 34 (1971), 12–39.

—— 'Portails, portiques, paradis: rapports iconologiques dans le Midi', *Les Cahiers de Saint-Michel de Cuxa*, 7 (1976), 35–43.

—— 'Terminology, Typology, Taxonomy: An Approach to the Study of Architectural Sculpture of the Romanesque Period', *Gazette des beaux-arts*, 88 (1976), 223–7.

—— 'Raymond Gairard and Romanesque Building Campaigns at Saint-Sernin in Toulouse', *Journal of the Society of Architectural Historians*, 37 (1978), 71–91.

—— 'La Table d'autel de Bernard Gilduin et son ambiance originelle', *Les Cahiers de Saint-Michel de Cuxa*, 13 (1982), 53–73.

MAGNOU, ELISABETH, *L'introduction de la réforme grégorienne à Toulouse (fin XIᵉ–début XIIᵉ siècle)*, Cahiers de l'association Marc Bloch de Toulouse: études d'histoire méridionale, 3 (Toulouse, 1958).

—— 'Le Chapitre de la cathédrale Saint-Étienne de Toulouse (fin XIᵉ–début XIIᵉ siècle)', *La Vita commune del clero nei secoli XI e XII. Atti della settimana di studio, Mendola, settembre 1959*, Pubblicazioni dell'università cattolica del S. Cuore, ser. 3. Miscellanea del centro di studi Medioevali, 3 (Milan, 1962).

MÂLE, ÉMILE, 'Les Chapiteaux romans du musée de Toulouse et l'école toulousaine du XIIᵉ siècle', *Revue archéologique*, 3rd ser., 20 (1892), 28–35 and 176–97.

—— *Religious Art in France: The Twelfth Century: A Study of the Origins of Medieval Iconography*, ed. Harry Bober, Bollingen Series, 90/1 (Princeton, 1978) (trans. of *L'Art religieux du XIIᵉᵐᵉ siècle en France: étude sur l'origine de l'iconographie du moyen âge* (Paris, 1922)).

MARTIN, DOM, *La Religion des Gaulois, tirée des plus pures sources de l'antiquité* (Paris, 1727).

MESPLÉ, PAUL, 'Recherches sur l'ancienne église de la Daurade', *Mémoires de la société archéologique du Midi de la France*, 31 (1965), 41–56.

MILHAU, DENIS, 'Les Cloîtres romans de Toulouse: l'art des chapiteaux', *Archeologia*, 77 (1974), 50–9.

—— 'Découvertes archéologiques au monastère des ermites de saint Augustin', *Mémoires de la société archéologique du Midi de la France*, 41 (1977), 39–88.

—— 'Haute-Garonne: découvertes archéologiques aux Augustins de Toulouse', *Bulletin monumental*, 135 (1977), 157–8.

Moissac et l'occident au XIᵉ siècle: actes du colloque international de Moissac, 3–5 mai 1963 (Toulouse, 1964; also published as special issue of *Annales du Midi*, 75 (1963)).

MONTÉGUT, JEAN FRANÇOIS DE, 'Recherches sur les antiquités de Toulouse', *Mémoires de l'académie des sciences, inscriptions et belles-lettres de Toulouse*, 1st ser., 1 (1782), 65–110.

—— 'Mémoire sur un tombeau qui étoit dans l'ancienne église de la Daurade, et sur une épitaphe gravée sur un marbre attaché au mur de cette église', *Mémoires de l'académie des sciences de Toulouse*, 2 (1784), 100–14.

MORALEJO, SERAFÍN, 'La Fachada de la sala capitular de la Daurade de Toulouse: datos iconograficos para su reconstruccion', *Anuario de estudios medievales*, 13 (1983), 179–204.

—— 'De Sant Esteve de Tolosa a la Daurade: notes sobre l'escultura del claustre romanic de Santa Maria de Solsona', *Quaderns d'estudis medievals*, 23–4 (1988), 104–19.

MORGHEN, RAFFAELLO, 'Riforma monastica e spiritualità cluniacense', in *Spiritualità cluniacense, Convegni del centro di studi sulla spiritualità medievale, 1958* (Todi, 1960), 33–56.

MUNDY, JOHN HINE, *Liberty and Political Power in Toulouse, 1050–1230* (New York, 1954).

—— 'Charity and Social Work in Toulouse, 1100–1250, Part I', *Traditio*, 22 (1966), 203–87.

PACAUT, MARCEL, *Louis VII et son royaume* (Paris, 1964).

PALOL, PEDRO DE, and HIRMER, MAX, *L'Art en Espagne du royaume wisigoth à la fin de l'époque romane* (Paris, 1967).

Bibliography

Patrologiae cursus completus. Series latina, ed. J.-P. Migne, 221 vols. (Paris, 1844–65).

PORTER, ARTHUR KINGSLEY, *Romanesque Sculpture of the Pilgrimage Roads*, 10 vols. (Boston, 1923).

—— 'Spain or Toulouse? and Other Questions', *Art Bulletin*, 7 (1924), 3–25.

PRESSOUYRE, LÉON, 'Les Apôtres de la salle capitulaire de Saint-Étienne de Toulouse', *Bulletin monumental*, 127 (1969), 241–2.

—— 'St. Bernard to St. Francis: Monastic Ideals and Iconographic Programs in the Cloister', *Gesta*, 12 (1973), 71–92.

Providence, Rhode Island, The Rhode Island School of Design, *The Renaissance of the Twelfth Century*, exh. cat. by Stephen K. Scher *et al.* (Providence, 1969).

QUARRÉ, PIERRE, 'Le Portail de Mauriac et la porche d'Ydes: leurs rapports avec l'art du Languedoc et du Limousin', *Bulletin monumental*, 98 (1939), 129–51.

RACHOU, HENRI, *Pierres romanes toulousaines: Saint-Étienne, la Daurade et Saint-Sernin* (Paris, 1934).

Recueil des historiens des Gaules et de la France, ed. M. Bouquet *et al.*, 24 vols. (Paris, 1738–1904).

REY, RAYMOND, 'Essai d'explication iconographique de l'ancienne porte capitulaire de la Daurade', *Bulletin de la société archéologique du Midi de la France*, 3rd ser. (1934–7), meeting of 19 Feb. 1935, 34–40.

—— *La Sculpture romane languedocienne* (Toulouse, 1936).

—— 'Le Sanctuaire paléochrétien de la Daurade à Toulouse et ses origines orientales', *Annales du Midi*, 61 (1949), 249–73.

—— *L'Art des cloîtres romans: étude iconographique* (Toulouse, n.d. [1955]).

RUDOLPH, CONRAD, 'Bernard of Clairvaux's *Apologia* as a Description of Cluny, and the Controversy over Monastic Art', *Gesta*, 27 (1988), 125–32.

RUPIN, ERNEST, *L'Abbaye et les cloîtres de Moissac* (Paris, 1897).

SAUERLÄNDER, WILLIBALD, 'Chefs-d'œuvre romans des musées de Province: Zu einer Austellung im Louvre', *Kunstchronik*, 11 (1958), 33–41.

—— 'Das sechste internationale Colloquium der "Société française d'archéologie": die Skulpturen von Saint-Sernin in Toulouse', *Kunstchronik*, 24 (1971), 341–7.

—— *Gothic Sculpture in France, 1140–1270* (New York, 1972) (trans. of *Gotische Skulptur in Frankreich 1140–1270* (Munich, 1970)).

SCHAPIRO, MEYER, *Romanesque Art* (Selected Papers; New York, 1977).

SCHILLER, GERTRUD, *Iconography of Christian Art*, i and ii (Greenwich, Conn., 1971) (trans. of *Ikonographie der christlichen Kunst* (Gütersloh, 1966)).

SCHMITZ, PHILIBERT, 'La Liturgie à Cluny', in *Spiritualità cluniacense. Convegni del centro di studi sulla spiritualità medievale, 1958* (Todi, 1960), 85–99.

SEIDEL, LINDA, *Romanesque Sculpture from the Cathedral of Saint-Étienne, Toulouse*. Outstanding Dissertations in the Fine Arts (New York, 1977); Ph.D. thesis, Harvard University (1964).

—— 'A Romantic Forgery: The Romanesque "Portal" of Saint-Étienne in Toulouse', *Art Bulletin*, 50 (1968), 33–44.

—— 'Romanesque Capitals from the Vicinity of Narbonne', *Gesta*, 11 (1972), 34–45.

—— 'Romanesque Sculpture in American Collections. X. The Fogg Art Museum, ii', *Gesta*, 11 (1972), 57–63.

—— 'The Façade of the Chapter House at La Daurade in Toulouse', *Art Bulletin*, 55 (1973), 328–33.

—— 'Installation as Inspiration: The Passion Cycle from La Daurade', *Gesta*, 25 (1986), 83–92.

SHEPPARD, CARL D., Jun., 'An Earlier Dating for the Transept of Saint-Sernin, Toulouse', *Speculum*, 35 (1960), 584–90.

STODDARD, WHITNEY, *The Façade of Saint-Gilles du Gard: Its Influence on French Sculpture* (Middletown, Conn., 1973).

—— *Sculptors of the West Portals of Chartres Cathedral: Their Origins in Romanesque and their Role in Chartrain Sculpture* (incorporating *The West Portals of Saint-Denis and Chartres*, Cambridge, Mass., 1952) (New York, 1987).

SWARZENSKI, GEORG, *Die Salzburger Malerei von den ersten Anfängen bis zur Blutezeit des romanischen Stils* (Stuttgart, 1969).

Toulouse, Archives départementales de la Haute-Garonne, *Exposition Alexandre Du Mège, inspecteur des antiquités de la Haute-Garonne, 1780–1862*, exh. cat. by Marcel Durliat (Toulouse, 1972).

—— Archives municipales, *Répertoire numérique des archives: Ancien Régime-Revolution*, ed. François Galabert and Odon de Saint-Blanquat, pt. 1, ser. AA-FF (Toulouse, 1961).

—— Musée des Augustins, *Les Grandes Étapes de la sculpture romane toulousaine*, exh. cat. by Denis Milhau *et al.* (Toulouse, 1971).

—— *Musée des Augustins, 1969–1984. Nouvelles acquisitions*, exh. cat. by Daniel Cazes, Denis Milhau, *et al.* (Toulouse, 1984).

VALOUS, GUY DE, *Le Monachisme clunisien des origines au xve siècle* (Archives de la France monastique, 39), i. *L'Abbaye de Cluny: les monastères clunisiens* (Paris, 1935).

VAN ENGEN, JOHN, 'The "Crisis of Cenobitism" Reconsidered: Benedictine Monasticism in the Years 1050–1150', *Speculum*, 61 (1986), 269–304.

VICAIRE, MARIE-HUMBERT, *L'Imitation des apôtres: moines, chanoines, mendiants (IVe–XIIIe siècles)* (Paris, 1963).

VIDAL, MARGUERITE, MAURY, JEAN, and PORCHER, JEAN, *Quercy roman* (La Pierre-qui-vire, 1969).

Ville de Toulouse: inventaire des archives communales antérieures à 1790, ed. Ernest Roschach, vol. 1, ser. AA, nos. 1–60 (Toulouse, 1891).

Vita comune del clero nei secoli XI e XII (La). Atti della settimana di studio, Mendola, settembre 1959, Pubblicazioni dell'universita cattolica del S. Cuore, Ser. 3. Miscellanea del centro di studi medioevali, 3, 2 vols. (Milan, 1962).

WETTSTEIN, JANINE, *La Fresque romane: la route de Saint-Jacques, de Tours à Léon*, Etudes comparatives II; Bibliothèque de la société française d'archéologie, 9 (Paris, 1978).

WILLIAMS, JOHN, 'San Isidoro in Leòn. Evidence for a New History', *Art Bulletin*, 55 (1973), 170–84.

—— ' "Spain or Toulouse?" A Half Century Later: Observations on the Chronology of Santiago de Compostela', *Actas del XXIII. congreso internacional de historia del arte: Espana entre el Mediterraneo y el Atlantico* (Granada, 1973), sect. 2, 557–67.

WOLFF, PHILIPPE, 'Civitas et burgus: l'exemple de Toulouse', *Die Stadt in der europäischen Geschichte: Festschrift Edith Ennen* (Bonn, 1972), 200–9.

—— *et al.*, *Histoire de Toulouse*, ser. Histoire des villes, under the direction of Philippe Wolff, (Toulouse, 1974).

INDEX

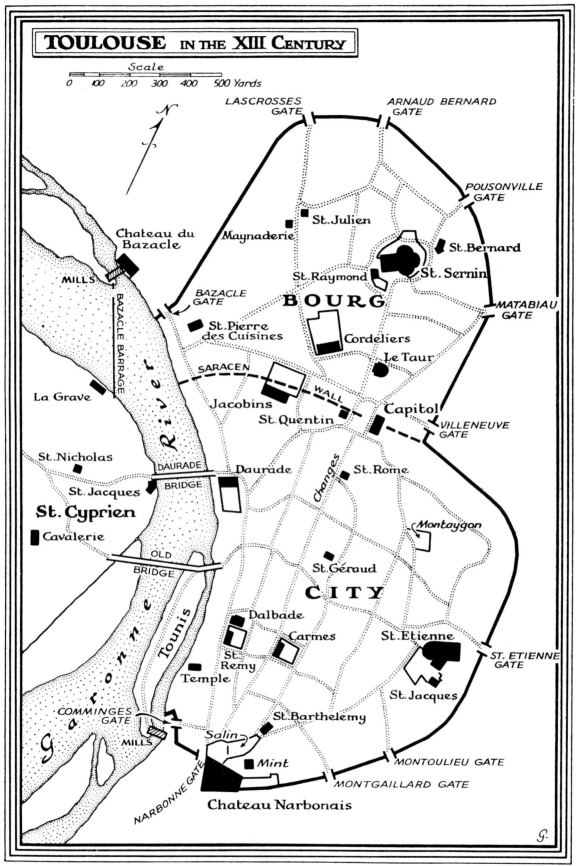

FIG. 1. Map of medieval Toulouse with principal churches of the city and the Bourg
(after John Hine Mundy, *Liberty and Political Power in Toulouse, 1050–1230*)

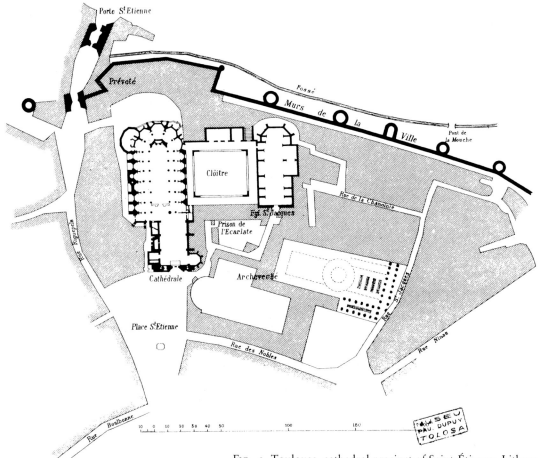

FIG. 2. Toulouse, cathedral precinct of Saint-Étienne. Lithograph by Délor after plan of 1750 of the city of Toulouse by Joseph-Marie de Saget (Photo: Musée Paul Dupuy, Toulouse)

FIG. 3. Toulouse, cathedral of Saint-Étienne. Plan of the existing cathedral by Debré and Braunweld (after Lambert, *Abbayes et cathédrales du sud-ouest*)

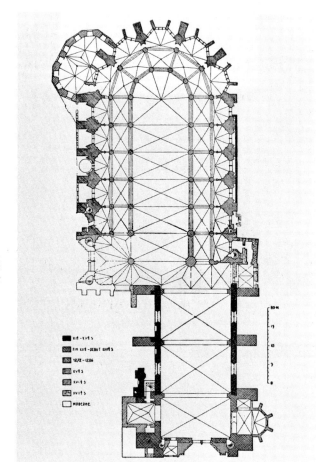

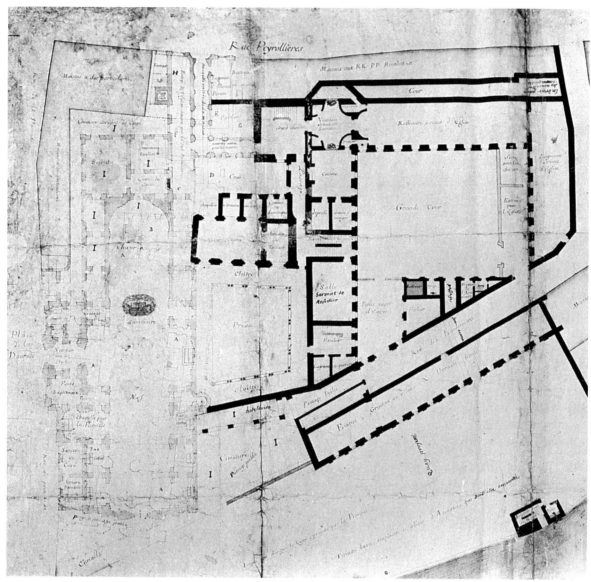

Fig. 4. Toulouse, La Daurade. Plan of the church and priory by François Franque. *c.*1764–5
(Toulouse, ADHG, Plan ancien 102) (photo: Toulouse, ADHG)

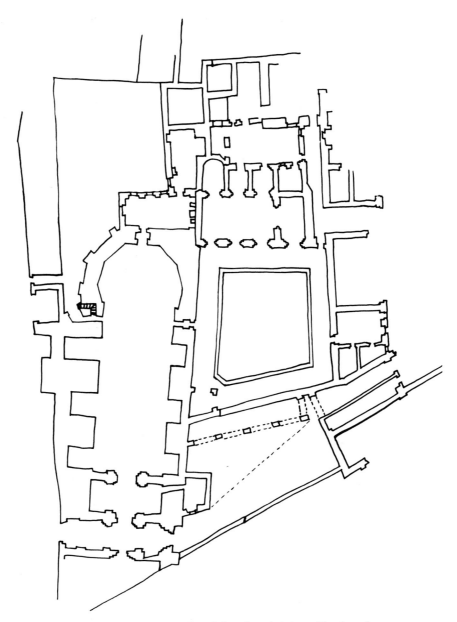

Fig. 5. Toulouse, La Daurade, medieval church and cloister. Tracing after plan by François Franque of *c.*1764–5 (Toulouse, ADHG, Plan ancien 102)

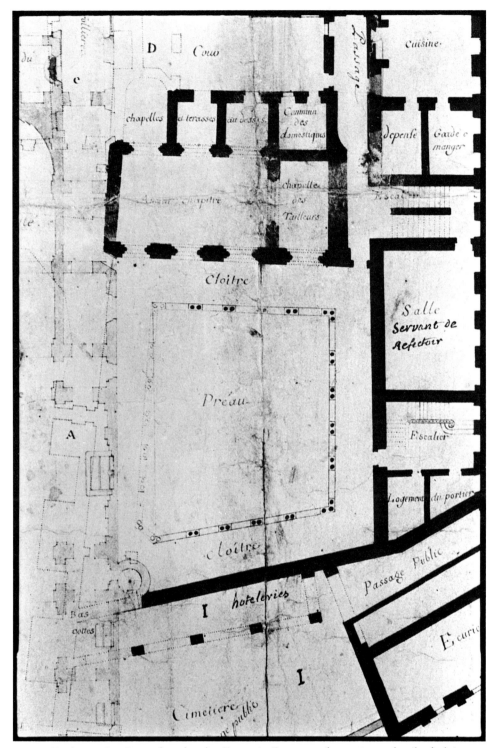

FIG. 6 Toulouse, La Daurade, plan by François Franque of *c*.1764–5, detail of cloister
(Toulouse, ADHG, Plan ancien 102)

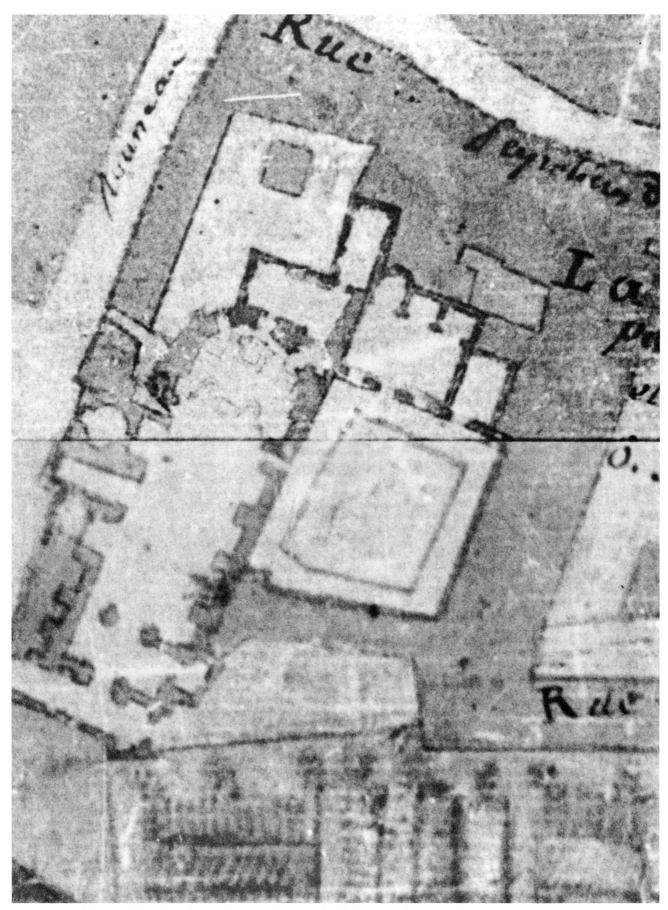

FIG. 7. Plan of the city of Toulouse by Joseph-Marie de Saget, detail of priory of La Daurade, 1750 (Toulouse, Bibliothèque municipale, Plan 34) (photo: Toulouse, Bibliothèque municipale)

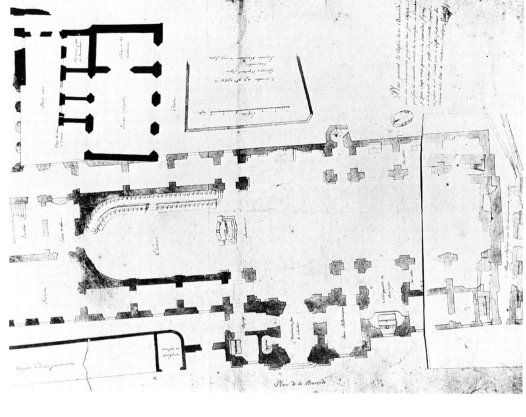

FIG. 9. Toulouse, plan of the church of La Daurade with projected changes by François Franque, 7 November 1765 (Toulouse, ADHG, Plan ancien 48–2) (photo: Toulouse, ADHG)

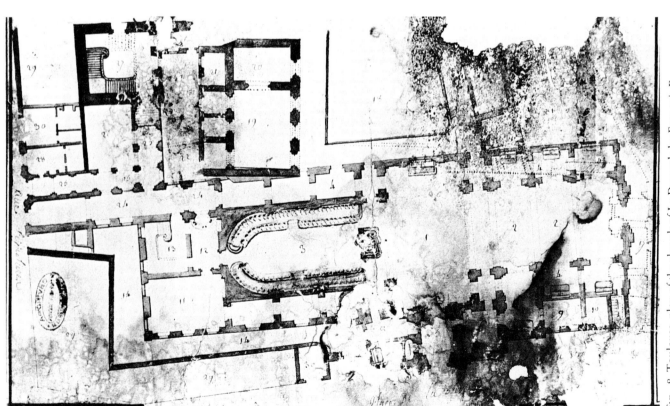

FIG. 8. Toulouse, plan of the church of La Daurade by François Franque, 1765 (Toulouse, ADHG, Plan ancien 77) (photo: Toulouse, ADHG)

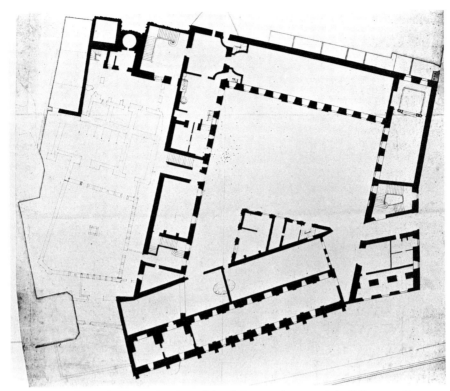

FIG. 10. Toulouse, La Daurade, plan of the cloister and monastic buildings, c.1811–14 (Toulouse, ADHG, Plan géométrique 965) (photo: Toulouse, ADHG)

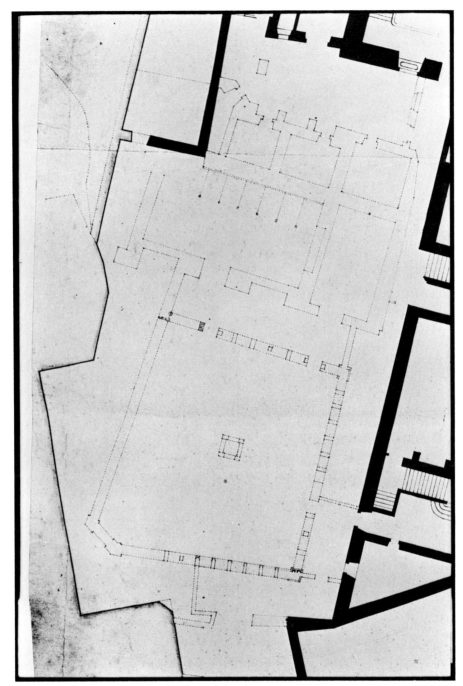

FIG. 11. Toulouse, La Daurade, plan of the cloister and monastic buildings, detail of cloister and chapter house, c.1811–14 (photo: Toulouse, ADHG, Plan géométrique 965)

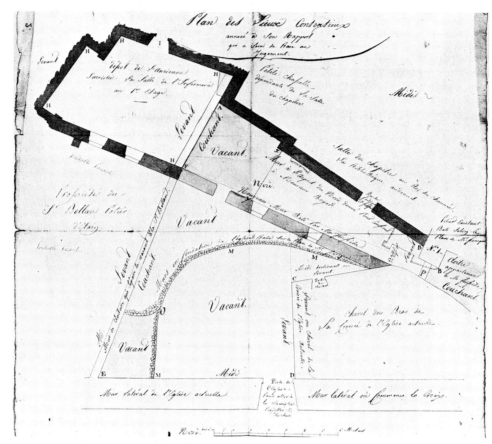

Fɪɢ. 12. Toulouse, La Daurade. Plan commissioned by Boyer-Fonfrède, showing terrain to north of former chapter house, 1804 (Toulouse, AMT 5 N 3) (photo: Toulouse, ADHG)

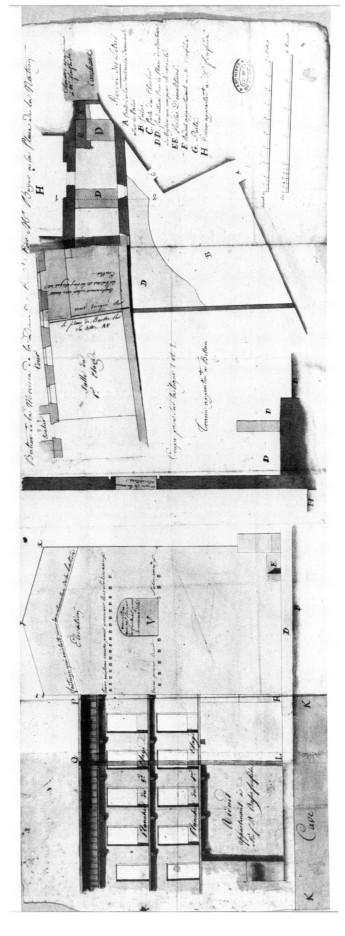

FIG. 13. Elevation and plan of the property of Boyer-Fonfrède in the former priory of La Daurade (left) Elevation of north wall of former chapter house (right) Plan of terrain to the north of former chapter house (H), 1804 (Toulouse, AMT 5 N 3) (photo: Toulouse, ADHG)

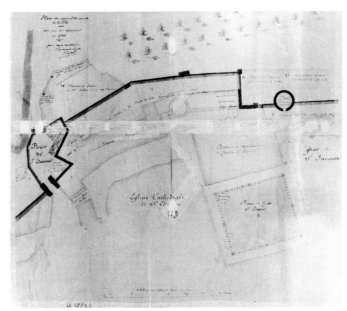

FIG. 14. Toulouse, plan of the rampart in the vicinity of the cathedral of Saint-Étienne. Copy by J. Suibal after plan of 1780 by Jacques Paschal Virebent (Toulouse, AMT 4 D 25 (2)) (photo: Toulouse, AMT)

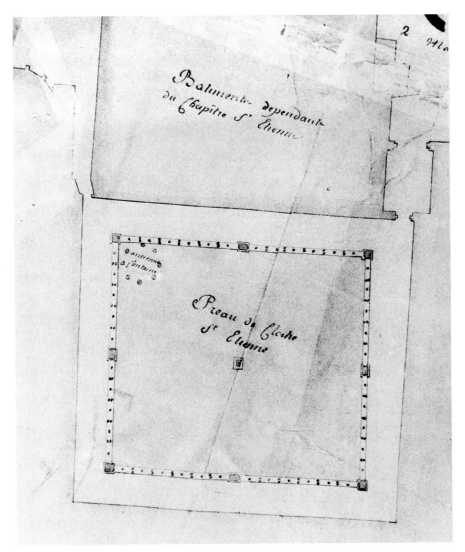

FIG. 15. Toulouse, plan of the rampart in the vicinity of the cathedral of Saint-Étienne, detail of the Romanesque cloister. Copy after Virebent plan of 1780 (Toulouse, AMT 4 D 25 (2)) (photo: Toulouse, AMT)

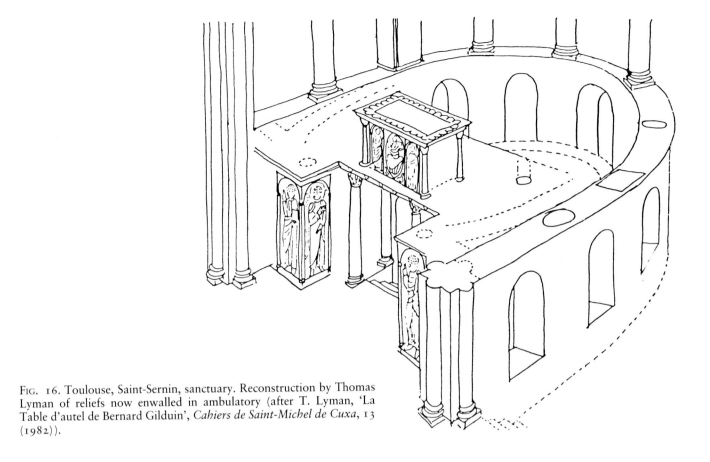

FIG. 16. Toulouse, Saint-Sernin, sanctuary. Reconstruction by Thomas Lyman of reliefs now enwalled in ambulatory (after T. Lyman, 'La Table d'autel de Bernard Gilduin', *Cahiers de Saint-Michel de Cuxa*, 13 (1982)).

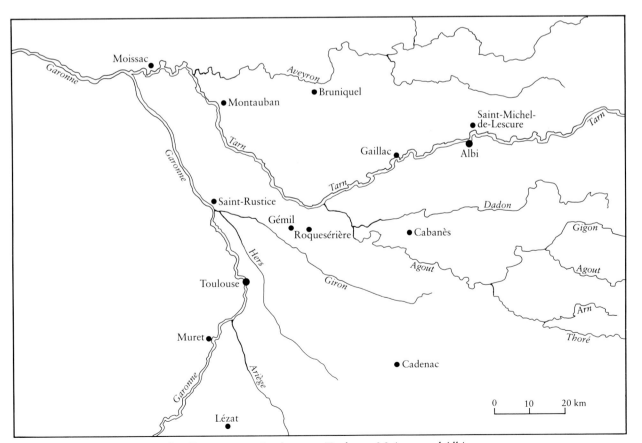

FIG. 17. Map of Haute-Languedoc. Romanesque sites between Toulouse, Moissac, and Albi

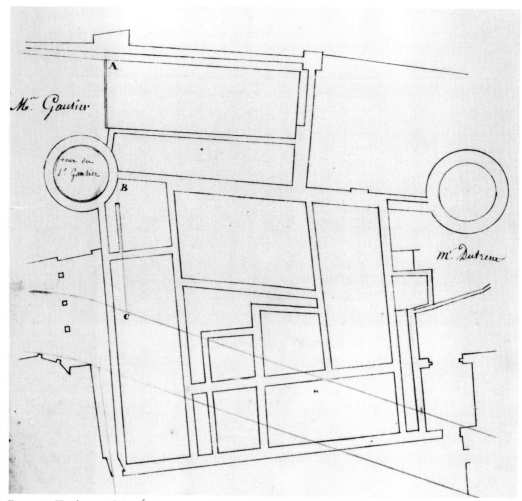

Fig. 18. Toulouse, Saint-Étienne, post-Revolutionary plan of the former chapter house (bottom) and adjacent structures (Toulouse, AMT, 2 M 3, dossier for 1791–1834) (photo: Toulouse, ADHG)

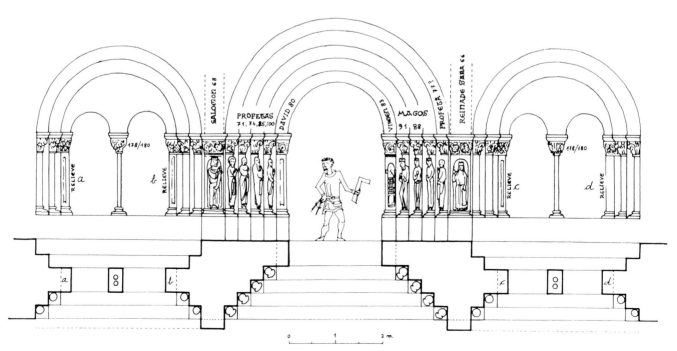

Fig. 19. La Daurade, chapter house, suggested reconstruction of façade by Serafín Moralejo (after S. Moralejo, 'La Fachada de la sala capitular de la Daurade', *Anuario de estudios medievales*, 13 (1983))

Fɪɢ. 20. La Daurade, chapter house, author's suggested reconstruction of façade.
(Drawing by Kathryn Horste and William Broom)

PL. 1. Toulouse, Saint-Sernin, interior, nave, north aisle, capital in 8th bay west of crossing
(photo: Thomas Lyman)

PL. 2. Toulouse, cathedral of Saint-Étienne, interior, west tribune, capital of the arcade
(photo: author)

PL. 3. Toulouse, cathedral of Saint-Étienne, interior, west tribune, capital of the arcade (photo: author)

PL. 4. Toulouse, Saint-Sernin, west façade, north portal opening, north jamb, capitals (photo: author)

PL. 5. Toulouse, cathedral of Saint-Étienne, interior, 13th-century nave, reused Romanesque capitals (photo: author)

PL. 6. Toulouse, cathedral of Saint-Étienne, interior, 13th-century nave, reused Romanesque capitals (photo: author)

PL. 7. Toulouse, Saint-Sernin, cloister, capital with lions (M. 220) (photo: James Austin)

PL. 8. Toulouse, Saint-Sernin, cloister, capital with birds (M. 224) (photo: James Austin)

PL. 9. Toulouse, Saint-Sernin, cloister, capital with human and animal combat in interlace (M. 212) (photo: James Austin).

PL. 10. Toulouse, Musée des Augustins, installation of the Romanesque sculptures between 1891 and 1928 (photo: Monuments historiques, Paris, Copyright 1990 ARS N.Y./SPADEM)

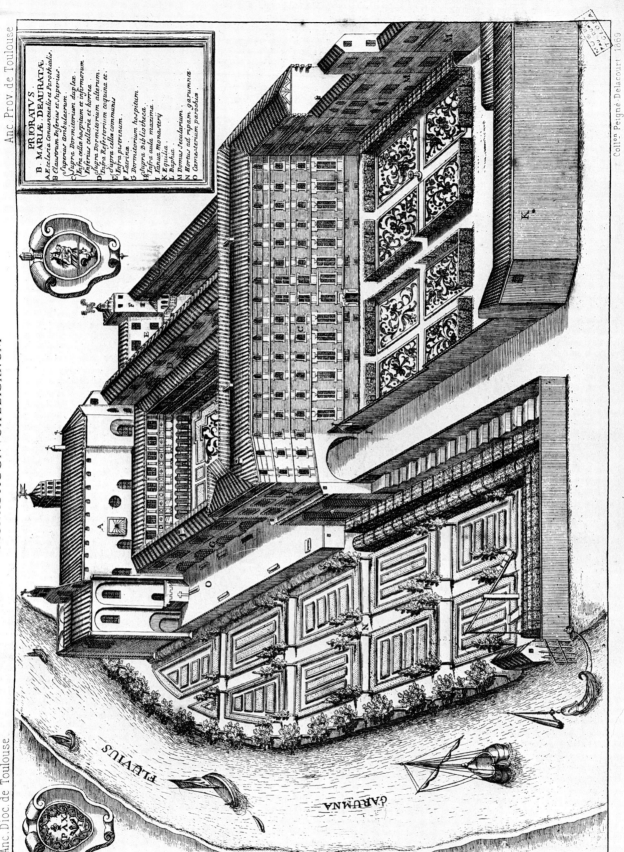

PL. 11. Toulouse, La Daurade, engraving of the church and priory in the seventeenth century (after M. Germain, *Le Monasticon Gallicanum*) (Toulouse, Musée Paul Dupuy D 60–6–22) (photo: Musée Paul Dupuy, Toulouse)

PL. 12. Toulouse, Saint-Pierre-des-Cuisines, sepulchral niche (photo: author)

PL. 13. La Daurade, capital for a corner column: *Sculptor at Work on a Capital* (M. 188) (photo: James Austin)

PL. 14. La Daurade, capital for a corner column: *Woman Combing a Child's Hair* (M. 184) (photo: James Austin)

PL. 15. La Daurade, cloister, fragment of impost excavated 1976 (Inv. 76–13–6) (left), matched with M. 194 (photo: Musée des Augustins, Toulouse)

PL. 16. La Daurade, cloister, fragment of impost excavated 1976 (Inv. 76–13–9), matched with M. 193 (photo: Musée des Augustins, Toulouse)

PL. 17. La Daurade, cloister, fragment of impost excavated 1976 (Inv. 76–13–10), matched with M. 195 (photo: Musée des Augustins, Toulouse)

PL. 18. La Daurade, cloister, impost for corner pier (M. 203) (photo: James Austin)

PL. 19. La Daurade, cloister, impost for corner pier (M. 200) (photo: James Austin)

PL. 20. La Daurade, cloister, capital for double applied columns: *Musicians of King David* (M. 102) (photo: author)

PL. 21. La Daurade, cloister, capital for double applied columns:
Musicians of King David, detail (M. 102) (photo: author)

PL. 22. Moissac (Tarn-et-Garonne), cloister, south gallery: *Musicians of King David*
(photo: author)

PL. 24. La Daurade, cloister, capital for double columns: *Daniel in the Lions'*
Den and *The Accusers of Daniel Devoured* (M. 104) (photo: author)

PL. 23. La Daurade, cloister, capital for double columns: *Daniel in the Lions'*
Den (M. 104) (photo: author)

PL. 25. Moissac, cloister, west gallery: *Daniel in the Lions' Den* (photo: author)

PL. 26. Moissac, cloister, east gallery: *Adoration of the Magi* (photo: author)

PL. 27. Moissac, cloister, south gallery: *Temptation of Christ*, detail of *Angels Administering to Christ* (photo: author).

PL. 28. Moissac, cloister, east gallery: *Miracle at Cana*, detail of *Wedding Feast* (photo: author)

PL. 29. Moissac, cloister, east gallery: *Miracle at Cana*, *Christ Turning Water to Wine* (photo: author)

PL. 30. Moissac, cloister, south gallery: *St Peter led from Prison* (photo: author)

PL. 31. Moissac, cloister, east gallery: *Washing of the Feet*, disciples (photo: author)

PL. 32. La Daurade, cloister, capital for single column: *Death of John the Baptist, Feast of Herod* (M. 107) (photo: author)

PL. 33. Moissac, cloister, south gallery: *Death of John the Baptist, Feast of Herod* (photo: author)

PL. 34. La Daurade, cloister, capital for single column: *Death of John the Baptist, Dance of Salome* (M. 107) (photo: author)

PL. 35. La Daurade, cloister, capital for single column: *Death of John the Baptist, Beheading of St John* (photo: author)

PL. 36. La Daurade, cloister, capital for single column: *Death of John the Baptist, Salome Presenting Head of St John to Herodias* (M. 107) (photo: author)

PL. 37. La Daurade, capital for double applied columns: *Christ and the Canaanite Woman*
(left) Fragment excavated 1976 (Inv. 76–13–3) (right) M. 113 (photo: author)

PL. 38. La Daurade, capital for double applied columns: *Christ and
the Canaanite Woman*, disciples (M. 113) (photo: author)

PL. 39. La Daurade, cloister, capital for single column: *Transfiguration*, disciples (M. 110) (photo: author)

PL. 40. Moissac, cloister, south gallery: *Transfiguration* (photo: author)

PL. 41. La Daurade, cloister, capital for single column: *Transfiguration*, Christ and Moses
(M. 110) (photo: author)

PL. 42. La Daurade, cloister, capital for single column: *Transfiguration*, the three pavilions
(M. 110) (photo: author)

PL. 43. La Daurade, cloister, capital for single column: *Incredulity of Thomas* (M. 110)
(photo: author)

PL. 44. Moissac, cloister, south gallery: *Descent from the Mountain after the Transfiguration*,
detail (photo: author)

PL. 45. La Daurade, cloister, capital for double columns: *Entry into Jerusalem* (M. 114) (photo: author)

PL. 46. La Daurade, cloister, capital for double columns: *Entry into Jerusalem*, disciples carrying palms (photo: author)

PL. 47. La Daurade, cloister, capital for double columns: *Arrest of Christ* (M. 114) (photo: author)

PL. 48. La Daurade, cloister, capital for double columns: *Arrest of Christ*, detail (M. 114)
(photo: author)

PL. 49. La Daurade, cloister, capital for single column: *The Last Judgement,* Weighing of the Souls (M. 116) (photo: author)

PL. 50. La Daurade, cloister, capital for single column: *The Last Judgement, The Blessed Making their Way to Paradise* (M. 116) (photo: author)

PL. 51. La Daurade, cloister, capital for single column: *The Last Judgement, Angel with Cross and Book* (M. 116) (photo: author)

PL. 52. La Daurade, cloister, capital for single column: *The Last Judgement, Christ in Majesty* (M. 119) (photo: author)

PL. 53. La Daurade, cloister, capital for single column: *The Last Judgement,*
Resurrection of the Dead (M. 119) (photo: author)

PL. 54. La Daurade, cloister, capital for single column: *The Last Judgement,*
Adoration of the Cross (M. 119) (photo: author)

PL. 55. Moissac, cloister, west gallery: *Adoration of the Cross* (photo: author)

PL. 56. La Daurade, cloister, impost: *Le Toilette du Prince* (M. 105) (photo: author)

PL. 57. Moissac, cloister, south gallery, two-row acanthus capital (photo: James Austin)

PL. 58. Toulouse, Saint-Sernin, interior, apse hemicycle, south side, south-west apsidiol, capital between south and south-eastern windows (photo: Thomas Lyman)

PL. 59. Toulouse, Saint-Sernin, interior, apse hemicycle, window capital between axial chapel and south-east apsidiol (after cleaning) (photo: Thomas Lyman)

PL. 60. Toulouse, Saint-Sernin, interior, apse hemicycle, south side, south-west apsidiol, capital between south and south-western windows (photo: Thomas Lyman)

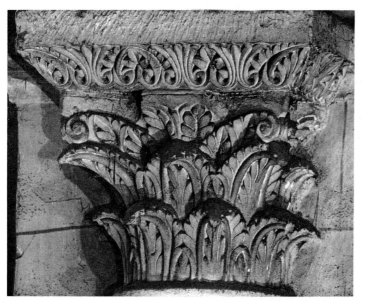

PL. 61. Toulouse, Saint-Sernin, interior, north transept (ground storey), west aisle, two-row acanthus capital (photo: Thomas Lyman)

PL. 62. Toulouse, Saint-Sernin, interior, apse hemicycle, north side, entrance into north-west apsidiol, east side, capital (Photo: Thomas Lyman)

PL. 63. Moissac, cloister, north gallery, foliate capital (photo: author)

PL. 64. Moissac, cloister, north gallery, foliate capital
(photo: James Austin)

PL. 65. Moissac, cloister, north gallery, foliate capital
(photo: James Austin)

PL. 66. Toulouse, Saint-Sernin, interior, south transept (ground storey), west arcade, pier capital (photo: Thomas Lyman)

PL. 67. Toulouse, Saint-Sernin, interior, south transept tribune, foliate capital (photo: Thomas Lyman)

Pl. 68. Toulouse, Saint-Sernin, interior, north transept arm, top of axial pilaster, foliate capital (photo: Thomas Lyman)

Pl. 69. Toulouse, Saint-Sernin, interior, north transept (ground storey), axial pier: *Incredulity of Thomas* (photo: Jean Dieuzaide)

Pl. 70. Moissac, cloister, east gallery: *Washing of the Feet* (photo: author)

Pl. 71. Lescure d'Albigeois (Tarn), Saint-Michel, west portal, north jamb (left to right): *Fall of Man, Sacrifice of Isaac, Addorsed Lions* (photo: author)

PL. 72. Lescure d'Albigeois, Saint-Michel, west portal, south jamb: *Punishment of the Rich Man* (photo: author)

PL. 73. Lescure d'Albigeois, Saint-Michel, interior, nave, south arcade: *Sacrifice of Isaac* (photo: Zodiaque)

PL. 74. Lescure d'Albigeois, Saint-Michel, interior, entrance to apse, south side: *Daniel in the Lions' Den* (photo: Zodiaque)

PL. 75. Lescure d'Albigeois, Saint-Michel, interior, entrance to apse, north side: *Meeting of Jacob and Esau* (photo: Zodiaque)

PL. 76. Bruniquel (Tarn-et-Garonne), Saint-Maffre, south portal, west jamb: *The Expulsion* (photo: author)

PL. 77. Bruniquel, Saint-Maffre, south portal, east jamb: *The Fall of Man* (photo: author)

PL. 78. Saint-Rustice (Haute-Garonne), church, capital for recessed column: *Christ in Majesty*. Toulouse, Musée des Augustins (photo: author)

PL. 79. Saint-Rustice, church, capital for recessed column: *Christ in Majesty*, angel holding mandorla. Toulouse, Musée des Augustins (photo: author)

PL. 80. La Daurade, cloister, capital for single column: *Washing of the Feet*, Christ and St Peter (M. 122) (photo: author)

PL. 81. La Daurade, cloister, capital for single column: *Washing of the Feet*, Christ (M. 122)
(photo: author)

PL. 82. La Daurade, cloister, capital for single column: *Washing of the Feet*, St Peter and
disciple (M. 122) (photo: author)

PL. 83. La Daurade, cloister, capital for single column: *Washing of the Feet*, disciples
(M. 122) (photo: author)

PL. 84. La Daurade, cloister, capital for single column: *The Last Supper*, Christ and St John (M. 125) (photo: author)

PL. 85. La Daurade, cloister, capital for single column: *The Last Supper* (M. 125) (photo: author)

PL. 86. La Daurade, cloister, capital for single column: *The Last Supper*,
St Martial (M. 125) (photo: author)

PL. 87. La Daurade, cloister, capital for single column: *The Last Supper*,
disciples (M. 125) (photo: author)

PL. 88. La Daurade, cloister, capital for single column: *The Last Supper*, Christ and St John
(M. 125) (photo: author)

PL. 89. La Daurade, cloister, capital for single column: *Christ in Gethsemane*, Christ praying
(M. 128) (photo: author)

PL. 90. La Daurade, cloister, capital for single column: *Christ in Gethsemane*, Christ
confronting the soldiers (M. 128) (photo: author)

PL. 91. La Daurade, cloister, capital for triple columns: *Arrest of Christ* (M. 131) (photo: author) .

PL. 92. La Daurade, cloister, capital for triple columns: *Arrest of Christ*, detail (M. 131) (photo: author)

PL. 93. La Daurade, cloister, capital for triple columns: (left) *Arrest of Christ* (right) *Flagellation* (M. 131) (photo: author)

PL. 94. La Daurade, cloister, capital for triple columns: *Flagellation* (M. 131) (photo: author)

PL. 95. La Daurade, cloister, capital for triple columns: *Christ before Pilate* (M. 131) (photo: author)

PL. 96. La Daurade, cloister, capital for triple columns: (left) *Christ speaking to the Women of Jerusalem* (right) *Peter striking Malchus* (M. 131) (photo: author)

PL. 97. La Daurade, cloister, capital for single column: *Deposition* (M. 134) (photo: author)

PL. 98. La Daurade, cloister, capital for single column: *Deposition*, St John (M. 134)
(photo: author)

PL. 99. La Daurade, cloister, capital for single column: *Entombment* (M. 134) (photo: author)

PL. 100. La Daurade, cloister, capital for single column: *Entombment* (M. 134) (photo: author)

PL. 101. La Daurade, cloister, capital for single column (left) *Entombment* (right) *Deposition* (M. 134) (photo: author)

PL. 102. La Daurade, cloister, capital for single column: *Entombment* (M. 134) (photo: author)

Pl. 103. La Daurade, cloister, capital for single column: *Christ in Limbo* (M. 140)
(photo: author)

Pl. 104. La Daurade, cloister, capital for single column: *The Blessed Led to Paradise*
(M. 140) (photo: author)

PL. 105. La Daurade, cloister, capital for single column: *Holy Women at the Tomb* (M. 137)
(photo: author)

PL. 106. La Daurade, cloister, capital for single column: *Resurrection of Christ* (M. 137) (photo: author)

PL. 107. La Daurade, cloister, capital for single column: *Holy Women at the Tomb* (M. 137) (photo: author)

PL. 108. La Daurade, cloister, capital for double columns: *The Apostles at the Tomb*, St John
(M. 143) (photo: author)

PL. 109. La Daurade, cloister, capital for double columns: *The Apostles at the Tomb*, St John
(M. 143) (photo: author)

PL. 110. La Daurade, cloister, capital for double columns: (left) *Apostles at the Tomb* (right)
Noli me tangere (M. 143) (photo: author)

PL. 111. La Daurade, cloister, capital for double columns: *The Apostles at the Tomb*, St John
(M. 143) (photo: author)

PL. 112. La Daurade, cloister, capital for double columns: (left) *Noli me tangere* (right)
Apostles at the Tomb (M. 143) (photo: author)

PL. 113. La Daurade, cloister, capital for double columns: *Noli me tangere* (M. 143)
(photo: author)

PL. 114. La Daurade, cloister, capital for double columns: *Journey to Emmaus* (M. 145) (photo: author)

PL. 116. La Daurade, cloister, capital for double columns: *Supper at Emmaus* (M. 145) (photo: author)

PL. 115. La Daurade, cloister, capital for double columns: (left) *Journey to Emmaus* (right) *Supper at Emmaus* (M. 145) (photo: author)

PL. 117. La Daurade, cloister, capital for double columns: *Traditio legis* (M. 148) (photo: author)

PL. 118. La Daurade, cloister, capital for double columns: (left) *Traditio legis*
(right) *Incredulity of Thomas* (M. 148) (photo: author)

PL. 119. La Daurade, cloister, capital for double columns: *Incredulity of Thomas* (M. 148) (photo: author)

PL. 120. La Daurade, cloister, capital for double columns: *Incredulity of Thomas* (M. 148) (photo: author)

PL. 121. La Daurade, cloister, capital for double columns: (left) *Incredulity of Thomas* (right) *Traditio legis* (M. 148) (photo: author)

PL. 122. La Daurade, cloister, capital for triple columns: *Ascension*, Christ (M. 151) (photo: author)

PL. 123. La Daurade, cloister, capital for triple columns: *Ascension*, angel addressing Apostles (M. 151) (photo: author)

PL. 124. La Daurade, cloister, capital for triple columns: *Ascension*, angel addressing Apostles (M. 151) (photo: author)

PL. 125. La Daurade, cloister, capital for triple columns:
Ascension, Apostles (M. 151) (photo: author)

PL. 126. La Daurade, cloister, capital for triple columns: *Ascension*, angel addressing the
Virgin (M. 151) (photo: author)

PL. 127. La Daurade, cloister, capital for double columns: *Pentecost* (M. 154)
(photo: author)

PL. 128. La Daurade, cloister, capital for double columns: *Pentecost* (M. 154) (photo: author)

PL. 129. La Daurade, cloister, capital for double columns: *Pentecost*, detail (M. 154) (photo: author)

PL. 130. La Daurade, cloister, capital for double columns: *The Four Rivers of Paradise*, Phison and Geon (M. 157) (photo: author)

PL. 131. La Daurade, cloister, capital for double columns: *The Four Rivers of Paradise* (M. 157) (photo: author)

PL. 132. La Daurade, cloister, capital for double columns: *The Four Rivers of Paradise*, Tigris and Eufrates (M. 157) (photo: author)

PL. 133. La Daurade, cloister, capital for double
columns: *Fantastic Birds* (M. 166) (photo: author)

PL. 134. La Daurade, cloister, capital for double columns:
Fantastic Birds (M. 166) (photo: author)

PL. 136. La Daurade, cloister, capital for double columns: *Vine Interlace* (M. 163) (photo: James Austin)

PL. 135. La Daurade, cloister, capital for single column: *Lions in Vine Stems* (M. 160) (photo: James Austin)

PL. 137. La Daurade, cloister, capital for double columns: *Vine Interlace* (M. 170) (photo: James Austin)

PL. 138. La Daurade, cloister, capital for single column: *Vine Interlace* (M. 171) (photo: James Austin)

PL. 139. La Daurade, cloister, capital for double columns: *Vine Interlace* (M. 169) (photo: James Austin)

PL. 140. Tavant (Indre-et-Loire), Saint-Nicolas, crypt: Seated figure (photo: Monuments historiques, Paris. Copyright 1990 ARS N.Y./SPADEM)

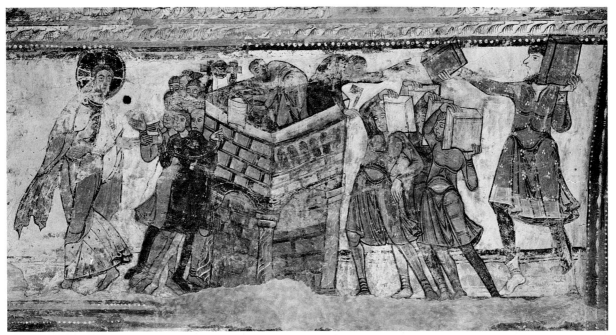

PL. 141. Saint-Savin-sur-Gartempe (Vienne), abbey church, interior, nave vault: *Construction of the Tower of Babel* (photo: Hirmer Verlag, Munich)

PL. 142. Saint-Savin-sur-Gartempe, abbey church, interior, crypt: *SS Savinus and Cyprian before the Judge Ladicius* (photo: Hirmer Verlag, Munich)

PL. 143. *Vita Radegundis:* (top) *Radegund Washing the Feet of the Poor* (bottom) *Radegund Feeding the Poor at Table* (Poitiers, Bib. mun., MS 250, fo. 29ᵛ) (photo: after E. Ginot, *Bulletin de la Société française de reproductions de manuscrits à peintures*, 4 (1914))

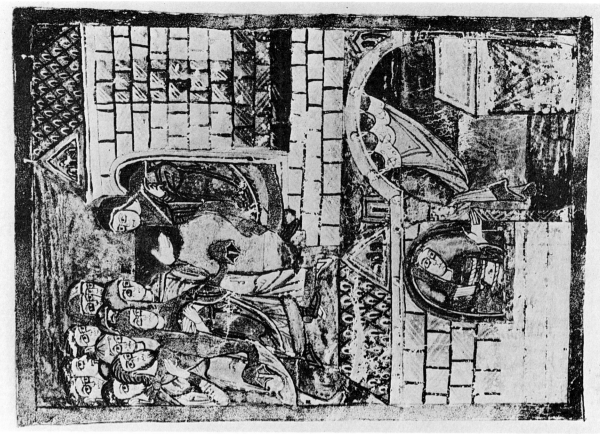

PL. 145. *Vita Radegundis: Radegund Retiring to her Monastery* (Poitiers, Bib. mun., MS 250, fo. 31ᵛ) (photo: after E. Ginot)

PL. 144. *Vita Radegundis:* (top) *Radegund before St Médard* (bottom) *Radegund Consecrated Deaconness* (Poitiers, Bib. mun., MS 250, fo. 27ᵛ) (photo: after E. Ginot)

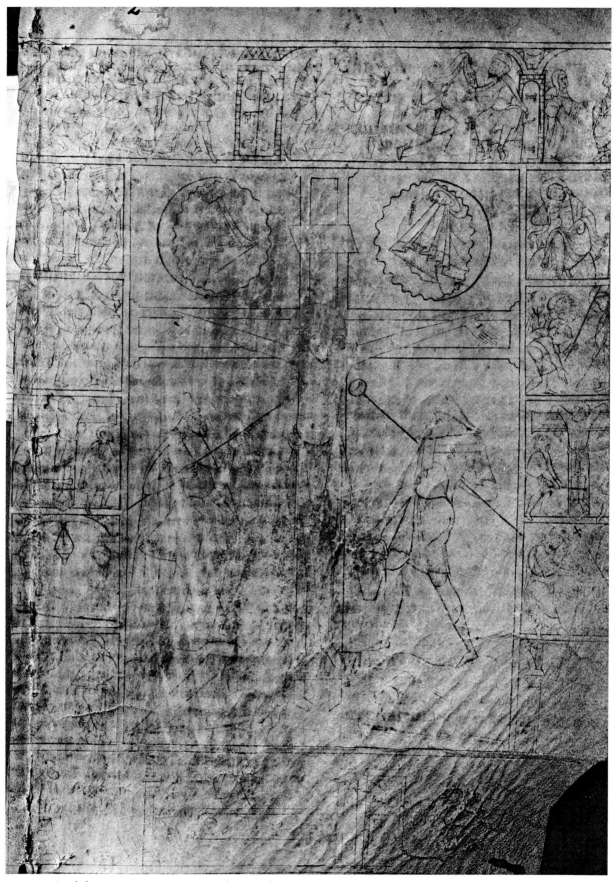

PL. 146. Leaf from a Romanesque Missal: *Crucifixion and Scenes of the Passion and Resurrection* (Auxerre, cathedral of Saint-Étienne, Treasury) (photo: Photographie Giraudon)

PL. 147. Leaf from a Romanesque Missal: *Crucifixion and Scenes of the Passion and Resurrection*, detail of Arrest of Christ (Auxerre, cathedral of Saint-Étienne, Treasury) (photo: after M. W. Evans, *Medieval Drawings* (London, 1969), pl. 41).

PL. 148. Sacramentary of Saint-Étienne de Limoges: *Ascension* (Paris, BN, lat. 9438, fo. 84ᵛ) (photo: Monuments historiques, Paris. Copyright 1990 ARS N.Y./SPADEM)

PL. 150. Sacramentary of Saint-Étienne de Limoges: (top) *Last Supper* (bottom) *Washing of the Feet* (Paris, BN, lat. 9438, fo. 46ᵛ) (photo: Monuments historiques, Paris. Copyright 1990 ARS N.Y./SPADEM)

PL. 149. Sacramentary of Saint-Étienne de Limoges: *Pentecost* (Paris, BN, lat. 9438, fo. 87ʳ) (photo: Monuments historiques, Paris. Copyright 1990 ARS N.Y./SPADEM)

PL. 151. Second Bible of Saint-Martial de Limoges: *Elias and the Envoys of the King* (Paris, BN, lat. 8, II, fo. 41) (photo: Bibliothèque Nationale, Paris)

PL. 152. Moissac (Tarn-et-Garonne), south porch, east wall: *Scenes of the Infancy of Christ* (photo: James Austin)

PL. 153. Toulouse, Saint-Étienne: Apostles, *St James* (M. 19) and
St Thomas (M. 5). Toulouse, Musée des Augustins (photo: author)

PL. 154. Toulouse, Saint-Étienne: Apostles, *St James*
(M. 19) and *St Thomas* (M. 5), profile. Toulouse,
Musée des Augustins (photo: author)

PL. 155. Toulouse, Saint-Étienne: *St James*, detail. Toulouse, Musée des Augustins
(photo: author)

PL. 156. Toulouse, Saint-Étienne: *St Thomas*, detail. Toulouse, Musée des Augustins (photo: author)

PL. 157. Toulouse, Saint-Étienne: Apostle, *St Andrew* (M. 22). Toulouse, Musée des Augustins (photo: author)

PL. 158. Toulouse, Saint-Étienne: *St Andrew*, detail (M. 22). Toulouse, Musée des Augustins (photo: author)

PL. 159. Toulouse, Saint-Étienne: (left) Unidentified Apostle
(M. 8) (right) *St Andrew* (M. 22). Toulouse, Musée des
Augustins (photo: author)

PL. 160. Toulouse, Saint-Étienne: Unidentified paired
Apostles (M. 1). Toulouse, Musée des Augustins
(photo: author)

PL. 161. Toulouse, Saint-Étienne: Unidentified paired
Apostles (M. 11). Toulouse, Musée des Augustins
(photo: author)

PL. 162. Toulouse, Saint-Étienne: Unidentified paired Apostles (M. 11), detail.
Toulouse, Musée des Augustins (photo: author)

PL. 163. Toulouse, Saint-Étienne: Unidentified paired Apostles (M. 24), detail. Toulouse, Musée des Augustins (photo: author)

PL. 164. Toulouse, Saint-Étienne: Unidentified paired Apostles (M. 24). Toulouse, Musée des Augustins (photo: author)

PL. 165. Toulouse, Saint-Étienne: *SS Peter and Paul* (M. 15). Toulouse, Musée des Augustins (photo: author)

PL. 166. Toulouse, Saint-Étienne, capital for double engaged columns: *Scenes from the Death of John the Baptist* (M. 31). Toulouse, Musée des Augustins (photo: author)

PL. 167. Toulouse, Saint-Étienne, capital for double engaged columns: *Beheading of St John* (M. 31). Toulouse, Musée des Augustins (photo: author)

PL. 169. Toulouse, Saint-Étienne, capital for double engaged columns: *Herod and Salome* (M. 31) (photo: author)

PL. 168. Toulouse, Saint-Étienne, capital for double engaged columns: *Salome presenting head of St John to Herodias* (M. 31) (photo: author)

PL. 170. Toulouse, Saint-Étienne, capital for double columns: *The Wise and Foolish Virgins*, Christ and Ecclesia (M. 34). Toulouse, Musée des Augustins (photo: author)

PL. 171. Toulouse, Saint-Étienne, capital for double columns: *The Wise Virgins* (M. 34) (photo: author).

PL. 172. Toulouse, Saint-Étienne, capital for double columns: *Wise Virgin* (M. 34) (photo: author)

PL. 174. Toulouse, Saint-Étienne, capital for double columns, fragment: *The Wise and Foolish Virgins*, Christ and Ecclesia (M. 37). Toulouse, Musée des Augustins (photo: author)

PL. 173. Toulouse, Saint-Étienne, capital for double columns: *The Foolish Virgins* (unfinished) (M. 34) (photo: author)

PL. 175. Moissac (Tarn-et-Garonne), cloister, looking south-east from the north gallery (photo: Zodiaque)

PL. 176. Beaulieu-sur-Dordogne (Corrèze), church of Saint-Pierre, south portal, tympanum, *The Second Coming* (photo: Hirmer Verlag, Munich)

PL. 177. Catus (Lot), Cluniac priory, chapter house, interior: *Traditio clavium* (photo: Monuments historiques, Paris. Copyright 1990 ARS N.Y./SPADEM)

PL. 178. Cahors (Lot), cathedral of Saint-Étienne, north
portal, tympanum: *Ascension* (photo: author)

PL. 179. Ydes (Cantal), Saint-Georges, west porch, north
wall: *Annunciation* (photo: author)

PL. 180. Collonges-la-Rouge (Corrèze), church, west portal, tympanum: *Ascension* (photo: author)

PL. 181. Collonges-la-Rouge, church, west portal, tympanum, lower right: *Ascension*, Virgin and Apostles (photo: author)

PL. 182. First Bible of Charles the Bald: *Christ in Majesty*, with four Prophets and the four Gospel writers. Carolingian, School of Tours (Paris, BN, MS lat. 1, fo. 330ᵛ) (photo: Bibliothèque Nationale, Paris)

PL. 183. Saint-Lizier (Ariège), cathedral, cloister, west gallery (photo: author)

PL. 184. Beaulieu-sur-Dordogne (Corrèze), Saint-Pierre, chapter house, façade (photo: author)

PL. 185. Catus (Lot), Cluniac priory, chapter house, façade (photo: Monuments historiques, Paris. Copyright 1990 ARS N.Y./Spadem)

PL. 186. Marcilhac-sur-Célé (Lot), chapter house, façade (photo: author)

PL. 187. Agen (Lot-et-Garonne), Saint-Caprais, chapter house, façade (photo: author)

PL. 188. Agen, Saint-Caprais, chapter house, entrance
opening, left jamb, *Angel of the Annunciation*
(photo: author)

PL. 191. Arles (Bouches-du-Rhone), Saint-Trophime, cloister, north gallery (photo: Hirmer Verlag, Munich)

PL. 192. Toulouse, Saint-Étienne, conjectural reconstruction of
the chapter house interior by Linda Seidel (photo: after Seidel,
'A Romantic Forgery', *Art Bulletin*, 50 (1968), fig. 15)

PL. 193. La Daurade, chapter house, crowned female
(Queen of Sheba?) (M. 66) (photo: author)

PL. 194. La Daurade, chapter house, crowned male
(Solomon?) (M. 68) (photo: author)

PL. 195. La Daurade, chapter house, Prophet displaying a book (Moses?) (M. 94) (photo: author)

PL. 196. La Daurade, chapter house, Prophet with scroll (Daniel?) (M. 97) (photo: author)

ERRATUM

Please note that Plates 193, 194 and Plates 195, 196
have been transposed.

PL. 197. La Daurade, chapter house, Prophet with scroll (M. 82) (photo: author)

PL. 198. La Daurade, chapter house, *King David tuning his Harp* (M. 80) (photo: author)

PL. 199. La Daurade, chapter house, *Virgin and Child Enthroned* (M. 83) (photo: author)

PL. 200. La Daurade, chapter house, *Virgin and Child Enthroned* (M. 83) (Photo: author).

PL. 201. La Daurade, chapter house, column statues: (left to right) Crowned male holding ampula; Nimbed male with scroll; Crowned male (M. 91, 71, and 88) (Photo: author)

PL. 202. La Daurade, chapter house, column statue: Crowned male holding ampula, profile (M. 91) (photo: author)

PL. 203. La Daurade, chapter house, column statues: Three Prophets holding unfurled scrolls
(M. 74, 77, and 85) (photo: author)

Pl. 204. La Daurade, chapter house, pilaster capital (M. 98) (photo: author)

Pl. 205. La Daurade, chapter house, fragmentary column statue (M. 100) (photo: author)

PL. 206. La Daurade, capital for double applied columns: Diminutive men and animals in vine interlace (M. 172) (photo: James Austin)

PL. 207. La Daurade, capital for double applied columns: Vine interlace with diminutive animals and humans in combat (M. 174) (photo: James Austin)

PL. 208. La Daurade, capital for double columns: *Hunt of the Siren and Centaur* (M. 178) (photo: James Austin)

PL. 209. La Daurade, capital for double columns: *The Story of Job* (M. 180) (photo: James Austin)

PL. 210. La Daurade, capital for double columns, fragment: *Oarsmen in a Boat (Les Barques)* (M. 176) (photo: James Austin)

PL. 211. Pontaut, Notre-Dame, chapter house as reassembled
at the Cloisters, New York (photo: The Metropolitan Museum
of Art, New York, The Cloisters Collection)

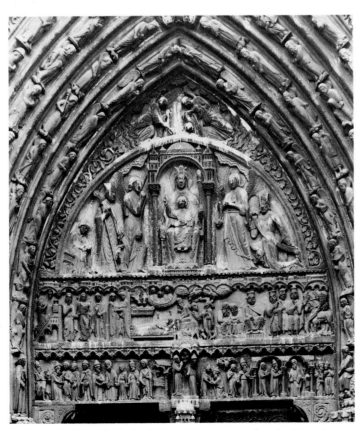

PL. 212. Paris, cathedral of Notre-Dame, west façade, Portail
Ste-Anne, the *Incarnation* (photo: Hirmer Verlag, Munich)

PL. 213. The Shaftesbury Psalter: *The Tree of Jesse* (London, British Library, Lansdowne 383, fo. 12) (photo: By permission of the British Library)

PL. 214. Mantes (Yvelines), collegiate church of Notre-Dame, west portal, center doorway, archivolts: *The Tree of Jesse* (photo: Hirmer Verlag, Munich)

PL. 215. Bourges (Cher), cathedral of Saint-Étienne, north portal: *Adoration of the Magi and Scenes of the Infancy of Christ* (photo: James Austin)

PL. 216. Bourges, cathedral of Saint-Étienne, south portal, east jamb: King and Prophets (photo: James Austin)

PL. 217. Toulouse, Saint-Étienne, capital for double columns: *Journey of the Magi* (M. 28)
(photo: author)

PL. 218. Toulouse, Saint-Étienne, capital for double columns: *Adoration of the Magi* (M. 28)
(photo: author)